CW01188133

A TENTATIVE INTERPRETATION OF IRAN'S MODERN HISTORY

Ali Murtaza Samsam Bakhtiari

MINERVA PRESS
MONTREUX LONDON WASHINGTON

A TENTATIVE INTERPRETATION
OF IRAN'S MODERN HISTORY
Copyright © A.M. Samsam Bakhtiari 1996

All Rights Reserved

No part of this book may be reproduced in any form,
by photocopying or by any electronic or mechanical means,
including information storage or retrieval systems,
without permission in writing from both the copyright owner
and the publisher of this book.

ISBN 1 85863 402 4

First published 1996 by
MINERVA PRESS
195 Knightsbridge
London SW7 1RE

Printed in Great Britain by
Antony Rowe Ltd., Chippenham, Wiltshire

A TENTATIVE INTERPRETATION OF IRAN'S MODERN HISTORY

This book is dedicated to my friend and brother-in-arms, martyr BIJAN ROSTAMI, takavar NCO of the Zulfaqar Division, fallen on the western front near Gilan-i Gharb, on December 6, 1981, while on a voluntary mission.

Respected and respectful, BIJAN was a true son of the Iranian nation – one of those who, with their blood, have written history.

ACKNOWLEDGEMENTS

First and foremost, my thanks go to my sister, Ms Fa'izeh Guiot, who typed all of the manuscripts and was with me from the very beginning till the end. I also have to thank my niece, Nathalie Guiot, for putting up with the changes in her family life.

My warmest thanks go to my cousin, Mr Farhad Samsam Bakhtiari, who always assisted me at critical junctures in the lengthy process.

I am extremely grateful to my children, Golbenaz and Amir Bahman, who showed a great deal of understanding during my long hours of research and writing.

I also take this opportunity to remember my former professor of history, the late Dr Carlo Mastelli (1918–1992), a genial man of encyclopaedic knowledge who taught me to respect history. I do hope that he would have approved of the present essay.

Finally, I am extremely grateful to the staff of Minerva Press for their vision and their masterful management of the whole project.

It goes without saying that the responsibility for all errors, inaccuracies, repetitions and misjudgements are entirely mine.

HISTORY... IS A NIGHTMARE FROM WHICH I AM TRYING TO AWAKE.
                        James Joyce, *Ulysses* (1,2)

HISTORY IS THE SCIENCE OF THINGS THAT NEVER REPEAT THEMSELVES.
                        Paul Valéry

HISTORY IS A MIRROR OF THE PAST AND A LESSON FOR THE PRESENT.   (Persian proverb)
                        General Sir Percy Sykes, *A History of Persia*

HISTORY CONSISTS FOR THE GREATER PART OF THE MISERIES BROUGHT UPON THE WORLD BY PRIDE, AMBITION, AVARICE, REVENGE, LUST, SEDITION, HYPOCRISY, UNGOVERNED ZEAL, AND ALL THE TRAIN OF DISORDERLY APPETITES.
                        Edmund Burke, *Reflections on the Revolution in France*

HISTORY IS A GRAVEYARD OF ARISTOCRACIES.
                        Vilfredo Pareto

L'HISTOIRE EST TOUJOURS CRUELLE.
                        Max Gallo, *L'Homme Robespierre*

HISTORIA MAGISTRA VITAE
                        Umberto Eco

TRANSLITERATION

The system of transliteration used throughout this book is the one adopted by the Royal Asiatic Society, as modified by Professor A.K.S. Lambton. It is exposed in detail in the introduction to Professor Lambton's book *The Persian Land Reform, 1962-1966* (Oxford: Clarendon Press, 1969). The only exception to that system introduced in the present work is the systematic use of the Farsi nominative form 'ul' in place of the Arabic definite article.

Furthermore, proper names (honorific titles, surnames or geographical names) are always used according to their historical context. For example, up to the year A.D. 1935 the name Persia will denote the country; thereafter the official name of Iran will be used.

As far as dating is concerned, the Gregorian calendar will be used throughout the book. In case a date is given using the Hejira solar calendar, it will always be followed by its Gregorian equivalent in parentheses.

ABOUT THE AUTHOR

The author received his Ph.D. in chemical engineering from the Swiss Federal Institute of Technology (ETH) at Zurich in 1970. Returning to Iran, he joined the National Iranian Oil Company (NIOC), and began lecturing at the Technical Faculty of Tehran University.

He took part in the Islamic Revolution of 1978/79, and served for seven months as a first lieutenant on the Iran-Iraq war front in 1960.

He has written dozens of articles, pamphlets and papers on the subject of the Iranian oil industry and OPEC.

He single-handedly wrote this present work during his spare hours.

CONTENTS

In the Name of God: Introduction	13
Chapter One: The Setting	17
Chapter Two: Decline	40
Chapter Three: Stalemate	65
Chapter Four: Constitutional Movement	108
Chapter Five: The Qajar Elite	143
Chapter Six: Change of the Guard	189
Chapter Seven: From Persia to Iran	217
Chapter Eight: The Second World War	265
Chapter Nine: Turbulent Times	295
Chapter Ten: Oil Nationalisation	346
ChapterEleven: American Clinic	394
Chapter Twelve: White Revolution	458
Chapter Thirteen: New Horizons	528
Chapter Fourteen: Transitions	578
Chapter Fifteen: Petrodollars	621
Chapter Sixteen: Iran Inc	689
Chapter Seventeen: Sacred Time	769
Conclusion	859

IN THE NAME OF GOD

INTRODUCTION

Some twenty-five centuries ago, Persia was an important empire. An empire that was, according to Hegel, "the first that passed away".[1] The German philosopher further added that Persia's inhabitants were the first "historical people"; comparing them to the other Asian communities, he wrote:

> While China and India remain stationary, and perpetuate a natural vegetative existence even to the present time, this Land [Persia] has been subject to those developments and revolutions, which alone manifest an historical condition...[2]

Since the legendary days of the Achaemenean kings, Persia has gone through a series of declines. From a superpower position, she was first downgraded to that of a world power, then to that of a regional power, and finally, to that of an almost powerless nation state: the predator had come full circle and turned into a prey. Notwithstanding this long downhill slide, Persia's past is rich in events and multidimensional changes. As historian C.R. Markham remarked:

> Persia is a land of many glorious memories. Bright and glowing visions are conjured by its very name...[3]

Yet another interesting and fundamental aspect of Persia (and one of the main causes of her vicissitudes) is her unique geographic location. She not only stands "on the highway of Nations",[4] but also on the line delimiting East from West.

"Is she the last frontier of the Occident or the first land of the Orient?" ventured Noel Baillif, before concluding "she is foremost a cross-roads; a cross-roads in Time and Space".[5] Due to her very special position, she happens to be the linchpin to the world's power-balance mechanism.

Add to that her universal poets (Hafiz, Firdousi, Moulavi, Saâdi, Attar and Khayyam, to name but a few), her language – which stands among the richest in world history – and her bountiful resources, and it becomes clear why Persia is a country unlike any other.

This might well be the reason for which the people of Persia have always kept their pride and have proven resilient beyond expression, surviving and enduring, during the long decline from empire, every challenge. Edouard Sablier, the renowned French journalist, has summarised this will to live in a nutshell:

> [Persia] ...a country old like the world, but constantly rejuvenated, and which, above all, is certain of living. When one has dominated the Greek conqueror, triumphed over Roman power, assimilated the victorious Arabs, survived the Mongol invasion, frustrated the Ottoman empire, and, a case almost unique in contemporary history, regained a province occupied by the Red Army, then, what can one fear from the future? The best argument in favour of this country's survival is that it could have existed up to this day...[6]

Today, towards the close of the twentieth century, Iran still ranks amongst the richest of the poor nations of the world. But, in order to sustain the livelihood of its rapidly increasing population, it relies heavily on exports of its crude oil. On the other hand, the support of its domestic currency is almost entirely secured by the famous treasure brought back from Delhi by the great Nadir Shah in 1739.

The present work is about the modern history of Persia. It begins with the folding of the Safavi dynasty and the rise to power of Nadir Shah Afshar, the last Persian king to have realised his dreams; and ends with the Islamic Revolution of 1978–1979 – covering roughly the last two and a half centuries. Part descriptive and part analytical, it is primarily an attempt to explain how Persia got from there to here.

The main interest will be concentrated on the three major actors of the Persian socio-political stage:

1) Her people as they were, and as they gradually became involved in politics.

2) Her elites, with her sub-elites and counter-elites, and their undeniable influence on historical change.

3) The World Powers who played the Persian Game and helped shape her future – for better or worse.

This book is subdivided into seventeen chapters, in addition to this introduction and a conclusion at the close. In Chapter One, an attempt is made to set the stage and briefly introduce the above actors. Then the two hundred and fifty years of history proper are covered. Chapter Two begins with the demise of the Safavi dynasty and ends in 1848; Chapter Three spans the reign of Nasir ul-Din Shah; the fourth Chapter deals with the Constitutional Movement; Chapter Five covers the First World War and its aftermath up to the *coup d'état* of 1921; the next two decades (1920s and 1930s) are the subject of Chapters Six and Seven; Chapter Eight is about the Second World War; Chapter Nine, the turbulent second half of the 1940s and Chapter Ten about the oil nationalisation of 1951-53; Chapter Eleven encompasses the 1953-60 period; Chapters Twelve and Thirteen relate to Iran through the 1960s; and Chapters Fourteen, Fifteen and Sixteen cover the seventies up to 1977; finally, in Chapter Seventeen, an attempt at understanding the Islamic Revolution of 1978/79 is made. A conclusion sums up the work and draws relevant lessons.

To our knowledge an essay on such a scale has not been published hitherto. Some scholars of Iranian affairs are of the opinion that, since all the bricks of Iran's descriptive history are not yet in place, any attempt at interpretative history is premature.[7] Notwithstanding such caveats, a massive fresco of the land and her inhabitants in modern times has been undertaken. We shall let the reader be sole judge of its shortcomings.

NOTES

1. G.W.F. Hegel, *The Philosophy of History* (New York: Dover Publications, 1956) p.173.
2. Ibid.

3. C.R. Markham, *A General Sketch of the History of Persia* (London: Longmans, Green and Co., 1874) p.V.
4. Sir Percy Sykes, *A History of Persia* (London: Macmillan, 3rd ed., 1951) Vol. II, p.367.
5. N. Baillif, *La Perse Millenaire* (Paris: B. Arthaud, 1958) p.9.
6. See introduction by Edouard Sablier in Inge Morath, *De la Perse a l'Iran* (Zurich: R. Delpire, 1958) p.5.
7. Nevertheless see the remarkable paper by P. Avery, 'Iranian Balances', *Middle Eastern Studies*, Vol. 19, no. 4, October 1983, p.486.

CHAPTER ONE:
THE SETTING

Iran is a large country: a huge mass of land, bordered by the Caspian Sea in the north and the Persian Gulf in the south; an endless conglomeration of mountain chains (the Alburz and the Zagros), with high plateaux and deserts in between. Thus, several different types of climate. And to every climate a specific type of life. Hence, an extreme diversity in the genetics, the languages and the customs of her inhabitants.

Over the centuries, this amalgam was hammered into a pseudo-unity. Due to these historical and cultural ties, a nation state eventually emerged. Nature and time have endowed Persia and its people with a set of unique characteristics. Persians are the result of a myriad of rich and varied experiences, and proud to be what they are. On this subject, R.G. Watson concluded that:

> He [the Persian] yet thinks in his heart that there is no land in the world at all comparable to the land of Persia...[1]

Indeed, he does. In retrospect, he sees his roots in centuries of sacrifice and survival; for him, as for his forefathers, sacrifice is a science and survival an art.

1.1. The People

Fundamentally, the Persian is an individualist. Only if compelled by circumstances will he deign to unite with some of his countrymen to form a homogeneous entity. Unfortunately for him, as soon as the unifying constraint subsides, a return to heterogeneity is the rule. The law of self-preservation, however, always overrules his narrow (but cherished) tendency towards individualism. That is why the sum of a number of Persians is always less than its parts. Only on special occasions do they forget their perennial Achilles' heel and work together towards a common goal: then they are unstoppable.

The common Persian is also highly flexible. History has genetically provided him with an unparalleled adaptability. He yields when necessary, but dominates forcefully when circumstances are in his favour; always seeking to optimise his gains according to the situation. He has learned to defer to superior authority (a deep-rooted cultural trait), biding his time for better days. Only a simpleton would take his apparent subservience at face value. As Prince Mosteazem Mirza, Countess von Rosen's hero, said:

> There is one thing the Persian absolutely refuses to do, and that is to drive in harness. He wriggles out sooner or later, but never with force...[2]

Furthermore, Persians tend to be extremists. As Arminius Vambery remarked:

> Persia is in fact that country in Asia which most clearly shows its Oriental character by representing the most opposite extremes...[3]

The Iranian easily passes from one exaggeration to the other. He is as capable of the best as of the worst; passing from one state to the other at the flick of an eye. Always ready to secure an advantage with his famous deceptions, he is also capable of agreeing wholeheartedly to some sacrifice. He can alter his spots at will, depending on his immediate environment – a real social chameleon.

The large majority of Persians are immensely gifted: "...a vivacious, intelligent people", Lady Shiel noted.[4] Furthermore, the nineteenth-century missionary, Rev. S.G. Wilson, was of the opinion that:

> Nor is the backward state of Persia due to any intellectual feebleness. The Persians have alert, active minds. ...[They] are a people clever and intelligent and more calculated to become great and powerful than any other nations of the East...[5]

Persians have a peculiar sense of humour. They can laugh at a serious matter and take to heart comic situations. For a layman, this approach can become highly confusing; but for the native it is a formidable weapon for ridiculing foes and mentally diminishing annoying matters.

Persians also happen to have a remarkable memory. They are good at remembering both positive and negative impressions. Once imprinted in their minds, pleasant as well as unpleasant memories are seldom forgotten. "Memories are long in Persia" correctly noted British Ambassador Sir Denis Wright.[6] Any ill encounter can become a dangerous time-bomb for its originator. Scores of foreigners have experienced, some with indescribable surprise, the results of delayed Persian reactions. Moreover, it should be pointed out that Persians, on top of their individual memories, rely on a formidable collective memory. Naturally, this latter type of memory is not only deeper but also much wider than the individual one.

The average Persian has a multi-layered personality, the crust of which is easily analysed. The core, however, is an intricate labyrinth of conflicting and overlapping mental characteristics, prone to effervescence. But, amidst this magma of preconceived ideas and shifting principles, there is a set of well-defined limits. The late Sir Reader Bullard, a subtle analyst of Persian mentality, correctly recognised one of these limitations, for he wrote:

> ...it struck on that part of patriotic resistance in the character of the Persian which surprises only those who judge him by his usual patience and indifference...[7]

In general, Persians do have a marked penchant for anarchy and they are, therefore, very difficult to govern. Shah Abbas the Great is supposed to have said that "Governing Persians is not only impossible, it is unnatural".

In his heart of hearts, though, the Persian is a fatalist. He believes in fate (*qismat* or *sarnivisht*) and in the supernatural. Vambery was quick in noting that:

> The Oriental is right, after all, in saying that Fate has her caprices, and it is childish to battle against them...[8]

In the land of Shi'ism and the twelve imams, the large majority of the people still believe that "We choose and God decides".

If, on the other hand, Persians have weaknesses, one of them is vanity – which, according to the father of the unforgettable Hajji Baba, James Morier, "is their most vulnerable point".[9] A few other negative aspects of their personality were enumerated by no less a person than Lord Curzon, in his final portrait of the Persian:

> ...light-hearted, nimble-witted, and volatile, but subtle, hypocritical and insincere...[10]

After the above qualitative schematisation, a quantitative note seems called for, especially because during the last two centuries Iran's population passed through different patterns of growth and multiplied by a factor of ten (see Table 1.1). The dramatic increase during the twentieth century was to have dramatic consequences on all aspects of Persian life and would play havoc with the "sense of group responsibility stemming from the corporate nature of Iranian life".[27]

But in the first half of the eighteenth century Persia was still a very underpopulated country, with fewer than three inhabitants per square kilometre. Just a few towns like Isfahan, Shiraz, Tabriz and Mashhad existed, with the majority of the population in small villages and nomadic tribesmen in their black tents. Agglomerations of people were separated by vast expanses of desolate land. Epidemics of cholera and plague struck regularly, with devastating effects upon a defenceless population.

Because of the poor quality of the kingdom's roads and tracks, travelling was only available to the very rich; ordinary folk could ill-afford to displace themselves. Suffice it to add that in the final days of the Safavi dynasty, Persians were still living as they had when the dynasty came to power.

1.2. The Elites

"In all societies, two class of people appear – a class that rules and a class that is ruled",[28] wrote Gaetano Mosca, the renowned Italian sociologist and one of the fathers of the modern elite theory.[29] Mosca further defined the class that ruled as the political class and went on to

Table 1.1. The population of Iran during the 19th and 20th centuries

Year	Number of inhabitants	Reference
1806	6,562,000	Jaubert[11]
1812	5,000,000	Drouville[12]
1838	6,000,000	Aucher-Eloy[13]
1839	5,000,000	de Sercy[14]
1866	5–10,000,000	Watson[15]
1868	5,000,000	Thomson[16]
1874	4–10,000,000	Markham[17]
1884	7,654,000	Houtum-Schindler[18]
1888	6,000,000	Zolotarev[18]
1891	9,000,000	Lord Curzon[18]
1894	7,500,000	Lebrun-Renaud[19]
1905	9,000,000	Anet[20]
1909	10,000,000	Medvedev[18]
1910	10,000,000	Berard[21]
1937	15,000,000	Furon[22]
1943	15,000,000	Vieille[23]
1956	18,954,704	1st nat. census[24]
1966	25,788,722	2nd nat. census[24]
1976	33,708,744	3rd nat. census[25]
1986	49,764,874	4th nat. census[26]
1992	60,000,000	author's estimate
1994	64,000,000	author's estimate

call it the elite. Yet another Italian sociologist, Vilfredo Pareto, took the theory a step farther. He proposed to subdivide "the higher stratum of society, the elite... [into] a governing elite and a non-governing elite".[30]

It is clear though that the two Italian sociologists agreed on the fundamental point that there is an elite in any society. Their respective analysis diverged, however, over the questions of counter-elites, circulation within the elite, and the homogeneity or heterogeneity of elites. Furthermore, their terminology and definitions were somewhat dissimilar. Thus, in order to clarify the subject, the following set of definitions – based on the works of Mosca and Pareto, and also on those of Professor Aron[31] and Bottomore[32] – are proposed here:

a) 'political class': the sum of those groups which exercise power or influence, while having competing interests. This class can further be sub-divided into a 'political elite' and a number of 'counter-elites'.

b) 'political elite': a smaller group within the 'political class' which comprises those individuals who actually wield the power in a society. This body is then split into two subdivisions: (i) a 'governing elite' – i.e. those members engaged in the decision-making process; and (ii) a 'non-governing elite' – i.e. members who do not directly control levers of power, but have an indirect influence over the polity.

c) 'counter-elites': groups within the 'political class' made up of leaders of political parties (or organisations), of representatives of new social interests, or even of intellectuals active in politics. These groups "may be engaged in varying degrees of co-operation, competition or conflict" with the 'political elite'.

d) 'sub-elites': bodies created by the elite to form a buffer between it and the masses.

The whole elite theory seems to fit Iranian society like a glove. As Marvin Zonis, an expert on the subject, put it:

> Persian society, then as now, was viewed as a progression of ranks, the members of each possessing successively more authority than the ranks below. While all societies can be viewed as a hierarchy of ranks, few people have been as consistent as the Persians in delineating and identifying intrasocial ranks or broad social classes or in having those perceptions of the social structure remain so constant over time...[33]

In Persia, the political elite was to be known under many different names: the aristocracy, the ruling class, the grandees, the Ruling Few,[34] the 'thousand families'[35] or even 'the Gang', an appellation conjured by the British Foreign Office.[36] However, and whatever its name, there is little doubt that there always was, in Iran, "a functional group of superior individuals with a high status in society",[37] which was nothing else than the Persian political elite.

In the course of Persian history, two very distinct types of elite members are encountered: 1) the lineage elitists, and 2) the exceptional individuals.

The first type of elite individual is part of a family tradition. At the outset, the familial line must have begun its ascent from some power base: either a tribe, a provincial centre or the royal court. It also must have had an initiator of uncommon talent. With time, the elite family gradually put down roots in its home ground. The roots' depth depended upon the family's personalities and characteristics. In order to fortify these roots, there were four major strategies the families usually followed. (i) The first and foremost strategy was to embark upon matrimonial links, as there is no stronger bond (for the Persian) than that of blood. On this subject, James Bill observed that:

> The power of national elite families has been considerably buttressed and expanded by inter-marriage...[38]

He also added that "families' bonds tended to be dyadic" and mentioned some unsociable pairings, such as, among many others, Adl/Panahi, Afkhami/Zulfaqari and Bihzadi/Kya. (ii) Unwritten alliances between families. Given the fickleness of the Persian character, these were usually short-lived and easily destroyed by the slightest wind of change in the socio-political environment. Paraphrasing Pareto, one could write that "Iran's history is a graveyard of broken family alliances". (iii) Allegiances of one family to another. Such contracts proved to be far more resilient than alliances. They even came to play such an important role that Iranian society could have become a model for Edmund Burke: "Society is indeed a contract... it becomes a partnership not only between those who are living, but between those who are living, those who are dead, and those who are to be born";[37] and, finally (iv) the use of financial clout to buy subservience. Monetary hand-outs are definitely useful at times, but not without their drawbacks as some just took the money and ran, or simply upped the ante at every opportunity. And however effective in the short term, the effect of money tends to diminish with time.

Having put down strong roots in its base by employing a mix of the above strategies, the elite family could then try to bid for a slot on the national stage. The quantum leap from the lower to the higher league was never easy, but repeated efforts were bound to be crowned with success. Once a foothold was secured within the national elite, the fortunate family could play on both levels, using the one to bolster the other and vice versa. Having made it nationally, a family would be deemed careless if it forgot its initial springboard. The select group of surviving national families are those who have, rain or sunshine, carefully tended their local roots.

If, however, Persian society did indeed fit so well the Mosca-Pareto elitist mould, it was mostly for historical reasons. The formation of Persia's four major sources of elites took place over centuries of history:

1) the institution of kingship and its court elite;
2) the highly stratified society of the nomadic tribes;
3) the strict hierarchy of the *Shiî* religious hierocracy;
4) the multi-layered structure of the *darvish* sects.

The background of each of the above groups will be succinctly reviewed hereunder.

(1) The Court Elite

The origin of the institution of kingship is lost in time immemorial. Karl Mannheim suggested that it must have had some "magic origin" and that "no person... can exert authority without being regarded as made of 'higher stuff' than the run of humanity".[40] Undoubtedly, dynasty founders must have had some exceptional qualities which helped them eventually make it to the top of the heap. Many of their descendants, though, were not as exceptionally gifted. Those kings made of the 'lower stuff' simply based their legitimacy on tradition and inheritance.

In Persia (as, for example, in France) a religious title was added early in the nineteenth century to the regal panoply: the *mujtahid* Mirza Abu'l-Qasim Qumi formulated the expression of 'Shadow of God on Earth' to designate the shah.[41] With or without title, it was clear that up to the Constitution of 1906 the Shah of Persia was "the State".[42] He monopolised all the powers of government – the executive, the legislative as well as the judicial. The shah's word was an order: it had to be obeyed. His was the right of life and death over every soul in his realm. Every fortune or position was at the mercy of his will and whims. Persian kingship was an archetype of the absolute monarchy.

But even within this frame of one-man rule, the shah needed a group of individuals to conduct the affairs of State, hence the inevitable formation of a national elite. The members of this elite were chosen by the shah from among (i) the princes of blood, (ii) the courtiers and court servants, or (iii) the Persian aristocracy. The highest and most sought-after position was that of *sadr-i âzam* (the chief minister); then, down the royal pecking-order came the *vuzara* (the ministers), the provincial *valis* (the governors) and the *mustoufis* (the chief revenue officers); at the court there was the head of the royal kitchen (*abdarbashi*) and the head of the royal stables, alongside a number of *munshis* (secretaries), of *sanduqdars* (clerks) and a few other lesser functions of the royal household down to the *khajehs* (eunuchs) of the royal harem. Besides these positions, there also were a number of *safirs* (ambassadors) and *amirs* (military commanders).

The struggle for that restricted number of positions was fought daily at court, with the shah as sole and ultimate arbiter. It was only natural that every courtier endeavoured to seek the king's favours. But, over and above personal rivalries, a much wider (and subtler) contest pitted the princes of blood against the traditional national aristocracy. On the sidelines of this formidable contest stood the courtiers; the members of this elite group catered to either side, always ready to change sides in accordance with the shah's changing moods. Seldom did a simple courtier succeed in dominating both the princes and the aristocracy at the same time, but in exceptional cases it proved possible.

The royal princes, by virtue of their lineage, insisted on being assigned major roles in the running of the country. They were usually offered more than they deserved, notwithstanding the apprehensions (carefully) voiced by the nobility. The more gifted princes (and those nearer to the shah's heart) were granted either high court functions or rich governorships. The crown prince (*valiâhd*) automatically received the governorship of the kingdom's richest province (either Fars or Azarbayjan). In consequence, the Persian nobility had to be content with the leftovers. For the realm's grandees the name of the game was survival. But while they bided their time, trying their very best not to fall into disgrace, they kept the princes under close watch, hoping for a blunder on their part or any other kind of opportunity to replace one of them with one of their own. The perceptive C.R. Markham recognised the nobility's predicament:

> The government of Persia being a pure despotism, and the highest nobles being liable, at the caprice of the sovereign to be put to death, robbed or even beaten, few fine qualities can be expected from a Persian Courtier and the throne is surrounded by fulsome flattery. Yet the nobles of Iran... have inherited their [ancestors'] talent and brilliant imaginations[43]... The Persian nobles are very handsome, hospitable and highly polished in their manners; but deceitful and haughty. Their bad qualities, however, are the fault of the wretched government under which they live...[44]

It was against such a background that the Persian nobles were shaped during the time of absolute monarchy. The constant court tension kept them continuously on their toes: by necessity they had to be alert, vigilant and flexible. Competition was fierce and rivalries merciless. In the relentless race for power, dice were loaded and rules broken. Adaptability and shrewdness were necessary to overcome the court's incessant whirlwind of intrigues. Sloth and apathy were synonymous with downfall and ruin. A tough environment, but also an incomparable stimulus for the strengthening of the arteries.

(2) The Tribal Elites

Tribes always were an important part of Persia; arguably, the "hard, central core of the Nation".[45] On this matter, Lady Sheil wrote: "Persia is overrun by tribes",[46] and R.G. Watson added "...a very great proportion of Persia is composed of wandering tribes".[47] In 1880, General Houtum-Schindler estimated that approximately "one quarter of Persia's population consists of nomads".[48] A sizeable minority.

In Persia, four large tribes dominated the nomadic ensemble. These were, from the north-west to the south-east of the Zagros mountain chain: the Kurds, the Lurs, the Bakhtiaris and the Qasqa'is.

These four tribal confederations, each consisting of tens of thousands of families, evolved over time a highly structured hierarchisation of their respective societies. It seems that the idiosyncratic features common to this type of life – dominated as it is by the yearly migrations from the winter grounds (*qishlaq*) to the summer ones (*yaylaq*) and vice versa – eventually led to the same general type of internal organisation within each tribal entity.

This common structure seems to be a natural necessity of tribalism, in order to "organise and control, in time and space, the occupancy of a limited territory by a large tribal population".[49]

The hierarchical pyramid that eventually crystallised within the tribes came to be dominated by an elite: the *khans*. All of the *khans* belonged to a single family, which had branched out over time to accommodate the geometric progression of successive generations. The founding member of that elite family must have been made of the 'higher stuff'; later, his sons and grandsons must have consolidated his legacy in such a way as to discourage any internal rebellion against their rule. In any case, the founder's work must have had a solid base, because in most instances the *khans*' family were able to rule for several centuries. For example, the Qasqa'i ruling family was established by Amir Qazi Shahlou Qasqa'i in the early seventeenth century; and the Bakhtiari dynasty was initiated by Haydar (nicknamed *kour*, the one-eyed), the son of a Lur leader who had left his own tribe to take refuge in the Bakhtiari territory, at around the same time as the Qasqa'is. Each of these families was still ruling in the second half of the twentieth century.

Every tribal elite had a supreme leader, chosen from among the *khans*: the *ilkhan* (i.e. the *khan* of the whole tribal confederation, the *il*).[50] There was no clear-cut process for the *ilkhan*'s selection and many different factors (tangible as well as intangible ones) influenced the appointment of this chief of chiefs. Suffice it to say that the seniority, wealth, personality and experience of the candidates were of paramount importance. Furthermore, outside sources such as the royal court had some leverage over the final choice. The function being neither hereditary nor for life, changes at the top were frequent; it was even possible for a single individual *khan* to assume the supreme role more than once in his lifetime, but it took an exceptional *khan* to remain *ilkhan* until his death. In most tribes, the *ilkhan* was seconded by an *ilbeg* – a right-hand man, a lieutenant and a shadow-

ilkhan all in one. In each tribe headed by such an inequable partnership, the latter function originated due to special historical precedents within the tribe in question.

A typical Persian tribe is made up of a confederation of *babs* (sub-tribes). The *bab* was further subdivided into *tayifehs* (clans), in which resided the real administrative power of the tribe. Then the *tayifeh* was segmented into a number of *tirehs* (sub-clans) and into *tashs* (groups) which, finally, were made up of *khanevars* (families), the basic building block of the tribe. However, some tribes (especially the smaller ones) did without some of the above subdivisions and a direct incorporation of families into *tayifehs* was possible. The hierarchical structure of command within the tribe derived directly from its organisational constitution. Or in other words, the second layer of the tribe's elite, below the *khans*, was formed by the heads of the tribal *tayifehs*, the *kalantars*. The *kalantars* wielded considerable power because they managed the day-to-day tribal affairs. They represented a typical case of a responsible and functional sub-elite. Their tenure was hereditary, barring exceptional events. They definitely had an implicit role in the selection of an *ilkhan* and acted as divisional commanders in case of war. Leading *kalantars* were wealthier and more powerful than many a lesser *khan*; but a *khan*, even destitute, was a *khan*, and a *kalantar*, however rich, just a *kalantar*.[51] Below the *kalantars* came the *kadkhudas*, the heads of the *tirehs* (or sometimes even heads of *tashs*). A number of *kadkhudas* reported to a single *kalantar*. Here again, the function was hereditary. Moreover, a deserving *kadkhuda* could hope to be promoted to *kalantar* rank. Completing the sub-elite, at either the *tireh* or the *tash* level, were the community elders or *rish-sifids* (lit. the 'white beards'). These elders were a real symbol of the tribal society's respect for seniority and seconded the *kadkudas* in tasks calling for traditional authority: a tribal precursor to the Western ombudsman.

In every tribal society, seniority rule is sacrosanct. As long as the old order thrives, the rule provides for continuity in tribal affairs. In times of transition, however, this rule always leads to catastrophe. "The value of tradition" goes the adage "is knowing when to break with it"; but it is easier said than done, for there is nothing as difficult to break with as centuries-old habits and ingrained reflexes. In the face of change, seniority rule is one of the major reasons behind the sudden collapse of tribal societies: tradition is of such paramount importance in the leaders' minds that they come to cherish it more than their own (and their tribe's) survival. And, if all societies are somehow wedded to their past, tribal ones are doubly so. Persian tribal elites were certainly no exception to these general rules and, in due time, they would also uphold seniority rule all the way to the abyss.

(3) The *Shiî* Religious Hierocracy

Every religious community usually develops a well-defined hierarchy. The Persian Shi'ite community was no exception to the rule as it developed its own idiosyncratic hierocracy: the rule of the *ûlama* (lit. 'the learned ones'). Within the *ûlama* ranks, one could find the *fuqaha* (specialists in Shi'ite jurisprudence) and the *mujtahids* (religious scholars who had received permission (*ijazeh*) to issue opinions on matter of faith). The *mujtahid* was "a religious expert having achieved the highest level possible in religious affairs"[52] because he was able to interpret the primary sources – i.e. the Holy *Quran* and the numerous *Hadis* (i.e. the reported sayings of the Prophet (S.) and the Imams (A.S.)[53]).

However, the rule of the *ûlama* took time to crystallise. Back in the fifteenth century, a religious scholar, Mulla Amin Astarabadi,[54] developed the *Akhbari* tradition which "rejected the *mujtahid*'s function as leader of the community as incompatible with the authority of the Imams".[55] Astarabadi held the view that each individual Shiî faithful should decide for himself the correct path to follow in religious matters. The *Akhbari* tradition was to be the dominating influence in the *shiî* community for almost four centuries – although religious leaders held positions of influence at the Safavis' court.

It was only towards the close of the eighteenth century that a leading Karbila scholar, Aqa Muhammad (Vahid) Bihbahani (1705-1803), a descendant on his mother's side of the renowned scholar Majlisi the Second,[56] launched a movement in direct contradiction of the *Akhbari* tradition. Bihbahani held that the masses could not, by themselves, interpret religious precepts and that, thus, they needed learned leaders (i.e. the *ûlama*) to guide them in these matters. His movement – which came to be known as the *Usuli* movement – clashed head-on with the *Akhbari* tradition. The ensuing struggle over the fundamental question of leadership ended with the total victory of the *Usulis*. The *Usulis*' triumph was also the *ûlama*'s: after centuries in the desert, they were back at the top. On the other hand, the *Akhbaris*' decline was irreversible: their movement would eventually branch out to give birth to Baha'ism and Shaykism, but would thereafter constantly fail to threaten the *ûlama's* firm grip over the minds of the *shiî* community. The logic behind the *Usulis*' preponderance was later underlined by a leading *mujtahid* thus:

> The reference of the ignorant to the learned one is a natural thing, and without it, society's order would be seriously perturbed...[57]

But also bolstering the *Usuli* tradition was the long and distinguished trail of *shiî* scholars, blazed in the tenth century by Abu'l Qasim Jâfar bin Muhammad bin Musa bin Qulivayeh Qumi Baghdadi (d. 978/9). Every passing century was to bring a few new lights to the *Shiî* scholastic firmament – with, among others, Shaykh Saduq (d. 999), Shaykh Mufid (d. 1022) and Shaykh Tusi (d. 1067). At any given time, the total number of superior *shiî* scholars never exceeded a dozen. Even during the nineteenth century, the *ûlama*'s membership remained restricted: a maximum of sixteen were registered, with nine residing in Persia and seven at the *Âtabat* (a name used to designate the region of the holy shrines of Najaf and Karbila).[58] By then, the *ûlama's* leadership had become an indisputable fact; and, furthermore, a scholar of genius, Shaykh Murtiza Ansari (d. 1865) – later to be known as the *Khatim ul-mujtahid*, the last of the *mujtahid* – was to take on Bihbahani's pioneering work and solidly fasten the last bolts of the *ûlama's* pedestal.

Thus was a *shiî* elite born. It possessed all the prerequisites to remain a superior group: (i) limited membership, (ii) excellence, and (iii) homogeneity through knowledge. Contrary to the court and tribal elites, it was not hereditary; and, although some familial patterns did eventually emerge (such as the Tabataba'is and the Bihbahanis), these were the exception rather than the rule. All in all, the hierocracy's meritocratic selection system, based as it was on scholarly excellence, was particularly well suited to protect the religious elite against degeneration – the ill that afflicts, sooner or later, all hereditary elites.

With time, in Persia, the *shiî* hierocracy was to become formally structured with the *Ayatullahs* (lit. 'sign of God') at the top, the *Hujjat ul-Islams* (proof of Islam) in the middle and the *talabehs* (the students in religious affairs) at the nadir.

(4) The *Darvish* Sects

A *darvish* is, by definition, 'a seeker of the way to God'. He also is a strict follower of Imam Âli (A.S.), the first of the twelve *shiî* imams, whom he believes to be 'The King of Both Worlds' (i.e. the worlds of the living and of the dead).

Like his venerated model, a *darvish* will try to shun worldly goods and pleasures, and will concentrate on purifying his 'self' (*nafs*).

Darvishes usually congregate in sects – although some independent *darvishes* are to be found. The sects gather in common, unprepossessing buildings (the opposite of mosques and churches) known as *khaniqas*. In Persia, the number of *darvish* sects was always rather limited and the number of *darvishes* in each sect never very large. However, they made up in quality what they lacked in quantity, so that, although a small minority within the Persian *shiî âmma*, it always represented a group to be reckoned with.

The *darvish* sects, like most religious congregations, have a strict hierarchy. Every sect has a single leader, the *Pir*, who rules for life. His orders (*nafas*) are binding for every member of his sect. Before his death (and any *Pir* should at least know exactly when he is to pass away) he will designate a successor. Thus, succeeding *Pirs* form a chain; hence the name of *silsileh* (lit. 'chain') to designate the Persian *darvish* sects. The longest *silsilehs* are known to stretch back to over sixty *Pirs*, all the way to the very first years of Islam.

The structural layer under the *Pir* is formed by the *Shayks*. Every *Shayk* is chosen by the *Pir* from among the *darvishes*' ranks. The senior *Shayk*, the *Shayk ul-Mashayikh* (or Shayk of Shayks), is second only to the *Pir* and is supposed to officiate in his stead in case of protracted absence. A *Pir* usually has no more than a dozen *Shayks* and, for every *Shayk* there are between one to two dozen *darvishes*. As the stress is on individual quality, recruitment is always naturally limited.

A *darvish*-inspired dynasty came to power in Persia when the Safavis ruled from 1501 until 1736.[59] The forerunner of the dynasty, Shaykh Safi ul-Din Ardibili, was a *Shaykh* (and the son-in-law) of that great thirteenth-century *Pir*, Shaykh Zahid Gilani (d. 1301).[60] Among other famous *Pirs* and prominent *darvishes* in Persian *Sufi* history worth mentioning are: Mansur Hallaj, Bayazid Bastami, Shaykh Kharaqani, Shams Tabrizi, Abu Saîd Abu'l Khayr, Najm ul-Din Kubra,[61] Junayd Baghdadi and Shaykh Suhrehvardi. During the twentieth century, Persian *darvish*-dom came to be dominated by yet another exceptional *Pir*: Hajj Âli Muhammad Mutahhar Âli Shah (1876–1983), the *Hazrat-i Darvish* of the Khaksar Jalaliyyeh *silsileh*, arguably one of the most extraordinary personalities of his epoch.

1.3. The World Powers

After the Arab, Turk and Mongol invasions, Persia had been left to lick its wounds without interference from World Powers. Then, at the onset of the Safavi dynasty's rule, a new threat was to come from the neighbouring Ottoman Empire, viz. the defeat suffered by the Persians at Chaldiran in 1515. But the Turkish invaders were eventually held in check by the loyal and exalted Safavi forces.

Far more ominous for Persian security were the forays of European explorers in the Indian Ocean. Since Bartolomeu Diaz had discovered a way around the Cape of Good Hope in 1486, Portuguese ships had sailed eastwards to find a route to India. Along the way, Portuguese captains had settled in Muscat (1507) and taken, after repeated attacks, the small island of Hurmuz, the choke point of the Persian Gulf. The conqueror of Hurmuz and future viceroy of the Indies (1509–1515), the great captain Affonso d'Albuquerque (d. 1515), ordered a fort and an entrepôt to be built on the island. The Portuguese also created settlements in Bahrayn and Ras ul-Khaymeh.

If the Portuguese came from the south, other European traders came in from the north. First among them were the British. In 1561, Anthony Jenkinson of the Muscovy Company (a company created at London in 1555) opened the way to the Persian market. Jenkinson's pioneering efforts paid off, as they led to the obtaining, for his company, of two royal *farmans* (decrees) sealed by the Safavi king, Shah Tahmasp (1524–1576). The first *farman*, delivered in 1566, spelled out commercial privileges for British merchants in Persia; the second *farman* (1568) added freedom of transit, as well as exemption from local customs and tolls for British traders.[62] It was on these promises that the Muscovy Company launched six trading expeditions to Persia via Russia (1562-1581). However, the hardships of such forays must have outweighed the resulting benefits, for thereafter the company discontinued its Persian ventures.

By the close of the century, yet another British group found its way to Persia. Sent by the Earl of Essex, two soldiers of fortune, the brothers Anthony and Robert Sherley, arrived at Shah Âbbas's court at Qazvin (1598), leading a troop of twenty-six Englishmen.[63] The Sherleys, acting as technical advisers, first attempted to reorganise the Persian Army. Through their gallant efforts, they soon gained the Shah's confidence. In 1600, Anthony was sent to the European courts as an Extraordinary Ambassador; and, although he carried a royal *farman* guaranteeing all Europeans extra territorial rights, his mission ended in failure. His brother Robert, however, met with more success in a similar effort undertaken in 1608/09. Robert's mission paved the way for the British East India Company[64] in Persia: in 1616 the company – through its representatives Steel and Crouther – received a *farman* from Shah Âbbas allowing it to set up factories (i.e. trading stations) at Gomroon (later on Bar Âbbas), Shiraz and Isfahan.

At that juncture, Shah Âbbas's aim of expelling the Portuguese from their Persian Gulf strongholds came to dovetail nicely with the East India Company's fortunes in the region. The Persians had already succeeded in driving the Portuguese out of Bahrayn in 1602. Then, in 1619/20, they displaced the Portuguese from Ras ul-Khaymeh. Finally, the Persian Army joined forces with the British to reconquer first the island of Qishm (January 1622) and then the island of Hurmuz by besieging the Portuguese fort, which eventually surrendered on April 23, 1622.[65] For the Portuguese it was the beginning of the end in the Gulf (they would eventually have to surrender their last station at Muscat in 1650); they had only themselves to blame (or rather their greed and ruthlessness) for having given away such a golden opportunity to dominate the Persian Gulf. On the other hand, for the British, it was only the beginning of a long and eventful adventure, that would lead to a long era of paramountcy in the Gulf and the 'Pax Brittanica'. Perhaps the knack the British had of keeping their possessions was due to their leaders' sense of mission and to their envoys' sense of diplomacy; their credo was best summed up by Lord Curzon of Kedleston:

> The Message is carved in granite, it is hewn out of the Rock of Doom, that our work is righteous and that it shall prevail.

As the Portuguese departed, the Dutch moved in with their own East India Company – the Vereenigde Oostindische Compagnie created at Amsterdam in 1595. The Dutch newcomers were soon to gain a position of commercial supremacy in Persia. In November 1623, the Dutch East India Co. was granted a *farman* which included in its twenty-three clauses all the privileges accorded its British counterpart.[66] The Dutch duly reciprocated by granting Persian merchants similar advantages in Holland, including extra territoriality, in a decree dated February 1631. The Dutch company would retain a toehold at the Kharaq (today, Kharg) Island until 1766.

The French too had decided to enter the Persian fray with their own East India Company – La Compagnie des Indes Orientales – established in 1664. Even though it had obtained two *farmans* (dated 1665 and 1671) similar to the ones granted to the British and the Dutch, its Persian venture ended in a fiasco. Even the mission of Ambassador Louis Michel to the court of Shah Sultan Husayn in 1708 failed to revive the French fortunes. As a result, the French company was the first to depart in the 1720s. The Dutch company followed suit after its loss of Kharaq Island in 1759; and the British East India was the last to leave Persia in March 1763 (after the French had, in 1759, destroyed their factory at Gomroon). Thus came to a close the commercial chapter of the East Indian companies in Persia.

At the dawn of the eighteenth century, yet another budding world power entered the Persian stage: Russia. Rejuvenated by Peter the Great's reforms and after regaining its self-confidence following its victory over the Swedes, the Russian Army dared to advance all the way down to Persia's Gilan province, which it easily conquered in 1723. After Peter's death in 1725, his next-but-two successor, Empress Anna, deemed it wiser to retreat and sign a treaty of amity, the Treaty of Rasht, with Persia in 1732. This pull-out was but a tactical move, a case of *reculer pour mieux sauter*, for it was clear since Peter's days that Russia's ambitions regarding Persia were one of the pillars of her global strategy of world domination. In this respect, Peter's will is self-explanatory – especially clause IX which reads:

>To approach as near as possible to Constantinople and India. Whoever governs there will be the true sovereign of the World. Consequently excite continual wars, not only in Turkey, but in Persia... And in the decadence of Persia, penetrate as far as the Persian Gulf, re-establish if it be possible the ancient commerce with the Levant, advance as far as India, which is the depot of the world...[67]

With the Russians readying themselves for an expansionist drive in the north and the British well-established in India and the Persian Gulf, the stage was set for the entry of Persia in the game of World Powers. The main rules of that game, as succinctly defined by scholar R.J. Barnet, are as follows:

>All great nations play the Game. There are only two principal rules. The first is that no rival nation or combination of rivals can be allowed to become powerful enough to threaten your own power. This is the time-honoured principle of balance of power. The second rule is that all the world is the playing field. To keep the game going you must be prepared to be flexible about your enemies, being prepared to change them when the game so requires. The 'name of the game' is to avoid losing 'influence' and if possible to gain more. It is much less clear what you do with the influence once you get it... But that hardly matters for the game cannot be justified in rational terms...[68]

Further enhancing the likelihood of an increase in the World Powers' activities in Persia was the Safavi dynasty's steep decline in the early decades of the eighteenth century. Under the rule of Shah Sultan Husayn (crowned shah in 1694), it had become clear that the ruling dynasty was terminally ill. Historian Lockhart made no mistake:

>As Shah Sultan Husayn became Shah... the doom of the Safavi dynasty was sealed...[69]

Still, only a single century separated the enlightened reign of Shah Âbbas the Great from that of his great-great-great-grandson; but even the strongly rooted Safavi dynasty could not survive the successive reign of two weak shahs.[70] It is, however, a proof of that dynasty's resilience that Shah Sultan Husayn reigned for some twenty-eight years before being brought down – and the Safavi dynasty with him.

NOTES

1. R.G. Watson, *A History of Persia* (London: Smith, Elder and Co., 1866) p.5.
2. Countess M. von Rosen, *Persian Pilgrimage* (London: Robert Hale Ltd., 1937) p.49.
3. A. Vambery, *His Life and Adventures* (New York: Arno Press, 1973) p.291.
4. Lady Shiel, *Glimpses of Life and Manners in Persia* (New York: Arno Press, 1973) as a reprint of the edition by John Murray, London (1856) p.89.
5. The Rev. S.G. Wilson, *Persian Life and Customs* (New York: Fleming H. Revell Co., 3d ed., 1900) p.167.
6. D. Wright, *The English amongst the Persians* (London: Heinemann, 1977) p. XV.
7. R. Bullard, *Britain and the Middle East* (London: Hutchinson University Library, 3rd ed., 1964) p.56.
8. A. Vambery, op. cit. (note 3), p.306.
9. J.J. Morier, *Hajji Baba in England*, p.VI.
10. G.N. Curzon, *Persia and the Persian Question*, (London: Frank Cass, 1892) Vol. I, p.496.
11. As cited in M.R. Fasha'i, *Takvin-i Sarmayehdari dar Iran (1796–1905)* (*The Creation of Capitalism in Iran*), (Tehran: Gutinbirg, A.H. 1360/1981) p.165.
12. G. Drouville, *Voyage en Perse fait en 1812 et 1813* (Paris: 2nd ed., 1825) p.50.
13. Aucher-Eloy, *Relation de voyage en Orient de 1830 à 1838* (Paris: 1842).
14. De Sercy, *Une Ambassade Extraordinaire* (Paris: 1840) p.140.
15. R.G. Watson, op. cit. (note 1), p.2.
16. Thomson, *La Perse, sa population, ses revenus, son armée, son commerce* (Paris: Bul. Soc. Geog., 5e série, Vol. XVIII, 1869).
17. C.R. Markham, *A General Sketch of the History of Persia* (The Netherlands: Kraus, 1877) as a reprint of the edition by Longmans and Green, London (1874) p.522.
18. G.N. Curzon, op. cit. (note 10), pp.491-494.
19. Lebrun-Renard, *La Perse politique et militaire du 19ème siècle* (Paris, 1894).
20. Cl. Anet, *La Perse en automobile* (Paris, 1905).
21. V. Berard, *Revolution de la Perse* (Paris, 1910).
22. Curon, *La Perse*
23. P. Vieille, *Teheran, le marche des terrains* (Paris, 1961).
24. *Iran Almanac 1978*, (Tehran: Echo of Iran, 1978) p.409.
25. *Iran dar A'yineh-yi Amar*, (Tehran: Markaz-i Amar-i Iran, 1363 (1984)) pp.8-9.

[26] See the results of the Fourth National Census of 1986; as published in the Bulletin of the *Markaz-i Amar-i Iran*, no.14, 3rd year, spring 1366 (1987).
[27] As quoted by M. Zonis, *The Political Elite of Iran* (Princeton University Press, 1971) p.334.
[28] In a letter to his friend Vettori, Machiavelli made use of the terms *nobile* and *ignobile* to denote these two classes without further dwelling on the subject.
[29] G. Mosca, *The Ruling Class* (New York: McGraw-Hill, 1939) p.50.
[30] V. Pareto, *The Mind and Society* (London: Jonathan Cape, 1935) Vol. III, pp.1423-4.
[31] R. Aron, 'Classe sociale, classe politique, classe dirigéante'; article published in the *European Journal of Sociology*, I (2), 1960.
[32] T.B. Bottomore, *Elites and Society* (Penguin Books, 1966) p.14.
[33] M. Zonis, op. cit. (note 27), p.119.
[34] C. Skrine, *World War in Iran* (London: Constable, 1962) p.XV.
[35] J.A. Bill, 'The Patterns of Elite Politics in Iran', in *Political Elites in the Middle East*, ed. by G. Lenczowski, (Washington D.C.: American Enterprise Institute for Public Policy Research, 1975) p.32.
[36] C. Skrine, op. cit. (note 34), p.XV.
[37] T.B. Bottomore, op. cit. (note 32), p.14.
[38] J.A. Bill, op. cit. (note 35), p.35.
[39] E. Burke, *Reflections on the Revolution in France* (Penguin Books, 1969) pp.194-5.
[40] K. Mannheim, *Essays on the Sociology of Culture* (London: Routledge and Kegan Paul, 1956) p.180.
[41] See S. Amir Arjomand, 'The Shi'ite Hierocracy and the State under the early Qajars', a paper presented at the Conference on State Society and Economy in Nineteenth-Century Iran and the Ottoman Empire (June 17-22, 1978) p.17. However, it should be noted that "the conception of the ruler as the Shadow of God on earth" was first made under the Âbbasids, later by Al-Ghazali and also by Nizam ul-Mulk in his *Syasat-nameh* (written in or after 1086-7), as mentioned in Professor A.K.S. Lambton's paper 'Concepts of Authority in Persia: Eleventh to Nineteenth Centuries A.D.', (IRAN, *Journal of the British Institute of Persian Studies*, Vol. XXVI, 1988, pp.95-103.)
[42] R.G. Watson, op. cit. (note 1), p.12.
[43] C.R. Markham, op. cit. (note 17), p.359.
[44] Ibid., p.360.
[45] W.O. Douglas, *Strange Lands and Friendly People* (New York: Harper and Brothers, 1951) p.55.
[46] Lady Shiel, op. cit. (note 4), p.393.
[47] R.G. Watson, op. cit. (note 1), p.6.
[48] G.N. Curzon, op. cit. (note 10), Vol. II, p.493.
[49] F. Barth, *Nomads of South Persia – the Basseri Tribe of the Khamseh Confederacy* (Oslo: Oslo Universitets Forlaget, 1964) p.76.
[50] J.P. Digard, 'Histoire et Anthropologie d'une tribu d'Iran', *Annales*, 28ème année, no. 6, Novembre-Décembre 1973, (Paris: Armand Colin) p.1427.
[51] It should be added that there was no intermarriage between the families of the *khans* and those of the *kalantars*. Only in the twentieth century would this unwritten rule be broken in exceptional cases.

52 M. Mutahhari, *Guftar-i Mah* (The Monthly Lecture), (Tehran: *Saduq*, 1340 (1961)) Vol. I, p.200.
53 Sayyid Mustafa Muhaqqiq Damad, *Usul-i Fiqheh*, (Qum: *Andisheh-ha-yi Nou dar Ûlum-i Islami*, 1341 (1962)) Vol. I, p.13.
54 M. Mutahhari, op. cit. (note 52), p.43.
55 H. Algar, *Religion and State in Iran – 1785-1906* (Berkeley: University of California Press, 1969) p.7.
56 S. Amir Arjomand, op. cit. (note 41), p.8.
57 Sayyid Abu'l Fazl Musavi Mujtahid Zanjani, *Bahsi dar bareh Marja^yat va Ruhanyat* (Tehran: *Shirkat-i Sahami Intishar*, 1341 (1962)) p.27.
58 S. Amir Arjomand, op. cit. (note 41), p.11.
59 As a matter of fact the Safavi dynasty lasted until the coronation of Nadir Shah Afshar in 1736; but in 1722, following the rout of the Persians by the Afghans, the dynasty had virtually ceased to rule.
60 When Changiz Khan, the Mongol leader, decided to destroy the thriving Persian city of Nayshabur, having heard of Najm ul-Din Kubra's great wisdom, he sent a special messenger to the septuagenarian *darvish* offering him a safe conduct to wherever he wished to settle, adding that he would be the only exception allowed. The old man told the messenger to thank Changiz for his generosity and to let him know that he couldn't leave his fellow citizens in this dire hour, "having lived amongst them for all his life", and that, "having shared with them his joys and sorrows, he preferred to share with them their last trial".
61 The name Zahid is his *darvish* name, given to him by his *Pir* Sayyid Jamal ul-Din Gili. His own name was Taj ul-Din Ibrahim. Shaykh Zahid is buried in an historical mausoleum located near the town of Lahijan in Gilan province.
62 J.C. Hurewitz, *Diplomacy in the Near and Middle East* (Princeton: D. Van Nostrand Co., 1956) Vol. I, pp.6-7.
63 See E. Denison Ross, *Sir Anthony Sherley and his Persian Adventure* (London: George Routledge and Sons, 1933).
64 The British East India Company was created in London in September 1599. Its initial capital of £68,873 was funded by two hundred and seventeen original subscribers. Its headquarters were located at Leadenhall Street. It was granted its first fifteen-year charter by Queen Elizabeth I in 1600 and thereafter went on to dominate India and the Persian Gulf for over two centuries until the Indian Mutiny of 1856/57, after which it was dissolved and the rule of India passed to the Crown.
65 On this period of history there are two remarkable sources which have been used extensively in this narrative. First and foremost J.G. Lorimer, *Gazetteer of the Persian Gulf, Ôman and Central Arabia*, (Calcutta, India: Superintendent Government Printing, 1915) Vol. 1, Part IA, and J.B. Kelly, *Britain and the Persian Gulf, 1795-1880* (Oxford: 1968).
66 J.C. Hurewitz, op. cit. (note 61), pp.16-7.
67 P. Sykes, *A History of Persia* (London: Macmillan, 3rd ed., 1951) Vol. II, p.245.
68 R.J. Barnet, *Roots of War* (Penguin Books, 1973) pp.96-7.
69 L. Lockhart, *Nadir Shah* (London: Luzac and Co., 1938) p.2.
70 It is interesting to note that on this subject Machiavelli wrote in his *Discourses*: "... a Weak Prince who succeeds another Weak Prince cannot hold any Kingdom" (Book One, disc. 19), and that the succession of the incapable Shah Sulayman (who ruled 1666-1694) and the 'meek and pious' Shah Sultan Husayn (whose weakness became proverbial) was a case in point. In his *Fall of the Safavi Dynasty and the*

Afghan Occupation of Persia (Cambridge Univ. Press: 1958), Lockart correctly stressed this double weakness as one of the major causes behind the dynasty's demise, alongside the "neglect of the Persian Army".

CHAPTER TWO:
DECLINE

On March 8, 1722, at Gulnabad, near Isfahan, some 20,000 Afghans routed the 50,000-strong Persian Army.[1] The Afghans, under their warlord Mahmoud, went on to occupy Isfahan, Qum, Kashan, Qazvin, and later, even Shiraz. The Persians had never before fallen to such an historical low. They had been invaded by world conquerors (e.g. Arabs, Turks and Mongols), but never by their weak Afghan neighbours. "The Persian nation had ceased to be virile..." concluded Sir Percy Sykes.[2]

Simultaneously with the Afghan invasion, the Russians occupied Rasht (1722), and the Turks advanced all the way to Hamadan (1724) and Tabriz (1725). Peter the Great even signed a treaty with the Ottoman Sultan for the 'dismemberment of Persia' (1724). But Peter's death in 1725 put a stop to the Russian aggression and the Afghans, under their new leader Ashraf,[3] were able to stop the Turks (1726).

Fortunately for the Persians, the Afghans were conquerors but not administrators: they were unable to establish themselves as rulers of Persia. Their tenuous hold on the land lasted for only seven years. As always in times of great hardship (or great shame), the Persians were able to come up with a fresh champion: a shepherd's son from Persia's north-eastern Khurasan province by the name of Nadir.

2.1. Nadir Shah Afshar

Nadir was no ordinary Persian. He was an exceptional leader of men, a formidable warrior and a great commander. A self-made man, he was both assertive and self-confident. He was also ruthless and did not hesitate to have his eldest son blinded. He ruled by the sword and died by it. When asked to name his ancestors, Nadir Shah is said to have replied: "I am the son of the Sword, son of the Sword, ...up to the seventh generation". He was clearly a 'one-man elite', with no roots and no successors. He climbed to the top on his own. Once there, he imposed his discipline throughout the nation. But his tenure was too short for him to put his stamp once and for all on

Persia: as soon as he was gone the country readily returned to its pre-Nadir disorders.

* NADIR SHAH AFSHAR (1688-1747), born in Dastgird (Khurasan province), son of a shepherd by the name of Imam Quli Khan; became servant to Baba Âli Beg, Governor of Abivard (Khurasan), married his daughter (1718), and upon his father-in-law's death (1723) inherited both the title and the fortune; with his Afshar tribesmen assisted Shah Tahmasib in occupying Mashhad (1726), eventually becoming head of the Imperial Guards (1726); subdued Abdalis (1729) before ousting Ashraf and his Galzai Afghans from Persia, with victories at Mihmandust and Murchehkhurt (1729) and finally Zargan (1730); undertook first campaign against the Turks, regaining Tabriz (1730); invested Herat after a ten-month siege (1732); signed the Treaty of Rasht with Russia (1732); crushed Bakhtiari uprising (1732); undertook second Turkish campaign, besieged Baghdad unsuccessfully, defeated at Jadida but took his revenge at Aq Darband (1733); suppressed Muhammad Khan Balouch's rebellion (1734); chastened Lazgi tribes of Daghistan before routing the Turks at Baghavard (1735) and taking Ganja, Tiflis and Erivan; signed the Treaty of Ganja with Russia (1735), thereby securing the return of Darband and Baku, and the Treaty of Constantinople (1736) with the Turks (never ratified), which recognised the Turko-Persian borders agreed at the Treaty of Zuhab of 1639; crowned shah at Dasht-i Mughan (1736); quelled a rebellion by the Bakhtiari chieftain Âli Murad (1736); attempted building a navy in the Persian Gulf with Latif Khan (who eventually invaded Bahrayn and Muscat in 1738), and another navy on the Caspian with the British Captain John Elton; reconquered Qandahar after a long siege (1738) and invaded India; won decisive victory against Muhammad Shah at Karnal (1739), occupied Delhi and took away India's treasures, including the Peacock Throne; went all the way to Sind province to bring Khudayar Khan to heel (1739); launched the Turkistan expedition, occupying Bukhara, Samarqand, Khiva and Merv (1740); made the Daghistan campaign to take his revenge on the Lazgis who had killed his brother Ibrahim in 1738 but was unable to defeat them conclusively, suffering one of his rare military setbacks (1741-43); had his eldest son Riza Quli blinded (1742) for allegedly ordering an attempt on his life in 1741 at Mazandaran; travelled through Persia, imposing the 'Nadir order' and raising ever heavier taxes which led to revolts in Persia (1743–44); undertook third Turkish campaign (1743–45), occupied Kirkuk, besieged first Mosul (1743), then Qars (1744) unsuccessfully, but decisively crushed Turkish Army near Baghavard (1745), leading to the Turko-Persian peace treaty of Kurdan (1746); showed increasing signs of mental fatigue (1746); his nephew Âli Quli Khan rebelled in Sistan, marched on Mashhad (1747); murdered at Khabushan by two prominent members of his inner circle (June 20, 1747).[4]

Nevertheless, Nadir Shah had shown that it takes a single individual, albeit exceptional, to make the difference in the East.[5] He had, single-handedly, revived Persia's fortunes, reversed the long decline that had afflicted the country since after the rule of Shah Âbbas the Great, ousted the Afghan invaders, defeated the Turks, tried his hand at building a navy, come to terms with the Russians, returned with a unique treasure from Delhi and had gone down in history as "the last great Asiatic conqueror".[6] But, in the end, all this might have been too much for the mind of the shepherd's son and Nadir Shah became so deranged that he had to be eliminated by the head of his own royal guards and the superintendent of his own royal household.

2.2. The Zand Interlude

In the aftermath of the Nadir Shah era, Persia returned to its usual affairs, as if nothing had occurred in the meantime. As Nadir had no evident successor, the main preoccupation was to find one. In 1847 there were four major contenders for the Persian crown:
- Azad the Afghan, one of Nadir Shah's generals
- Karim Khan the Zand,[7] a mere captain under Nadir Shah
- Âli Mardan Khan, the Bakhtiari tribal chief
- Muhammad Hasan Khan, the leader of one of the branches (the *Ashakhabash* branch) of the Qajar tribe.[8]

At the onset of the succession struggle, the Bakhtiari chieftain had taken the Zand captain as a second-in-command. But the leader had soon become disillusioned with his lieutenant, as the latter's military decisions usually carried the day. Âli Mardan Khan finally decided to have Karim Khan murdered. In the ensuing intrigue, the roles were suddenly reversed and it was the Bakhtiari chief who was eventually killed, leaving the Zand contender as sole commander-in-chief. Karim Khan's army didn't fare well in its first encounter with the Qajars: it was barely able to retreat after losing heavily. Against Azad, however, Karim Khan was successful and the Afghan Army was destroyed in the process. Further clashes with the Qajar troops came to an abrupt end as Muhammad Hasan Khan was assassinated by one of the leaders of the Qajar *Yukharibash* branch. Thus, Karim Khan the Zand, the least likely of the four initial contenders to succeed, was - *faute de combattants* - the eventual successor to Nadir Shah.

Karim Khan, not unlike Nadir, had no deep roots. He had risen gradually from the ranks due to his common sense, his humanism, the loyalty of his soldiers and a great amount of good fortune. During the long war of succession (1747–59), he had had the opportunity to witness the ravages caused by civil war and thus become a firm supporter of peace. He made Shiraz his capital, gave the honorific *shah* title to an obscure Safavi prince, left Shahrukh (Nadir's grandson) in charge of Khurasan province[9] and took for himself the title of *Vakil ul-Raâya* (lit. 'advocate of the peasants'). The two decades of Karim Khan's rule were peaceful. During these, Shiraz was greatly embellished, and fitted with a new bazaar (the *Bazar-i Vakil*), a new mosque (*Masjid-i Vakil*) and numerous new gardens.

Karim Khan, like Nadir Shah, was a one-man elite: he shouldn't have had his descendants establish a Zand dynasty (although his brothers and nephews thought otherwise and endeavoured to follow in his footsteps). As Nadir's era had been an exceptional era of Persian grandeur and conquests, so Karim Khan's time in power had been exceptional years of peace, rehabilitation and reconstruction.

Now, after the death of the wise *Vakil*, armed cohorts once again began to roam the country in fresh wars of succession. This time though, there were only two major contenders. On the one hand were Karim Khan's successors, his sons Abu'l Fath and Muhammad Âli (1779–1780), and, in between, his brother Zaki (for three months in 1779), then, successively, his brother Sadiq (1780–1782), Zaki's nephew Âli Murad (1782–1785), Sadiq's son Jâfar (1785–1789) and, finally, Jâfar's son Lutf Âli Khan (1789–1794). On the other hand, there was Aqa Muhammad Khan Qajar, the eldest son of the ill-fated leader Muhammad Hasan Khan.

The Zand leaders were safely ensconced in the safety of their capital Shiraz; but Aqa Muhammad Khan, after his timely escape from Shiraz upon Karim Khan's death, had to begin from scratch. The Qajar pretender first had to rally his Qajar tribesmen, then to force his rule upon the northern part of the country. In 1784 he even had to defend Astarabad against the onslaught of a 12,000-man strong Zand army. It soon became clear, though, that the Zand pretenders were, in the long run, no match for the iron-willed Qajar eunuch. Among the first to realise this fact was the powerful mayor of Shiraz, Hajj Ibrahim Kalantar, who, in August 1791, staged a coup and refused to allow Lutf Âli Khan entry to his own capital.

Thereafter, it was all downhill for the Zands. In 1792, Lutf Âli lost his last chance at the battle of Shahrak (in Fars), failing to press a night attack on the Qajar camp to a conclusion.[10] Two years later, Aqa Muhammad Khan did not let his chance pass away: he besieged Kerman, where Lutf Âli Khan had found refuge, and after four months duly occupied the town (October 1794). The Zand prince fled to the citadel of Bam, where he was finally captured before being blinded, sent to Tehran and killed. As for the town of Kerman, which had put up such a gallant defence, it was plundered, its inhabitants either butchered or sold as slaves. In a civil war rich in atrocities of all kind, Kerman's rape by Aqa Muhammad's troops must have been the culminating point of terror and horror.[11] Kerman would never really recover from that crushing blow of destiny.

2.3. Aqa Muhammad Shah

Aqa Muhammad Khan, who now stood as Persia's uncontested leader, was crowned Shah of Persia in 1796. Aqa Muhammad Shah* was ruthless, cruel, ugly, patient, superstitious, stubborn, avaricious, ambitious and indefatigable. "Agha Muhammad... un homme atroce", judged a French historian.[12]

* AQA MUHAMMAD SHAH (1742–1797), born in Astarabad, son of the Qajar *Ashakhabash* leader Muhammad Hasan Khan; as a young boy, taken prisoner by Âdil Shah (Nadir Shah's nephew and

ruler of Khurasan in 1747-48) and emasculated (1748); after his father's murder (1759) was taken as a hostage to Shiraz by Karim Khan; upon the latter's death (1779) rallied in three days his tribal Qajar lands (in the Alburz mountains) and began a civil war against the Zands that ended with the defeat of their last pretender, Lutf Âli Khan (1794); led campaign to Azarbayjan and Georgia, plundered Tiflis and sent thousands of prisoners to Tehran (1795); crowned shah at Tehran, the new Qajar capital since 1786 (1796); led an expedition to Mashhad and wrung Nadir's jewels from the latter's blind grandson Shahrukh (1796); had barely begun a fresh campaign against the Russians when he was murdered by three of his servants at Shousha (June 17, 1797).

Between Persia's new ruler and his two predecessors, Nadir Shah and Karim Khan, there was, however, a fundamental difference. Whereas they had been of the 'one-man elite' type, Aqa Muhammad was the protector of a strong tribal tradition. "The first object of his existence", Watson wrote, "was the exaltation of Qajars".[13] Before him, his grandfather Fath Âli Khan, who had made it to Shah Tahmasb's court at Mashhad, had paid with his life (1726) for his bid for power, consequent on the intrigues of an exceptional rival, Nadir Quli Afshar. Then his father, Muhammad Hasan Khan, had been killed by another Qajar *khan* (in 1759) before getting a chance to fight a last battle against Karim Khan Zand for the kingship. Finally he, Aqa Muhammad, had brought to fruition generations of aspiration. It goes without saying that his forefathers had paved the way for his successful bid by building up the Qajar tribe and developing deep familial roots within it. Yet it was his own peculiar characteristics – his thirst for revenge added to his uncommon resilience – which had allowed him to overcome all his enemies.

Aqa Muhammad Shah was murdered barely a year after mounting the Peacock Throne. Before his abrupt death, however, the cunning founder of the Qajar dynasty had had time to pave the way for his successors. First, he had wisely refrained from taking revenge on the rival *Yukharibash* branch for the murder of his father. Secondly, he had dictated that future Qajar shahs had to be the royal sons of a Qajar princess, thereby rejecting the law of primogeniture in favour of that of full-blooded Qajar monarchs.[14] These two crucial decisions by the dynasty's founder showed that he fully understood one of the basic conditions of the dynasty's longevity: the unity of the Qajar tribe. As long as the tribe was united, it would be a formidable support for any Qajar shah – especially because, henceforward, the power of the tribe was bolstered by continuous political and financial advantages flowing from the court at Tehran.

Not only had Aqa Muhammad Shah set the dynasty's basic rules, but he had also carefully chosen his own successor in Fath Âli Khan (surnamed *Baba Khan*), the eldest son of his full brother Husayn Quli Khan and had taken care to suppress any possible (future) contesting of his choice by having his own elder brother, Jâfar Quli Khan, assassinated.[15] Aqa Muhammad Shah was a ruler in the Machiavellian mould. Niccolò Machiavelli wrote on the subject of the wise ruler:

> The safety of a kingdom consists not in having a ruler who governs wisely while he lives, but in being subject to one who so organises it that it may continue to maintain itself after he passes away.[16]

Aqa Muhammad Shah also had the statesmanship to gather in his inner circle shrewd advisers. His right-hand man, Hajj Ibrahim Kalantar Shirazi, was a case in point. The Shah realised that Hajj Ibrahim's 1791 coup at Shiraz had heavily tilted the scales in his favour; therefore, he rewarded him with the title of Îtimad ul-Douleh and appointed him as his *sadr-i âzam* (lit. 'chief minister'). "A resourceful politician, with praiseworthy knowledge and experience", was Qajar biographer E. Pakravan's judgement of Hajj Ibrahim;[17] to which the historian Bamdad was to add: "A genius, a king-maker, a formidable manager".[18]

Certainly, the Qajar dynasty's founder was far from being a lovable creature. Yet he knew what he was doing for his family's future. After his death, the Qajars ruled Persia for another one hundred and twenty-eight years. Most of the credit is his. However, it should be pointed out that the Qajars were served by the fact that by the close of the eighteenth century the country was "worn out, exhausted and disabled" after a century of "constant change and unrest",[19] of civil strife and insecurity. Therefore people were looking for peace, continuity and security. For decades the Qajars profited from this general state of mind.

2.4. Fath Âli Shah

Persia at the beginning of Fath Âli Shah's reign was in a dismal state. Due to her remoteness from world events, her economic life was in a marked decline. Put in a nutshell: "The country was insecure, ...its cities weak, its commerce annihilated, its internal trade insignificant, its external trade non-existent".[20] In those days, Persian society was a typical example of a 'cold society'.[21] Persians were as far as can be from Hegel's 'historicity'; it should, however, be borne in mind that they were emerging from a tormented and war-ridden eighteenth century and that they were busy restoring spent energies and licking their deep wounds. Furthermore, the population was too scattered, lacking communications and travelling too hazardous for any concerted revival to take place. While Europe, spurred by the fallouts triggered by the French Revolution, was entering 'Le Grand Siècle', Persia was languishing in her backwater, content to finally have some peace and not caring too much about anything else.

As for Fath Âli Shah (1768-1834), Aqa Muhammad's nephew who was crowned at Tehran in March 1798, he was certainly not made from the 'higher stuff'. Pious and superstitious, he was essentially a *bon vivant* who had had the good fortune to succeed an exceptional uncle. He did have, though, some common sense and was also known to be a cautious administrator, but he did not possess the necessary qualities to put Persia's wrongs right. In spite of being a vain and voluptuous monarch, and possessing "one glaring vice of avarice",[22] the new Shah was in one way the perfect complement to his impotent uncle: he established a family that, to that day, must have been unique in world history:[23] "He at least had a total of a hundred and fifty-eight [legal] wives and some two thousand children" reported Lisan ul-Mulk Sipihr, the official Qajar historian.[24] Naturally, many of these children died in their early years; but still scores did survive: M.Q. Hidayat could list by name sixty-two surviving sons (born between 1788 and 1831) and forty-eight daughters.[25] Sipihr took stock of the royal family on the Shah's death in 1834 and came up with the following statistics:

- number of children (then alive): total of 101, of whom 57 sons and 44 daughters;
- number of grandchildren: total of 685, of whom 346 grandsons and 339 granddaughters. The sons sired 588 of them

(296 sons and 292 daughters) and the daughters had given birth to the other 97 (50 sons and 47 daughters).[26]

All these children and grandchildren add up to a grand total of 786 Qajar princes and princesses in 1834. Fath Âli Shah could rest in peace – he had more than done his duty. Through his extraordinary procreation, he had spread Qajar genes throughout the country and thus deeply anchored the dynasty's power in Persian society.

Another characteristic of Fath Âli Shah's reign was his continuous pursuit "of a Shiîte religious policy of momentous consequences".[27] During the eighteenth century, religious institutions in Persia, especially the *madrasehs* (religious schools), had suffered from official policies and the interregnum warfare. Leading Persian *ûlama* had even chosen to remain in the Iraqi *Âtabat*. The ascendancy of Aqa Bihbahani's *Usuli* movement (see Chapter One) and the genuine piety of Fath Âli Shah was instrumental in the revival of a *shiî* polity in Persia:

> He [Fath Âli Shah] built mosques and embellished shrines, and commissioned many works of theology. He exempted the inhabitants of the religious city of Qum from taxations, and built the important Fayziyyeh *madrassa* near the [Hazrat Mâsumeh] shrine. With his encouragement, Tehran became a centre of religious learning; and one of his courtiers, Muhammad Husayn Khan Marvi, founded a well-endowed school in the capital. Another nobleman, Hajj Muhammad Hasan Khan Sadr, built the famous Sadr school in Isphahan. Fath Âli Shah cultivated excellent personal relationships with the eminent *mujtahids* of his time, most of whom had been the students of Behbehani who had returned to settle in Iran at his invitation. He greatly favoured Mirza Abul-Qasim Qumi, who settled in Qum, Molla Ahmad Naraqi, who returned from the Arab Iraq to his native Kashan; and, with Hajji Ibrahim Karbasi, and Hajji Muhammad Baqir Shafti, who lived in Isphahan, revitalised its *madrassa* after the long period of decay...[28]

Thus Fath Âli Shah had reinstated the *shiî* hierocracy's power in Persia and revived the *madrasehs*, thereby shifting the centre of gravity of religious activity from the Âtabat back to Persia.[29]

If Fath Âli Shah was successful in greatly expanding the royal Qajar family and in reviving *shiî* religious *madrasehs*, he was far less assertive in his dealings with the European Powers' inroads on his kingdom. It was quite unfortunate for him that, as he mounted the Peacock Throne, Persia "suddenly and simultaneously focused the ambitions of Russia, the apprehensions of Great Britain, the Asiatic schemes of France".[30] In this respect, Fath Âli Shah was definitely the wrong man at the wrong place and at the wrong time: he was ill-equipped to deal with these Powers destiny had placed in his path. As E. Pakravan noted:

> He was put in contact with a world from which he ignored everything and with which he could certainly not contend...[31]

The French were the first to enter the Persian fray. In 1796, the naturalists Olivier and Bruguière came to Tehran on an unofficial mission. This was only an early move.

Persia had become pivotal in the long-term plans (viz. a land-driven invasion of India) of "the man who played with empires" – Napoleon Bonaparte. In 1805, the French Emperor dispatched Colonel Alexandre Romieu to Tehran, but the envoy died there in October of the same year, and was replaced by his deputy, Outrey.

In 1806, it was Pierre-Amede Jaubert's turn to make the trip to Tehran. From Persia he returned with the Persian envoy Mirza Muhammad Riza to the Emperor's camp at Finkenstein, where on May 4, 1807 a Franco-Persian treaty of alliance was duly signed. Among the treaty's sequels was the dispatch to Tehran of a mission consisting of some seventy French officers and NCOs under the command of General Claude-Mathieu de Gardane (1776–1817). The Gardane mission, which remained in Persia from December 1807 until February 1809, began training some units of the Persian Army and manufacturing its first modern armaments. But by 1809 not only had Napoleon lost his interest in India – and thus in Persia – but the British had finally also gained the upper hand at the court of Fath Âli Shah. French aspirations in the East were eventually dealt a death blow in

December 1810 as the British Navy occupied the French island of Île de France (later renamed Mauritius Island) in the Indian Ocean.

The British had, from the outset, taken Napoleon's Persian gambit seriously – as they would always take seriously any threat (even indirect) towards India. In 1798 they had sent Mihdi Âli Khan, the East India Company (EIC)'s resident in Bushire, to stir up the Persians against the Afghans, hoping thereby to neutralise the ambitions of the Afghan king, Zaman Shah.[32] The EIC's envoy was successful as Fath Âli Shah took the field in 1799, but "turned out a complete failure".[33] Then, by the close of 1800, Captain John Malcolm arrived in Tehran, in time to "counteract any possible moves by those villainous but active democrats, the French".[34] Malcolm spent lavishly (too lavishly for Sir Henry Rawlinson's taste) and secured the signature of the Anglo-Persian treaty of 1801 – "an eternal disgrace to our Indian diplomacy", commented the same Rawlinson.[35]

In his first official contact with the British, Fath Âli Shah had the good fortune to have in Hajj Ibrahim Kalantar an astute and wise chief minister, whom John Malcolm recognised to be the only capable administrator.[36] Hajj Ibrahim had first been *sadr-i âzam* to Aqa Muhammad Shah before serving in the same capacity under the second Qajar king. The founder of the Qajar dynasty had told his nephew "Always follow the Kalantar's advice". But Fath Âli Shah didn't trust the Kalantar: in 1801, he ordered his death – by having him thrown in a cauldron of boiling oil.[37] He also gave orders to have all his close relatives (many of whom held governorships throughout the country[38]) murdered or blinded. The Kalantar's fourth son, Âli Akbar, was the only one to escape the massacre. Whether the Kalantar's abrupt removal was triggered by the Shah's fear of his growing power or rather, as Bamdad suggested, by his staunch opposition to a British-sponsored invasion of Afghanistan[39] shall remain an unanswered question. In this tragedy, however, Persia had lost a formidable politician. Hajji Ibrahim Kalantar was the first *sadr-i âzam* to be eliminated on Qajar orders, though not the last one.

2.5. Ābbas Mirza

In 1805, the young crown prince of Persia, Âbbas Mirza (1789-1833), was appointed by his father governor-general of the province of

Azarbayjan – henceforward the usual sinecure of Qajar crown princes.[40] Âbbas Mirza, the Shah's fourth son, was then a good-hearted, inexperienced young man. He was already stricken by a devastating illness – bone tuberculosis, as Dr C. Cormick, the court physician, would later diagnose 41.

As the crown prince arrived in his capital Tabriz, his main concern was the Russian troops on Persia's northern borders.

A century earlier, the Russians had been led by Tsar Peter the Great. In those days, Russia's prime enemy was its western neighbour, Sweden. The Swedes, under the leadership of King Charles XII, had a first-rate army which defeated the Russians time and again.

However, Tsar Peter never despaired: he used to say: "The Swedes will defeat us until we learn how to defeat them".[42] Peter's long-term planning was vindicated in 1709, as the Russian Army humiliated its arch-enemy at Poltava. By then, it was at war with other leading European armies. Still, Peter had the wisdom to issue his famous 'Army Regulations' in 1716, setting in writing his military ideas and theories.

In 1723, Tsar Peter had taken advantage of the general breakdown in Persia to invade her northern province of Gilan. But his death in 1725 abruptly brought to a stop Russian ambitions in that direction. A decade later, Nadir Shah recaptured both Darband and Baku. Thereafter, Persia's north-western border had stabilised, for the small kingdom of Georgia had acted as a buffer between the two powers.

Towards the close of the eighteenth century, the fires of war were rekindled. First by Aqa Muhammad Khan's plunder of Tiflis in 1795; secondly by the demise of the House of Bagration in Georgia, King George XII of Georgia having been 'induced' to offer his crown to Tsar Paul I of Russia "by an instrument dated September 28, 1800".[43] Russia was now Persia's direct neighbour. Border skirmishes became routine. After a series of minor clashes, a Russian army under General Zizianov occupied Ganja by force in January 1804. The first encounter between the two armies, near Echtmiadzin, ended with a partial Persian victory, due to the impetuosity of its tribal cavalry.[44]

It was at this critical juncture that Âbbas Mirza arrived in Azarbayjan. His first action was to rescue Persian troops besieged in Erivan by the indefatigable Zizianov.

Notwithstanding this first success, Âbbas Mirza soon realised that he was confronted with a European army and that his Persian troops were, in the long run, no match for it. He correctly saw the undeniable military superiority, but probably failed to see that military power was only one of the facets of European superiority – the exposed tip of the iceberg. While Persians were still handling tools in a technology of craftsmanship, Europeans were building machines and weapons based on the technology of engineering science.[45] Military science was one of the avenues of European progress; among others, the Europeans had developed a new method for training their troops: they drilled them. Put in a nutshell, the 'drill' was the collective brainwashing of soldiers through repetitions: orders shouted at them by their commanding officers were repeated hundreds of times until the masses reacted as one, so that, even under fire, drilled troops would obey their officers' orders, all charging simultaneously, in a controlled manner, in the same direction.[46] Blended with modern management, organised logistics and the latest weaponry, this novel method of training yielded an ensemble that made obsolescent other types of armies, as for example the Persian one.

Pressed by these momentous events, Âbbas Mirza reached a conclusion he might have thought to be ineluctable: the only solution was to copy the Europeans. He had to bring discipline (*nizam*) to his irregular army and acquire new weapons, thereby hoping to close the gap between Persian and Russian forces. But he didn't appreciate that European armies were not to be copied. For Persians as a whole the process of imitation (or even adaptation) was hopeless because they were deficient in all crucial prerequisites: the theories, the skills, the technologies, the officers and the all-important *esprit de corps*. Nevertheless, the crown prince had taken his decision: his army would be trained *à l'Européen* by European officers. Thus was the first step to blindly copy Western military methods taken; and, as is well known, the first step is always crucial.

Neither the young and inexperienced Âbbas Mirza nor the Europeans officers, however, could envisage what this small step would entail – that it would open Persia's gates to Westernisation. As Professor Bernard Lewis summarised the overall process:

> The beginning was purely military... – a simple matter, so it seemed, of training and equipment, to be

> solved by borrowing a few instructors and attending to the appropriate supplies. Yet the task of running the new-style armies led inescapably to the building of schools to officer them – and the reform of education; to the formation of departments to maintain them – and the reform of government; to the creation and administration by the State of services and factories to supply them – and, very tardily, to the reform of the economy ...The military reformers had intended [as had their hosts] to open a sluice gate in the wall, with a limited and regulated flow. Instead they admitted a flood – a foaming, frothing flood that came seeping and bursting through a thousand cracks, bringing destruction and the seeds of a new life...[47]

At first, some Russian instructors were hired,[48] to be rapidly dismissed for obvious reasons of conflict of interests. Then, upon ratification of the Finkenstein treaty, the Gardane mission came to Tabriz. By the close of 1807, the mission's French officers began their training and support activities: while Captains Bontemps, Lami and Verdier drilled the Persian battalions and assisted in the erection of new, modern fortifications, Lieutenants Fabvier and Reboul established a cannon foundry and an arsenal at Isfahan. The French stayed only until mid-February 1809. The British were quick to replace them, with their representative Sir Harford Jones arriving in Tehran on the heels of the departing General Gardane.

On March 12, 1809, Great Britain and Persia signed a treaty of amity, known as the Preliminary Treaty. In 1810, Sir Gore Ouseley (1770–1844) replaced Jones in Tehran. Ouseley brought along some thirty military instructors and engineers, a consignment of twenty pieces of artillery and forty wagons of cartridges. Moreover, he paid a sum of 600,000 toumans to the royal treasury, the equivalent of three years of British subsidy to Persia.[49] Amongst the officers in his retinue there were Pottinger and Monteith, and two others who would distinguish themselves: the gallant Captain Christie, killed in action at the Aslanduz battle in 1812, and Sir Henry Lindsay Bethune (1787–1851), who eventually became commander-in-chief of the Persian Army.

Notwithstanding these British reinforcements, Persia's fortunes in its war with Russia were deteriorating. Even the *fatvas* (edicts) of the leading *mujtahids* of Najaf and Karbala calling, in 1809, for a *jihad* (holy war) against the Russian infidels,[50] had failed to reverse these fortunes. Peace offers advanced by the Russian commander-in-chief, Tormasov,[51] having been brushed aside, Âbbas Mirza and the Persian Army passed the Aras river in 1812 to confront the Russians. If only the young crown prince had had the foresight of his grand-uncle Aqa Muhammad Shah, who had told his right-hand man, Ibrahim Kalantar:

> Can a man of your wisdom believe that I will run my head against their [the Russians'] walls of steel, or expose my irregular army to be destroyed by their cannon and disciplined troops? I know better. Their shot will never reach me, but they shall possess no country beyond its range. They shall not know sleep; and let them march where they choose, I will surround them with a desert...[52]

Or, if only he had heeded General Gardane's advice "never to confront the Russian Army in a battle *en rase campagne*".[53]

However, Âbbas Mirza only listened to himself and met the Russian Army near Aslanduz on October 30 and 31, 1812. Naturally, the Persians were routed. Historian Watson reported that the crushing defeat was partly due to Âbbas Mirza's indecision and misjudgement.[54] In fact, at the root of the defeat was the national effort to imitate the Western armies. Sir Henry Rawlinson, for some time an instructor to Persian troops, remarked that:

> Truly then it may be said that in presenting Persia with the boon of a so-called regular army, in order to reclaim her from her unlawful loves with France, we clothed her in the robe of Nessus...[55]

And Sir Percy Sykes went a step further:

> This attempt to drill Persians on European lines, praise-worthy as it was, contributed to the ruin of their country...[56]

Efforts to introduce discipline to the Persian ranks were doomed from the outset: neither the officers nor the soldiers understood its *raison d'être*. "System was entirely wanting", wrote Rawlinson, "whether in regard to pay, clothing, food, carriage, equipage, commissariat, promotion or command".[57]

Persian troops were pale actors, not parts of a national army. "Internal discipline" noted Colonel Justin Sheil, "does not extend much beyond the knowledge of getting from column into line, with some awkward attempts at the formation of a square".[58] In the process, Persia had lost her only "natural defence, her clouds of irregular cavalry".[59] The logical conclusion about the Persian Army's predicament was drawn by Sir John Malcolm:

> A total change must take place before the new system of defence can do more than paralyse the old...[60]

But which change? Malcolm wisely kept silent on this point.

After losing the war at Aslanduz, Persia also lost the peace at Gulistan in October 1813. It was useless for her to rely on her new-found ally Great Britain, although they were legally bound by the Treaty of Tehran of 1812 (a treaty never ratified and later revised into the 'Definitive Treaty' signed on November 25, 1814). About Gulistan, Markham judged that:

> Sir Gore Ouseley does not appear to have acted, on this occasion, with much zeal for the cause of our defeated ally...[61]

In Ouseley's defence it must be said that for Great Britain and Russia the peace with Persia was but a minor problem in the light of the latest victories of Emperor Napoleon at Lutzen and Bautzen (April–May 1813). At Gulistan, the Persians experienced for the first time, the logical priority for the European Powers of their major global problems over minor local matters.

A decade later, the lessons learned at Aslanduz and Gulistan were totally forgotten. For the Persian rulers, it was an unforgivable blunder. The encouraging standing of Persian troops during the Perso-

Turkish war of 1821–1823 might have blurred their judgement; but that was no excuse. Neither was Fath Âli Shah's later claim to McNeil, the British envoy, that: "I did not want war with Russia, the mullahs brought me into it."[62]

It was true that in June 1826, Persia's major *mujtahids* led by Mulla Ahmad Naraqi-i Kashani, had visited Fath Âli Shahat at his summer camp of Sultaniyyeh and issued a *fatva* calling for *jihad* (holy war) against the Russians; and that both the Shah and Âbbas Mirza confirmed their religious edict. The crown prince, however, and his chief minister, Abu'l Qasim Qâim Maqam Farahani (the younger[63]), had misgivings about this second Russo-Persian war.[64] They were to be proven right. The first incident at the Gokcha Lake (an undefined region of the Gulistan Treaty) led to its occupation by Russian troops. After Gokcha, the Persians attacked. The Russian General Paskevich first defeated them at Ganja (October 1, 1826) – with the Persian Army retreating in disorder all the way to the Aras river. In 1827, Erivan and Tabriz were easily conquered by the Russian Army under Paskevich.[65] During this second war, Colonel John K. MacDonald, the East India Company's envoy, had played an ambiguous role by "ordering the British officers not to take part in the fighting".[66]

The end of this ill-fated war took place near the small village of Turkomancha'i. It was there that between February 10 and 22, 1828 a victorious Paskevich dictated the terms of the Russo-Persian peace treaty to a sickly Âbbas Mirza. Here again, Great Britain, Persia's ally, failed to soften the treaty's terms. Possibly the British stood to gain most of the same terms, as pointed out later by diplomat Sir Reader Bullard:

> This Treaty [of Turkomancha'i] is of general interest, because the privileges it granted Russia... were henceforth enjoyed by Britain and other Powers in virtue of most-favoured-nations rights...[67]

In any event, Turkomancha'i was a crushing blow for Persia. *Vae Victis!*: Persia's rich north-western provinces were lost; the Caspian Sea became a Russian lake; 'capitulations' (in other words, extra territorial jurisdiction for Russian subjects in Persia) were granted; fixed (five per cent) customs rights were imposed; and, finally, a formidable war ransom of five million *toumans* was to be paid. At

Turkomancha'i, Persia lost even more: she suddenly "ceased to be the entirely independent power that had been courted by France and England".[68] Three decades of Powers' involvement in her affairs and two wars with Russia had totally disqualified Persia as a nation. "[In 1829] we had awoke... to a sense of the worthlessness of Persia", wrote Rawlinson, before adding: "Our efforts to make her strong had but contributed to her weakness. We had been building on quicksand".[69] Thereafter, Great Britain looked upon Persia as a *quantité négligeable*, and was fully justified in doing so.

The sequels of the Turkomancha'i Treaty had an unpredictable twist. Under the treaty's terms (article XIII), people of Georgian origin taken to Persia as prisoners of war were to be returned to their motherland. A renowned young Russian dramatist, Alexander Sergeyevich Griboyedov (1795-1829), was Russia's ambassador to Persia. He was intransigent on the terms of the Treaty: all women of Georgian origin had to return to Russia. Under clouded circumstances, two women of Georgian origin from the harem of the head of the Qajar tribe, Asif ul-Douleh, had found their way to the Russian Embassy. The Qajar prince asked Tehran's leading *mujtahid*, Mirza Masih Astarabadi, to plead for the women's release. Griboyedov ignored the *mujtahid's* request. People alerted to the incident gathered around the embassy. The two women were finally set free. But the crowd had swelled to thousands – a Persian historian even advanced the number of 100,000,[70] a gross exaggeration – and became out of control after the Russian guards killed a Persian youth.[71] The crowd stormed the embassy, destroying everything in its way: thirty-seven of the embassy's personnel, including Griboyedov, were killed – only the secretary, Maltsev, survived the massacre.[72] On the Persian side, some eighty victims were reported.[73] Instead of using the case as a *casus belli* for a third war, the Russians simply accepted the official excuses taken to St Petersburg by Prince Khusrou Mirza. In an appeasement gesture, Mirza Masih Astarabadi (1779-1847) was exiled to the Âtabat, where he remained for the rest of his life. But for the first time in modern Persian history, a mass of Persians had shown that there were limits to what they were willing to accept and that no one could transgress them with impunity. In such instances, even an ambassador and his embassy were not above their law.

On October 21, 1833, Âbbas Mirza died, in Mashhad, from the bone illness that had afflicted him since his early childhood. As his father, Fath Âli Shah, died a year after him, he never got to be shah. Although he had failed in most of his enterprises, Âbbas Mirza had at least consolidated his family's power in Persia: article XII of the Turkomancha'i Treaty recognised him – and implicitly his descendants – as heir to the crown of Persia. Furthermore, his *nizam* army, although still no match for its European counterparts, had proven excellent for crushing internal rebellions: successful expeditions to Yazd (1830–31) and Mashhad (1832–33) underlined this fact.

2.6. Muhammad Shah

Upon Fath Âli Shah's death in October 1834, one of his sons rebelled at Tehran and had himself crowned shah. Two other sons joined forces in Fars province and openly revolted.

Simultaneously, Muhammad Mirza, Âbbas Mirza's son and crown prince, marched on Tehran; he was supported in his bid for the crown "by his father's veteran army, by many nobles of distinction and by the power of England".[74] The money required for the march on Tehran, some "70,000 toumans",[75] was loaned by Sir John Campbell, the British consul-general. Both the British and the Russian envoys accompanied Muhammad Mirza to Tehran: the Powers were thus displaying their increased clout in Persia's internal affairs.

After Muhammad Shah's coronation in January 1835, the 6,000-man strong royal troops, under the command of Lindsay Bethune, marched south and readily routed the Shah's rebellious uncles. Other uncles and even some of the Shah's brothers were rounded up, and either blinded or imprisoned at Ardabil or in the citadel at Tuysirkan.[76] After settling his score with his family, Muhammad Shah ordered the strangling of his own *sadr-i âzam* Mirza Abu'l Qasim Qâim Maqam Farahani, the man who had served his father for over two decades and had so wisely managed the transition of rulers. The Shah wanted Qâim Maqam out of the way in order to be able to appoint in his stead his former tutor, to whom he attributed "miraculous powers"[77]: the Russophile Hajji Mirza Aqasi, the self-proclaimed *darvish* from Erivan. Moreover, the Shah's Tabriz court "was transferred bodily to the capital. Toork [sic] governors sent in all the provinces. The native nobility were ground to the very dust".

For the thirteen years of Muhammad Shah's reign, Aqasi and his 'Toorks' would rule the country. This rule would have catastrophic consequences for Persia. Sir Henry Rawlinson's portrait of Aqasi perfectly summarises the man and his rule:

> Self-sufficient almost to fatuity; utterly ignorant of statesmanship, of finance, or of military science, yet too vain to receive instruction, and too jealous to admit a coadjutor; brutal in his language; insolent in his demeanour; indolent in his habits; he brought the exchequer to the verge of bankruptcy...[78]

Aqasi's only positive contribution was to develop agriculture in the dozens of villages he came to own and which he donated to the State upon his death. His 'Toork' governors failed to make any constructive contributions.

With such a weak ruler at the helm, the Powers had a free hand in Persia's affairs. And, unfortunately for the British, the winds were blowing in the Russians' sails. In the summer of 1837, Muhammad Shah had marched on Herat, at the head of 80,000 horsemen, encouraged by a timely 50,000 *toumans* loan from the Russian envoy, Count Simonich.[79] The siege of Herat was to last a whole year. The British brought pressure on Persia to bring the Afghan expedition to an end: they dispatched envoy McNeil to Herat to bring the Shah to reason; they debarked troops on the small Khark island in the Persian Gulf; they recalled their officers serving as advisors with the Persian Army and broke diplomatic relations with Persia. Herat held; Muhammad Shah had to retire at the beginning of autumn 1838; negotiations between Great Britain and Persia led to the commercial treaty of October 1841 (highly favourable for the British) and the departure of British troops from Khark in February 1842. As a Persian politician later summed up the Herat incident: "Persian and Afghans were fighting with bullets; British and Russians with diplomacy".[80]

But whereas Britain abided by its defence policy of containment, Russia proceeded with its policy of aggression. After her conquests west of the Caspian up to Turkomancha'i, she now turned her full attention to the East Caspian and Central Asia.

In 1837, the first Russians set foot on Ashouradeh Island, in the Bay of Astarabad, at the south-eastern tip of the Caspian Sea[81]; since 1838, the island had been used "for the rendezvous and refitting of her [Russian] marine"; and by 1846, Russians were erecting buildings on the island. When, in 1849, Great Britain, upon Persia's request, demanded a Russian withdrawal, she was rebuked. The island fell directly in line with Russian aggression plans, because, as a British historian noted, "it brings the northern invaders several hundred miles (the whole length of the Caspian) nearer to India".[82]

When Muhammad Shah died in September 1848 at the age of forty, Persia was in full-blown stagnation. The loss of independence was continuously getting worse: Britain and Russia had acquired such a dominating influence on the domestic scene that the Shah, the court and the elite were totally eclipsed by the Powers' envoys. The French, through their envoy, the Comte de Sartiges, had vainly tried a comeback which soon petered out, the French having no interest to defend. After only half a century of Qajar rule, Persia had been downgraded from a regional power to a mere pawn in the Powers' game. And, had it not been for British anxieties about India, Persia might well have suffered the fate of Georgia and other Russian annexations. For the Qajar shahs and princes, all these vicissitudes proved of secondary importance; their prime (and sole) ambition was to rule as long as possible over Persia.

NOTES

1. Sir P. Sykes, *A History of Persia* (London: Macmillan, 1930) Vol. II, p.226.
2. Ibid., p.226.
3. The Afghan warlord Ashraf mounted a successful coup against his chief Mahmoud, had him beheaded (April 1725) and took command of the Afghan troops in Persia (1725–1730). He later died while fleeing before the Persian troops in the south.
4. The synopsis of Nadir's life and conquests is a summary of L. Lockart's standard biography of Nadir Shah, (London: Luzac and Co., 1938).
5. Here is a typical anecdote summarising this fact: In early 1729, the Afghans decided to attempt a night attack on Nadir's encampment. The Afghans were easily fought off. Upon waking up, Nadir was informed of the skirmish and asked why he had not been woken up. "It wasn't necessary, sir, as we easily rebuffed them", came the reply. "Now, why couldn't you do likewise a couple of years ago?" "Oh, back then, sir, we didn't have you as a commander!"

6 See A. Vambery, *History of Bokhara* (London, 1873), p.339.
7 The Zands were a small sub-tribe of the Fayli Lurs of Luristan, see *Lughatnameh Dihkhuda*, letter Z, p.498.
8 The Qajar tribe was of Turkish origins. Under Safavi rule it was ordered to migrate to Astarabad (now Gurgan). Part of the tribe settled upstream of the Gurgan river, part downstream. Hence the names of *Ashakhabash* (or lower branch) and *Yukharibash* (or upper branch) for the two tribal branches. Muhammad Hasan Khan, the son of Fath Âli Khan, was the leader of the *Ashakhabash* branch.
9 The favour accorded to Shahrukh was a mark of Karim Khan's unwavering allegiance to Nadir Shah and his descendants, even after Nadir's death. See E. Pakravan, *Agha Mohammad Ghadjar* (Paris: Nouvelles Editions Debresse, 1963) p.27.
10 See H. Busse, *History of Persia Under Qajar Rule* (New York: Columbia University Press, 1972) pp.52-55.
11 Travelling through Persia in the early nineteenth century, Sir H. Pottinger, confronted with the hills of human skulls still to be seen around Kerman, wrote: "I feel inclined to look upon Persia at the present day to be the very fountainhead of every species of tyranny, cruelty, meanness, injustice, extortion, and infamy that can disgrace or pollute human nature, or have been found in any age or nation". Quoted in R.G. Watson, *A History of Persia* (London: Smith Elder and Co., 1866) p.11.
12 G.A. Olivier, *Voyage dans l'Empire Ottoman, l'Égypte et la Perse* (Paris: 1807) p.136.
13 R.G. Watson, op. cit. (note 11), p.102.
14 The only drawback to the rule calling for full-blooded Qajar monarchs lay in the probability of degeneracy in the long run. Possibly, Aqa Muhammad Shah had not meant that rule to be observed eternally. Nevertheless, all Qajar *shahs* would obey their founder's sacrosanct succession rule, regardless of its disastrous consequences.
15 "See how much blood I have had to have spilled so that you will be able to rule some day!" lamented Aqa Muhammad Shah to Fath Âli Khan, after he had had his loyal brother Jâfar Quli murdered. See E. Pakravan, op. cit. (note 9), pp. 187-189.
16 N. Machiavelli, *The Prince* Chapter III.
17 E. Pakravan, op. cit. (note 9), pp.135-136.
18 M. Bamdad, *Sharh-i Hal-i Rijal-i Iran* (Tehran: Zavvar, 2nd ed., 6 vols., 1357 (1978)), Vol I, p.22.
19 A.T. Wilson, *The Persian Gulf* (London: George Allen and Unwin, 1928) p.171.
20 Quoted from E. Pakravan, *Abbas Mirza* (Paris: Buchet/Chastel, 1973) p.8.
21 For a definition of a 'cold society', see C. Lévi-Strauss, *La Pensée Sauvage*, (Paris, 1962).
22 R.G. Watson, op. cit. (note 11), p.276.
23 S. Nafisi, *Tarikh-i Ijtimâi va Syasi-i Iran* (Tehran: Bunyad, 2nd ed., 1344 (1965)) Vol. II, p.2.
24 M.T. Sipihr [Lisan ul-Mulk], *Nasikh ul- Tavarikh* (Tehran: *Amir Kabir*).
25 M.Q. Hidayat, *Guzarish-i Iran*, (Tehran: *Nuqreh*, 2nd ed., 1363 (1984)), pp.53-56.
26 M.T. Sipihr, op. cit. (note 24).
27 S. Amir Arjomand, 'The Shi'ite Hierocracy and the State under the Early Qajars', a paper presented at the Conference on State, Society and Economy in Nineteenth-Century Iran and the Ottoman Empire (June 1978) p.6.

28 Ibid., p.9.
29 Ibid., p.10.
30 G.N. Curzon, in his introduction to J.J. Morier, *The Adventures of Hajji Baba of Isphahan* (London: 1895) p.VII.
31 E. Pakravan, op. cit. (note 20), p.9.
32 Sir D. Wright, *The English Amongst the Persians* (London: Heinemann, 1977) p.4.
33 Major General Sir H.C. Rawlinson, *England and Russia in the East* (London: John Murray, 1875) p.7.
34 Sir D. Wright, op. cit. (note 32), p.4.
35 Most probably, Rawlinson must have been shocked by the treaty's fifth and last article, which included the following: "...if any of the great men of the French nation express a desire to obtain a place of residence... [in] Persia, such request shall not be consented to...". (Anglo-Persian Treaty of January 1801). See H.C. Rawlinson, op. cit. (note 33), p.9.
36 E. Pakravan, op. cit. (note 20), p.47.
37 Sir P. Sykes, *A History of Persia* (London: Macmillan and Co., 3rd ed., 1951) Vol. II, p.302.
38 Two of the Kalantar's brothers held governorships; two of his sons too. Another one of his brother was mayor of Shiraz. All were arrested and executed on April 15, 1801. See H. Busse, op. cit. (note 10), p.99.
39 M. Bamdad, op. cit. (note 18), Vol. I, p.28.
40 Crown prince since 1799, Âbbas Mirza would later also become viceroy (*Na'ib ul-Saltaneh*) and would be known in posterity by the latter title.
41 E. Pakravan, op. cit. (note 20), p.14.
42 Voltaire, *Histoire de Charles XII*, (Paris: Classiques Larousse).
43 R.G. Watson, op. cit. (note 11), p.142.
44 E. Pakravan, op. cit. (note 20), p.41.
45 F. Rapp, *Analytical Philosophy of Technology* (Dordrecht, Holland: D. Reidel, 1981) pp.26-28.
46 J. Strachey, *End of Empire* (New York: Random House, 1960) p.38.
47 Professor B. Lewis, *The Middle East and the West* (Bloomington: Indiana University Press, 1964) pp.37-38.
48 Sir P. Sykes, op. cit. (note 37), Vol II, p.312.
49 See H. Busse, op. cit. (note 10), p.139.
50 These *fatvas* were bound by the *pishkar* (chief minister) to Âbbas Mirza (from 1799 until 1810), Mirza Îsa Farahani – the *Qâim Maqam*, nicknamed the *buzurg* (the older) to differentiate him from his son Abu'l Qasim, the *kuchik* (the younger) – in a pamphlet entitled *Risaleh-yi Jihadiyyeh*, allegedly the first book ever published in Persia. Mirza Îsa was also instrumental in sending the first five Persian students to England. See H. Busse, op. cit. (note 10), p.128.
51 Tormasov had succeeded Count Gudovich as commander-in-chief in 1809. Gudovich had taken over in January 1806 after General Zizianov was shot dead in battle.
52 See C.R. Markham, *A General Sketch of the History of Persia* (The Netherlands: Kraus, 1877), as a reprint of the original edition by Longmans and Green, London (1874) p.353. It is worth mentioning that the one who heeded such advice was Shamil (1797–1871), the legendary leader of Daghistan's Chechen tribesmen. For a quarter of a century (1834–1859), Shamil resisted, in his mountainous strongholds,

Russia's onslaught; faced with overwhelming odds, he eventually surrendered on September 6, 1859. See also: M. Grammer, 'Shamil in Soviet Historiography', *Middle Eastern Studies*, Vol. 28, no. 4, October 1992.

[53] E. Pakravan, op. cit. (note 20), p.113.
[54] R.G. Watson, op. cit. (note 11), pp.166-7.
[55] Sir P. Sykes, op. cit. (note 37), Vol. II, p.312.
[56] Ibid., p.312.
[57] Ibid., p.312.
[58] Lady Sheil, *Glimpses of Life and Manners in Persia* (New York: Arno Press, 1973) p.385.
[59] C.R. Markham, op. cit. (note 52), p.384.
[60] J. Malcolm, *History of Persia* (London, 1829) Vol. II, p.360.
[61] C.R. Markham, op. cit. (note 52), p.378.
[62] H. Algar, *Religion and State in Iran* (Berkeley and Los Angeles: University of California Press, 1969) p.89.
[63] Mirza Abu'l Qasim Qâim Maqam Farahani, the younger, (1779-1835), son of Mirza Îsa (see note 50). *Pishkar* to Âbbas Mirza (1811-1833), short disgrace (1823-1825), married Âbbas Mirza's full sister Gouhar ul-Mulk. Imposed new style for writing reports in his *Munsha'at*, the basis of modern Persian prose. Strangled on orders of the Shah (June 1835). See Mirza Abu'l Qasim Qâim Maqam Farahani, *Munsha'at*, (Tehran: *Sharq*, 1356 (1977)).
[64] E. Pakravan, op. cit. (note 20), p.237.
[65] Ivan Fedorovich Paskevich (1782-1856), (also Paskievitch), Count of Erivan (1827), promoted to field marshal of the Russian Army (1828).
[66] Sir D. Wright, op. cit. (note 32), p.18.
[67] Sir R. Bullard, *Britain and the Middle East* (London: Hutchinson University Library, 3rd (revised) edition, 1964) p.39.
[68] Sir P. Sykes, op. cit. (note 37), Vol. II, p.320.
[69] H. Rawlinson, op. cit. (note 33), p.44.
[70] See H. Busse, op. cit. (note 10), p.188.
[71] M. Bamdad, op. cit. (note 18), Vol. I, p.482.
[72] P. Avery, *Modern Iran* (New York: Praeger, 1965) p.44.
[73] M. Bamdad, op. cit. (note 18), Vol. IV, p.100.
[74] C.R. Markham, op. cit. (note 52), pp.471-472.
[75] See H. Busse, op. cit. (note 10), p.232. and also D. Wright, op. cit. (note 32), p.19., who mentions the amount of money advanced by Campbell as "£20,000".
[76] Muhammad Shah's rebellious uncles were Husayn Âli Mirza Farmanfarma and Hasan Âli Mirza Shujâ ul-Saltaneh. Both were captured in Fars and first imprisoned at Tehran. The former died in June 1835 and the latter was blinded and lived until 1852. As for Tuysirkan, it was the largest village in the midst of the Jalilvand tribal lands - situated some 40 km south of the city of Hamadan.
[77] H. Algar, *Mirza Malkum Khan* (Berkeley: University of California Press, 1973) p.22.
[78] H. Rawlinson, op. cit. (note 33), p.72.
[79] On the subject of Russian support for the Persian expedition against Herat in 1837 see G.N. Curzon, *Russia in Central Asia* (London: Frank Cass, 1967) p.325. "...[The] expedition against Herat in which Russian officers and engineers, as well as Russian money, played a prominent part".
[80] M.Q. Hidayat, *Guzarish Iran*, (Tehran: *Nuqreh*, 2nd ed., 1363 (1984)) p.64.

[81] H. Rawlinson, op. cit. (note 33), p.137. (Tehran: *Sharq*, 1356 (1977)). For further details on the Ashouradeh island – or rather its three small islands: the Great, Middle and Little ones – see: G.N. Curzon, *Persia and the Persian Question* (London: Frank Cass, 1966) pp.184-185.

[82] C.R. Markham, op. cit. (note 52), p.484.

CHAPTER THREE: STALEMATE

At the time of Muhammad Shah's death, his son and heir, crown prince Nasir ul-Din Mirza was in Tabriz. Mirza Taqi Khan, the head of his armed forces, rapidly took things in hand. He promptly borrowed the necessary funds and organised the crown prince's travel to Tehran. On October 19, 1848, he oversaw Nasir ul-Din Shah's coronation in the capital. Within a few short weeks, the forty-one year old Mirza Taqi Khan had shown his unusual mettle.

3.1. Amir Kabir

Shortly after mounting the Peacock Throne, the Shah appointed Mirza Taqi Khan *Atabeg* and then *Amir Kabir** (lit. 'grand commander') and he became Nasir ul-Din Shah's first *sadr-i âzam*.

* AMIR KABIR, Mirza Taqi Khan (1807-1852), born in Farahan, the son of Karbala'i Muhammad Qurban, the cook of the Qâim Maqam family; the younger Qâim Maqam (Abu'l Qasim), noticing the boy's natural gifts, had him educated with his own children and later introduced to court; part of Prince Khusrou's retinue to St Petersburg, to present official excuses for the Griboyedov incident (1829); joined the crown prince's court at Tabriz and rose to the function of *Amir Nizam* (1841); led Persian delegation to the Erzerum (Turkey) for the Turko-Persian border negotiations (1843-1846); appointed *sadr-i âzam* and *Amir Kabir* by Nasir ul-Din Shah (1848); attempted to reform, single-handedly, the whole system of the State (1848-1851); in 1849, married the Shah's full sister, Îzzat ul-Douleh (1834-1905); founded the Dar ul-Funoun school (1851); disgraced following court intrigues masterminded by the queen mother, Malik Jahan Mahd-i Ûlia' (d. 1873); exiled to Kashan and murdered on the Shah's written orders, by Âli Khan Hajib ul-Douleh Farashbashi, in the bath at Kashan's *Finn* gardens (January 1852).

Without any doubt, Amir Kabir ranks among the greatest personalities of nineteenth-century Persia – and even, arguably, modern Persia. Like Nadir Shah, he was an exceptional, self-made individual; like Nadir he tried his best (but unsuccessfully) to revive Persia's fortunes at a critical juncture. He placed his trust in the youthful Nasir ul-Din Shah; but the young, inexperienced Qajar monarch was not (like all the other Qajar shahs, save for Aqa Muhammad Shah) of his *sadr-i âzam*'s calibre. Finally, the Shah ordered his death. Thus, Amir Kabir became the third outstanding *sadr-i âzam*, after Ibrahim Kalantar and Abu'l Qasim Qâim Maqam, to be put to death upon the orders of a Qajar king. As R.G. Watson saw it:

> Amir Kabir was the only man who possessed at the same time the ability, the patriotism, the energy and the integrity required... to conduct the vessel of State...[1]

From the outset Amir Kabir was a nationalist; in other words, someone whose superior ideal was to promote, to the best of his abilities, his country's higher interests while disregarding his personal situation. His nationalism was on a direct collision course with the court's petty selfish advantages and vested interests. He did not belong to the elite and was bent on curtailing their unwarranted benefits: his vigorous anti-corruption campaign had wide-reaching effects. On the other hand, the courtiers, led by the queen mother, sensed the danger Amir Kabir represented to their privileges; between him and them was an unbridgeable gap. They got him before he could bring his reforms to bear. "Mirza Taqi Khan... proved too honest and able for Persian Court taste. A palace intrigue cost him first his post, and shortly after, his life",[2] eulogised Edward Burgess, the American-born editor of the official gazette. The great loser was Persia.

Nevertheless, in the three years (October 1848–November 1851) he had been in charge, Amir Kabir had found the time to leave his mark. He established the Dar ul-Funoun, the first establishment of higher education in Persia, as a polytechnic for military and engineering sciences; and sent Jan Davud Khan to Austria to recruit Austrian professors (which he did). He encouraged and supported the implementation of small industrial units: a textile workshop in Tehran, a velvet weaving plant in Kashan, a sugar factory in Sari, a shop for assembling coaches in Isfahan and units for the manufacture of porcelain and chinaware. He had even sent some trainees to Moscow and St Petersburg "to work in factories and learn new skills". He had the first official journal – the weekly *Vaqaiyyeh-i Ittifaqiyyeh* – published in Persia: it had a run of forty-one issues between January and November 1851. He also spurred on various other development projects in the fields of agriculture, mining and handicrafts.[3] All these domestic projects, started under his impulse, were either shelved or left to wither away after his untimely death: with him died the drive to implant local industries in Persia. A unique chance to catch the train of development was thereby irremediably lost.

In parallel to these small development projects, Amir Kabir endeavoured to reform domestic administrative practices, especially in the finance department (tax collection and the payment of rents) and local government (from the governors downwards), thereby greatly enhancing the efficiency of the internal governmental machinery. He revolutionised the postal services, with the reintroduction of relays (*chaparkhanehs*) for the replacement of horse, along the main national axis. Understanding that law and order was a *sine qua non* for his various reforms and developments to blossom, he invested heavily in security measures and inspired a royal decree calling for the creation of police stations in Tehran and other major urban centres in 1850.[4] "Mirza Taqi Khan was the son of Politics", concluded historian Hidayat.[5]

In his intercourse with the British and Russian envoys – respectively, Sir Justin Sheil and Prince Dolgorouki – Amir Kabir showed the full range of his statesmanship. For the first time in Persian history, a chief minister could hold his own *vis-à-vis* the Powers' career diplomats. He knew how far they could go and made sure that they did not try to go any further. But, although highly capable, Amir Kabir failed to realise that Persia's days in any power play were long over. In that respect he was either a century late or a century early. Nevertheless, he did try to hinder the Russians at Ashouradeh, by backing his governor at Astarabad; but he eventually had to give in to Russian pressures, accept their ultimatum and recall his governor. Amir Kabir would be the last prime minister in the nineteenth century to dare keep the Powers' envoys in check.

Furthermore, Amir Kabir revived yet another institution which had been forgotten, because of disuse during the last decade of

Muhammad Shah's reign: the army.[6] Even the mission of Colonel Passmore in 1834 (with such prominent officers as Rawlinson, later a general, Sheil (later ambassador) and Colonel Francis Farrant) to advise the Persian Army failed to reverse the steep decline. Under Amir Kabir, the armed forces were required to crush internal dissent, for example the rebellion of Hasan Khan Salar, the son of the prince (and brother of Fath Âli Shah's favourite wife), Allahyar Khan Asif ul-Douleh, the governor of Mashhad. The army, under the command of the Shah's uncle, Sultan Murad Mirza, marched on Mashhad, defeated the rebels, captured and executed Khan Salar. All of Asif ul-Douleh's assets were confiscated by the government to pay for the expedition. Sultan Murad Mirza was rewarded with the title of Hisam ul-Saltaneh. Amir Kabir's determination and sense of organisation had won the day and nipped in the bud the revolt, thereby discouraging other malcontents and repolishing the army's tarnished blazon.

Amir Kabir would also need the armed forces to quell the *babi* uprisings. The *babis* were the devoted followers of Sayyid Muhammad Âli Shirazi, the Bab, (1820–1850) a follower of Shaykh Ahmad Ahsa'i (1747–1826). Ahsa'i was first a student, then a teacher at the Âtabat before moving first to Yazd, then to Kermanshah, where he benefited from the patronage of the city's governor, Muhammad Âli Mirza, a son of Fath Âli Shah.[7] Put in a nutshell, Ahsa'i held that the Twelfth Imam (A.S.) was "a hidden celestial pole and some 'perfect' mortals, according to their higher talent and piety, could enter in contact with Him, thus becoming worldly poles".[8] He further held that believers could communicate directly with the Hidden Imam (A.S.) through these poles and that the role of the *ûlama* was superfluous; he also added that there was but one worldly pole for every generation, and that for the present generation it was (naturally) himself. The leaders of the *Usuli* movement responded by excommunicating him in around 1822. When Ahsa'i died in 1826, his successor Sayyid Kazim Rashti (1798–1844) took over. At Najaf, Rashti launched *shaykhism*, and after his death the new creed was taken to Kirman by one of his students, Hajj Muhammad Karim Khan Kirmani; it would thereafter remain localised in this region. The Shirazi Muhammad Âli, another of Rashti's students, also returned to his native Shiraz upon his teacher's death. Upon his arrival, he declared himself, on May 23, 1844, to be the *Bab* (lit. 'door') to the

Hidden Imam (A.S.); then asserted that he was "the one you have been waiting for a thousand years (i.e., the Twelfth Imam)"[9]; and, finally, declared that he was a prophet. The then *sadr-i âzam* Hajji Aqasi, not unhappy to see his rivals the *ûlama* embarrassed, first gave the *Bab* enough freedom to preach his credo[10]; but later, under the *ûlama's* pressures and the dangers of the rapidly spreading movement, he back-pedalled and had the *Bab* arrested and exiled to Maku in 1847. It was there, in the Chiriq citadel, that the latter was imprisoned, prosecuted and executed by a firing squad in 1850.[11] But within the short amount of time (three years) the *Bab* had been able to preach, he had met with considerable success and had solidly anchored *babism* in the lower strata of Persian society (who were looking for change). The first armed *babi* uprisings, led by *mulla* Husayn Basharvaiyyeh in Mazandaran, were put down by government troops, when the *babi* defenders retrenched in the fortress of Shaykh Tabarsi surrendered after a long siege. The two other open *babi* revolts, both ruthlessly crushed by the government armed forces, took place in Zanjan (led by the *mulla* Muhammad Âli Zanjani and the beautiful Qurat ul-Ayn) and in Nayriz of the Fars province (led by Sayyid Yahya Darabi). The dedication of the *babi* fighters aroused the admiration (if not the sympathy) of large sections of the population, further enhancing the movement. The orders to the armed forces had been directly issued by Amir Kabir who was, from the outset till the end, in control of events.

Amir Kabir had always been in control of all events. His capacity to manage, to delegate, to inspire and to bring about reforms was exceptional: he succeeded in putting his mark on every enterprise he tackled. He had given the Qajar dynasty and its elite a chance to change Persia, but, instead of accepting his revolutionary gambit, they had intrigued to destroy him, being by instinct allergic to change and bent on sticking at all cost to the *status* quo; the Great Powers too.

Amir Kabir was way ahead of his time: he tried to make a leap into the twentieth century with a country still living in the sixteenth. His untimely loss at the age of forty-five was a catastrophe for Persia. "The execution of Amir Kabir", concluded Sir Percy Sykes, "was indeed a calamity for Persia; for it arrested the progress which had been so painfully achieved and it had an equally disastrous effect on her external relations".[12]

3.2. Terminal Decline

To replace Amir Kabir, Nasir ul-Din Shah appointed Aqa Khan Nouri as *sadr-i âzam*. Nouri, a protégé of the queen mother, had been instrumental in the assassination of Amir Kabir.

Some Persian historians even alleged that he was "virtually a employee of the British Legation",[13] and, even if he wasn't, he had close ties to it. In his seven years at the helm, Nouri annulled all of his predecessor's achievements. First, the new *sadr-i âzam* had to deal with the sequels of the *babi* troubles. After the heavy losses sustained during the open rebellions, the *babi* leadership decided to go underground and switch to terrorist actions. On August 15, 1852 at Niavaran, three *babis* made an attempt on the Shah's life: Nasir ul-Din was wounded in the shoulder blade before the three assailants were neutralised.[14] The consternation in Tehran was general. If the Shah was not safe any more, who was? The threat was not lost on the Qajar elite and its response was swift: the *babi* leaders were rounded up and each one of them was handed over to a different group of elite members to be tortured to death.[15]

With this decisive action, the *babi* movement was decapitated in Persia. *Babi* followers fled to other neighbouring countries; one amongst them, the *Baha'ullah*, would later launch an international sect known as *Baha'ism*.[16]

During Nouri's tenure, Persian troops departed yet again on two disastrous foreign expeditions. The first was against Afghanistan, with the Herat as a perennial goal. Thus the Qajar elite showed that they had failed to learn the lessons of the first Afghan war of 1836–1838; furthermore they failed to honour their agreement of January 25, 1853 "not to send troops on any account to the territory of Herat". This time round, after the usual diplomatic messages, which again went unheeded, the British reply to the Persian invasion was as uncompromising as in 1836. While the Persians, under Hisam ul-Saltaneh, occupied Ghorian (March 1856) and Herat (October 1856), the British were once again shipping troops from India to the Persian Gulf. On November 1, 1856 Great Britain officially declared war on Persia and shortly thereafter British troops, under Major General Sir James Outram, stormed Reshire, occupied Bushire and marched on Muhammareh,[17] threatening further land advances if Persia failed to enter negotiations. Anglo-Persian peace talks began at once in Paris and resulted in the Paris Convention (March 1857) signed by Lord Cowley and Farrukh Khan (Amin ul-Mulk) Ghaffari. "A shameful convention", commented historian Bamdad[18]; but also the logical conclusion of a useless and uncalled-for venture. At Paris, Persia renounced all her rights over Afghanistan and accorded Great Britain all the advantages given to Russia at Turkomancha'i (including the 'capitulations'). For the Paris fiasco, many blamed Nouri and went as far as accusing him of treason.[19] Nouri, whom the court physician, Dr Polak, thought to be "an intriguer, sly and without scruples", was finally dismissed in 1859 and Nasir ul-Din Shah decided to do without a *sadr-i âzam*.

The second foreign venture was the dispatch in 1860 of a 60,000-man army, under the command of Mirza Muhammad Khan Qavam ul-Douleh and Hamzeh Mirza Hishmat ul-Douleh (one of the Shah's uncles), against unruly Turkoman tribesmen. In the arid steppes near Merv, the Persian military expedition was routed.

This fiasco was the final point in Persia's foreign ambitions: Merv was the last of Persia's ventures abroad for a long time to come. For Nasir ul-Din Shah, however, the message was clear and when advised to modernise his army, he replied: "What does Persia want with rifles? Let England and Russia fight it out".[20] Henceforward, the Shah would remain subservient to the Powers and try to "exploit either party as he thought profitable".[21]

Seen from the Russian point of view, the Persian military collapse meant that the way was free now in Central Asia. Their troops could conquer it piecemeal: they only had to overpower local tribes, without any fear of Persian or British interference. The Russian Army would not waste this unique occasion, and in due time it occupied the whole region – up to the Persian and Afghan borders.

3.3. Nasir ul-Din Shah's Elite

Half a century of Qajar rule, under Fath Âli Shah and Muhammad Shah, had spawned the first nuclei of the Qajar elite.

Fifty years under Nasir ul-Din Shah provided the necessary continuity for a Qajar aristocracy to crystallise. It came to consist of:

(i) Qajar princes, (ii) members of the Persian nobility and (iii) leading courtiers.

The elite was primarily selected by the shah; but the Powers' envoys had an ever-growing say in the selection process.

The main prerequisites for securing a place within the elite's ranks were: (i) noble birth; (ii) some administrative capability; (iii) the royal favour – depending on the candidate's wit, flattery, shrewdness and *présence d'esprit*; (iv) powers for survival – to be fitted with the necessary amount of cynicism, ruthlessness and persistence to remain alive in the court jungle, and, above all, avoid major blunders. Now, the foreign ambassadors, especially the British and the Russian, had their protégés among the elite and regularly promoted their interests at court in exchange for due services. The Shah was not fooled and knew exactly who belonged to which Power; he took full advantage of this state of affairs by playing off his elite members, neutralising each other and for sending messages to the envoys.

Since the early Qajar days, the rivalry between the Qajar princes and the old, aristocratic families overshadowed individual competitions. The most dangerous time for the latter came at dynastic transitions: the fresh shah, unaware of matters of State, would replace members of the aristocracy by mere favourites; it would take years for the nobility to make their comeback. The reign of Muhammad Shah proved a typical example, as initially the nobility was "ground to the very dust".

But Persia's nobles had survived under the most difficult circumstances and were used to the inevitable ups and downs of court life.[22] The Qajar princes, but for a few exceptions, were no match for the aristocracy. Having understood this basic fact, the Qajars endeavoured to 'qajarise' the nobility by multiplying matrimonial links between the royal blood and targeted families.

Nevertheless, the Qajar princes and especially the ruling shah's sons always held positions of choice, unless discredited. The eldest son was Sultan Masôud Mirza, Zill ul-Sultan (1850–1918). Not born of a Qajar mother, he could not succeed his father. But he could rule over provinces, and thus collected governorships; first those of Mazandaran and of Fars (1861–1874); then that of Isfahan (1874–1906), and simultaneously the governorships of fourteen southern provinces (1878–1887). In 1887, he was partly discredited at court for having received a G.C.S.I. from the British Government, but retained his Isfahan fiefdom. Beside being one of Persia's richest individuals, he also was ruthless and ambitious. Muzaffar ul-Din Mirza (1853-1907) was the Shah's second son; as the official crown prince (since 1862) he automatically received the governorship of Azarbayjan; but he held no real power, being simple, good-hearted and indecisive. On the other hand, the Shah's third son, Kamran Mirza, (1856-1928) was the favourite. Appointed viceroy (*Nayib ul-Saltaneh*) and governor of Tehran, he later added the Ministry for War (1884-96) to his vast responsibilities. A born intriguer, the wily Kamran Mirza was known to be his father's right-hand man; he would gather an immense fortune.

Among the Shah's brothers, the only one within the inner circle was the diminutive Âbdul Samad Mirza, Îzz ul-Douleh (1845-1929), the Shah's prime confidant. He held a record number of governorships and positions at court. And the only cousin of importance was the inoffensive and religious-minded Âli Riza Khan Âzud ul-Mulk, (1822-1910), the head of the Qajar tribe.

Among the Shah's uncles, four of them stood out:
1) Sultan Murad Mirza, Hisam ul-Saltaneh (1818-1883); commander of the armed forces, victor of Herat (1856) and loser to the Turkomans (1860); five times appointed governor-general of Khurasan.
2) Firouz Mirza, Nusrat ul-Douleh (1818-1886); Minister of War (not very successful) in 1868-1871 and 1873-1874; also held numerous governorships over the period 1834-1881.
3) Farhad Mirza, Mûtamid ul-Douleh (1818-1888); appointed as governor in Fars (1841); during a period of disgrace in 1855 sought refuge in the British Legation; recovered to become head of government during the Shah's first trip to Europe (1873); leader of coup against Sipahsalar (1873); again governor of Fars (1876-1881). The Shah's machiavellian *éminence grise* induced the Shah to have Zill ul-Sultan order the treacherous murder of Bakhtiari chieftain, Husayn Quli Khan, the *ilkhan*.
4) Âli Quli Mirza, Îtizad ul-Saltaneh (1819-1880); a son of Fath Âli Shah; Minister of Sciences (1866-1880); head of the Dar ul-Funoun; in charge of the telegraph project on the Persian side. A knowledgeable prince.

Intermingling with the above Qajar princes at court were the leading members of the Persian nobility. Among these noble families some had a pre-Qajar background and others were of Qajar stock; but it was almost exclusively from among these families that Nasir ul-Din Shah chose his inner circle. First and foremost among these leading noble families were the Qaraguzlus of Hamadan. Of Turkish origin, the Qaraguzlu tribe had dominated the district of Hamadan since the seventeenth century. One of the Qaraguzlu leaders, Muhammad Hasan Khan, had been among Aqa Muhammad Khan's first (non-Qajar) supporters; in consequence, the Qaraguzlus had always had a special place at the Qajar court and its leading *khans* had regularly been awarded governorships and sinecures.

Another prominent family was the Mustoufi ul-Mamaliks. The Mustoufis originated from Ashtian, a large settlement in the central province, some 180 kilometres south-west of Tehran.[23] Early in Muhammad Shah's reign, Mirza Hasan of Ashtian had been appointed Mustoufi ul-Mamalik (chief *mustoufi*, the equivalent of finance minister). Later his son, Mirza Yusuf (d. 1886) – nicknamed *Aqa* for his binding personality – would inherit both the function and the title. The second Mustoufi would climb even higher than his father, eventually becoming Minister of Court and *sadr-i âzam* (1881–1886).

Also from Ashtian were the descendants of Qavam ul-Douleh. Related to the Mustoufi ul-Mamaliks – both families having a common ancestor, Mirza Muhsin – the family founded by Mirza Muhammad Khan Qavam ul-Douleh, the unfortunate army commander routed by the Turkomans in 1860, would prosper beyond all expectations during the twentieth century, at times eclipsing all other elite families.

The Hidayats, a family of courtiers and scholars, were well placed at court. Family founder, Riza Quli Khan, was the court's official historian and his voluminous *Rouzat ul-Safa-yi Nasiri* (the history of Nasir ul-Din Shah's reign) ranks among the masterpieces of Qajar prose literature. Riza Quli Khan's son, Âli Quli Khan Mukhbir ul-Douleh, supervised the implementation of the telegraph lines throughout Persia. The Hidayats would also fare well during the twentieth century.

The Muâyyiris, originating from Bastam, were another prominent elite family, founded by Husayn Âli Khan, the *Beg* of Bastam, and Fath Âli Shah's son-in-law. His son (by another wife) Doust Âli Khan Muâyyir ul-Mamalik Nizam ul-Douleh (1821–1873) took over as the Shah's personal treasurer and thus became one of Persia's richest men. Doust Âli's son, Doust Muhammad Khan (1856-1912), would inherit the title and the function and marry the Shah's second daughter, Îsmat ul-Douleh. But Doust Muhammad was not up to scratch: an inveterate player, he gambled away the family fortune. The Muâyyiris never recovered from his gambling debts, although they still held on to their elite status for some time.

The family of Hajj Mirza Muhammad Khan Sinaki, Majd ul-Mulk, with its Mazandarani origins, was firmly placed within the elite. The founder's son, Âli Khan Amin ul-Douleh (1844-1904), became Nasir ul-Din Shah's perpetual private secretary (1866-1896), and the *sadr-i âzam* (1897-1898) of Muzaffar ul-Din Shah. His son Muhsin Khan (1876-1950) married Ashraf ul-Muluk Fakhr ul-Douleh, the daughter of Muzaffar ul-Dinand Hazrat Ûlya (the sister of Abdul Husayn Mirza Farmanfarma).[24] Muhsin Khan later took Amini for his family name.

The Ghaffari family from Kashan is worth a mention. Farrukh Khan Amin ul-Douleh Ghaffari, of 1857 Paris Convention fame, was appointed Minister of Court. His son, Ibrahim Khan Muâvin ul-Douleh, later became a minister and, among other posts, Minister for Foreign Affairs.

The descendants of Mirza Sâid Khan Mûtamin ul-Mulk formed the future Ansari family. Sâid Khan (1816-1884) began his career as Amir Kabir's private secretary (1848-1851) before becoming Nasir ul-Din Shah's Minister for Foreign Affairs for over twenty years.

Furthermore, two lesser families who both benefited from Amir Kabir's assassination were: (1) the Muqaddam Maragheh'i family, founded by Hajib ul-Douleh (Amir Kabir's murderer) and his fourth son, Muhammad Hasan Khan Îtimad ul-Saltaneh, (1843-1895) who became Nasir ul-Din Shah's Minister of Information and official translator, the author of detailed *Memoirs*; and (2) the Khajeh Nouri family, established by Amir Kabir's rival and successor as Persia's *sadr-i âzam*: Nasrullah Nouri, the Aqa Khan (1807-1865). After his dismissal in September 1858, Nouri was exiled to Isfahan where he died in March 1865.

Finally, a one-man elite of exceptional resilience and longevity in politics deserves a special niche: Hasan Âli Khan Garusi, the Amir Nizam (1822-1900), son of Riza Quli Khan, a minor Kurdish *khan* from the Kabudvand tribe (located around Garus, between the towns of Hamadan and Kirmanshah). He was a man who surprisingly did not found an elite family (his sole son dying young of cholera at Shiraz). This unique personality of nineteenth-century Persia held positions of influence for no less than sixty-three years – with, among others, the ambassadorship at Paris (1858–1865) and the chief ministership to Crown Prince Muzaffar ul-Din Mirza (1885–1896), with some periods of disgrace in between. During this final mission, he educated the realm's future court elite.[25]

Below the Qajar princes and the aristocracy, the courtiers formed a vast sub-elite. The hundreds of court attendants were a privileged class *vis-à-vis* the population at large, with opportunities for considerable advancement. No courtier, however, dared dream of competing for the higher positions with the princes and the nobles. Only a courtier of genius could dream to eclipse them all: one would towards the end of Nasir ul-Din Shah's rule.

3.4. The Governments of Nasir ul-Din Shah

Without any doubt, the elite's centre of gravity was the shah's governing elite at court, at most a dozen individuals hand-picked by the monarch himself. During Nasir ul-Din Shah's long reign (forty-eight years) not only did the faces of this inner circle change, but the structures did too. At the outset and towards the end of the reign, the vessel of State was in the hands of a single, supreme *sadr-i âzam*: first Amir Kabir, then Nouri, and towards the close, Âli Asghar Khan Amin ul-Sultan. In between, the Shah tried a number of variations.

In 1858, after dismissing the incapable Nouri, Nasir ul-Din Shah decided to do without a *sadr-i âzam* and rule directly with a board of six ministers: those of Interior, Foreign Affairs, War, Finance, Justice and Endowments (*Ouqaf*).[26] Furthermore, under the influence of the Armenian theoretician Malkum Khan,[27] the Shah ordered the creation, in 1859, of two advisory councils:

1) the *majlis-i shoura-yi doulati* (the governmental advisory assembly); a higher council, formed by eleven members, all selected by the Shah, with amongst others the six standing ministers.

2) the *maslahat khaneh* (the advisory house); a lower body of twenty-six members recruited from among the middle ranks of the bureaucracy and the court.

Both councils remained in the background for the rest of Nasir ul-Din Shah's reign, with altered appellation (e.g. the *dar-i shoura-yi kubra* in 1871 and *darbar-i âzam* in 1872), as well as changing membership and number of members. But, in practice, both councils failed to deliver constructive proposals. After all, their members were first and foremost Persian courtiers who said what the shah wanted to hear - no more, no less. It is thus not surprising that "neither body proved very effective".[28]

Then, in July 1864, the Shah abruptly reduced the number of ministers from six to only three. The remaining ministries were those of Foreign Affairs, War and Finance. The new triumvirate was dominated by the Minister for War, Mirza Muhammad Khan Sipahsalar.[29] Two years later, yet another ministerial reshuffle took place; the new arrangement lasted until 1872.

In the meantime, during a pilgrimage to the Âtabat in 1870, Nasir ul-Din Shah had met his ambassador to Istanbul, Mirza Husayn Khan Mushir ul-Douleh (1827-1881), and had come to appreciate his undeniable qualities. The latter's career at court was made: Minister of Justice and of Endowments (December 1870), Minister of War with the title of *Sipahsalar Âzam* (September 1871), appointed *shakhs-i avval* (first person) of a cabinet consisting of nine ministers - the six former ones, in addition to those of Court, Education and Commerce (November 1871). But Mirza Husayn Khan's meteoric rise to the very top was not to the taste of another top official, the Minister of Finance, Yusuf Khan Mustoufi ul-Mamalik, who resigned his ministry in protest and retired to his estate at Ashtian.

Mirza Husayn Khan's decline was to be as rapid as his rise. In September 1873, upon the Shah's return from his first trip to Europe, he was fired. But he was recalled three months later to the Ministry of Foreign Affairs. Mustoufi ul-Mamalik who, from Ashtian, had intrigued against him, was recalled to Tehran. A bizarre duumvirate ensued, with Sipahsalar in charge of all external affairs and Mustoufi overseeing internal matters. In 1880, with the addition of Prince Kamran Mirza, the Shah's third and favourite son, an uneasy triumvirate was established. With the death of Sipahsalar in 1881, the way was free for Mustoufa ul-Mamalik, who deservedly rose to the top, becoming *sadr-i âzam* in 1884 before dying in 1886.

Of the triumvirate there only remained Kamran Mirza. But even being his father's favourite was of little assistance against the man who would come to dominate the closing years of Nasir ul-Din's reign: Âli Asghar Khan Amin ul-Sultan, later, Atabeg-i Âzam. With the latter, the Shah had finally found the ideal solution he had been driving at with his different cabinets, his councils, his duumvirates and triumvirates: "an arrangement that would provide him with a cabinet that could at once ensure effective government and his control over the administrative machinery".[30]

3.5. The Great Game

During the nineteenth century two Powers dominated the large expanses lying between the Near East and India: Great Britain and Russia. From Constantinople to Calcutta, passing through Tehran and Kabul, these two Powers – through their envoys, officers and agents – played an intricate game of global chess for the domination of the East. It was later to be known as the Great Game.

And a great game it was indeed, played by the two greatest Powers of the nineteenth century. Russia was striving to push further south; Great Britain trying to keep her in check, protecting her own Indian Empire and pivotal paramountcy in the Persian Gulf. For the Russians, India was the ultimate price but she would have been amply satisfied with either Turkey or Persia, with the latter as the weakest link. In October 1835 Lord Palmerston had thus summarised Russian aims:

> Russia pursues the same system of strategy against Persia and Turkey; she creeps down the Black Sea and wants to do the same down the Caspian and to take both Persia and Turkey on each of their flanks...[31]

Russia, however, had to go on the offensive whereas Great Britain only needed to defend her possessions. Thus the British had, from the outset, the easier hand to play. Furthermore, in the Game, Great Britain had the undeniable advantage of a presence of historical longevity in Persia (since the mid-sixteenth century), whereas Russia was a newcomer, with at best a few decades of intercourse with Persia.

The British never have relished going to war. By principle they always prefer peaceful alternatives. In 1854 they were forced into waging war in Crimea to protect the Turks against the Russians: they had to show the belligerent Tsar Nicholas I that there were limits over which he couldn't trespass without triggering a stern British reply. It was the first time that armed forces from the two Powers directly met in the battlefield. The British allied with the French, the Turks and the Sardinians soundly defeated the Russians – both on the field and around the green table (viz. the clause in the Treaty of Paris of March 1856, a clause unilaterally repudiated in 1871, barring Russian naval vessels from navigation on the Black Sea). The Crimean incident taught the Russian once and for all not to overstretch themselves, especially *vis-à-vis* the British. The lesson also had a beneficial effect on Russia's elite, for thereafter any conflict with Great Britain was settled by peaceful means. And the long-awaited Russo-British war in Asia never took place.

Both Great Britain and Russia were first and foremost European Powers before Asian ones; and therefore their respective western policies had priority over eastern ones – to the eternal dismay of Persian politicians, who found it difficult to fathom the intricate European game, with all its nuances and fluctuating alliances. Even when the Persian diplomats had correctly analysed the European game, they were at a loss to deduce its direct bearing on the Powers' Great Game.

Since the earlier days of the nineteenth century, the Russo-British rivalry had taken shape over Persia. The bilateral relationship would always be based "on mutual suspicion". The British had first looked askance at Russian advances in the Caucasus, but after the Treaty of Turkomancha'i (1928) they had drawn a clear line: the Aras river was the natural limit allowed Russia in its southern reach. Limited on the western Caspian, the Russians turned their attention to its eastern side. Since 1837–38, the Russian Navy had used the small island of Ashouradeh as a watering point, and had even erected some buildings onshore. By 1846, it had *de facto* appropriated the small Persian island. Both British and Persian appeals for a Russian withdrawal from Ashouradeh in 1849 came to naught; and Amir Kabir's endeavours to re-establish Persian control on the island a couple of years later failed too. In 1866 Nasir ul-Din Shah had to recognise Russian claims on Ashouradeh during a visit to the island.

Far more menacing was the drive by Russia to annex all the territories of Central Asia. It had begun in 1839–40 with a resounding fiasco: a 5,000-man force commanded by General Perofski was destroyed by tribesmen in the deserts south of the Urals (a repeat of Prince Tcherkasky's suicidal raid against Khiva in 1717). But the Russians were far from deterred. Since 1847 they went at it systematically: first a series of forts was built as initial bases for expeditions in the south, with the main ones at Karabutak, at Orenburg, at Cazala (finished in 1850) and at Karmakchi (the Fort Perofski). Once the forts were ready and the Crimean War wounds healed, the Russian Army began its southern drive. This time round, the tribesmen were no match for the Russian juggernaut: advance was slow but irresistible. In 1863 Hazrat-i Turkistan was invested; a year later it was Chimkent's turn and in 1865 Tashkent fell to General Tchernaieff. In 1866 Bukara was occupied and two years later Samarqand followed suit. In 1869 the port of Krasnodovsk on the east Caspian was taken and in 1873 the large (4,000 square kilometres) Khivan oasis fell to the Russians. In the meantime, the British were given assurances through the Gortchakoff-Granville agreement of 1872–73, which contained the celebrated engagement that "the Emperor looked upon Afghanistan as completely outside the sphere within which Russia might be called upon to exercise her influence".[32] This agreement did not bring to an end plans for the invasion of India, or any halt to the Russian drive in Central Asia. The Turkomans were defeated and massacred at Geok Tepe in January 1881 by the gifted Russian General Mikhail Skobeleff (nicknamed 'Red Eyes') – who died prematurely in Moscow in 1882 at the age of thirty-nine. The capitulation of Merv in 1884 put an end to the successful Russian drive in Central Asia.[33] The eastern coast of the Caspian Sea was theirs. After conquering the western Caspian during the first half of the century, Russian troops had taken the eastern part during the second half; so, that at the end of the nineteenth century, Persia (and Afghanistan too) had but a single northern neighbour – Russia.

On the other hand, the British had observed the gradual Russian occupation of Central Asia with detachment. Grant Duff had "dismissed the Russian menace lightly" being certain that "England possessed the power to drive her rival out of Central Asia whenever it suited her to do so".[34] The British made sure to warn the Russians that at Merv (as at Turkomancha'i) they had reached their limits: any trespassing of the Persian or Afghan borders would immediately trigger British counter-measures – in other words, war. Instead of intervening, the British could let the Russians spend themselves in Central Asia. General Skobeleff had, in 1877, recognised the danger of immobility:

> A knowledge of this region, and of its resources, leads inevitably to the conclusion that our presence in Turkestan, in pursuance of Russian interests, is justifiable solely on the ground of an endeavour to solve the Eastern question in our own favour from this quarter [i.e. annex India]. Otherwise the hide is not worth the tanning...[35]

There was nothing to add to Skobeleff's logic, but the Russians did not have either the means or the nerves to undertake an invasion of India. As their pragmatic ambassador to London, Benckendorff, put it:

> Ces malheureuses Indes où nous n'irons jamais et où nous persistons à faire semblant de vouloir aller.[36]
> [Unhappy India, where we will never go, and where we persist in pretending we want to go.]

As Benckendorff predicted, the great Russo-British war in Asia did not come to pass. On the British side, Lord Salisbury had correctly judged the Asian rival: he had "always seemed unafraid of Russia's power", he "thought her 'feeble'" and remarked that "her diplomacy was so bad that we have no cause to fear its extension".[37] In 1905, the Japanese further justified Salisbury's judgement, by proving that the Russian colossus had feet of clay.

The last Persian politician to try and stand firm against the Powers' will was Amir Kabir. After his tragic murder, the case was clear for every elite member from the Shah down: the Powers' envoys were the arbiters of the domestic scene. The Shah not only learned to walk the tightrope between the two but became an expert at it. All the other elite members learned to please the one without displeasing the other. The Powers took advantage by developing its protégés within the elite: some became Anglophiles, others Russophiles. The Shah kept a careful mix at court to keep both Powers satisfied; and, when he needed a go-between to settle a problem with either side, he always had a couple at hand. With every passing year, the Powers' grip over internal politics tightened and the Shah became ever more attentive to the envoys' advice.

As on the global Asian scale, here too the British had an undeniable overall advantage over Russians. The former's diplomacy was incomparably superior to the latter's, and British representatives and agents regularly outsmarted their Russian counterparts. Over time, the Russian Foreign Office had developed an overall inferiority complex *vis-à-vis* its British counterpart in Persian affairs – as pointed out by Morier, the British envoy to St Petersburg.

Consequent to Great Britain's evident superiority, the Persian elite members, masters of the survival game, were generally more inclined to serve her interests than Russia's. With the British, the average elitist could rest assured that under no circumstances would he be let down – as long as he remained faithful to their cause. Such an insurance was not to be expected from the Russians. And for the Persian elitists playing for survival, insurance was crucial. Over the years both Powers were to develop strong links with Persian elite families, with the British clients clearly outclassing the Russians' – both in quantity and in quality. Some families preferred to play it safe by having at least a son in each camp, just in case one of the two Powers eventually took the whole prize; during the *status quo* the family could play both sides and maximise its benefits.

3.6. Era of Apathy

After the Griboyedof incident in 1831, the people of Persia had lapsed into their usual state of torpor. Neither the gross mismanagement of Mirza Aqasi, the murder of Amir Kabir nor the blunders of Aqa Khan Nouri could bestir them. A major reason behind this apathy was a general lack of adequate means of communications. In 1857, momentous events in India would come to revolutionise Persian communications.

"The Indian Mutiny", wrote Sir Denis Wright, "served to bring home as nothing else had done, the lamentable slowness of London's communications with an area that was at the geographic centre of Empire".[38] The solution to this problem was to set up a telegraph line from England to India via Persia. Invented in 1840 by Samuel F.B. Morse, the telegraph stood in those days as the *ne plus ultra* of long-distance communication technology.

The first line, connecting Washington to Baltimore, was inaugurated in 1844; London and Paris were linked in 1851. Then, in 1857, work on the line from London to India was begun. The first stretch, linking London to Baghdad, was completed in 1861 by the engineers of the Indo-European Telegraph Department. Legal matters related to the Persian stretch took the better part of 1862 and after much haggling between the two sides a formal agreement was eventually signed on December 17, 1862 which called for a telegraph line from Khaniqayn (on Persia's western border) to Bushire (on the Persian Gulf) via Tehran. British engineers began work on the 3,060-kilometre long line in early 1863 and completed it within two years. From Bushire underwater cables were laid to Jask and the last onshore stretch from Jask to Gavatir eventually linked London to the Indian telegraphic network.

Thus Persia had come to benefit from the latest innovation in world communications. The technology was rather simple and the Persian students of Dar ul-Funoun, assisted by their professors, were to install a Julfa-Sultaniyyeh-Tehran line shortly thereafter.[39] Then, in 1870, the commercial (double-wired) line built by a subsidiary of the Siemens Brothers, from London to Tehran via Germany and southern Russia, was inaugurated. All these telegraphic lines criss-crossing the country allowed for instantaneous communication between distant urban centres: abruptly, weeks had been replaced by minutes in the transmission of information in Persia. It was not only a dramatic technological quantum leap, but also the first inroad of Western technology (after the military advisers), with all its benefits and disadvantages. Neither the British nor the Persians could have envisioned that Persia's perennial problem of communications would be solved as a sequel to the 1857 Sepoy Mutiny. The telegraph was yet another example of the unrelatedness of cause to effect, as far as pawn-countries are concerned, on the chessboard of the Great Powers.

Western influence in Persia was also bolstered from yet another quarter – by Persians who had been educated in Europe. Crown Prince Âbbas Mirza had opened the door to European education by sending the first batch of Persian students abroad. And, although an onerous enterprise in those days, some private individuals had also sent their sons to study in Europe. Two of these fortunate youngsters came back to Persia and eventually climbed to the highest positions of the State: one was Mirza Husayn Khan*, the future *sadr-i âzam* and *Sipahsalar*, and the other Malkum Khan,** the gifted Armenian-born ambassador.

* MIRZA HUSAYN KHAN SIPAHSALAR (1827-1881), son of the talented Nabi Khan, a Qazvini servant to Qajar Prince Rukn ul-Douleh, who rose to become Minister of Justice, amassed a great fortune and had the presence of mind to use it to send both his sons (Husayn and Yahya) to Europe; Mirza Husayn studied in France (1848-50), embarked upon a diplomatic career, appointed consul at Bombay (1851-55) and at Tiflis (1855-59); received title of Mushir ul-Douleh, Minister (later ambassador) at Istanbul (1859-70); impressed the Shah favourably during royal pilgrimage to Âtabat (1870-71); appointed *sadr-i âzam*, given title of Sipahsalar (1871); accompanied Shah on his first journey to Europe (1873); dismissed upon return due to court intrigue, reinstated as minister (close of 1873); shared supreme power with Mustoufi ul-Mamalik (1876); finally dismissed in 1880, given governorship of Kurdistan, took part in subduing the Kurdish uprising of Shaykh Ubaydullah (1880); died in 1881 (possibly poisoned on the Shah's orders); left as a legacy the beautiful Sipahsalar mosque and school (the future *Majlis*).

** MIRZA MALKUM KHAN (1833-1908), born at Julfa (Isfahan), son of Yaqoub Khan, a teacher of French to Qajar princes; became a Muslim when young, studied in Paris (1843-52); translator to Dar ul-Funoun's Austrian professors (1852-56); founder of freemasonry in Persia (1860); exiled after the closing of his *faramoush khaneh* (1861); recuperated with Mirza Husayn Khan at Istanbul (1862-1871); launched the era of Persian concessions; ambassador to London (1873-1889); dismissed due to the lottery concession scandal (1889); published the anti-royalist newspaper *Qanoun* (1890-1898); returned in favour under Muzaffar ul-Din Shah, ambassador to Rome (1899-1908); died at Lausanne (1908).

The exiled Malkum Khan met Mirza Husayn Khan in Istanbul in 1862. From then on, the two were inseparable; the latter readily espousing all of the former's theories on Persia's predicament: progress and development along Western lines. Malkum was, in Professor Algar's words, "the first coherent advocate of Westernisation in Persia".[40] As prime minister, Husayn Khan Sipahsalar pushed through Malkum's ideas without encountering any resistance (except for Mustoufi ul-Mamalik) in the elite ranks. Algar further remarked that:

> It cannot be denied that many Iranian men of State of the time lacked any serious knowledge of economic and political matters, but one cannot escape the feeling that Malkum rejoices in the deficiency of their knowledge as a guarantee of his own status as would-be reformer...[41]

Under the joint efforts of Sipahsalar and Malkum, a new code of justice weakening the Islamic *shariâ* laws was readily approved and implemented, and a reorganisation of the government duly ratified. Malkum's proposal for "granting as many concessions to foreign companies as possible"[42] had the greatest impact, as it would open in Persia the 'era of concessions'.

The granting of wide-ranging concessions to foreigners opened a whole new chapter in Persian history. Concessions were the obvious alternative to Amir Kabir's failed attempt at Persianisation. It is only surprising that two decades had lapsed between his tragic death and the dawning of the new era. The idea of concessions, skilfully advocated by Malkum, made sense to Nasir ul-Din Shah and his elite, as these were supposed to be riskless ventures, with many benefits attached: down payments by the foreign investor, shares in the concessionary companies and a percentage of future profits. All in all, a free drive and a long-term rent – the Persian elite's dream. The concession might or might not prove a financial success, but in any event, the Shah and his elite were winners; with Malkum Khan the greatest winner of all, with his ambassadorship and his large fortune.

Before Sipahsalar and Malkum ushered in the era of concessions, some previous attempts had been made to secure Persian concessions. Two unfruitful approaches were made by the Austrian Jean Savalan[43] and the Prussian financier Dr Bethell H. Strousberg.[44] in 1864 and 1866, respectively. Then, in 1872, the Persian ambassador to London finally found a man of vision, or maybe, as Algar saw him: "an investor whose greed exceeded his caution"[45]: Baron Julius de Reuter. The baron bribed his way to a Persian concession, and what a concession: nothing less than the whole country and its resources for a period of seventy years: banks, roads, railways, mineral resources (except for gold, silver and precious stones) ...and the milking of all Persian customs duties for twenty-five years. Both the Russians and the British were dumbfounded by the news of the unique Reuter concession. Fortunately, an article in the legal document limited in time the set-up of the first project (a railway) and when it overran the limit, the contract was annulled and Nasir ul-Din could legally pocket (with his courtiers) the £40,000 token of good faith deposited by Reuter. Even though the Reuter venture had capsized (it would have a sequel), the world now knew that the Shah of Persia was ready to sell off his country, provided the royal treasury benefited.

With the mind-boggling Reuter concession, the era of Persian concessions was launched. The lesson was not lost on the Russians. After almost losing the whole of Persia to a single concessionaire, they woke up to the possible advantages of such one-sided agreements. First, in 1874, the Russian Government strongly backed a retired engineering officer, Major General von Falkenhagen, to obtain a concession for the Julfa-Tabriz railway line. But the deal fell through when the British intervened vigorously and the parties failed to find an operative compromise.[46] The Russians were more successful with Stepan Georgevich Lianozov (nicknamed the 'Russian Rockefeller'), who, in 1876, rented the Caspian Sea fisheries from Sipahsalar – the latter having rented them from the Shah. The Lianozov concession would prove a successful business and last some seventy-seven years (passing first to Stepan's son Martin, and then to the Soviet authorities) – a record for Persian concessions.

Besides the British and the Russians, other European investors were also eager to share in the riches of Persia. In 1882, the French Boital received a ninety-nine-year concession for gas works and electricity in Tehran, but the project never took off. A sequel of Boital's concession was the 1885 project for the construction of a Deauville railway for the capital city. The *Société des Chemins de fer de Perse* (with a capital of 5m Ffrancs, mainly subscribed by Belgian investors) was able to build ten kilometres of railway and six kilometres of tramway to link Tehran to Shah Âbd ul-Âzim; the line entering operation in July 1888.[46A] In 1884, yet another concession for oil and bitumen in the southern provinces was allocated to Messrs. Hotz of Bushire; after some borings at Dalaki near the famous bitumen pit proved unsuccessful, Hotz simply folded.[47] Furthermore, the French were to corner the concessions for antiquities in south Iran[47A], beginning with the Dieulafoy concession of 1884 – given for ten years, with fifty per cent of profits going to the Shah.

But the golden era of concessions spanned the years 1888–1891. Two individuals were to play key roles in this respect: the first was the Persian *sadr-i âzam*, the young and shrewd Âli Asghar Khan Amin ul-Sultan,* appointed by Nasir ul-Din Shah to the top position in 1886 after the death of Mustoufi ul-Mamalik; while the second individual was Lord Salisbury's special envoy to Tehran, Henry Drummond-Wolff (later Sir). Arriving at Tehran in 1887, Wolff (1830-1908) "was among the most powerful British diplomats of the 19th century". His first success was in striking up an excellent personal relationship with the Anglophile Amin ul-Sultan; his second was leading an all-out British offensive for key concessions, without worrying about possible Russian recriminations. Wolff's first master stroke secured the Karuom's navigation rights for Messrs. Lynch Bros.,[48] against serious Russian opposition. Unable to stop Wolff's offensive, the Russian decided to join the fray. They quickly obtained some successes: a road from the Persian border all the way to Qazvin (for ninety-nine years); an Astara-Ardabil road for fifty years; a transport and insurance company to Lazar Poliakoff (a Russian citizen)[49]; the northern olive trees and *shimshads* were rented to the Russian trading house of Kossis Theophylactos and a contract signed in 1900 gave it rights over Persia's northern forests for eight years. Finally, a railway concession to the Russian envoy Prince Dolgorouky failed to materialise – like all other railway schemes.

* ÂLI ASGHAR KHAN AMIN UL-SULTAN (1857–1907), grandson of Zal (an Armenian of Georgian origin), and son of Ibrahim Khan Amin ul-Sultan, Nasir ul-Din Shah's pantry superintendent and later court minister; upon father's death in 1883, was appointed court minister; upon Mustoufi's death in 1886 was named *vazir-i âzam* (grand minister), then *sadr-i âzam* (1893); greatly influenced the last decade of Nasir ul-Din Shah's reign; dismissed by Muzaffar ul-Din Shah in 1896, reinstated in 1898; instrumental in securing the two Russian loans, for which he was rewarded with the title of *Atabeg-Âzam* (1900); signed the oil concession to William Knox D'Arcy (1901) and the Russo-Persian commercial convention before being again dismissed (1903); travelled extensively to Japan and America before settling in Europe; recalled by Muhammad Âli Shah in May 1907 to disentangle the constitutional conundrum; shot dead in front of *Majlis* (August 1907).

Besides the small railway line linking Tehran to Shah *Âbd ul-Âzim*, no other railway would see the light in Persia for decades. Both economical and political reasons lay behind the railways' failure to materialise. Economically, such a venture across the vast Persian expanses would prove risky at best; the "unmatched authority" on Persian affairs, Sir Henry Rawlinson, called the idea of a profitable Persian railway "visionary".[50] Politically, such railways were unpalatable both to the British and the Russians. The latter even became so obsessed by the idea of a British railway criss-crossing Persia that they compelled the Shah to issue a secret moratorium on such projects in Persia. Thus "the inter-relations among Russia, Britain and Persia produced a stalemate... [as] the interests of all three governments were served by non-action so far as railways were concerned".[51] Consequently Persians had to wait another five decades before being able to construct a trans-Persian railway line.

Making no headway on the railway question, the crafty Drummond-Wolff turned to other ventures. In 1888 he introduced the New Oriental Banking Corporation in Persia. The bank opened branches in Tehran and several provincial towns. In 1889, during the Shah's third trip to Europe, an agreement was reached on the sequels of the 1872 Reuter concession, with Julius's son George.

According to the compromise of January 1889: i) the original £40,000 deposit was returned to Reuter, who lent it back to the Shah for ten years at six per cent interest; ii) a fresh concession for banking and a right to issue banknotes, along with wide-ranging mining rights, was granted to Reuter.[52] In order to implement the new concession, the Imperial Bank of Persia (IBP) was created with a capital of £1,000,000 in September 1889.[53] The IBP lost no time in buying out the established Oriental branches. With the competent management of J. Rabino, seconded by General A. Houtum Schindler, the bank rapidly expanded throughout Persia. In 1890 IBP sold its mining rights to the newly-formed British company Persian Bank Mining Rights Corporation Ltd. for £150,000.[54] The corporation issued 200,000 shares at five pounds each, which it successfully placed with Belgian and Russian investors. It also drilled three unsuccessful wells: two near Dalaki and one on the island of Qishm. The company went bankrupt in 1894, was dissolved in 1899 and liquidated in 1901.

The Russians also received a banking concession. It was granted for a seventy-five year period to Russian Jacques Poliakoff, and led to the establishment in 1890 of the Russian Banque d'Escompte de Perse, known in Farsi as the *Bank-i Istiqrazi*. The Russian bank never was a threat to the IBP's banking supremacy; it satisfied Russian interests, who were content to play second fiddle to the British bank.

In 1889, during the Shah's visit to Europe, the Persian ambassador Mirza Malkum Khan acquired from the monarch a concession for a Persian lottery against a £1,000 payment. The concession was issued in the name of De Cardoel, the French-born secretary of the Persian Embassy in London. De Cardoel and Malkum's brother, Mikhail, set up two companies – the Persian Investment Company and the Anglo-Asiatic Syndicate – to sell shares in the lottery concession on the London market. The companies were able to make over £40,000. Tehran got wind of the transactions in London and, after much haggling, Amin ul-Sultan (Malkum's arch-rival) induced the Shah to have the lottery concession annulled. But, even after the annulment, the unscrupulous Malkum and his accomplices continued selling shares to credulous investors in London. The whole venture ended in a scandalous court case. Malkum was fortunate to get away with "a court blame",[55] before his shameful lottery swindle came to a close.

Malkum Khan, Persia's leading proponent of Westernisation and an outstanding liberal thinker, had set an execrable example for future generations of Persian intellectuals. His overall message to Western-educated elitists was:

> Take full advantage of your privileged position; have no scruples: anyone in your position would do the same; if you fail to do so, the final loss will be yours, for someone will take your place and do as he should; as for the homeland, don't you worry; it will take care of itself.

Malkum's spiritual legacy to the Persian intelligentsia would indelibly mark this group for the whole of the twentieth century.

With their forced injection of Western capital into Persia, Malkum and Sipahsalar hoped to link Western interests to Persian security and simultaneously to bring about a revival of the moribund Persian economy. Malkum believed that "alone, Persia is irrevocably lost"; he was "close to offering England a protectorate over Persia" in March 1885. But the British diplomats, far from taking Malkum's proposal at face value, and as ever the eternal pragmatists, had their own ideas on Malkum and the local Persian position. For example, in December 1886, Nicolson wrote to Iddesleigh:

> The panaceas, which Malcolm Khan and a few others who assume they are the pioneers of progress, are never weary of proposing, are scarcely adapted to a country in the position of Persia. Tribunals, legal codes, and the other paraphernalia of civilisation would be of little avail. There is no indigenous material with which to work them...[55A]

As the British diplomats were not convinced, Malkum and Sipahsalar failed in both of their major goals. On the point of national security, Persia's independence in the nineteenth century (or thereafter) was never linked to economic well-being, as geo-strategic parameters overshadowed any economic interest; on the other hand, the concessions had very little impact on the domestic economy, as they were superimposed and had a life of their own, giving rise to a two-tier economy system (i.e. the foreign and the local), with very little linking between the two. This meant that, while some of the foreign concessions were thriving (a number of them also fell by the wayside), the local socio-economical scene was stagnating, and in some cases even declining.

3.7. Economic Decline

In the nineteenth century, agriculture was the backbone of Persia's anaemic economy. More than ninety per cent of its gross domestic product was produce of the land; the rest consisted of traditional handicrafts manufactured by master-artisans in the urban bazaars.

Millions of Persian peasants tilled the land, just as their forebears had: subsistence agriculture, with rudimentary production techniques and a perennial lack of sufficient water supply. The large majority lived in villages and worked for a landlord. There were five major types of land tenure in Persia:[56]

(1) the *amlak* type, with the village belonging to a specific landlord who had either inherited it or purchased it;

(2) the *tuyouls* (or *suyourghals*), lands or villages whose income was assigned to an individual by the shah for a year (usually a revolving grant, which could even become hereditary);

(3) the *khalisehs* or crown lands, whose income went into the shah's privy purse;

(4) the *vaqf* lands, whose income was "immobilised for some specific purpose" – most probably a charitable one, but usually pocketed by the trustee(s); and

(5) the *rayatis*, peasant-owned villages (quite exceptional).

In general terms, the share of crops handed over by the peasant to the landlord depended on local custom: it varied from one-third (the famous *sehkub*) to four-fifths of the total crop (when the five main crop ingredients i.e., land, water, seeds, oxen and labour were taken into account, and the peasant provided only his work: a meagre one-fifth).

Tribes had a life all of their own. They were self-sufficient but for their tea and sugar. The tribesmen migrated twice yearly as they had done since time immemorial with their sheep, their goats, their dogs, their cows, their mules and their horses.[57] They had very little contact with the outside world (and were thus able to keep both their purity and simplicity). The number of village settlements was extremely reduced, as they lived in their black tents, following their herds.

At the centre of every urban settlement stood a *bazaar*, the economic and social heart of the township surrounding it. During the second half of the nineteenth century, the main Persian *bazaars* were those of Tabriz, Tehran, Isfahan, Yazd, Kashan, Shiraz, Kirman, Hamadan and Rasht. In the small *bazaari* shops the traders, the merchants, the *sarrafs* (money-changers) and artisans thrived. The latter group included carpet-weavers, shawl-weavers, tailors, carpenters, saddlers, shoe- and boot-makers, potters, glass blowers and metalworkers (especially silver- and copper-smiths). Every master-artisan (*astad* or *ousta*) had in his shop a number of apprentices (*chagird*); the most gifted underlings would form the next generation of masters; the secrets of the trade were passed from the master's mouth to his successor's ear (never written; most of the artisans were analphabetes anyway). The merchants and artisans gathered in professional associations – the *sinf* or, in its plural form, *asnaf*, tightly-knit organisations with a leading merchant or artisan at its head, in some ways akin to the European guilds and German hansas. In the *bazaar*, elite status was not hereditary, although family ties were, naturally, of importance.

The *bazaar* shops remained artisanal, the masters being incapable of making the quantum jump to small industrial units. The setback of Amir Kabir's attempts at industrialisation was to mark the whole of Nasir ul-Din Shah's reign. Moreover, Persian artisans suffered from competition from Western industrial goods, and, instead of forging ahead, their abilities and capacities stagnated.

In the Tehran b*azaar*, one man rose above all others by his exceptional capacity to manage: Hajj Muhammad Hasan Amin ul-Zarb.*

* HAJJ MUHAMMAD HASAN AMIN UL-ZARB (1834–1898); moved in 1850 from his native Isfahan to Tehran with a capital of only 100 *Krans*; rose rapidly to the very top of the Tehran bazaar; entered into business with Mr Panayotti of Ralli and Agelasto, a leading Greek-British firm of international traders created in London in 1818; profitably exported opium to Hong Kong; purchased much-needed staple food from Russia during the great famine of 1871–72; after the first mint in Persia was established with European machinery (1877), became master of the mint and received his title of Amin ul-Zarb; always on excellent terms with Amin ul-Sultan and virtually private banker to the Shah; rented the *firouzeh* mines at Nayshabour from the Shah for a pittance; proposed the creation of a national bank to the Shah as early as 1879, but saw his efforts thwarted by the creation in 1889 of the IBP; invested a fortune in the ill-fated Mahmoudabad–Amol railway line (1886–88); acted as host to Asadabadi during both his stays in Tehran; rumours of falsified assays of gold, silver and copper coins led to his arrest and he was fined

800,000 *toumans* (1897); relaxed after his son (and successor) Hajj Husayn had paid 400,000 *toumans* cash and 365,000 *toumans* in promissory notes; died in December 1898. (His elite family would later choose Mahdavi as family name).

During the 1860s and 1870s, Persia's thriving silk sector (from the culture of silkworms to the weaving of silk shawls) went into a terminal decline. Within a few years, Persian silk was destroyed by the muscarine pest disease imported from Europe. After a record production of 2.2 million pounds in 1864, Gilan's silk output plummeted to a bare 200,000 pounds in 1873.[58] As the domestic silk industry was wrapped up, the culture of cotton (in the north) and opium (in the south) came in to fill the void created.

For any economic development in a country as large and as sparsely populated as Persia, transport is crucial. With its poor, unsafe roads and its total lack of railways, any economic revival was doomed. Well-protected caravans of camels and mules were the order of the day. Large distances between urban settlements impeded any lasting endeavour at trade expansion.

Furthermore, the poor state of transport facilities favoured the outbreak of famines on the national scale: the terrible famine of 1871/72 which indiscriminately decimated Persian towns and villages is a case in point. As Nasir ul-Din Shah, encouraged by Sipahsalar and Malkum, was signing the Reuter Concession, the average Persian was still starving to death.

As Sir Henry Rawlinson summarised Persia's predicament:

> Persia ...probably in a more depressed condition than she has ever before reached at any period of history. Scarcity and drought ...culminating in the famine of 1872 ...national atrophy ...appalling picture ...decrepitude...[59]

The usual lot of the people was not only famine but also epidemics: black plague, cholera, etc. During the nineteenth century, the plague appeared on at least ten occasions. In 1876/77 an outbreak of plague in Gilan wiped out the population: that of Rasht fell from 60,000 to between 15,000 and 20,000 within a year.[60] The deadly pandemics visited the country from time to time, leaving thousands of deaths in their wake. The people had almost no defence against such calamities; they only knew of a few traditional herbs to be used against common ills, but were totally powerless in the case of epidemics.

During the second half of the nineteenth century imports and exports did not play a major role in the Persian economy. Naturally, trade was always being carried out – especially in the south with Great Britain and India (accounting for well over fifty per cent of the total during the 1860s and 1870s, slightly declining thereafter) and in the north with Russia (gradually increasing in the 1880s and 1890s to reach half of the total in the early twentieth century). But the impact of international trade was always extremely limited. Main export goods consisted of silk (until 1864 the staple export), opium, rice, raw cotton, carpets, dried fruits, livestock and pearls (from the Persian Gulf); whereas main import items were cotton and wool textiles (roughly two-thirds of total imports[61]), tea and sugar.

Another calamity plagued Persia – a monetary one, which was not of her own making. Underpinning the disaster was the fact that the Persian monetary system was based on a silver standard[62] and that, with all the European and South American countries switching to the gold standard in the 1870s, the price of silver went on a long slide on the London exchange during the last two decades of the century. As the Western countries demonetised silver, Persia (totally unaware of the catastrophe) stuck to its standard (incapable of change) and drank its silver chalice to the last drop, leading to a dramatic readjustment in the *Kran*–pound rate of exchange from 27.8 *Krans* per pound in 1877 to 50 *Krans* per pound in 1897[63] (see Table 3.1. for details). The law changing Persia's monetary standard to gold was only promulgated in March 1932.[65] By then the harm had long been done. Taking the lessons of this monetary calamity, Persia's early financiers duly recognised that foreign financial policies could have a momentous impact on domestic matters.

The local and the foreign sections of the economy met in 1891 in the watershed event of the Tobacco Concession. Before this extraordinary concession, the two tiers of the Persian economy – the foreign (concessions) and the domestic – had almost totally ignored each other. But, with the sudden encounter between the two, sparks flew dramatically – the people eventually emerged from their torpor and the Qajar dynasty entered its long, terminal decline.

Table 3.1. The *Kran* to Pound Sterling Exchange rate and the Price of Silver on the London Exchange (for selected years of the late 19th century).[64]

Year	Exchange Rate of Pound to *Krans*	Price of Silver in London (in Pence)
1246 (1867/68)	25.0	60d. $9/16$
1256 (1877/78)	27.8	54d. $13/16$
1266 (1887/88	34.0	44d. $5/8$
1276 (1897/98)	50.0	27d. $9/16$

3.8. The Tobacco Concession

In the flurry of 1889/90 concessions, Drummond-Wolff went a concession too far: in March 1890 he obtained a fifty-year concession on the production, sales and exports of all Persian tobaccos for his friend, Major Gerald F. Talbot. Heavy bribes had been paid to the Shah (£25,000) and to Amin ul-Sultan (£15,000). For Wolff, after the Karoun river navigation rights and the IBP, the tobacco monopoly was to be the icing on the cake. Only a few among the Persian elite dared oppose Talbot's concession; one of them was Amir Nizam Garousi, who was summarily dismissed from his governorship for his misbehaviour.

Since 1884, in the neighbouring Ottoman Empire, the Turkish Tobacco Régie had operated smoothly. There was every reason to believe that the Persian régie would do likewise. The fifteen-article contract between Talbot and the Persian Government provided for a yearly rent of £15,000 and the payment to the latter of twenty-five per cent of the régie's profits. The Turkish agreement was slightly more advantageous to the host country and did not include exports, as pointed out by the Istanbuli newspaper Akhtar;[66] but, basically, the two concessions were roughly similar.

Major Talbot duly established the Imperial Tobacco Corporation of Persia in London with an initial capital of £650,000 before departing for Tehran in early 1891. Once there he duly created the Persian Tobacco Régie and decided to open its first shop in the tobacco-rich province of Fars. From the outset, dissonances were in the air: a local tobacco producer preferred to destroy his twelve thousand bags of tobacco rather than sell them at a reduced price to the Régie[67]; a leading Shirazi tobacco merchant, Hajji Âbbas Urdubadi, voiced his opposition to the Régie, and a prominent *mujtahid*, Hajj Sayyid Âli Akbar Fal Asiri, publicly denounced the tobacco concession, condemning to death all foreigners settling in Shiraz.[68] It was a far from propitious beginning for a long-term concession.

Fal Asiri was exiled to Basra for his outrageous remarks. There he met with another Persian man of religion in exile, Sayyid Jamal ul-Din Asadabadi.* According to Professor E.G. Browne, Asadabadi was:

> ...a man of enormous force of character, prodigious learning, untiring activity, dauntless courage, extraordinary eloquence, both in speech and in writing, and his appearance equally striking and majestic. At once, philosopher, writer, orator, and journalist, but above all a politician...[69]

Furthermore, Asadabadi was a man of ideas. He wrote articles and delivered lectures. He was instrumental in forming the next generation of Islamic thinkers – among others, Muhammad Âbduh. He had correctly understood the Muslim nations' predicament: a protracted decline, added to the challenge of the West's overall superiority. In a lecture delivered in 1872 at Calcutta, he said:

Ignorance and blindness have led the East to a decline; science and progress enabled the West to dominate it...[70]

He knew that the Westernisation of Muslims was not the way out of the decline; he foresaw the vicissitudes and pitfalls along this easy (but erroneous) way out. His counter-proposal was to unify the Islamic nations politically so that they could act as a counterweight to the West's scientific and technological superiority. Hence his message was pan-Islamism and the creation of the Islamic Union Party to achieve it.

* SAYYID JAMAL UL-DIN ASADABADI (1838-1897), born at Asadabad (near Hamadan), son of Sayyid Safdar; studied at Âtabat, under Shaykh Murtaza Ansari (1850-54); travelled widely: to India (1854-56), Afghanistan (1857-68), Bombay (1869), Cairo (1870), Istanbul (1871) and Egypt (1872-79), where he allegedly entered freemasonry (1876); after yet another stay in India (1880-82) he went to Europe: first to Paris, where he edited the monthly *Ûrvat al-Vusqa* (eighteen issues) with Âbduh, then to London (1883-86); his first visit to Persia (November 1886-April 1887) was far more successful than the second one (December 1889-January 1891), which ended in an humiliating expulsion *manu militari* after a six-month *bast* (sit-in) at Shah Âbd ul-Âzim; returned to London via Baghdad, edited the monthly *Zia al-Khafiqin* (five issues); finally settled in Istanbul (1892), where his relations with the Sultan rapidly deteriorated; fearing for his life, asked for British protection (1895); after Nasir ul-Din Shah's assassination, threatened with death (1696); died in 1897, allegedly poisoned by Persian agents.

Asadabadi was restless, travelling widely from India to Egypt to propound his Islamic message to the amirs, the shaykhs, the khedives and the shahs. He was, however, unable to light the religious fires of which he dreamt; instead, he "planted the seeds of an intellectual revolution".[71] He also travelled to the Western capitals to debate with western intellectuals such as W.S. Blunt, Ernest Renan[72] and Professor Browne, seeking 'mutuality' – which in Professor H.A.R. Gibb's words "means that you understand [one another]".[73]

Although staunchly against absolute power, it was, ironically, the monarchs and the princes whom Asadabadi courted, trying to win them over rationally. "Reason", he said, "doesn't appeal to the masses... its lessons are only understood by the intelligent elite".[74] To that statement he also added: "However, if reason and philosophy are for a minority, the religious ideal remains for the masses".[75] Towards the end of his life, Asadabadi regretted placing all his hopes in the elite; to a Persian friend he wrote:

> If only I had planted all the seeds of my new ideas in the fertile soil of the people's mind, instead of sowing them in the barren lands of royal courts. Whatever I sowed in the former came to fruition, whereas in the latter, the seeds rotted...[76]

A century later, his spiritual heirs would not make the same mistake. They moved the masses and were thus able to realise Asadabadi's dream of a "Theocratic Republic of Persia, ruled by the religious clergy".[77]

Meeting with the exiled Fal Asiri at Basrah, Asadabadi was informed of the new developments in Persia in the wake of the fresh concession. Correctly assessing the situation, he envisioned the predominant role to be played by the religious elite, and accordingly sent messages to the *Âtabat* and Persia. His first letter was to the leading *marjâ-i taqlid* of the *shiî* community, Mirza Muhammad Hasan Shirazi (d. 1895), to whom he wrote: "If these concessions are implemented during your tenure, without you opposing them, History will not be kind to the memory of your leadership".[78] The other *ûlama* addressed by Asadabadi were the leading Persian *mujtahids*, who included:
- Mirza Habibullah Rashti (1819–1895), one of Shaykh Ansari's students, residing at Najaf.
- Mirza Hasan Ashtiani, Tehran's leading *mujtahid*, who had also studied under Ansari.
- Mirza Javad Aqa, Tabriz's leading *mujtahid*.
- Shaykh Muhammad Taqi Bujnurdi, at Mashhad.
- Hajji Shaykh Muhammad Taqi Mujtahid Isfahani, known as 'Aqa Najafi', Isfahan's leading authority.
- Hajji Shaykh Hadi Najmabadi, at Tehran.

The religious network in Persia, spurred by Asadabadi, was going to show his idea to the population at large and orchestrate popular opposition to the tobacco concession. It was assisted in its effort by the Russian Legation, which had seized on this unique occasion to embarrass its British counterpart,[79] and was financed by the leading tobacco merchants who provided the necessary funds. After the initial Shiraz disturbances, trouble spread to Tehran in May 1891. During the summer Tabriz, Isfahan and Mash followed suit. For the first time in modern Persian history the people, shedding their usual apathy, took part in a widespread movement of protest. The anti-Régie movement reached its climax in December 1891 when Mirza Hasan Shirazi allegedly issued a *fatva* – "whether actually issued by Shirazi or published under his name, the result was the same", quipped Hidayat[80] – which read: "In the Name of Allah, The Compassionate, The Merciful. The user of tobacco, under all its forms, is in direct conflict with the Directives of the Twelfth Imam (A.S.). Signed: Muhammad Hasan al-Husayni [Shirazi]".[81] Thousands of copies of the *fatva* were reproduced in a matter of days. Tobacco was banned all over Persia *sine die*. The ban's success was dumbfounding: even court servants and maids stopped smoking.[82] The court and the elite were shocked by this popular discipline. No one could have predicted such a show of solidarity by these uncouth masses.

The people of Tehran went a step further. When rumours circulated that Mirza Hasn Ashtiani, Tehran's leading *mujtahid*, was to be exiled and that he had decided to depart the capital beforehand, Tehranis took to the streets. On January 4, 1892 some four to five thousand-strong, they even dared mob the *Ark*, Prince Kamran Mirza's palace, located north of the Tehran Bazaar.[83] Guards fired; casualties ensued: "between forty to fifty deaths" reported one source,[84] "between thirty-five and seventy", according to another.[85] This time, the court and the elite were shaken. The people had dared to challenge their authority. Incapable of finding a face-saving compromise, the Shah was eventually compelled to declare the ill-fated Tobacco Concession null and void (January 26, 1892).

Two weeks later another *fatva* from Shirazi allowed tobacco consumption in Persia. Things returned to normal and the British employees of the Imperial Tobacco Corporation returned to Great Britain.

The tobacco fiasco proved disastrous for both the Qajars and the British. They had gone one concession too far and were going to pay dearly for that blunder. The Shah had lost a great deal of his remaining prestige. Under popular pressure, he had back-pedalled; and to add insult to injury, he had to borrow £500,000 from the Imperial Bank of Persia (for forty years, at six per cent interest, against the customs revenues of Bandar Âbbas, Bandar Lingeh and Shiraz) to compensate the Imperial Tobacco Corporation. That unfortunate loan had opened a new source of revenues in Persian finances and future Qajar shahs would keep that door ajar.

For the British too the tobacco fiasco was a serious setback. For the next decade, it would adversely influence their options in Persia. Of course, the Russians took full advantage of this new situation and stepped aggressively into Persian affairs. They wasted no time in courting the Anglophile Amin ul-Sultan, who, disillusioned with the British, answered favourably to their overtures. The *sadr-i âzam's* change of heart was followed through by the Shah and the leading courtiers.

The British had certainly lost some goodwill but gained precious experience in this affair.

On the other hand, the tobacco merchants were the prime beneficiaries of the concession's annulment: they could now revert to their trade as usual. In the process, they had won a total victory over the court by entering the political arena. Their allies, the *ûlama*, to whom they were related matrimonially and economically, were the other great victors of the tobacco revolt. They had shown that they could lead the masses. Finally, on the victors' side, the Persian people had surprised everyone, including themselves, by their discipline and sense of solidarity. Coming out of their usual torpor, they had flexed their muscles and found out that they wielded more power than generally suspected. Of this newly-found consciousness of the masses, Professor Browne objectively concluded:

> ...that there was a limit to what they would endure, that they were not the spiritless creatures which they had been supposed to be, and that henceforth they would have to be reckoned with...[86]

After a century of decline under the Qajars, the people of Persia were proving once again the validity of their historical roots.

3.9. Regicide

The court was humming with the preparations of the ceremonies being envisaged to celebrate the Shah's fifty years' reign (fifty lunar years since the Persian calendar was based on lunar months). No Persian monarch since the Safavi shahs had achieved such longevity.

On his thanksgiving pilgrimage to the shrine of Shah Âbd ul-Âzim, south of Tehran, Nasir ul-Din Shah was shot dead by a single pistol shot fired point-blank by Mirza Riza Kermani.*

* MIRZA RIZA KERMANI (ca. 1848–1896), son of Mulla Husayn Âqda'i; went to Tehran, married Fatimeh, the sister of a secretary to Amineh Aqdas, one of the Shah's wives; sold clothes and textiles to wealthy courtiers; employed by Amin ul-Zarb; could never bring himself to serve the elite; on orders of Amin ul-Zarb, acted as Asadabadi's host during his visits to Tehran, becoming a devotee of his; jailed and tortured for protesting against Asadabadi's expulsion (1891); spent four years in prison (June 1891–June 1895), first at Qazvin and then at Tehran; after being set free, a sick and broken man, travelled to Istanbul to meet Asadabadi (1895); returned to Tehran in January 1896, buying a pistol and twenty-five cartridges along the way; shot Nasir ul-Din Shah dead in the Shah Âbd ul-Âzim shrine on April 30, 1896; jailed and tortured, sentenced to death and hanged on August 11, 1896.

An era had come to end. Nasir ul-Din Shah had passed away and a whole epoch with him. With his death, Persia had not lost much because with him on the throne there was no way out of the stalemate. During his lifetime he was more concerned with keeping his crown than with the welfare of Persia and Persians. In a time of industrial revolution across the world, he had condemned Persia to a stale *status quo*, appearing afraid of changes that might induce political troubles.

His uncle, Âbd ul-Samad Mirza Îzz ul-Douleh, wrote about his royal nephew in his diaries:

> The king is busy day and night living in pleasure. His attention is devoted to the care of his several cats; in his trips they are taken along in cages. Hunting is his utmost desire. He avoids meeting people and does not like them. Except in some festivals there are no *salams* (official group audiences), and even such audiences last [only] a quarter of an hour ...He is exceedingly infatuated with women. Every day he marries one; currently he has fifty wives. His conversation and inclination is with roguish and inane servants or else young pages. He has no desire for the companionship of others than them. He is excessively desirous of food and victuals; especially fruits, which he eats incessantly. He is very much given to primping himself up. At all times he is accompanied by a mirror and a comb, which [the servants] carry around with him in gardens or rooms. I swear to the Divine Pure Essence [of God] that I have written down [only] a few of the many of his manners and attitude... It is a pity that the King has no eyes for truth; it is not significant affairs which are the subject of his interest and preoccupation; he has contended himself with some trifles...[87]

One cannot doubt the sincerity of Îzz ul-Douleh, knowing that he was his nephew's confidant and had always been fairly treated by him,[88] thus had no axe to grind or revenge to seek. It should further be added that at the end of his reign the Shah had become even more "self-seeking, self-willed and obstinate",[89] and had not shied from appointing as general of the army his favourite, a young boy named Ghulam Âli (nicknamed Malijak), the nephew of his wife Amineh Aqdas, to whom he had already given the title of Âziz ul-Sultan and whom he had taken on his third trip to Europe in 1889.[90]

With the death of Nasir ul-Din Shah, the Qajar dynasty entered its terminal decline. During his reign, he had been far too cautious; it might have served him well for his own security, but his successors would have to pay the price of his prudence. Persia was worse off at the end of his long reign than at the beginning. Towards the end, he had increasingly discharged State affairs on his trustworthy and capable Amin ul-Sultan. His cynicism and misanthropy had deepened with time. During the last years he had felt discouraged and depressed. One day, during the 1890s, sitting alone in front of his mirror, he was heard muttering to himself: "Hopeless, hopeless, it is hopeless". One of his courtiers opened the door, thinking that the Shah had called for him; believing that he had been overheard, the Shah asked the nonplussed courtier, "Do you know what is hopeless?" and, before the courtier could react, he added: "Persia's predicament is hopeless!"[91] Thus thought Nasir ul-Din Shah, the man who for half a century had ruled over Persia. He had been the longest-reigning Qajar monarch. His ultimate goal had always been to maintain himself on the throne, regardless of consequences to his country and its citizens: in this regard alone one can say that he had been successful.

NOTES

[1] R.G. Watson, *A History of Persia* (London: Smith Elder and Co., 1866).
[2] C. and E. Burgess, *Letters from Persia* (New York: The New York Public Library, ed. by B. Schwartz, 1942) p.116.
[3] Â.A. Hashimi Rafsanjani, *Amir Kabir* (Qum: Daftar-i Intishirat-i Islami, 1363 (1984)) p.81.
[4] See H. Busse, *History of Persia Under Qajar Rule* (New York: Columbia Univ. Press, 1972) p.300.
[5] M.Q. Hidayat, *Guzarish-i Iran* (Tehran: Nuqreh, 1363 (1984)) p.76.
[6] Â. Mustoufi, *Sharh-i Zindagi-yi Man* (Tehran: Zavvar, 3rd ed., 1360 (1981)) Vol. I, p.70.
[7] D.M. Maceoin, *Changes in Charismatic Authority in Qajar C. Hillenbrand* (Edinburgh University Press, 1983) pp. 164-7.
[8] M.R. Fashahi, *Vapasin Jumbish-ha-yi Qurun-i Vusta'i dar Douran-i Fi'udal* (Tehran: Javidan, 1356 (1977)) pp.64-65.
[9] Ibid., p.85.
[10] M.Q. Hidayat, *Khatirat va Khatarat* (Tehran: Zavvar, 2nd ed., 1344 (1965)) p.54.
[11] On July 9, 1850, the *Bab* stood twice before the firing squad: the first time the bullets miraculously left him unharmed and free of his bonds. As the smoke cleared the *Bab* appeared to have vanished. He was found hiding under one of the citadel's staircases, brought back before the firing squad and this time shot dead.
[12] Sir P. Sykes, *A History of Persia* (London: Macmillan, 1930) Vol. II, p.346.

13 See, among others, F. Adamiyat, *Amir Kabir va Iran* (Tehran: *Khwarazmi*, 3rd ed., 1348 (1969)) p.196. M.Q. Hidayat, op. cit. (note 10), p.53. M.Q. Hidayat, *Guzarish-i Iran* (note 5), p.83.
14 See H. Busse, op. cit. (note 4) p.303.
15 Among those *babis* with lighted candles stuck in their open wounds was Sulayman Mirza, the son of Yahya Khan Mirakhuri Tabrizi. For further details see Îtizad ul-Saltaneh, *Fitneh-yi Bab* (Tehran: *Babak*, 2nd ed., 1351 (1972)).
16 The successors to the *Bab* were two half-brothers: 1) Mirza Yahya Khan Nouri, Subh-i Azal (d. 1912); 2) Mirza Husayn Âli Nouri, Baha'ullah (d. May 16, 1892). The former spawned the Azali movement from his Cyprus retreat and the latter, after his split with his half-brother, created Baha'ism – a religious sect said to believe in universal brotherhood – from his centre at Acre in Syria. Baha'ullah's sons Âbbas Effendi and Mirza Muhammad Âli helped spread Bahai'ism worldwide.
17 Major General Outram's expeditionary corps consisted of fifteen steamships. At Reshire, the British troops were met by some thousand Tangistani tribesmen under the command of Baqir Khan Tangistani. The British easily had the upper hand. On the Tangistani side, the major casualty was Ahmad Khan, Baqir Khan's eldest son. The British superiority was further evident at the battle for Muhammareh: Persian casualties amounted to two hundred against only five for the British. See H. Busse, op. cit. (note 4), p.320., and also J.B. Kelly, *Britain and the Persian Gulf, 1795-1880* (London: Oxford Univ. Press, 1968) pp.460-464.
18 M. Bamdad, *Shar-i Hal-i Rijal-i Iran* (Tehran: *Zavvar*, 1357 (1978)) Vol. III, p.83.
19 Taymouri, *Âsr-i bi Khabari*, (Tehran: *Iqbal*, 3rd ed., 1357 (1978)) p.260.
20 Â. Mustoufi, op. cit. (note 6), Vol. I, pp.93-94.
21 R.L. Greaves, *Persia and the Defence of India: 1884-1892* (London: University of London, The Athlone Press, 1959) p.49.
22 The aristocracy learned its lesson under Muhammad Shah and decided that in the future it would place some of its members in the court at Tabriz, so that the next shah would not throw them to the wind.
23 Ashtian was a large settlement in the central province, halfway between Arak and Saveh. It was on the summit of the geographical triangle (with roughly 30 km per side) formed by the villages of Ashtian, Tafrish and Farahan. This small region has provided a disproportionate number of elite members both in the nineteenth and twentieth centuries, from the Qâim Maqams and Amir Kabir downwards.
24 Muhsin Khan's first wife was the daughter of Muhsin Khan Muâyan ul-Mulk, Âli Khan's best friend. In 1897, as Amin ul-Douleh became *sadr-i âzam*, Muzaffar ul-Din Shah proposed to him to have his son Muhsin Khan marry his daughter Ashraf ul-Muluk. Amin ul-Douleh countered by making a request to which he thought the Shah would never agree: he asked as a dowry for the future bride the forty-two villages of Lasht-i Nisha (in Gilan, near Rasht), Persia's prime agricultural land. When the Shah readily agreed, the *sadr-i âzam* ordered his son to divorce his best friend's daughter and marry Ashraf ul-Muluk, which he naturally did. For the Amini family, Ashraf ul-Muluk – better known under her later title of Fakhr ul-Douleh (1882-1956) – was a godsend: she would not only safeguard the Amini's fortune but would also dominate twentieth-century Persian elite, along with her son Dr Âli Amini. Among other deeds, she pioneered the launch of private taxis in Tehran.

25 At the Tabriz court, the experienced Garousi found the time to educate the next generation of courtiers – among others, the Prince Âbd ul-Husayn Mirza Farmanfarma.
26 Â. Mustoufi, op. cit. (note 6), Vol. I, p.88. and also Sh. Bakhash, *Iran: Monarchy, Bureaucracy and Reform under the Qajars: 1858-1896* (London: Ithaca Press, 1978) p.92.
27 The primary source of inspiration for the twin advisory councils was a pamphlet Malkum had published in 1858: the *Kitabcheh-yi ghaybi*. In this work, Malkum proposed an eight-member council of ministers (*majlis-i vuzara*) and a twenty-six-member legislative council (*majlis-i tanzimat*), consisting of three princes, eight ministers and fifteen councillors. See Sh. Bakhash, *ibid.*, pp.7-8; and also the noteworthy reference by Ms. Z. Chajiî, *Vizarat va Vaziran dar Iran* (Tehran: Tehran University Press, 2535 (1976)).
28 Sh. Bakhash, ibid., p.92.
29 Ibid., p.79.
30 Ibid., p.138.
31 Quoted in Sir Charles Webster, *The Foreign Policy of Palmerston* (London: two volumes, 1951) Vol. II, pp.741-2.
32 G.N. Curzon, *Russia in Central Asia* (London: Frank Cass, 1967) p.326.
33 On the question of Russia's subjugation of Central Asia, beside the above reference, also see H.C. Rawlinson's outstanding *England and Russia in the East* (London: J. Murray, 1875).
34 R.L. Greaves, op. cit. (note 21), p.12.
35 Ibid., p.12.
36 P.C. Terenzio, *La Rivalité Anglo-Russe en Perse et en Afghanistan jusqu'aux accords de 1907* (Paris: Rousseau and Cie., 1947) p.141.
37 R.L. Greaves, op. cit. (note 21), p.46.
38 D. Wright, *The English Amongst the Persians* (London: Heinemann, 1977) p.128.
39 C. Issawi, *The Economic History of Iran, 1800-1914* (Chicago: The University of Chicago Press, 1971) pp.54-55.
40 H. Algar, *Mirza Malkum Khan* (Berkeley: University of California Press, 1973) p.18.
41 Ibid., p.17.
42 Ibid., p.112.
43 I. Taymouri, op. cit. (note 19), p.178.
44 H. Algar, op. cit. (note 40), p.114.
45 Ibid., p.115.
46 G.N. Curzon, *Persia and the Persian Question* (London: Frank Cass, 1967) Vol. I, p.615.
46A Ibid., Vol. I, pp.616-7.
47 Ibid., Vol. II, p.225.
47A Dieulafoy found the old city of Susa (Shushan) in 1886. Thereafter the French monopoly at Susa was unbreakable; the greatest beneficiary was the Louvre Museum in Paris. Dieulafoy remained at Susa from 1884 till 1896; he was then replaced in succession by archaeologist J. de Morgan (1897-1912), R. de Mecquenem (1912-1939), R. Ghirshman (1946-69) and J. Perrot (1969-1979).
48 Messrs. Lynch Bros. and Co., a transport firm based in Baghdad, and operating the Euphrates and Tigris Steam Navigation Company between Baghdad and Basra.

[49] I. Taymouri, op. cit. (note 19), p.352.
[50] On this subject see the interesting article by J.S. Galbraith, 'British Policy on Railways in Persia 1870-1900', in *Middle Eastern Studies*, Vol. 25, no. 4, October 1989. p.481.
[51] Ibid., p.497.
[52] I. Taymouri, op. cit. (note 19), pp.192-199.
[53] The IBP lost its monopoly of the printing of banknotes to the Bank-i Milli-i Iran in 1930. It later changed its name to the Imperial Bank of Iran in 1935 (according to the law); then, in 1949, altered it again to the British Bank of Iran and the Middle East; it extracted its capital from Iran in March 1951 and shortly thereafter it became known as the British Bank of the Middle East. It was eventually merged with the Hong Kong and Shanghai Banking Corporation (HSBC) in 1960. For the IBP's story see 'The History of the British Bank of the Middle East', in two volumes: G. Jones, *Banking and Empire in Iran* (Cambridge Univ. Press, 1986) Vol. I; and *Banking and Oil* (Cambridge Univ. Press, 1987) Vol. II.
[54] I. Taymouri, op. cit. (note 19), p.210.
[55] H. Algar, op. cit. (note 40), p.169.
[55A] Sh. Bakhash, op. cit. (note 25), p.236.
[56] On the subject of land tenure in Persia, see the magisterial work by A.K.S. Lambton, *Landlord and Peasant in Persia* (Oxford University Press, 1953).
[57] See the pioneering writings of Layard, covering his 1839–42 travels across the region, and especially in the Bakhtiari mountains; Sir Austen Henri Layard, *Early Adventures in Persia, Susiana and Babylonia* (London: John Murray, 1894). And also the unique film (and book) *Grass*, produced in 1924 by the American Merian C. Cooper, associated with Marguerite Harrison and Ernest Shoedsack (the cameraman).
[58] C. Issawi, op. cit. (note 38), p.231.
[59] H.C. Rawlinson, op. cit. (note 33), p.135.
[60] A. Seyf, 'The Plague of 1877 and the Economy of Gilan', in *IRAN, Journal of the British Institute of Persian Studies*, Vol. XXVII, 1989, pp.81-86.
[61] C. Issawi, op. cit. (note 38), pp.70-71.
[62] The Persian basic monetary unit was the *Kran*, originally introduced by Fath Âli Shah. At the outset the *Kran* weighed some 108 grains, but in 1877, when the modern mint was established it weighed only 71.4 grains (900 fine). See: E.B. Yaganegi, *Recent Financial and Monetary History of Persia*, (New York: Columbia University (Ph.D. thesis), 1934) p.60.
[63] Ibid., p.61.
[64] See Chams-ed-Dine Djazaeri, *La Crise Économique Mondiale et ses Répercussions en Iran* (Paris: Librairie Technique et Économique, 1938) p.163.
[65] Z.M. Chidfar, *La Réforme Monétaire et l'Étalon d'Or en Iran* (Paris: Éditions Domat-Montchrestien, F. Loviton et Cie, 1935) p.115.
[66] N. Keddie, *Religion and Rebellion in Iran* (London: Frank Cass, 1966) p.49.
[67] Shaykh Hasan Karbala'i, *Qarardad Rizhi 1890* (Tehran: *Mubarizan*, 2nd. ed., 1361 (1982)) p.46.
[68] I. Taymouri, *Tahrim Tambakou* (Tehran: Kitabha-yi Jibi, 3rd. ed., 1361 (1982)) p.71.
[69] Professor E.G. Browne, *The Persian Revolution of 1905-1909* (London: Frank Cass, 1966) pp.2-3.

[70] H. Pakdaman, *Djamal-El-Din Assad Abadi* (Paris: G.-P. Maisonneuve et Larose, 1969) p.199.
[71] Ibid., p.175.
[72] Ernest Renan, the French writer, met Asadabadi in Paris. Renan was a staunch anti-Islamist and convinced of Western superiority: "L'Islamisme perira par l'influence seule de la science l'Européenne, et ce sera notre siècle qui sera designé par l'histoire comme celui où commencerent a se poser les causes de cet immense événement".
[73] Professor H.A.R. Gibb in *The Near East and the Great Powers*, ed. by R.N. Frye, (Cambridge, Mass.: Harvard University Press, 1951).
[74] A.M. Goichon, *Jamal-el-din Al Afghani* (Paris: P. Geuthner, 1942) p.185.
[75] Ibid., p.185.
[76] Nazim ul-Islam Kirmani, *Tarikh-i Bidari-i Iranian* (Tehran: Agah, 3rd. ed., 1361 (1982)) Vol. I, p.87.
[77] Sir A. Hardinge to the Marquess of Lansdowne, September 6, 1901, FO 60/637.
[78] I. Taymouri, op. cit. (note 58), p.56.
[79] In a message dated July 17, 1903, Sir A. Hardinge wrote to Kimbell, the British consul at Shiraz: "The Russians, of course, used them [the ûlama] at the time of the Régie in a much more unscrupulous manner than would be consonant with our traditions of diplomacy, but I think we can profit by their example without resorting to such extreme methods as theirs." Quoted by H. Algar, op. cit. (note 40), p.236.
[80] M.Q. Hidayat, *Khatirat va Khatarat* (note 10), p.81.
[81] Shaykh Hasan Karbala'i, op. cit. (note 57), p.69.
[82] Shaykh Muhammad Riza Zanjani, *Tahrim Tambakou* p.103.
[83] N. Keddie, op. cit. (note 56), p.104.
[84] M.Q. Hidayat, *Khatirat va Khatarat* (note 10), p.81.
[85] Shaykh Hasan Karbala'i, op. cit. (note 57), p.117.
[86] Professor E.G. Browne, op. cit. (note 59), p.57.
[87] E. Yarshater, *Observations on Nasir al-Din Shah, in Qajar Iran* ed. by E. Bosworth and C. Hillenbrand, (Edinburgh University Press, 1983) p.10.
[88] Private communication by direct descendants of Prince Îzz ul-Douleh.
[89] Amin ul-Douleh, *Khatirat-i Syasi-yi Mirza Âli Khan Amin ul-Douleh* ed. by H. Farmanfarmayan, (Tehran: 1331 (1952)) p.24.
[90] Nasir ul-Din Shah made three visits to Europe: the first in 1873 (April 20–September 23); the second in 1878 (April 4–August 8); and the third in 1889 (April 14–October 20).
[91] M.Q. Hidayat, *Khatirat va Khatarat* (note 10), p.53.

CHAPTER FOUR:
CONSTITUTIONAL MOVEMENT

Until the very end, Nasir ul-Din Shah had been the centre of gravity around which the court and the State revolved. As long as he was there, the system somehow survived all mishaps – even weathering the Tobacco Concession fiasco; but, as he abruptly departed, "the curtain lifted on the elite, and behind the curtain everyone was found to be naked".[1] During Nasir ul-Din Shah's reign, the Qajar dynasty had reached the apex of its supremacy in Persia. Thereafter, it entered a prolonged and steady decline. The extended longevity of the dynasty after Nasir ul-Din Shah's departure was due to the loyalty of the Qajar elite rather than to the (non-existent) qualities of his successors.

The forty-eight-year rule of Nasir ul-Din Shah had been especially long for his son and successor, the crown prince, Muzaffar ul-Din Mirza. The latter had had to wait for his turn in his traditional fiefdom of Tabriz, where he had ruled for some thirty-six years, from 1860 until 1896. Upon his coronation in June 1896, he spoke *Farsi* with a marked *Azari* accent. Aged forty-three, the new Shah of Persia was already an old and sick man.

His father had toyed with the idea of altering the sacrosanct Qajar rule of succession in favour of his favourite son, Kamran Mirza; but without reaching a final decision while still alive. He had never liked nor trusted his crown prince and, when Îtimad ul-Saltaneh praised the latter in his newsletter, the Shah ordered him to delete the laudatory paragraph.[2] With a Kamran Mirza at the helm, the Qajars would have had a far better chance at survival. But Muzaffar ul-Din Shah it would be. Professor Browne found him to be "of kindly nature, weak health, ...lacking initiative and self-reliance"[3]; whereas Kermani was far harsher in his judgement of him: "simple-minded, easily persuaded, undecided and of a fickle nature... utterly devoid of prudence, judgement and foresight".[4]

The inexperienced Muzaffar ul-Din Shah was mounting the Peacock Throne at a turbulent time. The impact of Western inroads into Persia was beginning to be felt; a Persian intelligentsia had taken shape; the *ûlama* and the Bazaar still marvelled at their new-found status as giant-killers on the national scene and the people had finally shed their century-old torpor. It was amidst these dangerous currents and threatening socio-political eddies that the Shah was crowned. To guide him through these dangers, he had at hand the wily and experienced Amin ul-Sultan. His late father's and now his own *sadr-i âzam* knew Persia, Persians and politics better than any of his fellow citizens. Devoted to the Qajar cause and taking full advantage of his prerogatives, Amin ul-Sultan was the man in charge of the vessel of State. It was he who kept it going on an even keel, day in and day out. As long as he was invested with the royal responsibilities, the Shah could quietly attend to his capricious games and other liberties, and leave the affairs of State in expert hands.

4.1. Winds of Change

With the introduction of Western technology and ideas during the last decades of the nineteenth century, subtle changes were occurring in Persian society – especially in the major urban centres of Tehran, Tabriz, Isfahan, Mashhad, Rasht and Shiraz.

Among these changes were the gradual advances of the new educational system copied from the European schools. The very first step in that respect was taken by Amir Kabir in the early 1850s with the establishment of the Dar ul-Funoun School. A total of no fewer than 1,100 students would graduate from this institution in its first four decades.[5] Unfortunately, the recruitment by Malkum Khan of Dar ul-Funoun staff members in his freemasonry rendered Nasir ul-Din Shah suspicious of learning institutions and stopped him from further fostering the expansion of education in Persia. Notwithstanding this setback, the enlightened Prince Îtizad ul-Saltaneh, the Shah's uncle and long-standing Minister for Science (1858–1880), had the foresight to send forty-two Dar ul-Funoun graduates to Europe for further studies. Moreover he also had the yearly incomes of the districts of Malayir and Tuysirkan, of which he was governor, earmarked for the school's operating expenses.[6] Nevertheless, Persia had to wait half a century before a second school, the School for Political Sciences, was established in 1900 by the then Minister for Foreign Affairs, Nasrullah Khan Mushir ul-Douleh. A year later a college for agriculture was eventually created at Karaj. At the turn of the century Amir Kabir's pioneering efforts were still bearing fruit and he was being emulated by others.

Not only were Persian students educated in Persian schools, but an ever greater number were finding their way into European universities. At the beginning of the twentieth century, countries of academic preference for Persian students were England, Russia, France and Germany. Some of these were Dar ul-Funoun bursary-holders, but the majority were sons of the Qajar elite families. The attraction to foreign universities became so great that during the First World War approximately five hundred Persian students were enrolled abroad.[7]

In parallel to these developments, Persia's elementary educational system underwent a revolutionary change in 1894: Mirza Hasan Rushdiyyeh, a progressive cleric, opened the first lay school in Tabriz. Until then, the educational system had been the monopoly of the religious, who ran the traditional *maktab* system.[8] Two years later, Rushdiyyeh, supported by the *sadr-i âzam* Âli Khan Amin ul-Douleh, established Tehran's first lay school. Thus was the modern elementary educational system launched in Persia. The new tide overwhelmed the resistance of the religious community, and within a few decades replaced the *maktab* system. In Tehran new schools mushroomed: in quick succession the *Îlmiyyeh* School (directed by Mihdi Quli Hidayat), the *Sâadat* School (under Yahya Doulatabadi), the *Islam* School (founded by Sayyid Muhammad Tabataba'i) and the schools of *Sharaf*, *Danish*, *Adab* and *Shariât* were created, so that in 1900, a total of twenty lay schools – seventeen of them in Tehran (with a total of 1,300 pupils) – existed in Persia.[9] Most of these schools were in private hands; but in due time the Ministry of Science would take all of them under its control.

In parallel to education, printed matters and newspapers witnessed an exceptional development. It should be pointed out here that the first imported printing press was introduced in 1816 at Tabriz; Qâim Maqam's *Risaleh-yi Jihadiyyeh* must have been amongst the first pamphlets printed on it. Mirza Muhammad Saleh Shirazi made a first attempt in 1837 to publish a two-page (large size, printed on one face only) monthly, entitled *Akhbar-i Karaz*;[9A] but it ceased publication after only a few issues. In the field of journalism, too, Amir Kabir pioneered by launching a weekly, the court gazette entitled *Rouznameh Vaqaiyyeh-yi Ittifaqiyyeh* edited by the American-born Edward

Burgess. First issued in February 1851, Amir Kabir's weekly would survive its originator and run for 471 issues. Thereafter, the weekly changed its title to *Rouznameh Doulat-i Îlliyyeh-yi Iran* (until issue 668 in 1870) under the direction of Abu'l Hasan Khan Ghaffari. In the 1860s and 1870s, a number of wealthy elite members endeavoured, with mixed success, to publish their own newspapers: the Minister for Science, Âli Quli Mirza Îtizad ul-Saltaneh, published *Îlmiyyeh*, *Doulati* and *Millati* – the latter for thirty-four issues (over 1868–1872); Muhammad Hasan Khan Sanî ul-Douleh published the official *Iran* three times a week (from 1871); the Sipahsalar issued *Vatan* (only one issue), as well as the *Nizami* and *Mirrikh* for the Ministry of War; Muhammad Hasan Khan Îtimad ul-Saltaneh edited *Îlmi* (sixty-four issues, 1876–1880) and later the outstanding *Sharaf* (eighty-seven issues, 1883–1892); and Âli Quli Khan Mukhbir ul-Douleh published *Danish* (1882); Mirza Muhammad Husayn Khan Zuka' ul-Mulk (head of the School for Political Studies) edited *Tarbiyat*, and Sayyid Husayn Îdalat printed *Îdalat* at Tabriz. These forerunners paved the way for the journalistic explosion of the Constitutional Movement: since which journalism has become one of the pillars of Persian public opinion.

Besides the newspapers published in Persia, the *Farsi* ones printed abroad deserve a special mention. Not being subject to royal censorship and edited by capable editors, they had a tremendous impact in shaping Persian public opinion. India was a country of preference for the early *Farsi* newspaper. The oldest such paper was *Akhbar*, printed since 1798 in Delhi; *Marat ul-Akhbar* printed in Calcutta since 1822 was also of quality; other papers of Indian origin worth a mention were *Jam-i Jahan Nama*, *Shams ul-Akhbar*, *A'iyneh Sikandar*, *Chapak*, *Sultan ul-Akhbar*, *Mihr-i Munir* and *Jam-i Jamshid*.[9B] The most influential, however, was to be *Habl ul-Matin* published in Calcutta (1893–1930) by Sayyid Jalal ul-Din Husayni Kashani. But *Farsi* papers abroad were not an Indian monopoly. Istanbul was also a centre for such papers, with the high quality newspaper *Akhtar* published (1873–1896) by Hajji Muhammad Tahir Tabrizi. Cairo was another, with Mirza Muhammad Khan Kashani editing *Surayya* and *Parvarish*, and Mirza Mihdi Khan Tabrizi printing *Hikmat*. Finally, Malkum Khan's political paper *Qanoun*, published in London, ran for forty-two issues (1890–1898). Malkum being the best known of Persian intellectuals, the impact he had on his contemporaries was second to none.

Next to Malkum two other intellectuals were having their fair share of success in the circles of Persia's burgeoning intelligentsia. Both originated from the Azarbayjan–Caucasus region, an area always fertile in men of ideas due to its location on the crossroads between East and West. The first was Mirza Fath Âli Akhundof (1812–1878), a Russian correspondent of Malkum and, like him, a radical apostle of Westernisation. For a whole decade he had worked on a new, Latin alphabet for *Farsi* (as had Malkum) in order to bring about a change in the national Persian culture and thus pave the way for intensive Westernisation. The language of Firdousi and Hafiz, however, proved stronger than Akhundof and refused to be displaced. The second writer was Mirza Âbd ul-Rahim, known as 'Talbof', a Tabrizi liberal democrat with a considerable influence in his native Azarbayjan. 'Talbof' wrote books comparing the "backwardness" of Persia to the "progresses" of the West. He was even elected deputy from Tabriz in the first *Majlis*, only to be excommunicated by Shaykh Fazlullah Nouri for his highly controversial writings.

Yet another intellectual was Mirza Aqa Khan Kermani (1854–1896), a *Babi* writer from Kerman. With his friends Shaykh Ahmad Rouhi and Mirza Hasan Khan Khabir ul-Mulk, he had fled Kerman to seek refuge in Istanbul. There he collaborated with *Qanoun* and *Akhtar*, and made the pilgrimage to Cyprus to meet the *Babi* leader Subh-i Azal and marry one of his daughters (Rouhi married another). After Nasir ul-Din Shah's assassination all three were extradited to Persia and summarily beheaded in Tabriz on the orders of the new crown prince, Muhammad Âli Mirza.

After the printing press and the telegraph in the 1860s, the postal system was introduced in Persia. The great Amir Kabir had initiated an embryonic system of dispatching letters and goods, but had left the job unfinished. In the 1870s, the Austrian expert G. Riederer brought a modern postal system to Persia. In 1877, Persia joined the *Union Postale Universelle*, as she had joined the *Union Télégraphique Universelle* in 1869. In 1898, the first Belgian experts (Messrs. Naus, Priem and Theunis) arrived in Tehran to supervise the setting up of the Persian customs service. Four years later, the postal organisation was also brought under their supervision, with Camille Molitor at its head. In 1906, the Ministry for Post and Telegraph was created and

Persians gradually took over the two above organisations. Naus had to depart in 1907,[10] and the last Belgian expert left Tehran in 1915. In the field of transports very little was done. The revolutionary railway failed to develop in Persia. Roads were not being built; rivers were not used. There were only a few exceptions: the linking by Russians of their southern border to northern Persian centres (e.g. Tabriz); the opening of navigation on the Karoun river by Messrs Lynch; the creation by the same British company of the 430-kilometre long Ahvaz-Isfahan mule-track across mountainous Bakhtiari territory: the so-called Lynch Road.[11]

Efforts at industrialisation were discouraging. Local industrial units were not competitive because of low import tariffs (since Turkomancha'i) and a general lack of adequate technology and management. Non-existent means of transportation were yet another major impediment. Foreign investors did not fare much better than domestic capitalists in their Persian industrialisation schemes. In the 1890s, a Belgian company which had invested in a venture for gas lighting derived from coal went bankrupt. Other Belgian investments in a glass factory and a sugar refinery also came to naught. A Russian company which had established a match factory in Tehran had to close down, proving incapable of competing with cheaper imports. The only success came about in cotton ginning: in the northern provinces a whole industry developed, employing a total of four hundred and twenty workers in nine Persian-owned and seventeen Russian-owned cotton ginning factories.[12] Going one step further in cotton processing proved uncompetitive, as Sanî ul-Douleh, a Persian investor, experienced in 1893 as his cotton spinning venture folded soon after start-up. Mining projects did not fare any better than industrial ventures, as prohibitively high production prices proved higher than import prices; here again, Sanî ul-Douleh had some disappointing experiences.

Drastic changes in finance and money matters were introduced in the early 1890s by the two foreign banks: the British Imperial Bank of Persia (IBP) and the Russian Banque d'Escompte. The introduction of Western banking systems and banknotes brought some security and stability to Persian financial markets, and consequently an increase in commerce and trade. The new banks now had a considerable influence in the domestic economy – especially the IBP which had a monopoly on the issuing of Persian banknotes. The traditional Persian moneychangers – the *bazaar sarrafs* – lost part of their business but not all of it, because the *bazaar* and the people were reluctant to trust the foreign institutions. Nevertheless, together with the Tobacco Concession, the granting of banking rights to foreign outfits was yet another encroachment on the *bazaar*'s traditional prerogatives.

If not a direct threat to the small-time *sarraf*, the banks were going to thwart the development of nationwide trading houses and joint-stock companies. The most renowned of Persian trading houses was the Toumanians Trading of Tabriz, which had begun national and international (with Russia) trade and financing in the 1820s. In the 1880s, the Toumanians brothers had branched out in banking and moved their main business to Russia: the uneven competition from the new banks would weaken them and the Russian Revolution would ruin them. Two other national trading houses – the Jamshidian House, created in 1886 by Arbab Jamshid (a Zoroastrian), and the Jahanian House, established in 1895 by Khusrou Shah Jahan – both had their roots in Yazd, a town reputed for its shrewd businessmen. Both the Jamshidian and Jahanian expanded rapidly, borrowed from the foreign banks, over-expanded and eventually went bankrupt: the former in 1912 and the latter three years later.[13] The joint stock companies didn't do any better than the trading houses. The *Ittihadiyyeh* company, created at Tabriz in 1897 by Sayyid Mihdi Kouzeh Kanâni, Sayyid Murtaza Sarraf and a group of Tabriz *bazaaris*, was at first very successful; its interests later clashed with the IBP and it eventually collapsed in 1912.[14] In 1898, the *Shirkat-i Islami* was founded in Isfahan by Hajj Muhammad Husayn Kazirouni, a leading *bazaari*, with an initial capital of 150,000 toumans and with the support of the Prince Zill ul-Sultan and the religious authorities; dealing mainly in textiles, the *Islami* was initially successful but later went bankrupt. In 1899, seventeen Tehran *Bazaaris* joined forces to invest one million toumans in the Public Iranian Company; like its predecessors, this joint stock venture lasted five years before folding. In the end, neither trading houses nor public share companies were able to survive and flourish in late nineteenth- and early twentieth-century Persia. Such a massive failure of domestic capitalism was due mainly to: (1) the inability of domestic outfits to compete with the foreign banking institutions and (2) the seeming incapacity of Persian individuals (even *Bazaaris*) to co-operate in any enterprise. The *Bazaar*'s impotence at the national level sent their leading members back to their traditional shops, in the protective cocoon of their covered labyrinthine alleys (where no one could find them, let alone importune them), vituperating against the banks whose intrigues they held directly responsible for their losses.

In the military sphere too, after decades of stagnation, there had been some changes. The Persian Army, put on back burners by Nasir ul-Din Shah after the Herat invasion of 1856 and the Turkoman disaster of 1860, was barely capable of repressing domestic revolts. Because of the low influence and the lack of prestige associated with military careers, young elite members shunned the army and preferred going abroad to prepare for rewarding careers at court or in foreign affairs. To train the soldiers, the regime had to hire foreign officers. This it did, first in 1878 during the Shah's second trip to Europe, when ten Austrian officers (a colonel, a major, three captains and five lieutenants) were selected and sent to Tehran where they arrived in January 1879; some of these officers would stay (e.g. General Wagner). During the same trip, the Shah hired the forty year old Count of Monteforte to head the Tehran police and municipality; the Italian count managed his police well from 1878 until 1889, when he departed Persia. But the most important consequence of the second European trip was the acceptance by the Shah of the Cossack officers placed at his disposal by the Tsar to create a brigade of Persian soldiers under their command. Thus, in 1879, the so-called Cossack Brigade was born, initially acting as a special royal guard.[15]

Education, the printing press, the newspapers, the telegraph, the post, the mint, the concessions, the new banks, the efforts at industrialisation, the military officers: all these Western imports were bringing about changes on the domestic stage. Persian minds were being awakened to new ideas, new technologies and new habits. Communications were still hampered by poor transportation (Persia still had no railways), but Persians were getting used to communicating by the telegraph and the post. In these last years of the nineteenth century, traditional Persia was being shaken by its forced intercourse with the latest Western ideas and inventions.

4.2. Uneasy Reign

As long as Amin ul-Sultan held the power, he tried his best to serve both his country and his king. As only he knew how, he endeavoured to keep a delicate balance in Persian affairs. The continued rule of the prime minister might have been agreeable to the weak Muzaffar ul-Din Shah, but it was not to the members of his inner circle, who all had ambitions of their own. The Shah's inner circle consisted essentially of six men:

1) Âbd ul-Majid Mirza Âyn ul-Douleh; a Qajar prince (as a grandson of Fath Âli Shah); the Shah's *pishkar* (factotum); obstinate and arrogant.

2) Mirza Muhammad Khan Hakim ul-Mulk; from a long succession of *hakimbashis* (physicians); private doctor to the Shah like his father Mirza Âli Naqi; a capable, but greedy physician.

3) Husayn Pasha Amir Bahadur Jang; the Shah's personal security chief; arrogant and ignorant.

4) Sayyid Bahrayni; the Shah's spiritual confessor; whenever it thundered the Shah would hide under Bahrayni's long cloak.

5) Basir ul-Saltaneh; the Shah's private servant, his everyday companion and *souffre-douleur*.

6) Âbd ul-Husayn Mirza Farmanfarma, grandson of Âbbas Mirza on his father's side and great-grandson of Amir Kabir on his mother's side; both the Shah's brother-in-law and son-in-law; in a class all by himself; shrewd, ruthless and unscrupulous.

The six dominant courtiers were nicknamed the 'Turks' by the Tehran elite, because they had all come from Tabriz with the crown prince. They were to take full advantage of the weak Shah's generosity and rapidly depleted large parts of Nasir ul-Din Shah's legacy. For example, they convinced the Shah to give them his father's twenty-four gold-plated chairs, sold the whole lot and pocketed the proceeds.[16] As Amin ul-Douleh wrote in his memoirs:

> The 'Turks' ...were like hungry vultures fallen on the carcass of the kingdom...[17]

In November 1896, under pressure from the 'Turks', the Shah summarily dismissed Amin ul-Sultan and had him exiled to Qum. Amin ul-Douleh, a mild elite reformer, was called in to replace him.

Amin ul-Douleh tried his best to bring about reforms, but failed in most of his endeavours.[18] His only success was hiring the Belgian customs inspectors. When he failed to secure a £1,000,000 loan from the IBP, he was dismissed by the Shah in August 1898. Many had intrigued against the prime minister: among others, Amin ul-Sultan from his Qum exile, Farmanfarma from his Tehran governorship and Zill ul-Sultan from Isfahan.[19]

Having dismissed Amin ul-Douleh, who retired to his plush estate of Lasht-i Nisa, the Shah recalled Amin ul-Sultan.

The latter was charged with trying to secure a loan from the Russians so that debts could be paid and much-needed projects undertaken. Amin ul-Sultan, as the courtier for whom nothing was impossible, led the Russo-Persian rapprochement and eventually secured a 22.5 million roubles loan (equivalent to approximately £2.5 million). The conditions attached to this first Russian loan were: 1) repayment period of seventy-five years at an interest of five per cent; 2) all Persian customs revenues (except for the southern customs) as collateral; 3) reimbursement of 1.5 million roubles due to the Banque d'Escompte; 4) repayment of the IBP's £500,000 loan of 1892; 5) no other foreign loan for ten years; 6) prior Russian approval for the lowering of any customs tariffs. As soon as the loan was received the Shah and his courtiers departed for a seven-month visit to Europe (allegedly to attend the Exposition Universelle at Paris[20]). When they returned to Persia in November 1900, nothing remained of the first Russian loan. But a month later the deserving Amin ul-Sultan was duly rewarded for his services by being given the title of *Atabeg-i Âzam*.

The newly-appointed Atabeg persevered in his Russophile policy. In November 1901 he brought to conclusion a fresh Russo-Persian commercial convention (the first since Turkomancha'i), known as the Tariff Convention of 1902. The introduction of three fresh tariffs – 'A', 'B' and 'C' – not only drastically lowered all tariffs, but also provided "a frame entirely in favour of Russian goods". For example, duty on naphtha was reduced from five to one and a half per cent and that on sugar from five "to less than two per cent" – needless to say these were major imports from Russia.[21] The convention was applied from 1903 onwards with predictably dire consequences for the Persian traders and merchants. The British were to sign a roughly similar treaty with Persia shortly thereafter. But the harm had been done and over the next decade Russia would see its total trade with Persia greatly increase from 243m *krans* (1902) to 656m *krans* (1913), whereas Great Britain remained a distant second with only 235m *krans* in 1913.[21A]

And the Russo-Persian honeymoon was still on, as in 1903 Russia approved a second loan to Persia in the amount of ten million roubles – the conditions being the same as for the first loan, with a railway concession for the Julfa-Qazvin line (never implemented) added to the Banque d'Escompte. This time round, Muzaffar ul-Din Shah could not resist the temptations of a trip to Europe: departing in March 1903, he returned in October of the same year.[22] Thus were the funds of the second Russian loan squandered. The Atabeg, who had engineered both loans, later confided:

> In the management of Persia, I have not made many errors. Maybe the second Russian loan was the worst of them, because after the first loan which was earmarked for development and ended up being spent on the Shah's pleasures, I should have been better advised...[23]

At the close of Muzaffar ul-Din Shah's second European trip, the Atabeg was dismissed. He departed Persia to visit Europe, America and the Far East. Again the 'Turks' had succeeded in removing the man who had for two decades dominated Persian political life. Hidayat passed this judgement on the Atabeg:

> ...a fluent speaker and a good writer, ...a manager well versed in politics, but also a magnanimous and noble-minded individual...[24]

Atabeg left the Shah surrounded by "a wall of gloom and ignorance."[25]

The inner circle had finally decided to step into the political arena. It had learned all it could from the experienced Atabeg for the past five years; now it thought it could easily run the government without him. Âyn ul-Douleh was appointed as *sadr-i âzam* – an appalling choice (at this stage the imaginative Farmanfarma would have been a far better choice). Amir Bahadur Jang, the Shah's security chief, was to assist the prime minister in his task. The new leadership lacked competence, foresight and experience; it could only count on the Shah's backing. And as the Shah, unlike his father, was not capable of ruling, the Qajar Court was in a poor bind.

Between this politically weak court and the newly awakened forces in Persian society, the clash was almost inevitable. For these forces which had gained momentum since the Tobacco Concession, the time was ripe to flex their muscles: the power gradient *vis-à-vis* the regime was too propitious to let it pass by. Against the Shah and his 'Turks', they had the best possible opportunity for success.

4.3. Constitutional Movement (Part 1)

As soon as the new leadership was in place, troubles began. The first group to experience the heavy-handed policies of the fresh management were the religious: for a minor offence, some fourteen young *tullabs* (religious students) were bastinadoed and exiled to Ardabil for two months. The religious hierocracy pounced on the occasion and protested vehemently, arguing that the punishment was not in proportion to the fault committed. It was finally given satisfaction and the students returned, but the harm had been done and the religious sector of the population uselessly alienated.

As for the *Bazaar* merchants and traders, the religious sector's perennial ally, they were far from happy with the Belgians' handling of the customs. Naus and his compatriots taxed the traders to supply funds for the court's coffers and made payments only on the *sadr-i âzam's* orders.[26] The *Bazaaris* bided their time, until, in March 1905, they were given a golden opportunity to attack Naus: they secured a picture of the Belgian manager dressed as a *mulla* at a *bal masque*! The outcry was general. This time both the *Bazaar* and the hierocracy requested his immediate dismissal. In vain. Âyn ul-Douleh refused outright to sack his customs' chief, arguing that he would not yield under pressure.

The Naus incident was the drop of water that triggered the overflow of the malcontents' glass. In the spring of 1905, as the Shah was on his way to Europe, two leading Tehran *mujtahids* – Sayyid Âbdullah Bihbahani (1844–1910) and Sayyid Muhammad Tabataba'i (1843–1921) – accepted the leadership of the coalition of religious and

Bazaar forces ranged against the regime's caprices. With an articulate and respected leadership the anti-regime front now had a chance to make its voice heard throughout society. Moreover, under the aegis of the religious duumvirate, a whole slate of secret and semi-secret societies were gathering, to form the third (and not least) leg of the anti-regime coalition.

Known as *anjumans*, these semi-secret societies were a way for Persians to organise their covert networks: they were Persia's equivalent to European freemasonry (when the latter eventually developed branches there, it found the spadework done and simply incorporated whole *anjumans* within its lodges). In the *anjumans* one could not only find *mullas* and *Bazaaris* but also intellectuals, discontented bourgeois and even members of the lower nobility. The *Anjuman-i Makhfi* (Covert Anjuman) was essentially composed of clergymen under the direction of Tabataba'i's second son, Sayyid Muhammad Sadiq Tabataba'i – allegedly later a freemason like his father.[27] Another *anjuman* was the *Jamîyat-i Adamiyat*, launched at the turn of the century by one of Malkum Khan's fiercest disciples, Âbbas Quli Adamiyat. This latter society was extremely successful: it recruited some three hundred members (including in due time Muhammad Âli Shah himself[28]), and was also extremely rich, since entry fees ranged from ten to one thousand gold coins. Yet another remarkable and influential *anjuman* was the *Kumiteh Inqilab* (the Revolutionary Committee), formed by the friends of Sulayman Mirza Maykadeh and consisting of a total of fifty-four founding members.[29] The committee's leadership consisted of nine members, including personalities like Malik ul-Mutakalimin, Sayyid Jamal ul-Din Vâiz Isfahani, Sayyid Muhammad Riza Mussavat and Hajj Mirza Yahya Doulatabadi.[30]

The opposition was now prepared. It just needed a *casus belli* to enter hostilities. It was given it in December 1905, when the then governor of Tehran, Âla ul-Douleh, fined seventeen *Bazaar* sugar merchants for selling sugar over the fixed price, and had one of them, Hajj Sayyid Hashim Qandi, and his son bastinadoed. The next day, in the Shah Mosque, Sayyid Jamal ul-Din Vâiz vituperated against Âla ul-Douleh's inconsiderate act, calling for his dismissal. Clashes ensued in the mosque between royalist and opposition forces. When the royalists gained the upper hand, the opposition's leadership of Bihbahani and Tabataba'i decided to stage *bast* (sit-in) at Shah Âbd ul-

Âzim with hundreds of their followers. Simultaneously, in a sign of solidarity, the Tehran *Bazaar* closed down and sent the brothers Hajj Muhammad Taqi and Hajj Hasan Bunakdar to Shah Âbd ul-Âzim to assist the *bast* financially. Meanwhile Âyn ul-Douleh and Amir Bahadur Jang used all their powers to bring the *bast* to an end; but to no avail. Bihbahani and Tabataba'i had sent the Shah a list of requests, prominent among which was the creation of a House of Justice. Muzaffar ul-Din Shah eventually caved in and accepted all of the *bastis'* conditions. After twenty-eight days of *bast*, the Sayyids and their followers returned triumphantly to Tehran: they had won the first round. The only minor *quid pro quo* was that Jamal ul-Din Vâiz was to be exiled to Qum.

During the winter and spring of 1906 the struggle was carried on in the people's minds, with each side trying to win over the undecided. In this respect the religious had the formidable advantage of being able to harangue people daily in their mosques. The creation of a house of justice promised by the Shah had been completely forgotten. Then, on July 10, 1906, yet another incident occurred as guardsmen were taking an offending *mulla* to jail. Young religious students intervened to free him, guards fired, a student named Sayyid Âbd ul-Majid was shot dead. At his funeral mourners demonstrated, chanting slogans; guards fired to keep control of the mob: casualties ensued. The first blood had been drawn in the struggle between the religious and the regime. The point of no-return in the conflict had been passed.

The crass incompetence of Âyn ul-Douleh had brought the country to the verge of revolution and the Qajar dynasty to the brink of the abyss.

Bihbahani and Tabataba'i, realising that armed repression would leave them voiceless, decided on a tactical retreat to Qum. Shaykh Fazlullah Nouri, Tehran's third prominent *mujtahid* (although more dogmatic and less of a politician than the two Sayyids), decided to join them. In Tehran, the *Bazaar* naturally closed and the merchants thought of taking *bast* in order to ensure their own security *vis-à-vis* the royalist onslaught. The ideal setting was the sprawling British Legation located at the northern end of the city, where the royalist forces would not dare enter. The British authorities at first rejected initial *Bazaari* demands. But it was clear that the British would not side with a reactionary and declining regime and turn their back on the bullish *forces vives* of the nation. Moreover the court was filled with

Russophiles (since the two Russian loans), and the British were certainly not displeased to assist the opposition. Thus, on July 18, 1906, a first group of fifty *bastis* entered, unimpeded, the doors of the British Legation. Four days later they numbered eight hundred and sixty; within a week they were five thousand; and, on July 28, the number of *bastis* passed the fourteen thousand mark.[31] Discipline was perfect (yet another facet of the opposition's strength); the Bunakdar brothers supplied food directly from the *Bazaar*, and money; the British provided sanitary facilities[32] and water.

As in the first *bast*, a list of requests was sent to the Shah. The *bastis* asked for a constitution and a parliament (*Majlis*) and the dismissal of Âyn ul-Douleh. The abortive house of justice, which would have fully satisfied the opposition a few months earlier, was totally forgotten. Yet again the weak Muzaffar ul-Din Shah copped out: on July 30 he ordered Âyn ul-Douleh to resign and appointed his highly capable Minister for Foreign Affairs Nasrullah Khan Mushir ul-Douleh in his stead; then on August 5 he signed a royal *farman* (decree) to his fresh *sadr-i âzam* ordering him to set up a constitutional assembly.[32A] The *bastis* returned to their homes, triumphant; the self-exiled leaders returned victoriously from Qum. The opposition had won a decisive battle in its fight for a voice in national affairs.

Within a month the opposition's intellectuals had drawn up an electoral law including thirty-three articles and calling for a total of one hundred and sixty deputies, subdivided among six social classes.

The Shah and Mushir ul-Douleh duly signed the law's decree on September 9, 1906. Elections were rapidly carried out as foreseen by the law. On October 7, the first Persian *Majlis* was inaugurated (mainly with the Tehran deputies as the others still on their way). To accommodate the *Majlis*, the former Sipahsalar School was chosen as the venue. A total of one hundred and fifty-three deputies were elected. The breakdown of the elected deputies by actual social background (not the artificial classes proposed in the electoral law) clearly showed that the *bazaaris*, which had spearheaded the Constitutional Movement, were the big winners of the first popular consultation in Persia, with the religious activists, the landowners and the government employees filling the next places. Of the one hundred and thirty-three deputies whose main occupation was known, the following breakdown was compiled:[33]

Bazaaris:	49	deputies
Religious:	23	deputies
Landowners:	28	deputies
Civil servants:	21	deputies
Free professions:	7	deputies
Miscellaneous:	5	deputies
Total:	133	deputies

Persia's first *Majlis* enthusiastically got to work. The deputies had as their chief task to compile Persia's first constitution (taking the Belgian and French Constitutions as models). It came out as an ensemble of fifty-one articles. On December 30, 1906 it was signed by Muzaffar ul-Din Shah on his deathbed, and subsequently co-signed by Crown Prince Muhammad Âli Mirza and the *sadr-i âzam* Mushir ul-Douleh. On January 4, 1907, the Shah died. *In extremis*, he had conceded both a *Majlis* and a constitution: a considerable achievement for a Shah who was certainly not made of the 'higher stuff'. Because of his and his entourage's political weakness, what had started as a protest of sorts against the crass injustice of the administration (at the close of 1905) had ended with a parliamentary constitution (at the close of 1906). Thus, with the granting of a constitution and the death of the Shah, ended the first phase of the Constitutional Movement which had brought about tremendous changes, first in the minds and then in the lives of Persia's people.

The people had not been alone in their struggle and the British assisted them when and where needed to come to grips with Muzaffar ul-Din Shah's Russophile entourage. The huge *bast* in the legation's grounds was a turning point in the Movement's history. It was after the *bast* that the regime capitulated.

4.4. A Concession for the Better

As far as petroleum exploration in Persia was concerned, the background was not encouraging: Messrs Hotz were unsuccessful in the 1880s at Dalaki and the Persian Bank Mining Rights Corporation had to fold (at the turn of the century) after sinking a few fruitless wells. Nevertheless, an article published in *Les Annales Mines* in February 1892 and a book published in 1896[34] by the French archaeologist Jacques de Morgan, describing oil seepages in Persia, suddenly focused the attention of three individuals with long links to Persia: Sir Henry Drummond-Wolff, the former British envoy to Persia, Général Antoine Kitabchi Khan, a former director-general of Persian customs, and Edouard Cotte, a former Reuters agent in Persia.

The Wolff—Kitabchi—Cotte trio thought that, on the basis of the De Morgan reports, a fresh oil concession was well worth the risk. The only problem was that they lacked the necessary seed capital for the venture and that after the Tobacco Régie fiasco 'old' British money "was wary of investing further in Persian adventures".[35] But the resourceful Wolff found 'new' money with William Knox D'Arcy. D'Arcy (1849–1917), a solicitor's son, had gone to Australia when still young. There, he had formed a joint venture with the Morgan brothers in the Mount Morgan Gold Mining Company. The venture had struck gold and D'Arcy became a millionaire. He then retired as a *rentier* to London's plush Grosvenor Square. That is where Wolff had found him to persuade him to risk part of his fortune on a Persian oil concession. D'Arcy accepted.

D'Arcy's envoy to Persia, Alfred Marriott, paid the usual bribes (possibly as much as £10,000) to secure the oil concession. On May 28, 1901 the D'Arcy concession "for crude oil, natural gas, bitumen and natural wax" was signed by Muzaffar ul-Din Shah and witnessed by the *sadr-i âzam* Âli Asghar Khan Atabeg-i Âzam (Drummond-Wolff's old friend), the Minister for Foreign Affairs, Nasrullah Khan Mushir ul-Douleh, and the Minister for Mines, Nizam ul-Din Muhandis ul-Mamalik. The concession agreement, covering eighteen articles, was not of a high legal standard and some of the points were subject to diverse interpretations. The concession covered some 480,000 square miles of Persian territory[36] – in other words, the whole country, except for the five northern provinces, which had been excluded after vehement Russian recriminations. Furthermore, the concession was for sixty years; the Persian Government (or rather its representatives) would receive a £20,000 down-payment and some £20,000 in shares in the company D'Arcy was planning to establish to exploit the concession. In addition, 16% of the net profits of the said company or of any other company established by D'Arcy in regard to the concession would be paid to the Persian treasury.[37]

D'Arcy formed his company and dispatched George Bernard Reynolds as his site manager to Persia to commence with exploration.

G.B. Reynolds (1852-1925), an engineer formerly with the Indian Public Works, "then rising fifty and with experience in Sumatra and India",[38] was a happy choice. In a hostile and foreign environment, he proved indefatigable. He first began drilling at Shiah Surkh, near the Iraqi border (that parcel of land was returned to Iraq in 1913), with limited success as his sprouters soon dried up; he switched in vain to Mamatayn in the territories of the Bakhtiari tribe in the Zagros mountains, and for his last endeavour chose the Maydan-i Naftan (near a centuries-old seepage) north of Mamatayn. It was there that on May 26, 1908 – seven years almost to the day after the concession was granted – Reynolds discovered crude oil in commercial quantities at a depth of 1180 feet (his second well hit oil at 1010 feet a week later). After more than five years of uninterrupted efforts Reynolds had made history against all odds: he had by sheer perseverance struck oil in Persia (the first such find in the Middle East). The sprouter at Maydan-i Naftan was a triumph for him and also for D'Arcy, who had thus made two great fortunes in a lifetime. But both Reynolds and D'Arcy would remain the two "great unsung heroes in the history of oil"; were it not for the latter's money and the former's protracted labours, oil would not have been found there and then. At least a D'Arcy Exploration Company was created and Knox D'Arcy would receive his share of the concession's profits. But, as Sir Arnold Wilson remarked:

> The service rendered by G.B. Reynolds to the British Empire and to Persia was never recognised...

By 1908, however, D'Arcy was no longer the sole owner of his oil concession. Back in 1903, D'Arcy had formed a company to finance his huge exploration costs with an initial capital of £600,000: the First Exploration Company.[39] But by 1905, the capital had melted away and D'Arcy had even considered selling his concession to foreign interests. In the meantime, though, the economical and strategic importance of crude oil had dawned on a handful of British decision-makers. One of these was Lord John A. Fisher, the first sea lord, a firm supporter of having oil replace coal as the fuel of the Royal Navy's warships; another was E.G. Pretyman, the civilian chairman of the Oil Committee set up by Fisher to study the switch from coal to oil. Having got wind of D'Arcy's inclination to sell to non-British interests, the Oil Committee persuaded Lord Strathcona and his Burmah Oil Company[40] to bail out D'Arcy. Burmah obliged and partly refunded D'Arcy for expenditures incurred and in May 1905 created a new entity, the Concessions Syndicate Ltd., (CSL) to control the concession. Thus 'old' British money, taking advantage of D'Arcy's financial problems, was, by a timely action, snatching a controlling share in the prospective oil concession.

With Reynolds's discovery of 1908, money became secondary: the market was willing to provide as much as was needed, and even more. On April 14, 1909 as the Anglo-Persian Oil Company Ltd., (APOC) was established in London, its initial capital of £2,000,000 was oversubscribed fifteen times.[41] Simultaneously yet another company, the Bakhtiari Oil Company Ltd., (BOC) was created in London with an initial capital of £400,000.[42] The BOC controlled the one crucial square mile of land at the Maydan-i Naftan and was ninety-seven per cent owned by APOC; the remaining three per cent were distributed among the leading Bakhtiari *Khans* to secure their goodwill – after all, the black gold had been found in the ground beneath their tribal lands and, justly, they received some benefit from its commercialisation.

After Reynolds's historical strike at Maydan-i Naftan in 1908, not only would life never be the same for the Bakhtiari tribesmen, but neither would it be for the Persian nation. In twentieth-century Persia, in addition to the people, their elites and the Powers, a fourth vector – crude oil – would always be found lurching in the aisles of Persian politics.

4.5. Constitutional Movement (Part 2)

With the death of Muzaffar ul-Din Shah, his son and thirty-five year old crown prince, Muhammad Âli Mirza mounted the Peacock Throne. Crowned Shah of Persia on January 20, 1907[43] the sixth Qajar monarch differed physically from all his predecessors: whereas they had been lean and of average height, he was corpulent (even obese) and shorter. His unregal appearance was a sure sign that some degeneracy had set into the Qajar royal branch. Here again, as with the rivalry of Muzaffar ul-Din Mirza and Kamran Mirza, there were rumours that Muhammad Âli Shah's younger brother, Malik Mansur Mirza Shûâ ul-Saltaneh[44] (who, in turn, showed none of his elder brother's signs of degeneracy), had had a chance of being chosen to succeed his father. But, here again, the Qajars failed to break with their century-old tradition and went along with the crown prince. Thus, until the bitter end, the Qajars cowered before the sacrosanct rule of succession set by Aqa Muhammad Khan, unwilling to accept that the path to survival asks for a break with tradition. In their defence, it should be said that, in the case of Muhammad Âli Shah, the Russians strictly prohibited any other contender.

Politically, Muhammad Âli Shah had a Russophile background, having been educated by a Russian Jew, Shapsal Khan. Called to the crown prince's side as a private tutor, Shapsal had remained at his side ever since, as a confidant and top adviser. Thus, the Shah's education had been anti-democratic and reactionary, and now his goal was to return to an absolute monarchy. He was greatly encouraged in this objective by his reactionary courtiers: Amir Bahadur Jang, Amin ul-Mulk, Mufakhir ul-Mulk, Muvaqqar ul-Saltaneh and Mujallal ul-Sultan. The Shah and his advisers were too unimaginative to realise that "man's mind stretched to a new idea never goes back to its original dimension", and that the movement for democracy could not be reversed.

A power struggle was almost inevitable between the fresh *Majlis* and the court. The first round was fought in parliament over the national budget. The *Majlis'* finance commission had estimated the national revenues at around 7.5 million toumans and expenditure at 10.7 million toumans, resulting in a net deficit of 3.2 million. In order to fill the gap a number of measures were voted in by the *Majlis* in the autumn of 1907:[45] (1) the court's yearly allocation was halved, from 800,000 to 420,000 toumans; (2) yearly princely purses were allocated as per need; (3) provincial governors had to transfer to the central treasury the full amount of taxes received, not the nominal amount fixed decades before; (4) the proceeds of the sale of agricultural products was not acceptable (because of outdated price-fixing) therefore the products had to be delivered in goods; (5) the practice of *tuyoul* was henceforward abolished and former *tuyouls* had to be rented on the treasury's behalf. With such a set of decisions the *Majlis* had gone far on the way of reforms, but it had shied away from a revolutionary one, being a bourgeois *Majlis* with a large majority of moderate deputies, not a radical one. It had failed to implement the revolutionary land reform that would have really altered the balance of power within Persia. It dared not touch the royal *Khalisehs* and other private land holdings. In short, the basic problem of the Constitutional Movement was summarised here: it was merely a middle-class movement against royal prerogatives, not a revolution.

Among the first *Majlis* there were some revolutionary and extremist elements, but they were a tiny minority of four members: Sayyid Hasan Taqizadeh and Hajj Mirza Ibrahim Aqa (of Tabriz), Falak ul-Maâli (Rasht) and Yahya Mirza Iskandari (Tehran);[46] and, still, some of their members (like Taqizadeh) were far from being genuine revolutionaries. The real winds of revolution were blowing from the Russian Caucasus, especially after the abortive revolution of 1905. The Russian-inspired radical *Ijtimâyun-Âmmyun* party[47] found fertile ground in Persian Azarbayjan in which to branch out. Immigrants to the thriving Baku oil fields brought back with them the new ideas and ideals. And socialist ideas appealed to Persian intellectuals.[48]

Within a couple of months of his accession, the Shah decided to recall from exile the only man who could muzzle the *Majlis* – the crafty Âli Asghar Khan Atabeg-i Âzam. Obliged, the Atabeg came back to try to work out a *modus vivendi* between the movement and the court while simultaneously playing the various factions against each other. The Atabeg was about to succeed in his mission impossible[49] when he was assassinated in front of the *Majlis* on August 31, 1907. On Atabeg's death, historian A. Kasravi wrote: "A major obstacle was thus removed from the Constitutional Movement's path",[50] stressing the constitutionalists' fear of the Atabeg's undeniable capacities.

On the very same August 31, as the Atabeg was shot in Tehran, the Russians (Isvolsky) and the British (Nicolson) were signing at St Petersburg the partition of Persia into spheres of influence. The Russian northern sphere, inclusive of Kermanshah and Isfahan, came all the way down to Yazd before ending at the junction of the Russian and Afghan borders; the British south-eastern sphere was far less important, with a western delimitation along the Bandar Âbbas–Kerman–Birjand line; and the area in between the two spheres was a kind of no man's land (which was eventually allocated to Great Britain in 1914).

The 1907 Anglo-Russian convention was a direct consequence of European politics. Russia, after her defeat against Japan, had reverted to a second-rank power; incapable of threatening either India,

Afghanistan or Persia, still licking its wounds after Port Arthur and Tshimushi. If Great Britain was accepting such a partition, it was not from weakness but from strength, with the assurance that it could recover the northern Persian provinces whenever it pleased. If Great Britain was giving the Russians what they had been after for a whole century, it was with an eye on the rising European power of Germany and with the foreknowledge of deeply ingrained dislike between the German and Russian peoples.[51] Commenting, in a post-mortem on the 1907 partition, *The Nation* of London summarised thus the reasons behind it:

> Disastrous and foolish though we believe this [British] policy to be, we do not call it unintelligible. It is a consequence, and one of the worst consequences, of Sir Edward Grey's European policy. One simple and elementary principle has governed it from the first – his dread lest this or the other Power might be drawn into what he has called the 'orbit' of German diplomacy. Year in year out, we have been paying, chiefly in other people's goods, for the satisfaction of keeping certain powers from coming to any intimate understanding with Germany. To Russia we have given a free hand over Persia...[52]

Well, Russia had only been given a free hand over Persia's northern provinces. But even that much was difficult for the Persians to stomach. Unaware of European politics, Persian public opinion saw the convention as British weakness and the readiness of British politicians to sacrifice Persia's independence at will. Persians were "shocked by this alliance with the devil" and felt betrayed by the British, "to whom they had increasingly come to look upon as their protector against Russia".[53] As for the Russians, they would take full advantage in their own sphere and treat Persia's northern provinces as occupied territory – to the eternal dismay of Sir Edward Grey, who had not envisioned such Russian behaviour.

In the aftermath of the Atabeg's death, things were back to square one between the court and the *Majlis*. A special seven-member committee under Mirza Javad Khan Sâd ul-Douleh had been nominated to compile a supplement to the incomplete constitution; basing their work on the Belgian Constitution of 1831, the small group of enlightened deputies put together the 107 articles of the Supplemental Fundamental Laws. In October 1907, the Law was signed (after much tergiversation) by Muhammad Âli Shah, and, at a visit from the *Majlis* in November, the Shah swore once again that "he would endeavour to safeguard Persia's independence, ...and reign according to the Constitution".[54]

Apparently, a compromise between the Shah and the deputies was still a remote possibility. But, on February 27, 1908, terrorists struck, throwing a bomb at the royal motor car in one of Tehran's avenues. Some casualties resulted. The Shah, however, was not sitting in the targeted motor car but in the six-horse carriage; he escaped unhurt, only shaken. After this attempt (allegedly with some of the deputies in connivance with the terrorists, especially with bomb-thrower Riza Azarbayjani) compromise became impossible and confrontation inevitable. In March 1908, as the royalists were preparing their coup against the constitution, the *Majlis* added insult to injury by calling for the dismissal from court of six of the Shah's top advisers, with Shapshal Khan and Amir Bahadur Jang heading the list.[55]

At the beginning of June, the Shah surreptitiously left Tehran for his gardens of Bagh-i Shah outside the city limits (at a safe distance) and simultaneously appointed the thirty-five year old Colonel Liakhoff, the commanding officer of the Cossack Division, as the military commander of Tehran. In the early morning of June 23, the Cossacks, led by Liakhoff and supported by light artillery, machine-guns and the royal *Silakhuri* soldiers (of the warrior Lur tribe), marched on the *Majlis*. The poorly armed and amateurish defenders of the embryonic constitution were no match for the professional armed forces. At noon, the Cossacks were masters of the *Majlis*'s buildings. Most of the Movement's leaders were captured, chained and taken to the Bagh-i Shah headquarters. Some deputies, such as Taqizadeh (and five of his colleagues, including the young journalist Âli Akbar Dikhuda) were able to take refuge in the British Legation and thus avoided capture. Sayyid Muhammad Riza Musavat and Jamal ul-Din Vâiz were both able to escape from Tehran; Musavat safely reached Tabriz, but Vâiz was caught in Hamadan and taken to the Burujird prison, where he was murdered on the Shah's orders.[56]

Among the dozens of constitutionalists taken as prisoners to the Bagh-i Shah, two outstanding individuals were executed the next day:

the best constitutionalist tribune, Mirza Nasrullah Bihishti Malik ul-Mutakallimin, and the young and promising newspaper editor, Jahangir Khan Sourisrafil (the *babi* editor of *Sur-i Israfil*). The two Sayyids, Tabataba'i and Bihbahani, were soon released and exiled, the former to Mashhad and the latter to Karbala. Other captives were bastinadoed, put in chains and sentenced to various prison terms; among others, Malik ul-Mutakallimin's son, Mirza Muhammad Âli Khan (the editor of *Taraqqi*), Sultan ul-Ûlama (the editor of *Rouh ul-Qudus*) and Nâyib Baqir Khan (the *Majlis* door-keeper).

By its defeat the Constitutional Movement had proven that it was not a revolution, merely a movement: a revolution doesn't cave in after a couple of years, whatever the odds. Popular support had never been excessive, with the masses not directly involved in the reformist process. Moreover the split in the clergy, with the radical *mullas* led by Shaykh Fazlullah Nouri reverting to the royalist camp, had further weakened public interest in the movement's success. The lack of unity in the first *Majlis* and the assembly's timidity in voting decisive reforms (especially in matters of land ownership), due to its moderate majority, further weakened its hold on the people's hearts and minds. Finally, the movement's inability to set up a disciplined popular militia to defend itself proved crucial on the day of reckoning as the Cossacks and the *Silakhuris* proved once again that, in the short term at least, "*la raison du plus fort est toujours la meilleure*".

4.6. Constitutional Movement (Part 3)

Simultaneously with events in Tehran, royalist forces tried to occupy all other Persian towns. They succeeded everywhere, except at Tabriz. When they attempted to invest the constitutionalist districts of Tabriz, they were met with resolute defence and rebuffed. At Tabriz were men, or rather *mujahids* (warriors), capable of checking regular armed forces. The royalists could not accept such an exception to the rule: Tabriz had to be crushed too.

The battle for Tabriz had begun; upon it depended the future of Persia and of the budding Constitutional Movement.

If Persia is on the crossroads of nations, then Tabriz is its north-western outpost, where the paths from Europe and Russia meet. Always a must for international traders, Tabriz was a small town which always looked like a large village, with capable, work-loving people, open to all influences. Now, because of this openness, Tabrizis were more sophisticated and experienced than other Persians, and Tabriz was much better prepared than Tehran and other urban centres to counter the royalist backlash.

The centre of resistance in Tabriz was an *anjuman*: the *Anjuman-i Ghaybi* (the secret *anjuman*) headed by Âli Mussiou – a Tabriz merchant with a small porcelain factory, who had travelled throughout Europe and learned French, hence his surname of *Monsieur*, his real name being Karbala'i Âli.[57] Mussiou directed his *anjuman* with an iron hand and any member guilty of treason was ruthlessly eliminated. From his secret cellar, Âli Mussiou, assisted by his sons, managed the resistance of his cells during the royalist siege. In the field, two (*ad hoc*) commanders of troops were to lead the armed *mujahids*: Sattar Khan* and Baqir Khan.** Both were born leaders, Sattar the more so.

* SATTAR KHAN (1867–1914), son of Hajj Hasan Bazzaz Qaridaghi; had a politically active youth, ending several times in prison; travelled twice to Âtabat (1887–1901); became a horse trader in Tabriz (1901–7); charismatic *mujahid* field commander during the Tabriz resistance (1908–9); received triumphantly in Tehran, awarded title of *Sardar-i Milli* (national commander) by *Majlis* (1910); wounded in leg during assault on the Atabeg Park at Tehran (1910); infirm thereafter, living a secluded life at Tehran, supported by a monthly *Majlis* allowance until his death.

** BAQIR KHAN (1880–1916), son of Hajj Riza Tabrizi; a mason, living in the *Khyaban* quarter of Tabriz; assisted Sattar Khan during heroic defence of Tabriz (1908–9); received at Tehran with Sattar Khan, given title of *Salar-i Milli*; after attack on Atabeg Park, lived in Tehran on his monthly *Majlis* allowance of 300 toumans (1910–5); took part in *Muhajirat* movement (1915–6); killed in his sleep and robbed by his Kurdish hosts, in a village near Qasr-i Shirin.

With the battle for Tabriz, the Constitutional Movement entered its third and final phase. All national attention was concentrated on Tabriz, the north-western town representing the last flicker of hope for a cause many had come to believe forlorn. But Tabriz resisted valiantly. After the first month of battle, towards the close of July 1908, Âyn ul-Douleh was sent in as the fresh governor-general of

Azarbayjan. Accompanying him was a full-scale army commanded by the Mazandarani landowner Muhammad Vali Khan Sipahdar Âzam. For the whole summer royalist troops tried to storm the Tabrizi defences; time and again they were repulsed; at critical junctures Sattar Khan was always able to rally his *mujahids* and save the day.

By October, the royalist commander, Muhammad Vali Khan, impressed by the enemy's resilience and incensed by Âyn ul-Douleh's arrogance, resigned his command and retired to his Mazandarani estates: he had witnessed the power of popular will and the lesson was not lost on him.

In November and December 1908 a lull set in in the fighting around Tabriz. The town's 20,000 *mujahids*[58] were able to lick their wounds and prepare for the winter (usually harsh and bitterly cold in Azarbayjan). In January, the ruthless mercenary Samad Khan was dispatched to take command of the royalist troops. Having left a long track of blood in the defenceless villages along his way to Tabriz, Samad Khan arrived at Tabriz. For the whole winter he endeavoured to break the *mujahids*' resistance. In vain. In February there were some close calls, with Sattar Khan always available to step into the breach and carry his men. By early March, Samad Khan resigned, like other commanders before him, and retired, disillusioned. Skirmishes nevertheless continued, as food became scarce in Tabriz and hunger added to the defenders' woes. Until April the list of martyrs continued to lengthen as the fight continued; the name of a young American teacher at Tabriz's Memorial School, Howard C. Baskerville (1885-1909), was added to it in April.[59]

In April 1909 Russian troops invested Tabriz as royalist troops disbanded. The *mujahids* under Sattar Khan and Baqir Khan, supported by Âli Mussiou's secret *anjuman*, had by then resisted for ten long months, successfully repulsing all royalist attacks. Their heroic and historical defence, against all odds, had given the constitutionalists time to rekindle their movement's flame in two very different settings: Isfahan and Rasht.

In December 1908 the people of Isfahan, led by two *mulla* brothers, Aqa Najafi and Aqa Nourullah, rose against the tyranny of Zill ul-Sultan. The two leaders not only had excellent connections to the Isfahan *bazaar*, but also (then) to the leading Bakhtiari *Khans*. They had induced the latter to come down from their mountainous strongholds to provide armed support to the Isfahani constitutionalist movement. On the day following the popular uprising, some three hundred Bakhtiari warriors, commanded by Zargham ul-Saltaneh, duly entered the city and readily subdued the royalist defences.[60] Isfahan having surrendered, Najaf Quli Khan,* the Bakhtiari *ilkhan* (tribal chief), arrived triumphantly and placed his troops in the Constitutionalist camp. He communicated with Sattar Khan at Tabriz and had elections for Isfahan's provincial *anjuman* held.

* NAJAF QULI KHAN SAMSAM UL-SALTANEH (1852-1930), second son of Husayn Quli Khan, the *Ilkhani*; *ilkhan* of the Bakhtiaris (1903-1909); headed Bakhtiari warriors at Isfahan (1909); six times minister (1909-1911); prime minister, five cabinets (1911-12); again prime minister, two cabinets (1918); appointed governor-general of Khurasan (1921); sent on his last mission to pacify the Bakhtiari tribe by Reza Shah (1930); died upon his return to Isfahan.

Hitherto, the Bakhtiari tribe had never intervened in national affairs. It had always stuck to its territories in the Zagros mountains, with the tribesmen leading their nomadic life of transhumance. The tribe, like all Persian tribes, was dominated by its elite: the *khans*. A shrewd and capable *khan*, Husayn Quli Khan, had, in the middle of the nineteenth century, united the various sub-branches of the loose Bakhtiari confederation into a single entity. Appointed as official Bakhtiari *ilkhan* by Nasir ul-Din Shah in 1867, Husayn Quli Khan (thereafter known as the *Ilkhani*) greatly expanded his influence, to such an extent that the Shah, alarmed by his uncle Farhad Mirza's insidious reports, ordered the *Ilkhani's* murder, which was treacherously carried out by Zill ul-Sultan at Isfahan in 1882. After the *Ilkhani*'s death, his brother Hajj Imam Quli Khan *Hajjilkhani* succeeded him as Bakhtiari *ilkhan*. Since then the Bakhtiari have had two ruling families: the Ilkhanis (i.e. the descendants of the Husayn Quli Khan) and the Hajj *ilkhanis* (i.e. the descendants of Imam Quli Khan) – a case almost unique in Persia's tribal leadership.

The man who would enlist the Bakhtiari warriors on the constitutionalists' side was a nationalist, a politician and a scholar: Hajj Âli Quli Khan Sardar Asâd,* the younger brother of Samsam ul-Saltaneh. In Paris during the summer of 1908 for the treatment of his eyes, Sardar Asâd met some of the constitutionalists who had fled Tehran after the bombardment of the *Majlis*, and sympathised with their plight. Returning to the Persian Gulf via London, he debarked at Muhammarah in May 1909. There he met Shaykh Khazâl, the most powerful man in south Persia, to secure his goodwill and thus protect the Bakhtiaris' southern border during their army's northern march on Tehran. Then, joining the seven hundred-strong Bakhtiari army at Isfahan, he led it, with his brother Samsam ul-Saltaneh, on to Tehran. Along the way, royalist troops were no match for the skilled Bakhtiari horsemen and marksmen. Sardar Asâd's only problem was the Bakhtiari battalions serving on the royalist side under other Bakhtiari *khans* – among others, Amir Mufakham and Sardar Muhtashim. Sardar Asâd did his utmost to avoid Bakhtiaris shooting at each other; on the other hand, Amir Mufakham was more than willing to shoot on constitutionalist Bakhtiaris, and fought on the royalist side till the bitter end (being readily reintegrated within the *khans*' fold after the final Bakhtiari victory). Having surmounted all obstacles, the Bakhtiaris met, in July 1909, with the northern *mujahids* near Qasimabad. This first encounter was marred by the death of a number of *khans*, as Yeprem's *mujahids* mistakenly shot at them, believing them to be royalist Bakhtiaris.[61]

* HAJJ ÂLI QULI KHAN SARDAR ASÂD (1855–1917), fourth son of *Ilkhani*; had accompanied his father to Isfahan in 1882; put in jail after his father's murder (1882–3); upon Amin ul-Sultan's intervention, placed at the head of the Bakhtiari Guards at court (1883–1896); returned to tribal affairs after the Shah's assassination; instrumental in obtaining the Lynch Road concession, which would greatly enrich the Bakhtiari *khans* (1898); travelled to India and Egypt, made a pilgrimage to Mecca and sought medical help in Paris for his deficient eyes (1898–1903); after the death of his eldest brother (Isfandyar Khan), took the latter's title of Sardar Asâd (1903); second visit to Paris and London (1906–1909); led the Bakhtiaris to victory at Tehran (1909); five times minister (1909–10); went back to Paris for eye treatment (1911); returned to Persia against his doctor's advice (1912); began writing his monumental *History of the Bakhtiaris*; although totally blind, finished it by dictating to his secretary (1914); totally paralysed after a stroke (1916); died at the age of sixty-two.

As for the northern *mujahids* from Gilan and Mazandaran, their leader was no other than Muhammad Vali Khan Sipahdar Âzam,* the converted leader of royalist troops against Sattar Khan in Tabriz. During his retirement, Muhammad Vali Khan was asked by the 'Sattar Committee' - a committee created in Rasht by Caucasian revolutionaries, Armenian nationalists (under the formidable Yeprem Khan) and Gilan democrats (under Mûizz ul-Sultan, the future Sardar Muhyi)[62] - to lead the northern *mujahids* to Tehran. Sipahdar readily accepted. Being in the Russian sphere of influence, the new leader was naturally Russophile and thus could count on the Russians' tacit support. But the real fire behind the seven hundred northern *mujahids* was from the outset the indefatigable Armenian, Yeprem Khan.

In February 1909, Sipahdar, after being outlawed and deprived of all his titles by the Shah, marched on Rasht with five hundred armed Tunikabunis. In Rasht, the 'Sattar Committee' led by Mûizz and Yeprem, had assassinated the governor-general, Aqa Bala Khan Sardar Afkham, to pave the way for the Sipahdar's triumphant entry. After a stay of two months in Rasht, Sipahdar, ably assisted by his trustworthy lieutenant, Muntasir ul-Douleh, decided to march on Tehran. Meeting no major forces along the way, he reached Qazvin in May. At Qazvin, Yeprem Khan had shot dead the main royalist stalwart, Ghyas Nizam, the leader of the powerful Ghyasvand tribe.[62A] Yeprem further paved the way towards Tehran with hard-fought battles at Karaj, Shahabad and Âlishahavaz.[63] In early July, Yeprem's *mujahids* joined with the Bakhtiaris near Qasimabad.

* MUHAMMAD VALI KHAN SIPAHDAR (TUNIKABUNI) (1848-1926), son of Habibullah Khan Sâid ul-Douleh Sardar, a millionaire Mazandarani landowner; colonel in Tunikabuni army, then general in command (1886); title of Nasr ul-Saltaneh (1887); governor-general of Astarabad (Gurgan) (1889); leased Tehran Mint for 120,000 toumans per annum (1894); leased customs (1896); governor-general of Gilan (1899-1903); governor of Ardabil (1904); leased Telegraph for 230,000 toumans per annum, title of Sipahdar Âzam (1905); led royalist forces to repress Tehran constitutionalists (1906); commanded royal troops against Tabriz resistance (1908); resigned, retired, led northern *mujahids* to Tehran (1909); Minister for War (1909); prime minister, seven cabinets (1909-11), one cabinet (1916); title of Sipahsalar Âzam (1915); retired from politics to his Mazandaran estates (1917); committed suicide because of Reza Shah's encroachments on his estates (1926).

On their way to Tehran, the united Bakhtiari *mujahid* forces fought their last battle against the retrenched royalist forces (some four thousand-strong) around the small village of Badamak. For three long days the constitutionalist forces were unable to dislodge the royalists. Bakhtiaris on both sides were killed during the skirmishes.[64] On the evening of the third day, Sipahdar and Sardar Asâd decided to turn from Badamak and march directly on Tehran. The stratagem succeeded and on July 14 the constitutionalists entered the capital, which was for the next three days the scene of street battles between anti- and pro-royalist forces. Then, on July 17, Muhammad Âli Shah, sensing his cause lost, took refuge in the Russian Legation at Zargandeh.

The Constitutional Movement had finally won. Tehran and political power was in the hands of the victorious Bakhtiari and their *mujahid* allies. Sipahdar, Sardar Asâd and Samsam ul-Saltaneh were, as the victors of Tehran, the new arbiters of power. But they had to compromise with the old Qajar elite, which had rapidly imposed itself and taken things in hand. On the very first day, a twelve-member 'Higher Commission' assembled in the *Majlis*' building to assure the transition; it consisted of the Tehran victors and of prominent Qajar elite members. On the morrow, the commission was renamed 'Provisional Board of Directors', and the young Hasan Khan Vusuq ul-Douleh, one of the Qajar elite's young wolves, placed in the chair. Shortly thereafter the first provisional government was formed without a prime minister; the regent was supposed to oversee the cabinet's meetings. Sipahdar was Minister for War, Sardar Asâd in charge of Interior, Nasir ul-Mulk at Foreign Affairs, Mustoufi ul-Mamalik in charge of Finance and Farmanfarma at Justice. A well-balanced mix of the new and the old.

Muhammad Âli Shah was officially deposed. On August 30, he departed Tehran for Odessa in Russia, with a retinue of twenty-two courtiers, having finally accepted, "after much haggling, a yearly pension of a 100,000 toumans".[65] He was replaced by his twelve year old son Ahmad under the regency of the elder chief of the Qajar tribe, Âli Riza Khan Âzud ul-Mulk.

The Qajar dynasty had lost the war and was left badly mauled, but was still (legally) in power: a miracle given the circumstances and Muhammad Âli Shah's blunders. Nevertheless, the harm done to the dynasty should not be minimised: it had been dealt a mortal blow.

Only a superlative monarch could help it recover part of its former prestige. The young and slightly overweight Ahmad Shah didn't look as though he had the mettle to stand up to the momentous occasion.

The British could be satisfied with the turn of events: the victory of the constitutionalists, who were now in power at Tehran. The Russians were not unhappy either: although their Shah had lost, the Russophile Sipahdar was heading the new government.

The hotchpotch constitutionalist forces celebrated their triumph against the forces of absolutism. The *mujahids* of Sattar Khan and Baqir Khan, the secret fighters of Âli Mussiou, the Bakhtiari tribesmen, the northern *mujahids* and the Armenian nationalists were victorious. Even the religious hierocracy had reasons to be festive: its triumvirate of Najaf *ûlama* – Muhammad Kazim Khurasani (d. 1911), Shaykh Âbdullah Mazandarani (d. 1912) and Shaykh Husayn Khalil Tihrani (d. 1908) – had continuously and morally supported the constitutionalists with their flow of encouraging telegrams.

The winds of change had finally come to Persia. They had clashed with, and defeated, a weakened royal court. The Constitutional Movement had finally reached its goals: a *Majlis* and a constitution. A page was turned in Persia. There was no way back to the days of Nasir ul-Din Shah. It had taken the Persians some eighteen years and much internecine bloodshed, from the Tobacco Concession in 1891 to the victory at Tehran (1909), to attain their goals.

NOTES

[1] M.Q. Hidayat, *Guzarish-i Iran* (Tehran: *Nuqreh*, 2nd ed., 1363 (1984)) p.141.
[2] Îtimad ul-Saltaneh, *Rouznameh Khatirat* (Tehran: *Amir Kabir*, 1345 (1966)) p.226.
[3] Professor E.G. Browne, *The Persian Revolution of 1905–1909* (London: Frank Cass, 1966) p.98.
[4] Nazim ul-Islami Kirmani, *Tarikh-i Bidari Iranian* (Tehran: *Agah*, 3rd ed., 1361 (1982)) Vol. I, p.131.
[5] A.R. Arasteh, *Education and Social Awakening in Iran* (Leiden: E.J. Brill, 1969) p.31.
[6] M. Bamdad, *Sharh-i Hal-i Rijal-i Iran* (Tehran: Zavvar, 1357 (1978)) Vol. II, p.447.
[7] A.R. Arasteh, op. cit. (note 5), p.40.
[8] A *maktab* was a simple class where a clergyman (a *mulla*) taught a few pupils four main subjects: (1) reading; (2) writing; (3) religious matters; and (4) elements of arithmetic.

9   A. Kasravi, *Tarikh-i Mashrouteh Iran* (Tehran: Amir Kabir, 14th ed., 1357 (1978)) Vol. I, p.38.

9A   A number of historiographies of nineteenth-century Persian and *Farsi* newspapers were compiled by Iranian authors; the two most extensive are M. Sadr Hashimi, *Tarikh-i Jarayid va Majallat-i Iran* (Isfahan: Kamal, 2nd ed., 1363 (1984)) four volumes; and H. Moulana, *Sayr-i Irtibatat-i Ijtimaî dar Iran* (Tehran: *Danishkadeh Ûloum Irtibatat Ijtimaî*, 1358 (1979)).

9B   See the review article 'Az Akhbar ta Akhtar', in the monthly *Majlis va Pijouish*, 2nd Year, no. 7, *Farvardin 1373* (April 1994), pp.198-226.

10   Over their eighteen-year mission in Persia, sixty-five Belgian experts signed employment contracts with the Persian Government. The post of general manager of Persian customs was successively held by three of them: Nauss (1898-1907), J.J. Mornard (1907-1914) and J.B. Heynssens (1914-1915). Naus had the poor idea of putting on a *mulla*'s garb at a *bal masque*, where his photo was taken, copied and circulated in Tehran. He had to resign in February 1907 and depart Persia after a protracted and successful mission. See *Mustakhdimin-i Bilzhiki dar Khidmat-i Doulat-i Iran* transl. by M. Ittihadiyyeh, (Tehran: *Nashr-i Tarikh-i Iran*, 1363 (1984)).

11   The 'Lynch Road' became the standard link between the Persian Gulf and the north of the country: goods were taken by boat from Muhammarah to Ahvaz and then by mule from Ahvaz to Isfahan and Tehran. The prime beneficiaries of the Lynch Road were the Bakhtiari *Khans* who received one golden sovereign for every mule safely passing through their territory.

12   A. Ashraf, *Mavaneh Tarikhi Rushd-i Sarmayehdari dar Iran* (Tehran: Zamineh, 1359 (1980)) pp.98-99.

13   *Tarikhcheh Si Saleh Bank-i Milli-i Iran* (Tehran: Bank-i Milli-i Iran, 1338 (1959)) pp.50-51.

14   Ibid., p.53.

15   In 1878, Nasir ul-Din Shah signed at St Petersburg the contract for the dispatch of Cossack officers and NCOs to Persia for the formation of a Cossack regiment. In early 1879, Colonel Alexey Ivanovich Dumantovich (of the general staff of the Caucasian Military Command) arrived in Tehran at the head of the first Cossack contingent; for three years he remained in command and oversaw the initial development of the new entity before departing in 1881. From the outset the Cossacks' programme was on a correct footing: strict discipline and proper pay (with an initial budget of 97,000 toumans per year in 1879). The regiment was soon expanded to a brigade, with between four hundred and six hundred personnel. Until 1895 the Cossack brigade reported solely to the Shah and to the *sadr-i âzam*, thereafter being placed under the Ministry of War. Later, the Cossack brigade was upgraded to fifteen hundred men (in four squadrons of cavalry, two battalions of mounted artillery and one infantry battalion) with a yearly budget of 219,000 toumans, and on the eve of the First World War it was a full division with a total of roughly eight thousand men. On this subject see, among others, M.J. Shaykh ul-Islami, *Iran's First Experience of Military Coup d'état in the Era of her Constitutional Government* (Heidelberg: Ph.D. thesis, 1965); and also Sir Percy Sykes, *A History of Persia* (London: Macmillan, 1930) Vol. II, p.436.; and R. Ra'iss Tousi, 'The Persian Army, 1880-1907', in *Middle Eastern Studies*, Vol. 24, no. 2, April 1988, pp.219-220.

16 M.Q. Hidayat, *Khatirat va Khatarat* (Tehran: Zavvar, 2nd ed., 1344 (1965)) p.140.
17 Âli Khan Amin ul-Douleh, *Khatirat* (Tehran: H. Farmanfarmayan, 1341 (1962)) p.229.
18 See Shaul Bakhash, 'The Failure of Reform: the Prime Ministership of Amin al-Dawla, 1897-8', in *Qajar Iran*, ed. by E. Bosworth and C Hillenbrand, (Edinburgh University Press, 1983) pp.14-33.
19 Ibid., p.26.
20 The Shah's Paris visit might have brought about an end to his life because, on August 10, 1900 a French would-be assassin assaulted his carosse, only to find himself face to face with the Shah's personal physician and court minister, Mahmud Hakim, who managed to disarm the assailant.
21 I. Safa'i, *Rahbaran-i Mashroutiat* (Tehran: *Javidan*, 2nd ed., 1362 (1983)) Vol. I, p.342. And also E.B. Yaganegi, *Recent Financial and Monetary History of Persia* (New York: Columbia University (Ph.D. thesis), 1934) pp.49-51.
21A Ibid., pp.91-2.
22 Muzaffar ul-Din Shah made three trips to Europe – like his father. The first visit lasted from April till November 1900; the second from March to October 1903, and the third one from May until August 1905.
23 M.Q. Hidayat, op. cit. (note 1), p.158.
24 M.Q. Hidayat, op. cit. (note 16), p.118.
25 Ibid., p.137.
26 Â.H. Buzurg Umid, *As mast keh bar mast* (Tehran: *Danya-yi Kitab*, 1363 (1984)) p.182.
27 Nazim ul-Islam Kirmani, *Tarikh-i Bidari Iranian* (Tehran: *Agah*, 3rd ed., 1361 (1982)) Vol. I, pp.245, 463 and 580.
28 M. Katira'i, *Framasuniri dar Iran* (Tehran: *Iqbal*, 4th ed., 1361 (1982)) p.93.
29 M. Malikzadeh, *Tarikh-i Inqilab-i Mashroutiat-i Iran* (Tehran: *Ibn Sina*, 1328 (1949)) Vol. II, p.10.
30 Ibid. Interestingly, member number twenty-six, as given in the list of founding members by Malikzadeh, is Ardishir Ji, a Zoroastrian – the future Ardishir Reporter.
31 A. Kasravi, *Tarikh-i Mashrouteh Iran* (Tehran: Amir Kabir, 14th ed., 1357 (1978)) Vol. I, p.119.
32 The provision of necessary sanitary facilities for such a crowd is still a mystery. But, undoubtedly, those had to have been provided throughout the long *bast*! Could it be possible, as some Persians specialists believe, that the British, having foreseen the possibility of a massive *bast*, had prepared the necessary wells and facilities in advance?
32A There were in fact two decrees; the first dated August 5 and the second dated August 8. The second one, penned by the young Ahmad Khan Qavam ul-Saltaneh (he had received his new title in 1905), reinforced the first one and stressed the creation of a *Majlis-i Shoura-yi Milli-i Islami* (A national Islamic assembly).
33 Z. Shajîi, *Namayandigan-i Majlis-i Shoura-yi Milli dar Bist va Yik Doureh-yi Qanounguzari* (Tehran: *Intisharat-i Mu'asiseh Mutaliât va Taqiqat-i Ijtimaî*, 1344 (1965)), Table no. 2.
34 J. de Morgan, *Mission Scientifique en Perse* (Paris: Ernest Ledoux, 1896). An interesting book, with, for example, figure 142 (p.151) showing an old necropolis and entitled: "Nécropole située près des puits de naphte de Kent-e-Chirin" and

below his 'Planche VII' the following caption: "Kend-e-Chirin, sources de naphte à 480 mètres, sur le Tchiasorkh (rivière prenant source sur le Kouh-e-Bozinan)".

35 D. Wright, *The English Amongst the Persians* (London: Heinemann, 1977) p.107.

36 L. Mosley, *Power Play* (New York: Random House, 1973) p.19.

37 *Naft-i Iran*, a publication issued by the National Iranian Oil Company, Isfand 1344 (March 1966), p.3.

38 H. Longhurst, *Adventure in Oil* (London: Sidgwick and Jackson, 1959) p.20.

39 A. Jamalzadeh, *Ganj-i Shayigan* (Tehran: *Kitab-i Tehran*, 1362 (1983)) p.71. Jamalzadeh points out that the First Exploration's initial paid-up capital was £544,000 (with an eighty-eight per cent British shareholding), in 1925 increased to £1,244,000 (with a ninety-three per cent British shareholding). From the above information one can deduce that around £65,000 were in non-British, that is to say Persian, hands.

40 The Burmah Oil Co. Ltd., registered at Edinburgh on May 15, 1902. Headquartered at Glasgow. Set up by Scottish merchants to manage Burmese oil fields. Set up a refinery at Rangoon to market its products in India.

41 Of the £2,000,000 APOC shares issued, one million was in ordinary shares (all issued) and the other million in preference shares (£900,000 of which were issued). APOC's seven founding members received a thousand preference shares each: Lord Strathcona (Burmah Oil Co. Ltd.); John T. Cargill (Burmah Oil Co. Ltd., chairman); Charles W. Wallace (Burmah Oil Co. Ltd., director); William Knox D'Arcy (Mount Morgan Gold Mines Co., chairman); Francis of Teck; H.S. Barnes; W.M. Garson.

42 The Bakhtiari Oil Company (BOC) was created in 1909 with an initial capital of £400,000. It was raised to £500,000 (1915), £600,000 (1917) and finally to £700,000 (1920) before the company was merged with the First Exploration Company in November 1925. See Z. Mikdashi, *A Financial Analysis of Middle Eastern Oil Concessions (1901-1965)* (New York: Praeger, 1966) p.318.

43 At the coronation ceremony, a distraught Mushir ul-Douleh placed the *Kian* crown back to front on the Shah's head. Everyone present was dumbfounded. The superstitious courtiers took the mishap as a bad omen for Muhammad Âli Shah and the Qajar dynasty: they would be proven right. On this historical anecdote, see Âbdullah Mustoufi, *Zindigani-i Man* (Tehran: Zavvar, 3rd ed., 1360 (1981)) Vol. II, p.166.

44 Muzaffar ul-Din Shah had six sons and eighteen daughters. His three eldest sons were: Muhammad Âli Shah (1872–1925), Malik Mansour Mirza Shûâ ul-Saltaneh (1880–1920), and Abu'l Fath Mirza Salar ul-Douleh (1881–1959); the latter died at Alexandria in Egypt. Some Qajar courtiers suggested that Muhammad Âli's mother Taj ul-Mulouk (titled Um ul-Khaqan), who was the eldest daughter of Amir Kabir and Îzzat ul-Douleh (Nasir ul-Din Shah's only full sister), was not a full-blooded Qajar. In consequence, they contend that Shûâ ul-Saltaneh (his mother having irrefutable credentials) should have become shah in his stead (and Muzzafar ul-Din Shah had himself clearly favoured such an option). But behind Muhammad Âli's bid for the Peacock Throne were the Russians and the Prince Farmanfarma, who had married the crown prince's full sister, Îzzat ul-Saltaneh.

45 A. Kasravi, op. cit. (note 31), Vol. II, p.487.

46 F.R.C. Bagley, *New Light on Iranian Constitutional Movement*, in *Qajar Iran*, ed. by E. Bosworth and C. Hillenbrand, (Edinburgh University Press, 1983) p.52.

47 The *Ijtimâyun-Âmmyun* party was created in 1904 at Baku, as a Persian offshoot of the *Himmat* party formed by Dr Nariman as a Muslim Caucasian socialist party, that same year. It established branches at Tabriz, Rasht, Bandar Anzali, Tehran and Mashhad. Its basic programme was outlined in eight main points at its September 1907 congress at Mashhad: 1) unicameral parliament (elected by universal suffrage); 2) ministers individually responsible to parliament; 3) freedom of expression for all; 4) progressive direct taxation; 5) compulsory military service; 6) eight-hour working day; 7) public schools and hospitals to be set up; 8) public lands to be rented, and private lands to be sold (preferably to the peasants working on them).

48 The *Ijtimâyun-Âmmyun* gave birth to the Persian Social Democrat Party in 1909. The first central committee of the new party consisted of eight members: Sayyid Hasan Taqizadeh, Sayyid Muhammad Riza Musavat, Sulayman Mirza Iskandari, Mahmoud Mahmoud, Vahid ul-Mulk Shaybani, Mirza Baqir Aqa Qafqazi, Ahmad Amurluy'i and Rasoulzadeh. The major policies of the Democrat Party were spelled out in 1908 by Taqizadeh as: 1) separation of civil and religious powers; 2) distribution of lands among the peasantry; 3) unicameral parliament (opposition to senate); 4) compulsory nationwide education; 5) direct taxation instead of indirect taxation. Clearly in line with the *Ijtimâyun-Âmmyun* programme.

49 A. Kasravi, op. cit. (note 31), Vol. I, p.448.
50 Ibid., p.448.
51 See G.N. Curzon, *Russia in Central Asia* (London: Frank Cass, 1967) pp.21-23.
52 From *The Nation* (London) dated December 2,1911, as quoted by W.M. Shuster, *The Strangling of Persia* (London: T. Fisher Unwin, 1912) p.363.
53 D. Wright, op. cit. (note 35), p.30.
54 A. Kasravi, op. cit. (note 31), Vol. II, p.488.
55 Professor E.G. Browne, *A Brief Narrative of Recent Events in Persia* (London: Luzac and Co., 1909) p.11.
56 M. Malikzadeh, op. cit. (note 29), Vol. IV, pp.154-6.
57 See S. Sardarinya, *Âli Mussiou* (Tehran: *Dunya*, 1359 (1980)).
58 A. Kasravi, op. cit. (note 31), Vol. II, p.809.
59 Baskerville had joined the *mujahids* ranks against his consul's express orders. For months he fought, displaying praiseworthy courage. He now ranks among the very few American heroes in Persia.
60 M. Malikzadeh, op. cit. (note 29), Vol. V, pp.192-3.
61 Â.Q. Khan Sardar Asâd, *Tarikh-i Bakhtiari* (Tehran: *Yasavuli*, 1361 (1982)) pp.181-2. Among the victims was Âzizullah Khan Ilbag, the younger brother of Zargham ul-Saltaneh.
62 See Â.A. Khalât bari, *Sipahsalar-i Tunikabuni* (Tehran: *Nuvin*, 1362 (1983)) p.67.
62A See Yeprem's memoirs, *Yeprem Khan*, translated by *Narous* from the Armenian, (Tehran: *Babak*, 2536 (1977)) pp.36-40. The incident of Ghyas Nizam's death was confirmed to the author by his great-grandson (who had heard the story told by his grandmother): Yeprem, having made it to the roof of Ghyas Nizam's house, shot dead the latter, who was standing in the courtyard below.
63 Ibid., pp.42-52.
64 Â.Q. Khan Sardar Asâd, op. cit. (note 61), p.183.
65 Sir P. Sykes, op. cit. (note 15), Vol. II, p.421. Furthermore, the ex-Shah's brothers, Shûâ ul-Saltaneh and Salar ul-Douleh, were allocated an annual income of 25,000 toumans each.

CHAPTER FIVE:
THE QAJAR ELITE

With the young Ahmad Shah and his inoffensive regent as mere ciphers, the real political power now resided in an uneasy arrangement between the Tehran victors and the old Qajar elite. The latter entity was a rather homogeneous amalgam of princes, aristocrats and courtiers, linked together by a myriad of interconnecting matrimonial ties, common interests, invisible deals and a pervading will for the survival of their race. It was not formally hierarchised, but informally every member was made to understand exactly where he stood in the elite's pyramid. The common interest predominated over personal benefits, and, in case a member did not play the game, he was ostracised and punished for his selfishness. Promotion within the elite ranks was based on meritocracy and on wealth. The top elite layer was chosen by co-option of the existing members. Major decisions were taken by the top layer, whose numbers were not fixed – but usually consisted of five members. Highly pragmatic, it never placed all its eggs in one basket: it had members in both the British and Russian camps, and during the three years of the Constitutional Movement it placed more and more of its people in the other camp, just in case of defeat of the royalists.

Even if it had had no one in the other camp, the Qajar elite was sure that no one could rule Persia without its assistance. With the Shah's defeat, the elite had not hesitated to amputate (momentarily) its reactionary wing. On the other hand, it had hurried to place itself (and all its administrative assets) at the disposal of the victors. While serving the new masters, they also began to woo them, to win their confidence, eventually their friendship. After all the new masters of Tehran had won the war: they had proved acceptable to the Powers and their armed followers swarmed the capital's streets. On the other hand, the Qajar elite was among the side's losers, but, nevertheless, was still in power because of their Qajar shah, their Qajar regent and the Qajar court.

Fortunately for the Qajar elite, there were only three major individuals on the victors' side: the Sipahdar, the Sardar Asâd and Samsam ul-Saltaneh. Meanwhile they could still count on dozens upon dozens of higher and lesser Qajar elite members. Furthermore, all three were already wealthy and of aristocratic descent, therefore were that much easier to deal with and, possibly, in due time, to incorporate (if necessary) within the elite's ranks.

Above all, these two groups needed each other. The one had power but needed managers to rule; the other had the administrators but had to rely on those in power. All in all, maybe paradoxically, the elite was in a more favourable position than the victors: it had time and quantity (and also quality) on its side. As for the victors, Sipahdar did not have the resources to capitalise on his victory, whereas the Bakhtiaris had.

The Bakhtiari *khans*, however, also had two debilitating drawbacks that would, in the long run, foil their bid for protracted power on the national scale. The first was their glaring lack of unity. The *khans* were too attracted by deceit. "The Bakhtiari Khans are as full of intrigue as a nightingale's egg is pregnant with music" was the image described by G.B. Reynolds, who had to deal with them almost daily during the four years he drilled for oil in the Zagros. The *khans* were too short-sighted to sacrifice personal interests to the larger tribal cause (in this respect, the Qajar elite could have taught them a few lessons). It had required the unique charisma of Husayn Quli Khan Ilkhani to overpower tribal divisions and unify the "many-headed hydra of Bakhtiari leadership".[1] The ever-attentive British diplomats had correctly sized up the Bakhtiari *khans*: in January 1908, Captain D.L.R. Lorimer, the British consul at Ahvaz, had cabled Sir Cecil Spring-Rice at Tehran:

> At the best, they [the Bakhtiari *khans*] are a broken reed... [due] to their total lack of administrative capacity, their want of trustworthy underlings and their domestic quarrels...[2]

The *khans*' second disadvantage was their disastrous adherence to seniority rule in all circumstances. In times of continuity, seniority rule is a recipe for stability; in times of drastic change following tradition leads to catastrophe. In the specific case of the Tehran victors, Sardar Asâd, who had masterminded the Bakhtiaris' drive to Tehran, was compelled to play second fiddle to his elder brother Samsam ul-Saltaneh because of the seniority rule. Samsam, a nationalist leader with a lot of common sense, did not have the political acumen and the personal clout of his younger brother Asâd. When the premiership was presented to them, it was Samsam who took it outright; when the regency came up, the chances of the prime candidate, Asâd, were nullified by his own brother, who argued that he should become regent, although he well knew that (unlike Asâd) he could not gather the necessary votes. Thus, the Bakhtiaris let pass by a golden chance to rule Persia, or at least to place their very best *khan* in a position of supreme influence. They have only themselves to blame.

5.1. The Movement's Sequels

The situation of the new leadership was unique in Persian history: there was no absolute shah to take decisions and issue orders. They now had a collegiate-type forum for taking decisions and issuing orders. As a group the new masters of Persia did not know each other very well, if at all: circumstances had brought them together at the very top to decide a nation's future.

Their first task was to come to terms with the movement's consequences. And paramount among these was to judge some of the radical royalist elements captured after the occupation of Tehran (naturally, some had taken refuge with the Shah at the Russian Legation). The victors established an *ad hoc* higher court of ten members and had it judge its prisoners. Five of them – Mufakhir ul-Mulk, Sanî Hazrat, Muvaqqar ul- Saltaneh, Ajudanbashi and the brutal Mir Hashim Tabrizi – were sentenced to death and hanged. The court also had to pass sentence on the controversial sixty-six year old *mujtahid* Shaykh Fazlullah Nouri. The Shaykh had, at the outset, joined the movement and had even taken part in the Qum *bast* of summer 1906. Then, his relations with the two leading *mujtahids* Tabataba'i and Bihbahani deteriorated. Nouri is reported to have said: "The two Sayyids are not in favour of constitutionalism; they are against me",[3] before opposing the *mashrouteh* (i.e. conditional) concept of constitutionalism and advocating his own idea of *mashrouteh* (i.e. based on the Islamic *shariâ*). After the *mashrouteh*'s triumph, Nouri passed to active opposition and chose to side with the reactionary forces against his former colleagues, therefore being excommunicated in December 1907 by the Najaf *Ayatullahs*. He supported the coup of June 23, 1908 against the *Majlis*,[4] and also survived an attempt on his life made on January 8, 1909, by the thug Karim Davatgar.[5] The higher court eventually sentenced Nouri to death for his actions against the Constitutional Movement and his links to the royal court, from which he had accepted gifts. Nouri was duly hanged on Tehran's *Toupkhaneh* Square on August 2, 1909.

After settling accounts with the enemy, the victors had to reward their allies: Sattar Khan and Baqir Khan were invited to Tehran and given a triumphant welcome. A special decree was issued thanking the Tabriz heroes and awarded them the titles of *Sardar-i Milli* and *Salar-i Milli*. They were assigned the Atabeg Park[6] as a residence for themselves and their retinue of *mujahids*, and a monthly allowance was allocated them for their current expenses. However, contrary to appearances, the victors felt endangered by Sattar Khan and Baqir Khan, who, as successful rebels, were irreplaceable assets during the struggle, but heroic liabilities after the triumph. In a different context, but on a similar subject, T.E. Lawrence had these interesting insights into rebels:

> Rebels, especially successful rebels, were of necessity bad subjects and worse governors. Feisal's sorry duty would be to rid himself of his war-friends, and replace them by those elements which had been most useful to the Turkish Government. Nasir was too little a political philosopher to feel this. Nuri Said knew, and Nuri Shaalan...[7]

Before long the government of Mustoufi ul-Mamalik ordered the *mujahids* to deliver their arms to the authorities' representatives. When Sattar Khan refused to comply, Mustoufi ordered government troops (under Yeprem Khan) to assault the Park. Within a few hours the *mujahids* were crushed and the Park occupied *manu militari*; Sattar was badly wounded in the knee. The captured *mujahids* were disarmed and then sent back individually to their native Azarbayjan. The two unlucky rebels were assigned to a residence in Tehran: Sattar Khan died shortly thereafter in 1914, and Baqir Khan was killed in 1916.[8]

The victors' next task was to set up the second *Majlis*. On October 28, 1909 the decree calling for fresh elections was issued and on November 15 the *Majlis* was inaugurated with a contingent of sixty-four deputies. Unlike its first version, the elections to the second *Majlis* were not based on class quotas and candidacies were basically free. The result was a *Majlis* of only one hundred and eleven deputies, but clearly representative of the two major currents in the country: on the one hand, the conservative majority of the *Îtidalyun* (moderate) faction; and on the other, a minority of socio-reformist elements (some twenty members, led by Taqizadeh) reunited in the *Dimukrat* (democratic) faction – which later gave birth to the Democrat Party of Iran. A handful of independents completed the forum. From the outset, a sense of duty pervaded the Second *Majlis*'s atmosphere; the deputies sensed that they owed the movement's martyrs and the country at large their deputation, and took their mandate earnestly. The deputies' first act was to set, once and for all, the parliamentary rules and customs (based on the French model); its second action, to redesign the main hall as a chamber for debates, filling it with chairs and a tribune for the managing board and the secretaries; it then voted a national budget and allowed the government to borrow on the domestic market to finance its deficit; it reorganised the budding bureaucracy along efficient subdivisions; it voted to send graduates of Dar ul-Funoun and the School for Political Affairs abroad for post-graduate studies.[9]

In September 1910, Regent Âzud ul-Mulk having passed away, the *Majlis* had to choose a fresh regent. Sardar Asâd would have been the first and the best choice, but he was not a candidate for family reasons. The two main candidates were Abu'l Qasim Khan Nasir ul-Mulk and Hasan Khan Mustoufiul-Mamalik. The *Îtidalyun* deputies favoured the former and the *Dimukrat* faction the latter. Sardar Asâd, long undecided, eventually came to support Nasir ul-Mulk, thereby assuring his election to the regency by a 60 to 42 vote. Mustoufi, "a man of high reputation and great ability",[10] would have been a far better choice. With its poor choice of Nasir ul-Mulk, the *Majlis* (with the elite supporting it) had scored against itself: a blunder which was a first sign that the elite was not up to ruling the country. The regency was the key position in the kingdom, at least for the next four years (until Ahmad Shah's majority in 1914) and the regent could, by his very personality, influence almost every aspect of domestic life, from the Shah's education to the government's behaviour. The elite's only excuse for making the wrong choice was Nasir ul-Mulk's background at Oxford, but it should have known better. Morgan Shuster, who stayed in Tehran for just a few months, gave this opinion on Nasir ul-Mulk:

> He was more concerned with his own welfare and peace of mind than with the success of the difficult and complicated task which he had undertaken...[11]

Having reopened the *Majlis*, the government could tackle its foremost task: re-establishing law and order. The lifting of royal authority added to three years of fighting and disorders throughout the country and had exacerbated the problems of policing the provinces. To police the whole country, there were some two thousand Bakhtiari tribesmen under the command of Jâfar Quli Khan Sardar Bahadur (Sardar Asâd's eldest son), one thousand *mujahids* under Yeprem Khan,* and a few Cossacks; that was far from enough, especially because the main force of the Bakhtiaris was showing signs of lassitude and homesickness. Yeprem Khan was appointed chief of the Tehran police, and Jâfar Quli Khan led an expedition, towards the close of 1909, against the unruly Shahsavan tribe in eastern Azarbayjan; as a result, security was enhanced in Tehran and the Shahsavans were brought to heel. But these were only stopgap measures, not an overall solution. Moreover, in September 1910 a Bakhtiari force sent to Kashan to subdue the outlaw Na'ib Husayn Kashi (and his 1,200 brigands) was unable to bring its mission to a successful conclusion. Altogether, the Qajar elite looked askance at reinforcing either the Bakhtiaris or the *mujahids*; it calculated that in the long run either could become a dangerous phalanx and compromise their vested interests. The Tehran victors should have insisted on developing these forces which were their only trump card. But the elite had its way (as usual) and it convinced the government that a nationwide corps of gendarmes was needed and for its supervision and training foreign officers with experience were required. After reviewing possible alternatives, the government decided upon hiring Swedish officers for this purpose; the *Majlis* duly approved the necessary budget and in 1911, the first contingent of twenty Swedish officers under the command of Colonel Hjalmarson took up their assignment in Persia: the Persian Gendarmerie was born.

* YEPREM KHAN DAVIDIAN (1868-1912), born near Bursum, in the village of Ganstak; joined Armenian national revolutionary party *Hay Hiqapukhakan Dashnaktutyun* created in Turkey by S. Zorian (Roustoum), Ch. Mikâilian and S. Zavarian (1890); joined the armed group of Sarkis Gougounian at Tiflis (1890); arrested with twenty-five others, sentenced to fifteen years of hard labour in Siberia (1890); exiled to Sakhalin Island, escaped with Housip Mousisian, returned to Tabriz (1896); became a teacher, moved to Rasht; formed '*Sattar* Committee' at Rasht and '*Barq* Committee' at Anzali (1908); masterminded attack on Rasht and glorified himself in march on Tehran (1909); appointed chief of Tehran police (1910); led successful attacks on royalist forces, with his lieutenants Khachou (an ex-Tsarist officer) and the Armenian Kari Khan (1911); killed in battle against troops of Salar ul-Douleh, amid nebulous circumstances, at Shourjeh, near Hamadan (May 6, 1912). The most famous Armenian in Persia's modern times, nicknamed the 'Persian Garibaldi'.

Before the Gendarmerie could take shape, the Bakhtiaris and the *mujahids* had to come to terms with the former Shah's (Muhammad Âli Shah) last bid to regain the crown. Financed and supported by the Russians, the ex-Shah stayed for a few days at Gumishan (north of Gurgan) while his three armies advanced towards the capital. One army came from the north, another from the east (under his trusted Arshad ul-Douleh), and the third one from the south-west, with up to 30,000 Lur tribesmen, under his brother Salar ul-Douleh. At Tehran, the population panicked, but the government remained calm, sending its meagre troops to confront Arshad ul-Douleh, who was marching on Varamin. On September 4, 1911, the combined Bakhtiari-*mujahid* force met the rebels near Varamin and defeated them, thereby proving their worth yet again; Arshad ul-Douleh, wounded during the fighting, was court-martialled and executed on the morrow. Sardar Muhyi and his *mujahids* stopped the northern army and all the government forces together routed Salar ul-Douleh's large, but disorganised army near Saveh on September 27, 1911.[12] The ex-Shah's bid thus defeated, Muhammad Âli hurried back to its safe Russian exile; he would never return to Persia; he successively found refuge at Odessa (1911-9), Istanbul (1919-24) and San Remo in Italy (1924-5), dying in April 1925 in Savona (Italy), at the age of fifty-four; buried at Karbala, like his father. The first Shah of Persia to die in exile – not the last.

In July 1910, Sayyid Âbdullah Bihbahani was shot in his house by three bullets fired by Haydar Âmou Oughli and three of his accomplices. Bihbahani's assassination was a blow to the moderate faction of the *Majlis*, of which he was the mastermind.

There was little doubt that the leaders of the Democrat faction were involved in this act as they were the prime beneficiaries.[13] An even harsher blow was dealt to the ruling elite in February 1911 when one of its most capable administrators, Murtaza Quli Khan Sanî ul-Douleh, the Minister of Finance, was shot dead by two Armenians allegedly in the pay of Sardar Muhyi.[14] This loss was especially tragic because Sanî ul-Douleh was irreplaceable at Finance. After his untimely death, since no replacement could be found domestically, foreign financial experts were envisaged. The French expert Bizot, who had already come to Persia in 1908, was among the candidates. The final choice fell on the thirty-four year old American lawyer W. Morgan Shuster, a civil servant with experience in Cuba and the Philippines. A contract was drafted and approved by the *Majlis*. In May 1911 Morgan Shuster, accompanied by three American assistants, arrived in Tehran to take up his new post as treasurer-general of Persia. The range of Shuster's responsibilities was wide-ranging, extending from income taxes to treasury payments. From the outset Shuster acted as if he had been hired by the sovereign government of an independent country. There was a lot to be done to straighten out Persia's finances and bring them within a rational system. Unfortunately, the enormous effort Shuster was about to undertake was not to the taste of many actors, both domestic (i.e. the Qajar elite) and foreign (i.e. the Russians). Shuster's function and temperament would inexorably drag him into the midst of the Powers' Game.[15] What made Shuster's mission rather unique was the fact that it was the first time (except for the Belgian Naus) that a third Power expert had occupied a position of importance in Persia.

One of Shuster's innovations was the Treasury's Gendarmerie, a police force for collecting dues and taxes. At its head he appointed Major Stokes, the former British military attaché. With Shuster and Stokes in power, the Russians began to see the Shuster mission as a Anglo-American Trojan Horse for gaining control in Persia. They were thus waiting for Shuster's first *faux pas* to attack him. It was given them as Shuster legally decided to confiscate the properties of Prince Malik Mansur Mirza Shûâ ul-Saltaneh, the younger brother of

Muhammad Âli Shah. The prince was in exile and his properties in the escrow to the Russian Banque d'Escompte. Treasury gendarmes sent to confiscate the prince's house were met there by Russian officials and Cossacks; harsh words and even blows were exchanged. The Russians had their *casus belli* – they would not fail to capitalise on it.

Simultaneously sending troops to Anzali, the Russians sent the Persian Government two ultimata – respectively dated November 24 and 29, 1911 – asking for no less than: (1) the dismissal of Mr Morgan Shuster; (2) the consent of both the Russian and British legations for the future hiring by the Persian Government of foreign experts; (3) an indemnity to the Russian Government for covering the expenses of dispatching its occupation army to Persia. A beleaguered Persian Government called on the United States for assistance, but the latter invoked its isolationist Monroe Doctrine as an excuse for non-assistance. The British were called upon too; they gave "sage, though by no mean heroic, advice",[16] having their hands tied by the 1907 Convention. The *Majlis* refused categorically to accept the Russian ultimata, thereby placing the government of Samsam ul-Saltaneh in a difficult position. The Second *Majlis* legally came to an end on December 16, but the deputies refused to resign and remained in session. On December 22, Yeprem Khan, the Tehran police chief, on orders from the regent, closed the *Majlis*, as the elections for the Third *Majlis* were announced. Now the government could and did officially accept the Russian ultimata. As a direct consequence, on January 11, 1912, Morgan Shuster left Tehran with his assistants.

"Not the man to succumb without a struggle",[17] Morgan Shuster had tried to single-handedly counter the Russian threats and to awaken British public opinion to the Persian drama by, among other tactics, his open letter of October 21, 1911 to *The Times* of London. Although somewhat lacking in diplomacy and tact, he had been "a capable and energetic administrator";[18] under his stewardship Persian finances had been placed on the right tracks and positive results had been achieved.[19]

Notwithstanding these developments, Shuster's mission had been "doomed from its inception, ...[because] a prosperous Persia would have brought about a weakened Russian control".[20] After Shuster's departure, the Russian triumph was completed by the appointment of the Belgian J.J. Mornard, a Russian protégé, as treasurer-general of

Persia. Over the next three years Mornard would establish a quasi-monopoly over the Treasury.

While Shuster was sailing back to America, the Russian Army behaved in Azarbayjan as in a conquered territory, jailing, judging and executing whomever they believed to be a potential enemy in 'their sphere'. In Tabriz, on January 1, 1912 (the day of Âshoura, commemorating the martyrdom of Imam Husayn (A.S.)), the Russian forces hanged the Saqat ul-Islam, a religious personality, along with two of Âli Mussiou's sons and seven other freedom fighters; their crime was to have fought for the constitution.[21] The Russians committed many other atrocities during their occupation of Azarbayjan; some of these were related by Professor Browne in a pamphlet[22] and a number of articles, with among others: "...in the suburbs of Hukmabad which is chiefly inhabited by agricultural labourers, the Russians killed seventy-five persons, whose bodies they afterwards gibbeted ...while he [one of the would-be martyrs] was still alive they plucked out his eyes and cut his tongue, before they slew him".[23] In addition to the Azarbayjan massacres, the Russian troops shelled, on March 28, 1912, the Imam Riza Shrine at Mashhad, killing a number of innocent pilgrims and hitting the golden dome and the two minarets with no fewer than fifty-nine cannon balls. These Russian acts, whether at Tabriz or Mashhad, would never be forgotten nor forgiven by the Persians.

While the Russians were plundering, massacring, gibbeting and shelling holy shrines, not only the British but also Tehran remained silent (with only Professor Browne's pen to break the silence). If the British behaviour was excusable, Tehran's was not. The ruling elite lost many Persian hearts and minds during these 1912 months by being incapable of even protesting against these Russian atrocities. It buried its head in the snow hoping that the Russian nightmare might go away, arguing that: "[the] protests would have no effect but to offend the Russians".[24] Could it be that the total collapse of the Persian Government in the face of the Russian ultimata might have given them the feeling that they could get away with anything? In any event, the Tehran elite was collectively responsible for these dramatic events. The Russian atrocities of 1912 were yet a further sign that the elite in place at Tehran was seriously lacking in some crucial respects.

5.2. The Elite

In less than two years the Qajar elite had ended up co-opting the major leaders of the movement – both the initial leaders, the Sayyids Tabataba'i and Bihbahani (in order to reinforce their religious wing), and also the three Tehran victors, the Sipahdar, Samsam ul-Saltaneh and Sardar Asâd. In the meantime, the best and the brightest from within the Qajar ranks had been co-opted to the elite ranks, to make up an amazingly homogeneous ensemble of sixteen individuals. A gifted intellectual of *bazaari* origin was included to bring the total number of the new Persian elite – hereafter to be known as the Elite (with a capital E) – to twenty-two members.

These twenty-two Elite members, with their characteristics and the family name of their descendants, are listed in Table 5.1. An overall picture of each of these is given hereunder:[25]

1. The wealthy Sipahdar committed suicide in 1926, after realising that Reza Shah would appropriate all his Mazandarani lands and villages. His descendants, of the large Khalâtbari family, would remain on the fringes of the Elite.

2. Samsam ul-Saltaneh became the uncontested Bakhtiari leader and paved the way for his capable eldest son, Murtaza Quli Khan Samsam Bakhtiari (1874–1959) to become *ilkhan* of the Bakhtiaris and rank among the wealthiest men in Persia.

3. As Sardar Asâd died rather young, his eldest son Jâfar Quli Khan, took over his title and his political legacy. The latter had a great military career, but proved in the end not to have inherited his father's political genius.

4. Bihbahani was murdered in July 1910 for political reasons. His sons Sayyid Muhammad (the future Ayatullah Bihbahani), Sayyid Ahmad (ten *Majlis* deputations) and Sayyid Âli (eleven *Majlis* deputations) would continue in his footsteps.

5. Sayyid Tabataba'i's son Sayyid Muhammad Sadiq Tabataba'i enjoyed a long and successful political career, beginning with a deputation in the Second *Majlis* and culminating in the presidency of the Fourteenth, and ending with the Sixteenth *Majlis*.

6. The Russophile Âyn ul-Douleh, with his rather dull character and his lack of political flexibility, was an anomaly among the Elite –

owing too much of his career to royal favours. He did not leave any descendants of consequence.

7. With his immense fortune and his unequalled political skills, Farmanfarma would rise to the very top of the Elite, becoming its supreme arbiter during the 1920s and 1930s. His twenty-one sons and twelve daughters would later form the trunk of the Elite tree.

8. The veteran amongst the Elite, Âla ul-Saltaneh was ambassador to London for seventeen years (1890-1906). His son, Husayn Âla (1883-1964), Anglophile like his father, would collect ministerships, become premier and court minister, and senator.

9. Educated at Oxford's Balliol College, Nasir ul-Mulk, from the oldest Qajar aristocratic family, retired from politics in 1914 and lived in Europe until 1926. A plethora of younger Qaraguzlus would carry on the family presence in politics.

10. The highly capable Sanî ul-Douleh, son-in-law to Muzaffar ul-Din Shah since 1888, was among Persia's top administrators (especially for financial affairs). A bullet put an end to his ambitions: an irreplaceable loss for the Elite.

11. Mukhbir ul-Saltaneh, Sanî ul-Douleh's younger brother, would live longest among the twenty-two Elitists, up to the age of ninety-one. He had a protracted career, crowned by the premiership for six years in the late 1920s and early 1930s.

12. Muhtashim ul-Saltaneh collected ministerships and ended up as *Majlis* president from 1930 until 1943, spanning six different *Majlis* (i.e. Eighth till Thirteenth). He placed his Isfandyari family within the Elite's mainstream by his longevity.

13. Mustashar ul-Douleh, a prisoner at Bagh-i Shah after the *Majlis* bombardment, was fortunate to have his life spared. He remained in the political limelight until the end of the Second World War and placed his three sons within Elite ranks.

14. For years Minister for Foreign Affairs, Mushavir ul-Mamalik rose to become Persia's most respected diplomat. It was he who was dispatched to Moscow to negotiate and sign the Soviet-Persian treaty of 1921.

15. Hasan Khan Mustoufi ul-Mamalik, nicknamed *Aqa* like his father – a name he deserved too. A highly popular statesman, he was especially honest (known as the Incorruptible in Elite circles). Collected a record number of eleven premierships.

16. Hasan Khan Mushir ul-Douleh, the elder son of Nasrullah Khan, studied military history and law in Russia. His father launched him on a successful career in politics that spanned two decades. With Mustoufi, one of Persia's most popular statesmen.

17. Mutâmin ul-Mulk, the younger son of Nasrullah Khan, studied law and philosophy in Paris and London. He put his mark on the *Majlis* by presiding over it with an iron hand between 1914 and 1926 (Third, Fourth and Fifth *Majlis*).

18. Vusuq ul-Douleh, one of the most gifted of the Elite's up-and-coming generation. After the constitutionalists' victory, was among the Elite's leaders. Was a member of twenty cabinets in the period 1909–1919, as prime minister in four of them.

19. Qavam ul-Saltaneh, Vusuq's younger brother. As gifted as his brother. Began his career as private secretary to Muzaffar ul-Din Shah. Remained until 1919 in his brother's shadow. Rose to become Persia's greatest statesman of the twentieth century.

20. Hakim ul-Mulk, an M.D. (Paris) by profession, like his uncle (Mahmud Khan, the former private physician to Muzaffar ul-Din Shah) and his father (Abu'l Hasan Khan Hakimbashi). His long political career culminated in 1945 with two premierships.

21. Sardar Mansour, a wealthy landowner from Rasht, was more renowned for his money than for his political acumen. Functioned as the Elite's stopgap, and was satisfied with his role. His Akbar family would retain a foothold in the Elite.

22. Zukâ ul-Mulk was a curiosity among the Elite: the son of an Isfahani merchant, he was exceptionally gifted intellectually. Co-opted by the Elite's younger generation, he led five cabinets overall (his last two in the crucial year of 1941).

Over a period of 139 months – spanning August 1909 to February 1921 – no fewer than thirty-seven cabinets were formed to manage Persia's affairs: an average of one cabinet every four months. Only nine individuals (all of them Elite members) became prime minister. Of the total of 268 ministerships filled, 167 (i.e. roughly two-thirds) went to Elite members. Out of six *Majlis* presidents, four were from Elite ranks (the two others on the fringes of Elite). These simple statistics show how the Elite dominated Persian politics over the dozen years separating the constitutionalists' victory from the 1921 *coup d'état*. Yet another statistic worth noting in Table 5.1. is the average

Table 5.1. The twenty-two Elite members – with their full names, their best-known titles, their dates of birth and death, their future family names, and their respective number of premierships and ministerships between August 1909 and February 1921.[26]

Name and Title (Family Name)	Premierships	Ministerships	Dates
Muhammad Vali Khan Sipahdar Âzam (Khal âtbari)	8	10	1848–1926
Najaf Quli Khan Samsam ul-Saltaneh (Samsam Bakhtiari)	7	6	1852–1930
Hajj Âli Quli Khan Sardar Asâd (Asâd Bakhtiari)	–	5	1855–1917
Sayyid Âbdullah Bihbahani (Bihbahani)	–	–	1844–1910
Sayyid Muhammad Tabataba'i (Tabataba'i)	–	–	1843–1920
Âbd ul-Majid Mirza Âyn ul-Douleh	2	5	1845–1927
Âbd ul-Husayn Mirza Farmanfarma (Farmanfarmayan/Firouz)	1	7	1859–1939
Muhammad Âli Khan Âla ul-Saltaneh (Âla)	3	13	1838–1918
Abu'l Qasim Khan Nasir ul-Mulk (Qaraguzlu)	(regent)	2	1865–1927
Murtaza Khan Sanû ul-Douleh (Hidayat)	pres. *Majlis*	–	1856–1911
Mihdi Quli Khan Mukhbir ul-Saltaneh	–	3	1864–1955

(Hidayat) Hasan Khan Muhthashim ul-Saltaneh	–	13	1867–1945
(Isfandyari) Sadiq Khan Mustashar ul-Douleh	pres. Majlis	7	1865–1853
(Sadiq) Âli Quli Khan Mushavir ul-Mamalik	–	5	1869–1940
(Ansari) Hasan Khan Mustoufi ul-Mamalik	8	9	1874–1932
(Mustoufi ul-Mamaliki) Hasan Khan Mushir ul-Douleh	2	17	1874–1935
(Pirnya) Husayn Khan Mûtamin ul-Mulk	pres. Majlis	6	1875–1947
(Pirnya) Hasan Khan Vusuq ul-Douleh	4	16	1875–1951
(Vusuq) Ahmad Khan Qavam ul-Saltaneh	–	8	1877–1955
(Qavam) Ibrahim Khan Hakim ul-Mulk	–	13	1871–1958
(Hakimi) Fathullah Akbar Sardar Mansour	2	10	1867–1954
(Akbar) Muhammad Âli Khan Zukâ ul-Mulk	pres. Majlis	5	1875–1942
(Furoughi)			
Total of premierships and ministerships:	37	160	

age of the twenty Elite members who died a natural death (excluding the assassinated Sanî ul-Douleh and Bihbahani): a remarkable seventy-six years!

As for the six other families which were to join the twenty Elite families mentioned in Table 5.1, they consisted of the following families (with their base given in parentheses):

Imami (Tehran), Khazâl (Muhammarah), Qashqa'i (Qashqa'i tribe of Fars), Qavam ul-Mulk (Shiraz), Nizam Mafi (Qazvin) and Âlam (Birjand). Their general background is outlined hereunder:

1) The Imami family had its roots in the Safavi hierocracy. It began its climb to national status by taking wives from the famous Majlisi family. Mir Muhammad Husayn Khatunabadi married Muhammad Baqir Majlisi's daughter, and, when the latter died in 1699, succeeded him as Shah Sultan Husayn's *mullabashi* (or chief religious adviser). His brother, Mir Muhammad Mihdi, moved to Tehran and established the Tehran *Imam Jumêh* branch; it is this latter branch, the Imami family, which entered the Elite.

2) The Khazâl family was brought to prominence by Shaykh Jabir – "a very shrewd and calculating individual" according to Lord Curzon – who died in 1881. He was replaced by his eldest son Mizâl, who ruled until allegedly murdered in 1898 by his brother Khazâl, who replaced him. Shaykh Khazâl (1863–1936), from his base at Muhammarah, extended his grip over south-western Persia, virtually becoming its uncrowned king, and the richest man in Persia.

3) Ismâil Khan Soulat ul-Douleh (1873–1932) was the supreme chief (*ilkhan*) of the Qashqa'i tribe. He would be called to play a role in national politics, especially during and after the First World War. His four sons, Nasir, Malik Mansur, Muhammad Husayn and Khusrou, would later enter, with mixed success, the national fray.

4) The Qavam ul-Mulk of Shiraz were direct descendants of the formidable Ibrahim Khan Kalantar Shirazi (d. 1801) through his fourth son Âli Akbar (the only family member spared by Fath Âli Shah). With their vast land holdings in and around Shiraz, the family easily counted among Persia's wealthiest. The family's leader, the Qavam ul-Mulk, was, alongside the Qasqha'i *ilkhan*, the most powerful man of the important Fars province.

5) The Nizam Mafi family originated with the rise of Husayn Quli Khan Nizam ul-Saltaneh (1826–1909) from within the Mafi tribe – a Lur tribe displaced in the early nineteenth century to Qazvin. Husayn Quli Khan had collected governorships in southern Persia (Luristan, Fars, Bushire) before being called to the court and appointed prime minister in 1907–8 by Muhammad Âli Shah. His young son Husayn, educated in England, having mysteriously died in 1907, he was succeeded by his nephew Riza Quli, who received his title of Nizam ul-Saltaneh.

6) The Âlam family was the dominant family in Sistan and Baluchistan. Its main base was in Birjand and it possessed major lands in the Qâinat region. In 1905, Muhammad Ibrahim Khan Shoukat ul-Mulk (1880–1944) succeeded his brother as governor of Qâinat and as family leader. He had the wisdom to keep unity in the family by relinquishing some of his prerogatives to his nephews. Being a capable administrator, he later entered national politics and opened the Elite's doors for his family.

The above twenty-six families were to form the hardcore of the country's ruling elite. These Elite families, which were later to be (erroneously) called 'The Thousand Families', were at first a small nucleus of only twenty-six. With time, other families were naturally co-opted and accepted within the Elite ranks, but they never came to number one thousand, not even one hundred; at most there were fifty to sixty. Nevertheless the expression 'Thousand Families' has become a Persian standard to denote the Elite.

5.3. The First World War

In June 1914, the persistence of a young, twenty year old Bosnian student, Gavrilo Princip, finally paid off: the shots he fired at Sarajevo mortally wounded Archduke Franz Ferdinand and his wife Sophie. The spark triggered by the young student set Europe ablaze. The great European Powers declared war upon each other: by August, the First World War was underway.

For Persia and its Elite, the war was uncharted territory: there was no precedent to guide them. The best the Elite could come up with was to officially declare Persia's neutrality on November 1, 1914.

This move by the government of Mustoufi ul-Mamalik (in place since August 1913) was a defensive ploy, informing the belligerents that Persia supported no side, rather than a serious attempt at keeping its territory free from hostility. The latter hope was merely wishful thinking, because, firstly, Russians were already stationed in Azarbayjan and secondly, Persia did not have a deterrent force to defend her neutrality. At the beginning of the war, she had at most 8,000 Cossacks (with Russian affinities), 7,000 gendarmes[27] (with, mostly, German sympathies) and another 10,000 Persian soldiers scattered around the country. It was not with this hotchpotch force that Persia could hope to preserve her declared neutrality against belligerent Powers fighting a global war.

When, on October 29, 1914, the Ottoman Empire entered the hostilities on Germany's side, Persia's predicament looked even more precarious: the World War had come right to its western door. Now, with Turkey and Germany on one side and Great Britain and Russia on the other, it was evident that Persia would become a battlefield, with none of the foreign armies asking Tehran for permission to violate her borders. Of the four Powers involved, three were neighbours (with Great Britain as the Persian Gulf power) and habitués of the Persian Game (the Turks being out since the early nineteenth century). Germany alone was a newcomer.

It was barely two decades since Germany had been attracted to the Middle East and the Persian Gulf. The Germans' major effort was in Mesopotamia with their drive for oil concessions and the building of a railway from Europe all the way to Basra on the Gulf (hence the German-Ottoman *rapprochement*). These projects were managed under the umbrella of the Deutsche Bank which had set up (among others) the Baghdad Railway Company to build the railway line. Germans were also active in the Persian Gulf. It had begun in a benign way, with the opening in 1896 of an office by the Wonckhaus firm in Bandar-i Lingeh. Then, a year later, the first German consulate was established at Bushire. Wonckhaus gradually expanded first to Basra, then to Bandar Ābbas. In 1906, Albert Ballin's Hamburg-Amerika Linie began opening counters along the Gulf's shore. In the end, all these small developments came to little as they had to fold in 1914; their only use was to give German diplomats and then covert agents their first taste of Persia. After these preliminaries, the Germans' master plan was to conquer Persia by way of modern industrialisation.

Wilhelm Wassmuss was one of the German agents who had been consul at Bushire and used his cover to acquaint himself with south Persia. In 1914, he was back in Baghdad with a small group of selected German agents for covert missions in Persia and Afghanistan. His colleague Oskar von Niedermayer – "a Bavarian of outstanding ability and thoroughness"[28] – later joined by Otto von Hentig, departed for Afghanistan in April 1915; the Germans reached Kabul in August (after crossing Persia) and remained there until June 1916, but failed to convince the Amir Habibullah to enter into an alliance with Germany. Niedermayer used all his resources to cross Persia once again and make it back home; Von Hentig made it too, via China. Wassmuss, on the other hand, made south Persia his sphere of action: the region between Bushire and Fars, the land of the Tangistanis and the Qashqa'is. As Wassmuss found his way to his post at the beginning of 1915,[29] the Germans' other iron in the Persian fire, its official diplomatic network, was in place: at Tehran, Ambassador Prince Henri von Reuss, and his military attaché Graf Kanitz; at Tabriz, Schunemann; at Isfahan, Pugin and Seiler; at Bushire, Listermann; at Kerman, Zugmayer and Friesinger; at Yazd, Dr Biach; at Shiraz, Wustrow and finally, at Kermanshah, Klein.

All the Germans in Persia pulled their weight during the war years and created innumerable problems for their enemies. None of them, however, caused such havoc as did Wassmuss single-handedly. At first, in February 1915, the oil pipeline linking Masjid-i Sulayman to Abadan had been severely damaged and it took the British until mid-June to get it back on stream. It is not clear whether Wassmuss, who had passed the border in January 1915, had had a hand in this mischief, but it was put to his account. Wassmuss's main objective, however, was further south, near Bushire, the prominent port and customs centre, where, earlier, he had been a consul. In this respect Wassmuss arrived at the right time: the nationalistic undertones of the constitutionalist wave had reached the shores of the Gulf. At Bushire the right mix of *bazaar* traders and bureaucrats (teachers and civil servants) was ideal for propagating novel ideas. The nationalistic mood had taken, in the south, a definite anti-British turn, which was considerably accentuated in the hinterland, especially the region between Bushire and Shiraz: the lands of the Tangistani tribes, which were renowned for their independent ways, with memories of standing up to the British back in 1857. This was where Wassmuss would place his main effort, fuelling a rebellion spearheaded by three men:[30]

1) Ra'is Âli Dilvari, the courageous leader of the small village of Dilvar, located along the coast some forty kilometres south-east of Bushire;

2) Shaykh Husayn Khan Chahkutahi, a minor tribal chieftain, based in his stronghold of Chahkutah, a small town, situated some thirty kilometres north-east of Bushire;

3) Za'ir Khizir Khan, Amir-i Islam, a leading Tangistani personality of Ahrum, the unnamed capital of Tangistan, a small settlement consisting of roughly a thousand households, located fifty kilometres east of Bushire.

In July 1915, the first Tangistani drive on Bushire was repulsed by the British troops stationed there. Four navy ships on their way to Bushire bombarded the small village of Dilvar, causing considerable damage; however, a tentative attempt by British troops to disembark in Dilvar's date groves was valiantly repelled by Ra'is Âli and his men, at a cost of sixty to seventy casualties to the British (mainly Indian sepoys) troops.[31] In September, near Chughadak (a few kilometres east of Bushire), the combined Tangistani forces of Ra'is Âli, Shaykh Husayn and Za'ir Khizir Khan assaulted, *en rase campagne*, the well-entrenched British forces. The courage and sharpshooting of the tribesmen was no match for the trained and disciplined Indian troops commanded by British officers: the assailants were routed,[32] and their leader Ra'is Âli was shot in the back by a traitor.[33] Thus were the Tangistanis broken.

The centre of German activity thereafter shifted to Isfahan and Shiraz. At Isfahan, the Russian vice-consul was shot dead and the British consul narrowly escaped a similar fate. In Shiraz, the British vice-consul (a Persian national), was also shot dead in early September 1915. Then, in November, the consul himself, Lieutenant. Colonel Frederick O'Connor was taken prisoner, along with members of the British colony at Shiraz (which included six men and four women).[34] This unique coup had been achieved by a mix of gendarmes, liberal elements and Qashqa'i tribesmen, co-ordinated by Wassmuss and the Germans. The four women held captive were handed over to the British resident at Bushire and the men were incarcerated in Za'ir Khizir Khan's castle at Ahrum. After a year of captivity, the British prisoners were exchanged for Tangistanis and Germans held in India. The Persian adventures of the First World War ended with this exchange.

For three of its main actors, it had dramatic sequels. In April 1920, Shaykh Husayn Khan Chahkutahi was ambushed by members of a pro-British tribe and shot dead.[35] In April 1923, Za'ir Khizir Khan and his elder son Sam were murdered at Ahrum by an old friend paying them a visit.[36] As for Wassmuss, he continued harassing the British forces for the rest of the war, finally being caught in 1919 at Qum and eventually deported to Germany. In 1924, Wassmuss returned to Tangistan to work the land according to modern agricultural methods and earn enough money to pay the Tangistanis the £5,000 he had promised them back in 1915. At first his enterprise made some profits, but soon turned sour. In 1928, Wassmuss went bankrupt.[37] Three years later, dispirited and disillusioned, he returned to Germany, where he was to die in 1931. Single-handedly he had done much to disrupt British activities in south Persia, and was "in part responsible for Kut [al-Amara]'s catastrophic surrender [of April 1916]".[38] His actions were finally limited and circumscribed. Had Wassmuss been able to invest Bushire and Shiraz, with the help of his Tangistani tribesmen, he would have achieved, like Lawrence of Arabia, eternal fame; but, unlike Lawrence, who went all the way to Damascus, Wassmuss eventually failed in his undertakings.

By the close of 1914 the war had come to Persia. In the northwest, the Turk and Russian armies were fighting it out. On January 8, 1915, the Turks captured Tabriz; the Russians counterattacked and drove them out of it on January 30th.[39]

The defeated Turks retreated to the border, and the north of Persia became a Russian preserve. Then on March 18, 1915 the inter-Allied Constantinople Agreement was signed between Great Britain and Russia, giving Great Britain the lion's share of the 1907 agreement Neutral Zone (Russia getting its easternmost part) and giving Russia, as *quid pro quo*, full freedom in its northern zone. The Russian Army hurriedly landed troops at Anzali in May 1915 and in November invested Qazvin, threatening Tehran.

In Tehran, the closeness of Russian troops alarmed the politicians and the people. Prince von Reuss, the German ambassador, was finally able to convince Prime Minister Mustoufi to initial a twelve-point secret agreement between Germany and Persia (November 10,

1915). The Reuss-Mustoufi agreement was in direct violation of Persia's neutrality declaration (which had naturally long since been buried) and a sure sign of the Elite's total lack of a defined strategy in these highly turbulent times. With the Russians virtually at Tehran's doors, the exodus towards Isfahan, which was to become the new capital, was general. Even the young Ahmad Shah – he had been crowned shah on July 20, 1914 – was planning to leave. Prince Farmanfarma, the only politician to keep his head, dissuaded the Shah from departing at the very last minute: wise advice because a change of the shah's residence could well have triggered a change of dynasty. Moreover, a flight before the Russians would have meant a break with the Allies and an inevitable alliance with the Germans.

For the ones who had left Tehran, such as the radical *Majlis* deputies, the politicians, the gendarmes and the intellectuals, there was no other solution but to become Germany's allies. Stranded in Qum, they and the German diplomats had faced a vacuum. Prince Reuss had encouraged them to form a 'Committee of National Resistance' and assisted them in sending representatives to Arak, Isfahan and Shiraz. But a leaderless committee was worthless, and in any case its life was shortened by the advance of Russian troops towards Saveh, Qum and Hamadan. The refugees fled once again before the Russians, this time towards Kermanshah and the border. As for the Germans, they were still looking for a worthy leader to head their resistance movement.

Their first choice, Elitist Mukhbir ul-Saltaneh, politely refused. After this initial rebuff, they counted on the governor of Luristan, Riza Quli Khan Nizam ul-Saltaneh Mafi. Graf Kanitz for the Germans and Sayyid Muhammad Musavat, for the National Committee, went to Burujird to convince him to lead their movement. The forty-eight year old Riza Quli Khan accepted the German propositions and on December 26, 1915 signed a Protocol of Understanding with Graf Kanitz, including clauses calling for a German monthly subsidy of 20,000 toumans and a payment of 2,000,000 toumans to Nizam ul-Saltaneh's "private estate".[40]

Thus the provisional government of Persia for which the Germans had been angling was born. It would be known as the *Muhajarat* (the Migration), in the name of the Tehran migrants who were to play a prominent part in it. The Germans would provide money and armaments, Nizam ul-Saltaneh would recruit Lurs tribesmen to form a

40,000-man army. As the protocol was signed, Prince Reuss left Persia and was replaced by Dr Vassel. How had a man like Riza Quli Khan, "who found himself in strange circumstances, for by inclination he was Anglophile",[41] who had been governor in the south of Persia for decades, and who stood on the fringes of Elite (with his daughter married to Prince Farmanfarma's son and one of his close cousins the wife of Shaykh Khazâl) accept the German gambit? Was it for the money (the Germans promised and gave), or the hope that Germany would win the war, or the opportunity offered to lead a national movement? Or perhaps for all of these reasons? Even though both Farmanfarma and Khazâl coaxed him to go back on his decision, Riza Quli Khan refused adamantly. He formed his provisional government with Sayyid Mudarris at Justice and his own eldest son Muhammad Âli Khan at Foreign Affairs,[42] and gathered some tribesmen from the Kalhurs (2000), the Sanjabis (1000) and the Bakhtiaris (a few hundred). The total was far from the 40,000 he had promised the credulous Germans. Nevertheless, as soon as formed, the *Muhajarat* forces, led by a handful of professional Gendarmerie officers, were sent to stop the Russian advance which had engulfed Hamadan. In January 1916, Graf Kanitz, the architect of the movement, committed suicide, most probably in desperation. For the next five months, with skirmishes fought here and there, the Russians continued to progress while the *Muhajarat* troops retreated. In May 1916 the Russians occupied the border town of Qasr-i Shirin. The *Muhajarat* people had to find asylum on the other side of the border. The Provisional Government was taken to Baghdad, where it participated in the festivities following the fall of Kut al-Amara, where on April 29, 1916, the 13,000-man British army of General Townsend had surrendered to Field Marshal Kolmar von der Goltz Pasha – "the gravest disaster suffered by British arms in Asia".[43]

With the Germano-Turk success at Kut, the hopes of the *Muhajarat* were rekindled. *Geheimrat* Rudolph Nadolnyi had replaced Dr Vassel as chief German adviser to Nizam ul-Saltaneh and Colonel Bopp was his military attaché, commanding a dozen younger officers, among whom was Wipert von Blücher, the great-grandson of the Waterloo victor. In August 1916, a counter-offensive masterminded by General Gressman, the new German commander of the Iraqi and Persian front, and spearheaded by two divisions of the

13th Turkish Army under Âli Ihsan Pasha, advanced first to Kermanshah, then to Hamadan. This time the roles were reversed as the Russian troops of General Baratov were continuously retreating. In early 1917, the Russians were back to square one at Qazvin, for the Turks had stopped at Hamadan. The British Mesopotamian campaign of 1917 would come in time to foil the Germano-Turkish plans for Persia. In February 1917, the British had recaptured Kut al-Amara and by mid-March were in Baghdad. The Turkish troops in Persia, fearing that they would be cut off, retreated rapidly to the border, with the Russians on their heels. That was the end of the *Muhajarat* venture and of German actions in Persia: by the close of March, Nizam ul-Saltaneh was in Kirkuk and Nadolnyi recalled to Berlin. In April 1917, the British and Russian forces operated their junction along the Turko-Persian border.

After fifteen months of ebb and flow, the *Muhajarat* had folded. Its leadership took to an European exile; the tribesmen returned to their respective tribes; the gendarmes reintegrated into the national Gendarmerie. The *Muhajarat* never coalesced into a viable movement, for it was made up of too many disparate elements. It had hung on as long as it could to the Germans coat-tails; without German money, arms and support it simply collapsed. From the outset it had been a hopeless case, and it is not therefore surprising that it proved unsuccessful. As for the British and the Russians, the *Muhajarat* had been a blessing: it had kept all German (and Turkish) eggs in Persia in a single basket, which had been bound from the beginning to come crashing to the ground.[43A]

Meanwhile in Tehran, Mustoufi had finally resigned the premiership in December 1915. He was replaced by Prince Farmanfarma, who entered into negotiation with the British Legation to try to secure a general Anglo-Persian agreement. The Persian proposals of January 1916[44] were deemed unacceptable by the British: but they were serious and reflected the Elite's will to reach a general understanding with the Allies. After much pruning by the British diplomats, a totally revised protocol was submitted to Farmanfarma. It was akin to a joint Russo-British condominium over Persia. Farmanfarma could not sign such a document and had to resign in early March, having failed in his mission. The Prince later confided to Mukhbirul-Saltaneh: "As the grandson of Âbbas Mirza there are certain things I cannot indulge in..."[45] On the British side too there were limitations on what they could accept from the Persians, even from a Farmanfarma cabinet which was as pro-British as possible, being "virtually called into being by Marling (the British Envoy)".

Farmanfarma was replaced by Sipahsalar Tunikabuni at the head of government. The old Sipahsalar was confronted with the same problem as Farmanfarma, but, unlike his predecessor, he couldn't escape signing the agreement in August 1916 because of his known Russophilism. The only gimmick left to Sipahsalar was to "add to his signature on the agreement: "I am signing due to force majeure...".[46]

While following up the political negotiation in Tehran, the British were aware of their inherent weaknesses in south Persia. In view of the Constantinople Agreement of 1915, they decided that they needed an armed police force of their own in their sphere of influence – if only to counter the incursions and intrigues of the German agents. Therefore General Sir Percy Sykes, who had an excellent knowledge of Persia in general and especially of south Persia, was dispatched to build up the force. In March 1916, General Sykes disembarked in Bandar Âbbas accompanied by three British officers, three Indian officers, twenty NCOs and twenty-five Indian *sowars*.[47] From scratch, Sykes created the South Persian Military Police, better known under its name of South Persia Rifles (SPR), a Persian police force. The SPR would gradually develop to attain a maximum contingent of 8,000 men.[48] In September 1916, the SPR was officially recognised as a Persian security force by the government of Vusuqul-Douleh. A year later, this recognition was overturned by yet another government. During the last two years of the war the SPR kept law and order in the south of the country.

In the summer of 1918, the SPR was instrumental in quelling a Qashqa'i tribe rebellion. Once again, the Qashqa'i leadership had shot itself in the foot by launching a suicidal attack on Shiraz at the worst possible time. Already, during the Constitutional Movement, it had wasted a golden occasion to march on Shiraz and Tehran and secure a foothold on the national level (failing to heed the encouragement of Nizam ul-Saltaneh).

During the war, it had failed to flex its (undeniable) muscles when circumstances were ripe. Now, it acted as the British were at their apogee in south Persia and determined not to let anyone disturb internal security in their sphere – or, for that matter, in the Persian theatre as a whole, for the Bolshevik Revolution, by bringing about drastic changes in Russia, had altered the Great Game altogether. The SPR readily saw off the untimely Qashqa'i challenge.[48A] In January 1919, General Sir Percy Sykes finally departed Persia (after a presence covering a quarter of a century), having accomplished his last mission there.

In 1918 the shock waves of the October Revolution spread around the world, greatly influencing the nearby Middle East. With the Soviet Union replacing Russia, Lenin in place of the tsar, the Great Powers' rivalry in Persia was totally changed. In the short term, the Soviet Union, weakened by the war and the Revolution, would have to leave the Game; in the long term, though, it had stolen a march on all its rivals by acquiring an ideology: Marxist-Leninism. After signing the Peace Treaty of Brest-Litovsk (March 3, 1918) with Germany, the young Soviet Union was engulfed by a civil war between the Whites and the Reds. Great Britain had to post themselves on the Soviets' southern borders to contain the Revolution's southward overspill.

By filling the vacuum left by the Russians, the British were being prudent. They liaised with the Russian armies of General Baratov and Colonel Bicherakov, which were still occupying northern Persia. They also sent troops of their own to the north:[49]

1) A force under Major General L.C. Dunsterville, known as 'Dunsterforce', which consisted of twelve officers and a number of NCOs, dashed through Persia (from Hamadan) with four motor vehicles, thirty-six Ford vans and an armoured car, to Bandar Anzali and Baku in early 1918. It arrived too late in Baku to effectively stop the Turks' onslaught (at the end of October, the Turkish Army would turn back anyway) and in September Dunsterville returned all the way to Qazvin, to where he transferred his headquarters (from Hamadan). After his departure from Qazvin, his force became known as the 'Norperforce' (North Persian Force).

2) Commodore D.T. Norris organised a small navy on the Caspian Sea, comprising four vessels fully equipped and ready for action.

3) Major General W. Maleson led a small detachment from India to Mashhad in the summer of 1918. From his headquarters in Mashhad he tried to assist the Turkomans and the White Russians in Transcapia, but here too the Bolsheviks got the upper hand and the British force retired first to Charpui and then to Mashhad, eventually returning to India in the autumn of 1920. In support of Maleson's

drive, Lieutenant Colonel Etherton and Lieutenant Colonel F.M. Bailey[49A] were sent on special missions to Turkestan and Tashkent respectively.

The British also indirectly supported the White armies of General A.I. Denikin (in the south) and Admiral A.V. Kolchak (in Siberia). Denikin's 'Volunteer Army' fared well at first, occupying Odessa in July–August 1919. Its troops expanded to 150,000 men and his right wing was able to establish contact with Kolchak's left wing – total victory was near at hand. Then, the wind turned against Denikin as General Budenny defeated him and the Red Army took Kiev and Kharkov in December 1919.[50] By February 1920 Denikin's forces were totally routed and the defeated General transferred the remains of his South Russian Army to Crimea, gave it over to General P. Wrangel and retired to England.

After a full century of intercourse over Persia, the two Great Powers were abruptly reduced to one: only Great Britain was left to play the Game. For the first (and probably the last) time in the Game's history, a Power was left to play solitaire. This unique position would not be the sinecure many believed it to be.

5.4. Oil Industry Development

The seeds sown by W. Knox D'Arcy and the discovery of petroleum by G.B. Reynolds had spawned the establishment of the Anglo-Persian Oil Company (APOC) in 1909. Now the newly created company had to turn the petroleum in the Zagros mountains into a viable business.

The overall plan formulated by the APOC engineers was for (i) a number of production wells to be drilled at Masjid-i Sulayman (MIS), (ii) a pipeline to be laid between MIS and Abadan Island (the optimum site for exports in regard to MIS), (iii) a refinery to be built at Abadan to process the crude oil, and (iv) the erection of port facilities at Abadan to allow ships to berth and load refined products. At first APOC relied on contractors to manage its interests and appointed the Scottish firm of Lloyd, Scott and Co., (later Strick, Scott and Co.,) as its managing contractor. The contractor's headquarters were at Muhammarah.

The Strick/Scott-APOC relationship would endure until 1924, at which time the company decided to take direct control.

In 1909, APOC's overall plan unfolded in south Persia. Work began on the pipeline linking MIS to the coast: a six-inch pipe (lengths of which were screwed together) over a distance of 224 kilometres, with four major boosting stations in between:[51]

MIS to Tembi (OPLA): eight km.;
Tembi to Mullasani: sixty-one km.;
Mullasani to Kut Âbdullah: fifty-one km.;
Kut Âbdullah to Darkhuayn: fifty-six km.;
Darkuayn to Abadan: forty-eight km.

Two Scottish engineers, Charles Ritchie and James J. Jameson, assisted by "thirty British technicians and some thousand native hands", directed this unique enterprise and overcame all local problems to complete the line in a record time; by June 1911 it was pronounced "bottle-tight".[52] The MIS–Abadan pipeline had an initial capacity of 8,000 barrels per day (b/d); it had cost APOC £15,000. Ritchie was to die prematurely of smallpox in 1914; on the other hand, Jameson had a long career with APOC which took him to a directorship in 1939 until his retirement in 1952.

Simultaneously, at both ends of the pipeline, work was in process. At MIS development wells were being drilled to enhance petroleum output and storage tanks were built. At the coastal end, on the Abadan Island – an "island of sunshine, mud and flies" – the APOC refinery was being constructed on the square mile of land rented by Dr Young from the Shaykh Khazâl of Muhammarah at a cost of £650 per annum (June 1909).[53] At Abadan, R.R. Davidson was in charge, seconded by N. Ramsay, R. Neilson, J. Gillespie and J.H. Young. In August 1912 the first distillation unit went on stream.[54] During the next few months initial technical problems were ironed out and by early 1913 the refinery's stills were being operated near their full capacity of 2,400 b/d.

For the next decade, the burgeoning south Persian oil industry kept expanding, year in and year out, with only a minor hiatus in 1915, when for five months operations had to be interrupted due to the wartime sabotage of the pipeline.[55] After the war's end APOC claimed some £614,489 from the Persian Government for damages and loss incurred in the 1915 incident.[56] Meanwhile, new wells were being drilled at MIS; the pipeline capacity was being boosted; and fresh units were added at the refinery. Overall throughput constantly increased, from an average of 2,000 b/d in 1913, to 18,300 b/d in 1918 and to 35,400 b/d in 1921.[57] With its 13 million barrels of production in 1921, Persian oil amounted to 1.7% of total world oil output.

As APOC was finding its bearings in 1912-13, the British Government became directly interested in the Persian oil venture. Interest in oil had begun in the first years of the century, as Lord Fisher had decided to change the Royal Navy's fuel from coal to fuel oil. He was able to bring a number of politicians, among others Sir Winston Churchill, and bureaucrats (such as E.G. Pretyman) to his views. When Churchill became first sea lord he put two and two together and began his campaign to link the government, the navy and APOC in order to shore up larger British interests. Following his lead, a high-level Admiralty commission under the direction of Rear Admiral E.J.W. Slade – and including Professor John Cadman of Birmingham University and Dr E.H. Pascoe of the Geology Survey of India – was dispatched in August 1913 to south Persia to inquire into the oil fields and their potential. In January 1914, the Slade Commission issued its official report: it was highly favourable, if not enthusiastic.[58] On the strength of it, the government proposed a bill allowing it to invest in APOC; Parliament duly ratified it in May 1914 by a 254 to 18 vote; the government duly invested £2,000,000 in ordinary APOC shares and £1,000 in its preference shares, thus giving it a slight majority in a company then capitalised at £4m.[59] The government only asked for two *ex officio* directorships with limited veto rights. Shortly thereafter the Royal Navy signed a twenty-year agreement with APOC for the purchase of its fuel oil requirements at very advantageous terms (a maximum of 30 shillings per ton). As the First World War began, the trio of Lord Fisher, Sir Winston Churchill and Pretyman had achieved the goal of linking APOC's petroleum reserves to the Royal Navy; unsurprisingly "the British floated to victory on a wave of oil".[60]

While the British were exploiting their 1901 concession, the Russians were still trying to get even. In March 1916, they almost succeeded in getting their revenge: one of their citizens, Akakie Mephodievitch Khoshtaria (a close friend of the famous Calouste Gulbenkian), received from the Russophile premier, Sipahdar Tunikabuni, a seventy-year concession for oil exploration in the three northern Persian provinces of Gilan, Mazandaran and Astarabad (later Gurgan). The Khoshtaria concession was never ratified by the *Majlis*, and was thus for ever in a legal limbo. The cabinet of Samsam ul-Saltaneh even called it null and void in 1918, an annulment which was later confirmed in 1922 by the Fourth *Majlis*. Even so, the APOC was uneasy about the whole deal and preferred to buy out Khoshtaria (paying him £200,000 in March 1920). It immediately set up the North Persian Oil Company with a capital of £3m to exploit the concession;[61] the new company's board of directors consisted of three APOC directors, one Burmah director and, naturally, Khoshtaria. With the signing of the Sovieto-Persian Friendship Treaty in February 1921, the Khoshtaria concession would be dealt a deathblow.

As APOC was spreading its wings over south and south-western Persia, the enormous importance of this petroleum adventure was beginning to sink into the minds of a handful of Persian politicians. As early as in 1915, Prince Sulayman Mirza Iskandari, the leader of the Democrat faction in the Third *Majlis*, had stated in a public debate:

> Before oil was discovered we were a buffer State. Since the discovery of oil, Iran [sic] has become a puppet State...[62]

Prince Firouz Mirza Nusrat ul-Douleh, the eldest son and heir of Prince Farmanfarma, was another politician attracted by the growing importance of oil. He would be among the first to try and come to terms with the intricacies of the complex oil industry.

5.5. The Elite's Demise

The Elite had not fared well during its decade in power. Sir Arnold Wilson summarised his judgement of its tenure:

> Persia has been decaying for years. The Constitutional Movement, started by men who were trying to stop the rot, has hastened it...[63]

The Movement's victors had failed miserably on the key point of security throughout the country, especially the Bakhtiari *khans* and their tribesmen; perhaps the elder Sardar Asâd would have been able to redress a highly compromised situation, if given the chance, for he was the only administrator and statesman among his peers. However, by 1914 he was blind and incapacitated and none of the other *khans* had his capabilities. The *khans* had been given their chance. Instead of sacrifices to bring about law and order, they collected governorships and greatly enriched themselves. As an epitaph to the *khans*' inevitable tumble from power Sir Arnold Wilson wrote:

> Big men with big escorts and small minds... My only fear is that their ambitions lead them into courses which they have not the strength or inward unity to pursue to a successful conclusion...[64]

Indeed.

Neither had their co-victor, Muhammad Vali Khan Tunikabuni, who gradually faded before committing suicide. More surprising however, was the inability of the Qajar wings of the Elite (the older and the younger) to make good where the *khans* had failed. The former generation had had the formidable Prince Farmanfarma (a close friend of Sir Percy Sykes since 1895, as the latter was British consul at Kerman, 1895-1905[65]) and in the younger generation the likes of Vusuq ul-Douleh and Mushir ul-Douleh: they should have proved able to find stability. They too failed. It must be noted that Abu'l Qasim Khan Nasir ul-Mulk, regent from 1911 until 1914, had considerably weakened the Elite's cause. But, still, as a ruling elite they were collectively responsible for their own mismanagement and failures. They seemed to think that playing musical chairs with ministries and cabinets was enough to keep the ship going. They also gambled on the fact that there was no viable counter-elite to replace them; and on the fact that they had enough Anglophile pawns to keep the British (the only Power since the Soviet Revolution) satisfied. They failed in almost every enterprise they undertook. In their defence, it must be mentioned that (i) they were not used to ruling collectively (i.e. without an absolute monarch at their head); (ii) the circumstances at the end of the Constitutional Movement were not propitious for an easy government; (iii) the First World War aggravated disorders throughout the country; (iv) in the aftermath of the war, they were incapable of capitalising on the alternatives offered.

After the close of the Great War, the first rebuff the Elite suffered was at the Paris Peace Conference. Its delegation arrived with a long set of extravagant demands subdivided into three major parts. In the first section, Persian diplomats asked for the abrogation of the 1907 Anglo-Russian Treaty (a request by then superfluous!), the withdrawal of consular guards and the abolition of consular courts (the abolition of capitulations) – as if Persia had won the war and was dictating its conditions to a defeated enemy! In the second section, a simple restoration of Persia's imperial borders was asked for: in the east the Oxus; in the north-east Transcapia; in the north-west, Derbent, Baku and Erivan; in the west, Kurdistan and Mosul! Finally, in the third section, war reparations were claimed: no less than 436 million toumans![66] They had spread all their grievances thick on paper, assuming that they would be able to jettison most of their demands during the negotiations to secure the points they considered strategic. They had forgotten that in 1914 Persia had officially declared its neutrality, so that they were among neither the winners nor the losers: the Elite would have been wise to ponder the fact that hiding one's head in the sand is not always the best solution. Even the sympathies they awakened in the American delegation came to nothing. If at Paris, in 1919, the conference doors were closed to their delegation, the Elite had only itself to blame: with its multiple blunders in the realm of international politics, it had yet shown its weakest side.

But its woes were not confined to foreign affairs. Internally too it had been confronted with fresh challenges. The major one was the threat imposed by a small but incisive counter-elite: the so-called *Kumiteh-yi Mujazat* (lit. the 'Avenging Committee'). Created at the close of 1916 by two former Persian officers of the Cossacks brigade, namely Mirza Ibrahim Khan Munshizadeh and Asadullah Khan Abu'lfathzadeh, the *Kutimeh* was decisively anti-Elite. By means of terrorising second-string Elite members (accused of being traitors and agents of foreign powers), it believed that it could blackmail the Elite into appointing them at the head of the Cossacks brigade. They co-opted a third member, Muhammad Nazar Khan Mashkout ul-Mamalik, and hired a team of professional killers, including Karim Davatgar (Shaykh Fazlullah Nouri's unsuccessful assailant in 1909),

Husayn Khan Laleh and Rashid ul-Sultan. In February 1917 the *Kumiteh*'s first victim, Ismaîl Khan, the head of the Tehran grain silo, fell dead, shot by Karim Davatgar, who received 600 toumans for fulfilling his contract. In April, it was Davatgar himself who was shot dead by his accomplices, having become a liability for the *Kumiteh*. Then, in May, Âbdul-Hamid Saqafi Matin ul-Saltaneh, the thirty-nine year old editor of the *Âsr-i Jadid* newspaper and a leading intellectual linked to the Elite, was shot down. In June, it was the turn of Mirza Muhsin Mujtahid, a minor clergyman (close to Qavam ul-Saltaneh), to be gunned down. In July, it was Muntakhab ul-Douleh, the chief treasurer, who was murdered. Other prominent personalities on the *Kumiteh*'s list included Sipahsalar, Prince Zill ul-Sultan, Prince Kamran Mirza, Prince Farmanfarma and his eldest son Firouz Mirza.[67] Some of the Elite members approached by the *Kumiteh* duly paid the heavy bribes it demanded. Hasan Khan Mushir ul-Douleh, however, had the courage to stand up to Abu'lfathzadeh threats when the latter proposed his own appointment to head of the Cossacks brigade – the *Kumiteh*'s leaders having had the vision (the Elite remaining blind) to grasp the pivotal importance of this position. The Elite, at first uneasy before the *Kumiteh*'s bullets, found its footing and reacted by putting pressure on the police force and sending in its own servants to assist the officials. All of the *Kumiteh*'s leaders were arrested. Husayn Laleh and Rashid ul-Sultan were hanged. The others were either exiled or sentenced to prison terms. Abu'lfathzadeh and Munshizadeh were given fifteen years of exile at Kalat-i Nadiri; having arrived near Simnan they were discreetly murdered by members of their escort.[68] The *Kumiteh-yi Mujazat* had only lasted a few months, but it had clearly caught the Elite off guard. The limited success achieved by a handful of dedicated (albeit amateurish) counter-elitists had proved the Elite to be on the decline: had it been at its peak of power, it would have not have paid bribes to a gang of terrorists.

Far more ominous than the *Kumiteh* was the *Jangali* (Forest) Insurrection launched in the northern province of Gilan by Mirza Kouchak Khan, a team leader of the Constitutional Movement's northern *mujahids* (under Yeprem) in 1909. The region of Gilan was one of the most propitious places in Persia for a grass roots rural insurrection. The discontent of Gilani peasants had deep-rooted causes: it went back to the mid-nineteenth century when the Gilan silk output had dwindled from a high of 1,000,000 tonnes in 1864 to as low as 90,000 tonnes in 1873. Thereafter, the Gilan province was "still assessed at the same rate for the *maliat*, or land tax, as it was then",[69] creating a gross injustice for the peasantry. Therefore, Gilan was second only to Azarbayjan as the provider of cheap migrants for the oil industry at Baku and other industrial concerns in Russia: in 1903, Persian workers formed 22.2% of the workforce in the Russian oil fields.[70] The flow of ideas from southern Russia made its way to the Gilan minds and the radicals of the *Ijtimâ yun-Âmmyun* Party poured fuel on the red-hot coals of Gilani anger. It was the party's Bandar Anzali branch that organised, in 1906 at the Liazonov fisheries, the first ever workers' strike in Persia, followed by the fisheries' 3,000 workers.[71] The peasant revolt of 1906-7 in Gilan was also led by a group - the so-called *Anjuman-i Âbbasi* - linked to the *Ijtimâ yun-Âmmyun*.[72] Localised peasant revolts against the landlords became more frequent, and a 1909 revolt forced the powerful *khan* of Gurganroud to flee all the way to Rasht. The events of the Constitutional Movement had further enabled some of the peasants to turn into *mujahids*, thus acquiring martial skills and getting prepared for an armed insurrection.

The insurrection which was to became known as the *Jangali* Movement was launched at the outset of World War I, in September 1914, by Mirza Kouchak Khan,* with six companions and four guns. The movement gained widespread success as the majority of the Gilan peasantry readily identified itself with the *Jangalis*. Early police forces sent to subdue it while still in the bud were all soundly routed: the men of Asif ul-Douleh, Âbdul-Razzaq Shafti, Mafakhir ul-Mulk and Amir Muqtadir were repulsed one after the other.[73] Even a force of four hundred Cossacks had to retreat before them. The *Jangalis* were at home in the dense Gilan forests, knew the land and relied on a large indigenous network of informers. They had suppliers and financial support in Kasma', managed by Hajj Ahmad Kasma'i. At Rasht, Masouleh and Sumiêh Sara, they had secure bases. In Lahijan, Dr Ibrahim Hishmat was able to gather a force of five hundred armed *Jangalis*. Kouchak Khan's small initial band had developed into an army of hundreds of armed *Jangalis* across the province. The movement's logistics criss-crossed the province; it later had a newspaper *Rouznameh-yi Jangal*, and a training camp for fresh recruits at Gourab Zarmakh. It also could count on a dozen German and Austrian officers as military advisers, with, among others, Major von Pachen and Lieutenant Strich; also a group of Turkish officers, dispatched by Enver Pacha; a handful of Gendarmerie officers trained by the Swedish, with Sultan Mahmud Khan in command; and a few individuals who had joined it from all over Persia, such as the revolutionary Haydar Khan Âmou Oughli, the Kurdish leader Khalou Qurban and Ihsanullah Khan, a former member of the *Kumiteh-yi Mujazat*. By the end of 1916, the legend of Mirza Kouchak Khan was born: he was the hero of Gilan, the curse of the landowners and the peasants' champion.

* MIRZA KOUCHAK KHAN (1881-1921), born Mirza Younus, son of Mirza Buzurg, at Rasht; attended school in Rasht (until 1894); studied religion as a *tullab* at the Sadr school in Tehran; involved in Constitutional Movement (1906-8); joined *Kumiteh Sattar* in Rasht (1908); took part in march on Tehran as *mujahid* team leader (1909); entered military; wounded while fighting against royalist forces at Astarabad (1911); formed the *Ittihad-i Islam* (Islamic Unity) group (1914); leader *Jangali* insurrection (1914); headed Sovieto-*Jangali* Revolutionary Committee at Rasht (1920); Republic of Gilan issued stamps (1920); broke relations with Communists, because of his religious ideals (1921); failed to compromise with Reza Khan; in his hasty flight towards Ardabil, over mountains, froze to death in a snow storm (December 1921).

The *Jangalis* suffered their first defeat in early 1917 at Masouleh against seven hundred Russian Cossacks armed with long-range artillery and machine-guns. They suffered dozens of casualties and had to flee in disorder to their deep forest hideouts. They were saved *in extremis* from outright extinction by the Tsar's abdication and the notorious Army Order that followed it in March 1917.[74] In July, Russian troops stationed in the north of Persia were recalled to the homeland by Kerenski. Mirza Kouchak, who in the meantime had regrouped his forces, acted as an intermediary in the orderly retreat of Baratov's troops to their homeland via Rasht and Anzali.

In early 1918, Major General Dunsterville, on his way to Baku, met Kouchak Khan and proposed to him the official recognition of the *Jangali* movement by H.M. Government, provided that he was ready to co-operate with the British.[75] Kouchak Khan, not being a politician, refused the British hints and kept to his anti-imperialist stance, even refusing to set free his three British prisoners: Captain Noel (of the Intelligence Service), McLaren (the consul at Rasht) and Oakshott (the IBP branch manager at Rasht).[76] For Kouchak Khan, this was the penultimate chance for the movement to come out of its Gilan cocoon and enter the national stage; the last chance came up in June 1918, when Colonel Stokes, dispatched by Dunsterville, met the *Jangali* leadership to secure a free passage through Gilan for both the Russian Army of Colonel Lazar Bicherakov and the Norperforce. The *Jangalis* accepted letting the Russians pass through (they were returning home) but not the British, who, they argued, had no right or reason to be in Gilan. Not only had the *Jangalis* failed to seize their opportunity to march on Tehran during the favourable time stretching from late 1917 until early 1918, but they now refused to take account of realities. They couldn't carry on their stand against all and sundry for ever: they had to have a goal and it had to be Tehran, or in the long run they faced inevitable destruction – there was no third alternative. But Kouchak Khan was a religious, honest and nationalistic leader; he headed a vast popular movement who had shed much blood over the past four years; he had to decide for his thousands of genuine followers – although one of his favoured means of taking difficult decisions was to carry out an *Istikhareh* (asking for God's Will) on his *tasbiyh* (prayer pearls). Put in a nutshell, he was responsible and answerable both to the Gilanis and to history.

Mirza Kouchak nevertheless thought that he could fight both the Russians and the British. He let the last Russo-British ultimatum pass and on June 15 1918 the Russians attacked the *Jangalis* trenches at Manjil. Russian artillery and British planes caused havoc in the ranks of the three thousand *Jangalis* defending the valley. Armed only with rifles and light machine-guns, Kouchak Khan's army suffered a severe defeat, lost dozens of men and, had it not been for its forest hideouts, would have been squashed once and for all.

Once more, however, the *Jangalis* rebounded. Even the onslaught launched by Vusuq since late 1918 failed to bring the resilient movement to its knees – neither the treason of the *Jangali* treasurer and second-in-command Hajj Ahmad Kasma'i, lured into defection by Vusuq (and thrown in jail), nor the appointment of the decisive Sardar Muâzam Khurasani as Gilan's governor, nor the dispatch of thousands of Persian Cossacks. The surrender of Dr Ibrahim Hishmat and his group of two hundred and seventy *Jangalis* in the spring of 1919 and the subsequent hanging of the naive and kind-hearted doctor at Rasht (May 1919) were further blows to the movement. But, yet again, the *Jangalis*, fighting against an enemy superior in every respect, had the dense forests of Gilan as a last resort. They survived Vusuq's onslaught of 1919.

The spring of 1920 would bring the retreating Russian, General Denikin, to Anzali. In his wake were the Bolsheviks. Mirza Kouchak Khan, jumping on the occasion, struck a deal with the newcomers, entered Rasht triumphantly and created a joint *Jangali*-Bolshevik Revolutionary Committee that he himself headed. The Iranian Republic of Gilan was also created and even issued stamps. Kouchak Khan soon realised that there was an abyss between his ideals and the Bolsheviks': the divorce was as quick as had been the marriage. Meanwhile, in Tehran, Mushir ul-Douleh, who had replaced Vusuq as premier, saw the possibility of bringing a political solution to the Gilan conundrum: he tried his best to find a suitable compromise, with Kouchak Khan unwilling to yield as usual. Negotiations having failed, Mushirul-Douleh did what all his predecessors had done: he sent in the Persian Cossacks under the supreme command of Starosselski.

This time around, the *Jangalis* had the upper hand, and the Cossacks were lucky to break the irregulars' stranglehold and beat a hasty retreat all the way to Aqa Baba near Qazvin. Later, hints of Starosselski mismanagement (and even betrayal[77]) were dropped by the Persian officers. During the autumn of 1920, once again and for the last time, the road to Tehran was open to Kouchak and his *Jangalis*: the British were preparing to depart Persia for good and the bruised and tired Cossacks were licking their wounds at Aqa Baba. In Tehran, fears of an imminent *Jangali* takeover was spreading. Seen from the capital the situation looked so precarious that the IBP even considered transferring the bank's headquarters to Isfahan.[78]

Kouchak Khan's resilience was yet a further sign of the Elite's inability to deal with provincial troubles. In Tehran, the Elite had placed its last hope in its most brilliant individual: the ruthless and capable Vusuq ul-Douleh. The latter, appointed prime minister in August 1918, chose as his two key ministers two of the wealthiest heirs in Persia:[79] (1) Firouz Mirza Nusrat ul-Douleh, eldest son of Prince Farmanfarma, at Foreign Affairs; (2) Akbar Mirza Sarim ul-Douleh, son and heir of Prince Zill ul-Sultan, at Finance. Vusuq,

Firouz and Sarim formed a triumvirate and play the Elite's last trump card: finding a viable agreement with the British. The very same agreement over which Farmanfarma had stumbled in 1915, the one Sipahsalar Tunikabuni had signed invoking *force majeure* in 1916, the one Prime Minister Samsam ul-Saltaneh had unilaterally annulled in 1918. Lord Curzon was in command at the Foreign Office and he wanted a final agreement to bind, once and for all, the elusive Persia in the trammels of Empire. He had sent the highly capable Sir Percy Cox to Tehran to replace Marling. The time was right, the politicians and diplomats on both sides were right, it remained only to find the right agreement: it was to be the Anglo-Persian agreement signed on August 9, 1919.

The Anglo-Persia Agreement contained a preamble and six articles. In the first article the British Government reiterated its willingness to "respect absolutely the independence and integrity of Persia". The second and third articles provided for the "appointment of expert British advisers to the Persian Treasury" and "the supply of British officers to reorganise the Persian Army".[80] The fourth article called for a "substantial "British loan to Persia "for financing the reforms" (it later transpired that the loan amounted to £2m at seven per cent interest over twenty years). The fifth and sixth articles provided for British experts "to assist in the construction of Persian railways" and to revise "existing customs tariffs". The agreement was not an occasion for Persia to take advantage of British advances; Vusuq had reached a workable compromise. The problem was that the post-war mood in Persia was not favourable to the Elite and some of the counter-elitists, having grasped the link, were bent on destroying the agreement. Vusuq should have foreseen the backlash.

Nevertheless, with no *Majlis* available to ratify or reject the agreement, Vusuq simply went ahead with its implementation. The triumvirate asked for and received an advance of £131,000 on the loan, paid out during August and September 1919; the sum of money was at the triumvirate's disposal for any use it saw fit. "This is not merely exorbitant", Lord Curzon telegraphed his envoy in Tehran, "it is corrupt".[81] Over and above the money placed at their disposal, all three Persian ministers "were given written assurances of asylum in the British Empire".[82]

In the autumn of 1919 the two main British commissioners came to Tehran to take up their respective positions: Sydney Armitage

Armitage-Smith as financial adviser and Major General W.E.R. Dickson as head of the British Military Mission.

General Dickson lost no time in forming a mixed Anglo-Persian military board to reorganise armed forces in Persia, with the Cossacks to be dissolved and all military forces to be amalgamated into a national army under the Ministry of War.

Moreover all gendarmes and police forces were to be reunited in a national police force under the Ministry of the Interior. The suicide of Lieutenant Colonel Fazlullah Khan, a member of the mixed board, in March 1920, as a sign of protest against the agreement's application, "produced a deep impression" on Tehran's public opinion.[83]

As for Armitage-Smith, he decided to tackle the most pressing question bedevilling Anglo-Persian relations: the problem of the pending oil accounts. For the better part of the year 1920 he worked on finding solutions to the many problems created by the discrepancies which had arisen between the Persians' interpretation of the D'Arcy concession and the accounting methods of the APOC. Recommended by Armitage-Smith, the chartered accountant William McLintock, an expert reputed for his probity, was commissioned by the Persian Government to review the APOC books and give a report. In February 1920 McLintock delivered his report (not made public) to Foreign Minister Nusrat ul-Douleh; it is doubtful if the latter understood all of it, because the report is incomprehensible to the layman. But, to put it in a nutshell: the main question put to McLintock was whether the Persian Government had been paid the full amount it was due (i.e. sixteen per cent of net profits) and the accountant's answer "suggested that it was not".[84] In August 1920 Armitage-Smith was entrusted with the mission to bring about a final adjustment between the Persian Government and APOC. The British expert eventually negotiated an agreement in ten articles that he and the APOC chairman (Lord Greenway) signed on December 22, 1920. The 1920 agreement was a convoluted enterprise seeking the best possible compromise between the British and the Persian positions, while legally binding APOC on some of the most pressing Persian points – especially the sixteen per cent of profits from APOC's subsidiary companies.

Moreover, APOC had agreed to drop its £614,489 claim for war damages (a claim deemed excessive by McLintock) and to propose instead a £1m settlement for all Persian claims up to March 31, 1919. The 1920 agreement, never ratified by the *Majlis*, would remain a dead letter.

Although the agreement was signed and implemented in part, the struggle for its acceptance and approval was just beginning. Two Powers were opposed to the agreement: America and France. Their politicians could not understand British aims of turning "Persia into a private preserve".[85] For the French it was not unusual to attempt playing second fiddle in Persia (now that the Russians were out), but for the Americans it was rather new: so far, besides a few missionaries (since 1829 at Uroumiyyeh) and Baskerville at Tabriz, they had had little to do with or in Persia. The Americans were dumbfounded by the quasi-monopoly given to the British in the 1919 Agreement.

In turn, foreign apprehensions about the agreement fuelled internal opposition to it. It did not lack enemies in Tehran and the provinces. Public opinion – a new concept in Persia, born in the period between the Tobacco Concession and the Constitutional Movement – and the intelligentsia led by newspaper editors were strongly against it. Discontented Elite members and all the counter-elites were for its annulment. Among the latter, Âbdullah Mustoufi (no relation to Mustoufi ul-Mamalik) published a virulent pamphlet entitled *Ibtal ul-Batil* (the Annulment of Futility) taking the agreement to pieces.[86] Two popular religious personalities also opposed it in their sermons: in Tehran, it was the jovial and well-connected Sayyid Hasan Mudarris (on a comeback after being a minister in the *Muhajarat* movement); in Tabriz, it was a *mulla* by the name of Shaykh Muhammad Khiyabani. Khiyabani, a deputy affiliated to Taqizadeh's Democrat faction in the Second *Majlis* and editor of the *Tajaddud* newspaper, inflamed popular discontent in Tabriz. His numerous followers eventually stormed government offices and expelled the envoys who had been especially sent in from Tehran. Khiyabani's dream of a free Azarbayjan (or *Azadistan*) lasted only six months: in September 1920, amidst shrouded circumstances, he was shot dead by officers sent in to seize him on orders of the newly-appointed Governor-General Mukhbir ul-Saltaneh.[87]

Even Ahmad Shah had second thoughts about the 1919 Agreement. He did not realise that the agreement's annulment would almost automatically entail the end of the Elite's monopoly on power and thus, indirectly, the end of the Qajar dynasty. Officially invited to dinner by King George V, Ahmad Shah failed to grasp his last chance: he did not mention the agreement in his toast. Before the crucial dinner, Nusrat ul-Douleh, the Minister for Foreign Affairs, and Nasir ul-Mulk, his former regent, had hopelessly begged him to demur; seeing that the young Shah would not alter his stand, the latter prophetically told him:

> Your silence will eventually prove detrimental to your own cause...[88]

Meanwhile, the British were subsidising Vusuq's government to the tune of 350,000 toumans per month, paid through the IBP, just to keep it afloat.[89] But discontent with him and his agreement were growing louder by the day. And a politician as well-informed as Vusuq sensed that the agreement had stalled. On June 18, 1920, Ahmad Shah returned to Tehran from his European trip, and a tired Vusuq immediately tendered his resignation, being rapidly replaced by Mushir ul-Douleh.

The only victim of the agreement on the British side was the minister at Tehran, Herman Norman (replaced by Cox in June 1920) who had sent Curzon "courageous reports... [saying] that his proposed agreement was unlikely to succeed". Norman was recalled for his Cassandra-like attitude and "never employed again by the Foreign Office".[90]

On the Persian side, however, the agreement's failure had dramatic consequences. Its first victim was Vusuqul-Douleh, who had to give up politics once and for all, having been too closely associated with the ill-fated agreement. His early exit from politics was a serious loss for both the Elite and for Persia, because he was among the best and the brightest of his Elite generation. Henceforward, his younger brother Qavam ul-Saltaneh would carry the family colours in the Elite line-up. Both Nusrat ul-Douleh and Sarim ul-Douleh survived politically, only later being asked to repay the monies received for signing the agreement (which they did). For the Elite as a whole, the awakening (when it came) would be rough – abruptly its exclusive domination of Persian politics would be ended. For the Qajars 1919 was the beginning of the end: Ahmad Shah and the dynasty were both doomed. The final denouement was just a question of time.

After Vusuq's resignation, Persia was freewheeling. Neither Mushir ul-Douleh nor the stopgap cabinet of the innocuous Sipahdar Rashti could bring about any alteration. After Mushir ul-Douleh's resignation the British had even stopped their monthly payments of 350,000 toumans. Not that the British could not afford such a sum, but rather they did not see the reason to finance a cabinet to which they gave no future. For months now, the British position in Persia was sustained by Lord Curzon. The House of Commons had ordered the government to cut back on foreign exposure and expenditure (in the backlash following the end of the First World War) and Curzon had so far successfully argued for leaving untouched Persia's annual budget of £30m.[91] The failure of the 1919 Agreement had, however, cut the grass from under Curzon's feet and the withdrawal of all British troops from Persia had been fixed for April 1, 1921 [92].

If the British forces had to withdraw, they had to put in place, before retiring, a viable system to manage the country.

It had to be a Persian system. Not involving the Elite, which was on its way out. A system that could keep in check internal disorders, as well as preserve Persia's independence *vis-à-vis* its northern neighbour (the western neighbour having been dismembered during the war). The question was: if not the Elite, then which group (or groups) of Persian individuals should be placed at the helm? The general answer to that question had been supplied a few years earlier, within another context, by Dr David George Hogart, the keeper of the Ashmolean Museum at Oxford and the head of the Arab Intelligence Bureau during the war at Cairo. In 1917, Dr Hogart had written a *chef-d'œuvre* on the subject of 'Arabs and Turks', hinting, in a way, the solution to the question of Persia's future leaders:

> The policy of the Allies, declared, and presumably immutable, is to remove the Turks, as a governing people, ...It is not suggested hereby that our policy is wrong or should be revised. Circumstances not under our control have determined it. But after we have destroyed – or even while we are destroying – we have to construct, and we shall be in the better position if we have realised the faults as well as the merits of

those we are about to set up, and the virtues as well as the vices of those we are setting down...⁹³

These enlightening lines did not only apply to Arabs and Turks – they applied to any enlightened Power's systematic way of coping with inevitable change. In short, it was the practical application of Hegel's 'Begreifen ist Beherrschen'. In Persia too, change was inevitable. With only one Power in the Game, those in charge of "constructing while destroying" knew their potential options for Persia's future leaders: they had until April 1 1921 to set them up.

NOTES

1. G.R. Garthwaite, *Khans and Shahs* (Cambridge University Press, 1983) p.104.
2. Ibid., as quoted by G.R. Garthwaite, p.111.
3. F.R.C. Bagley, *New Light on Iranian Constitutional Movement*, in *Qajar Iran* ed. by E. Bosworth and C. Hillenbrand, (Edinburgh University Press, 1983) p.54.
4. Ibid., p.57.
5. V.A. Martin, 'Shaykh Fazlullah Nuri and the Iranian Revolution of 1905-09', *Middle Eastern Studies*, Vol. 23, no. 1, January 1987, p.47.
6. The Atabeg Park was the former residence of the *sadr-i âzam* Amin ul-Sultan. It later became the city residence of the Russian Embassy, which it still is.
7. T.E. Lawrence, *The Seven Pillars of Wisdom: A Triumph* (London: Jonathan Cape, 1935) p.649.
8. I. Safa'i, *Rahbaran-i Mashrouteh* (Tehran: Javidan, 1346 (1967)) Vol. I, p.412.
9. I. Safa'i, *Panjah Sal* (Tehran: Vizarat-i Farhang va Hunar, 1356 (1987)) pp.93-4.
10. W. Morgan Shuster, *The Strangling of Persia* (London: T. Fisher Unwin, 1912) p.211.
11. Ibid., p.215.
12. I. Safa'i, op. cit. (note 8), Vol. I, p.553.
13. "Mr Adamiyyat [the writer] is convinced that Taqizada (sic), despite his later denials, must have been privy to the assassinations of Bihbahani and Atabak", reported F.R.C. Bagley, op. cit. (note 3), p.63.
14. Sanî ul-Douleh (1856-1911), the son of Mukhbir ul-Saltaneh and the brother of Mihdi Quli Khan, had been a successful businessman before entering politics. Siding with the Constitutionalists, he became the first president of the First *Majlis*, resigning a few months later to become Minister for Public Works, then Minister of Finance. According to his brother, Mihdi Quli Hidayat, Sanî ul-Douleh was assassinated for refusing to reimburse 20,000 toumans to Sardar Muhyi for the expenses the latter had incurred during his march on Tehran. See M.Q. Hidayat, *Khatirat va Khatarat* (Tehran: Zavvar, 2nd ed., 1344 (1965)) p.220.
15. See W. Morgan Shuster, op. cit. (note 10).
16. Ibid.; see the reproduced leader from *The Nation* (London), p.363.
17. See article from *The Nation* cited by Morgan Shuster, op. cit. (note 10), p.362.
18. Ibid., quoted from the Resolution of the House of Commons, p.353.

19 Â. Mustoufi, *Zindagani-i Man* (Tehran: Zavvar, 1360 (1981)) Vol. II, pp.346-7.
20 From H.F.B. Lynch's speech of January 29, 1912, quoted by Morgan Shuster, op. cit. (note 10), p.358.
21 M.Q. Hidayat, op. cit. (note 14), p.241.
22 Professor E.G. Browne, *The Reign of Terror at Tabriz: England's Responsibility* (London: no ed., 1912).
23 See article in *The Manchester Guardian* of February 9, 1912 quoted by M. Afshar, in *La Politique Européenne en Perse* (Tehran: Fondation Dr M. Afshar, 2nd. ed., 1973) p.120.
24 Ibid., p.126.
25 The material and data used for these snapshots on the Elite members was taken from two main sources and a myriad lesser ones such as biographies, Persian history books and private communications to the author. The two main references are:
1) M.Bamdad, *Shar-i Hal-i Rijal-i Iran* (Tehran: Zavvar, 2nd ed., 1357 (1968)) all six volumes.
2) I. Safa'i, *Rahbaran-i Mashrouteh* (Tehran: Javidan 1346 (1967)) Vol. I & II.
26 Ibid.
27 Sir Percy Sykes, *A History of Persia* (London: Macmillan, 3rd ed., 1951) Vol. II, p.436.
28 C. Skrine, *World War in Iran* (London: Constable and Co., 1962) p.XIX.
29 On Wassmuss's adventure in Persia, see the excellent romanticised version of factual history: A. Ahrar, *Toufan dar Iran* (Tehran: Nuvin, undated) 2 Vols.
30 See M.H. Ruknzadeh-Adamiyyat, *Diliran-i Tangistani* (Tehran: Iqbal, 1352 (1973)).
31 Ch. Sykes, *Wassmuss* (Paris: Payot, transl. A.F. Vochelle, 1936) p.104.
32 Â.M. Farashbandi, *Gousheh-yi az Tarikh-i Inqilab-i Musallahaneh Mardum-i Mubariz-i Tangistan, Dashti va Dashtistan Âliyyeh Istîmar* (Tehran: Shirkat-i Sahami Intishar, 1362 (1983)) pp.103-113.
33 M.H. Ruknzadeh-Adamiyyat, op. cit. (note 30), p.191.
34 Ch. Sykes, op. cit. (note 31), p.112.
34 M.H. Ruknzadeh-Adamiyyat, op. cit. (note 30), p. 222.
35 Ibid., p. 238.
37 Ch. Sykes, op. cit. (note 31), pp.220-223.
38 Ibid., p.136.
39 G. Lenczowski, 'Foreign Powers' Intervention in Iran During World War I', in *Qajar Iran*, ed. by E. Bosworth and C. Hillenbrand, (Edinburgh University Press, 1983) p.77.
40 Ibid., p.83. Interestingly, on the very same page is Field Marshal Von der Goltz's impression of the Persian situation, expressed after his January 1916 visit to the Persian front: "Anarchy in Persia. Nothing to be done. Dust, cupidity and cowardice. Vast expenditure and no return". Indeed.
41 P. Avery, *Modern Iran* (London: Ernest Benn Ltd., 1965) p.195.
42 For the exact composition of the *Muhajarat*'s cabinets, see M. Sipihr, *Iran dar Jang-i Buzurg* (Tehran: Bank-i Milli-i Iran, 1336 (1957)) pp.296 and 308.
43 Sir Percy Sykes, op. cit. (note 27), Vol. II, p.454.
43A The undeniable advantage drawn by the Allies from the weak *Muhajarat* movement was so evident that some historians went so far as to suggest that the movement

was an Anglo-Russian plot! See Â.R. Salar Bihzadi, *Muhajarat*, in *Ayandeh*, Mihr-Azar 1372 (no. 7-9), p.636.
44 Wm. J. Olson, *Anglo-Iranian Relations During World War I* (London: Frank Cass, 1984) pp.130-3.
45 M.Q. Hidayat, op. cit. (note 14), p.290.
46 J. Zargham-i Burujini, *Doulat-ha-yi Asr-i Mashroutiyyat* (Tehran: *Idareh-yi Kull-i Qavanin*, 1350 (1971)) p.98.
47 C. Skrine, op. cit. (note 28), p.XXIII. and also D. Wright, 'Sir Percy Sykes and Persia', *Central Asian Survey*, Vol. 12, no. 2, 1993.
48 Sir Percy Sykes, op. cit. (note 27), Vol. II, p.477.
48A Ibid., the whole chapter LXXXIX (pp.499-517) extensively relates the Qashqa'i rebellion and its crushing by the SPR.
49 Ibid., pp.488-9; pp.496-7; pp.497-8.
49A About Lieutenant. Colonel Bailey's extraordinary odyssey, see the chapter 'All is known to Finkelstein' in F. Maclean, *A Person from England* (London: Jonathan Cape, 1958) pp.307-332.
50 Refer to P. Knightley, *The First Casualty* (Quartet, 1975) p.157. F. Kazemzadeh, *The Struggle for Transcaucasia (917-1921)* (New York: Philosophical Library and Oxford: George Ronald, 1951) pp.237-252.
51 J.W. Williamson, *In a Persian Oilfield* (London: Ernest Benn Ltd, 1927).
52 H. Longhurst, *Adventure in Oil* (London: Sidgwick and Jackson, 1959) p.44.
53 W. Mineau, *The Go Devils* (London: Cassell, 1958) p.57.
54 S.H. Longrigg, *Oil in the Middle East* (Oxford University Press, 1961) p.20.
55 B. Cadman and J. Rowland, *Ambassador for Oil* (London: Herbert Jenkins, 1960) p.79.
56 L.P. Elwell-Sutton, *Persian Oil* (London: Lawrence and Wishart, 1955) pp.26 and 32.
57 See *Our Industry* (London: The Anglo-Iranian Oil Co. Planning Dept., 2nd ed., June 1949) p.343. and also Z. Qadimi, *Tarikh-i Inqilab-i Naft-i Iran* (Tehran: *Majlis* Printing, 1332 (1953)) p.36.
58 H. Longhurst, op. cit. (note 52), p.51.
59 Ibid., p.51.
60 N.S. Fatemi, *Oil Diplomacy* (New York: Whittier, 1954) p.73.
61 L.P. Elwell-Sutton, op. cit. (note 56), p.36.
62 N.S. Fatemi, op. cit. (note 60), p.43.
63 Sir Arnold Wilson, *S.W. Persia* (London: Readers Union Ltd., Oxford University Press, 1942) p.206.
64 Ibid., 226.
65 See D. Wright, Sir Percy Sykes and Persia, in *Central Asian Survey*, Vol. 12, no. 2, 1993.
66 Sir Percy Sykes, op. cit. (note 27), Vol. II, pp.518-520.
67 On this subject, see J. Tabrizi, *Asrar-i Tarikhi-i Kumiteh-yi Mujazat* (Tehran: *Iran va Islam* and *Intisharat Firdousi*, 1362 (1983)); M. Sipihr, *op. cit.* (note 42), pp.416-430.
68 Ibid., p.430. Where the final episodes are described in detail.
69 C. Issawi, *The Economic History of Iran, 1800-1914* (University of Chicago Press, 1971) p.231.
70 Ibid., p.51., as cited by M.H. Malek, 'Capitalism in Nineteenth-Century Iran', *Middle Eastern Studies*, Vol. 27, no. 1, January 1991, p.68.

71 F.R.C. Bagley, op. cit. (note 3), p.60.
72 Ibid., p.59. The rebellion's leaders Mirza Rahim Shishehbur and Sayyid Jalal ul-Din Shahrashub were imprisoned and bastinadoed.
73 On this subject see the two major references: I. Fakhra'i, *Sardar-i Jangal* (Tehran: Javidan, 8th ed., 1357 (1978)). A. Ahrar, *Mardi az Jangal* (Tehran: Nuvin, 2nd ed., 1361 (1982)).
74 Sir Percy Sykes, op. cit. (note 27), Vol. II, p.486. The Army Order informed the soldiers that they no longer needed to salute their officers: an open door to indiscipline.
75 I. Fakhra'i, op. cit. (note 73), pp.117-8.
76 P. Avery, *Modern Iran* (London: Ernest Benn, 1965) p.214. McLaren and Oakshott were able to escape, but Noel had to remain in *Jangali* custody for a few months, having failed in his two attempts to flee.
77 I. Khajeh Nouri, *Bazigaran-i Âsr-i Tala'i* (The General Amir Ahmadi), (Tehran: Javidan, 1357 (1978)) pp.61-2.
78 M.Q. Hidayat, *Guzarish-i Iran* (Tehran: Nuqreh, 2nd ed., 1363 (1984)) p.356.
79 The only individual in Persia richer than these two young heirs was Shaykh Khazâl of Muhammarah.
80 The full text of the 1919 Agreement is to be found in Sir Percy Sykes, *op. cit.* (note 27), pp.520-1. Moreover, an excellent exposé on the reasons underlining its ultimate failure are given in H. Nicolson, *Curzon: The Last Phase, 1919–1925* (London: Constable and Co., 1934) pp.119-148
81 Wm. J. Olson, 'The Genesis of the Anglo-Persian Agreement of 1919', in *Towards a Modern Iran*, ed. by E. Kedourie and S.G. Haim, (London: Frank Cass, 1980) p.210.
82 D. Wright, *The English Amongst the Persians* (London: Heinemann, 1977) p.179.
83 H. Arfa, *Under Five Shahs* (London: J. Murray, 1964) p.91.
84 L.P. Elwell-Sutton, op. cit. (note 56), p.28.
85 Sir Percy Sykes, op. cit. (note 27), Vol. II, p.522.
86 Â. Mustoufi, op. cit. (note 19), Vol. III, pp.11-118.
87 On the Shaykh Khiyabani, see Â. Azari, *Shaykh Muhammad Khiyabani* (Tehran: Safi Âli Shah, 4th ed., 1354 (1975)).
88 M.Q. Hidayat, op. cit. (note 14), p.311.
89 J. Zargham-i Burujini, op. cit. (note 46), p.121.
90 D. Wright, op. cit. (note 80), p.31.
91 Ibid., p.179.
92 Ibid., p.179.
93 D.G. Hogart, Arabs and Turks, publ. in *The Arab Bulletin*, No. 48, April 21, 1917; as reproduced by E. Kedourie, *England and the Middle East* (London: Bowes and Bowes, 1956) pp.224-6.

CHAPTER SIX:
CHANGE OF THE GUARD

Every Persian politician was waiting for the end of the transition, waiting to see who would be Persia's new leaders. And every Persian politician hoped that, when the die was cast, he would naturally be among the happy few.

This time, though, it was wishful thinking. The seasoned politicians were in for a surprise because the system in Persia was about to undergo drastic change. The people wanted security and bread (bearing in mind the famine of 1917/18); the intelligentsia wanted to achieve the ideals of the Constitutional Movement; the *Bazaar* wanted to prosper amidst law and order; the urban bourgeoisie wanted its revenge over the unruly tribesmen; and the counter-elites wanted to be promoted into elites. For the last decade, all these urban social groups had seen their hopes shattered by the Elite's tragic impotence to satisfy national needs and dreams.

While the people and the politicians were waiting and hoping, the last preparations for the transition were being made.

The ultimate British deadline being April 1, 1921, there was little time left. The British arbiters, and particularly Godfrey Thomas Havard, the British Legation's oriental secretary and expert on Persian politics, were trying to find a suitable solution to the crisis. For the new set-up it was clear that two types of individuals would be required: professional military officers and younger intellectual politicians with no link to the former Elite. First and foremost, though, were the officers, because a military force would be needed to fill the gap left by the departing British troops.

The Persian officers required could come from either of the three existing professional formations: the Cossack Division, the Gendarmerie or the South Persia Rifles. The latter formation had the twin handicaps of being too young (only five years in service) and too British. As for the Gendarmerie corps, its officers were too educated and too nationalistic. There remained the Cossacks, with their *esprit de corps* and their four decades of experience behind them (it is undeniable that in Persia, more than elsewhere, time is needed to mould institutions).

Nevertheless no stone would be left unturned and all potential candidates would be considered.

As for the young politicians, the Constitutional Movement had witnessed the launch of many promising careers, with the candidates knocking in vain on the Elite's door for a place in the sun. Would these newcomers be ready to enter centre stage through the back door? In any event, they were available: young, bright, gifted and eager to be given a chance and to succeed. For both the officers and the politicians the fifteen years of constitutional monarchy had been enough to simultaneously prepare them and whet their appetite.

6.1. *Coup d'État*

On the night of February 21, 1921 some three thousand men of the Cossack Division entered Tehran. They had eight pieces of artillery and eighteen machine-guns. A few shots were fired but they encountered no serious resistance – no force in Persia was a match for the Cossacks. In the early morning hours of February 22, Tehran was duly occupied. In the afternoon Ahmad Shah appointed Sayyid Zia ul-Din Tabataba'i,* the thirty year old editor of Tehran's *Râd* newspaper, as his prime minister. In Tehran, personalities and politicians were being arrested in their homes and taken to the old Cossack garrison (later, the *Bagh-i Milli*): within a couple of days sixty to seventy of them would be rounded up, allegedly to forestall any countercoup. Prominent among the arrested Elite members were Prince Farmanfarma, Nusratul-Douleh and Sipahsalar Âzam. Only Mustoufi ul-Mamalik, Samsamul-Saltaneh, and the brothers Mushir ul-Douleh and Mûtaminul-Mulk would be spared the insult of imprisonment.[1]

On the morning of February 23, an order was found pasted on the walls of Tehran's main streets: it began with "I order", consisted of nine drastic martial law orders, and was in the name of "Reza, Head of the Cossack Division and Commander-in-Chief of the Armed Forces".[2] Within the first two days of the February 21 *coup d'état*, the identity of the coup's two leaders was clear: Sayyid Zia on the political side and Reza Khan for the military.

* SAYYID ZIA UL-DIN TABATABA'I (1891-1969), born in Shiraz, from a Yazdi father; schooled at Tabriz and Shiraz; first published *Nida-yi Islam* at Shiraz before editing *Râd* at Tehran (1914); during First World War encouraged politicians to side with Allies, after the war wrote leaders in the defence of the 1919 Agreement; participated in *coup d'état* of February 22 (1921); prime minister (February-May 1921); after dismissal, exiled to Palestine, took up farming near Haifa (1921-43); returned to Tehran (September 1943); created *Hizb-i Iradeh-i Milli* (National Will Party); deputy from Yazd in Fourteenth *Majlis* (1944); imprisoned on orders of Qavam (1946); quit politics after *Murdad 28*; built immense garden at Evin-Darrakeh in Shimiran to breed his exotic birds; engaged in vast agricultural project near Qazvin; died very rich (fortune estimated at over Rls 1,000m) at the age of seventy-eight.

Amongst the politicians, the choice had fallen on the Anglophile Sayyid Zia, who enjoyed excellent relations with the British Legation and Mr G.T. Havard. In addition to being educated and a capable writer, he also was a born politician. Furthermore, he was at the centre of a secret association, the *Kumiteh Ahan* (or Iron Committee), which regrouped young intellectuals and Gendarmerie officers.[3]

As for the choice of Reza Khan on the military side, one has to go back to early October 1920, as Major General Sir Edmund Ironside took command of the Qazvin-based Norperforce from Brigadier Hugh Bateman-Champain. Ironside, "an impressive professional soldier, ...a man of action and quick decisions",[4] lost no time in having the Russian officers of the Cossack Division dismissed by the Shah and replaced by an "ineffective political figure" in the person of Sardar Humayun. He also appointed Lieutenant Colonel Henry Smyth, a member of General Dickson's Military Mission, to be head of the Cossack Division's administration and finances.[5] After its retreat from Gilan, the mauled Cossack Division was left to lick its wounds at the small village of Aqa Baba, some twenty kilometres west of Qazvin. During a visit to the Cossacks' camp Ironside noted that "Reza Khan, the Commander of the Tabriz *atryad*, is certainly one of the best. Smyth recommends him as the practical head of the show, acting under the political commander, who was appointed from Tehran".[6] Besides this first meeting on November 2, 1920, Ironside and Reza Khan would meet three more times: on January 14 and 31, again at Aqa Baba, and on February 12 at Qazvin.

However, to have the opportunity to be noticed by Smyth and Ironside, Reza Khan had come a long way. Of unknown father, Reza began his career at the age of fourteen, as a stablehand in the Cossack Brigade.[7] He had no education, but, due to his exceptional physical strength, he rose gradually through the ranks. As an NCO, he was in charge of one of the Maxim machine-guns, becoming such an expert with it that he earned the nickname of 'Reza Maxim'.[8] He graduated to officer and climbed the officers' scale, until he was promoted to commander of the Hamadan *atryad* in 1915. Five years later, Reza Khan was, at the age of forty-three, among the Division's senior officers, with the rank of *Mir Panj* (colonel). In January 1921, Ironside sent Sardar Humayun on leave and placed Reza Khan in effective command of the Cossacks.

Sayyid Zia and Reza Khan had first met a week before the *coup d'état*, while the Cossacks were already on their way to Tehran. At the meeting, alongside Sayyid Zia were two members of his 'Iron Committee', both Gendarmerie officers: Colonel Kazim Khan (later, Sayyah) and Major Masûd Khan (Kayhan). Reza Khan had come to the meeting with his (devoted) second in command, Colonel Ahmad Aqa Khan (Amir Ahmadi). The two Cossacks sympathised with the three 'Iron' men, and, at their last encounter on February 19, at Shahabad, all five had "sworn to serve Iran" whatever may come.[9] General Ironside had confided to his diary on February 14 and 15: "Better a *coup d'état* for us than anything else".[10] Four days later, he left for Baghdad. It was in the Iraqi capital that he received the news of the Tehran coup: "I fancy", he wrote, "that all the people think I engineered the *coup d'état*. I suppose I did strictly speaking".[11] James McMurray, the IBP's chief manager, paid all participants a compliment by saying that the coup was "admirably made and carried out".[11A]

Now, the orderly withdrawal of 'Norperforce' could take place without undue apprehensions. In Tehran, Sayyid Zia and Reza Khan were in power, the former relying on his 'Iron Committee' and the latter on his Cossacks. For the British, it was a chapter closed; for the Persians, a new one was just beginning.

On February 23, 1921, Sayyid Zia was Prime Minister, Colonel Sayyah Minister for War, and Major Kayhan was the Military

Commander of Tehran. Reza Khan was only given the honorific title of Sardar Sipah. The 'Iron Committee' had won the first round, securing for itself the three key positions; however, the real power resided in the disciplined and seasoned Cossacks. Within the ranks there was no discussing the leadership of Reza Khan. The latter knew that his Cossacks were the new regime's only pillar, that time was on his side and that he had to become accustomed first to the new world of politics. Sayyid Zia needed him; he, on the other hand, didn't need anyone.

Sayyid Zia tried his best to expedite current affairs and was rather successful in his administrative endeavours. Muhbir ul-Saltaneh, the governor of Azarbayjan, reported that:

> For the very first time our telegrams were being answered and, for once, the replies [from Tehran] made sense.[12]

Sayyid Zia officially annulled the 1919 Agreement (long since a dead letter) and ordered the disbanding of the SPR, thereby closing the last two files left open by the British in Persia. It was also during his tenure that, in Moscow, the Soviet-Persian Treaty of Friendship of February 26, 1921, setting a new framework for bilateral relations, was signed by G. Chicherin and L. Karakhan for the Soviets, and Mushavir ul-Mamalik (Ansari) for Persia. But Sayyid Zia's honeymoon lasted only a month, for on March 27 his Minister of War, Colonel Sayyah, tiring of Reza Khan's independent ways, threatened to resign. The Prime Minister cajoled Sayyah into staying but the colonel couldn't remain much longer and eventually resigned on April 27, with Reza Khan replacing him at the Ministry of War. Not resting after this victory, Reza Khan forced Sayyid Zia to transfer the Gendarmerie from the Ministry of Interior to the Ministry of War – so that all the armed forces would be under his direct command (especially the Gendarme officers).

By the end of May, Sayyid Zia himself had to go. He had made too many enemies, especially among the old Elite. Moreover, his mission was fulfilled: he had assured a smooth transition. Reza Khan had been given the initial political platform he needed to get a firm grip on national affairs. Sayyid Zia's fall from power was yet another example of the impotence of loose forces (i.e. the Gendarmerie, the intelligentsia) in the face of an homogeneous constituency dominated by a single strong individual. Nevertheless, during his short tenure Sayyid Zia had shown that even a young journalist with no previous administrative experience could run the vessel of State properly. And that was, for Persia, a revelation.

With Sayyid Zia on the way to his Palestine exile, a fresh administration had to be formed. As it was too soon for Reza Khan and his Cossacks to hijack the whole state machinery, the old Elite had to be called in to act as stopgap. Qavamul-Saltaneh was appointed prime minister while still languishing in his prison, from where he was taken to court to be given his orders by Ahmad Shah! For Reza Khan, whether Sayyid Zia or Qavam was in power it didn't matter, as long as the country was administered and the bureaucracy lingered on. Reza Khan had to concentrate on building up his armed forces to undertake his first large task: the rule of law and order throughout Persia, the ultimate desire of all the forces that had propelled him to the very top. He was ready to compromise with the Elite, knowing that in the last resort he held all the trump cards and could play them whenever required, and that the Elite was smart enough to understand this.

The weathered Elitists knew the rules. They were quick in acknowledging the new situation and the powers that be. They would have to deal with Reza Khan in the future. Having recovered from the shocking mass arrests, they were satisfied with making a timid comeback. They had known that, sooner or later, Sayyid Zia's 'Iron Committee' would fold and that they would be called back to administer the country – they still were the only ones who knew how. But some of the Elite's leaders, foremost among them Prince Farmanfarma, had already begun to toy with the idea of a non-governing elite; in other words, of an anonymous elite which would remain on the sidelines yet nonetheless run the whole show by remote control, always ready to step in whenever called for by the circumstances. Why risk arrest and jail, when one could stay in the shadows and still govern? After all, the end justifies the means. Wasn't the essential to be able to take advantage of all circumstances and compel the governing elite to act in consequence? Moreover, this *modus operandi* had the advantage of keeping them out of the public eye: *ni vu ni connu*. The theory of this non-governing elite still had to be defined and its rules set; but Prince Farmanfarma, the Elite's uncontested leader, had found the key to Persia's new lock.

6.2. Domestic Law and Order

During 1921 Reza Khan had two major cases to settle. The first case was the sudden rebellion of Colonel Muhammad Taqi Pisian, the head of the Khurasan province Gendarmerie. The thirty year old Pisian was a bright, French-educated Gendarmerie officer. He had taken part in the *Muhajarat* movement, then spent two and a half years of exile in Germany before coming back in the summer of 1920 to Mashhad as Gendarmerie commander (not the first of the *Muhajarat* people to make a remarkable comeback and certainly not the last). At Mashhad, the newcomer Pisian had honestly served the powerful governor Qavam ul-Saltaneh. Even on the morrow of the February 22 *coup d'état*, the two had exchanged mutual assurances for the future. Then, in the early spring, when Sayyid Zia had ordered Pisian to have Qavam arrested and sent to Tehran *manu militari*, he had obeyed the central authority's directive (he could have delayed it) and sent a vexed Qavam under escort to the capital. Now, Qavam was prime minister and in cahoots with Reza Khan, and Pisian was feeling doubly threatened: once by Qavam who had neither forgotten nor forgiven the Mashhad incident (Elitists never do forget or forgive), and secondly by Reza Khan, who as a Cossack officer had little sympathy for a rising Gendarmerie officer and even less for a rebellious one.

At the head of a force comprising four thousand devoted gendarmes, Pisian was a potential threat[12], especially since he was also acting governor, until Qavam appointed Samsam ul-Saltaneh as Khurasan governor at the end of July. The latter never left for Mashhad, only communicating by telegram with Pisian. Finally, Qavam struck on the optimal solution of sending a fully accredited Gendarmerie mission to Mashhad, under the command of the Swedish Colonel Gleerup to relieve Pisian of his tenure. Pisian countered by having the officers of the Gleerup mission arrested – thereby putting himself outside the law. A Cossack battalion immediately departed Tehran for Mashhad and simultaneously the northern tribes of Zafaranlou and Shadlou were ordered to harass the gendarmes in

Khurasan. On October 4, 1921, at a major skirmish with the tribesmen near Qouchan, Pisian was killed;[13] the Khurasan rebellion had been put down with a minimum of time and bloodshed. With Pisian dead, the rebellion caved in, as every rebellion in Persia does after the loss of its leader.

In the background to the Pisian rebellion lurked the wider rivalry between the Cossacks and the Gendarmes. With the successful *coup d'état* of February 1921, the former institution had stolen a march on its rival. The young and (mostly) educated Gendarmerie officers would always feel frustrated at losing the ultimate contest. Insurrectional tensions would remain for years in the Gendarmerie ranks. After Pisian in 1921, Major Lahouti rebelled in 1922 at Sharafkhaneh and Colonel Mahmoud Pouladin attempted a general movement in 1926 in Azarbayjan (fleeing to Central Asia after his failure). All these belated attempts would be killed in the bud by the Cossack forces. The Gendarmerie had lost the war in February 1921: it had henceforward to play second fiddle to the Cossacks and Reza Khan. Any attempts at reversing the stream would prove futile and stale.

Having settled the Pisian revolt, Reza Khan turned his sights towards Gilan and the still simmering problem of Mirza Kouchak Khan and his *Jangalis*. This time, instead of attacking in Gilan along the Manjil-Rasht axis, Reza Khan had decided to attack from the east, sending his Cossacks through the Mazandaran province in early summer 1921 and turning them westwards toward Gilan. On the other side, Mirza Kouchak Khan had split his *Jangalis* into three main groups: the first around Lahijan, with roughly three thousand men under his lieutenant Ihsanullah Khan; the second at Rasht, consisting of eight hundred men commanded by the Kurdish leader Khalou Qurban; and the third in the Sifidrud valley around Roudbar, with two thousand *Jangalis* under himself. The Cossacks' expeditionary corps (under Amir Ahmadi) advanced in Mazandaran, first crushing the troops of the landlord Ismâil Khan Amir Mu'ayid Savadkouhi in June, then those of Âli Asghar Khan Sâidul-Douleh (the son of Sipahsalar Tunikabuni) in July. Towards the end of August, it clashed with Ihsanullah Khan's right wing; the *Jangalis*, lacking heavy weapons, were defenceless against the Cossacks' artillery. The heavy guns struck panic in *Jangali* ranks and sent them retreating in disorder. The news of the ignominious rout spread through the northern provinces. The *Jangalis'* morale suffered a heavy blow, and, from then on, they were in free fall. Systematically, the Cossacks pressed their military superiority, advancing inexorably towards Rasht. To add insult to injury, internecine struggles came to plague the *Jangali* leadership: at a reunion in September of the *Jangali* Revolutionary Committee at Mulla Sara, dissident *Jangalis* attacked and arrested Haydar Âmou Oughli. He escaped, was again arrested and finally killed by the dissident *Jangalis*; thus died at the age of forty-one a revolutionary who had bombed and shot his way to fame from the days of the Constitutional Movement.[14]

The month of October 1921 proved crucial in the war between Kouchak Khan and Reza Khan. The latter had come in person to the war front to oversee the final onslaught. The *Jangalis* were no match for the disciplined Cossacks. On October 11, Khalou Qurban accepted Reza Khan's conditions and surrendered with arms and troops, being gratified by the grade of colonel in the regular army.[15] Four days later, Reza Khan entered Rasht. The warring parties entered indirect negotiations. A *Jangali* envoy to Tehran was told by Premier Qavam: "I cannot do a thing for you because the northern question is the monopoly of Reza Khan".[16] Mirza Kouchak and Reza Khan exchanged messages; the latter wrote to the former:

> So far, your actions have been logical and correct, and for the benefit of the people. I also have to admit that your *Jangali* movement has been good for the country, and if capitalising on it, you would have marched on Tehran, no-one could have recriminated. Now I have taken power in Tehran. But as your goals are similar to mine, I propose you a worthy co-operation on the long common road that stretches ahead...[17]

On the strength of these exchanges, a tentative meeting was fixed, and a forty-eight hour ceasefire arranged. An incident occurred at Masouleh, during which three Cossack officers and fifteen soldiers were killed by a *Jangali* detachment (unaware of the ceasefire?). Given a *casus belli*, a furious Reza Khan, brushing aside Kouchak Khan's claims of a misunderstanding, ordered a general onslaught on the *Jangali* positions.[18] Unable to withstand the pressure, two other

Jangali commanders, Sayyid Muhammad Tulami and Sayyid Jalal Chamani, surrendered without conditions. Motivated by Reza Khan's presence in their midst, the Cossacks showed no mercy, killing and burning their way ahead. Ihsanullah having fled to Baku with his close collaborators, Mirza Kouchak Khan was left alone with his devoted German companion Kovack (nicknamed Houshang by the *Jangalis*). Having witnessed the débâcle of the Jangalis' response and knowing that the Cossacks were only after him, Mirza decided to take refuge in the Ardabil/Khalkhal region, where his ally, the formidable matriarch Âzimat Khanum-i Fouladi of the Fouladlous (a major Shahsavan sub-tribe), was awaiting him. Taking leave of his last group of faithful *Jangalis*, Mirza began his climb of the fierce Tavalish mountain range with Kovack. A snowstorm surprised them near the small village of Gilavan and they both froze to death during the last days of 1921. Thus ended the life of the man who for eight years had dominated the hearts and minds of the Gilanis, becoming their greatest hero.

Mirza Kouchak Khan's *Jangali* movement was, in many ways, a northern sequel to the Constitutional Movement. It was yet another expression of Persia's rising nationalism, as it had only counted on its own resources and rejected British and Russian proposals, with only a half-baked alliance with the Bolsheviks that had eventually turned sour. On the other hand, it was a revolt of the Gilan peasantry against the land-owning classes: the *Jangalis* were largely simple Gilani peasants and the majority of grand landowners, such as Amin ul-Douleh (taken hostage and ransomed by the *Jangali*), had always been a constant sore in the movement's flank. Every *Jangali* success was feasted in all of Gilan's villages and mourned by the landowners. During the eight years the movement lasted relations between peasant and landlord in Gilan had considerably changed: that was perhaps the *Jangalis'* most important victory. For the peasants, fighting and dying as *Jangalis* had been a point of honour: they were showing their landlords, their fellow Persians and the foreigners that they were ready to die for their cause and that therefore they had to be reckoned with.

The main problem of the *Jangal* had been its leadership. Mirza Kouchak Khan was too good a man to be a real political leader. He was an idealist with strong religious convictions. As long as he had been the chief of a group of rebels, he had somehow managed to stay in command, but, once the movement had spilled on to the national stage, he had been totally out of his depth, with no visionary adviser to show him the way. He had wanted an independent Republic of Gilan, free from foreign and domestic interventions. He couldn't see that this was impossible and that neither Tehran, London nor Moscow could allow it to be. Once in the national arena, he had but two alternatives: either march on Tehran or remain in Gilan and rot. He could not envisage the first option (although the British officers had time and again hinted at it in their meetings with him, even offering to close their eyes when he passed Qazvin), so he remained put in Gilan. A man who was his exact opposite came and ruthlessly destroyed him, his movement and a number of Gilani villages in the process. A new Persia was being shaped, in which there was no room for idealists like Colonel Pisian and Mirza Kouchak Khan.

After settling the two main pending problems of Pisian and Kouchak Khan within the year 1921, Reza Khan and his Cossacks could be proud of their initial results. The major lesson to be drawn from the Gilan expedition was that irregular troops could not hold their own against a regular corps led by professional officers. And, with time, the regular armed forces could only get more efficient, with a man like Reza Khan at the Ministry of War catering to all the needs of his troops in the field.

6.3. Sardar Sipah's Army

On November 17, 1921, Sardar Sipah officially founded the modern Persian Army. His Cossack Division had grown during the year from its initial strength of three thousand to over twenty thousand. These troops now required a fresh organisation with future growth in mind. Having been in the armed forces since his youth, Sardar Sipah was in the process of realising his dream of a regular Persian armed force with all the necessary gears of a national army. Not only would this instrument he was about to shape carry out his law and order programme, but it would act as his lever in political forays. He used his clout in the government to have the revenues of government stamps (i.e. indirect taxation) funnelled into the army budget; army pay had priority over other expenses; logistics were systematically given the correct administrative foundations so that soldiers' food, clothing and armaments would become standard.

In the enormous task Sardar Sipah had undertaken, of transforming an equalled division into a full-scale army, he was assisted by a dozen senior officers he personally knew. Needless to say, these officers were all young and devoted to his person: they had sworn "to follow and obey him".[19] The majority of these officers were naturally from within the Persian Cossacks, and prominent among them were the following:

– *Sartip* Ahmad Aqa Khan (later General Amir Ahmadi); Reza Khan's second in command, head of the Cossacks Division cavalry; virile and ruthless. The Army's first four-star general.

– Colonel Murtaza Khan (later General Murtaza Yazdanpanah); close to his leader; not impressive, but a soldiers' soldier, with a tenor's voice. The Army's second four-star general.

– *Yavar* Karim Aqa Khan (later General Karim Aqa Khan Buzarjuhmiri).

– Amir Touman Âbdullah Khan (later General Âbdullah Khan Amir Tahmasibi).

– Muhammad Khan (later General Muhammad Shahbakhti).

– Muhammad Husayn Ayrum (later general).

– Mahmoud Ayrum (later general).

– Husayn Aqa Khazaî (later general).

– Ismâil Khan (later General Amir Fazli).

– Amir Muvassaq (later General Muhammad Nakhjavan).

– Colonel Iraj Khan (later General Iraj Matboûi).

– Khudayar Khan (later General Khudayari).

– Mahmud Aqa Khan (later General Mahmud Amir Ikhtidar).

– *Yavar* Riza Quli Khan (later General Amir Khusravi).

– Sadiq Khan Salar Nizam (later General Koupal); Reza Khan's chief of staff.

Sardar Sipah would also use educated military officers like the future Generals Shaybani (St. Cyr) and Jahanbani, but without ever giving them the familial trust he had in his Cossack brothers-in-arms.

In Kurdistan and western Azarbayjan, the warlord Ismâil Khan Simitqou (also known as Simko), the redoubtable chief of the Shakkak tribe, seemed invincible. With his thousands of armed Kurdish tribesmen, Simitqou reigned supreme over north-western Persia. He had defeated regular troops sent against him time and again, thus acquiring a superiority complex. In the summer of 1922, Sardar Sipah had decided that the time was ripe to field his fifteen thousand-man expeditionary corps against Simitqou's Kurds. At its head he first placed General Habibullah Shaybani, one of the Gendarmerie's most promising young officers, but later promoted Shaybani to co-ordinator at the corps' Tabriz headquarters and replaced him with the Qajar prince, General Amanullah Mirza Jahanbani. Under Jahanbani, the regular troops fought their way to Simitqou's headquarters in the Chiriq fortress, routing the experienced Kurds, investing their stronghold and forcing Simitqou to seek refuge on the other side of the border. Two of Jahanbani's young battalion commanders distinguished themselves in this action: *Sartip* Husayn Muqaddamand *Sartip* Fazlullah Zahidi.[20] Festivities broke out in Tehran when the news of the army's successes in Kurdistan reached the capital in early August. Sardar Sipah's popularity took yet another quantum leap.

Meanwhile, in eastern Azarbayjan, General Âbdullah Amir Tahmasibi commanded the troops sent to subdue the Shahsavan sub-tribes which had invested Ardabil and were threatening Tabriz.[21] Clashes between regular troops and the tribesmen were most serious in the Ardabil/Khalkhal region, where the Fouladlou *khans* put up a desperate resistance. However, one after the other, the different sub-tribes were subdued. The leading *khans*, such as Amir Âshayir the Fouladlous' *ilkhan*, were publicly put to death *pour encourager les autres*. The commanding army officers had strict orders to quell any resistance and use all the means at their disposal to eliminate dangerous tribal leaders.

As his armies were accumulating successes in western and eastern Azarbayjan, Sardar Sipah received the good news that the supreme *khan* of Sistan and Baluchistan, Amir Shoukatul-Mulk, had wisely decided to put all his armed men at the disposal of the regular army. Thus the prudent Shoukat had both forestalled useless fighting against the superior army and won Reza's goodwill. Sardar Sipah was thus left facing the most difficult nut to crack: south-western Persia, with the Lurs and the Bakhtiaris, and the powerful Shaykh Khazâl of Muhammarah. There was no mission, however complicated or dangerous, from which the army's leader would shrink: he had to bring security to the whole country, with no exceptions allowed.

To Luristan, the most difficult of all regions, Sardar Sipah sent his number two, Ahmad Aqa Khan. Never having been brought to heel before – no central power had ever been powerful enough to conquer them – the Lurs' tribal *khans* rested assured that this newcomer would, like all his predecessors, try his best and eventually depart like all others, after suffering heavy losses. They were wrong. Having been given *carte blanche* by his commander-in-chief, Ahmad Aqa Khan knew that he had to succeeded. For this mission impossible, he had the required ruthlessness and stamina. In 1924, he began systematically taming the region's sub-tribes, not shirking bloodshed. He obtained results either by hook or by crook. He quelled rebellions by the Bianvand and Hasanvand tribes, capturing and putting to death their respective leaders: Shaykh Âli Khanand Mihr Âli Khan. In the process, Ahmad Aqa Khan earned himself the nickname 'Butcher of Luristan'[22] and also a considerable fortune from the spoils of war he accumulated. In the *Pusht Kouh* region, he even came to terms with the unruly Abouqadareh tribe. Within a span of three years, though, he had brought security to Persia's most unstable region[22A] and rendered Reza Khan an immense service (for which he would be rewarded with his fourth star in March 1929).

On the Bakhtiari side, Reza Khan had been given the necessary guarantees by his former commanding officer, Jâfar Quli Khan Sardar Asâd, the eldest son of the Constitutional Movement leader Hajj Âli Quli Khan Sardar Asâd. The young Sardar Asâd had a tremendous confidence in Sardar Sipah's future and believed that he could get a free ride on his coat tails for ever. He therefore even used his family clout to defuse a Bakhtiari plot against the life of his former subordinate.[23] When, in July 1922, a four hundred-man armed column tried to sneak through the Bakhtiari territory on its way to a secret mission in the south (against Shaykh Khazâl), it was ambushed at Shalil and destroyed by Bakhtiari tribesmen.[24] On receiving the news, Reza Khan erupted and it took all of Sardar Asâd's persuasion to stop him from sending an army to punish the Bakhtiaris. The alarm had been close, but the Bakhtiaris would be treated differently (and not suffer the Lurs' unenviable fate) as long as Sardar Asâd remained in favour.

Reza Khan's most daunting task, however, was the subduing of Shaykh Khazâl of Muhammarah. Here was an individual who ruled over the Arabs of Ârabistan (later renamed the province of Khuzistan), who sent assistance to the likes of Shaykh Jabir of Kuwait and Ibn Sâud of the Arabs, who could count on thousands of Arab warriors and the most colossal fortune in Persia, and who also was a *de jure* ally of the British Government, having signed a defensive treaty with Captain (later Sir) Percy Cox in October 1910 providing that: "His Majesty's Government will be prepared to afford you the support necessary for obtaining a satisfactory solution in the event of any encroachment by the Persian Government on your jurisdiction and recognised rights or on your property in Persia".[25] Clearly, the Shaykh officially was a British protégé. In November 1914 yet another treaty was signed to reinforce the bonds between the two parties. The strategic importance of the Shaykh during the First World War was underlined in *The Arab Bulletin* which mentioned: "...our principal Mesopotamian allies, the sheikhs of Muhammarah and Koweit,...".[26] It was not surprising that the Shaykh's "first loyalty was to the British; his duty to the Persian Government coming a poor second".[27] Such a state of things was heresy to Reza Khan, and had to be remedied.

In the impending and inevitable duel between Reza Khan and the Shaykh, the fresh British envoy to Persia, Percy Loraine (later Sir), had a difficult hand to play. Here was Loraine, a member of the Establishment, with fifteen years of service in the Foreign Office, the trust of Lord Curzon, and a cousin of Sir Lancelot Oliphant, the head of the FO's Eastern Department, embarked on the Persian adventure. From the outset, Loraine's options were extremely limited because, as Eyre Crowe was to spell it out in October 1923: "She [Great Britain] was a State disarmed ...with a public opinion opposed to all employment of force whatever – equally for a right as for a wrong cause".[28] Loraine's global strategy was, perforce, to be one hundred per cent in support of Reza Khan. He summarised it in a dispatch to Lord Curzon:

> It must, I think, be perpetually borne in mind that Tehran is the ultimate criterion of our relations with Persia, and that the cohesion of the Persian Empire as a whole is far more important to British interests generally and in the long run than the local supremacy of any of our particular protégés...[29]

The views of two prominent members of the British community in Persia differed from Loraine's. The first dissident view was that of

Sir Arnold Wilson who contended that "Britain had everything to gain by continuing the existing system";[30] and the second that of W. Smart, an influential and experienced hand at the Tehran Legation, who was sceptical about Reza Khan's chances of success and held that "we cannot throw away these southern trumps".[31] When Loraine's angle of approach finally prevailed, Wilson was bitter; in a 1925 letter he wrote to Loraine:

> With what stoicism a Government will rid itself of a burden of gratitude in the interests of higher cause...[32]

Loraine was too much of a professional diplomat to mix personal predicaments with the necessities of imperial foreign policy: he would not hesitate to sacrifice the former on the altar of the latter.

On the field, both sides were preparing for the coming showdown. Shaykh Khazâl had formed the *Saâdat* Insurrectional Committee, to which he had invited his usual partners of the southern triad: some Bakhtiari *khans* and the *Vali* of Pusht Kouh. In June 1924, after an exchange of messages between the Shaykh and the clergyman-politician Sayyid Hasan Mudarris,* the *Saâdat* Committee joined Mudarris's anti-Reza Khan coalition. Sardar Sipah countered by revoking the royal *Farmans* Muzaffar ul-Din Shah had granted Shaykh Khazâl back in 1903. In September 1924, Khazâl invited Ahmad Shah to return from his voluntary exile to Paris to Tehran, via Muhammarah (an invitation the Shah quickly turned down); he simultaneously sent a passionate anti-Reza Khan manifesto to the *Majlis* (for what good?). From its doubtful manoeuvres, it became evident that the Shaykh was at a loss, facing a superior and determined enemy.

* SAYYID HASAN MUDARRIS (1870–1938), born in Sarab-i Ardistan, son of Sayyid Ismâil; studied at *maktabs* at Qumsheh, then Isfahan (1876–1891); spent seven years at the Âtabat (1892–8); returned to Isfahan as a teacher; appointed by the Najaf religious leadership as representative to the Second *Majlis* (1910); elected deputy to Third *Majlis* from Tehran (1914); joined *Muhajarat* movement, named Minister of Justice in Nizam ul-Sataneh's cabinet (1916-7); first deputy president and majority leader in Fourth *Majlis*,

vigorously opposed Reza Khan (1921-3); elected to Fifth *Majlis*, opposed change of dynasty as anti-constitutional (1925); escaped terrorist attack, with minor wounds (1926); imprisoned (1928); exiled to Khaf, near Afghan border (1928-38); transferred to Kashmar and murdered (December 1, 1938).

When he launched his offensive against Shaykh Khazâl, Reza Khan attacked with all his forces. In November 1924 he ordered his 15,000-strong Southern Army to march southwards from its Tehran base. He also gave orders for elements of his Northern Army (Azarbayjan) and his Western Army (General Amir Ahmadi) to head in that direction in support. He himself travelled to Bushire via Isfahan and Shiraz, rattling his sabre along the way loud enough for Shaykh Khazâl to hear. In Bushire he was met by Havard, who tried to keep Reza's bellicosity in check. In Ahvaz, Loraine prevailed upon Khazâl to send Reza Khan a humble apology. The latter failed to reciprocate and Khazâl found himself on the defensive, with Loraine as a spectator.[33] With the British officials tergiversating, Khazâl finally broke under the unbearable pressure: he disbanded his Arab forces and retired to Muhammarah. On December 2, E.G.B. Peel, the British consul in Ahvaz, telegraphed Tehran: "His spirit seems now completely broken".[34] Khazâl's collapse was due to the fact that he had realised the British were leaving him on his own. As Sir Reader Bullard judiciously remarked with hindsight:

> ...the Shaik's [Khazâl] long immunity from interference by Tehran, and his friendship with H.M. Government, may well have persuaded him that his position was unassailable, and the discovery that it was not must have been very bitter...[35]

Indeed.

During the first half of December, the Shaykh and Reza Khan met in Ahvaz several times in the presence of Percy Loraine – "with the Shaikh eating out of Percy's hand", recalled Lady Loraine.[36] In the end they made each other an oath of friendship, swearing it on a copy of the *Quran*. Reza Khan returned triumphantly to Tehran, while his troops occupied Ahvaz and his governors took up their posts in Ahvaz and Abadan – totally ignoring Peel's protests. Four months later, on

April 19, 1925, Reza Khan, taking advantage of the fact that Loraine and Wilson were both on holiday, delivered his final estocade: he ordered his yacht *Khuzistan*, with Colonel Zahidi and fifty men on board, to accost the Shaykh's yacht *Ivy* on the Karun river in the middle of the night, capture Khazâl and his son Abdul Hamid and bring the two to Tehran. The Shaykh was kept under house arrest at Tehran for years. British demands for his eventual exile to Europe fell on deaf ears. In 1936, Shaykh Khazâl was strangled in his prison-house on orders of Reza Shah.[37] Thus ended the life of the man who had fallen victim to Reza Khan's will not to let any influential individual live in the country he wanted to rule. Khazâl's neighbours and vassals, Ibn Sâud of Arabia and Shaykh Jabir of Kuwait, would have a golden destiny; Khazâl's ill fortune was to have been a Persian.

With the defeat of Shaykh Khazâl, Reza Khan had brought to an end his programme of pacification in Persia. Naturally, here and there, troubles would still erupt from time to time, but now the iron collar was in place to quell any major eruption throughout the country. The national army was ready to nip any tribal ambitions in the bud.

6.4. Reza Khan, the Politician

While his armies were busy defeating unruly tribesmen and irregulars throughout the country, Reza Khan was mapping his way in Tehran's political labyrinths. His first discovery had been that Ahmad Shah and his crown prince brother, Muhammad Hasan Mirza, were mere ciphers, having neither authority nor power.

Secondly, the Elite was docile as long as it had a foothold in the national arena. Qavam ul-Saltaneh, Mustoufi ul-Mamalik and Mushir ul-Douleh took turns in the premiership, keeping Reza Khan at the Ministry of War (uninterruptedly from April 1921 until October 1923). The latter bided his time for his next logical step to the premiership. One single obstacle stood on his way: the Fourth *Majlis* which had convened on June 22, 1921 and had elected as president Mûtamin ul-Mulk, and as his deputies Sayyid Hasan Mudarris and Ibrahim Hakim ul-Mulk. The *Majlis* still was the Elite's last stronghold and it was dominated by Reza Khan's last (but not least) opponent: Mudarris.

Mudarris, besides being a simple *mulla*, was a man of talent, an excellent speaker, a courageous citizen and a mountain of common sense all rolled in one. From the *coup d'état* onward, he had feared Reza Khan's dictatorship and had tried at every turn to stop his meteoric career, even supporting to the hilt the candidacy of Qavam ul-Saltaneh (a man he didn't trust either) to the premiership, in the belief that, among all the politicians, only Qavam had the knack needed to stop Reza. Being the only individual daring to oppose Reza Khan publicly, Mudarris had united under his umbrella all the anti-Reza currents. From his *Majlis* pulpit, Mudarris launched virulent attacks on Reza Khan, with the military replying by staging military parades. But Reza Khan failed to get around the *Majlis* and had to wait for it to dissolve, in June 1923.

In the interim between the Fourth and Fifth *Majlis*, Reza Khan pushed with all his forces for the premiership.

Notwithstanding Mudarris's opposition and Ahmad Shah's reluctance to give him the post, Reza Khan eventually was appointed prime minister, presenting his first cabinet to the Shah on October 25, 1923. Ahmad Shah only asked him in return to give him a signed safe conduct so that he could leave on his golden exile, and quickly left Tehran for Baghdad in November 1923,[37A] leaving behind his brother Muhammad Hasan Mirza as viceroy. Ahmad Shah was never to return to Persia. He spent the rest of his life in France, shuttling between his suites at the Majestic Hotel in Paris and the Negresco at Nice. Some of his close relatives had advised him time and again to return to Persia and defend his Qajar crown,[38] but he had consistently refused to consider returning, being afraid of not being able to return to his French *dolce vita* and the fortune he had there.[39] Ahmad Shah, the seventh and last Qajar shah, did not care about his throne: he had never really wanted the role and had avowed himself that "he was unfit for the kingship".[40] Kidney problems were to mar the last two years of his life he spent in Neuilly, near the American Hospital where he was treated; in 1929 one of his kidneys was removed and in February 1930 he passed away at the age of thirty-four.

With the Shah out of the way and the Viceroy an empty figurehead, as his brother always refused to abdicate in his favour (Ahmad Shah wanted to die as Shah), the Qajars were now out of the contest. Between Reza and his ultimate power remained only the *Majlis*, or, more precisely, the Fifth *Majlis*. This time round, he had

had his regional military commanders supervise the vote and influence the outcome in provincial centres.[41] They had done a proper job so that when the Fifth *Majlis* opened in February 1924, out of the 139 deputies Reza Khan could count on the forty solid votes of the *Tajaddud* faction, led by Sayyid Muhammad Tadayyun, a school teacher totally devoted to Reza Khan, and on the sympathies of the fifteen deputies of the *Susialist* faction (the former Democrats), headed by Prince Sulayman Mirza Iskandari and Sayyid Muhammad Sadiq Tabataba'i. On the other hand, his nemesis Mudarris was minority speaker with six deputies and could count at most on a dozen independent votes, not enough to counter Reza Khan's overwhelming majority. Early in 1924, Reza Khan held all the trump cards to fulfil his dream of becoming the first President of the Persian Republic – thereby emulating his hero and *alter ego* Mustafa Kemal Atatürk, President of Turkey since 1923. This plan of his, however, foundered on two unexpected obstacles: the twin opposition of the religious hierocracy in Qum and of the British Legation in Tehran. The religious had opposed the Republic in their sermons; and Sir Percy Loraine had exposed his reservations to Mustoufi ul-Mamalik, who in turn had spread them around.[42] The opposition staged popular demonstrations and the mobs clashed with the armed forces. Disorders culminated on March 22, 1924, the day Reza Khan had chosen for the debate on the Republic in the *Majlis*. After receiving a brick on the neck and being severely reprimanded by the authoritarian *Majlis* president, Mûtamin ul-Mulk, for trespassing on his responsibilities within the *Majlis* enceinte (he later presented his excuses to the President),[43] Reza Khan decided to shelve once and for all his republican ambitions.

This fiasco had the effect of rejuvenating the opposition to Reza Khan. Spurred on by Mudarris, it started action.

It convinced Ahmad Shah to dismiss (from his Paris exile) the prime minister and order the *Majlis* to appoint a fresh premier. Reza Khan immediately resigned and left in self-imposed exile to Roudhin, a village east of Tehran he had recently acquired. Army commanders from all over Persia sent protest telegrams to the *Majlis*, threatening to march their troops to the capital if their commander-in-chief was not reinstated. The *Majlis*, caving in to the wave of threats, recalled Reza Khan and reappointed him prime minister. The Fifth *Majlis* had just shown that it was powerless against bayonets, thereby opening the road to absolute power for Reza Khan.

In January 1925, returning from his successful foray against Shaykh Khazâl, Reza Khan induced the *Majlis* to appoint him Supreme Commander of the Armed Forces – a title exclusively reserved for the Shah, as stipulated by Article 50 of the Supplementary Fundamental Laws. In March, the Prime Minister had the *Majlis* change the calendar from the lunar to the solar version, replacing the Arab months for Persian equivalents. A month later he had it vote the abolition of all Qajar titles like *Saltaneh*, *Douleh* and *Mamalik*; and also ratify the introduction of compulsory family names for all citizens, registered on identity cards to be issued from June 1925. Then, in the autumn 1925, Reza Khan began his last battle against the Qajars. On September 13, the *Majlis* ratified a bill limiting the Viceroy's assets; then on October 31 it voted by eighty votes for and five against (namely, Mudarris, Dr Muhammad Musaddiq, Sayyid Yahya Doulatabadi, Sayyid Hasan Taqizadeh and Husayn Âla) to make destitute the Qajar dynasty. Two days before this crucial vote, Sir Percy Loraine had met Reza Khan and told him that H.M. Government was determined to "leave Persia absolutely free to settle her internal affairs. This was the only possible attitude for a loyal friend. In return we did expect our questions to be taken in hand and settled as soon as possible".[44]

The final act was inevitable. A constituent assembly was rapidly brought together and on December 12 it duly approved, by 257 votes out of 260, to alter articles 36, 37, 38 and 40 of the Supplementary Constitutional Laws, replacing the Qajars with Reza Shah Pahlavi and his descendants. Reza Khan had become Reza Shah. Within a five-year span, the unknown Cossack officer had climbed the whole ladder of power, step by step, to come out at the top, to sit on Nasir's Peacock Throne.

6.5. Winners and Losers

On April 24, 1926, Reza Shah was crowned Shah of Persia; his eldest son, Muhammad Reza, was chosen as crown prince. Two months later Sir Percy Loraine departed Tehran for other diplomatic horizons. After the coronation he had written: "Reza Shah is my Shah, and we have scored a big hit".

And his friend Colonel W. Fraser duly congratulated him on his undeniable success: "It is quite obvious that the power that guided Persia during the last five years was Loraine-Reza".[45] Undoubtedly, Loraine's role in Reza Shah's irresistible ascent had been pre-eminent; he had believed in the Cossack officer from the outset and had been pleasantly surprised by his protégé's multi-faceted talents. Major General Sir Edmund Ironside, Lieutenant Colonel Smyth, G.T. Havard and W. Smart, among others, must have been satisfied to find out that they had all made a fortunate choice back in 1921.

When accused of having taken the crown from the Qajars by force, Reza Shah replied: "Not so, I found the Crown lying in the gutter!" He was correct: the Qajars had overstayed their time. They had belonged to the nineteenth century, not to the twentieth. The last two decades had seen the Qajars' pathetic and prolonged agony. Lucky for them that Reza Khan came along to cut it short.

After one hundred and twenty-nine years, the last chapter of Aqa Muhammad Shah's heirs was closed. Like all the other dynasties before it, the Qajars would not make a comeback. Their historical tombstone could well read: "With the Qajars Persia entered the most unromantic and unproductive period of her history".[46]

That Reza Shah Pahlavi had mounted the Peacock Throne was a blatant sign that things were not what they used to be in Persia. Two decades earlier, the very thought of a semi-literate Cossack officer becoming shah would have been unthinkable – now it was a fact. This was, in a way, an indirect result of the Constitutional Movement and its sequels. In an other way, it was a revenge for the people, especially for the urban bourgeoisie, who were weary of an Elite which could not cater for their basic wants, especially security. Reza Shah "gave them what for long they had lacked – a man".[47]

The dozen or so top army officers around Reza Khan were also among the winners. They had done their respective jobs against irregulars in the most varied climates and conditions, boldly risking their lives. Now they could enjoy the pleasures of fame and wealth in continuing to serve their leader Reza Shah. They would form his inner circle and be always assured of his backing. For example, when in 1928, General Yazdanpanah clashed with Farajullah Bahrami, Reza Shah's private (and capable) secretary since 1921, the outcome was easily foreseeable: Bahrami had to go, ending up in exile,[48] whereas Yazdanpanah remained.

From the outset of their formidable adventure in 1921, they had been the spokes of the spinning wheel of Fortune, all linked to the Reza Khan hub. Now that he had made it to the very top, he would not forget those officers who had made it possible; he would still get angry at them from time to time, but he would provide them with all they could wish: commands, honours, wealth, fame and, for the gifted amongst them, a place in his Pahlavi elite.

The Elite should be placed among the losers: it had lost its monopoly on power. But it was rapidly recovering, as it knew how. It still had kept intact its economic base (the hundreds of villages it controlled and milked) and through it could still influence elections and retain its political base within the *Majlis*; only revenues stemming from court allowances and royal patronage had been lost. But in the long run, the policies of Reza Shah were to prove highly beneficial to the Elite, both in the economic and political spheres. Economically, the law and order policy would increase and secure their revenues from the land. Politically, the breaking of regional and the tribes' powers was a boon to the Elite: with its "cold-blooded selfishness",[49] it was being able to get rid of despised regional rivals (i.e. Shaykh Khazâl, Simitqou, the tribal *Khans*), and side with the victorious urban masses, hiding its own nakedness behind the middle classes.

The real losers in the new Pahlavi system were Persia's tribes, first and foremost the tribesmen and, to a lesser extent, their *khans*. The latter group was to be blamed, not so much for failing to stop Reza's irresistible rise, but for failing to capitalise on the golden chance given it in the aftermath of the Constitutional Movement. Back in December 1911, Sir Arnold Wilson had passed the following judgement on the country's state of affairs:

> The country is in a miserable state and ready to accept any form of government which will give them security. ...[it will take] ten years before this country recovers from the anarchy of the last three.[50] Persia has been decaying for years. The Constitutional Movement, started by men who were trying to stop the rot, has hastened it.[51] Government by tribes and by great families was at an end: the system had broken

> down. What was needed now was government by a Government ...the Persian Government...[52]

The *khans* could only blame themselves for their greed and short-sightedness. Now they and their subordinates had to pay the consequences: occupation of their tribal lands by Reza's ruthless armed forces. Between the dwindling tribes and the growing urban masses the fight had been unequal from the outset. Urban Persia was now fully in control through its champion Reza Shah; it would extract its revenge from the tribes through its new-found military machine.

Among the winners were the intelligentsia's leaders. Standing at the summit of public opinion, they manipulated the urban masses at will. No other social group had increased (quantitatively and qualitatively) as had the Persian intelligentsia within the first two decades of the twentieth century. This hotchpotch of educated individuals had been one of the main pillars supporting Reza Shah's bid for absolute power. Representing a tiny minority among a large mass of analphabets, it controlled the national administration. Its membership came from within five main sub-groups: (1) the artists; (2) the journalists; (3) the liberal professions; (4) the educators; and (5) the civil servants. As a group, it loathed the tribes, which it believed to be "backward" as opposed to their own "forwardness"; it detested the Elite, which stood along its path and rise to the top;[53] it loved Reza Shah, who it thought to be both its creature and, as Malik ul-Shuâra Bahar put it:

> The middle classes saw in the person of Reza Khan the realisation of its goal...[54]

The intelligentsia could ride unimpeded on Reza Shah's coat-tails and assist him in shaping the Persia they wanted. In their post-coup dreams, the intelligentsia had forgotten that Reza Khan was a Cossack officer not an intellectual. The intelligentsia would soon wake up to its error of having taken its dream for reality, but too late to change the course of history, and it would console itself by coming to the conclusion that Reza Shah was still far better than either the Qajars or the old Elite.

Among the Cossacks, the Gendarmerie, the tribes, the Elite, the intelligentsia and the urban and rural masses, there now was but a single arbiter: Reza Shah Pahlavi. In five turbulent years on the national stage, he had shown his iron will and his political shrewdness, and imprinted the whole nation with his singular personality. Risen from the masses, he now stood at the very top. Alone. But to be alone is not a disadvantage, as long as you are the strongest, for, as Friedrich von Schiller concluded:

Der starkste ist am machtigsten allein. (The strongest is at its best alone)[55]

NOTES

1. Â. Mustoufi, *Sharh-i Zindagani-i Man* (Tehran: *Zavvar*, 3rd ed., 1360 (1981)) Vol. III, p.213.
2. H. Makki, *Tarikh-i Bist Saleh Iran* (Tehran: *Nashir*, 3rd ed., 1361 (1982)) Vol. I, pp.233-4.
3. Ibid., Vol. I, p.189.
4. Sir Denis Wright, *The English Amongst the Persians* (London: Heinemann, 1977) p.180.
5. Ibid., pp.180-1.
6. Ibid., p.181. In a footnote on the same page, Wright mentions that Ardishir Reporter (alias Ji), a Bombay parsee "who had come to Tehran in 1893" and "kept in close touch with the British Legation" (ibid., p.45.), had become a member of Malik ul-Mutakallimin's secret *anjuman* during the Constitutional Movement. He further stated "in his unpublished memoirs that he first introduced Reza Khan to Ironside".
7. H. Arfa, *Under Five Shahs* (London: John Murray, 1964) p.91.
8. The Maxim machine-gun, invented by Sir Hiram Stevens Maxim, was at the turn of the century the *ne plus ultra* in firing weapon technology. A single-barrelled automatic rifle, the Maxim could fire up to ten shots per second.
9. See Amir Ahmadi's memoirs, *Asnad-i Nakhustin Sipahbud-i Iran Ahmad Amir Ahmadi*, ed. by S. Saâdvandian (Tehran: *Mu'asiseh Pijouish va Mutaliât-i Farhang*, 1373 (1994)) Vol. 1, p.170.
10. D. Wright, op. cit. (note 4), p.184.
11. *High Road to Command - The Diaries of Major General Sir Edmund Ironside*, ed. by Lord Ironside, (London: Leo Cooper, 1972) p.117.
11A. F. Bostock, 'State Bank or Agent of Empire? The Imperial Bank of Persia's loan policy 1920-23', in *IRAN*, J. of the British Institute of Persian Studies, Vol. XXVII, 1989, p.105.
12. The Pisian family as a whole already had a reputation for creating trouble. Pisian's cousins, the brothers *Yavar* (captain) Âli Quli Khan Pisian and *Sultan* (lieutenant) Ghulam Riza Khan Pisian, both Gendarmerie officers at Shiraz, had taken part in the anti-British events of November 1915 that eventually led to the arrest of British Consul O'Connor. Defeated by Qavam ul-Mulk's armed men, the

two brothers were found dead – they had been either killed or had committed suicide.

13 On Pisian's rebellion see H. Makki, op. cit. (note 2), Vol. I, pp.455-480.

14 On the life and revolutionary acts of Haydar Âmou Oughli, see the biography written by Ismîil Ra'in, *Haydar Khan Âmou Oughli* (Tehran: *Javidan*, 1352 (1973)) 2 Vols. Educated as a an electrical engineer in the Caucasus, Âmou Oughli first came to the *Ijtimâyun-Âmmyun* Party and later ranked among the founding members of the Social Democrat party. Joined *Îdalat* Party, formed in Baku in May 1917 (by Asadullah Ghafarzadeh and Bahram Agayev, with Avetis Sultanzadeh as leading theorist and Jâfar Javadzadeh, alias Pishavari, as the editor of its paper *Hurriyyat*). At its first congress in Persia (at Inzili) in July 1920, *Îdalat* changed its name to *Firqeh Kumunist-i Iran* (Communist Party of Iran) and elected Âmou Oughli as its first secretary-general. In 1921, the latter left for Gilan (replaced at the secretariat by Karim Nikbin) to become Minister for Foreign Affairs in Mirza Kouchak Khan's Republic of Gilan (August 1921). See also M. Reza Ghods, 'The Iranian Communist Movement under Reza Shah', *Middle Eastern Studies*, Vol. 26, no. 4, October 1990. p.506.

15 I. Fakhra'i, *Sardar-i Jangal* (Tehran: *Javidan*, 1357 (1978)) p.372. The traitor Khalou Qurban (who owed everything to his leader Kouchak Khan) was shot in the back and killed a few months later, while leading government troops against irregulars in Azarbayjan. Yet another example that, in Persia, treason doesn't pay.

16 Ibid., p.735.

17 I. Ra'in, *Qyam-i Jangal* (Tehran: *Javidan*, 1357 (1978)) p.251.

18 I. Fakhra'i, op. cit. (note 15), p.

19 H. Arfa, op. cit. (note 7), p.110.

20 Muqaddam and Zahidi were the prototypes of the new younger generation of army officers: solid, devoted and courageous. Both of them would have long and successful careers.

21 Â. Mustoufi, op. cit. (note 1), Vol. III, p.366.

22 On the atrocities committed by Amir Ahmadi in Luristan, see W.O. Douglas, *Strange Lands and Friendly People* (New York: Harper and Brothers, 1951) pp.104-9.

22A See Amir Ahmadi's memoirs: *Asnad-i Nakhustin Sipahbud-i Iran Ahmad Amir Ahmadi* ed. by S. Saâdvandian, (Tehran: *Mu'asiseh Pijouish va Mutaliât-i Farhang*, 1373 (1994)) 2 Vols.

23 Upon the return of Ahmad Shah from his second European visit in December 1922, Sardar Sipah, then Minister for War, went to Isfahan to pay his respects. All the leading Bakhtiari *khans* were there too. One of them, Yusuf Khan Amir Mujahid (the *Ilkhani*'s fifth and youngest son), proposed to his fellow *khans* that they should use this unique opportunity to assassinate Reza Khan, arguing that: "It is our last chance to get rid of him. Later he will be too powerful. If we don't kill him now, he will get rid of us all in due time". Having got wind of the plot, Sardar Asâd threatened his uncle with unveiling the plot to Sardar Sipah, if he didn't stop conspiring. In the face of such a threat, Amir Mujahid backed down, but told his nephew: "You shall live to regret it". This prophecy would be fulfilled a decade later. This historical anecdote was reported to the author by a minor Bakhtiari *khan*, then in the retinue of Amir Mujahid.

24 G. Waterfield, *Professional Diploma*, (London: John Murray, 1973) p.70.

25 Ibid., p.77.

26 See *The Arab Bulletin*, no. 47, April 11, 1917, as reproduced by E. Kedourie in *England and the Middle East* (London: Bowes and Bowes, 1956) p.230.
27 G. Waterfield, op. cit. (note 24), p.96.
28 Ibid., p.77.
29 Ibid., p.78. Citing Loraine to Curzon (no. 551; September 4, 1922; FO 371/10134).
30 Ibid., p.78.
31 In a rather unique incident, W. Smart and his colleague R. Bridgeman were caught (by Reza Khan's secret police) on a night in March 1922 in the house of Tehran's leading courtesan, Âziz Kashi. They were both recalled to England. Perhaps in higher Persian spheres Smart's ideas were not appreciated? On this bizarre anecdote see: Â. Mustoufi, op. cit. (note 1), Vol. III, p.492.
32 G. Waterfield, op. cit. (note 24), p.107.
33 Rahimzadeh Safavi, *Asrar-i Suqout-i Ahmad Shah* (Tehran: Firdousi, 1362 (1983)) p.89.
34 Ibid., p.92.
35 Sir Reader Bullard, *Britain and the Middle East* (London: Hutchinson University Library, 3rd (revised) ed., 1964) p.125.
36 G. Waterfield, op. cit. (note 24), p.96.
37 Personal communication by a member of Shaykh Khazâl's last wife's family.
37A The hushed-up travel of the Shah and his small retinue from Tehran to the Iraqi border (via Hamadan and Kermanshah) looked more like an organised flight than a royal departure. Reza Khan in person accompanied the Shah all the way to Qasr-i Shirin, to make sure that he had rid himself of the last Qajar monarch for ever.
38 Personal communication by an elder Qajar prince.
39 Ahmad Shah had had time to transfer abroad considerable sums of money (mostly in gold and silver coins) and jewels. In 1921 he was already planning customs evasion on a large scale. He had not hesitated to ask the departing General Ironside, who had come to pay his respects before leaving Persia, to take along with him to Baghdad a large consignment of silver toumans – "about half a million sterling". Ironside recalled in his diaries: "The enormity of the crime he was proposing me to commit suddenly dawned upon me". To an outraged Ironside, who suggested that the silver should be kept in Persia, Ahmad Shah sheepishly replied: "Peut-être qu'oui, mon général, mais n'oubliez pas qu'au fond tout le monde est egoïste." (Maybe so, General, but don't forget that, at bottom, everyone is egotistically-minded). See Major General Sir Edmund Ironside's diaries, op. cit. (note 11), pp.152-3.
40 Quoted by M.Q. Hidayat, *Khatirat va Khatarat* (Tehran: Zavvar, 1344 (1965)) p.353.
41 Â. Mustoufi, op. cit. (note 1), Vol. III, p.606.
42 M.Q. Hidayat, op. cit. (note 40), p.364.
43 G.T. Havard, the oriental secretary of the British Legation, who always seems to be present at all critical junctures, was an interested observer of the *Majlis* happenings of March 22, 1924.
44 G. Waterfield, op. cit. (note 24), p.122. What were these questions Loraine was referring to? Could one of them have been about oil?
45 Ibid., p.138.
46 See G.B. Walker, *Persian Pageant* (Calcutta, 1950) p.71.
47 H.W. and S. Hay, *By Order of the Shah* (London: Cassell, 1937) p.238.

48 Â. Dashti, *Panjah Panj* (Tehran: *Amir Kabir*, 2nd ed., 1355 (1976)) p.140.
49 C. Skrine, *World War in Iran* (London: Constable and Co., 1962) p.XV. Skrine was extremely curious on the subject of Elite; he was highly interested by its composition and *modus operandi*. He became a specialist on this matter.
50 Sir Arnold Wilson, *S.W. Persia* (London: Readers Union Ltd., 1942) p.197.
51 Ibid., p.206.
52 Ibid., p.187.
53 A case in point is the journalist Rahimzadeh Safavi, the special envoy of Mudarris (and his Elite friends) to Ahmad Shah in Paris. In his memoirs (see note 33), Safavi clearly shows that he sympathises with Reza Khan and his ideals (pp. 41, 42, 72 and 169). Mudarris and his friends should never have used a journalist as a go-between with Paris: a young, amateurish Elite member might not have been as efficient, but would have been infinitely more reliable.
54 See M. Reza Ghods, 'Iranian Nationalism and Reza Shah', in *Middle Eastern Studies*, Vol. 27, no. 1, January 1991, p.43.
55 F. von Schiller, *Wilhelm Tell* I, 3.

CHAPTER SEVEN: FROM PERSIA TO IRAN

With the accession of Reza Shah Pahlavi to supreme power, the country returned to the one-man elite patterns developed during the eighteenth century by Nadir Shah Afshar and Karim Khan Zand. A self-made man of forty-six, the first Pahlavi was still vigorous and indefatigable: a veritable *force de la nature*. He had shown the whole gamut of his abilities during his rise to power, especially his incredible talent at filling any new role he chose.

However, the formidable task he had set himself of transmuting the old, decrepit Qajar Persia into a fresh, modern Pahlavi nation state seemed way over his head. But the dream was the size of the man. He knew his fellow Persians, he knew what they were capable of (if properly motivated), he knew they would obey him as his field commanders did, he knew they wanted him to succeed and he knew that he was their only hope. And he also knew how to choose his collaborators, perhaps Reza Shah's greatest gift: his ability to co-opt and work with different types of capable individuals – the sign of the great man. To the journalist Âli Dashti, who advised him to sideline all the Elite members and place in their stead individuals fully dependent on him, Reza Shah replied: "But where shall I find such people?"[1] Dependent or independent subordinates was not his worry: they all depended upon his will. He would simply choose them from among the best and the brightest of his generation, indifferent to their background. He wanted to construct, thus he needed capable builders not docile yes-men.

Reza Shah's plans were plain: adapt whatever was adaptable, create whatever was missing, and hammer the lot into a Pahlavi mould. On this route towards a modern nation state, he would naturally begin with the prime instrument of his power: his army.

7.1. The Pahlavi Army

Reza Shah had begun sharpening his army in 1921. He had to start everything from scratch, his only initial asset being his own Cossack Division. As Minister for War from April 1921 until

October 1925 (replaced at the latter date by General Amir Tahmasibi), he had catered to his troops' requirements and gradually expanded their budget, their scope, their armaments and their numbers. In 1922/3, Reza Khan had the army regulations compiled, ratified by the *Majlis* and implemented. In June 1925, he pushed through the *Majlis* the Compulsory Military Service Bill, thereby anchoring his institution in the civil society at large; thereafter, the armed forces would have a permanent officers and NCO corps, with a changing mass of conscript soldiers. He also created, in 1925, an army pension fund, for taking care of servicemen after their retirement, and the Sipah Bank (the army's bank), the first domestic banking institution (whose shares were owned by the army's pension fund) to cater for the armed forces' banking requirements.

Within the five year span 1921-25, the officer's image in the country had drastically improved from that of a poor, parasitic member of society to that of a superior and powerful member of a new elite. This trend would continue over the Pahlavi years. The best and the brightest began to flock to the officers' corps to benefit from an advantageous career and the enhanced status. Even the NCOs were recruited from amongst the strongest and fittest in the villages: the army's selection committee signed up those candidates who could do fifty push-ups non-stop on a fixed iron bar.[2]

As all ranks needed training, Reza Shah ordered a military school and a military academy to be established at Tehran, and a staff college; a war academy was to be created later (in 1936) by the French General Jean. Many junior officers were sent abroad, mostly to France (Saumur, St. Cyr and École Supérieure de Guerre) for specialised training. There were always too few cadres to man the fresh battalions, brigades and divisions. The Persian Army had doubled from some 20,000 men under arms in 1923 to 40,000 in 1925; and later expanded to a grand total of 183,000 in 1941,[3] inclusive of the air force and the navy.[4] The army's backbone consisted of five armies (namely those of the East, North-West, West, South and Gilan) and the two Tehran Divisions (the First and the Second).

These men needed food, clothing, armaments and medical services. An extensive system of logistics had to be set up: purchasing services, stores, accounting, dispatch and distribution - in short, the whole paraphernalia of modern army services. Modern armaments were purchased from abroad: tanks from the Czechoslovakian Skoda, mountain guns from the Swedish Bofors, machine-guns from Britain and many other needs were fulfilled by companies in Germany and France. Army factories proliferated as the armed forces wanted to become self-sufficient and received the necessary budgets, with German firms getting the lion's share: first came the ammunition and rifles (7.92) manufacturing units; then the vehicle repair shops and the light machine-guns (Brno model); Skoda factory (located in the east of Tehran); finally, the chemical units for producing explosives (located at Parchin, some twenty-five kilometres south-east of Tehran). Eventually these various industrial and services units were amalgamated into the *Sazman-i Sanayî Nizami* (the Military Industries Organisation). By 1941, Reza Shah's army had 500,000 rifles, 874 artillery guns, 7,500 light machine-guns, 1,000 heavy (Maxim) machine-guns and 100 Skoda tanks (fifty light 3.5 tonnes and fifty heavy 7.5 tonnes).

To facilitate and speed up the movement of troops, thousands of kilometres of roads were either repaired or freshly drawn. Garrisons had to be built in major towns so that divisions could be kept in secluded and safe conditions.

Tehran received more than its fair share of new barracks and military camps.

As Minister for War, Reza Khan had, in 1922, ordered his first combat aeroplane from Germany, a Junkers F-13. In 1924 the Persian Military Air Force was born. By 1926 the new air force consisted of twenty-six planes – mainly Junkers, French Breguets and British De Havillands (manufactured in the Soviet Union).[4A] In 1925, the Shahbaz factory had been established near Tehran by the British company Hawker to build, "under the direction of British technical experts", Adax-Tigermoth aeroplanes "with British designs and British engines". The airport of Qalêh Murghi was built in the south of Tehran for the air force.

A full decade after the air force was established, Reza Shah ordered two navies to be set up in November 1932. There was a small one on the Caspian Sea consisting of a few armed sloops and a larger one on the Persian Gulf stationed at Bushire, Bandar Shahpur or Muhammarah (later Khurramshahr), with two 750-tons Italian gunboats (the *Babr* and the *Palang*) and four 500-tons gunboats (the *Karkas*, the *Shahbaz*, the *Shahrukh* and the *Simurgh*),[5] a training ship

(Khazâl's former *Ivy* yacht), and four smaller vessels. The Southern Navy's father and commander-in-chief was Rear Admiral Ghulam Âli Bayandur, a former Cossack officer with a British wife.

With its army, air force and two navies, Reza Shah's armed forces became, within the short span of two decades, a new institution on the domestic socio-economical stage. Some 180,000 Iranian citizens were directly involved in this military institution, with thousands more in indirect support. This formidable machinery, built up from scratch, ranks among Reza Shah's major achievements. The army certainly proved unbeatable domestically: irregular forces were simply no match for it. The last major tribal uprising of 1928/9 was a case in point. In the autumn of 1928, the first clash occurred at Duragmadou between Boir Ahmadi tribesmen, led by Imam Quli Khan Rustam, and a small army detachment. Profiting from the surprise effect, the tribesmen scored a victory. Encouraged by his success, Rustam decided to march on Shiraz; he was joined by the Qashqa'is, the Mamassani and the Baharlous. At Shiraz, General Habibullah Shaybani, the commander-in-chief of the Expeditionary Corps assembled to counter the tribal threat, had to make use of the air force to stop the tribesmen.

The tribal leaders, witnessing the disastrous effects of these flying machines (widely used militarily for the first time in Persia), ordered a surprise attack on the Shiraz airport in June 1929: the tribal commando was able to destroy three of the planes and damage a number of others.[6] In July 1929 the Bakhtiaris, under Muhammad Riza Khan Sardar Fatih, joined in the fray but were easily stopped at the Battle of Sifid Dasht, putting a premature end to their diversion. On the other hand, the Boir Ahmadis, after holding their own at the Second Battle of Duragmadou, wiped out Shaybani's regulars (2,800-strong)[7] in August 1930 at the Tang-i Tamuradi, killing four officers and over three hundred NCOs and soldiers.[8] The Boir Ahmadis' champion and sharpshooter, Lurhasib, encouraged his men to pursue the retreating soldiers, but the tribesmen were already busy pillaging the reserves the army had left behind.[9] In the autumn of 1930, Lurhasib was shot and killed in an ambush – thus ended the last serious tribal rebellion during Reza Shah's reign.

It was not surprising that the formidable army machine built by Reza Shah was unbeatable domestically. The real surprise would come in 1941, when it had to face foreign armies in the field.

7.2. Reza Shah's Administrators

While refurbishing his army, Reza Khan had begun to think of the economy because of his need for ever-larger funds to finance his expansion of the armed forces. After the short-lived mission of Armitage-Smith, the Persian Government had hired the services of the American financial expert Dr A.C. Millspaugh in 1922. From the outset, Reza Khan backed the Millspaugh mission. In his six years in Persia (1922–27), the American expert carried out some useful work by putting the country's finances on the right track. During his tenure he would "centralise revenues, expenditure and accounting";[10] moreover, "accounts were streamlined, taxes claimed and the national budget balanced". Dr Millspaugh also helped pass through the *Majlis* the Civil Recruitment Bill and the Tea and Sugar Monopoly Bill of 1925 – which included the taxes on sugar (two-thirds of a rial per kilo) and on tea (two rials per kilo).[11] "The American adviser", wrote Sir Percy Sykes, "accomplished much sound work with the support of Reza Shah".[12] But, in 1927, Reza Shah clashed with the American adviser and it was clear which one had to resign. Reza Shah told him: "There can't be two Shahs in this country and I am going to be the Shah".[13] After the progress achieved over the previous years, Millspaugh's services were not needed as they had been. The American dutifully resigned in July 1927 and left Persia. He had succeeded where Morgan Shuster had failed because of his tact and because he had the support of Reza Khan.

By 1927 Reza Shah had had the time to pick the best and the brightest politicians and administrators to serve him.

First and foremost, as his Minister of Court he had chosen the brilliant Âbd ul-Husayn Taymourtash* (the former Sardar Muâzam Khurasani). Bright, good-looking and gifted, Taymourtash deserved the highest ranks in Persia (even the top one). During a cabinet meeting in 1927, Reza Shah had made things clear for all by openly stressing that "Taymourtash's word is my word".[14] In practice, Taymourtash was caretaker for all non-military questions: the *Majlis*, the government, the court, the economy and finances, the oil negotiations, etc.; the Shah took care of military affairs. Both men were among the ablest Persians in their respective spheres. "As long as Taymourtash was in charge", wrote M.Q. Hidayat, "the wheels of

State turned smoothly ...all institutions and especially the Court Ministry (a Ministership he was born to fill) ...were under control".[15] Taymourtash worked incessantly, deciding on everything, with no subject out of his scope. His negotiations with the British for a fresh agreement between APOC were his most ambitious enterprise.

After his last trip to London for meeting once again with APOC chairman Sir John Cadman (later Lord Cadman), Taymourtash returned to Tehran by way of Moscow. On the train back to Persia, some confidential documents (related to oil negotiations) were allegedly stolen from his attaché case[16] by "a spy with blue eyes". A few months after his return he was arrested. While he languished in his Qasr prison cell the fresh oil agreement was signed in Tehran. Even a last minute request by visiting Soviet official Leon Karakhan proved unsuccessful. While the latter was in Tehran, Taymourtash was murdered in his cell. Thus ended the turbulent life of a remarkable Persian, who had been instrumental in placing the Pahlavi nation state on the right track.

* ÂBD UL-HUSAYN TAYMOURTASH (1879–1933), son of Karimdad Khan Nardini Bujnurdi Muâziz ul-Mulk; trained at the Imperial Russian Nikolayevski Cavalry School (till 1907); entered Ministry of Foreign Affairs (1908); elected deputy from Khurasan, Second *Majlis* (1910); commander of Khurasan Army, title of Sardar Muâzam Khurasani (1912); governor-general of Gilan (1918); Minister of Public Works (1924–5); Minister of Court (1926–32); dismissed by Reza Shah (December 1932); under house arrest, imprisoned, two trials (sentenced to three and five years), murdered in Qasr Prison (October 1, 1933).

Another prominent individual co-opted by Reza Shah to take care of economic and financial affairs was Prince Firouz Mirza Nusrat ul-Douleh, yet another outstanding Persian.* A multi-millionaire and a second generation Elitist, Firouz had made his mark in foreign policy by negotiating the 1915 and the 1919 Anglo-Persian Agreements. The ill-fated 1919 Agreement he had signed almost proved to be his parting shot in politics - as it was for Vusuq ul-Douleh. But the versatile Firouz rebounded and nursed hopes to lead the political side of the February 1921 *coup d'état*.[17] These hopes were unrealistic because Firouz, a marked Elitist, had no chance to lead an anti-Elite coup. He resurfaced in the Fourth *Majlis* as deputy from Kermanshah and, when attacked on the 1919 Agreement in the Assembly, was vehemently defended by Mudarris himself. Back in the cabinet at Justice in 1925, he oiled the dynastic change and was rewarded with the Finance portfolio in 1927. He lost no time in forming a new triumvirate at the top with Taymourtash (at Court) and Sardar Asâd (at War). Two years later, he was abruptly dismissed by Reza Shah for alleged intrigues. Firouz Mirza never accepted that back in 1921 his Elite team had lost the game; he always hoped for a comeback. Reza Khan, however, was both extremely suspicious and extremely well-informed, and Firouz never stood a chance of toppling him. He was the first of the triumvirate to go to prison and the last of the three to be murdered.

* FIROUZ MIRZA NUSRAT UL-DOULEH (1890-1938), eldest son of Prince Farmanfarma; studied at Beirut (1897-1904) and Paris (1909-12); deputy to Minister of Justice (1913); assisted father during his premiership (1915); Minister of Justice (1918); Minister of Foreign Affairs, promoter of Anglo-Persian Agreement (1919); raised oil question during Armitage-Smith's mission (1920); imprisoned after 1921 coup, elected deputy to Fourth *Majlis* (1922); again Minister of Justice (1925); Minister of Finance, assisted Taymourtash during oil negotiations (1927-9); dismissed, imprisoned, brought to trial and set free again (1929-31); under house arrest until incarcerated anew (1936), exiled to Simnan (1937); murdered in Simnan (January 10, 1938).

Beside Taymourtash and Nusrat ul-Douleh, Jâfar Quli Khan Sardar Asâd* also had a brilliant career under Reza Shah. A second generation Elitist and the leading Bakhtiari *khan* in the new regime, Sardar Asâd lasted for seven years as Minister for War. He constantly restrained other Bakhtiari *khans* from fomenting uprisings. After the incident of summer 1922, they behaved docilely – with the exception of the Amir Mujahid disruption in support of Shaykh Khazâl in 1924 (easily muzzled) and the summer 1929 diversion at Sifid Dasht. But the fate of Firouz in 1929 and the arrest of Taymurtash in 1932 were ominous signs that the winds were not favourable to the War Minister. The latter, careless, intervened in favour of the imprisoned Taymourtash, thus showing himself to be a reliable friend but a poor politician. He never thought his own disgrace possible: his old friend Reza-Maxim wouldn't do that to him!

But the Shah did, for he believed that the *khans* planned to "bring back Muhammad Hasan Mirza [Qajar] and were passing arms through the Bakhtiari territory".[18] Reza Shah also ordered the arrest of another nineteen lesser Bakhtiari and Qashqa'i *khans*, four of whom were executed by a firing squad at the Qasr Prison and the rest given heavy prison sentences.[19] Sardar Asâd had finally been the victim of his own credulity; the Bakhtiaris in general and their *khans* in particular were also indirect victims of Asâd's misplaced blind faith in Reza Shah.

* JÂFAR QULI KHAN SARDAR ASÂD (1879–1933), eldest son of Hajj Âli Quli Khan Sardar Asâd; took part in the march on Tehran under his father's command (1909); commander of Constitutionalist troops during their first campaigns (1909–12); governor-general of Kerman (1919) and Khurasan (1922); Minister for Post and Telegraph (1924–5); Minister for War (1927–33); arrested in Babul at the annual horse races (November 1933); imprisoned in Tehran, murdered in his cell (no. 28) like Taymourtash, allegedly by Dr Ahmadi (March 29, 1934).

Another exceptional individual to serve under Reza Shah was Âli Akbar Davar.* Having earlier distinguished himself as a lawyer, a journalist, a party leader and a *Majlis* deputy, Davar embarked in 1927 on a successful career as a high civil servant. For ten years, first at Justice then at Finance, he worked hard (sixteen-hour days) to place both ministries on new tracks. He succeeded in both cases: first revolutionising the Persian justice system, imposing a new structure based on the French legal system, then rearranging the Finance ministries.

"Probably the ablest administrator among the Persians", Dr Millspaugh wrote of him.[20] Undoubtedly one of the founding fathers of the modern Iranian bureaucracy, Davar left his imprint on the next generation of high civil servants. Taking their first bureaucratic steps under him were: Allahyar Salih, Âbbas Quli Gulshayan, Muhammad Surouri, Dr Muhammad Sajjadi, Ibrahim Zandand Âbd ul-Husayn Hazhir. The likes of Âli Vakili and Âbdul-Husayn Nikpour began their careers in state corporations set up by Davar before switching to private businesses and becoming multi-millionaires. Davar became the new symbol for civil servants and intellectuals, somehow repolishing the images of these two groups in the public's mind.

* ÂLI AKBAR DAVAR (1888-1937), primary studies at Dar ul-Funoun; became a lawyer, appointed prosecutor (1911); continued law studies in Switzerland (1918-21); deputy (from Varamin) in Fourth *Majlis* (1922); established the *Radikal* Party and published newspaper *Mard-i Azad* (The Free Man); Minister of Public Works (1925); Minister of Justice (1927-33); Minister of Finance (1933-37); committed suicide by swallowing opium (February 9, 1937).

Finally, two veteran Elitists also served under Reza Shah as prime ministers. The oldest was Mihdi Quli Khan Mukhbir ul-Saltaneh (Hidayat).* Educated in Germany, Hidayat could well have further exacerbated his master's Germanophile tendencies. A scholar and an experienced administrator, Hidayat had the exact qualities Reza Shah was looking for: patience and political skills. Being very religious, Hidayat had, in 1928, warned the Shah about anti-religious elements at court and in government circles; it seems that on this point he was not very successful in view of subsequent events. After retiring from active civil service, he would enjoy over two decades of retirement.

* MIHDI QULI KHAN MUKHBIR UL-SALTANEH HIDAYAT (1864-1955), son of Âli Quli Khan Mukhbir ul-Douleh; studied in Germany (1878-80); made his mark during Constitutional Movement as Minister of Science (1906); thereafter sixteen ministerships; three times governor-general, Azarbayjan (twice) and Fars (1906-1927); Reza Shah's longest serving prime minister (July 1927-September 1933); among directors of non-governing Elite (1934-50); wrote memoirs and other historical books; died in September 1955.

The second older Elitist to work under Reza Shah was Muhammad Âli Khan Zuka' ul-Mulk (Furoughi).* A very gifted intellectual, he was rapidly co-opted into Elite ranks: the only exception to the rule. Discovered during the Constitutional Movement, he served almost continuously from 1906 until 1941 (save for a 1935-41 hiatus). A great scholar, he would be plagued at the end of his life by heart problems; the events of 1941 were to take their toll and finally his life.

* MUHAMMAD ÂLI KHAN ZUKA' UL-MULK FUROUGHI (1877–1942); grandson of an Isfahan *bazaari*, son of educator Mirza Muhammad Husayn Khan; studied Persian Literature and French at Dar ul-Funoun (1895–99); translated French bestsellers and taught French to Elite youngsters; upon his father's death, inherited title of Zuka' ul-Mulk (1908); deputy and president of Second *Majlis* (1910); Minister of Finance (1911); Minister of Justice (1912); head of Supreme Court (1913); many other ministries, including Justice (1917–8), Foreign Affairs (1922–3), Finance (1924–5) and War (1926–8); three times prime minister: in 1925-6, in 1933–5 and 1941–2 (thus Reza Shah's first and last premier); died of heart attack (autumn 1942), leaving behind Elite positions for his three sons.

To manage such a diverse group of individuals was no easy task. Only a man with Reza Shah's leadership qualities and self-confidence could have achieved such a feat. In a way he had to, because, being an analphabet himself, he needed capable administrators to realise the immense task he had set himself: to build a modern Iran.

7.3. The Golden Era

The nation's *forces vives* expected Reza Shah to make concrete all the seminal ideas formulated since the days of the Constitutional Movement: it was his *raison d'être*. And, as Reza Shah was a born achiever, he would channel all his formidable energy and the nation's untapped potential into this gigantic operation of internal renewal. No institution would be left untouched, no capable man left on the sideline and no stone left unturned. Within the short span of fifteen and a half years of his rule, Reza Shah would achieve more than his supporters had expected from him and less than he had set himself to do. One way or the other, the Iran he left was not the Persia he had inherited from the Qajars; by always putting "efficiency before luxury",[21] he partly achieved his dream of a strong, centralised government, leaving behind a nation state with a rigid framework and durable institutions.

After pacifying the tribes and sanifying national finances, Reza Shah first tackled the judiciary by placing Âli Akbar Davar at Justice with a free hand to rejuvenate the moribund judicial system with his team of young bureaucrats. In 1927, the fresh structure of the Justice Ministry and different subdivisions were put in place; simultaneously the Judicial Regulations (essentially based on French laws) were issued. With such a systematic approach to the judiciary, it was possible to bring to an end in May 1928 the antiquated extra-territorial judicial agreements known as 'capitulations' (dating from the Turkomancha'i Treaty of 1828). In October 1928, a cadastral system for land ownership was introduced and the registration of properties became compulsory. Finally, in 1930, the Persian Civil Code was published (an amalgam of the Napoleonic *Code Civil* and of the Islamic *Shariâ* laws) thus bringing to a close the construction of Davar's legal system.

Reza Shah really believed that "Persia should be administrated [sic] by Persians".[22] He knew that it was possible with a strong leadership and educated manpower. As he was an analphabet himself, he gave top priority to education. Already, before his time, the Teachers' Training College and the Ministry of Justice's School of Law had been established in 1918 and 1921 respectively; he would further encourage their development. In 1928, he revolutionised educational affairs by having the *Majlis* approve a bill authorising the Ministry of Culture to annually send one hundred of the best students abroad for graduate studies, at government expense; the first contingent being dispatched the very same year. As other ministries had also begun sending students abroad on scholarships and wealthy students went on their own, the trickle of Persian students into European universities had turned into a torrent. By the close of 1934, the Educational Act calling for the creation of a university was ratified by the *Majlis* and, in February 1935, Tehran University, the cornerstone of Iran's higher education system was created.[23] In the wake of Tehran University, twenty Schools of Higher Education were created over the years preceding the Second World War in various provincial centres.

In parallel to education initiatives, the first steps were taken by the government in the field of public hygiene and health.

In 1922, the Pasteur Institute opened a branch in Tehran. Credits and budgets were allocated to combat widespread diseases, especially in Tehran and the three northern provinces of Gilan, Mazandaran and Gurgan where malaria and other diseases were plaguing the population. Doctors were sent north to cure the defenceless population with the necessary assistance and pharmaceuticals. Within a relatively short time progress was made and the hitherto catastrophic situation redressed.

Transportation also received special attention, as it had both strategic and economical impact. Roads, or rather *chaussées*, were built on the main lines linking the capital to the main provincial centres (i.e. Isfahan, Tabriz, Mashhad, Hamadan, Rasht). The work itself was labour-intensive, as heavy machinery was not available and of a low technological level; moreover road building created employment for thousands of unskilled labourers. The first road to be inaugurated in 1924 was the one linking Tabriz to Zanjan. Thereafter and up to 1932 some 11,400 kilometres of road were completed – subdivided into first, second and third category roads, with 1,050 km, 6,000 km and 4370 km respectively.[24] During the same time, some 4,500 trucks were imported. These new facilities had an undeniable economic importance as the cost of transport dwindled from 3.2 rials per ton/kilometre in 1926 to 1.0 rial in 1932.[25] Then, during the five years 1932–1936, yet another 3,200 kilometres of roads were built, with the Tehran–Chalous road, crossing the Alburz mountains (and its extraordinary Kandivan tunnel), inaugurated in 1935. Besides the roads, ports and shipping were also being developed: on the Persian Gulf, the ports of Bushire and Bandar Shahpur and on the Caspian those of Bandar Anzali and Bandar Shah. Air transport made its debut in 1928 when the German company of Junkers came to link Tehran with European and domestic centres.

In the field of transportation, though, a master project eclipsed all other achievements: the construction of the Trans-Persian Railway (TPR), stretching some 1,394 kilometres from the southern port of Bandar-i Shahpur to the northern one of Bandar-i Shah – the line north of Tehran covering 461 kilometres. The TPR's completion took a total of eleven years: from September 1927 until August 1938.[26] An American engineering commission, under M. Poland, finalised the railway's design. A number of international contractors were at first awarded trial sections; these contractors included Ulen and Co. (New York), Julius Berger (Berlin), Stewart and McDonnell (London) and Société Batignolles (Paris).[26A] From 1932 onwards a Scandinavian group of Swedish and Danish companies, the Kampsax consortium, were involved in its finish. The main contractors were Italian, with more than a thousand Italian workmen imported, mainly for tunnelling and masonry. At its peak, "20,000 Iranian labourers were employed in the southern section and 10,000 on the northern". The mammoth undertaking necessitated the construction of 224 tunnels (with a total length of 83.7 kilometres) and the building of no fewer than 4,109 bridges. Total project costs had amounted to 2,195,180,700 rials and £3,587,448 – which added up to a total of roughly £31m. Approximately two-thirds of the rial portion (or exactly 1,395,961,654 rials) had come from the sugar and tea taxes[27] – or around 107 rials per capita (assuming an average population of 13 million Persians over the project's life). The railway dream of the Persian people had become a reality. Many had argued for a west–east line, but Reza Shah had decided on a south–north direction: it linked his cherished Mazandaran with the whole country and the warm waters of the Persian Gulf. The TPR was also inaugurated in August 1938, ready just in time to allow the transport through Persia of millions of tonnes of Allied material to the Soviet Union during the Second World War. Coincidence or prescience?

The rapid development of transportation, added to the element of security, gave a fresh impetus to trade and commerce. The introduction of new customs tariffs in 1928 further encouraged Persian trade. Persia's exports (exclusive of petroleum products) came to exceed its imports in 1931 for the first time in decades: with exports of Rls810m against imports of Rls741m.[28] In the same year, the national budget stood balanced (as it had been since 1928) at the Rls321m level.[29] It must be mentioned that from 1929 onwards the revenues derived from petroleum sales had been shifted to a special national reserve, set aside for the purchase of strategic armaments. The development and regulation of commerce and industry were further enhanced by a series of laws promulgated between 1928 and 1936, which included:
 – the 1928 Opium Monopoly Law;
 – the 1929 Tobacco Monopoly Law;
 – the 1930 Foreign Exchange Regulating Law; partly a consequence of the worldwide recession and the subsequent silver crash, the price of silver falling at the London Metal Exchange from 26.8 pence per ounce in 1928 to 14.6 pence per ounce in 1931). The

rial officially replaced the outdated kran. A new gold standard based on 0.3661191 grams of gold per rial was introduced. This standard was replaced in 1932 (after Great Britain had dropped its pound-to-gold parity) by a new standard of 0.07322382 grams of gold per rial. The one Pahlavi gold coin was launched with a weight of 7.322382 grams (equivalent to one hundred gold rials).

- the 1931 Companies' Registration Law;
- the 1931 Patents and Trademarks Law;
- the 1932 Persian Commercial Code;
- the 1932 Foreign Trade Monopoly; which would lead to the creation in 1934/5 of a spate of governmental companies for the state monopolies on carpets, cotton, silk, etc., in addition to the existing opium and tobacco companies.
- the 1933 Income Tax Law;
- the 1936 New Customs Tariffs (for the protection of local manufacturers).

In the domain of banking, another of the *Bazaar*'s dreams materialised when the monopoly of the IBP and the Soviet Banque d'Escompte (renamed the Russo-Persian Bank in 1923) was finally broken by the creation of the Bank-i Sipah in 1925. In May 1927, a bill calling for the establishment of a national bank was ratified and the Bank-i Milli-i Iran, with an initial capital of Rls150m, began operating in October 1928 as a commercial bank with German management (Dr Kurt Lindenblatt becoming its first manager). Two years later, Bank-i Milli became Persia's central bank as well when it paid IBP a sum of £200,000 for purchasing its right to print banknotes.[30] Two other public banks were founded in the 1930s: the *Bank-i Taâvun-i Kishavarzi-i Iran* (Agricultural Co-operative Bank of Iran) and the *Bank-i Rahni-i Iran* (Mortgage Bank of Iran), in 1933 and 1938 respectively. Alongside banking, insurance also opened up in Persia: first, branches of the Soviet Nedefa and Dafla Mercury insurance firms were launched and then the British Yorkshire (1929) and the Soviet Ingostrak made their entry into the Persian market. Finally, in 1935, a national insurance company, the *Bimeh Iran*, was established with an initial capital of Rls20m.

Large-scale introduction of industrial units was yet another feature of Reza Shah's modernisation programme.[30A]

After the fruitless efforts of Sanî ul-Douleh at the turn of the century to set up small industries and the German fiasco at Qazvin with the first textile mill (1908), industrial development was at a standstill over the 1910s and 1920s – with the exception of the APOC (capital estimated at around £20m in 1930) and of the Lianozov Caspian Fisheries (capital of roughly £2m).[31] To realise his ambition of diversifying into manufacturing, Reza Shah ordered in 1930 the creation of a general Industrialisation Administration as a new department within the Ministry of Public Works. Five years later, the new department had outgrown its mother and turned into a ministry of its own: the Ministry of Fine Arts and Industry. The three major industrial sectors of sugar, cement and textiles were given top priority – being import-substitution industries for which the main raw materials were available internally. For these and other sectors, projects were chosen by Persian technocrats and the execution – from technology and design to construction and start-up – was contracted to foreign companies. German and British firms got the lion's share; with the French, Americans, Czech (Skoda), Soviets and Danish (Kampsax) firms getting the rest. A summarised picture of the major industrial sectors and factories established in the 1920s and 1930s is outlined hereunder:

* The Sugar Industry

Utilising local beetroot, the first sugar refinery, with a capacity of 800 tonnes per annum, had been implemented at Kahrizak (south of Tehran) in the closing years of the nineteenth century but production was soon discontinued; in 1931, after a rehabilitation programme, it resumed operation.

Then, within the five-year time span 1932–6, the Czech Skoda firm built a total of nine sugar factories with capacities varying between 5 and 20,000 tonnes per annum at different locations. Consequently domestic sugar production rose from 1,000 tonnes in 1931 to around 35,000 tonnes at the onset of the Second World War. Domestic sugar consumption also rose accordingly, from 48,000 tonnes in 1932 to over 120,000 tonnes in 1940.

* The Cement Industry

The first cement factory (capacity of 100 tonnes per day[32]) was built in 1933 at Ray (south Tehran) by a Danish company. Four years later, a German company completed a 200 tonnes/day expansion at the same site. The output of the two units covered a large portion of domestic consumption.

* The Textiles Industry

The traditional silk industry of Gilan and Mazandaran was rejuvenated with the implementation by the French of two industrial workshops: a silk-reeling factory at Rasht and a silk-weaving unit at Chalous. Also in the northern provinces, some cotton gins (capacity of 5 to 10 tonnes/day) were added to the existing ones, mainly using American and Soviet equipment. Cotton spinning and weaving factories were established at Shahi (1929) (in addition to a bagging factory) and Bihshahr (1932). Meanwhile the wool industry chose Isfahan as its capital: Hajj Muhammad Husayn Kazirouni, a wealthy *bazaar* merchant, bought a complete textile factory (of British origin) from his friend and rival Âta ul-Mulk Dihish, who had gone bankrupt.[32A] In 1926, Kazirouni's *Vatan* factory began operations and was initially faced with poor sales. Reza Shah's timely directives to the army and the Ministry of Education to buy *Vatan* fabric solved all of Kazirouni's problems and made him the richest man in Isfahan, and one of the richest in Iran. The success of *Vatan* spurred further developments in textiles and the two large factories of *Risbaf* and *Zahyandehroud* joined *Vatan* in 1934 and 1935.[33] In Tehran, the *Chit Sazi* factory was implemented at Ray and proved highly profitable. By the close of the 1930s, Iran's textiles industry was among the country's leading new industrial sectors – both in terms of revenues and number of employees. The cotton factories produced annually some 20m metres of cloth and 870 tonnes of yarn, and the wool factories 1.6m metres of cloth and 220,000 blankets.[34]

* The Food Processing Industry

Among the first processing units introduced in the northern provinces were the rice milling factories. Tea processing units with a capacity of 5 to 10,000 tonnes per annum were also brought to Gilan.[34A] In Shahi a large food processing complex for the production of canned food was set up to furnish the army's requirements of canned rations and jams. A 2,000 tonnes per annum tuna fish factory was started up in 1939 at Bandar Âbbas. A vegetable oil factory was acquired from France in the same year, but, due to the outbreak of war, its equipment never made it to its site at Varamin (it would be completed and brought into operation after the war).

* The Glass Industry

The Qazvin plant of the *Shirkat-i Shisheh-yi Iran* was put into operation in 1939. It had a capacity of 60 tonnes/day and consisted of one furnace and three production lines, based on the Fourcault process. The plant was closed down in 1941 (for lack of spares) and restarted only in 1954.

* The Chemical Industry

A small chemical unit for the production of hydrochloric acid was organised at Ray, and nearby a glycerine and soap factory, created with German technology, opened in 1940.

* Miscellaneous Industries

Small units for the local production of crystal, leather, cardboard and matches (at Tabriz, with Swedish technology, since 1922) were created. At Shimshak there was coal mining. At Aminabad, some eight kilometres south-east of Tehran, Sanî ul-Douleh's small complex was refurbished and the Germans added a copper refinery (of 380 tonnes/annum) in 1939. Seven large grain silos were constructed by a German contractor, with the largest one at Ray (Tehran) and the six others in major provincial centres. Iran's first cigarette producing unit, with a capacity of 12.5m cigarettes, was put into operation in September 1937.

* The Steel Mill

Reza Shah's wish for a modern steel mill (another Persian dream) almost crystallised when in 1938 Iran signed an agreement with Krupp of Germany for the implementation of a project including two blast furnaces (150 tonnes/day each), a foundry, a wrought iron works, a coke crusher, a rolling mill, a wire-drawing mill, a lime plant, an ammonia and benzene plant, a tar distillation unit and all the necessary utilities.[35] Total investment was estimated by Krupp at Rls13m, with a workforce of 1,200 people.[35A] The site of the plant was chosen to be Karaj. The first provisional buildings were erected on site while the designs and engineering were being finalised. Reza Shah laid the first stone himself in 1939. The Second World War, however, would come to foil the completion of Iran's first steel mill.

The 'forced' industrialisation of Persia, carried out at a breakneck pace under Reza Shah's iron grip, was the urban middle classes' revenge over the Elite's former stagnation.

They held that industrialisation brought modernism and that, in turn, modernism necessarily brought progress and progress brought with it (Western) civilisation. Iran would be "proud of itself" and looking forward; in contrast to the old Persia which had been looking backward. Through their champion Reza Shah, they had achieved something: the TPR, the roads, the army, the modern industries. Thus they were able to take Iran to new heights so that it could regain its lost lustre and its rightful place in the concert of nations. Their only problem was that Pahlavi's achievements were but a veneer spread thin over the old entity and this veneer would readily crack or peel under pressure or heat: it had no roots in the country and its people.

According to analyst W. Floor, Reza Shah's industrial programme had indeed been "a big leap forward", which had cost the country some "$260m over the period 1930-1941 ...the burden of the price to be borne by the mass of the population".[36] And here was the catch: the people had indirectly paid for it, but did not "share [in] the benefits of development". Only a few of them (a small minority) were hired to man the factories: "in 1940, employment in selected urban economic activities accounted for 260,100 people",[37] mainly concentrated in the three centres of Tehran, Isfahan and Tabriz. The whole industry came from abroad: the technology, the equipment, the constructors and the spares. The only Iranians involved were either Reza Shah's technocrats or private capitalists. In the end, everything belonged to the government, and even the private firms somehow came to depend on government goodwill (e.g. the public rescue of the largest private factory in Iran, Kazirouni's *Vatan*).

During Reza Shah's era electricity came in a big way to Persia. After the small private generators of Hajj Husayn Amin ul-Zarb of 400 KW (AEG), in 1903, came the Anglo-Belgian diesel generators from 1923 onwards.[37A] The first municipal powerhouse began operation in 1937 in Tehran – four Skoda generators of 1500 KW each. By 1941, there were some 17,368 electricity subscribers in Tehran.

Cinemas and theatres also became major Tehran attractions as the urban middle classes found time for leisure.

After the pioneering efforts of Ibrahim Mirza Âkasbashi, who brought back the first cinématographe from France in August 1900 (he had been among Muzaffar ul-Din Shah's retinue), Mirza Ibrahim Sahafbashi was to show the first short films in 1904.

Thereafter, Russi Khan Aghayov's teahouse (1907), Ardashis Badmagirian's first cinema-house (1912)[37B] and George Smailov's cinema (1913) launched the film industry in Persia.

Solid and functional buildings were also added to the capital's skyline, especially the new ministries of Justice, of Finance and the masterpiece of Foreign Affairs: a Reza Shah style was born, massive and square, and very German *à la Bauhaus*. The Shah also built a couple of new palaces (*Saâdabad* and especially the Marble (*Marmar*) Palace); and commissioned the Frenchman Andre Godard, in 1928, to design the buildings of the *Kitabkhaneh-yi Milli* (National Library), inaugurated in 1937, and the *Iran Bastan* museum, completed in 1939.

Within the urban middle classes, among the winners of "Reza Shah's leap" stood the *Bazaar* merchants. Security, legal regulations, discipline, increased trade, banking and insurance facilities and the industrial development were all grist to their mills. For the first time in many decades, the wind was blowing for them: they might have been robbed of their democratic dreams during the Constitutional Movement and of their *Majlis* after 1913, but with Reza Shah they had taken their revenge over the selfish Elite and the unruly tribes. They had made a tacit (and temporary) alliance with the intelligentsia to support Reza Shah, leaving their perennial allies, the clergymen, in the cold.

The fifteen years of Reza Shah's reign were a boon for Iran's merchants and traders. They had the time to develop their neural centre at the Tehran *Bazaar*; to consolidate their northern and southern centres at Tabriz and Isfahan; to reinforce the arteries linking these three major *Bazaars* to the fifty or so provincial *bazaars*; to accumulate profits like never before; to fill their stores and coffers for the days of penury (the famous *Rouz-i Mabada*) and to take a much larger share of the national assets. After all, it was their right because: (i) their *Bazaars* were the economic heart of society; (ii) their network functioned better than any other national institution (inclusive of the army); and (iii) they were, as Sir Percy Sykes had noted, "the most trustworthy in Persia".[38]

As the *Bazaar* merchants got richer, they were faced with a dilemma. This new industrial world which was part of the Reza Shah package was alien to them; but they couldn't reject it without rejecting the whole. Used as they were to traditional crafts (coppersmiths, silversmiths, shoemakers and so on) in traditional *bazaar* workshops, the merchants were loath to invest their extra profits in the new factories. Nevertheless, the attraction of exorbitant profits proved stronger than *bazaari* solidarity and many were enticed to buy shares in the new industries. With time, a split was inevitable between the *Bazaar*'s 'traditionalists' and 'modernists' – for it was to prove extremely difficult to play both sides without getting fingers burned. The Reza Shah era seemed to favour the latter group, but Persia's history of unpredictable (and cyclical) ups and downs seemed to be on the side of the former group. The dilemma, however, would not go away: the *Bazaar* hands would have to live with it and choose their side: either or...

7.4. APOC's Apogee

The February 1921 *coup d'état* had the effect of throwing the oil question into virtual oblivion. The controversy over the share of APOC's profits due to the Persian Government were left in abeyance for some years. APOC and its subsidiary companies were doing very well indeed and Sir Winston Churchill could write about Persian oil:

> Fortune brought us a price from fairyland far beyond our expectations...[39]

Within a few years, the British Government's share in APOC had increased in value by more than 1,000 per cent and the total it received annually in dividends and income taxes from APOC amounted to over £14m (inclusive of savings on the Royal Navy's fuel).[40] Other APOC shareholders must have been greatly satisfied with their substantial dividends: a justified reward for their timely investment. As for the Persians, on whom these facts had not been lost, they were receiving during the 1920s an annual income fluctuating between £500,000 and £1,400,000. It was only a matter of time before the Persian grievances voiced in 1919-20 would be tabled again.

The time came in 1927, as the oil question re-emerged on the Persian agenda. Reza Shah needed fresh funds to finance his extensive programmes – i.e. the Trans-Persian Railway, the army's armaments and industrialisation. That he cared about the oil question was shown by the fact that he placed Persia's top administrator, Taymourtash, in charge of it; Nusrat ul-Douleh Firouz aiding the Court Minister in his labours. On the British side was Sir John Cadman (later Lord), the fresh APOC chairman who had replaced Lord Greenway in the chair in 1927. Cadman, a former professor of petroleum science at the University of Birmingham, a technical man involved in oil questions since the late 1890s and with Persia since 1913, was the right man at the right time to confront Persia's oil problems.

As serious negotiations began in 1928 in London, it became clear to APOC that the Persians' main grievances were:

(1) The perennial question of APOC's bookkeeping and accounting practices, which seemed detrimental to Persia's revenues.[41] Sir William McLintock, still retained by the Persian Government as its official oil accountant, had hinted in his report of 1920 at the unorthodox cross-sales of crude between APOC, the First Exploration Co. and the Bakhtiari Oil Co., which had the effect of diminishing Persian profits.[42]

(2) The legal status, as far as Persia's revenues were concerned, of APOC's subsidiary companies created abroad (e.g. the British Tanker Company, created in 1915 as a fully-owned subsidiary; and also British Petroleum, Petroleum Steamship, Homelight Oil), over which the Persian Government had no control whatsoever.

(3) The Persian Government's share of APOC's various accounting reserves (i.e. legal reserve, general reserve), which was never clarified.

(4) The settling of the sterling–silver and sterling–gold exchange rates mechanism in a way not detrimental to Persia.

But Cadman was both "intolerant of suggestion and unyielding in negotiation"[43] and didn't concede his points to Taymourtash. At the summit of his career, the APOC chairman, who had just wound up the

'As Is' agreement at Acnacarry Castle with H. Deterding of Royal Dutch Shell and W.C. Teagle of Standard Oil of New Jersey in July 1928,[44] was not to be pushed by Persian negotiators. He had already shown his unwillingness to accept being outsmarted by the Persians, for, when the Bakhtiari *khans* had tried to peddle their Bakhtiari Oil Company shares (given to them free, just to assure them a rent) on the London stock market, he had ordered the company to be merged with the First Exploration Company in November 1925.[45]

In 1929, Cadman visited Persia and had an interview with the Shah. It came to no conclusion; neither did the further rounds of APOC-Persian negotiations. Things came to a head in 1932, as APOC announced that Persia's revenues amounted to only £307,000 due to poor market conditions – against a record £1,437,000 in 1929 and £1,288,000 in 1930. With £1m less than expected, the blow was severe for Persian finances. On November 27, 1932, at a meeting of the cabinet chaired by the Shah, the D'Arcy Concession was unilaterally annulled. A few days later, as the British Government brought its case to the Council of the League of Nations, Taymourtash was consigned to his house. In January 1933, the Council held hearings for the British complaint: Sir John Simon, the British Secretary for Foreign Affairs, presented his government's case, and Âli Akbar Davar, the Persian Minister of Justice, replied for Persia. Davar had been told not to attack the British Government,[46] thereby hampering his defence. The result was that, although "the British argument was arrogant and unconvincing, the Persian rebuttal was weak, evasive and ineffective".[47] In the end the Council asked the two parties to renew bilateral negotiations in order to reach a settlement of their dispute.

The two sides were back to square one, without the D'Arcy Concession as a safety net. A new agreement had to be reached. On April 3, 1933 Sir John Cadman debarked in Tehran to enter the final round of negotiations before any reference to arbitration. He was assisted in this task by W. Frazer (an APOC director), Dr Young (in Persia since the days of G.B. Reynolds), Dr Idelson, Lefroy and Allen. On the Persian side were Â.A. Davar, H. Taqizadeh (Minister of Finance), M.Â. Furoughi (Minister of Foreign Affairs) and the American adviser Frederick G. Clapp.

On May 1st, 1933, Cadman departed Tehran for Baghdad, taking with him the freshly signed agreement (April 29) between the Persian

Government and APOC. For Cadman it was a resounding victory, and, for APOC, the apogee. The 1933 Agreement was the final result of a series of meetings between Cadman and Reza Shah between April 24 and 27. The Shah had asked for a minimum annual income of £2,700,000[48] – he got a meagre £750,000. Cadman had bargained for a seventy-five-year concession before settling for sixty years: he got it. Now, instead of D'Arcy's *terminus ad quem* of 1961, the fresh deadline stood at December 31, 1993. Cadman had even been willing at the last minute to go down to fifty-five years, to which the Shah had replied: "Today I have said that I cannot grant the sixty years, and I have made it clear that I can go no further. Does Sir John wish to bargain with me?"[49] But in the end, as Taqizadeh said, "the Shah allowed himself to be persuaded".[50] To which a British official later added: "The Shah, and only the Shah, made the agreement possible".[51] Moreover, Cadman was able to insert the highly controversial Article 21 in the agreement, which read: "The Concession shall not be annulled by the [Persian] Government and the terms therein contained shall not be altered either by general or special legislation in the future, or by administrative measures or any acts whatever of the executive authorities". On the other hand, the Persians obtained: (1) a reduction of the concession area from its original 480,000 square miles to 100,000 (to be chosen by APOC south of the so-called 'Violet Line'[52]); (2) a payment per ton (later defined as a metric tonne not a long ton) instead of the sixteen per cent of net profits (albeit at the low price of four shillings per ton); (3) a programme of 'Persianisation' of the company's workforce (formulated in 1936 in Davar's General Plan, but barely implemented due to the outbreak of the World War); (4) the development by APOC, through a subsidiary, of the Naft-i Shah oil field discovered in 1923, on the Turkish border west of Kermanshah.

If the 1933 Agreement had been a victory for Cadman, it had been a reverse for the Shah. The agreement must have been a bitter pill to swallow for Reza Shah, also at his apogee. The Shah of Persia must have had an Achilles' heel, some kind of debt incurred to the British (and known to Cadman) in the course of his meteoric ascension to the throne. From 1933 on, his relations with the British would continuously deteriorate, never lapsing back to the sunny Loraine days. Distancing himself from the British, he would turn to the Germans, with whom he found many affinities. Furthermore, the

1933 Agreement was not a satisfactory settlement of the oil problem for the Persian side. The major grievances had been shifted, not resolved; but as long as Reza Shah ruled no further alteration to the *status quo* was to be expected. The side-stepped problems would inevitably resurface at a later date.

While negotiating with the Persians, Sir John Cadman had to deal with the far more ominous threat posed by American oil interests in the Middle East and Persia. At the end of the war, the US had come out of its isolation and taken a global view. Although it still looked at the Middle East as essentially a British sphere of influence, it had "reacted violently to the 1919 Anglo-Persian treaty [,] denouncing it as a virtual annexation of Persia".[53] Its oil companies had reacted as violently to the 1920 sell-out of Khoshtaria to the APOC and the creation of the North Persian Oil Co., Ltd., to work the northern Persian provinces. The US Government contended that the APOC-Khoshtaria deal "paved the way for a monopoly of APOC in Persia",[54] and proposed the participation of Standard Oil (New Jersey) in this venture. Cadman went to America in 1920–21, as petroleum adviser to the British Government, to try to "dissipate some of the ill-feel[ing] ...that had long bedevilled Anglo-American [oil] relations".[55] The tangible result of Cadman's trip was an "open door policy in the Middle East" that landed Standard Oil a half interest in the Khoshtaria concession (for a £187,000 investment).[56] In addition, an American consortium, made up of five oil companies led by Standard Oil, was given a twenty per cent (later increased to 23.75%) interest in the Turkish Petroleum Company in 1922. These inroads in the Middle East didn't change the fact that "American oil interests in the Middle East looked with active jealousy on their British rivals".[57] Washington reminded London "that America had helped to win the war and was entitled to a share of the spoils";[58] simultaneously it told its own oil companies "to go out and get it".

The first US oil company to "go out" and push open the Persian door was Standard Oil of New Jersey. It courted the Persian premier, Qavam ul-Saltaneh, and obtained on November 21, 1921, a fifty-year oil concession covering the five Persian northern provinces – thus effectively displacing the Khoshtaria concession. The Fourth *Majlis* duly ratified the Standard Oil agreement contingent upon (i) a US $10m loan to Persia (the oil company even made "an advance payment of $1m in March 1922"[58A]); (ii) ten per cent of any oil produced to be the Persian Government's take; (iii) the transfer of any share in the concession to an outsider to be approved by the *Majlis*. Cadman, now adviser to APOC, convinced Standard Oil to let APOC have half of its northern concession: a 50/50 joint venture known as the Perso-American Oil Company was thus created. The *Majlis*'s 'no outsider' clause was violated and the assembly consistently refused to recognise the new venture. Thus the first US attempt to share in Persian oil folded on this note.

After Standard Oil's exit, the Sinclair Consolidated Oil Company entered the Persian fray. In November 1922, the *Majlis* approved of negotiations with Sinclair for a northern concession. The talks resulted in a fifty-year oil concession to Sinclair covering four of Persia's northern provinces (excluding Gilan so as not to displease the Soviets). The Sinclair Concession was approved in March 1924 by the *Majlis* with the conditions that: (i) twenty to twenty-eight per cent (depending on circumstances) of the profits accrued to the Persian Government; (ii) one fifth of the directors be Persian nationals; (iii) 85% of the concession area would be relinquished within eight years; (iv) a $10m loan was granted to Persia.

As the Sinclair experts were beginning their exploration in the Gurgan province, Major Robert Whitney Imbrie, the American vice-consul in Tehran, was murdered by a mob on July 18, 1924 in downtown Tehran. The vice-consul's imprudence in attempting to take pictures of the Aqa Shaykh Hadi *saqqakhaneh* (worshipping shrine) on a Friday morning was at the heart of the tragedy. A large mob of worshippers attacked his coach and badly wounded both Imbrie and his colleague Seymour before the coach made it to the nearest hospital. But the mob could not be calmed, and elements followed Imbrie all the way to his hospital room. Historian Mustoufi suggested that there was a marked difference between the worshippers objecting to Imbrie's photographing at the *saqqakhaneh* and the few "professional thugs" who followed him to his hospital room;[59] author D. Davoudi advanced the thesis of a conspiracy hostile to the Sinclair company as an explanation of the unusual tragedy.[60] Martial law was declared in Tehran. Six of Imbrie's assailants were arrested and tried and three of them were sentenced to death and executed. Ten days after Imbrie's tragic death, S. Sopor, Sinclair's representative in Tehran, folded the company's operations and precipitately departed

Persia. Thus ended the second US attempt at securing a share in Persian oil.

The third American attempt would come from the Amiranian Oil Co., a subsidiary of the Seabord Oil Company of Delaware. With a capital of $5,050,033 and Charles C. Hart as president and Frederick G. Clapp as vice-president, Amiranian seemed well equipped to make a breakthrough. The concession it sought covered some 200,000 square miles of the Khurasan and Sistan provinces. Conditions were roughly similar to those of the Sinclair Concession. A complementary concession was negotiated with another Seabord subsidiary, the Iranian Pipeline Company, for the laying of a pipeline from the proposed Amiranian oil fields to the Persian Gulf coast. Â.A. Davar led the Persian delegation during the six months of secret negotiations with Amiranian; he signed the agreements on January 3, 1937, and presented the twin bills to the *Majlis*, which readily ratified them on February 4 and 7. On the evening of February 9, Davar allegedly committed suicide by swallowing opium. Yet another death after a major oil concession – the suicide thesis was not universally accepted and doubt was rife in Tehran. "Davar's death is still shrouded in mystery", noted historian H. Makki.[61] After some preliminary work in Khurasan, Amiranian officials informed the authorities that, due to uncertain world conditions and unfavourable economics, it had to relinquish its concession.[62] Thus ended prematurely the third American venture in Persian oil.

During the rule of Reza Shah Pahlavi, two other foreign companies tried their hand at obtaining oil concessions in Persia. The first was the Société Franco-Persane de Récherches S.A., a joint venture formed in 1930, with a capital of 10m Ffrancs, among the Persian Government, Khoshtaria and the French Purfina Company[63] to work the Kavir-i Khuryan concession, initially granted in 1880,[64] in the Simnan Desert. French experts drilled a couple of exploratory wells before departing the site in 1932. The concession reverted then to the Soviet partners. The second foreign concession went to the Dutch Algemeene Exploratie Maatshappij N.V., an affiliate of Royal Dutch Shell.[65] The salient point of this last concession, granted in April 1939 for an area of Azarbayjan, was the 50/50 split of the venture's profits between the Dutch company and the Persian Government. The Second World War came to thwart this venture, which, if successful in finding oil, would have had an enormous impact on the whole Middle East. This Dutch concession was later cancelled in 1944.[66]

In short, at the outbreak of the Second World War, APOC was still the only outfit producing petroleum in Iran.

In the late 1920s and the 1930s, under the expert hand of Sir John Cadman, APOC chairman from 1927 until his death in 1941, the Anglo-Persian prospered in all fields. Oil production in Persia had gone from 45,000 b/d in 1921 to 109,000 b/d in 1927 and a pre-war record of 215,000 b/d in 1938.[67] The refining capacity of Abadan Refinery had increased by leaps and bounds from around 40,000 b/d in 1921 to over 200,000 b/d in 1939. APOC's profits had doubled from £4m in 1921 to £7.5m in 1937; payments to the Persian Government showed a much steeper rise with £585,000 in 1921 to £3,545,000 in 1937.[68] Intensive exploration for new fields in the Zagros mountains by the D'Arcy Exploration Company yielded fresh discoveries: the oil fields of Haft Kel (1927), Aqa Jari (1936), Gachsaran (1937) and Naft-i Sifid (1938), along with the gas field at Pazanan (1937). Aqa Jari and Gachsaran later proved to be super giant fields, with oil reserves of billions of barrels of oil.

In parallel with increased activities, the number of employees had considerably increased, both at Abadan and in the fields. In 1940 total manpower stood at 18,347 people at the refinery (of whom around one thousand were foreigners) and 26,123 people in the oil fields,[69] making a grand total of 44,470 people, with roughly 95% of them Iranian nationals. AIOC's management in Iran had difficulties controlling this huge personnel mass (more numerous than all other industries in the country). Workers' strikes were inevitable. The first occurred in 1922 over a demand for a 100% wages' increase, with the management granting 75% after firing hundreds of labourers; the second major strike took place in May 1929 (in the teeth of Pahlavi repression) with the five ringleaders imprisoned in Tehran (until 1941) and two hundred other strikers jailed at Khurramshahr.[70] Notwithstanding these minor hitches, AIOC reigned supreme in Khuzistan and in South Iran. From MIS down to Ahvaz, Khurramshahr and Abadan, the company's (*Idareh* or *Kumpani* in Farsi) word was law. Discipline existed like nowhere else in Iran. Living conditions of simple labourers were not good, not even adequate, but certainly better than in the rest of the country: their facilities, their food, their hygiene, their pay and their insurance was incomparably superior to any other employer in Iran (although Reza Shah's army was rapidly closing the gap). The company's workforce had two generations of experience and it was slowly beginning to realise that it belonged to a workers' elite, finding an *esprit de corps* rarely duplicated in Iran. In the 1930s the sense of pride derived from belonging to the *Kumpani* had begun to show in Abadan and the fields.

In 1936, Minister of Finance Davar had reached an agreement with APOC deputy chairman, W. Frazer, about the Iranisation programme for the company's qualified personnel, as foreseen by Article 16 of the 1933 Agreement. In letters signed on July 17 and 23, the company agreed to:

(1) The creation of a company secondary school at Abadan;

(2) The establishment of a technical school (the future Abadan Institute of Technology – AIT) at Abadan, duly inaugurated in 1938;

(3) The erection of new buildings and public accommodation by the company;

(4) The reduction of the company's non-Iranian (staff) employees from 27.5% in 1932 to 13.5% by the close of 1943; at the time of signing (July 1936), expatriate staff stood at around 2,050 people (around 17% of total staff).

The APOC was bending backwards to try to satisfy both the Iranian Government and its Iranian employees.

In 1933, in accordance with Article 9 of the fresh agreement, the APOC began implementing its plan for working the Naft-i Shah oil field. It registered a subsidiary, the Kermanshah Petroleum Company Ltd., (KPCL) in London in 1934 with an initial capital of £750,000 (in one pound shares all held by APOC). Then, KPCL drilled development wells at Naft-i Shah, and built a 3" diameter, 237 kilometre-long pipeline (the first welded pipeline in the Middle East) from Naft-i Shah to Kermanshah. It further erected a 4,500 b/d topping plant at Naft-i Shah and a 4,200 b/d refinery at Kermanshah.[71] In 1935, the KPCL was in full operation with a total personnel of approximately 1,000. The start-up of the Kermanshah operations proved timely because, due to the economic boom of the 1930s, domestic consumption of petroleum products had soared: from a lowly average of 550 b/d in 1927 to a respectable 3,300 b/d in 1937 (a six-fold increase within a decade).[72] Back in 1925, APOC had entered the domestic market displacing the Soviet 'Persazneft'; in 1928, it had opened its Tehran office and acquired its first road truck tankers (two of 1,900 litres and two of 3,600 litres each);[73] by 1937, the company had 153 tankers (105 company-owned and 48 belonging to contractors) and it ran five garages, the main one at Kermanshah and the four others respectively at Qazvin, Tehran, Mashhad and Shiraz.[74] Internal consumption of refined products was on the right tracks; a growing market would assure increased consumption.

In the meantime APOC had grown to rank among world oil's Big Three with Standard Oil and Royal Dutch Shell – albeit the smallest of the three. It controlled 23.75% of the Iraq Petroleum Company (since 1926) and 50% of the Kuwaiti concession (since 1934). It had subsidiaries in dozens of countries, a large fleet of tankers and a number of refineries beside Abadan (which towered among the largest refineries in the world). With its share capital of roughly £30m in 1939, the Anglo-Iranian Oil Company (AIOC) – Iranian had replaced Persian in 1935 – ranked amongst the largest British companies. Moreover it provided its home country's needs for refined products and the Royal Navy's fuel requirements. Entering the Second World War, AIOC knew that its role and its responsibility in the worldwide conflict would be of the highest importance: it remained for its British management and its Iranian workforce to face the challenge.

7.5. Dictatorship

"Reza Shah was by nature a dictator",[75] wrote his Prime Minister Hidayat, before adding that at a cabinet's meeting in the summer of 1929, the Shah had told his ministers: "Every nation has its own regime, ours is of the one-man type".[76] That was no idle boast – it was the crude truth, as the Shah clearly ruled and dominated Persian society. His was a true dictatorship with a single man of iron at the top, a small elite of devoted yes-men to carry out his orders and a sophisticated machine of repression to silence those who dared stand up to him.

On one important point, Reza Shah would deceive his early supporters (especially the intellectuals): he failed to do something for the Persian peasantry. In January 1926, he had begun adequately when "a uniform land tax was established throughout the country, and was to be assessed on the basis of a new cadastral survey".[77] But the survey was timidly started and soon discontinued. The 1926 decree was abrogated by a law of December 15, 1934 which decreed an income tax and a three per cent due on land revenues – with neither being put into widespread practice. Instead of initiating land reform, Reza Shah chose to become Persia's greatest landlord himself, and therefore the wealthiest individual in the realm. He created the *Amlak-i Shahanshashi* (the Crown Estates) to manage and expand his land holdings. Large and small landlords were compelled (by hook or by crook) to give, transfer or sell their villages or plots to the *Amlak*. All means were used to assure a smooth growth of the royal lands especially in Mazandaran (Reza Shah's province of preference, as he had been born there) and Gilan; tales of extortion and duress circulated in the northern provinces,[78] but to whom dared the victims complain? Soon he was the largest landowner on the Caspian seashore and also in Gurgan (around Gunbad-i Kavous), in Khurasan (Bujnurd), the central province (Varamin) and west of Kermanshah (Shahabad-i Gharb).

In his beloved northern provinces, the Shah did order the restructuring of all northern townships along a standard pattern: the creation of a large square in mid-town and the location of all major administrative buildings – the municipal bureaucracy, the local branch of the Gendarmerie, the post and telegraph centre, the Bank-i Milli branch, the civil registration office – around the square, so as to centralise the administration and facilitate bureaucratic affairs. Reza Shah had a dream project: to develop intensively the northern provinces' agriculture and transport the produce of the land to the Persian Gulf by train for export to world markets. To one of his *Amlak* managers he had lamented: "If only the Caspian seashore had an average of a hundred kilometres in width instead of its actual twenty kilometres; by God, then I could conquer the world!"[79]

If Reza Shah was by far the richest of all, his fellow Cossack officers from General Amir Ahmadi downwards were getting their fair share. Every single one of them had acquired a comfortable fortune, mostly in real estate in either Tehran itself or villages nearby. Amir Ahmadi had made his early fortune in Luristan and had built dozens of shops and a number of houses in Tehran as well as purchasing vast land holdings around Varamin; Khudayar Khan had no fewer than seventeen villages in the Shahryar-Budumak area;[80] many other Cossack generals and colonels had been given land in the southern part of Tehran, with a number of them planting orchards.

With their pay and fringe benefits, all Cossacks officers had been more than fairly rewarded by their royal master. With their newfound fortunes this elite in the making started mixing with the old Elite and intermarriages began to take place in the 1930s (when the Elite began to realise that these uncouth Cossacks were in power to stay not for years, but for decades).

The old Elite, henceforward to be known as the Qajar Elite (even though some of its members were not related) in contrast with the new Pahlavi elite, had come to terms with the fact that it was not governing any longer. A very small number of the old guard had rallied around Mudarris for a last ditch attempt against the Sardar Sipah, while the large majority had rolled with the tidal wave, knowing perfectly well that they stood little chance in direct opposition. Sir Lancelot Oliphant had "found it hard to believe that the old Princes and their supporters can tamely accept such an usurper".[81] Instead of trying to unsettle Reza Khan, the old Elite adopted a multi-pronged strategy of survival: (1) attempt to co-opt, or link matrimonially, as many Cossacks' officers as possible (as mentioned above); (2) form a non-governing, semi-visible elite of its own, based on the *doureh* (regular meetings[81A]) network systems; (3) place as many Qajar elite members as possible in the administration because these could be used to influence the system from within; (4) send a number of members into domestic exile (and out of the public's eye), for a comeback after the Pahlavi wave had passed.

Nevertheless it would be wrong to think that the Qajar elite was totally displeased with Reza Shah's policies. To three of them it whole-heartedly subscribed: (i) the establishment of law and order; (ii) the breaking of tribal power; and (iii) the assurance given to private (real estate) property. The Qajar Elite could sit back in its large estates, both in rural and urban settings, get legal titles for it through the new registration offices and at least enjoy its wealth. Reza Khan had let them save the family gold, jewels, furniture, antiques and houses and gardens. During his reign he took his share from some of the Qajar grandees, but the total sequestrated estates did not exceed two per cent of the total assets of the Qajar families. All in all, under Reza Shah, the Qajar Elite saw its fall from power largely compensated by security and real estate gains.

If the Qajar Elite should have been more than satisfied with its predicament, the intelligentsia was in heaven. Reza Shah had created a brand-new institution which was to be henceforward the fiefdom of the intelligentsia: the Persian Government. It goes without saying that such an institution had existed since time immemorial in Persia, but it was Reza Shah who gave it its new shape and placed it squarely on the national stage beside the people, the *Bazaar*, the religious hierocracy, the tribes, the army (the other institution Reza had created) and the *Majlis*. The government had to be run by a bureaucracy and a technocracy – in any case by an educated elite of civil servants – a group of individuals that only the intelligentsia could recruit. Thus the government became its domain, its lever, its fortified castle. But, in a way, Reza Shah had been obliged to institute such a centralised institution to manage his achievements. With time, the government would expand as any bureaucracy does and as it grew so did the domain of the intelligentsia and its prerogatives *vis-à-vis* society. An idea of the rapid expansion of the Iranian bureaucracy under Reza Shah is indicated by the inflation of the public budget, which rose from Rls248m in 1926 to Rls4,324m in 1941 (see Table 7.1 for detailed figures and a comparison with national trade statistics). Of the two creations of Reza Shah, the government was far more important than the army, and the real winner of the Pahlavi era was the intelligentsia.

But, once in charge of this formidable institution, the Persian intelligentsia was to show its true colours: disunity and selfishness (*à la* Malkum Khan). Its leaders, lacking vision, failed to grasp the enormous power Reza Shah had willy-nilly placed at their fingertips. They failed to use it to place all other institutions under their command. The Davars, Salihs, Gulshayans *et al* might have been highly educated, but they were not elite material or else they would have grasped the unique occasion and stolen the whole Pahlavi show. In this respect, the little-educated Cossacks officers were far more of an elite than they since they did far better with the little they had.

To complete his dictatorship Reza Shah needed a capable and efficient repression system, especially as the first Pahlavi was a very suspicious and untrustworthy man, even suspecting his closest associates. Therefore he surrounded himself with a strong and totally devoted police force; a force ready to spy, to intrigue, to blackmail, to inform and to physically eliminate anyone it was told to. A single word from the Shah was sufficient. He had tried a few chiefs at the head of his *Shahrbani* (police) such as Muhammad Aqa Dargahi and

Table 7.1. Annual Public Budgets During Reza Shah's Reign,[81B] With (for comparison) National Trade Statistics for Selected Years.[81C]
(Figures in millions of Rls)

Year	Public budget	Imports	Exports	Total Trade
1926	247.7			
1927	258.3			
1928	286.9	777	480	1257
1929	311.1			
1930	353.4			
1931	321.8	741	810	1551
1932	500.1			
1933	508.9	605	466	1071
1934	621.4			
1935	751.1			
1936	1000.1	866	677	1543
1937	1250.0			
1938	1527.0			
1939	2613.5	612	813	1425
1940	3211.0	864	952	1816
1941	4323.9	614	812	1426

even his own chief of staff, Sadiq Khan Koupal, but neither could do the job: their men had almost bungled the assassination of Mirzadeh Îchqi, the poet and editor of *Qarn-i Bistum* (The Twentieth Century) in July 1924.[82] He finally found the right man for the job in General Muhammad Husayn Khan Ayrum, whom he appointed police chief in 1927. Ayrum, a Cossack officer, eventually shaped the instrument Reza Shah wanted: an efficient police force, invisible, well-informed and ready for any mission. That Ayrum was amassing a personal fortune on the side by blackmailing opponents was not the Shah's problem as long as Ayrum was doing his job properly. For eight years the foxy Ayrum catered to all his master's whims, ordering during his tenure the cold-blooded murders of Taymourtash, Sardar

Asâd and Soulatul-Douleh, the Qashqa'i *ilkhan* (in early 1933); nipping in the bud plots against his master; harassing opponents; and creating a small, but highly efficient department by the name of *Karagahi* (the Commissariat) or *Pulis-i Syasi* (the Political Police), at the head of which he placed the redoubtable Captain Âbdullah Miqdadi. In 1935 Ayrum, sensing the tide turning, on the pretext of an imaginary loss of voice, departed for Germany for medical treatment, never to return. His life in exile was that of a rich retiree; he was one of the rare persons who could boast of having deceived Reza Shah and saved his own neck in the process.[83]

Ayrum was replaced by yet another efficient policeman, *Sarpas* (General) Rukn ul-Din Mukhtari. The newcomer further sharpened the blunt instrument left him by Ayrum and made Miqdadi his right-hand man. Mukhtari's police was directly responsible for the murders of Shaykh Khazâl, Nusrat ul-Douleh Firouz, Sayyid Hasan Mudarris, the poet and writer Muhammad Farkhi Yazdi[84] and, indirectly, for the execution of Muhsin Jahansouz.[84A] It was also at the forefront of the 1937 arrest of a group of fifty-three young men accused of holding Marxist-Leninist ideas, and thus having violated the law of June 1931 "banning any kind of communist teaching or activity".[85] The leader of the '53 Group' was Dr Taqi Arani,* a young high school teacher. The fifty-two others were either his direct pupils or their friends and relatives. The cream of the group were men in their twenties, educated at foreign universities: Dr Murtaza Yazdi, Dr Muhammad Bahrami, Buzurg Âlavi and Khalil Maliki at Berlin University; Dr Riza Radmanish at Paris University; Iraj Iskandari at Grenoble and Âbd ul-Samad Kambakhsh at Moscow University.[86] The categorisation of the '53 Group' according to their professions was:

- government employees   18
- teachers and writers   11
- high school students   15
- craftsmen   3
- workers   4
- peasant   1
- unemployed   1

In 1938, forty-eight of the '53 Group' were tried publicly for their adherence to a communist group. They were given sentences ranging from one to ten years. Aside from Dr Arani, who died in prison, all others would be freed in September 1941 and enter Iran's political fray – as veteran politicians.

* DR TAQI ARANI (1902–1940), born at Tabriz; went to Tehran (1907); studied at the Dar ul-Funoun, graduated top in his class (1920); sent to Germany for postgraduate studies on government scholarship (1922); Ph.D. in physical chemistry from Berlin University (1930); upon return to Persia, after short stint at the Ministry of Industry, became high school teacher; founded the magazine *Dunya* (World) (1934); helped launch the *Kanoun-i Javanan* (Youth Club); *Dunya* banned (1935); spread socialist ideals among his pupils; arrested with fifty-two others (May 1937); given a ten-year sentence (November 1938); died of ill-treatment at Qasr Prison (February 1940).

With the duo Mukhtari-Miqdadi at the head of his police (and secret police), Reza Shah could rest assured that no internal opposition could hope to break through the sophisticated system of safeguards they had put in place. As the Shah relied on his army commanders to keep the tribes at heel, he came to rely on his police to curb any urban dissent. It had *carte blanche* to do its job efficiently. The Shah wanted results and got them.

After Reza Shah's departure Mukhtari and Miqdadi had to pay for their acts: the former with six years of prison (1942–47) and the latter with his life (executed in 1942).

On his way to his modernisation of Iran, Reza Shah clashed with the religious hierocracy over the question of the women's *Kashf-i Hijab* (removal of the veil). With the army and government looming stronger by the day, the importance of the clergy was on the wane: its *mullas* acted only as dutiful listeners to the people's grievances against the exactions and injustices of the regime. In 1935, Reza Shah ordered an official change of dress (European suits) and hat (the Pahlavi military *casquette*) and the veil's interdiction; three measures he had, according to historian Hidayat, "brought back from his Turkish visit in 1934"[87] (he was a fervent admirer of his Turkish *alter ego* Atatürk's reforms). The public's first reaction to these measures occurred in March 1935 after the dance reception (without veils) given at Shiraz by the Minister for Religious Affairs and Industries, Âli Asghar Hikmat. The outcry from Shiraz was heard all the way to

Tehran, Tabriz and Mashhad. The religious leader of Mashhad, Ayatullah Hajj Aqa Husayn Qumi, left for Tehran to protest to the authorities but was unable to do so, being virtually under house arrest. At Mashhad, the wily Shaykh Muhammad Taqi Buhloul, a capable tribune, poured oil on the fire by haranguing the masses of pilgrims against the veil's interdiction; he then fled to Afghanistan before the police could catch up with him.

In yet another development at Mashhad, Muhammad Vali Khan Asadi, the popular *Na'ib ul-Touliyyeh-yi Ustan-i Quds-i Razavi* (Keeper of Imam Riza's Shrine) since 1926, had the courage to send Reza Shah a telegram asking for a temporary exemption from the veil's interdiction for the Holy City of Mashhad. The Shah flatly refused and tensions mounted at Mashhad. People began gathering at the Gouharshad Mosque. On July 11, 1935, troops encircled the mosque, but were unable to dislodge the protesters. After a lull on July 12, during which General Iraj Matbouî, Mashhad's commanding officer, was treated as "incapable" by Reza Shah and ordered to immediately "crush the resistance",[88] the entrenched protesters were machine-gunned during the early morning hours of July 13, resulting in dozens of casualties and hundreds of arrests.[89] A score of Mashhad clergymen were arrested in connection with the troubles, and either sent to prison or to exile. The Gauharshad bloodbath had the radical effect of cutting short all protests against the reforms and throwing the religious hierocracy which had led it on the defensive.

In a sequel to the Mashhad events, Asadi, the man Reza Shah had always held to be the main instigator of the troubles, was arrested in November 1935, court-martialled and executed. Prime Minister Furoughi, whose daughter had married Asadi's son,[89A] tried his best to interfere with the sentence on Asadi's behalf, but to no avail. When Asadi was executed, Furoughi resigned his premiership (after a twenty-seven-month tenure) and decided to retire from politics altogether. In early December 1935 he was replaced by his former Interior Minister, Mahmoud Jam. By his rash decision to have Asadi executed, Reza Shah had lost, with Furoughi, the last capable politician around him. From then on caretakers, not politicians, would serve him. In any event, from 1935 on, Reza Shah believed that he didn't need politicians to rule Iran and that he could manage with the support of his army and police.

7.6. Reza Shah's Exit

Reza Shah had not been as successful in his foreign enterprises as in his domestic ones; he was as ignorant about the world at large as he was knowledgeable about his own country. His only trip abroad had been a forty-day visit to Turkey to meet his *alter ego*, the Turkish President Mustafa Kemal Atatürk. The reforms and progress achieved by the Turkish leader deeply impressed him. Upon his return, the Shah decided to change his country's name from Persia to Iran – a decision officially announced in January 1935 and applicable from March 21, 1935. The Turkish trip also paved the way for the signing at the Saâdabad Palace, on July 8, 1937, of a loose non-aggression agreement among Turkey, Iraq, Afghanistan and Iran (hence called the Saâdabad Pact). This quadripartite treaty was the first attempt at creating on the Soviet Union's southern confines a vast buffer zone, later known as the 'northern tier'. The document had omitted "any clause of mutual defence"[90] and proved stale, thus rapidly lapsed into oblivion.

On the Powers' scale, Reza Shah's disenchantment with the British after the signing of the 1933 oil agreement, had led to his *rapprochement* with the Germans. German experts and companies had always been welcomed by Reza Shah. The experts at the Bank-i Milli and in the military industries; and companies such as Junkers, I.G. Farben and Krupp in commercial and industrial ventures. In 1929 Germany was placed on the list of most-favoured nations and during the 1930s trade with Germany boomed: from a meagre 8% of total Persian imports in 1932/33 it soared to 45% in 1940/41.[91] In November 1936 Dr Hjalmar Schacht, the German financial wizard and the Reich's Minister of Economy, was invited to Iran to discuss with Reza Shah about future bilateral co-operation. As a result of these talks, German technical advisers were dispatched to Iran to assist in the railways, the PTT and the armed forces' equipping.[92] Moreover political undertones came to reinforce the economic links and Reza Shah's Germanophile tendencies grew by the day.

On September 3, 1939 the Second World War began, with Great Britain, France, Australia and New Zealand declaring war on Germany. At the outset Iran, still far away from the European theatre of operations, decided to reiterate its Word War I stand and declare its neutrality. Notwithstanding these moves, Reza Shah's pro-German sympathies were an open secret and the signature of a fresh Irano-German Commercial Treaty in 1940 left little doubt about his leanings. The outbreak of hostilities had brought all of Iran's development projects to a standstill (e.g. Krupp's steel mill and the French vegetable oil plant at Varamin), but life was otherwise little changed. Then, with Hitler's surprise Operation Barbarossa of June 22, 1941 against the Soviet Union, Iran's balancing act became dangerously imperilled. With Great Britain and the Soviet Union allied against Germany, Iran had no chance of avoiding being somehow drawn into the conflict.

On July 19, 1941, the British and Soviet envoys presented their governments' notes to the Iranian Government.

The identical notes, while stressing the desire to maintain Iran's independence and freedom, underlined the Allies' interest in seeing the large resident German colony expelled from Iran.

Reza Shah, with no capable politician to advise him in this quagmire,[93] decided to procrastinate, believing that "Germany was superior militarily to the Soviet Union and that it would defeat her in the near future".[94] He had never read history to know about Napoleon's Grande Armée, about the Soviet Union's millions of square kilometres. He couldn't see the ominous threats behind the notes. He thought that the seven hundred or so German citizens in Iran[95] were a minority among a European community numbering around 4,600. He was given a last chance on August 16, as a joint Anglo-Soviet memorandum was handed over to the authorities, stressing the need for the expulsion of all German nationals. Three days later the Iranian Government gave a vague reply, deemed totally unsatisfactory by the Powers. There was no doubt that the next step was war. Only Reza Shah's wishful thinking could have misread the issue.

In the early morning hours of August 25, 1941, British troops from the south (8th Indian Division of Major General Harvey) and the west (10th Indian Division under Major General Slim), and Soviet troops from the north invaded Iran. The small German colony had been their *casus belli*. And German agents had definite plans to prepare the ground for their armies through the Caucasus to Iran; Shulze-Holthus, the German vice-consul in Tabriz, outlined some of these in his memoirs;[96] and the redoubtable pair of SD chiefs, Franz Mayr and Ramon Gamotta, were ready to create mischief throughout the country. The British had not forgotten the exploits of Wassmuss and Niedemayer during the First World War and were unwilling to witness a repetition, especially in view of the southern oil fields' and Abadan Refinery's crucial importance. Furthermore, the British hoped to "co-operate with the Soviets on a joint policy" - a view supported in London by decision-makers like Cadogan, Sargent and Cripps.[97] As for the Soviets, who had referred to the 1921 Soviet-Persian treaty, their main goal was to assure a land link with their allies. All in all, it became clear that "Iran's strategic situation was of vital interest to the Allies".[98]

Within forty-eight hours, the Allies had a total grip on the country. The only serious resistance they encountered had been in the south. At Abadan, General Muhammad Shahbakhti had put up a worthy defence. But the British Navy had rapidly sunk Iran's two main gunboats: the *Palang* at Abadan and the *Babr* at Khurramshahr.[99] Rear Admiral Ghulam Âli Bayandur, the Iranian Navy commander (a former Cossack officer), was killed in the ensuing hostilities;[100] among his personnel 7 officers and 616 NCOs and sailors had also died.[101] During the wave of occupation the Iranian armed forces suffered a total of 6,000 casualties,[102] most of them in the south. In the north and other locations, the 183,000-strong Iranian armed forces had simply collapsed, with many officers (even generals) and thousands of soldiers deserting their posts without firing a single shot. Tehran was panic-stricken by the news of the advancing Red Army. Whoever had the means was fleeing towards Isfahan. Reza Shah spoke of treason and even had a couple of his own generals (the Deputy War Minister General. Ahmad Nakhjavan and the head of Army Engineering General. Âli Riazi) placed under arrest.[103] That might have soothed the Shah's nerves, but he had to face reality: his cherished armed forces, on which he had spent twenty years and millions of toumans, had vanished into thin air at the first serious alert. On August 25 and 26, 1941, the verdict was passed on the formidable Pahlavi Army: it was only good for crushing internal rebellions led by rifle-toting tribesmen.

On the political stage events were moving as rapidly as on the military field. On August 26, Prime Minister Âli Mansour resigned. The next day, Muhammad Âli Furoughi (suffering badly from an heart ailment) was appointed in his stead. On the 28, Furoughi presented his cabinet to the *Majlis*, with Âli Suhayli at Foreign

Affairs. Having received parliamentary approval, he called on the Powers' envoys and secured an immediate ceasefire. On the 29, the BBC's *Farsi* service launched its first verbal attack on Reza Shah.[104] On the 30, martial law was declared in Tehran and General Amir Ahmadi appointed to enforce it. As usual in times of crisis in Iran, the best politicians and administrators had been given the power to handle the delicate situation.

Reza Shah, for once, was totally out of his depth. He only feared that he had to go. He told his ministers: "their [the Allies'] only aim is to get rid of me".[105] Many wanted him to go, including the Viceroy of India, Lord Linlithgow, who had gone as far as proposing a Qajar restoration.[106] The battle for the succession was wide open; the possibility of a republic with Furoughi as its first president was even envisaged. Sir Reader Bullard, the British envoy in Tehran, cabled the Foreign Office:

> Britain could possibly force Iran to accept [the Qajar] Prince [Muhammad] Hasan [Mirza] ...or anyone else...[107]

However, Bullard was not favourable to a Qajar comeback, on the grounds that "there were hundreds of Qajars in Iran and that they were all waiting for the return of the days when Iran had been bled not by one leech but by hundreds".[108] Moreover Furoughi had told Bullard that "he was not favourable to a Qajar reinstatement" and that "he could work better with Reza Shah's son, Muhammad Reza Pahlavi". On the subject of placing the Pahlavi pretender on the throne, Bullard had concluded: "Britain could always get rid of him if he proved unsuitable".[109] On September 13, 14 and 15, the BBC *Farsi* service aired programmes detrimental to Reza Shah, suggesting that "his autocratic Nazi-like Government was responsible for Iran's present troubles".[110] For Reza Shah it was the *coup de grâce*: on September 16 he abdicated in favour of his son and left for Isfahan. Before departing Iran he also legally transferred to his son his personal fortune in Iran (not his prestigious foreign assets and cash): his vast *Amlak* landholdings and his cash at Bank-i Milli, estimated at around Rls680m.

A chapter of Iranian history ended as Reza Pahlavi boarded the *SS Bandra* off Bandar Âbbas on September 28, 1941.

He left Iran with all his sons and daughters except for Muhammad Reza, who had remained behind in Tehran to become shah in his stead. The Pahlavi family's first destination was Karachi, where the Shah was not allowed to step down but placed aboard the larger *SS Burma* for the next leg to the Mauritius Islands. The climate on the islands not being to Reza Pahlavi's taste, he later asked for a transfer to South Africa. On March 27, 1942 he was eventually granted a transfer, to settle first at Durban, then Johannesburg. His exile didn't last long: on July 26, 1944 he died in his bed at the age of sixty-six. After Muhammad Âli Shah and Ahmad Shah, Reza Pahlavi was the third consecutive Iranian monarch to die in exile: not a bright sign for a two and a half thousand year old institution.

As Reza Pahlavi departed Iran, Iranians "breathed a collective sigh of relief and settled back into the traditional posture of self-interest and lack of cohesiveness".[111] The bitter taste left by the social injustice suffered during Reza Shah's reign was overwhelming in the people's memory. Back in 1933, the elder statesman Hasan Mushir ul-Douleh (Pirnya), in his last interview with Reza Shah, had bluntly replied to the Shah's long litany of achievements:

> Unfortunately, with the lightest knock, all the achievements you are so proud of will tumble like a flimsy house of cards ...for the simple reason that there is no social justice in the country...[112]

Mushir ul-Douleh didn't live long enough (he died in 1935) to see his prophecy come true and witness the collapse of the Pahlavi Army. But, achievements such as the roads, the Iranian Government, the Trans-Iranian Railway, the Tehran University, the Military Academy and the Bank-i Milli were there as landmarks of the Reza Shah era: solid and permanent. Another important legacy of Reza Pahlavi to his fellow Iranians was the nationalistic self-confidence that had characterised his reign: it was there to remain in the minds when all the rest would be forgotten.

As the historian Mommsen wrote:

> The brilliant attempt of great men to realise the ideal, although they do not reach their aim, forms the best treasure of nations...[113]

On the other hand, though, as British diplomat H. Nicolson judiciously noted, he had brought about a "fragmentation" of Iranian society, "which was beginning to lack its previous elasticity and its remarkable power of resistance", before drawing the conclusion that:

> The old [Qajar] Persia was a loose-knit pyramid resting on its base. The new [Pahlavi] Iran was a pyramid almost equally loose, but resting on its apex, as such it is easier to overthrow...[114]

In his days of power Reza Shah had endeavoured to achieve as much as he possibly could. He had laboured all his life, single-handedly. He had been a one-man elite, and as such, with no roots, he should have gone with no heir. He had never given much consideration to his family's future while ruling; maybe he had thought to take care of these aspects later. He had, in the late 1930s, arranged the marriage of Crown Prince Muhammad Reza to Princess Fouzieh of Egypt (King Faruk's sister) and that of his daughters, Shams to Firaydoun Jam (son of Prime Minister Jam), and Ashraf to Âli Qavam (heir to the Shiraz Elite family of the Qavam ul-Mulk), to try and anchor the Pahlavis in the elites; but, with him gone, all these artificial links would dissolve within a decade. It is a rule that one-man elites cannot put down roots. Reza Pahlavi was yet another example of this truth. Setting Muhammad Reza Pahlavi on the Peacock Throne was not one of the best decisions struck in the hurly-burly hours of September 1941.

NOTES

1 Â. Dashti, *Panjah va Panj* (Tehran: *Amir Kabir*, 2nd ed., 1355 (1976)) p.112.
2 Private communication from an old army NCO, recruited in Azarbayjan after he had pulled his head over the horizontal iron bar more than sixty times, before the recruiting officer had shouted: "Hired! Next."
3 *Iran Almanac*, 1974, (Tehran: Echo of Iran, 1974) p.119.
   R.A. Stewart, *Sunrise at Abadan* (Praeger, 1988) p.11.
4A See: *Tarikh-i Nirou-yi Hava'i-i Shahanshahi* (Tehran: Intisharat-i Nirou Hava'i, 1355 (1976)).
5 R.A. Stewart, op. cit. (note 4), p.81. And also A. Banani, *The Modernisation of Iran (1921-1941)* (Stanford University Press, 1961) p.71.
6 *Tarikh-i Nirou-yi Hava'i-i Shahanshahi*, op. cit. (note 4A), p.72. And P. Oberling, *The Qasqai Nomads of Fars* (Mouton, 1974).

7 General Shaybani was severely reprimanded by Reza Shah for the loss of life incurred at the disastrous episode at Tang-i Tamuradi. When reprimanded by Reza Shah for the severe defeat, Shaybani shot back: "Win some, lose some". Court-martialled, Shaybani was given two years before spending one in prison for having dared stand up to the Shah. In 1933 he went into exile in Switzerland before settling down in Berlin, where he died in 1945 during an Allied bombardment. However, General Jahanbani, who replaced Shaybani as the chief of the general staff in 1928, would keep Reza Shah's trust, remaining obedient long enough to secure a permanent niche in the military for his family.

8 P. Oberling, op. cit. (note 6), pp.155-8.

9 On the uprising of the southern tribes in 1928/9, see the remarkable book by K. Bayat, *Shourish-i Âshayir-i Fars* (Tehran: *Nuqreh*, 1365 (1986)).

10 A.C. Millspaugh, *Americans in Persia* (Washington D.C.: The Brookings Institution, 1946) p.23.

11 The taxes on sugar and tea, introduced to finance the Trans-Persian Railway, were initially propounded some fifteen years earlier by the then Minister of Finance Sanî ul-Douleh.

12 Sir Percy Sykes, *A History of Persia* (London: Macmillan, 3rd ed., 1951) Vol. II, p.549.

13 A.C. Millspaugh, op. cit. (note 10), p.26.

14 M.Q. Hidayat, *Khatirat va Khatarat* (Tehran: *Zavvar*, 2nd ed., 1344 (1965)) p.371.

15 Ibid., p.395.

16 See, among others, H. Arfa, *Under Five Shahs* (London: John Murray, 19) p.236.

17 H. Makki, *Tarikh-i Bist Saleh-yi Iran* (Tehran: *Nashir*, 3rd. ed, 1361 (1982)) Vol. I, p.163.

18 M.Q. Hidayat, op. cit. (note 14), p.403.

19 Of the nineteen arrested *khans*, four were sentenced to death, four others to life, four to ten years, and the rest (seven) received sentences ranging from four to eight years. The four death sentences were carried out by firing squad at the Qasr Prison at the close of November 1934; executed were: (1) Muhammad Riza Khan Sardar Fatih; (2) Muhammad Javad Khan Sardar Iqbal; (3) Âli Mardan Khan Chahar Lang; and (4) Aqa Gudarz Ahmad Khusravi. See *Ittilaât* newspaper of *Azar 6, 1313* (November 27, 1934).

20 A.C. Millspaugh, op. cit. (note 10), p.27.

21 H.W. and S. Hay, *By Order of the Shah* (London: Cassell, 1937) p.292.

22 Â. Dashti, op. cit. (note 1), p.16.

23 Asked to allocate a piece of land for the campus of Tehran University, Reza Shah stood on the freshly filled *Khandaq* (the moat, until then delimiting the city's northern boundary; later the *Shah Reza* Avenue, and today's *Inqilab* Avenue) and said: "Take one kilometre as a base on the Avenue and go all the way north up to the Alburz foothills!" The university's board of trustees was flabbergasted: expecting a few hectares, he was offering them some thirty square kilometres! Private communication from an old Tehran University professor.

24 *Tarikhcheh Si Saleh-yi Bank-i Milli-i Iran* (Tehran: Bank-i Milli-i Iran, 1338 (1959)) p.152.

25 Ibid., p.153.

26 M. Khan Malik Yazdi, *Arzish-i Masaî-i Iran dar Jang* (Tehran: Ministry of Agriculture Printing, 1324 (1945)) pp.161-2.

26A E.B. Yaganegi, *Recent Financial and Monetary History of Persia* (New York: Columbia University (Ph.D. thesis), 1934) p.44.
27 Ibid., p.166.
28 *Tarikhcheh Si Saleh...* op. cit. (note 24), p.155.
29 Ibid., p.151.
30 Ibid., pp.100 and 103. In addition, the Persian Government also waived its rights to its six per cent of IBP's annual profits and to an independent inspection of the bank's accounts.
30A On Persian industrialisation, the pearl is Violet Conolly, 'The Industrialisation of Persia', *Journal of Royal Central Asian Society*, July 1935, pp.454-463.
31 In 1923, Martin Lianozov ceded his rights to the Caspian fisheries to the Soviet Government. In October 1927, after protracted negotiations, a twenty-five year Soviet-Persian joint venture agreement for the fisheries' exploitation was signed: management remained in Soviet hands while Persia received an annual rent of Rls800,000m and the profits were to be split 50-50. See I. Taymouri, *Âsr-i Bi Khavari* (Tehran: Iqbal, 3rd ed., 1357 (1978)) p.307.
32 It is reported that the young technocrats in charge of formulating the project had recommended a maximum capacity of 30 tonnes/day as more than sufficient. Reza Shah had told them: "Don't be timorous, take one hundred tonnes/day. We shall need it". They did. By the time the unit was completed, it had to be expanded.
32A Mirza Fazlullah Khan (later Âta ul-Mulk; chose Dihish as family name) was the Isfahan representative for Lynch Bros., the major forwarding company in south Persia. Encouraged by the former German consul Schunemann, who had switched to private business at Isfahan, Âta ul-Mulk ordered the future *Vatan* factory. The equipment was duly delivered to Bushire but it proved too heavy for the tracks of the Lynch road across the Zagros mountains to Isfahan. The equipment had to be brought back to Bushire, transferred to Basra and carried by camels to Isfahan via Khaniqayn. Along the way the factory had changed hands for Âta ul- Mulk had gone bankrupt (because of the unforeseen delay) and had been forced to sell out to Kazirouni. Âta ul-Mulk would, however, recover, making a killing by pioneering urban electricity at Isfahan (with wood-burning steam-engines) and later by importing diesel generators to Iran. In the end, the Dihish-Schunemann collaboration ended on a happy note as both became extremely rich, and Âta ul-Mulk's son married the ex-consul's daughter.
33 H. Nour Sadiqi, *Isfahan* (Tehran: *Shirkat-i Matbuât*, Isfand 1316 (March 1938) pp.174-7.
34 *Tarikhcheh Si Saleh...* op. cit. (note 24), p.201.
34A The Prince Muhammad Mirza Kashif ul-Saltaneh (1861–1929) had gone to India as general-consul in 1896. He brought back tea seeds from his Indian mission. The climate of Lahijan (Gilan) proved ideal for the cultivation of tea. The first green leaves of Persian tea came to maturity in 1904 and a new product was launched which was to feed a whole new industry and make of Lahijan one of the richest towns in Iran. Kashif ul-Saltaneh died in a car crash near Bushire. His small mausoleum dominates the beautiful town of Lahijan.
35 W. Floor, *Industrialisation in Iran, 1900–1941* (University of Durham, Centre for Middle Eastern and Islamic Studies, 1984) p.35.
36 Ibid., p.35.
37 Ibid., p.27.

37A Among the major importers of diesel generators was Âta ul-Mulk Dihish (see note 32A above).
37B Ardashis Badmagirian (1863-1928) was among the fathers of cinema in Tehran. He opened the first cinema in Âla ul-Douleh Street (today, Firdousi) in 1912; transferred it to the salon of the Grand Hotel (on Lalehzar Street) in 1913; opened Cinema Khurshid in 1917; then, in 1920, pioneered the first summer (open air) cinema in a garden he had rented off Amiriyyeh Street; gravely ill, went to Paris in 1925 for treatment and died in 1928.
38 Sir Percy Sykes, op. cit. (note 12), Vol. II, p.385.
39 Sir Winston Churchill, *The World Crisis: 1911-1914* (London: Thornton Butterwork, 1961) p.132.
40 Ibid., p.134.
41 L.P. Elwell-Sutton, *Persian Oil* (London: Lawrence and Wishart, 1955) p.28.
42 Ibid., p.29., quoting: "Firstly, [the First Exploration Company] as the primary producer, sold its oil below cost price to the Bakhtiari Oil Company, whose sole function was to resell it to the APOC at the normal price".
43 J. Rowland and B. Cadman, *Ambassador for Oil* (London: Herbert Jenkins, 1960).
44 H. O'Connor, *The Empire of Oil* (London: John Calder, 1856) p.324.
45 In November 1925, the Bakhtiari Oil Company, with a capital of £700,000, was merged with the First Exploration Company, which had a capital of £544,000. Thus the latter's capital was readjusted to £1,244,000 and the former abruptly ceased to exist, for it had served its purpose. A few years later, Cadman ordered the four leading Bakhtiari *khans* to stop squabbling over the distribution of their oil revenues, or else... When the four *khans* continued to squabble, Cadman simply let the axe fall. The APOC chairman neither accepted nonsense nor gave second warnings. In 1936, the *khans* were forced to sell their remaining shares to the Iranian Government at face value.
46 H. Longhurst, *Adventure in Oil* (London: Sidgwick and Jackson, 1959) p.77.
47 N.S. Fatemi, *Oil Diplomacy* (New York: Whittier Books, 1954) p.172.
48 H. O'Connor, *World Crisis in Oil* (London: Elek Books, 1963) p.287.
49 J. Rowland and B. Cadman, op. cit. (note 43), p.131.
50 L.P. Elwell-Sutton, op. cit. (note 41), p.73.
51 D.N. Wilber, *Contemporary Iran* (London: Thames and Hudson, 1963) p.79.
52 The 'Violet Line' stretched in the west-east direction across Persia: starting in Kurdistan from Marivan, and passing through Burujird, Sâidabad (Sirjan) and Irafshan in Baluchistan. APOC had until December 31, 1938 to make its choice known.
53 R.C. Mowat, *Middle East Perspective* (London: Blanford Press, 1958) p.42.
54 N.S. Fatemi, op. cit. (note 47), p.77.
55 J. Rowland and B. Cadman, op. cit. (note 43), p.103.
56 H. O'Connor, op. cit. (note 48), p.284.
57 P. Graves, *Life of Sir Percy Cox* (London, 1941) p.258.
58 A. Sampson, *The Seven Sisters* (Coronet Books, 1975) p.83.
58A F. Bostock, 'State Bank or Agent of Empire? The Imperial Bank of Persia's Loan Policy, 1920-23', in *IRAN*, Journal of the British Institute of Persian Studies, Vol. XXVII, p.110.
59 Â. Mustoufi, *Sharh-i Zindigani-i Man* (Tehran: Zavvar, 3rd ed., 1360 (1981)) Vol. III, pp.620-3.

60 D. Davoudi, *Jang-i Makhfi Barai-i Naft* (Tehran: no ed., 1326 (1947)) pp.31-4.
61 H. Makki, op. cit. (note 17), Vol. VI, p.315.
62 M. Nakhai, *Le Pétrole en Iran* (Bruxelles: J. Felix, 1938) p.191.
63 L.P. Elwell-Sutton, op. cit. (note 41), p.42.
64 Originally granted in 1880 by Nasir ul-Din Shah to Hajj Âli Akbar Amin ul-Maâdin for 7,000 toumans, the *Kavir-i Khuryan* Concession was confirmed in 1924 by the Ministry of Public Works in the names of Mirza Âbd ul-Husayn Khan Amir ul-Maâdin and Hajj Âli Akbar Khan Sutoudeh. In 1925, the *Kavir-i Khuryan* Company was formed with a capital of 5m toumans and the participation of the Persian Government and Khoshtaria. In 1926, the French took a share in the venture. See L.P. Elwell-Sutton, ibid., pp.41-2.
65 Ibid., p.126.
66 S.H. Longrigg, *Oil in the Middle East* (Oxford University Press, 2nd ed., 1961) p.62.
67 *Iran Almanac 1969* (Tehran: Echo of Iran, 1969) p.331.
68 B. Shwadran, *The Middle East, Oil and the Great Powers* (New York: Praeger, 1955) pp.162-3.
69 I. Naraghi, *Social Problems Related to Oil Industry in Iran* (Tehran: Farvardin 1337 (April 1958)).
70 L.P. Elwell-Sutton, op. cit. (note 41), pp.68-9.
71 For details see: A.M. Samsam Bakhtiari, 'The Bakhtaran Refinery', in *Iran Oil News*, no. 68 (March-April 1992), (Tehran: NIOC Public Relations Department, 1992) pp.14-5.
72 Ibid., p.15.
73 A. Ittihadieh, 'The Haulage of Petroleum Products in Iran', in *The Bulletin of the Iranian Petroleum Institute*, no.1 (April 1960), p.2.
74 Ibid., p.3.
75 M.Q. Hidayat, op. cit. (note 14), p.373.
76 Ibid., p.386.
77 A.K.S. Lambton, *The Persian Land Reform 1962–66* (Oxford: Clarendon Press, 1969) p.34.
78 Dr. L. Barimani, *Asrar-i Amlak-i Shahanshahi* (Tehran: no ed., 1324 (1945)) pp.33 and 76.
79 Private communication from an old Cossack hand to whom the story had been reported.
80 From an article in *Itilaāt*, Mihr 26, 1321 (October 18, 1942), quoted in *Itilaāt, Bist va Hasht Hizar Ruz-i Tarikh-i Iran va Jahan*, p.628.
81 G. Waterfield, *Professional Diplomat* (London: J. Murray, 1973) p.123, quoted from Oliphant's letter to Loraine.
81A The *doureh* was an informal reunion of a group of Elite members, at most a dozen individuals. Participants in the *doureh* could be from the fringes of Elite. Reunions were held either weekly, bi-weekly or monthly depending on the *doureh*. At each reunion, matters of interest to the Elite were discussed. The *dourehs* were a genial way of networking the whole Qajar Elite, from its board of five directors down to the simple Elitist. The system was later copied by non-Elite groups.
81B *Nameh-yi Ataq-i Bazargani* (The Commercial Chamber's Letter), nos. 222-223, *Farvardin 1319* (April 1940), pp.46-47. The budget for 1941 is from *Iranshahr* (Tehran: *Chapkhaneh Danishgah*, 2 Vols., 1342/43 (1963/64)) Vol. II, p.1141.
81C *Tarikhcheh Si Saleh...* op. cit. (note 24), pp.155, 178, 196, 199 and 218.

82 A young and courageous poet, Îchqi didn't fear Reza Khan, whom he criticised at will in his newspaper. Although his newspaper was repeatedly seized, Îchqi carried on. His friend Malik ul-Shuâra Bahar had even lent him a pistol, just in case. Îchqi was the first victim of the Pahlavi terror system, but not the last.

83 General Ayrum would never return to Iran, although Reza Shah promised him the most grandiose rewards in case he came back. Ayrum knew his leader and refused all the inducements: he knew that a return was synonymous with death.

84 Editor of the *Toufan* newspaper since 1921, Farkhi Yazdi was a veteran of the *Muhajarat* movement. In 1928, he was elected deputy from Yazd. In 1930 he created the *Hizb-i Millyun* (Nationalists' Party), which had no impact. Imprisoned at Qasr, he was allegedly murdered by Dr Ahmadi on October 15, 1939. See Kh. Mûtazid, *Pulis-i Syasi* (Tehran: *Janzadeh*, 1366 (1987)) p.463.

84A Muhsin Jahansouz was a young extreme rightist youngster who had studied law at Tehran University (1934-38). While he performed his military service at the Military Academy, the secret police saddled him with conspiracy for a *coup d'état*, leading to his arrest and that of eighty-six other cadets and relatives in 1939. He was executed at Qasr Prison in February 1940.

85 L.P. Elwell-Sutton, op. cit. (note 41), p.69.

86 E. Abrahamian, *Iran between Two Revolutions* (Princeton University Press, 1982) p.158.

87 M.Q. Hidayat, op. cit. (note 14), p.405.

88 Private communication to the author.

89 See one of the rare works on the subject: S. Vahid, *Qyam-i Gauharshad* (Tehran: *Inthisharat-i Vizarat-i Farhang va Irshad Islami*, 1366 (1987)). Vahid writes of "thousands of people killed", "hundreds of wounded" and "over fifteen hundred arrested", but the Gauharshad Mosque could not have contained so many people on that tragic night. On the other hand, at his 1979 trial, retired General Matboûi admitted a total of "twenty-five killed and forty wounded" (p.83) before being sentenced to death and executed. The truth, as always, lies between these two sets of figures, probably nearer the ones given by Matboûi. For an eyewitness account see the extremely well written work by Gh.H. Baqiî, *Angizeh* (Motivation), (Tehran: *Rasa*, 1373 (1994)) pp.177-190.

89A Asadi's son, Âli Akbar, was jailed for six years (1935-41) in Birjand prison.

90 H. Arfa, *Under Five Shahs* (London: J. Murray, 1964) p.266.

91 A.W. Ford, *The Anglo-Iranian Dispute of 1951-1952* (University of California Press, 1954) p.27.

92 *History of the Second World War* (London: Purnell and Sons, 1966) Vol. 2, no. 10, p.726.

93 Â. Dashti, op. cit. (note 1), p.176.

94 F. Eshraghi, 'Anglo-Soviet Occupation of Iran in August 1941', in *Middle Eastern Studies*, Vol. 20, no. 1, January 1984, p.41.

95 H. Makki, op. cit. (note 17), Vol. III, p.29.

96 Shultze-Holthus, *Daybreak in Iran* (transl. by M. Savill), (London: Staples Press Ltd., 1954).

97 F. Eshraghi, op. cit. (note 94), pp.43-4.

98 *History of Second World War* (note 92), Vol. 2, no. 10, p.725.

99 R.A. Stewart, op. cit. (note 4), p.88.

100 Iranian businessman Majid Muvaqqar had told Bayandur about British preparations, but the rear admiral had "brushed aside the report". See note above, p.21. By

an incredible coincidence Bayandur's younger brother, a lieutenant in the Northern Iranian Navy, was also shot dead on the same day, but by the Soviets.
101 *Iran Almanac 1974* (Tehran: Echo of Iran, 1974) p.119.
102 N. Kemp, *Abadan* (London: Allan Wingate, 1953) p.21.
103 H. Makki, op. cit. (note 17), Vol. VII, p.395.
104 R.A. Stewart, op. cit. (note 4), p.184.
105 I. Khajeh Nouri, *Bazigaran-i Âsr-i Tala'i* (Tehran: the *Nida-yi Îdalat* newspaper, 1324 (1945)) Booklet no. 45, *Âli Suhayli*, p.400.
106 F. Eshraghi, op. cit. (note 94), p.338.
107 Ibid., p.338.
108 Ibid., p.338.
109 Ibid., p.339.
110 Ibid., p.341.
111 D.N. Wilber, op. cit. (note 51), p.81.
112 H. Makki, op. cit. (note 17), Vol. VII, p.531.
113 T. Mommsen, *Romische Geschichte*, as quoted by J. Strachey, *The End of Empire* (New York: Random House, 1959) pp.331-2.
114 H. Nicolson as quoted by R.W. Ferrier, *The History of the British Petroleum Company* (Cambridge: Cambridge University Press, 1982) p.589.

CHAPTER EIGHT:
THE SECOND WORLD WAR

As Reza Pahlavi departed Iran, he left behind a political vacuum. Professor Lambton preferred the term "spiritual" instead of "political", for she wrote:

> When Reza Shah went, and with him the hollow regime which he had built up, there remained a spiritual vacuum...[1]

But whether political or spiritual, there was vacuum. And as nature abhors a vacuum, someone or something naturally had to fill it.

Ailing with a heart disease that had been further aggravated by the hectic days of the September crisis, Reza Shah's last prime minister, Furoughi, was not the man to fill the vacuum. His son and heir, Muhammad Reza Pahlavi, was too young (only twenty-two) and too inexperienced to fill his father's shoes; the young Pahlavi's experience consisted of a five-year stint at Le Rosey School in Switzerland (1933-38) and a couple of years at Tehran's Military Academy (1938-1940). If neither the old premier nor the young Shah could fill the vacuum in Iran's power structure, all other domestic forces had a chance to do so.

8.1. Power Vacuum

One prime candidate for filling part of the vacuum was the *Majlis*. It was the first institution to awake from its protracted torpor. For the past fifteen years it had acted as a rubber stamp for policies formulated in the Shah's cabinets, docilely ratifying the bills forwarded to it. By the end of August 1941, though, sensing the wind shifting, the deputies had jumped into action. Under the leadership of their elder president, the Elitist Hasan Isfandyari (the former Muhtashim ul-Saltaneh),[1A] they reacted and drafted a letter to the Shah asking him to henceforward respect the constitution. The only hitch in their plan was that none of them dared deliver the letter to Reza Shah at court. It was the Shah who, having heard of the letter through his *Majlis* agents, telephoned Isfandyari to invite him to the palace to discuss its contents on September 16.[2] The historic meeting never took place, for on September 16 Reza Pahlavi was on his way to Isfahan.

Instead of the deputies going to court, it was the court, in the person of Muhammad Reza Pahlavi, who came to the *Majlis* on September 17, to swear the oath on the constitution. On October 30, 1941, the 12th *Majlis* was dissolved and on November 12, the 13th *Majlis* was inaugurated. As Premier Furoughi presented his cabinet to the new assembly, the deputies asked him to present his government's programme in detail so that it could be debated, and, if necessary, amended.[3] The deputies were adamant on the point that their *Majlis*, representing the will of the people, was all-powerful and that, in consequence, the executive power had to follow its directives and the Shah reigned according to the constitution. On all other points, opinions diverged. As deputy Dr Musaddiq would later say:

> In our Parliament each deputy has his own personal opinion and this is why bills, even the simplest, cannot be passed rapidly by this body...[4]

The Thirteenth *Majlis* was no exception to the rule. It barely had a common denominator, with roughly 80 of its 134 deputies landlords. But even between the landlords there were profound divergences. Other large professional groups in the *Majlis* were formed by the civil servants and the liberal professions. Four major factions were to emerge from it:[5] (i) the *Îdalat* (Justice) faction, the intelligentsia's group, led by veteran journalist Âli Dashti; (ii) the *Ittihad-i Milli* (National Unity) faction with some thirty deputies, under President Hasan Isfandyari, Murtaza Quli Bayat (a rich Araki landowner) and Sayyid Ahmad Bihbahani (the son of the Constitutional Movement's religious leader); (iii) the *Mihan* (Country) faction with Hashim Malik Madani, a rich Malayir landlord and a deputy since 1927; and, finally, (iv) the *Azarbayjan* faction, the exclusive club of the old Qajar elite. Lacking in unity and lacking in tribunes (the best still being the veteran Âli Dashti), the Thirteenth *Majlis* had little chance to fill the vacuum.

Another group with a claim to fill the vacuum was the old Qajar Elite. Quite a number of Elitists had survived the Reza Shah era;

some working for the dictator, like Mukhbirul-Saltaneh Hidayat and Isfandyari; some by retiring to their private estates, such as Qavam (Qavam ul-Saltaneh), Dr Musaddiq (Musaddiq ul-Saltaneh), Hakimi (Hakim ul-Saltaneh), Pirnya (Mûtamin ul-Mulk) and Sadiq (Mustashar ul-Douleh). They were now without their natural leader, Prince Farmanfarma, who had passed away in 1939, and were not in their prime any more, with their doyen Hidayat seventy-seven years old and the youngsters Qavam (sixty-four) and Musaddiq (sixty-two). In the meantime they had co-opted seventy year old Muhsin Sadr (Sadr ul-Ashraf), the son of a minor Mahallat clergyman, renowned for having judged the Constitutionalists at *Bagh-i Shah* in 1908. As for the Elite's younger generation it had quantity but not quality: its only promising candidates were fifty-eight year old Husayn Âla (the eldest son of Elitist Âla ul-Saltaneh) and the crafty thirty-eight year old Prince Muzaffar Firouz (the eldest grandson of Prince Farmanfarma). The older generation would have to fend for itself to find its place in the vacuum; working for them were their cohesion, their fortunes and their old network. They all knew that their best iron in the fire was the genial and experienced Ahmad Qavam ul-Saltaneh.

The two main pillars of the Pahlavi system, the army and the bureaucracy, only had a remote chance to fill the vacuum. Both institutions had been surprised and devastated by the events of September 1941. The army had lost its credibility and honour in the few days of the Allies' invasion. Within a week its total personnel had plummeted from 180,000 to 60,000. The remainder were totally demoralised. Then, on September 16, they had lost their supreme commander, the Shah. Its elite of generals, however, was still theoretically in command: Amir Ahmadi, Yazdanpanah, Shahbakhti, Buzarjumihri and Nakhjavan. But, like their junior officers, they had been shaken by the scale of the desertions. They had to carry out a thorough *post mortem*, and reconstruct their armed forces without Reza Shah: a Herculean task, which would take years. In the meantime the senior generals decided to bank on Reza Shah's young son, come what may. After all, the generals were at the service of the Pahlavi dynasty before being the servants of the nation. And even while licking their wounds, they knew that they still had the power to crush any insurrection, but that was not enough to fill the vacuum.

As for the government bureaucracy, it had lost the formidable man on whose coat-tails (or rather blue *shinil*) it had been riding. Without

Reza Shah it stood naked and vulnerable. Without his development projects (at a standstill since the beginning of the war), it was almost useless and completely powerless. Its elite, used to hiding under the umbrella of Reza Shah's power, was at a total loss for direction. Knowing only how to obey to orders from above, it was lost in a vacuum.

Some politicians envisioned the future Iran dominated by political parties, so they hurried to form their own parties. Atheist author Ahmad Kasravi formed his *Hamabad-i Azadigan* (Libertarian's Party, with *hamabad* meaning party) in 1941. Âbd ul-Qadir Azad created the *Hizb-i Istiqlal* (Independence Party) on a social platform, with engineer Natiqand Murtaza Razavi (of the '53 Group'). Mustafa Fatih, the AIOC's Iranian factotum, joined forces with Âbbas Naraqi (of the '53 Group') to establish the *Hizb-i Hamrahan* (Companions' Party) as a left of centre party (1942). The political revenant Sayyid Zia ul-Din Tabataba'i, returning in 1943 from his Palestinian exile, formed with Muzaffar Firouz the *Hizb-i Iradeh-yi Milli* (National Will Party), a reform-minded organisation. All of these were eclipsed by the leftist *Hizb-i Toudeh* (Masses' Party), founded in September 1941 by a number of renowned Iranian communists and socialists, with, among others, Prince Sulayman Mirza Iskandari, Iran's veteran socialist Qajar prince. Only the *Toudeh* would find a niche in the vacuum, the others either failing to take off or falling by the wayside.

Journalists were yet another social group hoping to benefit from the new-found liberty, after two decades of strict censorship. The urban middle classes (and especially Tehran's), which had fared better than others during the Reza Shah era, were ready to support the best editors: they had the money, the brains, the time and the education, and they formed what was generally called 'public opinion', an appellation they had come to take seriously. First and foremost was Âbbas Masûdi, a forty year old self-made man who had published his daily *Ittilaât* since 1925, thereby stealing the march of seniority on all his future rivals. Soon popular was Muhammad Masûd, forty-one, a professional journalist with a degree from Brussels School of Journalism (the first Iranian to have one), who launched his weekly *Mard-i Imruz* (Today's Man) in August 1942. Another daily which would acquire a regular clientele from its inception in 1942 was *Kayhan* (World), published by Dr Mustafa Misbahzadeh, a thirty-four year old lawyer with a degree from Paris University and with the brilliant writer-lawyer Âbd ul-Rahman Faramarzi, forty-two, as chief editor. Below these leaders, dozens of lesser editors and publishers could be found, with only a few worth a mention:

– Ahmad Dihqan, editor of *Tehran Mussavar* (Images of Tehran), a young, good-looking nobody from Isfahan, with close connections to Princess Ashraf (the Shah's twin sister).

– Jahangir Tafazzuli, editor of *Iran-i Ma* (Our Iran), a left-leaning newspaper, which would place its editor on a political orbit.

– Ahmad Kasravi, first edited his monthly *Payam* (Message) 1936–1942, then began publishing his daily *Parcham* (Flag) from 1941 on.

– Abu'l Hasan Âmidi Nouri, publisher of *Dad*, educated at Tehran's Faculty of Law, a highly controversial editor.

– Hasan Arsanjani, energetic and socialist editor of *Darya*, a capable manager and writer.

Most of these press captains had a *bête noire*: the old Qajar Elite. Some of them, such as Kasravi and Arsanjani, execrated the Elitists, whom they saw as the cause of Iranian society's many ills. Kasravi was to write in black and white what many other editors thought (but feared to write) about the Elite:

> A small selfish elite has been monopolising all power in our country for the last sixty years. Only its members can become Ministers, under-secretaries, Generals [sic] and heads of departments. They oppose progress, abhor the idea that we can catch up with the others, and hope to perpetuate the present unfortunate conditions, with the central government weak, the tribes up in arms, the ministries unable to enforce legislation, the people distrustful of the state, the majlis a picture of ridicule[6] ...this elite is powerful and well interconnected. Its members are not only in the ministries but also in all fields of life. They have not just appeared recently but were in power during the days of Qajar despotism, during the constitutional revolution, during the years after the Revolution, during Reza Shah's reign, and now during our own time. If we do not cut their roots they will always remain in power...[7]

This declaration of war dated from 1945, but the war between the Elite and the others over Reza Shah's legacy had begun in September 1941. Mounting the assault on the Elite were three counter-elites which had profited from the relative freedom of the vacuum (no repression) by expanding as fast as they could.

8.2. Counter-elites

In spite of its paramountcy over the executive and its large *Majlis* majority, there was no denying that the old Elite was in a sharp decline. Serious doubts were raised about its reservoir of future talent; the Elite's scions did go abroad to study but, instead of acquiring an education, they took advantage of the pleasures offered by the European way of life. On the contrary, the gifted students with just enough money to scrape by would rush through their degrees and return home an engineer, a Ph.D. or an M.D. The new channel to professional and political pre-eminence was education: not having one counted as an initial handicap. The exception to the rule amongst the Elite families were the children and grandchildren of Prince Farmanfarma (and there were still a total of thirty-two sons and daughters, not counting the murdered Nusrat ul-Douleh), who would all graduate because the patriarch had threatened to leave out of his will those who failed to do so.

Undoubtedly it was the declining elite that begat counter-elites. In the teeth of a strong national elite, groups in opposition would think twice before jumping into the fray. Sensing that the Elite had lost its former grip (or else it would have immediately filled the vacuum), the counter-elites had passed their respective Rubicons. A total of three counter-elites were making their debuts in the national arena: the religious, the leftist and the nationalistic.

The religious counter-elite had deep roots in the history and the minds of the people. Over two centuries of Safavi rule dominated by its *Shiî* creed, religion had left behind deep furrows. The Persian religious hierocracy had opened up a new chapter during the golden years of Fath Âli Shah Qajar's days and since then had always been under the tutelage of the *Âtabat mujtahids*. The Tobacco Rebellion had relied upon the domestic religious network but the directives had come from Mirza Hasan Shirazi at Samarrah. The Constitutional

Movement too, started by Bihbahani and Tabataba'i, had benefited from the backing provided by Shaykh Tihrani, Shaykh Mazandarani and Mulla Akhund Khurasani, at the *Âtabat*. Multiple marriage links between the religious families and the Qajars, as well as the introduction of the Bihbahani, Tabataba'i and Imami families into the Elite, had thwarted any counter-elite formation in the old religious network. Asadabadi and Mudarris were capable politicians but with few links to the hierocracy and thus no widespread religious backing. What was needed was a religious critical mass within the country and for shaping the mass a nurturing ground was required.

At the beginning of the First World War, the religious authorities of the small township of Sultanabad (today Arak), located some 220 kilometres south-east of Tehran, invited a fifty-four year old Persian *mujtahid* residing at Karbala, Hajj Shaykh Âbd ul-Karim Ha'iri Yazdi,* to start a *Houzeh Îlmiyyeh* in their town. Seven years later Ha'iri Yazdi moved to Qum, the burial ground of Hazrat-i Mâsumeh, the sister of Imam Riza (A.S.) the Eighth *Shiîte* Imam. Both on the Tehran–Isfahan and the Kashan–Sultanabad axes, Qum's geographical location was ideal for a *Houzeh Îlmiyyeh*, and Ha'iri Yazdi was the right man to set it up. "A mature and enlightened pragmatist",[8] Ha'iri even thought about having foreign languages and elementary sciences taught at the *Houzeh*. He thereby hoped to open new horizons to his students so that one day they could preach abroad.[9] The Tehran *Bazaaris*, having heard of the Shaykh's plans, travelled to Qum to tell him that "the *Sahm-i Imam* (the Imam's Share) they were paying was not for the students to learn the infidels' language and if he didn't shelve such projects, they would stop their payments".[10] The Shaykh had no choice: he forgot about his revolutionary plans. When he died in 1937, he passed over to his successors – the triumvirate of Sadr, Kouhkamareh'i and Khwunsari – a *Houzeh* with solid bases and a growing national reputation.

* HAJJ SHAYKH ÂBD UL-KARIM HA'IRI YAZDI (1860–1937), born in Maybud (near Yazd); studied at *Âtabat* under Mirza Shirazi, Sayyid Isfahani and Akhund Khurasani before taking residence at Karbala; created the *Houzeh Îlmiyyeh* at Arak (1914), then that of Qum (1912); co-signed telegram to Reza Khan disapproving of his republic (1924); sent Reza Shah another telegram

vehemently protesting against the veil interdiction (1935); died in January 1937.

Notwithstanding Shaykh Ha'iri Yazdi's efforts, the clergy's influence in Iran was on the wane. Reza Shah's reforms and modernisation programme had dealt the religious authorities heavy blows. Modern schools had displaced the religious *maktab* system of traditional schooling. Davar's overhauling of the Persian judicial apparatus had dissociated religion from justice. The 1934 *Ouqaf* (Endowments) Law, by placing all the endowed lands under the aegis of the Ministry for Religious Affairs, Endowments and Industries, had taken away one of the religious authorities' main power levers and traditional sources of income. The veil's interdiction had been the last insult and the Gauharshad *bast* was the last resistance to Reza Shah's *diktats*. "By the end of 1936", P. Avery could write, "Iran was legally almost entirely emancipated from religion".[11] Although religion was still in the hearts and minds of Iranians (especially the peasant masses), nationally, religious voices had been reduced to a whisper.

Contrary to other traditional cultures, the religious hierarchy was at its best with its back against the wall.

Coming out of the nightmarish Reza Shah years, the clergy opted for the offensive. The very first move was a measure for bringing the Islamic message to the masses: propaganda, a weapon not yet utilised. In Qum, Dr Shahabpour launched his *Anjuman-i Tablighat-i Islami* (Islamic Propaganda Society) in 1942; the society published religious pamphlets (31,000 in 1942/3 and 100,000 in 1943/4), books, a bi-monthly magazine: *Nour-i Danish* (Light of Knowledge), and also a yearbook.[12] At Mashhad, the *Kanoun-i Nashr-i Haqa'iq-i Islami* (Centre for the Publication of Islamic Truth) was established by a group of religious individuals under Muhammad Taqi Shariâti, and it began publishing Islamic pamphlets and booklets. Some Islamic *anjumans* were created in professional circles, mainly among students and artisans. Preacher Husayn Âli Rashid (b. 1897) distilled religious and moral teachings on Tehran Radio and in articles published by the *Ittilaât* newspaper. Religious preacher Muhammad Taqi Falsafi (b. 1910) was just beginning to impose himself as a first-class tribune in religious gatherings.

At the Qum *Houzeh Îlmiyyeh*, the bright students attracted by Ha'iri Yazdi were not satisfied with their triumvir leadership: Sadr ul-Din Sadr (d. 1954) was far too conservative, Sayyid Muhammad Hujjat Kouhkamareh'i (d. 1953) too lacklustre and Sayyid Muhammad Taqi Khwunsari (d. 1952) too radical. During the war years, as the top *Houzeh* students travelled through Iran, they also looked for a potential leader. They eventually found him in the small town of Burujird, in the person of the seventy year old Ayatullah Burujirdi, a descendant of the renowned Tabataba'i and Hakim families. They recommended him to the *Houzeh*'s teaching staff, who in turn invited him to Qum. In January 1945, Ayatullah Burujirdi was placed in charge of the Qum *Houzeh*. Such a transition between the triumvirate (in charge for eight years, 1937-1944) and Burujirdi was difficult to envision for other Iranian institutions but the religious hierocracy managed this shift rather smoothly. A *Houzeh* teacher, Rouhullah Mousavi Khomeini, when asked his opinion about the coming of Burujirdi, simply replied: "What if the three become four?"; but the teachers worried in vain as Burujirdi brushed aside the triumvirate and went on to reform the Qum *Houzeh*.

Two other Iranian clergymen would make their mark during the war. The first was Hajj Mirza Ahmad Khurasani Kafa'i (later, *Ayatullah* Kafa'i), who led "the Mashhad resistance to Soviet occupation during the war".[13] The second, Sayyid Abu'l Qasim Kashani, was a clergyman close to Reza Shah, successful during the 1930s, who was arrested by the British forces in 1941 and briefly imprisoned at Arak before being exiled to Kermanshah and released at the end of the war.

The leftist counter-elite would find a ready base in Dr Arani's '53 Group'. A majority of them formed the *Hizb-i Toudeh* in September 1941 at the house of veteran socialist politician, the Qajar Prince, Sulayman Mirza Iskandari (1872-1943). Thus the *Toudeh* leadership became essentially based on the '53 Group': notably Iraj Iskandari, Dr Riza Radmanish, Dr Muhammad Bahrami, Dr Murtaza Yazdi, Âbdul-Samad Kambakhsh (who joined it later), Zia' Alamuti and Ihsanullah Tabari. A few outsiders like Dr Husayn Joudat (involved in the *Jangali* movement), Dr Firaydoun Kishavarz and Dr Nour ul-Din Kianouri joined it.

Prince Iskandari's son Iraj acted as go-between with the Soviet authorities in Tehran, getting their permission to launch the new party.

For the Soviets, the creation of such a party was a boon, for sooner or later it would become their own Iranian asset. At the outset, though, they only gave Iskandari a five-point guideline to be applied by the *Toudeh*:[14]

1. It had to be an official and legal party;
2. It should not be said to have a communist ideology;
3. It should support the Allies and especially the Soviet Union in their foreign policies;
4. It should endeavour to recruit "national personalities", so that the Soviets could approach them through the party;
5. It should not harm Allied interests in Iran (especially the oil and armament industries), so as not to weaken the war effort.

The brand-new party immediately began bringing indirect pressure on *Majlis* deputies for the freedom of their still detained colleagues, and celebrated its first victory when the *Majlis* voted for a bill in October 1941 calling for the freedom of all political prisoners still held in prisons (a measure favoured by all factions then). The *Toudeh*'s main effort, however, was directed to its newspapers. The party created at least a dozen papers and indirectly supported another dozen. The first newspaper to be launched in 1942 was *Rahbar* by Iraj Iskandari, followed by *Razm* by Dr Kishavarz, *Azhir* edited by Sayyid Jâfar Pishavari, *Mardum* (Dr Radmanish), *Rasti* (M. Parvin Gunabadi) and *Zafar* (R. Rousta), to name but the major *Toudeh* publications during the war. All the *Toudeh* newspapers would naturally join the journalistic *Jibheh-yi Azadi* (Freedom Front), successfully launched by the *Toudeh* between August 1943 and September 1944.[15] Furthermore, the party decided in 1942 to develop its initial networks in the three provinces of Azarbayjan, Gilan and Mazandaran, the left's traditional strongholds and now under the occupation of the Red Army.

In September 1944, *Toudeh* held its first party congress. A total of one hundred and sixty-nine national delegates took part. A Central Executive Committee of ten members was elected, with seven of them belonging to the '53 Group'; an eight-member Control Commission was also nominated, with five of them from within the '53 Group'.[16] At the congress's opening session, Iraj Iskandari (one of the party's secretaries) spelt out its main objective: "To unite the exploited masses and forge a party of the masses".[17]

Thereafter the *Toudeh* concentrated on industrial labour and trade unions, leaving aside the peasant masses, which were too difficult to reach for purposes of efficient indoctrination. The organisation of Persian labour had begun in 1906 with the first strike in the northern (Liazonov) fisheries and the formation of Tehran's printing press workers into an initial nucleus. During the 1910s trade unionism gradually took root in Persia so that, in 1922, trade unions grouped around 20,000 workers were established in the main labour centres – the main centres being Tehran (with a total of 50,000 workers), Tabriz (30,000), Abadan (30,000), Rasht (15,000) and Bandar Anzali (15,000).[18] With Reza Shah in power the trade unions were doomed, being by nature unacceptable to a dictatorship. By 1928, Persian trade unions were "almost completely smashed, numbering only a paltry few hundred members scattered among a whole number of dwarfish unions".[19] The most prominent labour leader, Riza Rousta, was arrested in 1930 and spent the next eleven years (till September 1941) in prison; other trade unionists suffered the same fate. In 1942, fresh trade unions were created and started recruiting anew from among a greatly expanded labour base, which was a direct consequence of Reza Shah's industrialisation programme. The trade unions developed independently of each other until May 1st, 1943, when four of the leading trade unions were amalgamated into the *Shoura-yi Mutahhideh-yi Markazi Ittihadiyyeh-ha-yi Kargaran va Zahmatkishan-i Iran* (Central Council of United Trade Unions of Iranian Workers and Toilers – CCUTU). The CCUTU secretary-general was naturally Riza Rousta, by then also a leading *Toudeh* member.

The CCUTU was instrumental in the waves of strike that plagued Iran's largest industries during 1945 and 1946 – notably the July 1946 strike that hit Abadan Refinery and ended only after clashes had resulted in forty-seven killed and a hundred and seventy-three wounded.[20] In mid-1946 the CCUTU would reach its apogee, with some 250,000 members nationwide. With such a success, the demarcation line between the CCUTU and the *Toudeh* became increasingly blurred. In a report, E.P. Harries, the British representative to the World Federation of Trade Unions' Delegation in Iran (March–April 1947), noted that: "Unfortunately, the CCUTU became indistinguishable from the Tudeh party".[21] In that context, it became evident that: "Tudeh's most notable success was in organising labour".[22]

During the war, the *Toudeh* had two further successes. The first was the propaganda coup of being able to co-opt within its ranks (or on its fringes) a handful of prominent writers and poets, such as Dr Sâid Nafisi, Dr Fatimeh Sayyah, Jalal Al-Ahmad and Nima Yushij. These intellectuals acted as a potent catalyst for rallying the educated urban masses under the *Toudeh* banner. The second success was the covert formation of the *Toudeh* Officers' Organisation by one of its members, the gifted artillery officer Lieutenant Khusrou Rouzbeh. Recruiting talented young officers like himself, Rouzbeh single-handedly built a *Toudeh* network in the armed forces from scratch.

The nationalist counter-elite came into being as the reply of the right-of-centre intelligentsia to the creation of *Toudeh*. The young technocrats and bureaucrats wanted to form an institution in order to have a mouthpiece for their socio-economic group. The first logical step was the creation of the professional association *Kanoun-i Muhandisin-i Iran* (Engineers' Association of Iran) in October 1941. This professional institution proved to be a formidable lever in the field of industry and development, but of little avail in politics. In 1944 the technocrats established a legal political party with dues-paying members: the *Hizb-i Iran* (Iran Party). By giving their party the name of the country, they were taking a serious responsibility. Prominent among the founders were Engineer Ahmad Zirakzadeh, Engineer Ghulam Âli Farivar, Engineer Kazim Hasibi, Dr Âbdullah Muâzzami and Engineer Jahangir Haqshinas; veteran bureaucrat Allahyar Salih, a Davar protégé renowned for his honesty, later joined the party. Engineer Mihdi Bazargan, one of the leaders of the Engineers' Association,[22A] refused to enter party politics (saying it stood in contradiction to his religious beliefs). A large majority of the party's rank and file came from younger civil servants engaged in the bureaucracy, thus giving the new party the most educated following of all national parties – not necessarily the most politically-minded.

The *Iran* Party programme included "the defence of independence and democracy in Iran, social justice, increase of the standard of living, agrarian reform, promotion of education and hygiene, and development of trade and industry".[23] A wishful and thorough programme, but for which the party lacked two major inputs: (1) an ideology, not covered by its general social democrat and anti-Communist platform, nor by its main slogan of *Kar-Dad-Azadi* (Work-Justice-Liberty); and (2) a determined and capable leadership.

Moreover, as the elder politician Hasan Taqizadeh judiciously pointed out to a young party member: "A political party based on civil servants is not a viable proposition in Iran, because the careers of its members and their salaries depend on the ruling government's goodwill. The ruling power's 'Damocles Sword' is thus always over their heads".[24] Nevertheless the young technocrats went ahead with their *Iran* Party, having no plausible alternative means of gaining a share of national power. Even with all its evident drawbacks, it still seemed better than nothing.

In the crucible of the Second World War, Iran's three major counter-elites were taking shape, each of them in its own idiosyncratic way. All three represented a current in Iranian society: the religious had tradition on their side; the *Toudeh* counted on labour and the urban middle classes; and, the *Iran* Party drew on the support of the educated civil servants.

8.3. The Second World War

With the Allied invasion of August 1941, Iran was drawn into the global conflict. Soon Soviet troops occupied the northern provinces and British ones the southern part of the country. Iran had become the link between the two Allies in their common war against Germany. A small American observer mission had also come to Iran as early as September 1941 in the British zone; its commander was Colonel R. Wheeler. After the December 7 attack on Pearl Harbor, when the USA entered the war, their military mission in south Iran was greatly strengthened and placed under the command of Major General C.S. Ridley; another US mission headed by Colonel H.N. Schwarzkopf was brought in to reorganise the Iranian Gendarmerie[25] – the Gendarmerie having been reinstated as a separate organisation in 1941, after twenty years passed under the army's general command. In March 1942, Iran was declared eligible for the US Lend-Lease Act and a month later the Soviet Union received its clearance too. The Russian Front was of prime importance to the Allies and it had to be bolstered to resist the deadly blows of the German Wehrmacht.

The only safe way for Allied (i.e. Anglo-American) aid to reach the beleaguered Soviets was through Iran. In December 1942, 5,000 US troops landed in Iran's southern ports (without prior notification[26]) as the first contingent of the 30,000-strong US Persian Gulf Service Command (PGSC). Co-ordinating with the British troops and services in place (the British Middle East Supply Centre (MESC) which co-ordinated civilian needs[26A]), the PGSC began its task of transporting through Iran equipment and material destined for the Red Army.

Over a three-year span (September 1941–September 1944) some five million tonnes of goods were moved through Iran to the Soviet Union. The initial trickle of 1941 had developed into a spurt in 1942 and a flood in 1943. Included in the material were 5,826 aircraft, 5,480 tanks, 8,649 lorries, 325 million cartridges, 350,000 tonnes of food, 450,000 tonnes of raw material (such as steel, aluminium, tin, copper and rubber) and military clothing supplies.[27] The transport logistics from the southern Iranian ports to the Soviet border were an intendant's nightmare. Fortunately for the Allies, the Trans-Iranian Railway and its 35,000 employees was on hand. General D.H. Connaly, the US commanding officer in Iran (after General Ridley), noted in his memoirs:

> ...without the Iranian assistance and the Trans-Iranian Railway the shipment of war material to the Soviet Union would not have been feasible...[28]

Of the five million tonnes funnelled northwards, some 3.6 million went by rail (with the Iranian Railways incurring a loss estimated at Rls1,079m[29]), 600,000 tonnes were carried by the British U.K.C.C. overland and the remaining 800,000 tonnes by the American forces associated with Iranian private entrepreneurs.[30] Without this gigantic Anglo-American-Iranian war effort to supply the Soviet troops, Stalingrad would most probably not have held and the German panzer divisions could have reached the Caucasus oil fields and... All in all, Iran deserved its post-war fame as the Allies 'Bridge to Victory'.

Another crucial Iranian input in the war effort was in the form of the refined petroleum products manufactured by the Abadan Refinery. Average daily production rose from 135,000 b/d in 1941 to 345,000 b/d in 1945 (a 155% increase over four years).[31] In particular the production of the critical aviation gasoline (avgas) soared from a normal 820 b/d (1941) to over 23,000 b/d (1945) [32]. Over the same period total employment at Abadan almost doubled from 17,000 in 1941 to 33,000 in 1945, and in the fields it went from 26,000 to

46,000; in other words, total AIOC personnel, which had stood at around 43,000 at invasion time, had grown to a staggering 79,000 (including some 5,000 expatriates) at the end of the war.[33]

Within the country itself, the Allies had little difficulty with the tribes. The Bakhtiaris were firmly held in hand by Murtaza Quli Khan Samsam, a wise and consistent leader (and Samsam ul-Saltaneh's eldest son). The Kurds and the Lurs behaved themselves, while licking the deep wounds inflicted by Reza Shah's brutal anti-nomad policies. In Professor Lambton's opinion:

> The tribal policy of Reza Shah, ill-conceived and badly executed, resulted in heavy losses in livestock, the impoverishment of the tribes, and a diminution of their numbers...[34]

Only the Qashqa'is were tempted by hostile activities, with the German agents in Iran (especially Schulze-Holthus of the Abwehr[35]) pouring fuel on their intentions. Supreme leader *Ilkhan* Nasir Khan, the eldest son of Soulat ul-Douleh (another of Reza Shah's victims), decided to side with the Germans, who provided him with arms, money and "two secret airfields built by the Luftwaffe and well equipped with German aircraft".[36] In the early summer of 1943, the Qashqa'is, encouraged by the Germans, staged a full-scale uprising exemplified by the useless and stupid massacre in July of the garrison at Simirum. General Shahbakhti headed an expeditionary corps to the Fars province, and, assisted by the Allies, easily quelled the Qashqa'i rebellion. Judging from the 1943 outburst, it was clear that the Qashqa'i leadership would never learn from its mistakes: once again it sided with a loser and alienated the Allies and the national army for no eventual gain – both their antagonists would in due time take their revenge against them.

Another pro-German movement in Iran during the war was the Resistance Movement of Iran, composed of Iranian officers and politicians. Among the officers, the most prominent was General Fazlullah Zahidi; he was duly arrested by the British agent Fitzroy Maclean at Isfahan and sent to Sultanabad to spend the rest of the war in prison. Among the politicians, the most enterprising was Habibullah Noubakht, who went on to create the pro-Nazi *Hizb-i Kaboud* (Black Party) in Shiraz.

8.4. Iran During the War

The war, the atrocities of which Iranians had been spared, was taking its economic toll in Iran. At first, Premier Furoughi had had his hands full with the political transition and found neither the time nor the will to implement prudent economic measures. The exhausted Furoughi finally resigned in early March 1942 to take up the post of Minister of Court (he was to die in October). He was replaced as premier by his Minister of Foreign Affairs, Âli Suhayli, a man the Allies trusted. But Suhayli, more concerned with keeping the *status quo*, adopted a lax attitude towards economic affairs and pursued Furoughi's non-interventionist policy. In August 1942, Suhayli submitted his resignation to the Thirteenth *Majlis* to clear the way for the comeback of Iran's political grandmaster: Ahmad Qavam.

Whenever politicians and deputies were at a loss, they called on Qavam. This time, the main problem with which he had to come to grips was economic: inflation was unchecked and bread was scarce. But it was much too late to redress the balance, even for Qavam. Requisitions and spending by Allied troops had their negative impact on these domestic problems. "Everywhere in the Middle East", Sir Reader Bullard, the British envoy to Iran (1940–45), wrote, "heavy spending by the Allied forces tended to cause inflation, this process was perhaps seen at its worst in Iran".[37] Because of the laxity of the Furoughi and Suhayli cabinets, inflation was galloping in Iran (see Table 8.1.[38]). In a single month of autumn 1942, prices rose by an average of 50 to 60%.[39] The black market was flourishing: a kilo of sugar fetched 100 rials and a single car tyre commanded a price of between 15,000 and 20,000 rials.[40] By the close of 1942, bread was in short supply in Tehran and the quality of the bread available was execrable, as a little flour was mixed with all ingredients at hand: sawdust, pecan flour and lots of salt. This surge of inflation, unparalleled in Iran's history, was due on the one hand to the Allies' commandeering of all the means of transportation available and, on the other hand, to the abrupt drop in imports due to worldwide hostilities: Iranian imports fell from a high of over 400,000 tonnes in 1940 to only 250,000 tonnes in 1941 and between 125,000 to 150,000 annually during the years 1942–1946.[41]

Table 8.1.: Inflation in Wartime Iran – as per the Bank-i Milli's Cost of Living Index (1939–1945).[38]

Year	Bank-i Milli's Cost of Living Index
1937	100
1939	142.6
1941 (September)	250.8
1942 (March)	314.0
1943 (March)	778.3
1944 (March)	1085.0
1945 (March)	963.0
1946 (March)	877.0

Qavam had the law for printing and circulating banknotes worth a total of Rls800m ratified by the *Majlis* and carried out in September and October 1942 to ease the Allied troops' local currency problems. During the war years the amount of bank notes in circulation (see Table 8.2.) rose parallel to inflation. Then, in order to bring some order to Iran's financial policies, Qavam remembered Dr Millspaugh and in November 1942 the American expert was given a five-year contract (at $18,000 per annum) as Iran's administrator-general of finances. In January 1943 he arrived in Tehran and on May 4, 1943, the *Majlis* granted him full powers to reorganise internal finances and distribution.[43] The Iranians had expected the American expert to bring black-marketeers to heel (especially after the bad harvest of 1942 had led to bread riots at Tehran in December 1942[43A]); but he only succeeded partially in this endeavour. He was, however, "trying to help the Iranians more than they wanted to be helped at this juncture".[44] Dr Millspaugh's forty-strong team, with their hands in finance, treasury, customs, food and price stabilisation, had become a bureaucracy within the Iranian bureaucracy. The nationalist intelligentsia suffered this encroachment only as long as it had to.

When Dr Millspaugh ordered Abu'l Hasan Ibtihaj to resign from his top position at Bank-i Milli, the latter refused, defying the American expert, thereby creating a scandal (that overspilled in the press) and remained in his post. In January 1945, the *Majlis* rescinded Millspaugh's full powers and the American expert resigned and departed Iran in February 1945.

Table 8.2. Banknotes in Circulation in Iran – Statistics of the Bank-i Milli Iran.[42]

Year	Banknotes in Circulation (Rls million)
1937	849
1938	837
1940	1215
1941 (September)	1537
1942 (March)	1738
1942 (September)	2310
1943 (March)	3727
1943 (September)	4549
1944 (March)	6037
1944 (September)	6147
1945 (March)	6631

Prime Minister Qavam was also keen to be granted full powers by the *Majlis*. The Premier was on his way to becoming the supreme arbiter of Iran. With a shy Shah, a timid court and a weak army, the last hurdle remaining along Qavam's path to absolute power was the *Majlis*. On November 20, 1942, he sent it a bill asking for full prerogatives. But the national assembly, still unwilling to lose its newly-found clout and, under the spell of the intelligentsia's leaders such as Dashti and Masûdi, rebuked him. Years later Muhammad Reza Shah recalled this troublesome era and the power struggle between Qavam and the *Majlis*, in the process giving an insight into his own relations with the then British envoy:

"One day [in early December 1942], Sir Reader Bullard came to see me and told me that: "We have confidence in the present Premier [Qavam], but he cannot work with the present *Majlis*; so have the assembly dissolved." I replied: "I will not do so," and he asked: "Why won't you?" I then added that: " I do appreciate Great Britain's friendship and alliance, and know it to be to our advantage; however, an ally's friendship was most welcome to my country when independent"; and finally told him that: "It is none of your business to trust or not our government; rather it is mine and the *Majlis*'s to do so..."

I also remember that at around that time the British Military Attaché, General [WAK] Fraser, the British Political Attaché, [AC] Trott, and the AIOC's most senior Iranian manager, Mustafa Fatih, were all three trying to persuade me to relinquish my function of Supreme Commander of the Armed Forces. But I resisted their request. Why shouldn't I have? Why should I have relinquished my responsibilities? Whose business was it to meddle in these matters anyway?[45]

On December 8, 1942, a few days after the above meetings, serious riots took place in front of the *Majlis*. Troops had to intervene; a number of casualties resulted; martial law had to be imposed in the capital and public opinion was outraged. Qavam had lost to the coalition ranged against him: the Shah and a number of *Majlis* deputies. In the riots' aftermath, the official inquiry traced back some of the Shah's cheques to the Masûdi brothers of the *Ittilaât* newspaper, but the case was abruptly dropped to avoid a scandal.[46] On December 8, a dangerous precedent was set and a new phenomenon had come to the capital's streets: 'mobocracy'. The mobs came into being because no one could fill the vacuum and the streets were left to whoever could gather the largest mob. Thus the era of the street-fighters and knife-wielders (*chaqoukishan*) dawned upon Iran.[47] On December 23, Qavam called on General Amir Ahmadi to become Minister of War and bring law and order to the capital's streets.

Unabashedly a Qajar Elitist, Qavam had experience and patience on his side. He was immensely rich from the annual revenues of his large tea plantations at Lahijan. He had a thorough knowledge of the Iranian people and of the things they would or wouldn't accept. He knew the Great Powers, their Game and its rules. In the early 1940s, Qavam, who had just married a young Lahijani girl,[48] was at the summit of his extraordinary capabilities. Behind him were all the devoted Elitists and the young, capable politicians he (and only he) was able to attract under his wing. Sir Reader Bullard, a diplomat who was a fine psychologist too, held that Qavam was: "the most energetic, shrewd, skilful, courageous, ambitious and authoritative of the old statesmen".[49] No small compliment.

On the other hand, the young Muhammad Reza Shah, who had come to mistrust the old and crafty statesman, feared that the latter's overpowering political presence would make the monarchy redundant. The young Shah, still far from being in the royal saddle, was ready to ally with anyone to stop Qavam's drive. The Shah had inherited all his father's enemies and only his trusted generals as devoted supporters – he had bent over backwards and used all of his limited power to protect "from public hearings the field commanders who had deserted their posts in August 1941; [and] showered officers with promotions",[50] contrary to the practice of his father, who had distributed them reluctantly. The military high command was a rather thin cover for these turbulent times and therefore he "tried to secure as many friends as possible"[51] – a dangerous policy in Iran: because once going it was very difficult to stop. He promised the Allies "full co-operation, even offering volunteers to fight in Europe and remaining silent at the arrest of some fifty pro-German officers". His relations with the British were strained from the outset, as he held them responsible for his father's exile; later, when asked by a British politician whether he held grudges about this matter, he replied: "Forgiven, forgotten or do you mean I understand?"[52] Between him and Sir Reader Bullard, a British envoy of high calibre, things were never rosy and Bullard must not have appreciated the Shah's rebukes of early December 1943.

In the aftermath of the December 8 riots, the struggle between Qavam and the royalists was being conducted in the political arena. The final decision lay with the British and the Americans. The US Mission in Tehran had decided to side with the British, who were leaning towards Qavam; but "the War Department in Washington overruled the American military advisers in Tehran and swung US support behind the Shah and against the Prime Minister".[53] This was the first sign that American decision-makers wanted the young Shah to remain on the Peacock Throne; it was also the first indication that US decisions were not always unanimous (a dangerous precedent for a world Power). Eventually Qavam had to tender his resignation in February 1943 and was replaced by Âli Suhayli, the only other candidate acceptable to the Anglo-American camp. The royalists had won the first round; but for Qavam it was only *reculer pour mieux sauter*: he would wait for the next opportunity, as he had waited eighteen years on the sidelines for Reza Shah's exit.

In September 1943 Iran came out of its neutrality and finally declared war on Germany. The Persian Resistance Movement had been decapitated and General Fazlullah Zahidi imprisoned at Sultanabad (Arak); the last German agents, Mayr, Shulze-Holthus, and the SS officer Kurmis, were arrested.[54] The first German reverse came at El Alamein, near Cairo, in the fall of 1942; and the first catastrophic débâcle before Stalingrad (the war's true turning point) during the winter 1942/43.[55] Then, in late November 1943, the Tehran Conference took place between US President Franklin Roosevelt, British PM Sir Winston Churchill and Soviet leader Marshal Joseph Stalin.[56] Iran was not yet on the Powers' agenda as the Allied leaders still had to win the war. Thus, the Tripartite Declaration of December 1, 1943 was a mere formality, acknowledging Iran's contribution in "the war against the common enemy", restating the Powers' "desire for the maintenance of the independence, sovereignty, and territorial integrity of Iran", and agreeing to "make available to the Iranian Government such economic assistance as may be possible" to compensate Iran for war damages.[57]

8.5. The Fourteenth *Majlis*

Begun in early 1944, the elections to the Fourteenth *Majlis* were among the most bitterly contested in Iran's parliamentary history. The presence of *Toudeh* candidates on the electoral lists had altered the whole traditional voting system. A total of eight hundred candidates from centrist and rightist parties further blurred the issues,[58] as a high degree of "confusion, rivalries and complications"[59] surrounded these elections. Implicitly benefiting from the presence of Soviet troops stationed in northern Iran, the *Toudeh* had nine of its candidates elected – an unprecedented event for the Iranian polity.

On February 26, 1944, the Fourteenth *Majlis* was officially inaugurated with a total of 134 deputies. Its overall composition was not altogether different from the Thirteenth edition, as the bulk of the deputies (roughly sixty per cent) were landlords, some twenty per cent were civil servants and ten per cent businessmen.[60] Of the nine *Toudeh* deputies, only Sayyid Jâfar Pishavari had his mandate revoked by the assembly, leaving the eight remaining *Toudeh* deputies – five of whom were members of the '53 Group' – to form the *Toudeh* faction. The *Toudeh* entity was small but homogeneous, and well supported from outside by the *Toudeh* press, its intellectuals and its mobs. Beside the *Toudeh*, the Fourteenth *Majlis* counted seven other factions:[61]

1) The largest faction was the conservative *Ittihad-i Milli* (National Union) faction, with some thirty deputies (mostly court-leaning) led by Îzaz Bayat, Nasir Quli Ardalan, Faraj Assif, Sayyid Hisam ul-Din Doulatabadi and Sayyid Ahmad Bihbahani. The faction leaders also formed a political party, the *Hizb-i Ittihad-i Milli*, renamed *Hizb-i Mardum* (People's Party) in 1945.

2) The second largest faction was that of *Mihan* (Nation), with around twenty-six deputies led by the large landowner Malik Madani and the Yazdi businessman Dr Hadi Tahiri.[59] In June 1944 a *Mihan* Party was formed by Dr Mihdi Azar, Dr Karim Sanjabi, Jahangir Tafazzuli, Âbd ul-Qadir Azad, Dr Abu'l Hasan Maliki and Dr Marzban. Subsequent to the defections of Tafazzuli and Azad in 1945, the *Mihan* merged with the *Iran* Party.

3) Another influential faction, almost indistinguishable from the *Mihan* faction, was the *Vatan* faction led by Sayyid Zia' ul-Din

Tabataba'i. The former prime minister's abrupt return to active politics was due to the political acumen of a young politician, Muzaffar Firouz,* in search of a mentor. Impassioned by politics, like his father Nusrat ul-Douleh, the third-generation Elitist Firouz had gone all the way to Palestine to convince Sayyid Zia to come back; together they launched the *Hizb-i Vatan* (Fatherland Party) and a newspaper *Râd-i Imrouz* (Today's Râd) with Firouz as editor. In January 1945 their party was renamed *Hizb-i Iradeh-yi Milli* (National Will Party). Its goal was to counter-balance the *Toudeh* in all spheres. But the talented Firouz soon realised that Sayyid Zia was but a hollow figurehead unlikely to grab power, and switched to the buoyant Qavam camp, where he was welcomed.

4) Next came the twenty- strong *Azadi* (Freedom) faction, composed of old Qajar elite members, in principle opposed to the Pahlavis, and led by Muhammad Vali Farmanfarmayan (Nusrat ul-Douleh's younger brother).

5) The *Dimukrat* (Democrat) faction, formed of eleven southern deputies, was linked to Sayyid Zia's *Vatan*, with some prominent tribal chieftains such as Ahmad Quli Samsam Bakhtiari (the eldest son of Bakhtiari *ilkhan* Murtaza Quli Khan), Amir Jang Sardar Asâd (brother to Reza Shah's Minister of War) and Âbbas Qubadyan (the leader of the Kurd tribe of Kalhur).

6) The *Mustaqill* (Independent) faction was the intelligentsia's faction, claiming some fifteen deputies, with influential orators such as Âli Dashti and Âbbas Masûdi.

7) And, finally, the *Munfaridin* (Individual) faction, with sixteen uncommitted deputies, brought together by Dr Muhammad Musaddiq, including five members of the *Iran* Party.

The intercourse between the old Elitist and the young *Iran* Party technocrats within this Fourteenth *Majlis* faction was to pave the way for their future entente.

With the *Majlis* at the focus of Iranian political life and with all eyes on it, the stage was set for turbulent events in the assembly's arena. The first clash occurred between Dr Musaddiq, Tehran first deputy (always a special honour), and Sayyid Zia over the latter's parliamentary mandate.

Sayyid Zia had been elected in Yazd with the generous assistance of the wealthy Dr Tahiri. Musaddiq held that the Sayyid had come to power in 1921 with British backing and therefore was not qualified for deputation; in a speech delivered on March 26, 1944, Musaddiq disclosed that:

> [Reza] Pahlavi himself admitted in my own house, before Taqizadeh, Hidayat and Husayn Âla, that he had been brought to power by the British.[62]

Sayyid Zia, however, survived the onslaught and his right-wing friends dutifully approved his credentials.

The life of the Fourteenth *Majlis* was to be dominated by a number of major trends. The first of these was the return of an old Elitist to the premiership, and the constant rotation at the head of government (a strategy dear to Qavam). The second trend was the *Toudeh*-inspired street disorders and strikes to influence the assembly from the outside. The third was the perennial (and unavoidable) question of fresh oil concessions.

The old Elitists who took the prime ministership during the Fourteenth *Majlis* were to number five: Muhammad Sâid (three cabinets, eight months); Murtaza Quli Bayat (one, five months); Ibrahim Hakimi (two, three months); Muhsin Sadr (one, six months); Ahmad Qavam (one, for the *Majlis*'s last month). The youngest among them was Bayat, a harmless and colourless landowner, described by Sir Reader Bullard as "one of the most stupid men in Persia".[63] In comparison, Sâid, a politician seemingly naive[64] but far less stupid than he appeared, old Sadr and even Hakimi shone by virtue of their abilities (which were relative at best). As for Qavam, who was in a class all by himself, he had just entered the fray as the Fourteenth *Majlis* folded.

The Fourteenth *Majlis* also had to put up with the first *Toudeh*-inspired disorders. The worst incidents occurred in Isfahan in the spring of 1944; they were triggered by a lock-out staged by the owners of the large textile factories, who simply locked their factories' doors and left the city! The workers, finding the doors locked, wrought havoc in the city before order was restored. The 'workers' revolt' helped spread the fears of a communist takeover in Isfahan. The 'right to private property', guaranteed by the laws of Islam and the laws of Iran, had been seriously transgressed.[65] Isfahan was the beginning of the wave of subversion encouraged by the *Toudeh* in Iran.

The first wartime request for an oil concession was tabled in October 1943 by the Royal Dutch Shell group. In secret negotiations with Prime Minister Suhayli, the group's representatives asked for a concession in Iran's Baluchistan province. The Iranian Government decided to engage two American oil experts, namely A.A. Curtis and Herbert Hoover Jr.,[65A] to advise it on its oil affairs. As the two American experts arrived in Tehran in March 1944, two US companies (both with previous experience in Iran) applied for concessions: first, the Standard Vacuum Oil Co. – a joint venture between Standard Oil of New Jersey and the Socony Vacuum Oil Co. (later Mobil) – and a month later, the Sinclair Oil Company. The sudden arrival of American oil companies' representatives in Tehran prompted the British Government to enter into direct negotiations with the US Government in Washington. The Anglo-American negotiations yielded an agreement, signed on August 8, 1944, but never ratified by the US Senate.[66] The unratified agreement was the first shot of a protracted struggle between British and American interests over the oil riches of the Middle East, a struggle still ongoing half a century later.

The debate over fresh oil concessions became the focus of the Fourteenth *Majlis*, and it constantly made newspaper headlines. As if three pending concessions were not enough, the Soviets decided to jump into the fray too. A Soviet delegation, headed by Sergei I. Kavtaradzeh, the Soviet assistant commissar for Foreign Affairs, came to Tehran in September 1944 to make good Soviet promises on the defunct *Kavir-i Khuryan* concession. The thin pretext was, however, soon dropped to unmask the real cause of the mission: a Soviet oil concession covering Iran's five northern provinces. Kavtaradzeh put as much pressure as he could on Premier Sâid; *Toudeh* mobs demonstrated daily in the streets, *Toudeh* newspapers vehemently supported the Soviet initiative and the *Toudeh* faction in *Majlis*, led by the Machiavellian Kambakhsh and Radmanish, harassed the cabinet. A beleaguered Sâid came to the conclusion that the only way out of the quagmire was to grant no concession at all until the end of the war. On October 16, 1944, the Prime Minister officially notified all three Powers' embassies of the Iranian Government's decision to close the oil file until the end of the war.[67]

Insofar as Kavtaradzeh was concerned, Sâid's official message had fallen on deaf ears. On October 29, Dr Musaddiq, in an important *Majlis* speech, criticised the Soviet attitude. Then, a few days later, with Kavtaradzeh still undeterred, Musaddiq expounded his *Muvazineh-yi Manfi* (negative balance) theory in opposition to the positive balance applied so far in Iran, ending with a parable to stress his point:

> In order to achieve a balance a one-handed individual would certainly not agree to have his remaining hand cut off![68]

Dr Musaddiq thus rejected the Soviet proposals, insisting that it was the British D'Arcy concession which should not have been granted in the first place. As Kavtaradzeh still insisted, *The Times* of London suggested (in a November 2 leader) a tripartite conference among the Powers to achieve a permanent agreement with regard to Iran's oil resources;[69] the suggestion was left hanging in the air. In Tehran, Sâid, with no alternative left, resigned. The ball was then squarely in the *Majlis*'s court. The assembly offered Dr Musaddiq the Premiership, which he refused, suggesting instead his friend and relative Murtaza Quli Bayat, who was duly voted in as head of the next cabinet. Then, on December 2, Dr Musaddiq proposed a bill that stipulated:

> No Prime Minister or Minister was allowed to enter official negotiations for any oil concession with foreign Governments or companies; the penalty for trespassing the law ranged from three to eight years of solitary imprisonment[70]

(no mention being made of the war's end). The *Majlis* readily approved Musaddiq's bill, and thus the legislature had found an elegant way to protect the executive from further political pressures.

Thus, under the influence of Dr Musaddiq, the Fourteenth *Majlis* had legally closed the door to all new oil concessions.

The Dutch, the Americans and the Soviets would have to shelve their concession demands for the time being, waiting for more propitious days. Kavtaradzeh eventually left on December 9, bringing to a close another oil chapter in Iran's history. Before the chapter closed, however, the deputy for Qouchan, Ghulam Husayn Rahimian, took a bold step on December 3 and drafted a bill calling for the "cancellation of the D'Arcy concession and of the 1933 agreement with AIOC".[71] Dr Musaddiq refused to sign the draft, arguing that "the proposal was ill-timed".

Rahimian failed to gather the necessary fifteen signatures and his draft remained a dead letter. But the Rahimian initiative, although unsuccessful, was, for the British and AIOC, a warning that the attack on fresh concessions would sooner or later have a backlash on the only existing one: theirs.

8.6. The War's End

1945 would be the last year of the Second World War. The collapse of the Third Reich was formalised on May 7, when General Jodl signed Germany's unconditional surrender at Rheims.

Four months later, after the atom bombs on Hiroshima and Nagasaki, it was Japan's turn to sign the instrument of surrender on September 2, aboard the *USS Missouri* anchored in Tokyo Bay.

The war was finally over. The final date of September 2 had its importance for Iran for it automatically fixed – as foreseen in the Allies' Tripartite Agreement of January 29, 1942 – the date of March 2, 1946 as the deadline for the final withdrawal of all Allied troops from Iranian territory. With American, British and Soviet troops still occupying parts of its territory, Iran was not out of the war yet.

NOTES

[1] Professor A.K.S. Lambton, in 'Persia', *The Journal of the Royal Central Asian Society*, 13/1, January 1944, p.14.

[1A] Hasan Isfandyari, President of the *Majlis* for the Tenth, Eleventh, Twelfth and Thirteenth sessions, was by then seventy-four years old.

[2] J. Mihdinya, *Zindagi-i Syasi-i Razmara* (Tehran: *Giti*, 1363 (1984)) p.399.

[3] *Ittilaât* newspaper, supplement *Bist va Hasht Hizar Rouz-i Tarikh-i Iran va Jahan*, p.562.

[4] D.N. Wilber, *Contemporary Iran* (London: Thames and Hudson, 1963) p.50.

[5] E. Abrahamian, *Iran between Two Revolutions* (Princeton University Press, 1982) p.178.

[6] The quote from A. Kasravi, *Afsaran-i Ma* (Tehran: 1st ed., 1945) pp.25-6, was cited in *Towards a Modern Iran*, ed. by E. Kedourie and S.G. Haim (London: F. Cass, 1980) p.117.

7 The quote from A. Kasravi, *Dadgah*, p.44., ibid., p.118.
8 *Yadnameh Ustad-i Shahid Mutahhari*, ed. by Â. K. Suroush, (Tehran: *Intisharat va Amuzish-i Inqilab-i Islami*, 1360, (1981)) p.334.
9 M. Mutahhari, in *Bahsi dar Bareh-yi Marjaîyat va Rouhaniyat* (Tehran: *Shirkat-i Sahami Intishar*, 1341, (1962)) p.187.
10 Ibid., p.188.
11 P. Avery, *Modern Iran* (New York: Praeger, 1965) p.292.
12 *Majmouêh Intisharat-i Anjuman-i Tablighat-i Islami* (Tehran: *Taban*, 1323 (1944)) pp.11-12.
13 S. Akhavi, *Religion and Politics in Contemporary Iran* (Albany: State University of New York Press, 1980) p.73.
14 A. Khameh'i, *Fursat-i Buzurg as Dast Rafteh* (The Great Chance that was Lost), (Tehran: *Hafteh*, 1362 (1983)) p.17.
15 N. JAMI, *Guzashteh Chiragh-i Rah-i Ayandeh Ast* (Tehran: *Quqnous*, 1361 (1982)) p.190.
16 G. Lenczowski, *Russia and the West in Iran* (New York: Greenwood Press, 1968) pp.224-5.
17 E. Abrahamian, op. cit. (note 5), p.281.
18 C. Chaqueri, *The Condition of the Working Class in Iran* (European Committee for the Defence of Democratic Rights of Workers in Iran, 1978) pp.10-11.
19 Ibid., p.99.
20 L.P. Elwell-Sutton, *Persian Oil* (London: Lawrence and Wishart, 1955) p.147.
21 C. Chaqueri, op. cit. (note 18), p.138.
22 E. Abrahamian, op. cit. (note 5), p.292.
22A Engineer Bazargan's greatest coup was to use the post-war clout of the Engineers' Association to successfully negotiate with the old Elite the entry of non-Elitist engineering firms into the lucrative public consultancy business. Many young middle-class engineers thus came to owe their future fortune to Bazargan's skilful negotiation on their behalf.
23 G. Lenczowski, op. cit. (note 16), p.326.
24 Private communication made by the (then) young party member in question.
25 M.K. Sheehan, *Iran: The Impact of US Interests and Policies (1941-1954)* (New York: Th. Gaus, 1968) p.13.
26 Ibid., p.19.
26A The British MESC had been "set up in Cairo in 1941", under the "energetic and persistent director, Robert Jackson". Its objective was to "mobilise and reallocate Middle East production", acting as a "problem-solver"; the small British outfit played an important role during the war. See M. Wilmington, *The Middle East Supply Centre* (London: University of London Press, 1972).
27 A.H. Hamzavi, *Persia and the Powers* (London: Hutchinson, undated) pp.80-81.
28 As quoted by M. Khan Malik Yazdi, *Arzish-i Masaî-i Iran dar Jang* (Tehran: *Vizarat-i Kishavarzi* (Ministry of Agriculture), 1324 (1945)) p.171.
29 Ibid., p.170.
30 Many Iranian entrepreneurs made a fortune during the war transporting goods for the Allies. A handful ended the war as multi-millionaires. Among them was Desire Kettaneh, a wily entrepreneur of Lebanese origin.
31 *Our Industry*, The Anglo-Iran Oil Co., (London: The AIOC Central Planning Dept, 2nd ed., June 1949) p.343.

32 See A.M. Samsam Bakhtiari, 'Abadan Refinery', in *Iran Oil News*, Vol. 60 (October–December 1990), (Tehran: NIOC Public Relations Dept., 1990) p.38.
33 I. Naraghi, *Social Problems Related to the Oil Industry in Iran* (Farvardin 1337 (April 1958)).
34 A.K.S. Lambton, *Landlord and Peasant in Persia* (Oxford University Press, 1969) p.286.
35 Schulze-Holthus, *Daybreak in Iran* (London: Staples Press Ltd., 1954) pp.158-314. Schulze-Holthus would become military adviser to Nasir Khan Qashqa'i over the period 1942–1944, and advised the Qashqa'i tribal insurrection during these years.
36 E.H. Cookridge, *Secrets of the British Secret Service* (London: Sampson Low, Martson and Co., 1948) p.151. Also see: Schulze-Holthus, op. cit. above, p.182.
37 R. Bullard, Britain and the Middle East, (London: Longmans, 1951) p.138.
38 *Tarikhcheh Si Saleh Bank-i Milli Iran*, (Tehran: Bank-i Milli Iran, undated) pp.192 and 219.
39 *Ittilaât* newspaper, op. cit. (note 3), p.617.
40 Private communication by an older member of Iran's medical corps, reminiscing about his war years.
41 *Tarikhcheh Si Saleh...* op. cit. (note 38), pp.199 and 218.
42 Ibid., pp.216, 224 and 227.
43 A.C. Millspaugh, *Americans in Persia* ((Washington D.C.: The Brookings Institution, 1946) pp.273-5.
43A N.R. Keddie, *Roots of Revolution, An Interpretative History of Modern Iran* (Yale University Press, 1981) p.115.
44 M.K. Sheehan, op. cit. (note 25), p.18.
45 *Ittilaât* newspaper, op. cit. (note 3), p.949. Quoting from Muhammad Reza Shah's speech at the closing ceremony of the Nineteenth *Majlis* on June 5, 1960.
46 N. JAMI, op. cit. (note 15), p.175.
47 See G. Le Bon, *Psychologie des Foules*, (Paris: Felix Alcan, 1911).
48 By his young wife, Qavam would have a son Husayn, born in 1945, who was to commit suicide in December 1982.
49 E. Abrahamian, op. cit. (note 5), p.181.
50 Ibid., p.178.
51 Ibid., p.176.
52 P.C. Radji, *In the Service of the Peacock Throne* (London: Hamish Hamilton, 1983) p.34.
53 E. Abrahamian, op. cit. (note 5), p.183.
54 Schulze-Holthus, op. cit. (note 35), pp.316-318. General Zahidi was arrested by Fitzroy Maclean in 1943 and sent to the Arak internment camp. Franz Mayr was arrested in 1943 too. Schulze-Holthus and Kurmis were taken into British custody in April 1944 after Nasir Khan Qashqa'i first imprisoned and then betrayed them. SS officer Kurmis committed suicide by jumping from his hospital room's window (where he had been taken for a blood transfusion after slashing his own wrists), grabbing his guard in his fall. Both died. Schulze-Holthus was exchanged for a British officer and returned to Berlin via Switzerland in early 1945.
55 *The History of the Second World War* (London: Purnell and Sons, 1968) Vol. 3, no. 7 (El Alamein) ; Vol. 3, no.15 (Stalingrad).
56 Ibid., Vol. 4, no. 10.

57 E.A. Bayne, *Persian Kingship in Transition* (New York: American Universities Field Staff, 1968) pp.256-7.
58 E. Abrahamian, 'Factionalism in Iran: Political Groups in the Fourteenth Parliament,' in *Middle Eastern Studies*, Vol. 14, no. 1, January 1978, p.29.
59 Ibid., p.31.
60 Z. Shajiî, *Namayandigan-i Majlis-i Shoura-yi Milli dar Bist va Yik Doureh-yi Qanoun Guzari* (Tehran: 1344 (1965)).
61 M.Â. Safari, *Qalam va Syasat* (Tehran: *Namak*, 1371 (1992) p.106. And also: E. Abrahamian, op. cit. (note 58).
62 H. Kay Ustuvan, *Syasat-i Muvazineh-yi Manfi* (Tehran: *Muzaffar*, 1327 (1948)) Vol. I, p.93.
63 E. Abrahamian, op. cit. (note 58), pp.43-44.
64 At one of the sessions of the Sâid cabinet, the minister in charge of sports reported that national weightlifter Namjou had "broken yet another record", which attracted the following reply from the prime minister: "Well, for this time I accept paying for his misdeed from government funds, but tell him that next time he breaks anything he will have to pay for it out of his own pocket." Private communication from a civil servant who had it from the minister in charge of sports.
65 E. Abrahamian, op. cit. (note 58), pp.39-40.
65A Curtis and Hoover had previously (1943) been advising the Venezuelan Government on their oil concessions, and had then, for the first time, proposed a 50-50 split of profits between the oil companies and the host country. See L.M. Fanning, *Foreign Oil and the Free World* (McGraw-Hill Book Co., 1954) p.94.
66 Anglo-American Agreement of August 8, 1944 at Washington.
67 N.S. Fatemi, *Oil Diplomacy* (New York: Whittier Books, 1954) p.239.
68 H. Kay Ustuvan, op. cit. (note 62), Vol. I, p.193.
69 Ibid., Vol. I, p.198.
70 *Asnad-i Naft* (Tehran: *Puyan*, 1330 (1951)) p.24.
71 H. Kay Ustuvan, op.cit. (note 62), Vol. I, p.223.

CHAPTER NINE:
TURBULENT TIMES

With the guns now silent in Europe, the after-effects of the war were still to have an impact on Iran. The Soviet Red Army still occupied the northern provinces. In August of 1945, two noteworthy incidents were to occur in the Soviet northern zone.

The first incident happened in Khurasan where, at Mashhad, in the evening of August 16, a group of officers under the command of Major Âli Akbar Iskandani rebelled, stole a jeep and two trucks, and headed west. The first destination of Iskandani's small troop (nineteen officers and six soldiers) was Gurgan. In that northern town, Iskandani was joined by six *Toudeh* officers sent in from Tehran under the command of Colonel Azar.[1] The Gurgan *Toudeh* leader Ahmad Qasimi had been directed to assist the rebels, which he did.[2] As the small caravan was crossing the town of Gunbad-i Kavous on August 20, it was ambushed in broad daylight by a well-entrenched Gendarmerie battalion. Iskandani paid the price of his insouciance with his life, along with four of his officers and two soldiers. The remainder of the group was able to escape the ambush and surrender to Soviet forces. Thus ended a bizarre episode which must have had the Soviets' green light,[3] and whose alleged objective was to have Iskandani's group lead a force of 2,000 Turkoman warriors stationed near the Soviet border. Along the way, something must have gone wrong in the overall plan, for on August 19, at Gunbad, Qasimi had told Iskandani: "Your action is useless and negative ...there is nothing the party [*Toudeh*] can do for you"; and a Soviet major told the escapees "Your rebellion was a damnable action!"[4]

The second incident occurred in the small Azarbayjan village of Liqvan, where, at the instigation of three communist agents, the landlord Hajji Ihtisham, his wife and his three children, were murdered. When the conservative elements of the province, harassed and exhausted by four years of Soviet occupation, failed to react to the tragic Liqvan murders, the communists had an open field in Azarbayan.

9.1. North-western Secessions

The Azarbayjani communists would not hesitate to use any opening offered them. Naturally they had the blessing of the Red Army's command in their endeavours. In September 1945, a new organisation, the *Firqeh Dimukrat Azarbayjan* (Democratic Grouping of Azarbayjan) was established at Tabriz by Sayyid Jâfar Pishavari* and Mirza Âli Shabistari; the *Firqeh* set up an eleven-member central committee with Pishavari as secretary and Shabistari as his deputy. An armed *Firqeh* militia was organised, and its members took the name of *fada'yan*, in memory of Sattar Khan and Baqir Khan. Within a month, the *fada'yan* controlled all major towns in Azarbayjan.[5] The *Firqeh* published its own newspaper entitled *Azarbayjan*. On November 20 at Tabriz a People's Congress was brought together to appoint a thirty-nine-member national committee for supervising the elections to the national assembly of Azarbayjan. The deputies were promptly elected and the assembly inaugurated on December 12, with Shabistari as its speaker. The assembly's first act was to create a National Government of Azarbayjan (*Hukumat-i Milli-i Azarbayjan*), placing Pishavari at its head with a cabinet of ten ministers. Four days later, the Third Army of General Dirakhshani, garrisoned at Tabriz, was disarmed by the *fada'yan* with no attempt at resistance. The Riza'iyyeh garrison under Colonel Zanganeh resisted (as it had been ordered to by the general staff) before capitulating; Zanganeh was arrested and incarcerated.

* SAYYID JÂFAR PISHAVARI (1893–1949), born in Sadat, near Bhalkhal; studied at Baku (1905–11); high school teacher (1911–19); took part in October Revolution (1917); joined Communist Party of Iran (1920); organised trade unions in Tehran, published *Haqiqat* (1920–30); arrested, imprisoned at Qasr (1930–40); exiled to Kashan (1940-1); not founding member of *Toudeh*, published *Azhir* (1941–45); MP from Tabriz in 14th *Majlis*, his mandate was revoked (1944); created *Firqeh Dimukrat* at Tabriz (1945); led National Government of Azarbayjan, launched sweeping programme of reforms (December 1945–December 1946); retreating before the Iranian Army's onslaught, fled to Baku with 70,000 *fada'yan* (early 1947); uselessly begged the Soviets to rearm his men (1948); died under shrouded circumstances at Baku (1949).

The Iranian province of Azarbayjan had thus seceded, giving birth to an independent government, an event of unprecedented gravity for the Iranian nation state. A country that had maintained its integrity since 1828 was abruptly cut off from its main province: Iran without Azarbayjan was not Iran any more. In just a hundred days, Pishavari had, with tacit Soviet blessing, succeeded in his bid for secession. As soon as he was in power, he announced a programme of sweeping reforms with, for the first time in Iranian history, a drastic land reform. With this train of reforms, Pishavari's popularity, which was already high, soared. Pishavari was certainly sincere in his wish to reform, but, nevertheless, the game in which he had engaged Iran was dangerous: a Finlandisation of Azarbayjan or its takeover by Soviet Azarbayjan (leading to a 'Great Azarbayjan', the dream of the Soviet Azarbayjani leader Mir Jâfar Baqerof (a close friend of Beria's) and of his deputy Mirza Ibragimov) were two of the possible outcomes.

Following in Pishavari's footsteps were his neighbours the Kurds. The Iranian Kurds were but part and parcel of the great Kurdish family which had branched out into Iraq and Turkey after being denied the Kurdish State foreseen by the Treaty of Sèvres in 1920. Iranian Kurdistan, with its backward agriculture (some tobacco) and its hinterland in Iraqi Kurdistan, was ideally located for smuggling and armed rebellions. The use of all three Kurdistans by the Powers for their own ends further exacerbated the Kurdish predicament. In the summer of 1943, the attention of the Soviet command in northern Iran was drawn by a secret Kurdish society created in Mahabad: the Committee of Kurdish Youth,[6] better known as the *Kumileh Jiani Kurdistan* or simply *Kumileh*. This secret society, which admitted only Kurdish members, elected as its leader the reform-minded religious leader Qazi Muhammad of Mahabad. The organisation's military arm consisted of 3,000 *pishmirgas* (lit. 'those who don't fear death') under the command of the Iraqi Kurdish tribal leader Mulla Mustafa Barzani. Qazi Muhammad, following Pishavari's lead, founded the *Hizb-i Dimukrat-i Kurdistan* (the Kurdish Democratic Party – KDP) in August 1945, and in December, only three days after Azarbayjan, seceded too, establishing the National Government of [Iranian] Kurdistan, later known as the Republic of Kurdistan or the Republic of Mahabad. On January 22, 1946, the thirteen-member *Majlis* of Kurdistan elected Qazi Muhammad as its chief of government and Qazi's cousin Muhammad Husayn Sayf Qazi as its Minister of War.[7]

With all their common points, the Governments of Azarbayjan and Kurdistan had ample reason to join forces against any potential threat (especially in view of the fact that Baqerof had promised them total independence should his 'Great Azarbayjan' materialise). Surprisingly it took protracted negotiations between the two parties to hammer out a treaty of friendship (signed on April 23, 1946), including a clause for mutual assistance in case of aggression and calling for the joint approval of any agreement negotiated with Tehran.

In Tehran, the political class had grasped the gravity of the twin secessions – with Azarbayjan naturally eclipsing Kurdistan. Neither Premier Muhsin Sadr nor his successor Ibrahim Hakimi (he had replaced Sadr as premier on December 20) were thought able to handle such a secession. Hakimi's only plausible option was negotiations with Moscow; he therefore suggested such a visit to the Soviets, who readily turned it down, both Soviet Ambassador Maximov and his deputy Yaghoubov being recalled to Moscow for consultations.[8] Hakimi was in a political impasse: he had to go. On January 19, his last move was to instruct his ambassador to London, Taqizadeh, to file a complaint with the Security Council of the United Nations. On January 21, Hakimi resigned, leaving the field to the only Iranian statesman with a chance of solving the Azarbayjan conundrum: the inevitable Ahmad Qavam.

On January 26, the Fourteenth *Majlis* approved Qavam's premiership by a majority of one.[9] Once at the helm, Qavam lost no time in sending a telegram to Stalin, knowing perfectly well that the key to Azarbayjan (if there was one) was in Moscow. The Soviet leader replied by inviting him to Moscow. The Soviets believed then that they could 'do business' with Qavam; they knew him to be head and shoulders above the Iranian polity and hoped that he would play the old Qajar balancing game between them and the British, which was, in a way, their best alternative in Iran. The Security Council replied on January 30 to Iran's complaint by calling for direct Soviet-Iranian negotiations, in line with Qavam's Moscow trip. Qavam prepared himself without unmasking his batteries. He waited for the very last day (February 18) before his departure for Moscow and then went to the *Majlis* to present his cabinet. He told the deputies that he would table his programme after his return from Moscow, leaving suspense high. There was nothing the helpless deputies could do about the premier's coldly bypassing them: they knew that he held all the trump cards, and they had been given a first hint that henceforward he would play his hand as he wished, without caring about the Shah, the *Majlis* or public opinion. On the Azarbayjan question Qavam was the soloist who knew that the stakes were as high as they could be: he was playing for Iran and his own immortality. The part of his life.

Before Qavam's trip to Moscow, James Byrnes, the US Secretary of State, and Ernest Bevin, the British Foreign Minister, had been there to meet the Soviet leadership to discuss points of contention. The evacuation of Soviet troops from Iran was on the agenda. After the first round of talks with Stalin, Secretary Byrnes became highly suspicious about the presence of Soviet troops, because Stalin kept mentioning absurd excuses for keeping them there; for example, the Soviet leader contended that "saboteurs from Iran would infiltrate into Russia and set fire to the Baku oil fields".[10] Byrnes first warned, then even threatened, the Soviets – President Truman had sent him a memorandum urging him to use "strong language" and "an iron fist" at the Moscow conference[11] – but to no avail. Even Bevin's proposal for a tripartite commission to settle the Iranian problem proved unacceptable to the Soviets. As the American and British envoys departed Moscow, it had become clear that the Red Army's withdrawal from Iran would not be the formality everyone had thought it would be. Perhaps it could be said that the very first shots of the Cold War were exchanged between Byrnes and Bevin, on the one side, and Stalin and Molotov on the other, at Moscow, over the Iranian question.

If the official American and British representatives returned empty-handed from Moscow, Qavam's predicament looked grim at best. Nevertheless the Iranian premier was able to meet Stalin twice and Molotov a total of four times between his arrival in Moscow on February 19 and his departure on March 6. On March 2, Stalin told him that only Soviet troops stationed in the north-east (i.e. Mashhad, Shahroud and Simnan) would be withdrawn. Qavam replied by issuing a protest note to the Soviet Government for failing to remove their troops from Azarbayjan in accordance with the 1942 agreement – Great Britain and the United States also filed separate official protests on March 4 and March 8 respectively.[12] The Soviets answered that "they were going to remain in some parts of Iran until the situation had been 'elucidated' [sic]".[13] By not honouring their signed word, the Soviets had shown their true colours: even their closest allies (those alongside whom they had just won the Second World War) could not trust their signature. Such a state was not a good omen for the Soviet regime in the long term. Formal protests failed to move Stalin and Molotov. The latter made a last-minute proposal to Qavam for the creation of a joint Soviet-Iranian company to exploit Iran's northern oil resources for fifty years. Qavam, although under considerable pressure, kept his nerve[14] and refused to sign the proposal. He also refused to sign the final joint communiqué prepared by the Soviets (a watered-down version was later issued). If Qavam came back to Tehran on March 8 empty-handed, apparently he had not given away anything either.

In Tehran, Qavam gave a full report of his Moscow negotiations to a closed session of the Fourteenth *Majlis* on March 10, the day before its dissolution. From then on, Qavam, with no *Majlis* and no other internal watchdog to hinder him, was in full command of the whole situation. On March 18, he ordered his UN representative, Husayn Âla, to file a fresh complaint with the Security Council; but Âla, playing his own game, tergiversated and failed to follow Tehran's instructions, prompting Qavam to reprimand him in a nasty telegram[15] (rightfully so, because an envoy either carries out his government's orders or resigns). At the *Nowrouz* (New Year) of March 21, 1946, Tehran was full of rumours of a *Toudeh* coup, supported by the Soviet tanks. Endeavouring to make the best of a tense situation, Qavam relentlessly followed his policy of appeasement towards the Soviets. He had the Anglophile chief of the army general staff, General Hasan Ârfa, dismissed and imprisoned; other personalities suspected of being Anglophile, such as Sayyid Zia', Âli Dashti, Jamal Imami and Dr Tahiri, were also arrested.

Meanwhile, his trusted deputy Muzaffar Firouz carried on secret negotiations with Soviet Ambassador Sadchikov.

As Qavam followed his programme of conciliation, Radio Moscow announced on March 25 that within the next five or six weeks the withdrawal of all Soviet troops from Azarbayjan, begun the day before, would be completed. The multi-sided strategy of Qavam had brought about the final peaceful end to the issue that many had come to doubt. Perhaps American pressures, with President Truman sending Stalin a March 21 ultimatum "to get out or we would put some more people in there [i.e. Iran]",[16] had influenced the Soviets. Iranian historian K.A. Samii believes that President Truman's "peremptory message to Stalin"[16A] allegedly delivered by Bedell Smith "caused a reversal of Soviet policy", but "his contention is not convincing".[16B] On the other hand, American historian M.H. Lytle is highly sceptical about such claims,[16C] and is of the opinion that in 1946, America was far from taking a leading role in Iran. The British, however had risen to the danger, and were doing their best to jockey for a peaceful settlement.[16D] But all these speculations come to naught, when one looks at the conundrum from Qavam's point of view. Such a sophisticated statesman as Qavam would not have gone to so much effort with the Soviets if he had known or even suspected that the US (with its then nuclear advantage) was squarely behind Iran's moves. If Qavam eventually signed the agreement with Sadchikov (see below), it was because there was no other way out, even though that signature allowed him to be branded a traitor, and finally cost him his career when he had to perform political *hara-kiri* when the Fifteenth *Majlis* rebuffed both it and him. Thus it was Qavam, and only Qavam, who manoeuvred in such a diplomatically astute way that, by the close of March 1946, the Soviets had reached the point where they had more to win by leaving than by staying put. All the credit should go to the foxy old statesman for this diplomatic masterpiece; and the plaudits for any supporting role (if any) would have to go to the British diplomats, not to President Truman.

In Iran, all the credit was given to Qavam: he fully deserved all of it. At the close of January he had accepted this unique responsibility and brought it to a successful end by the close of March: mission accomplished. He had realised what many believed to be impossible: the withdrawal of the Red Army from a conquered province. With this indisputable victory, he dominated the whole Iranian polity. Finally it was he who had filled the vacuum created upon Reza Shah's departure. On April 4, reassured that the Red Army was really packing, he signed a three-point agreement with Soviet Ambassador Sadchikov calling for: (1) the creation of a joint Soviet-Iranian oil company for exploiting Iran's northern provinces oil resources over fifty years (with a 51% Soviet shareholding for the first twenty-five years and 50/50 thereafter), pending ratification by the Fifteenth

Majlis within the next seven months; (2) the evacuation of Iran by Soviet troops to be completed by May 6, 1946; (3) the Azarbayjan problem was deemed to be an internal Iranian affair.

So Qavam had finally had to agree to the all-important oil concession (point one) in a *quid pro quo* for the Azarbayjan province (points two and three): a relatively cheap price to pay – especially as the Soviet were paying cash, and Qavam in the future. The Qavam-Sadchikov agreement had most probably been reached secretly at Moscow, with Qavam making its final signature contingent upon the official Soviet declaration of withdrawal. That the agreement was in direct breach of the December 2, 1944 *Majlis* bill was no worry to Qavam: with the departure of the Red Army from Azarbayjan, he had already entered immortality.

9.2. Ahmad Qavam

In spite of his triumph in the negotiations with the Soviets, Qavam still had a long way to go. Not a man to let himself be carried away, he focused on the major problems he had to tackle to achieve the success of his scheme. First on his agenda was yet again Azarbayjan and the Pishavari Government; second, the *Toudeh* threat was hanging like a Damoclean sword over Iran; and third, the settlement of the Soviet oil concession. Qavam would concentrate on all three in parallel, playing a delicate game on the three distinct, albeit interrelated, boards. In his labours the Prime Minister was aided by the indefatigable Prince Muzaffar Firouz* who, possessing his own political dexterity (a serious match for Qavam), was also playing the game of his life.

* MUZAFFAR FIROUZ (1906–1988), son of Nusrat ul-Douleh and Daftar ul-Muluk (Dr Musaddiq's sister); educated in England (1912–29); joined Levant Service before his return to Persia; briefly with Ministry of Industries, then entered Foreign Affairs (1930); attaché to Washington Embassy; turned to politics (1941); engineered Sayyid Zia's comeback (1943–5), then joined Qavam's team (1945); appointed deputy prime minister and head of Propaganda in Qavam's first cabinet (1946); masterminded creation of *Dimukrat Iran* Party (1946); Minister for Labour and Propaganda in second Qavam cabinet

(1946); Ambassador to Moscow (November 1946–August 1947); self-exile to Paris; continued political activities, sending pertinent letters on Iranian affairs to various heads of state; compiled political memoirs: *L'Iran Face à l'Imposture de l'Histoire*; passed away in April 1988.

Qavam's overall strategy would always be hidden behind a smokescreen of apparent goodwill – goodwill towards Pishavari, towards the *Toudeh* and towards the Soviets. With Pishavari, he accepted entry into negotiations with a rebel government. The first round of talks, held in Tehran April 28–May 13 between Pishavari and Firouz, proved fruitless; the second round, begun on June 11 at Tabriz, finally yielded the Pishavari-Firouz agreement of June 15. The agreement met almost all of Pishavari's major demands, but was restrained to the province of Azarbayjan. Many came to believe that the settlement achieved "was undoubtedly a victory for the Communists".[17] In fact, though, Firouz and Qavam had given the Azarbayjani leadership enough rope to hang itself, by bringing it to limit itself to "an azarbayjanian Azarbayjan".[18] Failing to table his demands on the national scale, Pishavari had fallen into Qavam's trap of remaining a mere secessionist province. And that was what Qavam had been angling for, knowing that it didn't pay for a province to stand up to the central government.

The Azarbayjani leadership was not alone in falling into traps. The central committee of the *Iran* Party fell into one too. Fearing to miss the train, the purblind party leadership, under Engineer Farivar, Dr Sanjabi and Allahyar Salih, jumped on the *Toudeh* bandwagon by forming with it the *Jibheh Mûtalifeh-yi Ahzab-i Azadikhah* (the Coalition of Libertarian Parties) in the last days of June 1946. The threat posed by the coalition of the centrist and leftist counter-elites was not lost on Qavam: on June 30, he created his own party, the *Hizb-i Dimukrat-i Iran* (Democratic Party of Iran). For the first time in Iran's history a ruling prime minister was launching a political party. Qavam had even selected his party's name in direct opposition to Pishavari's, only substituting *Iran* for *Azarbayjan*. The Prime Minister was naturally party chairman, with Firouz as vice-chairman and Hasan Arsanjani as editor of the party newspaper, *Dimukrat Iran* (Democratic Iran). With his fresh party, Qavam was providing a refuge (against the Red wave) for all of Iran's right-of-centre politicians – a wide spectrum ranging from the old Elite to businessmen and tribal *khans*.

On August 1, 1946, Qavam had yet another stroke of genius as he offered the coalition of *Toudeh* and *Iran* parties four portfolios in his reshuffled cabinet. Three went to *Toudeh* leaders: Culture to Dr F. Kishavarz, Health to Dr M. Yazdi and Commerce and Industry to Iraj Iskandari; and the fourth to Allahyar Salih of the *Iran* Party (at Justice). Qavam was careful to keep the Interior and Foreign Affairs portfolios for himself and pack the other ministries with uncompromising anti-leftist elements: General Amir Ahmadi (War), General Muhammad Husayn Firouz (Roads), Dr Manouchihr Iqbal (PTT) and Âbdul-Husayn Hazhir (Finance). As for Muzaffar Firouz, he was appointed deputy prime minister in charge of the crucial Ministry of Labour and Propaganda. In this venture, the *Toudeh* had everything to lose and nothing to win; on the other hand, Qavam was scoring yet another double victory: (i) by muzzling the leftist opposition (how could it criticise a government in which it had three portfolios?); and (ii) by reawakening dormant rightist forces to whom the existence of *Toudeh* ministers was anathema. Simultaneously, Qavam had played for time, in order to bolster his own party.

For Iran's southern tribal leaders, communist ministers represented a *casus belli* against the central government which dared harbour them. Encouraged underhandedly by Qavam – through middlemen like Isfahan's Rashidians (father Habibullah[18A] and sons Asadullah, Qudratullah and Sayfullah) – the southern tribal leaders formed the *Nihzat-i Junoub* (Southern Movement). Prominent in this anti-leftist movement were Nasir Khan Qashqa'i, Murtaza Quli Khan Samsam Bakhtiari[19] (who had entered an alliance with Nasir Khan at Simirum in August 1944) and the highly capable Fathullah Hayat Davoudi (the *ilkhan* of the small Hayat Davoudi tribe whose tribal lands straddled the Persian Gulf seashore around Bandar-i Ganaveh and Bandar-i Rig); completing the loose movement were the Qavam ul-Douleh family at Shiraz and the Fatimi family (especially Nasrullah Sayfpour) at Isfahan. Ere long, the movement's leaders sent an ultimatum to Qavam calling for the dismissal of the three communist ministers. In order to underline their demands with action, the Qashqa'is and Hayat Davoudis swiftly occupied Bushire and Kaziroun, and besieged Shiraz. At Bushire, they "requisitioned 6,000 rifles, numerous machine-guns and millions of rounds of ammunitions".[20] This factual requisition made absurd the allegation that the southern tribes "had received arms from the British Navy in the Gulf";[21] although some British diplomats – including Colonel H.J. Underwood (in charge of tribal affairs at Ahvaz), A.C. Trott (consul at Ahvaz) and C.A. Gault (consul at Isfahan) – might have poured some fuel on the movement's fire.

As the southern tribesmen were storming Bushire and Kaziroun, the Bakhtiaris failed once again in their plan to occupy Isfahan. As usual, internecine dissensions between the leading *khans* jeopardised the plan. Abu'l Qasim Khan caught wind of the plot's preparations and alerted the Tehran authorities. Muzaffar Firouz had made a detour through Isfahan to order the arrest of Murtaza Quli Khan Samsam, his three sons (Ahmad Quli, Jahanshah and Amir Bahman), Habibullah Rashidian and his sons (Asadullah and Qudratullah), and the journalist Abutalib Shirvani (editor of the *Mihan* (Nation) newspaper),[22] and had them sent to Tehran.[23] Firouz also had Colonel Hijazi, the commander of the Khuzistan Army, arrested for colluding with the tribal *khans*. Here, the nervous Firouz had gone one arrest too far. In Tehran, the reaction to Hijazi's arrest was shattering: the Generals Amir Ahmadi (Minister of War), Razmara (chief of the general army staff) and Safari (head of police) tendered their resignation. Qavam naturally refused to accept the resignations, but went in person to the Ministry of War to present his apologies to the generals;[24] Colonel Hijazi having been released in the meantime. Alienating the army was the last thing Qavam wanted at this point in time, for (he knew) that it would soon have an important role to play in his master plan. Unfortunately, Firouz, a valuable lieutenant, did sometimes create problems by his excess of zeal.

One of the programmes Muzaffar Firouz had almost single-handedly pushed throughout 1946 was the compilation of labour regulation laws, which were severely missing from Iran's legal panoply. Up to 1946, only a total of three pieces of legislation (a directive and two laws) had been issued nationally for workers and work conditions:

(1) A Directive for Carpet Factories, issued in eleven articles, on December 16, 1923, by the then Governor-General of Kerman and Baluchistan, Sardar Muâzam, for the protection of factory workers.[25]

(2) The August 10, 1936 law regulating factories and industrial establishments, compiled in sixty-nine articles, but giving little consideration to workers' rights.[26]

(3) The November 20, 1943 law relating to workers' insurance and work-induced disability, issued in four articles by Âli Suhayli's cabinet.[27]

Firouz provided the original framework for a comprehensive and complete Labour Bill (48 articles[28]), ratified by the Council of Ministers (there was no *Majlis*) on May 18, 1946.

Later the bill, thought to be too socialist, was totally rewritten and reduced to twenty-one articles before being ratified by the *Majlis* in June 1949. Another of Firouz's labour coups was his marathon negotiations in Abadan and Ahvaz with the oil industry's trade unions in the aftermath of the bloody strike of July 1946, to reach a satisfactory settlement of the dispute. Firouz's last effort yielded the important Minimum Wages Regulation of October 1946. That was as far as Firouz went before November 1946, when he was finally given his marching orders to Moscow, where Qavam had appointed him ambassador.

Even without Firouz, the social programme he had launched was underway, and his Higher Council of Labour was the supreme arbiter in labour affairs. During the year 1947, the Council passed the following pieces of legislation:

February 22 – decree preventing the dismissal of surplus workers without the Labour Ministry's prior approval.

June 12 – establishment of the *Sazman-i Ta'min-ha-yi Ijtimaî* (Social Welfare Organisation) provided for in the Labour Bill (art. 37); placed under the supervision of the Higher Council of Labour.

July 12 – Regulations for workers' insurance, superseding the November 20, 1943 law.

July 14 – regulations for workers' education and training.

July 21 – regulations for the formation of workers' unions.

In May 1947, as the first National Workers' Congress met in Tehran, Iranian labour had a solid legal backing. This was by no means a small achievement of the Qavam/Firouz team as it cut the grass from under the *Toudeh*'s feet, and, furthermore, was a programme without which the rightist backlash would not have been possible.

While Firouz was busy formulating his labour laws in Tehran, Pishavari was hurrying to enforce his programme of reforms in Azarbayjan. Within a short timespan, the Azarbayjani leader was able to:[29]
- make it a legal offence for a public servant to take a bribe;
- found the University of Tabriz with two faculties: Literature and Medicine;
- control the prices of basic commodities;
- create health clinics for the destitute;
- legally set minimum wages and the maximum number of working hours;
- put the unemployed to work on regional infrastructure projects.

All these achievements were secondary to Pishavari's land reform programme. Many before him, from the Constitutionalists to the *Jangalis*, had envisioned it, but no one had ever dared push it through. Pishavari didn't hesitate: he placed it at the top of his agenda. On February 11, 1946 (less than two months after coming to power), he had the Azarbayjani Council of Ministers approve the Land Reform Bill; five days later, the Azarbayjani *Majlis* ratified it. Azarbayjan's Land Reform Law provided for the distribution of *khaliseh* (crown) villages to their peasants (with around 1,000 such villages in Azarbayjan) and the sequestration and distribution of the villages belonging to landlords who had fled Azarbayjan (an estimated 437 cases[30]). As for the landlords still in Azarbayjan, they were not particularly harassed and an April 11, 1946 law (22 articles) regulated their position *vis-à-vis* their peasants. In April 14, the first Azarbayjani Congress of Peasants, attended by some six hundred delegates, was inaugurated at Tabriz. Pishavari had opened a Pandora's box by awakening the dormant giant of Iranian society: the peasantry.

In Tehran, Qavam attempted to counter Pishavari's land reform by introducing a bill calling for the sale of all *khaliseh* lands and villages across the country and stipulating a 15% increase in the share of land produce accruing to the peasants. That was yet another commendable effort on the Prime Minister's part, but was too little too late. Later, nothing would remain of Qavam's bill, but Pishavari's land reform had stretched the imagination. The seed had been planted: land reform was possible. The sacred cow of Iranian political life had been slain by Pishavari in Azarbayjan.

But Pishavari's days were numbered, for in Tehran Qavam was engineering the last phase of his master plan for the recovery of Azarbayjan. Before entering the final straight, Qavam had wanted to make absolutely sure of the Soviets' non-intervention. For this specific purpose, he had attracted the up-and-coming *Le Monde* editorialist Edouard Sablier to Tehran for an exclusive interview.[31] In reply to the inevitable question on the Soviet-Iranian oil company, Qavam told Sablier that it was up to the Fifteenth *Majlis* to ratify the agreement (the seven months' deadline was already forgotten), and that the *Majlis* formation required elections, which in turn needed law and order, and that in this context Azarbayjan and Kurdistan had somehow to be brought back under the law. When the Soviets totally failed to react to the Sablier editorial in *Le Monde* (a kite sent up by Qavam), a reassured Qavam moved on to the final act.

On October 18, 1946, Qavam dismissed his three *Toudeh* ministers, apparently bowing to southern tribal pressures. In November, it was Muzaffar Firouz's time to go: he had begun to flirt with *Toudeh* (in case they suddenly grabbed power) and with the young General Razmara, chief of the general staff (with whom he planned a coup *à la* 1921 with himself as political leader and Razmara as the military one to topple the Pahlavis[32]). Qavam simultaneously ordered the release from prison of General Ârfa, Âli Dashti, Dr Tahiri, Jamal Imami and all the Isfahan conspirators. Thus the Prime Minister had completed his U-turn. Now he was ready for the invasion of Azarbayjan.

Qavam knew that he could rely heavily on General Razmara, the highly capable chief of the general staff. The Premier further paved the way for the national army by having his friends (of the old Qajar network) the Zu'lfaqari brothers of Zanjan – namely Mahmoud, Muhammad and Nasir, the three sons of Asad ul-Douleh, a wealthy Zanjan landowner since Qajar times (who had a total of nine sons and four daughters) – prepare the ground for the troops' initial advance. On December 7 and 8, the last Soviet contingent advising the Azarbayjan Popular Army departed Iran, taking their heavy weapons with them.[33] On December 9 and 10, Iranian Air Force planes dropped leaflets on Tabriz asking the population to co-operate with the national army which was coming to restore law and order to the province. On December 10, the government troops took Zanjan and moved on to Tabriz, which they reached after two days, encountering little resistance. It seemed that the military command of the Azarbayjani Popular Army had abruptly torn apart under pressure – even in peacetime there had been tensions between the educated (Khurasan rebellion) officers, the so-called 'Fars officers' under Colonel Azar and the *fada'yan* officers, who had gained their officers' stars on the battlefield.[34] Pishavari, his top military command and some 70,000 *fada'yan* were able to retreat all the way to the Soviet border. After Tabriz, it was the Kurds' turn. The national army took Mahabad on December 17. When negotiations between Mulla Barzani and General Razmara failed, the Kurdish leader began his long retreat along the Turko-Iranian border. Barzani and his *pishmirgas* repeatedly clashed with army detachments and finally reached the Soviet border near Mt. Ararat, in April 1947. Qazi Muhammad, Sayf Qazi and Sadr Qazi had refused to flee with them; they were arrested, court-martialled and hanged at Mahabad on March 30, 1947.[35] The hanging of the three Kurdish leaders was the last act in story of the secession of the two north-western provinces.

The rapid collapse of the secessionists was a severe setback for the whole communist movement in Iran. The *Toudeh*, after its apogee in 1945/46 (when it might have tried for a *coup d'état*), was to bear the full brunt of the rightist backlash. Its allies in the *Iran* Party (already showing their unabashed opportunism) hurriedly broke their links with it in the days following the fall of Tabriz. *Toudeh*'s clubs and offices were attacked by rightist gangs. In February 1947, the *Toudeh*'s trade union bastion of the CCUTU was banned, its offices closed and its secretary Riza Rousta arrested. Qavam replaced the CCUTU by four loyal trade unions (two previously founded and two fresh ones), namely:

(1) The *Ittihadiyyeh Sindika-ha-yi Kargaran-i Iran* (Union of the Workers' Syndicates of Iran), known by its *Farsi* abbreviation of ISKI; created in September 1946 as a semi-official trade union by Engineer Khusrou Hidayat, with Dr Mihdi Sharif Imami (Engineer Jâfar Sharif Imami's brother) as secretary.

(2) The *Ittihadiyyeh Markazi-i Kargaran, Pishavaran va Kishavarzan-i Iran* (Central Union of the Workers, Artisans and Farmers of Iran), abbreviated to IMKI; formed in April 1944, with Ashtiyani as secretary. A splinter group formed under another secretary, Engineer Maymand.

(3) The *Ittihadiyyeh Kargaran-i Naft* (Oil Workers' Union), created in January 1947, with at its head Yusuf Iftikhari, the veteran leader of the May 1, 1929 general strike at Abadan.

(4) The Dissident Committee of the CCUTU, created simultaneously with the ban on the CCUTU in February 1947, and headed by Sattar Ardashir and Ahmad Rahna.

Having solved the Azarbayjani question and greatly reduced the *Toudeh*'s national power base by shattering its trade unions, Qavam could tackle his last problem: the Soviet oil concession in the Fifteenth *Majlis*. On January 11, 1947, he ordered the *Majlis*'s elections to be initiated. He directly supervised the 135 electoral contests throughout the country.

His supervision was so thorough that, when the Fifteenth *Majlis* was inaugurated on July 16, Muhammad Masôud could, in his *Mard-i Imrouz*, entitle his issue 'Qavam's Majlis'.[36] Ha'irizadeh, himself a Fifteenth *Majlis* deputy, had told Masôud in an interview:

> Many of the present deputies are Qavam's servants and that is the only reason behind their election ...for example Arsanjani [Hasan], Nikpay [Îzaz] and Mashayikhi [Mihdi].[37]

As soon as the *Majlis* convened, the question of the Soviet oil concession hit the headlines yet again. Eventually, on October 22, 1947 (a full eighteen months after the Qavam-Sadchikov protocol, instead of the seven months foreseen), Premier Qavam presented the concession to the assembly for ratification. The *Majlis* rejected the proposal by a vote of 102 to 2. After the vote Qavam was reported, by *Le Monde* editorialist Edouard Sablier (yet again in Iran), to have said: "This is the biggest success of my political career!"[38] As indeed it was, because the last piece of his gigantic deception puzzle had just fallen into place. On December 9, all of his ministers but two resigned *en bloc*. The *Majlis* voted down Qavam, and, instead, on December 27, voted overwhelmingly for the cabinet presented by Premier Ibrahim Hakimi – the very same prime minister from whom Qavam had taken over in January 1946. The circle was completed: Iran's polity was back at square one.

For Ahmad Qavam, his two years, 1946/1947, in office had been extraordinary. He had guided Iran during the most turbulent years in her modern history. He had dealt with Stalin and Molotov, Pishavari and Qazi Muhammad, the Fourteenth and the Fifteenth *Majlis*, the *Toudeh* and the *Iran* Parties. He had been all alone at the very top, masterfully playing a difficult and dangerous game. When he left, in the closing days of 1947, he had achieved all his goals and saved Iran from the menace of communism and Soviet domination. During his tenure all Soviet troops had withdrawn from Iran, the secessionist provinces had been brought to heel, the *Toudeh* threat had been contained and reduced, a comprehensive legal framework had been given to the Iranian labour force and the rightist forces had been given the assistance required to flex their muscles – the whole country was finally free of the Second World War's aftermath. He had won on all fronts, against all his enemies.

For all his labours, Qavam received only an honorific title from the Shah: that of *Jinab-i Ashraf* (His Excellency). On the other hand, what is left, besides all his unforgettable achievements, was a legacy for the future generations of Iranian politicians: an overall theory for ruling Iran and Iranians, a theory he had put into practice over his two years in power, summarised here by the term 'Qavamism'.*

* QAVAMISM – An Attempt at Definition
- 'Qavamism' is a pragmatic (*realpolitik*) socio-political theory tending to maximise the basic interests of the Iranian nation state, with national unity and integrity as its prime objectives.
- 'Qavamism' is the art of the possible in a multi-dimensional national model, dominated by the Powers' equations and the result of domestic *forces vives*, with its fixed cultural, historical and geopolitical constraints.
- 'Qavamism' is a special brand of patriotism, mixed with just enough Machiavellianism, to be used by expert Iranian statesmen (with nerves of steel) in cases of national impasse.
- 'Qavamism' is based on a foreign policy "respectful of every Great Power and the constant endeavour to reach a practical balance with each of them separately" (Qavam *dixit* in February 1946).
- 'Qavamism' is a way of dominating the national stage by stretching all of the natural networks as far as possible and by co-opting any

capable dissident, while pressing for laws and actions benefiting the common lot of Iranians.
- 'Qavamism' is a set of simple rules for perpetual Iranian crisis management, including (1) showing a lot of patience, (2) planning every move carefully, (3) not relying on appearances, and (4) changing what can be, leaving the rest as such.

9.3. The Superpowers' Era

Lord Curzon's nineteenth-century conviction that "Turkestan, Afghanistan, Transcaucasia and Persia ...are the pieces of a chessboard upon which is being played out a game for the domination of the world" was still an actuality decades later; most probably, it always will be because this region, at the crossroads of the three large land masses of Europe, Asia and Africa, is the only area in the world with no predestined dominating Power.

Now, with the Allied victory in 1945 sealing the fate of the Second World War, the planet was entering the era of the two superpowers. Back in December 1790, the Franco-German diplomat Frederich Melchior, Baron de Grimm, had, in a letter written to his patron Empress Catherine II of Russia, proposed a long-term vision of the world:

> Two Empires will then share all the advantages of civilisation, of the power of genius, of letters, of arts, of arms and industry: Russia on the eastern side and America ...on the western side, and we other peoples of the nucleus will be too degraded, too debased, to know otherwise than by a vague and stupid tradition what we have been.[39]

One and a half centuries later, de Grimm's prophecy was about to be fulfilled: the US had emerged from the war strengthened, as the most powerful nation on earth, with the Soviet Union a potential second superpower.

Iran still belonged within the Western world, and this fact had been implicitly recognised by the Soviet leadership at the Yalta Conference. After the monopoly enjoyed by Great Britain during the

1920s and the German interlude during the 1930s, in the war's aftermath Iran was, for the first time in her history, the battlefield in a three-way game: Great Britain, the Soviet Union and the US The West, now bicephalous on the Iranian stage, had a numerical superiority of two to one over the Eastern Power; but the other side of the coin was that the two Western Powers did not necessarily share the same interests and the same views.

For the first time, too, Iran had witnessed the arrival on its territory of US forces: the 30,000 troops of the Persian Gulf Command. Iranians were curious about this newcomer to the Game. As for the Americans, they were discovering another new country. For the US Iran was still, until further notice, within the British sphere of influence. But "wars speed things up" and the American military was soon advising the Iranian Army (General Ridley's mission), the Iranian Gendarmerie (General Schwarzkopf's mission) and the Iranian Police force (a US mission under the civilian L.S. Timmerman). It had also taken over the management of the Trans-Iranian Railway from the British (in the summer of 1942[40]). Dr Millspaugh's team was in charge of Iran's Treasury. Soon some independent US advisers found their way into Iran too – notably Dr Harold B. Allen, of the Near East Foundation, a specialist on agricultural questions; Dr L.M. Winsor, an expert on irrigation; Dr B. Avery and Colonel A.A. Neuworth for assisting on problems related to public health. Added up, that made a lot of American influence in Iranian affairs.

During the war, the US had two centres for global decision-making in Iran: a diplomatic and a military one. In case of divergence, the latter usually overruled the former. This might explain the quick succession of changes occurring at the US Legation (upgraded to an embassy in December 1943) in Tehran. Minister Louis G. Dreyfus, a rather successful envoy[41] in position since 1939, was transferred to another country in November 1943, allegedly consequent on frictions with the US military command. After a seven month lapse, Dreyfus was replaced by Ambassador Leland B. Morris (1944), then came Ambassador Wallace Murray (1945–46), and in August 1946 Ambassador George V. Allen took over. Already all the Americans involved in Iran, whether diplomats or officers, had but one idea in mind: the US role in post-war Iran.

As early as 1942, the Americans were contemplating "running Iran".[42] Another American view was expressed by Dr Millspaugh in February 26, 1944, in a note written to President Roosevelt's special assistant Harry Hopkins:

> Iran because of its situation, its problems, and its friendly feeling towards the US, is (or can be made) something in the nature of a clinic – an experiment station – for the President's post-war policies ...a means of helping nations to help themselves, with negligible cost and risk to the US".[43]

Some of Millspaugh's ideas must have impressed US decision-makers for, in a major policy paper on post-war Iran issued by the State Department in July 1944, one could read:

> The President and the Department [of State] have considered Iran as something of a testing ground... America's position in Iran is not intended to lapse again in any way to that of relative unimportance. The US was adopting an active policy of bolstering Iran... and protecting its interests.[44]

American interests in Iran were further summarised as (i) the US's desire to have a share in Iran's commerce (in 1945 the US's share of Iran's trade already stood at around twenty-five per cent of the total[45]), (ii) to develop Iran's resources (i.e. oil), and (iii) to establish air bases on her soil due to her strategic location. Moreover, the main objective was to "render Iran strong and healthy enough so as to discourage any foreign power from intervening in her affairs", and in order to attain these objectives "every effort would be made to obtain British and Russian collaboration". In sum, a complete programme for effectively "running Iran".

As for the Iranians, they had every reason to look at the American Power with nothing but goodwill. So far they had seen their early missionaries, along with Baskerville, Morgan Shuster, Dr Jordan, Dr Millspaugh and Mr Dreyfus, as a succession of positive individuals. They had heard that America was the land of freedom and justice. Perhaps Iranian thinkers thought the US might be induced to play a positive role in the traditional Great Game. In March 1943, the dormant *Anjuman-i Iran va Amrika* (Iran-America Society – IAS), initially formed in 1925 by Hasan Khan Mustoufi ul-Mamalik and Hasan Khan Mushir ul-Douleh, was revived by Minister Dreyfus. An interesting combination of elder Elite members and younger counter-elite intellectuals were brought on to the IAS's board of trustees, with the following officers:

Chairman: Hasan Isfandyari (the former Muhtashim ul-Saltaneh);
Vice-chairmen: Dr Îsa Sadiq and Abu'l Hasan Ibtihaj;
Secretary: Âli Pasha Salih (also secretary of US Legation),
Officers: Husayn Âla, Murtaza Quli Bayat, Âli Asghar Hikmat, Allahyar Salih (Âli Pasha's brother) and Dr Millspaugh.

Notwithstanding the general goodwill, the Americans played second fiddle to the British during the war, conducting a policy of appeasement towards the Soviets. These relationships would be turned upside down in the post-war era: the British did not have the means to play first fiddle any longer, and the Soviets had proven (if proof was needed) at the December 1945 Moscow Conference that appeasement was not a language they understood. The Americans believed then that they had the resources and the power to take the pre-eminent role in Iran. They believed that if the British could pull it off, they could too. They never stopped to consider that they only had four years of experience in Iran against Great Britain's four centuries. *Vis-à-vis* the Soviets, the Truman Administration soon took its measure: the wartime ally had turned into what US Justice Douglas termed "the most virulent form of imperialism that has ever plagued the world".[46] Iran was not the only bone of contention between the two superpowers-to-be – there also was Greece and Turkey. US global strategy had become a determining factor in world affairs. On March 12, 1947 President Truman spelled it out in an historic speech that laid down global US foreign policy thereafter, beginning:

> I believe it must be the policy of the United States to support free peoples who are resisting attempts to subjugation by armed minorities or by outside pressure...

Truman did not mention Iran, only Greece and Turkey. The new doctrine stressed US readiness to contain communism all over the world and to defend the integrity and independence of all nations endangered by it. The Truman Doctrine was born; its message to the Soviets had its i's dotted and its t's barred.

The main initial thrust of direct US intervention in Iran was along military lines. The wartime US missions to the Iranian armed forces were there to stay. Acting Secretary of State Stettinius had written to Secretary of War Hull:

> A most practical way to implement this policy [the Truman Doctrine] is to strengthen Iran's security forces.[47]

The Americans believed that strong Iranian forces under their control would be a guarantee for controlling the country. On October 6, 1947, the bilateral agreement extending the contracts of the US Army and Gendarmerie missions in Iran up to March 20, 1949 was signed by US Ambassador Allen and Premier Qavam – the first of what was to become automatic renewals.

With its 1917 Revolution, the Soviet Union had stolen a march on its rivals by arming itself with an ideology. Marxist-Leninism was a formidable weapon, especially for influencing the masses. "It is comparatively easy", wrote Bertrand Russell, "to have an immense effect by means of a dogmatic and precise gospel, such as that of Communism".

However, the new ideology had brought no alteration in global strategic plans: Tsarist Russia and the Soviet Union shared the same goals as far the country's southern borders were concerned. As early as 1918, Soviet thinker K. Troyanovski had stated in the review *Vostok i Revolutsia*:

> India is our principal objective. Persia is the only path open to India. The Persian Revolution is the key to the revolution of all of the Orient ...this precious key to the uprising of the Orient must be in the hands of Bolshevism, cost what it may ...Persia must be ours; Persia must belong to the Revolution.[48]

Troyanovski also held that Persia, with its location at the centre of the triangle formed by the Ottoman Empire, the Hindu-Muslim subcontinent and the Arab world, and also with its powerful clergy and social-democrat tradition, was the ideal platform for the launching of the third "World Revolution".[49]

In Iran, the Soviets had little initial success with their Communist Party of Iran, but had the chance to witness the popularity of the '53 Group' and to help the *Toudeh* party build upon this base. Almost from the outset the *Toudeh* leadership was under the spell of the Soviet Embassy in Tehran, which furnished it with funds and advice.[50] It was evident that the Soviets could not let an Iranian socialist party develop independently of their will: they would rather have destroyed such a heresy. One of the most gifted and pro-Soviet *Toudeh* leaders was Âbd ul-Samad Kambakhsh, who had studied at Moscow University, and then had returned to Moscow during the war years, taking a leading position in the *Toudeh* upon his return to Iran.[51] But, besides Kambakhsh, the rest of the leadership was not as motivated and thus had difficulties in shedding its typical Iranian traits of selfishness and opportunism.[52] Furthermore, the eleven members of *Toudeh*'s executive committee lacked political experience, as Pishavari, who had met them in jail during the 1930s, would point out about the '53 Group': "like us they had not been exposed to the struggle's rough and tumble, and although most of them were fairly gifted and well-read, they lacked that indispensable experience".[53] The leadership's deficiencies would lead to constant internecine squabbling and the ensuing splits would eventually enfeeble the party.

A venture in which the Soviets were successful in Iran (a rare occasion) was the Irano-Soviet Society for Cultural Relations, established in the autumn of 1943. The joint society was able to attract the brightest stars in Iranian literature: its first two secretaries were Professor Sâid Nafisi and Karim Kishavarz (Dr F. Khishavarz's brother). In August 1944 the society launched its *Payam-i Nou* magazine, edited by Dr Fatimeh Sayyah, a literature professor at Tehran University. In 1946, the society's inaugurated its own *Khaneh-yi Farhang* (House of Culture) and held the highly successful First Congress of Iranian Writers in its premises from June 25 till July 2. The congress chairman was the Minister of Culture and poet Malik ul-Shuâra Bahar; the congress's executive board consisted of Karim Kishavarz, Sadiq Hidayat, Âli Akbar Dikhuda, Professor Badi ûl-

Zaman Fouruzanfar, Âli Asghar Hikmat, Dr Âli Shayigan and Mrs Surour Mu'asis. The father of Iran's *Shîr-i Nou* (New Poetry), Nima Yushij, and a cohort of younger poets read their poems; Dr Parviz Natil Khanlari, Dr Husayn Khatibi and Ihsan Tabari delivered papers on Iranian literature. Truly, 1946 was the year of the Soviet apogee in Iran.

1945 and 1946 were the last chances for any Soviet takeover in Iran. Soviet troops still occupied Iran's northern provinces; the *Toudeh* was young and buoyant; the trade unions and labour were behind *Toudeh*; the first strands of Rouzbeh's secret officers' organisation had come together. But the Soviets did not dare to show openly their expansionist intentions (perhaps fearing in their hearts of hearts that they couldn't "run Iran") or maybe thought that they could get what they wanted – either economic benefits or territorial gains – by other, less drastic, means. They soon lost their illusions: Kavtaradzeh's efforts for an oil concession were neutralised by Dr Musaddiq's timely Fourteenth *Majlis* bill; Soviet-inspired secessions in Azarbayjan and Kurdistan were crushed; Sadchikov's joint oil company was voted down by Qavam's Fifteenth *Majlis*. The Soviets had too little experience in Iran (roughly as long as the Americans: the war's duration). They had opposing them their arch-rival, the British, and also the Americans. Western assertiveness, added to Soviet vicissitudes, led to the logical conclusion "that after 1947 Stalin ceased to take an active interest in Iran".[54] The Soviet leadership was at least realistic, realising that with both the US and Great Britain in Iran, there was little room for a third player – even a superpower.

Last but certainly not least, came the third Power: Great Britain. She was no superpower any longer. But as far as Iran was concerned she had two unbeatable trump cards: (1) four centuries of intercourse, of which one and a half centuries were of active participation; and (2) deep roots in the various elites and the population at large (having been prudent enough not to put all her eggs in a single basket).

During the war the British had done their share of the Allied effort. They had dismantled the Nazi fifth column, arrested and imprisoned pro-Nazi Iranians, set up the Middle East Supply Centre (MESC), assisted in operating the Trans-Iranian Railway and managed the Anglo-Iranian UKCC transport facility. They also countered Soviet moves on the Iranian chessboard.[55]

"The British realised", G. Lenczowski wrote, "that direct Soviet propaganda and infiltration must be counteracted by direct British action, and that indirect Soviet activities must be met by similar indirect measures. Thus, despite the outwardly cordial co-operation on higher government levels, a local but very important 'cold war' was being waged in Iran between Russia and Great Britain during World War II".[56] Without this covert British engagement, the Americans would have been powerless to counter the Soviet moves in Iran.

At the end of the war, Great Britain began her long and step by step retreat from empire. The resources were simply not there any more to support global involvement. The British people faced economic crisis at home. And their American partners expected her to bring colonialism to a close – an implicit wish to which she responded by the granting of independence of India as soon as August 1947. Iran, however, was not and had never been a British colony. And for Iran, Great Britain was the only Power to actually have a policy. The following quote taken from scholar E. Kedourie does seem to clarify this proposition:

> The policy of a country towards another is, at best, a poor makeshift thing. It is conceived in the heat and the urgency of pressing affairs and, from the nature of the case, must be grounded upon ignorance, irrelevance and misunderstanding. Directed as it is to the attainment of advantage and the securing of interest, policy is heedless of things as they are, provided the advantage is attained and the interest secured. And yet a policy which survives through the years, which generations of statesmen and diplomats practise and modify, gradually begins to live and to fascinate; little by little it takes on the aspect of a dogma, and becomes independent of the purpose for which it was first devised, ruling the thoughts and actions of men, giving rise to hot metaphysical disputes in which temperament clashes with temperament, and belief with belief. So it is with English policy in the Middle East in the nineteenth and twentieth centuries.[57]

And with English policy in Iran.

As for the Powers with no defined policy, they tended to fall in line with the existing ones – and to dislike this forced subordination. "[Another] grave mistake", US Justice Douglas wrote in 1950, "has been our subservience to British policy in the Middle East".[58]

Not only did the British have a policy, they also had interests in Iran; first and foremost, the largest and most profitable industry in the country, the oil industry operated by the Anglo-Iranian Oil Company (AIOC), on which the other Powers looked with active envy; then, the oldest bank in the bank in the country, the fifty year old Imperial Bank of Persia (IBP), which was still printing Persia's banknotes as late as 1930. They had engineering and construction companies with extensive experience in Iran, for example the firm of Sir Alexander Gibb in charge of the Tehran potable water project.[59] And they were still Iran's first trade partner in 1946, gradually slipping to second place behind the US in the late 1940s.

Furthermore, Great Britain could rely on yet another precious asset other Powers lacked: she possessed centuries-old institutions that were responsible for shaping imperial statesmen, politicians, diplomats, scholars and agents. These institutions were somehow part of the Empire, but located on British soil. So, although she retreated, these Establishment institutions continued to churn out their quotas of imperial officers and servants – albeit at an ever slower pace. Thus, Foreign Office high-flyers, Levant Service graduates and Oxbridge Iranologists were still available year in and year out. In this respect Great Britain was decades ahead of any other Power and this tremendous superiority showed itself in the field. For the Powers-that-be, this situation of inferiority was difficult to bear. The alternative was to create equivalent institutions of their own, but there are things that even millions of dollars or roubles cannot purchase overnight.

In the first peacetime elections of July 1945, the Labour Party won a majority in the House of Commons. Clement Attlee became prime minister and Ernest Bevin secretary for Foreign Affairs. The new British government would develop a fresh strategy for the Middle East (inclusive of Iran): it would endeavour to support 'moderate Nationalists' instead of the discredited 'old gangs' (read 'Elite' for Iran), and, by trying to look "beyond rulers to peoples", seek to benefit "peasants not pashas".[60] It was indeed a commendable policy, well in tune with its times (as the wave of nationalisations managed by Attlee's cabinet had been the wish of the British people). In Iran, the nearest group to the "moderate Nationalists" was the so-called nationalist counter-elite made up of bureaucrats and technocrats. After the radical change in Great Britain's ruling party, changes in global British policy were only a natural consequence.

In the era of the two superpowers, Great Britain's active presence in the Middle East was a fact. Although no match for either superpower in economic or military terms, she still had plenty of assets. These she would put to use in the three-way modern Great Game, which had begun as soon as the Second World War ended.

8.4. Can Iran Plan?

At the end of the Second World War, Iran was economically where Reza Shah had left her in 1941. During the war only inflation and scarcity of goods had come her way. Despite Pahlavi's efforts at modernisation, work on the land still provided the livelihood of three Iranians out of four. The country could not only feed its citizens but even had a surplus for export. Reza Shah's programmes had mostly benefited urban dwellers and the northern provinces; other rural areas had been left almost untouched. In the 60,000 Iranian villages the general standard of living was very low and nothing much had changed there since the Qajar days: the land tenure, the housing, health problems and the working of the land were unaltered. Only the villages along the few main roads linking provincial centres or with the chance to have a railway station nearby had moved out of their centuries of torpor. As for the Reza Shah legacy – i.e. the Trans-Iranian Railway, the thirty-four larger industrial establishments (mainly sugar, cement and textiles factories) and the thirty-nine smaller ones (mostly tea, dyeing and rice milling)[61] – it had problems of operation because of the lack of spare parts and foreign expertise (except for the railway, which was operated under Allied supervision). The private sector, especially Isfahan's textile factories of *Vatan*, *Risbaf* and *Zayandehroud*, being more self-sufficient than the public sector factories, had fared well during the war and made outrageous profits. As for the two major projects begun before the war, the

Krupp steel mill was indefinitely shelved and the French vegetable oil factory at Varamin would be terminated in the late 1940s.

Now, underlining the whole question of Iranian development was the crucial mode of development. The technocratic elite, in charge of planning, failed to realise the importance of their decisions, still believing that development meant churning out a list of projects – as in the Reza Shah days. The basic question facing Iran was spelled out in a seminal article published by *The Economist* in 1950, appropriately entitled 'Can Persia Plan?':

> [Iran] must now choose between two patterns of social change – either the ruthless, methodical process now being imposed on China; or the more hesitant, unspectacular transformation that takes place when eastern feudalism accepts western aid for "social development"... Persia's landlord-politicians pay lip service to reform but most of them have complacently refused, hitherto, to see that a ruling class of the present pattern must inevitably choose the Western Way... So far, however, by no means all Persian politicians have faced the implication.[62]

It was clear. The only option was hesitant Western aid. Besides a handful of top Iranian intellectuals, no one realised the wide-ranging consequences for development, planning, the economy, the way of life and Iran's future. The only point of doubt lay not on the Iranian side but rather with the Western Powers, for there were two alternatives for Western aid: an Anglo-American one and a purely American one.

Among the few Iranian politicians able to grasp the choices ahead was Ahmad Qavam. As soon as he became prime minister in early 1946, he called for a Seven Year Plan for post-war reconstruction and development; he set up a Planning Commission and appointed his young cousin, Dr Âli Amini[63], at its head. The Commission tried its hand at planning, issued a £450m plan, then a £150m one, before shelving both.[64] In December 1946, the American firm of Morrison-Knudsen International Engineering Co., (MKI) was given a $250,000 contract to come up with a plan. In July 1947, MKI issued its *Report on a Program for the Development of Iran*, in which it proposed two plans: the first estimated to cost $500m and the other $250m.

Working on the basis of the MKI proposals, the Planning Commission came up with a plan of Rls21bn (equal to $650m), which it officially recommended to the government in January 1948 (for a breakdown of the Plan's major allocations see Table 9.1.). The plan's financing was to come from four sources:(1) oil revenues; (2) a Bank-i Milli loan; (3) the sale of public properties; and (4) a loan from the International Bank for Reconstruction and Development (IBRD) - later to be known as the World Bank.

Table 9.1. Breakdown of the First Seven Year Development Plan According to Major Economic Sectors.[64A]

Economic Sector	Capital Investment During Plan
Agriculture and Irrigation	5,000
Railways and Roads	5,000
Industries	3,000
Oil Development (outside AIOC)	1,000
Posts, Telegraphs, Telephones, Radio	1,000
Power supply, Cheap housing	2,500
Health services	1,500
Education	1,000
Scientific Research	1,000
Total	21,000

(Figures in Rls millions)

When the IBRD was approached for a preliminary loan assessment, the bank asked for a detailed independent appraisal of the plan. Max W. Thornburg, a former vice-president of the California-Texas Oil Co. and a wartime petroleum adviser to the State Department, with some experience of Iran, was chosen to co-ordinate the appraisal. Thornburg convinced MKI and ten other US engineering firms to form Overseas Consultant Incorporated (OCI) and to undertake for $650,000 per annum a revision of Iran's plans. Thornburg arrived in Tehran with some forty OCI specialists in January 1949 to start his review. On August 22, 1949 Thornburg and his OCI team issued five voluminous reports on their survey of Iranian development plans.[65] The OCI reports were more of a fact-finding mission than a final review or appraisal. Within eight months, the American specialists had not had enough time to get to know (even less understand) Iran. Their report left more questions unanswered than it answered. A member of the OCI team, R.K. Hall, sheds some light on the problems faced by both Americans and Iranians:

> There was clearly a very hazy basic philosophy of technical assistance, and widely divergent opinions as to an appropriate policy to be followed in detailed projects. Thus, the Iranian [Planning] Commission was badly divided as to whether the Plan should be directed towards a basic industrialisation of the country with major engineering projects, or towards a modest upgrading of the efficiency of existing techniques in agriculture and local industry. Little or no thought had been given to questions of the impact of nearly 650 million dollars of new investments on Iranian economy, nor to the impact of sweeping technological changes upon the mores and social structure of the country.[66]

After yet another eighteen months of haggling and squabbling between American experts and Iranian technocrats, the OCI contract was terminated and the American team departed in January 1951. During their two-year stay, Thornburg and OCI had gathered first-hand information about the land and its inhabitants, but their voluminous report would be shelved. On the other hand, Iranian planners had shown their extreme weakness in the planning field, and, as planning is essentially an elite occupation, this first encounter between the post-war elite and planning boded ill for the new Iranian elite in general and for the technocrats of the nationalistic elite in particular, because they should have jumped on the opportunity offered and used the Seven Year Plan as a lever to power.

As the OCI team was debarking in Tehran, President Truman was delivering his January 20, 1949 inaugural address at Washington. In it he envisioned a new course for US foreign policy. It had four points; and point four propounded "a bold new program for the United States to share its technical knowledge with other peoples to help them realise their aspirations for a better life".[67] In theory, a seemingly generous gesture, in practice, it became the US Technical Assistance Program, or simply 'Point Four', America's new channel for bringing assistance to underdeveloped nations. On October 19, 1950, Ambassador Henry F. Grady and Prime Minister Razmara signed the Point Four agreement for Iran. Unofficially, the three main goals of Point Four in Iran were: "(i) containing the process of [the] *Toudeh* party, (ii) achieve a quick increase in the National Income, (iii) assist in alleviating misery among Persian masses".[68] There probably were three other motives behind Point Four: (i) an attempt at propaganda for America (unsurprisingly even the Americans came to realise that "the Point Four Program was looked at by Iranians as pure propaganda"[69]), (ii) an opportunity for American experts to get to know Iran first-hand, and (iii) begin to prepare the peasants for the future shock of the land reform, about which US Iranologists such as Justice Douglas were adamant. "Land reform above all else", the latter wrote, "is the starting point for launching the counter revolution against communism. No program of reform can long succeed unless land reform is first carried through".[70]

The *Majlis*, however, had not waited for the Americans and had approved the Rls21bn Seven Year Plan proposed by the Planning Commission, after it was endorsed by the government on February 22, 1949. In parallel with the plan's ratification, the assembly had decided on the formation of a body independent of government, the Sazman-i Barnameh (Plan Organisation – PO), for implementing the plan. Although free from governmental supervision, the PO had a complex hierarchy: at its head was an administrator-general appointed by the Shah for three years (the first appointee in May 1949 was the Shah's brother Âbd ul-Riza Pahlavi), who reported to a seven-member Higher Planning Council nominated by the government; the PO's activities were finally under the control of a six-man supervisory board whose members were elected for two-year terms by the *Majlis* from a list of candidates submitted by the government. With the Plan's official launch, doubts were aired in the press about the "wisdom and the feasibility behind its projects".[71] A total of Rls21bn seemed enormous; for comparison purposes the total capital invested in 178 Iranian industrial establishments over the period 1929–1946 was cited as under Rls3bn (Rls 2,718m to be precise[72]).

Whether feasible or not, Iran's First Seven Year Plan had been approved and had legally to be executed by the PO. The last hurdle on its way was its financing. Of the four potential sources of funds envisaged the two Iranian ones had a very limited scope and the two foreign ones (i.e. oil revenues and the IBRD loan) depended on the goodwill of London and Washington respectively. The Iranians first turned their sights on Washington and even sent the Shah on a six-week (first) American tour (close 1949–early 1950) to convince the US to persuade the IBRD to grant a sizeable loan. But the Shah failed miserably, as the Americans told the Iranians that the plan should essentially be financed by the oil revenues and the residual requirements from a IBRD loan – not vice versa. The Americans had two good reasons to refuse Iran a large loan at the outset: the first came from the vivid memory of her poor experience with the millions of dollars it had uselessly given the ill-fated Chinese *Kuomintang*; the second was that after a substantial loan the Iranians would not be keen to battle for increased oil revenues. This meant that calculated US stalling on the IBRD loan left the Iranians with only a single option for financing its First Plan: enhanced oil revenues. Once again oil was at the dead centre of the Iranian Game.

9.5. Oil Revenues

Iran's oil revenues, paid by the Anglo-Iranian Oil Co. (AIOC), had increased from a flat £4m per annum during the war to £7.1m in 1946 and 1947, £9.2m in 1948 and £13.5m in 1949.[73] In parallel, Iranian oil production had risen from around 360,000 b/d in 1945 to 560,000 b/d in 1949. In between, the AIOC had decided to spend more money in Abadan and the southern fields as a consequence of the "severe shock of the July 14, 1946 general strike".[74] The company's local wages and expenditures rose steeply from a meagre total of £2.6m in 1943 to £10.3m in 1946 and £20.3m in 1949.[75] Furthermore, in the autumn of 1946 the company opened an AIOC information department under the direction of Iranologist Dr Laurence Lockhart.

After a very successful war, on top of its domestic and operational problems, AIOC had to attend to the new international threats which stemmed from the superpowers' desire to share in Iranian oil. The US and the Soviet Union would naturally have preferred a concession of their own (the cornerstone of their future Iranian empire), but both were ready to take shares in any concession. The Americans had been turned down once (in 1943) and the Soviets foiled twice (Kavtaradzeh in 1943, Sadchikov in 1946/47). Nevertheless, although Soviet pretensions seemed to be well-grounded, the American companies were still looking askance at the AIOC's monopoly. In order to place a framework on future Anglo-American co-operation for Middle East oil, an Anglo-American Petroleum Commission was formed in 1943 to "regulate post-war Middle Eastern oil production for the benefit of all concerned".[76] British representatives went to Washington and hammered out an agreement of co-operation, signed on August 8, 1945, but it was never put into practice because the US Senate failed to ratify it.

In order to officially rescind the clause on the joint oil company in the Qavam-Sadchikov agreement, the Fifteenth *Majlis* decided to approve a five-point bill proposed by Tehran deputy Rizazadeh Shafaq. This law, duly voted in on October 22, 1947, provided for: (i) the annulment of the Soviet-Iranian agreement; (ii) the sales of products to the Soviet Union in the case of oil being found in the northern provinces; (iii) the financing by the Iranian Government of oil exploration in Iran (outside the AIOC agreement area, naturally); (iv) an interdiction on granting concessions to foreigners and the creation of joint venture companies with foreign companies in oil exploration; and (v) the conduct of negotiations by the government "where Iran's rights over its natural resources was deemed to have been impaired" (viz. the southern oil fields).[77] This new law would have wide-ranging implications not only for Iran and the Soviet Union, but also for the AIOC and the Americans.

Having heard about the *Majlis*'s plans for exploration inside Iran, the Iranian technocrats jumped on the chance. On October 13, 1947, the Iranian Engineers Association had formed six sub-committees on oil affairs – 1) Exploration, 2) Exploitation, 3) Refining, 4) Transportation, 5) Engineering, 6) Legal – manned by twenty-two educated engineers, under the direction of Engineer Zirakzadeh and Engineer Haqshinas (both from the *Iran* Party). But the commendable effort (for once the technocrats had at least tried) soon fizzled out: genuine Iranian oil expertise was to be found at Abadan and the southern fields, not in Tehran. Nevertheless an Iranian Oil Company (the *Shirkat-i Sahami-i Naft-i Iran*) was the only palpable result of the technocrats' efforts. It was created by a law of February 1949 and established with an initial capital of Rls1,000m on October 20 of the same year.[78]

In the meantime, the AIOC was far from idle. In 1946, the oil company had decided to sell part of its Iranian oil interests to its American partners in the Iraqi Petroleum Co. (IPC), namely Standard Oil of New Jersey and Socony Vacuum. The overall sales scheme was announced in December 1946 and the actual twenty-year sales contracts were signed in September 1947 and March 1948 respectively.[79] The Standard Oil contract called for sales to begin in 1952 at the rate of 90,000 b/d for the first three years, 114,000 b/d for the next seven, with the amounts for the last ten years to be fixed later.[80] Socony was to be sold 70,000 b/d for the first ten years, the rest to be determined at a later date. These were not small quantities of oil, representing roughly 40% of the AIOC's 1947 production of 425,000 b/d of Iranian oil.[81] The American oil companies in Saudi Arabia, the ARAMCO partners, then stole an economic march on the AIOC, by bringing a new weapon to Middle East oil rivalry: the pipeline. In September 1947, ARAMCO began work on the Trans-Arabian Pipeline (TAPline), across the Arabian desert to the Red Sea. The TAPline would tremendously reduce the costs of transportation of crude oil to Europe, and ARAMCO could then undercut AIOC's prices. The British company responded by forming a joint venture with Standard and Socony dubbed Middle East Pipelines Limited – created in December 1947 with AIOC holding 60.9%, Standard 24.7% and Socony 14.4% – for the construction of a 34"/36" pipeline with a capacity of 535,000 b/d from the Persian Gulf to a Mediterranean port, via Iraq and Syria.[82] In the end, neither the sales' contracts nor the pipeline would be implemented. But the crucial point of the 1946/47 intercourse between AIOC and the American companies in the Gulf was to remain: the British were interested in giving the Americans a share (somewhere around 40%) of their Iranian oil production.

The negotiations with the AIOC stipulated by the October 22 law were another mammoth task: all the Iranian grievances dating back to the 1910s with Nusrat ul-Douleh, through the 1920s with Taymourtash and the 1930s with Davar, then eclipsed by the world war, would all resurface. Prime Minister Hahimi was not the man for such a Brobdingnagian undertaking. In June 1948, the young Âbd ul-Husayn Hazhir, a successful courtier, replaced Hakimi and placed the AIOC negotiations on his cabinet's agenda. The Shah's visit to London in July 1948 did not bring about any fresh developments. In August 1948, a bill presented by Âbbas Iskandari, the deputy from Hamadan (and a cousin of the *Toudeh* leader), to the *Majlis* on the nationalisation of the oil industry was defeated by a vote of 93 to 8.[83]

The first soundings for the AIOC-Iranian negotiations were made by Neville Gass (later Sir) in November and December of 1947 in Tehran. The first round of negotiations eventually took place in Tehran, between September 26 and October 13, 1948: a four-man AIOC delegation led by vice-chairman Sir Neville Gass (a former assistant to Lord Cadman) met the Iranian team led by the new Minister of Finance, Muhammad Âli Varasteh. On the Iranian team sat two French specialists: Professor Gidel and Jean Rousseau (with the American Max Thornburg also advising the Iranians). This time round (probably due to the two Frenchmen), the Iranians had done their homework: they tabled a twenty-five-point, fifty-page memorandum containing their revendications and constructed around two main topics: (i) the 1933 agreement was vague on many points; and (ii) Iran was not receiving her fair share of the oil revenues. The Iranian team had compared Iran's revenues on a per tonne basis with those of Iraq, Kuwait and Venezuela and it had found out that the others were receiving a higher income. The British asked for time to study the document and talks were adjourned. On November 8, Hazhir was replaced by the specialist of oil disputes, the old and inoffensive Sâid. Thus the year 1948 ended without the oil conundrum having been settled.

The second round of negotiations began in Tehran on February 9, 1949. Between February 13 and March 15, no fewer than twelve meetings would be held. The new Iranian Minister of Finances, Âbbas Quli Gulshayan, entered the talks with two shattering proposals: the management of oil operations in Iran by Iranians and a fifty-fifty sharing of the profits. Sir Neville Gass naturally rejected both propositions out of hand. Even Gulshayan's argument that Iran was not receiving a fair deal and that (1) Venezuela received $200m against Iran's $32m by producing only twice as much oil,[84] and (2) over the past fifteen years (1933–1947) the British Treasury had received £72.2m as against £60.1m to Iran,[84A] failed to convince the British delegation. A third round of talks were held in April, but were again inconclusive. It was then that the AIOC chairman, Sir William Frazer, decided to come to Tehran to negotiate with Premier Sâid.

On May 5, 1949, Chairman Frazer handed over to Sâid the AIOC proposal for a Supplemental Agreement (SA) to the 1933 Agreement. The SA was clearly a British platform for initiating negotiations: major Iranian claims had not been taken into consideration. In the SA, the royalty had been increased by 50% (from 4 to 6 shillings per tonne of crude), a global £8,767,449 down payment by AIOC was foreseen, and 20% of future AIOC General Reserve was allocated to Iran.[85] All in all, the SA was but a thin veneer over an obsolescent and unwelcome structure. From the outset the 1933 Agreement had been a makeshift ensemble, more or less palatable then, but totally out of touch in the late 1940s. The Iranians had wanted a fresh agreement, something to last well into the 1950s and 1960s, not just a rehash of the 1930s. They had wanted to deal with a second Cadman but got Frazer. The latter had neither the personality nor the vision of the former. Kenneth Younger, the British Minister of State, wrote of Frazer in an October 1951 memo:

> ...he struck me as a thoroughly second-rate intellect and personality. He has on many occasions explicitly stated in my presence that he does not think politics concern him at all.[86]

If Frazer had been concerned with politics he would have seen that there was no Reza Shah with whom he could deal, but a broad coalition of national forces including the counter-elites, the *Majlis* and public opinion. Furthermore he should have sensed that the late 1940s were in no way comparable to the early 1930s, especially now that, in 1948, Venezuela had finally got her fifty-fifty split of the profits approved (after the botched-up deal of 1943).

Frazer made it clear to Sâid: either the SA or confrontation and arbitration, take it or leave it. From the AIOC side the SA gambit made sense: if the Iranians accepted the strict minimum offered therein, AIOC would be safe for at least another decade and if they didn't, it was arbitration and Cadman's 1933 Agreement upon which to fall back. Frazer had chosen to use force and confrontation, but his inappropriate attitude prompted author R.C. Mowat to compare the AIOC to a "dinosaur".[87] Premier Sâid was at a loss regarding the SA. On June 8, 1949, he and Gulshayan presented the oil file to a closed session attended by members of the non-governing and governing elites – namely Mihdi Quli Hidayat, Âli Mansour, Murtaza Quli Bayat, Sardar Fakhir Hikmat (the *Majlis* president) and Âbd ul-Husayn Hazhir – and discussed the pros and cons of its acceptance. Having ruled out arbitration, the select group decided to accept (albeit reluctantly) the SA. So far things were going as Frazer had predicted. On July 17, Sir Neville Gass and Âbbas Quli Gulshayan signed the SA agreement, which immediately became known as the Gass-Gulshayan agreement.

On July 19, the agreement was sent to a mixed (Finance and Industry) parliamentary commission, which approved it by a narrow majority. On July 23, the agreement was sent to the general assembly for final approval; there remained only four days in the life of the Fifteenth *Majlis*: the 23, 24, 25, and 26, as the 27 was a holiday and the 28 was the day allotted for the closing ceremonies. Three deputies sympathetic to the *Majlis*'s nationalist wing, namely Husayn Makki, Sayyid Abu'l Hasan Ha'irizadeh and Dr Muzaffar Baqa'i Kermani, mounted a successful four-day filibuster and thus shifted burden of the approval of the Gass-Gulshayan to the future Sixteenth *Majlis*.[88] Premier Sâid went to London in October 1949 for a last plea on the Gass-Gulshayan agreement with AIOC's management, but met with no success. The Iranian Premier might have been soothed by the opinion given him by Calouste Gulbenkian (Mr Five Per Cent) over the SA: "...the best agreement so far granted by any oil company in the Middle East".[89] Probably the best, but not necessarily a good one.

9.6. Muhammad Reza Shah

Muhammad Reza Shah had lain low during 1946/47, which had been dominated by Ahmad Qavam. The Azarbayjan expedition was a triumph for his army, which was able to climb back a notch or two in the public's estimation from the lows of 1941. With the army's revival, the Shah was in the saddle again, as his fortunes were directly linked to that of the military pillar his father had erected. Another source of royal support was to be found in Washington: the American politicians time and again defended his position during the war days, especially against Qavam's piques. At the close of 1947, with Qavam's departure, the Shah could hope to find his rightful national place. But the Fifteenth *Majlis* and the twin problems of planning and oil eclipsed his comeback.

His July 1948 visit to London had been a dramatic disappointment for all concerned. He seemed to be unable to find his right footing either internally or internationally. Even his private life had become a shambles after his separation and divorce (1948) from his first wife Fauzieh, who consistently refused to return to Tehran from Cairo, leaving behind her small daughter Shahnaz (born in 1940). So the question was beginning to be asked: was the second Pahlavi a king after all?

On February 4, 1949, Muhammad Reza Shah's world was turned upside down. As usual on that day, the Shah went to Tehran University to take part in the ceremonies commemorating the inauguration of the university in 1935. Suddenly five shots were fired at him from a distance of a couple of metres by a photographer who had hidden a gun in his tripod-mounted camera. As the sixth shot became stuck, Nasir Fakhrara'i, the photographer, pulled the gun out of its hiding place and threw it at the Shah before going down in a hail of bullets fired by security officers. Of the five shots fired only two found their targets, causing only minor injuries to the Shah's right upper lip and his left shoulder. The Shah would soon recover in hospital.

Many versions about the hand that had armed Fakhrara'i circulated in Tehran; one saw the *Toudeh* behind it, alleging that the party leaders assembled in the city's southern cemetery to commemorate Dr Arani's death were readying themselves for a coup; another version saw General Razmara behind the attempt, and a source even alleged that the general was conspiring with his top officers while the shooting took place.[90] The real conspirator who had armed Fakhrara'i will probably never be known because of Fakhrara'i's death. What mattered was that the thirty year old Shah had faced certain death, for

Fakhrara'i had been a highly capable young man.[91] The Shah had miraculously survived an assassination attempt and this miracle would change his life.

On the evening of February 4, as he addressed the nation on Tehran Radio, the Shah was a winner. This time, the court did not let the golden opportunity slip away: "The Shah turned the assassination attempt into a Royalist coup".[92] Riding a conservative wave, fully backed by his father's old guard and rightist elements of the polity, he would strike at various targets simultaneously:

- First target was the *Toudeh* party, which was outlawed on February 16. Of the party's executive committee, six members were arrested and sentenced in April to heavy sentences: Dr N. Kianouri (ten years), A. Qasimi (ten years), Dr M. Yazdi (five years), Dr H. Joudat (five years), Engineer. A. Âlavi (three years) and M. Buqrati (three years). Three fled abroad: Dr Radmanish, Dr Kishavarz and Ihsan Tabari; with the last two going underground in Iran, Dr Bahrami and Dr Furoutan. In May, 18 other *Toudeh* leaders were tried *in absentia* and eight of them were sentenced to death. The *Toudeh* had been decapitated, its backbone broken, with only its covert officers' organisation unscathed.
- The second target was the press. A bill drastically restricting press freedom was presented to the *Majlis* in February and was easily approved. The main objectives had been the *Toudeh* and the liberal papers (except for the *Iran* Party papers), especially members of the *Jibheh-yi Matbouât Zidd-i Diktaturi* (Front of the Anti-Dictatorship Press), created in April 1948.
- The constitution represented the third target. The Shah had long entertained the wish of having a senate, and a royal prerogative for dissolving the chambers of Parliament. In May 1949, a Constituent Assembly of 272 deputies was set up. Its first act was to pave the way for a senate, as provided by the Supplemental Laws of 1908 (but never called): a higher legislative chamber composed of sixty senators, thirty elected and thirty nominated by the Shah, in each case with fifteen from Tehran and fifteen from the provinces. Its second act was to amend article 49 of the Fundamental Laws, allowing the Shah to dissolve the two chambers (separately or together), subject to the monarch's stating his reason for doing so and ordering fresh elections within three

months from dissolution. Moreover, dissolution could not be ordered twice in a row for the same reason.
- The fourth target was his father's *Amlak-i Shahanshahi* (royal estates) which the Shah wanted back. On July 6, 1949, the *Majlis* obliged, and voted for (after some squabbling) the return of the *Amlak* to the Pahlavi family. In a March 1951 interview the Shah provided an economic not a political explanation for the reversal: "The Estates' annual income amounted to Rls70m before they were turned over [in 1941] to the Government; by 1948, this income had plummeted to Rls6m. Therefore, I proposed to the *Majlis* that I should be allowed to manage the Estates directly, as before..."[93]

After Fakhrara'i's shots, Muhammad Reza Shah had come a long way. The Tehran University miracle had apparently made of him a winner. With no dominating statesman on the domestic stage, the Shah had been able to glow and grow like never before. Some were already asking themselves the question: why not the Shah as leader? After all, he already was on the Peacock Throne and his family had now ruled for almost a quarter of a century. There were some 'Pahlavists' in Iran and although the majority was in the armed forces, a few were to be found in other walks of life. Even the American politicians and millionaires had not disliked this young, sporting man when he had visited the US at the close of 1949 to lobby for the IBRD loan to Iran. He had not received the loan, but his first US trip had been a personal success for the Shah. He returned home with a typical American message for the Iranians: "The components for success are: Work, Unity and Social Reforms". Moreover President Truman's private remark to him – "Rule, your country needs it"[94] – must have been a boon for a man who had faced death a few months before.

The only shadow cast upon Muhammad Reza Shah's revival was a harsh open letter sent to him on March 17, 1950 by the only Iranian statesman who could allow himself such a *lèse-majesté*: Ahmad Qavam. Returning from a long convalescence in Europe, Qavam was flabbergasted by the change brought to article 49 of the Fundamental Laws in regard to the royal prerogative of dissolving the two chambers. In his historic letter he told the Shah that he had clearly overreached his powers, had threatened the fundamental rights of the Iranian people and, by thus introducing an era of dictatorship, he was exposing himself and his regime to the greatest dangers. Qavam concluded his letter with these prophetic words:

> I can see the day the bayonets and the prisons and the tortures won't be able to stop the defenders of the People's Rights and on that day, it will be much too late for despairs and regrets...[5]

9.7. Popular Writers

During the 1940s the people of Iran had to cope with unprecedented inflation and severe food shortages, especially in urban centres. But after Reza Shah's centralisation programme, it was these urban masses that dominated Iranian society, with the peasants and the tribes (still living as their forefathers had) as second-rate citizens. Among these centres Tehran, with the court, the government, the *Majlis* and a population approaching its first million (as against only 540,087 inhabitants in the 1940 census[96]), was indisputably the centre of national decision-making. 7 Tehran was the location of Tehran Radio (with broadcasts since 1940), the centre of the press, the centre where the elites and counter-elites converged, the centre of Iranian public opinion. Tehran was a showpiece of Westernisation with its embassies, its hotels, its cinemas, its hospitals, its bars, its cafes and its budding *thé-dansants*. Tehran's streets had become a formidable battlefield since the early clashes of 1942, with all political parties and factions relishing victories on this unique ground. Violence was not only on the Tehran streets, it had surreptitiously invaded the Iranian polity: political murders had become another parameter in the power equation in Iran.

Towards the close of the 1940s, the people of Tehran had found a new assertiveness. The causes for this new mood were multiple. Some of these stemmed from Reza Shah's legacy, which included education, economical stability, industrialisation and improved transportation. Other factors derived from the relative freedom enjoyed by a freer press in the turbulent 1940s. In a way Reza Shah's dictatorship had overpressurised society and the vacuum left after his exit had engendered the 1940s' wave of participation. Everyone wanted to know, to influence, to be part of the political process.

After all, the country was theirs too – they had some rights, the right at least to decide what they wanted or not.

Enhanced education among the middle classes had brought the best Iranian writers a wider public. During the 1940s, four of them clearly stood out, having been chosen by the people for their unique and exemplary achievements: a pioneering poet, Nima Yushij; an indefatigable lexicographer Âli Akbar Dikhuda; a genial writer, Sadiq Hidayat; and a courageous journalist, Muhammad Masûd.

Nima Yushij* was the pen name of Âli Isfandyari. Born in the small village of Yush in Mazandaran's Alburz mountains, Isfandyari would be known as Nima to posterity. A quiet revolutionary, he single-handedly revolutionised Iran's most cherished asset: her poetry. He proposed simply discarding rhymes, meters and rules, nothing less: in a word, the whole structure that underpinned Iran's most precious legacy, the poems of Hafiz, Firdousi, Saâdi and Moulana. Instead, he proposed a free, harmonic, unruled and open poetry, which he called *Shîr-i Nou* (New Poetry). In Nima's apparent disorder there was supposed to be an overall organisation of words, but, as there were no rules whatsoever, it was difficult to explain how the New Harmony was to come about. He even stressed that the new was more difficult to write than the old. Critics were not convinced, although some began comparing Nima's revolution to that brought about in France by the likes of Arthur Rimbaud and Paul Verlaine (Nima was educated at Tehran's St Louis School, an establishment run by French clergymen). In the 1940s the New Poetry made cultural waves, with detractors easily crushing supporters. But the people were beginning to read his simple New Poetry, and young poets were writing free poetry. Nima had acquired a niche and a name for being the first to propose changing the formerly sacrosanct traditions of poetry.

* NIMA YUSHIJ (1897–1960), born in Yush (Mazandaran province), as Âli Isfandyari; studied at the St Louis school at Tehran; fathered the *Shîr-i Nou* (New Poetry) (1921); published in *Music Journal*, later joining its board of editors (1938); sympathetic to the Toudeh party and a pillar of its cultural life; died at the age of sixty-four.

Âli Akbar Dikhuda* was first a journalist, then a politician and a civil servant before settling down to become Iran's leading lexicographer. In the early 1920s he began on his long road to compiling a universal dictionary (inclusive of common words, as well as historical, geographical and scientific names) which he named a *Lughatnameh* (lit. 'lists of words'). For the next thirty years, day in and day out, he would fill his *index verborum* with new words and expressions – only taking three days off for his mother's funeral. His method of work, based on the Littre system, was to fill a fresh card for every new word: he ended up with one million cards, all filled by his own hand (having achieved a remarkable average of roughly one hundred cards per day). Between 1929 and 1932, needing money to continue his work, he published his unique collection of Persian proverbs in four volumes, *Amsal va Hakam*. Towards the end of the war, his creditors, to whom he owed Rls2m, were threatening to expropriate his house. The matter came to the public's attention, and in January 1946 Dr Musaddiq brought the case to the attention of the Fifteenth *Majlis*, which rapidly voted two special bills (in January and March 1946) approving a budget for the completion of Dikhuda's work. From 1946 until 1955, work on the *Lughatnameh* was carried in Dikhuda's own house. In the autumn of 1955, Dikhuda appointed Dr Muhammad Muîn as his executor. When Dikhuda died on February 26, 1956, his monumental project was well on its way to completion. In 1958, Tehran University's Faculty of Literature took over the whole project and placed it in a Shimiran house on Pahlavi Avenue donated by the philanthropist Dr Mahmud Afshar Yazdi. After Dr Muîn's death, Dr Sayyid Jâfar Shahidi took over the project and with a dozen collaborators completed the three million cards of the dictionary and brought about the publication of the *Lughatnameh Dikhuda*, an Iranian masterpiece. Dikhuda had shunned power and chosen achievement: for an Iranian, a decision at odds with his culture. Even more remarkable than his extraordinary persistence and resilience was the fact that his fantastic dream finally materialised (a fact quite unique in Iran). For his modern safeguard of their most precious asset, the *Farsi* language, the people of Iran should be thankful to Âli Akbar Dikhuda.

* ÂLI AKBAR DIHKHUDA (1879–1956), born in Qazvin, the son of Khan Baba Khan; studied under Shaykh Hadi Najmabadi and at

Dar ul-Funoun; travelled to Rome and Baku; active in socialist circles and in the *Ijtimâyun-Âmmyun* Party; wrote in the *Sur-i Israfil* newspaper (under the pseudonym of *Dakhou*), advocating the peasant's rights to land ownership (1907-08); after bombardment of *Majlis*, took refuge at the British Legation before exile to Switzerland (1908-1909); after his return to Tehran (1909) elected to Second *Majlis* (1909-11); worked briefly for the Ministry of Culture and the Ministry of Justice (1912-18); head of the School for Political Sciences; undertook his monumental *Lughatnameh* (dictionary) (1921-1955); published Iranian proverbs in *Amsal va Hakam* (1929-32); the Fifteenth *Majlis* accorded financial facilities for publication of his life's work (1946); upon his death in 1956 his dictionary was already an institution.

Sadiq Hidayat*, a member of the Elite Hidayat family, had studied in France, at Besançon and Paris. He was a genius, and, like all geniuses, lived in a distracted world of his own. During his short life, he found the time to translate five old works from their Pahlavi original into Farsi and write twenty-one books of his own, with the *Blind Owl* and the *Strayed Dog* as his masterpieces. He excelled in short stories, the new genre pioneered in 1921 in Berlin by Muhammad Âli Jamalzadeh with his remarkable *Yiki Bud, Yiki Nabud* (lit. 'Once upon a time...').

Hidayat's prose was brilliant, refined and full of variety, but always with a dark, pessimistic background. His characters were picked from Iranian everyday life, ordinary folk like his unforgettable characters *Dash Akul*, *Kaka Rustam*, *Bibi Khanum* and *Îsmat Sadat*. He made them speak their own language, a fact that raised many eyebrows in the world of Iranian literature. Notwithstanding these reservations, the next generation of prose-writers would all follow in Hidayat's footsteps. If his work and his style were ever more successful, the writer himself was losing his mental balance: the genius had trapped himself. He used to say "I hate both the reader and myself", and he had said a few days before switching on the gas in his studio at the Rue Championnet at Paris on April 8, 1951: "I don't want anything any more. And there is nothing I can do about it".[97] Thus the Iranian people lost their most promising author, the one who had placed modern Iranian literature on its planetary orbit.

* SADIQ HIDAYAT (1903-1951), born in Tehran, a scion of the Hidayat family; studied in France; influenced by Kafka and Sartre; among the greatest prose writers of twentieth-century Iran, left a number of masterpieces; very pessimistic both in his writings and in life, committed suicide at Paris in 1951.

Muhammad Masôud (1901-1948) was the first Iranian to receive a degree in journalism, earned from the Brussels School of Journalism on a public scholarship granted upon a recommendation from Âli Akbar Davar. In August 1942, he published the first issue of his weekly *Mard-i Imrouz* (Today's Man). Success was immediate and widespread: publication rose above 30,000 issues. Masôud's editorials were acidic and bold and no one was spared: neither Elite members (Qavam was his favourite target, he even offered Rls1m to whoever would kill him) nor the royal family (including Princess Ashraf). He attacked corruption, injustice, political horse-trading and social ills. His political caricatures were unique. People loved it, for what they discussed privately Masôud printed in his paper. Attacks and popularity brought him his share of enemies, even deadly enemies. His *Mard-i Imrouz* was banned from publication time and again in its short lifetime of five and a half years. Masôud was an incorruptible idealist, a man with a mission; he wrote: "My only goal is to eradicate poverty and oppression in order to ensure the people's happiness". He came from the people, he wrote for them, lived for them and eventually died for them. The powers-that-be caught up with him on the evening of February 11, 1948, as he was sitting in his car before his printing house: a shot was fired point-blank behind his left ear and he died before his printers reached him. The people of Iran had lost a champion who had not been afraid of tilting at the terrifying windmills along his way, the very windmills which silenced him after he had long passed the limits allowed to common mortals.

Influenced by Yushij, Dikhuda, Hidayat, Masôud and many other second-tier poets, writers and journalists, the people were being educated politically and socially. Iranian society was still a highly hierarchical one, with its three distinctive and well-delineated classes: the first, a small elite of a few dozen families at the top; the second, a growing middle class, gradually stretching to its upper and lower levels; and the third, consisting of the large majority of illiterate people, either living below the poverty line or constantly being threatened with falling below it.

But in Iranian society things were changing. The powerful and directly opposing winds of the 1930s and the 1940s had significantly influenced the popular masses. One sign that things were not as they were was the order given by the court in the aftermath of the assassination attempt on the Shah in February 1948 – that every Tehran University student had to sign a statement undertaking not to engage in any political activities. The TU Chancellor, Dr Âli Akbar Syasi, resisted the inept order but was forced into acceptance after being threatened. Dr Syasi later confided that: "...the statements were finally the best compromise I was able to obtain. In case I didn't comply on this point, the 'higher' powers had intimated more forceful measures".[98] Students were being politicised, and that worried the court; if students were thinking of politics instead of their studies, it was because things were changing at the popular level: for students, as is well-known, are the people's enlightened vanguard.

NOTES

1. Colonel Azar had studied military cartography in France and was a lecturer at Tehran's Military Academy. A convinced Marxist, he survived the Iskandani rebellion and escaped to the Soviet Union before returning to Tabriz to join Pishavari's Azarbayjan Army in 1946 and become its commander-in chief. Exiled to the Soviet Union after his army's collapse, he spent the next thirty years there, eventually coming back to Tehran in 1976, to die at home in September 1978.
2. Especially A.H. Tafrishyan, *Qyam-i Afsaran-i Khurasan* (Tehran: *Atlas*, 1367 (1988)) p.70. And also: N. Daryabandari, *Beh Îbarat-i Digar* (Tehran: *Payk*, 1363 (1984)) pp.32-3.
3. N. JAMI, *Guzashteh Chiragh-i Rah-i Ayandeh Ast* (Tehran: *Quqnous*, 1361 (1982)) p.263.
4. N. Daryabandari, op. cit. (note 2), p.37.
5. N. JAMI, op. cit. (note 3), p.313.
6. W.O. Douglas, *Strange Lands and Friendly People* (New York: Harper and Brothers, 1951) p.57.
7. N. JAMI, op. cit. (note 3), p.355.
8. Ibid., p.363.
9. Qavam collected fifty-two votes against fifty-one to veteran Husayn Pirnya (Mûtamin ul-Mulk), who would certainly had declined the premiership had he won.
10. N.S. Fatemi, *Oil Diplomacy* (New York: Whittier Books, 1954) p.236.
11. M.K. Sheehan, *Iran: The Impact of US Interests and Policies (1941-1954)* (New York: Theo. Gaus, 1968) p.32.

12 G. Lenczowski, *Russia and the West in Iran* (New York: Greenwood Press, 1968) p.297.
13 N.S. Fatemi, op. cit. (note 10), p.296.
14 Qavam was submitted to all kinds of pressure in Moscow. The premier, who must have had nerves of steel, later related to one of his junior assistants upon his return to Tehran that at his first *tête-à-tête* with Stalin, the Soviet leader had failed to stop writing at his desk when he was ushered in. Qavam, unimpressed, made his way to the first tableau on the wall and was lost in contemplation until Stalin deigned to notice his presence... Personal communication by the junior assistant in 1982 (then a very old man – he died in 1986) to the author; and *si non è vero, è ben trovato* (if not true, then well made-up), adding yet another anecdote to Qavam's legend. It must be added that Qavam was himself a master in the field of intimidation: in his own office there was only a single chair (his own) and any visitor had no option but to remaining standing before a seated Qavam. Once a delegation, including the very old and weak Sadiq Sadiq, having come to visit him, Qavam ordered Akbar Khan (his factotum) to "bring one chair for the ailing Sadiq", adding *sotto voce* "but only one". Another personal communication, this time from a member of the Sadiq delegation.
15 M. Firouz, *L'Iran face a l'Imposture de l'Histoire* (Paris: L'Herne, 1971) pp.86, 90 and 157.
16 N.S. Fatemi, op. cit. (note 10), pp.306-7., quoting a press conference of President Truman reported by *The New York Times* of April 25, 1952.
16A K.A.Samii, 'Truman against Stalin in Iran: A Tale of Three Messages', in *Middle Eastern Studies*, Vol. 23, no. 1, January 1987.
16B K.A. Samii, *Involvement by Invitation: American Strategies of Containment in Iran* (Pennsylvania State University Press, 1987). and the critique thereof by M.E. Yapp, in *Middle Eastern Studies*, Vol. 24, no. 4, October 1988.
16C M.H. Lytle, *The Origins of the Iranian-American Alliance, 1941-1953* (New York: Holmes and Meier, 1987).
17 G. Lenczowski, op. cit. (note 12), p.302.
18 N. JAMI, op. cit. (note 3), p.295.
18A Habibullah Rashidian, former gardener and coach-driver at the British Embassy in Tehran, turned businessman and middleman. Made a fortune in the Isfahan *bazaar* and in real estate deals.
19 Murtaza Quli Khan Samsam Bakhtiari, the eldest son of Samsam ul-Saltaneh, was then the immovable Bakhtiari *ilkhan*. His fears of the Soviet-backed communist threat were, like those of the other Iranian tribal leaders, always genuine. In his visit to Iran in 1950, US Justice Douglas met with him at his sumptuous residence of Shalamzar and asked him, "Do you think that the Russians will invade Persia?" only to hear the old and wise *ilkhan* candidly reply: "One day the Communists from Russia will come like a flood and sweep all of Persia before them. They will shoot me and all like me, for I am the symbol of all they hate. I will not run away. I will stay right here and die with my people". Cited by W.O. Douglas, op. cit. (note 6), p.121.
20 Ibid., p.136.
21 *Iran Almanac 1961*, (Tehran: Echo of Iran, 1961) p.257.
22 N. JAMI, op. cit. (note 3), p.431.

23 Firouz had even envisaged having them all shot for plotting against the government, but had been *in extremis* dissuaded by Qavam, who had himself backed the plot from the outset.
24 N. JAMI, op. cit. (note 3), p.432.
25 C. Chaqueri, *The Condition of the Working Class in Iran* (European Committee for the Defence of Democratic Rights of Workers in Iran, 1978) pp.206-7.
26 Ibid., pp.367-77.
27 Ibid., pp.400-1.
28 Ibid., pp.326-34.
29 W.O. Douglas, op. cit. (note 6), p.44.
30 N. JAMI, op. cit. (note 3), p.366.
31 Private communication to the author by a junior aide at Qavam's prime ministerial office. Sablier had been invited to Iran with a number of foreign journalists. The whole group was even sent on a tour of Isfahan and Shiraz (to further whet their appetite for an interview). Just before the Frenchman's return to Paris (there weren't many flights then), the premier suddenly decided to grant Sablier an exclusive interview. The whole show had been put on by Qavam to make sure that *Le Monde* would send his kite up for the Soviets to see. It seems that Sablier later realised the totally unknowing role he had played in Qavam's plan, and confirmed the above story.
32 H. Arfa, *Under Five Shahs* (London: John Murray, 1964) pp.369-370.
33 N. JAMI, op. cit. (note 3), p.465.
34 N. Daryabandari, op. cit. (note 2), p.39.
35 A.R. Ghassemlou, *Le Kurdistan Iranien* (Paris: S.E.D.A.G., 1977) p.27.
36 *Mard-i Imrouz* newspaper, no. 116, *Tir 27, 1326* (July 18, 1947) p.1.
37 *Mard-i Imrouz* newspaper, no. 118, *Murdad 10, 1326* (August 1, 1947) p.3.
38 *Ittilaât* newspaper, supplement *Bist va Hasht Hizar Rouz-i Tarikh-i Iran va Jahan*, p.794.
39 P. Dukes, *The Emergence of the Super-Powers* (New York: Harper and Row, 1970) p.33.
40 R. Stewart, *Sunrise at Abadan* (Praeger, 1988) p.222.
41 Mrs Dreyfus with her charitable actions in favour of destitute Iranians would pull her weight too and share in her husband's successful tenure.
42 R. Stewart, op. cit. (note 40), p.221.
43 T.H. Vail Motter, *The Persian Corridor and Aid to Russia* (Washington D.C.: Office of the Chief of Military History, Dept. of the Army, 1952) p.445.
44 M.K. Sheehan, op. cit. (note 11), p.23.
45 N. JAMI, op. cit. (note 3), p.179.
46 N.S. Fatemi, op. cit. (note 10), p.XI.
47 T.H. Vail Motter, op. cit. (note 43), p.471.
48 As quoted in G. Lenczowski, op. cit. (note 12), p.10.
49 M. Ferro, 'Les Deux Sources de l'Islam Révolutionnaire', in *Le Monde Diplomatique*, January 1980, p.11; quoting from C. Chaqueri, *Naissance du Parti Communiste en Iran*, thesis, (Paris: *École des Hautes Études en Sciences Sociales*).
50 The leaders of the *Toudeh* party at their trial in 1983 admitted having been helped financially from their very first days by the Soviet Embassy in Tehran. Some of them, like Secretary-General Nour ul-Din Kianouri, even confessed to having spied for the Soviet Union. Close links between the Soviets and the *Toudeh* had never

been in doubt for Iranian specialists, but the 1983 trial of the *Toudeh* leadership lifted the veil, once and for all, on this relationship.

51 On Kambakhsh see A. Khameh'i, *Panjah Nafar ...va Seh Nafar* (Tehran: *Hafteh*, undated) pp.30-62. Author Buzurg Âlavi (from the '53 Group') further called Kambakhsh "the Stalinist", in comparison to Arani "the Liberal"; see *An Nist Keh Minimayad*, in *Adineh* magazine no. 80/81, *Khurdad 1372* (June 1993), p.14.

52 Private communication to the author from a (then) junior *Toudeh* official, who added that there had been long and heated discussions on the sharing out of the five party cars between party leaders!

53 N. JAMI, op. cit. (note 3), p.283.

54 E. Abrahamian, *Iran Between Two Revolutions* (Princeton University Press, 1982) p.246.

55 The British involvement is best shown in a masterpiece of historical romance about Iran in the 1946 crisis: J. Aldridge, *The Diplomat* (London: The Bodley Head, 1949).

56 G. Lenczowski, op. cit. (note 12), p.255.

57 E. Kedourie, *England and the Middle East* (London: Bowes and Bowes, 1956) p.9.

58 W.O. Douglas, op. cit. (note 6), p.320.

59 Sir Alexander Gibb managed the highly successful potable water project for Tehran which provided the Iranian capital with its excellent drinking water.

60 Wm. Roger Louis, *The British Empire in the Middle East, 1945-1951* (Oxford University Press, 1984).

61 G.B. Baldwin, *Planning and Development in Iran* (Baltimore: John Hopkins Press, 1967) p.102.

62 See *The Economist*, May 6, 1950, p.982.

63 Dr Âli Amini was the grandson of Muzaffar ul-Din Shah on his mother's side, and the grandson of Âli Khan Amin ul-Douleh on his father's side, was closely related to Qavam, whose mother had been the sister of Amin ul-Douleh and whose niece (the daughter of brother Vusuq ul-Douleh) was Amini's wife.

64 L.P. Elwell-Sutton, *Persian Oil* (London: Lawrence and Wishart, 1955) p.159.

64A O. Caroe, *Wells of Power* (London: Macmillan, 1951) p.228.

65 L.P. Elwell-Sutton, op. cit. (note 64), p.160.

66 J. Amuzegar, *Technical Assistance in Theory and Practice* (New York: Praeger, 1966) p.101; quoting from R.K. Hall, 'Seven Year Plan in Iran', in *Yearbook of Education*, 1954, p.283.

67 W.E. Warne, *Mission for Peace* (Indianapolis and New York: The Bobbs-Merrill Co., 1956) p.16.

68 J. Amuzegar, op. cit. (note 66), p.48.

69 *Iran - Country Survey Series*, (New Haven: Human Relations Area Files, 1957) p.100.

70 W.O. Douglas, op. cit. (note 6), p.322.

71 J. Amuzegar, op. cit. (note 66), p.101.

72 J. Bharier, *Economic Development in Iran, 1900-1970* (Oxford University Press, 1971) p.173.

73 *Iran Almanac 1969*, (Tehran: Echo of Iran, 1969) p.333.
74 L.P. Elwell-Sutton, op. cit. (note 64), p.150.
75 Ibid., p.157.
76 See Wm. Roger Louis, 'Musaddiq and the Dilemmas of British Imperialism', in *Musaddiq, Iranian Nationalism and Oil*, ed. by J.A. Bill and Wm. Roger Louis, (London: I.B. Tauris, 1988) p.152.
77 *Asnad-i Naft* (Tehran: Puyan, 1330 (1951)) pp.25-26.
78 F. Naficy, 'Oil Exploration in Iran', in *The Bulletin of the Iranian Petroleum Institute*, no. 2, October 1960, p.12. All the shares of the Iran Oil Co., were transferred to NIOC in January 1954.
79 L.P. Elwell-Sutton, op. cit. (note 64), pp.131-133.
80 Standard Oil company of New Jersey, *Report to Shareholders* (1950), p.26.
81 Interestingly enough, the magical share of forty per cent for the American companies was already on the cards by 1946/47.
82 S.H. Longrigg, *Oil in the Middle East* (Oxford University Press, 2nd ed., 1961) p.147.
83 L.P. Elwell-Sutton, op. cit. (note 64), p.164.
84 N.S. Fatemi, op. cit. (note 10), p.328.
84A In an article, R.W. Ferrier gave the following figures for benefits over the period – HM's Government: £194.1million ("22.5m in dividends) – Iran's Government: £100.5million – other shareholders: £17.4million. Thus Iran's share stood at 32.2% of the total. See R.W. Ferrier, 'The Anglo-Iranian Oil Dispute: a triangular relationship', in op. cit. (note 10), p.171.
85 For the full text of the SA, see N. Kemp, *Abadan* (London: Allan Wingate, 1953) pp.260-5.
86 A. Sampson, *The Seven Sisters* (London: Coronet Books, 1976) p.134.
87 R.C. Mowat, *Middle East Perspective* (London: Blanford Press, 1958) p.54.
88 H. Makki spoke longest of all three; he also published the complete proceedings of the filibuster in his work, *Istizah* (Tehran: *Amir Kabir*, 1357 (1978)).
89 L.P. Elwell-Sutton, op. cit. (note 64), p.171.
90 N. JAMI, op.cit. (note 3), p.540.
91 The twenty-eight year old Fakhrara'i, a *Toudeh* party member, was a jack of all trades, an adventurer, a resourceful fellow and also a genuine sportsman. In his school days, Fakhrara'i never accepted discipline and always had to do things his own way, even if it meant going up a five-metre high wall instead of going through the main door. He fully deserved his nickname of *Nasir Fanar* (Springy Nasir). It is amazing that such a man missed his close-range target three times out of five, and, moreover, had his last bullet jam the gun! These general facts about Fakhrara'i were communicated to the author by one of Fakhrara'i 's school friends. See also: *Ittilaât* newspaper, no. 6853, *Bahman 16, 1327* (February 5, 1949), p.8.
92 E. Abrahamian, op. cit. (note 54), p.250.
93 N. JAMI, op. cit. (note 3), p.546.
94 E.A. Bayne, *Persian Kingship in Transition* (New York: American University Field Staff, 1968) p.66.
95 Qavam's open letter of March 17, 1950 was reprinted along with the Shah's insulting reply calling Qavam "a thief and a murderer" in the day's newspapers. It was reprinted verbatim in July 1952 as Qavam's name once again hit the headlines,

as for example in: *Hizb-i Millat-i Iran* newspaper, dated Tir 29, 1331 (July 20, 1952) pp.1-2.

[96] P. Avery, *Modern Iran* (London: Ernest Benn, 1965) p.243.

[97] R. Jaccard, 'Au Cabaret du Néant', in *Le Monde*, March 19, 1993.

[98] N. JAMI, op. cit. (note 3), p.533.

CHAPTER TEN:
OIL NATIONALISATION

Under Reza Shah every citizen obeyed and did what he was ordered to do. On the contrary, during the relatively free 1940s, evolving in a political vacuum, the people of Iran (and especially Tehran) wanted to participate and somehow become part of a political process dominated by no single individual or institution. The relative liberty of the press further added to society's evolution. After all, the country was the people's too – they had some rights, at least the right to decide what they wanted. The early signs that popular mentality was altering had become evident towards the close of the 1940s. There was a new assertiveness, a newly-found self-confidence which had been spawned by the turbulent post-war years and the fact that the future was wide open. If the popular crisis had originated from multiple causes, it would trigger multiple crises.

10.1. Multiple Crises

At the dawn of the year 1950 not only were the people in crisis, but the other three major parameters in Iran's overall equation – the Powers, the elites and the oil industry – were too.

For the Western Powers, the crisis was due to the fact that the British hegemony dating from the post-World War I days was not yet dead and the new post-World War II arrangement concerning Iran were not yet birthed. It was clear that the new order would have to be born from an Anglo-American arrangement. The British monopoly on Iranian oil was not viable in a two-superpower world. Moreover, without the US, the British could not hope to contain the Red threat to Iran single-handedly.

The Americans had their military missions in Iran, but little else – no other direct involvement, no precise policy either: in 1948–1950 there was even a period of bizarre ambivalence towards Iran. Their only vague guideline was to always stand behind the Shah. But indubitably they had the desire to be in Iran, understanding that no world Power (even less superpower) could afford to shun the Iranian Game. They could have acquired a financial lever in 1949 with a timely loan, but their decision not to grant one was in line with American (bottom line) logic: Iran had the resources to finance her development herself, so she shouldn't bank on American generosity. Simultaneously, by closing the IBRD's door to the Iranians, the US had indirectly shifted their attention to oil revenues and to their allies (and rivals) the British. Since the early 1920s US oil companies had been fighting for a share of Iran's oil resources without ever reaching their goal. Why should they now make the British an present? In the global war for oil (either overt or covert) such things as niceties don't exist.

As for the Soviet Union, since 1947 she had been on the sidelines, hanging on to the 1921 agreement and to the hope of one day getting that oil concession in the northern provinces.

The Soviet-backed *Toudeh* party was at its lowest ebb, with only two irons still in the fire: (i) its intact secret officers' organisation and (ii) its highly disciplined rank and file. But, as usual, there was a rather poor leadership across the whole spectrum.

The Iranian elite was also facing a crisis, because the old Qajar Elite was at the end of its tether. Behind Qavam, the younger Elite generation seemed incapable of taking the relay baton. The crafty Muzaffar Firouz was in exile at Paris; hopefuls Husayn Âla and Dr Âli Amini were not leaders; the rest was a large mass of foreign-educated bureaucrats, *Majlis* deputies and businessmen: all Indians, no chief. The days of the likes of Sâid, Hakimi and Sadr were long past. To defend the Elite's tarnished colours there remained only two septuagenarians: the inimitable Ahmad Qavam, seventy-three, and the popular Dr Musaddiq, seventy-one.

The late Reza Shah's elite of army generals was doing only slightly better than the old Elite. Similarly, it only had two veterans at the top: Generals Amir Ahmadi, sixty-two, and Yazdanpanah, fifty-six. Amir Ahmadi, as Minister of War (1946–49), had been in charge of refurbishing the armed forces. Within a short time, with the assistance of the American missions (and their gifts of equipment), he had overseen an unexpected recovery. He had been greatly helped in his task by the timely Azarbayjan invasion, the type of internal police action against irregular troops always relished by Reza Shah's army. The swift march on Tabriz had given back the army its self-confidence and its lost popularity. Quantitatively too, the armed forces had rebounded from a low of 65,000 men at the end of 1941 to number

102,000 in 1946 and 120,000 in 1949.[1] Among the officers' corps, the Ârfa brothers, Ibrahim and Hasan, had rapidly risen through the ranks – Hasan to the command of the Imperial Guards, and Ibrahim to become the armed forces' logistics tsar. The latter was killed in a military plane crash in January 1943 and the former rose to become chief of the army general staff in December 1944. General Ârfa's tenure lasted only until April 1946, as he was arrested during Qavam's wave of imprisonment of personalities who were suspected of harbouring anti-Soviet feelings. Freed after seven months, Ârfa went to see Minister of War Amir Ahmadi and related the meeting in his memoirs:

> Entering the Minister's office I saw there beside General Ahmadi, Generals Yazdanpanah and Razmara. Ahmadi did all the talking ...During all this the other two Generals did not utter a word...[2]

Ârfa was eventually compelled to retire from the army in February 1947.[3]

Ârfa's long-time rival General Hajj Âli Razmara had finally triumphed. For years the race for the position of chief of the general staff (the army's key post) had been a private duel between them. Razmara had won the first round (1943–44) and Ârfa the second (1944–46), but with the latter's exit, Razmara had secured the third and decisive round (with the help of his close friend Muzaffar Firouz) in time to lead the crucial Azarbayjan invasion. "Although outwardly vivacious", Ârfa would say of his rival in his memoirs, "Razmara was a shrewd and intelligent man who seldom acted on impulse".[4] Razmara was not made from the common stock: he was courageous, assertive and indefatigable (he hardly slept a couple of hours at night). He was a man of iron, fit for elite status. His four brothers and four sisters had aptitudes above the average. Born into a military family, most of them had remained in the military: elder brother Husayn Âli was head of the army's Geographical Department, and another was a colonel; while two of his sisters were, respectively, the wives of Generals Gulpira and Parsa; his own wife was the sister of General Âbdullah Hidayat.

While the political and military elites were in a marked decline, the counter-elites were busy expanding. The *Toudeh* was recruiting through its secret officers' organisation, headed by its originator Khusrou Rouzbeh and the doyen Colonel Syamak. Its *Sazman-i Javanan Hizb-i Toudeh* (*Toudeh*'s Party Youth Organisation) was targeting the best and brightest high school students through its myriad of *Toudeh* teachers (especially in Khuzistan province where the high wages paid by the AIOC attracted the best Iranian teachers, the majority of whom had links to *Toudeh*). The rank and file distributed communist propaganda received from Soviet sources or printed on clandestine presses in Tehran. Even decapitated and without official outlets such as clubs or trade unions, the *Toudeh* continued to expand – albeit at a much slower pace than during the 1940s.

The nationalistic counter-elite was attracting to its new fold of the National Front some individuals like the tribune Husayn Makki, the politician Dr Baqa'i Kermani and the journalist Dr Husayn Fatimi, who had reunited in his newspaper *Bakhtar-i Imrouz* (The West Today), which was launched on July 29, 1949 with his cousin Sayyid Muhammad Riza Jalali Naini, a plethora of young stars: Dr Rahmatullah Mustafavi, Muhammad Âli Safari, Sipihr Zabî and Nasrullah Shifteh. The *Iran* Party, still the main NF pillar, had not expanded. Never after quantity, the leaders of the *Iran* party strove to attract quality. Thus they didn't bother with theory, ideology, or recruitment and their propaganda was limited to a couple of pamphlets. They had themselves and that was enough for supporting Dr Musaddiq and his cause.

The religious counter-elite was slowly but surely forming fresh support at the central Qum *Houzeh Îlmiyyeh*, where the leadership of Ayatullah Burujirdi* had worked wonders. Discipline, study and excellence were the order of the day. Burujirdi, a conservative both by birth and by nature, was a proponent of dialogue with the central government. In return for his non-intervention in political affairs, he expected the politicians (i) not to intervene in his *Houzeh*'s affairs, and (ii) to listen to his advice on religious and moral matters.

Under Burujirdi's wise leadership the Qum *Houzeh*'s reputation progressed by leaps and bounds. Four years after taking over the *Houzeh*, Burujirdi was ready to receive Iran's leading religious personalities at Qum. In February 1949, some 2,000 clergymen gathered in the first congress of its kind, to debate the state, politics, religion and the clergy's role in society. It was decided at this historic meeting that henceforward the religious hierocracy would shun direct engagement in politics.⁵ After the congress, Qum and Burujirdi were at the very centre of Iran's religious community.

* AYATULLAH HAJJ AQA HUSAYN TABATABA'I BURUJIRDI (1875-1961), born in Burujird, son of Hajj Sayyid Âli and descendant of the famous Âllameh Sayyid Muhammad Tabataba'i (1679-1747); studied at Burujird, Isfahan and Najaf; leading Burujird *mujtahid*; became head of Qum *Houzeh* (1945); renovated the *Masjid-i Aâzam* (the Great Mosque), refurbished the *Madraseh Khan* (the Khan School) and ordered the erection of the Hamburg Mosque; reformed *Houzeh* and placed it on its modern tracks; died at the age of eighty-six in 1961.

On the fringes of the community, a small splinter group known as the *Fada'yan-i Islam* had formed in 1945 under the charismatic leadership of Sayyid Mujtaba Navvab Safavi.* Inspired by the Egyptian *Ikhwan al-Muslimin* (Islamic Brotherhood) of Hasan Al-Bana and Sayyid Qutb, the young Navvab Safavi was a firebrand radical. Supported at the top of the hierocracy by the Ayatullahs Khwunsari and Kashani, his *Fada'yan* was "an unabashedly mass organisation".⁶ It was not, however, well received in Qum, where Burujirdi placed them on the *persona non grata* list. But the latter was always careful not to discredit them publicly.⁷ This did not stop Navvab from gathering in Tehran and Abadan a dozen devoted followers, with the brothers Vahidi as his chief lieutenants. Their first coup was the 1945 attempt by Navvab Safavi himself to eliminate the atheist author Ahmad Kasravi; he failed and was arrested, but a year later, in March 1946, *Fada'i* Sayyid Husayn Imami killed Kasravi in the Ministry of Justice. In an era of political violence and murders, the *Fada'yan* were adding their own grain of salt: interestingly, in such an environment, a small group of fanatical youngsters could make a great deal of hay, placing the enemies of Islam on the defensive.

* SAYYID MUJTABA NAVVAB SAFAVI (1924-1956), born at Tehran's Khaniabad district, son of Sayyid Javad Mirlouhi; after his father's death, lived with his maternal uncle Safavi; educated at the *Hakim Nizami* school and the German industrial school of Tehran (till 1941); hired by AIOC at Abadan (1943); went to Najaf for religious studies (1944); returned to Iran, detained after unsuccessful attempt on

Ahmad Kasravi (May 1944); created *Fada'yan-i Islam*; his *Fada'yan* executed Kasravi (1945); created *Majmah-i Musalmanan-i Mujahid* as the political arm of the *Fada'yan* (1948); ordered Hazhir's execution (1949); involved his men in Razmara's assassination (1951); arrested under Musaddiq (1952); condemned murder attempt on Dr H. Fatimi, ordered by his lieutenant Vahidi (1952); ordered attempt on Premier Âla (1955); arrested, with his lieutenants, by General Taymour Bakhtiar's security forces; tried and executed on January 17, 1956.

Ayatullah Kashani, a firm supporter of the *Fada'yan*, was an exception in the Iranian hierocracy. With tenuous links to the Qum elite and an active political past which had included a role as close adviser to Reza Shah, a stint in the British camp at Sultanabad (Arak) during the war, five months of prison under Qavam's premiership in 1946, and two exiles, the first to Qum (1946–47) and the second to Beirut via Damascus from February 1949 until June 1950, Kashani was a religious maverick. With his checkered background, the clever clergyman had gathered a team of advisers and a popular following in Tehran. Sporting strongly anti-British colours – intensified by his brushes with the British authorities during the war – the sixty-five year old Kashani was prepared to enter any coalition opposed to their interests in Iran.

After the crises of 1920 and 1932/33, the question of Iranian oil was back on the main national agenda. Negotiations with the AIOC had yielded the Gass-Gulsha'yan Supplemental Agreement (SA), which had not satisfied the technocrats of the *Iran* Party. Their oil affairs specialist, Engineer Kazim Hasibi, took apart the SA in a lengthy presentation delivered at the *Iran* Party offices on April 9, 1950. During his lecture he had even accused Gulsha'yan of 'treason'.[8] Hasibi had based some of his points attacking the SA on the various 'Notes' delivered during 1949 by the French advisers of Iran's Ministry of Finance, Professor Gilbert Gidel and Jean Rousseau.[9] The Frenchmen had even drafted a counter-proposal to the SA in fourteen articles, with a minimum revenue of £12m per annum for Iran (art. 4) and the right for Iranian citizens to acquire fifty per cent of any new AIOC shares issue (art. 8). It goes without saying that this draft was rejected out of hand by AIOC.

The dialogue between Iran and AIOC was one of the points of the oil agenda, while the other was the question of the American oil companies, which wanted an oil concession of sorts in Iran – as though it were their automatic right. Thus, until the Iran-AIOC difference over the SA and the American companies' concession were settled, Iran's oil affairs would be in crisis. As a workable solution to the two above files was not easy to envision, even less so to bring about, there were still many sparks to expect from these potential friction points.

10.2. The Sixteenth *Majlis*

As usual in Iran, the elections to the Sixteenth *Majlis* held in September 1949 were rigged. The Tehran elections had seen a royalist list come out of the ballot boxes. Dr M. Musaddiq had been elected from Tehran, but not his friends from the *Iran* parties and other individuals he had supported. On October 10, at a reunion of opposition personalities in Dr Musaddiq's house, it was decided to hold a protest at the royal palace. Word of mouth spread and the silent protest held on October 14 was a large popular success. The Shah, taken aback, was forced to receive a delegation to hear the protesters' requests. Dr Musaddiq and eighteen others (among whom were Dr Âli Shayigan, Dr Shams ul-Din Amir Âla'i, Dr Karim Sanjabi, Dr Husayn Fatimi, Dr Muzaffar Baqa'i Kermani, Engineer Ahmad Zirakzadehand Husayn Makki) were ushered in to meet the Shah. Dr Musaddiq requested the annulment of the Tehran elections and fresh elections under a new, impartial government. The Shah asked for time to review the question. On October 23, the palace protesters formed the *Jibheh Milli* (National Front), a loose political grouping of political parties and leading personalities, with, at its head, naturally, Dr Musaddiq.

Then, on November 4, came the watershed, as Âbdul-Husayn Hazhir, the Minister of Court (whose marriage to Princess Ashraf was said to be imminent), was shot dead by Sayyid Husayn Imami, a member of the *Fada'yan-i Islam* (the assassin was executed a few days later). On November 11, the Shah back-pedalled and announced the annulment of the Tehran elections and the holding of another round of voting. Dr Musaddiq's protest had borne fruit and the National Front had begun rolling and gathering steam. The fresh Tehran elections returned seven deputies from the National Front – namely Dr

Musaddiq (once again the capital's top vote-winner), Dr Shayigan, Dr Baqa'i, Nariman, Azad, Makki and Ha'irizadeh – and when the Sixteenth *Majlis* was inaugurated on February 10, 1950, the Front's faction counted eight deputies (its Tehran deputies, in addition to Allahyar Salih elected from Kashan) out of a total of 131 deputies. Simultaneously with the Sixteenth *Majlis*, the first ever Iranian Senate was also inaugurated, in accordance with the 1949 law.

The first act of the new *Majlis* was to dismiss Premier Said and replace him with a stopgap, Âli Mansour. The days of compromise which had led to the choice of elder statesmen capable of withstanding the Powers' pressure was over. Public opinion and the *Majlis* wanted politicians able to solve problems (especially the oil imbroglio) at the helm. After two months of tergiversations, Mansour hit upon a solution agreeable to everyone: create a special oil commission in the *Majlis* to review the Supplemental Agreement.

Mansour's solution might have been elegant, but it was extremely time-consuming as the Oil Commission would take months. Nevertheless on June 20 the *Majlis* approved of the Commission and duly elected its eighteen members: the National Front succeeded in getting five (out of eight) of its deputies on the commission – besides Dr Musaddiq as head of the commission and Makki as secretary, also Dr Shayigan, Salih and Ha'irizadeh.

The Oil Commission was a godsend for the Front because, from 8 out of 131 in the *Majlis*, it now had the favourable ratio of 5 out of 18 in it, with the added bonuses of the commission's two key posts and of the extreme diversity among the other thirteen members, whose large majority was greatly inferior intellectually to the Front members.

As soon as the Oil Commission began its work, the *Majlis* forced Mansour to resign on June 26 and replaced him with General Hajj Âli Razmara,* the hitherto chief of the general staff. The choice was of the best man available: if someone in Iran had the energy and the resources to solve all the crises without breaking too many eggs, it was Razmara. Behind him stood the ramrod-straight Iranian armed forces from Amir Ahmadi downwards. Among the best and the brightest of his generation, the general had only two drawbacks for the task ahead: (i) his unbounded and unlimited self-confidence (an advantage for any other individual) and (ii) his lack of vision in international affairs (if only Muzaffar Firouz had been at his elbow!). The only internal sphere of power annoyed by his nomination was the court. Razmara did not hold the Shah in esteem, thinking him weak and vacillating (Robin Zaehner of the British secret service MI6 thought along the same lines[10]), and told whoever wanted to hear that "someday I shall eventually get rid of the Shah".[11]

* HAJJ ÂLI RAZMARA (1901–1951), son of Muhammad Razmara, a retired army colonel; educated at the French school *Alliance*, at the Dar ul-Funoun and the Military Academy (graduated first of his class); second lieutenant (1920); first lieutenant (1921); captain (1922); Saint-Cyr (1923–25); major (1927); lieutenant colonel (1929); colonel (1935); general (1939); the favourite of the old generals; chief of the general staff (1943–44); head of Military Academy (1944–45); again chief of the general staff (1946–50); prime minister (1950–51); shot dead in the *Masjid-i Shah* on March 7, 1951.

Once in power, Razmara began to open all files at once. His first effort was to bring the stalled bill on regional councils before the *Majlis*, only to have it rejected yet again by the assembly in which landlords, opposed to official councils in their lands, had an unbeatable majority of 76 out of 131 deputies. The Prime Minister's second effort was to rekindle the anti-corruption effort first launched by Premier Sâid and left pending under Mansour. He set up a commission to review the prepared lists of corrupt officials – categorised into lists *Alif* (A), *Beh* (B) and *Jim* (C), with the latter listing the most corrupt – only to witness commission members resigning one after the other. By the end of August 1950, the government finally published the three lists with a grand total of 269 names, with the crucial (C) list (which automatically entailed life banishment from public service) of 110 names[12] – led by the names of Ahmad Qavam, Sardar Fakhir Hikmat, General Shahbakhti and Dr Manuchihr Iqbal. The lists were deemed an unacceptable farce by the political establishment (no one had ever been fingered, let alone arrested, for corruption in Iran) and they were filed away without any further ado. With this second successive failure in domestic reforms, Razmara decided to turn his sights towards the international stage, where the critical oil file awaited him.

Razmara's foreign strategy was extremely simple: bend backwards to satisfy all three Powers at once.[13] His negotiations with Soviet Ambassador Sadchikov culminated in November 1950 with the signature of a generous Soviet-Iranian trade agreement. As a *quid pro quo* he tried to induce the Soviets to repay Iran its debt for war reparations without any success. He also had rumours circulated regarding a possible Soviet oil concession for the northern provinces. He tried his best not to stand in the way of the *Toudeh* rank and file, while they carried out their anti-AIOC propaganda. Finally, he closed his eyes (and maybe lent a hand) when, on December 15, 1950, ten *Toudeh* leaders escaped from jail with their janitors, First Lts. Muhammadzadeh and Qubadi.[14] Prominent among the ten escapees were Dr Kianouri, Dr Joudat, Dr Yazdi, Engineer Ãlavi and Khusrou Rouzbeh.

At first, "the US Embassy had openly supported Razmara's candidacy [to the premiership]",[15] believing that this strong military figure could usher in reforms while keeping a lid on lawless elements. A couple of days after Razmara's official appointment, a new US ambassador, Dr Henry F. Grady, an expert on aid to small nations, had arrived in Tehran. After a short honeymoon, during which the 'Point Four' agreement for Iran was signed (October 1950), relations between the US. Embassy and Razmara rapidly deteriorated. Not only had the premier failed in his domestic reforms, but clashes had occurred between Iranian military forces and the US military missions, prompting an official protest from the embassy. In December, the contracts of Max Thornburg and his OCI experts were rescinded and the American team left Iran at the beginning of the new year. By then, the US was totally disillusioned with Razmara and ready to throw its support behind the young technocrats whom they understood and whom they held to have the best chance of straightening out Iran's affairs.

10.3. Oil Nationalisation

The British were expecting the Gass-Gulsha'yan SA to be ratified by the Sixteenth *Majlis*. The ball was now in the Oil Commission's court and Razmara tried his best to convince Dr Musaddiq and its colleagues to endorse the SA. The Oil Commission, on the other hand, was adamant about having a copy of the Minister of Finance's secret oil file. The tug of war between Dr Musaddiq and Dr Husayn Pirnya, the delegate of the Ministry of Finance, lasted for a few weeks before the latter capitulated and handed over the file to the commission in September. In October, the National Front members decided upon a presentation of their opinion on the oil question to the *Majlis*; at four sessions – on October 12, 15, 17 and 19 respectively – four speakers presented the Front's case: Ha'irizadeh developed the political aspects, Salih the social implications, Makki the technical problems, and Dr Musaddiq himself touched upon the legal points.[16] In a wide-ranging reply the prime minister could only deplore the sweeping attacks on the AIOC and the SA, and reiterated his defence of the latter document. Dr Husayn Fatimi, taking advantage of the oil debates on the *Majlis* floor, proposed openly in two editorials published in his own *Bakhtar-i Imrouz* "the nationalisation of the oil industry in the whole country"[17] – a concept he had been the first to formulate in an informal meeting at Mahmoud Nariman's house.[18]

The wave of nationalisations implemented by Attlee's post-war Labour Government – which included the Bank of England, the National Health Service and a number of basic industries such as coal, railways, airlines, electricity and gas – had caught the eye of the very 'moderate Nationalists' Attlee and Bevin had wanted to set up in developing countries. Now that Dr Fatimi had launched the oil nationalisation train, it only needed to gather steam. In November it was Dr Baqa'i who seconded Fatimi's proposal in a *Shahid* editorial. On November 25 the Oil Commission finally concluded that the SA was unacceptable and on December 12 officially presented its conclusion to the *Majlis*, which officially rejected the agreement five days later. In the meantime, the National Front members had failed to convince the Oil Commission to support their nationalisation proposal. A National Front draft to have nationalisation of the oil industry debated by the *Majlis* gathered only twelve signatures, three short of the minimum required. On December 13, it was *Ayatullah* Kashani's turn to favour nationalisation in a long communiqué which concluded that:

> ...oil nationalisation in Iran is the only alternative left to pull us out of our wretchedness...[19]

Two months later *Ayatullah* Khwunsari joined the fray by issuing a *fatva* supporting oil nationalisation. The nationalisation train was gaining momentum.

Iranian public opinion was further exacerbated in early January 1951 as the news hit Tehran that ARAMCO had signed a fifty-fifty agreement with Saudi Arabia on December 30, 1950. The supporters of nationalisation had a field day asking: "If the Arabs can get 50-50, why can't we?" At that stage, a *Majlis* (and a public) majority would have embraced any 50-50 proposal from AIOC, but the company and its chairman Fraser were unwilling to consider anything but Gass-Gulsha'yan. A question of taxation seems to have been behind the AIOC's failing to fall in line with a mode of agreement which would inevitably become a world standard. As oil expert Dr Frankel wrote:

> Actually one of the reasons why Anglo-Iranian did not match in time the advantages offered by ARAMCO to Saudi Arabia, a fact which lost her the Iranian concession, was to a great extent due to the UK tax authorities being slow in adapting themselves to the American pattern.[20]

Thus, the American oil companies, with their tax deductions on royalties paid to host countries, had stolen a march on their British rivals. Chairman Fraser tried his best to convince the British Treasury to make " a special dispensation in respect of dividend payments to the Iranian Government", but "the Chancellor of Exchequer, Sir Stafford Cripps, was not prepared to make an exception".[20A] The British authorities would eventually be obliged to follow suit a couple of years later. But in 1951 the British were not interested, and, when George McGhee came to London to explain to AIOC officials the workings of the new fifty-fifty agreement, he was "told to mind his own business".[21]

However, yet another reason behind nationalisation was that the AIOC "had offered too little, too long; ...in 1951 Iran was getting eighteen cents a barrel on its oil, while Bahrein got thirty-five cents, Saudi Arabia fifty-six and Iraq sixty".[22] Furthermore, the benefits accruing to the British were almost double those of the Iranians. BP's late historian R.W. Ferrier estimated that "between 1932 and 1950: £194.1million (inclusive of £22.5m in net dividends) to His Majesty's Government as against £100m to the Iranian Government (and £17.4m to other shareholders)".[22A] In other words, of the total benefits estimated at £312m, Iran had received 32.2%, roughly one-third.

In any event, the ARAMCO deal poured welcome fuel on the National Front's campaign for nationalisation. On January 11, the Oil Commission was prolonged for another two months. A fortnight later, Front leaders addressed a 10,000-strong crowd at the Tehran *Bazaar* on the subject of nationalisation. Meanwhile Razmara was still trying to convince the British to grant 50-50 (with no success[23]), while weighing the nationalisation option by evaluating the possibility of Iranians operating the industry. The Prime Minister asked three young Iranian oil graduates to assay the technical, financial and legal feasibility of the option. When all three gave him negative replies, he went on March 3 to the Oil Commission and stated that Iran could not consider nationalising its oil industry because it didn't have the expertise to manage it and wrapped up his statement by asking the commission: "How can we set our sights on the oil industry when we can't even manufacture a *lulahing* (mud-ewer)?"[24] Here the Prime Minister had gone a sentence too far; running a country was not like running a garrison.

By then, Razmara was the last obstacle on the way to nationalisation. On March 7, the *Khatm* (funeral service) of *Ayatullah Fayz Qumi* was being held at the Shah Mosque. Razmara was reminded of the event by his Labour Minister, Asadullah Âlam, who had come to his office to accompany him. As Razmara and Âlam entered the mosque, shots were fired and Razmara fell, hit three times: "one bullet from the left penetrated through his neck and came out of his forehead (destroying his brain), two bullets from the right through his chest and shoulder, said Dr Mirsipasi, the head of the *Pizishk-i Qanuni* (Legal Medical Office)", who was in charge of the autopsy.[25] Khalil Tahmasibi, a member of Navvab's *Fada'yan*, was caught gun in hand and admitted having shot at Razmara. But Razmara's real assassins were three of his NCO bodyguards (the single gunman theory doesn't stand up): Latif Tahouni, Allahyar Jalilvand and Mustafa Bazouki.[26] Further evidence that the conspiracy was way above the *Fada'yans*' head came to light in a letter written by Colonel Habibullah Dayhimi, a former secretary of the Shah's *Daftar-i Nizami* (Military Bureau), to the Shah asking for assistance by writing: "As His Majesty knows perfectly well, in the assassination of General Razmara, no one had a greater share than I, after Âlam".[27] Razmara was dead for having failed in all his ventures and especially for his utter failure on the oil question, in which he had alienated all of the players. He had not been able to fill Reza Shah's shoes: he had been a good soldier, not a politician. The powers-that-be had destroyed him because he had not been able to defeat them.

As the gun shots echoed through the Shah Mosque, the Oil Commission was in the midst of a crucial meeting. Its members were busy editing the final text of the oil nationalisation bill.

At noon, the information slipped into the closed conference room that Razmara had been shot dead. Pandemonium broke out in the commission as half a dozen members asked to leave the session. Dr Musaddiq kept his composure: "Gentlemen", he said, "we are here to do our duty, and until we are through with it, no one will leave this room. It is in no one's interest to do so anyway".[28] Finally, only Javad Âmiri resigned on the spot and Dr Musaddiq opened the closed door for him to leave. In the afternoon, the bill's text – a single sentence simply calling for the nationalisation of the oil industry throughout the country - was unanimously approved and signed. The Oil Commission had signed a bill which eight months earlier would not have had the shade of a chance of being adopted. The train launched by Dr Fatimi in October had reached its first major station.

On March 8, the Nationalisation Bill was presented to the *Majlis* which ratified it on March 15; the next day it charged the Oil Commission with the task of drafting yet another bill regulating the nationalisation process. Against a background of intense social disorders, while martial law was being applied in Tehran, the Senate endorsed the *Majlis*'s ratification on March 20, 1951. The oil industry in Iran had been nationalised, the royal signature on the Nationalisation Law was a formality which the Shah would perform "reluctantly on May 1".[29] The oil industry itself was in a crisis too, as the company had withheld the payment of a special yearly allowance and the authorities had had to place Abadan under martial law on March 24.

The Anglophile Husayn Âla had been elected as a stopgap premier in Razmara's stead. Totally eclipsed by the momentous events taking place in Iran, Âla was the symbol of an Elite in decomposition. There was nothing Âla could do but occupy the premiership, waiting for the first occasion to resign.

As the Oil Commission came up with its nine-point bill regulating oil nationalisation on April 25, Âla lost no time in presenting his resignation on the morrow. On April 27 the *Majlis* took two decisive steps: it ratified the Nine-Point Bill and elected Dr Musaddiq prime minister with seventy-nine votes for and twelve against. On April 29, the Senate also endorsed the Nine-Point Bill. The new law proposed a wholesale transfer of the whole southern oil industry from the AIOC to the newly-created National Iranian Oil Company (NIOC) under the supervision of a Mixed Parliamentary Board (consisting of five senators, five deputies and the Minister of Finance or his deputy). A new era was dawning for Iran's oil, almost exactly half a century after the granting of D'Arcy's concession. The road ahead was traced in the Nine Point Law of April 29, 1951. In the driver's seat was the man who had brought the train so far against all odds: the seventy-two year old Dr Muhammad Musaddiq, the former Musaddiq ul-Saltaneh.

10.4. Dr Muhammad Musaddiq

Dr M. Musaddiq* was the last of the Elitists. Being of the select Qajar aristocracy by birth and by marriage (having married an Imami, the family from which Tehran's *Imam Jumêhs* issued), he was also a member of the intelligentsia by education (an exception among the Qajar nobility). Once at the top, instead of promoting his Qajar Elitist friends, he brought into his cabinet the National Front leaders who had assisted him in his struggle for oil nationalisation. He was, indeed, acting as a stepping stone for the counter-elitists who were replacing the Elite at the top. A man like Qavam could understand that, but the rest of the Elite would never forgive Musaddiq his 'treason' to their cause. The divorce between the Qajar Elite and the prime minister was sealed when the five elder members of the Elite's board of directors went to see him (in 1951) and "argued that as the oil concession would be terminated in ten years [they meant D'Arcy's] Musaddiq should reconsider his nationalisation scheme", but the Prime Minister told them "about the 1933 Agreement and the December 31, 1993 deadline" and that "he knew exactly what he was doing" and "politely thanked them for their consideration".[30] The leaders of the Qajar Elite would not forget this affront and took their revenge in due time.

* DR MUHAMMAD MUSADDIQ (1879–1967), son to Mirza Hidayat Vazir Daftar and Princess Najm ul-Saltaneh (Prince

Farmanfarma's sister); educated at Tehran; high civil servant in Ministry of Finance, posted to Khurasan province (1897–1906); went to Europe, studied at Paris and Neuchâstel, received his Ph.D. in law (1914); Minister of Justice (1920); Governor-General of Fars province (1920–21); resigned after the February 1921 coup; minister in the three Qavam cabinets (1921); Tehran deputy in Fifth and Sixth *Majlis* (1924–28); retired to his Ahmadabad property outside Tehran (1928–40); detained at Tehran, exiled for six months to Birjand (1940–1); returned to politics (end 1941); deputy from Tehran in Fourteenth and Sixteenth *Majlis*; leader National Front (1949–53); chairman of *Majlis*'s Special Oil Commission (1950–1); prime minister (April 1951-August 1953); his legal government was overthrown by *Murdad 28* coup (August 19, 1953); stood trial, received three year sentence, served them before being exiled to his Ahmadabad property; supported from afar the National Resistance Movement and the Second National Front (1953–62); died on March 5, 1967.

In his supporting cast, Dr Musaddiq had wanted from the outset a loose coalition, like the National Front, which could accommodate both individuals (like Makki and Dr Fatimi) and political parties or associations (like the *Iran* Party). Moreover, in a Front, one could include extreme-rightists like Darioush Furouhar's Pan-Iranists (a section only of the party, the rest, under Muhsin Pizishkpour, having refused to join the Front); right-of-centre Tehran *Bazaar* personalities such as Hajj Muhammad Hasan Shamshiri, Hajj Mahmoud Manian, Haj Âbdul-Âzim Hajjian and Hajj Muhammad Suhayli Kishbaf (Musaddiq's trustworthy leader of the *Bazaar* financial supporters); the centrists with the dominant *Iran* Party and its leaders Allahyar Salih, Dr Azar, Dr Siddiqi, Dr Sanjabi, Engineer Zirakzadeh and Engineer Haqshinas, but also Muhammad Nakhshab's small *Jamîyyat-i Azadi-i Mardum -i Iran* (JAMI) (Association for the Liberty of Iran's Peoples); the left-of-centre parties, from the modest *Khudaparastan-i Susyalist* and the compact *Jamîyyat-i Havadaran-i Sulh* (Association of the Supporters of Peace) created in June 1950 by Malik ul-Shuâra Bahar with Dr Shayiganand Ha'irizadeh to the impressive *Hizb-i Zahmatkishan-i Millat-i Iran* (Toilers' Party of the Iranian Nation), created in May 1951 by Dr Baqa'i and Khalil Maliki (a member of the '53 Group'), before Maliki left in 1952 to launch his own political organisation: the *Nîrou-yi Sivvum* (the Third Force).[31] In addition to covering all these, the Front could accommodate a loose religious wing led by Ayatullah Kashani, his lieutenant Shams Qanatabadi and top civilian adviser Dr Mahmoud Shirvin; itself linked to Navvab Safavi's *Fada'yan-i Islam* (through co-ordinator Shaykh Mihdi Doulabi) and to Tehran's *Majmâ-i Muslamanan-i Mujahid* (Association of Moslem Freedom Fighters) and the *Ittihad-i Muslimin* (Islamists' Union) created in 1948 by Hajj Saraj Ansari and Aqa Riza Faqihzadeh.

Dr Musaddiq had always dreaded a party or an individual directly linked to his name, because he feared that a scandal tainting them would inevitably tarnish his own reputation – that is to say his probity, his honesty and his incorruptibility, which were his main assets. These were the basis of his success with the newly-awakened Iranian middle classes, who would listen to his protracted radio monologues and have the satisfaction of hearing a politician who was not treating them like children and was not lying to them: they believed deeply that he was fighting for their colours, that he needed their support (he really did), that he sincerely wished them and their country well. He was more than their hero and their champion, he was their dream come true – the majority of the people of Iran stood behind him as they had never stood before. And Dr Musaddiq, the Qajar Elitist and *Docteur en Droit*, was going to forget all he had learned during half a century of political experience, even Machiavelli's "he who builds on the people, builds on mud". And he would live his dream, despite all his detractors and enemies, who were in a numerical minority, but who controlled the totality of resources.

Dr Musaddiq's game with the Powers was simplified to the extreme: on the one hand were the British, from whom he had little to expect; on the other were the Americans, who were sympathetic to his cause, especially US Ambassador Dr Grady, who was ready to intervene in Iran's favour if necessary, and who held that the AIOC policy was "obsolete and certain to be ineffectual" and felt irritated by the company's "stubborn uncompromising attitude".[32] In sum, Dr Grady was mostly interested "in helping the Iranians find more money".[33] Undoubtedly, at the outset, American sympathies went to the National Front which was advancing along lines most favourable to US policy in Iran. Dr Musaddiq and his supporters were even given the impression that the Americans were firmly behind them (and would always be) in their struggle with the AIOC, and maybe that the brothers Salih – Âli Pasha Salih, the secretary of the US Embassy in Tehran, and Allahyar Salih, the future ambassador to Washington – were for something in the *atomescrochus* between the Front and the Americans. Furthermore, some of the junior staff at Tehran's US Embassy (e.g. Richard Cottam[34]) were definitely sympathetic to Iran's cause in its struggle with the AIOC.

On April 30, 1951, Dr Musaddiq began his mammoth task of nationalising his country's largest industry. First the National Iranian Oil Company (NIOC) was established (its official statutes would only be approved by the *Majlis* on November 26, 1952) and its first provisional board of directors chosen, with Tehran University's physics professor Dr Mahmoud Hisabi appointed as chairman. Hisabi resigned before beginning and was readily replaced by another Tehran University (Technical Faculty) professor, Engineer Mihdi Bazargan. The Mixed Parliamentary Board was formed with Deputy Finance Minister Engineer Kazim Hasibi in charge of five elected senators (Dr Matin Daftari, M. Surouri, Dr Shafaq, Najm ul-Mulk and Murtaza Quli Bayat) and five elected deputies (A. Salih, Dr Muâzzami, Makki, Dr Shayigan and Nasir Quli Ardalan)[35] who were sent to the south to supervise the orderly transfer of assets from AIOC to NIOC, with Dr Amir Âla'i, the Minister of National Economy, dispatched by Dr Musaddiq as the government's observer.

In the south, the NIOC directors and the Mixed Board were faced with British intransigence. The smooth takeover planned in Tehran was not to progress as planned because the AIOC deemed it illegal. Confrontation was inevitable. On June 25, E.C. Drake, AIOC's general manager in Abadan, left Iran. On July 1, the private house of Richard Seddon, AIOC's representative at Tehran, was searched by the police, assisted by members of Dr Baqa'i's Toilers' Party: all documents found in Seddon's house were impounded.[36] Crude oil throughput at Abadan Refinery was gradually reduced, until total shut down occurred on August 2. On September 20, Dr Musaddiq issued an ultimatum to British staff members to leave Iran within a week. On September 27, Iranian troops occupied the Abadan Refinery and four days later all British employees left Iran. Thus, within a five month span, Dr Musaddiq had fulfilled the first part of the initial task: the physical takeover of the oil industry – albeit at the price of confrontation with the company. Seen from a British point of view, that of historian S.H. Longrigg, the first phase looked like this:

> The nationalisation (in fact confiscation) ...offered a sad record of practical ineptitude ...[the] result of excitement, naive irresponsibility, and a 'political' atmosphere of violence, malice and fear. ...The view of the Company, the British Government and world opinion was [that] the Company's assets in Persia remained its property.[37]

While events developed in the south, the formidable legal war between the government of Iran and the AIOC had begun.

The company had fired the first shots by sending official notes (on March 14 and April 27) to Iran protesting at the illegality of the two oil nationalisation laws, referring to article 21 of the 1933 Agreement[38] which stated: "This Concession shall not be annulled by the Government [of Iran] and the terms therein contained shall not be altered either by general or special legislation in the future, or by administrative measures or any acts whatever of the executive authorities".[38A] To the contrary the Oil Nationalisation Law of March 20 was not precise about the "nationalisation of the oil industry throughout Iran" and the final semi-sentence "that is to say that all operations of exploration, extraction and exploitation shall be managed by the Government" – with refining not specifically stated – was added later and did not feature in the law itself.[39] The Nine Point Law of April 29 was also subject to differing interpretation, with the participation of foreign companies in the Iranian oil industry left unclarified. It was on the basis of the 1933 Agreement (for AIOC) and the two nationalisation laws (for Iran) that the dispute exploded on the international scene.

Protracted negotiations between the two embattled parties began in early May 1951 and lasted for the better part of two years. American intermediaries did their best to find a suitable arrangement. Three international institutions were dragged into the process: the International Court of Justice (ICJ) at The Hague, the Security Council of the United Nations (UNSC) in New York and the International Bank for Reconstruction and Development (IBRD) in Washington. On May 2, British Foreign Secretary Morrison sent Dr Musaddiq a message proposing a negotiated settlement. When the Iranian premier failed to answer, Great Britain immediately appointed its arbitrator, Lord Radcliffe, and, when Iran failed to reciprocate, decided on May 26 to take the case to the ICJ according to Article 22 (arbitration) of the 1933 Agreement. Two days later Iran declared that it didn't recognise the competence of the ICJ in its dispute with AIOC, contending that the different was not between two nations but rather between a nation (Iran) and a company (AIOC), and hence not within the ICJ's jurisdiction. This line of defence was successfully followed during the ICJ's hearings of the case in The Hague (June 9–23, 1952) by Dr Musaddiq, Iran's agent Husayn Navvab, and Iran's advocate, the Belgian professor of international law, Henri Rolin, against the British case pleaded by Sir Eric Beckett and Sir Lionel Heald. On July 22, 1952, the ICJ by a vote of nine to five concluded that "it had no jurisdiction to deal with the case" and dismissed the British application. For Iran, the Hague victory was practically a Pyrrhic one, for it had solved nothing; and the question would always remain that if the ICJ had arbitrated what kind of judgement would it have reached? The worst it could have done was to impose an indemnity on Iran, which would certainly not have been to Iran's detriment. Paradoxically, it seems that Dr Musaddiq might well have been better off had the case been heard by the ICJ.

During the two years of protracted Anglo-Iranian negotiations, a total of five major proposals were made to Iran by either the Americans or the British or jointly. The first of these proposals was proffered by AIOC vice-chairman Basil Jackson during his mission to Tehran (June 10–22, 1951): "On June 19, the Company offered an immediate payment of £10m and £3m a month from July onwards during the negotiations. ...the offer also provided for the vesting of the Iranian assets of the AIOC in the NIOC, on condition that the latter would grant to a new company established by the AIOC the exclusive use of those assets".[40] The offer was rejected as inconsistent with the Nine Point Law. Nevertheless it stood as an indication of the distance travelled by AIOC between March and June 1951.

The way for the second proposal was paved by President Truman's special envoy to Iran, Averell Harriman.[41] Arriving in Tehran on July 14, 1951, Harriman and his oil adviser Walter Levy (and interpreter Colonel Vernon Walters) negotiated with Dr Musaddiq and his oil specialist Engineers Kazim Hasibi. Great Britain had officially recognised the Oil Nationalisation Law on July 30[42] and this proved to be the cornerstone of Lord Privy Seal Richard Stokes's mission to Tehran. Arriving on August 3, Lord Stokes unveiled his proposal two days later to the Iranian negotiating team – consisting of K. Hasibi, A. Salih, Dr Shafaq, Dr Matin Daftari, Dr Shayigan, Dr Sanjabi and M.Â. Varasteh. The second British proposal, while explicitly recognising the act of nationalisation, was along the same line as the first one: in a nutshell it foresaw the transfer of AIOC installations to NIOC (after indemnification) and the lease of the same by NIOC to a new entity set up AIOC and other partners. Iran countered by suggesting a package of: (i) direct purchase of oil by Great Britain; (ii) indemnification of AIOC; (iii) transfer of British technicians to NIOC. Neither proposal was agreeable to the other side and talks broke down. Lord Stokes departed on August 23 and Harriman on the 25.

The only sequel to this second round was the American disillusionment with Iran's attitude: Harriman failed to see "businesslike practicality" and "goodwill" on the Iranian side and knew that without these a settlement was hopeless. The first signs of American dissent with previous policy were heard in the summer of 1951, when Max Thornburg proposed to Secretary of State Dean Acheson "a bold course" to establish "a responsible government" in Iran.[43] In September Dr Grady, the ambassador sympathising with Iran's cause, was removed and replaced by the far less sympathetic professional diplomat Loy Henderson.

On October 1, 1951, the U.N. Security Council decided by a vote of nine to two (those of the USSR and Yugoslavia) to place the British complaint against Iran (for expelling its nationals) on its agenda. On October 8, Dr Musaddiq arrived in New York to attend the UNSC hearings, which, after five days of heated confrontation (October 15–19), were adjourned, pending the final ICJ decision of 1952. Dr Musaddiq later went to Washington to meet President Truman and Secretary of State Dean Acheson. Furthermore, between October 8 and November 18, Assistant Secretary of State George McGhee "had approximately eighty hours of conversation" with the premier, discussing all the issues at hand but without the talks yielding any concrete solution.[43A] Dr Musaddiq also raised the question of an American loan to Iran, which received the "most careful attention". But the US was still loath to lend to Iran, and decided instead to send two IBRD teams to Iran: the first under Hector Prud'homme in

December 1951 and the second headed by the bank's vice-president Robert Garner, in February 1952.

Meanwhile in Britain the Tories had won the October 1951 general election and Sir Winston Churchill was PM once more. In Tehran, the IBRD teams presented Iran with its third proposal: for a temporary (two year and renewable) reactivation of the Iranian oil industry. In order to operate the industry, until the dispute was settled, the IBRD would set up a new organisation totally independent of the two parties. Iran's negotiators wanted this organisation to act legally as its agent, with the IBRD team insisting on its independence. After weeks of negotiations, with the bank's top executive, Eugene Black, becoming involved from Washington, the IBRD team announced on March 17 that it had failed to reach a solution and departed from Iran. The IBRD proposal was yet another positive solution for Iran which was left to fall by the wayside. In Tehran, conspiracy theorists were on hand yet again, arguing that "the British had purposely sabotaged the IBRD negotiations because they neither wanted the dispute to be settled while Dr Musaddiq was in power, nor did they want to have an international third party getting involved in Iranian oil affairs".[44]

In London, Foreign Secretary Sir Anthony Eden concluded that the IBRD's failure "would bring the US Government to accept that only a change in the Iranian Government can lead to a settlement of the oil dispute"[45] – Eden also had earlier bluntly observed that "without United States's encouragement he doubted whether Musaddiq would have survived so long".[45A] The new strategy followed by PM Churchill was to convince the Americans that the regime in Iran, which had even ordered the closure of all British consulates in January 1952, had to be changed. After the failures of Harriman and the IBRD, the US State Department announced (on March 24) that it would refuse Iran a loan as long as the oil dispute remained unsettled. However, the Americans had not despaired of finding a solution and some high-level meetings with the British yielded the fourth proposal to Iran in August 1952 (known as the Truman-Churchill proposal). Once again Dr Musaddiq rejected this proposition, stating at a September 7 press conference that "it was inferior on some points to the previous ones". Anglo-Iranian relations further deteriorated, leading on October 22 to a complete break of diplomatic relations initiated by Iran. On November 1, the last British diplomats departed Iran: bilateral relations had sunk to an all-time low.

In November 1952, General Eisenhower was elected president of the United States and on January 20, 1953 he took over from President Truman. The change was momentous, radically altering Iran's Great Powers Game. This American switch from a Democratic to a Republican administration, coming on the heels of the British Labour to Tory switch of October 1951, boded ill for Iran's chances of keeping the two Powers apart, especially as President Eisenhower and PM Churchill knew each other extremely well since their victorious co-operation during the Second Word War. But, even while envisaging confrontation, the new US administration wanted to give Iran a last chance: hence the fifth proposal hammered out in London between Foreign Secretary Sir Anthony Eden and US Secretary of State John Foster Dulles.

This last proposal, known as the Anglo-American proposal and by far the best deal offered to Iran, was delivered to Dr Musaddiq on February 20, 1953. It could be summarised in four points:[46]

1. Total liberty for Iran to manage its oil industry;
2. Acceptance by Iran of entry to negotiations with an international organisation (including AIOC among its shareholders) to sign a long-term oil sales agreement for a substantial part of its production;
3. AIOC's indemnification for its Iranian assets would be set by the ICJ, according to nationalisation as practised in England, as chosen by the company. The indemnification would be paid either in cash (25% of annual oil revenues) or in oil (25% of annual production);
4. As soon as the indemnification was set, the US Government would provided a loan (repayable with oil) for reactivating Iran's oil industry.

The fifth proposal, qualified by its architects as "the most equitable", was clearly to be the last: it was either take it or leave it. There would be no sixth proposal.

The fifth proposal was deemed acceptable by Dr Musaddiq, except for the indemnification question. On March 7, the Americans and the British issued a joint communiqué in London stating that Iran's apprehensions about indemnification were totally unfounded. On March 10, four senior NIOC managers, all renowned for their professionalism and integrity – namely Engineer Âbbas Parkhideh, Fu'ad Rouhani, Engineer Hasan Razavi and Engineer Âta'ullah

Ittihadiyyeh[46A] – sent a message to Dr Musaddiq (through one of his top advisers) with their opinion that "the proposal was not in contradiction with the Nine-Point Nationalisation Law and should be accepted".[46B] The four technocrats never received any feedback, and were left only with the impression of having done their duty and given their professional opinion to their head of government. Instead it was Dr Shayigan, by then Dr Musaddiq's top adviser, who let slip in an interview: "Mr Eden has said that he will persevere until Iran accepts the joint proposal, and we say that we shall persevere until it is declined".[47] In view of such inconsiderate statements, it was a foregone conclusion that in his March 20 speech Dr Musaddiq would reject the fifth joint proposal, and so he did. And thus came to an end the attempts at finding a negotiated settlement to the Anglo-Iranian oil dispute.

Intertwined with the legal war opposing the AIOC was the battle Dr Musaddiq was conducting on the oil market front for the export of Iranian crude oil. If Iran could sell enough oil in world markets, it would earn money to reactivate its industry and economy, and would simply bypass AIOC and let the dispute drag on. The strategy had its merits, but it had to prove effective. And it proved to be a difficult game to play for the Iranians, trying to sell oil in a world dominated by the Seven Sisters of Oil – in other words, AIOC, Royal Dutch/Shell and the five American Sisters: Esso (later Exxon), Mobil, Texaco, Gulf and Socal (later Chevron). At the very onset of its dispute AIOC "enlisted the support of the other six sisters, to make sure they would not buy [Iranian] 'hot oil'".[48] The US Sisters willingly played AIOC's game, apprehensive of nationalisations in other countries (in case of an Iranian breakthrough) and not losing "sight of their own ultimate interest".[49] As for the smaller US oil companies, they were dissuaded by their government from buying any Iranian oil.[50] In view of this solid anti-Iranian front, oil pundit Frankel concluded that: "Dog bites dog, but dog doesn't eat dog". Having formed its coalition, AIOC announced officially in September 1951 that it would take legal action against any company purchasing Iranian oil. NIOC, with nothing to lose, offered discounts of up to fifty per cent on the official Gulf of Mexico prices, and went out looking for customers. Any Iranian expectation that "people and markets are waiting for us"[51] would lead to disappointments.

In spite of the Seven Sisters' embargo, the NIOC was able to sell some oil: a total of 118,700 tonnes over 1952/53.

Its very first sale was to the Italian company Ente Petrolifero Italia Medio-Oriente (EPIM), owned by the Count Della Zonca. On May 30, 1952, EPIM's ship, the *Rosemary*, loaded 700 tonnes of Iranian crude at Bandar-i Mahshahr; on June 18, it was forced to dock at Aden by British warplanes; its cargo was arraigned on orders of AIOC, and finally seized after an Adeni court gave a verdict favouring the British company (on January 10, 1953). EPIM later took another 5,000 tonnes before its contract was annulled. Instead, another Italian company named Supor signed a contract with NIOC for 12.5% of its exports at a fifty per cent discount of the FOB price. Supor's ship, the *Miriella*, loaded 5,000 tonnes of crude oil at Abadan on January 19 and made it to Venice on February 14, where its cargo was impounded on AIOC's orders. A Venetian court gave a verdict in favour of Supor on March 10, but the Italian authorities refused to issue it an entry permit and the oil had to be stored at the port. After taking a total of 49,000 tonnes of Iranian crude oil, Supor terminated its contract with NIOC. The third company to buy oil from Iran was the Japanese company of Idemitsu Kosan, whose managing director Keisuke Idemitsu took the decision to do so. Idemitsu sent its large ship (18,774 dwt), the *Nissyo Maru*, to Abadan: its first cargo arrived in Tokyo on May 9, 1953. On May 27, the Tokyo District Court rejected AIOC's application for disposition of the *Nissyo Maru*'s cargo.[52] Idemitsu would take a total of 64,000 tonnes of crude oil during 1953. Its Iranian success had even prompted American independents to suggest to Idemitsu that he act as their intermediary with Iran, but it was already too late, as it came in the middle of summer 1953.

Besides the actual buyers of Iranian oil, two captains of oil had toyed with the idea of coming to Iran's aid. The first was Enrico Mattei, the managing director of Italy's AGIP (incorporated into the Ente Nazionale Idrocarburi (ENI) in 1953). Mattei, tempted by cheap Iranian oil, was too clever by half: he correctly predicted Dr Musaddiq's demise and opted to wait for the aftermath, declaring he "would have nothing to do with Iran and 'stolen oil'".[53] Mattei believed in a just reward for his 'good' behaviour, forgetting that his country had lost a world war less than a decade before: ENI would not be given a share in Iranian oil. The second captain was Alton Jones, the chief executive of the US company Cities Services (also representing Sinclair Oil Company). Jones came to Iran in August 1952 with the grand idea of reactivating its oil industry, but later made a U-turn and abruptly shelved his grandiose plans. It later came to light that AIOC and Gulf had given Cities Service a twelve-year contract at discounted prices (around half the posted price) for roughly 20,000 b/d of Kuwaiti crude oil.[53A]

Another vector of the Seven Sisters' multi-pronged strategy against Iran was to compensate for lost Iranian oil by increasing oil output in the other Middle Eastern states. Between 1951 and 1953, Iraq's output rose from an average of 167,000 b/d to 565,000 b/d; Kuwait's from 561,000 b/d to 862,000 b/d and Saudi Arabia's jumped from 762,000 b/d to 845,000 b/d.[54] Thus, within two years, the three Arab states had added almost 800,000 b/d to their regular production, largely filling the gap left by Iran's failure to produce. The increases thus achieved in the Arab states "was to be a source of some shame to them ever afterwards".[55]

Oil pundit Paul H. Frankel was of the opinion that in the long term Iran and Dr Musaddiq might have had a chance to sell oil, provided they could have lasted long enough:

> The failure of Dr Mosaddeq's experiment, though an indication of the difficulties involved, is no conclusive proof that such enterprise would have been impossible. He was handicapped in the first instance by legal problems which made 'stolen' oil unacceptable to buyers and to authorities alike – although a similar interceptive campaign had failed thirty years earlier in the face of Soviet resources and resourcefulness. The plain fact was that Dr Mossadeq's regime was not up to the task it had set itself and that it folded up before the laws of economic gravity had a chance of making themselves felt...[56]

Dr Musaddiq was not only fighting an oil war against AIOC and its Sisters – he was also fighting an internal war against his own Elite, the court, the army and all the other counter-elites. His only support in these domestic vicissitudes were the people of Iran.

10.5. Internal Struggles

One of Dr. Musaddiq's major problems was to be the continuous trickle of defections from his own National Front ranks. Having decided upon a loose organisational structure from the outset, he had to live with its disadvantages as well as with its benefits. One of the former was that every group or individual was directly linked to the top (i.e. Dr Musaddiq) and at the slightest misunderstanding or divergence of interest, the group or person injured would bolt from the structure. As one of the junior government members would later reminisce in an apt figure:

> In the Front we had good bricks, some were even excellent. But we always lacked an adequate mortar to hold them together. Each of them was attached by a wire to the apex; when the wire snapped, the brick crashed...[57]

The first departures from the Front's fringes came early from Âbd ul-Qadir Azad and the journalist chameleon Âmidi Nouri: both defections were of little importance, but were a sign of things to come.

Another constant irritant for the liberal Dr Musaddiq was the repeated street demonstrations staged by *Toudeh* or *Toudeh*-inspired mobs. On July 14, 1951, in commemoration of the Abadan strike of 1946 and coincident with the arrival in Tehran of the Harriman mission, the *Jamîyyat-i Milli Mubarizehba Shirkatha-yi Istimari Nafti dar Iran* (National Association of Struggle against Imperialistic Oil Companies in Iran), a *Toudeh*-related organisation, was able to bring some 20,000 demonstrators to the Baharistan Square (before the *Majlis*). Armed troops sent in to control them starting shooting into the crowd, as a result twenty people were killed and two hundred wounded according to the official communiqué.[58] Then, on December 5, 1951, *Toudeh*-linked student organisations called for a demonstration at which they clashed with both the police and the extreme-rightist groups – Munshizadeh's pro-Nazi *Sumka* and Dariush Furouhar's Pan-Iranists – and at which Colonel Nourishad was also killed. On March 28, 1952, yet another *Toudeh* offshoot, the Kanoun-i *Javanan-i Dimukrat* (the Democratic Youth Centre), organised a mass rally that was quelled after two died and over fifty were injured.

The Sixteenth *Majlis* was due to close on February 18, 1952, so Dr Musaddiq had to handle the elections for the Seventeenth *Majlis* in the spring. Faithful to his principles, the prime minister decided, in the face of advice from his closest associates, to have fully democratic elections, refusing prepared lists of National Front candidates. In Tehran, he had no problem, as the Front's candidates were duly elected; but in the provinces the landlords associated with gendarmerie officers still had the upper hand and used their influence to get conservative elements elected, hostile to Musaddiq. Dr Musaddiq realised at the eleventh hour the deadly danger of a conservative, anti-democratic *Majlis* and he ordered the provincial elections to be stopped, amidst vociferous protests from the opposition, after only a total of seventy-nine deputies had been elected. Out of the rump parliament of seventy-nine (instead of 134), some thirty-eight deputies were landlords and twenty-two of them civil servants, with the opposition controlling roughly half of the assembly; prominent among their ranks were Dr Hasan Imami (Tehran's *Imam Jumêh* from Abhar),[59] Hajj Aqa Riza Rafî (from Bandar Pahlavi),[60] Dr Tahiri (from Yazd) and Sayyid Mihdi Mir Ashrafi (from Mishginshahr).

Inaugurated on May 29, the Seventeenth *Majlis* would elect Dr Imami as its president by thirty-nine votes on July 1, with the Front's candidate Dr Âbdullah Muâzzami getting thirty-five. From the outset, the *Majlis* would prove a thorn in Musaddiq's side; after trying to come to an understanding which never materialised, he bypassed it totally after making it vote, on October 23, 1952, the closure of the First Senate (a worse bedrock of opposition filled with ultra-royalists); but this didn't stop the opposition from using the *Majlis* as one of its institutional bastions against the regime.

Dr Musaddiq's experience in democracy was proof that it was still a lure as far as Iran was concerned. It can be said that both the Shah and Musaddiq could have learnt something from Qavam: the latter had unabashedly rigged the Fifteenth *Majlis* elections and they would have been wise to rig the elections leading to the Sixteenth and the Seventeenth respectively.

Dr Musaddiq's main internal headache stemmed from the armed forces and their subservience to the shah. As both the minister of War and the chief of the general staff were appointed by the Shah, they naturally reported directly to him, bypassing the prime minister. The latter had tried in vain to have them obey the government's orders. In the summer of 1952, Dr Musaddiq's patience reached its limits and on July 16, for three hours he debated the matter with the Shah. When Muhammad Reza Shah failed to agree, Musaddiq handed over his resignation, mentioning the reason behind his decision. The next day, the Shah called on veteran Ahmad Qavam to form the new cabinet. The Western Powers both seem to have been behind Qavam's nomination.[61] After he received the *Majlis*'s vote of confidence, Qavam issued a harsh communiqué calling for the respect of law and order, ending it with the famous tirade: "The Captain hath on a new course decided".[62] The old Qavam was back at the helm, ready to play yet again his role of supreme arbiter, with a premeditated plan for getting rid of the Shah once and for all.[63]

The people of Tehran would spoil Qavam's parting shot by taking to the streets on July 21, in one of the largest riots the capital had witnessed. Present on the streets that day, besides the nationalists, were Kashani's supporters, Dr Baqa'i's Toilers, Furouhar's phalanxes, the *Bazaar* forces and also the *Toudeh* rank and file (with their uniform of white shirts and grey pants[64]) – who had not forgotten the deadly blows Qavam had dealt their party in 1946 and were now extracting their revenge (they might well have tilted the scales in the streets' favour). Troops fired on the people, killing some twenty and wounding dozens, but in the late afternoon the popular riot stood victorious. Qavam fled, taking refuge in Dr Âli Amini's house and resigned. Dr Musaddiq made a triumphant comeback: he was the day's great winner, around whom the people had rallied – "Long Life to Musaddiq!" The two houses of the Iranian Parliament hurried to confirm the streets' wish by re-electing him prime minister – the *Majlis* on July 22 by sixty-one for and only two against, the Senate on the morrow by a score of thirty-three to eight.[65]

It was at this juncture that Dr Musaddiq would show one of his greatest personal failings: the incapacity to strike at political opponents. Here he was, voted back to power in a unique display of popular political activism, the most powerful man in Iran, given the unique chance to muzzle the opposition, with the people crying for revenge. Instead of finally unsheathing his sword, he seemed to be content with cosmetic and protracted legal measures: Kashani was rewarded with the presidency of the *Majlis* as Dr Imami left for foreign parts; the *Majlis* enacted the Full Powers Act on August 11, giving the prime minister the power to rule by decree for six months (later extended to one year); the Ministry of War was renamed Ministry of National Defence, Musaddiq keeping that portfolio for himself (the bone of contention leading to his resignation); an eight-member *Majlis* commission with Dr Baqa'i as chairman and M. Nariman as vice-chairman was charged with the investigation of the July 21 riots; Princess Ashraf and the Queen Mother were sent on 'extended vacations' abroad. The main culprits of the July 21 events – namely Qavam, General Âbbas Garzan (chief of the general staff) and General Muhammad Âli Âlavi Muqaddam (Tehran's military commander) – were not brought to account. Efforts to impound Qavam's properties languished in the *Majlis*. Generals Garzan and Âlavi Muqaddam were briefly detained in the Officers' Club, then forced into retirement, along with General Shahbakhti and ten other generals.[66] Dr Musaddiq ill-advised leniency in the aftermath of July 21 (only explicable by his dual status of simultaneously belonging to the old Elite and leading the new one) would encourage his enemies and disappoint his allies, leading to further desertions from the National Front.

In early 1953, Dr Baqa'i deserted Dr Musaddiq and the Front, rejoining the ranks of the opposition with his Toilers' Party. His apparent motive for doing so was Dr Musaddiq's unwillingness to severely discipline the individuals responsible for the July 21 killings. In the wake of Baqa'i's desertion, his friends Makki and Ha'irizadeh followed suit. Makki had been hoping to place some of his friends in the Front's power structure; when the nationalist elite made it clear that he alone was acceptable, Makki offered his services – which he had always grossly overestimated: "a man of mediocre abilities" Cottam quipped[67] – to the opposition. Thus the 'three musketeers' of April 1949 fame left the camp they had helped to set up. Their departure was not disastrous for the Front, nor was that of Front deputy Yusuf Muchar in November 1952.

The split between Dr Musaddiq and *Ayatullah* Kashani, however, by striking at the top, would have dire consequences. As the leader of the regime's religious wing, Kashani was the second most important individual in Iran. His spiritual power and his links to the *Bazaar*, the *Fada'yan* and other religious organisations were not to be underestimated. His presidency of the *Majlis* after July 21, although he failed to attend the assembly and left his faithful lieutenant Shams Qanatabadi to act as his mouthpiece, was a further asset. However Kashani's people had made only minimal headway in Dr Musaddiq's secular government; one of his sons-in-law, Dr Mahmoud Shirvin, an M.D., was director-general of the *Ouqaf* (Endowments) Department at the Ministry of Culture. In the autumn of 1952, Dr Shirvin crossed swords with the Qum establishment when he attempted to have the administrator of the *Astaneh-yi Hazrat-i Mâsoumeh* at Qum, Abu'l-Fazl Touliyyat, replaced by his own nominee, Dr Mishkat, a professor of law at Tehran University. On December 9, Dr Shirvin and Dr Mishkat left for Qum to officiate over the transfer of power on the spot.[68] In the meantime, the Qum hierocracy discreetly approached Dr Musaddiq stressing the fact that Touliyyat's tenure was hereditary and that he had been Qum's deputy in the past seven *Majlis*. Dr Musaddiq, reluctant to alienate Qum's *Ayatullahs*, refused to back Mishkat's bid. Returning empty-handed from Qum, Dr Mishkat and Dr Shirvin could only resign. Touliyyat remained as administrator. But, for Ayatullah Kashani, the loss of face, added to the lost opportunity to gain a foothold in Qum, must have been hard to swallow. He lost little time in hitting back, attacking Dr Musaddiq's request for the renewal of the Full Powers Act of August 11, pointing out that full powers were for an exceptional period, not to be granted for ever. Nonetheless the *Majlis* extended the Act for a full year on January 19 by fifty-nine out of sixty-seven votes. A week later, a reconciliation meeting was arranged at Dizashib between Dr Musaddiq and Ayatullah Kashani, with everyone eager to assist at a *rapprochement* at the top. But the harm had been done and the divorce between the two leaders finalised and any number of meetings couldn't alter this basic fact.

From vocal opposition to political counter-action was only a step, a step that Kashani took at the worst possible time for Dr Musaddiq: on February 28, 1953 as the Shah was packing his suitcases to depart Iran. Since the events of July 21, the prime minister had angled to bring about the Shah's departure for "an extended vacation". Kashani associated with Elitist Sayyid Muhammad Bihbahani to lead the movement thwarting the Shah's departure on the fateful day. Kashani issued a communiqué asking the people to resist "by all means" the Shah's departure, "which could lead to chaotic and regretful events",[69] and wrote a personal letter to the Shah "begging him to reconsider his plans and advising him to remain in Iran".[69A] Some retired officers, led by Generals Amir Ahmadi, Shahbakhti and Gilanshah,[70] also went to see the Shah to ask him to postpone his trip.

Some of the officers even had plans to kill Musaddiq as he was leaving the palace, but they were frustrated and their attack on the prime minister's house (located near the palace) was repulsed by the security forces.[71] The indecisive Shah, encouraged by the extraordinary turn of events, finally decided to report his trip *sine die*. Dr Musaddiq's plan for removing the opposition's central focus had failed at the last minute. Kashani had, on this occasion, sided with the royalists.

Without the support of its religious wing, the regime's chances of remaining afloat were greatly diminished. The technocrats of the *Iran Party* were now the sole masters on board the vessel of State, as Dr Musaddiq's apparatus of government rested essentially on their shoulders – with only a couple of exceptions such as Dr Fatimi. The problem facing Iran's technocratic governing elite was that its members were not elite material. There was no doubt that Dr Grady had correctly judged that these "Nationalist leaders were the least corrupt and most dedicated group in modern Iranian history and were sincerely concerned with achieving independence for their nation and modernising it".[72] They were honest, educated, knowledgeable, cultivated and, to a certain extent, patriotic. But, on the other side of the coin, they had all the general characteristics that have bedevilled Iranian technocrats (and bureaucrats) since the days of Malkum Khan: ingrained selfishness, lack of civil courage, inevitable self-aggrandisement and visionary blindness.

They were much better critics than rulers, although they had been able to obtain palpable results in domestic affairs: first and foremost, they had managed the economy with almost no oil revenues, enacting enlightening import-export regulations[72A] and issuing national bonds. They had failed to secure an American loan (the US limiting itself to Point Four assistance) and the Soviet Union repayment of war reparations, but still had succeeded in balancing foreign trade (see Table 10.1.) and the national budget (Table 10.2.).

Moreover, a first and important step was taken in the field of land reforms: in this respect, Dr Musaddiq issued two decrees on October 6 and 11, 1952 respectively. "The first laid down that 20% was to be

Table 10.1. Iran's Foreign Trade for the Years 1330 (1951) to 1332 (1953) – Exports Not Including Crude Oil.[73]
(Figures in Rls millions)

Year	Imports	Exports	Balance
1330 (1951)	7,404	4,390	– 3,014
1331 (1952)	5,206	5,832	+ 626
1332 (1953)	5,756	8,425	+2,669

Table 10.2. Iran's National Budget for the Years 1330 (1951) to 1332 (1953).[74]
(Figures in Rls millions)

Year	National Income	National Expenditure	Balance
1330 (1951)	9,804	9,804	
1331 (1952)	7,786	11,118	– 3,332
1332 (1953)	11,944	11,639	+ 305

deducted from the landowner's share of the income from an agricultural estate, 10% of which was to go to the peasants cultivating the land, and 10% to the development and co-operative funds which were to be set up under the decree", wrote Professor Lambton about the first decree.[75] The second decree limited the rights of the landlord over the peasants ("abolishing feudal dues and forced labour in the villages[75A]). Although the decrees "did nothing to give the peasants security of tenure", which, according to Professor Lambton, "was fundamental to reform",[76] they did manage to alienate all of Iran's landlords and turn them against Dr Musaddiq's regime. Justice Douglas further commented that:

For the first time in Iranian history, institutions of self-government were introduced at the grass roots level...[77]

And although the farmers' co-operatives failed to take off, it was indisputably a sterling first attempt.

Dr Musaddiq's regime had also forced the British Bank of Iran and the Middle East (the sequel to the Imperial Bank of Persia) to close its doors in July 1952. The Soviet concession over the northern fisheries reverted back to Iran in February 1953. And the Shah had to relinquish (yet again) the ownership of his father's *Amlak-i Shahanshahi* in May 1953, with the government earmarking its income for the newly-founded *Sazman-i Shahanshahi Khadamat-i Ijtimâi* (the Imperial Organisation of Social Services).

Unfortunately for the young technocrats of the *Iran* Party the key problem facing them was not the domestic reform programme but the oil question. They collectively failed to realise that it was the settlement of the oil nationalisation problems on which their tenure hinged. They did not envision the enormous forces behind the power struggle that nationalisation had unleashed. They either did not perceive or perhaps they closed their eyes to the contradictory interests of their leader and their own political future on this capital point: he was seventy-four years old, at the very end of his career and on his way to achieving immortality with his nationalisation of the Iranian oil industry; they were young, riding the popular nationalisation wave and were the first counter-elite in modern Iranian history able to displace the established older Elite. They should have known that the Americans would not put up with their intransigence for ever. They should have seen the writing on the wall with the coming to power of the Tories in Britain and the Republicans in the States, further underlined by the premiership of Churchill and the presidency of Eisenhower, both conservatives. They should have realised that large quantities of Iranian 'hot' oil could not readily be sold on world markets and that the Seven Sisters could not afford to let Iran get away with it. There had to be some kind of an arrangement in the end. In the technocrats' defence it should be mentioned that some of them were paralysed by the idea of compromise; one of them confided to author Âli Dashti:

> But if we compromise what will the people think? And then, this national whirlwind which has arisen and brought about the oil nationalisation will vanish into thin air, and the honour of the Iranian Nation would have been put to shame...[78]

The young technocrats had won power on Dr Musaddiq's coat-tails, their leader having grabbed power through a unique opening. Due to their incapacity to analyse the alternatives and take decisive measures in consequence, they would lose everything.

10.6. *Murdad 28*

Dr Musaddiq's mercifulness in the aftermath of the July 21, 1952 events would encourage all of his enemies to conspire for an eventual *coup d'état*. Due to his regime's immense popularity, only a forceful coup could topple him. In early October 1952, the first conspiracy was unveiled (which led to the break of diplomatic relations with Great Britain): the two Rashidians, father Habibullah and son Asadullah, were apprehended in this respect, interrogated and released after a few days following pressure from the court. They had confessed to meetings at Senator General Zahidi's house at Hisarak (near Tehran). On October 13, at a press conference, Dr Fatimi further implicated in the Hisarak conspiracy General (retd.) Hijazi, General Bahram Aryana (later exiled to Paris), General Hajji Ansari, Asadullah Âlam and seven senators and four deputies.[79] Here again, with the first nucleus of Iranian conspirators assembled, the regime would be far too lenient: it could have (and should have) nipped this conspiracy in the bud.

As long as the conspiracy was confined to Iranians it had not a single chance of success: in a country like Iran, with its people's innate subservience to established authorities, it is extremely difficult to topple a government by force, let alone a genuinely popular government. But the thaw in Anglo-American relations over Iran had begun in Tehran with the arrival of US Ambassador Loy Henderson in May 1952; as C.M. Woodhouse, the MI6 officer in the British Embassy at Tehran, wrote in his memoirs:

> Loy Henderson changed the atmosphere in the US
> Embassy towards sympathy with the British case...[80]

Towards the close of 1952 (with the new Republican administration getting ready to take over) the relations had warmed to the point of holding a joint preliminary meeting at Washington for a coup project in Iran, codenamed 'Ajax'. A second meeting in January and a third meeting on February 3, 1953 followed. At this last encounter, the British proposed the American CIA agent Kermit (Kim) Roosevelt (a grandson of President Theodore Roosevelt) as the field commander for 'Ajax'.[81] Roosevelt later prepared a twenty-two-page paper (based on an earlier British draft) setting forth the project.

Both the British and the Americans had their own reasons for embarking upon 'Ajax'. "Their [the British's] motivation", wrote K. Roosevelt, "was simply to recover their oil concession. We were not concerned with that but with the obvious threat of Russian take-over... The Soviet threat is indeed genuine, dangerous and imminent".[82] The communist threat was not only on Roosevelt's mind, it was on that of most US decision-makers: President Eisenhower mentioned it,[83] Justice Douglas too,[84] and CIA director Allen Dulles, in a *a posteriori* justification of 'Ajax', stated that:

> When there begins to be evidence that a country is slipping and Communist take-over is threatened ...we can't wait for an engraved invitation to come in...[85]

Undoubtedly the *Toudeh* street mobs had attained a high degree of preparedness; its secret officers' network had grown exponentially to around six hundred officers in the armed forces. Nonetheless, a communist takeover in Iran was not a possibility for the simple reason that the Soviets were not willing to support such a move. This was, firstly, because their supremo Stalin had passed away on March 25, 1953. The second that the new Soviet leadership feared President Eisenhower: as ex-President Lyndon Johnson told President Nixon in 1969, "The Russians feared Ike; they didn't fear me".[86] And third was the fact, correctly underlined by French expert Hélène Carrere d'Encausse, that Soviet leverage in the Middle East was by then non-existent; even when asked for assistance by Dr Mussadiq, they declined the offer to help:

> Dr Mossadeq s'adresse finalement a l'URSS pour lui demander de l'aide. Moscou repousse cette possibilité d'intervenir en Iran, comme refusa quelques semaines plus tard de répondre a l'appel du Tudeh qui se proclame maître du pouvoir. L'URSS n'a plus aucune influence au Moyen-Orient a l'époque...[87]

Communist threat or not, the Americans had embarked upon 'Ajax'. They had accepted the operation's leadership, chosen the coup's Iranian leader as General Fazlullah Zahidi (imprisoned by the British during the Second World War) and undertaken to fund the whole operation. As is well known, the one who pays the piper is allowed to choose the tune.

The prelude to 'Ajax' had taken place during the spring of 1953 in Tehran. On the evening of April 20, Dr Musaddiq's loyal police chief, General Muhammad Afshar Tous, was kidnapped in Dr Husayn Khatibi's house by a group of retired army officers including the retired Generals Mazini, Munazzah, Bayandur, Major Balouchqara'i and a number of civilian acolytes, prominent among whom were Khatibi and Dr Baqa'i.[87A] Afshar Tous was drugged, transported to a cave in the hills of Tilou (north-east of Tehran), tortured and killed on April 22. After his body was found, the official inquiry began. A number of politicians were implicated in the affair, including Dr Baqa'i and Ardashir Zahidi (the general's son). Baqa'i was a close friend of Khatibi, who was a member of his Toilers' Party.[88] As a deputy, Baqa'i benefited from parliamentary immunity, and was able to convince the special commission investigating his case not to lift it; he eventually resigned under pressure on May 19, 1953. As for the younger Zahidi, after answering the inquirer's questions he left on a pressing visit abroad. Thus, without undue complications, the assertive and competent Afshar Tous, the only military stumbling-block to the success of 'Ajax' had been removed. By eliminating the police chief, the conspirators had also decapitated the newly-created *Sazman-i Guruh-i Milli* (National Organisation of Nationalist Officers), the successor to the *Guruh-i Afsaran-i Nasiunalist*

(Nationalist Officers' Group),[89] in both of which Afshar Tous had held a leading role.

On June 25, in Washington, Secretary of State John Foster Dulles gave 'Ajax' the green light.[90] On July 3, President Eisenhower answered Dr Musaddiq's strongly-worded letter of May 28 by letting him know that no US assistance would be forthcoming. On July 14, the National Front deputies resigned *en bloc* and the *Majlis* sessions were suspended. A fortnight later, Dr Musaddiq announced a referendum (a system of popular vote never before used in Iran) concerning the dissolution of the Seventeenth *Majlis*. On August 3, Tehran gave the referendum a massive yes by 155,544 votes against 115; six days later, the provinces gave dissolution 1,830,000 votes against 1,092.[91]

"Dr Musaddiq", noted L. Mosley, "did not need to manipulate the referendum, for the masses were with him even if the army, police and landowners were not".[92]

While the Iranians were voting, the preliminaries for 'Ajax' were unfolding as planned. On July 19, Roosevelt arrived in Tehran after legally crossing the border at Khaniqayn on July 6. Another American visiting Tehran was General Norman Schwarzkopf, the former head of the US Mission to the Iranian Gendarmerie (1942–1948), who had come to renew old contacts for 'Ajax', of "which he was a part",[93] and leave Iran before the coup. On July 25, Princess Ashraf debarked incognito in Tehran, travelling under the name of her husband Shafiq; the purpose of her short visit was to encourage her connections in the army to support the impending coup, but her cover was rapidly blown and she had to depart Tehran for Switzerland on July 30. It was in the Swiss Alps that the Princess allegedly met with CIA Director Dulles and Ambassador Henderson on August 10, while the last pieces of the coup were falling in place.

'Ajax' was not a single coup, but rather a series of three escalatory actions to be carried out until the downfall of Dr Musaddiq. The first action was an all-Iranian *coup d'état*; the second was a staged pro-Shah uprising to take place in Tehran; the third was the conduct of civil war in Tehran by the two Iranian armoured divisions of Isfahan and Kermanshah.

Colonel Nimatullah Nasiri, the commander of the Imperial Guards, was in charge of the Iranian coup. On August 12 he had been to meet the Shah at the latter's summer retreat at Kilardasht in the

Alburz mountains. The Shah gave him two blank sheets of paper, bearing only the Pahlavi coat of arms and his own signature. Nasiri took these back to Tehran and had them filled in by the Shah's private secretary Hirad: the first decree, dated August 13, appointed General Zahidi prime minister, the second, dated August 15, dismissed Dr Musaddiq (thus accordingly Iran had two premiers for two days!).

On the evening of August 15, the Iranian coup began with the arrests by the Imperial Guards of Dr Fatimi (Minister of Foreign Affairs), Engineer Haqshinas (Minister of Roads) and Engineer Zirakzadeh (of the *Iran* Party) and their detainment at the Guards' Saâdabad headquarters. General Taqi Riahi, the chief of general staff, alerted in the afternoon by a young officer of an imminent coup,[94] had left his home for the security of the general staff headquarters. Undaunted Nasiri, armed with his decree dismissing Dr Musaddiq, made his way with his four trucks of guardsmen, two Jeeps and one tank to the prime minister's house at 109 Kakh Street. He presented his decree and was immediately arrested, along with his subordinates Colonels Akhavi and Azmoudeh – Nasiri later said that Colonel [Farhang] Khusroupanah had arrived two minutes late with his reserve forces for him to open hostilities. On August 16, at seven o'clock in the morning, Radio Tehran announced the coup's failure. Dr Fatimi and Engineers. Haqshinas and Zirakzadeh were freed and went to Dr Musaddiq's house to attend an extraordinary Council of Ministers. The Imperial Guards were to be disarmed by regular troops. Major Dr Îllmiyyeh began the interrogation of Colonel Nasiri and his arrested accomplices in the coup. Maybe the news of the Shah's flight to Baghdad and Rome might have lured the ministers to believe that everything was over, for once again, on August 16, they failed to react decisively: it took them two days to issue warrants for the arrests of General Hidayatullah Gilanshah and Colonel Âbbas Farzanigan; General Mudabbir, the police chief, was relieved of his office only on August 19. Junior *Iran* party officers (such as Dr Shahpour Bakhtiar) would never forgive Dr Musaddiq for not decreeing martial law. Dr Shayigan would later recognise the government's laxity in dealing with the August 16 coup.[95]

The Shah, hearing the news from his Kilardasht retreat, decided to flee aboard his private plane to Iraq. On the flight to Baghdad, he had gloomily confided to his wife, "Now, everything is finished." Surraya Isfandyari, his wife since February 1951, replied, "Don't worry, in a week we shall be back." "You don't believe it yourself," the Shah had concluded.[96] In Tehran, on August 17, the streets overflowed with jubilant crowds tearing down the statues of Reza Shah and Muhammad Reza Shah.

Then, on August 19 (*Murdad 28*), the stick-wielding mobs led by the mercenary thugs Shâban Jâfari, Tayib Hajj Riza'i and Ramazani Yakhi (all three leading throngs of the Tehrani *demi-monde*) launched the second act of the coup. Their troops first assaulted the offices of the *Iran* Party at ten o'clock in the morning. At eleven they were joined by truckloads of armed soldiers and police as the first tanks rumbled on to the capital's streets. Hundreds of copies of the decree naming Zahidi prime minister (photocopied in the 'Point Four' offices[97]) were distributed in the streets. Around noon, a number of groups converged on Dr Musaddiq's house; the well-armed defenders and their two tanks put up a fierce resistance that caused numbers of casualties on both sides and lasted until five in the afternoon, when a heavy tank destroyed the house's metal door and the rioters poured in to ransack the prime minister's house.

While the loyal Colonel Mumtaz fought the rioters, Dr Musaddiq had had time to escape to the adjacent house of Dr Muâzzami with his last handful of top advisers (all of them *Iran* party members): Dr Shayigan, Dr. Muâzzami, Dr Siddiqi, Nariman, Engineer Zirakzadeh (who broke his leg in the process), Engineer Razavi and Engineer Hasibi. The supine chief of the general staff, General Taqi Riahi, was incapable of organising his loyal troops to contain the mobs: "I was acting like an automaton," he later admitted.[98] At two in the afternoon, a small group led by Sayyid Mihdi Mir Ashrafi and Jamal Imami took Tehran Radio. They had to wait until four for successful repairs to the transmitting equipment, which had been destroyed in time by a faithful Musaddiqist. Mir Ashrafi spoke first, then Pirasteh, Faramarzi and Dr Shirvin (Kashani's in-law) before General Zahidi arrived and announced Dr Musaddiq's downfall. The people of Tehran, lacking a rallying centre (Musaddiq had always been loath to create one) and surprised by the mercenary mobs, totally failed to react. Nevertheless "at least three hundred Iranians died in street fighting" on that day.[98A] It was the end: the second coup had brought down Dr Musaddiq's regime.

There was no need for the third action, the crushing of any popular resistance by the armoured division from Kermanshah.

Colonel Âbbas Farzangan had gone to Kermanshah on behalf of Zahidi to enrol the division's commander Colonel Taymour Bakhtiar in the coup.[99] The latter had accepted and his first tanks had rolled into Tehran on August 20. But the second act had already sealed the victory on *Murdad 28* and Bakhtiar's third act was now superfluous. The millions of US dollars (or their Rial equivalent) distributed among Tehran's thugs and soldiery had tipped the scales in the coup's favour. The figure of "many million dollars" mentioned by N.R. Keddie[100] after "having interviewed direct participants in the coup" seems to be the best estimate so far available.

Besides the dollars which tipped the scales, the *Murdad 28* coup was run by a large cast of actors, the principal individuals being:

The US cast: Allen Dulles (director of CIA), K. Roosevelt (CIA), Joe Goodwin (CIA – Roosevelt's assistant), Ambassador Loy Henderson (who had returned to Iran on the eve of the coup), Dick Manville, Fred Zimmerman, and reporter Kennett Love.[101]

The British cast: Major Jackson, C.M. Woodhouse, Samuel Falle (the 'Oriental Counsellor'),[102] Dr Robin Zaehner.[103]

The Iranian cast – for the military: General Fazlullah Zahidi, General Hidayatullah Gilanshah, General Nadir Batmanqilich, General Muhammad Daftari (Musaddiq's relative), General Hasan Ârfa, Colonel Âbbas Farzanigan (a key element, alias 'Mohsen Tahuyi'in Roosevelt's countercoup), Colonel Zand Karimi, Colonel Khalâtbari, Colonel Iskandar Azmoudeh, Colonel Taymour Bakhtiar, Colonel Zargham, Colonel Muhammad Vali Qaranay (commander of Gilan Army), Colonel Muhsin Hashiminijad (Imperial Guards).

For the civilians: Shâban Jâfari, Ardashir Zahidi (alias 'Mustapha Vaysi'), the Rashidians (Habibullah and sons Asadullah, Qudratullah and Sayfullah – the 'Boscoe brothers'), Engineer Hurmuz Shahrukhshahi ('Point Four' executive – 'Cafron'), Parviz Yarafshar ('Nossey'), Sayyid Mihdi Mir Ashrafi, Sayyid Muhammad Âli Shustari, Jamal Imami, Mustafa Muqaddam, Sadiq Naraghi, Kashanian, Âbd ul-Rahman Faramarzi (of *Kayhan*).[104]

For the religious: Sayyid Muhammad Bihbahani and son Sayyid Jâfar Bihbahani.

And also Shahpour Reporter[105] and Ernest Perron.[106]

The mobs chanting "Long live the Shah" on *Murdad 28* could not have been part of a genuine popular expression asking for the Shah's return: true Iranians would never go out in the streets to support a former leader who had fled his country a few days earlier. On *Murdad 28*, the Iranian nation was the victim of a rape. In its modern history it had never experienced such a devastating collective blow. Thereafter nothing would ever be the same again in the country of Hafiz and Firdousi. Iran had abruptly made in 1953 the transition from her traditional way of life to the new (inhuman) technological age. It would take decades for her to remove the *Murdad 28* tragedy from her nightmares.

The actual passage of power from the declining but still capable British to the up-and-coming but brutal Americans was beginning on a sour note. And US Justice Douglas, seeming not to understand why, noted in 1961: "We united with the British to destroy him [Dr Musaddiq]; we succeeded; and ever since our name has not been an honoured one in the Middle East".[107] On this point George McGhee could have taught Justice Douglas a lesson, as he had concluded:

> Neither Truman nor Acheson nor I would in the early 1950s have accepted the policy of overthrowing Musaddiq made by Eisenhower and Dulles in 1953...[108]

With this candid conclusion, McGhee proved once again that, seen from a Third World angle, Democrats are preferable to Republicans in the US White House.

But, whether Democrats or Republicans, the Americans had still everything to learn in Iran. In the meantime the next generation of Iranians would not (could not) forget *Murdad 28*, and would, in due time, take their revenge.

NOTES

1. E. Abrahamian, *Iran between Two Revolutions* (Princeton University Press, 1982) p.246.
2. H. Arfa, *Under Five Shahs* (London: J. Murray, 1964) p.376. For any Iranian it would have been evident that the set-up in Amir Ahmadi's office was a sign that the two Cossack army leaders had chosen Razmara over Ârfa.
3. After his retirement from the army, the well-connected Ârfa would embark on a successful diplomatic career, ending his career as ambassador to Istanbul.
4. H. Ârfa, op. cit. (note 5), p.375. Coming from a rival, a nice compliment indeed.
5. S. Akhavi, *Religion and Politics in Contemporary Iran* (Albany: State University of New York Press, 1980) p.63.
6. Ibid., p.66.
7. See *Houzeh* magazine, nos. 43 & 44, Farvardin-Tir 1370, (April–July 1991), special issue on Ayatullah Burujirdi (commemorating the three decades since his death), (Qum: *Houzeh*, 1370 (1991)) pp.37-8. And also: *Yadnameh Shahid Ustad Murtaza Mutahhari*, ed. by Â.K. Suroush, (Tehran: *Sazman-i Intisharat va Amouzish-i Jumhiri-i Islami*, 1360 (1981)) p.340.
8. The full speech delivered by Hasibi was reprinted in Bulletin no. 9 of the *Iran Party* (no ed., undated) p.
9. Among other 'Notes', Professor Gidel had delivered one on the AIOC Reserves (dated April 14, 1949) and which presented the company's reserves at the close of 1947 as:

General reserve:	£ 14m
Preferred Stock reserve:	£ 5m
Reserve for war contingency and deferred repairs:	£ 2.7m
Total	£21.7m

Gidel had also included the Reserve for taxation, amounting to £11.9m, but he shouldn't have done so as it was for 1947 only and would have to account for tax payments.

10. Wm. Roger Louis, 'Musaddiq and the Dilemmas of British Imperialism', in *Musaddiq, Iranian Nationalism and Oil*, ed. by J.A. Bill and Wm. Roger Louis, (London: I.B. Tauris, 1988) p.234. Quoting: "Zaehner was contemptuous of the Shah, whom he viewed as vacillating, indecisive and opportunistic."
11. Private communication from a (then) young Iranian politician in the early 1970s, a friend and solid ally of Razmara's in the Iranian polity, who had heard him, more than once, proffer his coup threats before the handful of people present, without any fear of these being reported to court; "he even seemed at times willing to let the Court know of his coup plans!" the politician added.
12. J. Mihdinya, *Zindagi Syasi-i Razmara* (Tehran: Giti, 1363 (1984)) pp. 130-139.
13. H. Makki, *Khal-î- Yad* (Tehran: *Bungah-i Tarjumeh va Nashr-i Kitab*, 1360 (1981)) Vol. I, p.60.
14. Lieutenant Qubadi, who had fled with his prisoners to the Soviet Union, was extradited to Iran in 1963. Court-martialled and sentenced to death, he was executed at the Hismatiyyeh shooting range on July 13, 1964.
15. E.A. Bayne, *Persian Kingship in Transition* (New York: American Universities Field Staff, 1968) p.153.

[16] F. Rouhani, *Tarikh-i Milli Shudan-i Sanât-i Naft-i Iran* (The Nationalisation of the Oil Industry in Iran), (Tehran: *Kitab-ha-yi Jibi*, 2nd ed., 1353 (1974)) pp.85-87.
[17] *Bakhtar-i Imrouz* newspaper, issues of *Mihr 21/23, 1329* (October 13 and 15, 1950).
[18] Dr Musaddiq recorded this historic event in a note reproduced by N. Shifteh, *Muhammad Masôud* (Tehran: *Aftab-i Haqiqat*, 1363 (1984)) frontispiece.
[19] M. Dihnavi, *Majmuêh az Maktubat, Sukhanraniha va Payamha-yi Ayatullah Kashani* (Tehran: Chapakhsh, 1361 (1982)) Vol. I, pp.90-93.
[20] P.H. Frankel, *Oil – The Facts of Life* (London: Weidenfeld and Nicolson, 1962) p.9.
[20A] R.W. Ferrier, 'The Anglo-Iranian Oil Dispute: A Triangular Relationship', in op. cit. (note 10), p.170. An excellent review of the Anglo-Americano-Iranian triangle on the events of 1951-53.
[21] Heard on a BBC World Service programme on Iranian history, produced by Roger Hardy and broadcast on July 22, 1991.
[22] H. O'Connor, *The Empire of Oil* (London: John Calder, 1956) pp.324-6.
[22A] R.W. Ferrier, op. cit. (note 20A), p.171.
[23] M.Â. Safari, *Qalam va Syasat* (Tehran: *Namak*, 1371 (1990)) pp.412-3. One of the best books available on this period. Safari reported that Dr Husayn Pirnya had told journalists that Razmara had shown him an AIOC letter including some kind of fifty-fifty deal, telling him to keep it secret. This seems rather implausible because if Razmara had really received such a miraculous proposal he would have tabled it and thus brought about a settlement of the oil conundrum.
[24] J. Mihdinya, op. cit. (note 12), p.354.
[25] M. Turkaman, *Asrar-i Qatl-i Razmara* (The Secrets behind Razmara's Murder), (Tehran: Rasa, 1370 (1991)) p.486. Also see J. Mihdinya, ibid., pp.372-3.
[26] M. Turkaman, ibid., p.486.
[27] Gh.R. Mussavar Rahmani, *Khatirat-i Syasi* (Tehran: *Ravvaq*, 1363 (1984)) p.275.
[28] J. Mihdinya, op. cit. (note 15), p.345.
[29] G. Lenczowski, *Russia and the West in Iran, the Supplement to* (New York: Greenwood Press, 1954) p.34.
[30] Private communication from the wife of one of the five Elitists (one of the non-governing Elite five directors), who added to the tale she had heard from her husband: "I think that Dr Musaddiq should have listened to them; after all ten years is not such a long time, is it!"
[31] A man incapable of standing still, Maliki had first joined the *Toudeh* Party before created a schism in 1948 and branching out with Jalal Al-i Ahmad and Anvar Khameh'i. Re-emerging in 1951 with Dr Baqa'i, he again walked away to create his own Third Force (1952) and, in 1960, the Socialist League.
[32] Dr H.F. Grady, *US Foreign Policy Bulletin*, December 15, 1951.
[33] L. Mosley, *Power Play* (Random House, 1973) p.201.
[34] Cottam's sympathy for the Front is evident in the pages of his memoirs: R. Cottam, *Nationalism in Iran* (University of Pittsburgh Press, 2nd ed., 1979).
[35] F. Rouhani, op. cit. (note 18), p.119.
[36] Some of these documents were published in the book by I. Ra'in, *Asnad-i Khaneh Sedan* (The Documents of Seddon's House), (Tehran: *Bangah-i Tarjameh va Nashr-i Kitab*, 2nd ed., 1358 (1979)).
[37] S.H. Longrigg, *Oil in the Middle East* (Oxford University Press, 2nd ed., 1961) pp.172-3.

38 See reproduction of 1933 Agreement in N. Kemp, *Abadan* (London: Allan Wingate, 1953) pp.251-65.
38A The international validity of Article 21 was put into doubt by Iranian legal expert M.Â. Mouvahhid. In his book *Naft-i Ma va Masa'il-i Huqouqi-i An* (Tehran: *Khwarazmi*, Isfand 1349 (March 1971)) p.342, Mouvahhid invoked the 'Calvo Clause' to undermine the article's international legality.
39 F. Rouhani, op. cit. (note 18), pp.112-3.
40 See *United Nations Bulletin*, Vol. XI, no. 8, October 15, 1951, pp.335-8.
41 Averell Harriman (1891–1986), the millionaire son of a legendary railway baron, was among the *ne plus ultra* of US diplomats. He was dispatched by President Roosevelt as a special envoy to Churchill and Stalin during the Second World War. His intervention in the Iran-AIOC dispute as special envoy of the US President was a proof of the importance attached to the dispute by the Americans.
42 Reported with details in *Kayhan*, no. 2482, *Murdad 12, 1330* (August 3, 1951), pp.1 and 8.
43 N.R. Keddie, *Roots of Revolution* (Yale University Press, 1981) pp.136 and 288.
43A G.C. McGhee, 'Recollections of Dr Muhammad Musaddiq', in op. cit. (note 10), p.296.
44 F. Rouhani, op. cit. (note 16), p.255. For the ultimate conspiracy theory, see J. Jumhiri, *Asrar-i Milli Shudan-i Naft* (The Secrets of the Oil Nationalisation), (Tehran: *Chap-i Danish*, undated) 84p; in which Jumhiri (probably a pen name) contended that the British would benefit from nationalisation, thus they had engineered the oil nationalisation process!
45 N. JAMI, *Guzashteh Chiragh-i Rah-i Ayandeh Ast* (Tehran: Quqnous, 1361 (1982)) p.631. Quoting from *Ittilaât* newspaper, no. 7771, Isfand 28, 1330 (March 19, 1952).
45A R.W. Ferrier, op. cit. (note 20A), p.186.
46 F. Rouhani, op. cit. (note 16), pp.333-4.
46A This quartet of senior managers, in addition to Fathullah Nafisi and Dr. Riza Fallah, were to launch NIOC on the right tracks. They were educated and dedicated young men: a worthy pioneering elite for the national oil company.
46B F. Rouhani, op. cit. (note 16), pp.335, 340 and 526.
47 Ibid., p.338.
48 A. Sampson, *The Seven Sisters* (Coronet Books, 1976) p.135.
49 P.H. Frankel, *Mattei* (London: Faber and Faber, 1966) p.102.
50 M.K. Sheehan, *Iran: The Impact of US Interests and Policies (1941–1954)* (New York: Th. Gauss, 1968) p.72.
51 P.H. Frankel, op. cit. (note 49), p.131.
52 See K. and M. Katakura, *Japan and the Middle East* (The Middle East Institute of Japan, undated), in which the tale of the intercourse in 1953 between NIOC and Idemitsu is given in detail. An interesting point is the admission, with *Murdad 28* hindsight, of Keisuke Idemitsu that: "If we had known the real power the majors [i.e. the Seven Sisters] could exercise as they wished, we would not have gone to Tehran for oil negotiations under pressure of the oil crisis".
53 P.H. Frankel, op. cit. (note 49), p.95.
53A The Alton Jones affair came to light in June 1956 when Gerald Waldren, chief executive of Consolidated Brokerage brought a $110m lawsuit against Alton Jones in a US court, contending that this was the amount it had lost because Jones had not kept his promises to carry out the deals to which he had agreed in Iran.

54 M.Â. Mouvahhid, op. cit. (note 38A), pp.117-8., citing *The Washington Evening Star* of May 21, 1968.
55 W.A. Leeman, *The Price of Middle East Oil* (Ithaca, New York: Cornell University Press, 1962) p.296.
56 A. Sampson, op. cit. (note 48), p.151.
57 P.H. Frankel, op. cit. (note 20), p.7.
58 Private communication to the author.
59 General Baqa'i, in command of the troops, was severely reprimanded and relieved of his command for ordering soldiers to shoot without having been given permission to do so.
60 The royalist Dr Hasan Imami, a member of the powerful Imami family and a nephew of Dr Musaddiq's wife, was among the directors of the non-governing Elite. He also was Tehran's *Imam Jumêh*. He had entered the political fray in order to control the *Majlis*. On the aftermath of the July 21 events, he would relinquish his *Majlis* presidency and leave for a vacation in Switzerland. Imami had been the victim of a murder attempt on August 22, 1950 by the policeman Akbari, escaping with minor knife injuries.
61 Hajj Aqa Riza Rafi, Qa'im Maqam ul-Mulk, a member of Reza Shah's inner circle. A wily royalist politician, he was for over three decades a *Majlis* deputy – from 1924 to 1953, only missing four assemblies between the Fifth and Seventeenth *Majlis*. He became famous for being Iran's top political matchmaker. Placed his Rafi family within the Pahlavi elite.
62 E.A. Bayne, op. cit. (note 15), p.157.
63 Qavam's letter dated March 17, 1952 and the Court Minister's reply were reproduced by *Tuloû* newspaper, *Farvardin 20, 1329* (April 9, 1950).
64 *Iran-i Ma* newspaper, no. 97, *Murdad 17, 1331* (August 8, 1952), in article by 'D.T.' from Paris.
65 See the report of a journalist eyewitness in M.Â. Safari, op. cit. (note 23), p.631.
66 Ibid., p.645.
67 Dr Musaddiq held the view that through army purges, he could straighten out the military. The officers had to compile lists of 'undesirable' elements themselves. The process yielded first a list of two hundred officers, then of a hundred and thirty-six officers who were sent to early retirement. The exclusion process might well have been democratic, but it was not a way to do things in Iran.
68 R.W. Cottam, op. cit. (note 34), p.277.
69 S. Akhavi, op. cit. (note 5), p.62.
70 M. Dihnavi, op. cit. (note 19), Vol. III, pp.261-2.
69A M.Â. Safari, op. cit. (note 23), p.738.
71 Gh.R. Nijati, *Jumbish-i Milli Shudan-i Sanât-i Naft-i Iran* (Tehran: Shirkat-i Sahami Intishar, 1364 (1984)) p.258.
72 See: M.Â. Safari, op. cit. (note 23), p.744. On that day, a plot against Musaddiq's life failed. A group of retired officers, accompanied by a few thugs, wanted to attack the premier as he was leaving the palace, but the latter left through a back door. Frustrated, the group then marched on the premier's house and attempted to storm it. Dr Musaddiq, along with Dr Fatimi, had to find refuge in a nearby house, fearing for their lives (in case the assailants broke through the meagre defences). Iran still was a country where the prime minister had to effectively jump a wall in order to secure his own safety.
73 R.W. Cottam, op. cit. (note 34), p.273.

72A On April 4, 1952, a governmental decree was issued "allowing the use of foreign exchange earned from the export of 1st class and 2nd class goods for imports".
73 Official Iran's Customs Statistics for the years 1330, 1331 and 1332, as cited by *Kayhan*, Day 5, 1364 (December 26, 1985) p.8.
74 *Iranshahr* (Tehran: *Chapkhaneh Danishgah*, 2 Vols., 1342/43 (1963/64)) Vol. II, p.1158.
75 A.K.S. Lambton, *The Persian Land Reform, 1962-1966* (Oxford: Clarendon Press, 1969) p.37.
75A H. Ladjevardi, 'Constitutional Government and Reform Under Musaddiq', in op. cit. (note 10), pp.80-81.
76 A.K.S. Lambton, op. cit. (note 75), p.40.
77 W.O. Douglas, *West of the Indus* (New York: Doubleday, 1958) p.296.
78 Â. Dashti, *Panjah va Panj* (Tehran: *Amir Kabir*, 2nd ed., 2535 (1976)) p.211.
79 M.Â. Safari, op. cit. (note 23) pp.668-9. Also see N. JAMI, op. cit. (note 45), pp.647-8.
80 C.M. Woodhouse, *Something Ventured* (London: Granada, 1982) p.250.
81 K. Roosevelt, *Countercoup* (McGraw Hill, 1979) p.120.
82 Ibid., pp.3 and 11.
83 F. Rouhani, op. cit. (note 16), p.375.
84 W.O. Douglas, op. cit. (note 77), p.287.
85 V. Marchetti and J.D. Marks, *The CIA and the Cult of Intelligence* (Coronet Books, 1976) p.54. Quoting a Dulles letter to *Washington Post* correspondent Chalmers Roberts.
86 *Time Magazine*, July 29, 1985, no. 30, p.40. Interview with ex-president Richard Nixon.
87 H. Carrere d'Encausse, *La Politique Soviétique au Moyen-Orient, 1955-1975* (Paris: *Presses de la Fondation Nationale des Sciences Politiques*, 1975) p.15.
87A See *Ittilaât*, no. 8082, *Urdibihist 12, 1332* (May 4, 1953).
88 M. Turkaman, *Toutiêh Raboudan va Qatl-i Sarlasghar Afshar Tous* (Tehran: Rasa, 1363 (1984)) p.8.
89 Gh.R. Musavvar Rahmani, op. cit. (note 27), pp.101 and 109.
90 K. Roosevelt, op. cit. (note 81), p.18.
91 Gh.R. Nijati, op. cit. (note 70), p.291.
92 L. Mosley, op. cit. (note 33), p.216.
93 D. Wise and T.B. Ross, *The Invisible Government* (New York: Vintage Books, 19774) p.112.
94 K. Roosevelt, op. cit. (note 81), p.173.
95 N. Pakdaman, *Muqaddameh barayi, Musaddiq dar Muhakimat-i Nizami* (unpublished hand-written manuscript) p.66.
96 S. Esfandyari, *Ma Vie* (Paris: Plon, 1963) p.123.
97 W. Warne, *Mission for Peace* (Merrill, 1965) pp.243-4.
98 Gh. R. Mussavar Rahmani, op. cit. (note 27), p.137.
98A J.A. Bill, op. cit. (note 10), p.285.
99 N. Pakdaman, op. cit. (note 95), p.41. The enrolment of General Zargham at Isfahan did not go through for unclear reasons; on the other, the Gilan Army under General Muhammad Vali Qaranay sided with the coup and would have been ready to intervene if it had proven necessary.
100 N.R. Keddie, op. cit. (note 43), p.288. (note 69). Keddie's estimate was partly confirmed by the cashing of Bank-i Milli cheque no. 703352 for Rls32,643,000

(equivalent to $390,000) by a Mr Edward G. Donnaly on August 18 (see C. Julien, *L'Empire Americain*, (Paris: Grasset, 1968) p.318), and also the fact that the conspiracy had to use the services of American currency specialists.

101 K. Love, a reporter for *The New York Times* in Tehran during the summer of 1953, was accused in 1980 by the magazine *CounterSpy* of having somehow taken part in the coup. See *The International Herald Tribune*, September 27, 1980. Another American who assisted by introducing Kim Roosevelt to leading Iranian politicians was fingered as 'Professor Roger Black'. See J.A. Bill, op. cit. (note 10), pp.285-6.

102 Wm. Roger Louis, 'Musaddiq and the Dilemmas of British Imperialism', in op. cit. (note 10), pp.236-7.

103 Dr Zaehner, "extremely successful in covert propaganda in 1944", was informed of "palace politics through the Shah's *eminence* Ernest Perron" and was directly "linked to the Rashidian brothers". See Wm. Roger Louis, ibid., pp.233-4. In the 1950s, spycatcher Peter Wright even came to suspect Zaehner of being a double agent, but after a short interview found him to be 'clean'. See P. Wright, *Spycatcher* (Viking, 1987) pp.244-6.

104 N. Pakdaman, op. cit. (note 95), p.24.

105 Shahpour Reporter (later Sir), the son of Parsee Ardishir Ji, one of Britain's top MI6 agents in Iran. See P. Wright, op. cit. (note 103), p.348. "He [Lord Victor Rothschild] maintained his links with British Intelligence, utilising his friendship with the Shah of Iran, and running agents personally for Dick White in the Middle East, particularly Mr [Shahpour] Reporter, who played such a decisive role in MI6 operations in the 1950s". In other words: in the operations leading to *Murdad 28*.

106 Ernest Perron, Muhammad Reza Shah's strikingly good-looking confidant. Had been an humble employee at *Le Rosey* school in the 1930s, in charge of gardening and general house-cleaning. He had extraordinary power over Muhammad Reza Shah. See M. Pourkian, *Irnist Pirun* (Ernest Perron), (Berlin: *Ghamgusar*, undated)

107 Musaddiq, 'Iranian Nationalism and Oil', op. cit. (note 10), p.288.

108 G.C. McGhee, op. cit. (note 43A), p.304.

CHAPTER ELEVEN: AMERICAN CLINIC

In the evening of August 20, Dr Musaddiq and his closest advisers were apprehended at Dr Muâzzami's house and taken into custody at the Officers' Club. On August 22, Muhammad Reza Shah returned triumphantly to Tehran, with Prime Minister Zahidi and the full cabinet waiting for him at Mihrabad Airport. On August 23, Roosevelt paid his last visit to the Shah, before departing for Washington via London. In both capitals, the victorious 'Ajax' field commander would tell his tale: in London to Sir Winston Churchill and in Washington to President Eisenhower and the Dulles brothers. Roosevelt was nicknamed 'Mr Iran' in the CIA for his *Murdad 28* coup, and "was secretly awarded the National Security Medal"[1] and praised by President Eisenhower.[2]

The Americans had won: they had unsettled Dr Musaddiq's regime and replaced Muhammad Reza Shah on the throne, whom President Eisenhower believed would prove "an effective leader of his people".[3] Yet another proof of how little even the brightest Americans knew about Iran and Iranians. In the aftermath of *Murdad 28* there were many other winners in Iran. Losers too.

11.1. Winners and Losers

Paradoxically, the first and foremost winner of *Murdad 28* was Dr Muhammad Musaddiq. The old statesman himself could not have engineered his exit more favourably. He had achieved immortality with his nationalisation of the Iranian oil industry. He had been *Time Magazine*'s 'Man of the Year 1951' (the first Iranian to achieve such fame). He had decided not to compromise come what may. His record as prime minister stood unblemished: he had remained incorruptible, never lying to his people, till the bitter end. Iranian opponents had been unable to mount a successful coup against him, and in order to remove his legal and popular regime foreigners had been required, specialists who had spent months in planning and millions of dollars in the process. His National Iranian Oil Company (NIOC) stood well rooted, with no one daring to question it.

Naturally, he had made mistakes along the way, squandered golden opportunities, uselessly antagonised allies, been too lax or inflexible. But soon all these would be forgotten, and what would always remain were his achievements in history, remembered as such by the people of Iran. He was the symbol of Iranian nationalism; any future Iranian nationalist movement or leader would have to refer to him and be measured against his achievements (how many times can Iran nationalise its oil?) and his incorruptibility; even his enemies would find themselves chasing his shadow, like Muhammad Reza Shah who would bend backwards to try and emulate him. Musaddiq was now old and sick, and the powers-that-be could do what they wished with him – put him on trial, exile him to Ahmadabad, call him "old Mossy" or "the man in pyjamas", even kill him. Nothing mattered any more. He had won: he had moved the hearts and minds of the Iranian nation, set a standard example for posterity. The rest was literature.

Dr Musaddiq, as the Shah had told K. Roosevelt on August 23,[4] was court-martialled along with General Taqi Riahi, from November 8, 1953 until May 13, 1954 (inclusive of both first instance and appeal). Both men received three-year sentences, as the Shah had predicted. Dr Musaddiq used his trial to defend himself and his administration and thank the people of Iran for their support. Alongside him during his trials was yet another winner, his fierce advocate, the lawyer Colonel Jalil Buzurgmihr, who compromised his military career, refused the benefits offered him and stood up to threats and insults to defend the man he thought worth defending.[5]

Among the losers were the *Iran* Party technocrats and some National Front members. Dr Shayigan and Dariush Furouhar were sentenced to a maximum of ten years, with the former released from prison in 1956 and the latter in the early sixties; others, such as Engineers Razavi, Zirakzadeh and Haqshinas, were given lighter sentences and released a few months later. Of Dr Musaddiq's inner circle only Dr Fatimi,* who had gone into hiding on *Murdad 28*, was arrested and executed, after surviving a savage attack by Shâban Jâfari's knife-wielding thugs. "He was the most vituperative of them all", the Shah had told Roosevelt; "he will be executed".[6] National personalities and politicians intervened with the Shah, begging him to accord Dr Fatimi a royal pardon; the Shah proved inflexible on this point, as if such an act was out of his power. Dr Fatimi was the only

Elitist among Dr Musaddiq's collaborators and he also was the only one to be executed. Of all the individuals involved in the oil nationalisation era, only the names of Dr Musaddiq and Dr Fatimi would find a place in the collective memory of Iranians.

* DR HUSAYN FATIMI (1917-1954), born in Naîn, the youngest brother of Misbah Fatimi, Nasrullah Sayfpour Fatimi and Muhammad Mâsumi; schooling at Naîn and the British School at Isfahan; journalist at Tehran's *Sitareh* newspaper (1937-41); editor of his brother Nasrullah's paper *Bakhtar* (1942-45); studied at Paris, Ph.D. in law, dispatched articles for his friend Muhammad Masôud (1945-48); upon return to Iran, launched his own paper, *Bakhtar-i Imrouz*, joined the National Front (1949); proposed oil nationalisation (1950); appointed deputy premier and government speaker by Dr Musaddiq (May 1951); shot in the stomach by Âbd Khuda'i of *Fada'yan* (February 1952); hospitalised for six months in Tehran and Hamburg; elected deputy in Seventeenth *Majlis* from Tehran; Minister of Foreign Affairs (October 1952 - August 1953); went into hiding after *Murdad 28*; arrested (February 1954); after assault by Shâban's thugs, court-martialled, sentenced to death, and executed on November 10, 1954.

Another victim of the post-*Murdad 28* revenges was the courageous journalist Amir Mukhtar Karimpour Shirazi, the editor of *Shourish* (Riot). He was arrested in his hiding place on October 18, 1953, and imprisoned. Then on March 15, 1954, he was taken to hospital with third degree burns on his head, neck and torso. The next day he died. The official version had it that "he had burnt himself while trying to escape"; it later transpired that he had been transformed into a live torch by orders allegedly emanating from circles near to the court.[7]

Dr Musaddiq's four supporters in the Tehran *Bazaar* were imprisoned and exiled – namely Hajj Muhammad Hasan Shamshiri (the *Bazaar*'s leading Chilau Kabab owner), Hajj Mahmoud Manian, Hajj Âbdul-Âzim Hajjiyyan and Hajj Muhammad Suhayli Kishbaf.[8] Hajj Shamshiri was exiled to the island of Kharg in the Persian Gulf for a few months.

Hajj Shamshiri would be joined in Kharg by the first batch of the group who lost the most in the royalist coup: the *Toudeh* rank and file.[9] Used to the excessive freedom of the Musaddiq years, the communists were unprepared for the whirlwind that was to hit them. In the aftermath of the *Murdad 28* coup, they had their first encounter with the new repressive system, with fear, prison, torture, exile and death. The *Toudeh* rank and file were too numerous to emigrate to the Soviet Union (or Eastern Europe) like the leaders; moreover, they didn't have the means to go abroad. The Second Armoured Division and Tehran's Military Command were at the centre of the gigantic repressive system rapidly put into place to crack the *Toudeh* nut, with General Taymour Bakhtiar at its head.

Muhammad Reza Shah might appear one of the winners of *Murdad 28*. The successful coup had transmuted an ex-monarch in exile into a shah who had hitherto never been so powerful. The crowds on *Murdad 28* had rallied to the phrase, "Long live the Shah!"

This time round there was no Qavam or Musaddiq, or even a Razmara, to loosen his grip on power. Squarely backing him were his American saviours, who were now as much linked to him – for the worse or the better – as he was indebted to them. At his service were General Zahidi (who had climbed into his plane at Mihrabad and kissed his hand in a sign of subservience[10]), his court and his family, and a hotchpotch of individuals who had taken part in the coup. But the tragic *Murdad* events had left deep scars on the Shah – they had shattered his self-confidence and brought their fill of bile and hatred: for example, courtiers were not allowed to use the name of 'Musaddiq' in his presence, as the Shah had told his Court Minister Husayn Âla that he was "allergic to it".[11] But the fact that, once again, Muhammad Reza Pahlavi had survived was in itself a miracle, the second one to come his way after February 1949.

The Shah was, however, not the only Pahlavi to benefit from *Murdad 28*. His twin sister, Princess Ashraf, had a share in the comeback. Exiled by Dr Musaddiq after the July 21, 1952 events, Ashraf had thrown herself into the battle against him with all her powers. Energetic and courageous, the princess, who deserved her designation of 'Black Panther', had a great influence over her weaker twin brother, "being a more determined and scheming person".[12] She was ruthless, without scruples, and thrived on controversy: her three marriages (to, successively, Âli Qavam Shirazi, Ahmad Shafiq and Dr Mihdi Bushiri) and her multiple romances (e.g. Hazhir) were the talk of Tehran. During the 1940s, she had slowly begun her career in international public relations, having been invited by the American Red Cross in 1947, and meeting Stalin in 1948 (he gave her a mink coat). She had pulled more than her full weight in the *Murdad 28* coup. Now she was a player in her own right, not just the Shah's sister any more.

Suddenly, the court had became the centre of gravity of Iranian politics. After the lacklustre 1940s, the 1950s were smiling on every courtier. Besides the Shah and Ashraf, all other Pahlavi princes and princesses were back in society. Prominent among the princes was the Shah's only full brother, Prince Âli Riza Pahlavi, whose house had been a political beehive during the 1940s. The prince was to die prematurely in 1954 when his private plane crashed during a return trip from the Caspian Sea shore to Tehran (the possibility of the sabotage of his plane should not be discarded).

Ernest Perron, the man closest to the Shah, rose to prominence too. Before his death in 1961, Perron was the court's most powerful individual, mixing in politics, in court affairs and even (the only individual daring to do so) in the Shah's private affairs. As the ex-Queen Surayya Isfandyari related in her memoirs:

> Peron [*sic*] came to my room and asked me indiscreet questions on my marital relations with my husband. I told him to "remember whom he was talking to"...
>
> I didn't know what were the exact relations between the Shah and Peron... (after eight years of living with the Shah!)[13]

Behind the throne was the capable General Husayn Fardoust, a close aide to the Shah since his Le Rosey schooldays, who had assisted Colonel Nasiri in his failed coup of August 16,[14] and was the Shah's top adviser on security questions. Old-timers Sulayman Bihboudi and Abu'lfath Atabay were in charge of the royal household. General Dr Âbd ul-Karim Ayadi, the Shah's *baha'i* private physician since 1948, was already lurching in the aisles of power, ready to fill the niche left vacant after Perron's death.

The Shah had incurred debts to a series of individuals and interest groups during the coup. These were all among the winners of *Murdad 28* and would ask for their share of the pie. Heading the list were the

Zahidis, father General Fazlullah and son Ardashir. Having married one of the daughters of Elite member Husayn Pirnia (Mûtamin ul-Mulk), the general had strong links to the old Qajar Elite. Such links had come in handy during the *Murdad* events[15] as General Zahidi had been able to co-ordinate the efforts of the Americans, the British and the Elite, all three bent on removing Dr Musaddiq. His son Ardashir had close links to the Americans since his days at the American University of Beirut and the University of Utah; upon his return to Iran, he had joined Point Four, rising to the position of assistant and translator to its director, W.E. Warne. From 1953 onwards, Ardashir would either be ambassador (to London or Washington) or Minister of Foreign Affairs. In October 1957, he became the Shah's son-in-law by marrying Princess Shahnaz, the Shah's daughter from his first marriage to Queen Fouziyyeh; the couple would have a daughter, Mahnaz, before divorcing in September 1964.

The Shah was also heavily indebted to his armed forces, with four officers (besides Zahidi and Fardoust) standing out:
- Colonel Nîmatullah Nasiri, the leader of the August 16 coup attempt; promoted to general on August 22 by the Shah.
- Major Muhammad Khatami, the Shah's private pilot (since 1946), at the controls of the royal plane in the *Murdad* exile flight; replaced General Gilanshah as commander-in-chief of the Imperial Iranian Air Force in October 1958, married the Shah's sister Princess Fatimeh in November 1959 (after her divorce from Vincent Hillyer).
- Colonel Taymour Bakhtiar, commander of the Kermanshah Armoured Division, after *Murdad 28* placed in charge of Tehran Military Command.
- Colonel Âbbas Farzanigan, among K. Roosevelt's close aides during coup; promoted to general, appointed Minister of PTT in the first Zahidi cabinet.

Two other groups had benefited tremendously from the anti-Musaddiq coup: Iran's trade union leaders and Iran's underworld. The Americans had not hesitated to approach both with fistfuls of dollars to tap their muscular power. The labour unionists and the professional thugs had spearheaded the coup. Not content with the dollars they had received, they now wanted their fair share of the - rewards. On the labour side were people such as:

- Parviz Khwunsari, a Tehran University graduate of law turned into specialist of labour problems, controlled the trade unions for Premier Razmara in 1950, later moved to SAVAK.
- Byouk Sabir, a successful trade union leader, head of the *Sindika-i Kargaran* (Workers' Syndicate) an anti-*Toudeh* outfit, created Iran Labour Consultants and the newspaper *Syasi* (Politics). After *Murdad* moved to the big league of middlemen, making millions of dollars in the process.
- Âbbas Shanhadeh, editor of *Farman* (Decree) since 1942, with extensive connections in the underworld, took the right turn in *Murdad*, thereby assuring his family an enviable niche in the Pahlavi elite.

Among the underworld, a number of tough gang leaders emerged on *Murdad 28*, adding a fresh dimension to Iranian politics:
- Shâban Jâfari, known as Shâban bi Mukh (the Brainless), became a wealthy owner of a *Zourkhaneh* (sports club), wielded enormous power on the Tehran streets, ready for any action against any designated foe.
- Tay'ib Hajj Riza'i, a powerful giant, one of the leaders of the *Maydan* (Tehran's fruit market), with his partner Hajj Âli Nouri.
- Husayn Ramazan Yakhi, a redoubtable and famous knife-wielder of the Tehran underworld.

There were also lesser gangsters such as Zaki Turkeh, Nasir Jigaraki, Mustafa Divaneh, Amir Rustami (involved in General Afshar Tous's murder), Husayn Mihdi Qasab, Husayn Farzin, Baqir Furoutan (nicknamed *Kachal* (Bald)) and Husayn Aqa Mihdi, one of the very best strongman on Tehran's streets.[16]

The old Qajar Elite could also be classified among the winners of *Murdad 28*. Back in 1951, impressed by the nationalist wave, it had contemplated throwing its weight behind Dr Musaddiq to crush the *Toudeh* threat. However, after the regime was given the thumbs down by its boards of directors, Elitists in positions of power began working against it. The events of July 21, 1952 proved the watershed: the Elite unveiled its batteries and joined the Shah/army opposition. The decrees of October 1952 concerning the revenues of land further alienated the old Elite, whose major income came from the produce of land. But, whichever side it chose, the Elite was in a losing position. Its two last stars, Qavam and Musaddiq, were out for good; the next generation counted on the elderly Husayn Âla and an astute newcomer, Amir Asadullah Âlam, to prop them up. The Elite's religious wing of the Imamis and the Bihbahanis (with both families active on *Murdad 28*) still seemed better off than the rest. The danger, however, for the Elite would not come from the Shah/army coalition; rather it would come from within, as its decline seemed irreversible, and the first symptoms of degeneracy had set in. Moreover, it had little to expect from the new American masters, whose interests and values were diametrically opposed to its own.

At the other extreme of the Iranian spectrum, the people of Iran were the ones who had lost the most in the August coup. They had lost the only natural leader they had known; lost an honest elite, which would have liked (if it knew how) to render service; lost a unique occasion to take the soft road to reform and a rejuvenation of Iran. On *Murdad 28* the people had lost a good deal of their political innocence. They had witnessed for the first time ruthlessness on a grand scale, and repression on a even greater scale in the coup's aftermath. The new order that was being imposed on them by a foreign force, far superior to their own, was definitely not their cup of tea. But the people of Iran are adaptable realists, and, once past the first shock of the coup, they collectively realised that there was little they could do about it, the odds being stacked in favour of the armed forces backed by the Americans. They would have to wait to get to know the powers-that-be; wait to see what kind of a system and which elite would be imposed on them. And then, but only then, see what they could do about it.

Amongst the winners, the Americans seemed to have won the most. Finally, with *Murdad 28*, the US ambivalence of the 1940s had given way to a total involvement in Iranian affairs. Why should they play second fiddle to the British? They didn't need them any more – they were strong and rich enough to 'run' Iran by themselves. They would turn it into a 'clinic', an American clinic, a showpiece of how to bring reforms, progress and development to a poor and backward country. Show the world the American way to do things in such countries. On September 5, 1953, President Eisenhower announced an emergency grant of $45m to Iran. This was a considerable amount of money for an economy like Iran's, when compared with her total 1953 import needs of Rls5,756m (equal to $178m). American military missions were buttressed; American experts in agriculture and economics were sent in; Point Four was reactivated; funds were made available for all kinds of projects; Iranian studies courses were launched in some US universities. The number one superpower was structuring its Iranian 'clinic', as though it were any other multi-million project, such as the TVA or the Manhattan Project.

After their abrupt departure of 1951/52, the British were back in Iran. Among the winners, but playing second fiddle now.

The Iranian winners were looking at the Americans for their direction, not to the British any more. The long decline from Empire, begun after the end of the Second World War, had come to Iran too. If the Americans had power and money, the British had experience and knowledge; they were aware of how difficult it was to control the smart Iranians. And they still had their roots, tended with care for the past century, which were not to be uprooted by a single event such as oil nationalisation. And now that Dr Musaddiq was out of office, they still had their oil concession in the south, nationalised but nevertheless theirs until December 31, 1993, as stipulated in the last (valid) agreement signed between the AIOC and the Iranian Government in 1933. It went without saying that the AIOC would somehow have to share its Iranian rights with the American oil companies; but it was preferable to have them as partners in a British-owned concession than have them as rivals in a concession of their own.

11.2. Oil Consortium

Herbert Hoover Jr., the American oil expert, acted as a co-ordinator for the Seven Sisters on the settlement of the Iranian oil question. It was he who first thought up the idea of a consortium, inclusive of all major oil companies, to operate the Iranian oil fields. After protracted negotiations, the Iranian Oil Consortium was finally made up of the Seven Sisters, with forty per cent going to AIOC, fourteen per cent to Royal Dutch/Shell and 40% to the five major American oil companies – 8% each to Esso, Texaco, Mobil, Gulf and Socal. The remaining 6% was given to the French oil company Compagnie Française des Pétroles (CFP).

The second step of the settlement had to be reached between the Consortium and the government of Iran. A team under the leadership of Howard W. Page of Esso, including Herbert Hoover Jr., Harold

Snow of AIOC and John Loudon of Shell, met the Iranian negotiating team in Tehran, made up of Dr Âli Amini, the Minister of Finance, NIOC's chairman and managing director Murtaza Quli Bayat and the NIOC directors. Both teams knew that they had to come up with a workable arrangement. The main obstacle along the way was the nine-point Oil Nationalisation Law of 1951. Eventually a highly complex legal structure was set up that gave, in the end result, an almost total control of Iran's oil industry to the consortium. The final agreement was signed in September 1954 (with both the US and British ambassadors present) and quickly ratified by the Eighteenth *Majlis* on October 21 and by the Senate on October 28.

The Consortium Agreement was set to last for twenty-five years and three extension periods of five years each, subject to mutual accord. The agreement roughly covered the 100,000 square miles of AIOC's concession area. Profit-sharing was to be on a fifty-fifty basis. Abadan Refinery and other installations were NIOC's properties, but they could be used by the Consortium with no restrictions. Crude oil produced on behalf of NIOC in the agreement area was to be sold to the trading companies set up in Iran by the Consortium members. Only the distribution and sales of refined products in Iran, and services not related to manufacturing (the so-called 'non-basic') were to be NIOC's preserve. Thus the Consortium "was given sufficient control of oil operations".[17] "The final formula", concluded chief negotiator H. Page, "was as effective as ownership".[18] In retrospect, this agreement, seen from the Iranian point of view, was far inferior to the joint Anglo-American proposal of February 20, 1953. In the proposal the two crucial points of the industry's operations and export sales had been NIOC's responsibility, whereas in the Consortium Agreement they were squarely under the foreign companies' umbrella.[19] From his exile in Ahmadabad, Dr Musaddiq said of the agreement that "it assured the enslavement of my country for the next forty years".[20] On October 30, 1954, the first Consortium tankers were at Abadan to load their first crude oil shipments.

To operate its agreement area, the Consortium set up two affiliated companies (registered in Holland): (1) the Iranian Oil Exploration and Production Company (IOEPC), for managing the oil fields; and (2) the Iranian Oil Refining Company (IORC), for operating Abadan Refinery. The twin companies together formed the Iranian Oil

Operating Companies (IOOC) and their shares were held by a holding company registered in London, the Iranian Oil Participants Ltd. Another London-based company, the Iranian Oil Services Company (IROS), was in charge of purchasing and forwarding equipment and materials for both IOOC and NIOC.

In 1955, a group of twelve smaller American oil companies (the so-called independents) wrung a 5% interest from the five American majors, using the tight US anti-trust laws as a lever. Each of the US majors were forced to chip in 1% of their respective 8% Consortium share. The twelve companies, each with a $^5/_{12}$ of one per cent share, formed the Iricon Group. The initial twelve were: American Independent Oil Company, Atlantic Refining Company, Cities Service Oil Company, Continental Oil Company, Hancock Oil Company, Pacific Western Oil Corporation (later Getty Oil), Richfield Oil Corporation, San Jacinto Oil Company, Signal Oil and Gas Company, Sinclair Oil Company, Standard Oil Company (Ohio) and Tidewater Oil Company. The twelve would be reduced to ten as Cities Service and Sinclair, the companies linked to Alton Jones, readily sold their shares to Richfield; Iricon would later be reduced to eight and finally to six companies following buy-outs and mergers.[21] Each $^5/_{12}$ share had cost its holder $625,000.[2] On April 29, 1955 the *Majlis* ratified the Iricon Group's entry into the consortium.

On December 17, 1954, AIOC changed its name to that of one of its subsidiaries, British Petroleum (BP). The defunct AIOC had produced some two and a half billion barrels of Iranian crude oil during its forty-five years of existence. Its legacy to BP included some forty subsidiaries in Great Britain and thirty-five affiliated companies in twenty-three other countries.[23] BP also inherited valuable assets: a 40% share in the Iranian Oil Consortium, a 50% stake in Kuwait's oil resources and a 23.75% interest in the Iraq Petroleum Company. BP was also compensated for its Iranian concession by a £25m payment over ten years (first instalment in January 1957) and £21m for transferring its installations at Naft-i Shah and Kermanshah and its internal distribution system to NIOC. BP was to further receive a $90m down payment from its Consortium partners and ten US cents per barrel of Iranian crude oil exported until the accumulated account reached $510m.[23A] "It was indeed a remarkable improvement", PM Sir Anthony Eden wrote in his memoirs, "on what might have been expected three years before, when we were out of

Abadan with only an indefinite prospect of ever returning there".[24] The London Stock Exchange quotation of AIOC's shares reflected this improvement: from $4^1/_2$ per share in 1951 they recovered to £6 in September 1953, soared to $£9^1/_2$ (January 1954) and £12 (May 1954) before ending up at £19 in November 1954. AIOC had gratified its shareholders "with a four hundred per cent bonus on its ordinary share by capitalising £80,550,000 from its general reserve"[25] before turning itself into BP. As John Strachey underlined: "The last British Empire, the empire of oil, has 'paid' better than any other".[26] Indeed.

On the ground at Abadan and in the oil fields, the Iranian oil industry was back in operation. During the years 1952 and 1953, the under-trained Iranian workforce had done more than a fair job of properly maintaining the industry's facilities. Iranian hands had even been able to start up the Abadan lube oil plant and produce motor oil for internal consumption. Western experts visiting Abadan were surprised by the quality of the maintenance job done, and even S.H. Longrigg had to recognise that the plants had "indeed, been adequately maintained".[27] In its first three months of operation under the IORC, Abadan was able to refine over one and a half million long tons of oil:[27A] a sure sign that it had been in working order in the first place.

In the meantime, the Iranians had also begun to make headway in their own oil exploration. The public company *Shirkat-i Sahami-yi Naft-i Iran* (Iran Oil Company – IOC) was established in October 1949 with a capital of Rls1,000m to carry out oil exploration in regions outside the AIOC area. With the assistance of Swiss geologists, the IOC (first under the management of Fathullah Nafisi, then Engineer Baqir Mustoufi) began its investigations in the Balouchistan, Qum and Caspian Sea areas.[28] IOC's first exploratory well was spudded in the so-called Alburz area near Qum on June 18, 1951. On July 3, 1953 oil was discovered at the Alburz No. 3 well; on August 26, 1956, the Alburz No. 5 blew out. Between these two milestones, the IOC had been merged with NIOC in January 1954. Altogether, some 25,000 metres had been drilled near Qum by the end of 1957; most of the drilling had been contracted out to the Drilling and Exploration Company (DEC) of Los Angeles. In 1958, a gas/condensate field was discovered at Sarajeh near the Alburz field. The commercialisation of the Alburz field at 35,000 b/d and of a refinery was proposed and investigated: the feasibility study proved the project not to be economically viable. The Alburz and Sarajeh wells were shut: in Alburz three out of thirteen wells sunk were producers, whereas at Sarajeh five out of seven wells produced gas and condensate.

With the arrival of the consortium's mixture of Dutch, American and British oil managers in southern Iran, the Iranian oil industry was to witness drastic changes, not always for the better. The first palpable alterations were soon felt as the American 'high wage, low obligation' industrial approach gradually (but surely) began displacing the British 'paternalistic' type of management practised for almost half a century by the AIOC. Efficiency and bottom line results were the new orders of the day. In consequence, the number of expatriates was considerably reduced: from 4,250 (of whom 2,725 were British nationals)[29] in March 1951 to only 321 in 1955 and 510 in 1957. The Iranian labour force was also trimmed from 65,106 Daily Rated Employees (DREs) in 1951 to around 40,000 in 1957; Iranian staff numbers, however, remained fairly constant at around 5,000.[30]

During the second half of the 1950s, the Iranian oil industry expanded in all dimensions. First, Iranian oil production rose to unprecedented heights, quadrupling within an eight year span: from a daily average of 328,900 b/d in 1955 to 1,334,500 b/d in 1962[31] - a mind-boggling 22% cumulative yearly increase (see Table 11.1). In parallel, exploration and drilling activities were sharply increased in the Agreement Area (leading to two major fires[31A]). As thousands of square kilometres were explored, drilling operations rose from a meagre 3,500 metres in 1955 to 81,000 metres in 1962.[32] In the eight year span 1955-1962, the IOEPC spudded a total of 119 wildcats, 62 of which hit oil: a touch above 50% success. This feverish exploration drive led to the discovery of a score of new oil and gas fields:

- In 1958, the supergiant field of Ahvaz (both in the Asmari and Bangistan formations);
- In 1959, the small Binak field;
- In 1961, the Bibi Hakimeh field, the Pazanan dome gas and the Kharg Island field;
- In 1962, the Ramshir field.

By December 1962, a total of 544 oil wells had been drilled in the Consortium area and 178 of these were oil producers.[32A]

Table 11.1. Crude Oil Production in the Consortium Area (1955–62).[31]
(Figures in b/d)

Year	Production
1955	328,900
1956	541,800
1957	719,800
1958	826,100
1959	928,200
1960	1,067,700
1961	1,202,200
1962	1,334,500

The Consortium decided to implement a small topping plant (capacity of 20,000 b/d) at Majid-i Sulayman which was put into operation in 1955 – and expanded thrice to 80,000 b/d (before being totally shut down in 1979/80). It also made its first foray to Kharg Island (forty kilometres off the coast) by laying a 160 kilometre-long 26"/28" pipeline from the Gachsaran field to Ganaveh and linking it to a 30" submarine pipe from Ganaveh to Kharg. On the island a crude terminal and a T-shaped jetty were erected and inaugurated in 1960 as the first tanker loaded crude oil from the island.

Finally, the gap existing in the profit margins per barrel made by Iran in comparison to its neighbours had been closed by the late 1950s, as Iranian profit per barrel caught up with that of Saudi Arabia and Kuwait (as illustrated in Table 11.2).

As the Consortium was gradually settling in south Iran, two men were planning their revenge. The first was Enrico Mattei, the mercurial chairman of Italy's national oil company ENI. Mattei was still sore at being left out of the Consortium by the *Sette Sorelle* (the Seven Sisters – an expression he had first coined to denote the major oil companies), even though he had 'behaved' during the Iranian oil boycott, but CFP had been given a share. And Mattei knew a share's

Table 11.2. Profit Margins per Barrel of Crude Oil Exported From Iran, Kuwait and Saudi Arabia, for the years 1955 and 1958.[33]

Exporting Country	Profit Margin per Barrel Exported (in US cents)	
	1955	1958
Iran	75	89
Kuwait	80	85
Saudi Arabia	76	81

worth, having told oil pundit Frankel that a share in the Consortium "was like getting a licence to print money".[34] In 1957 Mattei took his revenge on the Sisters by proposing a revolutionary type of agreement to NIOC: the so-called '75-25' agreement (in contrast to the traditional 50-50). In a nutshell, the operator (ENI) would finance the venture up to the discovery of commercial oil reserves, then for exploitation it would form a fifty-fifty joint venture with NIOC and, as the venture had to pay 50% of its profits to the Iranian Government, Iran stood to reap 75% of total profits. It was an offer which NIOC could not refuse. Naturally, at the joint venture's inception, NIOC had to reimburse the operator half of his exploration outlay.

The second man with vengeance to take was the Shah of Iran. He wanted to get even with Dr Musaddiq. And even though the US ambassador had "tried to discourage the Shah from entering into this new kind of agreement [with ENI]",[35] he could not afford to reject this golden opportunity to show the NIOC technocrats and Iranians at large his own patriotism in oil affairs (and on the side make some money for himself[35A]). NIOC formulated a Petroleum Act, allowing it to enter into joint ventures with foreign companies and had it ratified by the *Majlis* on July 31, 1957. Three days later the historic '75-25' agreement was signed by NIOC and AGIP Mineraria (an ENI subsidiary) and approved by the *Majlis* on August 24, giving birth to the Société Irano-Italienne des Pétroles (SIRIP). Mattei's revolutionary idea was to be copied in Iran and throughout the world. In Iran, NIOC entered into two other '75-25' agreements in 1958, with the American Standard Oil of Indiana (AMOCO) and the Canadian oil company Sapphire (all three '75-25' agreements are summarised in Table 11.3). In 1960, SIRIP discovered oil at its Bahrigansar offshore station; the NIOC-AMOCO joint venture struck oil at its Darioush and Cyrus offshore structure; the Canadian venture proved unviable and soon folded.

Table 11.3. NIOC's First Three '75-25' Agreements

1. Société Irano-Italienne des Pétroles – SIRIP
   - Between NIOC and AGIP Mineraria (August 1957)
   - Agreement areas: (1) in Zagros mountains: 11,300 km^2
                     (2) on Makran coast: 6,000 km^2
                     (3) continental shelf: 5,600 km^2
   - Agreement period: 25 years (from start of sales), plus three possible 5 year extensions
   - Exploration period: 12 years (from effective date of October 1957)
   - Minimum exploration expenditure: $22m

2. Iran-Pan American Oil Company – IPAC
   - Between NIOC and Pan American Petroleum Corporation, a subsidiary of Standard Oil of Indiana – AMOCO (April 1958)
   - Exploration areas: two offshore areas, totalling around 25,000 km^2, in upper Persian Gulf region, off Kharg Island
   - Agreement and exploration periods: same as SIRIP, with the effective date of June 1958
   - Minimum exploration expenditure: $82m
   - Cash deposit: $25m

3. Iran-Canada Oil Company – IRCAN
   - Between NIOC and the Canadian Sapphire Company (June 1958)
   - Exploration areas: a 1,000 km^2 strip of land, partly onshore and partly offshore, on Iranian coast off the Oman Sea
   - Agreement and exploration periods: same as SIRIP

Following Mattei's '75-25' revolution of 1957, another revolutionary move would occur in 1960 in the world of oil: the creation in September at Baghdad of the Organisation of Petroleum Exporting Countries (OPEC) by Iran, Iraq, Kuwait, Saudi Arabia and Venezuela. OPEC was fathered by the far-sighted Venezuelan Oil Minister Juan Perez Alfonso and the radical Saudi minister Shaykh Âbdullah Taraki. The organisation was a defensive counter-move against the multinational oil companies' strategy of lowering the oil's 'posted price' (i.e. the price for computing the royalties paid to producer countries). In February 1959, the companies had reduced the posted price for Venezuela by between five and twenty-five US cents per barrel and for the Middle East by an average of eighteen US cents. On August 9, 1960, the companies engineered further cuts of between four and fourteen US cents per barrel without warning the producers. These cuts translated into a fiscal loss for the Middle East countries of $93m over eighteen months.[36] But the second (less obvious) reason behind the formation of OPEC was that Venezuela could not maximise (unlike the Middle East producers) its oil revenues by volume (of exports), and therefore it had to maximise by price: hence it convinced the Middle Eastern producers to form OPEC so that the organisation would push for a maximisation by price. At first, the new organisation passed unnoticed, although Perez Alfonso announced at Baghdad:

> We have formed a very exclusive club... Between us we control ninety per cent of crude exports to world markets, and we are now united. We are making history...[37]

History would indeed be made, but only a decade later.

11.3. Repression

In Iran, the era of the 1940s' *laissez-faire* was gone. In the 1950s, the United States needed law and order to enable it to carry out its reforms and its assistance programmes, so as to shape its Iranian 'clinic' as it saw fit. The people of Iran were to face strict repression, in order to allow the Americans to bring them the benefits of progress.

The first domestic group abruptly to experience the armed forces repressive mood was the students at Tehran University. In 1953/54, the university students – a small minority of some 10,000 – were mostly concentrated in Tehran University (with an enrolment of 8,300), and the rest scattered among the Isfahan Medical Faculty (later, Isfahan University) created in 1947 and the first faculties at Shiraz, Mashhad and Tabriz, established in 1949. The 1940s, and especially the Musaddiq years, had politicised the student body. Teachers and high school pupils were also attracted to street politics. But Tehran University (TU) remained the ultimate bastion of education in a country with a literacy rate of only 14.9% (33.3% in urban centres and 6.0% in rural areas.[38] Within TU, the Danishkadeh Fanni (Technical Faculty) was the faculty where the *crème de la crème* enrolled.

And Fanni was the place the army decided to strike on December 7, the day before the arrival in Tehran of the US Vice-President Richard Nixon, to make an example. From the beginning of December tension had been in the air at Tehran University. The army dispatched a contingent of its elite Janbaz Guards to bring the university under control. At Fanni the officers insulted the students and when a couple of them reacted pandemonium broke loose: soldiers around the faculty's (large) main hall opened fire.[39] Students shouted "Either death or Musaddiq!" When the smoke cleared three students lay dead, namely martyrs Mustafa Buzurgnia, Mihdi Shariât Razavi and Nasir Qandchi, some forty others were injured and twenty-seven were taken to prison by the Janbaz Guards.[40] On December 8, Nixon arrived in Tehran as scheduled; during his visit he was invited to Tehran University where he was awarded an *honoris causa* doctorate of law, adding insult to the blood spilled on December 7. War had been declared between the Shah's armed forces and the Tehran University students. The Janbaz had won the first round, but the students would never forget the cruel show of force of December 7: there was blood between the Shah and them.

Every year thereafter the first week of December would bring Tehran University and Fanni to a state of ebullition.

The next group to fall victim to the armed forces' repression was the secret *Toudeh* Officers' Organisation. To ferret out this secret entity, the Americans had chosen General Taymour Bakhtiar, Tehran's military commander, and his deputy General Shahshahani (a former air force officer), in addition to the redoubtable General Farhad Dadsitan, and a special team consisting of Colonel Muhsin Mubassir, Lieutenant Colonel Mustafa Amjadi, Major Moulavi and Captain Âmid. Having done its homework (under the direction of US anti-terrorist specialists), the special team entered action by arresting on August 12, 1954 ex-captain Abu'l Hasan Âbbasi and three other officers as they were leaving one of their hideouts with a trunk full of documents. Âbbasi, expelled from the army some years earlier for his leftist ideas, was a prize catch, as he was simultaneously a member of the secret Officers Organisation's seven-man Higher Council[40A] (and thus knew all of the secret network's group heads), the keeper of the organisation's secret list of members (compiled in a complex code of trigonometric functions kept in a green-covered booklet) and a link between the council and the *Toudeh*'s Executive Committee. Dr Joudat, the Executive Committee's member in charge of military affairs, had taken the green booklet to a safer place some ten days earlier, but on second thoughts had returned it a week later to Âbbasi – decidedly, some decisions made by *Toudeh* leaders were a boon for their enemies. Rouzbeh, informed of Âbbasi's capture, was sure that he would never divulge his secrets, and he was right to a point. Under the tortures inflicted on him by the Military Command's specialists – Colonel Ziba'i', Captain Syahatgar and Captain Zamani – Âbbasi held his tongue, but, when they threatened to bury him alive, he cracked and eventual gave Colonels Mubassir and Amjadi enough clues to enable them to decipher the trigonometric formulae. The names of 434 *Toudeh* officers were thus uncovered.[40B] On August 25 and 26, the organisation's officers on the green booklet's list were arrested; only a very few (including Rouzbeh) were able to escape the Military Command's dragnet (masterminded by American specialists).

The *Toudeh*'s second secret military network, that of the NCOs and soldiers, failed to be uncovered, due to the foresight of Lieutenant Colonel Muhammad Âli Mubashshiri of the Higher Council. Falling into the trap set in Âbbasi's hideout, Mubashshiri deceived his gaolers after a failed suicide attempt: in return for seeing his wife, he promised to tell them all he knew. They readily accepted the favourable deal, and, during his wife's visit Mubashshiri ordered her to go immediately to Khurramabad to alert Major Bahrami, the head of the Khurramabad Army's G-2, of the wave of arrests in Tehran. Mubashshiri knew that Bahrami was the sole head of the *Toudeh*'s second network of NCOs and soldiers. Informed by Mubashshiri's wife, Major Bahrami didn't hesitate: he destroyed his archives and shot himself in the head. The *Toudeh*'s second network would never be uncovered.

By the close of 1954 the *Toudeh* officers' court-martials were initiated. Seventy-four officers were sentenced to death, fifty were given life and 179 others sentenced to prison times ranging from eighteen months to fifteen years.[40C] Then the Military Command presided over its first mass execution: the first ten senior officers, including Colonel Îzzatullah Syamak, Colonel Muhammad Jalali, Lieutenant Colonel Âli Mubashshiri, Major Jâfar Vakili and Abu'l Hasan Âbbasi faced the firing squad. Public opinion was outraged. The last six officers to be executed were Suroushyan, Muhaqqiq, Mukhtari, Nasiri, Marzvan and Bihzad.[40D] That brought to a total of thirty-two the number of executed officers. The formidable pressure exercised by public opinion forced the regime into commuting the forty-two remaining death sentences into life imprisonment.

For all opposition members in Iran, the trial and execution of the *Toudeh* officers was a cataclysm. The officers had formed the *Toudeh*'s backbone. It had consisted mainly of elitist officers: educated, honest, charismatic and capable.[40E] The *Toudeh* militants were inconsolable: they had lost their legendary secret organisation. A song came out at the right time – 'Mara Bibus' (Kiss Me), the goodbye of a father to his little daughter – and people attributed the poignant lyrics to one of the *Toudeh* officers, preferably Mubashshiri. In fact the music had been composed by Majid Vafadar to lyrics written by Haydar Riqabi. Nevertheless, militants cried out their tears listening to the timely song, immortalised by the non-professional singer Hasan Gulnaraqi.

In July 1957, the *Toudeh*'s Officers' Organisation founder and mastermind Khusrou Rouzbeh was finally captured. Sentenced to death, "after having done his best to defend his life in the military tribunal",[41] Rouzbeh was executed in May 1958. Thus was the last nail driven into the *Toudeh*'s Officers' Organisation's coffin.

The next group to succumb to the Military Command's repressive fury was Navvab Safavi's *Fada'yan-i Islam*. In the coup's aftermath, Navvab had chosen a semi-clandestine status in spite of his mentor Ayatullah Kashani moving to the royalist camp – as proven by Dr Shirvin's Tehran Radio speech on *Murdad 28* and Kashani's son

(Sayyid Mustafa) and his right-hand man (Shams ul-Din Qanatabadi) being elected to the ultra-royalist Eighteenth *Majlis*. The *Fada'yan* would strike again on November 16, 1955 after years of inactivity. Their target was Premier Husayn Âla, who had taken over in April 1955 from General Zahidi, who had fulfilled his mission and could enjoy a cushioned retirement in his Montreux villa (until his death in September 1963). On November 16, 1955 at the Shah Mosque, the *Fada'i* Muzaffar Âli Zu'lqadr fired a single shot at Âla, the bullet only grazing the top of the latter's head. The shot had caused more noise than harm, but Bakhtiar's Military Command had been given a *casus belli* to move against the *Fada'yan*. Within a week the whole *Fada'yan* leadership was rounded up. On November 28 it was announced that Navvab's lieutenant Sayyid Âbd ul-Husayn Vahidi (captured at Ahvaz) had died at the Command's headquarters – not the first nor the last to face sudden death there.[42] The other prominent *Fada'yan* were court-martialled and four of them – Navvab Safavi, Sayyid Muhammad Vahidi (Âbd ul-Huusayn's younger brother), Khalil Tahmasibi and Muzaffar Âli Zu'lqadr – were sentenced to death and executed by firing squad on January 17, 1956. Lesser *Fada'yan* were sentenced to terms ranging from three to five years and Muhammad Mihdi Âbd Khuda'i, captured later, to eight years. The *Fada'yan*'s organisation had thus been crushed. But it had given the religious hierocracy, which had always looked obliquely at this ragbag group of zealous terrorists, the idea of an armed wing. Navvab's charismatic conduct had fired the imagination of more than one of Qum's younger students: in time, the *Fada'yan* would find new disciples.

In his repression drive against the nationalist, leftist and religious groups, General Bakhtiar had been greatly assisted by "Captain J.J. Leonard, a veteran of the Chicago police force who had served as a counter-intelligence chief in Hawaii and then Korea, [and who had, in the cadre of Iran's Military Command] assembled and trained a staff in the use of FBI techniques for penetrating civilian subversive organisations".[43] The Military Command, however, being part of the military, was a bridging measure. What was needed was a special organisation for the upkeep of internal security.

The *Sazman-i Amniyyat va Ittilaât-i Kishvar* (National Organisation for Security and Information) better known by its acronym of SAVAK, was created in 1956 as part of the Prime Minister's Office, and the reliable General Bakhtiar was naturally placed at its head. "The CIA created SAVAK, the Iranian police force [*sic*]" said William Colby, a veteran of the OSS and CIA director (1973-1976), in a speech in 1978, "and taught it proper methods of intelligence".[44] With quasi-unlimited assistance from the CIA and the discreet help of Israel's secret service agency Mossad, SAVAK was shaped within five years into an efficient instrument for institutionalised repression. Advised by international experts, SAVAK soon made inroads into all domestic organisations, placing its agents in crucial positions. It had also begun making inroads in the minds of Iranians (with a carefully planned propaganda scheme to persuade Iranians that SAVAK knew all, saw all and controlled all) and had succeeded in instilling a new dimension to Iranian life: the constant fear of SAVAK. A state within the state was in the making.

The problem was that it was Bakhtiar's preserve, the general being smart enough to recruit his very own men. By the late 1950s, Bakhtiar held Iran's top power position. At any time he could have attempted a coup against the Shah, if given the green light by the CIA[45] (and he could also have done it without American approval, presenting the CIA with a *fait accompli*). But Bakhtiar had come to think erroneously (like so many before and after him) that he was indispensable and could bide his time. He would find out the reality in March 1961, as national dynamics required a softer SAVAK image, and he was given his marching orders to a golden exile in Switzerland (like Zahihdi), to be replaced by the intellectual General Hasan Pakravan. The Shah was careful to place his close friend General Fardoust as Pakravan's deputy, so as to be able to recover for his own ends this precious organisation which had been so closely identified with Bakhtiar.

11.4. Point Four

The clinic the Americans were trying to set up in Iran could not be all repression, especially since the Americans believed in the 'stick and carrot' approach. As well as the Military Command and the SAVAK 'sticks', there had to be a 'carrot' of American assistance packages and reform programmes. US decision-makers knew very well how to wield the sticks, but were far less adept at throwing carrots. The Americans' first problem was that they knew little about the country; their second problem was that they would not admit it, and their third problem was that they nevertheless forged ahead. During their brief intercourse with Iranians, their main representatives had learned about it, but their views on her future needs were not necessarily concordant. Justice Douglas, for example, had come back from two trips to Asia and Iran a declared foe of "greedy landlords who have nightmares when they think of bringing schools and first aid centres to the villages"[46] and a staunch supporter of reform: "Land reform above all else is the starting point for launching the counter-revolution against communism".[47] Others, such as press attaché T. Cuyler Young (later a professor at Princeton), with his direct exposure to the Azarbayjani events of 1945/46, proposed generous assistance and extensive reforms so as to cut the grass from under the communists' feet;[48] he had, however, warned that the "landed and mercantile classes" and the "conservative clerics" might actually sabotage the entire US effort, "perceiving it as a threat to their privileges". Some perspicacious American diplomats, such as Richard Cottam and Dr Taylor Gurney, had begun to understand some of the internal workings of Iran's Byzantine polity, and had reported their findings to Washington.

In America itself, meetings, seminars and conferences were being held to discuss the Middle East and Iran so that academics and the Establishment could be educated about her problems. The organisers of a conference on the Near East held at Harvard University in August 1950 invited Sir Hamilton (H.A.R.) Gibb to speak, the eminent don of Oxford's School of Oriental Studies, who had formed a whole generation of British Orientalists (among others, Professor Lambton). At the conference, Professor Gibb attempted to educate his select American audience on ways of properly playing its hand in the Middle East:

> ...the problems of the Near East, and an adequate and accurate knowledge about them, are more vital to the United States than most Americans realise...[49]
>
> I do wish to emphasise... that the whole problem of a cultural program is to establish mutuality. Mutuality does not mean necessarily that you and the other man completely agree on each and every subject. It means

that you understand, sympathise with, and comprehend the other man's problems and attitudes from the inside, and that he understands your problems and attitude from the inside also...[50]

...I do not think it has yet got across in Western Europe, and certainly not in Asia, that what the American Government and the American people are trying to do is serve not their own interests pure and simple, but to serve the interests of the peoples who are benefiting by the immense effort they are making. The suspicion that prevents this from getting across is, I think, due to the fact that they are not associated with democracy as a body of ideas which aims to serve the interests of the world, but interpreted as the action of a country with a particular form of democratic government which is interested in securing, first and foremost, its own political objectives...[51]

Was Professor Gibb's select audience listening?

In any event, Americans had money and they were extremely generous to Iran during the 1950s. After the $45m emergency loan granted in September 1953 by President Eisenhower, more loans, grants and aids were forthcoming. For example, total US aid to Iran in 1955 amounted to $128m. This aid can be compared to total Iranian imports during 1955 worth Rls10,896m (equal to $144m) and to Iran's oil revenues (1955) of $90m. US financial assistance flowed into Iran during the second half of the 1950s and the first half of the 1960s, until December 1965, when Iran was declared to be a 'developed country' not in need of financial assistance[52] (by then oil revenues were sufficient to keep Iran afloat). Over the post-war period until June 1963, the US poured $1,416m into Iran,[53] subdivided into $632m in military aid (exclusive of the $53m-worth of US military stock excesses) channelled through the American ARMISH-MAAG[54] command in Tehran, and $784m in technical and economic assistance.

In 1953, the US had a ready vehicle for technical assistance to Iran: the 'Point Four' programme.[55] The American technical assistance programme was, in the words of its director W.E. Warne, "conceived as a continuous rope pulling that country forward".[56]

According to an Iranian Point Four manager, the programme had three major objectives:[57]
   1) to contain the *Toudeh* Party's progress;
   2) to help the Iranian Government achieve a quick increase in its national income;
   3) to help alleviate misery among the Iranian masses.
In order to achieve its aims, Point Four had established ten technical co-operation centres in major Iranian towns: namely at Tehran, Isfahan, Tabriz, Mashhad, Shiraz, Ahvaz, Rasht, Kerman, Kermanshah and Babulsar. American experts were generously distributed among these centres, with a total of 114 US nationals manning them in 1952.[58] Dozens of local staff were hired to support the expatriate management; these local hands might well have been the main beneficiaries of the programme,[59] as many of them unscrupulously took advantage of American inexperience and made fortunes for themselves. "Too many advisers may be as harmful as too few", Sir Reader Bullard wrote, "to judge by the effects of the effects of the overstaffed Point Four programme".[60]

Point Four was highly instructive for the Americans in getting to know Iran. Some were amazed by the Iranians' ways: "It is remarkable what they can do with what they have got"; another became doubtful about the mission: "I find a universal belief that though hundreds of millions of dollars have been spent on the program of this mission, virtually nothing has been accomplished except furthering the wealth and interests of the so-called 'thousand families of Iran'"[61] while a third came to grips with realities: "We Americans out here are amateurs, rank amateurs...".[62] In this process, though, they also became acquainted with a number of young Iranian technocrats on whom they could count – besides Ardashir Zahidi, prominent were the Amuzigar brothers, Jamshid and Jahangir; with the former as Point Four's chief sanitary engineer, and also:
   - Abu'l Qasim Raji, Warne's close friend and the Plan Organisation's deputy managing director;
   - Engineer Khalil Taliqani, Point Four's chief interpreter and Minister of Agriculture under Dr Musaddiq; later became Iran's hydraulics tsar, fronting for the US firm of Justin and Courtney;
   - Dr Muhammad Muqaddam, educated at Princeton, professor at Tehran University, adviser to Point Four.

It required a great deal of temerity for Point Four managers to attack grass roots problems existing at the Iranian village level. There were some 60,000 villages, scattered across the Iranian landscape, with disastrous conditions in almost every respect: agriculture, hygiene, education and sanitation. The Rural Improvement Program (RIP) was devised by Point Four to try and remedy these myriad ills. Under the direction of Dr Franklin Harris, the RIP began its projects: the fight against typhoid; the control of insect pests and plant diseases; the control of locusts (six planes for spraying insecticide were brought in); the poultry improvement programme (thousands of American hens were imported); the construction of community centres and training of domestic hands completed the picture. And not to forget the most spectacular of the RIP's projects: the DDT spraying of thousands of Iranian villages, with huge red markings (still to be seen) recording the date of the spraying on the villages' mud walls. All in all, Point Four was undoubtedly pioneering in Iranian villages. If some of the methods it used were not suitable for Iran, it is undeniable that they achieved something: Iran's sleeping giant, its long-forgotten peasantry, had been given its first fillip.

Next to the RIP, Point Four had taken on more than it could possibly handle. "The Americans wanted too much progress, too fast, too efficiently",[63] forgetting sometimes that they were in Iran, where things usually advance at a snail's pace, if at all. Of a total of 162 projects, Point Four eventually completed roughly half. Besides the RIP, the programme addressed itself to some of the industrial projects included in the First Iranian Seven Year Plan which had not implemented due to a lack of funds:

– cement plants (completion of Fars, expansion of Ray plant);
– sugar factories (three: at Fasa, Chinaran and Kerman);
– canning factory (near Bandar Âbbas);
– cotton mill (expansion of Tehran's Chit Sazi);
– dams (at Karkheh (Khuzistan) and at Gulpaygan; plus the Kouhrang irrigation tunnel);
– deep water wells (some twenty such wells were drilled).

In the wake of Point Four, philanthropic American organisations had opened windows into Iran:

> The Ford Foundation, in addition to sponsoring the Harvard Advisory Group, supported Franklin

> Publications in its task of publishing reference books, assisted the National Teachers' College for training librarians, helped the Shiraz Agricultural College and Nezamee [Namazi] Vocational School, had an active program for integrated rural development, and provided individual scholarships for study abroad. The Near East Foundation ...was offering technical aid to the Khuzistan Development Authority, the University of Ahwaz and a few other minor agencies. The Rockefeller Foundation was assisting the Shiraz Medical School. CARE was supplying food, tools and equipment to Iranian rural areas. The American Friends of the Middle East helped Iran with a library of professional periodicals, and guided Iranian students in their choice of schools in the US. The Oil Consortium had a contract with Lafayette College to man a Technical Institute of Petroleum Studies [AIT] at Abadan...[64]

Furthermore a score of United Nations agencies, including UNTA, UNESCO (United Nations Educational, Scientific and Cultural Organisation), ILO (International Labour Organisation), WHO (World Health Organisation) and IAEA (International Atomic Energy Agency), were financing independent projects in Iran; over the period 1958–1964 they allocated around $2m for their Iranian undertakings. In the execution of Point Four there had been much genuine goodwill on the Americans' part. However, at the Iranian end many looked on the programme as "pure propaganda".[65] One of the reasons behind local misgivings was that:

> ...few phenomena are more unsettling than masses of energetic and high-minded Americans intent on doing good...[66]

At the Iranian-American interface there was tremendous friction, which led to sparks. The first spark occurred at Shiraz on March 16, 1953, as mobs attacked Point Four offices in Shiraz; the mission head, E.C. Bryant, and his colleagues were lucky that Qashqa'i tribesmen came to their rescue and gave them asylum in their Bagh-i Iram garden, saving their lives. In March 1957, in yet another incident, Kerman's Point Four mission head, Caroll, was shot dead by Balouchistani leader Dadshah and his men. For the next two years special army and Gendarmerie forces pursued Dadshah and his small guerrilla force, without being able to subdue them. Finally, in early 1959, Dadshah and his lieutenant, Ghulam Razmi, were lured into an ambush by Balouchi politicians (who had sworn not to harm them) and cold-bloodedly murdered, thus bringing to an end Dadshah's mini-insurrection.

Point Four and other American assistance programmes filled the gap between revenues and demand during the mid-1950s. They also paved the way, especially with RIP, for future land reforms. However, the Americans' frontal attack on Iran's most pressing problems was not a viable solution, as it fostered undesired side-effects and led to dangerous imbalances. All in all, the Americans had shown that they still had a lot to learn about Iran: the first lesson they had received was that it was in no way comparable to their own Far West – it was not an almost uninhabited virgin land.

11.5. Development Plans

Iran's First Seven Year Plan (1949-1955) had fallen victim to American unwillingness to finance it. Planning was later totally eclipsed by oil nationalisation problems. In 1952, the technocrats of the Plan Organisation had nevertheless revised the First Plan's total budget from the initial Rls21bn to Rls26.3bn, showing once again how ill-prepared they were for this elitist occupation (and foreshadowing their loss of elite status a year later). Of the total predicted budget only a fifth, or Rls5.1bn, was finally invested in actual projects (for details see Table 11.4.). Among the star projects stood the Tehran potable water network, completed in October 1955 by the British firm of Alexander Gibb.

By 1954, the new US-backed regime needed planning not only to boost the economy but also for more fundamental reasons. As Professor Vatikiotis argued:

> Planning in many under-developed states helps to legitimise ...the attainment of power by force... the

problems of direction and control are crucial, since what the ruling elite seeks is loyalty to a regime whose legitimacy is in question... Planning becomes one of the means, if not the chief instrument, of social control...[68]

There was the need, the will and the Plan Organisation created in 1949. It only remained to find a capable managing director. The Americans found the mercurial Abu'l Hasan Ibtihaj and enthroned him as Iran's planning tsar in September 1954. A banker by profession, Ibtihaj had first been director of the Bank-i Milli (1943–50), then, after a short stint as ambassador to Paris, he had become an assistant to the IMF's managing director (1952) before heading the Fund's Middle East Department in 1953. IBRD chairman Eugene Black, "the Banker to the World", had said of Ibtihaj: "A dedicated, enthusiastic man. He is a live wire. He is a difficult fellow. He makes a lot of enemies".[69]

The energetic Ibtihaj lost no time in putting his stamp on the Plan Organisation (PO). He paid lip-service to the seven-man Higher Planning Council (a sinecure for political appointees) and the six-man Supervisory Board (another sinecure). He set up a Technical Bureau, placed Hector Prud'homme of the IBRD (who had headed its first mission to Iran in 1952) at its head and filled half of it with expatriate experts and the other half with Iranian graduates fresh from US universities. A Division for Economic Affairs was created to evaluate the feasibility of potential projects. Under Ibtihaj the PO became a closed, elitist organisation, independent of mainstream government institutions – and thus prone to envy from the public sector, which loathed exceptions to its rules. Ibtihaj and his team came up in 1955 with an initial blueprint for the Second Seven Year Plan (1956–1962). The plan called for a total investment of Rls70bn, while addressing the completion of some First Plan projects and making an effort in social affairs. It further presented two major priorities: transportation – roads and railways – and water resources – dams and irrigation– (see Table 11.6). Approved by the *Majlis* in March 1956, the plan promptly got underway with timely loans from the IMF ($17.5m) and the IBRD ($75m). The plan's initial take-off was so rapid that expenditures surpassed initial projections and the total plan envelope had to be revised upwards by 20% from Rls70bn to Rls84bn (and

Table 11.4. Synopsis of Iran's First Seven Year Development Plan (1949–1955).[67]
(All figures in Rls billions)

First Plan revenues (initial forecast 1949)

1) Oil revenues	7.8
2) Sales of government assets	1.0
3) Loan (Bank-i Milli)	4.5
4) Loan (IBRD)	6.7
Total	21.0

First Plan expenditure

	Initial Plan (1949)	Revised Plan (1952)	Final spending (1955)
Agriculture	5.3	7.3	1.0
Infrastructure and Communications	5.7	7.7	1.5
Industry and Mines	3.0	4.3	1.2
Iranian Oil Co. (capital)	1.0	1.0	1.2
Social affairs	6.0	6.0	0.2
Total	21.0	26.3	5.1

rearranged as shown in Table 11.5). The plan was nothing more than a series of projects, executed in four standard phases, as in the days of Reza Shah: (1) an Iranian project team was formed; (2) the team chose the foreign technology, the foreign consultant and the foreign contractor (usually from guidelines dictated from higher up); (3) machinery and equipment were purchased from abroad, while local civil engineering firms prepared the site; and (4) the manufacturing facilities were erected by the main contractor (and his sub-contractors), before being started up and handed over to the Iranians for operation and maintenance. For the Iranians, the process was 'effortless' as the foreigners did most of the work. The problem with this type of development is that it translates into almost no indigenous progress. As for the foreigners, the Second Plan saw the US, West Germany and Great Britain take the lion's share of the projects, with France, Holland, Japan, Italy and Denmark taking the rest.

The major achievements of the Second Plan can be summarised as follows:

1) Agriculture and Irrigation
- Of the Rls23.5bn invested in this sector, some three-fourths, or roughly Rls18bn, was spent on five dams.
- Two smaller dams dating back to the First Plan were completed, namely the six metre high Karkheh Dam and the fifty-one metre high Gulpaygan earth dam).
    - Three larger concrete dams were built: i) the Karaj Dam was erected by the American firms of Hazra and Morrison-Knudsen to a height of 185 metres, and was completed in 1961 at a cost of $64m. It was designed to provide Tehran with 400 million m^3 of water annually, to irrigate 20,000 hectares of land and yield 75 MW of hydropower; ii) the Sifidroud Dam was constructed at Manjil by a French Consortium(SASER) led by Campenon-Bernard, and reached 106 metres in height. It was inaugurated in 1961, cost a total of $60m, and was designed for the irrigation of 240,000 hectares of prime land and the production of 87.5 MW of electricity; iii) the Diz Dam was built over a Karoun tributary, towered 203 metres above the ground, and provided water for 120,000 hectares of land with a total capacity of 520 MW (eight generators, installed step by step between 1962 and 1971) costing $94m (see details in Table 11.6.) and was started up in 1962.

Table 11.5. Synopsis of Iran's Second Seven Year Development Plan (1956–1962).[70]
(All figures in Rls billions)

Second Plan Projects: Initial Plan (1955)

	Completion of First Plan Allocation	Second Plan Projects	Total Plan Projects
Agriculture & Irrigation	6.2	12.0	18.2
Infrastructure & Communications	5.4	17.4	22.8
Industry & Mines	2.8	7.8	10.6
Social Affairs	2.8	15.6	18.4
Total	17.2	52.8	70.0

Revised Second Plan (1958) and Results

	Revised Plan Initial	Revised Plan Rearranged	Final Plan Realisations
Agriculture & Irrigation	21.8	25.1	23.5
Infrastructure and Communications	27.4	34.0	30.0
Industry & Mines	12.7	9.4	8.8
Social Affairs	22.1	15.5	13.0
Total	84.0	84.0	75.3

Second Plan: revenues and expenditures

Revenues		Expenditures	
Oil revenues	61.0	Projects (see above)	75.3
Loans (foreign)	25.7	Loan repayments	7.6
Advances from Bank-i Markaz	3.7	Loan interest	3.7
Miscellaneous	4.2	Miscellaneous	2.2
		Reported to 3rd Plan	2.7
Total	94.5	Total	94.5

2) Infrastructures and Communications
- Roads and railways received top priority in this sector. Of the Rls30bn invested, 18bn was spent on roads and 5bn on railways.
- Roads: some 2,000 kilometres of asphalted roads were laid, with the major 1,181 kilometres north–south axis linking Bandar Pahlavi to Khurramshahr completed; and 3,500 kilometres of first- and second-class roads drawn.
- Railways: the Tehran–Mashhad line was inaugurated in 1957 (ten years after initiation), and the Tehran–Tabriz line finished in 1958.
- Tehran's Mihrabad Airport was expanded and refurbished; provincial airports were modernised, with special attention given to Abadan, Isfahan and Shiraz.
- The ports of Bandar-i Pahlavi (north) and Bandar-i Shahpour and Khurramshahr (south) received some funds.
- A modern communications system with exchanges for 180,000 automatic telephones was installed.

3) Industries and Mines
- The three types of industry launched under Reza Shah (i.e. cement, sugar and textiles) were given priority: of the Rls9bn spent, they received 80%.

- Six new cement factories were built, boosting cement production capacity from 82,000 (for the two existing plants) to 1,200,000 tonnes per annum.
- Three new sugar factories were implemented, two using sugarbeet and the third, at Haft Tappeh (in Khuzistan), using sugar cane (see Table 11.5).
- Four public textile factories, three in the northern provinces and one at Tehran, were expanded and modernised.
- Mines were only allocated 1% of total funds.

4) Social Affairs
- Highest priority was given to urban services, which accounted for over half the Rls13bn invested. The electrification of 167 urban centres, a potable water network in 172 centres and inner roads in 73 provincial towns were the main results achieved.
- The second priority was given to health and hygiene (where much needed to be done), with the construction of new hospitals, dispensaries, nursing schools and training centres. The DDT sprayings initiated by Point Four were extended to the whole country.
- In the field of electricity generation, Iran had by the end of the Second Plan an installed capacity of 440 MW (inclusive of 295 MW hydropower from the three dams and 50 MW from the Tarasht plant built by the French company Alsthom).
- Schools and high schools were built and a new university was established at Tehran (the Tehran Polytechnic – today, Amir Kabir University), set up by Engineer Habibullah Nafisi and a team of Belgian and Iranian professors.
- In 1956, the first national census was carried out (with the help of IBM machines): Iran was said to have 18,954,704 inhabitants.

The adventures of David E. Lilienthal and Gordon R. Clapp and of their Development and Resources Corporation (set up with $10,000 in 1955 in association with Lazard Freres of New York) are a salient feature of the Second Plan. The major event was the battle for the future of Khuzistan, Iran's oil province and also its most promising area.

Both former TVA (Tennessee Valley Authority) chairmen, Lilienthal and Clapp were invited to Tehran by Ibtihaj (after a first meeting in Istanbul in September 1955) to propose specific projects to be included in the Second Plan. The two experts also went to meet the Shah, who became highly interested on DRC's ideas on the development of Khuzistan. He ordered the creation of a seven-man commission to review DRC's proposals: the Preparatory Commission for the Khuzistan Region Development. Lilienthal and Clapp had a grand vision for Khuzistan: dams for hydropower and irrigation; agri-industrial projects on its flat and fertile lands; hundreds of thousands of tonnes of sugar being produced from sugar cane; huge fertiliser and petrochemical plants fed on the natural gas being flared downstream on all the crude oil production units. In other words, a mammoth TVA for Khuzistan. At the outset, though, there had to be the dams to provide water and power: a total of fourteen were proposed, with seven on the Karoun itself, two on the Diz, three on the Karkheh, one on the Maroun and the last one on the Zuhreh. The fourteen dams would have a total hydroelectric capacity of 6,600 MW.

Both the Shah and Ibtihaj were enthusiastic about DRC's vision. They gave DRC the green light to go ahead with the first phase, which consisted of the construction of the Diz Dam, a sugar cane project with a sugar refinery, a fertiliser unit and a petrochemical plant. In summer 1957, the Plan Organisation and DRC set up their subsidiaries in Khuzistan: respectively, the Khuzistan Electric and Gas Energy Company (KEGEC) and the Khuzistan Development Services (KDS). DRC cut a few corners to accelerate the projects' advancement (see major projects in Table 11.6.). One corner was at the IBRD, which had balked at providing a $42m loan for Iran's Diz Dam and finally agreed, after Lilienthal's personal pitch to Black and the spelling out in the loan contract that "DRC [not the Government of Iran] is responsible for the planning, execution and initial operation for this program which includes, besides the Dez project, a sugar cane plantation, mill and refinery near Haft Tappeh, and an electrical line from Abadan to Ahvaz". The second corner to be cut came with the inviting of the Italian company Montecatini (which had previous experience in south Iran[72]) to survey the gas potential around Ahvaz and propose chemical plants downstream thereof. Montecatini gave the fertiliser file to the Belgian L'Union Chimique Belge S.A. (UCB), which, in March 1957, came up with a proposal for a complex producing urea (102 tonnes/day) and ammonium sulphate (150 tonnes/day) for either Ahvaz or Abadan, with an investment of between $17m and $19m (UCB had estimated Iran's imports of fertilisers at 2,050 tonnes for 1956). As for the petrochemical plants, Montecatini proposed a small caustic/chlorine unit and a PVC unit (capacity of 4,000 tonnes/annum). The project's only hitch was the natural gas feedstock: it was the consortium's property, and neither the PO's or DRC's to allocate.

Table 11.6. Summary of DRC's activities in Iran (1956–1961).[71]

1) Total DRC staff at peak: 1,345 people
of whom   45 in New York
           1,300 in Khuzistan: 100 expatriates
                       1,200 Iranians

2) DRC's accounts (1957–61):
Received from Plan Organisation: $ 111,623,655
Expenditures incurred on projects: $ 102,732,468
(of which DRC's fees $ 933,750)

3) Major projects supervised directly by DRC, with capital investment and main contractor:
- Diz Dam: $33m; Impresit-Girola-Lodigiani, Italy; consulting engineer: Georgia Inst. of Technology, US.
- Diz Dam approach roads and tunnels,: $8.3m; Morrison-Knudsen, US
- Diz Dam power generation: $3.5m; Siemens, W. Germany, Hitachi, Japan, GE, Canada
- High voltage power line Ahvaz-Abadan: $4m; SAE, Italy
- Sugarcane project: $21.4m; R.M. Parsons and C. Brewer, US
- Sugar mill and refinery: $14.3m; Gebr. Stork and Werkspoor N.V., Holland, with a 300,000 tonnes/annum mill and a 30,000 tonnes/annum refinery

4) Final total investment estimated at $155m, including the IBRD loan of $42m secured for the Diz Dam project by DRC

From the outset, the Consortium had not appreciated the DRC's encroachments on its Khuzistan *châsse gardée* – and this Ibtihaj had known from the beginning because he had been behind a similar (albeit smaller scheme) in 1946 and had been told then by the oil company that his "scheme did not suit the AIOC's book".[72A] Now Lilienthal and Clapp wanted the Consortium to surrender its gas resources so that they could produce fertilisers and petrochemicals! There were limits to the oil companies' patience and the DRC had clearly ridden rough-shod over these. The Consortium refused categorically to lease its gas for the DRC projects. Montecatini and UCB left Iran empty-handed. The mainstream bureaucracy came in with its own fertiliser project proposed by the Ministry of Industry: a $34m complex based on a sizeable ammonia unit (100 tonnes/day) to be built by the French ENSA (Empain Schneider) group, to be located near Shiraz (out of the consortium's area) and fed on associated gas from the Gachsaran oil field. The Consortium readily accepted to allocate the necessary gas (the project being outside Khuzistan) and the project was included in the Second Plan, eventually being inaugurated in 1962 as the first Iranian fertiliser complex. The caustic/chlorine unit (which needed no gas, only salt), with a capacity of 2,800/2,500 tonnes/annum, was built near Abadan by the Pazargad Company, set up by the Farmanfarmayan family. After heavy initial losses, the Farmanfarmayans were bailed out by NIOC, which took a commanding 66.6% share in the Pazargad plant (an almost unique case of NIOC bailing out a private outfit). That was how two of the three remaining DRC projects were implemented without its participation.

In the wake of its success with the fertiliser complex, the main bureaucracy launched its frontal attack on the PO. In February 1959, the *Majlis* voted down Ibtihaj's full powers and placed the PO under the Prime Minister's Office, with a deputy prime minister at its head. Ibtihaj resigned and was replaced by Engineer Khusrou Hidayat. DRC's actions and accounts came under close scrutiny. PO asked DRC to cut back on the profits it was asking for work done in Iran, and, after long negotiations, Lilienthal agreed to a reduction, only to have PO officials accusing him of making excessive profits. The whole DRC operation came into question, leading to a scandal that Engineer Hidayat did his best to conceal. Hidayat's successor as head of PO in February 1961, Ahmad Aramish,[73] had the file reopened and publicly accused Ibtihaj and DRC of misappropriations, bringing about a legal case against Ibtihaj, who spent seven months in prison (November 1961–June 1962). Later Ibtihaj got his revenge – it was Aramish's turn to spend seven years in jail, while Ibtihaj was making millions in private banking. The DRC case was the subject of a hearing in the US Senate in 1962, which ended with the case being shelved. Lilienthal remained a friend and adviser to the Shah.

The first sugar came out of the Haft Tappeh Refinery in 1961. Inaugurated in 1962, the Diz Dam was subsequently renamed the Muhammad Reza Shah Dam. The PO also renamed its Khuzistan Electricity and Gas Energy Company (KEGEC) the Khuzistan Water and Power Authority (KWPA). The vision of Lilienthal and Clapp had partially seen daylight. Oil, however, still dominated Iran's south-western province.

11.6. Iranian Capitalism

One of the major beneficiaries of the US policy of bringing Iran into international finance's orbit was the Iranian private sector. During the Second Plan, the authorities bent over backwards to attract foreign and domestic capital to all branches of the economy, especially banking and industry.

In order to encourage foreign investors the Law for the Attraction and Protection of Foreign Investment in Iran was approved by the *Majlis* in November 1955 and the Regulations thereof in September 1956. These legal incentives created the most propitious framework international capital could hope to find in a developing country: capital was readily transferable; there was no limit on profits' repatriation; government protection was guaranteed; private companies were assured the same treatment as that given public companies; in the event of expropriation, foreign capital was guaranteed fair compensation, and the right of appeal to Iranian courts. Between 1957 and 1961 some $8m of private foreign funds found its way into banking and industry, most of it in the form of joint ventures, with American firms dominating, since the American Government had, in 1957, taken the unusual step of guaranteeing investments made in Iran.

Domestic entrepreneurs were given all facilities required: from the initial capital down to government protection. Possibilities for producing goods to replace imported items were practically unlimited. All that was required was a minuscule seed capital to secure soft loans from a buoyant banking system. Land was readily available at bargain prices off the Tehran-Karaj road. Technology and equipment were easily purchasable from anywhere in the world. Manpower was in oversupply. Effortless and riskless capitalism was the name of the game in the Iran of the late 1950s. Many would become extremely wealthy by seizing the occasion at the right time.

The greatest winners were those who entered private banking. The first private Iranian bank was set up in 1949 by the crafty Tehran *Bazaar* money changer Mustafa Tajaddud, who broke the rules and (almost illegally) launched his Bank-i Bazargani-i Iran (the Commercial Bank of Iran). In the wake of Tajaddud's pioneering efforts, five other private banks were created in 1952: the Bank-i Tehran, Bank-i Pars, Bank-i Sadirat-i Iran (the Export Bank of Iran), Bank-i Bimeh Bazarganan (the Merchants' Insurance Bank) and the Bank-î Umran (the Development Bank), with the latter being the Pahlavi Estates' banking arm. In 1955 a Banking Law was ratified to regulate private banks' activities and a public Banking Control Council set up as a watchdog.

In 1956, the PO set up its own bank, the Bank-i Îtibarat-i Sanâti (the Industrial Credit Bank), with an initial capital of Rls600m (later increased to 900m), and handed out a total of 110 industrial loans to the amount of Rls880m to entrepreneurs over the Second Plan period.[74] In May 1957, it was Bank-i Milli's turn to enter the soft loans market, when according to the Note Cover Amendment Act – re-evaluating the gold and foreign exchanges held by Bank-i Milli from the previous rate of 1$ = 32.25Rls to the new (February 1955) rate of 1$ = 75.75Rls – it placed the accruing difference of Rls3,609m in the market. Also in 1957, the first foreign banks entered the Iranian banking system as the French banks of Banque de Paris et des Pays-Bas (later Paribas) and the Banque Ottomane purchased a 30.3% share in Bank-i Tehran's capital.

The years 1958 and 1959 were exceptional for Iranian private banking: twelve new banks were established, six in each year. In 1958, three of them benefited from foreign participation: (1) Bank-i Îtibarat-i Iran (the Credit Bank of Iran), with Crédit Lyonnais (35%);

(2) Bank-i Iran va Ingilis (the Iranian-British Bank), with the Standard Chartered Banking Group (35%); (3) Bank-i Tijarat-i Khariji-i Iran (the Foreign Trade Bank of Iran), with American, German and Italian banks (40%); the other three were all-Iranian banks: (4) Bank-i Kar (the Work Bank); (5) Bank-i Asnaf-i Iran (the Iranian Guilds' Bank), later renamed Bank-i Iranshahr; (6) Bank-i Bimeh-yi Iran (the Insurance Bank of Iran). In 1959, of the six new banks, five had foreign shareholdings: (7) Bank-i Iranva Khavar Myaneh (the Bank of Iran and the Middle East), with the British Bank of the Middle East – formerly IBP – (35%); (8) Bank-i Iranian (the Iranians' Bank), with the American Citibank (35%); (9) Bank-i Tijarat-i Iran va Hulland (Mercantile Bank of Iran and Holland), with the Dutch Algemene Bank (35%); (10) Bank-i Baynulmillali Iran va Zhapun (International Bank of Iran and Japan), with a Japanese bank group (31.5%) including the Bank of Tokyo (9%); (11) Bank-i Tousiêh-i Sanâti va Madani-i Iran (Industrial and Mining Bank of Iran – IMDBI), with twenty Western institutions, led by the American Lazard Freres and Chase Manhattan; and the last bank was set up with Iranian capital: (12) Bank-i Îtibarat-i Taâvuni Touzî (the Distributors' Co-operative Credit Bank), owned by the Rashidian brothers (of *Murdad 28* fame) and their acolytes.

Finally in 1960, Iran's central bank, the Bank-i Markazi-i Iran, was created and Bank-i Milli-i Iran, which had hitherto acted as central banker, transferred all its non-commercial activities to the new outfit, in order to concentrate on its commercial affairs.

In Iran's new banking world a number of individuals were to make a name for themselves. First were the brothers Muhammad Âli and Riza Mufarrah who managed the formidable expansion of the Bank-i Sadirat-i Iran from scratch to the second place in Iran after the Bank-i Milli in capital, revenues and profits, and to the top spot for the number of branches countrywide. Next to the Mufarrahs came Abu'l Hasan Ibtihaj, the man behind the Bank-i Iranian after his PO resignation; Mustafa Fatih, the managing director of Bank-i Tehran after years as the AIOC's Iranian factotum; Abu'l Qasim Khiradjou, the tsar of IMDBI (one of the best managed outfits in Iranian banking); Houshang Ram, the guardian of the Pahlavi safe at Bank-i Ûmran; the millionaire Muhammad Ibrahim Nikpour at Bank-i Pars and Yusuf Khwushkish, the immovable governor at Bank-i Milli since 1961.

Another group benefiting from the economic boom of the late 1950s was the Tehran *Bazaar*. In line with their traditions, *Bazaar* gnomes were shy of boasting and kept to their usual low profile. But there was little to hide as the numbers spoke for themselves. From a low of Rls5.3bn in 1953, Iranian imports had doubled to Rls10.9bn in 1955, and increased every year thereafter, soaring to a record-breaking Rls52.6bn in 1960.[75] During these seven years of 'fat cows', the *Bazaar* found time to add a few layers of fat and fill its hidden stores to saturation. It also found the time to strengthen its grip on the provincial *bazaars* and on its networks of Tehran retailers, letting every downstream merchant, trader and dealer know that the Tehran *Bazaar* was the heart of the system and woe to anyone who thought of bypassing it: the Tehran gnomes would boycott him.

As private investment boomed nationwide, the Total Fixed Capital Investment jumped from a respectable Rls10bn in 1955 to 23.3bn and 30.5bn in 1958 and 1959 respectively.[76] Some of the *Bazaar* people were lured out of their traditional ways by these fabulous profits and fresh opportunities. The stronghold of this new breed of *Bazaaris* was the Tehran Chamber of Commerce (TCC). Its president from 1931 until 1955 was the super-rich Âbd ul-Husayn Nikpour (1894–1968), who was replaced by the phenomenal Âli Vakili (1892–1964), a legend in his own time[77] and the main Iranian distributor of foreign films. Next to Vakili in the TCC were the following prominent businessmen: the brothers Akbar and Muhammad Khusroushahi (the latter becoming the TCC's president upon Vakili's death); Âli Akbar Mahlouji; Muhammad Mihdi Lari; Ali Muhammad Bunakdarpour; Hasan and Kazim Kurous; Abu'l Qasim Lajivardi; Husayn Qasimiyyeh; Muhammad Qurayshi; and the trio of car importers Ahmad Soudavar, Sulayman Vahabzadeh and Jâfar Akhavan.

The demarcation line between the old breed of Tehran *Bazaar* importers and the new breed of industrialists soon became blurred as the former group diverted part of its momentous profits into industrial ventures. Ever-larger numbers of individuals jumped on the industrial bandwagon. Five large groups were to bloom in the 1950s' wave, later to be known as the 'First Wave' of private industrialisation:

(1) The Sabit Pasal group, founded in 1948 by a twenty-eight year old Jewish technician, Habib Sabit (the S in Pasal), in association with a forty-four year old engineer from an old Tabriz merchant family,

Âli Asghar Panahi (the P of Pasal), and a forty year old lawyer, Muhsin Lak (the L of Pasal).

Sabit, who had done business in the US during the war, set up an Iranian empire of importation, industrial and distribution units. Its major activities consisted of importing Volkswagen cars, bottling Pepsi-Cola (Zamzam Co.), operating the first Iranian TV channel (since October 1958), and representing a myriad US multinationals: RCA, Rockwell, Union Carbide, Johnson and Johnson, etc. It also had a hand in banking (the Bank of Iran and the Middle East); and would later (in the sixties) join the US General Tire Co. in producing tyres, and manufacture motor oils in co-operation with Esso.

(2) The Bihshahr Industrial Group (BIG), managed by the Lajivardi family, brothers Abu'l Qasim and Ahmad, and cousin Akbar Lajivardiian. From their native Kashan, the family branched out to Bihshahr (Mazandaran) in the 1940s. Their small cotton ginning factory soon developed into an industrial complex producing soaps, chemicals, detergents, vegetable oil, draperies, cardboard and poultry feed. In the 1960s, BIG built a similar complex near Tehran, while simultaneously branching out into new ventures, creating a total of twenty-two subsidiaries. In the 1970s, it joined the super-league by implementing, with the American firm Du Pont, the $400m synthetic fibres Polyacryl factory at Isfahan.

(3) The Ray Textile group, an Iranian giant in its sector, dominated by the Kurous family, Hasan, Îsa and Kazim Kurous. Sole importers of British textile machinery since the 1930s, the Kurouses launched Ray Textile in the fifties. The concern flourished. With the fabulous profits, the family acquired prime real estate in the centre of Tehran and later made a second fortune in this field.

(4) The Plasco Group, Iran's pioneer in mass plastic products, managed by the four Ilqanian brothers, Habibullah, Nourullah, Âtaullah and Sion. The Jewish quartet reaped tremendous profits from their pioneering efforts in plastics. They built Iran's first skyscraper (the Ilqanian Building) and later diversified into refrigerators and home appliances (General Steel Co.).

(5) The Jahan Group, the conglomerate managed by Muhammad Sadiq Fatih and his wife's family, the Ghazanfars. Having made his fortune in the Yazd *Bazaar*, Fatih moved to Tehran and first associated with the Kurouses in Ray Textile, but soon sold his 30% share in Ray and bought a huge estate at Hajjiabad near Karaj where

he set up his own Jahan complex: chit production and wool-weaving, alongside his Jahan tea and Jahan vegetable oil. The group later went into oil products with Internol and Interlop, and into the construction business with Hasan Fatih's successful Paradis company.

A few scattered industrialists left their mark on some provincial centres. In Kashan, Hasan Taffazuli's textile factory, established in 1936, was continuously expanded; in Yazd, the Yazdbaf and Afshartex textiles, controlled respectively by the Tahiri and Afshar Yazdi families, made enormous profits; in Isfahan, where the Kazirounis' Vatan was faltering because of poor management, it was the brothers Âli and Husayn Hamadanyan who struck gold with their superb management of their 500 tonnes/day cement kiln created in 1955,[78] then the largest kiln in the private sector.

With all the public projects envisaged in the Second Plan (and some private enterprises), a new breed of capitalists – that is to say, the consultants, the architects and the contractors needed to implement these projects –were finding their place in the sun.

Âbd ul-Majid Aâlam's Tessa company soon came to dominate the lot, followed by Asad-Ecbatane, owned by the trio of Tashakkuri, Naraqi and Sadiq (with close links to General Zahidi), the Musalas owned by Engineer Kazim Jafroudi and Qubad Zaffar Bakhtiari (both close to the court), Rankin, with its Baha'i shareholders who took its share of military contracts and Armeh, managed by the Yazdi Malikzadeh, which would irresistibly rise to the top of Iran's construction world, eventually even surpassing Tessa.

Two families, however, were to reap the largest benefits from the 1950s economic boom. The first family was formed by the direct descendants of Elite Qajar Prince Âbdul-Husayn Mirza Farmanfarma (1855–1939) who would choose either Farmanfarmayan or Firouz as family names. The prince had thirty-three children, twenty-one sons and twelve daughters; his four eldest sons were all born to his wife Îzzat ul-Douleh, the daughter of Muzaffar ul-Din Shah and the granddaughter of Amir Kabir on her mother's side: (1) Firouz Mirza, Nusrat ul-Douleh; (2) Âbbas Mirza, Salar Lashgar; (3) Muhammad Vali Mirza; (4) Muhammad Husayn Mirza (General Firouz). Later children were born from either permanent or temporary marriages entered into by the prince. The prince, who had amassed during his lifetime one of the most fantastic fortunes in Iran, envisioned a future in which education would be of primary importance, and encouraged all of his children to go to university, under the threat of not receiving their share of the family fortune if they failed to get a degree. They all returned from abroad (the US or England) as graduates. His second advice to his children was to keep united, because he (correctly) held that unity was a *sine qua non* source of success in Iran.

In the 1950s, the second and third generations of Farmanfarmayans and Firouzes began their multi-pronged conquest of Iran. In the industrial sector, alongside the Pazargad chemical company in Khuzistan, the family came to own the Pak Dairy, the first (and best) of the Iranian dairy products companies, created by Farouq Farmanfarmayan with the US Foremost Dairy Co.; the motor oil company Naft-i Pars (Pars Oil), in a joint venture with the Shell company, organised by Âbd ul-Âli Farmanfarmayan (an Oxford graduate); and Iran Khalij (founded by Iskandar Firouz), Mazandaran Textiles, ASEA Iran, Nayr Pars formed by Âlidad Farmanfarmayan.[78] In the construction business, it was represented by Narsi Firouz's Firouz Construction Company, set up in 1960. In consulting, Âbd ul-Âziz's Wilmafar, a joint venture between the William Company and the H. & R. Farmanfarmayan Company, managed by Haroun al-Rashid and Hafiz Farmanfarmayan, a former Tehran University professor and owner of a major publishing house, was at the top. In banking, the family had Âli Naqi as managing director of the PO's ICB, and also directorships for Khudadad, Haroun al-Rashid (Bank-i Tehran) and Ghaffar Farmanfarmayan. In the civil service the family had Dr Sabbar (Dr Musaddiq's Minister for Agriculture and head of Tehran's Pasteur Institute); Manuchihr (an NIOC senior manager and IORC director, educated at Birmingham); Jamshid (an expert in labour affairs, head of the Social Insurance Organisation); Khudadad (educated at Stanford, future PO managing director); and Bahram (educated at Pennsylvania and Michigan, a director-general at the Ministry of the Interior). In education, Miss Sattareh (an USC graduate), was since 1958 director of Tehran's School of Social Work and later accumulated the chairwomanships of the Family Planning Organisation and the Community Welfare Centre.

The Farmanfarmayans were one of the rare old Persian families able to exist comfortably in the new Iran. Their matrimonial links were with the old families – Qaraguzlu, Nizam Mafi, Âla, Pirnya, Imami, Isfandyari, Doulatshahi, Mirdamadi, Naraqi and Amir

Sulaymani – as well as with the new ones: Namazi, Soudavar, Mahlouji, Parkhideh, Sabiti, Ittihadiyyeh, Asar and Ra'is. Their fabulous wealth was, in a similar fashion, made up of old villages and landholdings acquired by the prince in the provinces of Kermanshah, Hamadan, Fars, Khuzistan and the Tehran region as well as by the new assets of factories, consultancies and contracting firms. Their assets abroad, especially in Switzerland and England (with, among others, whole sets of apartment blocks), were said to be worth millions of dollars.

The second family to share in the boom was the Pahlavi family. The August 1953 shock suffered by the Shah – of ending in exile with meagre financial assets – had left its mark on the monarch. Once back on the throne, one of his first thoughts was to set aside eggs for the next time round. The best vehicle at hand was his father's *Amlak*, which only needed some face-lifting. In May 1958, the Bunyad-i Pahlavi (Pahlavi Foundation) was established and all the family's visible assets were transferred to it, a total of some Rls4bn (see Table 11.7. for breakdown). It was the first and the last time that the foundation would provide a list of its assets. From then on it was a race to expand in all directions (domestic and foreign) under the expert hands of Muhammad Jâfar Bihbahanian and Houshang Ram. Under the table cash 'gifts' from NIOC, the PO and other public institutions further added to the foundation's riches. In the autumn of 1961, the Shah, in order to underline the foundation's charitable 'orientation', placed it under a board of trustees consisting of nine members under the chairmanship of Asadullah Âlam, its managing director (replaced by Jâfar Sharif Imami in July 1962), and comprising Dr Âli Amini, Husayn Âla, Muhsin Sadr, Sardar Fakhir Hikmat, Muhammad Surouri, Valiullah Shahab Firdous, Dr Parviz Natil Khanlari, Îmad Turbati and Sayyid Jalal ul-Din Tihrani.

The whole Pahlavi family was after money and not coy about it: British Minister A. Nutting, visiting Tehran in 1958, noted that:

> ...[members of] the Royal Family are known to be waist-deep in commercial activities of all kind. Not only do they possess large quantities of land, they also own hotels, night-clubs and railways. Inevitably this association of the Shah and his relatives with the entrepreneurs and others, who are known to take their

cut of the moneys voted by Parliament for national development, is too easily represented by left-wing propagandists out to create trouble as proof that the wealth of Iran's oil is being squandered by her rulers, or used to enrich themselves by investment and speculation abroad. The prodigious coups of the Shah's sister Princess Ashraf at the gaming tables of Monte-Carlo [sic] do not exactly help to counter this seditious chit-chat...[80]

Table 11.7. Breakdown of the Pahlavi Foundation's Assets at its Inception in 1958.
(Rls millions)

Asset	Net Worth
Shirkat-i Kishtirani-i Iran (Iran Shipping Co.)*	2,612
Hotel chain (in northern provinces)	600
Holdings in factories	531
Bank-i Ûmran (Development Bank)	37
Orphanages	186
Total	3,966**

* Essentially two oil tankers (32,500 dwt each) carrying crude oil to Holland, and two cruise ships (1,000 dwt each).
** Equivalent to roughly $52m.

11.7. Royal Rule

With no more Qavam (who had died on July 22, 1955) or Musaddiq (safely exiled to Ahmadabad), Muhammad Reza Shah could finally rule as President Truman had advised him to, back in 1949. Now even his American adviser E.A. Bayne was telling him to do so.[81] With full US backing, ruling might even have seemed a rather easy and pleasant occupation for the Shah – especially as he could get his revenge on former enemies and reward trusted servants.

General Zahidi had to relinquish the premiership in April 1955, having fulfilled his mission. The septuagenarian Husayn Âla was again appointed as a stopgap premier (April 1955–April 1957). Âla was the apparent leader of the old Elite, but not on its board of directors. He was not held in high esteem by his peers.[82] Nevertheless, the old man would do his job properly and get Iran into the Baghdad Pact, when, in 1955, the US and Great Britain decided to revive the defunct Saâdabad Pact of 1937 after they had ironed out (to a certain extent) their regional conflicts of interest and "signed a secret treaty of understanding concerning American aid to Iraq [$10m loan], which assured Britain's... paramountcy in Iraq".[83] On February 24, Iraq and Turkey signed the initial pact; Great Britain joined on April 5 (thereby terminating the bilateral Anglo-Iraqi treaty of 1930), transferring the Habbaniya Air Base to Iraq; Pakistan and Iran became signatories to the pact on September 23 and November 5, respectively. The US, however, failed to join officially, preferring to only participate in some of its activities.

Nevertheless, the Soviet Union was extremely perturbed by this new defensive set-up, drawn up along the lines of Secretary of State Dulles's 'Northern Tier' concept. The Soviets had put pressure on the Shah not to join the Baghdad Pact. In vain. On the other hand, they were able to stop other Arab countries (except for Iraq) from joining it, with a special mention to Egypt where Nasser "by preventing the consolidation of the Baghdad Pact thereby earned a debt of gratitude which the Kremlin acknowledged in the 1955 arms deal and has continued to pay through the financing the Aswan Dam and equipping the Egyptian army".[84] The Soviets must have been satisfied in the end that the Pact "proved an abject failure".

Insofar as Iran was concerned, the pact failed to provide her with a direct defensive link with the Americans. When, in January 1957, the

Eisenhower Doctrine failed to address itself directly to Iran while encompassing the Arab states, American lapses further exacerbated Iranian nervousness and "hardly seemed an appropriate reward for Iran's participation in the Baghdad Pact". Iraq withdrew from the pact after the bloody *coup d'état* of July 1958 and the four remaining members renamed it the Central Treaty Organisation (CENTO), moving its headquarters to Turkey. It was at Ankara that on March 5, 1959, US Ambassador Fletcher and the Iranian envoy, General Ârfa, signed a bilateral American-Iranian Mutual Aid Agreement; the document had an extremely limited value, not having been ratified by the respective parliaments, but it seemed better than nothing for the Iranians. Its first article stipulated that:

> In case of aggression against Iran, the Government of the United States of America ...will take such appropriate action, including the use of armed forces, ...in order to assist the Government of Iran at its request...[85]

The Soviets reacted angrily to the agreement and Soviet leader Nikita Krushchev publicly vented his discontent "by making two personal attacks on the Shah".[86]

If the Soviets could only influence Iranian affairs indirectly, a new regional power was doing its best to enter the Iranian fray: the State of Israel. The Israelis had begun cultivating Iranian politicians since the late 1940s, through their fifth column: the influential and wealthy Jewish Iranian community (some 100,000 strong). In 1948, a Jewish Agency had been opened in Tehran, with Nathan Shadi at its head. In the agency's wake, the first Mossad agents found their way to Tehran: Shlomo Hilleh, Tzion Cohen and Moshe Tchervinsky. The new State of Israel had then been totally isolated in the Middle East and was looking for non-Arab friends. It first secured Turkish recognition, followed by the establishment of diplomatic relations in September 1949. Then it targeted Iran for recognition. It achieved a partial success with the official *de facto* recognition of Israel by Iran in March 1950, after sizeable bribes of (at least) Rls13m had been paid to Premier Sâid and members of his cabinet;[87] as Mossad's Tchervinsky had realised early, "It was possible to achieve almost anything in Iran through bribery".[87A]

Then, in the post-*Murdad 28* era, the Iranian-Israeli *rapprochement* was further engineered by members of the old Elite (purchased by wealthy Iranian Jewish families, for example the Machian family) and of the intelligentsia (e.g. Dr Arsanjani) who argued that "on balance-of-power grounds such a rapprochement made sense".[88] The Shah's personal antipathy towards Egypt's President Nasser further pushed the court into Israel's arms. Iran decided to secretly provide crude oil to Israel and began delivering in April 1957 the required feed to the 8" 217-km long Israeli pipeline linking the port of Eilat on the Red Sea to Beersheba.

As a *quid pro quo* the Israelis provided Iran's SAVAK with first-class training by Mossad. In late 1958, Mossad created a formal (secret) trilateral liaison with both SAVAK and Turkey's National Security Service (TNSS), called the Trident Organisation – thus the region's three non-Arab states had acquired covert links, leading to "continuing intelligence exchange plus semi-annual meetings at the chief of service level":[89] another triumph for Mossad. Furthermore, Mossad had been authorised to create three covert 'stations' in Iran, in the provinces of Khuzistan, Ilam and Kurdistan, to gather information on Iraq and the Arab countries of the Persian Gulf. These three stations, which came to number an average of a hundred agents each,[89A] were under the supervision of Mossad ace Jacob Nimrodi. The Israeli agents remained on site until 1965-66, when they left for Israel, as they were now capable of running the stations by remote control. Within their seven to eight years of continual presence, with SAVAK's benediction, Mossad and Nimrodi had time to spread their networks not only in the south and west, but all over Iran.

Things came near to an Iranian *de jure* recognition of Israel when, on July 23, 1960, the Shah declared at a press conference that Iran might send a diplomatic mission to Israel. Nasser took this pretext to break off diplomatic relations with Iran. As for the Israelis, they had had an unofficial diplomatic mission in Tehran since late 1956, headed by Dr Zvi Doriel. The legal status of Israeli diplomats was always unclear: Israeli operations were "almost clandestine"[89B] and Israeli diplomats were not issued with special diplomatic cards (given to all accredited diplomats) by the Ministry of Foreign Affairs. Dr Doriel committed the imprudent act of giving an official reception for the diplomatic corps in Tehran in May 1962 – his first and last official invitation. Dr Doriel's prime strategy was to use Iranian newspapers to disseminate pro-Israeli material in the local press; his initial contacts were through Âbbas Shahandeh (editor of *Farman*) and Âbdullah Vala (publisher of *Tehran Musavvar*).[89C]

On the domestic scene, the Shah had been told to try and win back the bureaucracy from its unlawful love affair with Dr Musaddiq and the National Front, turning it into the second pillar of his internal base after his military pillar. With the funds available in the late 1950s, the Shah had no problem with the expanding bureaucratic maze; overlaps and duplications were necessary for the Shah to 'divide and rule' his fresh constituency. Moreover the development of the civil service was appreciated by the Americans who saw it as a useful reservoir for the middle classes they wanted to foster. The Iranian intelligentsia treated the growing public service as its personal domain and placed its members wherever it could, writers, journalists, even artists. A post as a civil servant had become a kind of distinction in Iranian society: a secure life tenure, with a comfortable salary, many perks (loans, foreign trips, free lunches, and in many positions cars, bonuses and possibly commissions), plus an aura of serving the nation. Young graduates were even paying 'entry fees' to managers (yet another perk) for hiring them.

The Shah wanted to place his own men at the top of his bureaucracy: capable technocrats-cum-politicians, personally devoted to him. A prime candidate was the young Dr Manuchihr Iqbal (born in 1909), an MD, educated at Paris, with a French wife, who entered the civil service in the late 1930s. Iqbal became a minister in the 1940s with his first portfolio in 1944 (in PM Sâid's third cabinet), governor-general of Azarbayjan in 1950 and a senator in 1954; since 1955 he had been simultaneously chancellor of Tehran University and Court Minister; in April 1957 he was appointed prime minister, a post he would keep until August 1960. Another candidate was Asadullah Âlam (born in 1919), whose father Ibrahim Shoukat ul-Mulk had come to yield considerable power towards the end of Reza Shah's reign[90] and whose wife (married in 1939, on orders from Reza Shah) was Maliktaj Qavam ul-Mulk Shirazi; after studies at the Karaj Institute of Agriculture, Âlam managed his vast landholdings at Birjand before entering politics as governor-general of the Sistan and Balouchistan province under Premier Qavam; his first ministerial position came in 1949 (Interior, under Sâid); he became very close to the Shah, for whom he rendered multiple services. The third possibility was Jâfar Sharif Imami (born in 1911), a railway engineer educated in Germany and Sweden, who had joined the technocracy in 1931 and had married Îshrat Muâzzami (the only sister of the six Muâzzami brothers, the children of the richest Gulpaygani landowner, Muhammad Khan Muâzzam ul-Sultan); made a career in the railways, then as chairman of the PO Higher Council; elected as a senator in 1954 and appointed Minister of Industry and Mines in 1957.

When the Shah was told in 1957 that the time was ripe for an apparent return to democracy, he ordered the creation of two political parties: the *Hizb-i Milliyoun* (Nationalist Party) and the *Hizb-i Mardum* (People's Party), and naturally named the loyal Iqbal and Âlam as their respective secretary-generals. On April 27, 1957, in a speech before the joint *Majlis* and Senate, the Shah explained the creation of the twin royalist parties: "The essence of democracy is the people's freedom to form political parties. Now that we have parties ...we also have democracy".[91] The people were not fooled by these gimmicks and quickly dubbed the two parties the 'Yes' and the 'Of Course' parties. It was clear to the people that the Shah ruled Iran with the US's blessings and that these parties were political gimmicks to please the Americans.

11.8. Dissonances

As the Shah's nominations reinforced his own position, sounds of dissent were to be heard. In February 1958, General Muhammad Vali Qaranay, a *Murdad 28* hero and head of the army's counter-intelligence division (the G-2) as a result of his participation in the coup, was arrested and court-martialled for conspiracy "against the security of state" and sentenced to three years' imprisonment. Implicated in the unsuccessful Qaranay coup were Dr Âli Amini, Iran's ambassador to Washington (who was recalled on March 4) and his brother General Mahmoud Amini; Dr Hasan Arsanjani, Qavam's former factotum and the coup's eventual "political leader",[91A] who was detained for a few days; and Ahmad Âli Sipihr (Muvarikhul-Douleh), a second-string Elite member with considerable experience in internal politics, briefly interrogated for his part in the conspiracy; and also General Hasan Akhavi, Ahmad Aramish, Muhammad Dirakhshish, Hasan Nazih and Ahmad Madani.

From his ideal position at the head of G-2, the capable and ambitious General Qaranay had been planning a coup. Through intermediary Isfandyar Buzurgmihr, a man with close links to the Americans and the CIA, he had received the green light from the US Embassy at Athens (then the centre for decisions on the Middle East).[91B] Qaranay himself had been to the US in 1956 and had direct contact with diplomat John Bowling in October 1956 and January 1957. But the conspiracy was uncovered before Qaranay had the time to act. It was either General Bakhtiar[91C] or General Fardoust [91D] who tipped off the Shah and triggered the wave of arrests. Maybe too a section in the CIA which did not favour the Qaranay coup had informed the Shah: it wouldn't be the first time that the CIA was pulling in two different directions simultaneously. In any event, the Americans were not seen at their best in the Qaranay fiasco, especially when, after Qaranay's arrest, they tried to hush up the whole incident. With hindsight, though, the Americans would have been better off if they had backed Qaranay to the hilt.

Years later, General Qaranay would recall these 1958 events in the last interview he gave, a few days before being gunned down:

> Then, the Americans didn't need me because they had the Shah and this very obedient servant of theirs would execute any of their orders, without the slightest hesitation or resistance...[92]

As the domestic threats multiplied, the Shah reinforced further his repressive and information network. In October 1958, he added the Bazrisi Shahanshahi (Imperial Inspectorate) to his security panoply. Reporting directly and exclusively to him, the new institution had the authority to follow up any public complaint and thus to investigate at will any civilian or military organisation. The Shah placed the old and trustworthy General Murtaza Yazdanpanah at the head of his Inspectorate – a post the Cossack general would occupy until his death in August 1972. Another bureau set up by the Shah in 1959 was the *Daftar-i Vizheh-yi Ittilaât* (Special Intelligence Bureau), at the head of which he appointed the reliable General Fardoust (the latter retaining this post until January 1979).

Notwithstanding the setting up of the Inspectorate, further conspiracies were being plotted against the Shah. In April 1959, in a *New York Times*'s leader, C.L. Sulzberger reported that:

> Indications now point to a ...plan to upset the Iranian Shah's regime. Outside Iran, the conspiracy would be hatched in Iraq ...Inside Iran [it] would be led by the powerful Kashgai tribe. Émigré leaders of the Kashgais recently met in Munich to decide on whether to declare war on the Shah ...They are trying to work out a national-front alliance with the Bakhtiaris ...with southern tribes, who resent the imprisonment of their head, Hayat Davudi; ...and with frustrated Kurds...[93]

If true, this fresh conspiracy was a boon for the Shah, for it was well known that the Qashqa'is usually side with losers.

The Shah, however, must have reacted strongly to an article by British Minister A. Nutting in *The International Herald Tribune* (written after his visit to Iran), in which he implied that the Shah was redundant. Nutting later commented:

> It was ...suggested that my article showed that the British Government no longer had any use for the Shah ...I can assure [everyone] that everything I said was my own personal opinion and in no way represented the view of the British Government...[94]

But he did not shy away from a direct warning:

> If the Shah persists in his ways and if Dr Eqbal [the Prime Minister] fails to move him, an explosion must sooner or later result... [which] could well flare up into real revolution...[95]

Nutting's critical view was echoed in November 1959 by CBS's Ed Murrow, who told DRC's D.E. Lilienthal, after filming the Shah in Tehran for a special transmission for five hours: "I would say it is a rather brittle regime".[96]

To further reinforce his regime, Muhammad Reza Shah was forced by his family and close courtiers to divorce his second wife, Surayya Isfandyari, after some seven years of married life on March 14, 1958, because she couldn't bear children. The final decision must have been hard on the Shah, but *raisons d'état* won over private considerations. On December 21, 1959, the Shah married his third wife, the twenty year old Farah Diba. And on October 31, 1960, his first son Riza Pahlavi was born in Tehran and proclaimed crown prince: the Pahlavis finally had an heir to the Peacock Throne.

As dark clouds were multiplying over Iranian skies, Muhammad Reza Shah had one great advantage going for him: the disarray of his opponents.

Among Iran's old Elite families things were at their worst. Elitists took advantage of all their privileges (rural and urban rents, *dolce vita*, night-life, trips to Europe and America) and failed to shoulder their responsibilities (no charity, no *noblesse oblige*, rents collected by paid managers). The Elite's scions were rich and wanted to have a good time; after the harsh 1940s and the shocks of the oil nationalisation, that was their right. Of the Elite's insouciance of the late 1950s, Nutting noted:

> Where national affairs are concerned, the rich and ruling classes exhibit an indolence and irresponsibility that is really frightening in this day and age. The parallel with the attitude and behaviour of their counterparts in pre-Revolutionary France and Russia is too close to be comfortable...[97]

Had the Elitists read any history at all?

The Elitists told anyone wishing to hear that, with SAVAK's savage uprooting of the communist threat, they had nothing to fear any more, as General Bakhtiar, who had ruthlessly destroyed the *Toudeh*'s cells, was still in charge. The Elitists were making the same mistake as former elites in Persia: believing that in their country there is such a thing as a free ride. Whenever there is one, it is always ephemeral, brought about by special circumstances (e.g. SAVAK's defanging of all potential threats). But a special situation can never be expected to last long.

If the Iranian leftist counter-elite had virtually been obliterated by 1956, the religious hierocracy had fared extremely well given the circumstances. In Qum, Ayatullah Burujirdi's wise management of the *Houzeh* was beginning to bear fruit. His reorganisation of the scattered religious activists in the provinces within a network of representatives in charge of collecting the *Sahm-i Imam* (the Imam's dues, which covered the *Houzeh*'s expenses) had brought a degree of order unknown before. Compiling the list of provincial envoys was a small step indeed, but a significant one, for "this new order had been brought about in an environment that had systematically refuted it. It had been obtained in the teeth of traditional religious circles which held that the institution's secret of survival was its lack of precise books and accounts – or, in other words, that systematic planning was a liability, not an asset".[98] In 1953, Burujirdi had given free rein to the opponents of the leftist-leaning Sayyid Âli Akbar Burqiî,[99] who was exiled from Qum, and had thus beheaded the *Houzeh*'s left before it could gather steam. He had also created two new departments within the *Houzeh*: (1) the Dar ul-Tabligh (Propaganda Department) and (2) the Dar ul-Taqrib (Reunification Department) and appointed two promising clerics, the Ayatullahs Sayyid Kazim Shariâtmadari and Muhammad Taqi Qumi, their respective heads. He fully supported Qumi's mission to Cairo's Al-Azhar University and was rewarded for his choice when in 1959 the University's rector, Shaykh Shaltout, issued a *fatva* (decree) recognising *Shiîsm* as one of the legitimate sects of Islam.[100] Also in 1959, Burjirdi dispatched a young relative of his,[101] the thirty-one year old Sayyid Mousa Sadr, the gifted son of Sadr ul-Din Sadr, to Tyre in Lebanon, to revitalise the dormant Lebanese *Shiî* community.

Burujirdi had maintained excellent relations with Ayatullah Sayyid Muhammad Bihbahani and his son Sayyid Jâfar in Tehran. After *Murdad 28*, the Shah and the army were indebted to the Bihbahanis for their active participation in the coup. Burujirdi kept them as a covert channel to the Shah. The Qum–Tehran axis of Burujirdi and Bihbahani first flexed its muscles during the anti-*Baha'i* drive spearheaded by tribune Abu'l Qasim Falsafi. In May 1955, upon the latter's request, the military destroyed Tehran's *Baha'i* centre and occupied their Shiraz centre.[102] Reza Shah had had a particular aversion for the sect, but his son had closed his eyes to their activities. Maybe he had been influenced in this instance by his personal physician General Dr Ayadi, who was "from a baha'i family" and whose "mother was a leader of that sect", as the Shah himself told Queen Surayya.[103]

In the wake of the anti-*Baha'i* drive, a Mashhad cleric, Shaykh Mahmoud Zakirzadeh Tavalla'i (later to be known as Shaykh Mahmoud Halabi), registered in 1956 an official organisation, the *Anjuman-i Hujjatiyyeh*, to keep the *Baha'i* expansion in check. The Hujjatiyyeh had from the outset strong links to the Tehran *Bazaar*.

Yet Burujirdi's greatest achievement was his ability to create in his Qum *Houzeh* an atmosphere propitious for intellectual development. Out of these nurturing grounds, a young, dedicated and educated religious elite would blossom. The first manifestation of this fresh intellectual elite occurred in 1960, when Murtaza Mutahhari, a Qum teacher who had migrated to Tehran, organised his *Anjuman-i Mahaneh Dini* (the Monthly Religious Society), whose main goal was to "rejuvenate religious thinking". Around Mutahhari and doyen Âllameh Muhammad Husayn Tabataba'i, a dozen religious thinkers gravitated: the nationalist Sayyid Abu'l Fazl Mujtahid Zanjani; the popular Sayyid Mahmoud Taliqani; the passionate Sayyid Murtaza Jazayiri; and also Sayyid Murtaza Shabistari, Hajj Mirza Khalil Kamareh'i, Sayyid Muhammad Baqir Sabzivari, the young Sayyid Mousa Sadr and Sayyid Muhammad Bihishti, alongside Dr Muhammad Ibrahim Ayati, Engineer Mihdi Bazargan and Âli Ghaffouri. Beginning in September 1960 (until March 1963), the *Anjuman* held monthly seminars at which one of its members presented a lecture on prominent religious questions facing the *Shiî* community, such as *ijtihad*, property in Islam, the task of the younger generation. It was a revolution and a revelation. For the very first time, religious thinkers were debating topics of burning relevance and having them published in the *Guftar-i Mah* (Monthly Lectures) series.[104] For the Iranian hierocracy, the creation of an intellectual wing was in itself a formidable leap forward.

Among the religious intellectuals, Sayyid Mahmoud Taliqani was an exceptional figure. Born in 1903, Taliqani was the son of Ayatullah Sayyid Abu'l Hasan, a minor Tehran cleric who had been close to Mudarris. In the early 1940s Taliqani took over as prayer leader of the Hidayat Mosque in Tehran and founded the *Kanoun-i Islam* (the Islamic Centre) which published the magazine *Danishamouz* (Student). Active during the oil nationalisation movement, he was the most nationalistic of the new religious generation. His closest friend was Engineer Mihdi Bazargan, the most religious among the nationalists. In the aftermath of *Murdad 28*, they created, together with Dr Yadullah Sahabi (another TU professor), the *Nihzat-i Muqavimat-i Milli* (the National Resistance Movement – NRM). Other prominent NRM members were Engineer Mansour Âta'i, Rahim Âta'i and the young lawyer Hasan Nazih. The NRM's main goal was to keep the opposition's flame alight: it issued communiqués on major problems and published a semi-clandestine leaflet entitled *Rah-i Musaddiq* (Musaddiq's Way). Life was not without risks for the NRM leadership, with Bazagan being imprisoned in March 1955 and Taliqani being incarcerated in December of the same year for giving asylum to Navvab Safavi after the unsuccessful attempt on the life of Premier Âla (Taliqani was the only person who dared to harbour the fugitive *Fada'yan*). In 1957, both Bazargan and Taliqani were again arrested. Nevertheless they had shown that resistance was possible even in the teeth of SAVAK's ruthless repression. By so doing they had placed their NRM in the vanguard of the opposition to the Shah.

With the communist counter-elite on the sidelines, and the nationalists still reeling after the *Murdad 28 débâcle*, the only viable counter-elite in Iran was the religious one. The latter's revival came at the right time for any future role in domestic politics: the wounds inflicted by Reza Shah had healed and Qum's *Houzeh* had been transformed by Burujirdi's fine management into a centre capable of delivering the human material required to allow a comeback by the clerics. Minister Anthony Nutting, in his concluding remarks on the Middle East, had candidly presented Islam as one of the powers-to-be, not only in the Middle East but also in the world at large:

> If the West, and especially Britain can redeem its pledges and help the Moslem world to regain its unity and cohesion, we shall not only have established an unbroken line of resistance to Communism from Casablanca to Karachi; we shall have gained the friendship and the esteem of one of the greatest powers in world politics for generations to come – the reawakening strength of united Islam...[105]

NOTES

1. T. Powers, *The Man Who Kept the Secrets* (New York: A.A. Knopf, 1978) p.85.
2. Ibid., p.338. Roosevelt resigned from the CIA in 1957 and joined Gulf Oil as a vice-president. He would leave Gulf in 1963 to set up his own consultancy, Kermit Roosevelt and Associates, with the Northrop Corporation among its clients.
3. K. Roosevelt, *Countercoup* (McGraw-Hill, 1979) p.208.
4. Ibid., p.200.
5. In return for his defence of Dr Musaddiq, Colonel Buzurgmihr asked only to be given exclusive possession of the memorabilia of the two trials. For a quarter of a century he kept these documents hidden in a safe place, and after the 1978/79 Islamic Revolution published five books on Dr Musaddiq and his trials: (1) *Taqrirat-i Musaddiq dar Zindan*, with I. Afshar, (Tehran: Sazman-i Kitab, 1359 (1990)); (2,3) *Musaddiq dar Muhakimat-i Nizami* (Tehran: Nashr-i Tarikh-i Iran, 2 Vols., 1363 (1984)); (4) *Duktur Muhammad Musaddiq dar Dadgah-i Tajdid-i Nazar* (Tehran: Shirkat-i Sahami Intishar, 1365 (1986)); (5) *Az Duktur Muhammad Musaddiq* (Tehran: Nahid, 1373 (1994)). For his defence of Dr Musaddiq, Colonel Buzurgmihr was forced into early retirement on October 31, 1955. He and five other officers so penalised were rehabilitated in November 1979 by the Revolutionary Council of the Islamic Republic of Iran. The five other officers were Colonels Husayn Quli Ashrafi and Husayn Quli Sarrishteh, and Captains Mousa Mehran, Murtaza Shirdil and Iraj Davarpanah, who were reintegrated into the army with back pay from the day of retirement. See reference (5) above, p.193.
6. K. Roosevelt, op. cit. (note 3), p.200.
7. Allegations made in *Javan* magazine, no. 15, Isfand 25, 1357 (March 16, 1979), pp.42-3.
8. *Ittilaât* newspaper, Mihr 10, 1332 (October 19,1953).
9. See K. Kishavarz, *Chahardah Mah dar Kharg* (Fourteen Months at Kharg), (Tehran: Payam, 1363 (1984)).
10. *Ittilaât*, Murdad 31, 1332 (August 22, 1953).
11. Private communication from a source near to the Âla family who had heard the anecdote several times.
12. R. Graham, *The Illusion of Power* (New York: St. Martin's Press, 1978) p.65.
13. S. Isfandyari, *Ma Vie* (Paris: Plon, 1963) p.102.
14. Gh.R. Nijati, *Jumbish-i Milli Shudan-i Sanât-i Naft-i Iran* (Tehran: Shirkat-i Sahami Intishar, 1365 (1976)) pp.329 and 474.
15. For example, at five o'clock on the morning of *Murdad 28* General Zahidi came out of the house of Dr Husayn Pirnia, the former director-general of Oil Affairs at the Ministry of Finance and Professor of Economics at Tehran University, where he had been hiding. Yet another instance of how family connections help in Iran. See N. Pakdaman, *Muqaddameh barayi "Musaddiq dar Muhakimat-i Nizami"* (unpublished hand-written manuscript) p.50.
16. Private communication to the author by a former member of the underworld, with only good things to say about Husayn Aqa Mihdi, whom he personally considered to be among the underworld's top five in the 1960s and 1970s. The Iranian underworld has a tradition all of its own: its own elite, hierarchy, rules of honour and its own laws. On this subject see M. Âraqi, *Na Gufteh-ha* (Things Not Said), (Tehran: Rasa, 1370, (1991)).

17 A. Eden, *Full Circle* (London: Cassell, 1960) p.218.
18 H. O'Connor, *The Empire of Oil* (London: John Calder, 1956) p.331.
19 F. Rouhani, *Tarikh-i Milli Shudan-i Sanât-i Naft-i Iran* (Tehran: Kitab-ha-yi Jibi, 2nd ed., 1353 (1974)) p.342.
20 M.K. Sheehan, *Iran: The Impact of US Interests and Policies (1941-1954)* (New York: Theo Gauss, 1968) p.66.
21 Among many other reshufflings of Iricon shares along the years, Signal bought out Hancock, Continental took over San Jacinto, and Atlantic Refining and Richfield merged to form Atlantic Richfield Corporation (ARCO), Getty Oil and Tidewater (both Getty companies) were later merged. By 1977, the Iricon Group was reduced to six companies dominated by ARCO (four shares), American Independent (two shares) and Getty Oil (two shares).
22 H. O'Connor, *World Crisis in Oil* (London: Elek Books, 1963) p.294.
23 *Oil and Petroleum Yearbook 1955*, (London: W.E. Skinner, 1956) pp.49-50.23A. The deadline for crediting the $510m account was set for 1970. The target sum was reached by 1966.
24 A. Eden, op. cit. (note 17), p.218.
25 L.P. Elwell-Sutton, *Persian Oil* (London: Lawrence and Wishart, 1955) p.328.
26 J. Strachey, *End of Empire* (New York: Random House, 1959) p.173.
27 S.H. Longrigg, *Oil in the Middle East* (London: Oxford University Press, 2nd ed., 1961) p.279.
27A L.P. Elwell-Sutton, op. cit. (note 25), p.327.
28 F. Nafisi, 'Oil Exploration in Iran', in *The Bulletin of The Iranian Petroleum Institute*, no. 2, October 1960, p.11.
29 A.W. Ford, *The Anglo-Iranian Oil Dispute of 1951-1952* (University of California Press, 1954) p.249.
30 G. Lenczowski, *Oil and State in the Middle East* (Cornell University Press, 1960) p.313. Exact figures for expatriates, and Iranian labour and staff are given for the years 1955-57.
31 *Annual Statistical Bulletin 1966* (Vienna: OPEC, 1967).
31A The two major fires during the 1950s occurred at: (1) Rig 20 at Naft-i Safid (May 1951), which burned for forty-three days before being put out by Myron Kinley; (2) Ahwaz no. 6 (April 1958), which burned for fifty days before Kinley blew it out and brought it under control. See: S.H. Longrigg, op. cit. (note 27), p.280.
32 *Oil Industry in Iran* (Tehran: Iranian Petroleum Institute, June 1963) p.40. And other IPI. publications.
32A Ibid., p.32.
33 W.A. Leeman, *The Price of Middle East Oil* (Cornell University Press, 1962) p.65.
34 P.H. Frankel, *Mattei: Oil and Power Politics* (London: Faber and Faber, 1966) p.96.
35 C. Tugendhat, *Oil - The Biggest Business* (London: Eyre and Spottiswoode, 1968) p.153.
35A See Â. Aruzi, *Khatirat-i Abu'l Hasan Ibtihaj* (Tehran: Îlmi, 1371 (1992)) pp.785-6. Quoting "the Shah benefited through [Dr Ahmad] Maybud from the AGIP Mineraria oil concession deal".
36 F. Rouhani, *A History of OPEC* (New York: Praeger, 1971) p.77.
37 A Sampson, *The Seven Sisters* (Coronet Books, 1975) p.170.
38 *Statistical Yearbook 1968* (Tehran: Plan Organisation, Statistical Centre of Iran, June 1971) p.222.

[39] M. Chamran, *Shanzdah-i Azar* (Tehran: Nihzat-i Azadi Iran, 1361 (1982)) pp.11-13.

[40] Ibid., p.17.

[40A] See O. Miyata, 'The Tudeh Military Network During the Oil Nationalisation Period', in *Middle Eastern Studies*, Vol. 23, no. 3, July 1987, p.315. According to Miyata, the Executive Council consisted of:
(1) Ex-Captain Khusrou Rouzbeh;
(2) Gendarmerie Colonel Îzzatullah Syamak;
(3) Artillery Lieutenant Colonel Muhammad Âli Mubashshiri;
(4) Air Force First Lieutenant Manouchihr Mukhtari Gulpaygani;
(5) Artillery Captain Ismâil Muhaqqiq Davani;
(6) Ex-Captain Abu'l Hasan Âbbasi;
(7) Infantry Major Jâfar Vakili.

[40B] Ibid., p.316.

[40C] Ibid., p.325.

[40D] One of the forty-two *Toudeh* officers who saw his death sentence commuted to life was Major Ghulam Husayn Baqiî, who later wrote his memoirs: *Angizeh* (Motivation) (Tehran: Rasa, 1373 (1994)). On pages 448 and 449, he details the execution of these last six officers.

[40E] The life and character of some *Toudeh* officers, especially Rouzbeh and Mubashshiri, and the difficulties of underground life in the Tehran of the 1950s is told by Maryam Firouz (the daughter of Prince Farmanfarma and wife of Nour ul-Din Kianouri) in her book, *Chireh-ha-yi Dirakhshan-i Mubarizan-i Iran* (The Brilliant Faces of Opponents in Iran) (Tehran: Pishrou, undated).

[41] Contrary to the legends later publicised by the *Toudeh* about the unflinching defence of its heroic officers, it later came to light that both Rouzbeh and Colonel Syamak (the *Toudeh* officers' outstanding leaders) had pleaded their very hardest in court to save their own necks – naively believing that the regime would give them the shadow of a chance. That was better than Dr Bahrami and a host of others who had signed "letters of repentance". See: M. Bihnoud, 'Shukouh-i Jam-i Jahani Bin Shikast', in *Adineh* magazine, no. 80/81, Khurdad 1372 (June 1993), p.29.

[42] Deaths were not a surprise at Bakhtiar's headquarters. The *Fada'yan*'s biographer even advanced that Vahidi was shot and killed by Bakhtiar himself. See S.H. Khwushniyyat, *Sayyid Mujtaba Navvab Safavi* (Tehran: Manshour-i Baradari, 1360 (1981)) p.171. In a private communication to the author, a cousin of Bakhtiar with links to the *Toudeh* reported that he had met the general at a family gathering in the mid-fifties and had begun to tell the assembled family about the insidious rumours about the Military Command's 'accidental' deaths; after a while, the general became angry, stood up and shouted at him: "Be careful about your words – if you are not, I might well shoot you right here!"

[43] J.C. Hurewitz, *Middle East Politics: the Military Dimension* (New York: Praeger, 1969) p.283.

[44] K. Roosevelt, op. cit. (note 3), p.9. Quoting Utah's *Logan Herald Journal* of November 10, 1978 which reproduced Colby's speech delivered at Utah State University.

[45] G. de Villiers, *SAS contre CIA* (Paris: Librairie Plon, 1965).

[46] W.O. Douglas, *West of the Indus* (New York: Doubleday, 1958) p.286.

[47] W.O. Douglas, *Strange Lands and Friendly People* (New York: Harper and Brothers, 1951) p.322.

48 T. Cuyler Young, 'The Race between Russia and Reforms in Iran', in *Foreign Affairs*, January 1950, p.287.
49 *The Near East and the Great Powers*, ed. by R.N. Frye, (Cambridge: Harvard University Press, 1951) p.10.
50 Ibid., p.87.
51 Ibid., p.194.
52 J.C Hurewitz, op. cit. (note 43), p.293.
53 *Iran Almanac 1966* (Tehran: Echo of Iran, 1966) p.283.
54 ARMISH-MAAG was the acronym given to the US military mission in Iran. First came ARMISH (short for ARmy MISsion Headquarters) and GENMISH (GENdarmerie MISsion Headquarters), then the MAAG (Mutual Assistance Advisory Group). But as ARMISH and MAAG were acting in parallel, the two organisms came to use one abbreviation. In 1959, a total of seven hundred US military personnel worked in Iran under the aegis of ARMISH-MAAG. See *Echo Reports*, no. 11 (198), March 20, 1959, (Tehran: Echo of Iran).
55 Administratively speaking, Point Four changed skins a number of times during its short life. It originated in the State Department as Technical Co-operation for Iran (TCI); in summer 1953, the Foreign Operations Administration was set up independently of the State Dept. and TCI turned into the US Operation Mission in Iran (USOM/I); in July 1955, Foreign Operations reverted to the State Department, under the aegis of a semi-autonomous entity: the International Co-operation Agency (ICA); finally, an independent agency, the US Agency for International Development (USAID) was created to cover US assistance programmes abroad.
56 W.E. Warne, *Mission for Peace* (The Bobbs-Merrill Co., 1956) p.58.
57 J. Amuzegar, *Technical Assistance in Theory and Practice: the Case of Iran* (New York: Praeger, 1966) p.48.
58 W.E. Warne, op. cit. (note 56), p.61.
59 J. Amuzegar, op. cit. (note 57), p.20
60 R. Bullard, *Britain and the Middle East* (London: Longmans, 1951) p.183.
61 J. Amuzegar, op. cit. (note 57), pp.9-10. Quoting from R.P. Loomis's completion of tour report.
62 Ibid., p.218.
63 *Iran – Country Survey Series* (New Haven: Human Relations Area Files, 1957) p.134.
64 J. Amuzegar, op. cit. (note 57), p.107. CARE did especially well in getting flour, vegetable oil, clothes and other essentials to needy Iranians. In the distribution phase, Iranian middlemen naturally shifted large amounts of their consignments to the more lucrative black market, but nevertheless a fair share of the total trickled down to the poor and hungry – who really needed these free staples (private communication to the author from one of the honest Iranian middlemen in Khuzistan province).
65 Op. cit. (note 63), p.100.
66 P.Y. Hammond and S.S. Alexander, *Political Dynamics in the Middle East* (New York: American Elsevier, 1972) p.383 quoting S.P. Huntington, in *Military Intervention, Political Involvement and the Unlessons of Vietnam.*
67 *Guzarish-i Ijra'i-i Barnameh-yi Haft Saleh Duvvum* (Report on the Realisation of the Second Seven Year Plan), (Tehran: Plan Organisation, 1343 (1964)).
68 Professor P.J. Vatikiotis, 'The Modernisation of Poverty', *Middle Eastern Studies*, Vol. 12, no. 3, pp.193-5.

69 W.H. Forbis, *The Fall of the Peacock Throne* (Harper and Row, 1980) p.253.
70 *Guzarish...* op. cit. (note 67),
71 Report entitled *Activities of the Development and Resources Corporation in Iran*, discussed at a hearing before the Commission on Foreign Relations in the US Senate, March 20, 1962, (Washington, D.C.: US Government Printing Office, 1962) p.19.
72 Back in 1953 Montecatini had already studied the feasibility of chemical units for the production of fertilisers (90,000 t/a), DDT (1,875 t/a) and acetyl salicilic acid (168 t/a) in a single complex. Investment estimates amounted to $13.5m. Feed to the small complex was sour natural gas (with a 14% H²S content), to be piped from Lali to Ahvaz in a 140-km long pipeline. For all its past efforts, Montecatini would be rewarded with the urea unit (capacity of 52,000 tonnes/annum) in the Shiraz fertiliser complex.
72A See Â. Aruzi, op. cit. (note 35A), pp.792-3. In a letter dated July 29, 1987 to Helen Lilienthal, Ibtihaj disclosed that in 1946 he had contacted Colonel Bridges (retd.) for a joint Anglo-Iranian project "to build dams and carry out irrigation and agricultural development in Khuzistan". Colonel Bridges, to be on the safe side, had contacted the AIOC to get its opinion on the project, and received the above reply from AIOC's chairman Frazer.
73 Ahmad Aramish (1908-1973) was a very special individual. Discovered when still rather young by Qavam (who had the knack of finding and promoting the best and brightest), he made his debut as Minister of Labour in the crucial year of 1946.
74 *Guzarish...* op. cit. (note 67), p.48.
75 *Tarikhcheh Si Saleh Bank-i Milli Iran* (Tehran: Bank-i Milli Iran, undated) p.
76 *Guzarish....* op. cit. (note 70), Table 6 of Appendix.
77 Âli Vakili was the driving force behind the eleemosynary organisation *Mu'asiseh tibari Danishgah* (University Credit Institution) he had set up in 1959 with a handful of TCC colleagues. The institution's initial fund provided interest-free loans to needy university students, with the beneficiary repaying the *Mu'asiseh* after they had found employment. The institution assisted hundreds of students through their studies and is still operating today. After Vakili's death in 1964, it was well managed by Mahmoud Dihdashti (as per the founder's will) until 1978. After the Revolution the institution was managed by political appointees.
78 When told by a soil specialist that the factory's clay and limestone reserves were good enough for "at least a hundred years", Husayn Hamadanyan shot back: "What shall we do after that?" (Private communication from a close friend of the Hamadanyan family).
79 The fact that a Nayr Pars executive, Engineer Ghyasi, was able to retire to Los Angeles in 1978 with a fortune estimated at between $20m and $30m will serve to underline the magnitude of the Farmanfarmayans' fortunes. (Private communication from a Tehran socialite very knowledgeable about who transferred how much).
80 A. Nutting, *I Saw for Myself* (London: Hollis and Carter, 1958) p.52.
81 E.A. Bayne, *Persian Kingship in Transition* (New York: American Universities Field Staff, 1968).
82 Private communication from a younger Elite member who had gone with an Elite 'director' to visit the premier. During the courtesy visit, the director, although four years younger than the premier, "was not particularly respectful and even, at times, slightly contemptuous of the Prime Minister".

83 R.L. Lasse, 'The Baghdad Pact: Cold War or Colonialism?' in *Middle Eastern Studies*, Vol. 27, no. 1, January 1991, pp.140-3.
84 A.S. Klieman, *Soviet Russia and the Middle East* (John Hopkins Press, 1970) p.35.
85 E.A. Bayne, op. cit. (note 81), p.259.
86 R.K. Ramazani, 'Iran and the Arab-Israeli Conflict', in *The Middle East Journal* Vol. 32, no. 4, autumn 1978, p.416.
87 U. Bialer, 'The Iranian Connection in Israel's Foreign Policy 1848-1951', in *Middle East Journal*, Vol. 39, no. 2, spring 1985. Bialer mentions "Ahad Wahab Zadeh" (most probably Ahmad Vahabzadeh), a merchant close to Premier Sâid, as the middleman between the latter and Israeli agents (p.302). He also mentions an Israeli payment to politician Sayyid Zia ul-Din Tabataba'i (p.313).
87A Ibid., p.299.
88 R.W. Cottam, *Nationalism in Iran* (University of Pittsburgh Press, 2nd ed., 1979) p.362.
89 *Asnad-i Laneh-yi Jasousi* (Documents from the Spies' Den), number 11, (Tehran: 'Muslim Students Following the Line of Imam', undated) p.25.
89A See General Fardoust's memoirs, *Zuhour va Suqout-i Saltanat-i Pahlavi* (Tehran: Mu'asiseh Mutaliât va Pijouish-ha-yi Syasi 2 Vols., 1369 (1990)) pp.364-71.
89B *Asnad-i* ... op. cit. (note 89), no. 36, p.48.
89C See 'America: Supporter of Usurpers of the Gods', in the series *Documents from the U.S. Espionage Den* (Tehran: Muslim Students Following the Line of the Imam, undated) p.1. In a message labelled "secret" and dated January 28, 1957.
90 The super-rich and reasonable Shoukat ul-Mulk had gone a long way in the Pahlavi system. Apparently Minister for PTT, he was in charge of many other departments; one of his responsibilities was to cater to the old Elite's grievances. An Elite member from Hamadan had approached him because the army had taken some four hectares of his land near Hamadan without compensation, asking for redress. Shoukat said no problem, and promptly offered him some 40,000 square metres in Tehran instead, which the Elitist bluntly turned down – to his eternal regret. Such was the power Shoukat held in those days. (Private communication from the Hamadan Elite member).
91 From *Majlis* minutes, as quoted by *Umid-i Iran* magazine, no. 3, Bahman 23, 1357 (February 12, 1979), p.18.
91A Gh.R. Nijati, *Majira-yi Koudita-yi Sarlashgar Qaranay* (The Qaranay Coup d'état), (Tehran: Rasa, 1373 (1994)) p.88. In an interview with Colonel Tahir Qanbar.
91B Ibid. p.54. In the translation of an article by M.J. Gasiorowski, published in *The International Journal of Middle East Studies* (1994).
91C See B. Rubin, *Paved with Good Intentions* (Penguin Books, 1981) pp.108-9. Rubin was told by Kim Roosevelt in a 1980 interview that in 1958 General Bakhtiar's SAVAK had uncovered the Qaranay plot and had informed him and Allen Dulles about it. The latter had told the Shah, who had ordered Qaranay's arrest.
91D In his memoirs, General Fardoust writes that he tipped off the Shah about the impending coup. See *Zuhour va...* op. cit. (note 89A), p.330-1.
92 Qaranay's exclusive interview of April 28, 1979, a few days before his assassination, was published in *Javan* magazine, no. 21, Urdibihisht 14, 1358 (May 4, 1979), p.13.
93 C.L. Sulzberger, 'Danger Signs in the Middle East', in *The New York Times*, April 27, 1959, p.26.
94 A. Nutting, op. cit. (note 80), p.49.

[95] Ibid., p.55.
[96] D.E. Lilienthal, *The Harvest Years 1959–1963*, the fifth volume of Lilienthal's Journals, (Harper and Row, 1971) p.21.
[97] A. Nutting, op. cit. (note 80), p.51.
[98] *Bahsi dar bareh-yi Marjâiyyat va Rouhaniyyat* (Tehran: Shirkat-i Sahami-i Intishar, 1341 (1962)) p.248.
[99] Sh. Akhavi, *Religion and Politics in Contemporary Iran* (Albany: 1980) p.65.
[100] Ibid., p.99.
[101] The old families of Burujirdi and Sadr were related in more than one way. An important addition to their links occurred when Burujirdi's first degree cousin, Muhammad Baqir Tabataba'i, married Mousa Sadr's sister. Five children resulted from this union: four sons and a daughter. The eldest son was to become Dr Sadiq Tabataba'i and the daughter, Fatimeh Sultani Tabataba'i, was to become the wife of Ayatullah Khomeini's second son, Sayyid Ahmad.
[102] Sh. Akhavi, op. cit. (note 99), p.80.
[103] S. Esfandiary, op. cit. (note 13), p.103.
[104] *Guftar-i Mah* (Monthly Lectures) (Tehran: Sadouq, 3 Vols., 1340/41 (1961/62)).
[105] A. Nutting, op. cit. (note 80), p.103.

CHAPTER TWELVE: WHITE REVOLUTION

The American 'clinic' set up in Iran during the 1950s was based on a tripod consisting of (i) the Shah, (ii) SAVAK's repression, and (iii) a forced economic development programme. With unconditional US support (after the Qaranay incident), Muhammad Reza Shah grew increasingly powerful, gradually placing himself, his family and his court at the centre of gravity of internal politics. As for SAVAK, it was extending its long tentacles into the furthest domestic recesses. But the third leg of the tripod, the unprecedented economic boom fuelled by American aid and the Second Plan investments, was not faring as well as expected.

Too much liquidity had overheated Iran's anaemic economic base. After years of price stability (with annual inflation below 5%), prices soared as inflation shot into two digit figures in 1958 (see Table 12.1). Alarmed, the IMF stepped in and ordered all economic brakes to be applied. A strict credit squeeze ensued: imports dwindled and investments plummeted. Abruptly, the development drive turned into recession, in 1961/62. In 1960, following the IMF's impulse, the Bank-i Markazi-i Iran (the Central Bank of Iran) was created to implement national monetary policies, taking over from the Bank-i Milli, which was left to cater to commercial operations. The Iranian private sector was hit hardest, being caught flat-footed in the midst of an historic development (the public sector, relying on increasing oil revenues, suffered much less). In the Tehran *Bazaar* bankruptcies were the order of the day; provincial *bazaars* suffered too, but on a scale proportionate to their exposure.

12.1. Crises

The sudden economic crisis naturally triggered social unrest. In June 1959, brick-kiln workers (among the worst paid of Iran's labour) went on strike after their demands for a 35% wage increase were turned down.[2] When SAVAK moved in to arrest twenty-six of their ringleaders, the workers rioted. Armed troops were sent in to crush the uprising and killing a dozen of the defenceless workers, injuring

Table 12.1. The Economic Crisis of 1961/62 in Figures.[1]
(Figures in Rls billions)
(Cost of Living Index Basis: 1955 = 100)

Year	Investments		Total	Imports	Cost Of Living Index
	Public	Private			
1958	21.4	23.3	114.8	44.7	33.5
1959	20.5	30.5	129.7	51.0	41.6
1960	27.2	21.9	140.1	49.1	52.6
1961	25.6	13.0	143.4	38.6	47.2
1962	17.8	13.0	143.8	30.8	41.9
Total	112.5	101.7		216.8	

another fifty. That made an example, but at a heavy price: if further strikes were thus stifled, it was at the price of alienating the workers' body.

The economic crisis had not only unleashed a social crisis, but a political one too. The Nineteenth *Majlis* had folded on June 4, 1960, so politicians were able to enter the fray for the elections to its Twentieth edition. In July, the two official parties, the *Milliyoun* and the *Mardum* entered the arena, when their respective secretary-generals, Dr Nusratullah Kasimi and Asadullah Âlam, presented their lists of candidates. The Shah failed to foresee the impending crisis; on the contrary, he "was so confident of his ability to control the election and still maintain a democratic motif that he permitted an influx of correspondents from the world's press".[3] With foreign reporters present, the opposition had a field day.

On July 21, the resuscitated National Front (known as the Second NF in contrast to its first edition under Dr Musaddiq) announced its formation and entered the elections. The fresh Nationalist coalition was spearheaded by the inevitable *Iran* Party led by veteran Allahyar Salih. Its Central Committee consisted of Engineer Ahmad Zirakzadeh, Engineer Kazim Hasibi, Dr Shahpour Bakhtiar, Nasirul-

Din Mousavi, Dr Âbd ul-Husayn Danishvar, Engineer Firaydoun Amir Ibrahimi; with alternate members Engineer Nizam ul-Din Muvahhid and Hasan Izadi. Other smaller entities in the coalition were: (i) the *Jibheh Susialist-i Iran* (Socialist Front of Iran) created in 1960 by Muhammad Âli Khunji from the remnants of Khalil Maliki's *Nirou-yi Sivvum*; (ii) the *Hizb-i Millat-i Iran* (the Iranian People's Party), an offshoot of the right-wing Pan-Iranist Party, with Darioush Furouhar at its head; and, (iii) the minuscule *Hizb-i Mardum-i Iran* (the Iranian People Party) under Muhammad Nakhshab. On the Front's fringes, Dr Baqa'i's rejuvenated Toilers' Party, renamed *Nigahbanan-i Azadi* (the Freedom's Guardians), also made its comeback – with former personalities like Husayn Makki and the remnants of Ayatullah Kashani's organisation joining its ranks (Mustafa Kashani, the Ayatullah's son, was placed in charge of the party's youth). For the Twentieth *Majlis*, the Shah and Premier Dr Iqbal "argued that although elections were free, 'traitors' could not be permitted to run".[4] The Front's litmus test for election freedom turned negative when its candidate for Isfahan, Dr Âbdul-Rahman Buroumand, was promptly arrested after announcing his candidacy. The Front threatened to boycott the elections. The electoral process nevertheless went ahead as planned. According to the law of April 1957, the official number of deputies was increased from 136 to 200 and the *Majlis*'s term from two to four years. On July 30, the first deputy to the Twentieth *Majlis* was elected and another 156 deputies were elected during August. Gross irregularities during the (customary) rigging process gave a buoyant opposition enough ammunition for sweeping attacks against the elections' results; even some *Mardum* Party elements joined in the protest. Under pressure, the Shah once again caved in, ordered all the deputies to resign and had the elections annulled on August 27, calling them "the second worst elections in Iran's history, after the elections to the 17th *Majlis*". The elections' fiasco led to Dr Iqbal's resignation after forty-one months in office (a post-war record) and his replacement by Engineer Jâfar Sharif Imami. A few days later, Asadullah Âlam was appointed managing director of the Pahlavi Foundation, leaving the *Mardum* Party's secretariat to Dr Yahya Âdl, the Shah's private surgeon and personal friend. General Nîmatullah Nasiri was placed at the head of the *Shahribani* (the police), an appointment showing the regime's will to further strengthen its iron grip on the cities. Fresh elections for the Twentieth *Majlis* were postponed to early 1961.

The winter of 1960/61 was a turning point in more than one way. First and foremost, America had a new president, John F. Kennedy. After eight years of Republican administration, the Democrats were back in the White House. The president's inaugural speech on January 20, 1961, contained dangerous omens of change for America's Iranian 'clinic':

> We observe today ...a celebration of freedom, ...those human rights to which this nation has always been committed, ...to those people in the huts and villages of half the globe ...we pledge our best efforts to help them help themselves, ...a new world of law, where the strong are just and the weak secure...[5]

After eight years of benevolent Republicanism under President Eisenhower, a new era was dawning for America and the world at large.

Simultaneously with President Kennedy's inauguration, the fresh elections for the Twentieth *Majlis* were launched. The National Front and Dr Baqa'i's Freedom Guardians held separate meetings for the boycott of the elections; the Front's club was closed down by the authorities and its leadership had to seek refuge in the Senate. Dr Baqa'i was arrested. The students at Tehran University (TU), encouraged by their nationalist professors, demonstrating vehemently. On January 31, 1961, police entered the campus and arrested dozens which in turn led to a students' strike. On February 4, the regime ordered TU to be closed down for a week, thereby trying to cool tempers. But the stratagem failed, and on February 21 riots flared up again, leading to further arrests among the students. Two days later, Dr Iqbal's car was set on fire and the TU rector was lucky to escape the students' ire by fleeing through a back door, assisted by his trustworthy servant Amir Navidi.

Tehran University had turned into the regime's *bête noire*. In order to dilute its influence, the Shah's advisers thought of drowning it in a larger pool of fresh centres of higher education. In 1959, the Teachers' Training College was dissociated from TU and set up as an independent organism; in 1960, Shiraz University was refurbished by generous financial assistance from the Rockefeller Foundation, and was renamed Pahlavi University; during the same year, the Tehran Polytechnic was launched by Engineer Habib Nafisi; finally, in February 1961, the privately-owned *Milli* (National) University was set up with funds from the Pahlavi Foundation and began admitting fee-paying students. Notwithstanding these new institutions, Tehran University, propitiously located on the capital's main avenue (the Shah Reza Avenue), remained the focus of Iran's higher education and the cradle of the nation's best and brightest. The Shah's *bête noire* was alive and kicking.

It was before 165 deputies (out of a total of 176) that the Shah eventually inaugurated the Twentieth *Majlis* on February 21, 1961. The only opposition deputy was Allahyar Salih, elected by his home town of Kashan. The regime had finally won the *Majlis* contest, but not without paying a heavy price for its victory. In the process, it had showed that, notwithstanding American backing, it was still subject to caving in under the slightest pressure.

March 1961 was the time chosen by Queen Elizabeth and Prince Philip of Great Britain for their official five-day visit to Iran (March 2nd to 6th). On the British royal family's heels, it was the turn of General Dudley, the commander-in-chief of the British forces in the Middle East, to arrive in Tehran as the guest of General Âbdullah Hidayat, the capable chief of the Iranian general staff.

Simultaneously with General Dudley's arrival, Generals Hidayat, Taymour Bakhtiar (head of SAVAK) and Hajj Âli Kia (head of the army's counter-intelligence division G-2) were abruptly dismissed and forced into early retirement.[6] Hidayat was replaced by General Âbd ul-Husayn Hijazi and Bakhtiar by General Hasan Pakravan. The sudden dismissal of the armed forces' pillars was related to General Dudley's visit and rumours spread in Tehran of possible connivance between the British commander and the three Iranian generals (especially the Anglophile Hidayat). Talk of a military *coup d'état* was rife in Tehran. It was in March 1961, that the first signs all was not entirely rosy between the Americans and the British in Iran came to light: they certainly could not be ignored any longer. Totally displaced by the American monopoly over Iranian affairs, not even allowed to play her natural role of second fiddle (a role that might have proved satisfactory) Great Britain was undoubtedly exploring possibilities for a comeback – especially because her politicians (rightly) believed that the high road taken by the Americans in Iran was not, in the long term, in the West's or even Iran's best interests. The Americans, however, were not taking British doubts seriously, and stuck to their own strategy – right or wrong.

At the end of this eventful month of March 1961, Iran's religious leader Ayatullah Burujirdi passed away. His death would have momentous consequences for the Qum *Houzeh* and also for overall domestic policies. On the local scale, his diligent and rational management would not be easily replaceable (if at all). On the national scale, his departure lifted the last major hurdle on the path of long-awaited reforms.[7]

12.2. Rumblings of Reform

Since the late 1940s, the Americans (led by Justice Douglas) had been advocating a sweeping land reform scheme for Iran. The reform's theoretical groundwork had been laid down by Professor Lambton in her magisterial 1953 essay entitled 'Landlord and Peasant in Persia', which she had concluded with:

> The question at issue is not the need for reform, which is abundantly clear, but the means by which it is to be carried out. Any measures which fail to relieve the peasant of his poverty, to dissipate the prevailing distrust, or which neglect the importance of the provision of security for all, are unlikely to succeed. Moreover, it is futile to suppose a movement of reform can be brought about by an act of the legislature alone. Its successful accomplishment presupposes changes so great as to amount to a social revolution.
> This, too, assumes an element of leadership, but it is by no means clear whence this is to come...[8]

The question of leadership was indeed crucial. In 1952, Kermit Roosevelt, the Americans' man on the ground, had only two alternatives in a similar reform case: "[Either] a 'peaceful revolution' wherein King Farouq himself would supervise the liquidation of the old and its replacement by the new, ...[or], if this failed, he was to look around for a handsome front man, a strong man, or some formula combining the two".[9] In Egypt, Roosevelt finally opted for the second solution, after trying to convince the hopeless Farouq. That led to the rise to power of the Neguib-Nasser combination. In Iran, the same options as in Egypt were available: the liquidation of the 'old' by the Shah himself or the emergence of a 'strong man'. The latter had been the ill-fated General Muhammad Vali Qaranay. Thus the Shah was given the green light.

Accordingly, in 1958, the latter "began to speak sharply in press conferences and speeches about the large landowners who had refused to follow his example [of selling the Pahlavi Foundation's lands to the peasants]... He said that he had decided to limit the size of individual landholdings and stated that the former owners would receive considerable sums which they could later reinvest profitably in productive enterprises".[10] The Shah was thus following the reformist line now favoured by the Americans.

But, before embarking on the revolutionary path, the reformers had given the landlords in *Majlis* (around 60% of deputies being landlords) the chance to do the job themselves – notwithstanding Professor Lambton's prediction that:

> The landlords are hardly likely to come forward as the standard-bearers of a movement the immediate effect of which is likely to be a reduction in their privileges. The experience of the past and the present situation hold little hope that they will even seek to maintain the substance of their privileged position by a compromise...[11]

Nevertheless, no one could say later that such a remote possibility had been overlooked. The whole process had begun in December 1955, when the Eighteenth *Majlis* had ratified a first reform bill regulating the sales of *Khaliseh* (formerly crown) lands to the peasants tilling it, with instalments to be paid over twenty-five years. This law remained a dead letter until 1958, when suddenly sales shot up. In July 1956, the Nineteenth *Majlis* ratified the Rural Community Bill calling for the establishment of village councils and made it mandatory for the landlords to pay 5% of their revenues to these councils. The enforcement of this law was to be supervised by the Community

Development Department at the Ministry of Interior (first under Bahram Farmanfarmayan, and later under Akbar Zad). With considerable assistance from the American ICA, the Near East Foundation and the Ford Foundation, the department was able to set up some 17,000 village councils in 1957/58, but this attempt at creating grass roots institutions in the basic rural units proved an overall failure (with only a few isolated cases of peasant leaders envisioning the councils as a first step to future reforms[12]). Finally, in December 1959, the Nineteenth *Majlis* came up with a complete land reform bill entitled 'On the Limitation and Reform of Landed Property'. Iranian landlords were thus given a last chance to tailor the now inevitable land reform according to their own interests: they failed to this by piling amendment over amendment until the bill became barely recognisable. The *Majlis* nevertheless approved the emasculated bill in March 1960 and the Senate followed suit in May. Professor Lambton had been right in her 1953 prediction, and the popular proverb 'When the swamps need cleaning, you simply don't call in the frogs' had been once again confirmed.

The landlords thought that by drowning the bill they had won the war. They could not imagine a power undermining them. They counted especially on their right-wing clerical allies, especially Ayatullah Burujirdi and *Majlis* deputy Sayyid Jâfar Bihbahani. Burujirdi had sent a letter (February 13, 1960) to Bihbahani complaining about the land reform question being debated on the *Majlis* floor. To further dot his i's, Burujirdi had declared at Qum on March 14 his personal opposition to any landholding limitation in Iran. With Burujirdi's death in March 1961, the reform scenario being readied since 1958 could now unfold.

In early 1961, Iranian high school teachers had also become restive. The teachers' discontent (something new for Iran), due to high inflation, was channelled through its two trade unions: (1) the Teachers' Trade Union headed by Muhammad Dirakhshish, the director of the *Mihrigan* Club; (2) a smaller union, under Riza Mârifat, an official in Dr Iqbal's *Milliyoun* Party. On March 8, the teachers staged a silent strike to underline their salary ambitions. Premier Sharif Imami made some promises, but failed to keep his word and disruptions followed which culminated in a mass rally held on May 2: teachers clashed with police, and the latter fired, killing Abu'l Hasan Khanâli, a teacher at the Shahristani school, and injuring three of his colleagues. In the event's aftermath, Dirakhshish was arrested, the Ministers of Health and of Justice resigned and the *Majlis* voted a monthly payment for Khanâli's family. The incident had triggered a political crisis. On May 6, Sharif Imami resigned and was replaced by Dr Âli Amini. As the latter presented his cabinet, the Shah dissolved the Houses of Parliament according to Article 48 of the Constitution. The door to reforms thus stood wide open, with no domestic power to oppose it.

Dr Amini, fifty-six, an old Qajar Elitist and a large landowner himself (with forty-two villages at Gilan's Lasht-i Nisha, arguably the best agricultural land in Iran), was the right man for the job[13] – although it was a paradox having the most prominent member of an aristocracy being lured to drive the last nail into his own class's coffin. In spite of not being a "servant of the court", he had solid backing, especially in Washington[14] where he had served two years (until 1958) as Iranian Ambassador and where oil executives remembered his diligent supervision of the 1954 Consortium Agreement. Internally, he could rely on the Elite's remnants to behave as long as he was premier. The cabinet he put together was a carbon copy of the cabinet foreseen by General Qaranay back in 1958, with Dr Hasan Arsanjani in the key post of Minister of Agriculture. Furthermore, Dirakhshish had been given the Culture portfolio to soothe the teachers; Ibtihaj, just released from prison, later said that he had been offered the Finance portfolio but declined,[15] so the post went to Âbd ul-Husayn Bihnya. Once in the saddle, Amini's programme was clear-cut: while pursuing the economic stabilisation drive begun under Sharif Imami, he had to tackle simultaneously the anti-corruption campaign and the land reform plan.

While Arsanjani systematically prepared his land reform programme, Amini tried his hand at rooting out corruption. He had questionnaires distributed among Iran's 205,000 civil servants, asking the size of their fortune and its provenance.[16] The whole project was not taken seriously since there was no organisation to follow up the matter, and it was soon forgotten. Therefore it was a real shock to Tehran when, on May 13, Amini, who had stated that "corruption had exceeded all limits", made a series of arrests:

- General Mihdi Quli Âlavi Muqaddam, the former chief of police and Minister of Interior (under Sharif Imami), was accused of misappropriations concerning Tehran's United Bus Company.

- General Hajj Âli Kia, the former head of the army's G-2 unit, was detained over a twelve-storey apartment building (dubbed the "where-did-you-get-it-from building") located on the Old Shimiran Road, which he had built at a cost of Rls80m.
- General Âli Akbar Zargham, the former Minister of Finance, was arraigned for embezzling some Rls750m from the Civil Supplies Department.
- General Rouhullah Navisi, former head of the Northern Fisheries, was arrested in connection with millions of Rials which were allegedly missing.

Dozens of other personalities, such as General Ajudani and former Tehran mayor F. Furoud, were arrested during 1961. Arresting the suspect officials was one thing, bringing them to trial and convicting them another. In 1961, the Northern Fisheries' case was brought to trial, with General Navisi and his subordinates being acquitted in September 1964. Âlavi Muqaddam and Zargham were set free in March 1962 and Kia came out in July 1962, all of them without being convicted. By then, Amini's campaign had petered out. Like Razmara in 1950, the prime minister soon realised that corruption was not limited to a few generals and that its ramifications went all the way to the court and the old Elite. No one in Tehran was willing to see skeletons falling out of closets, and the Pandora's box opened by Amini was rapidly closed again. Even the Senate Building scandal, a case of blatant irregularities (the colossal sum of Rls660m had been spent on it!), led only to the arrest of two project engineers and their release in August 1962 after a whitewash.

12.3. Land Reform

Dr Hasan Arsanjani, forty-nine, was the unanimous choice for leading the land reform schedule. A lawyer by training and a journalist by profession, he had developed a deep-rooted hatred for the landowning class, which he held responsible for all the country's social ills (and for marring his own political career). Recruited as an up-and-coming politician by Qavam in 1946, he had remained faithful to the latter's camp, and thus to Dr Amini. He had shown his sympathies in his weekly *Darya* (created in 1944) when in 1950 he published in a series of articles entitled 'The Caged Lions',[17] reprinting the letters of imprisoned *Toudeh* leaders to their families. As an "exponent of Iran's ambitious, hard-working younger generation",[18] Arsanjani thought that land reform was a precursor to the reform of the whole society: "feudalism is being abolished, the middle class grows and a democracy of the bourgeoisie is established", he had written.[19] Every group in Iranian society (except for the landlords, of course) wanted land reform, but none of them was willing to bell the cat – except for Arsanjani, with his missionary zeal to achieve the goal of his life. Even the Shah and the court at first hid behind Arsanjani's small, but powerful frame, waiting to see developments before committing themselves. As for Arsanjani, he had been committed even before being appointed.

By the close of October 1961, Arsanjani was ready to move, having done his homework. He forwarded his proposals for reform to the Shah, via Amini. The Shah replied by issuing a *farman* (decree) "ordering the government, *inter alia*, to execute, if necessary in a modified form, the Land Reform Law of May 17, 1960".[20] As the opposition protested noisily that the decree was unconstitutional, Arsanjani presented to the cabinet his 38 article amendment. On January 9, 1962, the cabinet reluctantly approved the proposed amendment, which was in fact "a new law" as Professor Lambton correctly pointed out:

> It differed from the old law in the following respects: (i) it limited holdings to one village, (ii) fixed the compensation to be given the landowners on the basis of the taxation they had paid, (iii) allocated the land to the peasants cultivating the land without upsetting the field lay-out of the village, and (iv) made membership of a co-operative society a condition of the receipt of the land...[21]

On January 15, 1962, Arsanjani appointed a five-man Land Reform Higher Council to oversee the new law's implementation (the council held one hundred meetings between January 1962 and August 1963).

Simultaneously, the opposition launched its last-ditch stand against the land reform as disorders hit Tehran and especially the TU campus. Sardar Fakhir Hikmat, the former *Majlis* president, wrote in an open letter that the land reform programme was against the teachings of Islam. Sayyid Muhammad Bihbahani and his son Jâfar echoed Hikmat's statements, leading to Jâfar's arrest. On January 22, Tehran University exploded, leading to violent clashes between students and paratroopers. It was alleged that General Taymour Bakhtiar had had a hand in pouring fuel on the university's fire (playing *la politique du pire*), and the general was sent to Swiss exile four days later.

In February it was the turn of Najaf's ayatullahs to officially condemn Iran's land reform programme. On the other hand, Arsanjani was not without supporters, as proven by the congratulatory telegram sent him on February 28 by the US Secretary for Agriculture, Orville L. Freeman. But Arsanjani needed no encouragement to forge ahead on his crusade against the landlords. He had an easy time (being a seasoned journalist), taking full advantage of the propaganda machine at his disposal, issuing inflammatory declarations to the media against the landlords. He had the good fortune of being able to benefit from the latest revolution in communication: the small portable transistor radio, made cheaply by Japanese companies (like Sony's model TR-610), that even some peasants could afford and on which the illiterate rural masses could listen to Arsanjani's fiery and emotional speeches. A transistor radio hanging on the horn of a cow became a new feature of Iranian villages: the peasants thus got to know their chief defender. Hasanjani, they called him. And if anyone needed a vigorous advocate in Iran, it was the peasant masses.

The plight of the Iranian peasantry was appalling. The average peasant was still living as his forebears had for centuries before. None of the technological innovations of the nineteenth and twentieth centuries (except for transistor radios) had come to improve his simple existence: no elementary hygiene, no basic pharmaceuticals, no electricity and no potable water. The projects of Point Four and the Second Plan had made but a small dent in his daily routine. His usual lot was days of still hard work to eke out a bare subsistence, with three Damoclean swords continuously hanging over his head: (1) illness; (2) poor weather; and (3) the landlord's ire. Health problems meant diminished productivity and possibly massive medical expenses in Tehran or Isfahan at best; death at worst. A year of drought was a catastrophe – for a peasant who had to struggle in an average year to make ends meet, a bad year was a crippling blow. Having no personal reserves (but his pair of cows, without which he couldn't till the land), he either had to rely on temporary assistance from his landlord (some wheat for his yearly bread and for next year's seeds) or enter the never-ending spiral of indebtedness (paying usurious interest rates, without ever becoming capable of repaying the principal). After centuries of tightrope walking, peasants had naturally become callous, defiant and saw things in terms of relative strengths, in black and white. The landlord was the major element against which the peasant had to guard. Naturally, there were not only inhuman landlords: as in every other social group there was some distribution between the extremes, but with the worst landlords definitely outnumbered the best. One thing was clear though: any landlord had every right *vis-à-vis* any of his peasants. The peasants, however, were not totally defenceless, being able to migrate to another village in the last resort. Before reaching that point, they used their ingrained astuteness, their inherited flexibility and their highly developed sense of survival to fend off the landlord. Besides these obvious landlord–peasant matters, there was an indefinable cloud of intangibles between the two, a set of unwritten rules that both sides could not break without impunity. After all, both the master and the peasant were only human.

Between the landlord and the peasant stood a buffer: the village dignitaries, headed by the *kadkhuda* (the village mayor). This village elite, essentially made up of the landlord's appointees, formed an upper class, usually wealthier than the average peasant by a factor of five to ten. The dignitaries acted as a two-way conduit, communicating the landlord's orders to the peasantry and channelling the petitions from the bottom to the top. For their labours they also got paid twice: by the landlord for services rendered and by the peasant for favours obtained. In the process, some *kadkhudas* became very rich indeed, but it was their due, for they were somewhat their villages' elite.

In the 1950s, more and more landlords had developed the damaging habit of letting their villages for a fixed sum to professional managers. From the owner's point of view it was a good deal: a fixed income with no personal input and the possibility of blaming the manager for any wrongdoing. For the manager it was also a fair deal: he would squeeze the maximum out of the peasantry (to whom he had no link) and end up getting a sizeable discount from the landlord on the agreed rent (under a myriad of pretexts). Naturally the great losers in this deal were the peasants – whereas they had some collective (even individual) lever over their landlord (gradually developed over the years), they were almost powerless against a yearly manager. For the landlords renting might have been an easy way out, but it was a clear discharge of responsibility (keeping the privileges) and nullifying their *raison d'être*. On the other hand, the professional managers were gaining experience while getting rich; this experience would come in handy when they would turn, a decade later, into factory managers supervising the same peasants turned workers, in a safer and more regulated environment.

On March 1, 1962, Dr Arsanjani had the cabinet approve a decree placing the land reform programme under the sole responsibility of the Ministry of Agriculture. Two days later, he finally launched his land reform scheme (later known as 'the first phase'). He had carefully chosen his first battlefield: Maragheh in Azarbayjan. Knowing the north-west to be the toughest nut to crack (agreeing with Justice Douglas's opinion of Azarbayjani landlords as "the most callous I know..."), he had carefully planned his first strike. Realising the crucial impact of this first test on the country at large, he had secretly sent a small hand-picked team of close collaborators to Maragheh as early as October 1961. On March 7, he was on the spot himself to oversee the orderly transfer of property to peasants: the Maragheh landlords had co-operated (hoping to hold on to the best single village allowed them by the law). On March 12, the Shah came to Marageh for the formalities of handing over the deeds to the peasants. Having won in Maragheh, Arsanjani was confident of ultimate victory: therefrom the snowball was rolling and no power could now stop it.

On May 27, it was the deeds to Lasht-i Nisha which the Shah distributed among Amini's peasants. By mid-July Amini duly resigned, under the pretext of a $80m budget deficit. He had done his duty as the figurehead for land reform. Asadullah Âlam, the Shah's confidant, replaced him in the premiership. Arsanjani remained at Agriculture to complete the land reform plan. In the summer of 1962, the land reform programme was rolling full steam ahead: from Azarbayjan to Khuzistan, from Khurasan to Sistan. Single-handedly the tenacious Arsanjani had bulldozed his way over all obstacles, realising his dream: defeating, or, better, crushing, the landlords he abhorred. During the reform schedule his hate had turned to contempt for the landlords: he had expected them to put up a better fight against him.[22]

In the face of land reform, the landlords had been defenceless. "At no time", wrote Professor Lambton, "did the landowning class make a concerted stand against it".[23] A Dutch observer was flabbergasted by this fact:

> A very few isolated cases of individual opposition – evasion of law, embezzlement or concealment – are reported. The landlords ...when summoned to declare their landed property, come; one after another. Their collaboration becomes so great that the Ministry of Agriculture feels compelled to interrupt his flow of accusations against them for a word of praise. This performance of the landlords is astonishing. The whole programme is aimed to bring about their annihilation and they co-operate![24]

The landlords had failed to develop (unlike the clergy) an intellectual wing which could have formulated a concerted action plan in the face of the reform. Their Landlords' Association, set up in Tehran, turned out to be an empty shell. Their "immensely important position in society" and their "great influence in the political field",[25] emphasised in the early 1950s by Professor Lambton, had crumbled within a decade under the weight of almost one billion dollars of US assistance and over one and a half billion dollars of oil revenues. The landowning class was isolated, despised, lacking a leader and a worthy elite. Moreover many landlords had deserted ship by selling cheaply in the late 1950s and reinvesting in Tehran real estate, or by purchasing agricultural machinery and setting up 'mechanised' units (which were exempted from the land reform law as per its article 3[26]). But the large majority of landlords bent with the wind, fearing the worst and hoping for the best, always on the defensive.

From mid-1962 onwards, Arsanjani was not thinking of the land reform any longer (as it now moved under its own steam), but rather thought of his own political ambitions. He had realised the immense potential power of Iran's peasant masses. He would use his enormous popularity amongst them to bring them together, forming a huge national lever he would use to turn the whole Iranian society like a pancake, with himself ending up at the top. Masking his ambitions behind the successes of the land reform schedule, he organised elections for the First National Congress of Peasants in Tehran. Inaugurated on January 9, 1963, his congress was attended by no fewer than 4,700 rural delegates from across Iran. The best and the brightest of the peasantry attended it. Arsanjani had debated lengthily with the peasants' leaders about his idea of incorporating them in a *Hizb-i Dihqan* (Peasants' Party), with himself as secretary-general and them as party leaders. Finally, Arsanjani was near his ultimate goal.

But the Shah and his advisers were not idle. They had ascertained Arsanjani's master plan and decided that the best defence was to attack. The land reform had been a great success and it was high time for the Shah to wrest the plaudits for it from Arsanjani. Thus he would (i) take the credit, (ii) link the peasants to the monarchy, (iii) pull the brakes on a reform which had gone further than expected, and (iv) hand over the controls of the reform to docile managers. On January 9, at his inaugural speech to the peasants' congress, the Shah unveiled his batteries with a six-point reform programme (drowning the land reform in his own reform flood):

1. Land reform;
2. Nationalisation of forests and pastures;
3. Sale to the public of state-owned factories (for financing the land reform);
4. Profit-sharing of workers in industrial establishments;
5. Right to vote for women;
6. Creation of the *Sipah-i Danish* (the Literacy Corps).

On January 26, 1963 the six-point reform programme were submitted to the people's approval in a nation-wide referendum, the outcome of which was never in doubt and which ended with a total of 5,603,626 votes cast – 5,598,711 in favour:[27] a 99.9% majority. President Kennedy sent the Shah a telegram of congratulations underlining this "event of historical importance". By the timely launching of his 'White Revolution',[28] the Shah had cut the grass from under Arsanjani's feet. With the land reform on track, the Agriculture Minister was now redundant and could be jettisoned (before he launched his Peasants' Party). On March 7, 1963, Arsanjani was abruptly dismissed and sent off to Italy as ambassador (displacing Jamal Imami Khwu'i). In his stead, a no-nonsense (and reliable) fifty-nine-year old career officer, General Ismâil Riahi, was appointed Minister for Agriculture. Within two months, the Shah had turned a compromised internal situation in his favour and in the process Arsanjani's dangerous plans had been thwarted.

Without Arsanjani, the land reform rapidly lost its initial impetus, the first phase almost grinding to a halt.

The authorities tergiversated over its continuation, under the pretext that they were waiting for the Twenty-First *Majlis* and the Fourth Senate to convene. When the Houses of Parliament assembled in October 1963, they tackled the question of the land reform programme's second phase, coming up with a 47-article law, which was ratified in May 1964 by the *Majlis* and in July by the Senate. Put in a nutshell, the landlords had to liquidate the single village they had originally been allowed to keep:

> Landowners were given a choice of five possible courses. These were tenancy, sale to the peasants, division of the land between the landowner or landowners and the peasants in the same proportion as the division of the crop under the existing crop-sharing agreement, the formation of an 'agricultural unit' by the landowner or landowners and the peasants to run the property and the purchase by the landowner of the peasants' rights...[29]

The land reform scheme's second stage was launched in the summer of 1964 amidst increasing doubts over the practicality of the various options. Willy-nilly, the reform went ahead, albeit at an ever-slower pace, a pace inversely proportional to the size of the expanding land reform bureaucracy. The two options favoured by the landlords were: (1) outright sale to the peasants at a price set by the Land Reform Organisation (to be paid in twelve annual instalments); and (2) the partition of land, with the landlord receiving between thirty-three and forty per cent of the total acreage in most cases. But without Arsanjani the land reform was going backwards instead of forwards. As Professor Lambton concluded with hindsight:

> The first stage of the land reform marked a genuine change in the political and social life of Persia. Its aims were clear and unambiguous and its operation, in

the whole, rapid and effective. The second stage was not merely, or even mainly, a consolidation of the ground already won; it was rather a weakening of the original purpose...[30]

The third stage of the land reform programme was launched in January 1966. The aims of the last phase were to increase agricultural production in order to improve the condition of the peasants and bring about a stabilisation of food prices.[31] Now that the landlords had been evicted, the problems of running the villages without them had to be solved. Some loose structure was required to fill the void and as a means of channelling outside assistance to the peasants. Peasants' co-operatives were created in the framework of the rural community development model, copied from the similar organisation set up in 1952 in India.[32] Co-operatives mushroomed throughout Iran to reach, at the close of 1970, a total of 8,928 units (covering 27,250 villages and 1,606,083 rural households[33]). The co-operatives, however, were in stark opposition to the Iranian peasant's marked individualistic character. They proved a failure.[33A] As soon as the pressure (and the financial assistance) behind a co-operative was withdrawn, the entity slowly disintegrated, proving incapable of managing itself. Even trained managers were unable to reverse this trend as the peasants could fool any of them (after all, not so long ago, they had fooled their all-powerful landlord).

In October 1967, the Land Reform Organisation, hitherto a division within the Ministry of Agriculture, was upgraded into a ministry: the Ministry of Land Reform and Rural Co-operatives.

The director-general of the organisation since January 1965, Colonel Âbd ul-Âzim Valian, was promoted to ministerial rank. On January 19, 1969, the last land reform law (in 19 articles) was ratified by the Houses of Parliament. Its aim was to legislate in unsettled or disputed cases, and make it mandatory for landlords who had failed to come forward to do so or face judgement *in absentia*. Over the next thirty-two months, the new bureaucracy matured into a full-blown ministry as it eventually settled the few pending cases. On September 23, 1971, Iran's land reform agenda was brought to a close and its ministry renamed the Ministry of Co-operatives and Rural Affairs. According to Minister Valian, the whole reform programme had cost a total of only Rls24bn (equivalent to around $317m), with approximately Rls10bn being spent on the all-important first phase. In his concluding remarks Valian noted that:

> Today, ...there is not a single farmer in the country who does not own the land he tills...

That was not true – although a majority of peasants tilled their own land, this group was far from all of them.

For propaganda purposes, statistics were continuously updated to show the remarkable achievements of the White Revolution. But numbers were rough (to say the least), with the statistics of a single village difficult to come by, let alone a district or a whole province. Numbers were there to impress the foreigners and the gullible. The real and palpable consequences of the land reform were that:

(1) The bastions of the old Elite had been conquered. In the process the landlords had been compensated (to a larger extent than they had envisioned at first), but they had irretrievably lost their power and their economic bases, if not their self-confidence. A whole tradition and a special way of life was dying.

(2) A sleeping giant had finally been awakened: the Iranian peasantry. When it was finally to flex its muscles, shockwaves were to be sent through the whole country. Whatever it lacked in quality, it would make up for in quantity: with two out of every three citizens, it not only was a majority – it was Iran.

The man who had made it all possible by sheer willpower, playing the role of his life, Dr Hasan Arsanjani, would be cast off. Recalled in the autumn of 1964 from Italy after calling the embassy "an official stew" in an official report, he reopened his Tehran law practice and inherited a fortune.[34] In 1969, he died at the age of fifty-seven. "Few Iranians believed his death to be a natural one", Cottam concluded.[35]

The man who received Arsanjani's legacy was Muhammad Reza Shah. He was able to launch his White Revolution on the basis of the land reform successfully engineered by Arsanjani.

12.4. Active Oppositions

The murder of Engineer Shahpour Malik Âbidi, the head of the Land Reform station at Firouzabad in Fars province, on November 12, 1962, was a sure sign that land reform was not to everyone's taste. Among the unhappy few were the tribal *khans*, who had correctly foreseen that the land reform scheme's sequels would inevitably lead to their own ruin and their tribes' subservience to the state. In the plan's aftermath, the Shah would certainly endeavour to pursue the tribal policies begun by his father.

The *khans* were not well-equipped to resist this new threat. They had lost Murtaza Quli Khan Samsam, the old and uncontested Bakhtiari leader, on December 26, 1959. His successor was his fourth son, the forty-five year old Amir Bahman Khan. The Qashqa'i Ilkhan Nasir Khan was in exile. There remained as the natural leaders of Iran's *khans* only Fathullah Khan Hayat Davoudi,* the leader of the small Hayat Davoudi tribe (located in South Iran, around Bandar Rig and Bandar Ganaveh), and Âbdullah Khan Zarghampour,** the chief of the Boir Ahmadi tribe. They joined forces and set up a tribal coalition including the Hayat Davoudis, the Boir Ahmadis, the Mamasanis, the Qashqa'is and the Bakhtiaris, of which they took command, the former as political leader and the latter as military commander.

* FATHULLAH KHAN HAYAT DAVOUDI (1905-1964), son of Haydar Khan; like his father, tribal *ilkhan*; occupied Bushire during the Southern Rebellion (1946); led protracted legal battle against NIOC and the Consortium over Kharg Island, which was part of his tribal lands (1950s); masterminded tribal rebellion, chairing leaders' meetings at Tehran (1962); political leader of rebellion (1963); arrested, tortured (1963), court-martialled, sentenced to death, executed on October 5, 1964, with five of his fellow tribal *khans*.
** ÂBDULLAH KHAN ZARGHAMPOUR (1912-1963), son of a Boir Ahmadi tribal chief who was executed on Reza Shah's orders (1929); for twelve years under house arrest in Tehran (1929-41); took part in attack on Simirum (1943), in Southern Rebellion (1946) and also in *Murdad 28* coup (1953); arrested for defying authorities (1957); sentenced to fifteen years by court martial and imprisoned (1957-61), then under house arrest in Tehran (1961-63); fled with

Nasir Tahiri (another Boir Ahmadi chief) to set up southern tribal headquarters and led military rebellion (February–June 1963); shot dead on June 8, 1963.

After a year of preparations the tribal uprising began (prematurely) on February 28, 1963, with the storming of the Dadinjan Gendarmerie post by Boir Ahmadi tribesmen. The armed rebellion quickly spread throughout the southern provinces. Gendarmerie posts were attacked, the tribesmen needing the weapons therein. The rebellion's main forces consisted of 1,200 Boir Ahmadis under Nasir Khan Tahiri, 1,000 Mamasanis led by Husayn Quli Khan Rustam and 500 Qashqa'is of the Surkhi sub-tribe, commanded by Habib Khan Shahbazi. The Bakhtiaris' uprising failed to materialise as its leader, Amir Bahman Samsam, was arrested in Tehran before being able to enter the fray. On March 5 and 6, air force jets strafed tribal encampments in the south, causing numerous casualties among the defenceless nomad population. On March 10, General Karim Varahram was appointed Governor-General of Fars with full powers. Two days later, General Bahram Aryana arrived in Shiraz to take command of all armed forces – known as the Southern Expeditionary Army, which consisted at its peak of four full army divisions, Gendarmerie units and an air force squadron. The Shah's army was in its element against rifle-armed tribesmen (lacking ammunition and heavy weapons). With no rearguard support and no outside help forthcoming, the tribesmen were at the mercy of the army corps, whose commanders wanted the rebellion to last long enough for them to get their promotions, war bonuses and medals. From the outset, there was no doubt about the inevitable outcome.

In early April 1963, army columns began the systematic invasion of tribal territory. On April 14, the army chalked up its first success by arresting chieftain Husayn Quli Khan Rustam. But on April 22, it was the tribesmen's turn to score against the government forces: a handful of tribesmen ambushed a full battalion in the valley leading to the Tang-i Gachistan and wiped it out, killing and wounding some four hundred of its men (only a few were able to flee the rebels' deadly cross-fire[36]). The rebels' morale soared. The army licked its wounds, taking its revenge on simple, defenceless tribesmen. Notwithstanding the army harassment and air force bombings, the rebellion held steady its mountain strongholds. On June 8, 1963, its supreme chief, Âbdullah Zarghampour, was shot dead by his own cook. Thereafter the whole rebellion collapsed. Rebel leaders were either captured or had to surrender. Nasir Khan Tahiri gave himself up at Yasouj on June 21. In July, General Aryana returned triumphantly to Tehran while the now redundant Southern Expeditionary Corps was disbanded.

The last act of the failed tribal rebellion of 1963 took place at Shiraz in the summer of 1964 when its eleven tribal leaders were court-martialled. On August 6, the court passed six death and five prison sentences. All eleven defendants appealed and on September 16, the appeals court confirmed the initial sentences – except that Vali Kiani's death sentence was altered to a ten-year sentence (after the accused admitted in court having tipped off SAVAK about the rebels' plans),[37] and Khudakaram Zarghampour's prison sentence was changed to a death sentence (to re-establish the initial six), notwithstanding that the young Zarghampour (Âbdullah's son) was incurably ill: a rather unique legal precedent. Along with Kiani, Suhrab Zarghami Kashkuli, Firaydoun Javidi, Amir Bahman Samsam and Muhammad Husayn Khan Qashqa'i were sentenced to prison times ranging from ten to two years. Finally, on October 5, 1964, Fathullah Khan Hayat Davoudi, Nasir Khan Tahiri, Husayn Quli Khan Rustam, Jâfar Quli Khan Rustam, Habibullah Khan Shabazi and Khudakaram Khan Zarghampour were executed at Shiraz. There now was blood between the Pahlavis and Iran's tribes.

The collapse of the 1963 tribal rebellion sounded the *khans*' death knell. The tribes' and tribesmen's times were long past on the domestic stage. From then on the Shah's army, his Gendarmerie and his SAVAK would look at tribal lands as occupied territories. Given *carte blanche* by Tehran, officers would treat simple nomads as third-class citizens. Any armed resistance was implacably crushed. The successful armed guerrilla group launched in 1964 by the young idealist Bahman Khan Qashqa'i (the courageous son of the formidable Farrukh Bibi, the sister of Nasir Khan) was a case in point. Bahman Qashqa'i led a successful campaign, but eventually surrendered after being given a promise of safe conduct by the Pahlavi University rector, Amir Asadullah Âlam,[38] and was summarily executed within hours of giving himself up, in November 1966. Bahman's effort was the last serious attempt by tribesmen to mount a viable rural guerrilla campaign (with all the hardships and tortures such a movement meant for the nomad population). During the late 1960s, the few remaining Qashqa'i rebels were weeded out and mercilessly destroyed.[39]

The *khans'* greatest loss, though, was Fathullah Khan Hayat Davoudi: he had been the best and brightest of them all. At his court-martial he had not budged when sentenced to death. During the trials he had dominated the group of defendants; in prison he had kept his spirits; when given a lie detector test "administered by an American technician"[40] he had lied (knowing all the details of the conspiracy) and deceived the apparatus; even when tortured by the Military Command's henchmen he had refused to talk. Hayat Davoudi was an inspiration to the *khans*: a great personality, a leader of men, a vivid intelligence and possessing legendary courage. He lived and died like a man. There were not many like him: the Shah and his generals could rest assured that no *khan* would fill his shoes. On the other hand, the Shah's supporters should have been worried that in a country where a Muhammad Reza Pahlavi could order the execution of a Fathullah Khan Hayat Davoudi there was bound to be a very deep flaw somewhere: sooner or later, this basic fault had to surface and rip the whole fragile fabric at the top.

Another group that feared a return to the ways of Reza Shah was the Qum religious hierocracy: it could see the pattern of dictatorship re-emerging. Moreover it had lost Ayatullah Burujirdi and no single leader had surfaced from among potential candidates, who numbered Najaf's four Grand Ayatullahs: Muhsin Hakim, Sayyid Mahmoud Shahroudi, Khwu'i and Sayyid Âbdullah Shirazi; Qum's triumvir of Sayyid Muhammad Kazim Shariâtmadari, Muhammad Riza Gulpayigani and Shahab ul-Din Marâshi Najafi; and the Mashhad duo of Hadi Milani and Ahmad Kafa'i Khurasani. Ayatullah Kashani, who had died in March 1962, never ranked among the contenders. During 1962, the clerics' intellectual wing freely debated the question of leadership, but failed to come up with a recommendation.[41]

As the land reform schedule made headway during 1962, tensions between Tehran and Qum increased. When Premier Âlam announced in early October that elections for the provincial and town councils were imminent, Qum's hierocracy reacted vehemently – these elections were a direct threat to the supremacy of the religious faction in rural areas. On November 6, a sixty year old teacher at the Qum *Houzeh*, Ayatullah Rouhullah Khomeini,* did something highly unusual: he sent a strongly-worded protest telegram to Prime Minister

Âlam.[41A] After some tergiversations, the Shah eventually decided to back down and the elections were cancelled a month later. Having won the first round and found a worthy leader – Khomeini – in the process, Qum's younger clergymen were ready to fight the Shah's six-point referendum of January 1963. Here, though, the clerics faced a dilemma: on the one hand, they couldn't let these reforms pass without a protest (knowing it to be the first step towards dictatorship) yet on the other, they had to be careful not to antagonise the millions of peasants and workers standing to (theoretically) benefit from it. As a compromise they decided to attack the referendum's illegality and the unacceptable issue of votes for women. Tensions continued to increase between Tehran and Qum.

* AYATULLAH ROUHULLAH AL-MOUSAVI AL-KHOMEINI (1902–1989), born in Khumayn, the youngest of the three sons of Sayyid Mustafa, a rural clergyman murdered in 1903; studied at *maktab* in Khumayn; entered Arak *Houzeh* (1919); followed mentor Shaykh Âbd ul-Karim Ha'iri Yazdi to Qum *Houzeh* (1920); married daughter of Ayatullah Saqafi (1929); wrote *Kashf ul-Asrar* (Uncovering the Secrets), (1940s); teacher at Qum *Houzeh*; led religious opposition to the Shah's regime (1962–63); his arrest on June 5, 1963 triggered widespread riots; imprisoned (June–October 1963); under house arrest (November 1963–March 1964); returned to Qum, spoke up against 'new capitulations', exiled to Turkey (November 1964), took up residence at Najaf (1965); wrote *Vilaiyyat-i Faqih* (1971); led Islamic Revolution from Najaf, then Paris (1978–79); returned to Iran (February 1979); founded Islamic Republic of Iran (April 1979); Iran's uncontested Supreme Leader (1979–1989); died on June 4, 1989.

On March 22, 1963, in a response to the attacks by the religious community, the regime dispatched a paratroopers' battalion to Qum's *Madraseh Fayziyyeh*, the school where Khomeini taught. During the punitive raid, a young student, Sayyid Younis Roudbari, was killed and several others seriously injured. From then on, Khomeini was on a collision course with the regime. On May 1, the fortieth day of the *Fayziyyeh* raid, Khomeini issued a caustic communiqué accusing the Shah of wanting "to eradicate Islam and its bases in Iran".[42] Then, on June 3, in a public sermon, he directly attacked the Shah, calling him "a poor, deficient thing".[43] The insults led to Khomeini's arrest in the early morning hours of June 5 and his transfer to Tehran; arrested on the same day were Ayatullah Mahallati Qumi, the tribune Muhammad Taqi Falsafi and a dozen lesser clerics, with Ayatullah Hasan Tabataba'i Qumi being arrested on the morrow, and the Ayatullah Sayyid Âbd ul-Husayn Dastghayb being apprehended the next day in Shiraz.

News of Khomeini's arrest spread throughout Iran and triggered mass riots in Tehran, Qum, Isfahan, Mashhad, Shiraz and Varamin. In Tehran, thousands of demonstrators took to the streets in the south of the city. Empty-handed youths, although some wielded wooden sticks, battled armed policemen, soon reinforced by regular army units of the Martial Law, under the command of General Nîmatullah Nasiri. In the city centre, a police station was besieged by five thousand people; the twenty or so policemen defending it ran out of ammunition and were saved *in extremis* by army reinforcements; three other police stations were unsuccessfully besieged. Shâban Jâfari's traditional *Zourkhaneh* was set on fire and the offices of the unpopular *Ittilaât* newspaper ransacked. Facing determined troops, the demonstrators were unable to take any strategic centre, and they were crushed in a bloodbath of unprecedented proportions in Iran's history, with hundreds of casualties. Demonstrators marching from Varamin to Tehran were intercepted by a battalion along the way and mercilessly mown by machine-gun fire. On June 6, riots broke out again in Tehran, but were soon quelled by fresh troops – ordered on to the streets by the Shah after Premier Âlam had threatened to resign.[44] The Tehran garrison had been badly depleted by their heavy contribution to the Southern Expeditionary Corps, but was still strong enough to stop mainly unarmed rioters. The inexperienced riot leaders had made the mistake of sending their troops on to the streets two days in a row: even mobs need time to find their second wind. The June 5 and 6 riots had met with failure. But they had made of Ayatullah Khomeini a national hero and leader. His peers in Qum lost no time in asking publicly for his release from jail, although wondering in private: "For what has all this blood been shed?"[45] The regime did not dare court-martial Khomeini and transferred him in October from his prison at the Second Armoured Division garrison to house arrest at Hajji Roughani's home on Doulat Street. In April 1964 he was allowed to go back to Qum, the regime believing that he had been neutralised. The June 5 riot leaders Tayyib Hajj Riza'i and Hajj Ismâil Aqa Riza'i (not related to each other) were not as fortunate: they were tortured,[46] tried and executed on November 2, 1963 [47]; other leaders were sentenced to heavy prison terms.

The troubled events of January 1962 were the occasion for the nationalist counter-elite to resurface behind the screen of the Second National Front (NF II). In 1961 their Tehran *Bazaar* pillar, Hajj Hasan Shamshiri, had passed away, thereby weakening their grip in the *Bazaar*. His successor Hajj Mahmoud Manian did not possess the same clout. But, at Tehran University, they still had some support among the faculty and the students – whose slogan on January 23, 1962 at Tehran University had been 'Reforms, Yes. Dictatorship, No'. On May 28, 1962, NF II would reach its zenith with the enormous success of its meeting at the Jalaliyyeh racetrack, attended by some 100,000 people. The NF II failed to capitalise on such a unique following. Its problem was certainly not popularity but the calibre of its leadership. Instead of Dr Musaddiq (still in forced residence at Ahmadabad), the Front had opted for the arch-conservative Dr Allahyar Salih to lead it. Lacking a strategy and clear objectives, the leadership failed to listen to its younger, radical elements.

The two tendencies within the NF II clashed in the open at its congress held at Tehran between December 20, 1963 and January 6, 1964. Dr Salih preached "patience and hope" to a radical rank and file whose priority was action. When the students tried to make inroads into NF II organs, the elder politicians, fearing a radical hijack, closed ranks and systematically excluded the students from executive institutions. The students, rebuffed, took their case to Dr Musaddiq himself and the elder leader proved more far-sighted than his old guard by siding squarely with the students. In a letter dated May 19, 1964, Dr Musaddiq asked for the Front's statutes to be revised to allow the students a say. The Central Committee, feeling let down by their leader, resigned *en bloc*. That was the end of NF II. The elder politicians would retire to their ivory tower, hoping for an elusive comeback. The students, disillusioned by the nationalist counter-elite, would begin looking for fresh political avenues.

On March 5, 1967, Dr Musaddiq would pass away at the Najmiyyeh Hospital at the age of eighty-seven. He had been unique, his first National Front and his oil nationalisation too.

The NF II leaders could have learned a lesson or two from Ayatullah Taliqani and Engineer Bazargan. On May 15, 1961, the religious-nationalist duo had found the time ripe to change their outdated National Resistance Movement shell and launch their *Nihzat-i Azadi Iran* (Freedom Movement of Iran – FMI), correctly placing emphasis on 'movement' and 'freedom'. They had understood that the days of political compromise were long over and that in the 1960s, there were only two alternatives: one was either for or against the Shah's regime. For the FMI the choice was clear. Its leaders had the courage of their convictions, as they were to prove time and again. They issued a harsh communiqué entitled 'The Dictator Draws Blood' after the June 5 riots and were quickly arrested and court-martialled in the autumn of 1963. On January 7 and on March 2, 1964, the first and the appeals court passed the same prison sentences: Sayyid Mahmoud Taliqani and Engineer Mihdi Bazargan, ten years each; and between two to six years for Dr Âbbas Shaybani, Dr Yadullah Sahabi, Ahmad Âlibaba'i, Îzzatullah Sahabi, Abu'l Fazl Hakimi, Mihdi Jâfari, Âbbas Radnia and Parviz Îdalatmanish.[48] All were eventually released within months, only Taliqani and Bazargan remaining incarcerated until 1967.

As for Dr Baqa'i, he was arrested in March 1961, sentenced in June to two years' imprisonment and released in October 1961.

His Guardians of Freedom Party was disbanded and he regained his tenure at Tehran University. He was out of politics, almost for good.

12.5. Transitions

In October 1963, General Nasiri gave a grand gala function at Vanak's plush Police Officers' Club to celebrate the end of martial law in Tehran – and the multiple victories of 1963. The cream of the armed forces attended Nasiri's soiree, including a total of fifty-nine generals (thirty-one from the army, eleven from the Gendarmerie, seven each from the police and SAVAK, and three from the Military Command) and eighty-one senior officers, mostly colonels.[49]

All the up-and-coming younger generals were present: Ayadi, Aryana, Fardoust, Uvaysi, Azhari, Khusrouvani, Pakravan and Hashiminijad. They had a good reason to celebrate this year of 1963 which had seen them kill a great number of their internal enemies with their sophisticated US equipment, and paved the way for their Shah's dictatorship.

The victorious generals needed only a handful of amenable politicians to use as a political façade for the people. They had first thought of Ahmad Aramish and his *Guruh-i Taraqqikhwahan-i Iran* (Progressive Group of Iran), but, instead of serving them loyally, he had rocked the boat (he would eventually have to be imprisoned in 1965 for not toeing the line). Then, in 1963, the powers-that-be had discovered the *Kanoun-i Mutaraqqi* (the Progressive Centre), a small group of some forty technocrats led by the son of former Premier Âli Mansour, Hasan Âli Mansour. In June 1963, the Shah appointed all the members of the Progressive Group to his private think-tank: the Royal Bureau for Economic Research. The appointment was strongly encouraged by the Tehran CIA station chief, Colonel Yatsevich.

After twenty-two years on the Peacock Throne and weathering the crises of 1963, Muhammad Reza Shah could afford to choose his pawns. His trustworthy General Yazdanpanah had reported to him that, at a meeting of high court officials on June 6, called by Court Minister Husayn Âla, some of the attendees had dared to criticise the Shah's handling of the riots and his attacks on the Qum hieroracy.[50] At the meeting, besides Âla and Yazdanpanah, there were present: Muhammad Âli Varasteh (former Finance Minister), Âbdullah Intizam (NIOC's managing director), Âli Asghar Hikmat (a former minister), Sardar Fakhir Hikmat (former *Majlis* president, 1947-61), Muhammad Surouri (head of the Supreme Court) and Jâfar Sharif Imami (head of the Pahlavi Foundation). The Shah decided to punish the malcontents. In October, Âla was dismissed and appointed to the Senate; he died in July 1964. Intizam was also dismissed and replaced at NIOC by a political revenant, Dr Iqbal, recalled from his Paris exile. Surouri was retired, as were the two Hikmats. Only Sharif Imami emerged unscathed (he had kept his tongue at the fateful meeting), to be rewarded with the presidency of the Senate in October 1963.

Having dismissed the old, the Shah could bring in the new. This he did in March 1964, by first asking Âlam to resign the premiership[50A] and then appointing Hasan Âli Mansour in his stead. A few months earlier, in December 1963, Mansour had had the prescience to transform his Progressive Centre into a genuine political party – the *Hizb-i Iran Nuvin* (the New Iran Party) – so as to attract as many technocrats as possible. Many of them, sensing that the technocratic train was gathering steam, jumped on his bandwagon.

Mansour's first act was to bring to fruition in July 1964 the signing of the Regional Co-operation Development (RCD), the economic association linking Iran, Turkey and Pakistan. Then he was confronted with the US Status of Forces Bill, the plan proposed by the Americans to extend to all their military personnel and advisers in Iran some kind of diplomatic immunity, giving them "the protection and immunity foreseen by the paragraph 6 of Article 1 of the Vienna Convention of April 18, 1961"[51] (as a *quid pro quo* the US proposed a $200m commercial loan to Iran). Mansour did his best to jockey along this delicate bill in the Houses of Parliament: the Senate ratified it in July 1964 and the *Majlis* did too (after much cajoling) in October. Some deputies opposed to the bill even mentioned that the US Supreme Court had proclaimed in 1948 that "The principle of sovereign immunity is an archaic hangover not consonant with modern morality".[52] But the Americans were determined to have legal security one way or the other.

At Qum, Ayatullah Khomeini could not remain silent and demonstrated considerable courage by pouncing on the "damnable Bill". The only other individual daring to put his neck out was Dr Baqa'i, who published a pamphlet entitled 'Is It Or Is It Not?' [capitulations]. But, whereas Dr Baqa'i played on words, Khomeini, in a major sermon at Qum on October 26, squarely accused the Shah of reintroducing 'capitulations'. This time round, the Shah could not accept such insulting remarks and Khomeini was exiled for having "instigated against national interests". Exile was an honourable exit for Khomeini; he had been fortunate not to end up before a firing squad, like so many of the Shah's enemies. As for the regime, it thought that it had got rid once and for all of the inflexible and obstinate teacher from Qum. Khomeini and his family remained for a year in Turkey before taking up permanent residence at Najaf.

Premier Mansour did not seem unduly worried about becoming unpopular – an uncommon approach for an Iranian premier. On the heels of the damaging US Forces Bill and the consequent forced exile of Ayatullah Khomeini, he recklessly decided to increase the price of domestic petroleum products: petrol price was doubled from five to ten rials per litre and kerosene went from 2.5 to 3.5 rials. The popular outcry was general; disorders spilled over into Tehran's streets. Mansour had to back-pedal, reducing the petrol price to eight rials per litre and cancelling the mark-up on kerosene. On November 24, 1964, the daredevil prime minister presented his programme to the *Majlis*: a National Crusade for Progress. He would not find time to implement it for, on January 21, 1965, Mansour was shot in front of the *Majlis* by the young Muhammad Bukhara'i and died five days later of his wounds in Tehran's Pars Hospital. His *alter ego* and second in command, Amir Âbbas Huvayda,* was appointed as a stopgap premier.

* AMIR ÂBBAS HUVAYDA (1919-1979), son of career diplomat Âyn ul-Mulk; educated in Beirut, Brussels and at university in Paris; return to Iran (1940), military service (1940-42), entered foreign service (1942); posted to Paris embassy, expelled from France for alleged involvement in drug-ring (1946); posted to embassy in Bonn (1947-51); department head at UNHCR in Geneva (1952-56); counsellor to Ankara embassy (1956-58); NIOC director (1958-63); co-founder of Progressive Centre (1960) and New Iran Party (1963); Minister of Finance (1964); Prime Minister (1965-77); married Layla Imami Khwu'i, the sister of Mansour's wife, Farideh (1966), and divorced (1970); Minister of Court (1977-78); imprisoned (1978); judged and sentenced to death by Revolutionary Tribunal (1979); executed in April 1979.

In the aftermath of Mansour's assassination, the Shah dismissed the benign General Pakravan from SAVAK, replacing him with the brutish but loyal General Nimatullah Nasiri. General Muhsin Mubassir took Nasiri's place as head of police. In bringing Nasiri to SAVAK, the Shah was endeavouring to get a firm grip on the secret service, which still was more General Bakhtiar's than his. Nasiri and Mubassir collaborated to arrest Mansour's killers: they swiftly rounded up thirteen members of the *Hay'at-ha-yi Mûtalifeh-yi Islami* (the United Islamic Groups), loose religious associations created in the early 1960s by the lower *Bazaar* class.[53] Their court-martial was carried out and resulted in four death sentences, six life and three prison sentences. Condemned to death and executed on June 16, 1965 were Muhammad Bukhara'i, Murtaza Niknijad, Sadiq Amani Hamadani and Riza Saffar Harandi (also sentenced to death *in absentia* was Sayyid Âli Andarzgou, the only group member to have slipped through SAVAK's dragnet); life sentences were given to Mihdi Âraqi, Hashim Amani Hamadani (Sadiq's brother), Habibullah Askarouladi, Âbbas Mudarissifar, Abu'l Fazl Haydari and Muhammad Taqi Kalafchi. After Navvab Safavi's *Fada'yan*s, another small religious group had reminded the politicians that they had to be reckoned with.

Even with General Nasiri at its head, SAVAK was not able to uncover a plot to assassinate the Shah himself. On April 10, 1965, a young guardsman at the royal Marmar Palace, Riza Shamsabadi, made his attempt on the Shah's life. He had planned to machine-gun the monarch as he stepped down from his car, but arrived too late, as the Shah and his entourage had already entered the palace's main hall. He entered too, and opened fire as soon as he was in the hall. Two young NCOs standing in the hall, Muhammad Âli Baba'yan and Ayatullah (his first name) Lashkari, drew their guns and returned fire. When the smoke cleared, all three were dead. Once again, due to the quick reflexes and self-sacrifice of two guardsmen, Muhammad Reza Shah had escaped another attempt on his life. Fourteen members of an alleged Marxist-Leninist cell were rounded up, accused of having armed Shamsabadi and court-martialled. The cell's leaders, namely Parviz Nikkhwah, Ahmad Kamrani and Ahmad Mansouri, were sentenced to death. Following petitions and pressure from students' organisations abroad (one of them signed by no fewer than forty-nine British Labour MPs), the three death sentences were commuted to life. Nikkhwah repented, made a full *mea culpa* on national television and ended up being co-opted by the regime (not the first, and certainly not the last communist to enter the Shah's service). He later masterminded royalist propaganda on TV and in the media.

12.6. Black Gold

The locomotive pulling the Shah's court and his elite ahead on golden tracks was the formidable revenues reaped from the oil industry. The 1960s were the most exceptional decade in Iran's oil history. The Consortium had turned Iran's oil heartland in Khuzistan into a mammoth industrial machine. From this extraordinary effort there resulted the unprecedented euphoria of new discoveries, new production records, increased refining throughputs and higher exports and revenues year after year – the sky was the limit. Within the span of a decade, production trebled to almost four million b/d in 1970 and oil revenues sextupled to nearly two and a half billion dollars at the close of the decade (see Table 12.2). Posted prices had essentially remained constant at $1.80 per barrel, although the spot price had plummeted from $1.57 in 1961 to $1.21 in 1970.

Table 12.2. Iran's Average Daily Oil Production and Total Oil Revenues for Selected Years (1962–1970)[55]

Year	Production (average in b/d)	Revenues (in $ million)
1962	1,334,500	706.0
1964	1,710,700	1109.0
1966	2,131,800	1149.0
1968	2,839,800	1688.0
1970	3,829,000	2358.0

In order to sustain the fantastic expansion, drilling, exploration and development were all boosted during the decade.

Thousands of square kilometres of Khuzistan were subjected to fresh geological and seismic investigations. Drilling rates jumped from an annual rate of 80,000 metres in 1962 to 120,000 metres in 1965 and around 200,000 metres in 1970. Such a formidable output led to more wildcat strikes than ever before and to the discoveries of a record number of twelve new oil fields, including the supergiant Marun field (see Table 12.3). Furthermore three gas fields were discovered: Pazanan in Khuzistan (1961), Tang-i Bijarin Kurdistan (1966) and Khangiran, near Sarakhs in Khurasan (1968). Subsequent to these multiple discoveries, Iran's proven reserves of oil jumped from 35 billion barrels in 1960 to 55 billion barrels in 1970 and gas reserves more than doubled in the same time span, from around 2,500 billion cubic metres (1960) to 5,664 billion cubic metres (1970).

Table 12.3. New Oil Fields Discovered in the Consortium Agreement Area During the 1960s.[56]

Year	Oil Fields Discovered
1961	Bibi Hakimeh; Pazanan; Kharg
1962	Ramshir
1963	Mansuri; Karanj
1964	Marun; Paris; Par-i Siah; Rag-i Sifid
1965	Kupal
1968	Lab-i Sifid

Four major reasons were behind this massive expansion in southern Iran:

(1) The steep rise in the worldwide demand for oil, fuelled by the Vietnam War and the industrial boom it entailed. A large part of added crude oil capacity had to come from the Persian Gulf and Iran. While world demand for oil increased by 116% during the decade, Iran's production soared by 259%.

(2) The consortium's urge to develop its concession area. Its horizon was either 1979 (twenty-five years) or 1994 (twenty-five years plus three five-year extensions). With things getting worse, it had only two decades to investigate the oil potential of its area. During its first decade, it naturally ploughed ahead, using all the means at its disposal.

(3) The Shah's insatiable thirst for increased oil revenues. 'Oil for Development' turned into his favourite leitmotiv. In fact, larger revenues meant more gifts to favourites, more projects to be implemented, more armaments to be bought and, naturally, more dollars in Swiss bank accounts. Shaykh Taraki of Saudi Arabia was

no dupe and in a June 1969 open letter he "called on the Shah to put an end to this ridiculous comedy".[57]

(4) The Shah's uphill battle with the Saudis for oil production supremacy in the Persian Gulf. Such a rivalry with a neighbour possessing reserves at least three times Iran's was pointless and detrimental to Iran. Nevertheless the Shah wanted to prove to the world that he could match the Saudis' output barrel for barrel. During the sixties, he got away with it (see Table 12.4).

Table 12.4. Comparison Between Iran's and Saudi Arabia's Oil Production During the 1960s.[58]
(Figures in thousands of b/d)

Year	Iran	Saudi Arabia	Difference
1960	1067.7	1313.5	- 245.8
1962	1334.5	1642.9	- 308.4
1964	1710.7	1896.5	- 185.8
1966	2131.8	2601.8	- 470.0
1968	2839.8	3042.9	- 203.1
1970	3829.0	3799.1	+ 29.9

Not only was NIOC getting ever-increasing revenues from the consortium, but it was forging ahead with new '75-25' type agreements. During 1965 it signed six fresh offshore deals with a total of twenty-four foreign companies – twelve Americans, eleven European and one Indian (see Table 12.5). Every newcomer was a fresh shareholder in the Iranian oil pie. Of the six new entities only two became oil producers – namely IMINOCO and LAPCO. By 1970, NIOC's four offshore joint ventures were producing a total of over 320,000 b/d (see Table 12.6).

Table 12.5. Agreements of the '75-25' Type Signed by NIOC During 1965.[59]

Joint Venture's Name	Foreign Companies	Offshore Minimum Area (km^2)	Outlay ($m)
Dahestan Offshore Petroleum Company – DOPCO	Royal Dutch/Shell (Anglo-Dutch)	6,036	18
Iranian Offshore Petroleum Company – IROPCO	Tidewater Oil, Sun Oil, Skelly Oil, Superior Oil, Kerr McGee Oil, Cities Service, Richfield (all US)	2,250	16
Iran Marine International Oil Company – IMINOCO	AGIP (Ital.), Philips Petroleum (US), Oil & Natural Gas Commission (Ind.) – 33.33% each	7,960	48
Lavan Petroleum Company – LAPCO	Atlantic Refining, Sun Oil, Union Oil, Murphy Oil (all US) – 25% each	8,000	15
Farsi Petroleum Company – FPC	Bureau des Récherches de Pétrole S.N.P. Aquitaine, Régie Autonome des Pétroles (all Fr.)	5,759	22

Joint Venture's Name	Foreign Companies	Offshore Minimum Area (km^2)	Outlay ($m)
Persian Gulf Petroleum Company – PEGUPCO	Deutsche Erdol, Deutsche Schachtian und Tiefbor, Preussag, Scholven Chemie, Wintersahll, Gelsenkirchner Bergweks (all German)	5,150	10
Total		35,155	119

Table 12.6. NIOC's Successful Offshore Joint Ventures, with Oil Fields Discovered and Average Daily Production in 1970.[60]

Joint Venture	Major Oil Fields (Date of Discovery)	Oil Production (b/d)
SIRIP	Bahrigansar (1960) Nourouz (1966) Handijan (1968)	32,000
IPAC	Darioush (1961) Sirous (1961) Firaydoun (1966)	92,500
IMINOCO	Rustam (1967) Raksh (1969)	55,000
LAPCO	Sasan (1966)	142,000
Total	Nine offshore fields	322,000

In 1966, NIOC came up with yet another revolutionary type of exploration agreement: the so-called 'contract agreement'. The contractor first advanced NIOC an interest-free loan (repayable over fifteen years) for paying the contractor's exploration expenditure. This type of agreement gave NIOC a 100% ownership at the wellhead (a theoretical concept cherished by Iran's oilmen since oil nationalisation). The first such agreement was signed in December 1966 with the French Enterprise de Récherches et d'Activités Pétrolières-ERAP for 254,000 km^2 onshore and 21,500 offshore (more than twice the Consortium area). ERAP had gone one better than AGIP to get its hands on a fabulous piece of land (roughly a sixth of Iran), with NIOC paying for the exploration – and it was NIOC that shouted victory! In case ERAP found oil in commercial quantities then, and only then, would the following apply: (i) 50% of the discovered reserves to be placed for NIOC in a 'national reserve' (a mouth-watering concept that allowed mind-boggling but stale calculations on paper); (ii) ERAP would advance a loan (maximum interest of 9%, repayable over five years) to NIOC for paying ERAP's commercial development expenditures; (iii) ERAP would be entitled to purchase between thirty-five and forty-five per cent of oil produced over twenty-five years; (iv) NIOC's sale price to ERAP would be calculated according to the formula 'production cost + 2% + tax (on posted price)', an advantageous proposition; (v) ERAP agreed to export at NIOC's demand, and on its behalf, up to 3m tonnes of oil annually (first five years) and 4m tonnes (second five years), earning a 2% sales commission. At the close of 1967, after protracted negotiations, the Consortium came to relinquish "a quarter of its concession area to mollify the Shah".[61] The relinquished area in South Fars was readily 'contracted' out along ERAP lines in 1969. The larger western part went to a group of European companies (EGOCO) and the smaller eastern one to the US Continental Oil Co. (for details see Table 12.7). Of the three, ERAP would find some offshore oil near Sirri Island and EGOCO would find gas at a number of locations, but no oil.

Table 12.7. Summary of the Three 'Contract Agreements' Signed by NIOC in 1966 and 1969

Contractor	Foreign Companies	Allocated Area (km²)
Société Française des Pétroles d'Iran – SOFIRAN	ERAP (onshore) (offshore)	254,000 21,500
European Group of Oil Companies – EGOCO	ERAP (32%) AGIP (28&) Hispanoil (Sp.) (20%) Petrofina (Bel.) (15&) O.e.m.v. (Austral.) (5%)	36,000
Continental Oil Company Iran – CONIRAN*	Continental Oil Company (US) (onshore)	14,000

* In 1973, Continental sold half of its shares to Philips Petroleum (US) and a quarter to Cities Service (US). The contractor was renamed Philips Petroleum Company Iran – PHILIRAN.

While NIOC was signing its new agreements, the Consortium had to face two major problems caused by its massive expansion drive. The first concerned the exports of ever-larger quantities of crude oil, the second the wasteful flaring of important amounts of by-product associated natural gas. It found the following solutions to these two problems:

(1) For its crude exports the Consortium found the small Kharg Island, located some 40 kilometres off the coast. This insalubrious island had excellent berthing capacities. In the late 1950s, a first experiment was made with a first 160-kilometre long, 26"/28"/30"

pipeline from Gachsaran to Kharg via Bandar-i Ganaveh, for direct exports of Gachsaran oil. On Kharg, some twelve storage tanks with a total capacity of 2.736 million barrels were erected, and an L-shaped jetty with four berths for tankers up to 100,000 dwt was built. Also an embryonic village for housing oil industry employees was set up, along a 1,500 metre-long airstrip. In the early 1960s, a decision was taken to greatly expand Kharg's export facilities: the $43.4 Cham Project was implemented over 1964–1966. Cham's main facilities were:
- A second Gachsaran-Ganaveh pipeline (26"/30") parallel to the first one, with a tie-in for Bibi Hakimeh crude oil.
- A large 42"/170 km-long pipeline from Aqa Jari to Ganaveh – a new world record for the size of an oil pipeline.
- The Gurreh (near Ganaveh) booster station, with a total power of 33,000 hp.
- Three 30"/42 km-long submarine pipelines linking Ganaveh to Kharg.
- Eleven new 500,000 barrels floating-roof crude storage tanks, taking the island's store capacity to over 8.2 million barrels.
- Expansion of the four-berth L jetty to a ten-berth T-shaped jetty capable of handling up to 200,000 dwt tankers.
- Modern living quarters for Consortium and NIOC employees, with sweet water (desalination), electricity and other facilities.

In March 1966, when the new installations were inaugurated, Iran took possession of the largest and most modern crude oil terminal in the world. The consortium's export problems were solved: every quantum leap in exports would hereafter be matched by additions to Kharg. For example, in 1968–69, the Gurreh booster station capacity was doubled, a submarine pipeline to Kharg was added on and three one million-barrel storage tanks erected. One direct consequence of the Kharg development was to render the terminal at Bandar-i Mahshahr obsolete, so it was transformed, at a cost of £18m, into an export facility for refined products from Abadan. The necessary changes were made to the Abadan–Mahshahr pipelines, a microwave communications system was installed and thirty-two new storage tanks were built at Mahshahr so that a total of thirty-eight products could be exported from the port's six jetties (accommodating 50,000 dwt tankers).

(2) Increased oil production resulted in larger quantities of associated gas being produced. As there was little use for the gas, it was mostly flared (the cheapest way to dispose of it). With time, the quantity flared reached enormous amounts: from an average 1962 gas production of 882 million standard cubic feet per day (MMSCFD) roughly two-thirds were flared; by 1968 production stood at 2,333 MMSCFD, of which 83% was flared (see Table 12.8). In 1964, the subject of uses for gas resources was on the consortium's agenda: at a seminar held at Tehran in December 1964, a seminar paper presented jointly by NIOC and the Consortium and entitled 'Present Status of Natural Gas in Iran' addressed the problem and advanced solutions for its use "for possible export or other third party projects".[63] The door for the use of southern flared gas was opened.

Table 12.8. Associated Natural Gas Produced in the Consortium Area (1962–1968), with Percentage Being Flared (Exclusive of Mechanically Used Gas).[62]

Year	Daily Average Gas Production (MMSCFD)	Daily Average Flared Gas (MMSCFD)	Percentage of Gas Flared
1962	882	591	67
1964	1,131	798	71
1966	1,821	1,474	81
1968	2,333	1,934	83

The *rapprochement* begun in late 1962 (in the aftermath of the Cuban missile crisis) between Iran and the Soviet Union came to dovetail nicely with the consortium's new gas policy. *Vis-à-vis* the USSR, Iran had made the first conciliatory gesture by convincing the Americans (in the late 1950s) to station their missiles in Turkey (an OTAN member), not in Iran. The second gesture was to have Dr Murtaza Yazdi and sixteen other *Toudeh* released from prison in

October 1962. Six months later an Iranian-Soviet trade agreement was signed and in July 1963, the first technical co-operation agreement, for the construction of a dam on the Aras river and the construction of eleven silos in Iran, was signed. In November 1963, Soviet President Leonid Brezhnev made his first official visit to Iran. In 1964 Princess Ashraf reciprocated by going to Moscow and in June 1965 it was the Shah's turn to travel to the Soviet Union. These visits paved the way for a massive venture in four major areas between the two neighbours, signed at Moscow in January 1966 and ratified by the *Majlis* on February 13, 1966:

- The construction by the Soviet Union of a steel mill (initial capacity of 600,000 tonnes per annum) near Isfahan;
- The establishment by Soviet companies of a large machine tools plant at Arak;
- A Soviet loan of 260m roubles (with 2.5% interest over twelve years), equivalent to $286m, to Iran for financing the projects;
- Export by Iran of natural gas to the Soviet Union, at a c.i.f. (cost including freight) delivery price of $0.186 per million BTU (equivalent to $6.60 per thousand cubic metres).

As a result of the 1966 Iranian-Soviet agreement the Iranian gas industry had to materialise, if only to fulfil its obligation to export gas to the USSR (a project given the green light by the consortium). In March 1966 the National Iranian Gas Company (NIGC) was established, as a fully-owned subsidiary of NIOC, to manage and supervise all aspects of the new industry. In December 1966, NIOC and the Consortium signed a memorandum stipulating that gas reserves were to be put aside for NIGC's exclusive use. NIGC immediately began, under managing director Engineer Taqi Musaddiqi, to tackle the project of designing and laying the first Trans-Iranian Gas Trunkline (known as IGAT I) from the southern oil fields to the Soviet border at Astara.

The IGAT I project was a mammoth undertaking which included: (i) a gas gathering scheme; (ii) a gas treating plant; (iii) the pipeline proper with its compressor stations; (iv) an upstream pipe manufacturing factory; and (v) a downstream Natural Gas Liquids (NGL) refinery at Bandar-i Mahshahr (see Table 12.9 for overall description of these sub-projects). Ultimate pipeline capacity was foreseen at 1,650 MMSCFD (line pressure between 1030 and 1065 psig), with 1,050 MMSCFD earmarked for exports and 600 MMSCFD for domestic consumption. Gas flow to the USSR was inaugurated in October 1970. Total investment for the whole project amounted to $678m.

Table 12.9. Description of the IGAT I and Two Related Projects.[64]

(i) Gas Gathering

Natural gas from the four oil fields of Aqa Jari, Marun, Karanj and Paris were earmarked for IGAT I. The gases (mainly first and second stage gas) from the production units were routed to six new NGL plants (three near Aqa Jari, three near Marun) where the gases' liquids were separated, formed into a raw NGL stream and sent to the Mahshahr Refinery (see (v) below), and the resulting methane-rich gas compressed before being sent to the gas treating plant. William Bros., (UK) and Entrepose (France) were contracted for this project.

(ii) Gas Treatment

Located at Bid-i Buland (10 kilometres east of Aqa Jari), the plant consisted of five identical trains capable of desulphurising and dehydrating 240 MMSCFD of raw gas each. A 60-tonne per day sulphur unit was included. Design was by J.F. Pritchard (US) and construction by Costain and Press (UK). Total investment amounted to $44m. The plant was commissioned in December 1970.

(iii) The Pipeline

Stretching 1,123 kilometres across Iran, with a diameter of 42" from Bid-i Buland to Tehran (628 km) and 40" from Tehran to Astara (495 km). In addition some 656 kilometres of spur tracks (6"-30") were routed to Shiraz, Isfahan, Qum and Tehran. Design was by IMEG (UK), and William Bros.; Entrepose was in charge of the first section, the Soviet Naftekhimprom Export in charge of the second and of the 34 turbo-compressors required (for $110m). The eight original compressor stations were built by Mannesmann (W. Germany) for $28m. The French Compagnie Générale provided the microwave system for $5.4m.

(iv) The Pipe Mill

In order to manufacture the pipes of IGAT I, a modern pipe mill was erected by NIOC near Ahvaz. Two mills with a combined capacity of 1,000 tonnes/day and using the High Frequency Welding process, were purchased from Torrance Machinery and Engineering of California: the first for 6"-16" pipes and the other for 18"-48" pipes. The mill was in operation by 1967, but the 350,000 tonnes of IGAT I pipes were nevertheless imported from West Germany.

(v) The Mahshahr NGL Refinery

Design capacity was of 57,600 B/D of raw NGL, routed from the six NGLs to Mahshahr via a 12" pipe. Its main products were propane, butane and C5+ (total design production capacity of 48,000 b/d), which were exported by the Consortium member companies at a highly favourable price, allowing for a very lucrative business.

In parallel to the gas industry, the Iranian petrochemical industry also took off. After being pulled to and fro between NIOC, the Plan Organisation and the Ministry of Industry and Mines, it eventually ended up in NIOC's lap. On December 27, 1964, the National Petrochemical Company (NPC) was established as a fully-owned NIOC subsidiary, and Shiraz Fertilisers was transferred to it for a flat fee of $24m. In July 1965, the *Majlis* enacted a law for the development of the petrochemical industry in Iran, thereby legally allowing NPC to enter joint venture agreements with any foreign company it saw fit. NPC entered negotiations with international chemical companies for possible co-operation. Hitherto, the French had a special interest in Iran's fertiliser and petrochemical industries, as shown by their involvement in the Shiraz complex. Most early studies made for NPC were carried out by French institutions (especially the Institut Français du Pétrole), so it was to a number of raised European eyebrows that NPC's managing director, Engineer Baqir Mustoufi, announced in 1966 that three joint ventures for the erection of three major complexes in southern Iran had been entered into with three American companies (see Table 12.10 for a synopsis of the three complexes).

Table 12.10. Synopsis of the Three Chemical Complexes Built by NPC Joint Ventures.[65]

(i) The Abadan Petrochemical Company
  NPC 76%, B.F. Goodrich 24%)
Feeding on waste gases from Abadan Refinery and on natural salt, the APC complex was built adjacent to the refinery.
It was designed to produce PVC (20,000 tonnes/annum), DDB (10,000 t/a) and caustic soda (24,000 t/a).
Licensees included Goodrich, UOP, Lummus, Olin and Chevron (all US)
Managing contractor: Lummus
Total cost: $31m
Inaugurated in November 1969
APC created its Polika subsidiary at Karaj for producing PVC pipes and granules (6,000 t/a)

(ii) The Kharg Chemical Company
  (NPC 50%, Amoco 50%)
NPC joined NIOC's partner in IPAC to erect a small chemical complex for treating the sour gases flared on Kharg Island by IPAC and NIOC.
Products to be recovered were propane, butane and C5+ (7,000 b/d), and sulphur (580 tonnes/day).
Designed by J.F. Pritchard and Amoco (both US) and efficiently constructed by Chiyoda of Japan (the first Japanese foray into the Middle East).

Total cost: $42m
Inaugurated in November 1969

(iii) The Shahpour Chemical Company
(NPC 50%, Allied Chemicals 50%)

Built on thirty-two hectares of recovered mud flats near Bandar-i Shahpour, the huge fertiliser complex fed on sour gases (25% H^2S) from Masjid-i Sulayman – routed to the complex through a special alloy 20"/170 km-long pipeline with a maximum capacity of 170 MMSCFD. Raw water to the plant came from the Karoun river via a 40" 81 km-long Darkhuayn–Shahpour pipeline.

M.W. Kellog was managing contractor for the complex, which consisted of: a gas treating plant; a sulphur recovery unit (1,540 t/d); units for sulphuric and phosphoric acids; ammonia (1,000 t/d) and urea (500 t/d) units and a DAP unit.

Total cost: $217m; a further $15m was spent on the new town at Mahshahr for housing the 1,200 company employees.

The SCC complex was inaugurated in November 1970

Furthermore, NPC had set up, in 1967, a domestic subsidiary, the Fertiliser Distribution Company (FDC), for the importation and distribution of fertilisers throughout the country. With fertilisers being sold in Iran at a very low price to the peasants (aided by government subsidies), consumption had soared during the 1960s (see Table 12.11), the provinces of Gilan and Mazandaran taking the lion's share. The meagre output of the Shiraz fertiliser plant was not sufficient to meet the internal demand and the fertilisers produced at SCC in 1970 went directly to domestic consumers.

Meanwhile, the mother company of NIOC was not idle, for it too was expanding in all directions:

– Twenty-four of its top managers had founded in March 1959 the *Anjuman-i Naft-i Iran* (the Iranian Petroleum Institute – IPI). Launched in February 1960, the IPI was a technocratic forum for airing ideas. It was also a counterweight to Sharif Imami's

Table 12.11. Fertiliser Consumption in Iran – Selected Years Between 1956 and 1970.[65A]

Year	Annual Fertiliser Consumption (Thousands of Tonnes)
1956	2.9
1958	15.2
1960	36.0
1962	47.3
1964	71.2
1966	124.3
1968	185.0
1970	243.0

Engineers Association of Iran, which had hitherto monopolised technocratic opinion in the country. The IPI was an instant success, membership (mostly NIOC staff) climbing to over three hundred. It soon built its own two-storey headquarters and began issuing a high-quality technical quarterly bulletin. Its first president was the gentle Âta'ullah Ittihadiyyeh (an excellent first choice).
– NIOC built its own fifteen-storey main office in the city centre, which became one of the capital's landmarks.
– NIOC's refined products' distribution system (the company's main occupation) was expanding fast. It had to accommodate a 150 per cent increase in overall consumption during the 1960s: from 73,500 b/d in 1961 to 187,000 b/d in 1970 (see Table 12.12). Products' pipelines criss-crossed the country, railroad and road tankers multiplied, storage depots were erected in every province, service stations mushroomed in the cities and the company's contracted vendors were adding up in the countryside – NIOC's Distribution Division was in a constant flux of expansionist changes. As it provided over 95% of the people's energy needs, it had to be highly efficient and keep its millions of consumers satisfied.

Table 12.12. Iran's Domestic Consumption of Refined Products Daily Average (rounded up) 1961–1970.[66]

Year	Domestic Consumption (in b/d)
1961	73,500
1962	77,000
1963	80,900
1964	93,100
1965	102,000
1966	115,800
1967	133,700
1968	150,900
1969	170,100

– NIOC's first ever refinery in the south of Tehran (near Ray), with an initial design capacity of 85,000 b/d, was designed and constructed by the Fluor-Thyssen (US-W. Germany) joint venture. Begun in mid-1965, the refinery was inaugurated in May 1968. Some $92m had been invested in it and a further $58m went to the Ahvaz-Ray 16"/20" pipeline. Soon after start-up, the refinery was debottle-necked to 100,000 b/d.

– Following on its Tehran success, NIOC decided to build a new 15,000 b/d refinery at Kermanshah to replace the existing one, which was obsolete after thirty-five years of service. For a total cost of $18m UOP (US) designed the units and Continental Engineering Company (Holland) erected the refinery. In 1970, as the old units were shut off, the new ones were brought into operation.

– Adjacent to Tehran Refinery, NIOC set up a small research centre in 1967. France's IFP had drawn up the pilot unit's initial blueprints. By 1970, some two hundred scientists and technicians were engaged in research activities at the centre. But Iranians were ill-prepared to tackle scientific research. The centre's location was far from ideal (it was rumoured that the sale of the land had determined the centre's choice). It soon turned into a

large analytical laboratory, simply because it had the best equipment for chemical and physical analysis in the country.
- In 1966, NIOC launched a new subsidiary, the National Iranian Tanker Company (NITC), for managing the two 32,500 dwt tankers it had been 'invited' to purchase from the Pahlavi Foundation. NITC ordered two 53,000 dwt tankers and, by the close of the decade, it managed a small fleet of 170,000 dwt
- NIOC's internal communications had deteriorated over the decade, so to remedy the problem it paid Philips (Holland) $20m for a private microwave network of ninety-three stations. By November 1970, NIOC's private grid was operational.

NIOC was not solely expanding domestically – it also invested in joint ventures abroad. Its first external foray was in India, where it took a 13% share in the 50,000 b/d Madras Refinery, with the government of India holding 74% and the American firm Amoco 13%; NIOC further agreed to supply the refinery's crude oil requirements, beginning commercial production in September 1969.

Two years later NIOC acquired a 24.5% stake in the Madras Fertiliser Complex, adjacent to the refinery. NIOC similarly entered into a deal with the government of South Africa (52.5%) and the French company CFP (30%), taking a 17.5% share in the 45,000 b/d Sasolburg and accepting to supply at least 70% of its crude oil. In May 1971, NIOC's third venture abroad was inaugurated.

Another of NIOC's forays abroad was with the Israelis. Since 1957 it had provided crude oil for the Eilat–Bersheeba pipeline (later duplicated) and supplied over 80% of Israel's domestic oil, which stood around 140,000 b/d in the mid-sixties. The whole Israeli oil operation was strictly confidential (with only a handful of NIOC managers involved) and semi-covert, even though by 1966 four large oil tankers flying the Liberian flag ran the Kharg–Eilat shuttle service.[67] In 1968, the Iranian-Israeli oil connection was further reinforced when the Shah was lured into taking a 50% share in the new Trans-Israeli Pipeline – TIPline (42"/1,000,000 b/d capacity) – linking the port of Eilatto Ashkelon on the Mediterranean. Over 1968–69 the TIP project was completed at a cost of $200m. Iran's participation in the project was handled for NIOC through a number of bogus front companies, such as Rainbow and the Canadian APC Holdings (of Montreal), as the managing director of the TIPline, Ben Dor, readily admitted.[68] Due to Iran's unswerving support (250 to

350,000 b/d delivered from Kharg[69]) the TIPline proved a success, as its throughput surpassed the 800,000 b/d mark in the 1970s.

Oil was by far the most important Iranian-Israeli connection, but not the only one. There were also political, military and commercial connections. Many Iranian politicians and journalists were encouraged to visit Israel (free of charge); besides pioneers Shahandeh and Vala, there were also the chameleon Âmidi Nouri, Dr Shariât, Mihdi (Moush) Shaybani and especially Mahmoud and Âbdullah Gurji.[70] Israeli agricultural experts were engaged to manage the Qazvin Agricultural Development Organisation, set up in the area of Bu'in Zahra after it had been destroyed by an earthquake on September 1, 1962. The number of Israeli experts in Qazvin grew to over forty, so that "Israel had more technicians in Iran than in any other country".[71] Israeli companies were taking advantage of the Iranian economic boom, with Iranian Jews acting as middlemen. Israeli contractors were even making inroads into Iran's lucrative real estate and industrial projects. Some of Iran's generals became closely linked to Mossad and Shin Bet agents in Iran, leading to close links between the Iranian Army and Israeli Military Industries (IMI), the Israeli Defence Navy (IDF Navy) and to Israel's largest industrial conglomerate, Koor Industries.

Israeli assistance in military training (especially for the special paratroopers and anti-terrorist units) and technical courses became almost routine. Furthermore, military purchases from Iran expanded rapidly and, for example, the firm Soltam, a Koor subsidiary, came to manufacture ammunition almost exclusively for Iran. In return, Iran assisted Israel in emergency cases such as in the Six Day War of 1967, when Egypt's SAM missiles surprised Israeli jet fighters and Iran provided replacement F4 and F5 jets (just changing the planes' insignias from the Iranian tricolour to the Star of David did the trick). Egyptian President Nasser had always abhorred the Shah, and his assistance to Israel during the war further incensed him; after the end of the war, Nasser prophesied that: "The Iranian tyrant will die, like his father, in exile and infamy".[72] It is not surprising that "between 1966 and 1970, Cairo replaced Moscow as the centre of danger in [official] Iranian eyes".[73] Nasser's open animosity towards the Shah partly helped to explain the Iranian-Israeli honeymoon of the 1960s.

12.7. The Third Plan

In May 1961, Premier Amini appointed the lacklustre Safi Asfia at the head of the Plan Organisation (PO) to replace the capable but unruly Aramish. The forty-eight year old Asfia, a graduate of the prestigious French Polytechnique, had been a deputy to the flamboyant Ibtihaj during the Second Plan. Unlike his two predecessors, Asfia was a tame intellectual. During his protracted tenure (till November 1968) at the helm of PO, he would oversee the metamorphosis of this elitist think-tank into a bloated bureaucratic rubber stamp. Through him, the civil service had brought back within its fold an institution which had had the arrogance to be outstanding; the PO never recovered from this deadly blow. Under Asfia, the PO was gradually stripped of its executive functions, projects costing under Rls5m were taken away from it, and the PO's executive teams departed for their respective ministries. The PO was left with the clerical function of allocating funds and tallying up expenditure. Under Asfia the PO was what the Shah and his elite wanted it to be: a docile and subservient technocracy apportioning oil revenues as told by the executive. For his labours, Asfia was rewarded with a portfolio for life and a place on the board of the lucrative Southern Fishing Corporation of Iran, a new outfit he had himself helped to launch in 1963.

To assist Asfia in formulating the Third Plan "an independent team of [American] experts, the "Harvard Advisory Group", financed by the Ford Foundation and directed by a Harvard university official"[74] was brought in. The plan's duration was reduced from seven to five years – from March 1963 till March 1968. It consisted yet again of a series of unrelated projects, with a wide scope and an initial budget of Rls140bn. As Iran came out of the economic slump, the PO revised the budget upwards, to Rls185bn (1963), then to Rls200bn (1964) and finally to Rls222bn (1965).[75] Oil revenues were to finance sixty-five per cent of it, the rest coming from loans. The plan's target was an average GNP growth of six per cent per annum. The plan's priorities were to be: (i) water and power; (ii) infrastructure; and (iii) the private sector industries. The plan's number of economic chapters was increased to ten, up from only four in the Second Plan. The Third Plan's major achievements are summarised hereunder, chapter after chapter:

1. Agriculture and Irrigation
   (Rls47.3bn invested)
   - Rls22bn was spent on land reform, rural development, subsidies for fertilisers, and 15,000 tractors purchased from Romania in August 1966.
   - Another Rls22bn went on completing the Second Plan's dams (i.e. Sifiroud (Rls4.8bn), Latian (3.8bn) and the Diz's downstream (5bn)) and initiating half a dozen new ones, such as the Zayandehroud, Aras and Jajiroud Dams.

2. Industry and Mines
   (Rls17.1bn)
   - Rls2bn was invested in traditional industries - cement, sugar and textiles.
   - Rls9.6bn was spent on modern, capital-intensive industries such as petrochemicals.
   - Rls4.4bn was given as credits to private industries - Rls1.8bn and 0.8bn through the IMDBI and the ICB respectively.
   - An attempt was made to revive traditional Iranian crafts, leading to the creation of the Iran Handicrafts Organisation in 1964.
   - The Tehran Stock Exchange was established in October 1967.

3. Energy and Fuel
   (Rls32.0bn)
   - Rls15bn was invested in electricity generation and distribution, with installed power capacity doubling from 440 MW to 900 MW; and the placing of 2,500 km of high voltage and 5,000 km of low voltage cables.
   - Rls17bn for three major oil industry projects: (i) IGAT I; (ii) Tehran Refinery; (iii) the Ahvaz–Tehran crude pipeline.

4. Communications
   (Rls53.8bn)
   - Rls36bn was allotted to road building: 4,000 km of asphalted roads, 3,000 km of secondary roads were completed, with 6,000 km in progress.

- Rls6bn was spent on railways: the Kashan–Yazd (419 km) and Sharafkhaneh–Qatur (233 km) lines were given priority.
- Rls4bn was spent on the ports, especially Bandar Âbbas, developed with $20m in US assistance.
- Rls3bn was spent on airports – ten provincial airstrips were upgraded a national airline was launched, Iran Air (see details in Frame 12.1).
- Rls4.5bn was invested in telecommunications: (i) the Iranian section of the CENTO Microwave Network, linking Ankara to Karachi, completed in 1965; (ii) 8,000 km of telephone cables laid, 77,000 automatic telephone exchanges installed; (iii) the creation of the National Iranian Radio and Television (NIRT) (see Frame 12.2).
- Completion of the National Meteorological System, with the creation of 282 new stations.

5. Culture
(Rls17.3bn)
- Rls11bn was allocated to primary school education: 582 new schools and 23,700 new teachers hired, with 680,000 new pupils.
- Rls3.4bn went to universities: (i) Rls1.2bn for Tehran University, which acquired a pool-type AMF 5 MW nuclear reactor for research purposes (it went critical in November 1967); (ii) Rls1.1bn for Shiraz's Pahlavi University; (iii) the establishment of the Aryamihr Industrial University in Tehran in 1966.
- Subsidies for the first Shiraz Art Festival (autumn 1967), a pet project of Empress Farah and her sycophants.
- Funds for tourism, with tourist numbers soaring from 87,000 (1963) to 212,000 (1968).

6. Hygiene and Health
(Rls13.2bn)
- 4,200 new hospitals (taking the total to around 31,000 beds, or an average of 11.7 beds per 10,000 inhabitants).
- 185 new dispensaries were created throughout the country.
- Rls8bn was spent on the anti-cholera and anti-malaria campaigns, which, however, failed to stop a cholera epidemic

in the summer of 1965 which resulted in at least eighty-five deaths.

7. Labour and Manpower
   (Rls2.8bn)
- Funds poured down the bottomless hole of technical and vocational training. In 1963 there were ninety-six schools with 10,500 trainees; in 1968 one hundred and thirty-eight schools with 16,300 apprentices.

8. Urban Development
   (Rls7.2bn)
- Master plans for fifteen cities (including Tehran) were drawn up.
- One hundred and forty provincial urban centres were provided with drinking water.
- The internal roads of one hundred provincial centres were asphalted.

9. Statistics and Planning
   (Rls1.5bn)
- The establishment of the *Markaz-i Amar-i Iran* (the Statistical Centre of Iran), under the PO's aegis, in 1966.
- The second national census was carried out in 1966,[76] with the following results:

    a) Iran's population was 25,078,923; 6 million more than 1956.

    b) The literacy rate (for ten years of age and older) stood at 28.1%, compared with 14.9% in 1956.

    c) Iran's under-19 population was 54.6% of the total population (up from 49.7% in 1956).

    d) Iran had an urban population of 39.1% of the total (up from 31.4% in 1956).

10. Construction and Housing
    (Rls12.2bn)
- Some 500,000 persons were employed in the construction industry.

- Rls4.3bn was spent on twenty-three large government building projects.
- Rls3.4bn was allocated for 3,000 housing units for the armed forces and civil servants.
- Rls4.5bn was spent on camps and garrisons for the armed forces.

Frame 12.1. The Birth of Iran Air

During the 1950s, two private airline service companies were created in Iran, the Persian Air Services, a leasing company created in 1954 and owned by Princess Ashraf's second husband Ahmad Shafiq, and the Iranian Airways Company, a small outfit owned by Mahmoud Afshar. In February 1962, the two companies were merged into United Iranian Airways. As the merged company still couldn't get over its financial problems, the government decided to take a 50% share in it (buying out the happy shareholders) and in February 1963 took over the whole firm, thus nationalising the company and renaming it Iranian Airways, or Iran Air for short. At the outset, Iran Air controlled a fleet consisting of six DC3s, three DC6s and three Viscounts. It employed 667 people. A veteran air force officer aged fifty, General Âli Muhammad Khadimi, was placed at the head of the new airline.

In 1963, Iran Air signed SAS (Scandinavian Air Services) to guide it into the world of international airlines and secure European routes. But the Scandinavian flirtation didn't last long, for Iran Air was taken to the altar (initially for three years) by the American PanAm company in 1964. In 1965 Iran Air rented three Boeing 727s, and purchased four 727s in 1967 and two 707s in 1969. Under PanAm's wing Iran Air developed rapidly from carrying a total of 218,000 passengers in 1964 to 531,000 in 1968.

Frame 12.2. The Birth of NIRT

The private (and limited) television channel operated by the Sabit Pasal group in October 1958 was nationalised in early 1967, when radio and television were officially turned into a state monopoly – a unique exception being made for the US Armed Forces' channel, the AFTV. A first cousin of Empress Farah, the twenty-nine year old French-educated Riza Qutbi, was placed at the head of NIRT. In March 1967, NIRT began broadcasting on radio and television.

The final and official accounts of the Third Plan are presented in Tables 12.13 and 12.14.

Table 12.13. The Official Accounts of the Third Five Year Development Plan.[77]
(All figures in Rls billions)

Chapter	Budget Forecast	Allocation Paid Out
Agriculture/Irrigation	47.9	47.3
Industry & Mines	27.3	17.1
Energy & Fuel	35.1	32.0
Communications	57.0	53.8
Culture	17.6	17.3
Hygiene & Health	13.3	13.2
Labour & Manpower	2.9	2.8
Urban Development	7.3	7.2
Statistics & Research	1.6	1.5
Construction/Housing	12.4	12.2
Total	222.4	204.4

Table 12.14. The Plan Organisation's Revenues and
Expenditures During the Third Plan Period (1963-67).[78]
(All figures in Rls billions)

Revenues		Expenditures	
Oil revenues	154.5	Development projects	204.4
Domestic loans	37.7	Loan repayments	9.9
Foreign loans	31.3	Loan interests	9.4
Other revenues	5.5	Other expenses	5.3
Total	229.0		229.0

The Third Plan was to the economic crisis of 1961/62 what the Second Plan had been to the political crisis of 1951/53: an expensive tranquilliser. Nevertheless great strides forward were achieved in a number of fields. Overall growth during the plan had been 6.4% (roughly according with the initial 6% forecast). Growth, however, was fuelled more by the average 18.6% surge in oil revenues than by the plan's achievements. In the wake of the buoyant oil revenues, the industrial sector had grown by an average of 12.5%, services by 7.7% and agriculture by an anaemic 3%.

Agriculture, little capable of profiting from the oil bonanza, was Iran's sick sector. On the bright side were the facts that domestic wheat production had increased from 2.5 million tonnes in 1963 to 3.3 million in 1967,[79] and that Iran's agricultural exports were still positive at the end of the plan – a Rls7bn surplus in 1967, as against 6bn in 1963. On the other side of the coin, the peasants were ill-prepared to manage their own affairs, and it took time for them to adapt to the new conditions. Furthermore, scores of Armenian peasants (whole villages) left for Armenia or for the urban centres (Tehran, Tabriz and Isfahan getting the lion's share). Moreover, the best and the brightest among the peasants decided to use the transition period to try their luck in the cities (selling their land or leasing it to a relative). The year 1964 was also catastrophically dry and the winter of 1964/65 unusually cold.

Massive Iranian imports of basic staples from America date back to 1964: in September 140,000 tonnes of wheat and in October 25,000 tonnes of corn were imported. It is nevertheless surprising that the combined new inputs (i.e. water from dams, fertilisers, tractors and soft bank loans) had not brought about a revolution after the success of the land reform scheme. One of the reasons behind the partial agricultural failures of the 1960s was the lack of incentive for the average peasant: the price of land produce was extremely low; with no payment to the landlord his survival chances had soared but even if he could make extra money what could he purchase with it? It was no surprise that the gap between rural and urban incomes (already quite wide) continued to widen, encouraging migration to the towns and cities.

If 1964 was not a good year for agriculture, it was a good one for the institutions of the White Revolution and for its *Sipah-i Danish* (the Literacy Corps) – created according to the sixth revolutionary point. It was in the summer that the first contingent of 2,460 diploma-holders left for their respective villages. At first there was some friction between the sceptical and cunning peasants and the young urban newcomers, but pupils of the younger generation accepted them readily as teachers. A pioneering spirit also helped during the first years and the corps proved to be a successful enterprise, allowing and even compelling two different faces of Iran to communicate, a thing they had never done before. The lessons of this experience would not be lost on the younger peasant generation, the so-called *Dihqanzadehs* (lit. 'the peasants' children'). In 1969, university graduates and women would also be allowed in the corps, further enhancing its general standing. By the close of 1977, a total of some 150,000 corps members would have passed through the villages, with a definite cumulative effect.

In the wake of the Literacy Corps's success, the regime, seeing the fantastic propaganda it could reap from such a dirt cheap experiment, decided in late 1964 to repeat it with the creation of the *Sipah-i Bihdasht* (the Health Corps) and the *Sipah-i Tarvij* (the Development Corps) as the seventh and eighth points of the White Revolution. In January 1965, the first contingent of four hundred and twenty-three freshly graduated medical students were dispatched to the villages, inevitably enhancing hygiene standards. By 1977, the Health Corps had seen a total of 13,618 medical students progress through its ranks.

The Development Corps, providing agricultural graduates, was the least successful and, although a total of 32,080 youngsters served in it, it had a lesser impact than the other two corps.

In October 1965 the ninth point of the White Revolution was unveiled as the creation of *Khaneh-ha-yi Insaf* (the Houses of Justice) in villages – an attempt at creating a grass roots judicial system of five elder peasants in every village to arbitrate in local disputes in place of the former landlord and the ex-*kadkhuda* (mayor). The system never took off, and in most villages the elders' committee was just a formality. In January 1967, some 500,000 copies of the Shah's book *Inqilab-i Sifid* (The White Revolution) were issued[80] and, shortly thereafter, the appellation was altered to the *Inqilab-i Shah va Mardum* (The Shah and People Revolution), in an attempt to break all barriers between the Shah and the people. Finally, in October 1967, three more revolutionary points were piled on to the list, bringing the total to twelve points:
- Tenth point: nationalisation of water resources
- Eleventh point: national plan for urbanisation and reconstruction
- Twelfth point: administrative and educational reform.

School children across the country had to memorise the twelve points of *The Shah and People Revolution*: history was turned into instant propaganda by the regime. In retrospect, however, only the Land Reform and the Literacy Corps would remain from the Shah's grandiose plans of the 1960s: these two had a real impact and the mountains they were supposed to move would take only time.

The third objective of the Third Plan had been to assist the private sector. The first wave of 1950s industrialists made use of the multifaceted assistance given to consolidate their budding empires. Next to these pioneers, a second wave of industrialists profited from the plan's easy credits and incentives to the private sector. Another boon to both waves was the willingness of foreign investors to place their capital in Iranian joint ventures. The accent was on import-substitution industries and the mechanism for setting up factories with Western technology was similar to the one used in the 1950s. Under such favourable conditions industrialisation surged forward. Domestic industrial production soared from Rls84bn in 1963 to 183bn in 1968; total industrial added value also increased (albeit at a slower pace) from Rls38.4 to 66.6 over the same period.[81] Employment in industrial occupations reached the 1,335,000 mark – a partial explanation for the new jobs of migrating peasants. But growth was erratic, without any master plan, with factories mostly producing consumer goods from imported semi-finished products.

A case in point is the erratic development of the car assembly industry in Iran. It began in 1960 with the launch of four assembly plants, putting together knocked-down automobiles:

(1) The Fiat Iran Company out together Fiat 1100 models, sold as taxis;

(2) The Iran Jeep Company assembled Jeeps under licence from the Kaiser Jeep Company (US);

(3) The Murattab Company put together Land Rovers under licence by the Rover Company (UK);

(4) The Khavar Automobile Manufacturing Company (initial capital: Rls1350m) assembled light Mercedes-Benz trucks under a Daimler-Benz licence.

A couple of years later, the Iran Jeep Company switched to assembling Rambler 220 (Shahin) and Rambler 440 (Arya) models under licence from the American Motor Company (US) and Fiat Iran folded (allegedly for having failed to introduce a minimum of local components). In 1962, the British Leyland Company opened up a plant for assembling double-decker buses; in 1964, the Zamyad Company was established to produce four hundred Volvo (Sweden) trucks per annum and in 1966 Kaveh Company duplicated the experience for Mack (US) trucks. Finally in 1968, the Pars Louks Company began assembling buses under licence from the German KHD-Magirus company.

In May 1967, the first *Paykan* (Arrow) rolled off the assembly line of the Iran National Manufacturing Company. This first passenger car to be assembled in Iran was a replica of the Hillman model developed by Rootes Motors of Birmingham (UK). Brothers Mahmoud and Ahmad Khayyami, scions of a Mashhadi family of garage owners, held a majority of shares in Iran National.

Their *Paykan* was an immediate success: simple technology, sturdy mechanics, the right size and shape for Iran's middle-class families and a reasonable (initial) price of Rls140,000. Prime Minister Huvayda drove one and had promised "a Paykan for every Iranian". Although output records were broken every year (from 8,000 units in 1967 to 34,000 in 1971), demand clearly outpaced production. Soon every Iranian mechanic could fix a *Paykan* blindfolded. Operating in a quasi-monopoly, Iran National could hike the price every quarter: in 1972 the basic model retailed for Rls236,900 and the export price stood at Rls130,000[82] – a hefty discrepancy due to booming internal demand and export subsidies. As the Khayyamis reaped infamous profits, they both vertically integrated their automobile business from components to the finished product (creating dozens of affiliated companies) and diversified into assembling minibuses and buses (under a Daimler-Benz licence) and also vans. The Khayyamis would also launch the highly successful Kuroush retail chain and forge links with the Asia Insurance Company In the 1970s, Iran National was the largest private industrial conglomerate in Iran with annual sales approaching the Rls6000m mark (equivalent to roughly $870m), and the Khayyamis were among the richest families in Iran.

In the late sixties, Citroën Iran was created to assemble a car for the lower middle classes: the *Zhian*, an Iranian copy of the Citroën 2CV. Major shareholders in the Iranian company S.A.I.P.A.[83] were the Armenian brothers Charles and Alfred Aysseh. Like the *Paykan*, the *Zhian* was a national success.

Besides the Khayyami and Aysseh families, some nineteen other families (or individuals) climbed high in the second wave of private sector tycoons launched during the Third Plan: sixteen came from the industrial sector and three from mining activities:

1. The Soudavar family

Founder Samad Soudavar began in the Mashhad *Bazaar* and married into the town's richest family, Hajj Aqa Malik's daughter. Owner of the Mirrikh company, exclusive importer of Mercedes-Benz in Iran (their cash cow), the Soudavars diversified into assembly with Khavar (light trucks) and Doucharkheh va Mutursiklit Sazi-i Iran (two-wheels), and textiles with Fuminat, the new units being managed by Samad's sons Husayn Âli and Âbd ul-Âli; his daughter was married to Âbd ul-Âli Farmanfarmayan.

2. The Vahabzadeh family

Founder Sulayman Vahabzadeh headed the Vahabzadeh Commercial Conglomerate, exclusive importers of BMW cars, and representatives of Philips, Brown-Boveri, with an interest in the Bank of Iran and Holland. Sulayman's sons Ahmad[84] and Rasoul took over the expansion with, among other interests, the Pakdis wine bottling complex at Riza'iyyeh.

3. The Akhavan family

Jâfar Akhavan was the managing director of the Iran Jeep Company – later changed to General Motors Iran (a joint venture between General Motors (US), the Akhavans and the Pahlavi Foundation). Jâfar's brothers, Mustafa and Murtaza, managed the Akhavans' import-export company and their other ventures, such as the Moulin Rouzh Group and film producing.

4. The Riza'i family

The brothers Âli and Mahmoud Riza'i began in mining; the latter managed the family's chromite mines and with the British Selection Trust discovered the Sarchishmeh copper field while Âli branched out into iron products, forming the Shahryar Industrial Group and setting up four rolling mills in Ahvaz with Germany's DEMAG (total capacity of 400,000 tonnes/annum), a cable factory (with SKF), a wire rod mill, two scrap iron foundries and two pipe mills (diameters of 1/2" to 6"). His conglomerate turned Riza'i into Iran's iron tsar.

5. The Arjumand family

Syavoush Arjumand expanded the small family flagship Arj factory (home appliances) tenfold and placed its quality products in Iranian homes; by 1969, Arj employed some 2,200 persons and produced 1,200 units a day, placing it at the forefront of its sector in Iran and the Middle East. Brothers Darioush and Kourush launched a factory for steel roofs and oil tanks, and another for screws and bolts; they also set up a joint venture with the Swedish carrier company, Thermo Frig Carrier.

6. The Khusroushahi family

Patriarch Muhammad was president of the Tehran Chamber of Commerce during the 1960s; his brother Kazim founded the KBC group in 1963, its main thrust in pharmaceuticals, with Toulid Darou and Cyanamid KBC, and other companies were Kayvan, Afshureh, Pyazar, Polychem, Payvar and Khurak; brother Âli Akbar created the Pars Group, with its flagship Minou, Iran's largest producer of candies and chocolates. The family was majority shareholder in the Abgineh glass factory and represented a score of foreign firms, *inter alia*, L'Oréal, Sandoz and Beatrice Foods.

7. Muhammad Rahim Iravani

Created the Milli Shoe Group in 1961; built his first factory with German technology and went on to add unit after unit with various partners. Producing mass quality shoes, Milli came to dominate the domestic market and began making inroads into shoe exports.

8. Âli Akbar Mahlouji

He controlled Iran's sole nylon producer, the Alyaf company, in which West Germany's Bayer firm held a fifty per cent share. Initial plant capacity stood at 3,000 tonnes/annum, and was expanded over the years to 11,000 t/a; all caprolactam raw material was imported from West Germany.

9. Muhammad Taqi Barkhurdar

A cunning Yazdi businessman with a knack for hiring (and keeping) the best managers, he began in 1962 with his Pars Electric Manufacturing Company (renamed Pars Toshiba in 1969) and never looked back, ending up on the boards of four banks (i.e. IMDBI, Iranians, Iran and the Middle East, and the Bank-i Shahryar) and with no fewer than seventy-two companies.

10. Muhsin Azmayish.

A self-made man, he started with a small workshop in Tehran and managed to nurture his Azmayish Industries into the second slot of Iranian home appliances, behind Arj; in the mid-1970s, he was on his way to surpassing his rival with a mammoth appliance complex at Marvdasht near Shiraz, capable of producing 3,800 units per day.

11. Murad Aryeh

The Jewish businessman famous for his timely August 1953 blank cheque to the Shah in Rome, he established the Chini Iran company, manufacturer of Irana tiles, and passed on his businesses to his sons Rafiûllah and Iskandar, who kept the Aryeh family among the wealthiest of Iran's Jewish community.

12. Muhammad Tahiri

Scion of the renowned Tahiris of Yazd, he skilfully managed the family's Yazdbaf textile factory and diversified into home appliances (Philver), plastic goods (Palastrin), motorcycles (Kawasaki Iran) and chemicals (Rangin Industrial and Chemical Company).

13. Âbdullah Muqaddam

Built an imposing textiles factory on his sprawling estate at Nazarabad, located near the Tehran–Qazvin highway. Inaugurated in 1961, the plant came to employ some 1,700 people. Muqaddam Textiles became renowned for their high quality and profits poured in; Âbdullah was later assisted in running the company by his brothers Mustafa and Murtaza.

14. Husayn Qasimiyyeh

Founder of the Pars Manufacturing Group, a conglomerate initially based on cotton ginning. Pars diversified into vegetable oil (Swan), margarine (Golden Atlas), detergents (Tide), soap (Camay) and other derivatives; the Pars Group was second only to the Bihshahr Group in its field.

15. Mansour Yasini

The uncontested king of the Iranian glass industry and head of the Iranian Glass Syndicate. His Qazvin Glass Company set up a 12,000 tonnes/annum line with Pan Alliance (US) in 1968; its second and third lines (respectively 18,000 t/a and 36,000 t/a) were with the Japanese firm Nippon Glass; Yasini later gobbled up Abgineh and the Mumtaz textile factory.

16. Muhammad Abu Nasr Azud.

An eccentric Qajar prince related to the Farmanfarmayans, he fathered the sugarbeet industry in Khuzistan province; his Ahvaz Sugar Refining Company started operations in 1961 and became official supplier to a number of Iranian institutions, such as Iran Air; in the seventies, he also came to head Iran's Private Sugar Industry Syndicate.

17. Murtaza Rastigar Javahiri

A professor of mining at Tehran University's Technical Faculty, who pioneered in private mining, he created the firms of Simiran, Kalsimin and the Bafq Mining Company. Rising to the top of his profession, he managed to accumulate profits and diversify into downstream industrial projects.

18. Âli Asghar Payravi

A former track-and-field champion, he entered private mining with his Iran Barite firm, formed the Copper Smelting Company and the Iranian Oil Drilling Company. His mining empire came to cover twenty-one companies and 4,000 employees.

19. Qanbar Rahimi

A self-made mining tycoon, who had begun life at the bottom in mines, he climbed to the top of Iran's marble and travertine industry, remained his simple self and became known as Arbab Qanbar, with a large following throughout Iran. He discovered Iran's best marble mines, and provided the creamy-white marble stones for the Shahyad Monument (later Azadi), which became Tehran's symbol.

These were the new generation of captains of Iran's industry and mining, coming from the most varied backgrounds. During the Third Plan years, they made their mark by proving that they were capable managers. They had the good fortune to start at the best possible juncture: the Iranian economy was being pulled ahead by ever-increasing oil revenues and the Americans were determined to make a success story out of Iran's private sector.

12.8. Malaises

Notwithstanding the American successes in Iran during the early 1960s, everything was not for the best in the American clinic. There were some strains in the system, momentarily placed on the back burner (an act at which the average Iranian is expert), but nevertheless palpable in the Iranian society and polity for any connoisseur. The best expression for defining these strains was "a profound malaise", used by Martin F. Herz, the political counsellor at the US Embassy in Tehran, in his remarkable dispatch of June 15, 1964, entitled 'Some Intangible Factors in Iranian Politics'. In a nutshell, Herz had recognised that, although the future seemed bright for the Shah's regime and the opposition was weak and divided, there was a malaise. He couldn't put his finger on it (hence its description as intangible), but, even seeing parts of the intricate puzzle, he, at least, knew that it was there – an almost unique feat for an American diplomat in Iran and a reason behind his eventual recall from Tehran.

Another facet of the Iranian malaise was brought to the attention of the general public in America and the world by an extraordinary article entitled 'The Billion-Dollar Mystery' by F.J. Cook in *The Nation*.[85] Cook presented a photostat of a *relevé de compte* dated June 30 1962 made by the Union de Banques Suisses – UBS (Geneva Branch) – of the Pahlavi Foundation's account (number 214895.20H), with payments of millions of US dollars made from it (roughly $46m over February and March 1962) to Iranian and international personalities – in the former group were the Shah's brothers and sisters, Empress Farah and Ardashir Zahidi, and in the latter former US Ambassadors Henderson and Allen, Point Four's Warne, and the former CIA chief Allen Dulles. Some sources came to view the photostat as a fake, but the fact that it was never challenged by either the UBS or the Pahlavi court clearly speaks in favour of its authenticity (in any event, the photostat closely resembles a genuine UBS document). Cook goes on to tell the tale of Khabir Khan and his adventures in obtaining a copy of the UBS photostat before retiring to American exile. Some American representatives were even sent to Tehran to investigate, but failed to uncover the truth (or preferred to look the other way).

Decidedly, the year 1965 was not the most propitious for the Shah. Back in February he had been booed and insulted by a crowd of two hundred demonstrators in Vienna during an official visit.

Then, in May, after a quick tour of Argentina and Brazil (where it was alleged that the Pahlavi Foundation had heavily invested in real estate in São Paulo), the Shah went directly to Canada and then to France to meet the Canadian Governor-General and President de Gaulle respectively. The Shah probably failed to stop over in the USA because of the scandal unleashed by the Cook article, which was, however, to catch up with him in both Ottawa and Paris:

> ...copies of the Cook article were sent to the Governor-General in Ottawa and to General de Gaulle in Paris, the Shah's next stop. The Canadian Governor-General, obviously perturbed, confirmed the contents of the article with President Johnson, and when the Shah arrived in Ottawa his reception was distinctly cool. The Shah took off in a huff for Paris on June 2nd, where General de Gaulle, also in receipt of the article, refused to see him. After sulking in a Paris hotel for a few days, the Shah returned to Tehran...[86]

Back in 1962, during the official visit made by De Gaulle to Iran, the elderly president had advised the younger man "to keep his independence". Muhammad Reza Shah had failed to listen to the wise piece of advice, placing all his eggs in the American basket. By 1965, it was clear to the Powers that even the Cook article could not derail the American train in Iran and bring down its sole conductor: 'America's Shahanshah'.

NOTES

1 *Guzarish-i Ijra'i-i Barnameh-yi Haft Saleh Duvvum* (Tehran: Plan Organisation, 1343 (1964)) Tables 6 and 10. Also *Statistical Yearbook 1968* (Tehran: Markaz-i Amar-i Iran, June 1971) p.186.
2 C. Parham, *Inqilab-i Iran va Mabani Rahbari-i Imam Khomeini* (Tehran: Amir Kabir, 1357 (1978)) p.19.
3 R.W. Cottam, *Nationalism in Iran* (University of Pittsburgh Press, 2nd ed., 1979) p.297.
4 Ibid., p.298.
5 T.C. Sorensen, *Kennedy* (London: Pan Books Ltd., 1965) pp.274-7.
6 *Iran Almanac 1961* (Tehran: Echo of Iran) p.39.
7 On Burujirdi's opposition to reforms, especially the land reform, see *Houzeh* magazine, no. 43/44, (special issue on Ayatullah Burujirdi), Farvardin-Tir 1370 (April-July 1991), pp.18-21. To the Shah, who sent him the message, "In Iran reforms are necessary, like everywhere else in the world", Burujirdi sent the reply: "Everywhere else, first a republic is set up then reforms are launched" (p.21).
8 A.K.S. Lambton, *Landlord and Peasant in Persia* (Oxford University Press, reprint, 1969) p.395.
9 M. Copeland, *The Game of Nations* (London: Weidenfeld and Nicholson, 1969) p.51.
10 D.N. Wilber, *Contemporary Iran* (London: Thames and Hudson, 1963) p.184. And for an optimistic view on the role played by the Bank-i Ûmran in the collection of monies from the sales of the royal villages, see D.R. Denman, 'Land Reforms of Shah and People', in *Iran under The Pahlavis*, ed. by G. Lenczowski, (Stanford, Calif.,: Hoover Institution Press, 1978) pp.257-60. It should be added that during the 1960s the Bank-i Ûmran would gross billions of rials by selling its landholdings along the Caspian Sea littoral to private individuals.
11 A.K.S. Lambton, op. cit. (note 8), p.395.
12 Personal experience of the author. In a region of some thirty villages (in central Iran), only one village council was actually formed. It asked for its five per cent from its landlord, getting a harsh rebuff. But hostilities between this single council and the landlord had begun and would continue into the 1960s and 1970s. Even if rural councils proved a failure, they had been yet another spark for kick-starting the rudimentary moor of Iran's rural community.
13 The other possible candidate amongst the old Elitists was Muhammad Âli Nizam Mafi, the eldest son of Riza Quli Khan, the leader of the *Muhajarat* movement during the First World War. But, aged seventy-four and unwilling to make enemies among his fellow landlords, he had turned down the offer. Private communication to the author.
14 When *Newsweek* reporter Arnaud de Borchgrave asked the Shah in a November 1977 interview whether the allegation that, back in 1961, President Kennedy had used a $35m US aid package to push him into accepting Dr Amini as prime minister was correct, the Shah replied: "It's past history, but correct." Quoted by F. Hoveyda, *The Fall of the Shah* (New York: Wyndham Books, 1980) p.54.
15 In his memoirs, Ibtihaj wrote that "the CIA's [Tehran Station chief, Colonel] G. Yatsevich came to see me in the summer of 1962 (after my release from jail) to propose me the post of Finance Minister. He came again in summer 1963 to

propose me the Premiership. I asked him: 'Who are you speaking for?' He replied: 'For Washington.'" In the early 1960s, no one in Tehran doubted that Yatsevich took most of the major decisions in Iran. See Â. Aruzi, *Khatirat-i Abu'l Hasan Ibtihaj* (Tehran: Îlmi, 1371 (1992)) pp.525-6.

16 *Iran Almanac 1967* (Tehran: Echo of Iran) p.57.
17 N. JAMI, *Guzashteh Chiragh-i Rah-i Ayandeh Ast* (Tehran: Quqnous, 1361 (1982)) p.583.
18 C. Op't Land, 'Land Reform in Iran', in *Persica II (1965–6), Annuaire de la Société Neerlando-Iranienne,* (Holland: 1966) p.95.
19 D.N. Wilber, op. cit. (note 10), p. 187.
20 A.K.S. Lambton, *The Persian Land Reform (1962–66),* (Oxford: Clarendon Press, reprint, 1969) p.63.
21 Ibid., p.63.
22 Private communication from a Ministry of Agriculture civil servant, personally chosen by Arsanjani to lead the land reform in a crucial province (his native one).
23 A.K.S. Lambton, 'Land Reform and the Rural Co-operative Societies', in *Iran Faces the Seventies,* ed. by E. Yarshater, (New York: Praeger, 1971) p.21.
24 C. Op't Land, op. cit. (note 18), p.99.
25 A.K.S. Lambton, op. cit. (note 8), p.274.
26 Article 3 of the original law delimited the exceptions (or Mustasniyyat) to the law. Besides "all lands farmed by mechanised methods", exceptions numbered orchards, tea plantations (a boon for the Qavam family) and coppices, as well as all buildings and installations on the land that belonged to the landlord: no small loophole!
27 *Persica II,* op. cit. (note 18), p.135.
28 'White Revolution', an expression first coined by Dr Mahmoud Afshar Yazdi in articles published in his journal *Ayandeh* (the Future) back in 1946! A man of ideas, the late Dr Afshar Yazdi was also a wealthy philanthropist. See Ayandeh, *Third Series* no. 14/15/16, Bahman-Isfand 1324 (February–March 1946), (Tehran: 2nd ed., 1352 (1973)) pp.767-770.
29 A.K.S. Lambton, op. cit. (note 20), pp.194-5.
30 Ibid., p.356.
31 Ibid., p.354.
32 A.M. Eghtedari, 'Management of Rural Community Development', in *Tahqiqat-e-Eqtesadi* (The Journal of the Institute for Economic Research), Vol. IV, nos. 11 & 12, January 1967, (Tehran: Tehran University, 1967) p.64.
33 Quoted from *Iran 1971,* a special issue of the *Iran Trade and Industry* magazine, September–October 1971, (Tehran: Echo of Iran) p.73.
33A D. Craig, 'The Impact of Land Reform on an Iranian Village' in *The Middle East Journal,* Vol. 32, no. 2, Spring 1978, p.147.
34 The wildest rumours circulated around Arsanjani's fortune, because, having begun poor, he had become extremely rich, living comfortably in his huge mansion at Vilinjak.
35 R.W. Cottam, op. cit. (note 3), p.363. Most probably, Arsanjani was poisoned at a plush party he had given at his Vilinjak mansion. Private communication from a close relation to Arsanjani.
36 On the Southern Tribal Rebellion of 1963 see P. Oberling, *The Qahqa'i Nomads of Fars* (Mouton, 1974) pp.210-215. Oberling reports that five officers, three NCOs and forty-five soldiers were killed, and that two officers, eight NCOs and thirty-

37 three soldiers were wounded in the encounter, which lasted twenty-one hours. (p.213).
37 Vali Kiani's son Nasir had not been as fortunate as his father. Having killed two gendarmes and stolen their rifles, he was caught trying to sell the rifles back to the Gendarmerie. Too clever by half, he was court-martialled and executed in June 1963.
38 Âlam had sworn on the Holy *Quran* that Bahman's life would be safe. Bahman's mother, to her eternal regret, had trusted Âlam's word of honour. Private communication to the author.
39 P. Oberling, op. cit. (note 36), p.214-5. As Oberling reports, Gendarmerie NCOs refusing to torture rebels were court-martialled on the spot and executed. He cites the case of two such NCOs "refusing to obey orders" and being executed.
40 Ibid., p.211.
41 In January 1963, the intellectual wing published its ideas in *Bahsi dar Bareh-yi Marjâiyyat va Rouhaniyyat* (Discourses upon Questions Related to the Clergy and its Leadership), (Tehran: Shirkat-i Sahami-i Intishar, 1341 (1962)) 261p.
41A See *Sahifeh-yi Nour*, (Tehran: Shirkat-i Ufsit, 1361 (1982)) Vol. 1, p.15.
42 Dihnavi, *Qyam-i Khunin-i Punzdah-i Khurdad 1342* (Tehran: Rasa, 1360 (1981)) p.34.
43 Ibid., p.65.
44 Âlam's threat to resign on the evening of June 5 forced the Shah's hand in ordering fresh troops to take to Tehran's streets on June 6 and "shoot to kill". See M. Zonis, *The Political Elite of Iran* (Princeton University Press, 1971) p.66.
45 Dihnavi, op. cit. (note 42), p.185.
46 M. Âraqi, *Na Gufteh-ha* (Things Not Said), (Tehran: Rasa, 1370 (1991)).
47 The families of the two condemned men begged Khomeini to ask the Shah for a grace. Khomeini summoned SAVAK chief General Pakravan to an interview, with the latter arriving only after the executions had been carried out, advancing as an excuse for being late that he had been on a mission.
48 See *Asnad-i Nihzat-i Azadi Iran* (Tehran: Nihzat-i Azadi Iran, 1363 (1984)) Vol. 3. (Proceedings of the court martial).
49 Dihnavi, op. cit. (note 42), pp.218-223.
50 *Ittilaât* no. 15871, Khurdad 14, 1358 (June 4, 1979).
50A Although eventually rewarded with the Court Ministry in December 1966, Âlam would always be sour about his 1964 demotion, after all he had done for the Shah.
51 *Persica II*, op. cit. (note 18), p.147.
52 G. Lenczowski, *Oil and State in the Middle East* (Cornell University Press, 1960) p.96.
53 The United Islamic Groups were formed by the coalition of three major *Bazaar* religious *Hay'ats*: groups charged with organising the mourning ceremonies for the martyrdom of Imam Husayn (A.S.), which were not supposed to mix in politics. These *Hay'ats* were:
(1) The *Shaykh Âli Hay'at*, under Sadiq Amani Hamadani and Asadullah Lajivardi;
(2) The *Amin ul-Douleh Mosque Hay'at*, led by Mihdi Âraqi and Habibullah (Mihdi) Shafiq;
(3) The *Isfahanis' Hay'at*, with Mahmoud Mirfindiriski and Âla' ul-Din Mir Muhammad Sadiqi.
The *Hay'ats* had been brought together under orders from Khomeini, and were partially supervised by the young Bihishti. They had elected a twelve-member

Executive Committee, which included the six *Hay'at* leaders, and which held its meetings in the house of H. Shafiq.

54 Arrested in Switzerland for alleged heroin smuggling, Davallou alerted the Shah, who was vacationing at Saint Moritz, who intervened in his favour, pretending that he had diplomatic immunity. The Swiss authorities let Davallu depart freely on the Shah's private plane. See *Le Monde*, March 5/6, 1972. In an article signed by I. Vichniac and entitled 'À Genève: Le Prince et la Drogue', one could read: 'Mr Pierre Weber, le juge charge de l'affaire ...conclut donc: "Le prince X, ...qui se trouvait dans le benefice des privilèges d'immunité diplomatique, ...a pu quitter librement le territoire suisse".' See also the pertinent articles published by the Geneva weekly *La Pilule*: among many others, 'Un Sharmant Procès', no.40, December 7, 1971, pp.1-6; 'L' Immunité Crapulomatique', no. 55, March 21, 1972, p.2. Swiss justice, instead of bringing the Prince X to court, allowed the Shah to sue *La Pilule* – a case unique in Swiss legal history. The court imposed a fine of 500 Fr(Sw.) on its courageous editor Narcisse-René Praz. An affair of which the Swiss justice system must certainly not be proud today.

55 *Annual Statistical Bulletin 1980* (Vienna: OPEC) pp. XVIII and XXVII.
56 *Oil and Gas Journal*, December 25, 1972, p.113.
57 P. Terzian, *OPEC: The Inside Story* (London: Zed Books, 1985) p.106.
58 Op. cit. (note 55), p.XXVII.
59 *Iran Almanac 1967* (Tehran: Echo of Iran) pp.360-4.
60 *The Bulletin of the Iranian Petroleum Institute* (IPI), nos. 39-42, June 1970–March 1971.
61 J.B. Kelly, *Arabia, the Gulf and the West* (London: Weidenfeld and Nicholson, 1980) p.330.
62 *The Bulletin of the IPI*, various issues, 1963-1971.
63 'Present Status of Natural Gas in Iran', in *The Bulletin of the IPI*, no. 18, March 1965, p.630.
64 S. Naghavi and N. Manouchehri, 'The Iranian Gas Trunkline Project', in *The Bulletin of the IPI*, no. 27, June 1967.
65 *Petrochemical Industry in Iran* (Tehran: National Petrochemical Company, March 1977).
65A The statistics on fertilisers were compiled from early National Petrochemical Company reports (years 1856–60) and from the *Statistical Yearbook 1973* (Tehran: Markaz-i Amar-i Iran, June 1976) p.185.
66 Extracted from the report *Barrisi-i Âmaliyyat-i Qismat-i Pakhsh dar Sal 1970* (Tehran: Public Relations Dept. of NIOC, 1970).
67 *Asnad-i Laneh-yi Jasousi* (Tehran: Muslim Students Following the Line of Imam, undated) no. 36, pp.47-8.
68 Ibid., p.14.
69 Ibid., pp.58 and 61.
70 *Asnad-i...* op. cit. (note 67), no. 36, p.8.
71 Ibid., p.14.
72 *Afrique Asie* magazine, no. 219, August 4, 1980, p.47.
73 L.M. Pryor, 'Arms and the Shah', in *Foreign Policy*, no. 31, summer 1978, p.59.
74 J. Amuzegar, *Technical Assistance in Theory and Practice: the Case of Iran* (New York: Praeger, 1966) p.105.
75 *Guzarish-i Âmalkard-i Barnameh-yi Ûmrani-i Sivvum, 1341–46* (Results of the Third Development Plan, 1962–67), (Tehran: Plan Organisation, 1347 (1968)).

76 *Statistical Yearbook 1968*, op. cit. (note 1), pp.13-24.
77 *Guzarish-i...* op. cit. (note 75).
78 Ibid.
79 *Statistical Yearbook 1968*, op. cit. (note 1).
80 Muhammad Reza Shah's first two books were *Mission for My Country* (London: Hutchinson, 1960) and *The White Revolution* (Tehran: Kayhan Press, undated)
81 *Iran in the 1980s*, ed. by A. Amirie and H.A. Twitchell (Tehran: Institute for International Political and Economic Studies, 1978) pp.418-9.
82 *Iran Trade and Industry* magazine, April 1972, p.25.
83 Aysseh had the cunning to name his company the Société Anonyme Iranienne de Production Automobiles, thereby its acronym was S.A.I.P.A., which also happened to be the abbreviation of the full title (in French) of Princess Ashraf: Sa Altesse Impériale la Princesse Ashraf, an acronym her close friends used, among others Parviz Raji. See P.C. Radji, *In the Service of the Peacock Throne* (London: Hamish Hamilton, 1983).
84 Most probably the go-between who linked Israeli agents to the Iranian cabinet in 1950, which led to the *de facto* recognition of Israel by Iran in March 1950 (see Chapter 11); and U. Bialer, 'The Iranian Connection in Israel's Foreign Policy, 1948-1951', in *The Middle East Journal*, Vol. 39, no. 2, spring 1985, p.302.
85 F.J. Cook, 'The Billion-Dollar Mystery', in *The Nation*, April 12, 1965.
86 *MERIP Reports*, 'America's Shah, Shahanshah's Iran', no. 40, p.15.

CHAPTER THIRTEEN: NEW HORIZONS

During the second half of the 1960s, the path ahead for the Shah's regime was already traced: invest the increased oil revenues in development projects, thereby trying to content a majority within society. Since the beginning of the century Iranian society had been spilt into three major classes: (i) the upper class (the court, the elites); (ii) the middle class (the merchants, liberal professions); (iii) the third class (the masses, whether urban or rural). Since the inception of the American clinic, the goals had been to relieve the misery of the lowest class while trying to promote the highest number into the middle class: it was by the eradication of poverty and the promotion of a hard-working bourgeoisie that the Americans were planning to bring stability and prosperity to the country. The problem was that the links between popular welfare and massive industrial projects were rather tenuous, and certainly not direct. Nevertheless there was no other means of reinvesting oil revenues in the domestic economy. Thus, following the Third Plan, the Fourth Plan was to be yet another step in that overall direction.

13.1. The Fourth Development Plan

As the Third Plan was nearing completion, Iranian planners and their American advisers turned their sights to the next plan. In 1966/67 the initial blueprints of the Fourth Development Plan (March 1968–March 1973) were on the drawing board. The path to the Fourth Plan was traced when the American economist W.W. Rostow "concluded at the close of the Third Plan that Iran had passed the stage of 'economic take-off' and was readying for the fourth stage of development – the age of high mass-consumption".[1]

The die was cast. The Fourth Plan was based on the key forecast that oil revenues during the plan period would amount to Rls385bn, against Rls155bn during the Third Plan; and that plan expenditure would rise in parallel with these revenues: Rls480bn on Fourth Plan projects as against the 204bn spent during the Third Plan. These outlays called for an average annual GNP increase of 9% (against 6%

during the Third Plan). The aims of the new plan seemed extremely ambitious, when bearing in mind that the Third Plan had already stretched local potential to its limits. The young (forty year old) economist Khudadad Farmanfarmayan was brought in from Bank-i Markazi to replace Asfia as the head of the PO. The opening of a 'recurrent expenditures' item in the Fourth Plan allowed for manipulation of expenses and paved the way for the plan's eventual 'budgeting'. A Committee for Long-Term Planning saw its report filed *sine die*, no one being interested in looking too far down the road. Finally, the number of plan chapters was increased from ten to seventeen for the Fourth Plan.

The plan's major achievements are summarised here, chapter after chapter:

1. Agriculture
(Rls48.8bn invested)
– Once again the plan failed badly in this sector, with oil revenues not finding their way into rural Iran. Investments fell twenty per cent short of forecasts.
– All staple products output for 1972 were far off the plan targets: domestic wheat output fell one million tonnes short, and rice, cotton, sugar and tea didn't fare much better.[2]
– For Iran, the Fourth Plan was a turning point with regard to agricultural products since, for the first time in her history, she turned into a net importer.
– Farming corporations were introduced, but, although forty-three such corporations were set up, the scheme met with little success because the Iranian peasant wanted land of his own, not shares.
– The origins of Brobdignagian agro-businesses date back from 1968, when the *Majlis* approved a by-law for leases of land to such business. A minimum of 1,000 hectares for a maximum of thirty years was allotted – they would see the light in the early 1970s.

2. Industry and Mining
(Rls112.8bn)
– With 20% of total allocations, this area was the plan's top priority.

- Ninety per cent of funds was spent on public factories, while the rest went to the private sector.
- Steel mill was inaugurated at Isfahan with a capacity of 600,000 tonnes/annum, with a 1,033m^3 blast furnace. It was designed and construction by Soviet contractors; begun in March 1968, inaugurated in March 1973.
- Petrochemical plants at Abadan, Kharg and Bandar-i Shahpour were completed.
- In 1967 the Industrial Development and Renovation Organisation of Iran (IDRO) was established by an act of the *Majlis* as a holding company (modelled on Italy's IRI). In 1972, IDRO controlled twenty-three companies with a total capital of Rls15bn; it had its own consultancy (Technolog) from 1969, and its four major industrial complexes were:

  1) The Tabriz machine tools plant, producing lathes and drilling machines, was set up with Czech technology with an investment of Rls5.6bn, and began operations in September 1972.

  2) The Tabriz tractor plant, was built with Romanian know-how, and had a capacity of 3,500 tractors per annum (later expanded); it began producing in March 1970.

  3) Arak machine tools and heavy engineering complex was constructed with Soviet assistance, had an output of 30,000 tonnes/annum of machinery, costing the sum of Rls6.1bn, and began production in September 1972.

  4) Iran Aluminium Company (IRALCO), was located in Arak, had a capacity of 45,000 tonnes/annum, and was implemented with partners Reynolds Company (20%) and Pakistan (5%), with German machinery (HKD and BBC).

- In 1972, there were 5,000 large factories (i.e. employing more than ten people) in Iran. Out of a total industrial output of Rls421bn, they accounted for 240bn; the hundred and forty-four largest plants employed a total of 120,000 people;[3] three of these were built by the private sector:

  1) The Iran Telecommunications Manufacturing Company (ITCM) was a joint venture between the Ministry of PTT (30%), Siemens (40%) and IMDBI (30%); with a plant at Shiraz, its annual production amounted to 30,000

exchange units and 45,000 telephones, employing 700 persons.
2) Iran Transfo, which implemented a factory for assembling transformers at Ray, had a capacity of 500,000 KVa/annum, and employed 1,200 people.
3) The Pars Paper Mill, at Haft Tappeh, fed on the sugar mill's bagasse, had a capacity of 35,000 tonnes/annum; had an initial investment of $23m, and started up in October 1970, although there were technical hitches.

3. Oil and Gas
   (Rls67.5bn)
– The lion's share of funds was allocated to the Trans-Iranian Gas Trunkline (IGAT I), with its first phase (1,050 MMSCFD) being put into operation in October 1970.
– Rls5bn went to the Shiraz Refinery, built on a location twenty-five kilometres north of Shiraz, with a capacity of 40,000 B/D. Designed by UOP (US) and constructed by Snam Progetti (It.), it started up in summer 1973.

4. Water resources
   (Rls43.7bn)
– Six major dams were completed during the plan period:
   1) The Shah Âbbas Dam on the Zayandehroud river was 150 kilometres upstream of Isfahan; had a height of 95 metres; power generation of 60 MW; downstream irrigation of 116,000 hectares.
   2) The Aras Dam on the Aras river; built by the Soviets; cost of Rls 6bn; began operating in December 1970; power generation of 44 MW; irrigation of 90,000 hectares in the Dasht-i Mughan.
   3) The Cyrous Dam on the Zarrinehroud (Azarbayjan); cost Rls2.7bn; power generation of 10 MW; irrigated 65,000 hectares of land downstream.
   4) The Darioush Dam on the Kur river, north of Shiraz; an earth-filled dam (5.4 million m³ earth); investment of Rls9.1bn; water for Shiraz, the fertiliser complex and 76,000 hectares of land.
   5) The Shahpour I Dam at Mahabad; Rls1.7bn invested.

6) The Gurganroud Dam in Gurgan province; Rls1.1bn invested.

5. Power
   (Rls43.0bn)

- Rls18bn was allotted to power generation; installed capacity more than doubled from 900 MW (1967) to 2,100 MW in 1972; and output of electricity more than trebled from 1,842m KWh (1967) to 6,870 KWh in 1972.
- Rls17bn was spent on distribution networks: 1,000 kilometres of 132 KV and 2,150 km of 230 KV cables were laid.
- A study made by Edison Electric Institute (US) called for a national electric grid, a ten-year programme at a cost of Rls97bn.

6. Communications and Transport
   (Rls84.3bn)

- Rls51bn was allocated to highways and first-class roads, among others, the Tehran–Karaj highway (built by Asad-Ecbatane) plus 2,600 kilometres of first-class roads and 7,760 kilometres of second-class roads.
- Three major railway links were completed: (1) the Kashan–Zarand line (750 km); (2) a spur from the Qum–Yazd line linking Sagsi to the Isfahan Steel Mill (112 km); (3) the line linking Sufian to the Turkish border (195 km).
- Among the Persian Gulf ports, Bandar Âbbas (Rls1.7bn) and Bandar-i Shahpour (Rls1.5bn) were given priority; although Khurramshahr was still the largest port, handling 66% of cargoes.
- A $12.5m contract was given to a British Consortium for renovating twelve provincial airports.
- A public shipping company, the Arya National Shipping Company, was created (see Frame 13.1).

7. Telecommunications
   (Rls44.4bn)
- Iran's first satellite communication station was installed at Asadabad (near Hamadan) by Page Communication Engineers, a subsidiary of Northrop (US).
- The Integrated National Telecommunication System (INTS), a microwave network 13,700-km long linking six hundred relay stations and fifty-eight major urban centres, was built by a Consortium led by Page-Northrop and including Siemens (W. Germany), Nippon Electric (Japan), General Telephone (Canada) and Electronics International (Italy). The first phase of INTS was completed in 1973, the second in 1974. In 1975, the project was hit by a momentous bribery scandal.[3]
- A fifteen-storey national communications centre was completed in Tehran's Sipah Square.
- Rls12bn went for increasing telephone lines from 240,000 to 530,000 units.
- In 1972, NIRT's radio programmes reached 75% of the population, and its TV broadcasting around 60% of households.

8. Rural Development
   (Rl010.1bn)
- Rls3.5bn was spent on providing drinking water to dozens of villages.
- Rls2.4bn was spent on local hygiene and the building of public baths (with showers).

9. Urban Development
   (Rls7.6bn)
- Drinking water for urban centres.
- Internal road asphalting for provincial towns.
- Reorganisation of municipalities and master plans for development, including the fresh Tehran Master Plan.

10. Construction and Housing
    (Rls36.4bn)
- Around Rls20bn was spent on garrisons and buildings of the armed forces, and on housing complexes for officers and NCOs.
- Rls9bn was allotted to governmental buildings throughout the country.
- Rls6bn was spent on public housing schemes.

11. Education
    (Rls37.3bn)
- Two-thirds of the budget was spent on current expenses: Rls13bn on primary education and 6bn on secondary.
- Rls9bn went to vocational and technical schools. Enrolment stood at 66,000 in 1972 compared with 19,000 in 1967.
- Rls6.5bn went to the universities. The number of students doubled from 59,800 (1967) to 115,000 (1972), and graduates trebled from 9,000 to 26,300 over the same period.[4]

12. Culture and Arts
    (Rls1.5bn)
- Budgets were allotted for fresh stock in museums.
- Money was spent on the restoration and upkeep of historical monuments (e.g. renovation works at Persepolis).
- Grants were given to local movie producers.

13. Tourism
    (Rls3.7bn)
- Rls3bn went on the erection of standard provincial inns and offices by INTO (the Iranian National Tourism Organisation).
- Number of foreign tourists reached 411,000 in 1972.

14. Health and Sanitation
    (Rls16.5bn)
- More than Rls7bn was spent on 'recurring costs'.

– Rls8bn was spent on new hospitals, dispensaries and medical posts. Nine thousand hospital beds were made available, bringing the total to forty thousand.

15. Social Welfare
(Rls4.8bn)
– Rls2.5bn was spent on youth welfare, and on the building of some ninety new schools for handicapped children (from a base of fifteen schools in 1967).
– Rls2bn was spent on social insurance.

16. Statistics and Research
(Rls1.9bn)
– Recurrent costs were allocated to the statistical Centre of Iran for the partial 1971 census and other surveys and plans.
– Large sums were spent on research centres, for the hardware.

17. Regional Development
(Rls3.7bn)
– A timid try at decentralisation: in May 1970 the *Majlis* revived the law calling for elected township and provincial councils (as per the constitution) and elections were held in August 1970 (the Americans' wish to go to the grass roots) for the councils (from a minimum of five members to a maximum of fifteen) of 151 townships (*shahristans*) and twenty-three provinces (*ustans*).
– Over Rls1bn was invested in extensive development studies and twenty-year regional development master plans.

Frame 13.1. The Arya National Shipping Company

Created in July 1967 with a capital investment of Rls10m, Arya was initially designed to carry cargo and passengers in the Persian Gulf. It began life with two small vessels, the *Razi* and the *Ibn Sina*.

In May 1968, private investors were accepted and an expansion programme devised; major new shareholders were the Bank-i Bazargani-i Iran, NWK Shipping Lines, Faravard Dried Fruit Company and Iranian Oil Drilling Company

In 1970, Arya owned five ocean-going ships (three of 12,000 dwt, one each of 10,000 and 16,000 dwt) and three smaller vessels for the Gulf (respectively 1,000, 1,600 and 1,800 dwt) and had become Iran's leading maritime cargo transporter.

The breakdown of the Fourth Plan's planned and actual investments can be seen in Table 13.1.

Table 13.1 The Fourth National Development Plan (1968–1972) – **Planned and Actual Investments.**[5]
(Figures in Rls billions)

Plan Chapters	Planned Investments — Public Sector	Private Sector	Recurrent Costs	Actual Total Investments	
Agriculture	24.0	20.0	21.0	65.0	48.8
Industry & Mining	84.7	6.0	8.3	99.0	112.8
Oil & Gas	26.3	—	—	—	67.5
Water	47.4	1.1	—	48.5	43.7
Power	36.3	1.7	—	38.0	43.0
Communications	78.0	2.0	—	80.0	84.3
Telecom	19.1	1.2	—	20.3	44.4
Rural Dev'ment	8.1	1.0	—	9.1	10.1
Urban Dev'ment	7.0	—	—	7.0	7.6
Construction	20.1	—	2.9	23.0	36.4
Education	14.7	20.3	—	35.0	37.3
Culture/Arts	1.8	—	—	1.8	1.5
Tourism	3.6	0.2	—	3.8	3.7
Health	4.9	7.3	1.6	13.8	16.5

Social Welfare	3.0	1.5	0.1	4.6	4.8
Statistics	—	1.0	—	1.0	1.9
Regional Dev'l	1.2	2.6	—	3.8	3.7
Total	380.2	65.9	34.9	453.7	568.0

Altogether the Fourth Plan had been overambitious, supporting far too many projects. The weak and ill-equipped Iranian bureaucracy had almost caved in under these extreme loads, wasting tremendous amounts of money paying for its multiple deficiencies. Iranian project teams deteriorated qualitatively (and quantitatively), thereby lowering the quality of the projects' execution. Average annual increases of 30% in oil revenues had allowed the PO to brush aside any problem by simply throwing dollars at it. Fuelled by these oil dollars, GNP had grown at an average rate of 12% (at constant prices) – an unprecedented record for Iran's economy. Inflation held within the 2-3% bracket during the plan's first three years, but slipped to between 5–7% during the closing years. The plan's main beneficiaries were the industrial and services sectors, with respective annual growth of 13.8% and 14.7%. The main laggard was yet again agriculture: its share of GNP fell from 14.6% in 1968 to 10.5% in 1972. The perennial difficulties of agriculture had further widened the gap between average rural and urban per capita consumption – from a ratio of 2:22 in 1967/68 it had jumped to 3:22 in 1971/72 (for details see Table 13.2).

Table 13.2. Per Capita Consumption Expenditures of Iranian Urban and Rural Households, for Selected Years (1959–1972).[6]
(Figures in constant 1959 Rials)

Year	Urban Consumption	Rural Consumption	Rural:Urban Ratio
1959/60	14,923	7,012	2:13
1961/62	15,857	7,400	2:14
1963/64	16,213	7,443	2:18

1965/66	16,277	8,375	1:94
1967/68	19,197	8,648	2:22
1969/70	24,659	8,134	3:03
1971/72	25,866	8,036	3:22

13.2. Rural–Urban Migration

The ever-steeper gradient of difference between rural and urban incomes was pushing higher number of peasants towards the cities in general and Tehran in particular. In the villages peasants could only hope to survive, but in the cities they could hope to find a place in the sun. The early months of city life were always the most difficult and they required special resilience and capacity for hardship, a challenge for the most sturdy peasants. Two categories of villagers left for the cities: (1) the best and the brightest of the peasant masses, who sold their plot of land (at between 50,000 and 100,000 Rials in the sixties) or rented it to their kin; and (2) the younger peasant generation, who had little attachment to the land and was readier than the older generations to accept the initial urban challenge, to brave its hardships and the inevitable city sharks. In the cities, with their booming economies, the possibilities were almost unlimited: every business needed new, capable hands; there were the expanding bureaucratic institutions; the private sector companies required workers and janitors; the foreign companies' employees needed servants, guards and factotums; the new bourgeoisie wanted couples from the countryside to keep their households for food, shelter and a monthly pittance; there were the new municipal services (e.g. waste disposal) and the new private services (e.g. garages and restaurants); the expanding armed forces needed NCOs; and, finally, the booming urban construction sector never seemed to find enough unskilled and semi-skilled cheap labour.

Iranian rural–urban migration, like any other human mass migration, developed its own network system: the first one to find a solid position in Tehran would do his utmost to get his next of kin a job (any job would do). Soon the inhabitants of one village were entrenched in a company, another in a construction site and a third filled the key slots in a factory. The new capitalist elite was incorporating the peasants into their novel structure: industry, housing construction and services. On the other hand, the workers were satisfied with the easy work (relative to working the land), the secure daily or monthly pay, the material advantages of urban life and the savings they could send back to the village or exchange for gold. In the sixties, they were ready to obey any order from their new masters: they needed the job and the pay to survive the shock of migration and find a new footing. Over the decade 1966-1976 at least some 2.3 million peasants migrated to the cities[7] – an average of 230,000 per annum. But, looking at the figures of the 1966 and 1976 national censuses, total urban population growth was in the order of 6 million (from 9.8m in 1966 to 15.8m in 1976) and thus it can be concluded that around 40% of the new urban population was made up of rural migrants, especially if the contemporary demographic and sociology studies are to be believed: "Economic migrants were mostly men 20-24 years of age. After 25, migration fell steeply and the population 35 and over was almost sedentary".[8]

Rural-urban migration was not a consequence of land reform, but rather a phenomenon resulting from the fact that the domestic benefits of oil revenues were to be found in the cities, not the villages. Both the migrants and the non-migrants could witness this basic truth, as the economic standards of the former rose year after year and those of the latter remained stagnant (at best). The stagnation of agricultural produce prices was due to the basic fact that American economic experts wanted them strictly aligned to international prices (why?). On the other hand, the steep increases in the price of manufactured goods (e.g. the *Paykan* car) further added to Iran's rural and urban dichotomy. During the 1960s, although migration was in full swing, things were running extremely smoothly: all groups involved, from the captains of industry to the migrants, were satisfied with their position, and all benefited from the booming economy of the late 1960s.

The 1960s' economic boom and the rural-urban migration was to give birth to a novel economic sector, hitherto dormant in Iran: real estate. Land speculation in a country with so much barren land and a population density of only sixteen inhabitants per square kilometre in 1966 seemed illogical and almost certain to fail. The first attempt at launching such a new national sport had been made in Tehran back in 1958-59 on the back of the boom engineered by the Second Plan; but the 1960-61 economic crisis had turned the real estate bull market into a bear market and dozens of imprudent speculators crashed into bankruptcy.

The second attempt dated from 1968-69. Circumstances then were highly propitious for a real estate revival in Tehran:

(1) Great amounts of idle money were ripe to enter real estate deals because investments in agriculture yielded poor returns, if any, and in industry the first and second wave of industrial capitalists had already monopolised the most profitable activities.

(2) The first waves of rural migrants had found their way to Tehran and joined the large numbers of middle-class Tehranis ready to invest their savings in real estate.

(3) Rates of return in Tehrani real estate were far above other potential investments as the economic boom was in full swing and, with substantial oil revenues, a repeat of the 1960-61 recession was improbable – especially with the Bank-i Markazi as a vigilant watchdog.

(4) Furthermore, a small group of large urban landholders, owning dozens of hectares in and around Tehran, were manoeuvring to keep the artificial real estate investment fever as high as possible.

These major Tehrani families were:
- The Farmanfarmayans/Firouzes (with holdings in Punak, Rustamabad, Farmaniyyeh, Kamraniyyeh and all over Tehran);
- The Aminis (Illahiyyeh);
- The Nizam-Mafis (Jinatabad, Kan);
- The Vusuqs (Sulaymaniyyeh);
- The Mansours (Zafiraniyyeh);
- The Shaybanis (Darrous);
- The Mustoufi ul-Mamaliks (Vanak);
- The Muâyyiris (Lavizan);
- The Imamis (Vilinjak);
- The Khazanehs (Shahr-i Ray).

These families (all of them from the old Qajar Elite, except for the Khazanehs – whose wives were from the Qajar Elite) were supported in their efforts by dozens of second-string Elite families owning only thousands of square metres in Tehran. This was the way the Elite had found to stay on top of the heap (probably initially an idea of the late Prince Farmanfarma, who came to own the largest estates): through control of the land, it could control the whole of society for decades.

The first ripples of real estate speculation were felt in 1969 when rents throughout the capital began moving upwards. The increases were sudden and unprecedented. The official rate of rents' inflation was reported at 12.2% for the year 1969[9] – an average that masked reality in the capital's residential areas, where mighty rises of 30–40% were reported.

Increases in rents spurred increases in land prices and vice versa, giving birth to a self-winding inflationary spiral. An army of dealers, middlemen, go-betweens and clerks were busy pouring fuel on the fire with their rumours and stories of instant fortunes: speculators were assured that buying land was the surest investment because it was solid and today was always cheaper than tomorrow. Worthless land was being sold first at three rials per square metre, then for five and even ten – the pump of land speculation was well primed and lubricated by dozens of Elite hands. Nothing could stop the real estate wave. For land prices, the sky was the limit – and the old Elite families would make sure that it remained so.

13.3. The Shahanshah Aryamihr

If 1965 had been a year to forget for the Shah, 1967 would be a year to remember. Oil revenues had passed the $750m mark, allowing for much leeway in budgets and expenditures. He and his family were immensely rich (the nightmares of Rome 1953 were long forgotten). The opposition was still ruthlessly muzzled by SAVAK. The army and air force were expanding daily, propped up by American advisers and state of the art armaments. The development plans were moving ahead. The urban middle classes were busy consuming (or rather learning how to), saving and investing like never before. Nothing could go wrong.

In early spring, the Twenty-First *Majlis* had been persuaded to thrust upon its successful sovereign the pompous title of *Aryamihr* (lit. 'Light of the Aryans'): henceforth the Shah would officially be known as His Imperial Majesty Muhammad Reza Shah Pahlavi, Shahanshah Aryamihr – nothing less. Referring to him as simply the King or the Shah was deemed a crime of *lèse majesté*.

The Shah's second achievement of 1967 was to legally secure his own succession. In August he ordered the convention of a 277-

member constituent assembly for settling the question. On September 2, the constituent assembly unanimously ratified the Regency Bill, according to which, in the case of the Shah's demise before Crown Prince Reza Pahlavi reached the age of maturity (twenty-one years of age), Empress Farah would become regent, at the head of a Regency Council consisting of eight other members: the prime minister, the head of the Supreme Court, the presidents of the *Majlis* and the Senate and four elder statesmen, to be nominated by the court.

The Shah's third major achievement was to have himself and his wife Farah crowned Emperor and Empress of Iran on October 26, 1967, the date of his own forty-eighth birthday. After twenty-six years on the Peacock Throne, the Shahanshah Aryamihr suddenly felt that the time was ripe to put on his great coronation show. Poorly copied from traditional British royal protocol (with the royal carosse being pulled by eight white horses), millions of dollars were spent on the occasion – with the Parisian jewellers Van Cleef and Arpels getting their fair share of the bounty for crafting the Empress's crown, complete with 1,469 diamonds "after months of painstaking work".[10] Among the foreign dignitaries invited to the ceremonies was American diplomat and lawyer George W. Ball, who was clearly not impressed by the extravaganza, and wrote in his memoirs:

> It was pure factice [*sic*] – a flamboyant attempt to give bogus legitimacy to the parvenu Pahlevi Dynasty... What an absurd, bathetic spectacle![11]

After a quarter of a century of survival, Muhammad Reza Shah had found time to develop his own elite: the courtiers, the politicians and the technocrats he had grown to personally trust over the years. In the 1940s and 1950s, he had not had a choice of using trusted friends to help him govern, but now, in the mid-1960s, he did. And he would use his prerogatives to keep 'his elite' running the vessel of State for him. The Shahanshah Aryamihr's elite was essentially made up of the following seventy-one individuals:

i) The Imperial Court (ten members)
– Asadullah Âlam, court minister (November 1966–August 1977), the only courtier who dared speak his mind to the Shah, albeit

occasionally, and who kept repeating that "If His Majesty would order it, I would gladly cut the head off my beloved children myself!"[12]

- General Dr Âbd ul-Karim Ayadi, the Shah's personal physician, a Baha'i, the Shah's *éminence grise*, also his factotum and business associate, who controlled shrimp production in the Gulf.

- Sulayman Bihboudi and Abu'l Fath Atabay, old family servants of the Reza Shah generation, trustworthy members of the household, both wielding considerable influence.

- Muhammad Jâfar Bihbahanian, the Shah's treasurer, who kept count of all the Shah's investments and accounts, both in Iran and abroad.

- Hurmuz Qarib and Rustam Amir Bakhtiar were the men in charge of protocol and ceremonial at the Pahlavi court, the latter being a leftover from Queen Surayya's days.

- Professor Yahya Âdl, the Shah's private surgeon (among Iran's best), his personal friend and belote partner,[12A] an amateur politician in Âlam's *Mardum* Party.

- Shujâ ul-Din Shafa, deputy court minister for cultural affairs, and in fact the Shah's private pen (a good one).

- Nusratullah Mûinian, the Shah's personal secretary, a capable bureaucrat, but out of his depth in the court's minefields.

ii) The Royal Influence-Peddlers (six members)

- Amir Houshang Davallou Qajar, an old Qajar princeling, in a class by himself, immensely rich and powerful, who held a monopoly over Iran's caviar exports; involved in a drug-smuggling scandal in Switzerland.[13]

- Abu'l Fath Mahvi, related to the Diba family, frontman for a number of American oil companies (e.g. AMOCO) and head of Iran's 'Air Mafia'[14] and of many more mafias (e.g. computers).

- Dr Ahmad Maybud, one-time diplomat, representative of American oil and shipping companies, the Shah's go-between in oil deals (e.g. the 1957 AGIP-NIOC agreement) and, since 1960, 'special adviser to the Imperial Court'.

- Felix Aqayan, an Armenian lawyer educated in Switzerland, leader of Iran's Armenian community, the uncrowned king of Iranian sugar imports, who became a senator; his brother Alexander thrived in his wake.

— Shahpour Reporter (later Sir), the Shah's close friend, who oversaw the Chieftain tanks deal; he represented Neill-Price[15] and a dozen other firms in Tehran; he invested (too late) in Vanak real estate.

— Byouk Sabir, a former trade union leader, who had made his name in the *Murdad 28* coup; the regime's jack of all trades, always useful, who made a fortune before retiring to the French Riviera.

iii) The Armed Forces (twelve members)

— General Husayn Fardoust, the Shah's closest friend since his school days, who always kept an extremely low profile – was never in the public eye – but held key positions in SAVAK and in the Imperial Inspectorate.

— General Muhammad Amir Khatami, pilot of the Shah's personal plane, who flew him to Baghdad and Rome in August 1953; he was commander-in-chief of the Iranian Air Force (1957), and married Princess Fatimeh in 1959; he was member of Iran's 'Air Mafia'.[15A]

— General Ghulam Âli Uvaysi, an officer's officer, from a family of landlords, who was linked by marriage to the old Kashan family of Ghaffari; he was trusted by the Shah and became head of the Gendarmerie (1965).

— General Hasan Toufanian, deputy minister of war in charge of logistics and arms procurement, the future tsar of Iran's fabulous armament purchases, who directly oversaw deals worth at least $26bn.[15B]

— General Âbbas Qarabaghi, who, after graduating from the Military Academy, was promoted by the Shah and appointed chief of the Army General Staff in 1968.

— Generals Jâfar Shafaqat, Ghulam Âli Azhari, Âbd ul-Âli Badreh'i and Manouchihr Biglari were four senior army officers on whom the Shah could rely.

— General Parviz Khusrouvani was an officer turned sportsman who made millions out of his *Taj* (crown) Sports Club.

— General Manouchihr Khusroudad, the rising star in the special paratrooper and helicopter *Havanirouz* forces.

— General Nadir Jahanbani, captain of the Acrojet team which flew in aeronautical shows, who was the future commander-in-chief of the air force.

iv) SAVAK (seven members)
 - General Nîmatullah Nasiri, of *Murdad 28* fame, SAVAK's third chief since 1965, after Taymour Bakhtiar and Hasan Pakravan.
 - Parviz Sabiti, a civilian, SAVAK's number two, who was presented on TV as "a security official", redoubtable and feared.
 - General Nasir Muqaddam, Nasiri's deputy at SAVAK, who was capable but not made for the secret service fold.
 - General Âli Mûtazid, the chief of SAVAK's forays abroad, the right man for the job, who kept a low profile.
 - General Âbd ul-Âli Mahoutyan, the most secretive among Iran's secret men and the co-ordinator of SAVAK's secret branches.[15C]
 - General Mansour Qadar, SAVAK's Middle East specialist, who was usually based in Lebanon.
 -Parviz Khwunsari, SAVAK's representative in Europe, who controlled student opposition groups from his Geneva headquarters.

v) The Houses of Parliament (two members)
 - Engineer Jâfar Sharif Imami, president of the Senate (1963-78), who had a hand in the Pahlavi Foundation and was a freemason leader.
 - Engineer Âbdullah Riazi, president of the *Majlis* (1963-78) and former (successful) rector of Tehran University Technical Faculty.

vi) The Government Bureaucracy (seventeen members)
 - Amir Âbbas Huvayda, prime minister (January 1965-August 1977), a record for constitutional premiers.
 - Ardashir Zahidi, the general's son, either foreign minister or ambassador to Washington (1967-78).
 - Dr Jamshid Amuzigar, minister of finance (1965), Iran's OPEC representative, a former Point Four manager.
 - Mansour Rouhani, minister since 1965, minister of agriculture from 1971 onwards.
 - Mihrdad Pahlbud, altered his Minbashian family name when he married Princess Shams (in 1945), minister of culture (1965).
 - Houshang Ansari, minister since 1966, at Economy since 1968, a second-rate diplomat who caught the Shah's eye, and later mystified American politicians.

- Âbd ul-Majid Majidi, minister of labour (1967-72), then Iran's planning tsar at Plan Organisation.
- Hadi Hidayati, minister of education (1965-68), later minister of state.
- Âta'ullah Khusrouvani, minister of labour (1961-67), secretary of New Iran Party (1965-69), head of NIOC Inspectorate (1969-79).
- Safi Asfya, head of Plan Organisation (1961-68), minister of state for development affairs (1968-78).
- Âbd ul-Âzim Valian, minister for land reform and rural co-operatives (1965-74), Governor-General of Khurasan (1975-78), one of Davallou Qajar's protégés.
- Ghulam Riza Nikpay, minister of state (1965-8), Tehran mayor (1969-77).
- Dr Husayn Khatibi, managing director of Red Lion and Sun Society (1954-78); General Afshar Tous was kidnapped in his house.
- Âbd ul-Riza Ansari (not related to Houshang), managing director of the Imperial Organisation for Social Services - IOSS (1969-78), began his career in KWPA, became a top protégé of Princess Ashraf and very rich in the process.
- General Âli Muhammad Khadimi, managing director of Iran Air (1963-78).
- Dr Tahir Zia'i, minister and senator (1967-78), president of Chamber of Commerce, Industries and Mines (1967-78), the uncrowned king of the Ramsar resort on the Caspian Sea.
- Firaydoun Huvayda (Amir Âbbas's brother), Iran's permanent UN delegate.

vii) The Oil Industry (five members)
- Dr Manuchihr Iqbal, chairman of the board and managing director of NIOC (1963-77), a trusted servant of the Shah.
- Dr Riza Fallah, deputy chairman of NIOC (1963-77), with solid roots in the southern oil industry since the 1940s.
- Aqa Khan Bakhtiar, NIOC director for personnel and finance (1964-78).
- Baqir Mustoufi, NIOC director and managing director of the National Petrochemical Company (1964-78).
- Taqi Musaddiqi, NIOC director and managing director of the National Iranian Gas Company (1966-78).

viii) Universities (two members)
- Dr Jahanshah Salih, brother of Allahyar and Âli Pasha, chancellor of Tehran University (1963-68), and Empress Farah's gynaecologist, later a senator (1971-78).
- Dr Houshang Nahavandi, minister of housing (1964-68), chancellor of Pahlavi University (1968-71) and Tehran University (1971-75), head of Empress Farah's Special Bureau (1976-77).

ix) The Banking and Insurance Sector (four members)
- Yusuf Khushkish, managing director of Bank-i Milli Iran (1963-77), governor of Bank-i Markazi Iran (1977-78).
- Houshang Ram, managing director of Bank-i Ûmran (1963-78), and the Pahlavi Foundation's money-changer.
- Abu'l Qasim Khiradjou, managing director of IMDBI (1963-78), and private adviser to most of Iran's captains of industry.
- Javad Mansour (Hasan Âli's brother), minister (1965-68), managing director of Central Insurance (1972-78).

x) The Mass Media (six members)
- Âbbas Masôudi, publisher-owner of the *Ittilaât* group of newspapers, who was succeeded by his eldest son Farhad after his death in June 1974.
- Mustafa Misbahzadeh, publisher-owner of the *Kayhan* group of newspapers (1943-78).
- Riza Qutbi, Empress Farah's cousin, and head of National Iranian Radio and Television - NIRT - since its inception (1966-78).
- Manuchihr Azmoun, the regime's chief ideologue, who moved between the Ministry of Interior, the NIRT, the Pars News Agency, the Endowments Organisation and the *Majlis* (1966-78).
- Mahmoud Jâfarian, Azmoun's assistant at NIRT and head of the Pars News Agency.
- Parviz Nikkhwah, NIRT's chief propagandist and selector of political programmes and debates (1967-78).

These seventy-one individuals were the regime's decision-makers, who pulled the visible levers of power in Iran. They were all trusted by the Shah, who had chosen every single one himself. This select group was frozen into power by the Shah in the mid-1960s and would rigidly remain in position for the next decade and a half. The Shah was loath to change a reliable player for an untried one. Never before had the Iranian elite been frozen in such a way (not even in the Elite's golden days of the 1910s). But the basic problem of the Aryamihr elite was not its stagnation, but rather its quality: it was not made up of the best and brightest. Instead, it was made up of capable yes-men, of individuals able to play the Iranian power game and not foul up, of egotists good at showing their strengths and hiding their faults. It lacked an *esprit de corps*. It also had too few leaders (Fardoust, Khatami), too few strong-willed individuals (Sharif Imami), too few intellectuals (Shafa) and hardly a single man of vision: the Shah would never have accepted such prima donnas in case they stole attention from his solo performance. If people like Generals Fardoust and Khatami had made it to the top, it was due to the extraordinary nature of their role in the Shah's life. In the final summary, this elite was not a viable elite: as long as the Americans and SAVAK could prop it up it would sail along with the Shah at the wheel, but it was not made to weather strong winds, let alone storms. Furthermore, with time it would grow more corrupt and richer, hence weaker and less flexible. Security of tenure for life never was a boon for Iranian elites, in whatever period.

13.4. The Armed Forces' Revival

In the aftermath of their double victory of 1963 against the southern tribal rebellion and the street mobs in Tehran, Iran's armed forces were back in the saddle. They were ready to share in the bonanza unleashed by the enormous oil revenues. In the framework of the Fourth Plan, the armed forces were not only given an allocation for housing and garrison constructions, but defence subsidies were included in the general governmental budget, under the headings of (i) Ministry of War, (ii) Gendarmerie and (iii) Police. The defence outlay averaged 18% of the public budget over the period 1968-1972 (see Table 13.3 for details).

In parallel with their increased budget, the armed forces had begun expanding again: from 185,000 men in 1965 "to a total military strength of 221,000 in 1969/70".[17] Since the mid-fifties, the Iranian Army had benefited from armaments given to them by the US Army: tanks, trucks, jeeps, howitzers, machine-guns, combat rifles and ammunition. It was with this American equipment that it had taken part in the CENTO military exercise (code name 'Shahbaz') of November 1959. For the joint Iranian-American project of April 12–15, 1964 (code name 'Delaware'), the Iranian armed forces was much

Table 13.3. The Share of Defence Expenditure in the Public Budget for the years 1968–1972.[16]
(All figures in Rls billions)

Year	Total Public Budget	Defence Expenditure	Defence's Share (%)
1968	189.4	36.3	18
1969	221.9	37.7	17
1970	271.8	45.0	17
1971	356.2	58.7	17
1972	386.9	77.5	20
Total	1426.2	255.2	18

better equipped; its units defended the Nadir line on the Zagros, separating the invading northern army occupying 'Sunland' (northwest Iran) from the forces stationed in 'Freeland' (south-west Iran). In 1964, the Iranian Army also began purchasing (cheaper) military equipment from the Soviet Union: the first consignment, worth $110m, included jeeps, Zil trucks and Katyusha multiple rocket-launchers. In 1967, the army's helicopter unit, the *Havanirouz* ('army's wings') came into being when one hundred Agusta Jet Ranger AB 206 helicopters were purchased from Italy. In 1968, forty American Iroquois helicopters were added to the new unit's hardware. It was also in the late 1960s that its first helicopter-borne regiment, the *Tip-i Nouhid* (short for *Tip-i Nirou-yi Vizheh Havaburd* – the Special Helicopter-borne Forces' Regiment), was created: the army's crack regiment of hand-picked NCOs and officers (no soldiers), a cross between the British SAS and the American Green Berets.

The Iranian Imperial Air Force (IIAF), under General Muhammad Khatami, was witnessing a unique transformation from a support force into the armed forces' spearhead. The best American fighter jets had become a must for the IIAF: from the T-33 (in 1956) to the 90 F-5 (Northrop) in 1965 and the F-4 Phantom (McDonnell Douglas) in 1968 – with, in between, the F-84 Thunderjet (1957) and the F-86 Sabre (1960).[18] In 1963, twelve C-130 Hercules (Lockheed) transport planes were added to the force. Besides the main squadron wings stationed at Tehran's Mihrabad Airport, two further wings were formed: one at the new Vahdati[18A] military air base near Dizful in Khuzistan, built by Morrison-Knudsen (US) and Iranian sub-contractors (1957–61); the other at the Shahrukhi[19] base near Hamadan, inaugurated in 1963. Later a fourth wing would be added, based at Tabriz. It should be noted that three out of the four air force bases were on Iran's western border.

In 1967, the IIAF faced a problem over the technical services of the highly sophisticated amount of flying hardware it had acquired: it required high-skilled technicians. But it only had two subdivisions, either officers or NCOs. In which category should the new technicians join? General Khatami cut the Gordian knot by creating a new entity within the air force: the *Humafars*. Neither fish nor fowl, the fresh group was left in limbo between the officers and the NCOs. Someone should have had the courage to tell the autocratic Khatami that in Iran's large institutions there was a place for two distinct subdivisions, but never three. Consequently, he should have fitted his technicians within either of the existing two (the interested technicians naturally eyeing the officers' group) for, by so doing, Khatami would have saved the IIAF many resultant problems.

The Iranian Navy's expansion was noteworthy too. Iranians had never had the knack of forming a real navy. This time round things were no different from past experience. In 1965, the British Navy had presented its Iranian counterpart with three modern frigates: the *Bayandur*, the *Naqdi* and the *Qishm*.[19A] The navy also purchased four modern missile-firing frigates and six minesweepers on its own. In 1968, it acquired the first hovercraft squadron in the world: no fewer than eighteen hovercraft (SAN-6), made in Great Britain. To complete its small flotilla, the navy ordered two small destroyers from the Southampton Naval Works. The first, *Sam*, was delivered in 1968 and the second, *Artemis*, (the navy's flagship) in July 1970.

Meanwhile dozens of young Iranian officers had been trained in Italy and Great Britain. In 1970, the Iranian Navy was ready to play its limited role in the Persian Gulf.

In November 1969, Robert McNamara, the World Bank's president, came to Iran and announced that "the Bank would extend a $400m loan for strengthening the Iranian Army". The Vietnam War was still dragging on then, and the Americans were anxious to strengthen local forces. The loan was quickly ratified by the *Majlis*, and the armed forces could rejoice at this providential shot in the arm. The extraordinary amount of this jumbo loan was roughly equivalent to all loans hitherto advanced to Iran by the World Bank since December 1945 (see Table 13.4).

Table 13.4. World Bank Loans to Iran (1945–1969), Exclusive of the 1969 $400m Jumbo Loan.

Loan Recipient in Iran	Loan Amount ($ million)
Ministry of Agriculture	85.5
Diz Dam	42.0
Ministry of Roads	125.2
Industrial Projects	104.7
Miscellaneous	48.3
Total	405.7

13.5. Iranians Say No

While the Shah's 'constructive base' was being reinforced, the opposition was in total disarray. Within its ranks, the leftist counter-elites had been practically obliterated by SAVAK. Its cadres had fled into exile and its second-line managers had either opted for private businesses (where they could put into profitable practice the skills they had learnt managing *Toudeh* cells) or aim for a place in the bureaucracy (the Shah being willing to put to use their expertise in middle management).

The nationalist counter-elite would do likewise after the fiasco of its Second National Front. Some branched out into the private sector, arguing that an income would make them independent of the system (and, at the same time, take full advantage of the opportunities provided and become rich![19B]) while others found ready niches in the bureaucracy and only a tiny minority (e.g. Dr Shams ul-Din Amir Âla'i, Dr Shahpour Bakhtiar) retired to an ivory tower.

Of the three perennial counter-elites, the religious one was still faring better than its rivals. Although suffering a severe setback in the 1963 riots, its radical wing was continuing its struggle. Ayatullah Khomeini's exile had been a further blow, with the radical leadership in Qum left leaderless and disoriented. It was still able to strike, though, as shown by Premier Mansour's assassination. At Qum, a small group of Khomeini supporters had re-formed under his lieutenant Husayn Âli Muntaziri, his son Muhammad Âli Muntaziri, and the *hujjat ul-Islam* Shaykh Âli Mishkini and Rabbani-i Shirazi. In March 1966, the Muntaziris (father and son) were arrested and spent eighteen months in prison before being exiled to Masjid-i Sulayman. On January 9, 1971, the senior Muntaziri was appointed Khomeini's official representative in Iran, in charge of collecting the *Sahm-i Imam* (the religious dues); Khomeini had sent him a note from Najaf: "His [Mutaziri's] signed receipts are equivalent to mine".[20] In Tehran, Ayatullah Taliqani, the LMI leader, also refused to compromise with the regime and therefore was continuously harassed, imprisoned and exiled (among other places, to Zabul and Baft).

In 1964, inspired by the young *hujjat ul-Islam* Muhammad Javad Hujjati Kermani, a group of youngsters calling themselves the *Hizb-i Millat-ha-yi Musalman* (the Islamic Nations' Party) began organising for armed struggle. Before it had time to strike, the group was uncovered by SAVAK in January 1966 and fifty-five of its members were arrested (only one, Ârabshahi, escaped the dragnet). The would-be guerrillas, aged an average of twenty-one years, were court-martialled in April 1966. The court handed down one death sentence (to their leader Muhammad Kazim Musavi Bujnurdi, the son of a leading Bujnurd clergyman), seven life sentences, forty-six prison sentences and one acquittal. Prominent among Bujnurdi's lieutenants were Abu'l Qasim Sarhadizadeh, Âbbas Aqa Zamani (a.k.a. Abu Sharif), Âbbas Duzduzani and Muhammad Mir Muhammad Sadiqi. The death sentence given to Bujnurdi was later commuted to life by the Shah. After all, the group had not committed any crime.

A forty-one year old *hujjat ul-Islam* made history by publishing, in May 1970, a pamphlet denouncing the Iran Investment Conference, held in Tehran between Iranian technocrats and top American executives.[21] The author, the young *Hujjat ul-Islam* Muhammad Riza Sâidi, a unconditional supporter of Khomeini, had just taken up his appointment as prayer leader of Tehran's Mousa Bin Jâfar Mosque. He was immediately arrested by SAVAK. Eager to induce a retraction and wanting to make an example, SAVAK's strongmen tortured him to death: Sâidi died on June 10, 1970 "while his skull was being crushed and boiling water forced into his intestines".[22] Until the very last, Sâidi had proclaimed his fidelity to Khomeini and his ideals: an heroic supporter.

All *Hujjat ul-Islams* were not *Sâidis*. Many of them had been lured into the golden nets spread by the *Sazman-i Ouqaf* (Endowments' Organisation), set up as an independent institution in 1964. The new *Ouqaf* mission was to control all the funds flowing from the *Vaqfs* (Endowments) and channel them to 'friendly' clergymen while trying to squeeze 'unfriendly' ones. Here again the regime was using finance as a carrot, a strategy it relished, especially in connection with the SAVAK stick. It must be said that it knew of no other mechanism for its intercourse with the opposition.

The last noteworthy move by a religious leader during the late 1960s would come from its intellectual wing. In 1969, three of its leading scholars, namely Âllameh Tabataba'i, Murtaza Mutahhari and Sayyid Abu'l Fazl Mousavi Zanjani, simultaneously opened three bank accounts in Tehran, asking people to place therein their donations for helping the Palestinian struggle. The regime could not denounce such a humanitarian move without being accused of siding with the Israelis and decided to look the other way on this minor issue.

The university students had been taken aback by the events of 1963. In the aftermath, the students' leadership had concluded, once and for all, that attempts at conciliation with the regime were futile and that its divorce from the impotent Second National Front back in 1962 had been a correct decision.

Any protest would henceforward be met with brutal force. Even the SAVAK, after a couple of years of restraint (1961–62), had regained its old brutish habits, even when General Pakravan was still in command.[23] By then SAVAK had found a rival in ferality and sadistic treatment: the army's Public Prosecutor Office. In July 1964, *Le Monde* published a letter addressed to the Shah by the International League for Human Rights, in which "the serious violation of civil and political rights by the military regime" were denounced. In the same newspaper, Lord Bertrand Russell condemned Iran's "deplorable conditions of persecution" and "the suppression of every critical liberty". All these rightful criticisms were but pinpricks to the regime, for the Shah failed to understand that worldwide opinion-makers would not give up their criticisms of a regime which used naked brutality to maintain itself in power. Instead of trying to accommodate his influential critics, the Shah went his own way, even placing the ruthless General Nasiri at the head of SAVAK.

The first to taste Nasiri's brutish ways were to be the students. In 1964, some 25,400 students were enrolled at domestic universities, with 14,000 of them at Tehran University. In addition to these, some 17,400 young Iranians were studying abroad: roughly 5,900 in the US, 4,700 in West Germany, 2,800 in Great Britain and the others mainly in France, Italy and Austria. The students had no counter-elite to join or support, no footprints ready to tread on, no domestic example to follow. Their only inspiration came from abroad, from Fidel Castro's suicidal attack on the Moncada and subsequent victorious rural guerrilla campaign in the Sierra Madre, from Ernesto 'Che' Guevara, the legendary guerrilla hero (killed in Bolivia on October 8, 1967) and whose *Guerrilla Warfare* was the classic text for the world's revolutionary leaders, with its basic advice: "The guerrilla must be an ascetic fighter". Other examples came from the Algerian urban guerrilla in the Algiers *Kasbah* and Ali la Pointe; from Brazil's Carlos Marighella; from Colombia's Camillo Torres and his United Front; from Uruguay's resilient Tupamaros; and, nearer to home, the Palestinian freedom fighters of *Al Fath* and the FPLP, to whom the Iranians would eventually turn for their training.

In Iran, though, the students' leaders had to start from scratch. As all the political options were dead, they had to turn to armed struggle. In order to undertake it, an organisation was needed. In the mid-1960s, three such guerrilla groups were formed. The first was the

Sazman-i Mujahidin-i Khalq-i Iran (the Organisation of the People's Warriors of Iran), with its acronym of SMKI, established in September 1965 by three young graduates who had just completed their military service:

(1) Sâid Muhsin, twenty-six, was a student at Tehran University's Technical Faculty (TUTF), a militant in the LMI's ranks and an employee at the Ministry of Interior.

(2) Âli Asghar Badîzadigan, twenty-five, a TUTF student, gravitated towards the Second National Front, then took up a job as laboratory supervisor at TUTF.

(3) Muhammad Hanifnjad, twenty-seven, a student at Karaj's Agricultural College, joined LMI and was imprisoned for seven months for political activities in 1963, working on agricultural projects.

The base of the SMKI's ideology was Islamic, but with some Marxist-Leninist overtones – leading to blurred insights into a series of crucial issues. At first, the founding trio worked on their ideology and theories for armed struggle and thus progress was made at a snail's pace. Recruitment among Tehran University students advanced more rapidly, as the best and the brightest of the non-communist students flocked to the SMKI banner. The new organism grew slowly while it developed the necessary subdivisions: technical, propaganda, financial support, armaments and information-gathering. It would take the SMKI five years to come out of its cocoon and began 'confiscating' bank branches in Tehran in 1970 to secure necessary funds for its operations.

In comparison to the slow SMKI, the first Marxist group founded in 1964 by twenty-seven year old Bizhan Jazani,* a veteran of leftist struggles, was quick off its blocks. Jazani founded his first cell with three fellow students, publishing the clandestine paper *Payam-i Danishjou* (The Students' Message). The group was soon uncovered and Jazani spent nine months in prison. In 1965 Jazani teamed up with his friend Hasan Zia Zarifi, a TU law graduate, to form the Jazani-Zarifi group. Jazani's charismatic leadership coupled with Zarifi's precise mind yielded a solid basis for the fresh entity. Recruitment went swiftly ahead in student circles longing for action. Jazani's plans was for a rural guerrilla campaign, to begin in the fertile Gilan province, copying Mirza Kuchik Khan. He first set up his Tehran nucleus, the so-called 'city team', before shaping the 'mountain team' which would carry out the armed struggle in Gilan. Finally he created teams to handle logistics, technical aspects and communications to support his front line guerrillas. Each team was quasi-independent, and only Jazani and Zarifi knew the team leaders and their key members. The main priority was physical fitness, and long climbing expeditions were organised in the Alburz range, with cross-overs to the Caspian seaside to further enhance group cohesion.

* BIZHAN JAZANI (1937–1975), born in Tehran; the eldest son of Husayn Jazani, a senior *Toudeh* member with a D.Phil. (from Germany); joined the *Toudeh* Youth Organisation (1947); imprisoned several times after *Murdad 28* (1953–55); entered Tehran University (1960); joined the Second National Front (1961), later expelled (1962); graduated in philosophy from TU (1963); founded his first underground cell (1964), then the Jazani-Zarifi group (1965); arrested (January 1968), kept his secrets under torture, court-martialled, sentenced to fifteen years' hard labour (1968); led the political prisoners' resistance movement from his prisons of Qasr, Qum, Qizil Qalêh and Evin (1968–75); shot down in cold blood on the hills above Evin prison (April 19, 1975).

In 1967, the group acquired two handguns and was ready to initiate its first coup when its leadership was arrested by SAVAK acting on tip-offs from two undercover agents who had infiltrated the infant organisation: Nasir Aqayan and Âbbas Shahryari. Aqayan would pay for his betrayal with his life when the guerrillas executed him in 1974, while Shahryari, a former CCUTU veteran and Tehran's *Toudeh* antenna, would go on to tip off SAVAK about many other covert dissidents.[24] Thus, in early 1968, Jazani was arrested with his two lieutenants, Âbbas Suriki and Âziz Sarmadi. In February, Zia Zarifi and Ahmad Jalil Afshar were caught and in July 1968 SAVAK completed its round-up with the capture of Mâshouf (Sâid) Kalantari and Muhammad Chupanzadeh. At their court-martial, Jazani received fifteen years, the others ten years each, except for Chupanzadeh, who got eight years. The Jazani-Zarifi group had abruptly been decapitated because of two traitors among its ranks, but some parts of the group remained intact (due to Jazani's and Zarifi's silence under torture), especially parts of its 'mountain team', under the leadership of Âli Akbar Safa'i Farahani (they had gone to Lebanon to train with

Al Fath) and parts of its 'communications team', managed by a lowly young member, Hamid Ashraf. The first wave of would-be guerrillas were amateurs (some of them still believed in semi-covert activities!). The second wave, more experienced, would be more cautious and less amateurish, especially when they faced SAVAK's highly trained professionals.

The guerrillas' direct enemy was SAVAK. From the outset the struggle was unbalanced. On the one hand were the poorly armed guerrillas, on the other were the SAVAK agents benefiting from the latest in communications technology, eavesdropping methods and psychological warfare techniques developed in the US and Israel. SAVAK must have had its own Dan Mitrione.[25] In its arsenal, SAVAK had a major weapon which it greatly sharpened in the late 1960s: torture. Defined by the World Medical Association as "the deliberate, systematic, or wanton infliction of physical or mental suffering by one or more persons ...to force another person to yield information, to make a confession, or for any other reason", torture was pursued by SAVAK to achieve three major objectives:

(I) to obtain information, as fast as possible, on the guerrilla's connections in order to map out his team's network;

(ii) to punish and humiliate those who dared defy the system;

(iii) to leak grim horror torture stories to the outside, so as to discourage would-be guerrillas (for example, the raping of guerrillas with bottles, even turned into jokes by younger elite members).

As the guerrillas became better organised, SAVAK multiplied its capacity to torture, turning it during the 1970s into a major industry, with ever more sophisticated techniques and apparatus.

The second Marxist-Leninist group was formed in early 1968 by a handful of Tehran University students, prominent among whom were:

(1) Masôud Ahmadzadeh, twenty-two, the son of Tahir Ahmadzadeh (a leading Mashhad opponent of the regime, close to Muhammad Taqi Shariâti), who took up mathematics at TU in 1965 and there repudiated his Islamist background to embrace communism, writing *Armed Struggle: Both a Strategy and a Tactic* in 1970. His younger brother Majid Ahmadzadeh was always at his side, albeit with less charisma.

(2) Amir Parviz Pouyan, twenty-two, also a Mashhadi, had studied literature at TU since 1965. With his brilliant mind he was the

group's theoretician, and wrote the movement's reference pamphlet *On the Necessity of Armed Struggle and Refutation of the Survival Theory*.

(3) Âbbas Miftahi, twenty-three, born in Sari, was a student at TUTF 1963–1967, and the group's operations leader, a courageous fighter. His younger brother, Asadullah, would also join the group.

The Ahmadzadeh-Pouyan-Miftahi group had come to the conclusion that an urban guerrilla strategy was more suited to Iran's conditions than a rural guerrilla one (the opposite of the Jazani-Zarifi group). Its contacts with the remnants of the Jazani-Zarifi group (especially Hamid Ashraf) in late 1968 came to naught because the latter was geared for rural action in Gilan. In 1970, Safa'i Farahani, back from an eighteen-month training stint with *Al Fath*, met Miftahi in Sari. The leader of the 'mountain team' was able to convince the latter to send him ten trustworthy men as reinforcements. Miftahi would send him only one, but he was an excellent warrior: Ahmad Farhoudi.

Other groups were also trying to get off the ground, the most prominent being:

– Shukrullah Paknizhad's so-called Palestine Group, which intended to train in Lebanon with *Al Fath*. Paknizhad was caught at the Chalamcheh border post in January 1970 as he tried to cross over to Iraq. His whole group of a dozen members was all rounded up – the Palestine Group had gone belly up before entering the fray. Paknizhad remained in prison until January 1979.

– The group set up by Cyrous Nahavandi. The latter had trained in China and upon his return in 1968 to Tehran had begun recruiting guerrillas. After a successful Rls2.9m hold-up of an Iranian-British bank branch, Nahavandi created regular businesses, such as the Mikhak Farm, to finance the group's activities. One of his team almost succeeded in kidnapping the US ambassador. Suddenly all of the group's members (some thirty-five of them) were arrested. It later emerged that Nahavandi had been a SAVAK *agent provocateur* from the outset, with SAVAK thus trying to tread in Feliks Dzerzhinski's footprints.

– The *Saka* group of communists, created by the 1969 merger of two small splinter groups. It grew rapidly to include some fifty members, but was indecisive about entering armed struggle. Its

Isfahan team bungled a bank robbery. SAVAK eventually arrested all of its members, half of whom were later sentenced to heavy prison terms in court.

– Two exiled *Toudeh* leaders, Ahmad Qasimi and Dr Furutan, thought that they could run an underground cell from abroad. They sent Hasan Saâdati to Iran to form the pro-Chinese *Toufan* group. Within three years (1969–71) the group lost some forty of its members (either shot dead, imprisoned for life or executed). Thereafter the group concentrated on infiltrating student organisations abroad.

For Iran's budding guerrilla groups, 1970 was to be known by the double significance of bank hold-ups and hijacking. The nearest route to untraceable money was robbing a bank branch. As there were plenty of branches, the guerrillas could choose their target. The first to launch this new fashion in funding one's organisation was a young Tabriz guerrilla leader by the name of Muhammad Taqi Sarkarati, who in late 1969 acted all by himself and failed in his attempt.[26] In Tehran, the first hold-up occurred in August 1970: the Bank-i Milli branch on Vuzara Street was 'confiscated'. In September, the guerrillas struck twice, both times getting away with millions of rials. Each hold-up not only embarrassed the regime in the eyes of public opinion, but also worried its anti-guerrilla specialists, who reasoned that: (i) if guerrillas could raid bank branches in broad daylight and get away with it, they must have reached maturity in their logistics and operations; (ii) having secured their war chest, they could gear up their subversive plans. It was also in August and September when the first two hijack attempts were made, but both failed. The third one (made on November 9, 1970) was a success when nine guerrillas ordered an Iran Air flight flying the Dubai–Shiraz route to go to Baghdad.[26A] Thereafter hijacking lost much of its appeal as the risks incurred outweighed the benefits. Nevertheless, with all their 1970 activities the guerrilla groups had shown that within a few years they had graduated to being capable teams, now somehow more professional.

If the students at home were active, Iranian students abroad were not idle. In 1959, they had created in Great Britain the *Kunfidirasyun-i Jahani Muhasilin va Danishjouyan-i Irani* (the Confederation of Iranian Students, which later evolved into a National Union – giving it its final acronym of CISNU). The CISNU soon became the umbrella for all student activities abroad and rose to prominence as a leading opposition organ to the Shah.[26B] The CISNU's main bases soon turned out to be West Germany (Frankfurt) and Italy (Milan, Perugia), with strong branches in England and the US The CISNU was behind the demonstrations in the major European cities which the Shah visited, beginning with Vienna (February 1964), Zürich and Geneva. But the crunch was to come during the Shah's official visit to West Germany in 1967, when a young German student, Beno Ohnesorge, was shot dead in West Berlin on June 2 during an anti-Shah demonstration which was repressed by German policemen assisted by Parviz Khwunsari's mercenary phalanxes. World opinion was shocked, Germans angry at the killing of one of their students, and the CISNU was given its widest coverage to date.[26C]

By the late 1960s, communist and radical tendencies, such as those affiliated to *Toudeh* or *Toufan*, came to dominate the CISNU's government. The nationalists and moderates were constantly outmanoeuvred. The religious interest was hardly represented, having too few students abroad; instead they set up their own Muslim Student Organisation (for example, the Berkeley MSO which eventually published a paper, *Al-Bayan*). In spite of their inherent weaknesses the nationalists and the religious activists had a handful of capable individuals on whom they could rely:

– Âli Muhammad Sayfpour Fatimi (surnamed Shahin), Dr Fatimi's nephew, who was elected head of the CISNU's US branch: "the power behind the two Nationalist-oriented Iranian student publications Irannameh and Danishjou". He successfully fought off [with his uncle's assistance] an attempt by the State Department to have him deported in 1963.[27]

– Sadiq Qutbzadeh was another prominent opponent to the Shah studying in the US. His Iranian passport was not renewed and he was expelled from the US, from where he went to the Middle East and Paris, taking up a Syrian passport.

– Dr Mustafa Chamran, an honours student at TUTF, was sent on a scholarship to Berkeley, where he received his Ph.D. in electrical engineering (1962). A friend of Qutbzadeh and Dr Ibrahim Yazdi, he was affiliated, like the latter, to Taliqani's LMI.

– Dr Ibrahim Yazdi was a Houston-trained MEd and founder of the Moslem Students' Association in Houston in 1963. Went with Chamran and Qutbzadeh to Egypt in 1964–66 (the bastion of anti-Shah conspiracies) for courses in guerrilla warfare. Was a research fellow at the Baylor Medical College of Houston (1967), and went to Najaf to meet Ayatullah Khomeini on behalf of the US opposition.

- Bahman Niroumand was among CISNU's most prominent opponents in West Germany. He wrote two books – *Iran: The New Imperialism in Action in 1969*[28] and *Feuer unterm Pfauenthron* in 1974.[29] He also travelled throughout Europe to lecture students on the Shah's regime.

- Abu'l Hasan Bani Sadr was the Paris-based son of Ayatullah Sayyid Nasrullah Bani Sadr of Hamadan. A student under the Iranologist, Professor Paul Vieille, he failed to complete his Ph.D. thesis. Instead he wrote articles and pamphlets, sometimes jointly with his mentor Vieille.

Back at home, the regime was bent on squeezing the students in their main base at Tehran University. In 1967, TU chancellor, Dr Jahanshhah Salih (in place since March 1963), had the idea of introducing tuition fees for all TU students: Rls8,000 per annum for humanities students and Rls10,500 for science students (who had to use laboratories). This was hitting the students below the belt, especially because a large majority of provincial students had problems making ends meet – living on shoestring budgets, taking on menial jobs and sometimes feeding exclusively on cheap foods such as potatoes or eggs. Dr Salih had left an option for students to nullify the tuition fees: if they proved that they were in need, they could submit a request for assistance and the tuition fee would be paid by the university. But the threat of payment suspension in case of the student taking part in political activism was a Damoclean sword held over his head, a guarantee of good behaviour. That the institution of tuition fees had little bearing on the university's financial status was underlined by the fact that total tuition fees of around Rls155m amounted to roughly eleven per cent of the total TU annual subsidies of Rls1,400m. For students ready to face SAVAK's mediaeval tortures, a tuition fee was no problem, but for the average student it was and Dr Salih had found a legal way to maintain control.

There was no doubt that the students, especially those from TU, were the regime's main problem. The Shah himself was involved in trying to find adequate solution to this problem. In October 1967, a twelfth point was added to his Shah and People' Revolution – administrative and educational reforms. The Shah introduced the new point in these terms:

> The essential goal of this movement is to uplift the personality of youth and their sense of self-confidence in every respect, so that the future destiny of the country may be handed over to people who should be really prepared and well-equipped to cope with their responsibilities...[30]

The twelfth point had little impact, but paved the way for the First Ramsar Conference on Educational Revolution (August 6-8, 1968) chaired by the Shah himself and involving all of the kingdom's educational and academic lights (with any constructive criticism really welcome). The conference spawned a Revolutionary Educational Charter in forty-three articles. The main recommendations were to create more institutions of higher education (thereby diluting the water of the TU fish) while opening the door to privately-owned universities. In consequence, within the following four years the total number of students doubled while TU studentship stagnated (see Table 13.5). The charter had also given added powers to university chancellors, giving them a free hand in choosing their subordinates; more pay and incentives to the teaching staff (so that they wouldn't side with the students); and approved scholarships for meritorious students and other financial incentives for the student corps (the carrots of the regime's strategy).

Table 13.5. Number of Registered Students in Iran's Institutions of Higher Education (1968–1972).[31]

Academic Year	Total Number of Higher Education Students	Total Number of Tehran University Students
1968/69	58,194	18,100
1969/70	67,268	17,079
1970/71	74,708	17,292
1971/72	97,338	17,147

However, the regime's educational policies failed to rally the students to its banner. In February 1970, when the government raised the price of bus tickets from Rls2 to Rls5 apiece, the students pounced on the occasion and took to the streets, grabbing this golden opportunity to show the urban masses which side they were on. Buses were boycotted, a few were smashed and a couple were even set on fire. High school students came out of their classrooms to support their seniors. Police intervened and clashes resulted: hundreds of students were arrested, taken to police stations, given a sound thrashing and set free after a brief detention. Every evening Tehran papers listed the names of the day's detainees. After three days of clashes and detentions, the government back-pedalled (as usual in this kind of situation) and bus tickets were set back at Rls2. The students celebrated their victory. They had proven that their latest *cri de guerre* (introduced by TU students) of "Ittihad – Mubarizeh – Pirouzi" (Unity – Struggle – Victory) was a sure recipe for success.

In December 1970 the struggle turned more political when eighteen students (including members of Paknizhad's Palestine Group and CISNU affiliates) were court-martialled for alleged communist activities. Unrest erupted at TU (December 7th also being the ritual commemoration of the 1953 martyrs) and on foreign campuses across the world, in a well-orchestrated CISNU campaign. The military nevertheless issued harsh sentences, ranging from three years to life. On December 23 and 28, Parviz Sabiti, SAVAK's anti-guerrilla specialist and on this occasion the regime's public relations mouthpiece, explained the latest events at televised conferences: the occurrences of the last month were apparently the results of a collision between the CISNU, the *Toudeh*, pro-Chinese elements and the Iraqi government. The main target remained the CISNU, for a month later the army's public prosecutor, General Farsiou, officially gave confederation members two months to resign their membership or face legal consequences upon their return to Iran, in accordance with the anti-communist law of 1931.

In 1970 the regime reached the conclusion that there could be no compromise with the students and the guerrilla groups: henceforward it would be confrontation and repression, while building up Iran's 'consumption society'. After the carrots distributed during the late 1960s, it would turn to its SAVAK sticks.

If the regime had failed to convince the students, it had chalked up two successes in 1970. The first success was in its economic policy, when it had to confront a bad budget deficit: the Central Bank went on a borrowing spree,[31A] getting, among others, bridge loans of DM200m from the Deutsche Bank in January, $160m from London banks in June and $60m from the World Bank in October, and thus keeping its ship on an even keel. The second success came in its confrontation with General Taymour Bakhtiar, who from his Iraqi base planned to overthrow the Shah with Iraqi assistance and his former SAVAK men. When asked how he would neutralise the armed forces, Bakhtiar replied: "That's the least of my worries, because the Iranian Army is a 'paper tiger'!"[32] But, before Bakhtiar had the chance to launch his offensive, he was shot dead on August 18, 1970 near the Iraq-Iran border by SAVAK elements he had come to trust, but who had (influenced by the Shah's foreign friends) turned their coats and undertaken to murder their former leader.

13.6. Four Popular Heroes

Iranian youth's hearts and minds were neither on the wavelengths of the Pahlavi family nor on those of any elite members. During the 1960s the heroes of the younger generation were four exceptional and highly gifted individuals, in order of seniority: (1) a writer, Jalal Al Ahmad; (2) a scholar, Dr Âli Shariâti; (3) a sportsman, Ghulam Riza Takhti; and (4) a teacher, Samad Bihrangi. All four were trusted to be from the people and for the people. They never bowed to the regime (although it had bent over backwards to accommodate all four of them) nor did they stop criticising it: they were all on a collision course and all four were to die young.

(1) Jalal Al Ahmad

For a quarter of a century, Jalal Al Ahmad* did not stop writing and teaching. During his long and fruitful career, he had written in his simple and flowing style what he thought to be right. As his fellow author Âli Asghar Hajj Sayyid Javadi remarked: "He never lost his sincerity ...never compromised on his principles ...never was afraid of being unjustly criticised".[33] In his remarkable essay on the increasing Westernisation of Iranian society, simply entitled *Gharbzadigi* (Westernisation) and written in 1961-62, he attacked the evils of Western influences on his fellow intellectuals and the formidable inferiority complex shown by the latter in front of Western cultural dominance.[34]

In his voluminous literary testament *Dar Khidmat va Khyanat-i Roushanfikran* (On Services and Treasons of Intellectuals), written between February 1965 and August 1969, he again shocked Iran's intellectuals by candidly pinpointing their numerous shortcomings and concluding that they had ominously failed in their mission[35] (which was true).

* JALAL AL AHMAD (1923-1969), son of a minor clergyman; initially a *tullab*, switched to Dar ul-Funoun, from where he graduated (1943); joined the *Toudeh* (1944); met Nima Youshij, wrote for *Mardum* and graduated from the Teachers' College (1945-46); began teaching in high schools (1947); followed Khalil Maliki after his defection from *Toudeh* (1947), joined Dr Baqa'i's Toilers' Party (1950), reverting later to Maliki's *Nirou-yi Sivvum* (1952); edited the monthly *Îlm va Zindagi* (Science and Life) (1960); invited to a Harvard seminar on Iran (1965); met Samad Bihrangi and Bihrouz Dihqani at Tabriz (1967) and Dr Shariâti at Mashhad (1968); created the *Kanoun-i Nivisandigan-i Iran* (Iranian Writers' Centre) (1968); died suddenly at his Asalam retreat in Gilan (September 8, 1969).

From Al Ahmad's point of view, nothing was more dangerous than artificiality and inauthenticity. In a 1972 interview, he threw some light on his stand with a couple of examples:

> The peasant didn't need a motorcycle, but 'Point Four' wanted him to have one, which he, in turn, could not have adopted. In our society, things have to bubble out from within. Or, in other words, the peasant must have felt the need for a motorcycle before being given one...
>
> ...There is a plan to redistribute Iran's 50,000 villages into two to ten thousand provincial 'poles' ...this

> would lead to a national catastrophe ...now, for example, if on its migration route the Basiri tribesmen have three large villages, it is because their migrating herds require them at that very location...

"Even the Mongols have not done so much harm to us", he concluded.[36]

To confront Westernisation head on, Al Ahmad conceived a return to the lost identity of Iranians. In the crusading *Bazgasht beh Khwistan* (Return to the Self), he dotted his i's. A political chameleon, he tried all hues of the political spectrum from the left to centre-right before ending up making the Hajj pilgrimage and returning to his own religious origins, just before his death.

Notwithstanding his capacity to write and criticise, Al Ahmad was far from being perfect. He was a nervous critic, praising or damning rather too promptly. In many of his analyses, superficiality was the order of the day, leaving the reader with the feeling that he lacked depth in these subjects. Some of his works (especially his autobiographical ones) are prone to repetitions and monotony. But he nevertheless was the uncontested *chef de file* of the new generation of Iranian authors – his lifelong wife, writer Simin Danishvar, assisted him in his leadership. In April 1968 he passed his Rubicon by refusing to the attend the court-sponsored Artists' Congress and, instead, opted to create the Writers' Centre with his friends and colleagues Dr Ghulam Husayn Sâidi, Manouchihr Hizarkhani, Firaydoun Tunikabuni, Mahmoud Îtimadzadeh (a.k.a. Beh Azin), Muhammad Âli Sipanlou, Nadir Nadiripour and Nasir Rahmaninizhad. From then on clashes with the system were inevitable: some of his books were censored and SAVAK's Sabiti and Husaynzadeh summoned him to proffer thinly veiled threats.[37] A few months later he was dead.

Al Ahmad's intellectual honesty and sincerity were his most precious legacy to the coming generations of Iranian intelligentsia. During his lifetime he had said and written all of his major thoughts. His Writers' Centre would live on, continuing in the path he had laid out for it, a bastion for *engagé* authors. In 1970, his younger friend, the talented F. Tunikabuni, published his *Yaddashtha-yi Shahr-i Shulough* (Notes on a Hysteric City),[38] a work which exactly caught the indescribable atmosphere of the Tehran at the time in a series of critical short stories: realistic and nerve-racking. Censorship immediately impounded the book (only a few copies being circulated *sous le manteau*) and SAVAK duly arrested the author, treated him to a severe beating and left him for a few months in solitary confinement. This time round, Iran's writers closed ranks and dared publish a petition, signed by no fewer than fifty-two of them, asking for Tunikabuni's prompt release. Instead of back-tracking, SAVAK arrested the movement's leaders, Beh Azin, Sipanlou and Rahmaninizhad, then Dr Sâidi, Hizarkhani, Nîmat Mirzazadeh (a.k.a. M. Azarm), Jâfar Koushabadi, Rahman Hatifi and Sâid Sultanpour among others. The writers had shown courage and self-denial in their stand in the teeth of SAVAK and their original leader could be proud of them, since, unlike former Iranian intellectual groups, they had not bolted at the first blow. That the Shah's regime was compelled to close down the Writers' Association in May 1970 was a further victory for Al Ahmad's colleagues, promoting them to the very first ranks of opposition and showing the people at large that they were intellectuals ready for sacrifice – a novelty for Iran (and a fact which the regime and its strategists should have noted in red).

(2) Dr Âli Shariâti

The young Shariâti* was an outstanding pupil at Mashhad's Firdousi School. In his free time, he took an active part in his father's *Kanoun-i Haqayiq-i Islami* (Centre for Islamic Truths). In high school, he flirted with Muhammad Nakhshab's God-worshipping Socialists, before supporting Dr Musaddiq's oil nationalisation movement. After *Murdad 28*, he joined the National Resistance Movement branch at Mashhad created by Asayish and Tahir Ahmadzadeh, leading to his arrest in 1958. Finishing at the head of his class, he was awarded the top students' scholarship (albeit having to wait two years for its approval). Before departing for France he married Pouran Razavi, the sister of the TUTF 1953 martyr Mihdi Shariât Razavi.

* DR ÂLI SHARIÂTI MAZINANI (1933–1977), originally from small Khurasan village of Mazinan, son of Muhammad Taqi Shariâti (1907–1987) a religious personality of Mashhad; received his diploma (1951); entered Mashhad University's Literature Faculty (1952–58); imprisoned for eight months (1958); left for France to study sociology

at the Sorbonne, received his Ph.D. (1963); lecturer at Mashhad University (1963-72); delivered weekly lectures at Tehran's *Husayniyyeh Irshad* until the centre was closed down by the authorities (early 1970-November 1972); imprisoned (1973); set free due to Algerian pressures at the Algiers Conference (March 1975); lived in semi-retirement (1975-77); left for England, having deceived SAVAK with his Âli Mazinani passport (May 1977); found dead at his Southampton flat (June 19, 1977);[39] buried at Zaynabiyyeh Cemetery in Damascus.

It was in France and Algeria that Shariâti acquainted himself with Sartre, Camus and especially Franz Fanon and his *Les Dames de la Terre*, which he would translate into Farsi. He was quick to see the parallel between Fanon's exhortations to sacrifice and the martyrdom preached by the initial *Shiîte* imams, Hazrat Imam Âli (A.S.) and Imam Husayn (A.S.). He had his basic idea for an Islamic revival: martyrdom. "The Martyr", he wrote, "is at the heart of History". His caption for the Islamic struggle was a simple catechism spelled out in eight words: Agar Mitavani Bimiran – Jihad (If you can, kill – Holy War), Agar Natavani Bimir – Shahadat (If you can't, die – Martyrdom). During the 1960s, in his Mashhad retreat, he was busy readying his explosive amalgam of revolutionary ideas and *Shiîte* ideals. In 1970 he delivered his first lecture at Tehran's *Husayniyyeh Irshad*, the Centre for Islamic Studies and Conferences – created in 1965 on the Old Shimiran Road by donations from the philanthropist Muhammad Humayoun and a handful of others. In his high-pitched voice, he preached a modern, revolutionary *Shiîsm*, thereby reconciling Iranian youth with historical Islam. His lectures were an immense success; taped, they were transferred on to cassettes and printed as books.

Dr Shariâti had come to the conclusion that the Western and the Islamic *Weltanschauung* were not compatible, being in many respects if not contradictory, then at least very different from each other. His opinion of these two distinct views is summarised in Table 13.6.

(3) Ghulam Riza Takhti

Takhti* was a *force de la nature*, an excellent wrestler and an exceptional champion. He had won one Olympic gold medal, two world championships, and a couple of Asian and Iranian titles in middleweight wrestling. But he was not only a great champion – he was a national hero. The Takhti phenomenon was unique and difficult to explain: the only such case in modern Iranian history of a sportsman rising to national prominence. It was a fact that the

Table 13.6. Dr Âli Shariâti's Observed Differences Between Western and Islamic *Weltanschauungen*.

Western *Weltanschauung*	Islamic *Weltanschauung*
REALIST	IDEALIST
POWER-ORIENTED	VALUE-ORIENTED
CENTRED ON SOCIETY	CENTRED ON THE INDIVIDUAL
TENDS TOWARDS CIVILISATION	TENDS TOWARDS CULTURE
RELIES ON TECHNOLOGY	RELIES ON IDEOLOGY
SEEKS KNOWLEDGE OF THE WORLD	SEEKS KNOWLEDGE OF THE SELF
PROFIT-MINDED	SPIRITUALLY-MINDED
STRESS ON SOCIAL BEHAVIOUR	STRESS ON HUMAN BEHAVIOUR
SOCIETY IS THE END, THE INDIVIDUAL A MEANS	INDIVIDUAL IS THE END, SOCIETY THE MEANS
GOALS ARE HAPPINESS AND SECURITY	GOALS ARE SELF-PERFECTION AND BEAUTY
SCIENTIFICALLY-MINDED	WISDOM-MINDED
CONTROL OVER ENVIRONMENT	CONTROL OVER SELF
LOOKS FOR WHAT IS	LOOKS FOR WHAT SHOULD BE

honours and the medals had not gone to his head; that he had retained his simplicity and honesty of his humble Khaniabad origins; that he was generous and warm-hearted and polite; that he had refused millions to turn film actor (like fellow wrestler Habibi and national trainer Bulour).[39A] He had a high sense of moral rectitude both in sports and in life. The Iranian people loved him, they identified with him: when he entered the arena they were with him, and when he won they won. They didn't care whether he won gold or silver: he had won, and that was enough for them. Even when, in 1966, he finished fourth (being past his prime), he was fêted upon his return to Tehran as though he had won gold. His name became synonymous with that of Pourya-i Vali, Persia's legendary fourteenth-century wrestling champion.

* GHULAM RIZA TAKHTI (1930–1968), born in Tehran's southern suburb of Khaniabad; studied at Khaniabad's Manouchihri School; joined the Poulad Wrestling Club (1946); trained by Iran's greatest wrestling specialist Hajj Âbd ul-Husayn Fayli and later by national team trainer Habibullah Bulour (1946–52); silver medal at Helsinki Olympics (1952); gold at Melbourne Olympics (1956); gold at Tokyo's Asian Games (1958); world champion in Tehran (1959); silver at Rome Olympics (1960); world champion in Yokohama (1961); silver at Toledo (1962); took fourth place in his fourth Olympics at Tokyo (1964); pointlessly took part in 1966 world championship; retired and married (1966); his son Babak was born in 1967; found dead on January 6, 1968 in Tehran's Atlantic Hotel.

In the aftermath of the Qazvin earthquake of 1962, Takhti began collecting funds for the survivors. Due to his formidable popularity he was able to gather millions of rials for the stricken areas. At a wrestling championship in 1964, the crowd stood up as Takhti entered the stadium shouting "Takhti! Takhti!" but when, a few minutes later, Prince Ghulam Riza Pahlavi entered, it was amidst a polite silence: in their own special way the Iranian people had said all they had to say. Such incidents and popularity were not made to ingratiate him with the court. He made no mystery that his political sympathies were with the nationalists (he was even elected a delegate at the Congress of the Second National Front in January 1963) and Ayatullah Taliqani, whom he had met a couple of times. Having retired from competition, he intended to devote himself to promoting sports on a national level. He had his own ideas on the subject: "Sports in Iran is under-developed ...our youngsters are weak and lacking self-confidence ...their moral deficiency is a direct consequence of their physical inability".[40] He hoped to launch a sports crusade, bringing about "the eradication of tobacco, alcohol and opium consumption in Iran". No one doubted that Takhti could have moved mountains, to the extent that even the regime was worried about his future plans: he was a time-bomb ticking much too near an emotive younger generation lacking heroes and close to finding one of its own.

But Takhti's Achilles' heel would be his wife, the beautiful Shahla, whom he had married in 1966. Frictions were evident in the couple's relationship, with quarrels all too frequent. Even the birth of their son Babak didn't bring much-needed peace. Shahla's father had some harsh words with his son-in-law; three days later Takhti was dead. There were many who sustained the thesis of a SAVAK-engineered murder, pointing to the location of the Atlantic Hotel, a renowned SAVAK base. Had Takhti found the time to launch his crusade, the regime might have been forced to eliminate him, but such a move was still premature. Takhti was a man of honour and there were limits to what he could accept, so it may have been that he had preferred to take his own life before the authorities were stirred to action. Naturally, public opinion never doubted that SAVAK had had a hand in their champion's abrupt death.

Whether murder or suicide, it made little difference to the Takhti cult that would emerge: Iran's only national champion sportsman was turned into a national hero. He deserved it.

(4) Samad Bihrangi

There were hundreds upon hundreds of primary school teachers in rural Iran. One amongst them was an extraordinary individual, the Azarbayjani Samad Bihrangi.*

Besides his teaching of primary school youngsters, Bihrangi began writing articles for the weekly magazine *Bamshad* in the early 1960s. His first effort was a series of crisp articles on the deficiencies of the local educational system – later collected into book form.[41] His criticism of the existing conditions was harsh and uninhibited, writing in black and white what others were too shy to say: attacking the futile attempts made at transferring Western educational methods to Iran, pointing to the lack of materials in rural schools, analysing the plight of young teachers in far-flung rural outposts (even touching upon the taboo question of homosexuality), denouncing bureaucratic red tape and damning the bureaucrats for their impotence.

* SAMAD BIHRANGI (1939–1968), born the fourth of six children of a rather poor Tabrizi family; after getting his diploma (1956), attended Tabriz's Teachers' Training School before taking up teaching in rural Azarbayjan, in the Azarshahr district, touring the villages of Mamqan, Qadjahan, Gavgan and Akhirjan (1958–1967);

established contacts with leftist elements through his colleague and friend Bihrouz Dihqani; wrote short stories for children, among others his masterpiece *Mahi Syah-i Kouchulou-i Dana* (The Small Knowledgeable Black Fish), published in 1968, with which he won first prize at the Bologna and Bratislava book fairs (1968); moved to Tehran to work on a simple Farsi alphabet for the Movement Against Illiteracy (1968); allegedly drowned during a swim in the Aras river (September 1968).

If Bihrangi's socio-educational writings had struck home as far as Tehran, it was in storytelling that he would best express his indisputable talent. During his short career, he gathered thirty-nine Azarbayjani fairy-tales (published with Bihrouz Dihqani in two volumes[42]) and wrote eleven short stories, with his *The Small Knowledgeable Black Fish* standing out as a jewel of modern Iranian literature. It brought him considerable success, even international recognition; in this story for children there were profound thoughts, for example this piece on the subject of death in one of the book's monologues:

> Death could very easily come upon me at any instance; but, as long as I can live I shall not think of death. In case I should have to face death – as I eventually will have to sooner or later – it shall not be of importance; the important point would rather be how my life and death have influenced other peoples' lives...[43]

If his Black Fish was receiving the acclaim it was justly due abroad, winning prizes and being translated into a dozen languages, at home it was banned: people caught with a copy of Bihrangi's masterpiece were liable to imprisonment and questioning by SAVAK. The few existing copies were only circulated with extreme caution *sous le manteau* among close friends.

At the age of twenty-nine, the gifted Bihrangi eventually faced death. No one believes his end to have been an accidental drowning. But it was useless speculating over it: the fact was that a writer of genius, with a long career before him, was no more – a tremendous loss for Iranian literature. "His loss was irreplaceable", wrote poet

Ahmad Shamlou in 1972, adding that "he was that very rare phenomenon, a committed intellectual defending a treasure: the people's liberty and their rights to live... in other words, the indomitable spirit of the people of Azarbayjan".[44] Besides his literary successes, or rather because of them, Bihrangi had a tremendous impact on the thousands of young teachers scattered throughout rural Iran: before Bihrangi, every one of them dreamed only of a transfer to Tehran, but after Bihrangi they shunned transfers, focusing on their rural pupils, trying their hand at what they did best. If they could not emulate Bihrangi in his writings, they could endeavour to copy him in the classroom. Suddenly rural teachers saw their job in a new light, forgetting their problems and limitations: it was a mission. Bihrangi's death had spawned a national revolution in Iranian villages: he had had an impact both with his life and his death which would have far-reaching consequences.

In the end, the four national heroes all died young amidst suspicious circumstances: Al Ahmad at forty-six, Shariâti at forty-four, Takhti at thirty-eight and Bihrangi at twenty-nine. Had they been less popular, probably they would have lived much longer. But they lived in the era of a regime that could not accept or accommodate Al Ahmad's Writers' Union, Shariâti's lectures at the *Husayniyyeh Irshad*, Takhti's formidable popularity and Bihrangi's *The Small Knowledgeable Black Fish*. Between a regime which cannot accept the people's champions and the people themselves there is bound to be an ever-growing gap. The distance between the two can only grow in time, with misunderstandings and resentments multiplying *ad infinitum*.

NOTES

1 *Annual Report 1968* (Tehran: Bank-i Markazi-i Iran, 1348 (1969)).
2 *Iran Trade and Industry* magazine, April–May 1973, p.9.
3 From its inception the whole INTS project had an aroma of misappropriation and price-fixing. In October 1975, the scandal exploded in public and the Consortium partners were accused of wrongdoing and mismanagement of funds, although Page-Northrop and Siemens denied all charges categorically. But Siemens accepted that it had deposited $2.05m in a numbered Swiss account: what for, if not for covert pay-offs? See *Iran Almanac 1976* (Tehran: Echo of Iran) pp.175-6. It is worth noting in this context that the Northrop representatives in Iran were (1) Prince Shahram Pahlavinya, the eldest son of Princess Ashraf, and (2) General Khatami,

the commander-in-chief of the air force. See F. Halliday, *Iran: Dictatorship and Development* (Penguin Books, 1979) p.99.

4   *Statistical Yearbook 1973* (Tehran: Markaz-i Amar-i Iran, June 1976) pp.84-5.

5   *Barnameh Chaharum-i Ûmrani-i Kishvar 1347–1351* (The Fourth National Development Plan, 1968–1972), (Tehran: Plan Organisation, 1968); and also *Barnameh Panjum-i Ûmrani Kishvar, 1352–1356* (The Fifth National Development Plan, 1973–1977), (Tehran: Plan Organisation, 1973).

6   N. Momayezi, 'Economic Correlates of Political Violence: The Case of Iran', in *The Middle East Journal*, Vol. 40, no. 1, winter 1986, p.75. (Table 4). Quoting from: M. Parvin and A.N. Zamani, 'Political Economy of Growth and Distribution: A Statistical Interpretation of the Iranian Case', in *Iranian Studies*, no. 12, winter/spring 1979, p.47.

7   See the study (albeit with a biased conclusion) on Iranian rural-urban migration: M.G. Majd, 'On the Relationship between Land Reform and Rural-Urban Migration in Iran, 1966–1976', in *The Middle East Journal*, Vol. 46, no. 3, summer 1992, pp.452-3. F. Kazemi reports that during 1966–1976 period "2,111,000 individuals migrated from rural areas to the cities" in F. Kazemi, *Poverty and Revolution in Iran* (New York: New York University Press, 1980) p.28.

8   M.G. Majd, ibid., p.454.

9   This sudden surge in inflation came after years of a flat market (one to two per cent increases) in housing rents. See *Iran Almanac 1971* (Tehran: Echo of Iran) p.263.

10 G.W. Ball, *The Past has Another Pattern* (W.W. Norton, 1982) p.435.

11 Ibid., p.435.

12 Private communication to the author by a senator who had heard Âlam say so more than once.

12A Besides Professor Âdl, the Shah's other usual belote partners were Âbd ul-Majid Aâlam (the contractor), Hajibi and Parviz Bushiri – the court jester and one of the rare individuals allowed to be informal with the Shah, whom he called Patron.

13 Among others, see *Le Canard Enchaîné*, March 22, 1972.

14 *Asnad-i Laneh-yi Jasousi* (Tehran: Muslim Students Following the Line of the Imam) no. 17, pp.45-7. H.A. Ferguson Jr., in a report to the US ambassador (dated April 27, 1971), wrote that Iran's 'Air Mafia' consisted of five individuals: three generals, Muhamad Khatami (commander-in-chief of the air force), Âli Muhammad Khadimi (managing director of Iran Air) and Âli Asghar Rafât (managing director of Pars Air), and two civilians, Abu'l Fath Mahvi and Amir Husayn Zangineh. Ferguson added that these five individuals "control all aviation activities in Iran".

15 Neill-Price had made an initial bid of $105m for the Ahwaz-Ray pipeline. Another company had bid $58m. Neill-Price was declared the winner. Junior NIOC managers leaked the bids and the scandal broke. Neill-Price was forced to lower its bid to $75m. The junior managers' leader was expelled from NIOC (for divulging confidential information); on the other hand "39 [NIOC] officials" touched by the scandal had to be given early retirement. See *Asnad-i Laneh-yi Jasousi*, no. 17, p.78.

15A On 'Air Mafia' see note 14 above.

15B The rough figure of $26bn came from a private communication from an Iranian expert on arms deals and procurement.

15C General Mahoutyan was Iran's most secretive man according to secrecy specialist General Fardoust. He was in charge of SAVAK's Special Information and Special

Missions Bureau. He ran the ultra-secret Mahoutyan Network in the northern provinces, allegedly "directly for the British MI6". See *Zuhour va Suqout-i Saltanat-i Pahlavi* (Tehran: Mu'asiseh Mutaliât va Pijouish-ha-yi Syasi, 2 Vols., 1369 (1990)) Vol. 1, pp.347-353.

16 *Statistical Yearbook 1973* op. cit. (note 4), p.463.

17 *World Almanac and Book of Facts 1971* (New York: Pharos Books, 1971) p.350.

18 See *Tarikh-i Nirou-yi Hava'i-i Shahanshahi* (History of the Imperial Air Force), (Tehran: Intisharat-i Nirou Hava'i, 1355 (1976)).

18A The Dizful military airport was named Vahdati in honour of Major Vahdati and Captain Vahdati, two brothers, test pilots, who had been killed in service.

19 The base at Hamadan bore the name of Colonel Shahrukhi, an ace pilot, killed in 1950 while testing the air force's latest plane.

19A The British had already presented the Iranian Navy with two brand-new destroyers after the war – the *Babr* (2,000 tons); and the *Palang* (1,650 tons) – in a gesture of making good the destruction of the original ones in 1941. On the history of the Iranian Navy from its early days up to the Reza Shah years, albeit deficient on the 1960s and 1970s developments, see F. Rasa'i (admiral), *2500 Sal bar rou-yi Darya-ha* (2500 Years on the Seas, (Sitad-i Farmandeh'i-i Nirou-yi Darya'i-i Shahanshahi, undated) 496p.

19B One junior *Iran* Party member speculated in Karaj real estate, acquiring thousands of square metres. His holdings were estimated to be worth at least Rls5 to 6bn in 1993.

20 M. Izadi, *Faqih-i Âliqadr* (Tehran: Suroush, 1361 (1982)) p.59.

21 The Iran Investment Conference of May 1970 was held in Tehran, with, on the American side: David Rockefeller (Chase Manhattan), David Lilienthal (DRC), John Arpet (Alcoa), Henry Wingate (International Nickel), H.J. Heinz II (Heinz), Najib Halaby (PanAm) and thirty other executives.

22 On Sâidi's being tortured to death, see, among others, H. Algar, 'The Opposition Role of the Ulama in Twentieth Century Iran', in *Scholars, Saints, and Sufis: Muslim Religious Institutions Since 1500* ed. by N. Keddie, (Berkeley: University of California Press, 1977); and also the testimony of international jurist Dr Heinz Heldmann, who was expelled from Iran, as *persona non grata*, for his declarations, especially about Sâidi's hell.

23 See the open letter sent by Professor P. Vieille (an expert in Iranian affairs) on the activities of SAVAK under General Pakravan in *Le Monde*, November 9, 1978, p.2. And also see Pakravan's letter dated January 5, 1972 (then ambassador to Paris) and published in *Le Monde* on January 11, 1972, "strongly denying that any torture was being inflicted on political prisoners in Iran".

24 Shahryari, the *Toudeh*'s antenna in Tehran, was the first one informed of the return of exiled Iranian officers from the Soviet Union. He simply passed on this information to SAVAK.

25 On the subject of Dan Mitrione, the American CIA agent in charge of training Uruguay's anti-guerrilla special squad, who was kidnapped by the Tupamaros and executed, see A.J. Langguth, *Hidden Terrors* (Pantheon Books, 1979).

26 Muhammad Taqi Sarkarati had tried to rob a bank branch single-handedly. Everything was going according to plan until an old man, who had been passively sitting in a corner, broke a chair on Sarkarati's head. The latter, bleeding profusely, rushed out of the bank, shot a man who was trying to stop him and was finally arrested by the people. The man who had been shot later died. The

authorities at first thought Sarkarati to be a thief and murderer, and sentenced him accordingly. Only a few months later, after some of his guerrillas had been caught and named him, under torture, as their leader, did SAVAK realise its blunder. Sarkarati was tortured, court-martialled, sentenced to death and executed. His execution was reported in *Le Monde*, April 8, 1971. (Private communication from a cousin of Sarkarati who was in his second year at the Military Academy in Tehran, and was expelled indefinitely for being related to the guerrilla leader).

26A *Iran Almanac 1972* (Tehran: Echo of Iran) p.164.

26B *Parehi az Asnad-i Savak* (Some Documents from SAVAK), (Tehran: Amir Kabir, 1357 (1978)) p.

26C See *The Observer*, June 4, 1967 (report from Berlin by Neal Ascheson).

27 *Asnad-i Laneh-yi Jasousi*, op. cit. (note 14) no. 56, p.123.

28 B. Niroumand, *Iran: The New Imperialism in Action* (New York: Modern Reader Paperback, 1969).

29 B. Niroumand, *Feuer unterm Pfauenthron* (Berlin: 1974).

30 A.P. Saleh, *Cultural Ties between Iran and the United States* (Tehran: Shhirkat-i Ufsit, 1976) p.361.

31 *Statistical Yearbook 1972/Statistical Yearbook 1973*, (Tehran: Markaz-i Amar-i Iran, 1975/1976).

31A Minos Zombanakis, the head of manufacturers Hanover's London branch, put together the first syndicated Eurodollar loan ($80m) for Iran in 1969. The door to loans was thus opened. See A. Sampson, *The Money Lenders* (Coronet Books, 1982) p.127.

32 Private communication to the author. The source further added that "the collapse of the Shah's armed forces on February 11, 1979, confirmed the General's prophecy".

33 Â.A. Hajj Sayyid Javadi, *Hikayat Hamchinan Baqist* (Tehran: Chavash, 1357 (1978)) p.26.

34 J. Al Ahmad, *Gharbzadigi* (Tehran: Ravvaq, 1341 (1962)).

35 J. Al Ahmad, *Dar Khidmat va Khyanat-i Roushanfikran* (Tehran: Khwarazmi, 1357 (1968)) Vol 2., pp.74-78.

36 In an interview with Dr Javad Majabi, published in the magazine *Chapar*, winter 1350 (winter 1972), pp.142-4.

37 *Yadnameh-yi Jalal Al Ahmad*, ed. by Â. Dihbashi, (Tehran: Pasargad, 1364 (1985)) p.20.

38 F. Tunikabuni, *Yadashtha-yi Shahr-i Shulough* (Tehran: Pishgam, 2nd ed., 1357 (1978)).

39 The circumstances of Dr Shariâti's death are shrouded in mystery. The Iranian scholar was very probably murdered. Rumours in Tehran had it that the London SAVAK chief, the young General Mûinzadeh, had had a hand in the scholar's silencing. Interestingly, Mûinzadeh's brother was also a high-ranking SAVAK officer in Tehran.

39A A famous razor blade company offered him one million rials for a single photo of him shaving but he refused. Takhti's Mercedes-Benz (given him as a reward for his Olympic medal) was so battered that a group of mechanics stole it, returning it after a week freshly painted, refurbished and with new tyres. On the windscreen was a small note: *Excuse the inconvenience. But it was cheap for a hero like you to drive such a battered Benz.* (Anecdote from a Takhti family friend).

40 *Ghulam Riza Takhti* (Tehran: Farhang-i Varzish-i Iran, undated) p.11.

[41] S. Bihrangi, *Kand va Kav dar Masa'il-i Tarbiati-i Iran* (Inquiries about Iran's Educational Problems), (Tehran: Bamdad, undated).

[42] S. Bihrangi and B. Dihqani, *Afsaneh-ha-yi Azarbayjan* (Azarbayjani Fairy Tales), (Tehran: Nil, 4th ed., 1357 (1978)).

[43] S. Bihrangi, *Mahi Syah-i Kouchulou Dana* (Tehran: Kanoun-i Parvarish Fikri Koudakan va Noujavanan, 8th ed., 1356 (1977)) p.33.

[44] Samad Bihrangi: *Ba Mouj-ha-yi Aras beh Darya Payvast* collection of articles (Tehran: Aban, 2nd ed., 1357 (1978)) pp.28-9.

CHAPTER FOURTEEN: TRANSITIONS

1971 was to be a year of transition for the whole Middle Eastern sub-continent because it was the year Great Britain had chosen for pulling most of her remaining troops stationed east of Suez – with the exceptions of the Crown Colony of Hong Kong and the strategically critical Shaykhdom of Oman. Unable to bear the financial burden any more, the British had decided upon retirement in 1967, and PM Harold Wilson had announced a 1971 deadline for the withdrawal in an historic speech to the House of Commons on January 16, 1968. From 85,000 British troops in 1967, the total would dwindle to 15,000 in 1972.

For the Persian Gulf and its adjoining states, the departure of the British after some three and a half centuries of constant presence was in itself revolutionary. However, the vacuum so created was only partial, for, although her soldiers were departing, the British spirit of *Pax Brittanica* would linger on for a long time to come. Back in 1902, Lord Curzon during a visit to the Gulf's littoral states had clearly spelled out the Imperial vista:

> We were here before any other power... We created order... We have not seized or held territory. We have not destroyed your independence, but have preserved it. We are not going to throw away this... costly and triumphant enterprise; we shall not wipe out the most unselfish page in history...

Nevertheless, the British retirement of 1971 was bound to unleash forces and rivalries hitherto kept under control – due to the sophisticated balance of power exercised by weathered British diplomats.

Some naïve minds came to believe that the Persian Gulf was up for grabs. The Shah of Iran was not devoid of pretensions in this respect. After all, Iran was the Gulf's most populous and powerful state. Moreover, her bid for supremacy had been bolstered by the new doctrine formulated by US President Richard Nixon in July 1969 on the island of Guam. The Nixon Doctrine was a direct consequence of

American vicissitudes in Vietnam and was intended to encourage friendly nations to assume a greater share of their own defence, by promoting "protected clients into regional partners". Now the Gulf was a perfect example for applying the doctrine, as the Americans would inevitably have to fill the void left by departing British troops; and Iran was the perfect future partner.

Applied by National Security Council chief Henry Kissinger, the Nixon Doctrine gave rise to America's 'twin pillar' policy in the Persian Gulf: the pillars were to be Iran and Saudi Arabia. In fact, the Americans counted more on the Iranian pillar (based on culture and people) than on their Saudi one (based on sand and oil). Thus they encouraged the Shahanshah Aryamihr to assume virtual power over the region, gradually easing him into the role of 'Gendarme of the Gulf', and thereby playing to misplaced complexes of superiority. Naturally the American partner would provide training, armaments and logistics to its regional partner, and also provide back-ups in the way of its US Navy units in the Indian Ocean and its brand-new military base in the island of Diego Garcia (its first 8,000 feet runway was begun in 1971 and became operational in March 1973; it would later be expanded to 12,000 feet; and the island's communication systems were linked to Washington and the rest of the world).

However, the year 1971 would not only be the year of the British military withdrawal from the Gulf – it would also be the year of momentous events in Iran's history. First of all, the question of oil resurfaced after a long decade in abeyance.

14.1. 1971 and Oil

During the 1960s the oil business had been sheer routine. Market crude oil spot prices plummeted from an initial $1.63 per barrel in 1960 to $1.42 in 1965 and to as low as $1.21 in 1970.[1] However, 'posted prices' for crude (the price on the basis of which taxes and royalties were calculated) remained constant at their 1961 level of $1.80 per barrel throughout the decade. The successful defence of the 'posted price' (although there were some bilateral and unofficial reductions) represented a major achievement for the little-known Organisation of Petroleum Exporting Countries (OPEC).

In Iran, relations between NIOC and the Consortium were very cordial and the two organisations worked hand in hand to successfully develop the Iranian oil industry. Minor NIOC requests, for example its 1967 demand to barter 20 million tonnes of crude oil with Eastern European countries, were readily given the green light by the Consortium(due to the Suez Canal closure of 1967, only some 10 million tons were finally bartered). In addition, three Supplemental Agreements were added to the original Consortium Agreement of 1954: the first, with an effective date of January 1, 1964, addressed (in nine articles) minor tax amendments; in the second (effective date May 27, 1967) the Consortium relinquished around 25% of its concession area of 254,112 square kilometres; and with the third (effective date November 14, 1970) the level of taxation for oil trading companies in Iran was increased from 50% to 55% of net income.

Moreover, in all three agreements mergers and acquisitions among Iricon members were legally registered.

Change in the stagnating oil business would come from the most unexpected of OPEC members – Libya. Back on September 1, 1969, a bloodless *coup d'état* staged by a group of young officers, led by thirty year old Colonel Muammar Qaddafi, had toppled the old and senile King Idris. Overnight the kingdom was turned into an Islamic republic. Once in power, the young officers' first priority was to renegotiate the oil concessions granted by the previous regime. As an initial target they chose the weakest link amongst their concessionaires: the Occidental Oil Co. Negotiations between the two parties began in 1970 and, after protracted discussions interspersed with production cuts and snarled Libyan threats, ended on September 2 with the capitulation of Occidental: the oil company accepted an increase in its Libyan 'posted price' from $2.23 to $2.53 per barrel, as well as a raise in its tax rate from 50 to 58%. All other Libyan concessionaires were to sign a similar agreement – except for Royal Dutch/Shell, which adamantly refused to do so and was therefore forbidden to lift any more oil from September 22. Colonel Qaddafi and his young officers had resoundingly won their first round.

In Iran, NIOC had been following the Libyan gambit with interest. As soon as victory was in sight, Dr Iqbal had gone to London to hold talks with Consortium representatives. NIOC argued that, if the Libyans could get away with such advantageous terms, the Consortium could make an effort too. At the next round of NIOC-Consortium negotiations at Tehran, an agreement was signed on November 14, 1970, which gave the Iranian side full satisfaction. The 'posted prices' for Iranian light and heavy export crudes (FOB Kharg Island) were respectively raised by 6 and 9 US cents per barrel (to $1.79 and $1.72), and the tax rate was increased from 50 to 55%. In January 1971 the *Majlis* dutifully ratified the new agreement.

Other OPEC members, however, couldn't duplicate the Libyan and Iranian successes. They came to realise that their best chance lay in global negotiations between OPEC and the oil companies. At the OPEC Conference of December 1970 in Caracas, they tabled such a proposal and its approval paved the way for the Tehran Conference. Thus, on January 11, 1971 negotiations began in Tehran between the ten OPEC members and the twenty-two major oil companies. The Shah and advisers were to play a pivotal role in the protracted negotiations, benefiting from the goodwill of both the British and the American sides. As Persian Gulf expert J.B. Kelly pointed out:

> Neither the British nor the American Governments wished to run the risk of provoking him [the Shah] and thus jeopardising the attainment of their own separate goals – the British to make as smooth and comfortable an exit as possible from the Gulf at the end of the year, the Americans to build the Shah up as the guardian of the Gulf's security after the British departure...[2]

Nevertheless the Americans knew from the outset that they could get Iran to agree eventually to almost any compromise, for, in a December 1971 report issued by the State Department, it was concluded that:

> There is very little that we could do in most OPEC countries, except Iran, in case they did not accede to our demands...[3]

On January 17, US Under-Secretary of State John Irwin II arrived in Tehran to meet the Shah and Finance Minister Jamshid Amuzigar. Irwin was given the assurance that "any agreement entered into with the oil companies would be honoured for the full terms".[4] In return, Irwin was asked to agree to dual stages in the negotiations, with the

Persian Gulf countries meeting the oil companies in Tehran and the other OPEC members meeting them in Tripoli in Libya. After checking with Secretary of State Rogers, Irwin gave his approval. When Lord Strathalmond, BP's managing director, and George T. Piercy, Exxon's chief executive, debarked in Tehran two days later they were faced with a *fait accompli*. Consequently, Lord Strathalmond remained in Tehran to lead the team meeting the Persian Gulf countries while Piercy left for Tripoli to head the other team. "With this concession", Kelly noted, "the slide began and it was not to stop until the companies had given way on nearly every issue".[5]

In Tehran the negotiations led to the agreement of February 14, 1971, which was to run until December 31, 1975 and provided for the following:

(1) An increase in the 'posted price' of the Persian Gulf marker crude, from $1.80 to $2.10 per barrel;

(2) An automatic addition of 5 US cents per barrel to the 'posted price' every year;

(3) A 2½ per cent raise in the 'posted price' every year (to offset inflation);

(4) A tax rate of 55% (instead of 50%) for all OPEC Persian Gulf countries.

In Tripoli, the talks were concluded on April 2 with a final agreement which gave Libya a 77 US cents increase per barrel on its 'posted price' (from $2.53 to $3.30 per barrel) and giving proportional rises to non-Gulf OPEC members. It goes without saying that the Tripoli agreement also incorporated all the other concessions granted by the companies in Tehran.

The results of the Tehran Conference were only confirming the fears of Shell's chairman Sir David Barran, as stated at a meeting at the US State Department on September 25, 1970 (just after his company had been shut out of Libya):

> The dangers to our own and the consumers' interests lay much more in yielding than in resisting the demands made upon us ...our conclusion is that sooner or later we, both oil company and consumer, will have to face an avalanche of escalating demands from the producer Governments and that we should at least try to stem the avalanche...[6]

Barran's fears were well founded. First in Tehran, then at OPEC's September 1971 meeting at Beirut, the avalanche he had foreseen was set in motion. In Beirut, OPEC put forward the case for the 'participation' of producing countries in the operating companies. In Geneva, in January 1972, it asked for an across-the-board participation of 20% for its members. Before the close of 1971 it had asked for, and was granted, an 8½% increase in 'posted prices' as a compensation for inflation. This last request was the first infringement on the promises given to Irwin in January 1971 in Tehran, Kuwait and Riyadh – the promise made had not held a full year.

For the international oil industry, 1971 was the watershed: the industry would never be the same thereafter. The chapter of concessions and sacrosanct agreements was being closed. A revolution was in the making. OPEC, which was still "widely treated as a joke", had shown that it had muscles which it would flex. After a decade of preparations, it could finally play its role on the international oil stage. A minor role, but a role nevertheless.

As for Iran, with its economy heading towards asphyxiation, the Tehran Conference was a welcome balloon of oxygen. The average Iranian income per barrel of crude jumped from $0.838 in 1970 to $1.183 in 1971. The bill for food exports was on the way up and would hit $400m for 1971. In the spring of 1971 butter shortages had hit Tehran and other urban centres,[7] pointing to problems of importation and distribution. The new view in Tehran was that increased oil revenues would solve all of Iran's problems, and that this situation would arise soon, as a result of the Shah's masterly playing of his hand *vis-à-vis* the oil companies, without antagonising them or their governments. On the other hand, the regime's critics advanced the thesis that the Shah had simply followed Colonel Qaddafi's lead and that it was the Libyan leader who deserved all the kudos for placing the OPEC train on the right tracks.

14.2. Syahkal

After his return in the summer of 1970 from his training stint in Palestine, Âli Akbar Safa'i Farahani gathered the eight members of his 'mountain team' and began its first training drive in the Alburz mountains of Mazandaran (moving towards Gilan), in September. Safa'i's plans were for a spring offensive in May 1971, when the trees' foliage would provide adequate cover for his guerrilla team. Until then, he wanted to train and blend his small team into a military unit hardened to life in the dense northern forests. He forced his team-mates to undertake long walks and daily physical training. With the first snowfalls, he lost a man in the forest and never found him again. From Tehran, he was sent (as arranged with Miftahi) Ahmad Farhoudi, who had just returned from an *Al Fath* training camp in Jordan. Farhoudi proved so valuable that Safa'i promoted him to deputy team leader. Under the duo's command, the 'mountain team' became a cohesive unit. Communications with the 'town team' were smooth. The 'logistics team' was busy placing food and arms in special mountain caches. Everything was going ahead according to the plan for the beginning of operations in 1971.

The team's preparations in Gilan would be disturbed by events unfolding in Tehran. The chain of events began rather benignly with students' demonstrations at Tehran University on December 7, 1970. Police intervened and arrested dozens of students, who were delivered to SAVAK. This time round, the security forces had done their homework well, and the students were carefully pressured. One of them, Abu'l Hasan Khatib, awakened suspicions and a search of his house yielded subversive pamphlets and a complete set of mountain-climbing gear. Under torture, Khatib gave the name of Ghafour Hasanpour Asil as the owner of the incriminating gear. Hasanpour, a recent polytechnic graduate, was doing his military service in Shiraz. He was immediately arrested, brought to Tehran and placed in the hands of SAVAK's torture specialists.

Hasanpour's arrest triggered danger signals throughout the 'town team', for, if Khatib was a simple soldier, Hasanpour was a prominent team member, in possession of precious secrets. The 'town team' found it wiser to pull in its horns for some time. But, surprisingly, after SAVAK's Sabiti told a press conference that the latest round of arrests had not resulted in any significant catch, the team let itself be deceived and resurfaced. SAVAK had realised from the outset Hasanpour's value and the young guerrilla was continuously being tortured. After twenty days of the worst tortures (and SAVAK's torture experts were among the most imaginative as well as the most ruthless) the young guerrilla cracked, giving away his secrets. On February 2, SAVAK launched its surprise onslaught against the guerrilla teams: within the first twenty-four hours five key Tehran leaders and three regional co-ordinators for Gilan were arrested. As the freshly captured guerrillas were sent to SAVAK's torture chambers to divulge further names and addresses, the whole organisation was in disarray. All regular links had to be severed and nowhere was deemed safe any longer, with members were scrambling to their deepest underground hideouts. Communications between the 'town' and 'mountain' teams were cut off.

Fortunately for Safa'i Farahani, one of the members of the 'town' team was able to contact the 'mountain' team on February 6 and inform them of SAVAK's onslaught. Realising the seriousness of the situation, Safa'i decided to initiate action before SAVAK's juggernaut caught up with his 'mountain team'. Accordingly, he made the last preparations before heading for the deep Gilan forests. Among others, he dispatched one of his men, Hadi Bandeh Khuda Langaroudi, to the nearby village of Shab Khuslab (a tiny village on the fringes of Alburz, a few kilometres from Syahkal), to inform its young teacher Iraj Niri of the latest events and warn him to be cautious – the teacher was a crucial asset, for, besides being the brother of team member Houshang Niri, he had co-ordinated the placing of food reserves at the secret Kakouh mountain location. Iraj Niri, however, had already been arrested on February 2 (after tips from Tehran) and Langaroudi fell into the trap set by the local Gendarmerie in Niri's house. Taken to the local Gendarmerie post at Syahkal, Langaroudi committed the imprudence of telling the commanding officer that "my friends will soon come to free me"; this was enough for the officer to take Langaroudi to Rasht for further questioning by SAVAK about "his friends".

Safa'i Farahani, informed of Langaroudi's capture (but not of his transfer to Rasht), decided on the spot to attack the Syahkal Gendarmerie post the same evening and free him. Syahkal is a typical Iranian village, situated in the dense Gilan forest some seventeen kilometres off the main Rasht–Lahijan road, nearer to the latter. Its

Gendarmerie post was an unprepossessing, two-floor brick building. Nothing predisposed Syahkal for entering history, only the predilection of the Gilan province for being Iran's historical centre of gravity. Thus, on the evening of February 8, 1971, eight courageous guerrillas came out of their forest to requisition a passing shaky Ford minibus, and took it to Syahkal. These eight young guerrillas, who were about to initiate armed struggle in Iran, were:

(1) Âli Akbar Safa'i Farahani, thirty-one, the 'mountain team' leader; a graduate of Narmak Industrial College, trained by *Al Fath* in Jordan (earning the surname of Abu Âbbas), had written a booklet in 1970 entitled *An Cheh Yik Inqilabi Bayad Bidanad* (What a Revolutionary Should Know);

(2) Ahmad Farhoudi, twenty-nine, deputy team leader; trained in guerrilla tactics in Jordan, a civil servant until joining the armed struggle;

(3) Jalil Infiradi, thirty, a former master welder with a long career in underground activities;

(4) Âbbas Danish Bihzadi, twenty-eight, a graduate of Tehran University's Veterinary Faculty;

(5) Muhammad Âli Qandchi, twenty-five, also a TU Veterinary Faculty graduate;

(6) Mihdi Ishaqi, twenty-five, a graduate of the Pahlavi University at Shiraz;

(7) Muhammad Rahim Samâi, twenty-three, a graduate of Tehran's Polytechnic University;

(8) Houshang Niri, twenty-two, a Gilani, who had also trained in Jordan with *Al Fath*.

Safa'i split his small force into two. He placed two of his men before the offices of the Forestry Centre, and took the other five under his own command to attack the Gendarmerie building to find out Langaroudi's whereabouts. Safa'i's team easily took the Gendarmerie post, killing in the process the head of the Syahkal Justice House (there to supervise things in the absence of the commanding officer) and its leading NCO. Their only casualty was Niri, whose right elbow had been hit by a bullet. Finding no trace of Langaroudi, they seized the Gendarmerie's weapons (a total of nine rifles and machine-guns) before departing on the minibus. After reaching the forest, they paid the driver Rls6,000 for his services and rapidly took off. Here, Safa'i decided again to split his forces: he and Infiradi would accompany the wounded Niri to safety while the five others would go to the food reserve under Farhoudi's command and wait for them there.

The same evening the national armed forces were prompt in reacting (even overreacting) to the extraordinary Syahkal incident. All the region's armed forces were ordered to converge on Syahkal to capture the eight fugitives. Gendarmerie commander-in-chief General Ghulam Âli Uvaysi arrived the next day to set up his headquarters in the devastated Syahkal post. From there he summoned the whole Gilan Division, all available Gendarmerie reserves and a dozen helicopters to search for the guerrillas.

Iran's armed forces were playing their favourite game: crushing internal dissidence. This time round, they unashamedly used their heaviest sledgehammer to crack a nut, because their honour (and jobs) were at stake in the case of their failure to find the fugitives.

Notwithstanding Niri's wound, Safa'i's small group successfully dodged army patrols and made it to the small village of Chihil Sutoun. The wounded Niri badly needed medical treatment. The three armed men made it to the house of the village *kadkhuda* (mayor) to find assistance. Safa'i and Niri entered the house while Infiradi was left to guard its entrance. The tired guerrillas were given tea and bread while villagers came flocking to the mayor's house to see the armed guerrillas. Some of the entering villagers had hidden sticks and kebab skewers in their clothing. As Infiradi imprudently left his station before the door to enter the main room, the villagers assaulted the three guerrillas. A stick knocked Niri down, a skewer was stuck in Safa'i's stomach and Infiradi was set upon and subdued. None of the three had used their firearms against the villagers, trusting them to the bitter end. The callous villagers, on the other hand, would show no mercy to their prisoners: they threw them on the ground, pulled sheets over them and started beating them with spades and sticks. The three guerrillas were half-dead when they were saved *in extremis* by the village teacher, who pleaded with the villagers for their lives. They were imprisoned and Gendarmes later came to fetch them to take them to Rasht for interrogation by SAVAK. For Safa'i it had been deeply paradoxical to be captured and almost beaten to death by the very people for whom he was supposed to be fighting. A basic knowledge of Iranian peasants had led him to trust them: the innocent guerrillas had a long way to go to become a large fish in Iran's problematic rural waters!

Farhoudi's group easily found the foodstuff reserves on Kakouh mountain. But they were unaware that Iraj Niri had revealed its exact location under torture. The five guerrillas only realised that they were not alone when they had already been surrounded by a vast military force, armed with machine-guns and mortars. Called on to surrender, Farhoudi decided to fight it out. For two whole days and nights, the five were able to keep a full regiment at bay, inflicting heavy casualties. Eventually the contest proved too uneven: Ishaqi and Samâi had been killed and the others were captured; the last one to hold out was Farhoudi, finally captured in a half-frozen state on February 28. It had taken Uvaysi and the Gilan division twenty days to bring the guerrillas' adventure to an end. The general had been fortunate to receive the assistance of the Chihil Sutoun villagers: if Safa'i and Infiradi had been able to leave Niri safely behind, they would have gone a long way. The six surviving guerrillas were the subject of the harshest tortures by SAVAK specialists before being executed by a firing squad on March 17, 1971. Alongside the six, seven other guerrillas were executed on the same day: the first was Hadi Bandeh Khuda Langaroudi, thirty, the ninth member of Safa'i's team; the second, Iskandar Rahimi, twenty-three, a Gilani teacher; and the five others were all Tehran Polytechnic graduates and members of the 'town team' – namely Ghafur Hasanpour Asil, twenty-eight; Shuâû ul-Din Mashidi, twenty-eight; Ismaîl Mûini Âraqi, twenty-eight; Nasir Sayf Dalil Safa'i, twenty-seven; Muhammad Hadi Fazili, twenty-six. The only survivor of Syahkal was Iraj Niri, who was sentenced to life imprisonment, although today he quietly runs his own garage in the town of Lahijan.

The extermination of the 'mountain' and 'town' teams had been the price to pay for the Syahkal operation. But Syahkal had been a triumph! It had brought pride and self-confidence to the hearts of all of Iran's opponents wherever they were: in the prisons, living underground, abroad. That Safa'i and his men had dared was enough. Even public opinion, not particularly communist- or guerrilla-minded, was admiring of the stark courage of the young men of Syahkal. Moreover, Syahkal had broken the stalemate (in Farsi, the *tilism*) that had stalled Iran's armed struggle movement during the 1960s. It had given the Pahlavi regime, always so arrogant, a well-deserved black eye. It had shown the world that Iranians were no sheep and shown Iranians at home that some youngsters were ready to face torture and death to fight the Shah's dictatorial regime. Safa'i's men had put an ugly crack in the nice, white-washed Pahlavi façade.

The Syahkal incident had shocked the regime to its deepest foundations: it had never thought it possible that guerrillas would dare attack it practically bare-handed. After overreacting militarily, the regime would overreact psychologically (revealing its vulnerability) by banning the very name of Syahkal, ordering the destruction of the Gendarmerie building (which could become a place of pilgrimage), censoring any writing or poem alluding to trees and leaves, and any painting depicting forests;[8] the roads leading to it were guarded by Gendarmes and motorists were discouraged from continuing to Syahkal, the authorities fearing that it would become a national attraction. But nothing could stop the name of Syahkal from becoming the symbol of anti-Pahlavism. Nothing could stop the legend of the small guerrilla team from entering Iranian popular history. At Syahkal, amidst the dense Gilan forest, something had altered on that evening of February 8, 1971. Pahlavi Iran would never be the same. If only for Syahkal, 1971 was a very special year.

14.3. Persepolis Festivities

Far from learning his lesson from the incident at Syahkal the Shah went on with his project to throw a gargantuan party at Persepolis for his fellow heads of state, his jet-set friends, his worldwide business connections and his local acolytes. Officially the Shah's feast was dubbed the Celebrations of the 2,500th Anniversary of the Iranian Monarchy. The lavish and costly masquerade was a way for the parvenu Pahlavi to confer upon his family a degree of legitimacy which only sycophants and bootlickers were ready to bestow upon it. The Shah had even tried to make his people believe that it was their festival, telling them in a televised allocution:

> You must not forget that this shall not be an imperial or government festival alone. It shall be a festival belonging to the whole nation...[9]

Iranians are no dupes; they are most hospitable but hate pointlessly showing off: it was the Shah's private party and they had nothing to do with it.

With or without the people, the festivities went ahead as scheduled on October 12, 1971. In comparison, the 1967 coronation had been a pale dress rehearsal. The commemorations opened with a Congress of Iranologists, giving them a cultural note, and providing a forum for Iranian participants to be given the opportunity to praise the Shahanshah Aryamihr. Simultaneously, the Shah opened his programme with a visit to Cyrus the Great's tomb at Pasargadae, where he ended his speech with these unforgettable words: "Cyrus, rest in peace for we are awake!" There were limits even for Muhammad Reza Pahlavi, and it seemed that at Pasargadae he had surely exceeded his.

On October 13 the Shah's guests arrived one after the other at Shiraz airport, the most prominent, such as the Ethiopian Emperor Haile Selassie, being welcomed by the Shah in person. From there they were taken to the tented camp erected by the Parisian decorator Jansen (chief decorators Pierre Delbee and Pierre Deshays) at the foot of the Persepolis ruins, in the shape of a pentacle. This scheme, approved by the Shah, was not Empress Farah's cup of tea, who said, "I detest those tents ...they are so un-Persian".[10] On the evening of the 14th, the great gala dinner was served in the special reception tent for nine hundred selected guests. Louis Vaudable, Maxim's president, was orchestrating the dinner with thirty-five cooks and a hundred and fifty *maître d*'s, with the food, the wines and the 5,000 bottles of champagne having come from Paris by charter. Two of Princess Ashraf's close associates, her third husband Dr Mihdi Bushiri and her trusted friend Âbd ul-Riza Ansari, had been respectively appointed chief and deputy chief of the Celebrations Council, with *carte blanche* to provide the best; besides Jansen and Maxim's they had selected Lanvin (dresses), Truffaut (flowers), Quiry (fountains), Baccarat (glass), Porthault (tablecloth), Ceralene (table services), Robert Havilland (tea service), Carita and Alexandre (for the guests' hairdressing), Elizabeth Arden (for make up), et cetera, et cetera.[11]

On October 15, costumed Iranian troops, impersonating soldiers from the Achaemanean days up to the present, paraded in front of the Shah and his guests on the large Persepolis esplanade. For some three months special units of the Iranian Army were trained for the show;

their costumes and perruques had been purchased from specialists in France and Italy. In the evening the Shah's guests were treated to a *son et lumières* (produced by Alain Castelot and directed by Pierre Arnaud) in the Persepolis ruins. The spectacle was closed with a giant fireworks display to please the guests. The only people annoyed by all this *brouhaha* were probably Guiseppe and Ann Britt Talia, the archaeologists at Persepolis, who would do commendable work during their extended stay from 1965 until 1979, but could have done without the harm to the ruins caused by the electric cables, the projectors and the special stand built exclusively for the 'un-Persian' *son et lumières*.

On October 16 the whole show moved to Tehran for the inauguration of the brand-new, 45-metre high *Shahyad* monument (renamed the *Azadi* (Liberty) monument in 1979). Built with creamy-white marble stones provided by Iran's marble king Qanbar Rahimi, the Pahlavi era's most prominent work of art was located at Tehran's western gate, near Mihrabad Airport, so that any passing tourist was obliged to glimpse the Shah's monumental legacy (today, Tehran's global symbol). The only cloud that day was the news that Iranian students had set the Iranian Consulate in San Francisco on fire.

On October 17 and 18, the Shah's guests departed from Tehran, each of them taking home one of the 2,000 tins of golden caviar specially prepared for the occasion. Some local events took place on October 19 and on the next day the 2500th Anniversary festivities were officially closed.

To his numerous critics in the international press – among others was Jacques Rolland, who had written a leader in a Swiss journal, "hoping to launch a single bomb on the Persepolis gala night, to rid the planet of all the villains reunited there"[12] – who attacked the useless luxury and expenses, the Shah angrily replied that "I could not very well offer [my guests] bread and radishes".[13] He had neither listened to his domestic critics nor to Iranian public opinion, both of whom had been first flabbergasted then disgusted by the wasteful and ostentatious display. The total cost of the Persepolis junket must have been over $100m (although the court mentioned only $16.8m). But the people of Iran were not impressed. On the contrary, they had come to abhor the whole extravaganza, with some beginning to ponder the new catchphrase some opponents of the regime had the courage to repeat in public: "Two and a half thousand years of monarchy ...is enough".

14.4. Three Persian Gulf Islands

The withdrawal of the British troops from the Gulf by the close of 1971 was far from being a problem-free exit. The British were doing their best to settle what they could before taking their troops home. They would keep only a few thousand men stationed in Oman – "still the key to command of the Gulf" according to expert J.B. Kelly.[14] There, on July 28, 1970 the young, Sandhurst-educated Sultan Qabus staged a bloodless coup to oust his father, Sultan Sâid Ibn Taymour Al Bu Sâid.

On the southern shores of the Gulf the British had few problems. Adjacent to Oman, they had united the seven small shaykhdoms of Abou Dhabi, Dubai, Sharjah, Umm ul-Quwayn, Fujayrah, Ras ul-Khaymah and Ajman into the United Arab Emirates (UAE). The island of Bahrayn, recognised as "independent" by Great Britain since 1861, was firmly under the rule of the Al-Khalifah family (Iran officially recognised Bahrayn's independence in 1970). Qatar, a full OPEC member, was in the hands of the Al-Thani family. Even offshore boundaries (the source of future disputes) had been demarcated:[15] between Saudi Arabia and Bahrayn (1958), Saudi–Iran (1968), Abou Dhabi–Qatar (1969), Abou Dhabi–Dubai (1969), Iran–Qatar (1970) and Iran–Bahrayn (terminated in 1972).

The major problem was Iran, with the Shah trying to take advantage of the crisis, knowing that the Americans would support him in his plans ("Protect me" was the Shah's request of Nixon in May 1972[16]). The British special envoy to Iran, Sir William Luce, would need all his tact to accommodate the Iranians' Gulf ambitions. Having finally relinquished all her claims to Bahrayn in 1970, Iran was now eyeing the three islands of Abou Musa and the two Tumbs (the Greater and the Lesser) in the southern part of the Gulf, and the Shah had threatened "to refuse to recognise it [the UAE] unless he gets the islands".[17] Protracted negotiations ensued, interspersed with incidents such as the May 1971 flare-up between British aircraft and Iranian naval units in the Gulf. In August and September 1971, Iran duly established diplomatic relations with Oman, Bahrayn and Qatar. Iran–UAE relations were settled during November, with Sir Luce acting as supreme arbiter. The case of the main island of Abou Musa, hitherto under Sharjah's sovereignty, was solved by a six-point memorandum accepted by both Sharjah and Iran (with the British

Foreign Office acting as intermediary), which, put in a nutshell, split the island into two (neither party giving up its claim on the whole island) – Iranian troops could occupy the Iranian half, and the island's offshore oil resources remained with the Buttes Gas and Oil Company, with which Sharjah had entered into an agreement.

As the last British battalions left the Gulf on November 30, 1971, Iranian paratroopers occupied the three Gulf islands, presenting the Arabs with a *fait accompli*. Iraq protested vociferously and severed diplomatic relations with Iran. Iranian-Iraqi relations had already taken a turn for the worse when, back in April 1969, the Shah denounced the 1937 Saâdabad Treaty with Iraq and repudiated the border settlement over the Shatt al-Arab (i.e. the low water mark on the Iraqi side), calling on this occasion the up-and-coming Iraqi politician Saddam Husayn "a young man with a bold imagination".[17A] Libya's leaders hurled a flurry of insults at Iran and promptly nationalised BP's share in the Sarir oil field, "ostensibly in reprisal for the British Government's complicity in the Persian occupation of the Gulf Islands".[18]

The Shah had succeeded in getting away with his occupation of the islands. He may have antagonised his Arab neighbours, but they would never be pleased. On the other hand, he had boosted his regional prestige and secured the goodwill of nationalistic circles at home. The fact that the Shah had begun his new role of Gulf gamekeeper as a poacher showed the extent of his ambitions on his southern shores.

For the time being both Persian Gulf Powers (i.e. Great Britain and the US) were satisfied with the present developments. The former had retired without breaking too many eggs; the latter was letting the Shah place his large umbrella over the Gulf, waiting to see how the situation there would evolve.

14.5. Guerrilla Warfare

Of all the momentous events of 1971, the Tehran oil conference and the Syahkal incident would be the most consequential. The oil negotiations had brought a major change to the small world of oil, but its consequences would be felt a few years off, whereas Syahkal would have direct consequences, triggering off a covert (but no less real) civil war between, on the one hand, the guerrillas and their student supporters and, on the other, the Shah's armed forces and SAVAK.

In the aftermath of Syahkal, Tehran's universities were once again in a state of ebullition. By the end of February 1971, the National University students went on strike, ostensibly because of high tuition fees. Even the regime's higher education strongholds were turning to opposition. Tehran University was in a state of high buoyancy, with the police forces compelled to intervene daily to stop riots spilling over into the capital's streets: from mid-March onwards, police occupied the campus permanently. At TU, relations between the professors belonging to the ruling elite and the students degenerated into a war of words.[19] By early April, the students at Tehran's Polytechnic and Aryamihr University were also rioting, demanding an end to the TU's occupation by the police. Furthermore, Tabriz's Azarabadigan University was the scene of widespread rioting during the spring of 1971; violent clashes occurred between police troops and the students and some of the students were thrown out of windows and truckloads of bricks emptied on them. TU was not the education system's black sheep any longer, for the other universities were joining the opposition's camp. The guerrillas could count on their student supporters to unleash riots to alert public opinion.

In the aftermath of Syahkal, the remnants of the five teams forming the Jazani-Zarifi group were decimated. Besides the executed guerrillas, another fifty were still in prison awaiting trial. Only a handful of team leaders had managed to escape the SAVAK's onslaught (e.g. Hamid Ashraf, Ahmad Zaybram). These had been extra-vigilant, probably keeping a safe house known to no one else. SAVAK nevertheless had their names and pictures. The other leftist guerrilla group, led by Ahmadzadeh, Miftahi and Pouyan, had essentially remained untouched and was now ready and eager to enter action.

On April 3, a squad of the Ahmadzadeh-Miftahi-Pouyan group assaulted the soldier standing guard at Qulhak police station, shot him (he later died) and took away his machine-gun.

Four days later, three of their guerrillas under the command of Iskandar Sadiqinizhad machine-gunned the abhorred army public prosecutor, General Zia' ul-Din Farsiou, (who had condemned the thirteen Syahkal guerrillas to death) and his seventeen year old son

Farzad as they stepped out of their house: both died of their wounds. The successful attempt on Farsiou was a rude shock for the regime, the armed forces and SAVAK. The elite was suddenly facing a real danger: if the guerrillas could so easily gun down Farsiou, none of them was safe any more. SAVAK reacted by publishing nationwide the photos of the nine most wanted guerrillas (a first in Iran), with a one million rials reward per head. The nine were: (1) Hamid Ashraf; (2) Ahmad Zaybram; (3) Javad Salahi; (4) Âbbas Miftahi; (5) Amir Parviz Pouyan; (6) Rahmatullah Payrounazari; (7) Iskandar Sadiqinizhad; (8) Muhammad Saffari Ashtyani; and (9) Manouchihr Baha'ipour.

As SAVAK was mustering all its means to ferret out the fugitives, Masôud Ahmazadeh (surprisingly not on the most wanted list) and Miftahi were meeting Ashraf and Zaybram (of Jazani-Zarifi) to bring about the fusion of the two parallel groups. They reached an accord in April 1971 which led to the creation of the Marxist-Leninist *Sazman-i Chirik-ha-yi Fada'i-i Khalq-i Iran* – SCFKI (Organisation of the People's Guerrillas of Iran). The communist counterpart to the Islamist-Marxist SMKI was thus created. Henceforward, Iran's guerrilla movement would be bicephalous: the SMKI (with its *Mujahids*) and the SCFKI (and its *Fada'yan*).

SAVAK was on a war footing and its strategy for ensnaring the guerrillas was two-pronged: (i) keep torturing the ones it held, hoping to uncover new safe houses; (ii) and sending its well-organised 'hunting squads' on the streets of Tehran, to capture guerrillas on the loose. Results were soon achieved by SAVAK's pros against the guerrilla amateurs – who were in the dark about SAVAK methods for capturing them. On April 14, Javad Salahi was recognised and shot dead in Tehran's Paminar district. In May the SFCKI succeeded in holding up the Bank-i Milli branch on Eisenhower Avenue, getting away with around Rls6m. But during the same month SAVAK was arresting more and more SFCKI guerrillas, among them the sister and brother Ashraf and Bihrouz Dihqani (Samad Bihrangi's friend). The brother died in SAVAK's torture room,[19A] but the sister spectacularly escaped from Qasr Prison in March 1973.[20] Another SFCKI member to fall into SAVAK's clutches was Hamid Tavakkuli, who was Amir Parviz Pouyan's best friend. After Tavakkuli's arrest, subordinates begged Pouyan to leave the now-doomed Nirou-yi Hava'i safe house, but Pouyan wouldn't budge, arguing, "I know Tavakulli well, he will never talk". Tavakulli kept his tongue only for the first twenty-four hours (as prescribed by underground regulations, to give the others time to change safe houses), but no longer. On May 24, Amir Parviz Pouyan and Rahmatullah Payrounazari were trapped at their Nirou-yi Hava'i flat. For two hours they returned the SAVAK agents' fire, eventually committing suicide rather than be captured alive. Thus ended the life of Amir Parviz Pouyan, one of the best brains amongst Iran's guerrillas.

During 1971, the mini-war so far fought covertly came to the streets of Tehran. On May 25, three guerrillas assaulted two armed NCOs in the street to secure their handguns; in the action two of the guerrillas and one NCO died, the other NCO, although wounded ,arrested the third guerrilla. Not only were guerrillas desperate for weapons and money, but they had also taken to making and detonating bombs. During the summer a bomb destroyed the Mukhbir ul-Douleh police station and in September another exploded at the Ministry of Finance. On Firdousi Avenue a bomb went off prematurely in a taxi, blowing to smithereens both the taxi driver and the amateur bomb-maker. In Shiraz, two Pahlavi University students were killed and a third badly wounded when the bomb they were assembling exploded. In January 1972, it was American institutions in Tehran that were targeted: a bomb went off in the US Embassy's restaurant, another at the Iran-America Cultural Centre. By then, it was clear to everybody that something was going on and people began counting the shots and listening to rumours about the ongoing civil war.

While the guerrillas were taking risks to strike at the regime's pillars, SAVAK teams, getting more experienced by the day, caught them in their nets. During the summer of 1971, first, a series of SCFKI's sub-unit commanders were arrested: Hajian Sepileh, Sâid Aryan, Muhammad Suvaluni, Bahman Ajang and Shahrukh Hidayati. Then group leaders Masôud Ahmadzadeh and Âbbas Miftahi were trapped: the former's name was given by his own team member under torture, the latter's by a treacherous new recruit; their brothers Majid Ahmadzadeh and Asadullah Miftahi were also caught. All four leaders were brutally tortured, with Masôud Ahmadzadeh, SAVAK's prize catch, given the worst treatment. During the autumn of 1971, the SCFKI members were brought to court-martial. In January 1972, thirteen of them faced the firing squad; in February another six, and in March a group of eleven, including the two Ahmadzadeh and the two

Miftahi brothers. Within one year of its inception, the SCFKI had been bled white; it only had two major commanders still on the run, Ahmad Zaybram and Hamid Ashraf.

Ahmad Zaybram, the son of a Caspian Sea fisherman, was renowned as a master of disguise and known by SAVAK as the man "with a hundred faces". He had had a hand in the logistics of Syahkal, the execution of Farsiou and the hold-up of a number of banks, the latest being the January 11, 1972 Bank-i Milli Safaviyyeh branch (during which branch manager Muhammad Âli Tashid and an bank employee were shot dead). SAVAK had long been on his tracks in southern Tehran. None of his fellow guerrillas knew of his hideout. On the morning of August 19, 1972, SAVAK hunt squads finally caught up with him when he was on a motorcycle and they shot him in the leg, followed him to his safe house and sharpshooters finished him off. There remained at large only Hamid Ashraf.

During the 1970s, Hamid Ashraf* would become a living legend: for eight and a half years "the most wanted man in Iran" evaded SAVAK's crack anti-terrorist advisers (the world's very best). His record time on the run should be compared with the average survival time of four to five months for ordinary guerrilla leaders. He had survived the 1968 arrests of his leaders Jazani and Zarifi, and the Syahkal aftermath; had begun almost from scratch in 1971/72 to rebuild SCFKI cells according to his own system of doubly safe security. He was Iran's Scarlet Pimpernel. He was said to have sprung no fewer than fourteen SAVAK traps.[21] He was also the pride and hope of the whole guerrilla movement: as long as he was alive the movement was too. When SAVAK finally caught up with him on June 29, 1976, Iran's guerrilla movement also came to a crashing end.

* HAMID ASHRAF (1946-1976), born in Tehran; his father was a national railway employee; elementary school at Tabriz (1953-59); returned to Tehran for secondary schooling (1959-65); entered TU Technical Faculty (1966); joined budding Jazani-Zarifi group (1968); head of small 'communication team', linking the 'town' and 'mountain' teams (1970-71); co-founder of SCFKI (1971); supreme commander of SCFKI forces (1973-76); became Iran's most famous guerrilla; killed in a shoot-out on June 29, 1976 in the South Mihrabad district.

While the SCFKI's *Fada'yan* were being decimated in the war's front line, the SMKI's *mujahids* were still dormant. By August 1971, its leadership finally believed its organisation to be ready to spring into action. SAVAK, informed all along about SMKI by the traitor Dilfani, waited until the last minute; then, on August 23 and 24, 1971, it pounced on its unknowing prey and arrested some fifty SMKI members, including its three founders and some 90% of its officers.

The SMKI remnants (those guerrillas lucky enough not to have been in the mainstream, or to have safe hideouts) decided to carry on with the three operations planned by their leaders. All three failed. The first was the kidnapping of Princess Ashraf's eldest son Shahram in the centre of town; the guerrillas had managed Shahram into the getaway car, but their plan was foiled by a street urchin who grabbed the car's door handle and would not let go, shouting at the top of his voice. The guerrillas had to set their captive free in order to flee. The second operation had been a botched-up attempt at hijacking an air-taxi plane. The third one was to have been the bombing of the main Tehran Power station during the 2500th Anniversary festivities. A group of three Tehran Power Board employees, linked to the SMKI, were to assist Engineer Nasir Samavati in carrying out the explosion. However, on operation day, a simple policeman on duty at the power plant noticed Samavati's abnormal behaviour and alerted his superiors. Samavati and the three employees were arrested and handed over to SAVAK. It was rumoured that Samavati had withstood the worst tortures (even the flogging of his little daughter in front of him[21A]) without giving away his secrets. The Samavati incident prompted the government to have the *Majlis* vote a bill severely punishing terrorist actions against public installations and buildings, another bill to penalise arms smugglers (carrying a sentence of three to ten years) and a third bill stipulating the death penalty for drug smugglers (a few kilograms of opium could now legally justify any death).

By the close of 1971, only the professional SMKI guerrilla Ahmad Riza'i stood free. SAVAK had the brilliant idea of using his brother Riza Riza'i, captured in August, as bait. Riza played the game so well that in December 1971, using a public bath with a back door, he fled.[21B] Nevertheless SAVAK eventually caught up Ahmad Riza'i in his hideout on January 31, 1972, but, as the two SAVAK officers and two subalterns placed him in the SAVAK car, Riza'i exploded the two grenades hidden in his armpits and killed his four captors in his suicide action.

In May 1972, just prior to President Nixon's visit to Iran, the nine top SMKI leaders faced the firing squad, and were executed on May 19 (first four) and May 25 (last five). These included the three SMKI founding members – Sâid Muhsin (thirty-three-years old), Âli Asghar Badîzadigan (thirty-two) and Muhammad Hanifnizhad (thirty-four); and six major lieutenants, Âli Mihandoust (twenty-eight), Nasir Sadiq (twenty-eight), Mahmoud Bazargani (twenty-six), Âli Bakiri (twenty-nine), Âbd ul-Rasoul Mishkinfam (twenty-six) and Mahmoud Âskarizadeh (twenty-six). Âskarizadeh had been the brilliant head of the SMKI's counter-intelligence unit.[22] Of the nine young guerrillas, eight were graduates: five from the TUTF, two from the Karaj Agricultural School and one from the School of Commerce.

The SMKI was decapitated, but not totally out of action. On May 31, 1972, one of its teams placed a small bomb under the car of senior US ARMISH-MAAG officer, General Harold Price. The bomb went off severely wounding Price in the legs but failing to kill him. A month later the youngest Riza'i brother, twenty year old Mihdi Riza'i, was surrounded in the street by SAVAK agents; in self-defence he shot and killed Captain Javidmand, a crack SAVAK anti-terrorist expert, before his gun jammed and he was caught. SAVAK torturers exacted a bitter revenge on the young guerrilla for having killed Javidmand; after his trial and death sentence, they allegedly finished off Riza'i in a last torture session. On August 13, 1972, SMKI guerrillas shot dead the police general, Tahiri; the two guerrillas who had carried out this mission were later arrested and executed on January 11, 1973. In the autumn of 1972, three other prominent SMKI lieutenants were arrested: (1) Mahmoud Shamikhi, allegedly killed under torture; (2) Sayyid Kazim Zu'lanvar, a TU graduate, caught in 1971 but, having escaped from jail, became a prominent SMKI leader before being recaptured, and then directed his SMKI cells from within the prison; (3) Mustafa Javan Khushdil, the leading intermediary, on the SMKI side, with the religious groups – the SMKI being the sole underground group acceptable to radicals within the religious community.[23] According to SMKI reports, Khushdil was "the most tortured mujahid" (because of his precious information on contacts with religious opponents of the regime) and had allegedly challenged his torturers: "I know, but won't tell you".

By the close of 1972, the only remaining SMKI leader was Riza Riza'i.* He was to the *mujahids* what Hamid Ashraf was to the SCFKI. But, unfortunately for the SMKI, Riza'i lacked Ashraf's coolness under pressure and the latter's planning skills. Riza'i's last operation would be the execution of US officer Lieutenant-General. Hawkins (June 1973). A fortnight later, SAVAK (and its US advisers) caught up with him in his safe house. He jumped from a second-floor window, broke his leg in the fall and was shot dead by SAVAK sharpshooters. Thus ended the career of the last leader of SMKI's first wave.

* RIZA RIZA'I (1946–1973), born between brothers Ahmad and Mihdi; attended Tehran University's Dentistry Faculty (1965–69); joined SMKI (1968); left for Jordan with four other *mujahids*, for military training (1970); upon return promoted to SMKI Central Committee (1971); arrested (August 1971), escaped (December 1971); testified about SAVAK tortures to Western press (1972); masterminded assassination of US Lieutenant-Colonel Lewis G. Hawkins (June 1973); trapped and shot dead by SAVAK agents (June 15, 1973).

With the loss of its last leader, the SMKI entered a deep crisis. It still had a large reservoir of would-be guerrillas, but no leaders to organise them in the uneven battle against SAVAK. Even worse, the organisation lacked theoreticians, both on ideology and on warfare. In the summer of 1973, the very disciplined SMKI cells were standing as still as they could, waiting to see how the second-string leadership would weather the crisis, and who would eventually emerge to claim the overall leadership. In short, SMKI was up for grabs.

14.6. SAVAK's Ways and Means

Mistreatment of prisoners was as common in Persia as it was in other Eastern countries. But Persian gaolers were not especially renowned for their cruelty because, in serious cases, they would rather kill their victims. Under Reza Shah, the worst instrument available to the 'political police' was the *dastband-i qapuni* (handcuffing of the hands behind the back, one hand over the right shoulder and the other under left one) which caused terrible muscular pains; it was used on some of the '53 Group' members.

Torture as such in Iranian prisons began with the creation of SAVAK. In the late 1950s the first cases of using acids and heaters to burn suspects and to obtain information were reported.[24] In the 1960s, their methods became more and more sophisticated as the use of torture against Iran's first urban guerrillas became widespread: sleepless nights, lashing the soles of feet with electrical cables, cigarette burns on sensitive body parts, nail pulling and suspension by the hands or the feet.

In the 1970s, torture was turned into one of SAVAK's major weapons: it became a scientific and systematic means of obtaining information. For SAVAK torture had become a full-time job, with specially trained officers, extra-strong bullies (torture sessions were usually carried out by one officer – stipulated by regulations – and two or more strongmen), psychologists and doctors (to keep the suspect alive). A small group of officers and executioners would come to form the expert nucleus of SAVAK's chief tormentors, working directly under the supervision of anti-terrorist chief Parviz Sabiti. Among these were: Bizhan Niktab (an extremely vicious officer, executed in 1974 by a guerrilla action squad); Houshang Azqandi (a.k.a. Manouchihri); Muhammad Nuvid ('The Doctor'); Iraj Jahangiri; Assar ('Dr Javan'); Bahram Nadiripour (alias *'Tihrani'*); Firaydun Tavangari (*'Arash'*); Riza Âtapour (*'Azudi'*); the football star Humayoun Bihzadi; Husaynzadeh (*'Âta'i'*); the redoubtable gorilla-like Shâbani (*'Husayni'*); Kamalgar (*'Kamal'*); and also Suvati, Faraji, Mustafavi *inter alia*.[25]

SAVAK specialists had thoroughly studied the best methods for getting the fastest results in information extraction (bearing in mind the guerrillas' "first 24-hour protocol"); they had come to the conclusion that at first the suspect should be taken to the 'football room' where for a couple of hours half a dozen thugs would kick and hit him around (hence the room's name).[26] Now the groggy and totally disoriented suspect was ready for interrogation. The first phase consisted of the traditional means (leaving healable scars): sole flogging, cigarette burns, hanging of weights from parts of the body, nail pulling. The second phase was much harsher: the application of boiling water, or immersion in boiling oil, acid burns (especially on the penis), electrical shocks to sensitive parts, rapes with broken bottles or being forced to walk on broken glass. The third phase was reserved for the toughest guerrillas: it included the sending of boiling hot eggs up the prisoner's rectum (the tremendous amount of heat released internally destroying his internal organs, such as the liver and kidneys[26A]), the pressing of his head by a pressure-controlled apparatus (the one used on *Hujjat ul-Islam* Sâidi), and three sophisticated torture systems very dear to SAVAK specialists, who boasted of having 'invented' and 'perfected' them.

(1) The Heated Bed: a metallic bed which could be heated up electrically and on which the guerrilla was attached – with either his torso or his back touching the red-hot metallic surface. Engineer Âli Asghar Badîzadigan was allegedly attached for five hours to the bed, ending up half-paralysed; Masôud Ahmadzadeh also passed a few hours on the SAVAK bed, long enough to develop "large (9 inches long) scars on his torso and his back".[27]

(2) The Apollo: a metallic chair lengthened by a long table, heatable (like the bed), and in which the guerrilla was seated with his hands manacled to the arms and his stretched-out legs bound to the end of the table; thus, the guerrilla was entirely at the torturers' disposal for flogging, burning or electric shocks. The ultimate mark of ingenuity (and the source of the chair's name) was a heavy metallic hood that was placed over the guerrilla's head, causing the victim's screams to reverberate within his head, thereby multiplying his agony.

(3) The Cage: the guerrilla was placed in a small wire-mesh cage, only 150 centimetres high, so that he was forced into a hunched position, with his back squeezed against the ceiling's mesh; the floor was made of bricks that could be heated up, burning the victim's soles and sending him into a frenzy – the SAVAK specialists liked to watch the guerrilla 'dance'. The system, wired for high voltage, was mounted on a turning table: as it rotated, a wire extending from it touched a live connection every three seconds, sending electric shocks through the whole structure.[28]

Given these incredible means of inflicting pain, it is not surprising that many died, others were maimed, marked for life or went totally crazy. SAVAK thus destroyed the brains and the bodies of the best and the brightest among the guerrillas.

Many among them were never to be seen again; there is little doubt that some must have died (among others, the SCFKI's Bihrouz Dihqani and the SMKI's Mahmoud Shamikhi) in its torture rooms (some hearts resist less than others); and it was understandable that SAVAK "would not let live the ones it totally crippled", as one of its senior officers candidly told *Time Magazine*.[29] Some students not involved in the warfare suffered more heavily under torture, because, having no information to give, they could only shout their innocence, and among these some were mentally destroyed for life; SAVAK's lame excuses to their families did not bring them back to normal.[30]

If SAVAK's use of torture was systematic and yielded results, it was not the only iron in the fire. It also could count on the close co-operation of the armed forces, the police and the Gendarmerie through the *Kumiteh Mushtarak-i Zid-i Kharabkari* (the Joint Anti-Terrorist Committee) created in January 1972 to co-ordinate anti-guerrilla suppression nationwide.

All directives to public and private institutions and companies were channelled through the *Kumiteh*, which had in its different sub-committees representatives of all pertinent agencies and organisations.

The *Kumiteh*'s headquarters were in a four-storey high circular building situated in the centre of town. A highly sophisticated, state of the art communications systems connected it to the army, police and Gendarmerie HQs, and to the SAVAK main building in Sultanatabad. It was also linked with special action squads, patrolling the Tehran streets in groups of three men, with *carte blanche* to enter any premises, question anyone and arrest any suspect. The action squad members developed rapidly to include a total of some two hundred and fifty specialists selected from SAVAK or the armed forces, and trained in sharpshooting, car driving and the martial arts (with squad leaders attending training stints at Israel's renowned anti-terrorist school). With time, the action squads came to spearhead the regime's anti-terrorist efforts.

Suspects captured by the action squads were brought to the *Kumiteh*'s detention centre (small individual cells of 160 to 190 cms, where up to four guerrillas were detained in times of crisis – with only three of them sleeping at night lying down, and the fourth squatting next to the door[31]) and handed over to the prepared torture rooms (on the third floor). All night long (many torture sessions began at one or two in the morning) shouts and cries could be heard through the whole building, giving nightmares to all the inmates and further sapping their morale. The *Kumiteh* torturers, led by Niktab (before his execution) rivalled the Evin and Qizil Qalêh teams.

For the ones who survived the *Kumiteh*'s hell, the next step was incarceration, either in the Tehran detention centres of Qasr, Evin, Qizilqalêh or in provincial prisons such as those of Shiraz, Bushire or Khurramabad. In the prisons the struggle was pursued, albeit in other forms. Prisons were turned into universities and debating schools, as well as centres for the exchange of experiences of underground life. Every freed guerrilla was an experienced guerrilla ready to reintegrate into the underground. Information gathering was another major occupation.

Prison officers and guards were there to make life as hard as possible for the inmates. When the guards went too far, the prisoners' main weapon was the hunger strike, a general sacrifice that always placed the management in a difficult position for yielding was a negative action and a protracted strike was bad publicity. Most hunger strikes ended in a compromise, with the prisoners getting some of their grievances redressed and the management not losing face.

Prison propaganda by the freed prisoners was another of the guerrillas' weapons, keeping their image clean and virtuous, in contrast to SAVAK's vicious reputation. They went out of their way to report that all the guerrillas had fought like lions before being captured; that most of them had heroically borne the worst tortures – with the names of weaklings like Tavakkuli (who had revealed Amir Parviz Pouyan's address) or Manaf Falaki (who had betrayed the time and place of his rendezvous with Masôud Ahmadzadeh) simply and collectively blotted out of the guerrillas' popular legend. Traitors like Ardashir Davar, who had worked on the revival of the rural guerrilla campaign in Simnan province under the orders of Âbbas Miftahi and pioneered a SCFKI-SMKI *rapprochement* before trading his secrets to SAVAK for a sinecure in the Ministry of Economy, were turned into villains who had sold out to SAVAK. But the worst blow the guerrillas' well-kept image could suffer was the public recantation by former guerrillas on national television and radio, melodramatically staged by Sabiti. For the guerrilla such a TV appearance was the only unforgivable sin and each of them knew how detrimental these were to the guerrillas' public image. SAVAK was able to lure only a handful of insignificant opponents (with no former guerrilla willing to participate) to radio or televised conferences. In June 1971, it was Bahman Moulla'i Daryani, a former *Toudeh* member who had risen within the CISNU ranks in America before being expelled from that country (a very controversial individual); in December 1972, it was Dr Kuroush Lasha'i, a former *Toudeh* ideologue, whose sister, a painter, was employed at court; in 1975, it was Khalil Dizfuli, a minor SMKI turncoat. For Sabiti, it was a meagre result for years of efforts and a belated triumph for Iran's guerrilla's movement.

Nevertheless, the SMKI and the SCFKI, even in prison, were still rival organisations (a rivalry encouraged by SAVAK).

As the two groups' prime goal was similar, in prison cells the ideological debate went on. At the ideological level, the SMKI, with its Islamic ideology tainted with various hues of socialism, was at a marked disadvantage *vis-à-vis* the SCFKI's straightforward communist gospel. The SMKI was also inferior to the SCFKI in the leadership race because, behind bars, it lacked a leader of Bizhan Jazani's stature and, in the underground opposition, it had no one who could rival the legendary Hamid Ashraf. Whereas the leadership rivalry outside prison was academic (because of secrecy), in prison it was a highly important affair, because of its consequences to the mass of imprisoned guerrillas – estimated at around 2,000 to 2,500 in 1973. Hence, Jazani's role was gaining in importance daily.

Throughout all his prison days, Bizhan Jazani was indefatigable. Always somehow bolstering the spirit of his fellow detainees, he endeavoured not to let them gently sink into the torpor of prison routine. A master at sports and educational activities, he was the imprisoned guerrillas' uncontested leader.

He found time to paint (rather well), to think and to write. His thoughts were directed mostly to the guerrilla warfare he had helped launch: its successes, its failures and its future. By early 1973, he had arrived to the conclusion that guerrilla warfare, however successful, would not bring the movement to its ultimate revolutionary goal. In his view, the movement had failed in its "most important vocation which was to pave the way for the mobilisation of the masses".[32] He also held that the movement should "act as a detonator for the masses' revolution – not just foster unending terrorism", severely criticising "guerrilla leaders who put all their eggs in the armed struggle basket".[33] He had realised, from the relative quietness of his cell, that armed struggle was a blind alley, not the road to power. Consequently, he: (1) advocated smaller guerrilla teams, which were more homogeneous and therefore less at risk; (2) stressed constant ideological training for all group members; (3) urged the experienced guerrillas to "put down arms" and "focus on the formation of socio-political groups – involving the society's lower middle classes: teachers, minor employees, students, ... – in view of ultimately forming a political wing for the guerrilla movement"; (4) demanded the institution of "committees in foreign centres, to carrying out worldwide propaganda and formulate strategic planning, ...and publish well-written publications".[34]

In short, Jazani had perceived that it was time for the guerrillas' ship to change course: he had told his successors why and how. But for the guerrilla leaders, on the Tehran streets, always on their toes because of SAVAK's roving squads, that was difficult to see. With a continuous flow of students still trickling into the guerrilla ranks, the leaders had to manage day-to-day operations: urban guerrilla warfare had become their way of life, their very *raison d'être*. Jazani's timely vision and judicious advice would go unheeded. Another reason for this lack of response from the underground was the lesser quality of the leadership: more radical, more experienced in survival, but there were no more great theoreticians like Pouyan, leaders like Jazani, or great warriors like Safa'i Farahani and Ahmadzadeh.

Besides Hamid Ashraf, all the great guerrillas were either dead or in prison. Among those imprisoned, a small group had coalesced around Jazani, forming under his direction a nucleus of leadership. Among these individuals were six of Jazani's team members: his second in command Hasan Zia Zarifi, Âbbas Suriki, Mashôuf Kalantari, Âziz Sarmadi, Ahmad Jalil Afshar and Muhammad Chupanzadeh, in addition to two SMKI team leaders, Sayyid Kazim Zu'lanvar and Mustafa Javan Khushdil. SAVAK kept a close eye on all nine and rotated them among Iran's prisons, not giving them time to stay too long in a single prison and influence the other political prisoners – for example, the general hunger strike Âbbas Suriki had been able to organise at Shiraz's Âdilabad prison, which had to be broken up by elements of the Shiraz paratroopers division, or the actions of Zu'lanvar, who had provided SMKI teams with the addresses of Colonel Zamani (the abhorred guardian of Qasr Prison's political prisoners) and Zhyanpanah (a prison official), and ordered their executions (which were duly carried out).

During March and early April 1973, the top nine guerrilla prisoners were transferred to Evin Prison. Then, on the evening of April 18, 1973, they were taken together to the barren hills above the prison compound by a few SAVAK torturers and shot dead.[35] The next day, Tehran newspapers announced in a short official communiqué that nine prisoners had been shot dead while trying to escape from a bus during a prison transfer.

SAVAK had grown wary of Jazani's group's growing influence. They had been the guerrillas' natural leaders (except for Hamid Ashraf). In a fell swoop, SAVAK had cold-bloodedly eliminated the best and the brightest of those in the state prisons. For the guerrilla movement the loss was devastating. It had come to count on Jazani and his group as a safe reserve, as a future political elite. It would never really recover from the blow suffered on April 18, 1973; a deadly blow, but, as SAVAK used to say: "In wars, no candies".

14.7. Uneven Fight

Equally alarming to SAVAK was the fact that, besides the major SMKI and SCFKI groups, smaller groups and determined individuals were doing their best to enter the anti-regime struggle.

A smaller group of a dozen individuals, based on a core of five NIRT junior employees, entered the dangerous arena of anti-royalist conspiracy. It failed in its enterprise, but nevertheless made waves in Iranian society. The loose group of artists and civil servants planned the abduction of Empress Farah and Crown Prince Reza on the occasion of the Second International Film Festival, to be staged in November 1973 at Tehran. One of the group's members, Kiramatullah Danishyan,* was to provide the handgun for the kidnapping. A friend of his, Amir Fitanat, a former SCFKI guerrilla he had met in 1970 in prison, had told him that he would get him one. But Fitanat had turned his coat in prison and was thereafter on SAVAK's payroll – a blatant example of a guerrilla going over to the other side (not the only one to do so). Fitanat betrayed his friend; SAVAK was able to track the group's comings and goings, eventually arresting its eleven members (including Danishyan) in October 1973 before they were to carry out their planned kidnapping.

* KIRAMATULLAH DANISHYAN (1946–1974), son of a Shiraz Army NCO; after getting his diploma, studied at the Hotellerie School (1965), before switching to the NIRT-sponsored School for

Photography and Cinema (1966); directed movie *Doulatabad*, on one of Tehran's shanty towns (1966-67); school teacher at Masjid-i Sulayman (1967-69); arrested for anti-regime declarations, spent a full year in jail (1970); entered into a conspiracy with his former NIRT colleagues to kidnap the Empress and the Crown Prince but was arrested and court-martialled, and surprised everyone by his strong, anti-regime stand at the trial, sentenced to death (1973-74); executed, with poet Khusrou Gulisurkhi, on February 18, 1974.

There was no reason for the arrest of the NIRT group to make any waves: it was a minor rebellious spark which had occasioned no fire. But SAVAK pounced on the case, trying to turn it into a showcase of intellectuals participating in terrorist acts. Its ultimate goal was to embarrass the regime's liberal wing (under Empress Farah) which was directly opposed to its crude methods, and thus prove to the Shah that liberal bastions such as the NIRT (headed by the Empress's cousin Riza) and the *Kanoun-i Parvarish-i Fikri Koudakan va Noujavanan* (the Centre for Intellectual Development of Children and Youngsters), headed by Farah's close friend Lily Amir Arjumand, were dangerous liberal-communist nests nursing future terrorists. In order to increase the group's intellectual content, SAVAK added to it the famous, thirty-two year old poet Khusrou Gulisurkhi who had been arrested in spring 1973, and thus could not have been part to the conspiracy but fitted SAVAK's plan to hit various targets with one show trial. SAVAK had the court proceedings televised, with ten of the defenders recanting publicly, but Gulisurki and Danishyan defended the people and their Marxist-Leninist faith (their speeches were naturally not screened). The ten recanters were sentenced to long prison terms (three of them getting death, but granted a commutation to life by the Shah), while Gulisurkhi and Danishyan were sentenced to death and executed in February 1974, to the disbelief of the Iranian intellectual community, which had thought that the regime would not execute an innocent poet (although it knew SAVAK abhorred and feared poets most of all[35A]) and a sympathetic member of Iran's newly educated youth. In the process, SAVAK had scored a stunning victory against the liberals around the Empress. The price the regime had to pay for SAVAK's harsh ways was the alienation of intellectuals within the middle classes (who would not easily forget the gratuitous execution of one of their members) and also that of a large number of young, newly educated youngsters who later came to look on Danishyan as one of their heroes.

Another group of seven high school students planning to enter armed struggle was uncovered in the town of Nahavand by SAVAK. Based on Islamic ideology, the group had named itself *Abuzar*. Six of its members – the three brothers Âbdullah, Mashaûllah and Rouhullah Sayf, Âbdullah Khudarahmi, Bahman Manshat and *Hujjat* Âbduli – were executed at the Chitgar shooting range,[36] as a warning to all provincial amateurs to think twice before entering armed struggle. Only the group's leader, Mahmoud Talibian, escaped death, receiving a life sentence.

Yet another Islamic anti-regime group was set up by Shaykh Âli Andarzgou, the only 1965 escapee of the group who had staged Prime Minister Mansour's execution. Andarzgou's goal was to assassinate the Shah using a long-range rifle. Members of Andarzgou's small group were arrested before acting, and thereafter formed yet another entity in prison. A sub-branch of the group, under the command of Asadullah Lajivardi, attempted to fire-bomb the El Al (Israeli airline) office in Tehran in 1973, but failed, as its two-man squad was stopped before entering action: one was shot dead and the second one arrested. The whole Lajivardi cell (a dozen individuals with religious backgrounds) was rounded up by SAVAK and, after suffering the usual SAVAK tortures, (Lajivardi himself received the worst treatment and was left to bear the scars) were given long prison sentences, joining the small group of religious prisoners in the Shah's jails.

As for individuals and scattered groups who opposed the Shah's regime, there were many. Among these, two individuals are outstanding:

(1) Houshang Tizabi (1943–1974) in 1962 entered Tehran University's Medical School and joined the *Toudeh* Party; arrested in 1963 for his political activities, he was tortured and given a five-year sentence; freed in 1967, he began editing the clandestine *Toudeh* newspaper *Beh Sou-yi Hizb* (Towards the Party); disobeying party directives, which interdicted participation in the armed struggle (recommending instead the training and indoctrination of simple workers[36A]), he was disowned by the party; arrested and tortured, Tizabi was executed in June 1974; the *Toudeh* Party only recognised him as one of its heroes after the 1978/79 Revolution.

(2) Muhammad Riza Kamyabi (1954–1976), an exceptionally gifted student, finished seventh in the National University Entrance Examination (1972); entered Aryamihr Industrial University and finished at the head of his physics class (1976); while studying, had begun teaching in schools in southern Tehran, politicising his young pupils; in April 1976, SAVAK officers sent in to arrest him shot him dead.

Notwithstanding the smaller groups and individuals, the mainstream SMKI and SCFKI remained the guerrillas' major iron in the fire, as their active guerrillas still formed the large majority of the anti-regime underground. For a few months after Riza Riza'i's death, the SMKI was in limbo. But it had recovered in 1974, when a new leadership, consisting of Vahid Afrakhteh and his lieutenant Muhsin Khamoushi, emerged.

At first Afrakhteh's actions were crowned with success. SMKI execution squads first shot dead Gendarmerie NCO Hamzeh Mousavipour (June 28, 1974), then General Riza Zandipour, Sabiti's right-hand man at SAVAK, in the Office for Captured Terrorists (March 16, 1975).[37] By the spring of 1975, having secured a majority in SMKI's Central Committee, Afrakhteh whose sympathies had always been more leftist than Islamist, hijacked the organisation and squarely placed it under Marxist-Leninist ideology. The only snag hit by Afrakhteh was that two Central Committee members – Majid Sharif Vaqifi and Murtaza Samadiyyeh Labbaf – refused to shed their Islamic beliefs and even challenged the Central Committee's decision. A committee meeting to debate the question was set for May 6, 1975; Sharif Vaqifi arrived first and was killed there and then, his body being later dumped at Misgarabad and set on fire, making it unrecognisable. Samadiyyeh Labbaf arrived later, sensed the trap and fled, only to be caught two days later by SAVAK acting on a tip-off from Afrakhteh's men. In meetings with the SCFKI's Hamid Ashraf, Afrakhteh and Khamoushi had been advised by the SCFKI leader to compromise and run both SMKI's Marxist and Islamist branches in parallel. The SMKI leadership refused and decided to cut off its Islamist arm, severing all its relations with religious organisations and informing SAVAK of its religious branches, among others one of its main contacts with the religious groups at Qum – Âli Akbar Hashimi Rafsanjani. The latter was caught, tortured and jailed.

Following this internal struggle, Afrakhteh decided to deliver a master blow: in the early morning of May 21, one of his top SMKI hit squads blocked the car of two US Army officers, Colonel Paul Shaffer and Lieutenant-Colonel Jack Turner, and shot both of them dead, sparing the life of their Iranian chauffeur. For the new SMKI, this was indubitably the coup that placed the group at the forefront of guerrilla activities in Iran. Its next strike fell on July 3, when an Iranian translator at the US Embassy by the name of Hasan Husnan was shot and killed – Tehran newspapers hailed the execution as a mistake, but guerrillas seldom take the risk of killing the wrong man (Husnan was probably engaged in some covert activity).

In any event, Husnan was to be Afrakhteh's last victim, for, by the end of July, the SMKI leader was arrested in Tehran by SAVAK along with six of his top lieutenants, including his right-hand man, Khamoushi; at Tabriz, Dr Murtaza Labbafinizhad was also caught. In the autumn of 1975, the eleven members of the new SMKI leadership were court-martialled: nine received death sentences and two prison sentences – namely Mihdi Ghayouran (life) and Tahireh Sajjadi Tihrani (fifteen years). On January 24, 1976, the nine SMKI leaders were executed by firing squad: Vahid Afrakhteh; Muhsin Khamoushi; Muhammad Tahir Rahimi; Murtaza Labbafinizhad; Muhsin Bata'i; Sasan Samimi; Âbd ul-Riza Muniri Javid; Murtaza Samadiyyeh Labbaf and Manizheh Afsarzadeh (one of the few women to face a firing squad).

If Afrakhteh's tenure at the head of SMKI had barely lasted three months, his short time at the top was to leave a durable impact on the guerrilla organisation. While he and his co-defendants were being tried, SMKI published a 250-page leaflet entitled *Bayaniyyeh Îlam-i Mavazeh-yi Idehuluzhik-i Sazman-i Mujahidin Khalq-i Iran* (Pamphlet Announcing the SMKI's Ideological Line). It was an attempt at justifying the organisation's sharp ideological turn to the left. Simultaneously, the organisation published another booklet with marked socialistic tendencies: the *Juzveh Sabz-i Amuzishi* (Green Training Booklet). Islamic elements within the organisation (for there were still some, especially in the lower layers) were taken aback by the ruthless leftist hijack of the organisation. The SMKI being a highly disciplined organisation, most members followed the new directives, some even under the threat of death.[37A]

For the ones unable to cope, one of the alternatives was a link-up with the religious movement. They knew that its leader, Ayatullah Khomeini, was in Najaf. They went there. After a few weeks of indirect contacts, Khomeini refused to receive the SMKI's breakaway fraction, and the latter returned empty-handed to Iran. But the comings and goings had the Tehran *Bazaar* on tenterhooks and they decided to clarify the situation by putting a written question on SMKI to Khomeini at Najaf. The latter's reply in June 1977 was clear: he "never had any links to any Marxist or pseudo-Marxist groups and never would have, ...as, anyway, these groups were against Islam".[38]

Before Khomeini's official rejection of their group, the SMKI delivered its last punch in August 1976. On the 28th, the car of three American employees of Rockwell International (an American multinational corporation widely believed to be involved in a master scheme for tapping Tehran's telephones – a pet SAVAK project) was ambushed in the Tehran streets and all three Americans shot dead by a SMKI squad led by Bahram Aram and consisting of Hasan Aladpoush and Mir Mihdi Mirsadiqi. The story behind the killings was reported as follows by an Israeli diplomat:

> The terrorist group was really after just one of the men – a CIA Major who had landed in Iran about fourteen hours before the killing, ostensibly with a complete scheme for tapping Tehran's telephone lines. The other two people were shot for drawing revolvers...

His American interlocutor (a political officer), however, denied the story, calling it "an obvious propaganda attempt".[39]

The American-backed SAVAK was quick in catching up with Aladpoush and Mirsadiqi and shooting both dead in October 1975. A few days later Aladpoush's sister Surour was arrested.

During 1976 SAVAK mercilessly hunted down the remaining SMKI cells and shoot its members dead. Layla Zumurrudian was gunned down in January 1976. Aladpoush's wife, Mahboubeh Muttahidin,[40] and her team-mate were next in February. In October 1976, a number of guerrillas were shot dead: Nargis Qajar Âzudanlou (the sister of future SMKI leader Maryam); Parviz Davoudi; Touraj Haydari, Mujtaba Aladpoush (Hasan's brother); Âli Riza Ulfat;

Simintaj Jariri; and Akram Sadiqipour. In November it was Bahram Aram's turn to die fighting. In December 1976, safe houses belonging to the Cuban-trained group *Parviz Vaîzzadeh* were destroyed, resulting in nine dead guerrillas and eleven arrests. Then, during 1977, the shoot-outs gradually subsided. In February 1977, Masoumeh Tavafchyan, Mahvash Jasimi, Âli Akbar Nabavi Nouri, Bahman Amir Davani and Saba Bizhanzadeh were killed. The last major SMKI underground leader, Ahmad Ahmad, was captured in March 1977. One of the last major battles of the Iranian civil war occurred on May 16, 1977, when two safe houses were assaulted, resulting in the death of all the guerrillas inside but not before they had shot dead seven SAVAK officers.

With guerrillas like Aram and Aladpoush, the Islamists gradually regained control of the SMKI. In 1977, the group's left wing decided to break away, giving birth to a new faction: the *Sazman-i Paykar dar Rah-i Azadi-i Tabaqeh-yi Kargar* (Organisation Struggling for the Liberty of the Proletarian Class) or simply *Paykar* (Struggle). But although the Islamists seemed to have won the last round, their final ideology was still blurred, with socialist ideas and ideals still blossoming among its economic programme. The regime was correct in denouncing the Marxist-Islamists as a common denominator of the Red and Black conspiracy arrayed against it. The SMKI kept its options open by building on both Islam and Marxism, without ever being to draw a line between the two: this ideological indecision was to form its perennial Achilles' heel. And as long as the SMKI failed to straighten out its ideology, it stood little chance of appealing to the Iranian masses, which would always choose Islam over any of its red-tainted amalgams.

The SMKI's rival, the SCFKI, had ideological or leadership problems: Marxist-Leninism and Hamid Ashraf were still in place. While building up his organisation, Ashraf had not shunned action and chosen his targets from amongst the most unpopular individuals in Iran, namely:

– Captain Yadullah Nourouzi, the brutal head of the Aryamihr University guardsmen, was shot dead in March 1974.

– Muhammad Sadiq Fateh, the family's patriarch and founder of its Jahan industrial empire, was machine-gunned on August 11, 1974 on the Tehran–Karaj highway, in reprisal for the twelve

Jahan Chit workers shot down in April 1971 on the same highway, while on a protest march to Tehran.
- SAVAK Captain Bizhan Niktab, the abhorred Kumiteh torturer, was killed in December 1974.
- The traitor Âbbas Shariari (a.k.a. 'Islami') was killed for betraying dozens of guerrillas to SAVAK, in March 1975.
- Husayn Nahidi, SAVAK's chief torturer in Mashhad, was assassinated in February 1976.

Like SMKI, SCFKI had had to face SAVAK's new anti-guerrilla strategy of 'search and destroy' since early 1975. By then, SAVAK's statistics had shown that the odds for a freed guerrilla returning to the underground with considerably more experience were overwhelming. General Nasiri was ordered to simply blot them out instead of repressing them, a dead guerrilla being far better than a captured guerrilla (with just the drawback of lost information potential). For doing the job, SAVAK had its sharpshooters, its anti-terrorist experts and its explosives specialists (e.g. Jalil Sadr Isfahani). Woe to the captured guerrilla, for, if by some miracle he came out alive from the torture sessions (geared to get rid of him), he would eventually be disposed of. From 1975, SAVAK was unwilling to keep guerrillas alive.

In 1975, SCFKI's safe houses fell one after the other. Five of them located at Qazvin, Karaj, Isfahan, Tabriz and Tehran fell in quick succession. The final score was fifteen guerrillas killed, two seriously wounded and two captured alive.

But Hamid Ashraf continued to evade and nag SAVAK during 1975, continuously adding to his flourishing legend. It was only in June 1976 that SAVAK would deliver the *coup de grâce* to SCFKI: within ten days, twenty *Fada'i* would be killed. The bloodbath began on June 21, when two trapped guerrillas, Âli Rahimi Âliabadi and Husayn Mousavi Doustmuchali, were shot dead. Two days later another, Nastaran Al-i Aqa, was killed in a shoot-out (the guerrillas, knowing of SAVAK's new 'search and destroy' tactic, preferred to fight it out, rather than be mown down after surrendering). On June 28, Maryam Shahi was shot dead. Then, on the same evening, SAVAK surrounded a SFCKI safe house in the South Mihrabad district, where a meeting of the group's leaders was to take place. In the early morning hours of June 29, SAVAK initiated its assault on the house, the uneven fight lasting for four hours, but the final blow was allegedly dealt by RPG-7 rocket-launchers. In the house, the assailants found the body of Hamid Ashraf and nine of his team leaders: Muhammad Husayn Haqnavaz; Muhammad Mihdi Fuqani; Yunis Qanîkhushkeh Bijari; Ghulam Riza Layiq Mihrabani; Ghulam Âli Khuratpour; Âli Akbar Vaziri; Muhammad Yasribi; Fatimeh Husayni; and Tahireh Khurram. On June 30 and July 1st, five other SCFKI members were killed in shoot-outs (mostly beginning in the early hours and lasting until dawn – usually finished off with a RPG-7 charge): Hamid Aryan; Nadireh Ahmad Hashimi; Afsar ul-Saâdat Hasani; and Simin Tavakkuli.

So SAVAK had finally caught up with Hamid Ashraf, 'Iran's most wanted man' since 1971, who had spent some eight and half years in hiding. As the people refused to believe that their hero had finally been destroyed, SAVAK was compelled to publish the picture of his dead body in the newspapers[41] (like Guevara's): there was no doubt that it was Hamid Ashraf. Without its Scarlet Pimpernel, Iran's guerrilla movement stood headless. The next generation of Jazanis and Ashrafs was in the making, but it would take a few years for them to become far more radical and go deeper underground to make their own mark. But with Ashraf's death, it was a whole glorious chapter of Iran's guerrilla movement that was closed.

Thereafter, every two months or so, a morning shoot-out told Tehranis that another guerrilla safe house was being besieged by SAVAK forces. But guerrilla activities had almost become extinct. "At the onset of 1977", the Shah recollected in his memoirs," something surprising happened: terrorist acts abruptly stopped".[42]

14.8. The Guerrillas' Legacy

SAVAK seemed to have won the unequal war pitting it against the SMKI and SCFKI guerrillas. The mini civil war waged by a small number of guerrillas (never more than five hundred active ones at any given time) had never risked spilling over into general disorder. However, these activists had always been a thorn in the regime's side, with the Shah declaring in 1975 to a *New York Times* reporter: "...the terrorists are the only negative factor in Iran".[43]

There were, however, ominous parallels between the Iranian guerrillas and their no less famous predecessors in Algeria. Same methods, same tortures, same shoot-outs, practically the same heroes, Algeria's Scarlet Pimpernel being Amara Âli (a.k.a. 'Âli la Pointe'). After the blowing up of Âli's safe house in the *kasbah*'s Abderames Street (no. 5) on October 7, 1957, terrorism in Algiers was virtually brought to a standstill. Two years after his death, the first popular explosion occurred in Algiers. Now, in Iran's parallel case, adding two years to Hamid Ashraf's demise, one would get 1978.

The SMKI and SCFKI guerrillas might well have lost the war but they had left their mark, both domestically and internationally. In Iran, the two organisations had triggered off new ideas and ideals in the minds of the masses and thereby developed deep roots in the urban middle classes, which recognised them as their heroes and champions, as their worthy leaders, as their elite. They had earned the unwilling admiration of all classes, even the ruling royalist elite, with their sense of self-sacrifice, their stark courage and their heroic resistance. The exploits of their leaders had clearly overshadowed all the betrayals, weaknesses and failures. What remained in the hearts and minds of the people were the legends, especially those of Bizhan Jazani, the Syahkal group, the Riza'is and Hamid Ashraf.

During their mini war, the guerrillas had lost their best and brightest. Officially, the number of political opponents executed (a large majority of guerrillas) during Premier Huvayda's tenure (1965–1977) stood at around five hundred and fifty individuals (half as many again should be added for those who were killed in shoot-outs and for those who 'disappeared'). Their average age was computed to be twenty-four years old and roughly 80% of them were students.[44] The quantitative loss was, however, not in proportion to the qualitative loss: Iran's elite would have to wait a long time to witness the likes of Jazani and Ashraf. They were the results of three interlinked, unique events: (1) the bitterness of the popular defeat of *Murdad 28*; (2) a unhealthy, stagnant polity, dominated by the Shah (due to his unshakeable American support); and (3) an unprecedented economic boom (giving a large majority the basic means of subsistence).

The guerrillas, through their trials and tortures, had attracted the attention of international organisations, especially those dealing with human rights.[45]

But the most damning document to date had been the Amnesty International (AI) Report published in November 1976, which had compiled and documented SAVAK's total disregard for human rights and human life. Since the early 1970s, the AI had become the Shah's *bête noire*, for its officers could not be bought (like captains of industry or foreign reporters) – they had to be vilified. "They are Communists", the Shah told F. Huvayda back in 1970.[46]

The guerrillas might have lost the war on the ground but they had won morally: in the eyes of public opinion (whether domestic or abroad) they had defeated SAVAK. The Shah's elite, hiding behind SAVAK's muscular back, had hinted at a single solution: brutal repression – although Qavam ul-Saltaneh had warned them (back in 1950) that such a solution is not viable in the long term. A sclerosed elite had not bothered to try any strategy *vis-à-vis* the guerrillas' menace: it had sown violence in its prisons, on its campuses, in the streets and it could reap only violence.

If the guerrillas had won morally, they were incapable of turning their victory into power, as the FNL had done in Algeria. They lacked political experience and vision.

In the end, they were the forerunners of a new model for Iranian youth: ascetic, spirited, valiant, resilient, motivated and ambitious. With these assets they had won the minds and hearts of the next generation. When the latter tried to emulate its heroes, it would bring about a revolution.

NOTES

1. *Petroleum Intelligence Weekly*, April 12, 1982, p.11.
2. J.B. Kelly, *Arabia, the Gulf and the West* (London: Weidenfeld and Nicholson, 1980) p.356.
3. *The International Oil Industry Through the 1960s*, report issued by the US State Department, December 1971, p.80.
4. Ibid., p.24.
5. J.B. Kelly, op. cit. (note 2), p.353.
6. Ibid., p.338.
7. *Iran Trade and Industry* magazine, April-May 1971, p.31.
8. The renowned Iranian painter and calligrapher Riza Mafi had drawn his 'Syahkal' tableau (roughly 150 x 90cms.) in 1971 with thousands of Farsi letters depicting trees. Some of his Farsi Kaf Alif combinations were immeasurably large. I asked him why the empty spaces were so large during a visit to his house in 1979 (a week before his untimely death). He replied: "Oh! These are the eyes of the guerrillas looking out for the enemy!" The tableau had naturally never been for sale: it was the only piece of his own art Mafi kept for himself!
9. *Iran Almanac 1971* (Tehran: Echo of Iran, 1971) p.52.
10. See article by Sam White in *The Evening Standard*, October 15, 1971, p.17.

11 R. Vincent, 'Un Nouveau Camp du Drap d'Or', in *France-Soir*, April 2, 1971.
12 See article in *Le Monde*, September 7, 1971, extensively quoting Jacques Rolland's leader.
13 See article by Sam White, article cit. (note 10).
14 J.B. Kelly, op. cit. (note 2), p.504.
15 See W.D. Swearingen, 'Sources of Conflict over Oil in the Persian/Arabian Gulf', *The Middle East Journal*, Vol. 35, no. 3, summer 1981, p.329.
16 G. Sick, *All Fall Down* (New York: Random House, 1985) p.14.
17 *The Economist*, March 6, 1971, p.34.
17A *The Middle East: Oil, Conflict and Hope*, ed. by A.L. Udovitch, (Lexington Books, 1976) p.453.
18 J.B. Kelly, op. cit. (note 2), p.340.
19 The following anecdote will reveal the state of relations at TU: An old economics professor (from the Shah's elite) asked his students: "What would you do, that we are not already doing, if you were in power?" One of his students replied: "First we would have all professors like you executed by a firing squad!" (Private communication to the author by the student in question, a diplomat under the Islamic Republic).
19A Ashraf Dihqani recalled her brother's death (Bihrouz) in her memoirs, *Hamaseh Maqavamat* (The Apogee of Resistance), (Tehran: Mardum, undated) pp.80-4. Her book was also translated into English, under the title *Torture and Resistance in Iran* (London: Iran Committee Publication, 1977).
20 Ibid., Dihqani recalls her tortures, and the introduction of snakes into her cell to frighten her (she threw the snakes out), and of her escape in March 25, 1973 amidst a group of mothers who had come to visit the political prisoners at Qasr prison for the New Year.
21 Rumours and hearsay on Hamid Ashraf's exploits were endless; everyone in Tehran's younger generation had his own anecdote on his legendary brushes with SAVAK. Here are a sample, confirmed by various sources:
(1) Ashraf had a rendezvous with a subordinate in front of Cinema Empire on Pahlavi Avenue. Acting on information from its torture rooms, SAVAK was there in force. Ashraf noticed that something was wrong and hurriedly entered the cinema, with the agents on his heels. For hours the whole block was searched. In vain, for Ashraf had vanished into thin air.
(2) SAVAK surrounded a safe house where Ashraf was supposed to meet some subordinates. When the shoot-out ended, SAVAK found a number of dead guerrillas but not Ashraf.
(3) SAVAK set a trap in Muhsini Square on Mirdamad Avenue. Ashraf was able to break free in his car, shooting two top SAVAK officers in the process, one of whom remained crippled for life.
Another anecdote revealing SAVAK's nervousness (not to say obsession) *vis-à-vis* the famous guerrilla is the true story of student Hamid Ashraf (no relation to the guerrilla) who, while returning from America to Iran through Mihrabad Airport, was arrested by SAVAK and questioned for twenty-four hours (but no torture was used) before he could prove that he was not the guerrilla for whom they were looking (private communication).
21A Private communication from a political prisoner close to Samavati.
21B Riza Riza'i 's escape was related in *Le Monde* of February 12 and 17, 1972.

[22] Âskarizadeh's counter-intelligence unit filed reports on dozens of top SAVAK officers, because it wanted to wage a systematic and direct war against the top SAVAK echelon.

[23] See M. Alviri, 'Hasan Misaq-i Fallah', in *Kayhan-i Farhangi*, no. 6, Shahrivar 1365 (September 1986), p.41. Many religious radicals flirted with SMKI during the early 1970s, providing it with financial and logistical assistance. The honeymoon came to an end in 1975/76.

[24] B. Niroumand, *The New Imperialism in Action* (New York: Modern Reader Paperback, 1969).

[25] Among many others, see *Le Monde*, February 12, 1972., and *L'Express* magazine, no. 1077, February 28-March 5, 1972, p.49.

[26] *Dar Vietnam* (no author, no publisher, no date) p.3. One of the stencilled books on sale in 1978 in Tehran streets; probably compiled by former guerrillas with experience of SAVAK tortures and internment; the best source on the subject.

[26A] See R. Savin, *Vakil Abad Ira* (Edinburgh: Canongate/QPress, 1979).

[27] F. Halliday, *Iran: Dictatorship and Development* (Penguin Books, 1979) p.87. See also *Le Monde*, February 24, 1972.

[28] See the memoirs of a guerrilla who has been in 'The Cage', in *Keyhan International*, January 23, 1979, p.2.

[29] See *Time Magazine*, February 19, 1979, p.18. In an interview with D.S. Jackson, SAVAK's number two man confided that: "...we could easily have got rid of him. We would not have let him live as a document of torture"; thereby implying that SAVAK normally got rid of any "document of torture".

[30] Private communication from a Yazdi family whose son was among the innocent victims. The youngster was turned into a vegetable by SAVAK. Any report of the blunder was strictly prohibited. The usual excuses were presented to the family: "It had been a terrible mistake. They had thought him to be a leader. They were terribly sorry, but these things happen, unfortunately".

[31] Private communication from a former *Kumiteh* inmate.

[32] B. Jazani, *Chiguneh Mubarizeh Musalahaneh Toudeh'i Mishavad?* (How Will the Armed Struggle Turn into Mass Struggle?) (Tehran: Mazyar, 1358 (1959)) p.57.

[33] Ibid., pp.38-39.

[34] Ibid., pp.20-24.

[35] In the post-Revolution trials of captured SAVAK torturers Bahram Nadiripour (alias 'Tihrani') declared in court that he had been one of the execution squad in charge of shooting the nine guerrillas dead, using Uzi light machine-guns.

[35A] Poets were SAVAK's nemesis. Wherever the secret police uncovered an opposition poet, it went out of its way to either buy him off or silence him.

[36] The Chitgar shooting range, situated west of Tehran, in the wilderness of the Alburz mountain foothills, was a regular army practice range, used for the executions of regime opponents and guerrillas. In 1980, five wooden stakes were still to be seen in the midst of the site's wilderness. Bullet holes could be seen in the wooden posts.

[37] SMKI squad leader on this occasion was Murtaza Samadiyyeh Labbaf. Zandipour's chauffeur, Asadullah Utufi, was also shot dead in the process.

[37A] See the memoirs of Tahireh Baqirzadeh, a damning condemnation of the SMKI's ways by a long-standing member. Being basically from a religious background, she especially suffered during the forced turn to the left of the mid-1970s: T.

Baqirzadeh, *Qudrat va digar hiych* (Power and Nothing else), (Tehran: Ittilaât, 1372 (1993)) pp.39-46.

38 *Payam-i Inqilab* (The Revolution's Message), a collection of Ayatullah Khomeini's speeches and communiqués, (Tehran: Payam-i Azadi, 1360 (1981)) Vol. I, p.167.

39 *Asnad-i Laneh-yi Jasousi*, no. 11, p.37.

40 A twenty-seven year old teacher in the south Tehran area, Muttahidin met Aladpoush in 1971 while attending Dr Shariâti's lectures. In 1972, the two married, with their professor attending. Muttahidin was extremely popular in the poor quarters of south Tehran.

41 On July 3, 1976, *Kayhan* newspaper also mentioned a letter found in Ashraf's hideout, from the Palestinian (FPLP) leader George Habash, dated February 4, 1976, and congratulating Ashraf on the fifth anniversary of the historic uprising at Syahkal.

42 M.R. Pahlavi, *Réponses à l'Histoire*, (Paris: Albin Michel, 1979)   p.220.

43 See *The New York Times*, October 5, 1975.

44 *Islamic Revolution* magazine, May 1979, Vol. 1, no. 2, p.3.

45 Besides the prominent AI, there were also a number of humanitarian organisations and individuals: (1) Le Comité de Défense des Prisonniers Politiques Iraniens, based in Paris, supported by Jean-Paul Sartre, Vladimir Jankelevitch (its president), Jean Rostand, Simone de Beauvoir, Louis Aragon, Jacques Madaule, Rezvani and many other French personalities. See *Le Monde*, December 22, 1971 and May 11, 1972; and *Le Nouvel Observateur*, March 6–12, 1972, the damning article by author Rezvani: *Un trône rouge de sang*. (2) La Ligue Suisse des Droits de l'Homme, under Marie-Louise Dumuid. (3) The International Association of Jurists, with Me Christian Bourguet, Me Thierry Mignon, Me Dr Heinz Heldmann, Me Nouri Albala, Me Henri Libertalis and Me Christian Grobet, among others. (4) Individuals, prominent among whom stood Lord Bertrand Russell. The decisive engagement of all these great personalities was a real moral support for Iran's political prisoners.

46 F. Hoveyda, *The Fall of the Shah* (New York: Wyndham Books, 1980) p.110.

CHAPTER FIFTEEN: PETRODOLLARS

After the momentous winds of change during 1971 and the 'participation' wave of 1972, the international oil industry was trying to regain some form of stability. It was then, towards the close of 1972, that the question of the Iranian Consortium's future popped up on Iran's oil agenda. With only seven years left until the 1979 *terminus ad quem*, the time was ripe for reviewing their options. During secret meetings between the Shah and Consortium representatives in Tehran and Kish Island, the Iranian proposal for scrapping the Consortium Agreement and replacing it with a twenty-year crude oil sales agreement was discussed. The new sales proposal killed two birds with one stone: it gave Iran full *de jure* ownership of its oil industry (not merely *de facto*), and simultaneously provided for a thirteen year extension of the former agreement (without saying so). In January 1973, the Iranian proposal hit the Tehran newspaper headlines. The American and British reactions to it were totally dissimilar: the former held that such a move was premature as the Consortium had another seven years of life before utilising the three five-year extensions, whereas the latter was rather favourable to it, with the proviso that Iran should be flexible on some of its points. In January 23, 1973, at one of the press conferences he relished, the Shah sent an ultimatum to the Consortium members, saying that:

> There are two courses of action open to us. [Either the Consortium companies] continue their operations for the next six years, up to 1979, ...[and then] stand in a long queue to buy Iran's oil, with no privilege over the other customers. [Or they] return to Iran all responsibilities not at present in Iran's hands, ...[and stand] to become a long-term customer...[1]

There was an attitude of arrogance towards the Consortium which had not been there before: the Shah saw himself as the new sole ruler, tending to forget that he owed his throne and his immense fortune to the Consortium companies. The final round of negotiations took place at St. Moritz, during the Shah's winter vacation, on February 26,

1973. The next day a short communiqué announced that the Shah and the companies' representatives had reached an overall understanding regarding the framework of the new twenty year crude sales agreement.

15.1. Oil Bonanza

To hammer out the new agreement details with the consortium's executives, Dr Iqbal went to London in March 1973, at the head of a high-powered NIOC delegation. Two months later the new Twenty-Year Crude Oil Sales and Purchase Agreement was ready and duly signed on May 24, 1973 by the NIOC and Consortium representatives – with an effective date of March 21, 1973. The agreement was ratified by the *Majlis* and the Senate on July 24 and 30 respectively. Put in a nutshell, the new agreement provided for the following:[2]

– Total ownership of the oil industry and management of oil resources to rest with Iran;

– All of the industry's fresh capital requirements and operating funds were to come from NIOC;

– The consortium's subsidiaries hitherto operating Iran's oil industry were to be replaced by a single, private and non-profit-making organisation, the Oil Service Company of Iran (OSCO), in charge of assisting NIOC technically in exploration and exploitation.

– NIOC was to export on its own state quantities of crude oil: from an initial 200,000 b/d in 1973 to a maximum of 1,500,000 b/d from 1981 onwards.

– On October 1st of each year, Consortium members would inform NIOC of their crude oil requirements and their refined quantities at Abadan Refinery (up to a maximum of 300,000 b/d).

– All domestic LPG consumption was to come from the products of the Bandar-i Mahshahr plant; the surplus was to be sold at cost to the Consortium companies, which would in turn pay back 55% of profits realised to NIOC.

The Shah exulted over the deal, believing that he had finally realised Dr Musaddiq's dream of Iranian ownership over her own oil resources. In fact, and no one was duped, it was the Consortium which had scored a fantastic victory, disengaging itself from Iran, but retaining full control through OSCO, passing all the burden of effort and expense to NIOC. In the wake of the new agreement, Iran's overall oil strategy for the next twenty years (1973-1993) also came to light when Dr Riza Fallah, NIOC's deputy chairman and director for International Affairs, unveiled the production levels for the next two decades: Iran would produce some 42.5 billion barrels of crude oil, which would be divided as follows: (1) sales to the Consortium companies - 29.3bn barrels; (2) to the domestic market - 6.0bn barrels; and (3) on exports by NIOC - 7.2bn barrels.[3] Iran's oil production would peak at 7.6m b/d for eight years (1977-1984) and dwindle gradually thereafter to 1.5m b/d in 1994 - then barely enough to satisfy internal consumption. The picture drawn by Fallah meant that over the next twenty years Iran would extract all the oil it could and totally disregard future requirements; it all sounded it a bit like 'Après moi, le deluge', to paraphrase Madame de Pompadour. Seeing the plan for the first time, some of the junior NIOC managers were flabbergasted (to say the least); they thought the Fallah scheme (the company's official credo) was highly questionable, and their first question to the top management was roughly this: would not a slower rate of extraction maximise Iran's gains and allow for a longer and smoother period of production? As usual, they found a way to channel their questions to the top, but they never received an answer.

Then, in 1972, the report 'The Limits to Growth' was published by the Club of Rome.[4] The project, which covered the simulation of future world scenarios for planetary development, using a dynamic model developed by Professor Jay W. Forrester of MIT, was a joint European-American effort, headed by Dennis L. and Donella H. Meadows, and launched with a $200,000 grant from the Volkswagen Foundation. Its results had the effects of a bombshell:[5] put simply, the report concluded that, if the planet carried on at its present rate of economic development, it would face sever shortages and catastrophes during the twenty-first century. Due to these results, The Club of Rome warned against "irresponsible exploitation of natural resources" and proposed "a new planetary equilibrium".

Extrapolating the Club's caveats, analysts came to the conclusion that the only way to control growth was to limit resources and this could only be done by raising prices.

Furthermore, world energy consumption was going through the roof, fuelled as it was by cheap raw material prices e.g. crude oil at around $2 per barrel, which was about half the price it was in 1950 ($1.50 per barrel) if deflated to 1950 dollars.

World crude oil consumption had increased by leaps and bounds from 1938 onwards (see Table 15.1): doubling during the 1940s, doubling again during the 1950s and more than doubling during the sixties to reach 47.7 million b/d in 1970. In the seventies, the rapid pace of the late sixties failed to abate and still roughly three million b/d were being annually added to worldwide consumption, so that by 1973 another 9 million b/d had been added, to yield a total consumption of 56.8 million b/d. Such a trend could not go on. Especially now that the third industrial revolution (i.e. electronics, robotics, bioengineering) was knocking at the door, and, with these extra-cheap energy prices, the heavy sectors of the second industrial wave (such as the automobile, steel and chemicals industries) would not give way. Moreover, the two main players in the oil business – the Seven Sisters and OPEC – stood to increase their profits and rents in case of a price hike. So why should they stand in the way of a revolution that the brains of the industrial world had found necessary for the planet's future?

Table 15.1. Worldwide Crude Oil Consumption and Percentage of Oil in Total Energy Consumption – for selected years between 1938 and 1970.[6]

Year	Worldwide Crude Oil Consumption (b/d)	Approximate % of Crude Oil in Energy Consumption
1938	5,600,000	22
1950	10,890,000	28
1955	16,190,000	31
1960	21,980,000	34
1965	31,740,000	37
1970	47,740,000	44

The winter of 1972/73 was particularly cold in the USA and, for the first time since the 1940s, American schools and factories had to "close down for lack of heating oil".[7] But even these imbalances between supply and demand in the world's largest petroleum products market failed to trigger off the avalanche every analyst was excepting. The crunch came on October 6, 1973 when President Sadat of Egypt declared war on Israel. On October 8, the six OPEC Gulf states meeting the oil companies in Vienna asked for a rise in the posted price of around $2 per barrel, but the companies balked and countered by offering $0.25 per barrel. The talks broke down. A week later, the Gulf states' representatives meeting at Kuwait unilaterally raised the marker crude (Arabian Light) posted price from $3.01 to $5.11 per barrel[8] – which translated into a posted price of $5.34 for Iranian Light crude. This was a revolution: for the first time in history a group of exporters had decided upon a new price and boldly gone ahead with it; the steep increase of 70% was also revolutionary.

Two weeks after the beginning of the Israeli-Egypt war, Arab oil exporters decided on October 19 and 20 to stop crude oil exports to the US, South Africa, the Netherlands and other Israeli allies. This oil embargo further dramatised the oil supply picture of Western countries, especially because, this time round, the US had "no surplus to meet the shortfalls".[9] A small drop of only ten per cent in worldwide oil production was enough to bring havoc to the markets. The West had been caught off guard and it took the oil-consuming nations time to concert their strategies – the lack of preparedness and the gap in co-ordination would later be remedied with the creation in September 1974 of the International Energy Agency (IEA) which regrouped the major Western crude oil importers. The extent of oil consumers' panic was brought to light in December 1973 when NIOC announced the results of its oil exports auction conducted in November: the company received bids as high as $16.00/b for its Heavy and $17.34/b for its Light crude. There was indubitably an abyss between the posted price and what the market was ready to bear.

At the December 22, 1973 OPEC meeting in Tehran, representatives, encouraged by Iran, decided to close the wide gap by doubling the marker crude posted price from $5.11/b to $11.65/b – Iranian Light being thus priced at 11.875/b. "It was", concluded author A. Sampson, "the impulsive greed of the Shah of Iran, more than any unified Arab stand, that caused the redoubling of the oil price at the end of 1973".[10] The markets duly accepted OPEC's new price, and the posted price would oscillate between a low of $11.25/b and a high of $12.70 during the next five years.[11] Moreover, OPEC, during 1974, imposed fresh increases on the companies' royalty rates (from an initial 12.5%, to 14.5%, 16.66% and finally 20% in December 1974) and on the companies' income taxes (from an initial 55% to 65.75% and eventually 85% in December 1974).

The new sky-high crude oil prices would generate billions upon billions of petrodollars. These huge sums of monies would make many rich and many poorer. Among the main beneficiaries were first the OPEC members, then the Seven Sisters and finally the multinational banks and the arms merchants.

All OPEC members ran the danger of drowning in petrodollars, with Saudi Arabia and Iran taking the greatest gulp, contributing respectively around 25% and 20% of OPEC's exports. In Iran, the petrodollars were manna from heaven for the Shah and his elite: from around two billions' income annually in 1971 and 1972, it had jumped to around $18 billions for 1974 (see Table 15.2). The Shah now believed that these enormous amounts of petrodollars would buy him anything, including an infallible insurance against any catastrophe – should one come along he would keep throwing millions at it and even (why not?) billions. He now could bribe anyone bribable in Iran and both silence his critics and rein in unruly elitists, for, after all he had made it single-handedly and he alone deserved the biggest share. Abroad he could buy people, gold, armaments, shares and even (why not?) whole companies, lend one billion (under favourable terms) to any country he wanted to, thereby buying goodwill for himself and his family. What a long way he had come from the (almost) penniless exiled monarch of 1953, to the multi-billionaire godfather of 1973. Now, with all these billions at his disposal, he could also put aside (once and for all) the Pahlavi treasure in Swiss banks, American trusts, South African mines and Brazilian real estate.

Also benefiting from the oil price boom were the Seven Sisters and all the other, lesser oil companies. In 1974, the added net profits of the Seven Sisters passed the $10bn mark, Exxon making more than $3bn, Shell $2bn and the five others around one billion each.[13] The multinational banks also stood to win: these immense amounts of petrodollars would have to be transmitted through them and be

Table 15.2. Iran's Oil Production and Revenues from Oil (1971–78).[12]

Year	Average Daily Oil Production (thousands b/d)	Oil Revenues ($ millions)
1971	4,539.5	1,851.1
1972	5,023.1	2,396.0
1973	5,860.9	4,399.2
1974	6,021.6	17,821.8
1975	5,350.1	18,433.2
1976	5,882.9	20,242.9
1977	5,662.8	21,210.2
1978	5,241.7	19,300.0
Average & Total	5,447.8	105654.4

recycled in loans to importing countries, thereby generating plush and sure profits; some banks, such as Chase Manhattan, would use the Iranian Government's own deposits as collateral for their loans to Iran, pocketing the difference between the interest they paid Iran and the interest they received on the loan (only a couple of percentages, but it was a foolproof loan). The third group which stood to profit indirectly from the oil bonanza was the international mafia of the arms merchants: inevitably a large part of the Gulf's petrodollars would be channelled into arms purchases as the *nouveaux super-riches* had to defend, or rather put on a show to pretend that they could and would defend, their riches. Arms middlemen were scrambling to open offices in Tehran, Kuwait, Riyadh and Dubai.

All these developments and activities would take place in the framework of the Fifth Development Plan, as the Fourth Plan came to its conclusion in March 1973.

15.2. The Fifth Plan(s) (1973-1977)

There were to be two Fifth Plans: the first conceived before the oil price quadrupling of 1973/74, and the second in the wake of it.

The finishing touches to the first Fifth Plan were added in the autumn of 1972 by the Plan Organisation (PO). In early 1973, after being approved by the Council of Ministers, it was sent for final ratification to the *Majlis*. Simultaneously, the PO's managing director Khudadad Farmanfarmayan was replaced by the then Labour Minister Âbd ul-Majid Majidi. The change in personnel was a clear victory for Premier Huvayda, who had finally succeeded in placing one of his protégés of the first water in this key position; the change was also in line with the Shah's policy to have a new PO head for every plan; after Ibtihaj (Second Plan), there was Asfia (Third) and Farmanfarmayan (Fourth), and Majidi took over on the eve of the Fifth. With Majidi at the helm, the PO underwent momentous transformations: (i) it was brought within the governmental fold (the PO's managing director becoming a minister of state); (ii) its statutes were altered to bring under its aegis the national yearly budgeting procedures (thereby uniting planning and budgeting activities); and (iii) its name was changed to the Plan and Budget Organisation (PBO) to reflect its fresh responsibilities.

In February 1973 the *Majlis* readily ratified the Fifth Plan Law (March 1973-March 1977). The plan foresaw oil revenues of $21bn and development expenditures of roughly the same amount. The plan consisted of twenty-one chapters, as a new feature entitled Current Operational Credits was introduced to cover operational costs – an aberration in any development plan (see Table 15.3). Another new feature of the plan was the introduction of private sector fixed investments to its fold – not the best procedure (see total plan revenues and outlays in Table 15.4). All in all, the first Fifth Plan was to the Fourth Plan what the Fourth Plan had been to the Third edition; public sector investments of $23.0bn in the Fifth were roughly treble the Fourth's $7.5bn, which were in turn almost treble the Third's outlays of $2bn. Projects in the Fifth Plan would be much larger than previous ones, allegedly taking advantage of 'economies of scale', the PBO's newly found theory. It also gave the regime and its media lackeys the occasion to parade the plan's forecasted macro-economic achievements – a record GNP growth of 11.4% per annum (a world

Table 15.3. The Original Fifth Plan of 1973 – Projected Public Sector Investment and Current Operational Credits.
(Figures in Rls billion)

Chapter	Public Sector	Current Credits	Total
Agriculture	208.0	58.9	266.9
Water	108.0	2.7	110.7
Industry	183.9	10.6	194.5
Mining	46.5	0.9	47.4
Oil	130.7	—	130.7
Gas	29.0	—	29.0
Electricity	53.5	1.0	54.5
Communications	180.0	20.2	200.2
Telecommunications	41.2	18.2	59.4
Urban Development	33.0	1.8	34.8
Rural Development	36.0	0.8	36.8
Gov'tal Buildings	90.8	0.4	91.2
Housing	82.8	0.4	83.2
Education	230.0	175.0	405.0
Culture	9.4	6.5	15.9
Tourism	7.7	1.3	9.0
Health	52.0	64.5	116.5
Public Welfare	16.0	38.5	54.5
Physical Education	10.0	20.9	30.9
Research	6.2	10.5	16.7
Regional D'ment	5.3	0.6	5.9
Total	1560.0*	433.7	1993.7**

* The public sector total of Rls1560bn included Rls115.8bn earmarked for loans to the private sector.

** The grand total of fixed investments and current credits added up to $26.3bn – using the new (February 1973) revalued dollar rate of 1$ = 67.6Rls (as against the previous rate of 1$ = 75.75Rls).

record), growth subdivided among the four major components as follows: 5.5% for agriculture; 11.8% for oil; 15.0% to industry and mining; and 11.5% for services. Per capita income was to double from $495 to $925 per annum. American businessmen had pledged $543m for private sector investments over the duration of the Fifth Plan at the Second Conference on American Investments in Iran, held at New York in January 1972; the World Bank had promised at least $500m; Japan another $500m and West Germany $50m. The oil price quadrupling of 1973/74 was to catch up with the Fifth Plan, turning its blueprints to ashes. In January 1974, the Shah gave Huvayda and Majidi twelve months to come up with a fresh Fifth Plan, taking into account the latest oil revenue projections.

Table 15.4. Summary of Forecast Revenues and Expenditures During the Original Fifth Plan.
(Figures in Rls billion)

Revenues		Expenditures	
Oil Revenues	1577.4	Development Projects	1560.0
Domestic Taxes	788.6	Current Credits	1498.4
Foreign Loans	433.4	Interest on Loans	156.2
Bank Credits	310.0	Amortisation of Loans	129.4
Others	234.6		
Total	3344.0	Total	3344.0

Fixed Investments by Public Sector:	1560.0
Fixed Investments by Private Sector:	900.0
Total Fixed Investments:	2460.0
	(equal to $36.4bn)

In January 1975, the second Fifth Plan prepared by Majidi's PBO was approved by the *Majlis*. It was to the original Fifth Plan what the latter had been to the Fourth Plan; in other words, within two years two quantum jumps along the ladder had taken place. The PBO had simply piled more butter on the same piece of bread. Majidi's team of young technocrats had done its best to fit plan expenditures to accommodate the mind-boggling petrodollar revenues. The plan's total envelope had almost trebled in size (compare Tables 15.4 and 15.6); its number of chapters had jumped to thirty-five (as against twenty-one in the original version); public investments had increased by an average of 116% – with records in the fields of electricity (+358%), government buildings (+251%) and statistics (+228%); current operational credits were up by a striking 547% (the planners shifting masses of routine credits under the plan's rug); and, for the very first time, credits were included for defence affairs and domestic security (i.e. SAVAK and the police), adding up to roughly one-third of the plan's total outlay – as can be seen in Table 15.5. Every department, however large or small, would have a piece of the enormous Fifth Plan cake: all and sundry would share in the petrodollars' spoils; with a place in the sun, no one was given a reason to complain that he was left out in the cold. The plan's only novelty was the Foreign Investment allocation of Rls745.1bn (equal to $11bn), which had been favoured by the Shah (and, naturally, Huvayda) but was hotly debated by the PBO's young guard (led by Dr Manuchihr Agah, who was rapped on the fingers for not toeing the official line); but, eventually, the Shah got his $11bn to spend on the foreign markets and quickly spent $7bn during 1974.

The projected consequences of the revised Fifth Plan were almost unbelievable: a forecast average annual GNP growth of 25.9% (more than trebling over five years)! The only loser in the sweepstake would be agriculture, the economic sector most immune to petrodollars and least likely to benefit from it (as shown in Table 15.7). Per capita income was expected to skyrocket from $495 in 1972 to $1520 per annum! All the figures in the revised Fifth Plan seemed Brobdingnagian in a Lilliputian country. In order to control the immense machinery envisaged being set in motion by the fresh plan, the PBO needed an army of effective and capable administrators in the McNamara mould. All it had, however, was a handful of conceited Iranian bureaucrats, who were neither very effective nor very capable; they soon lost control over the 14,400 projects spawned by their plan, and just sat there looking at machinery which did not answer to any of their directives, the rat race for petrodollars having engendered forces far superior to any of the PBO's.

Table 15.5. The revised Fifth Plan of 1974 - projected public sector investments and current operational credits. (Figures in Rls billion)

Divisions and Chapters	Public Sector	Current Credits	Total
I) PUBLIC AFFAIRS			
1. Imperial Court	—	10.2	10.2
2. Legislature	—	5.1	5.1
3. General Admin.	4.9	30.5	35.4
4. Judiciary	5.3	28.9	34.2
5. Domestic Affairs	2.2	9.4	11.6
6. Domestic Security	8.5	221.2	229.7
7. Int'l Relations	—	21.8	21.8
8. Financial Admin.	6.4	36.3	42.7
9. Statistics	35.4	19.4	54.8
10. Information, Mass Media	46.2	16.2	62.4
11. Gov't Buildings	319.5	0.6	320.1
12. Manpower Management	2.0	3.3	5.3
Subtotal	430.4	402.9	833.3
II) DEFENCE AFFAIRS			
13. Military	—	1967.4	1967.4
14. Civil Defence	—	1.3	1.3
Subtotal	—	1968.7	1968.7

III) SOCIAL AFFAIRS			
15. Education	334.4	216.8	551.2
16. Culture	20.6	11.1	31.7
17. Health	160.1	76.6	236.7
18. Welfare	30.6	50.4	81.0
19. Physical Education	26.6	6.2	32.8
20. Urban D'ment	48.6	1.4	50.0
21. Rural D'ment	61.8	4.6	66.4
22. Housing	230.0	—	230.0
23. Environmental Protection	11.9	2.0	13.9
24. Regional D'ment	16.4	—	16.4
Subtotal	941.0	369.1	1310.1
IV) ECONOMIC AFFAIRS			
25. Agriculture	296.8	72.7	369.5
26. Water	161.2	3.5	164.7
27. Electricity	247.8	2.1	249.9
28. Industry	357.1	11.0	368.1
29. Oil	333.0.	—	333.0
30. Gas	51.0	—	51.0
31. Mining	63.4	2.0	65.4
32. Commerce	1.7	2.0	3.7
33. Communications	400.0	25.6	425.6
34. T'communications	73.0	11.9	84.9
35. Tourism	12.4	1.1	13.5
Subtotal	1997.4	131.9	2129.3
Grand Total (I+II+III+IV	6241.4	3368.8	2872.6
Grand Total (in $bn**)	49.8	42.5	92.3

   * Including Rls179.6bn for loans to private sector
   ** At the 1975 exchange rate of 1$ = 67.6Rls

Table 15.6. Summary of Forecast Revenues and Expenditures During the Revised Fifth Plan.
(Figures in Rls billions)

Revenues		Expenditures	
Oil Revenues	6628.5	D'ment Projects	3368.9
Domestic Taxes	1215.0	Current Credits	2872.6
Foreign Loans	150.0	Repayment of Foreign Loans	405.0
Bank Loans	—	Investments Abroad	745.1
Others	303.0	Others	905.0
Total	8296.5	Total	8296.5

Fixed Investments in Public Sector: 3368.8
Fixed Investments in Private Sector: 1400.6
Total Fixed Investments: 4769.4
(equal to $70.6bn)

Table 15.7. Projected Rate of Growth and Shares of the Major Sectors of the Iranian Economy (1972 and 1977).

Economic Sector	1972 Share of GNP (%)	Projected Annual Growth (%)	1977 Share of GNP (%)
Agriculture	16.2	7.0	8.0
Oil	23.3	51.5	48.7
Industry & Mines	18.0	18.0	16.1
Services	42.5	16.4	27.2
Total (average)	100.0	(25.9)	100.0

Even the best econometric and economic models developed by Western specialists failed to assist the PBO's young technocrats. They had ordered a score of Iran models, the main ones developed being:

(1) The OMAR Model formulated by Professor J.A.C. Brown of Bristol University in 1972 (later updated to 1977). OMAR was a multi-sectoral model (with the four usual sectors) linking input–output tables with sets of macro-economic demand equations and identities; there were three players (i.e. the government, the urban and rural private sectors) and four major exogenous variables dominated by oil revenues.

(2) The econometric model developed by Shahshahani and Dowling, and used to forecast the behaviour of the Iranian economy 1975–1985.

(3) The Iran Model developed by M. Mesarovic and E. Pestel of the Club of Rome and produced by a team of French specialists co-ordinated by the Frenchman M. Guernier.

(4) The Apadana Model (econometric) of the Iranian economy (with its five major blocs) developed over 1976–78 by Brussels University Professor J.P.A. Verbiest and his UNIDO (United Nations Industrial Development Organisation) assistant, Nak Kwan Kim, adviser to Iran's Ministry of Industry and Mines.

With time, Iran's technocrats found out that their country is unmodellable; they would still, however, go through the modelling motions and sessions, not daring to admit that all their technocratic paraphernalia was almost (if not totally) useless.

In the field, however, the projects of the Fifth Plan were gradually unfolding – some for the better, some for the worse. The relative degree of success of each project depended on its Iranian project team and on its foreign managing contractor (or, rather, was directly proportional to the two entities' capability and honesty). The 14,400 projects of the Fifth Iranian Development Plan unfolded inexorably: the end result would inevitably be a reflection of the capacities of the Shah's elite to manage their nation's development, a development made possible by the massive influx of petrodollars. It was only natural that one of the sectors on which the technocratic elite would focus was the Iranian oil industry itself.

15.3. Developments in Oil

The golden goose was the southern oil fields operated by OSCO under loose NIOC supervision. The fields had to provide the average five and a half million b/d required by the insatiable Shah to keep the petrodollars coming in (with the Consortium not unwilling to take its share while it still could). Over the eight years spanning 1971 to 1978, these fields would produce a cumulative 16 billion barrels of oil – more than the 12.4 billion barrels they had produced between 1912 and 1970. These figures loom large when compared to the estimated amount which could ultimately be recovered from the fifty-seven Iranian onshore oil fields – roughly 66 billion barrels (the best figure available[14]): within the eight years 1971-78, no less than a quarter of known Iranian reserves had been produced!

The reckless rate of production in Khuzistan had begun to seriously worry OSCO's Iranian engineers and planners in 1974. They could witness the effects of a 6m b/d output on the state of the fields: pressures were dropping faster than predicted and the higher salt content in the crude oil produced (due to a higher degree of seepage from the water layer, a consequence of coning). This state of affairs triggered a $300m project to install twenty-six desalters (of either 55,000 or 110,000 b/d capacity, for a total desalting throughput of 2.5m b/d) on production units. They were arguing that, with such outputs, some of the future produceable oil in place was being irretrievably lost; that the wells were being unnecessarily damaged; that one should back-pedal to sustainable rates of between 3m to 4m b/d. But the grumblings of Iranian experts had no impact on decision-making, as the Shah was not to be deterred from his goals just to please a couple of NIOC or OSCO employees. In 1975 OSCO was busy studying two alternatives for the future: 6.8m b/d and 7.2m b/d.[15] Instead of being reduced, the output would be slightly increased, and it still could go somewhat higher, bearing in mind that Dr Fallah had proposed 7.6m b/d, and that former US Ambassador James Akins had predicted in 1971 a 12m b/d production for Iran,[16] downgrading this number two years later:

> The estimated production for Iran in 1980 is 10m b/d ...[although] Iran has said that its production would level off at 8m b/d....[17]

In any event the Kharg Island oil terminal was readied for these high Iranian oil export rates. A new two-berth jetty, dubbed the Sea Island, was erected in eighteen months (1971-2) at a cost of $15m to accommodate two VLCCs simultaneously (up to 300,000 and 500,000 dwt for each of the berths). Moreover, nine one million barrel storage tanks were built on the island, boosting total reserve capacity past the 20m barrels mark. More sophisticated measurement instruments were fitted in the control rooms. Thus, on January 23, 1973, as the whole system was being tested, a new twenty-four hour record for Kharg exports was set at 8,802,031 barrels.

To silence the Iranian oil industry grumblers, the Shah's oil managers had two trump cards up their sleeves: (1) gas reinjection in the oil fields; (2) an all-out effort in exploration and drilling. After thoroughly studying the respective cases for water and gas injections, OSCO had come to favour water over gas, but NIOC's Exploration and Production Directory was of the opposite inclination. Therefore it convinced the NIOC board to form a team of experts to study the question with foreign consultants (chief consultant was Terramar of the US). The NIOC team's mathematical models (a set of tri-dimensional, implicit non-linear partial differential equations) were run on a state of the art CDC-6400 computer (later doped) specially purchased by NIOC for Aryamihr University. The team came up with excellent results for simulated gas injection and NIOC was able to bring round OSCO to its view on gas over water. As both OSCO and NIOC concurred, gas reinjection projects were planned and the first two experimental projects implemented: (1) gas from the Naft-i Sifid dome (400 million standard cubic feet per day – MMSCFD) was compressed and injected into the Haft Kel reservoir; (2) wet gas from the Pazanan dome (530 MMSCFD) in the Gachsaran field. At a total cost of $650m, these projects were launched in the spring of 1976 and 1977 respectively.

The preliminary results of these two gas reinjections having yielded highly successful results in line with theoretical computations, NIOC and OSCO experts were convinced that gas reinjection was a profitable proposal. A number of such projects were formulated. First in line were the NGL 900 and NGL 1000, to be implemented by Fluor Corp. (US), for drying Pazanandome gas and reinjecting it into the Gachsaran and Marun oil fields, at rates of 600 and 500 MMSCFD respectively; two other smaller projects were for the gas reinjection of oil fields' associated gases into the field itself: at Lab-i Sifid (37 MMSCFD) and Aqa Jari (200 MMSCFD). Some $500m had been spent on these four reinjection projects when the Revolution of 1978/79 came along, to bring them to a total halt.

As for NIOC management's second iron of exploration and drilling, the budgets were almost limitless. Geological and seismic surveys broke all previous records – whether in the Consortium area or other NIOC areas. But these efforts were eclipsed by the explosion in drilling activities: annual metreage reached the 450,000 metre mark (see Table 15.8). Drilling companies (mostly American) mushroomed in Ahvaz, for instance Sedco, Santa Fe, Reading and Bates, Zapata, Intairdril, as drilling rigs mushroomed in southern Iran. There were up to a total of sixty-four rigs at its peak of 1977: forty-four were operated by contractors (dominated by Sedco's eight and Santa Fe's seven), seven by NIOC and thirteen by NIOC's venture partners and service contractors.[19] The mammoth drilling programme of the 1970s (with near to two and a half million metres drilled) gave birth to a mouse; it was not so much the quantity of oil fields which left a great deal to be desired, as twenty-two were duly discovered (to add to the twenty-one discovered previous to 1971), but rather their quality, with meagre average outputs in the 10 to 12,000 b/d range (compared with 300,000 b/d for the older fields) and a total collective output of 244,000 b/d (for details of the 1970s' new fields see Table 15.9).

Instead of confronting the oil industry grumblers with its intensive exploration programme, the NIOC management had proven to its Consortium partners that its area certainly did not contain any more super-giant fields of the Aqa Jari, Gachsaran, Ahvaz and Marun stature. At the best it contained small fields, with a much higher production cost than the much larger ones. At least the Consortium members were now aware of the potential of their own area very precisely. The 1970s had clearly demonstrated that Iran's oil heartland was far from the black gold El Dorado many had expected: it was not comparable with the treasures of Saudi Arabia, not even at the level of Kuwaiti or Iraqi reserves. Suddenly the country which had long gunned for the position of top seed among Middle Eastern oil producers (posing as a rival to Saudi Arabia) was to be ranked among the unseeded. This inevitable downgrading would have momentous consequences for the whole Iranian Question.

Table 15.8. Drilling Activities in Iran (1971-78).[18]

Year	Total Metres Drilled	Wells Sunk	Wells Completed	Wildcats	Discoveries
1971	150,000	104	n/a	6	0
1972	88,000	61	n/a	2	0
1973	225,000	81	62	18	7
1974	325,000	100	n/a	27	5
1975	340,000	140	n/a	26	6
1976	440,000	182	n/a	26	3
1977	450,000	185	138	25	4
1978	440,000	180	140	10	0
Total	2,458,000	1033	n/a	140	25

NIOC's fortunes in gas and oil exploration on its own, with its ventures partners or service contractors, were also ploughing ahead. On its own, NIOC's Directorate for Exploration and Production was pursuing its systematic geological seismic and drilling programmes, mainly carried out by Swiss students. Exploratory drilling was performed in Khurasan, Azarbayjan and mainly Fars. Discoveries were made, mainly of gas: at Sarakhs (East Khurasan), Tang-i Bijar (Kurdistan) and Sarkhoun (Bandar Âbbas); with a meagre oil discovery (maximum of 20,000 b/d) in 1973 at Sarvistan in Fars province.

NIOC fared better in its 75-25 type of joint ventures, signing three new agreements in 1971 (see Table 15.10), bringing the total number of such ventures to twelve (with the first three signed in 1957-58, then six in 1965 - see Chapter 13). Such joint ventures were all grist to NIOC's mill: it allowed the company to train its cadres in exploratory operations while actually attempting to discover oil; at the same time, the regime was satisfied to have found a fresh potential partner in the Iranian oil pie. Of the twelve ventures, only four - namely SIRIP, IPAC, IMINOCO and LAPCO - would strike gold and develop viable

Table 15.9. Twenty-two Oil Fields Discovered in the Consortium Agreement Area During the 1970s, with Years of Discovery (where available) and Projected Field Output.

Name of Oil Field	Year Discovered	Projected Output (b/d)
Dehluran	1972	55,000
Cheshmeh Khush	1972	20,000
Ab Taymour	1973	18,000
Sarkan	1973	14,000
Dal Pari		14,000
Nargessi		14,000
Sulabedar	1970	10,000
Chillingar	1973	10,000
Kilour Karim	1974	10,000
Kaboud	1974	10,000
Siamkan		10,000
Shadegan		10,000
Qaleh Nar		7,000
Danan		6,000
Kouh Koki		6,000
Zeloi		5,000
Karoun		5,000
Vizenahar		5,000
Maleh Kouh		5,000
Golkkhori		4,000
Paydar		4,000
Khaviz		2,000
Total		244,000

commercial oil exports, all offshore, with SIRIP adding its Zagros onshore finds. The four ventures exported an average of 322,000 b/d in 1970, around 460,000 b/d in 1972 and a record 706,000 b/d in February 1978 (for a breakdown and details of the major venture oil fields, see Table 15.11).

Table 15.10. Three New 75-25 Agreements Signed by NIOC in July 1971.

Joint Venture Name	Foreign Partner	Allocated Area (km^2)	Minimum Expenditure ($m)
Iran Nippon Petroleum Co. - INPECO	Japanese consortium (onshore): Mitsui; Teijin; Luristan; Mitsubishi; North Sumatra Oil D'ment Co.	8,000	25
Bushire Petroleum Co. - BUSHCO	Amerada Hess (US) (offshore)	3,715	22
Hormuz Petroleum Co. - HOPECO	Mobil (US) (offshore)	3,500	11

* Later, one third of the concession was sold by the Japanese Consortium to Mobil (US), and the latter became the operator.

As for fresh service contracts, six were signed in 1974 (see Table 15.12 for details), to make a grand total of nine for such agreements – the first three having been entered into in the 1960s. The six new ones, however, differed from the initial ones in three main contractual points:

(1) After the contractor had found oil in commercial quantities, the contract was annulled and NIOC took over as operator (reimbursing the contractor for expenses incurred);

Table 15.11. Major Fields and Ultimate Record Production of NIOC's Four Successful 75-25 Joint Ventures.[20]

Joint Venture	Commercial Fields (Discovery Year)	Total Average Production (b/d February 1978)
SIRIP*	Offshore: Bahrigansar (1960) Nourouz (1966) Handijan (1968) Onshore: Kouh-i Rig (1968) Doudrou (1968) Shourum (1972)	42,000
IPAC	Darius (1961) Cyrus (1961) Firaydun (1966) Ardishir (1969)	430,000
IMINOCO	Rustam (1967) Rakhsh (1969)	46,000
LAPCO	Sasan (1966)	188,000
Total		706,000

* SIRIP's onshore crude exports were scheduled to begin at the close of 1978 (via a gravity pipeline to the coast) at an initial rate of 64,000 b/d, gradually increased to a maximum output of 120,000 b/d; however, the Revolution came along and upset these export plans.

(2) A fifteen year sales agreement was signed by NIOC and the former contractor for between 30% and 50% of total production (depending on location and production quantity);
(3) The sale price of crude oil would be the posted price minus three to five per cent – the price advantage accorded to the three initial contractors was not renewed here.

Of the nine contractors only the French company, SOFIRAN, the pioneer, was successful offshore. It struck oil *in extremis* some thirty kilometres west of Sirri Island; their 1975 strike occurred on their fifteenth wildcat, drilled by Atwood Oceanics (a Houston-based affiliate of Helmerich and Payne), in the final months of their contract (close of December 1975). The Sirri 'C' and 'D' structures were delimited, fifty-six wells were drilled and water reinjection provided for. Their joint reserves were estimated at 320m barrels; two other structures, 'A' and 'E' were said to contain some 250m barrels. In June 1978, Sirri 'D' began producing at 16,000 b/d. In September 1978, SOFIRAN's terminal at Sirri Island became operational, with its three one-million storage tanks and a loading berth accepting VLCCs of up to 330,000 dwt. Carriage of oil from Sirri began in December 1978, but was rapidly stopped by the revolutionary strikes. In 1979, Sirri 'C' came on stream at an initial rate of 24,000 b/d 21.

The French joint venture company of Elf-ERAP, however, was horribly unlucky with its onshore contract (it held a majority in the European Group of Companies – EGOCO), in a 36,000 km^2 concession of southern Fars. Between 1974 and 1977, EGOCO found no fewer than five large gas fields, Bandubast, Nar, Kangan, Aghar and Dalan – with possible reserves of up to 42 trillion cubic feet. EGOCO asked NIOC to substitute the word 'gas' for 'oil' in the service contract and let it develop its gas fields, but NIOC was adamant that oil is oil and gas is gas, and in June 1977 thanked EGOCO, undertook to pay it $173m for its exploration expenses (not provided for in the original contract) and asked it to depart the concession as per contract stipulations. NIOC quickly took over all operations and awarded its first contract for the Nar field development to R.M. Parsons of Los Angeles. The only (minor) concession NIOC gave its former contractor was to let it form a new entity (named SEGIRAN) to act as its supervisor in the gas fields' development. The NIOC rebuke would not be easily forgotten by the French oil companies of Elf and ERAP, which had dreamed of creating their own

Table 15.12. Six New Service Contracts Entered Into by Foreign Oil Companies with NIOC in July/August 1974.

Contractor's Name	Foreign Oil Company	Allocated Area (onshore) km^2	Minimum Expenditure ($m)
Deminex Iran Oil Company – DEMINEX	Deminex (W. Germany)	i) 6,704 (Shiraz) ii) 7,810 (Abadan)	32
Total Iran – TOTAL	CFP (France)	8,000 (Western Lar)	40
Ultramar Iran – ULTRAMAR	Ultramar (USA)	7,800 (Eastern Lar)	14
AGIP Iran – AGIPIRAN	AGIP (Italy)	7,150 (Central Lar)	20
Lar Exploration Company – LAREX	Ashland Oil (USA)	7,274 (Northern Lar)	25
Total		44,738	167

gas empire in south Iran, as AIOC had done with oil in Khuzistan! The French should have pondered the fact that Shell had discovered the giant gas field of 'C-Structure' (later renamed 'North Pars') in their DOPCO 75-25 joint venture and, similarly, had been denied the fruits of their (gas) discovery by NIOC.

Domestically, NIOC's major task consisted of satisfying a rapidly increasing internal demand for refined products. Growth rates of 20% to 25% were not rare for consumption during the 1970s (see Table 15.13). NIOC could either expand its older refineries or build new ones; and it did both in the 1970s, having terminated the new Kermanshah Refinery in the late 1960s.

Table 15.13. Iran's Domestic Consumption of Refined Products for the 1970s (even years).[22]

Year	Average Daily Consumption (b/d)
1970	187,000
1972	225,200
1974	303,900
1976	406,100
1978	457,900

NIOC's first new refinery was a 40,000 b/d effort some 25 kilometres north of Shiraz. Designed by UOP (US) and built by Snam Progetti (Italy), NIOC's fourth refinery came on stream in the summer of 1973, with crude oil from Gachsaran. Simultaneously the Lavan Island 20,000 b/d topping plant, built by a Yugoslav firm for the NIOC joint venture LAPCO, was brought into operation, but the plant was bogged down in multiple technical problems from the outset and never operated as scheduled, its output averaging around 12,000 b/d. In the summer of 1974, Tehran Refinery's 100,000 tonnes/annum lube oil plant was started up (NIOC's second lube unit after Abadan). A year later, the refinery's 100,000 b/d expansion, managed by Fluor-Thyssen, was completed on schedule, and began delivering its products to the capital city's market; to feed the twin Tehran Refineries a new, 736 km-long, 30"/26" Ahvaz–Tehran pipeline (capacity of 280,000 b/d) was laid.

After Shiraz and Tehran, NIOC concentrated on its fifth and sixth refineries. The 80,000 b/d fifth refinery at Tabriz was designed by UOP and constructed by Snam Progetti (like that at Shiraz). Work on site began in June 1975 and three years later the refinery stood mechanically completed; crude oil feed came through a Tehran–Tabriz pipeline. The 200,000 b/d sixth refinery was located at Isfahan; a duplicate of Tehran Refinery's twin trains, it was contracted out to Fluor-Thyssen, and was begun in 1976. The refinery was between 90% and 95% complete by the close of 1978, when the revolutionary strikes began; after the Revolution, the Iranian staff finished the job in 1980 (with hands-off assistance from Fluor-Thyssen and discreet payments by NIOC from its German accounts[23]). Crude oil feed came from Marun via a 432 km-long, 32"/30" Marun–Isfahan pipeline (built by Saipem of Italy); Isfahan Refinery went on to break all Iranian refining records with over-capacities of over 50%.

Furthermore, NIOC decided to build a new Crude Distillation Unit for Abadan Refinery: the 130,000 b/d CDU 85. A new Ahvaz–Abadan, 126 kilometre long, 24" pipeline was laid, and the whole project was completed in early 1978, boosting the refinery's total capacity to 590,000 b/d. As the CDU 85 was being inaugurated, NIOC began planning for its seventh, 250,000 b/d refinery at Bandar Âbbas; it contracted out the project to Cities Service (US), but the Revolution killed this project in the cocoon.[24]

Besides the flurry of fresh refining capacities, NIOC had to develop its nationwide distribution network. New products pipelines were laid, bringing the total to some 8,000 kilometres in 1978; railroad and road tankers were added to the transport stock, boosting totals to 1,100 and 6,000 respectively; retail outlets (for kerosene) jumped from 8,000 in 1971 to 12,500 in 1978; service stations (for petrol and gas oil) came to number four hundred and thirty-five in 1978.

Not all NIOC divisions fared as well as Refining and Distribution. For example, NIOC's Research Division, which was started in the early 1960s in the laboratories of Tehran University's Technical Faculty, and was later transplanted to Ray on a plot of land adjacent to the Tehran Refinery (far from ideal for research), rapidly sank into a mortal torpor. A fully-equipped research centre was erected there between 1967 and 1972 (with initial technical assistance from the French IFP), but it ended up being more of a showpiece than a scientific institution. It soon became Iran's prime centre for chemical and physical analysis (not the initial goal, but a worthwhile activity nevertheless). In 1976, NIOC and Shell signed a three year agreement for joint research projects; after a couple of good experiences, even Shell's goodwill failed to bring NIOC Research out of its torpor, and the Revolution brought the joint venture to a fitting end. Another venture embarked upon by the Research Centre was that for the production of industrial catalysts (capacity of 3,000 tonnes/annum), with Haldor Topsoe of Denmark and the National Petrochemical Company of Iran (each holding 33.3% of the shares), but this was torpedoed by the Revolution.

Much more successful was the National Iranian Tanker Company (NITC), set up by NIOC in the mid-1960s. Benefiting from the petrodollar bonanza, NITC went on a shopping spree. In 1974 it ordered Japan's IHI two 228,700 dwt VLCCS; by 1975 the *Azarpad* and the *Kharg* were carrying crude oil for NITC. In May 1976, NITC began an important joint venture agreement with BP Tanker which provided for: (i) the purchase by NITC of two VLCCs and three product carriers (price tag of $60.5m for total of 513,807 dwt) from BP Tanker; (ii) the pooling of these five NITC tankers with five similar BP tankers in a 50-50 joint venture (initial capital of $100,000) under British management: the British-Iranian Ship Services Company (BISSC); (iii) the formation of two BISSC affiliates in Tehran and London. The joint venture proved to be highly profitable, and NITC gained valuable experience in the world of shipping and crude carriage. By 1978 NITC controlled a fleet of ten tankers with a capacity of 1,119,000 dwt.

NIOC also entered into four joint ventures abroad:

(1) In 1972, NIOC and BP (50-50) won a forty-year concession for two offshore areas in Scottish waters, with BP as operator. In 1975, NIOC's chairman, Dr Iqbal, disclosed in his annual report that the venture had struck oil.[25]

(2) In 1975 NIOC repeated its action in Western Greenland's waters, with BP, SAGA (Norway) and Chevron (US) – each holding 25%. The four associates were awarded ten blocks in three different offshore areas.[26]

(3) Also in 1975, NIOC formed the IRASENCO 50-50 joint venture with Senegal's National Oil Company, for building a refinery and participating in the development of the Taiba phosphate mines. When these failed to materialise, IRASENCO entered refined products retail sales in Senegal by purchasing 50% of the Shell Senegal Distribution Co. and creating IRASENSHELL.

(4) In October 1975, NIOC signed an agreement with South Korea for the joint construction of a 60,000 b/d refinery in Onsan province;

crude oil was to be delivered by NIOC. Contractor Foster Wheeler terminated the job in 1979, at a cost of $170m.

If the four above ventures came through, a number of prospective deals did not. Prominent among those falling by the wayside were: the 1973 agreement with America's Ashland Oil to purchase a refinery and petrochemical complex at Buffalo and one hundred and eighty service stations in New York State, in return for a 100,000 b/d contract; NIOC's purchase of 6.25 million Occidental shares at $20 each; the three 500,000 b/d export refineries (respectively entered into with Shell, a Japanese Consortium and American oil companies) that never took off; and, last but not least, the Iranian-Japanese-American project to build a mammoth crude oil storage facility at the Palau Islands in US-administered Micronesia.[27]

15.4. Gas and Petrochemicals

NIOC had given birth in the mid-1960s to two daughters – the National Iranian Gas Company (NIGC) and the National Petrochemical Company (NPC) – to respectively develop its gas and petrochemical downstream sectors.

NIGC, inspired by Engineer Taqi Musaddiqi, a former Abadan Refinery engineer, had quickly got off the ground with the supervision of the IGAT I trunkline and export gas sales to the USSR. During the 1970s, with the enormous gas discoveries made throughout Iran, proven gas reserves had more than doubled from 150 trillion standard cubic feet (tscf) in 1971 to 375 tscf in 1976 (for the detail of proven, probable and possible Iranian gas reserves in 1976, see Table 15.14). With such gas reserves estimated at around 18% of global reserves, Iran ranked second in the world only to the USSR.

For OSCO, NIOC and NIGC, the prime *casse-tête* in the 1970s was the use of ever-greater amounts of associated gas produced in Khuzistan oil fields. These fields, with their average gas to oil ratio ('gor') of 800 to 850 SCF gas per barrel of crude produced, naturally yielded larger amounts of gas as the crude output rose towards 6 million b/d. From a total daily gas output of 3,000 million SCF (mmscfd) in 1970, associated gas output rose to over 5,000 mmscfd in the mid-1970s, culminating in 5,336 mmscfd in 1978 (for details see Table 15.15). Two major outlets were examined by NIGC for the

Table 15.14. Iran's Estimated Natural Gas Reserves in 1976.[28]
(figures in trillion standard cubic feet)

Fields	Proven	Probable	Possible
Khuzistan fields	210	210	210
Khangiran (Sarakhs)	18	18	18
Qhishm Island	4	6	8
Nar	14	17	21
Kangan	11	15	21
Pars:			
'C' Structure	54	65	75
'B' Structure	25	50	89
'F' Structure	9	17	66
'G' Structure	7	15	39
Other smaller fields (6)	23	32	46
Total	375	445	593

rational use of associated gas: domestic consumption and exports to the USSR and Western Europe. As for the huge reserves of dome gas, they would be fed to large liquefaction units and exported as Liquefied Natural Gas (LNG).

Begun in 1970, gas exports to the USSR through the IGAT I pipeline had come to rest on a plateau between 1,200 and 1,300 mmscfd in 1976–1978. Gas prices had increased slowly with time: from a meagre $0.186 per million BTU (mmbtu) in 1971 to $0.76 per mmbtu in 1978. In parallel to these exports, some of the natural gas carried by IGAT I was consumed in Iranian cities and industrial parks along the trunkline's path: beginning at 17.5 mmscfd in 1970, this domestic consumption multiplied by twenty to reach 350 mmscfd in 1977. Notwithstanding this gradual development of the domestic market for gas, it seems that more could and should have been done to boost its rapid domestication.

If the Iranians had one good reason to be satisfied with IGAT I,

Table 15.15. Iran's Natural Gas Average Daily Production in Khuzistan Oil Fields and Uses in Selected (even) Years of the 1970s.[29]
(Figures in mmscfd)

Year	Produced	Used	Flared	Flared (% of total)
1970	2,978.1	1,183.9	1,794.2	60.2
1972	4,026.7	1,725.1	2,301.6	57.2
1974	4,837.0	2,153.7	2,683.3	55.5
1976	4,874.3	2,174.7	2,699.6	55.4
1978	5,336.0	2,846.7	2,489.3	46.7

the Soviet Union had many – it was delivering natural gas to Europe at between $2.50 and $3.00 per mmbtu, while paying Iran far less than one dollar for it.[30] It was therefore not surprising that the Soviets were back in 1973 for an encore: the IGAT II scheme for Iranian gas exports to Europe via the USSR. For the best part of 1974 and 1975, protracted multi-party negotiations between Iran, the USSR and the European end-users took place. Finally, on November 30, 1975, the multi-party IGAT II project was signed, which called for the construction of a 1,358 kilometre-long gas trunkline (56") linking the southern fields of Nar and Kangan to Astara, to be built by the Italians and the French (up to Saveh) and the Soviets (Saveh-Astara); the exportation of 1,650 mmscfd of Iranian gas for twenty years (1983–2002); the repartition of the gas to: (1) Sojuzgasexport (USSR), 200 mmscfd (mostly at a transit fee of $0.50 to $0.70 per mmbtu); (2) Ruhrgas (West Germany), 550 mmscfd; (3) Gaz de France (France), 370 mmscfd; (4) OMV (Austria), 180 mmscfd; and (5) Metalimex (Czechoslovakia), 350 mmscfd (added in 1976). In the final analysis, the deal's supreme beneficiary was the Soviet Union. Analyst M.I. Goldman could not hide his admiration:

> Note the beauty of the scheme. The Soviets would receive one million tons of oil for building [part of] the

Iranian pipeline, 3.5 billion cubic metres [equal to 1.2 tscf] in part as a transit-fee, and the entire cost would be underwritten by the West Europeans...[31]

The USSR stood to gain even more in the long term, sitting comfortably in a monopolist negotiating position, controlling both ends of the scheme: the seller and the buyers. The project was never brought to completion because of the Revolution of 1978/79; the Italians of SAIPEM were roughly halfway to Isfahan on their part of IGAT II linking Nar-Kangan to Isfahan, a 632 kilometres stretch they had contracted out for $183m, and the Nar gas treating plant was still at the design stage.[32]

NIGC's second iron in the fire was its LNG export schemes. NIGC had received a dozen proposals for joint LNG projects, but the gas company wanted to study the projects thoroughly before committing itself (NIGC Projects and Planning director, Dr M. Shirazi, was a cautious and capable administrator). After careful examination, three major LNG projects made it to the detailed study stage: (1) the 1973 Transco project for producing 1.6m tonnes/annum of LNG and 5m tonnes/annum methanol (shelved after eighteen months of studies); (2) the joint El Paso (US)/Distrigaz-Sopex (Belgium) project for the liquefaction of 2,000 mmscfd of gas (which fell through after two years of feasibility studies); (3) the Kalingas LNG project, a multinational project for liquefying 800 mmscfd of gas for export to Japan, involving the following partners: NIGC (50%), a Japanese consortium of seventeen companies, led by Nissho-Iwai (15%), Crinavis of Spain (10%), F. Olsen and Halfdan Ditlev-Simonsen of Norway, two builders of LNG carriers (7.5%) and four US companies with a 17.5% holding (ISC, Enserch, Natural Gas Pipeline Company, and Chicago Bridge and Iron Company). By 1978, only NIGC (82.5%), the Japanese (15%) and Chicago Bridge (2.5%) were still at it, toying with the $3bn project; talks with Columbia Gas (US) for LNG sales and Kvaerner (Norway) for a skid-mounted LNG plant led nowhere; the Revolution merely put the last nail in the Kalingas (and Iranian LNG projects') coffin. Iran and NIGC were fortunate to miss the LNG train altogether: with its high upfront capital investment and poor returns, LNG projects were never profitable propositions for dome gas (associated gas has a slight advantage, but its economics are doubtful too).

If NIGC failed to complete IGAT II and missed the LNG train, it succeeded in developing the small (sour) gas field of Khangiran, near Sarakhs in the extreme north-east of Iran. Begun in 1976, the Khangiran gas treating plant (3 x 270 mmscfd trains) was completed at a cost of $800m in 1980 by Iranian engineers after the personnel of its managing contractor, Davy Powergas (GB), had to leave Iran in 1978. The Khangiran gas was piped to Mashhad and all the way to Neka on the Caspian Sea shore (through a pipeline built by Entrepose of France). In yet another domestic project, NIGC brought on stream the two gas fields of Gavarzin (sweet gas) and Salakh (sour) at Qhishm Island; their gas was piped to Bandar Âbbas (85 kilometres, 12" pipeline) and to the Sarchishmeh Copper complex (440 kilometres, 24" line); the Iranian branch of the British firm IMEG carried out the design and engineering, and the Land and Marine Company (GB) joined Tehran Junub (Iran) in laying the pipelines.

Besides oil and gas, petrochemicals came to form the third leg of Iran's oil industry tripod. Managed since 1964 by its wily tsar, Engineer Baqir Mustoufi, the NPC had begun to expand slowly. By 1970, it controlled four plants: two fertiliser complexes (the small Iran Fertiliser Company near Shiraz and the large Shahpour Chemical Company at Bandar-i Shahpour), a PVC complex at Abadan and a LPG unit on Kharg Island.

Then, in the 1970s, NPC began firing on all pistons, expanding erratically and taking on board much more than it could handle. But the Shah himself was squarely behind the momentous expansion, encouraging Mustoufi to forge ahead come what may. Petrochemicals had become the Shah's *cheval de bataille*: "Oil is a noble material", he used to repeat *ad nauseam*, and therefore "it should not be used for thermal purposes; it should be devoted to more profitable uses, such as a feed for the chemical and petrochemical industries". Although some among the NIOC directors (including Dr P. Mina) were sceptical about NPC's ambitious plans, Mustoufi went straight ahead with a series of expansions, a hotchpotch of smaller ventures and the largest industrial complex in the Middle East: the mammoth Iran-Japan Petrochemical Company (IJPC) complex at Bandar-i Shahpour.

NPC's expansions occurred in three of its existing plants:
(1) At the Iran Fertiliser Company plant at Marvdasht (near Shiraz)

- A soda ash unit (63,000 tonnes/annum), built with Romanian technology by a Romanian contractor, Petrom (1971-74).
- STPP (30,000 t/a) and NPK (50,000 t/a) units, had Israeli (IMI) and Spanish (Foret) licensees and an Israeli (Flare Corporation) contractor; completed in 1975, these units never operated properly.
- A major expansion project, consisting of four major units: ammonia (1,200 t/d), urea (1,500 t/d), nitric acid (600 t/d) and ammonium nitrate (750 t/d); begun in 1974 with mainly French and British licensees and contractors (Davy Powergas was chosen as managing contractor in 1975), the Shiraz expansion proved to be a catastrophe; its initial budget, which had stood at $140m in 1974, increased by leaps and bounds to $625m in 1978 - such a standard fertiliser project should cost around $250m to $300m at most.[33]

(2) At the Shahpour Chemical Company fertiliser complex, where, in 1972, NPC had bought out its joint venture partner Allied Chemical Company (US)
- A major expansion project, including four main new units, ammonia (1,000 t/d), urea (1,500 t/d), sulphuric acid (2x950 t/d) and monoammonium phosphate (600 t/d), was planned, also the refurbishing of the existing units. The managing contractor was Stone and Webster (the London branch of the US firm); and, due to a capable Iranian supervisory team (under Engineer N. Kouhyar), the project was completed in 1978 at a cost of $353m.

(3) At the Abadan Petrochemical Company complex
- The capacity of the PVC unit was trebled (from 20 to 60,000 tonnes/annum) with the introduction of an oxyhydrochlorination unit, built by the company of Badger (US); thereafter PVC output averaged 40,000 tonnes/annum.

NPC also tackled four smaller projects during the 1970s. The first was for a carbon black plant (16,000 t/a) at Ahvaz, with the $11m capital split between the American Cabot Corporation (50%), NPC (20%), IMDBI bank (10%), the International Finance Corporation - a World Bank subsidiary (10%) - and private Iranian investors (10%). Cabot provided the technology and Simon-Carves (GB) built the plant; operations began in 1975 and the first dividends were paid out in 1976. The second was a 50-50 joint venture between NPC and two Japanese *sogo-soshas* (Nissho Iwai (26%) and Mitsubishi (24%), respectively) to set up a plasticiser unit, with a DOP production capacity of 40,000 tonnes/annum, at Bandar-i Shahpour; some $85m was invested in the small plant constructed by the Mitsubishi company, which was brought into operation in March 1977. The third was a 50-50 Iranian-French joint venture between NPC and the Gaz Ocean Company for entering worldwide LPG transportation; a 70,000 m^3 LPG carrier named *Razi* was built by the Chantiers Navals de la Ciotat, and put to sea in December 1977. However, LPG trade hit a low, and revenues and leasing fees were not as expected, so Iran-Ocean was virtually bankrupt by 1978 (*Razi* was sold after the Revolution to pay back debts, and Iran-Ocean was liquidated). The fourth project was for a vast phosphate rock prospecting programme over 80,000 square kilometres of Iranian soil by the French Bureau de Récherches Géologiques et Minières (BRGM). Launched in 1975, the project scope was later limited to five areas of roughly 1,000 square kilometres each. The whole programme yielded little worthwhile results (besides the useful data accumulated by BRGM regarding Iranian geology) and folded in 1978 after a total expenditure of roughly $12m. Dozens of other small and large projects had been proposed by multinational corporations, but none of them materialised, the partners usually dropping negotiations after a few months of comings and goings and the outcome of the feasibility studies. Among these multinationals were the German firm Bayer, the American companies Dow Chemical, Union Carbide and the group of Philips-Ashand-Goodrich.

The formidable IJPC project eventually came to eclipse all these minor developments. Initially, the joint petrochemical project was part of the Iranian-Japanese collaboration package of the early 1970s, based on the 8,000 square kilometre INPECO 75-25 concession granted to the Japanese in Luristan province. On October 19, 1971, the project's basic agreement was signed between NPC (50%) and Japan's Mitsui (50%), calling for the erection of a petrochemical complex in Bandar-i Shahpour consisting of three major units: an olefin plant (300,000 t/a), a chlor/alkali plant (232,000/262,000 t/a) and an aromatics plant (351,000 t/a benzene); a large raw NGL fractionation unit, a 1,500 hectares salt from sea water field (390,000 t/a salt) and of ten (smaller) downstream manufacturing units for plastics (e.g. polyethylene, polypropylene and PVC) and synthetic rubbers (e.g. styrene-butadiene rubber); capital investment was roughly estimated at $358m. In December 1971, Mitsui formed a consortium with affiliated and allied Japanese companies to share in its 50% interest in IJPC. The consortium, registered as the Iran Chemical Development Company (ICDC), consisted of: Mitsui (45%); Mitsui Toatsu (22%); Toyo Soda (15%); Mitsui Petrochemicals (13%); and Japan Synthetic Rubber (5%). On April 29, 1973, after many comings and goings and an extended feasibility study (carried out in 1972, coming up with an investment of $800m for the project) IJPC was officially formed by NPC and ICDC.

During 1974, on the one hand, main licensees (a total of fifteen, mostly American and Japanese) were selected and agreements signed. On the other hand, work was begun on the Shahpour site (adjacent to Shahpour Chemical) with the walling of the 240 hectares of mud-flats and its subsequent filling in with six million cubic metres of suitable earth fill by local companies Batiman Beton, owned by the Batmanqilich family, and Gama. Site preparation was then completed by the pre-loading and the sinking of 47,600 steel/concrete piles in the site area to enhance its resistance. Then, in November 1974, ominous rumours spread in Tokyo that investment estimates for IJPC had trebled to $2400m!

Doubts plagued the project, and, although Mitsui came out with a fixed $942m figure to silence the sceptics, rumours would always abound about the Brobdignagian venture, for example the mind-boggling amount of 1,000 billion yen advanced in December 1975 by a serious Japanese daily.[34] By then, IJPC had become the largest project in the whole Middle East, the largest project ever undertaken by Japanese companies abroad, a multi-billion affair in which Japanese honour and superiority had somehow become involved.

In January 1976 it was MITI's boss himself, Toshio Komoto, who came to Tehran to finalise the mode of execution and the project's financing. As far as execution was concerned, Mitsui had (since the onset) told its Iranian partners that they should let the Japanese carry on with the job, intermingling as little as possible (a difficult thing to ask the ever-curious Iranians) but no one among the Iranians dared give the Japanese a blank cheque for execution according to the 'Japanese Way'. The matter went all the way to the Shah, who ordered his special bureau to give NPC the green light in acquiescing to the Japanese demand. Having gained a free hand for his Japanese companies, Komoto turned to Iran's financial wizard Hushang Ansari to finalise the project's financing for an investment now estimated at

550 billion yen ($1,833m); a complex finance scheme involving Japanese loans for ICDC and Eurodollar loans for NPC (with cross insurance by both parties) was set up by the two men. Towards the end of summer 1976, the IJPC complex was ready to forge ahead.

The Japanese project's manager, K. Okada (an impressive manager), moved to Bandar-i Shahpour to direct a formidable workforce of 12,500 people (at peak), of whom 2,500 were Japanese. The four major Japanese engineering companies of Chiyoda, Toyo, Hitachi and Mitsui had split all responsibilities; the firms of Taihei Dengyo and Kajima were involved in construction activities and dozens of smaller Japanese outfits were involved in support and special affairs. In the 240 hectares under construction a forest of four hundred steel towers was soon to be seen; 1,200,000 tonnes of equipment and machinery had been brought in from Japan (99% Japanese) and the construction schedule had been arranged to last four years, from September 1976 to September 1980. Investment was still climbing during the construction period: it passed from 550bn yen to 610bn, to 643bn, to end up in the autumn of 1978 at 656bn yen. Project expenditures were also climbing up much faster than expected and by the close of 1978 amounted to over $2100m.

Besides the complex itself, a dozen other supporting projects had to be implemented to service the mammoth petrochemical complex. Among the supporting projects, worth a mention were:

(1) The twin Natural Gas Liquids plants (the NGL '700' and '800') were being erected by R.M. Parsons (US) for OSCO near Ahvaz at a cost of $750m; the NGLs would process 430 mmscfd of associated natural gas from the Ahvaz and Marun oil fields to produce 120 mmscfd of gas and 120,000 b/d of raw NGL for the IJPC complex's fuel and feed requirements; two 12" pipelines were built (one for the gas, the other for NGL) to link the NGLs with the IJPC site; by 1978 the pipelines were in operation, but the NGL units were only half-finished.

(2) The one hundred kilometres long water channel-cum-pipeline linked the Karun river (at Kut-i Amir) to the IJPC site; the waterway's capacity was 430,000 m^3/day, with 315,000 m^3/d earmarked for IJPC and the remaining 105,000 m^3/d was to go to neighbouring urban and rural settlements. The project was managed by the Ministry of Energy, with the Iranian Tehran-Boston as consultant; prime project contractor was Campenon

Bernard-Cetra (France), supported by Degremont (France) for water treatment, Siemens (W. Germany) for electrical requirements and KSB (W. Germany) for pumps. The total forecast investment of $270m had been totally eaten up by the time the Franco-German contractors left behind a half-finished waterway in 1978.

(3) The 'New Town' to be built on the banks of the Jarahi river, some 30 kilometres north of the IJPC site, was designed to house the IJPC operating staff, and was masterminded by the architecture consultancy Mandala (owned by Dr Nadir Ardalan[35]) in association with architects Skidmore, Owings and Merrill (SOM) of the US It consisted of four thousand housing units, and a special organisation, the Khuzistan Urban Development Organisation (KUDO), was set up by the Ministry of Housing to supervise the 'New Town' development. KUDO hired a subsidiary of General Electric (US) to erect the fifteen hundred housing units forming the first phase of the project; in 1978, a half-finished project was left behind, after some $40m had been spent on it.

In 1978, not only were the half-finished supporting projects left behind to rot in the Khuzistan sun and humidity, but the mammoth IJPC complex inevitably suffered the same fate: work stopped and the Japanese decided (reluctantly) to depart, leaving behind a technological graveyard and the last of their naive illusions about Iran. For the Japanese the choice must have been hard: their overseas prestige was at stake in the construction of the sprawling petrochemical complex, the loss of face being far more difficult to swallow than any financial loss. In a decade during which the Japanese had shown the world their economic power, their technological skills and their all-conquering spirit, IJPC would stand as the spike that had punctured their aura of invincibility.

In 1977 NPC received an unexpected proposal from the small Swiss chemical firm of Inventa to build a $6bn petrochemical complex (dubbed the 'Aryamehr Complex') adjacent to IJPC at Bandar-i Shahpour. Inventa was backed by a consortium of European chemical companies and Swiss banks. The financing of the complex would be secured by Iran with a 200,000 b/d contribution during the six-year duration of the complex's construction (1978–1983). The project showed up in the official Iranian-Swiss protocol of co-operation signed on July 13, 1977, between Economy and Finance Minister Hushang

Ansari and the Swiss minister Ernst Brugger. After preliminary studies, Inventa proposed the setting up of a joint (50-50) Inventa-NPC company with an initial capital of Sfr5m at Zug to undertake a detailed study of the proposed complex. The Swiss proposal got stuck in the quagmire of Iranian bureaucracy, and 1978 came in time to kill yet another potential white elephant.

By then, Iran had developed a whole herd of white elephants, arguably the largest collection in world history.

Its largest specimen was undoubtedly IJPC, but there were many, many others, in almost every field of industry or mining. All of them would be helplessly stranded after the Revolution of 1978/79.

15.5. White Elephants

In 1978, there were white elephants of all sizes and denomination to be found in Iran's technological jungle. In the oil industry, the Isfahan Refinery was saved *in extremis* by the capable NIOC engineers from joining the herd; but the NGLS '700' and '800' joined, as did IGAT II on behalf of NIGC and IJPC, and the Shiraz expansion for NPC. Almost every other sector of the Iranian economy had its own specimens. Hereunder, while briefly reviewing the overall achievements of the Fifth Plan in each of the major sectors, the white elephants are pointed out.

The Steel Industry

To bolster the internal production of steel during the Fifth Plan the PBO had proposed two projects: (1) the expansion of the Isfahan steel mill from 600,000t/a first to 1,200,000t/a, then to 1,900,000t/a; and (2) the construction of a complex dealing with the direct reduction of iron ore. A third project for the production of special steel (capacity of 60 to 80,000 t/a), to be carried out with the co-operation of Creusot Loîre (France), gave birth to the Iran Special Steel Company, but failed to materialise.

The first project, being an expansion project, had little chance of developing into a white elephant, but it very nearly did. Executed by Soviet contractors (like the original complex), the expansion began with an initial credit of 230m roubles, but ended up costing more than $1500m and extending well after 1978. Furthermore, the Isfahan steel mill sputtered along, seldom producing more than a million tonnes annually. Talks on further expansion plans to 4m and 6m tonnes/annum never got off the ground.

The second project, though, clearly ended among the white elephants. It had begun in the early 1970s with high-powered teams of Iranian technocrats surveying the existing plants, which were based on the two existing direct reduction technologies – namely, the Midrex process, developed by Midland and Ross (US) and licensed by Korf (W. Germany), and the HYL process, thought up by a Mexican steel producer of the same name. Their very cautious reports (typical of Iranian survey teams, unwilling to openly take sides) failed to favour either the American moving bed or the Mexican multiple fixed beds system.[36] So the Shah (hoping to please everyone) ordered the National Iranian Steel Industries Company (NISIC), created in February 1973, to build units of 500,000 t/a each from both technologies at its Ahvaz site. The West German firm, Thyssen, which had recently developed its own direct reduction process, promptly sent a high-ranking team to St Moritz to convince the Shah to let them build their own 400,000t/a unit at Ahvaz, asking for payment only if the unit was made to operate properly; needless to say the Shah (naturally) accepted, and Thyssen implemented its unit double-quick at Ahvaz (ready when the other two were only 70% to 80% completed), rounded up the necessary signatures and left Ahvaz as rapidly as it had come.

At Ahvaz, the NISIC complex, with its three different main processing units, its common utilities, its common facilities and auxiliary units, such as the iron pelletiser unit given to Lurgi (W. Germany) for $100m, was yet another white elephant. With fifteen thousand skilled and semi-skilled workers on site, it was a manager's headache. By 1978 a total of $1500m had been invested, and the PBO estimated that another $900m would be required to complete the complex. Due to Iranian technocracy's lack of backbone, added to the Shah's inclination to please all and sundry (come what may), Iran was saddled with a three-headed industrial hydra, which would create a myriad of problems in the region and devour millions upon millions of dollars. Iran had also accepted the responsibility of investing some $630m in India's Kudremukh iron ore mines, to provide the necessary feed to the Ahvaz complex, a total of 150m tonnes of ore concentrate over twenty years. Of the $630m total Iran had loaned India some $255m before 1978.[37]

As if the Ahvaz fiasco was not enough, NISIC decided to implement two other major direct reduction complexes in Iran: the first at Bandar Âbbas and the second at Isfahan. The contract for the Bandar Âbbas project, some 2,500,000 tonnes/annum based on the Midrex process, had been awarded to the Italian firms of Finsider (IRI group) and Italimpianti for an estimated $2bn; the site had been chosen, readied and even fenced off when the Revolution took place.

After the Revolution the two projects at Bandar Âbbas and Isfahan would be merged and taken to the site of Mubarakeh, some 50 kilometres south of Isfahan.

Nevertheless, in 1977, Iran still had to import some 6 million tonnes of steel.

The Copper Industry

The copper mountain at Sarchishmeh, 120 kilometres south of Kerman, was discovered in 1969 by a joint Iranian-British prospecting group – on its Iranian side the group was dominated by the Riza'i family and on its British side it was funded by Selection Trust Iran, an affiliate of the British Selection Trust (60% of shares) and the Consolidated African Selection Trust (40%). First borings showed a reserve of 400 to 800 million tonnes of copper ore deposits, with the ore having an average copper content of 1.12% by weight. In 1970, the Riza'i and Selection Trust group formed Kerman Copper Industries to carry on prospecting at the site and build a 25 t/d copper pilot plant at Sarchismeh, but, in view of the undertaking's immensity, decided to interest the government in the scheme. The latter duly stepped in, bought out the Riza'is and Selection Trust (April 1971), formed the public company Sarchismeh Copper Mining Company, and later renamed it the National Iranian Copper Industries Company (NICIC).

In 1972, NICIC selected Anaconda (US), a company with considerable experience in Chilean copper mining, as a consultant in the development of the Sarchishmeh mine. Anaconda prepared the plans for developing the open mines (cutting through the mountain) and the blueprints for the 158,000 tonnes/annum copper smelter and refinery. In April 1973, NICIC hired the Parsons-Jurden Corporation (US) as the managing contractor of the $1,400m project. Krupp

Industrie (W. Germany) and Mechim (Belgium) were awarded the contracts for the 158,000 t/a cathode copper plant, the two continuous casting mills and the rolling wire mill; Krupp was also to deliver the Dore plant, for the recovery of nickel sulphate and precious metals. Krupp received some 4.5 million tonnes of oil (worth around $400m[38]) and Mechim $68m. Natural gas for running the gas turbines was brought in from Qishm Island and the turbines (5 x 25 MW) were installed by Alsthom (France). The enormous amounts of water required by the complex was a problem: engineer-in-chief Thomas decided to have twenty deep wells sunk in the plain and their water output pumped all the way up the mountain to the complex (a 1,200 metre head) – drying up the plain below Sarchismeh. On the eve of the Revolution some $1bn had been spent on Sarchishmeh but the complex was far from being ready: yet another white elephant decorated the Iranian wilderness.

In copper ventures, the smaller joint Iranian-Japanese effort based in the Qalêh Zari copper mines, located some 120 kilometre south of Birjand, was much more successful then the Sarchishmeh project, although far less spectacular.

IDRO's White Elephants

The Industrial Development and Renovation Organisation of Iran (IDRO) was created in 1967 as a copy of Italy's IRI. IDRO developed during the Fourth Plan into a full-sized conglomerate, as projects lacking an institutional sponsor and orphaned projects were thrown into its lap. By 1972, IDRO had invested some Rls14.6bn (equal to $193m) in twenty-three industrial companies: a manageable portfolio. During the Fifth Plan, IDRO would become overblown, with assets totalling Rls121bn (equal to $1,715m) in a hundred and thirty-five companies – sixty-eight of which were subsidiaries (IDRO holding up to 51%), and sixty-seven affiliates (IDRO holding less than 50%). An attempt at putting IDRO's house in order yielded the following list of interests:
- 33 companies in the mechanical and metallurgy sectors;
- 17 companies in the electrical and chemical fields;
- 16 companies in leather and textiles products;
- 38 companies involved in construction materials;
- 11 companies in mining activities;
- 20 companies engaged in all kinds of services.

Thus IDRO came to manufacture ships (in a $200m joint venture, located west of Bandar Âbbas), wagons (in a $150m facility at Arak, employing 2,500 people), tractors (either Romanian ones or Massey-Fergusons at Tabriz[39]), combines (John Deere machines, at Arak), heavy equipment (Hepco), fork-lift trucks (Sahand), lathes (Tabriz Tools), water pumps (at Pumpiran, a joint venture with West German KSB), compressors (at Compidro, a venture with British Compair), electromotors (Motogen), aluminium (at the Arak Iralco, set up with the American firm Reynolds), ball bearings, asbestos, etc. All these production units were assisted by IDRO's in-house consultancy outfit, Technolog.

Two of IDRO's major projects ended as white elephants: the two wood and paper complexes set up on the Caspian seashore:

(1) The Choub va Kaghaz Sazi-i Iran complex (named 'Chouka'), near Asalam in Gilan province. Feeding on 232,000 hectares of prime Gilani forests, Chouka was a 1973 joint venture between IDRO (60%) and the Ministry of Agriculture (40%). Austroplan (Austria) had designed the complex with the following annual production capacity: 53,000 m^3 of wood, 6,640 m^3 of plywood, 35,000 tonnes of paper and 115,000 tonnes of cardboard. The Canadian firm of Stadler Hunter International (the Montreal-based subsidiary of the US company International Systems and Controls Corporation) had been awarded the managing contractorship, the Canadian Export Development Corporation lubricating the award with a loan of Can.$102.6m; by the close of 1977, some $312m had been spent on Chouka but the installations were not yet ready.[40]

(2) In 1975 Chouka created a wholly-owned subsidiary to duplicate its Gilan project in Mazandaran, giving birth to the Sanayî Choub va Kaghaz Sazi-i Mazandaran complex located at Neka, hence to be known as 'Nekachoub'. Feeding on 150,000 hectares of Mazandarani forest, Nekachoub was even larger than Chouka, with the following annual capacities: 62,000 m^3 of wood, one million m^2 of plywood, 50,000 tonnes of paper and 170,000 tonnes of cardboard. A Romanian company acted as managing contractor and equipment was purchased from Romania, Canada and Finland; Nekachoub fared better than Chouka, as its main contractor stayed put during the Revolution and passed over control of the installations to the Iranian management in an orderly way.

In 1975, IDRO launched two other gigantic projects, namely the Isfra'in $2bn metal works project (capacity of 500,000 t/a) in north Khurasan and the Reza Pahlavi Industrial Park, costing an estimated $3bn, at Shahriza, south of Isfahan. These two enormous projects never really got off the ground and only a few million dollars were spent on preliminary studies and design; had they materialised, they would have easily made the white elephants list.

Even without these late additions, IDRO was a monumental failure itself. In 1976, with total sales of Rls24bn ($340m), it had chalked up losses of Rls1.6bn ($22m); in 1977, things got worse with losses of Rls2.3bn ($33m) on sales of Rls28bn ($400m). IDRO was awash in red with assets worth over $1.7bn, and a return to the black could not be expected in the near future, with all these autonomous companies doing more or less what they wanted. Furthermore, IDRO had become a bone of contention between the regime's radical wing (i.e. SAVAK) and liberal wing (i.e. Empress Farah's clique); SAVAK had won important points by grabbing the top IDRO post for the brother of its star Parviz Sabiti, Hushang Sabiti, and had placed at the head of Chouka the young Dr Bihrouz Mûtazid, the son of SAVAK's number two man General Âli Mûtazid; the liberal wing countered these moves by having NIRT tsar Riza Qutbi nominated as chairman of both Chouka and Nekachoub. But the latter nominations could not alter the basic fact that IDRO was securely in SAVAK's grip and acted as its window on the world of technology, industry and development.

The Nuclear Power Plants

In order to complete the Iranian national power grids, conventional power generating plants and transmission lines were another of the Fifth Plan's priorities. Steam turbines were installed at Isfahan (a 340 MW expansion by GIE of Italy, and started up in 1974 and 1979), at Ahvaz Zargan (145 MW by GEC of Great Britain, 1975), at Ahvaz Ramin (315 MW by Technopromexport of USSR, 1979) and gas-fired steam turbines at Neka (3 x 440 MW, built by the German consortium of Deutsche Babcock-Wilcox, Brown Boveri Company, and Bilfinger and Berger, 1979–1980). Gas turbines were used for the Ray power station (1,235 Mw) with five suppliers: AEG (W. Germany), ASK (Belgium), Fiat (Italy) and the Japanese firms Hitachi and Mitsubishi (1977–78). Hydraulic power was to come from the Karun River Dam, built over the Goudar Landar, where 4 x 250 MW units by

Alsthom (France) were installed (started up in 1977). Moreover, some 2,120 kilometres of 400 kV lines, namely Karun–Tehran and Neka–Tehran – the latter's contract was awarded to Furukawa Electric of Japan for $230m) – and 2,400 kilometres 230 kV lines, as well as 132 kV, 66 kV and 63 kV lines, were installed to complete the national grid. Thus Iran's electrical capacity was considerably enlarged during the Fifth Plan, as shown by relevant statistics in Table 15.16.

Table 15.16. Iran's Power Generation Capacity and Electricity Production and Consumption at the Beginning and End of the Fifth Plan.[41]

	1972	1978
Total Installed Power Capacity (MW)	2,100	7,000
Maximum Load (MW)	1,500	3,500
Electricity Production (mill.kWh)	6,870	17,386
Electricity Consumption (mill. kWh)	5,723	14,345

As if this gigantic conventional effort was not enough, the Shah surprised the large majority of his technocrats by abruptly announcing in a March 1974 interview that Iran would install a number of nuclear reactors capable of generating some 23,000 MW over the next twenty years. The prime motive behind the Shah's surprise decision was not power generation but rather the harnessing of nuclear power by Iran with, as a by-product, another means of spending excess petrodollars. In April 1974, the Atomic Energy Organisation of Iran (AEOI) was duly created and the forty-four year old, Swiss-educated (ETH Zürich) Dr Akbar Îtimad was placed at its head.

Dr Îtimad lost no time in launching the AEOI on its tracks. In November 1974 he signed a first contract with the firm Kraftwerk Union (KWU) of West Germany, worth DM7.8bn, for the keynote delivery of two 1,200 MW nuclear reactors of the pressurised water reactor (pwr) type; the contract foresaw the supply of enriched uranium by KWU for the first ten years. The site selected for the twin KWU reactors (named Iran 1 and Iran 2) was at Halileh, a small village 12 kilometres south of Bushire. The construction of two sea water desalination units (100,000 m³/day each) were contracted out to the Japanese trio of Sasakura-Mitsubishi-Sumitomo for $270m. In 1976 KWU began construction of the two units at Halileh; by 1978, Iran 1 and 2 were respectively 80% and 50% completed. DM5.8bn had been invested in the reactors and DM137m in the enriched uranium supply.[42] The Halileh nuclear reactors, on which some $3bn had been spent, were another pair of Iran's white elephants.

In parallel with these Iranian-German nuclear relations, there had been an Iranian-French nuclear connection from the outset. As early as in June 1974 (only three months after the Shah's plunge into the nuclear fray), Iran had advanced a $1bn (soft) loan to France's CEA (Commissariat de l'Énergie Atomique). On the same occasion, the AEOI purchased a 10% share in Eurodif, the holding company building a state of the art uranium enrichment plant at Tricastin in France.[42] Then in September 1976, the AEOI took another direct 20% share in yet another French uranium enrichment venture: Coredif.[43] The improved Iranian-French relations further led to the signing in October 1976 (by Economy and Finances Minister Hushang Ansari) of a contract with the French firm Framatome (an affiliate of the Groupe Schneider) calling for the construction of two 935 MW pwrs nuclear reactors in Iran. Framatome was joined by Alsthom and Spie Batignolles in Framatec, the outfit in charge of erecting twin Iranian reactors (named Iran 3 and 4), on the Karun river near to Ahvaz. The total price for the momentous contract was Ffr10.6bn, with a separate account for enriched uranium deliveries. The AEOI made a Ffr1.5bn down payment for the reactors and a payment of Ffr264m for early enriched uranium supplies. The revolutionary strikes of 1978 nipped Framatec's early efforts in the bud. In early 1979, the Framatome contract was officially cancelled, after Iran had spent some $500m on the doomed reactors. Iran 3 and Iran 4 just failed to make the white elephants list; they died a natural death just in time not to.

Besides KWU's semi-finished Iran 1 and 2 reactors, the Shah's foray into nuclear energy and fuels had a series of interesting side effects. First, there were the two well-furnished atomic research centres at Tehran and Isfahan. The Tehran unit, directed by Dr Âli Sikhavat,[44] was German-sponsored; the Isfahan unit, built at a cost of $70m and directed by Dr Saîdi, was sponsored by the French. Second, there was the Uriran company, set up in 1976 with a $300m capital to prospect for uranium deposits in Iran; Uriran hired the best geologists available (by offering them double what they made elsewhere) and found some uranium before the Revolution placed its activities on the back burner. Thirdly, in October 1974 Austrian President Bruno Kreisky proposed turning Iran's deserts into cemeteries for nuclear wastes, but the matter was leaked to the press and pandemonium broke out among Iranians, with even the regime's staunchest supporters being shocked! The question nevertheless remained on the Iranian-Austria agenda until 1978, when the Egyptian deserts were eventually chosen as the depository for Austrian nuclear waste.

In the span of five years, 1974–1978, Iran had sunk over $4bn into its nuclear adventure. Were it not for the Revolution, the final bill for the nuclear option could have become much more expensive, the Shah seemingly bent on realising the 23,000 MW he had proposed in 1974. By the close of 1978, negotiations for sixteen fresh reactors were being conducted by the AEOI with KWU (four pwr 1,200 MW, two at Isfahan with maximum air coolers), Framatome (two pwr 935 MW), the German BBC (two undefined reactors) and the American firm Westinghouse (eight similar reactors).[45] By then the Shah's nuclear dreams had been nipped in the bud; Iran 1 and 2 were rotting in the Persian Gulf's warm saline humidity and Dr Sikhavat had left Iran.

Infrastructures

With the massive influx of imported goods in 1974 and 1975, the Persian Gulf port facilities were in the first line of fire. In 1975 alone, over $1bn had to be paid to shipping companies in demurrage charges. The ports were the bottleneck, and they had to be given top priority, especially because the high level of imports was foreseen as continuing in the future. Suddenly the Ministry of Finance's Ports and Shipping Organisation (PSO) found itself at the forefront of the logistics battle being fought in the south to get the goods disembarked. If the PSO was caught napping, it was not entirely its fault; an interim report entitled 'Iran Ports Masterplan', issued in April 1973, had foreseen a quiet decade ahead: total southern ports' imports of 5.2

million tonnes (worth some Rls170bn) in 1972 were predicted as increasing in stages to 7.0 million tonnes (Rls288bn) in 1977. The oil price quadrupling, however, upset the PSO's apple cart: in 1977 some 16.9 million tonnes were imported (worth Rls1,034.2bn, equal to $14.7bn) and some 1.1 million tonnes were exported (worth Rls45.5bn, equal to $645m). In the south, three ports took the brunt of these massive imports: Khurramshahr, Bandar-i Shahpour and Bandar Âbbas.

Bandar Âbbas, the latest site being developed, received top priority. An immense expansion project including new jetties and a container discharging facility, priced at $2bn, was undertaken by an Italian consortium (named Italcontractors) led by Condotte d'Acqua and including Finsider (of the IRI group), Italedil, Dragomar, Mantelli and Bolivica; with Holland's NEDECO supervising the construction for a $24m fee. At Bandar-i Shahpour, twenty-four new jetties were to be built (the first six on a crash basis) according to a $763m contract awarded to the association of Dumez-Hadish-Hamoun. Finally, at Khurramshahr, four new jetties were erected. In 1977 the three major southern ports received close to 75% of all Iranian imports; during the 1970s Iran's Persian Gulf ports had witnessed an unprecedented activity: their capacity had increased by sixfold (see Table 15.17). If neither the ports at Bandar Âbbas nor Bandar-i Shahpour had ended up being numbered among the white elephants, it was because they had to operate and expand come what may: without these port facilities Iran could not import the goods it had purchased abroad with its petrodollars.

Table 15.17. Iran's Different Importation Capacities, 1967 and 1977.[46]
(Figures in million tonnes of capacity)

	1967	1977
Khurramshahr	1.2	3.9
Bandar-i Shahpour	0.7	5.6
Bandar Âbbas	–	3.2
Other Iranian Ports	0.3	2.3
Inland Imports	0.6	2.1
Total	2.8	17.1

Once the ports' bottleneck problem was solved, the next bottleneck developed on the transport system carrying the goods from the southern ports to the consumption centres in the north, especially Tehran (the Tehran *Bazaaris* insisted that, however inefficient the system, all goods had somehow to be transited through their stores). By the close of 1976, some 1.4 million tonnes of goods lay in the Khurramshahr yard, waiting in the sun, to be forwarded northwards. A solution to the transport problem was a six lane highway linking Bandar-i Shahpour (and Khurramshahr) to Tehran.

In 1976 the contract for the construction of this formidable 1,100 kilometres long work of art across Iran (passing through the Zagros mountains) was awarded for $2.5bn to an American-French association of Morrison-Knudsen (US) and the French companies Jean Léfèbre and Razelle (associated with other French contractors in Cofraran[47]). The contract stipulated that the highway had to be completed within forty months. It was simply impossible. The French tried their best to involve all their Iranian allies (mainly Armeh and Tessa) in the project, they bought all the existing earth-moving equipment available and tried to get on with the job, but it was an immense fiasco. In 1978, a Morrison-Knudsen expert had computed that, if they carried on at their average historical rate of progress, instead of forty months the project would take no fewer than two hundred and fifty-two years![48] For the super-highway, the Revolution arrived just in time to bury it, with just a couple of hundred million dollars spent; in this case Iran was fortunate not to have yet another white elephant on her hands.

In the water sector, six dams and a major tunnel were constructed during the Fifth Plan. The tunnel was 8,700 metres long, at Kouhrang in the Bakhtiari mountains. Linking the Karoun basin to the Zayandehroud river, it was capable of delivering some 8 m³/second. The largest of the six dams was the 203-metre high Reza Shah dam on the Karoun, near Masjid-i Sulayman, built under the supervision of Hazra International (US); completed in 1977, one year behind schedule, there had been serious negligence during construction which eventually led the Iranian Government to blacklist Hazra.

In the field of communications and telecommunications striking advances were realised during the Fifth Plan. In the field of national television, NIRT introduced its second channel in October 1975, and colour television (Henri de France's SECAM system) in October 1977

– CSF-Thomson (France) receiving the lion's share of the infrastructural installations. In telecommunications, the Telecommunications Company of Iran (TCI) embarked on a ten year development plan with the technical assistance of Bell International, a subsidiary of AT&T (US). Iran's telephone network was to grow from 800,000 to 5,000,000 units. The Bell contract was worth at least $5bn; in 1978, Bell had 850 expatriates working in Iran – their yearly cumulative salary of $190m was superior to the $180m TCI paid its 28,500 Iranian employees. Other TCI contracts went to: (i) GTE (US) for the delivery of 675,000 line-switching equipment (worth $600m); (ii) Nippon Electric Company (NEC) of Japan for hardware; and (iii) the British-American Fortres-Icas Continental (FIC) for the design, installation and maintenance of Tehran's telephone cable network (for $320m). Iran's domestic and international telecom network became a tangible reality during the Fifth Plan. It might have been expensive but it worked properly (for the first time in Iran). Foreign calls became routine: from a daily average of 400 calls in 1976 to 40,000 daily calls in 1978. Iranian telecommunications turned out to be a grey instead of a white elephant.

Tehran's White Elephants

Since 1958 there had been rumours about an underground train system for Tehran. The promoters of the scheme were France's RATP and Sofretu companies: in 1966 they proposed their 70 kilometre network for Tehran, pricing it at $150m. German and Japanese proposals were also reviewed, but it was with the French that Tehran Mayor Ghulam Riza Nikpay signed a letter of intent in 1970. One had to wait until 1975 for the *Majlis* to approve, on May 6, the creation of the Tehran Underground Railway Company (later renamed Tehran Metro Company – TMC) as a subsidiary of the municipality of Tehran. In March 1976, RATP/Sofretu proffered its latest 63 kilometre network scheme, with a price tag of $1.3bn; the contract was duly signed with the TMC and in early 1978 the French began digging at twelve different locations in Tehran. By the end of the year, investment had ballooned to $2bn; in early 1979 the French simply left: another white elephant was born. It is still alive and kicking.[49]

The metro was not to be Tehran's only white elephant, for it was soon joined by the second Tehran airport. Rumours about this new project began in 1972, as if Mihrabad Airport was obsolete (which it was not). A 2,500 hectare plot of land located between Sharyar and Saveh, some 36 kilometres south-west of the capital, was nevertheless purchased for the future airport. Then, on December 5, 1974, subsequent to a heavy snowfall, the roof of Mihrabad Airport's main hall collapsed.[50] While repairs were made at Mihrabad and two new wings were added, the second airport plan was put on ice. In 1976 it was revived, and the winning design (a copy of the Dallas-Fort Worth Airport) was submitted by Âziz Farmanfarmayan, associated with the designers of Dallas-Fort Worth, the American firm of Tippetts, Abbett, McCarty and Stratton. In June 1976 the PBO approved the project as one of the Sixth Plan projects, slapping an $850m ceiling on its first phase, shifting the second phase to the Seventh Plan. The first phase (1977-1982) consisted of five main terminals and would lift Iran's airport capacity from 2.5m passengers in 1976 to 12m in 1982. Moreover a twelve-lane highway would need to be built to link the airport to the capital. By 1977, overall first phase investment had passed the $1bn mark (even before the start of construction activities on site); as for the site itself, its size had grown from 2,500 hectares to 15,200 hectares (with a score of insiders making a killing).[51] In March 1978 the Saveh site was inaugurated and preliminary work began. The project was nipped in the bud by the Revolution, but it would, like the Tehran metro, be revived in the eighties.

The third Tehran white elephant was among the Shah's pet projects: the Pahlavi Shahistan (lit. 'the Pahlavi City'). The grass roots urban ensemble was to be developed on 111 hectares of prime virgin land in the hills of Âbbasabad, at the very heart of Tehran. Llewelyn-Davies International (GB) was put in charge of the Shahistan in 1977 and the New York architect J. Robertson was appointed as the project's director. The city would cost between $5 and 10bn to build, taking around twenty-five years, the Shah was told. He balked not over the price but over the schedule – he might not be alive in a quarter of a century's time – so he asked for shorter schedules, the contractors first agreeing to fourteen, then to eleven years. That would take him to 1988, when he would only be sixty-nine-years old: he could then see his Shahistan, with its 18.4 hectares of diplomatic enclave (reserved for Tehran's embassies), its governmental ministries (for his bureaucrats), its residential areas (for his elite) and its commercial and cultural centres. In 1977, Shujâ ul-Din Shafa, the deputy court minister in charge of cultural affairs, co-ordinated the international architectural competition for the first Shahistan landmark: the Pahlavi National Library. Its first prize of $50,000 was won by a design from the West German firm of Von Gerkan, Marg and Partners. A couple of high-rise buildings were begun in the southern part of the Shahistan by the Khaneh contractor but the Revolution brought the Shah's pet project to a halt.

Kish Island

Another of the Shah's pet projects was the development of the Kish Island international resort. Kish Island, one of the Persian Gulf's medium-sized islands, is situated some fifteen kilometres off the Persian coast at Bandar-i Charak. It was the property of SAVAK, although how the secret service received its deeds is unknown. SAVAK created an 80-20 joint venture with the Bank-i Ûmran (of the Pahlavi Foundation) to develop the island, the Sazman-i Ûmran-i Kish (Kish Island Development Organisation – KIDO), with General Nasiri and Hushang Ram signing the organisation's statutes. On KIDO's board of directors the following personalities were appointed:[52]

– chairman: Amir Asadullah Âlam (Minister of Court);
– director: Jâfar Bihbahanian (the Shah's treasurer);
– director: Hushang Ram (head of Bank-i Ûmran);
– managing director: Muhammad Munsif, the son of Muhammad Âli Munsif, a close Âlam associate, a *Majlis* deputy from Birjand for two decades (1933-1953).

From the outset, the activities surrounding this company were extraordinary. For its financing KIDO received funds from SAVAK, Bank-i Ûmran and the Holy Shrine of Imam Riza at Mashhad (if only the Holy Shrine knew what it was financing!).

Moreover, KIDO received two loans from Bank-i Markazi for Rls2bn and Rls7bn respectively – after Court Minister Âlam had, in the spring of 1976, written a letter to the then Bank-i Markazi's governor, Hasan Âli Mihran, implying that the bank's loan to KIDO was an order from the Shah (a typical example of the court's placing pressure on the private sector[53]). As for the government, it only disbursed Rls411m ($6m) for KIDO. All these monies were needed to develop the island from scratch, using foreign contractors and foreign goods to attract foreign guests. These developments yielded the following ensemble on the island:

- An international airport, where the first Concorde landed in January 1978, complete with a duty-free shopping centre;
- Three luxury five star hotels, with Mme Claude's girls available in the lobbies;
- Two standard international casinos, to be operated by Ladbrokes of London;
- An eighteen hole golf course;
- 1,200 plush villas, 500 of which were ready in 1978;
- Special barracks for the Imperial Guards detachment to the island.

But why would a multi-billionaire monarch want to set up a luxury vacation resort for millionaires? There were only three rational answers to this question: (1) to set up 'warm' winter quarters (as an alternative to 'cold' St Moritz) for himself, his family and his elite; (2) to emulate the Aqa Khan, and compete with the latter's Costa Smeralda; (3) to entice Gulf shaykhs to come and spend their petrodollars in Kish's casinos and on girls (instead of going abroad), with the profits thereof going directly to SAVAK and the Pahlavi Foundation. Nevertheless, the whole bizarre KIDO idea sounded tragi-comedic, and by the autumn of 1977 even the Shah found it necessary to unload the whole project on to NIOC and Iran Air (50-50), albeit at a nice profit; each of the buyers chipping in $400m. This final transaction never took place, as Dr Iqbal categorically refused to be a part of this disgraceful deal and died a couple of days thereafter.[54]

Stuck with their KIDO, SAVAK and Bank-i Ûmran tried their best to encourage tourism on Kish by pushing the elite families to show the way and launch a Kish fashion, but it flopped.

It then tried to sell exclusive Kish Club membership cards at Rls100,000 each and Kish credit cards with Rls1m denominations to Tehran's jet set, but these flopped too. The Revolution arrived to wash off all of KIDO's red ink. Managing director Munsif fled Kish Island on KIDO's private jet; arriving safely in Bahrayn, he allegedly sold off the jet and retired to his golden exile, leaving behind KIDO and its innumerable problems.

KIDO was the last and the most bizarre of Iran's white elephants – an elephant with the strangest all of bedfellows, its owner SAVAK and entertainer Mme Claude.

15.6. Agribusinesses

To cure Iranian agriculture, the "sick man of the national economy", the Shah was sold on the idea of developing agribusinesses in Khuzistan province: economies of scale added to intensive mechanisation and water from the Diz Dam would work miracles. After co-operatives and farm corporations, this new panacea would turn Khuzistan into the Middle East's granary (as in millennia before) and wipe out Iran's food imports – estimated to be worth $400m for 1970/71.[55]

Two men were to spearhead agribusiness in Iran: the Iranian *émigré* Hashim Naraqi, who had succeeded in Californian agribusiness; and the American George Wilson, head of TransWorld Corporation. In late 1969 Naraqi formed Iran's first agricultural business, H.N. Agro-Industries of Iran and America; and Wilson established his Iran-California Corporation in March 1970 (see Table 15.18 for details). In their wake came other businesses, consecutively, Dizkar, Shellcott, International Agrobusiness of Iran and Galleh. One of the most original couplings was that of Royal Dutch/Shell with the London brokerage firm of Mitchell Cotts. As a Shell executive later put it:

> In 1970 ...Iran was not a particularly wealthy country, so we said OK, we'll make a gesture which will be appreciated and help the Shah in his farming policy ...that was the basic rationale [behind Shellcott]...[57]

Table 15.18. The Six Major Agricultural Companies Engaged in Khuzistan (1969–1978).[56]

1. H.N. Agro-Industries of Iran and America
   Created in 1969 with initial capital of Rls100m
   Shareholders – Hashim Naraqi (operating agent): 51%
               – First National City Bank 30%
               – Bank-i Iranian 10%
               – Private Iranian investors 9%

2. Iran-California Corporation
   Established in March 1970, initial capital of Rls95.3m
   Shareholders
   - TransWorld Corporation (operating agents) 30%
   - Bank of America 20%
   - Agricultural Development Bank of Iran (ADBI) 20%
   - John Deere 10%
   - Dow Chemical 10%
   - Khalil Taliqani and partners 10%

3. Dizkar
   Formed by a group of retired army generals in 1970; folded shortly after formation.

4. Shellcott Corporation
   Founded in 1971, with an initial capital of Rls60m
   Shareholders
   - Shell International 70.5%
   - ADBI 15%
   - Bank-i Ûmran 10%
   - Mitchell Cotts (operating agents) 4.5%

5. International Agrobusiness Corporation of Iran
   Created in 1971, with an initial capital of Rls610m
   Shareholders
   - Hawaiian Agronomics (operating agents) 15%
   - Chase Manhattan 15%
   - Diamond A Cattle of New Mexico 15%
   - KWPA 15%
   - ADBI 15%
   - Ahvaz Sugar Beet Company 15%
   - Mitsui 5%
   - Bank-i Milli 5%

6. Galleh
    Formed in 1972, by Princess Ashraf and her associates

Within a couple of years, the Iranian agribusiness myth lay shattered, the five operating agribusinesses making tremendous losses. In 1974, pioneers Naraqi[58] and Wilson threw in the sponge and sold out, returning to greener pastures in California. The ADBI stepped in to restructure the two ailing ventures, taking direct interests in both. In 1976, it was Princess Ashraf's entry Galleh which folded. By the summer of 1977, of the 69,000 hectares allocated by KWPA to agribusinesses some 51,000 hectares had been returned to the public authority (see Table 15.19). Only Shellcott and International were left to forge ahead, piling up losses. International had made a Rls350m loss in 1974 alone, instead of projected profits of Rls50m; as for Shellcott it forecast a net loss of Rls166m in 1978 (see Table 15.20).

Table 15.19. Land Allocation and Cropped Areas Downstream of the Diz Dam in Khuzistan Province.
(Figures in hectares)

Companies	Total Allocated Area	Total Cropped Area (at peak)	Returned to KWPA by June 1977
Iran/America	20,485	10,290	14,363
Iran-California	10,536	6,740	10,536
Shellcott	17,399	5,770	8,134
International	16,744	6,860	14,162
Galleh	4,010	2,180	4,010
Total of the Five Agribusinesses	69,174	31,840	51,385

– Farm Corporations	11,888
– Private Mechanised Farms	5,450
– Haft Tappeh (sugar cane)	11,100
– Others	1,536
Total Land Allocated	99,148

Table 15.20. Shellcott's Profit and Loss Forecast for 1978, assuming 5,000 hectares of crops.
(Figures in Rls millions)

Gross Margin (i.e. gross sales minus direct costs)	2.5
Overhead Costs	168.9
consisting of: General Costs	68.9
Depreciation	25.5
Interest	74.1
Net Profit/Loss (i.e. gross margin minus overheads)	-166.0

Within a few years, agribusiness on a large scale had proven to be a failure in Khuzistan: the much-vaunted fantastic profits had simply not materialised. There were some evident reasons behind the unexpected fiasco (which, for once, could not be blamed on the Revolution by royalists), with each pulling its full weight:

(1) The basic assumption that economies of scale applied in Iran was erroneous. Whether in industry or agribusiness, scale-related benefits were more than counterbalanced by inefficiencies due to the lack of capable management, deficient technological support and the absence of necessary infrastructure (these three ingredients being the *sine qua non* of thriving Western enterprises). Moreover, the thousands of hectares chosen for the Khuzistan projects appeared excessive, especially when seen in light of the fact that even in California's San Joaquin valley "producers of cotton, alfalfa and barley ...were found to obtain their lowest average cost at about 640 acres [equal to around 260 hectares]".[59] And the inefficiency of Iranian support was further illustrated by the fact that KWPA's maintenance costs per hectare jumped from $15 in 1969 to $102 in 1977 – a trebling in constant dollar terms!

(2) Crop yields on the large estates could not duplicate the yields obtained on an experimental basis, thus further weakening profitability. A simple comparison of the results obtained at the US-sponsored Safiabad Research Centre and the forecasts of DRC with the factual results on the field confirm these discrepancies as shown in

Table 15.21, further underlining the abyss between theory and practice in Iran.

Table 15.21. Yields Predicted and Achieved in Khuzistan for Various Crops by the DRC, Safiabad Research Centre and Agribusinesses.
(Figures in tonnes per hectare)

Crop Study (1968)	DRC Feasibility (1966-75)	Safiabad	R.C. Agribusinesses Shellcott (1975-6)	Average (1977)
Alfalfa (dry)	12.5	9–17	3.5	8.0
Cotton	2.2	4.6	n/a	1.1
Maize (corn)	3.3	5.4	n/a	2.2
Wheat	1.1	3.7	2.3	2.0
Sugarbeet	35.0	55–60	38.9	38.0

(3) Sale price of agricultural products in Iran rose much more slowly than overall inflation, thereby increasing the gap between revenues and expenses. American experts, who implicitly influenced Iranian economics, held that domestic prices had to be in line with international prices, and thus wheat sold at around Rls11,000 per tonne (with a guaranteed 1976 ceiling of Rls11,800[60]), barley at Rls8,000 and alfalfa at Rls12,000 per tonne. At such prices, agriculture in Iran (let alone agribusinesses) was not a feasible economic proposition.

(4) Last, but not the least factor in the agribusinesses' ultimate fiasco, was the fact that they were artificial islands operated by foreigners in a sea of smallholding Iranian peasants who resented their presence and viewed them as the cause behind the displacement of thousands of their brethren (for the displaced tenants numbers of 17,000 to 50,000 were mentioned). The displaced peasants had been

paid for their expropriated land and resettled in one of the five modern villages set up by the KWPA; but after having spent their monies, they longed only to get back on their land, looking at daily paid labour in the agribusinesses as akin to slavery. Fortunately for the evicted Khuzistani peasants, the large-scale projects folded and, with the Revolution, they were able to get back on their land: in any event, artificiality (for a reason or another) never lasts long in Iran. The agribusinesses were a case in point.

Left to pick up the debris from the crumbling agribusinesses was the government-owned Agricultural Development Bank of Iran (ADBI). Created in 1968 to finance agricultural ventures in Iran, the ADBI loaned some $400m to the private sector share during the 1970s[61] The man who presided over this distribution of public funds was a chartered accountant in his fifties, Mihdi Sami'i; after stints as the head of the Bank-i Markazi (1963–68) and the PO (1968–69), Sami'i had come to ADBI in October 1973. It was under his management that the bank became nursemaid to ailing agribusinesses and financier to the Pahlavi family's agricultural projects. Topping the list was Princess Shams with loans of Rls3,223m ($45m); Princess Ashraf received Rls826m ($12m) for her Galleh company in Khuzistan; Prince Mahmud Riza was loaned billions of rials for his ambitious projects near Kerman and at Minab on the Persian Gulf; Prince Âbd ul-Riza received over Rls500m, and Prince Ghulam Riza Rls919m, and Prince Sharam Pahlavinia (Rls256m) were also among ADBI's beneficiaries. Senators were among the ADBI's favourite clients:[62] senators Muhammad Âli Mahdavi and Amir Husayn Khuzaymeh Âlam respectively received Rls1,134m and 312m. Another ADBI client was the Ziaran association (industrial sheep-breeding) between the Pahlavi Foundation and the combination of Nadir Salih and Qutbi (Empress Farah's uncle),[63] which received Rls370m.

The ADBI had also lent some Rls1,200m to a mammoth agri-industrial enterprise in Khuzistan: the Kisht va Sanât-i Karun (Karun Agro-Industries). The Karun venture, launched in 1974, was an repeat of sugar cane plantations and sugar refining in the Haft Tappeh mould, but three times the size: no less than 55,000 hectares in the Daymcheh area (12 kilometres from Shustar), a sugar refinery of 250,000 tonnes/annum capacity (to be provided by Stork Werkspoor (Holland) and West Germany's Ziegler), with by-products of 750,000 tonnes/annum of bagasse (to be transformed into 200,000 tonnes of paper) and 95,000 tonnes/annum melasse. The whole project was initially estimated as costing $433m, but it must have ended costing more than double that. Being a public company, Karun ended up as a white elephant, especially as the Revolution caught it in full swing, with some 7,000 workers employed on its immense site.

Some 150 kilometres north of the Daymcheh site, yet another agri-industrial unit (albeit on a much smaller scale) was being simultaneously launched in 1974: the Mujtamî Sanâti-i Gousht-i Luristan (the Luristan Industrial Meat Complex). Located some 15 kilometres from Khurramabad on a 1060 hectares site, the $60m project for raising sheep in Luristan (capacity of 400,000 sheep slaughtered annually) was officially a Ministry of Agriculture project, but in fact the consulting firm of Taliqani-Daftari[64] called the shots, because Khalil Taliqani's son-in-law, A. Ardakani, was project manager, and ordered around the project's main contractor (a Hungarian firm) and sixteen sub-contractors. Most of the project's equipment and machinery came from Hungary and East Germany, under an oil counter-trade agreement. By 1977 the project was 70% complete, after costs estimated at over $200m; the project's Golden Meat retail shops were ready to open their doors in twelve major provinces. The Revolution would kill the Luristan meat complex: the project's cattle herds were disbanded and the machinery sold off. By the close of 1979 the project ceased to exist (but like many other ventures of the 1970s it was revived during the 1980s, albeit on a smaller scale).

Agribusiness had not been envisaged as the panacea to revive the moribund Iranian agriculture. Other solutions were needed to revitalise this badly sick sector of the economy, some of which were listed in a report on Iran[65] regarding the lifting of the following limits to its growth:

(1) limited access to markets, due to inadequate road and rail communications;

(2) limited technical capability, because of poor seeds and poor techniques of cultivation;

(3) limited by natural constraints, such as inadequate water, soil salinity, high soil temperature and dryness;

(4) limited by lack of capital, and low product prices leading to low agricultural incomes and to undercapitalisation.

The predicament of the Iranian peasantry was bleak indeed. Still numbering some 3,800,000 active peasants,[66] the huge mass of rural Iranians was heading for stagnation and oblivion. Rural Iran was not receiving its share of the petrodollars; those benefiting from the Shah's grandiose projects were the urban higher and middle classes.

Urban per capita income was five times that of rural areas, and urban families were incomparably better off than rural ones (see comparative Table 15.22). In July 1976, a High Council for the Rural Research Institute was created to try and evolve down-to-earth solutions to rural problems: it achieved nothing constructive. The first rural problem was the extremely low price of produce of the land; the second was the lack of consumer goods Without proper roads, electricity (see numbers of villages provided by electricity in Table 15.23) and running water, what could they purchase beside motorcycles? Even the consumption of fertilisers began to plateau off after fifteen years of continuous growth: 616,000 tonnes in 1974, down to 624,000 in 1975 and 601,000 in 1976.

Table 15.22. National Statistics on Goods and Services in Urban and Rural Iran (1977), in Percentage of Households using them.[67]

Goods	Urban (%)	Rural (%)
Automobiles	16.9	1.4
Motorcycles	8.3	9.7
Radios	78.1	57.8
Televisions	52.2	3.2
Refrigerators	73.0	7.6
Services		
Running water	79.5	11.7
Electricity	91.6	16.2
Telephone	16.2	0.4

Table 15.23. Numbers of Iranian Villages Officially Provided with Electricity (1969–1978).[68]

Year	Number of Villages
1969	46
1970	49
1971	117
1972	109
1973	162
1974	359
1975	566
1976	810
1977	1215
1978	752

The great villain of the 1970s' agricultural recession was Minister Hushang Ansari. Being in charge of the whole Iranian economy, Ansari had opted for make or break industrialisation. In his overall plans agriculture was a dead end, and all of Iran's agricultural products' deficit could easily be imported using petrodollars. Hence, in the 1972 tariffs issued by his Ministry of Economy, tariffs on food imports were either annulled (e.g. for margarine, peas, lentils, beans, powdered milk) or drastically reduced (butter from Rls20 to 10 per kilo, cheese from Rls28 to 15 per kilo, and canned meat from Rls110 to 20 per kilo).[69] These new regulations, combined with greatly increased consumption and stagnating local production, had the effect of sending Iran's importation bill of 'natural goods' sky-high: from $129m in 1970 to over $1,600m in 1976 (see Table 15.24 for details). Cheap imports of staple foods shot up: between 1973 and 1975 wheat imports trebled, and they doubled for barley, rice, sugar and vegetable oils, being multiplied by ten for meat (see Table 15.25). Frozen chicken had to be imported from France and West Germany, whereas eggs were purchased from Holland at the rate of 2,000 tonnes per month (in 1977/78), with every day a special KLM plane (dubbed the 'egg jumbo') delivering its fresh consignment of eggs to Mihrabad Airport. By 1978, the government was spending at least Rls67bn

($955m) on food subsidies and another Rls11bn ($156m) on red meat subsidies.

Table 15.24. Iran's Import Bill for 'Natural Goods'* Imported in Even Years of the 1970s.[70]

Year	Imported 'Natural Goods' Bill ($ millions)
1970	129
1972	283
1974	901
1976	1635
1978	1328

* 'Natural goods' is a special subdivision of Iranian Customs, under which agricultural products and other natural products are classified.

Table 15.25. Iran's Importation of Selected Basic Foodstuffs for 1973[71] and 1975.[72]
(Figures in thousands of tonnes)

Imported Item	1973	1975
Wheat	578	1463
Barley	106	204
Rice	160	286
Vegetable oil	117	226
Tea	n/a	12.3
Sugar	280	596
Meat	12	117

The peasants' only alternative was to migrate to the town. And migrate they did. A simple comparison of the 1966 and 1976 censuses reveals the migration drive's magnitude: whereas overall population had increased at an average annual rate of 2.68%, urban and rural growth had respectively averaged 4.75% and 1.10%.[73] As the flow of migrants to Tehran reached epidemic proportions, the acute housing shortage grew worse and *halabiabads* (slums) mushroomed around Tehran. In 1977 at least thirty-nine major shanty towns were counted in and around Tehran. Worse than the war and the need to make ends meet (not too problematic in the booming 1970s, but already more difficult during the 1977/78 recession) was the culture shock suffered by the younger migrant generations. These young men and women had grown up in small, closely connected villages and were ill at ease in the impersonal and imposing city. A potentially dangerous imbalance.

15.7. An Industrial Cemetery

In less than a decade, Iran had been transformed into the largest industrial cemetery ever known to mankind. The unfinished skeletons of projects worth billions of dollars lay around the country. It is sufficient to mention the IJPC site ($2bn), the nuclear reactors, Iran 1 and 2 ($3bn), the Ahvaz (direct reduction) steel complex ($2bn), the Sarchishmeh copper refinery ($1bn), the Shiraz fertiliser expansion ($1bn), the northern wood processing complexes ($1bn) etc. Many observers would later place the blame their collective failure upon the Revolution, arguing that, had they been completed and brought into operation, they would have generated tremendous profits and propelled Iran into the industrialised nations league; nothing is less certain, because it can as well be argued that any of these projects would have been awash in red ink from the outset and would have had to rely on petrodollars (i.e. current credits) to keep operating – in fact, an IDRO multiplied by hundred. As far as the Shah's fantastic projects were concerned, the Revolution might well have been a blessing in disguise. But the whole debate over 'ifs and buts' is rather stale, the basic fact being that the overall scheme ended in an undeniable fiasco.

It should be mentioned, though, that everything didn't go down the drain: left behind were the roads, the few highways, the airports, the ports, the houses, the buildings, the skyscrapers, the military garrisons, the huge arsenal, the foreign investments, and, especially, the thriving and booming oil industry (which by itself pulled many economic levers). But all these undeniable achievements were little to show for the one hundred billion dollars taken in during the 1970s. And the industrial cemetery left behind was irrefutable as well.

Before getting on the Fifth Plan road, the Shah's American supporters would have been well-advised to read once again what should be considered as the Westerners' main reference book on Persia, namely Lord Curzon's *Persia and the Persian Question*, and more particularly its visionary conclusion:

> I feel compelled, however, to end with a word of caution. Colossal schemes for the swift regeneration of Persia are not in my judgement – though herein I differ from some other authorities – to be thought of, and will only end in fiasco. Magnificent projects for overlaying the country with a network of railways from north to south, and from east to west, and for equipping it with a panoply of factories and workshops and mills, can only end in financial disaster, and bring discredit upon their promoters...[74]

This one of Lord Curzon's prophecies was proven right eight decades later.

NOTES

1. 'Iran Announces New Oil Policy' in *Iran Trade and Industry* magazine, February 1973, p.5.
2. 'The 1973 Oil Sales and Purchase Agreement' in *The Bulletin of the Iranian Petroleum Institute*, no. 52, 3Q 1973, pp.2-69.
3. See 'Iran 73', a special report of *Iran Trade and Industry* magazine, August 1973, p.47.
4. Created in April 1968 under the leadership of Italian Aurelio Peccei and Scotsman Alexander King, the Club of Rome became a loose assembly of managers and thinkers. The Club got its name because of its offices being located in Rome's Accademia dei Lincei.

5 D.H. and D.L. Meadows, J. Randers and W.W. Behrens III, *The Limits to Growth* (New York: Universe Books, 2nd ed., 1974).
6 For 1945, 1950 and 1955, see from 1960 onwards: *BP Statistical Yearbooks*
7 *The New York Times*, January 22, 1973.
8 The Arabian Light marker posted price had been first raised to $2.18 per barrel at the Tehran Conference in February 1971, then to $2.48 and $3.01 at the First and Second Geneva Conference of January 1972 and June 1973 respectively.
9 G.W. Ball, *The Past has Another Pattern*, p.465.
10 A. Sampson, 'Stupidity Caused the Oil Crisis', in *Newsweek* magazine, September 12, 1983, p.4.
11 In 1977, a two tier pricing system even developed within OPEC.
12 *OPEC Annual Statistical Bulletin 1984*, (Vienna: OPEC, 1984) pp.15 and 34.
13 See the *Petroleum Economist*, May 1975.
14 Private communication from a reliable source in the staff of the Iranian oil industry.
15 Ibid.
16 *The International Oil Industry Thru 1980*, p.11.
17 J.E. Akins, 'The Oil Crisis: This Time the Wolf is Here', in *Foreign Affairs*, April 1973, p.480.
18 See *International Petroleum Encyclopaedia*, for the years 1972-9, (Tulsa: Petroleum Publishing Company). Statistics retrieved from the *Bulletin of the Iranian Petroleum Institute* over the 1971-1976 span indicate a total of thirty-eight wildcats for nine discoveries. See the *Bulletin of the IPI* (nos. 42-65); the IPI numbers add up to a 24% rate of success as against 18% for the IPE. above.
19 The *Bulletin of the Iranian Petroleum Institute*, no. 68, 4th Quarter 1977, p.36.
20 Ibid., no. 70, 2Q 1978.
21 The SOFIRAN saga did not end there. In May 1980 SOFIRAN was abruptly absorbed overnight by NIOC. Then, in 1983, the final point came when NIOC sent Elf-Aquitaine a cheque for $330m (by normal mail) for settlement of the nullified contract (officially and unilaterally annulled in August 1980).
22 Ibid., no. 64, 4th Quarter 1976, p.12 (for up to 1976) and other NIOC publications for 1978.
23 See *The Financial Times*, October 9, 1986, p.4.; quoting from a report published by *Der Spiegel*.
24 The Bandar Âbbas project was resuscitated by NIOC in the mid-1980s, as its eighth refinery (the number seven being built at Arak). The new capacity stood at 262,000 B/D
25 See 'NIOC's Annual Report 1975' in *The Economist*, August 28, 1976, p.19. (in its 'Special Survey of Iran').
26 The *Bulletin of the IPI*, no. 59, 2Q 1975, p.23.
27 The Palau Islands (capital Koror) are part of the US Trust Territory of the Pacific (since 1980, known as the Republic of Belau). Located east of the Philippines, the islands of living reef coral stretched over 100 kilometres. The crude storage and trans-shipment project was thoroughly studied by consultants, but when the oil crisis subsided the whole project was shelved.
28 U.-J. Pasdach, 'Natural Gas Projects in Iran', in *OILGAS International Edition*, II/77 (2Q 1977), p.25. Pasdach gathered his statistics directly from NIGC.
29 These statistics were retrieved from various issues of the *Bulletin of the IPI*, dating from 1970 until 1979.

30 The figure of near to $3.00 per mmbtu for USSR exports is advanced by J.D. Davis in: J.D. Davis, *Blue Gold: The Political Economy of Natural Gas* (London: Allen and Unwin, 1984) p.145.
31 M.I. Goldman, *The Enigma of Soviet Petroleum: Half-Full or Half-Empty?* (London: Allen and Unwin, 1980). It should be mentioned that Goldman got his details wrong: it would cost much more than one million tons of oil to build part of the pipeline, but, on the other hand, 3.5 billion cubic metres of gas for the transit fee was on the high side (2.0 billion cubic metres would probably do).
32 The IGAT II gas trunkline was designed by Snam Progetti (Italy) and Sofregaz (France). The feasibility study for the utilisation of the Nar and Kangan gas fields was carried out by Elf-Aquitaine. The contract for the erection of the Nar gas treating plant was given to R.M. Parsons (US). The pipeline itself was split into three parts:
   1. Nar-Kangan to Isfahan, contractor SAIPEM (Italy);
   2. Isfahan to Saveh, contractor Spie-Capag (France);
   3. Saveh to Astara, contractor from the Soviet Union.
33 The ill-fated Shiraz expansion project was finally completed in 1985 after well over $1,000m – probably between $1,200m and 1,300m – had been spent. From the outset the Iranian team in charge of supervising the project had been extremely weak: the importance of this element of co-ordination is crucial in all Iranian projects.
34 Japanese daily reference to 1,000bn yen.
35 Dr Nadir Ardalan had excellent connections, among others to Empress Farah, and his Mandala outfit was commissioned to design the Bu Âli University campus at Hamadan, to supervise the construction of Tehran's Olympic stadium and to build the headquarters of the Kanun-i Parvarish Fikri Koudakan va Noujavanan on a plot of land located to the south of Tehran's Intercontinental Hotel.
36 Having visited the different existing direct reduction plants, the high-ranking Iranian delegation delivered a five page report to the Shah's Special Bureau; the report was a mine of ambiguous statements, with no outright recommendation.
7 The Kudremukh project would resurface in 1989 (like so many other pre-Revolutionary projects), when a new Iranian-Indian agreement was reached on the delivery of ore concentrate – effective from 1990 for fifteen years.
38 See the *Middle East Economic Survey*, November 7, 1977.
39 The deal for assembling 30,000 Massey-Ferguson tractors per annum at Tabriz was signed in 1974 by Hushang Ansari, bypassing both the Ministry of Agriculture and IDRO, although both institutions readily accepted the contract signed by Ansari. Ansari later rescinded on a contract to assemble Perkins motors (from GB) at an IDRO subsidiary.
40 Stadler Hunter International later went bankrupt, creating further problems for the ill-fated project; and the American mother company (ISCC) placed a $220m complaint with The Hague ICJ after 1979, only to have it rejected.
41 *Sanât-i Barq-i Iran dar Sal-i 1359* (The Iranian Power Industry in 1980), (Tehran: Ministry of Energy, 1360 (1981)) pp.3-4.
42 To purchase its Eurodif share, AEOI had first taken a participation stake of 40% in the Sofidif joint company, created with Cogema (a CÉA affiliate) which held the other 60%. Then Sofidif took a 25% share in Eurodif. Other shareholders in Eurodif (established in November 1973) were: AGIP Nucleare (12.5%), Italy (12.5%), Spain (11.1%), Belgium (11.1%) and the French CÉA (27.8%).

43 The shareholders of Coredif' were: Eurodif' (41%), the French CÉA (29%) and Iran's AEOI (20%). Therefore Iran had a total share of 25.1% in Coredif: 5.1% through its holding in Eurodif and 20% direct shareholding.

44 Dr Sikhavat had ambitious plans for expanding his research activities: he wanted to establish a brand-new laboratory at the Aryamihr University (the preferred site for sensitive research activities), but the Revolution would cut the grass from under his feet. The question remained, though, of why Sikhavat required two research centres, one German-sponsored and the other Iranian (SAVAK?) sponsored.

45 The *Middle East Economic Survey*, November 13, 1978.

46 *Iran Almanac 1978*, (Tehran: Echo of Iran, 1978) pp.325-6.

47 Cofraran was a poor choice because *cofr* (or *kufr*) means 'infidel' in Farsi.

48 Private communication from an employee of the American-French association, who reported the expert's prediction *verbatim*.

49 Eventually in 1986 Sofretu came back with a $10m study contract and the whole scheme was revived. Construction was to be carried out by Iranian firms, with the French advisers lurking in the wings.

50 The scandal unleashed by the roof's collapse led nowhere, as the Danish consultants, Kampsax, the airport's construction supervisor, were exculpated and the blame shifted on the airport's maintenance services. As usual in Iranian scandals, no one was ultimately indicted and after a few weeks the affair was laid to rest.

51 On an area of 152m square metres one can build at least a dozen airports. The second Tehran airport didn't require so much land; speculators with inside information made an easy profit.

52 H. Arzangi, *Gharatgari dar Iran* (Tehran: at the author's expense, 1358 (1979)) p.29.

53 Ibid., pp.31-2; where a photocopy of Âlam's letter is reproduced.

54 Dr Iqbal looked extremely pale as he came to my office, straight out of his last meeting with the Shah. He asked me for a glass of water. After drinking a full glass, he thanked me and said he would leave. He suddenly looked very old and dispirited to me. I was left with the impression that the last meeting with the Shah had not gone well. Later I heard that the Shah had told him that he had "gotten old and stupid", I also heard rumours of KIDO's sale to NIOC.

Private communication from the daughter of a high court official, who had the story directly from her father.

55 M.G. Weinbaum, 'Agricultural Policy and Development in Iran', the *Middle East Journal*, Autumn 1977.

56 H. Richards, 'Land Reform and Agribusiness in Iran', *MERIP Reports*, no. 43, December 1975, p.14. Some of the table's details have been taken from other sources.

5 Ibid., p.17.

58 The mysterious death of Naraqi's son after a brawl following a traffic incident in Tehran must have been the last straw for the agribusiness entrepreneur.

59 H. Richards, op. cit. (note 56), p.18.

60 M.G. Weinbaum, op. cit. (note 55).

61 *Keyhan International*, February 21, 1979, p.4.

62 A former senator who needed a personal loan of Rls10m for his private estate was told by ex-colleagues: "We can get you a loan from the ADBI for Rls200m or

300m, but not 10m"; the former senator declined and got the needed millions from a relative.
63 The pair of Salih and Qutbi manoeuvred through their M.G.S. holding company, through which they controlled a dozen outfits including Ziaran and Maxal. If Qutbi was connected to the court through his niece Empress Farah, Salih was connected to the Minbashians through his first wife Anvar, who was Pahlbud's sister, to the Mansurs (his second wife was Surrayya Mansur) and to the Majidis, his son Hurmuz having married Zaza Majidi, the daughter of PBO tsar Âbd ul-Majid.
64 The Taliqani-Daftari consultancy was created in 1960 by Engineers Khalil Taliqani and Jamshid Daftari. Both men made a colossal fortune out of it. Taliqani had begun his career with Point Four and had worked for the American water dam specialists Joe Justin and Robert Courtney (the fathers of many Iranian dams). In the sixties and seventies, besides his consultancy, he had a finger in many pies: he was vice-chairman of IDRO's Higher Council, chairman of Manem consultants, chairman of TransWorld Corp. of Iran, chairman of B.F. Goodrich Iran, and had a dozen directorships in various American-Iranian outfits.
65 'Iran – Oil Money and the Ambitions of a Nation', a special report by *The Hudson Letter*, (Paris: 1975) p.13.
66 See the table on 'Economically Active Population by Major Economic Sector" (1972), with a "Grand total active population of 9,195,000, and 320,000 unemployed", in W. Elkan, 'Employment, Education, Training and Skilled Labor in Iran', *The Middle East Journal*, spring 1977, p.178.
67 *Salnameh Amari Kishvar 1358* (National Statistics 1979), (Tehran: Markaz-i Amar-i Iran, 1360 (1981)) pp.1048 and 1056.
68 *Haftehnameh Utaq-i Bazargani va Sanayî va Maâdin-i Iran* (weekly magazine of the Iranian Chamber of Commerce, Industries and Mines), no. 20, Isfand 12, 1364 (March 3, 1985), p.100.
69 *Iran Trade and Industry* magazine, April 1972, pp.7-8.
70 *Nahveh Touzî Kalaha-yi Varidati dar Gruhha-yi Sanayî Shimia'i va Sanayî Pichideh – 1357* (Imported Goods for Chemical and Sophisticated Industries – 1978), (Tehran: Ministry of Culture and Higher Education, 1360 (1981)) p.12.
71 Sh. Haqiqat, op. cit., p.206.
72 *Salnameh Amari Kishvar 1356* (National Statistics 1977), (Tehran: Markaz-i Amar-i Iran, 1357 (1978)) p.234.
73 Ibid., pp. 34-5
74 G.N. Curzon, *Persia and the Persian Question* (London: Frank Cass, 1966) Vol. II, p.633.

CHAPTER SIXTEEN: IRAN INC.

In 1974 Muhammad Reza Shah Pahlavi ruled supreme in his kingdom. No one dared oppose his sovereign grip on all the levers of Iranian power. With over thirty years on the Throne, it seemed as though he had always been there and would always remain. His pictures and posters were affixed everywhere: the latest copies had captions such as 'The Shadow of God on Earth' and 'The Father of the Nation'. Such an exaggerated status was due neither to his sagacity nor to his diplomacy but rather to the oil price quadrupling of 1973/74. With annual oil revenues estimated at around $18bn, Iran now was a very wealthy country indeed. As the cost of her basic requirements averaged around $3bn annually, that meant an annual surplus income of $15bn. The Shah was the sole man to decide upon the investing of this money: he had orchestrated the February 1971 Tehran Conference; invited the international jet set to Persepolis; reached an agreement with the Consortium in St Moritz in February 1973 and engineered the Tehran Conference of December 1973. No one dared dispute with him for the role of ultimate arbiter in the distribution of the windfall petrodollars. Assured of the United States' unflagging support (his US standing had never been better than under the Nixon/Kissinger leadership), he was secure at home with a personal elite he had chosen himself, with the counter-elite kept in check by SAVAK; furthermore, Iran's invisible government (made up of the leading quintet of its non-governing Elite) had decided to cater to the Shah's dreams of self-aggrandisement, to give him all the credit (and even more), while they scrambled to line their own pockets (and their Swiss bank accounts) riding his coat-tails, because, in case things went sour, they had a ready scapegoat at hand.

16.1. The Top Echelon

Given unlimited degrees of freedom in his own kingdom, Muhammad Reza Shah Pahlavi could choose to do anything he wanted. He could finally indulge his lifelong dream of becoming the enlightened autocrat of Iran, to try his best for his thirty million citizen-shareholders, who had no voting rights). To fulfil his dream, he set up Iran Incorporated, the corporation he needed to oversee the spending of Iran's surplus petrodollars (and incidentally the management of the country). At the very top of Iran Inc., he naturally cast himself as chairman (for life) and chief executive officer; the corporation's board of directors consisted of seven main members. Two vital functions were directly given his personal attention: the Pahlavi Foundation and SAVAK (see Figure 16.1); then came the corporation's main divisions: (1) the military; (2) the bureaucracy; and (3) the private sector. Two of the bureaucracy's main departments were of special importance to the chairman: oil and foreign affairs.

Figure 16.1. Iran Inc.'s Overall Structure

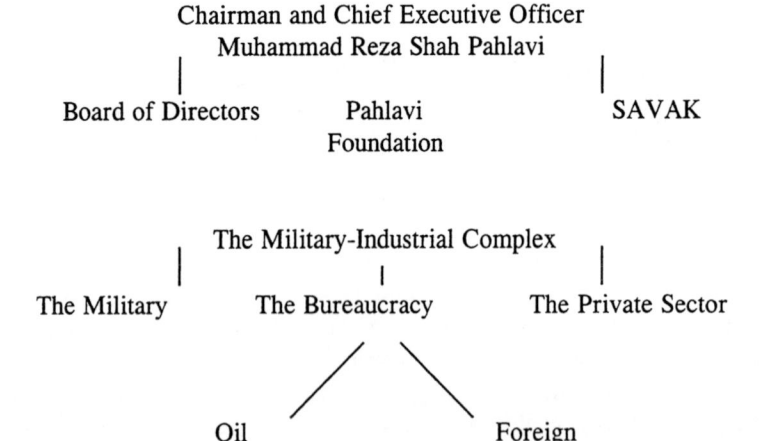

Chairman and Chief Executive Officer
Muhammad Reza Shah Pahlavi

Board of Directors — Pahlavi Foundation — SAVAK

The Military-Industrial Complex

The Military — The Bureaucracy — The Private Sector

Oil Affairs — Foreign Affairs

In 1974, aged fifty-five, the Shah, at the summit of his power, relished his role as Iranian chairman. He could not stop himself from lecturing Western national leaders over their societies' decadence and showing off his own Iranian 'Shah-ternalistic' model as an example to follow. Blinded by the flow of petrodollars, the Shah failed to realise that, if it were not for the West's support, he would not be in power and able to spout incessant bombast and broadcast lengthy rodomontades. It must be said in his defence that statements such as David Rockefeller's "the Shah's leadership could be a pattern for the world" and Henry Kissinger's "we attach a great importance to the advice of the Shahanshah" – both uttered during the Shah's official visit to the US in May 1975 – did not help to keep him modest. On the other hand, another American politician, Treasury Secretary William Simon, "publicly described him as a 'nut' and as 'irresponsible and reckless'",[1] striking the only false note in the symphony of American praise.

For his board of directors, the Shah chose a mix of seven characters:

(1) Princess Ashraf Pahlavi, fifty-five, the Shah's twin sister: a ruthless dynamo, as energetic and decisive as her brother was vacillating and soft; nicknamed 'the black panther',[2] she was not popular among Iranians, but never cared much about her popularity; she had her own supporters well-entrenched in SAVAK, the army and the bureaucracy; she was immensely rich in her own right, with interests in any profitable venture she could get her hands on; "that she and her entourage monopolised most of the country's business was a common belief", noted F. Huvayda in his memoirs;[3] her name was more than once linked to high stakes drugs-trafficking, since November 1960, when she had had a brush with the Geneva police "about two suitcases containing some $2m worth of heroin";[4] her third husband, Dr Mihdi Bushihri, was also successful with his Technisaz company and his multiple chairmanships (e.g. chairman of Sulzer Iran Co.); her eldest son Shahram Pahlavinia was unabashedly making a killing in his jockeying for US multinationals in Iran (e.g. Northrop) and his exclusive sales to NIOC through his Guide company (managed by a former NIOC employee, Dr Mihdi Mashayikhi); her second son Shahryar Shafiq, reputed for his honesty, was the Iranian Navy's up-and-coming officer;[5] young, good-looking boys were among her best friends, such as Gulisurkhi, Îtimadian, Raji and Amini – she had Raji and Amini posted as ambassadors to London and Tunis respectively, and Parviz Sipahbudi too ("Ashraf Ambassadors", as Raji puts it in his memoirs[6]); she also acted as Iran's super-envoy in China, the USSR and France (her second home), and as head of the Iranian delegation to the UN – being appointed to the head of the UN

Commission on Human Rights (a paradox in view of SAVAK's widely known actions!).

(2) Empress Farah Diba, thirty-six, the Shah's third wife and first empress (*Shahbanou*); her power stemmed mainly from the fact that, should the Shah pass away, her son, Reza, would reign and she would head the Regency Council; gravitating around her were a handful of close friends, headed by her cousin Riza Qutbi, the low-profile tsar of NIRT,[7] Lily Amir Arjumand and her private secretary, Karim Pasha Bahaduri; she tried her best to shape her public image in that of a caring mother, a patron of the arts and as a court member from the people and for the people – upon her thirty-sixth birthday she had proclaimed: "My family is the Nation"; but she had never been able to put down strong roots of popularity among the people from whom she said she came, and her natural timidity didn't help her in her quest for popularity; her beloved Shiraz Arts Festival (staged annually under NIRT's auspices and Riza Qutbi's personal management) proved a liability before turning into a catastrophe; her fully-pledged support also went to the Aspen Institute for Humanistic Studies, an American non-profit-making think-tank created in 1949, which had caught her eye, and had staged the Persepolis Symposium in 1975;[8] altogether, the Empress and her coterie of genteel liberals were no match for Princess Ashraf and her power-minded acolytes.

(3) Amir Asadullah Âlam, fifty-five, court minister and the Shah's right-hand man; over three decades at his sovereign's side, he had won his absolute trust – "Alam is the only remaining person", Radji correctly noted, "who could still permit himself to speak openly to His Imperial Majesty on all subjects";[9] he had come to learn (from experience) the checks and balances of Iranian society; married to a daughter (Nimtaj) of the Qavam ul-Mulk Shirazi Elite family, he had risen within the Elite's ranks, but not far enough to make it to membership of the top five-man directorate; rebuffed in his ambition, he endeavoured to siphon off Elitists to a breakaway elite dominated by himself and his supporters; he was immensely rich, having inherited a colossal fortune and taken his cut from all the deals he had lubricated; but he was struck by a grave illness and early treatments in 1974 and 1975 at the American Hospital at Neuilly had failed to stop the deadly illness spreading; still he carried on as first courtier.

(4) General Husayn Fardoust, fifty-five, the Shah's longest standing friend and *alter ego*; the Pahlavi regime's *éminence grise*, he

was practically invisible because he was so low profile (most pictures of him dated back to the 1940s), but he wielded enormous power behind the scenes at the head of the Imperial Inspectorate, a loose watchdog organisation with a lean (fifty at most) and capable staff, and almost unlimited powers to investigate anyone, anywhere and at any time; his personal telephone calls were dreaded by all top military commanders and senior civil servants; he was arguably the most knowledgeable man in Iran,[10] and hence one of the most powerful; a hard worker, he was definitely amongst the best and the brightest of the Shah's elite.

(5) General Âbd ul-Karim Ayadi, fifty-nine, the Shah's private physician and financial partner; in the 1970s he oversaw Bihbahanian's investments on behalf of the Pahlavi Foundation and the Shah's (growing) private purse; from 1974 onwards, their million-dollar deals turned into billion-dollar projects, the court developing a parallel bureaucracy overlapping and giving orders to the regular, public service, thereby exacerbating anti-royalist feelings in the latter's ranks (for example in the case of Ayadi's Swiss petrochemical deal, which was sabotaged by the bureaucracy); as a *Baha'i* leader, he oversaw the *Baha'i* renaissance in the 1970s and encouraged the emergence of businessmen such as Huzhabr Yazdani.

(6) Ardashir Zahidi, forty-six, the Shah's former son-in-law and most secure link to the Americans since 1953; the *Murdad 28* coup had secured his position for life (as did his Iran Inc. directorship); self-confident to the point of speaking to Empress Farah on the very limits of *lèse-majesté* and openly denigrating Premier Huvayda,[11] whose Minister for Foreign Affairs he had been from October 1967 until September 1971; in the summer of 1971, after an open clash with the Premier – leading to Huvayda's resignation, refused by the Shah – he had to leave for Washington as the Shah's 'Ambassador for Life'; the Shah must have been satisfied with his choice for in 1976 he told F. Huvayda (his ambassador to the UN): "In any case, Ardeshir has all the American senators in his pocket"[12] (not a very wise remark, grossly overestimating the limited Zahidi's abilities[13] and grossly underestimating American senators); but his Washington parties were truly the best in town, with caviar, champagne, opium and beautiful girls available,[14] and it is very plausible that a senator or two might have taken advantage of the goods offered at the Iranian Embassy by their 'dear friend' Zahidi.

(7) Jâfar Sharif Imami, sixty-four, was an intelligent and capable engineer; he had strong masonic links – was founding member of the Sitareh-i Sahar Lodge in 1960[15] (a branch of the German-related Independent Grand Lodge of Iran), and was listed in 1964 as one of its leaders (with Abu'l Hasan Muâdil and Qasim Lajivardi[16]) and later he allegedly rose to the top of the Independent Grand Lodge, following in the footsteps of Husayn Âla (its first Grand Master) and Hasan Taqizadeh (its second GM)[17] – moreover he was chairman of governors, multiple districts 354 of Lions International; and collected positions of power, such as the presidency of the Senate (1964–78), deputy custodian of the Pahlavi Foundation, chairman of the IMDBI bank and head of the Iranian Engineers' Association.

In the gigantic machinery of Iran Inc., two special entities were directly linked to the Shah: the Pahlavi Foundation and SAVAK.

The Pahlavi Foundation, supervised by two board members – General Ayadi and Engineer Sharif Imami – was managed in a masterly manner by Muhammad Jâfar Bihbahanian and Hushang Ram. Its Iranian base of real estate (in Gilan and Mazandaran), hotels, service companies, construction firms, sugar refineries, agribusinesses, mines and factories[18] made enormous profits; the development of its *Sharak-i Gharb* (the Western City) on the western fringes of Tehran made billions of rials for the Bank-i Ûmran, as did other urban developments in which it had a hand. Official grants allocated to it by governmental agencies (see Table 16.1) further filled its coffers; unofficial payments, or rather differential payments, made by NIOC (as hinted by R. Graham[20]) also enriched it. In the 1970s, however, the foundation became international: real estate in Brazil, development projects in New Orleans, shares in the NYSE, a thirty-six storey skyscraper on Manhattan's Fifth Avenue (and 52nd Street), an interest in the Geneva Société de Développement Financier and a 5% stake in the First Wisconsin Corporation (for which H. Ram received a seat on the FWC board), just to mention the visible tips of the foundation's iceberg abroad. In 1976, the Bank-i Ûmran, the foundation's bank, "was recognised as the largest single direct foreign investor in the US for the year":[21] a confirmation of the foundation's growing American empire, an empire the assets of which Bihbahanian had been cautious enough to shift into unassailable trust funds, just as he had been prudent enough to stash all of the foundation's cash in impregnable Swiss banks.

Table 16.1. Official Grants Made by Government Agencies to the Pahlavi Foundation (March 1977–March 1978).[19]

Agency or Ministry	Grants Allocated	
	Rls Million	$ Million
Ministry of Economy and Finance	250	3.5
NIOC	200	2.8
Bank-i Markazi	120	1.7
Plan and Budget Organisation	100	1.4
Imperial Sports Organisation	90	1.3
Ministry of War	60	0.9
Total	820	11.6

SAVAK was far too important to be left unchecked. Under the trustworthy General Nasiri, the Shah had been able to get a better grip over Iran's major secret services, but not a complete one, as foreign cells (American and Israeli ones), and even General Bakhtiar's men, were now so well-entrenched as to be immovable.

With its almost unlimited funds and its ever-increasing domestic clout (not failing to remind all and sundry that it was in the front line of the anti-terrorist war and was also keeping in check all of the regime's foes), SAVAK was busy expanding within the bureaucracy (during the 1970s, almost overtly) and the whole provincial power apparatus. Similarly to the Pahlavi Foundation, having done its utmost internally, SAVAK began setting its sights on the international stage: it had the means and (so it thought) the brains, so why not? It first targeted the CISNU and its Iranian students: instead of passively waiting for them in Iran, it would apply preventive measures and checkmate them on their Western campuses. In Europe, Parviz Khwunsari was masterminding the anti-student struggle from his Geneva base; Mansur Rafizadeh was in charge of US operations from Washington.[22] All Iranian embassies abroad had been turned into SAVAK strongholds, with non-SAVAK ambassadors closing their eyes to these covert operations. In May 1974, *The Sunday Times* revealed that Jahanbin, a first secretary in Iran's Embassy in London had been caught recruiting informers to spy on Iranian students in Great Britain.[23] This was a real blunder on SAVAK's part, which led to a full warning to all Western countries that SAVAK was subversively operating on their turf: a shocking piece of news, to say the least.

Outside its own borders, SAVAK was vulnerable. A coalition of Iranian students abroad and an outraged Western press would wage war. On June 1, 1976, thirteen Iranian students (having come from West Germany, Austria and Italy) stormed the Iranian consulate in Geneva and confiscated some 2,800 documents proving beyond doubt SAVAK's involvement in wide-ranging covert activities throughout Europe.[24] The Swiss and Western press were quick in reporting the students' finds, and their public campaign of exposure gave SAVAK a red face. The affair led to the expulsion from Switzerland of the first secretary to Iran's UN Office in Geneva (SAVAK's Geneva antenna), Dr Ahmad Malik Mahdavi, declared *persona non grata*. But this setback didn't stop SAVAK from pursuing its activities and expanding abroad. In London, SAVAK's young General Javad Muînzadeh was highly active; somehow he was implicated in the mysterious death of Dr Âli Shariâti at Southampton, and in the checking by SAVAK agents of the two Labour MPs, Stanley Newens and William Wilson in 1976 (which ended in a scandal).[25] In Paris, SAVAK agent Humayoun Kaykavousi (officially second secretary) was shot at and wounded by "unknown gunmen" on November 2, 1976. In America, Rafîzadeh had purchased a ranch (through Hushang Namvar Tihrani, his sister's husband) to house SAVAK's American headquarters.

16.2. The Military

Of the tripod of military-bureaucracy-entrepreneurs on which Iran Inc. rested, the military apparatus was by far the most important leg, being both the creature and the ultimate guarantor of the Pahlavi dynasty. Reza Shah had always told his son to give his army top priority. Now, Muhammad Reza Shah, with his billions of petrodollars, would show his hand-picked generals that he was his father's son: he would buy them the best there was worldwide, give them free rein to expand at will, and shower them with honours, promotions, medals, bonuses, perks, lands and money. This strategy of military development *à outrance* triggered an expansion of the Iranian armed forces unparalleled in the country's history and second in world history only to the forced expansion of the German Wehrmacht over 1933-1939.

The ensuing inflation of Iran's military machine was shocking, if not obscene. In less than a decade, the number of men serving under the flag (always in the rough proportion of 30% professional officers and NCOs to 70% conscripts) more than doubled from 220,000 to almost 500,000 in 1978 (see Table 16.3. for detailed numbers). Still manpower expansion was almost negligible when compared with the erratic purchase of all kinds of modern weaponry and armaments. Iran's annual defence budget would multiply by ten during the seventies, totalling some $43.3bn over 1971-1978 (see Table 16.4). In the span of seven years, 1972-1978, Iran bought some $19.5bn worth of arms from the US;[29] the exact breakdown per quarter of goods and services bought for the $2376m and imported from the US during 1977 (an average of $6.5m per day!) is shown in Table 16.5; in 1978 there were still some $11.5bn worth of armaments in the US pipeline to Iran, some of which were ready for shipment in American storehouses. The lion's share of the Iranian armed forces' hardware purchase naturally went to the US, but the USSR, Israel, France, Italy, Great Britain, West Germany and a number of East European countries also received substantial orders. Notwithstanding these extra non-US purchases, the Iranian armed forces had, during the seventies, become an appendix to the US armed forces and were totally dependent on them as far as waging war was concerned; this fact was recognised by the US Senate after extensive hearings which led to the publication of a fully documented report.[31]

Iran's impressive arms build-up had begun in 1972 with an approval by the *Majlis* of a foreign loan for Rls40bn (equal to $528m) to purchase military hardware, mostly helicopters. The helicopters to be purchased were of the type AH-1J Cobras attack helicopters (manufactured by Bell Helicopters, a Textron subsidiary, of Fort Worth, Texas) and the type AB 214 Hueys (manufactured by Agusta, of Milan, Italy, under licence from Bell Helicopters – the initials AB standing for Agusta-Bell). However the Agusta company held exclusive rights over all helicopter sales in Iran, be it helicopters from Bell, Boeing or Sikorsky; this exclusivity stemmed from the Shah's

Table 16.3. Number of Men Serving in Iran's Armed Forces in 1970[26] and 1978.[27]

Forces	1970	1978
Army	135,000	285,000
Air Force	22,500	100,000
Navy	9,000	28,000
Gendarmerie	55,000	74,000
Total	221,500	487,000

Table 16.4. Iran's Defence Budget for the years 1971–78.[28]

Year	Defence Budget ($ Millions)
1971	1,016
1972	1,329
1973	1,978
1974	5,515
1975	7,583
1976	8,028
1977	7,959
1978	9,930
Total	43,338

friendship with Prince Vittorio Emmanuele of Savoy, dating from the 1950s (after the Shah had divorced Surrayya, it was rumoured that he might marry the Italian Prince's sister) and his cousin Prince Agusta. Since 1968, Iran had began buying AB 206s, then in 1971 switched to AB 212s, before going over to AB 214s in 1972. In February 1974, Agusta was awarded a further contract worth $100m for the 1976

Table 16.5. Iran's Purchase of Military Goods and Services from the United States during the year 1977.[30] (Figures in $ millions)

	1Qtr '77	2Qtr '77	3Qtr '77	4Qtr '77	1977
Goods	386	612	379	356	1,733
Services	141	104	216	182	643
Total	527	716	595	538	2,376

delivery of six Agusta Sea Kings (copies of Sikorsky's SH-53D) made under Sikorsky licence; in February 1977 Iran agreed to transfer 5 million tons of crude oil to Italy's ENI (worth roughly $425m) in exchange for fifty Agusta Chinooks (copies of Boeing Vertol's CH-47D) made under Boeing licence.

Agusta also acted as a middleman in the 1974 $500m deal to have Bell Helicopters assemble helicopters at Isfahan.

The signing of the Bell contract was made in such a hurry that it broke all records for multi-million dollar contracts in Iran; another $150m was slapped on top of it for the extra assembly of fifty AB 214 A and three hundred and fifty 214 ST (twin turbine) helicopters; Air Taxi of Iran received a $2.9m commission on the deal;[32] Agusta must have received its normal commissions on all sales to Iran. The 3,600 American employees of Bell Helicopters formed the largest community of US private sector firms' employees in Iran; most of the American families were housed in separate quarters at the Shahin Shahr town,[33] some 30 kilometres north of Isfahan itself. The Americans played havoc with local customs and morals in the Isfahani community,[34] which strictly observed Islamic rules; Bell's contract was among the very first contracts cancelled by the Iranian Government towards the close of 1978 for "causes of *force majeure*".[35] By then, Bell's Iranian project had ballooned to costing $4bn. All in all, it produced a few dozen helicopters for the Iranian *Havanirouz* (the army's Aviation Command), which in 1978 controlled a total of nine hundred units – it would have been much cheaper to purchase these helicopters, and it would have caused less disruption in Isfahan.

The air force was another domain where the Shah and his brother-in-law General Khatami went for the best the US could provide. In the 1960s and early 1970s, the Imperial Iranian Air Force (IIAF) had acquired two hundred and twenty F4-Phantoms (McDonnell Douglas), one hundred and seventy F5-Tigers (Northrop), twenty-four Boeings (707s supply planes and 747s transporters) and fifty-seven C-130 Hercules from Lockheed. In January 1974, the Shah chose the new F-14 Tomcat, manufactured since 1972 by the Grunman Corporation for the US Navy as the IIAF new attack fighter-interceptor, ordering a first batch of thirty units (price tag: $900m). With its Mach 2.34 performance at 40,000 feet, its excellent rate of climb, its tight turn radius and its auto-wing sweep, the F-14 was a quantum leap over existing interceptors; moreover, its Hughes AWG-9 long-range multi-mode radar and up to six AIM-54C Phoenix long-range (100 nmi) state of the art air-to-air missiles made it an almost invincible foe in the air, which could lock in on six different targets simultaneously. In June 1974, the Shah ordered another fifty F-14s (at a cost of $950m) and a couple of months later he told Bank-i Milli to open a $75m credit line for the cash-strapped Grunman Corporation. By the close of 1978, the IIAF possessed some seventy-eight F-14s and around five hundred Phoenix missiles.

The IIAF also purchased some other missiles: (1) Sidewinders (AIM-9 G/H) air-to-air (by Raytheon/Ford Aerospace); (2) Sparrows (AIM-7 E/F), air-to-air (by Raytheon/General Dynamics); (3) Harpoons, air-to surface (by McDonnell Douglas); (4) Mavericks, television-guided air-to-surface (by Hughes).

In December 1975, a scandal over bribes and commissions was to mar Iranian-Grunman relations: General Toufanian, Iran's vice minister for war and the armed forces purchasing tsar, publicly accused Grunman of having paid $28m in commission to the three Lavi brothers (Hushang, Parviz and Mansur) on the F-14 deal; also party to the deal were the Eastern International Corporation (controlled by the Lavis and the Rashidian brothers[36]) and the Shalam S.A. company owned by Albert Fuze. General Toufanian publicly asked Grunman to reimburse that sum to the Iranian Government, arguing that Grunman had slapped it on top of its contract price; to bury the Lavi affair, Grunman promised to provide the IIAF with some $24m worth of F-14 spare parts free of charge. In February 1976, it was Northrop's turn to accept an $8m penalty deduction.[37] The Grunman and Northrop scandals had shown the enormous amounts of money to be made in arms sales. Individuals such as Albert Hakim and families such as the Indian Hinduja would take umpteen millions acting as go-betweens during the 1970s – the Hindujas even becoming billionaires.

For his army, the Shah turned to Great Britain to modernise its armour. To replace the obsolete American M-47 and M-60 tanks, his eye had fallen on the Chieftain tank, manufactured by the Royal Ordnance Factory at Leeds. The original contract was signed in January 1971 for a first series of 760 Chieftains at £100,000 each, and an ultimate order of 2,250 units.[38] The basic design for the two later series was altered in consequence of experience in Iran's hot weather, and modified Chieftains were renamed Shir Iran (the first step on the way to the future Challenger). Some 1,350 units of Shir Iran were ordered at £1m each, but none delivered before the Revolution.

Some two hundred and fifty smaller Scorpion tanks (also British made) and twenty-five Vickers (GB) armoured recovery vehicles (worth £80m) made it to Iran, taking the army's armour to over 1,900 units. The Royal Ordnance also set up tank-repair shops at Masjid-i Sulayman and Duroud – the latter, a £160m project, was half-complete in 1978.

In the field of defence, the basic anti-tank weapons acquired by the army were the simple, Soviet-made RPG-7 (with assembling facilities set up in Iran) and the sophisticated TOW rocket (made by Hughes). Orders for 15,000 TOWs were placed and a contract signed for assembling 2,000 TOWs annually at Shiraz. Some 10,000 Dragon rocket-launchers were also ordered from the US. In the anti-aircraft field, the lighter weapons were of Soviet origin. As for the anti-aircraft missile systems, two were envisaged: the American Hawk and the British Rapier (to replace the older Tigercat system). The former system became operational with 37 batteries and 1,800 Hawk missiles (from Raytheon, at a cost of $700m plus $34m for the training programme), but the Rapier 9 (from British Aerospace) fell by the wayside and the order was cancelled in January 1979.

In 1974, the Shiraz Iran Electronics Industries company (IEI) was created with the young Admiral Abu'lfath Ardalan at its head.

The IEI was set up to make a foray into the production of electronic boards and silicon chips. It also had a (covert) military mission: to assemble some 2,000 TOW rockets and 5,000 television-guided Mavericks annually (its further mission to assemble 75 Rapier tracked-missiles per month fell through when the whole system was cancelled). Such mixed civilian-military forays into high-tech operations proved a failure, a useless waste of funds.

The installation of a large-scale ordnance complex at Isfahan made more sense than the Shiraz IEI. Begun in 1977 by Millbank Technical Services (a subsidiary of Britain's Crown Agents), with Wimpey Laing Iran as main contractor, the £700m complex consisted (initially) of three major units:

(1) An assembly unit for manufacturing Chieftain tank spares and 120mm guns and ammunitions thereof, to be built by the International Military Services, a subsidiary of the British Ministry of Defence;
(2) A chemical plant for producing explosives (ammonium nitrate, tri-nitroglycerine and TNT), to be set up by Bofors Nobel Chemateur of Sweden;
(3) A small arms and ammunitions production unit was to be set up by the specialist firm Omnipol of Czechoslovakia. Only the explosives plant eventually went ahead, as over 95% of the equipment had been delivered to the Isfahan site (with no contract for later assembly). Later the contract was signed and the plant erected, albeit after the Revolution.

Another noteworthy military project was Project IBEX, also known as Trackman 2, the sharpest US 'eye and ear' operation concerned with Soviet missile and satellite launches from its (semi-covert) listening post of Bihshahr and Kilarabad, and the super secret $500m 'Big Ear' station of Kabkan (some 130 kilometres north-west of Mashhad, near the Soviet border), with a highly sophisticated relay station at the Tehran Doushan Tappeh Air Force base. IBEX was reported to have cost $1,300m. Rockwell International was managing contractor (signed up in June 1975) and major sub-contractors (naturally all from the US) were Ford Aerospace, Watkins-Johnson, E-Systems (especially ECI Division), Itek Corp., Syltech, Quest and Touche Ross companies.

The Americans also had a highly ambitious project for placing some special, ultra-sensitive radar detection equipment on forty-one

Iranian mountain tops at a cost of $32bn (the ideal remote control tripwire system). Code named Seek Sentry, the project's bill was too much to stomach, even for the Shah. The project was downgraded to sixteen then to twelve locations, but it still proved far too expensive. It was finally shelved after special Iranian teams had climbed and studied the most difficult mountain tops. A total of $50m had been spent on the far-fetched project.

After the F-14s for the IIAF and the Chieftains for the army, the Shah concentrated on the third leg of his military: the navy. Perennially the Iranians' weakest military spot, the navy was a *sine qua non* for the Shah's wish to be 'Gendarme of the Gulf'. It only had its hovercraft squadrons for the mudflats and obsolete patrol boats; it now needed fast attack missile patrol boats. The Shah took note of the Israelis' orders from France (and their hijacking of their own boats from Cherbourg) and decided to similarly order twelve Combattantes from Constructions Mécaniques de Normandie, and had them mounted with Harpoon sea-to-sea missiles (to replace the outdated Seacat (GB) and Seakiller Mk2 (Italy)). Faced with a *fait accompli*, the Iranian Navy officers were unable to cash in on their commissions and had to ask for changes in all of the boats' equipment (naturally at hefty extra charges) to get their commissions from the parts' manufacturers – in the end, only the hull was French.[39]

The man the Shah had hand-picked in 1972 to oversee the navy's expansion, Admiral Ramzi Âbbas Âta'i, was eventually arrested in 1975[40] with a dozen of his senior officers, one of whom, Captain Shafa'i, committed suicide in prison. On February 24, 1976, Âta'i was given a five year sentence and fined Rls258m (equal to $3.7m) and his deputy, Commodore Hasan Rafiî, received a similar sentence and a Rls25m fine while the other officers got away with lighter sentences; in March 1978, Âta'i wriggled out of prison (after having signed a *mea culpa*) just in time to escape abroad and enjoy a golden retreat.

When Vice-Admiral Kamal ul-Din Mir Habibullahi took over from the disgraced Âta'i, the Shah had looked out of the Gulf to see... the Indian Ocean: he needed an ocean-faring navy to keep safe the routes leading to the Strait of Hurmuz! The Shah embarked on the wildest of all expansions for his navy, ordering:

- twelve frigates, eight of which were to come from Rotterdam's Rijn-Schelde Vrome shipyard (at a cost of $1,300m) and the four others from West Germany;
- sixteen submarines: six 1,000-ton 209 class submarines were contracted out to the firm of Howaldtswerke-Deutsche Werft of Hamburg and Kiel, and three Tang class submarines from the US Navy;
- nineteen MK-III (class '65) patrol boats from the US Navy;
- eighteen new fast attack patrol boats;
- nine hunters and four naval support ships, from British shipyards;
- four 7,600-ton Spruance type destroyers (modified US DD 963s) from Litton Industries for $1,400m.

Moreover, after setting up Gulf naval bases at Bushire, Kharg Island and Bandar Âbbas, the Shah ordered the mammoth Kunarak Navy Base to be built at Chah Bahar, as his telescope on the Indian Ocean. Contracted out to Brown and Root (US) for $2bn, the project began in April 1978 with the dredging of Kunarak Bay and the construction of a harbour. Payments for the project were made through a 100,000 b/d consignment of crude oil to the New England Petroleum Company (Nepco). Adjacent to the naval base, a garrison town of 7,000 housing units was being constructed by Costain (GB). The Revolution brought the naval base and the garrison township to a stop, thus adding a naval white elephant to the civilian ones.

If the Shah could simply buy whatever military hardware he chose, he was unable to choose the best and the brightest among his top officers due to drawbacks of his own personality. He had two generals among his inner circle, Fardoust and Ayadi, but they were not in the military any more. At the top of the military echelon there were many generals whose independence or intelligence he could not stomach and of whom he had rid himself: among others General Taymour Bakhtiar (murdered), General Fouladvand (imprisoned and retired), General Firaydoun Jam (exiled), General Qaranay (cashiered) etc. His generals were supposed to attend to their functions and not be too imaginative, especially because the Shah's armed forces were splintered in such a way as to render a military *coup d'état* almost impossible (tripwires having been inserted at every corner). That left him with two military leaders on whom he could rely: air force commander-in-chief General Muhammad Amir Khatami and army commander-in-chief General Ghulam Âli Uvaysi.

General Khatami, the Shah's brother-in-law, was the immovable air force tsar and chief of Iran's so-called Air Mafia.[40A] In the 1960s, he had created the *Humafars*, the air force's technical staff, as a third group somewhere – in an unenviable position – between the officers' corps and the NCOs, but with none of their respective facilities, even creating special ranks for them. The *Humafars* became a thorn in the air force's side with their constant grumbling, their avowed goal being an amalgamation (even with loss of pay and benefits) with the officers' corps, but Khatami wouldn't budge: his no was final. A fanatical sportsman, with water-skiing and tennis his favourite activities, Khatami had taken to gliding: on September 12, 1975, at the Diz Dam, the rope pulling his glider snapped seconds after take-off, hurling him against the lake's stony shores and killing him instantly. It is difficult to imagine that Khatami was the victim of an accident (glider ropes are tested to withstand the worst treatment),[41] but, in any event, the Shah and the Pahlavi regime had abruptly lost one of its most precious assets.

As for General Uvaysi, who had graduated from the Officers' Academy in the same class as the Shah (1938), he was a soldiers' soldier who had climbed the military ladder step by step to become commander-in-chief of the army in 1972 (after seven years as the head of the Gendarmerie). Belonging to the landed Kashan aristocracy, he was rich enough (and his wife too[42]) to be scrupulously honest in a highly corrupt environment. A hard worker, he accepted no nonsense from his subordinates, whether general or soldier. The rest of the Shah's generals and colonels were rather lacklustre: real estate deals (in Tehran or Gunbad-i Kavous), socialising (with Tehran's high society) or travelling abroad (to acquire the best of everything) left them no time to perform their military duties.

If the generals had an excuse for their professional sloth, it was the overprotection provided them by the American officers of the ARMISH-MAAG missions. Dependence on American arms, technology and personnel had developed at an increasing rate, so much so that it was the US Senate which became worried about excessive American involvement in Iranian military affairs – its August 1976 report, *US Military Sales to Iran*, concluded that:

> Iran is now so heavily dependent on American personnel that it could not go to war without US

support on a day-to-day basis... the report further estimated that almost 20,000 Americans are now in Iran ...and projected 50,000 to 60,000 by 1980...[43]

For example, the air force logistics programme and its Mihrabad Aircraft Maintenance Centre, put together by Lockheed (US) for $138m, was essentially operated by American officers (under General Secord[44]) and the Iranian staff was solely there in a secondary support function.

With every fresh sale of American hardware to Iran, a contract was signed to train Iranians in the bases of the respective manufacturer in the US. Thus hundreds of young Iranian diploma holders selected in national tests and sent to California and Texas to be trained in the technology of the new hardware. The artificiality of the whole effort, with two cultures clashing on American soil instead of on Iranian, made it a losing proposal from the outset. It was not through a few weeks in a Pasadena classroom that the Iranian Air Force would become familiar with the sophisticated equipment of an F-14; neither, in this way, could the Iranian Army accept a weapon like the TOW anti-tank rocket. At its peak some 3,000 young Iranians were being trained in the US, in an intensive training programme supervised by Dariush Farzaneh; the usefulness of these programmes came to be doubted, for the youngsters took advantage of the situation and came to look on them as free American vacations. The training of the IIAF jet fighter pilots, however, was an exception to the rule, as their American training was the best available and highly efficient.

The deluge of new, modern armaments was simply too much for the average Iranian NCO and soldier to get used to and, after all, these were the men who had, ultimately to use the new weapons. An army geared to rifles, machine-guns and mortars was given electronic and optically-guided weapons. It could easily adopt a simple, unsophisticated piece of machinery such as the Soviet-made RPG-7, but not a TOW (it would take a full decade for the Iranian Army to warm to the TOW). There was an abyss between the US Army, gearing for world domination, and the Iranian one, still thinking of subduing unruly tribesmen. But the Shah wanted the hardware, thought he had the necessary personnel, that the petrodollars would eventually solve his specialised manpower problem, and that Iran's armed forces under American tutelage would become the world's fourth strongest military power. Thus the Shah believed that he could buy invulnerability for himself and his regime: who would dare attack him? Who could defeat his forces when they were armed with the best weapons in the world? On land there were his Chieftains' in the air his Phoenix-fitted F-14s, in the Gulf waters his Combattantes: no other could match his firepower. His detractors could deride his generals, his troops, his weaknesses; on paper, at least, he knew that he had the very best and let the one who dared try to prove him wrong.

16.3. The Bureaucracy

For a record 4,581 consecutive days, Premier Amir Âbbas Huvayda remained at the head of Iran's government and civil service. Huvayda was only head of government in name, the Shah being the chief executive – the latter ordered and the former obeyed: this was the whole secret of his longevity in the premiership. After experiencing domineering PMs like Qavam, Musaddiq and Razmara, Muhammad Reza Shah had been delighted to have a subservient and malleable premier, who could, moreover, squeeze results out of the unruly bureaucracy. Everyone was pleased with Huvayda's first-class performance: he was the elite's dupe, keeping the boat from rocking. With all his powers, he was incapable of developing a following, at best a few minor technocrats and a couple of journalists, especially *Kayhan*'s future editor-in-chief, Amir Tahiri.[45] At a dinner given in 1973 by Princess Fatimeh Pahlavi, the Shah quipped to his premier: "I think that we shall retire at the same time, you and I".[46] The Shah was almost correct on this one.

At the head of the bureaucracy, Huvayda had to contend with two ministers who had more clout than he: Hushang Ansari and Jamshid Amuzigar.

Hushang Ansari was a shortish, balding wizard, who had placed Iran's private industrial train on the right tracks (and maximum profits) between 1969 and 1974; he was assisted in his performance by the trio of Engineer Farrukh Najmabadi (a former NIOC employee), Dr Âbbas Quli Bakhtiar (also ex-NIOC) and Dr Hasan Âli Mihran – all three educated in Great Britain, respectively at UMIST, Imperial College, University of London, and the University of Nottingham.

The Namazis (of Shiraz) and the Lajivardis (Bihshahr group) had been instrumental in his early ascension; later the Panahis of Sabit-Pasal had taken over when Ansari married Maryam Panahi (a cousin of Engineer Âli Asghar Panahi). In 1974 Ansari amalgamated the Economy and Finance ministries to create a single ministry for himself: henceforth he was in charge of Iran's economy, bypassing everyone but the Shah. 1976 was his vintage year: he signed his usual score of joint venture deals; he finalised the IJPC financing package with Japan's MITI minister (January); he met President Ford *tête-à-tête* at the White House (March 29); he signed a trade agreement worth $3.5bn with the French authorities in Paris (May 15) and he crowned the whole on August 7, with a $15bn Iranian-American trade protocol signed with Henry Kissinger.

The second minister, Jamshid Amuzigar, had had solid American backing since his early days with Point Four. A minister since 1966 and Minister of Finance until 1974, he also acted as the Shah's representative at OPEC. With Amuzigar at OPEC meetings, the Shah pursued his strategy of 'divide and rule' in national oil affairs. With time, he had even given total freedom to Mustoufiat NPC in petrochemical affairs and to Musaddiqi at NIGC in gas (both men having fought hard for their independence), thus leaving Dr Iqbal with a barebones NIOC and diminished power. Premier Huvayda tried to keep an eye on NIOC through Majidi's PBO. In 1974, when Finance was taken over by Ansari, Amuzigar was given the Ministry of the Interior, keeping, however, his OPEC assignment and his assistant Dr Muhammad Yiganeh.

During the 1970s the government had acquired a special importance of its own: it had not only become a major player on the domestic stage, but even the primary player. Placed in charge of distributing the petrodollars, its financial clout was supreme; people realised that the government and its bureaucracy were playing an ever-larger role in their life, even in their day-to-day routine. Every other national player wanted to have its men in the bureaucratic fortress: SAVAK began at IDRO, the liberals at NIRT, the Pahlavi family across the board.

The Iranian bureaucracy was expanding as rapidly as it could. From a few thousand staff in the 1950s, it had grown to 300,000 in 1968/69, to 440,000 in 1972/73 and had passed the 700,000 mark in 1977/78[47] – these were exclusive of special independent institutions such as the oil industry, accounting for some 60,000 people all by itself. With such numbers of people it had clearly attained critical mass. At the top of the bureaucracy was a thin layer of Pahlavi elitists, but the bulk of it was formed by the middle and lower middle classes, whose bastion it was. At the same time it was the stronghold of the intelligentsia, with the large majority of writers and artists holding a sinecure in one of its institutions, as if it were their due. In 1976, the Iran Inc. board realised that it had been too liberal with its open-ended bureaucratic expansion policy when times were propitious: it had created large masses of busy, satisfied and controllable civil servants, maybe too many. Orders went out to put on all the brakes, and Huvayda dutifully executed them, announcing on November 24, 1976 that "22% of governmental positions had to be cut", as well as a total ban on new recruitment. The employment expansion could not be reversed so abruptly; the reduction of the bloated Iranian bureaucracy was but wishful thinking for too many constituencies had vested interests in the public service and the service itself was best geared to accommodate orders in such a way as to cause the least harm to itself (a game at which it had become expert).

But all of the regime's efforts to create a meritocracy out of its bureaucracy were faltering over two stumbling blocks. The first was the Iranian's unalterable individualism. Every department head, each division manager and all ministers wanted to shape their fiefdom as he pleased; every change was followed by total alterations, according to the wishes of the fresh management. The only exception to this general Iranian rule was to be found in the oil industry, where there was a rigid, rational structure set by the industry's pioneers and to which the Iranian servants had to adapt. The second stumbling block was due to the Shah's almost paranoiac fear of change leading to inveterate immobilism at the top of the bureaucracy, exemplified by Huvayda's record tenure – with the Shah contending that you don't change a winning team. Senior ministers and managers had become sclerotic and shallow; nepotism was creating ever-deeper ravages; merit could easily be counterbalanced by a bribe or a beautiful girl. Too long a stay in power had corrupted even the least corruptible. Higher civil servants with backbone were rare; the majority preferred to do something at which (all) Iranians were expert: "store the unpleasant things they came across, in some safe, faraway corner of their minds".

The freeze at the bureaucracy's top, however, created pressures and friction in the lower ranks, with junior managers arguing that without change there would be no promotion. Ministers tried their best to create new top positions by expanding but there were limits to that too. Down in the ranks frustrations were released in the form of either demands for better pay and more perks, or in the form of criticism directed to ever-higher levels. Junior management was clamouring ever louder for more benefits, in fact asking for more power, something which the regime's men were unwilling (or not allowed) to give. A couple of reshufflings in either 1975 or 1976 would have reduced the tensions that were continuously building up; even if changes wouldn't have satisfied all ambitions at once, it would have given them all reason to hope that the train of change would stop at their door too. But the Iran Inc. board was not willing to bow to the ranks' demands, believing bureaucratic dissatisfactions and discontent to be way below them.

16.4. The Private Sector

If the Shah and Iran Inc. controlled the military and the bureaucracy, their hold over the third leg of their supporting tripod – the private sector – was extremely tenuous. The regime had bent over backwards to seduce the captains of industry with soft loans, incentives and favourable regulations; in a word, it had created them, their factories, their fortunes, their fame; but the recipients were loath to admit their debt to their creator. The realisation of the entrepreneurs' lack of recognition of their benefactors' generosity and goodwill would come as a rude shock to the Iran Inc. board.

Even in the application of the White Revolution's fourth point, the participation of workers in their factories' profits, the regime had been more than conciliating: first excluding the factories with fewer than twenty workers and then accepting the industrialists' payment of a thirteenth month of wages in lieu of profit-sharing. But, protected and pampered as they were by the regime, which depended on them for employment and production of Iranian goods, the industrialists were making excessive profits. To further ensure their vast net incomes they usually either took a foreign partner (to fall back on his clout in case of a clampdown on industry) or a silent partner from within the ranks of the Pahlavi family or the Iran Inc. directors.

Paying taxes was anathema to the entrepreneurs: it would lower their sacrosanct profits. So they found ways around it, even pretending that they had operation losses, cooking their books unabashedly. They also readily bribed customs officials to get the lowest tariffs possible on their imports, and bureaucrats to get the highest sales prices for their products. They used every trick in the book to maximise profits, their only goal. After the first wave (1950s) and the second wave (1960s), there was no third wave in the 1970s: the first two had blocked all major newcomers, letting in only the small fish. In the early 1970s, Iran's industrial elite could count its members: they knew each other and would not tolerate major newcomers on their turf. As and when new opportunities arose, they took them in their stride, enlarging their own cake. Outsiders would be treated to the breadcrumbs. Iran Inc.'s third leg was now as strong as its other two, since it was made of solid gold; but it was a rogue leg that failed to heed advice and obey orders.

Tensions between the private elite and the regime came to a head in May 1972. After multiple warnings, the latter began its onslaught on the entrenched and arrogant entrepreneurs. The Shah abruptly "proposed" that "the larger enterprises divest themselves from a third of their shareholdings", selling their shares to the public, with priority purchasing opportunities being given to the enterprises' staff and workers. He also appointed an eight-member government commission, chaired by Hushang Ansari (and consisting of the Minister of Labour, the Deputy Minister of Court, the Deputy Minister of Economy, the president of the Iran Chamber of Commerce, Industry and Mines, the Bank-i Markazi governor; and the managing directors of the IMDBI and ICB banks). The bureaucracy was called in to supervise the private sector in a 'voluntary' programme of divestment. For the captains of industry the traumatism was high: the Shah had dared attack their golden goose. Unlike the landlords, flattened by the land reform, the entrepreneurs were no dupes: they had read between the royal decree's lines and saw in it the first shot in a protracted war that they would have to fight to defend their profits against Iran Inc. Still, a sense of moderation dominated as the programme was 'voluntary', but the undertones in the leader of a specialised Tehran monthly left no doubt about the programme's final objective:

> Iran's White Revolution has set a tradition of moderation. No extreme measures are applied against any group. The transformation of the industrial ownership will be carried out as moderately and reasonably as that of land reform...[48]

Iran's robber barons were no better than the landlords, but more homogeneous, far richer and still kicking. They would fight. And fight they did, with all legal means at their disposal. When the Ansari commission drew up a list of the eighty-six major Iranian enterprises (total value estimated at Rls54bn – equal to $713m) to be part of the programme, the owners invoked differences in legal statutes to retard execution. Ansari accepted that any of the eighty-six enterprises not yet public had first to be transformed into a public shareholding company and decided to begin with those that were, giving time to the others to transform legally. Thus the programme unfolded in four phases:
(1) September 1972: a first batch of eight companies, with, prominent among them, the Farmanfarmayans' Pars Oil Co. and Âli Riza'i's Ahvaz rolling mills;
(2) October 1972: seven companies, among which was the Pars Paper Company;
(3) December 1972: thirty-three companies, led by the heads of Iranian industry – the Khatyyamis' Iran National, the Lajivardis' Bihshahr group, Iravani's Milli Shoes, Barkhurdar's Pars Electric, the Soudavars' Khavar, the Akhavans' Jeep Company and the Arjumands' Arj;
(4) June 1973: the last batch of thirty-eight companies, including Azamyish appliances, Muqaddam textiles, Khalili's Butane, Kaveh Iran, the Mufid group, the Ittahadiyyeh Company and Jahan textiles.

This first half-hearted attempt by the executive to ask its industrial elite to shoot itself in the foot soon petered out. The industrialists engineered a concealed buying up of the shares' sales, buying with one hand what they had sold with the other. Thus they easily fended off the Shah's gambit. Having also learned their lesson, they began placing their own men in the bureaucracy and buying off even larger numbers of civil servants in order to be ready for the second round, whenever it would come. In the meantime, the industrialists were in no mood for defensive action, but, rather, buoyant for attack. It was proven by a sensational declaration from one of their spokesmen, Âli Riza'i, at a seminar in May 1973: Riza'i dropped his bombshell by "strongly attacking foreign investments in Iran, claiming that foreign investment had done nothing for the national economy – with the exception of oil and petrochemicals"[49] and he further argued that Iran needed only foreign technology, and neither foreign investment or foreign managers. The Iranian industrial puppets had grown rich beyond their wildest dreams and thought that they could revolt against their foreign puppeteers, forgetting that without them there would be no Riza'i and no Khayyamis. Some of them came to believe they were Iran's Rockefellers, Mellons and Morgans, forgetting that they had achieved in a short decade of overprotection and expert foreign assistance what their illustrious models had realised in the rough and tumble of early, unregulated industrialism. Iran's industrial elite was forgetting its humble origins, its debt to foreign investors, its subservience to Iran Inc.

To the Shah, his captains of industry had become too rich for their own good for they didn't respect anything any more. Moreover, the fiasco of his 'voluntary' 1972 programme still stuck in his gullet. In the early 1970s, the dangerous inflation phenomenon had, in the wake of increased oil revenues and public expenditures, raised its head again and grown to double digits. The Shah decided to use inflation as a *casus belli* against the industrialists. His first attempt was fended off by Dr Husayn Pirnia, a senior professor of economics at Tehran University with wide Elite connections and close links to the industrial elite, who argued, in 1972, that inflation was the result of imports and propounded a re-evaluation of the rial against the dollar to offset 'imported inflation'. The regime decided to follow Pirnia's advice, although it was pure nonsense, and altered the rial exchange rate from 75 to 68 per dollar. The measure made no dent in inflation (as local importers and retailers naturally failed to lower their prices, pocketing the difference instead) as was predictable, and it only benefited those engaged in capital flight by raising the value of the dollars they could buy by ten per cent. Another of Dr Pirnia's proposals, spelled out in April 1972, had been to "stop capital evasion by promulgating appropriate laws and regulations"; evidently this proposal was rejected out of hand as everyone in power in Iran was interested in keeping the freedom of exchange laws, so they were still able to transfer their profits (not yet assets) into their safe Swiss accounts.

In 1973, Iran Inc. decided to use more drastic means to bring profiteers to heel. In December it even sent a bill to the *Majlis* "for stamping out hoarding and profiteering through military tribunals". The farcical bill was forgotten in the euphoria following the oil price quadrupling. But the inflation fuelled by the oil price boom had its full effect in 1975. The regime, alerted to the dangers, prodded the bureaucracy into action. In July 1975, a bill was ratified by the *Majlis* "penalising any butcher or baker caught overpricing".

Simultaneously, the private sector agreed to lower its prices by an average of ten per cent provided that the government did too; the bureaucrats accepted, but when many industrialists failed to comply (raising their prices by ten per cent instead), a clampdown became inevitable. On July 28, a series of spectacular arrests were made; prominent among those arrested was Habibullah Ilqanian, the Jewish king of Iranian plastics. Ilqanian was set free after his son Firaydoun agreed to lower the price of his plastics. On August 17, it was BMW's Muhammad Vahabzadeh's turn to be detained for a couple of days before being set free. But the harm had been done, the war hatchet brought out. The industrialists would fight if forced to, for it was not by intimidation and arrests that the regime could bring them to their knees.

After the unsatisfactory result of the July 1975 anti-profiteering campaign, the regime had to fall back on its contingency plan. On August 6, the Shah suddenly unveiled his batteries by declaring total war on "industrial feudalism" (with the evident parallel with the land reform scheme). To make sure that the wily captains of industry wouldn't wriggle out of the plan this time, he had his diktats encapsulated as fresh revolutionary – 'Shah and People' – principles. New point thirteen called for "the expansion of industrial ownership base", decreeing that the country's largest industrial and mining corporations must sell 49% of their shares to their workers and the general public (the percentage for shares sold jumped to 99% for large public companies); and principle fourteen promulgated a nationwide campaign to "control inflation and prices". This was a general 'participation' programme, like the one dear to General de Gaulle, which would break the industrialists' power and make many happy shareholders – or so thought the Shah. The industrial sector quickly responded by transferring some $2bn abroad during the two months of August and September 1975, mainly to Swiss bank accounts.

As in the 1972 'voluntary' attempt, the Shah set up a nine member committee, once more chaired by Hushang Ansari, in charge of executing Principle Thirteen; besides Ansari, there were to be five ministers on the committee (those for Industry and Mines, Labour, Justice, Commerce and Agriculture) in addition to the heads of the PBO, Bank-i Markazi and the Chamber of Commerce, Industry and Mines. A total of three hundred and twenty of Iran's largest companies (minimum capital of Rls100m; fixed assets of at least Rls200m and annual sales exceeding Rls250m) were to be put on the sales block; the companies' total value was estimated at around $2bn. For the pricing of each company's shares, the company's pre-tax profits as stated in their tax returns for the last three years would be used as a reference point (a measure reminiscent of the land reform programme tactics); for the financing of the workers' shares purchase, a Financing Organisation with an initial capital of Rls1bn, set up within the Ministry of Economic Affairs and Finance, would provide them with interest-free loans.

Furthermore, a new government-sponsored entity for purchasing part of the companies' shares, the National Investment Company of Iran (NICI), was created with an initial capital of Rls10bn (equal to $142) and the young and inexperienced playboy, Khusrou Shahabi, was placed at its head. Originally NICI's shares were to be split 35%-65% between the banks and the public, but finally 83% was sold to four banks (Bank-i Markazi, Bank-i Milli, IMDBI and ADBI), 10% was held by two major insurance organisations (Bimeh Markazi and Bimeh Iran) and the remaining 7% went to the public. Finally, in the application of Principle Thirteen, two points were included to please the industrialists: the first carrot being a 20 to 25% tax exemption for those companies which complied with the decree; the second being a limitation of foreign investment in Iranian companies to a maximum of 25% (and 35% in exceptional cases), with foreign investors who held more than 25% shares in Iranian companies having to divest themselves of their surplus in the 'participation' market.

By March 1976, the first batch of 106 companies was put on the block, the next two batches of 108 and 106 being scheduled for March 1977 and March 1978 respectively. By the close of 1976, it was officially announced that 107,000 persons had acquired some Rls5bn of shares in the first batch of 106 companies; as for the NICI, it had purchased for Rls4.6bn shares worth, at par, Rls3.0bn! This time the wolf was here for Iran's industrial elite. There was no easy way out as in 1972. The Shah had dared attack them directly. The blow was severe, and their grip over their industrial estates severely compromised.

The Shah, who needed them more than they needed him – or so they wrongly thought – should not have pulled Principle Thirteen on them; by doing so he had shot himself in the foot, losing the captains of industry in the process and failing to win over the workers who, by staging wildcat strikes in April and May of 1976, showed their growing discontent with their predicament.

Since the early 1970s the wily captains of industry had branched out into lucrative banking; besides the evident benefits, they could supervise their own deposits and instantly transfer any of their assets abroad. Many of the twenty-three industrial elite families had members on the private banks' boards, as for example: Bank of Tehran (Ghaffar and Rashid Farmanfarmayan); ICB (chairman since 1960, Alinaqi Farmanfarmayan); IMDBI (Habib Sabit, Muhammad Khusroushahi, Isa Kurous, Muhammad Tahiri, Muhammad Taqi Barkhurdar); Bank-i Îtibarat-i Iran (Hasan Kurous, Habib Ilqanian); Bank of Iran and Japan (Mustafa Misbahzadeh of *Kayhan*, Sayyid Mahmud Lajivardi, Âli Akbar Lajivardi, Âli Akbar Mahluji, Farid Khusroushahi); Bank of Iran and Holland (Sulayman and Ahmad Vahabzadeh); Iranians' Bank (Rahim Iravani, Muhammad Taqi Barkhurdar); Bank of Iran and the Middle East (Habib Sabit, Muhammad Taqi Barkhurdar).

Then, in February 1973, the Bank-i Markazi decided to liquidate two limping banks: the Bank-i Asnaf-i Iran (Iran's Guilds' Bank) and the Bank-i Bimeh Bazarganan (Traders' Insurance Bank). The Guilds' Bank was replaced by a new outfit, the Bank-i Iranshahr (Iranshahr Bank), and the Traders' Insurance Bank was taken over by Bank-i Milli, with its former managing director, Husayn Shirafat, indicted on eleven counts of fraud and sentenced to a Rls107m fine. The defunct bank was replaced in 1973 by two banks set up by leading industrialists:

(1) Bank-i Shahryar, with an initial capital of Rls3bn, increased to 5bn within days by Âli Riza'i who thus became chairman; other

directors were Ahmad Khayyami, Husayn Qasimiyyeh, Siavoush Arjumand, Muhammad Taqi Barkhurdar, Mansur Yasini and Muhsin Azmayish; its first managing director was Jalil Shuraka, soon replaced by Îzzatullah Mumtaz;
(2) Bank-i Sanayî Iran (Industries' Bank of Iran) had an initial capital of Rls3bn, raised to 5bn; industrialists led by Mahmud Khayyami were also directors, such as the courtier Husayn Danishvar and influence-peddler Mihdi Amir Sardari; the bank's managing director was Khudadad Farmanfarmayan, the former PO tsar.

A few months later, the industrial elite established its own investment bank, the Bank-i Tousiêh va Sarmayehguzari Iran (Development and Investment Bank of Iran – DIBI), with an initial capital of Rls2.1bn; instrumental in its formation were its directors Faruq Farmanfarmayan, Ahmad Vahabzadeh, Iskandar Arjumand, Javad and Kazim Khusroushahi, and Habib Lajivardi. Finally in 1974 and 1975, three more banks completed the list of Iran's banking establishment (taking the total number of private Iranian banks to thirty-two):
(1) Bank-i Dariush, 1974, with 35% owned by Japanese and American interests; Iranian investors included Jâfar Akhavan, Abu Nasr Âzud and Rafiûllah Aryeh;
(2) Bank-i Baynulmillali-i Iran (International Bank of Iran), 1975, with 35% owned by Chase Manhattan; and Âlinaqi Farmanfarmayan as a director;
(3) Bank-i Iran va Arab (Iran-Arab Bank), 1975, with 33% owned by BCCI and with the redoubtable Aqa Hasan Abedi as vice-chairman and industrialist directors Kazim Khusroushahi and Âli Riza Sahib.

On top of creating banks to control their liquidities, the industrial elite decided to form its future managerial cadres in Iran and therefore created, in 1972, the Iranian Centre for Management Studies (ICMS) in a corner of the new Shahrak-i Gharb. The centre's campus for boarding sixty students was designed by Dr Nadir Ardalan and his Mandala team, slightly Iranising the Harvard Business School. Students were duly selected from among Iranian graduates, both male and female, with only a couple of foreigners. The ICMS cursus was for one year. The curriculum was a copy of Harvard's, as most of the teachers were from Harvard, with only a couple of Iranian lecturers with a Harvard MBA. The first class, which graduated in the summer of 1973, was a very special group of young men: as usual in Iran, new institutions attract the best and the brightest, then over time the initial quality deteriorates. The whole group was snapped up by the industrial groups and the 'first ICMS' graduates would climb to the very top of their new profession as industrial managers. Six other classes would follow, all of its graduates ending up in major Iranian enterprises.

Another part of the private sector was the Tehran *Bazaar*, old maybe, decrepit maybe, but it had made a killing during the protracted economic boom of the 1960s and 1970s.

In its anti-inflation fight, Iran Inc. had not only turned its guns against the industrial elite, but also against the *Bazaaris*. In the latter case, its offensive campaign gained better results because its guilds courts could easily fine and harass large traders as well as the small retailers, who, unlike the industrialists, had no relatives or allies in the bureaucracy and the military to plead their causes. In July 1975, Jahangir Anvari Muqaddam, the vice-president of the powerful Fresh Fruits Wholesalers Union, was arrested and only released after paying a heavy fine. In addition, some 5,000 *Bazaar* retailers were turned over to special 'guilds courts' (up to two hundred and seventy such courts at the peak) and fined according to their assets. The blow was hard to swallow for the (still) defenceless *Bazaaris*. Naturally, they had benefited more than anyone else from the economic boom of the 1970s, second only to the industrialists. In their entire history they had never had it so good: they had made billions, as practically all imports (with exceptions made for NIOC and limited direct government imports) had to pass through their hands; they were at the heart of the economic system, with links to three hundred and sixty-five provincial centres (i.e. towns with more than five thousand inhabitants); they had filled up their reserves and their stores; they had expanded at rates previously unheard of; had bought their fill of gold, carpets and land; the moneylenders had made the most fabulous killings, some of them becoming dollar millionaires. And now, the regime was coming in to spoil it all, harassing and fining them at will. After a decade passed in the quietness of easy and plentiful battening, the *Bazaar* was again pulled into politics, against its will. Again it had been unjustifiably harassed by the political power. But the *Bazaaris* were far from being sheep: they wouldn't allow the regime to chop off their head without a struggle, as it had done to the ill-fated landlords.

The *Bazaar* was rich, immensely rich, with a turnover which was said to stand at around 40% of total domestic consumption. It could purchase some power, some positions within the system, just enough to protect itself from injustice and the arbitrary. So this the *Bazaaris* tried, but in vain, for neither the top echelon nor the bureaucracy answered their demands; their money was readily accepted, but not their bargaining for power; they didn't have technocrats to place in the institutions, no engineers, no academics, no intellectuals since, from time immemorial, the *Bazaar*'s sons turned into either *bazaaris* or *mullas*. They even tried getting in through the 'old money' Qajar network (usually more flexible than the new Pahlavis) but there was no way in here either. They tried the industrialists, who told them that they had enough worries themselves. They tried the royal family (through their jewellers), but with no palpable result. They even sent their pleas to the Shah, through their guilds' representatives at the royal *salams*, without receiving the shade of a ministership or a directorship. For the second half of 1975 and the better part of 1976 they tried their best to make some headway in a world in which they ignored all, but where they had to get a foothold for this was where the petrodollars were, and hence the power. The *Bazaar* leadership, which consisted of some fifty leading traders (among whom were the heads of the twenty-nine guilds) and a dozen money-changers,[49A] was smart enough to see things clearly; it thought that the regime would clearly see as that it was in its best interest to compromise, giving them the little for which they were asking. Soon the *Bazaar* leadership woke up to the fact that, instead of compromising, the regime was trying to bypass them, and although public penalties were still the order of the day (a record 11,600 shopkeepers were fined in June 1976!), the *Bazaar* stood its ground – as long as the economy was booming, for confrontation with a regime which could rely on an annual income of $20bn seemed, at best, a losing proposition.

Iran Inc.'s masterplan for bypassing the troublesome *Bazaar* and confining it, once and for all, to its Tehran ghetto was based on (i) direct imports by international traders and companies, and on (ii) outright support of large industrial estates and harassment of small *Bazaar* and *bazaar*-related workshops. Consequently, foreign outfits began expanding their Tehran offices (at minimal cost) and importing directly, thus pocketing the commissions previously paid to the *Bazaar* middlemen and controlling the whole process from start to finish. On the other hand, the bureaucracy, strictly obeying orders coming from above, began passing laws and regulations favouring the larger establishments to the detriment of the small ones. With its petrodollars behind it, no entity, not even the super-rich Tehran *Bazaar* – worth at the most around four to five billion dollars – was a match for a government with an annual income of $20bn.

16.5. Foreign Policies

In Iran's foreign affairs, Muhammad Reza Shah took all the major decisions himself. To fill in the details, since September 1971 he had had as his Minister for Foreign Affairs, the honest and hard-working Âbbas Âli Khalâtbari, one of the best and brightest among his ministers. The Shah's foreign policy credo, shaped by thirty-odd years in the Game, was rather simple: stay in line with the US, cater to America's allies and try to keep all the others satisfied by giving them a piece of the rich Iranian cake (proportional to their international standing).

As long as President Nixon was in power, the Shah had little problem in keeping in line with the US for the two men understood each other. Nixon oversaw with pleasure Iran's transformation from client state to reliable regional power. The Shah would bend over backwards to get American armaments, technology and military assistance: the Washington–Tehran link was the platform on which his whole strategy rested. In May 1972, during Nixon's visit to Tehran, the Shah obtained from him all that he asked for; George Ball's summary of the agreement was:

> ...applying his so-called Nixon Doctrine, the President decided to entrust the security of the Gulf to the Shah, who would act as the protector of all Western interests. ...but, [the Shah] stipulated he would undertake the assignment only on certain conditions, of which two were particularly important.
> The first was that the US assist the Kurds in their revolt against Iraq in order to keep the Iraqis off balance. We agreed and later provided a substantial amount of money to Mustafa al-Barzani, the Kurdish

> leader, and sent military advisers to help the Kurdish forces. The second condition was that we give the Iranian government access to our most sophisticated military equipment. That we also agreed and, Kissinger ...directed that, regardless of the views of our Government departments, they should sell the Iranian Government whatever it desired (short of nuclear weapons)...[50]

Nixon's agreement to the Shah's two conditions was a great achievement for the latter, an achievement that placed Iran in a firm American orbit.

It was in this orbit that the Shah met three American allies willing to have closer bilateral relations with Iran (for her oil, her petrodollars and her growing market): (1) West Germany; (2) Israel; and (3) South Africa. So Iran became the fifth wheel of a select club of four dominated by the US. Always on a quest for added security, the Shah reasoned that four links gave a higher degree of insurance than just one.

Three diplomats played a crucial role in encouraging the Shah to join the select club of four. The first (and foremost) was the formidable West German Ambassador Georg von Lilienfeld,[51] posted to Tehran from 1968 until 1976. It became clear that Von Lilienfeld was not just "another Ambassador", when, in 1971, the CISNU (Confederation) issued death threats against him and his press attaché, Hans Koester. The sturdy and unflappable ambassador remained at his post, carrying out a highly successful mission in Iran, and was later rewarded with a seat on Krupp's board of directors.

The second influential ambassador was Richard Helms, who had attended the same Le Rosey school (1929-30) as the Shah; for thirty years he had been involved in the American secret services, the last seven as CIA director (1966-1973); posted to Tehran between February 1973 and December 1976, Helms helped consolidate bilateral ties. The third diplomat was the Israeli chief of (covert) missions in Tehran, Uriel Lubrani; between 1973 and 1977, Lubrani developed Israeli networks in Iran and fostered Israeli-Iranian co-operation in the military, industrial and construction domains, also trying his best to secure markets for Israeli products (such as avocados).

Iranian relations with West Germany dated back to the days of Reza Shah, when German goods and technology were dominant in Iran. Similarly, in the early 1970s, West Germany headed the list of Iranian importers, slightly ahead of the US and Japan. On the other hand, roughly 20% of crude oil requirements came from Iran; furthermore additional Iranian gas had been earmarked for export to Germany via IGAT II and the USSR. The West Germans had decided to sponsor the University of Gilan (outside Rasht) as a sign of goodwill. In order to tighten German-Iranian links, the Shah's forays into foreign investment of petrodollars[52] began, in July 1974, with the purchase of a 25.04% interest (for DM300m) in Fried. Krupp Huttenwerke, the limpig steel subsidiary of Fried. Krupp GmbH. Then, in April 1975, Iran acquired a 25% share in Deutsche Babcock and Wilcox from the firm's British mother company, later increasing it to 33.92%. And in October 1976, Iran put in a bid for a 25.01% share of the holding (mother) company of Fried. Krupp GmbH; the Iranian offer was accepted and Iran disbursed a total of DM870m (equal to $425m) over 1977 and 1978, to secure its shares at a 400% premium.[53]

For DM250m, Iran also purchased an interest in two of Krupp's Brazilian subsidiaries. Thus joint German-Iranian interests developed in a satisfactory way for both partners, and the Shah could feel secure about the Bonn–Tehran connection.

Israeli-Iranian relations had begun in 1950 with Iran's *de facto* recognition of Israel under the Sâid government. In the 1950s extensive SAVAK-Mossad links had developed, with Mossad teams quietly spying on the Iran-Iraq border.[54] In the 1960s, Israeli technical assistance began, with Tahal involved in Qazvin Agricultural Development. In the 1970s, Israeli contractors found their way into Iran, for example Solel Boneh International, Flare (at Shiraz petrochemicals) and Iscovitch and Shapira (Hilton Hotel's third tower and Eskan apartments). Iran, for its part, invested in the Trans-Israeli Pipeline and provided crude oil well in excess of Israel's domestic consumption of 90,000 b/d. But the military links came to eclipse all other aspects of bilateral co-operation. First the Zablodowitzs (father and son) set up a mortar factory in Iran for the manufacture of their Salgad model; talks were also underway with Zablodowitz's Finnish subsidiary to include a 155mm gun production line in the Isfahan complex. The Israeli Soltam company, a subsidiary of the Koor conglomerate,[55] manufactured ammunitions almost exclusively for the Shah's army, with annual sales of $150m. But this was small change when compared to the $800m advanced by Iran to Israel (as part of a $1bn oil for arms deal) for the development a jet fighter for the 1980s, codenamed LWF-4 (later known as Lavi). Another major joint project was Operation Flower, the best-kept secret in the Middle East, a scheme for developing a ground-to-ground missile capable of carrying both non-nuclear and nuclear "750-kg warheads up to a distance of 200 km"[56] – far enough to hit Baghdad from Iran. Based on the American Harpoon missile, purchased by both the Iranian Air Force and Navy, an Israeli prototype was ready by the summer of 1977; General H. Toufanian, Iran's logistics tsar, met both General M. Dayan, Israel's Foreign Minister and General Ezer Weizman, Israel's Defence Minister, on July 18, 1977, to specifically discuss Operation Flower.[57]

As for South Africa, the fourth wheel, it was much closer to Tel Aviv than to Tehran. Iran had only a minority stake (17.5%) in South Africa's 50,000 b/d Sasolburg Refinery and provided it with crude oil; in return, the latter had few interests in Iran. Its links with Israel however, were more substantial, for example the joint Iskoor tin factory in Israel; the marketing of South African agricultural products in the US by Israel's Agrexco;[58] and, last but not least, the nuclear collaboration between the two countries:

> Official Israeli-South African co-operation – on the basis of South African raw materials and Israeli manpower on joint projects – dates back to April 1976 and Prime Minister Vorster's visit to Israel. ...This was a straight technology-for-uranium deal, ...and most importantly, Vorster repeated the offer of South African territory [the Kalahari Desert] for Israel to test a nuclear device... According to documents in the early hours of September 22, 1979, a US Air Force intelligence satellite, the 'Vela', recorded a double flash of light emanating from the South Atlantic–Indian Ocean area. Such a double flash can be the signature of a nuclear explosion...[59]

On the same subject, *Time Magazine* commented that: "[US] State Department officials insist they are '95% sure' that some kind of nuclear explosion did occur".[60]

In 1974, to keep France and Great Britain at arm's length, the Shah played the magnanimity card. In June, a $1bn loan was extended to the French CÉA and in July, a $1.2bn credit line was opened for British institutions – $400m was paid to the National Water Council in October 1974 and two further $200m allocations were disbursed in June and September 1976, although the last $400m was never paid out.[61] All in all, during 1974, Iran spent some $2.4bn on foreign loans and grants, with grants totalling $953.7m – heading the list were India ($133m), Pakistan ($125m) and Egypt ($50m).[62] In 1975 Iran's generosity was considerably lessened as grants amounted to only $160m, $126m of which went to Pakistan.

A common Iranian-Pakistani headache was the budding guerrilla movements of Balouchistan, financed and supported by drug traffickers. On the Iranian side, the arrest of thirty-one armed guerrillas put a stop to Balouchi troubles; but in 1973, flare-ups on the Pakistani side developed into a mini war[63] and it took the Pakistani Army, assisted by nine Iranian helicopter gunships, six months (December 1973–May 1974) to quell the rebellion.[64]

Iranian-Pakistani relations were as good as the Iranian-Iraqi ones were bad. Since 1969, when the Shah had flexed his muscles, rejecting the Saâdabad Treaty of 1937 and the accepted settlement on the Shatt ul-Ârab waterway, tensions on the border had been daily worsening. With time, these escalated into incidents and later into skirmishes. In April 1972, Iraq signed a treaty of friendship with the USSR, further distancing itself from Iran and its American patron; as a *quid pro quo* for deliveries of modern armaments, the Soviet Navy was allowed use of the Iraqi naval base of Ûmm ul-Qasr. In northern Iraq, Mustafa Barzani *peshmergas*, supported by CIA experts and Iranian funds, proved a sore thorn in Iraq's side. During 1973 sabre-rattling on both sides of the border reached its climax and on February 10, 1974, a full-scale battle erupted near Mihran, occasioning severe casualties on both sides (at least forty-two deaths on the Iranian side). But skirmishes were unimportant, the main question now being: would an all-out Iranian-Iraqi war break out?

The Shah commissioned the capable General Uvaysi to investigate the outcome of an Iranian invasion of Iraq. Uvaysi toured all the border garrisons in a fact-gathering mission and concluded in his report to the Shah that Iran could not easily defeat the Iraqi army, in view of Iraq's well-trained armour and its efficient engineering corps.[65] Uvaysi's secret report paved the way for the March 6, 1975 accord between the Shah and Iraq's Saddam Husayn, the peace treaty being signed on March 18. There would be no Iran-Iraq war. Stabbed in the back, the Kurdish rebellion collapsed. The Iranian administration did its best to resettle the fleeing *peshmergas* in the Qazvin region, but the Kurds were not to forget Muhammad Reza Shah's treacherous ways.

The Shah also mended his fences with Egypt. The replacement of Nasser by Anwar Sadat had brought about an Iranian U-turn. The economically weak Egypt would be on the receiving end of Iranian generosity. On May 25, 1974, the signing of a groundbreaking protocol, worth $1bn, for a series of joint ventures, including the reconstruction of Port Said and the widening of the Suez Canal, set Iranian-Egyptian relations on a new footing. In January 1975, the Shah went on a official visit to meet Sadat. Thereafter the Misr-Iran Development Bank was established, with four major shareholders – Bank of Alexandria (37.5%), Egypt Insurance (37.5%), Bank-i Milli (12.5%) and IMDBI (12.5%) – and in 1976, the Egyptian-Iranian Maritime Company was created with an initial capital of $1m for joint shipping ventures. The Tehran-Cairo connection had become one of the most solid links of the 1970s.

A small portion of Iran's petrodollars was used to keep the USSR and the Eastern Bloc countries satisfied. The Soviets even had reason to be appreciative of their economic relations with Iran: they provided the Iranian Army with its light ordnance, its anti-aircraft defences, its multiple rocket launcher systems (*Katyousha*) and its RPG-7 (for which it had built an assembly line in Iran); the Isfahan Steel Mill and the Arak machine tools plant were being expanded by Soviet experts; cheap IGAT I gas flowed in and the future IGAT II would prove even more lucrative. The USSR's Eastern allies were given oil for goods counter-trade agreements, with Romania (tractors), Czechoslovakia (machine tools, small arms) and Poland (ships, textile machinery) leading the pack.

Iran was not only dealing with West or East, but also standing on the front line of the North-South dialogue, revived because of OPEC's petrodollar clout. In September 1974, the industrialised countries formed the International Energy Agency (IEA) as a counterweight to OPEC. The preparatory commission for the North-South conference met in April 1975 at Paris to discuss the conference's agenda. The seven southern hemisphere countries attending were Iran, Saudi Arabia, Venezuela, Algeria, Brazil, India and Zaire. The 'North' wanted energy resources on the agenda, the 'South' finance and development. At the General Conference at Paris, in December 1975, representatives of twenty-seven countries (eight for the 'North', nineteen for the 'South') compromised by forming four sub-committees on (i) energy, (ii) raw materials, (iii) finance and (iv) development. For the next eighteen months reports and papers piled up in the four committees, the 'North' being cautious not to give anything away. By 1977, the energy crisis had been totally forgotten and the North-South conference slowly died down on June 2, 1977. Nothing had been achieved, and nothing between North and South would ever be achieved around a green table – as every sensible observer knew by experience.

Whether west or east, north or south, Iran's position was forthright. Only in one direction of the compass was it ambivalent: towards London. Under Muhammad Reza Shah's rule, bilateral relations with the British had a chequered past. Since the days of Sir Reader Bullard, the British Ambassador to Tehran during the Second World War, there had been no love lost between the Shah and Her Majesty's envoy. And if Iranians have long memories, so does the British Foreign Office, especially in the seventies, when Sir Reader's son Julian was deputy head of the FCO, holding the title of political director. The Shah delighted in reminiscing in public about past brushes with British ambassadors (not the wisest thing to do), and at a press conference given on January 24, 1971, on the eve of the Tehran Oil Conference, he reported the words of one of them (most likely Sir Reader Bullard):

> ...For Iran it is to be regretted that she had never been a colony, because if she were she could have built the necessary infrastructure ...It is completely natural that one-third of the revenues from your oil should accrue to you, one third to the oil company, and the remaining one-third to us...[66]

But, notwithstanding the bad blood, the British and the Iranians were getting along very well during the 1970s, economically speaking. As author Anthony Sampson observed:

...Before 1979 [the British Embassy at Tehran] looked more like a trade fair, full of brochures, posters and travelling salesmen...[67]

Besides the extensive arms sales (Chieftain tanks), many British firms were doing extremely well in Iran: the exclusive Albermarle Nursing Service had placed fifty nannies in high society families (and hoped to double that number); Chrysler UK's sales of *Paykan* kits to Iran National were worth more than $200m per annum; the National Freight Company had almost monopolised the installation of cold storage areas in Iran; the auditing firms of Whinney Murray (senior partner Sir Byron Nelson), Coopers and Lybrand (J.M. Thompson) and Peat, Marwick and Mitchell (B.G. Mitchell) had cornered industrial accounting in Iran (and took the pulse of its private sector); Range Rovers were the higher middle class's new status symbol; British companies had invested in joint ventures for dairy and beef businesses; Acrow Engineering Company had set up a heavy engineering complex at Ahvaz with IDRO, Acrowsaz; British Industrial Plastics had a 40% stake in Persepolis Industrial Plastics (a melamine manufacturer near Shiraz); contractor Marples Ridgeway had a $200m contract for part of the Tehran to Pakistan border highway; Davy Powergas was managing contractor of the expansion of Shiraz Fertilisers; Perkins Motors and Massey-Ferguson were established at Tabriz; and there were also BICC, Leyland's double-decker buses, Johnny Walker Scotch whisky. Furthermore, at the Iran-British Investment Conference at Persepolis, in November 1973, British businessmen, led by Peter Walker, the Secretary of State for Trade and Industry, and Lord Thorneycroft, pledged another $250m towards investment in Iran.

If the Americans, the West Germans and the Israelis had sent their very best diplomats to Iran during the critical 1970s, the British had too: they had Sir Anthony Parsons. Arriving in Tehran in 1973, Parsons left in 1979. During his protracted mission he had a difficult hand to play, not on the economic side but on the political one. At home, critics were not mincing their words: Amnesty International

(AI) was constantly attacking human rights violations in Iran's prisons, having fully exposed SAVAK's and the *Kumiteh*'s actions in its *1973 Annual Report*; Sussex University's Tavistock Institute for Human Relations was highly critical of Iran's human rights record; and the Bertrand Russell Peace Foundation (headed by the formidable Ken Coates) was definitely not in the pro-Pahlavi league; but the Shah's *bête noire* was the British Broadcasting Corporation, the BBC. In October 1973, in its highly regarded *Panorama* television programme, in a transmission entitled 'Barrels and Guns', the BBC had drawn a highly critical picture of the Shah's policies and aspirations; it had "ridiculed Iran's ambitions to achieve in a decade or two what had taken the Western countries centuries to accomplish", "denigrated the Shah's expansionist aims and his wishes to revive the Achaemanean Empire", and finally "attacked land reform in Iran, [adding] that farmer co-operatives resembled prison work parties"![68] The Shah, as to be expected, exploded on seeing the BBC transmission: the BBC office in Tehran was closed *sine die* and its representative in Iran, John Bierman, expelled with the briefest of delays. Between the Pahlavi Shah and the BBC the hatchet would never be buried; the problem for the Shah was that a large majority of Iranians listened to the BBC's daily Farsi broadcasts.

Notwithstanding political differences, Iran was to co-operate fully with Great Britain in their joint struggle in Oman, assisting its sultan to crush the Marxist-Leninist rebellion in Dhufar. "A veil of secrecy", noted Persian Gulf expert J.B. Kelly, "was drawn over the war in Dhufar for political as well as for military reasons".[69] On the Omani side, the elite British Special Air Service (SAS) was engaged in supporting the Sultan's Armed Forces (SAF) against the Marxist guerrillas of the Popular Front for the Liberation of Occupied Arabian Gulf (PFLOAG) – later 'Occupied' was replaced by 'Oman and'. By mid-1970, PFLOAG had come to control two-thirds of the Dhufar province and threatened to occupy the last third. On July 23, in a bloodless coup, Qabous ibn Sâid displaced his ailing father Sâid ibn Taymur and became Sultan of Oman. In February 1972, secret Iranian-Omani negotiations culminated in an undertaking of military assistance to Oman. By his willingness to send troops and equipment to Oman, the Shah seemed to follow three objectives: (1) to show the Gulf shaykhs that he would intervene wherever necessary against Marxist guerrillas; (2) to try and ingratiate himself with the British, proving that in times of trial he was on their side; and (3) to give his crack troops some real action training.

In 1973, the first Iranian helicopters (with complete crew) duly arrived in Oman and the first contingent of 1,200 men of the crack *Tip Nouhid* paratroops unit debarked at Salalah. In December 1973, the Iranians' action to clear the Salalah-Thamarit highway, occupied by the PFLOAG since October 1970, was a first success.[70] Nevertheless, some senior British officers had a poor opinion of the capabilities of Iranian troops: one of them told a Lebanese reporter: "Although the Iranian soldier is one of the best-equipped soldier in the world (next to the American soldier), he has no fighting experience and that, in comparison, the Omani soldier is a better fighter".[71] In December 1974, another general offensive took place, and the Iranians were able to capture the coastal town of Rakhyut, in PFLOAG hands since August 1969. Consequent to this victory, the Iranian contingent (by then 3,200 strong[72]) began the construction of the 35 kilometre long Damavand Line, a defensive rampart perpendicular to the coast and parallel to the British Hornbeam Line, made to prevent PFLOAG guerrillas from crossing over from Yemen into Oman.

In the autumn of 1975, the remnants of PFLOAG received the *coup de grâce*. A combined British-Iranian-Omani assault out of the Sarfeet base against Hauf was crowned with success, after the position had been strafed by Iranian F-4 fighter-bombers (refuelled in the air). By early 1976, PFLOAG's back had been broken, but, during the twelve months encompassing March 1975–March 1976, Iranian troops had suffered heavy casualties: twenty-five officers and a hundred and eighty-six NCOs and soldiers were killed,[73] and at least three helicopters shot down.[74] By January 1977, it was announced that the Iranian contingent was pulling out of Oman, "leaving behind only radar and anti-aircraft operatives".[75] The very last Iranian officers came back in March 1979,[76] ending a six year Iranian involvement in Oman.

Thus, with some Iranian help, Britain had held on to the "key to command of the Gulf and its seaward approaches",[77] in other words Oman. Sultan Qabous could engage in prospecting for oil and gas reserves throughout his vast country unimpeded by leftist guerrillas. As for the Shah, although he had failed to noticeably alter general British antipathy towards him – author A. Sampson still thinking that: "[He] was a bad advertisement for kingship..."[78] – he had succeeded in making his point to the Gulf shayks and in giving his armed forces (expressly rotated every three months in Dhufar) a chance to lose their fighting virginity.

16.6. Iran's *Rastakhiz*

With the oil price quadrupling of 1973/74, the Shah was swept up in the euphoria of the moment and, envisioning an annual income of above $15bn, had overreached himself in many fields. One of these areas was internal welfare. The Shah thought that Iran was affluent enough to copy Sweden; in February 1974, he had issued an Imperial Decree declaring the first eight years of schooling free and compulsory for all Iranian children; the decree further stipulated a free midday snack to be served to all schoolchildren nationwide, consisting of either milk/biscuits, or eggs, or dates, or nuts, or sandwiches. The system was simply not ready to cope with such an enormous distribution service and the waste and the corruption engendered were correspondingly enormous, costing the government some $150m per annum, and making another few millionaires of the happy contractors. But although in some north Tehran schools the eggs and the milk cartons were used as projectiles, it would seem that in the south of Tehran and in provincial centres some children received a few extra hundreds of calories once a day. So, despite all the wastage, the far-fetched programme had some benefits. In April 1974, secondary schoolchildren were provided with free tuition too, provided that they promised to work for the government twice the number of years of free education after gaining their diploma.[79] Then, in a logical follow-up, all private schools were nationalised in September 1974: in one go thousands of teachers and school employees had been added to the public sector (not a very sensible move).

The next step was to declare higher education free. At the beginning of the academic school year 1974/75, this was done with the same proviso of the students spending twice as many years as spent on their free education working for the government. For students wishing to pay their way through university, annual tuition fees ranged from Rls70,000 to Rls300,000 (equal to a $1,000 to $4,300 range), depending on the university and the faculty attended.[80] Naturally over 97% of students chose the free option (being incapable of paying such sums). The government also approved a whole train of fringe benefits for students: living allowances, housing subsidies, low-interest loans, and summer camps fully paid for.

These measures would have two other direct consequences. The first was the multiplication of destitute rural students, who could now afford to attend universities if accepted through the all-important National University Entrance Test (*Kunkour*). Mostly with Islamic backgrounds, this new category of students was able to outnumber the nationalist groups on campus and dent the quasi-monopoly of the Marxist majority; in October 1977, the Islamist students were strong enough to ask for the segregation of female students on campuses. The second consequence was the proliferation of private establishments of higher education. Paid a fixed, generous sum for every student per year, these profit-making institutions made horrendous profits 1974-1978, and yet another bunch of (unhappy) millionaires.

With these private universities and the new universities at Hamadan and Gilan, the number of Iranian students increased by leaps and bounds to reach the 160,000 mark in 1977/78 (see Table 16.6); meanwhile the studentship of Tehran University stagnated at around 17-18,000. But the regime's twin strategies of diluting the radical students in a flood of fresh students and of 'buying-off' the students both failed. As they arrived on campus the fresh students were indoctrinated and rapidly taught the basic rules of rioting and battling the security forces (as a fourth year Tehran University Technical Faculty student put it: "We might not be the best in engineering, but in evading police forces we are number one in the world"[81]).

As for being bought off, the students had twenty years of almost uninterrupted struggle against the Pahlavi regime which could not be that easily forgotten; on the contrary, all the extra benefits given them in 1974 and 1975 allowed them to devote less time to earning money and more time to the anti-regime struggle.

On December 24, 1975 the Shah felt confident enough to engrave three new principles in his Shah and People Revolution:
- Principle Fifteen: free and compulsory education for schoolchildren up to the age of fourteen (as per the Imperial Decree of February 1974).
- Principle Sixteen: free nutrition for all babies up to the end of their second year.

– Principle Seventeen: social security and life insurance for all Iranians, inclusive of villagers.

Table 16.6. Total Number of Higher Education Students in Iran, and the Studentship at Tehran University (1970–78).

Academic Year	Nationwide	Tehran University Enrolment
1970/71	74,708	17,292
1971/72	97,338	17,147
1972/73	115,311	17,489
1973/74	123,114	17,617
1974/75	135,354	17,379
1975/76	151,905	18,866
1976/77	154,215	18,183
1977/78	160,308	17,069

This was pure demagogy. A welfare system copied from European models could not run for ever on petrodollars. The danger was in raising too rapidly the people's expectations, especially if (as in Iran) the delivery of promises given took time and the end result was not always up to scratch. The Shah himself soon came to realise that he had gone too far too quickly: at the Ninth Annual Education Conference at Ramsar in September 1976, he sheepishly admitted that "there was solid evidence that increased welfare benefits and spending in education had not guaranteed better results, [and that] it was time to have future spending directed where better results could be ensured". For back-pedalling, however, it was much too late.

Having had to bring out the obsolete 'Shah and People' framework once again was a sure sign that the Shah and his elite were at a loss for fresh ideas and ideals. They had tried to co-opt new blood, by, for example, propelling the forty-six year old civil servant Nasir Âmiri to the top of the *Mardum* Party (Âlam's personal fiefdom); but, not playing the electoral game according to rules, he had to be abruptly dismissed (amidst a flurry of insulting newspaper editorials) on December 29, 1974, and died in a car crash near Rasht on January 30, 1975. After the *Mardum* Party alternative had ended in a fiasco, the regime's masterminds – Parviz Nikkhwah, Dr Manouchihr Azmun, Mahmoud Jâfarian, Firaydoun Mahdavi *et alia* – put on their thinking caps and got the first point right: change was needed. For their change they came up with an idea most befitting the Iran Inc. structure: the creation of a unique party, the *Rasthakhiz* (Resurgence) Party, a unique, all-encompassing pyramid placed under the Shah and his board of directors (with Dr Azmun allegedly preparing the first draft of its organisation). They sold the idea to the Shah, who readily bought it, seeing the logic behind it.

On March 2, 1975, in an historic declaration at Niavaran Palace, the Shah trumpeted the creation of the *Hizb-i Rastakhiz-i Millat-i Iran* (the Iranian People's Resurgence Party), explaining that:

> Today, we lay the foundation of this new political structure. Every Iranian ...who believes in the Monarchy, the Constitution and the Sixth of Bahman ['Shah and People'] Revolution must definitely join this political organisation. All will be equal, all [*sic*] will have a single structure...[82]

In the wake of the declaration, Iran's four legal parties – the *Iran Nuvin*, the *Mardum*, the Iranian and the Pan-Iranist parties – scuttled to the Shah's shadow and dutifully announced their and their members' adherence to *Rastakhiz*. Premier Huvayda was appointed provisional secretary-general of the party[83] and two party wings were created: the Constructive and the Progressive wings, with respective leaders Houshang Ansari and Jamshid Amuzigar. Hence, the bureaucracy's top troika was leading the new party too. A fifty-five member Executive Board and a twenty-seven member Political Bureau (inclusive of twelve members elected by the Executive Board and eight ministers appointed by the prime minister) completed the party's administration. On March 3, 1975, the first issue of the party's newspaper, entitled *Rastakhiz*, was published, and two months later, two monthlies were added: the *Rastakhiz-i Kargaran* (the Workers' Rastakhiz) and the *Rastakhiz-i Rousta* (the Rural Rastakhiz).

According to the NIRT's monthly magazine *Tamasha* (edited by the dynamic German-educated Firouz Fouladi), "Rastakhiz was the national forum for airing thoughts; or, in other words, the indispensable mechanism for the participation of people in social affairs, and the conduit for informing people about national policies, and the catalyst for forming a consensus that would be reported to the highest authorities of the country". In theory, a wonderful programme for tapping new ideas from the Iranian masses; in practice, a total failure, a caricature of Huvayda's *Iran Nuvin* but bigger, an empty showcase. Although official membership, which was compulsory for civil servants, was said to have exceeded five million in the autumn of 1975, the large majority of Iranians had not been gulled by the Shah's artificial party. *Rastakhiz*'s litmus test came in the summer of 1975, when the elections to the Twenty-Fourth *Majlis* were held. The elections were naturally declared 'free', but people were not free to become candidates as pre-selection was drastic; they were only 'free' to vote for any of the 'selected' (royalist) candidates. In the end, the 268 *Rastakhiz* deputies would form a *Majlis* as tame as the Twenty-First, Twenty-Second and Twenty-Third editions. The case was heard and closed: the *Rastakhiz* trap was too simple to ensnare Iranians. It eventually proved a catastrophe, and in his memoirs even the Shah recognised the blunder:

> ...L'expérience devais malheureusement montrer que ce parti [*Rastakhiz*] fut une erreur...[84]

With *Rastakhiz* taking water from all sides in 1975 (already), the regime's masterminds decided to embark on a fresh ship, an unsinkable one this time: Iran was going to become the fifth world power within the next two decades. Even Premier Huvayda didn't shy away from declaring, in an interview to Eric Rouleau: "In some three decades Iranian per capita income would have outgrown the Japanese one".[85] Official propaganda began harping on the fact that extrapolations showed Iran "could do it", could become an industrial nation and catch up with the Western countries (with the first target, Italy, not far away).

Well, here was an international endeavour to fire Iranian youth's minds, the masterminds thought; but that was not to be, for Iran's younger generation did not trust its leadership, it could not dream realistically of becoming the world's fifth biggest industrialised country, and it was not even clear whether it cared, let alone having sufficient ambition. In 1975 a French-based think-tank looked seriously at Iran's official ambitions and came to the conclusion that:

> ...Iran's economy in 1985, even on the best projections, remains not much beyond what India's will be in ten years. ...Half of its [India's] exports are manufactured products. ...Iran's principal non-oil export is the Persian carpet...[86]

Nevertheless, the regime's propagandists went on to coin an expression for Iran's future goal: the *Tamaddun-i Buzurg* (the Great Civilisation). Intermittently used by the Shah since 1974, in 1975 it became his leitmotiv in the sense of the new frontier he was promising his people. Ideologue Mahmoud Jâfarian even found a way to link it to the unique party, declaring that: "Rastakhiz is the bulldozer paving the way for the Tamaddun-i Buzurg".[87] But people had to work hard to reach it, or, as the Shah outlined it in an interview:

> ...The Great Civilisation cannot be created in a paradise of sloth and indolence, it can only emerge when there is Great Patriotism, ...dedication and conscientious work...[88]

The only problem was that the paradise was for the Iran Inc. officers and the hard, dedicated work for the rest. With time, the ideologues introduced the new concept of the Great Civilisation's *Darvazeh* (Gateway), which "could be seen on the horizon". The *Darvazeh* became popular laughing material – after any mishap or snag in the Iranian daily routine, an ironic illusion allusion was made to the 'Gateway'. Thus an instrument of official propaganda had been turned into an instrument for ridiculing the regime. Notwithstanding the ridicule, the Shah went ahead with his third book, entitled *Beh Su-yi Tamaddun-i Buzurg* (Towards the Great Civilisation), which duly came out (late) in January 1978, in a first print run of one million copies!

The consecutive flops of *Rastakhiz*, of the international dream and of the Great Civilisation were a sure sign that the Shah, his elite and his ideologues had run out of ideas and ideals. They wanted only to remain at the top of the heap to decide how to spend petrodollars while lining their pockets. It was also a sign that Iran's brains were not thinking for the regime any more (having rejected the *Rastakhiz* trap); this second sign was far more ominous than the first one for, if they were not thinking for it, then they could only be thinking against it.

16.7. The Petrodollar Elite

With the petrodollars flood of 1974 and 1975, the Shah's elite was being overwhelmed by a new type of elite, the elite of money – also known as the petrodollar elite. Naturally, the higher members of the former elite were to be found in the latter, as they too benefited directly from the petrodollars, that is to say royal family members, royal influence-peddlers, higher court servants, top military brass and a handful of wealthy government members. The fresh 1970s money elitists (all quite independent of the court, albeit benefiting from its tacit support) can be grouped into four categories:
(1) captains of industry;
(2) large urban landowners;
(3) grand real estate developers;
(4) ex-*Bazaaris* in international business.

In the 1970s, urban land, and especially land in and around Tehran, was the new source of Iranian wealth. Having begun during the late 1960s, the first Iranian land price boom would be sustained until the close of 1978. The boom's dimensions were mind-boggling. According to the Middle East Economics Research Centre, urban land prices had multiplied by an average of sixteenfold over the decade 1968–1977.[89] In the north of Tehran, areas with a five-hundredfold to thousandfold price jumps were quite common, for example the Vanak area, owned by the heirs to Mustoufi ul-Mamalik (the former prime minister), where average prices in the mid-1960s stood at around Rls10 to 15 per square metre, by 1970 had jumped to the Rls80 to 110 bracket, in 1973 stood at Rls400 to 500, and ended up in 1977/78 at anywhere between Rls15,000 and 25,000 per metre (equal to $215 to $360), and sometimes even higher than that. The Vanak area was not an exception.

Everyone was sucked into the well-oiled real estate machinery set up by the larger landowners and their myriad agents and hangers-on. Among the large landowners the greatest winners of the 1970s were essentially those of the 1960s (see above Chapter 16) – first and foremost the thirty-two heirs to Prince Farmanfarmayan, their children and grandchildren; the Nizam-Mafi family, under their patriarch Muhammad Âli Nizam ul-Saltaneh; the Mustoufi ul-Mamaliks; the Shaybanis of Darrous; the Imamis of Vilinjak; the Âbbas Khazaneh of the Khazaneh district in south Tehran, added to the new breed of the Amir Sulaymanis of the upper Sayyid Khandan district; the Takish family's holdings around Âbbasabad and the Vuzara' Avenue; and Davoud Mânavi of Davoudiyyeh, just to name a few of the largest.

Under pressure from the middle classes the government tried time and again to bring land speculation to a halt, always only to witness its half-hearted efforts squashed by the power of the real estate machinery. In 1971, the government threatened to sell the urban lands it owned to break the land price inflation: when it failed to deliver on its threat another quantum jump in prices occurred. In January 1974, it took a Anti-Land Speculation Bill to the *Majlis*, asking for (i) the nationalisation of all coastal and riverside land lots, (ii) the one-time only sale of vacant lots, (iii) the fixing of special area prices (indexed on inflation); and (iv) the fixing of strict city limits. The bill languished in the *Majlis* and, when it was eventually ratified, with a number of amendments, it was rendered almost unworkable. In 1976 and 1977 more useless legal battles were fought, as land speculation continued unabated, until people took things into their own hands and began building illegally.

The ownership of land was one source of profit (large enough for the Farmanfarmayans or the Nizam-Mafis), but developers soon found out that building on it was also a very lucrative occupation – especially in times of high inflation.[89] Thus, cities and towns (Tehran leading the pack) became huge construction centres, with billions of rials being poured into this thriving new business. From Rls70bn in 1972, investment in construction rose to over Rls461 in 1977 – a cumulative total of Rls1311bn (equal to $18.6bn) in six years (see Table 16.7 for details). For the national economy that meant thousands of new jobs, increases in fixed investment and fresh housing units which could be offered to the middle classes and the rural migrants.

Paraphrasing the French, the Tehrani developers could say: "Quand le bâtiment va, tout va...".

Table 16.7. Investment in Iran's Construction Business (1972-77).[90]
(Figures in Rls billions)

Year	Urban Construction	Rural Construction	Total
1972	60.2	9.7	69.9
1973	83.1	12.5	95.6
1974	108.1	16.6	124.7
1975	187.1	21.3	208.4
1976	312.0	40.3	352.3
1977	411.1	50.2	461.3
Total	1161.6	150.6	1312.2

The development of Tehran's prominent skyscrapers was carried out by a handful of major developers:
- The three ASP towers were built by a French contractor, for Âlinaqi Asadi and Murad Panahpour, in association with the Bank-i Sadirat;
- The triple Auto-Tehran block was constructed by Desiree Kettaneh in the centre of town (in lieu of the former Dodge garage/parking lot). Kettaneh also built the three Khuvardin towers, in the Shahrak-i Gharb, in association with the Bank-i Ûmran;
- The towers built at Vanak were constructed by Sir Shahpour Reporter;
- The Vanak projects of Malikzadeh Yazdi: 'Parc des Princes' and 'Vanak Parc';

- The three octagonal towers of Iskan were erected by the Israelis, just above Vanak Square, for a group of Iranian investors led by Engineer Jâfar Sharif Imami;
- The multiple towers in the Sharak-i Gharb, known as the Zumurrud complex, were built by the American Starrett Housing Company;
- The Ûmran Tiklar towers were constructed by a Greek developer;
- In the middle of the town centre the 35-storey Bank-i Sadirat main building was erected by ASP (a great disservice to Tehran);

Large-scale housing projects, the building of artificial townships with thousands of housing units on very cheap land outside Tehran's city limits, also became a favourite investment and prominent projects included:

- The Ikbatan *cité-dortoir* of 12,000 flats was built in the neighbourhood of Mihrabad Airport by developers Muhammad Âli Gulzar and Husayn Danishvar (a courtier who probably acted as a front for the Shah);
- The 5,000 housing units were due to be built near the village of Kan (15 kilometres north-west of Tehran) for NIOC employees, by the contractors Nedeco (Holland), Goehner (Switzerland) and Raftar (Iran), but it was never started;
- The 14,100 units to be erected by the firm of Levitt and Sons (US) near the Sharak-i Gharb for $600m;
- A group of nineteen towers, was to be built by a French contractor, in the east Tehran Lavizan area, for army officers and NCOs (only half-finished in 1978 and terminated thereafter);
- The Vavan township plan, with thousands of villas and flats, on a plot of land some 22 kilometres south-west of Tehran which belonged to members of the Pahlavi family, was undertaken by a development Consortium consisting of Stahlbau and ARG (West Germany) and KLM (Holland). Investors paid up when the project began, but the developers fled with the funds during the Revolution and the government had to partly indemnify the investors.

If Tehran took the lion's share of urban and township development, some provincial centres witnessed febrile construction activities too. A development township, some 20 kilometres north of Isfahan, named Shahin Shahr, made the news: it was developed by the Rashidian brothers (Asdullah and Qudratullah), of *Murdad 28* fame, on land belonging to the Buroumand brothers (most famous of whom was Dr Âbd ul-Rahman Buroumand, the Nationalist politician). Shahin Shahr was a success. Inaugurated by the Shah, the township became home base for Bell Helicopters employees. Prices for land and flats in the township rose weekly.

The Rashudians and the Buroumands made millions, which flowed into the bank they virtually owned, the Bank-i Îtibarat-i Taâvuni Touzî. Founded in 1959, the private bank (one of the rare totally private banks in Iran, with 1976 assets of Rls16.2bn (equal to $230m)) had Asadullah Rashidian as chairman and managing director, and Dr Buroumand as director.

By the mid-1970s, two men had come to dominate building contractors, namely Âbd ul-Majid Aâlam and Amir Malikzadeh Yazdi. Aâlam had launched his Tessa civil engineering company in the early 1950s and upon this successful base he had then built an engineering empire; he had teamed up with Fluor Constructors and Engineers (of Los Angeles) to form Fluor Iran; with Ahmad Vahabzadeh and Sperry Rand (US) he had created Univac Iran; with Âziz Farmanfarmayan he had created the Khaneh joint venture for developing the Pahlavi Shahistan; and he had even joined forces with his rival Malikzadeh Yazdi to form the largest construction company in Iran, Armeh-Tessa, to take part in the erection of Tehran's 100,000-seat Olympic-size stadium, built for the Seventh Asian Games of 1974; in addition to his construction activities, Aâlam was on a dozen boards as director and on three banks' boards: Bank-i Kar, Bank-i Sakhtiman and the Mercantile Bank of Iran and Holland (with the Vahabzadehs).

As for Malikzadeh, a shrewd self-made Yazdi, he was sole owner of his Armeh empire, alongside his sons Shahrukh and Shahram; he owned thousands of square metres in Tehran, half a dozen major buildings in the centre of town (e.g. the IPAC tower), skyscrapers in Vanak and a dozen affiliated companies (e.g. Kamsaz, Paziran and the Rock Crusher Co.).

Besides the captains of industry, the real estate moguls and the developers, a fourth group was bidding for a place in the petrodollar elite: the Tehran *Bazaaris* were trying to bridge the gap between the 'old' *Bazaar* and the new world of international business, betting on both. One of the most successful among this new breed was Hajji Mufid who, from his *Bazaar* headquarters, had played the Tehran real estate and the import-export cards, making tens of (dollar) millions. Another such trader was Khamnehpour, a *Bazaari* with extensive matrimonial links to the Mufid family. There were many others who made use of their *Bazaar* experience to deal in domestic real estate and international affairs.

For the petrodollar elite, the Great Civilisation promised by the Shah was at hand. The new elite could enjoy one of the highest and brightest qualities of life available on the planet. Only the international jet set and chief executive officers of large multinational conglomerates could rival their lifestyle.

For the petrodollar elitists it was paradise on earth:

– They owned plush, beautifully built villas in Shimiran multi-hectare gardens which were exquisitely decorated with *bibelots*, French statues, original Gobelins, miniatures, Iranian tableaux either Qajar or modern Iranian (preferably Zendehroudi, Tabrizi, Reza Mafi, Tanavuli or Iran Darroudi), Nai'n carpets, Boulle *sécretaires* and Chinese lacquer screens, all set in the *ne plus ultra* of modern comfort, with the latest electronic gadgets. Swimming pools and Finnish saunas were a must; tennis courts and private cinemas were still a status symbol. A cohort of servants and maids, cooks and chauffeurs, gardeners and housekeepers whirled around the villa and its gardens (the older the money, the more silent they were). A fleet of cars (ranging from Nizam Âmiri's Lamborghini to Âli Fouladi's eleven automobiles) were always available for family members

– At their fingertips was the best food available in the world, from Iranian kebabs to French champagnes and Israeli avocados, to be eaten in cosy and chic restaurants (Xanadu, Chez Michelle, The Cellar, or Léon's) or at private dinner parties (usually numbering from a dozen to thirty guests), which was the craze of the time, with the elite's motto seemingly, "J'invite, donc je suis" – with the 'Party of the Year' (a must) given annually by Mrs Mirdamadi in her Shimiran garden

– After their dinner parties, they could dance their nights away in Tehran's two exclusive discos: the Key Club and La Cheminée, the former for the younger generation and the latter for the older one.

– They had their own private club, the sprawling Imperial Country Club (ICC), north of Vanak, managed by the sexagenarian Jamshid Buzurgmihr (a former water-skiing instructor); ICC membership was a must, as it was to be seen on its tennis courts or golf course.

— More select than the discreet ICC was the French Club (*Le Cercle des Amitiés Franco-Iraniennes*) situated in town, off Firdousi Square; there an older, quieter crowd gathered to have dinner and play bridge, possibly cutting as partner the club's sympathetic manager Jean Claude Bachou.

— They spent summers in their Caspian Sea villas (Ramsar was tops) or on the French Riviera; winter skiing took place either at Dizin or St Moritz (like the Shah); New Year celebration was either at Kish or Kharg Island (NIOC connection needed).

— They could travel to any location in the world at the blink of an eyelid: to rest at their villas in Grasse or Cannes, to attend a party in New York, to go on a buying spree in Harrods, to be pampered at Alexandre's or simply to get out of Tehran for the sake of going somewhere else.

— They cheered their tennis heroes at the Aryamihr Tennis Cup, held each autumn since 1972 at the ICC; the cup had reached a $175,000 purse in 1977 and a double-A rating (grand slam venues being triple-A) on the Commercial Union circuit.

— They applauded their favourite showjumpers at the Aryamihr International Showjumping Competition, held in Tehran for the first (and last time) in November 1977; the first prize of $8,300 going to Harvey Smith (GB), the second to Capitan Piero d'Inzeo (Italy) and the third to Jean-Michel Gaud (France).

— They placed their bets on horses at the Farahabad Stadium (30,000 seats), inaugurated in 1977; owned by the Tehran Racing Association (a joint venture between the Pahlavi family and Macao businessmen), the show was managed by Bahman Shahandeh, the former *Majlis* deputy, caterer to Tehran's Western embassies, representative of the Deutsche Press Agentur and the in-crowd's jack of all trades.

— They gambled in stylish casinos, on the Karaj Dam Lake, at the Ab-i Ali ski resort, at the Ramsar Hotel, at Isfahan, at Kish and at the Namakabroud Hyatt Regency (on the Caspian); three of the six casinos were owned by the Pahlavi Foundation.

— They watched the best movies at the International Tehran Film Festival, begun in 1972; with tickets (in 1976 and 1977) for the Roudaki Hall sold *en bloc* to elitists, who did not have time to attend.

— They flocked to Shiraz every autumn to yawn away at Empress Farah and Riza Qutbi's Shiraz Art Festival (another must); after staging Maurice Béjart's *Heliogabale* and *Golestan*, the festival ended in its eleventh edition (August 1977), after two actors performing *théâtre-verité* in the streets of Shiraz actually engaged in sexual intercourse; the poetic Shirazis, not easily shocked, were left dumbfounded.

– They could indulge in cultural activities at the new Tehran museums set up by the Empress Farah Art Foundation (president, Âbd ul-Majid Majidi) and supervised by the Empress's Special Cultural Bureau (chief, Aydin Aghdashlou):

(1) Tehran's Museum of Modern Art (MOMA), designed and erected by an all-American team, under the control of Kamran Diba, a cousin of the Empress and owner of the design outfit Kash;

(2) the National Carpet Museum, designed by Âbd ul-Riza Farmanfarmayan, located north of the MOMA and opened in February 1978;

(3) the Riza Âbbasi Cultural and Arts Centre, where 141 Pre-Islamic art objects, 116 artefacts of the Islamic era and some 10,000 calligraphic and lithographic documents had been put on display (since September 1977).

– They sent their sons and daughters to the Le Rosey school, the Shah and his brothers had attended; the list of Iranian Roseens of the 1970s reads like a petrodollar elite who's who: Khayyamis (four family members), Barkhurdars (four), Azmayishs (three), Akhavans (three), Mansurs (three), Vahabzadehs (three) and so on.

Observing such a fabulous quality of life, it was not surprising that many Iranians were ready to do their utmost to join the new elite, even engaging in fraudulent acts. Seeing corruption take on endemic proportions in the 1970s – "even the Shah himself might not be totally innocent in this respect", hinted *Le Monde*'s Jean Gueyras[92] – and being told that bribes and bribery were needed in a anti-communist society (and were also needed by the petrodollar elite to keep as many as possible corrupt and satisfied), many Iranians gave and received bribes. Almost everyone had a price. The tiny incorruptible minority were treated by the elite as "incapables and idiots".

Corruption scandals in Iran were few, because of the risk involved of stepping on elitist or royal toes. Rare scandals exploded in public when an individual had tried to take more than his share or when honest citizens (the tiny minority) blew the whistle on corrupt elitists. Besides the Navy Scandal (Admiral Âta'i taking too many millions, see Chapter 16), a score of smaller scandals were uncovered, making little waves:

– Baqir Âmili, the managing director of the Rural and Urban Consumers' Co-operative Organisation, and a handful of his direct subordinates were arrested for embezzlement.

– Mustafa Îlm Mutllaq, Iran's Ambassador to Sudan, was recalled to Tehran and detained for having falsified expense accounts, one of them by at least $140,000.

– Retired General Mahmoud Nâimi Rad, head of the Âbbasabad Land Development Project, an outfit set up to buy back land tracts sold earlier (at low cost) to officers and NCOs in the Âbbasabad hills, was convicted of having received bribes and was sentenced to four years in 1977 and fined Rls1m; he was set free in 1978.

– Âbd ul-Husayn Parviz Nava'i, head of the Meteorological Organisation, was convicted of misappropriation of funds and fined Rls10m.

– General Kyumars Salih (of the eight Salih brothers), the head of the army's Logistics division, was arrested with a dozen other Logistics officers; one of the latter committed suicide in prison and all the others were gradually set free without further ado.

With millions of dollars changing hands in 1974 and 1975, wafts of higher corruption scandals had reached the public. In January 1976, the Shah, knowing that the best defence was to be on the offensive, fulminated against corruption:

> There is thing we cannot accept in this country and that is administrative corruption... What we do is based on respect for the individual, individual rights, the absence of exploitation of man by man [sic] and derivation of the greatest benefit from personal initiative, perseverance and hard work...[93]

Nevertheless, three major administrative scandals made headlines and waves in Tehran:
(1) The Ouqaf (Endowments) Scandal. Since its inception in 1964, the Ouqaf organisation had always been a very sensitive socio-political phenomenon, at the borderline between governmental and

religious affairs. During Nasir Assar's tenure from 1964 until 1972,[94] it had become one of the elite's milch cows, with close links to the Empress Farah Foundation. Two examples shall suffice: the first involved 81,000 square metres of the Mustoufi ul-Mamalik endowment being placed at the disposal of the Empress's Special Cultural Bureau; and the second example concerned 1,000 hectares of land, located near Karaj, which was offered to Mahin Hashiminizhad (the wife of General Hashiminizhad, the Shah's general-adjutant), who transferred half of it to businessman Huzhabr Yazdani in 1971.[95] In July 1975, a fresh Endowments Law, which gave Ouqaf a fuller control over all endowments, was ratified (thus cutting off the clergy's and the various trustees' tenuous hold), so that Ouqaf and the Empress Farah Foundation could connive to sell and milk profitable endowments (a business worth billions of rials). In 1977, the Ouqaf Scandal hit the headlines when the organisation's director-general Iraj Gulisurkhi and four officers were arrested for embezzlement; Gulisurkhi received a four year sentence and a Rls1.3m fine, the four others getting lighter sentences; it was rumoured that the five had not been arrested for embezzlement, but rather for not having played by the rules.

(2) The Sugar Scandal. In 1975, Iran's Ministry of Commerce bought 250,000 tonnes of sugar from Britain's Tate and Lyle company at the highest price reached in history: around $800 per tonne (equivalent to a $200m deal). A public outcry ensued and two deputies to the Commerce Minister Firaydoun Mahdavi, Muhammad Âli Sayrafi and Husayn Âlizadeh, were arrested. Minister Mahdavi was not implicated and was only quietly demoted to minister without portfolio in February 1976. Sayrafi and Âlizadeh were brought to trial and proclaimed their innocence, saying that they had acted on orders from above but refusing to divulge any names. The name of Felix Aqayan (and of his brother Shahin) surfaced during the case; Aqayan, an influence-peddler with close links to Sir Shahpour Reporter,[96] was said to be the head of Iran's sugar mafia. Finally, after a protracted trial, Sayrafi and Âlizadeh were eventually acquitted in November 1977.[97]

(3) The Civil Aviation Organisation (CAO) Scandal. When, in 1977, Houshang Arbabi, the CAO chief (since 1960), was arrested along

with eight of his subordinates, it was a clear case of revenge for Iran's Air Mafia (see Chapter 16) because Arbabi was an honest individual.[98] He was nevertheless tried, found guilty, sentenced to five years and fined $1.57 m.[99] A real scandal.

16. 8. Dangerous Inequalities

Below the upper class of the petrodollar elite, there was a middle and a lower class of Iranians. Iranian society was a petrified society. Movement from the middle class to the elite was down to a trickle, as millions of rials were needed as an entry card and, with the state of control at the top, this was not easy to achieve (even outright dangerous). The only movement was from the third (lower) class to the middle class. Naturally, the few thousands of the elite were to be compared with the three to four millions of the middle classes and the rest of the third class.

The problem was that subdivisions of petrodollars among the three classes occurred in reverse proportion to the class's numbers.

The 'trickle down theory' was not functioning in Iran. There was an explanation for this, as an expert in the field pointed out:

> ...Theoretically, the benefits accruing [from oil revenues] should trickle down to the lowest classes, but in a hierarchically organised society [such as Iran] benefits inevitably are sucked sidewise into private channels instead...[100]

No statistical data was capable of describing the light years separating the Shimiran elitists from the shanty town dwellers of Doulatabad. For this last group, the Shah's hollow promises of a Great Civilisation or his fabulous nuclear reactors and fantastic petrochemical complexes did not mean a thing. They had to make ends meet; they had to fight to pay the extravagant rents that shot up much faster than the double-digit inflation; they were the prey of narrow-minded landlords, ruthless loan sharks (charging as much as 60% interest), bribe-hungry police officers and, if needed, even of SAVAK thugs and torturers; they had to fight disease and epidemics: by September 1977, the El Tor cholera strain had officially caused forty-seven deaths,[101] and infant mortality still stood at around 120 deaths per thousand live births (a figure mentioned by Minister of Health and Social Welfare Shaykhulislamizadeh in a December 1977 interview[102]) – with 114.8 per thousand the number given by the UN for 1979.[103]

A young and bright Iranian economist, Muhammad Hashim Pisaran,[104] head of the Statistics Department at Bank-i Markazi-i Iran (BMI), tried to analyse the trend in Iran's income distribution using household expenditure statistics from the BMI and from the Statistical Centre of Iran (SCI). Pisaran's investigation showed mixed results (see Table 16.8) as the data from BMI and SCI were contradictory (but official), and he concluded that:

> ...It appears that until 1971/72, the inequality in income distribution in Iran was increasing. But over the period 1971/72 to 1973/74 there seems to have been a general tendency for inequality in household expenditure to stabilise or even decline slightly...[106]

That was as far as Pisaran could or would go: he had clearly proven that according to the regime's official statistics the trickle down theory didn't apply in practice. He couldn't add that the SCI statistics were doubtful at best, that unofficial statistics were much more biased than that, that these were expenditures not assets, that foreign (Swiss bank) accounts were not included, that if he had detailed statistics about the top one per cent (instead of deciles) etc.

Inequality, even gross inequality, was not something new in Iran: it had always existed. But in the 1970s, the social inequalities seemed more unequal than others: more visible, more oppressive and more unjust. More visible, because, unlike the more reserved former elites, the petrodollar elite, like all parvenu elites, wanted to show off its wealth to all and sundry, letting everyone know that they had made it: building replicas of Le Petit Trianon, losing millions in the casinos without batting an eyelid, having their exploits reported in the papers' social columns, and showing off their dresses, their cars, their wives, their mistresses and even their dogs. More oppressive, because of the total breakdown in traditional Iranian channels linking the very rich to the very needy. The petrodollar elite looked with disdain and arrogance towards the poor (a prominent member, whose father had

Table 16.8. Statistical Data from BMI and SCI Used by Dr Pisaran, and the 'Gini-co-efficients' Obtained for Urban Income Distribution in Iran 1969-1974.[105]

Year	Percentage Share of Households with Top 20% Income		Gini Coefficients Derived for Urban Iran	
	(BMI)	(SCI)	(BMI)	(SCI)
1969/70	52.91	49.24	0.4710	0.4161
1970/71	54.30	47.83	0.4849	0.4227
1971/72	55.48	48.33	0.5051	0.4152
1972/73	55.33	47.11	0.4916	0.4032
1973/74	55.56	n/a	0.4946	n/a

made a killing in real estate, even regularly asked "God to send to Hell all the poor and hungry folk"). In the former elites, the rich knew that they had to participate in the assistance of the needy, that there existed the concept of *noblesse oblige*: all the small rivulets flowing (directly or indirectly) to relieve utter poverty made a large stream of social assistance. The new elite had not had time to learn, thinking that it already knew everything, because it could buy everything. In the old days, as pressures from below increased, the rich had had to disburse more and more to maintain an even pressure: this was incomprehensible to the petrodollar elite, with only a Soudavar here and a Kurous there to understand (and that was due to their half a century of experience). If, finally, the inequalities were more unjust now, it was due to the fact that quality in the lower classes was higher and quality in the higher elite lower; this quality imbalance was the crucial point, towering over visibility and oppression: the lower classes did not look up to the elite as they used to.

The Pahlavi regime had endeavoured to institutionalise social assistance. After the Red Lion and Sun Society (the Iranian Red Cross) was established in 1923 (and still managed in the 1970s by the efficient and controversial Dr H. Khatibi), it had formed the Imperial

Organisation for Social Services (IOSS) in 1947. The IOSS was headed in the 1970s by a Princess Ashraf protégé, Âbd ul-Riza Ansari (no family link to Hushang Ansari), was catering to some five million people nationwide. It controlled the mammoth Darou Pakhsh pharmaceuticals manufacturer and Franklin Publications, started in 1954 as a small, non-profit-making subsidiary of Franklin, New York; Iranised to Noumaghz in 1977, it ended in IOSS's lap.

Another Pahlavi institution involved in social services was the Farah Charitable Foundation. It had begun life in 1954 as the Surayya Charitable Foundation under the expert management of the then Queen's *éminence grise* Furough Zaffar, a formidable Bakhtiari matron, who had hand-picked a group of rich and young elite women to support her activities; in order that the high society ladies did not transform her charity meetings into a dress show, Furough Zaffar had ordered them to put on an uniform, and they had all obeyed. In 1958, when Farah Diba became queen, the courtiers simply changed the Foundation's name from Surayya to Farah – naturally without Furough Zaffar and her rich young ladies. Under Farah's (and maybe her mother's) direction the foundation would become a large bureaucratic ensemble of people thinking not of charitable actions but rather of finding ways to expropriate vulnerable endowments and line their own pockets; in this respect the Farah Foundation management worked hand in glove with the unscrupulous Ouqaf employees.[107]

Another sincere effort to further institutionalise social welfare and services in Iran were the results of the actions initiated by Sattareh Farmanfarmayan. With her University of Southern California master's degree in social work, she founded the Tehran School for Social Work in 1958, with A.A. Âlam as chairman of the board of trustees. She then established in quick succession the Family Planning Association of Iran and the Community Welfare Centre of Iran.[108] With her forays into bureaucratised social assistance, she might well have created a disservice both to her class and to the ones she eventually wanted to help, for this was not (yet) how things were done in Iran.

Her institutions were islands of artificialities in a sea of Iranian social misery; Furough Zaffar's system seemed better suited for Iran.

On April 13, 1976, none other than Princess Ashraf entered the fray with her own foundation "to promote peace, welfare and human rights [*sic*]". Having sensed that some charitable work was called for, the Princess had tried to draw the petrodollar elite into spending some of their dollars on someone other than themselves. In vain. On August 7, 1976, in a speech she "chided the wealthy for an insufficient response to the call for a nationwide charity movement". The elitists were not going to give away money for the Princess Ashraf Foundation to succeed in Iranian charity. Even if they had, it was much too late to fill the social abyss left during the 1970s by an insouciant and arrogant petrodollar elite.

The people who had promoted this elite would have been well-advised to read Burke's "If rare merit be the rarest of all rare things, it ought to pass some sort of probation".[109]

In the case of Iran's 1970s' elite, there was little rarity and there had been no probation. Iran's elitists would have been well-advised to read Sir Walter Raleigh's 'Preface to the History of the World':

> ...if we truly examine the difference of both conditions, to wit, of the rich and the mighty whom we call fortunate, and of the poor and oppressed whom we account wretched, we shall find the happiness of the one and the miserable estate of the other so tied by God to the very instant, and both so subject to interchange as the one hath nothing so certain whereof to boast, nor the other so uncertain whereof to bewail itself. For there is no man so assured of his honour, or his riches, health or life, but that he may be deprived of either or all at the very next hour or day to come.

16.9. Changes

1976 was supposed to be a good year for Muhammad Reza Shah and his regime. It was the fiftieth anniversary of the Pahlavi dynasty's foundation. Half a century of Pahlavi rule: fifteen years for his father, thirty-five for himself. His propaganda services had foreseen grandiose festivities to commemorate the Pahlavis' Golden Jubilee.

In 1976 the American were also commemorating – their Revolution's bicentennial anniversary. The Iranian regime was doing its utmost to take part in the momentous commemoration. In 1975, a

National Committee for Participation in the Bicentennial Celebrations of the American Revolution had been duly set up, with Empress Farah in the chair. Americanophile personalities sat on the National Committee and on its four sub-committees (i.e. cultural, festival, future horizons and advisory), with, prominent among many others, the Salih brothers (Âli Pasha and Jahanshah), Jahangir Amuzigar, Mahmud Zia'i, Sayyid Husayn Nasr, Sirus Ghani, Khalil Taliqani and Farhad Mishkat; in addition to some of the Empress's people such as Riza Qutbi and Nadir Ardalan.

During 1976 the third national census was carried out throughout Iran. In November 1976, a first approximation for the total population was placed at 33,662,176 (the final tally published in 1980 stood at 33,708,744). Further statistics put Iran amongst the youngest countries in the world, with over 55% of its people under the age of twenty and an average (median) population age of seventeen and a half years. Tehran's population was said to have passed the 4.5m mark, and was still growing at an average of 6% per annum. Finally, the literacy rate for seven year olds and older age groups stood at 47.1% – urban literacy 65.2% and rural literacy 29.7%.

However, 1976 began with a political bombshell: a letter dated February 16 sent by author Âli Asghar Hajj Sayyid Javadi* to the Shah's private secretary Nusratullah Mûinian.

Sayyid Javadi's letter (some fifty typed pages) was a polite but highly critical message, taking his cue from references made by the Shah to corruption in his January 26 televised speech; it fulminated against corruption throughout the administration, bureaucratic incompetence, and the disasters brought about by censorship as people were unable to voice their criticisms; he proposed the creation of inquiry committees to look into corruption affairs and demanded an end to censorship and a return to constitutional liberties, as a means to cure all the ills he had unveiled. Although the letter was not an 'open' letter, copies of it circulated *sous le manteau*. It was difficult to say who was more surprised by it, the regime or Iranian intellectuals, since both groups were dumbfounded by Sayyid Javadi's great courage. The latter, realising the extreme risk he was taking, had added at the end of his letter: "...in case I, myself, should retract the above writings, in the press or on radio and television, it would be against my free will and certainly under extreme duress".[110] He knew that he was jeopardising his freedom and maybe his life. But the regime and SAVAK failed to react, a fact even more surprising than the letter itself. Maybe the Shah wanted to use the intelligentsia as a lever in his anti-corruption crusade so Sayyid Javadi was fortunate to make the right move at the right time, thus becoming overnight the intelligentsia's new-found champion, the hero who had abruptly spearheaded its comeback in the political arena. With his courage, he had put to shame all Iranian intellectuals, if not all of Iran's non-armed opposition. With a single letter, he had shaken both out of their torpor: the fifty or so photocopied pages of his letter were the hottest document in Iran.

* ÂLI ASGHAR HAJJ SAYYID JAVADI (1925–), born in Qazvin, the son of a nationalist *mulla*, Sayyid Zia ul-Din (d. 1963); Ph.D. in philosophy, Sorbonne University, Paris (1956); editor-in-chief of *Ittilaât* newspaper (1957–62); author and journalist (1962–76); sent first letter to Mûinian (February 1976), second letter followed (December 1976); authored indictment of Premier Huvayda and his ministers (July 1977); replied to General Husayn Azmoudeh's biased writings against Dr Musaddiq (August 1977); elected secretary-general of the Committee for the Defence of Political Prisoners (April 1978); editor of *Jumbish* weekly (March 1978–May 1980); thereafter, lived in self-exile in France.

A month after Sayyid Javadi's letter, a second bombshell rocked Iranian society: the new official Imperial Calendar, proposed by the court and approved on March 14 by the Houses of Parliament. Based on the coronation of Cyrus the Great some twenty-five centuries ago, the Imperial version replaced the two *Hejira* calendars (i.e. the lunar and solar versions) in use in Iran; hence the solar *Hejira* year 1355 became Imperial year 2535.

This asinine decision, intended to reinforce the monarchy's legitimacy, alienated the large majority of Muslims, and the large majority of Iranians. People were flabbergasted by the regime's nonsensical decision and protests against the new law were widespread; if people did not dare voice their opposition directly, they did it indirectly. Much more fundamental was that the abyss between the regime and the people, instead of narrowing, was widening.

Another blow to hit Iran Inc. during early 1976 was the wave of workers' strikes shaking Iran's industrial and mining communities.

After a full decade of labour docility, unrest and management problems were at the top of the agenda. Subversive groups in factories were reaping what they had sown; secret SAVAK informants were ostracised; strikes were held. As soon as an establishment went on strike, SAVAK moved in, isolated it, took in the workers, used any means to uncover the ringleaders and tried to turn them to working for SAVAK thereafter; the ones who accepted were returned to work. Because of the total information blackout on strikes in Iran, it was difficult to form an overall picture of the strike. However, some of the major strikes of the first half of 1976 were later reported to have been:[111]
– February: the Shahbaf textiles factory at Rasht.
– April: Parsabad agribusiness workers in the Dasht-i Mughan.
– May: i) a total of 10,000 brick-kiln moulders at Tabriz, Ardabil and Marand.
ii) 4,000 miners at the Sangroud coal mine near Shahroud, with seventy leaders being taken into custody.
iii) 3,000 workers of the Tehran Chit factory struck; soldiers besieged the factory and clashes resulted in heavy casualties, the strike lasted a fortnight.
iv) Container Corporation of Iran, of the Bihshahr group, went on strike.
– June: i) the Hamadanian factory at Isfahan closed for four days.
ii) Simin and Shahnaz textiles of Isfahan on strike.
iii) the Aladin factory (two hundred workers) went on strike.
iv) the Minou factory, the jewel of the Khusroushahi empire, closed down.

In a November 1976, in a *Briefing on Iran*, Amnesty International was correct in revealing that "the workers had entered the opposition's ranks". Neither the law of 1963 which gave workers a share of the profits nor the law of 1975 giving them shares of their establishment had succeeded in buying them off.

Even the Imperial Commission, belatedly set up in November 1976 by the Shah to follow up Sayyid Javadi's allegations of corruption and incompetence, fell short of its ambitions. Headed by the Shah's private secretary Mûinian, the commission briefly came under the spotlight, as its initial sessions were televised. Mûinian had his fifteen minutes of fame, but, not being a dragon-killer, he failed to take his chance, fearing to rock the boat beyond the limits he knew that he could not pass with impunity. He praised Dr Ganji, the Education Minister, for having kept his promises in relation to the printing of school books; he gave out mild criticism, falling short of passing sentences; the furthest he went was to declare in January 1978 that: "several hundred Fifth Plan projects remain incomplete because unrealistically planned".[112] That was repeating the obvious – everyone knew. The Imperial Commission was one step behind Sayyid Javadi, and it always remained there. When it failed to indict Âbd ul-Majid Majidi, the man ultimately responsible for the planning *débâcle*, the chapter on the Imperial Commission was closed – and as soon forgotten.

The last bombshell of 1976 was by far the most important of all: the election on November 2, 1976 of the Democrat James Earl (Jimmy) Carter as the Thirty-Ninth President of the United States. Gerald Ford, the Republican incumbent candidate, had been favoured by the Shah, who had allegedly spent umpteen millions of dollars on his re-election only to be defeated by a few thousand votes. The Iran Inc. management, from the Shah downwards, were shocked by the election's outcome: Democrat presidents were not their cup of tea and memories of the Kennedy presidency came back to haunt them, especially because Jimmy Carter was a known advocate of human rights, a man who believed in "combining support for our more authoritarian allies and friends with the effective promotion of human rights within their countries", and also was reputed to be "a man who measured accomplishment in terms of the lifting of the human spirit, the revival of hope, the absence of fear, the release from prison, the end of torture, the reunion of a family, the new-found sense of human dignity",[113] a man who "emphasised human rights as a high-priority principle of US foreign policy". With SAVAK's skeletons rumbling in their cupboards, these declarations of the President-Elect boded no good; after the smooth Nixon and Ford years, the petrodollar elite was bracing itself for the worst.

As if 1976 had not brought its load of disasters, 1977 began on a disastrous note: the blooming Iranian economy, the Shah's certified panacea for curing all ills, had suddenly run out of steam. Although Ansari, Iran's economy tsar, still tried to fool the AP envoy in Tehran by telling him that "Iran is quickly moving away from economic dependence on oil and within twelve years will have the industrial production of a developed West European country",[114] no one was

duped any more. The locomotive (i.e. the oil revenues) pulling the Iranian economic train had reached saturation speed, with all its wagons having reached their expansion limits:
- Imports of goods – worth $11.5bn in 1975 and $12.8bn in 1976 – had attained their upper limit of $1bn per month; the system was already overstretched, with 1.4m tonnes of goods piled up at Khurramshar and almost as much in all the other Iranian ports.
- The industrial establishments of Iran's import-substitution era had reached a dead end because the profitable niches had been exploited by the leading industrial elite, with marginal projects left for the courageous newcomer; the Iranian 'miracle' had lasted a decade (roughly as long as the textbook example of Italy); all good things have to end some day.
- Land speculation had lost its early appeal; as prices rose exponentially returns were, although still substantial, lower and lower; the limits were being reached when Tehran prime real estate became worth between Rls100,000 and 150,000 (equal to $1,400–$2,200) per square metre.
- Developers were also becoming constrained, for there was a limit on projects they could handle; moreover competition had become fiercer (lowering the returns) as foreign construction firms entered the fray and small 'build-and-sell' contractors began to expand up the scale.
- There was no recovery to be expected from the moribund agriculture sector; incapable of compromising on living standards, for fear of reneging on promises, the regime was forced to continue subsidising food; hence, it had earmarked Rls9bn ($128m) for meat subsidies and announced the importation of 200,000 live sheep from Australia, Romania and Bulgaria.

In March 1977, the budget was fixed at $34bn, with a $7bn deficit. Some timid economic measures were implemented: (i) petrol prices were hiked (from Rls6 and 7.5 for normal and super, to Rls8 and 10); (ii) daylight saving time was introduced in 1977 for the first time; (iii) postal prices were raised by 30% to 100%, depending on services; (iv) the price of foreign cigarettes was increased by Rls3 to 5 per pack.

This was all too little and too late to have an impact. Iran's trade deficit shot through the roof in April–May 1977 with a record deficit of Rls153.6bn ($2,165m). As a result of economic stagnation and unbridled (subsidised) domestic consumption, soaring inflation came back to the Iranian economy for the first time since 1961/62. Officials such as Firouz Vakil, deputy head of the PBO, wanted to minimise inflation, which was running at around 30%, by "estimating it at around 17%".[115] In order to stop inflationary tendencies, Bank-i Markazi engineered a credit squeeze that sent the dollar to a record street rate of Rls74, against an official rate of Rls71.

The Iranian lion had "clearly stopped roaring"[116] and, whatever the official loudspeaker said, both Iranians and foreigners concurred on this point. To kick-start the economy, a number of economists proposed borrowing heavily, preferably in the London Eurodollar market. Proponents argued that the banks were willing to lend to Iran, whose total debt was negligible and creditworthiness excellent, that the Western banks were ready, as most of them had opened shop in Tehran – a total of sixty representative offices, fronting for no fewer than seventy-six banks, inclusive of eighteen American, twelve British, eight German, eight Japanese, seven French, five Italian and the three Swiss banks.[117] Iran's first syndicated Eurodollar $80m loan had been packaged in 1969 by Minos Zombanakis, the head of Manufacturers Hanover (US) London branch. Since then, Eurodollars had been little needed. But in 1975 some $250m was borrowed, $1,000m in 1976, $2,000m in 1977 and $1,300m in 1978 (before London's Eurodollar doors closed in the autumn): a total of roughly $4.5bn in four years, with the largest Iranian borrowers being (1) the National Petrochemical Company (NPC) with $880m (see Table 16.9 for details on loans); (2) the Government of Iran, $500m; and (3) the IMDBI bank, $480m. On the other side, the main lead managers were Chase Manhattan (with $1,700m) and the Iranvest Consortium (with over $1,000m). It was clear that David Rockefeller had taken over where his (subordinate) friend Doctor Henry Kissinger had left off.

In Iran, Rockefeller's nickname was 'Iran is in my pocket' and it was no secret that Iran's surplus funds were deposited, on the Shah's orders, in the Chase Manhattan Bank, so that in fact Rockefeller was lending Iran her own money, risklessly reaping two harvests. On the Iranian side, the charming (but incompetent) Jamshid Ashrafi, the Deputy Finance Minister, would have carried on and on, if unimpeded.

Table 16.9. Major Foreign Loans Advanced to Iranian Institutions (1975-1978).

Year	Borrower	Loan Amount ($ million)	Lead Manager
1975	IMDBI	100	Iranvest*
	IMDBI	30	Iranvest
1976	National Petrochemical Company	250	Iranvest
	IMDBI	200	Iranvest
	ADBI	100	Iranvest
1977	Gov't of Iran	500	Chase M'ttan
	NPC	310	Chase M'ttan
	National Telecom.	250	Chase M'ttan
	ADBI	130	Chemical Bank
	Industrial Credit Bank	120	Chase M'ttan
	Polyacryl Company	110	European American Bank and Trust
	Iran Air	72	Iranvest
	NPC	50	Kuhn Loeb, Lehman Bros., SG Warburg
1978	ADBI	99	First Boston
	National Iranian Gas Company	300	Chase M'ttan
	NPC	270	Iranvest
	ICB	200	Chase M'ttan

Year	Borrower	Loan Amount ($m)	Lead Manager
1978 (cont.)	IMDBI	150	Canadian Imperial
	ADBI	74	Japanese group
	ADBI**	80	DG Bank, Tokai, Dai Ichi Kangyo

* Iranvest stands for Iran Overseas Investment Bank, a consortium of ten banks – two Iranian banks held 25% each (Bank-i Milli and IMDBI), and eight Western banks holding the other 50% (Bank of America, Manufacturers Hanover, Midland Bank, Barclays Bank, Deutsche Bank, Société Générale, Bank of Tokyo and Industrial Bank of Japan).

** This loan was the first Iranian one that didn't come through. Arranged by Blyth, Eastman & Dillon in London, it had to be withdrawn in October 1978.

On February 26, 1977, Prime Minister Huvayda brought about changes in his cabinet for the eighteenth and last time. He gave the Science and Education portfolio to the capable Isfahan University chancellor Dr Qasim Mûtamidi and the Energy Ministry to the forty-two year old Parviz Hikmat (the scion of the super-rich Hikmat family of Shiraz and son-in-law of Engineer Âli Quli Bayani, the former *Iran Party* ideologue). The choice of Dr Mûtamidi was as wise as that of Hikmat was ill-advised: the former had proven his management talents at Isfahan, whereas the latter was inexperienced, untried and rather weak in management – on top of all that, he seems to have been rather unlucky as well.

The summer of 1977 would prove to be a very hot and a trying one for the young Hikmat; on June 27, he imprudently "ruled out the possibility of water and power rationing",[118] acting as though things were under control; but pandemonium broke out a few days later when electricity blackouts hit Tehran; two to three hours every day, with peaks of four hours depending on the location. For the regime which had wanted to compete with Western powers, the disgraceful power cuts were first an irritant, then an embarrassment and finally ended in a catastrophe, as sweating Iran Inc. officers began to realise that somewhere something was very wrong if they could not master simple electric power. On July 8, the government stepped in to launch a crash programme for easing power shortages. It was too late. The palliatives of reduced broadcasting by NIRT and the closing down of one hundred factories (placed on forced summer vacations) barely made a dent in the blackouts. The first 250 MW generator of the Reza Shah Kabir Dam was started on a crash basis by the French technicians of Alsthom; the authorities, looking for a scapegoat, tried to saddle Alsthom with the blame for unwarranted delays at the dam, with the French contractor was unwilling to do so. By the end of July, the best the Energy Ministry could achieve was an average reduction in the daily cuts from three to two hours.

By the end of July, it seemed evident that Prime Minister Huvayda had to go: the power cuts were the straw which had broken his back. The changing of the guard was long overdue. On August 6 Huvayda tendered his resignation; he was offered instead the Ministry of court, in place of Âlam, who was stepping down for reasons of personal health. On August 7, Dr Jamshid Amuzigar, the Americanophile technocrat, was appointed prime minister. Amuzigar kept eleven previous ministers (the 'old guard') and introduced seven fresh young ministers (the 'new wave'), by order of age:

(1) Muhammad Riza Amin, fifty, Minister for Industry and Mines, of Isfahani origin, former manager of the steel company NISIC;
(2) Dariush Humayun, forty-nine, Minister for Information and Tourism, a journalist with a leftist background, married to Ardashir Zahidi's sister Huma;
(3) Ahmad Âli Ahmadi, forty-eight, Minister of Agriculture, a long-standing expert in agricultural affairs;
(4) Manouchihr Agah, forty-seven, Minister of State and head of PBO, Iran's new planning tsar with a PBO background;
(5) Taqi Tavakkuli, forty-seven, Minister of Energy, a scion of the Tabriz match manufacturing family;
(6) Firouz Toufiq, forty-three, Minister for Housing and Town Planning, from the PBO's nursery;

(7) Murtaza Salihi, thirty-nine, Minister for Roads and Transport, the cabinet's youngest member.

Gone were Hushang Ansari and his lieutenant Farrukh Najmabadi, the trio of Azmun, Mahdavi, Taslimi, and also Dr Hidayati and Dr Shadman. Tehran mayor Ghulim Riza Nikpay was promoted to senator from Isfahan (his father's former position[119]) and replaced by Javad Sharistani.

All these changes amounted to very little, as they did not affect the top tier of Iran Inc. Âlam's departure totally eclipsed all of the cabinet's comings and goings. Being struck by a devastating and incurable illness, the fifty-nine year old Âlam had been treated time and again at the American Hospital in Neuilly. In vain. He eventually died after much discomfort in New York on April 14, 1978. His replacement Huvayda was not the man to fill his shoes. At court, the former premier would be a bewildered onlooker; he told his brother: "You cannot know what the court is like: a rat race and a hive of corruption"[120], and confided to Raji: "If the Government is corrupt, the court is a nest of vipers".[121] In a world in which Âlam thrived, Huvayda, the obedient bureaucrat, was at a loss.

At court, the one who stood to gain most from the void created by Âlam's departure was Empress Farah. While the cabinet changes were unfolding, she was on a three week solo tour of America (July 29 until August 17). At Aspen she took part in the board of trustees meeting (chaired by ARCO chairman Robert O. Anderson) of the Aspen Institute for Humanistic Studies. She met former President Gerald Ford and Mrs Ford at Vail, and First Lady Rosalyn Carter at the White House. In the view of her husband's illness, first diagnosed by French doctors in 1974 and later confirmed by Viennese experts, Empress Farah could someday become Regent of Iran, and that was a possibility which had the Americans taking an interest in her. But the Empress failed to impress her interlocutors as someone who "could take charge"; moreover she was not very popular in Iran. At the head of the Empress's special bureau, Dr Hushang Nahavandi, the former chancellor of Tehran University, had taken Karim Pasha Bahaduri's place in November 1976; however, he would not remain there long and returned to the political fold in 1978, being then replaced by Dr Sayyid Husayn Nasr.

Just ten days after the change of prime minister, on August 17, the Shah added two more principles (the last ones) to his 'Shah and People' Revolution:
- The Eighteenth Principle: the official fixing of land prices by area, with yearly increases in line with the official rate of inflation, but not exceeding it;
- The Nineteenth Principle: the disclosure of personal and family wealth became mandatory for high civil servants, and this point also forbade them from keeping interests in private businesses and forced them to transform any shares they might hold into government bonds.

The Eighteenth principle would be applied, leading to a two-tier land price system: an official, artificially low price and a free rate, artificially high price, with both systems co-existing side by side without influencing each other. The official prices having failed to influence the increasing land prices, the gradient forcing individuals to take risks and start building outside city limits on cheap land – illegal though it was according to Article 100 of Tehran Municipality's Laws and Regulations for Erecting Buildings, which authorised the bulldozing of any building built outside the limits – became steeper and steeper. Building activities took on vast proportions, and the municipality had to intervene; clashes ensued, casualties resulted and a worker died of his wounds, leading to a scandal reported by the press. By the end of August the government back-pedalled and ordered the municipality to allow small plot owners to build a single house outside city limits: necessity had won over legality. As for the Nineteenth principle, it was a masquerade: Iran was not America. In this case, reality won over legality: no civil servant would declare what he owned because it was nobody's business. With corruption existing at all levels of the bureaucracy (especially at the top), the principle became society's laughing stock.

Principles Eighteen and Nineteen were a half-hearted attempt to find a temporary solution to real problems. What was needed was a basic overhaul of the whole Iran Inc. machinery: new people, for fresh ideas, for a drastic shake-up. It might kill the patient, but it was the only serious way out. The regime had new faces available: the young, untainted and capable middle managers who were ambitious and ready to serve, albeit on their own terms. The problem was neither availability nor possibility: it was rather the inability of the

Iran Inc. leadership to analyse the situation, draw the correct conclusions, accept the inevitable, plan changes accordingly and get on with the job. But this was asking much too much from the Shah and his inner circle: they lacked both the vision and the courage. And they thought that they could muddle through these difficult times, hold on until the next wave came their way to lift them up again. And if not them, then whom? Who could manage Iran without them? And, finally, if the worse came to the worst, American assistance would always be there to protect them from any predator, domestic or foreign. Was not the USA the greatest of all great superpowers?

NOTES

1. See *Time Magazine*, November 4, 1974, p.23.
2. Black Panther was the Princess's popular nickname, see Firouz.
3. F. Hoveyda, *The Fall of the Shah* (New York: Wyndham Books, 1980) p.32.
4. The quote is from: 'America's Shah', *MERIP* Reports, no. 40, p.15. There are many other sources on Princess Ashraf drug-related stories; among them *Le Monde*, March 5/6 1972 and *Le Nouvel Observateur*, March 27, 1972.
5. The popular young Shafiq was shot dead during his Paris exile in December 1979. He was aged thirty-four: "it's always the best who depart first...".
6. P.C. Radji, *In the Service of the Peacock Throne*, (London: Hamish Hamilton, 1983) p.272. For years Parviz Raji had been a top adviser to Amir Âbbas Huvayda, first at NIOC and then at the Prime Minister's Office; as for Iraj Amini, the son of Elitist Âli Amini, he had officially been Princess Ashraf's Special Adviser.
7. During his ten year tenure at the head of NIRT, Qutbi had kept such a low-profile – not a picture, not a single interview, only a single NIRT award distribution, with always at least ten metres between him and the nearest camera – that during the 1978 mass demonstrations in Tehran he roamed freely through the streets, camera in hand, posing as a junior NIRT reporter and getting away with it. Private communication from a reliable eyewitness who had recognised him in the midst of Shah Reza Avenue.
8. See the Persepolis Symposium proceedings in: *Iran: Past, Present and Future*, ed. J.W. Jacqz, (Aspen Institute for Humanistic Studies, 1976) pp.3-6.
9. P.C Radji, op. cit. (note 6), pp.54-5.
10. See Fardoust's memoirs: *Zuhour va Suqout-i Saltanat-i Pahlavi* (Tehran: Mu'asiseh Mutali^at va Pijouish-ha-yi Syasi, 1369 (1990))
11. F. Hoveyda, op. cit. (note 3), p.46. In his memoirs, Premier Huvayda's brother affirmed that: "Zahidi was motivated by personal animosity towards the Prime Minister".
12. Ibid., pp.110-1.
13. As for Ardashir Zahidi's intellectual level, the following exchange he had in 1978 with Frank Giles of *The Sunday Times* speaks for itself: On October 31, 1978,

Zahidi had asked Giles to tell him, as a friend, what the authorities back in Iran were doing wrong:
Giles: "Ardeshir, it might help if the soldiers didn't fire live bullets into unarmed crowds so easily."
Zahidi: "Really, Frank? You think that's important?"
Giles: "..."
Zahidi: "I shall inform His Imperial Majesty of this immediately."
As quoted by P.C. Radji, op. cit. (note 6), p.247.

14 Private communication of two young Iranian students who had attended the parties and seen the young, beautiful girls in question on more than one occasion.

15 I. Ra'in, *Faramoushkhaneh va Framasunri dar Iran* (Tehran: Amir Kabir, 3 Vols., 4th ed., 1357 (1978)) Vol. III, p.660.

16 Ibid., Vol. III, p.526.

17 Ibid., Vol, III, pp. 528-533.

18 P. Balta, 'L'ex-chah ou le tourist errant', in *Courrier de Politique Étrangère*, 11e année, no. 223, du 15 au 30 juin 1978, pp. 1, 2 and 6.

19 Ibid., p.1.

20 R. Graham, *The Illusions of Power* (New York: St Martin's Press, 1978) p.154.

21 *Middle East Economic Digest*, December, 1977, p.16.

22 It later came to light that Rafizadeh worked for both SAVAK and the CIA. From 1979 onwards, however, he was fully on the agency's payroll. See *Time Magazine*, February 2, 1987.

23 *The Sunday Times*, August 1, 1976.

24 *Pareh'i az Asnad-i Savak*, compiled by CISNU, (Tehran: Amir Kabir, 1357 (1979)) p.266.

25 *The Times* of London, July 23, 1976, pp.1 and 7.

26 *The Economist*, October 31, 1970.

27 *Military Balance 1978*, a report published by the International Institute of Strategic Studies in London.

28 These statistics were retrieved from various issues of the *Iran Almanac*, published by Echo of Iran over the years reported.

29 G.W. Ball, *The Past has Another Pattern* (New York: W.W. Norton, 1982) p.455.

30 *Asnad-i Laneh Jasousi*, no.6 (secret report on US arms sales to Iran), p.14.

31 See 'US Military Sales to Iran', a Staff Report to the Sub-Committee on Foreign Assistance, published by the Senate Committee on Foreign Relations, August 2, 1976.

32 Air Taxi of Iran, a private outfit, was presided over by Zanganeh, with General Khatami as a silent partner. See note 40A below on Iran's Air Mafia.

33 Around the American compound a wall had been built to separate it from Iranian quarters; the curious Iranian youngsters had drilled holes in the wall to see how the expatriate youth lived on the other side. The wall was smashed down in 1979, when the American families were departing, selling their belongings at a fraction of the normal price, with the wily Isfahanis taking full advantage.

34 See *Keyhan International*, February 25, 1979, p.4, 'Bell Completes Evacuation Lift': "Only eight Bell employees remain in Iran ...3,600 [Bell] employees and 3,200 dependants ...In addition to 400 employees and 170 dependants of Bell sub-contractors ...left Iran over past four months". Also see *Keyhan International*, March 10, 1979, p.4., quoting in full a UPI cable dated Friday March 9 from Cincinnati: "Dr Abbas Amirie, the former head of the Institute for International

Political and Economic Studies (IIPES) said: "They [Bell employees] did more damage to your interests and to your image in Iran than your entire Government ...These were the people who served in Vietnam. They would bring prostitutes from Vietnam to serve them and they would take them on the streets and everybody knew what these people were". Dr Amirie concluded by further advising Americans to filter their people, next time round, "very, very carefully".

35 *Middle East Economic Survey*, January 1, 1979.
36 International Services was yet another company fronting for the Rashidians. It received $2.48m from the Lavi brothers on the Grunman deal.
37 *The New York Times*, February 22, 1976.
38 The commission on the Chieftain deal was worth (at least) several million pounds sterling. When it later came to light in a British court, Shahpour Reporter (later Sir) had received (at least) one million pounds for his part in the deal. See: *Middle East Economic Digest*, November 11, 1977.
39 Private communication from a young (and honest) navy officer.
40 The last item leading to Âta'i's arrest was allegedly the multi-million stone-studded ring which his wife had had the imprudence (or the arrogance) to wear at a court function (exciting jealousy).
40A The Air Mafia is described in detail in *Asnad-i Laneh Jasousi*, no. 17, p.45. Quoting directly from the report: "The so-called Iranian Aviation Mafia was created in 1963 with the founding of Iran Air. The following are members:
1. General Mohammad Khatami, commanding general IIAF; chairman of the High Aviation Council; president of Iran Air; part-owner of Air Tax;[*] silent partner In Iran Helicopters[**]; and a silent partner in Iranian Aircraft Industries (IAI)[***].
2. General Âli Mohammad Khademi, managing director of Iran Air; silent partner in Air Taxi and IAI.
3. Abol Fath Mahvi, a relative of the Queen; Boeing Corporation and Allison Engine representative; owner of Iran Helicopters; president of Pars Air;**** and titular head of IAI.
4. General Ali Asghar Rafaat, head of the Civil Aviation Club; managing director of Pars Air; silent partner in Air Taxi and IAI.
5. Amir Hossein Zanganeh, president of Air Taxi; AVCO, Aero commander and Lycoming engine representative; and silent partner in IAI.
The five people listed above control ALL aviation activities in Iran".
End of quote; here are the notes:
* Air Taxi was formed in 1958 as a private outfit for monopolising private air transport throughout Iran; it controlled some twenty-five aircraft: Fairchilds FH 227Bs, DC 3s, Falcon 20s, Cessnas and Aero Commanders.
** Iran Helicopters, a private firm set up with two dozen French Alouette helicopters, provided the only heliported service in Iran (except for the oil company's helicopter services in the Gulf).
*** IAI was created in 1970 as a joint venture between Iranian investors (51%) and Northrop-Page (49%) "as basically an overhaul outfit designed to be a major depot maintenance centre"; at first for the IIAF and Iran Air, then also for Saudia, Kuwait and Ariana (Afghanistan's) Airlines. A real gold mine.
**** Pars Air, established in 1969, came to own eleven aircraft, playing second fiddle to Iran Air on domestic routes.

41 A close friend of Khatami, who used to water-ski barefoot on the Diz Dam Lake with Khatami and General Nadir Jahanbani, was "99% sure that the General's kite rope had somehow been tampered with". Private communication to the author.

42 Moreover, Uvaysi had married the daughter, Shirafat, of the Sharif ul-Douleh (later family name Bani Adam), a very wealthy Kashan landlord; Shirafat's sister, Shoukat ul-Muluk, had been married to Âli Pasha Salih, the perennial Iranian secretary of the US Embassy. After Shirafat's death in the late 1960s, Uvaysi remarried the young daughter of Colonel (later general) Mustafa Sarmad.

43 L.H. Gelb, 'Arm Sales', in *Foreign Policy*, no. 25, Winter 1976/77, p.17.

44 General Secord and his associate Albert Hakim of Irangate fame.

45 On the evening before his execution, Huvayda asked the few journalists present the whereabouts of Amir Tahiri. When told that the *Kayhan* editor-in-chief had fled abroad, Huvayda is said to have relaxed and muttered a "Thank God, he is safe". Could it be that Amir Tahiri is the depository of Huvayda's premiership secrets? But even if these secrets do exist, they won't reveal much that is not already known.

46 F. Hoveyda, op. cit. (note 3), p.47.

47 *Iran Almanac 1978*, (Tehran: Echo of Iran, 1978) p.463.

48 *Iran Trade and Industry*, Vol. VIII, no. 6, June 1972 (Tehran: Echo of Iran) p.4.

49 Ibid., Vol. IX, nos. 6 and 7, June-July 1973, p.11.

49A The whole *Bazaar* itself is shrouded in secrecy, with a non-*Bazaari* easily getting lost in it; it is therefore not surprising that its top echelon is said to be formed by an ultra-secret group of five individuals; each of the top men has his own group of four lieutenants, who do not know each other and (naturally) do not know the other leaders; each lieutenant has four lesser merchants under his control, and so on all the way down the line. So every *Bazaari* (except for the top five) has one hierarchical superior and four lieutenants; and this system is said to be behind the *Bazaar*'s homogeneity and its agile manoeuvrability in cases of crisis. Private communications from a couple of old *Bazaari* hands, with the gaps (?) filled in by the author.

50 G.W. Ball, op. cit. (note 29), p.454.

51 A prisoner of war of the Soviets in Siberia, the Wehrmacht officer Von Lilienfeld escaped all the way back to Germany (a unique feat). After the war he married an American heiress and made his mark on Iran.

52 During 1974 many foreign investment deals were proposed to or by Iran, and all fell through; prominent among these deals:

a) the purchase of 25% of General Electric (US);

b) Iran's bid for an interest in Fiat (Italy) was turned down, although it was later sold to Libya, who made a substantial return on it.

c) Iran's offer to buy the bankrupt Leyland-BMC (GB); the company ended up nationalised;

d) the purchase of a 13% stake in PanAm (US).

e) the purchase of 20% of Union Carbide Caribe, the Puerto Rican subsidiary of Union Carbide (US), as part of a joint venture with the American multinational.

53 *Middle East Economic Digest*, December 1977, p.16.

54 See the memoirs of General Fardoust, note 10 above

55 Koor, Israel's largest conglomerate, is a Histradrut Labour Federation holding company.

56 M. Bailey, 'The Blooming of Operation Flower', in *The Observer*, February 2, 1986.
57 *Asnad-i Laneh Jasousi*, no. 19, pp.5 and 19 (the minutes of Toufanian's meetings are reproduced).
58 *Inquiry* magazine, January 1987, p.69.
59 *Arabia* magazine, Vol. 4, no. 48, August 1985, p.29.
60 *Time Magazine*, September 12, 1979, p.31.
61 R. Graham, op. cit. (note 20), pp.112-3.
62 *Iran: Past, Present and Future*, ed. by J.W. Jacqz, (Aspen Institute of Humanistic Studies, 1976) pp.323-5.
63 S.S. Harrison, 'Nightmare in Baluchestan', in *Foreign Policy*, no. 32, Fall 1978, p.139.
64 Sh. Haqiqat, Iran: La Revolution Inachevee et l'Ordre l'Americain, (Paris: Editions Anthropos, 1980) p.33.
65 Private communication from a junior officer close to General Uvaysi.
66 Keyhan International', January 25, 1973, p.3.
67 A. Sampson, The Changing Anatomy of Britain, (Coronet Books, 1983) p.264.
68 Keyhan International', October 6, 1973, p.3.
69 JAB. Kelly, Arabia the Gulf and the West, p.143.
70 Sh. Haqiqat, op. cit. (note 64), p.120.
71 The Persian Gulf and Indian Ocean in International Politics, ed. by Â. Amirie, (Tehran: IIPES, 1975) p.307.
72 J.B. Kelly, op. cit. (note 69), p.147.
73 Ibid., p.148.
74 *MERIP Reports*, no. 43, December 1975, p.23.
75 *The Financial Times*, January 21, 1977.
76 *Keyhan International*, March 1, 1979, p.4.
77 J.B. Kelly, op. cit. (note 69), p.504.
78 A. Sampson, op. cit. (note 67), p.6.
79 *Iran Almanac 1974* (Tehran: Echo of Iran, 1974) pp.413-4.
80 *Iran Yearbook 1977* (Tehran: Keyhan Group, 1977) p.395.
81 Personal communication on the Tehran University campus, after an afternoon of clashes with paratroopers.
82 *Keyhan International*, March 3, 1975, p.2.
83 The Rastakhiz party had three secretary-generals:
(1) Premier Huvayda, March 1975–October 1976;
(2) Jamshid Amuzigar, October 1976–August 1977 and also January 1978–September 1978;
(3) Dr. Muhammad Bahiri, August 1977–January 1978.
84 M.R. Pahlavi, *Réponses à l'Histoire* (Paris: Albin Michel, 1979) p.202.
85 *Le Monde*, October 4, 1976.
86 'Iran: Oil Money and the Ambitions of a Nation', a special report of *The Hudson Letter*, (Paris, 1975) p.8. The report further underlined "Iran's fragile economy", "her lack of an industrial base", "the limits on her agriculture", "her high infant mortality: 139 per thousand", "her high rate of illiteracy: 77%", "her low GNP per capita: $490 in 1972" and "her restrained working population: 8,079,000 people in 1971".
87 *Rastakhiz* newspaper, Day 5, 1355, December 26, 1976.
88 *Keyhan International*, October 25, 1976, p.6.

[89] It was so attractive that foreign managers of multinational companies (e.g. Boeing) found development projects were far more rewarding than their expatriate salaries (plus all the fringe benefits allocated while they were in Iran).

[90] *Hisabha-yi Milli-i Iran* (National Accounts of Iran), (Tehran: Bank-i Markazi-i Iran, (1360) (1981)) p.444.

[91] The French Bouygues was the stadium designer and consultant on the project was Âziz Farmanfarmayan. Initially estimated at $60m, the stadium ended up costing three times as much. A year after the games, cracks had developed throughout the stadium's concrete, extensive repairs were required and Âziz Farmanfarmayan was attacked in the press for negligence. As for the Seventh Asian Games, the Shah's dress rehearsal for the 1980 or 1984 Tehran Olympics, they proved quite a success, being organised in a masterly fashion by the games' tsar, Hasan Rasouli, and his wife, Layla, in September 1974. Iran's Olympic hopes, however, were premature (to say the least) and after three years of useless efforts, Tehran retired its candidacy in 1977.

[92] See *Le Monde*, October 3, 1978. The exact quote being: "Si l'on tient compte de l'Empereur lui-même n'est pas à l'abri de tout reproche dans ce domaine [de corruption]".

[93] *Keyhan International*, January 27, 1976, p.8.

[94] Nasir Assar owed his Ouqaf position and his subsequent career at Foreign Affairs to the fact that he married a Farmanfarmayan heiress.

[95] S. Akhavi, *Religion and Politics in Contemporary Iran* (Albany: State University of New York Press, 1980) p.133.

[96] *Asnad-i Laneh Jasousi*, no. 17, p.69, on the link between Reporter and the Aqayans, and the Aqayans' access to court.

[97] Many bureaucrats came to believe Sayrafi and Âlizadeh to be totally innocent then; the latter's excellent life in his London exile brought doubts to some bureaucratic minds.

[98] About Arbabi's honesty there was little doubt. An expert on Iran's civil aviation affairs confirmed to the author that "he had not the shade of a doubt about Arbabi being an honest and capable administrator". See also *Asnad-i Laneh Jasousi*, no. 17, p.37, in which an US Embassy officer characterises Arbabi as "an honest man".

[99] *Middle East Economic Digest*, May 6, 1977, pp.22-23.

[100] L.S. Stavrianos, *The Promise of the Coming Dark Age* (San Francisco: W.H. Freeman and Company, 1976) p.179.

[101] *Iran Almanac 1978* (Tehran: Echo of Iran, 1978) p.45.

[102] *Middle East Economic Digest*, December 16, 1977.

[103] *UN Demographic Yearbook 1982*, p.317.

[104] Educated in England on a Bank-i Markazi scholarship, Dr Pisaran received his Ph.D. in economics from Cambridge University. Among the most gifted bureaucrats of his generation, he went on to become Deputy Minister of Education (under Minister Dr Manouchihr Ganji) in charge of Social and Welfare Affairs. He engineered the formation of the Bank-i Farhangian (The Educationalists' Bank) with shares held by teachers and ministry employees and managed by an honest and talented chartered accountant (a Bank-i Milli officer), Bahman Sadr Hashimi. After the Revolution Dr Pisaran departed for English academia, with his English wife and three young sons.

[105] M.H. Pessaran, 'Income Distribution in Iran', in *Iran: Past, Present and Future*, op. cit. (note), pp.278-280.
[106] Ibid., p.277.
[107] The author was a direct witness of the case of an endowment involving prime provincial real estate, which Ouqaf and the Farah Foundation wanted to sell, totally disregarding the grave misgivings of the endowment's legal heirs. The Revolution arrived in time to foil their plans.
[108] On the meagre achievements of Farmanfarmayan's social efforts, see C.S. Prigmore, *Social Work in Iran since the White Revolution* (The University of Alabama Press, 1976). The photograph on p.68 is especially revealing in respect of artificiality.
[109] E. Burke, *Reflections on the Revolution in France* (Penguin Books, 1982) p.140.
[110] Â.A. Hajj Sayyid Javadi, *Namehha* (The Letters), (Tehran: Mudarris, 2nd ed., 1357 (1978)) pp.51-2.
[111] T. Jalil, *Workers say No to the Shah – Labour Law and Strikes in Iran* (London: Campaign for the Restoration of Trade Union Rights in Iran (CRTURI), April 1977) pp.82-5.
[112] See previous note no.77
[113] *Time Magazine*, October 18, 1982, p.18, quoting from J. Carter, *Keeping Faith* (Bantam Books, 1982).
[114] *Middle East Economic Digest*, January 7, 1977, p.17.
[115] *Iran in the 1980s*, op. cit. (note 81 above) p.147. The young Bank-i Milli economist Dariush Malikpour countered Vakil's estimate by mentioning that the Bank-i Markazi consumer price index "stood thirty points higher in July 1977 in comparison to July 1976". People in the streets, however, felt much higher effects than 30% inflation (as 30% was for a standard basket).
[116] 'Iran: The Lion that Stopped Roaring', *Euromoney*, June 1978, p. 108
[117] Ibid., p.133.
[118] *Iran Almanac 1978* (Tehran: Echo of Iran, 1978) p.43.
[119] Nikpay's disgrace was partially due to his father Îzaz shooting dead a vagabond who was eating fruits from his orchard.
[120] F. Hoveyda, op. cit. (note 3), p.32.
[121] P.C. Radji, op. cit. (note 6), p.99.

CHAPTER SEVENTEEN: SACRED TIME

In 1977, the people of Iran began their collective transition from 'Profane Time' to 'Sacred Time' – to use Romanian historian Mircea Eliade's terminology. In other words, they began to tread the path that would take them from their usual daily routine to the special events which shaped history.

It was during 1977 that the new mood first became palpable. At first it was almost imperceptible: an attitude, a nervousness, an unusual reaction.[1] But as the year advanced, these signs multiplied exponentially. The snowballing effect was the logical result of a series of events which had overlapped to provoke it. Prominent among these events were: (1) the stalling of the Shah's economic machine; (2) the inauguration on January 20 of America's President Jimmy Carter (Mr Human Rights); and (3) the campaign launched (in January) by Amnesty International (AI) to champion the cause of political prisoners in Iran. Although AI's secret plan for a massive February show in Holland was unveiled by a West German jurist (and made headlines in the Tehran press of January 16, 1977[2]), AI had made its point and would pursue its international fight in favour of the forgotten political prisoners in Iran. When on October 10, 1977 AI was awarded the Nobel Peace Prize, one of the repercussions was a boon for the humanitarian organisation and its director Martin Ennals, and also an indirect victory for all of the world's political detainees, especially Iran's prisoners. On the other hand, neither the Shah nor SAVAK must have appreciated the well-deserved accolade given to their AI nemesis.

The Shah didn't fear AI (although he was seriously irritated by its impact on public opinion), but he was seriously worried about Carter and his message about human rights. Hence, Iran Inc. adopted a defensive strategy from early 1977 onwards.

Treatment of political prisoners changed for the better (for the first time since 1953); a first visit on April 18, 1977 by a delegation of the International Committee of the Red Cross (ICRC) to the notorious political prisons of Evin and Qasr was a momentous event for Iran's political detainees.[3] Something was changing for the better in Iran:

the defenceless political prisoners had both the AI and the ICRC looking into their case.

As usual, the first Iranian constituency to catch the new national mood were the students. Since the beginning of 1977 daily disorders had occurred on Iranian campuses, especially those of Tehran University (TU) and the Polytechnic. Student dormitories throughout the capital were buoyant. In May, the Polytechnic dorm was stormed at night by paratroopers and the students were given a thrashing; a month later, TU's dorm at Amirabad suffered the same fate. In June the universities of Tabriz and Aryamhr joined the fray (on the 23rd and 25th respectively), when the TU students staged a sit-in in the Tehran *Bazaar*: an imaginative gambit by the youngsters. Summer vacations would cut the grass from under the students' feet and the regime's staging of fully-paid summer camps in ideal locations in the countryside further cooled their spirits (but failed to buy them off).

On September 13, 1977, a bizarre incident occurred on the French Riviera when Princess Ashraf's Rolls-Royce, driven by the young Îtimadian, was forced to stop off the Corniche above Nice by another car. Armed gunmen stepped down from the latter car and shot dead Ashraf's *dame d'honneur* Furough Khajeh Nouri, sitting in the back seat. Îtimadian rapidly disengaged the car and made off at full speed. In Tehran, the incident was interpreted as a warning by international drug-trafficking gangs to Princess Ashraf not to enter their turf, Khajeh Nouri being widely known in Iran as being involved in hard drugs deals. The incident was given wide publicity abroad, giving the Pahlavis a bad press at a time when they least needed it, notwithstanding the millions of dollars paid to PR outfits to cajole the media.

The reopening of Iranian universities in the autumn proved troublesome. On October 9, the TU students at Amirabad turned violent: they smashed the dorm's windows and went on a rampage around the premises, damaging three buses and setting a fourth on fire before the security forces could cordon off the area and bring it under control.

Amazingly, it was a peaceful event that sent the first noticeable tremors through the Pahlavi regime's foundations: the Evenings of Poetry, organised from October 10 until 19 (ten consecutive nights) at Tehran's Goethe Institut. The event was sponsored by the Iranian-German Cultural Association and, inaugurated by the Institut's director Dr H.H. Becker, turned into a popular explosion of cultural and political communication.

Attended by some 62,000 people[4] (mostly students and educated youngsters), the unbelievable happening, held in an atmosphere of freedom unseen in Iran for a whole generation, was a triumph for Iran's poets: Ahmad Shamlou, Mihdi Akhavan Salis, Siavoush Kasra'i (the *Toudeh*'s chanteuse) and Âli Mousavi Garmaroudi. Also present were the intelligentsia's vanguard, authors Beh Azin, Tunikabuni, Hizarkhani, Khwu'i, Shams Al-i Ahmad (Jalal's brother) and Jalal's wife Simin Danishvar; playwright Dr Sâidi and theatre director Sâid Sultanpour.[5] All of them were, to different degrees, opponents of the regime, and the anti-Pahlavi shivers running in the Goethe Institut (and all the streets around it) night after night were unmistakable. SAVAK could merely look on, learning to play its new defensive role – certainly not relishing these prospects. Were it not for Carter and AI and the timely departure of Ambassador Von Lilienfeld (who would never have allowed Dr Becker to go ahead with his Nights, as the new ambassador, Dr G. Ritzel, had done), Iran's intelligentsia wouldn't have been given this golden occasion to count itself and cast its first anti-Pahlavi vote. In Iran, when the best brains and minds are not on your side, it is because you have already lost. Maybe the Shah and his petrodollar elite failed to get the message from the Goethe's Nights of Poetry, but it was clear: the intelligentsia, so long and so ruthlessly restrained by SAVAK, was restless and freedom-thirsty. The Nights had been the catalyst needed to crystallise the new mood for change.

The forces of opposition were still rejoicing from the triumph of the ten glorious Nights, when the news of the death of Mustafa Khomeini, the eldest son of Ayatullah Khomeini, which had occurred on October 23 in Najaf (Iraq), reached Tehran. The sudden passing away of the forty-seven year old Mustafa (a member of a family known for its longevity) was perplexing at best, and rumours of poisoning circulated in Tehran (although the cause of death was never made public). During his exile in Najaf, Mustafa had acted as his father's secretary and lieutenant, with the latter declaring him to be "one of the brightest hopes of contemporary Islam". Mustafa's death revived the memories of 1963 in Iran. At Qum, large crowds gathered for the rituals of Mustafa's *Haft*,[6] at which the clergymen Rabbani Amlashi, Shaykh Sadiq Khalkhali, Shaykh Abu'l Qasim

Khazâli and Shaykh Muhammad Javad Hujjati Kirmani delivered their sermons. From all over Iran telegrams of condolences were cabled to Najaf.

Mustafa's enigmatic death had the effect of reviving Iran's religious community, for there was little doubt that Mustafa had fallen victim to the Pahlavis' vengefulness.

17.1. The Forces of Opposition

If the groups and leading individuals forming the petrodollar elite were pretty well-known, Iran's counter-elites were far more shadowy. By the close of 1977, the main stem of opposition still consisted of the three main counter-elites: communist, nationalist and religious (see Figure 17.1). With their star Hajj Sayyid Javadi and the Ten Nights of Poetry, the intelligentsia had stolen a march on the rest of the opposition. In April 1977, the intellectuals formed the Iranian Association for the Defence of Freedom and Human Rights (IADFHR); a few weeks later, the Iranian Lawyers' Association (ILA), dominated by *engagé* lawyers Hasan Nazih, Âbd ul-Karim Lahiji and Hidayatullah Matin Daftari, was revived. On July 11, it issued its first communiqué demanding "a greater say in national justice". Shortly thereafter, the Iranian Writers' Association (IWA), Al-i Ahmad's brainchild, came out of its seven year purgatory and organised elections for its board of directors, with five leftist authors being elected: Mahmud Îtimadzadeh (alias Beh Azin), Manouchihr Hizarkhani, Muhammad Âli Sipanlou, Baqir Parham and Firaydun Tunikabuni. The intelligentsia's fourth organisational pillar saw the light in April 1978 when the Committee for the Defence of Political Prisoners (CDPP) was created by members of the three existing pillars (after a hunger strike by political prisoners begun on March 11), naturally with Hajj Sayyid Javadi as secretary-general. On April 10, the CDPP sent its first petition to the ICRC and UNCHR on the plight of Iranian political prisoners; it bore the signatures of four hundred Iranian intellectuals. The intelligentsia had rapidly capitalised on his head start, but it lacked both a strong leadership and devoted troops; Hajj Sayyid Javadi was a courageous journalist but not a leader of men; as for the opposition's natural troops, the university students, they were already way ahead of their would-be leaders, at the cutting edge of the struggle.

Figure 17.1. Schematic Representation of the Main Groups Within the Iranian Opposition of 1977/78, with the Three Major Counter-elites at the Top.

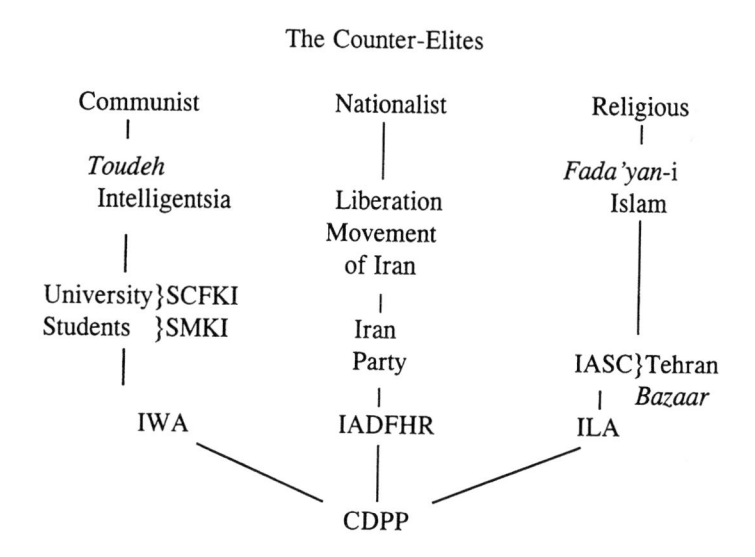

The Counter-Elites

```
    Communist          Nationalist         Religious
        |                   |                  |
     Toudeh                                Fada'yan-i
    Intelligentsia      Liberation           Islam
        |               Movement
                         of Iran
    University}SCFKI        |
    Students  }SMKI       Iran
        |                 Party          IASC}Tehran
                            |              |  Bazaar
       IWA               IADFHR           ILA
              \             |             /
                          CDPP
```

Abbreviations used:
SCFKI: *Sazman-i Chirikha-yi Fada'i-i Khalq-i Iran*
SMKI: *Sazman-i Mujahidin-i Khalq-i Iran*
IASC: Iranian Association of Struggling Clergymen
IWA: Iranian Writers' Association
IADFHR: Iranian Association for Freedom and Human Rights
ILA: Iranian Lawyers' Association
CDPP: Committee for the Defence of Political Prisoners

To the right of the intelligentsia and actively supporting its pillars (especially IADFHR and CDPP), was the LMI. Headed by Ayatullah Taliqani, Engineer Bazargan and Dr Sahabi, the elitist religious-nationalist entity was all Chiefs and no Indians. Prominent among the LMI lieutenants were Engineer Îzattullah Sahabi (the doctor's eldest son), Hashim Sabaghian and Muhammad Tavassuli.

Rahim Âta'i, an active member, was to die in July 1977, at the age of fifty-seven. Three other lieutenants were engaged abroad – Dr Mustafa Chamran (in Lebanon), Dr Ibrahim Yazdi (in the US) and Dr Sadiq Tabataba'i (in West Germany).

The *Iran* Party had roughly the same characteristics as the LMI, without the religious links and the courage to fight.

Its gerontocratic leadership, composed of A. Salih (eighty years old), Dr Amir Âla'i (seventy-seven), Dr Shayigan (seventy-five), Dr Sanjabi (seventy-three), Dr Sadiqi (seventy-two), Engineer Hasibi (sixty-eight) and the youngster Dr Shahpour Bakhtiar (sixty-three), was out of touch with Iranian realities. The nationalist counter-elite still had neither an ideology nor troops. Unprepared and unfit, they met to analyse the situation, hoping for a miracle. Their first action was an open letter to the Shah in June 1977 "asking for an end to dictatorship ...and a return to constitutional principle", walking in Hajj Sayyid Javadi's footprints and alerting the Shah to their presence. The next action was an adventurous rally staged at villa in Karavansara Sangi (between Tehran and Karaj) on November 22, 1977; some three hundred baton-armed (SAVAK) thugs broke up the meeting and Dr Bakhtiar, one of the main speakers, broke his arm when he fell off a wall during his flight. After the botched-up meeting, the *Iran* Party leaders found it safer to return to their ivory tower.

During the first half of the 1970s, the religious counter-elite had been hibernating. In Qum, the conservative triumvirate of Grand Ayatullahs Shariâtmadari, Gulpaygani and Marâshi Najafi was sitting on its fence, trying to keep channels to the royal power open (among others, through Ayatullah Muhammad Taqi Qumi in Tehran). On June 5, 1975, to commemorate the 1963 uprising, Ayatullah Khomeini's supporters staged a massive demonstration at the Fayziyyeh school in Qum. On June 7, paratroopers invested the school and fell upon the religious students: forty-five casualties and three hundred arrests ensued. The Ayatullahs Muntaziri (Khomeini's representative at Qum) and Taliqani were arrested; lesser clergymen such as Shaykh Âli Tihrani and Shaykh Sadiq Khalkhali were sent off to exile.

In Isfahan, an internecine religious struggle ended with the murder of Ayatullah Shamsabadi on April 7, 1976. The alleged murderer, Sayyid Mihdi Hashimi, a native of Qahdrijan (a large village near Isfahan), was linked matrimonially to Ayatullah Muntaziri (the latter's daughter was the wife of Hashimi's brother Sayyid Hadi) and twenty-one accomplices – all members of Hashimi's *Hadafiha* (lit. 'those with a goal') group – were duly arrested by SAVAK. The reason behind the incident seems to have been the victim's lack of caution in a pamphlet attacking Khomeini's theory of *Vilayat-i Faqih* (the Rule of the Knowledgeable): his murder would have any would-be critic thinking twice. Hashimi and his acolytes were tried in Isfahan and convicted of Shamsabadi's murder; on March 31, 1977, Hashimi and five others were given death sentences but none of them was executed. In prison, the unusual Hashimi developed contacts with both SAVAK and PLO leader Yasser Arafat.

In Iran's political prisons, the greatest event of 1976 was a decree jointly issued by the Ayatullahs Taliqani and Muntaziri (both prisoners themselves). The decree said that "real Muslims could not live side-by-side with atheist communists". The directive to the "real Muslims" was a death blow to their relations with the imprisoned guerrillas of the SCFKI and even the SMKI (also tainted red, the Ayatullahs said). Imprisoned clergymen such as Muhammad Riza Mahdavi Kani and Âli Akbar Hashimi Rafsanjani had to obey, as had the *Bazaaris* such as Mihdi Âraqi and Habibullah Âsgarouladi; the separation was easiest for right-winger Asadullah Lajivardi (who abhorred all communists) and most painful for Muhammad Âli Rija'i, a top political adviser to the imprisoned SMKI leadership, and Muhsin Rafiqdoust, who had close friendships with the guerrillas. After a full decade of active support to the SMKI, the religious hierocracy had suddenly decided to cut its links to the guerrillas and set up its own shop.

Once the break-up was finalised, a large number of "real Muslims" were set free (after taking part in a televised enactment). In August 1977, some thirty-five of the 'freed Muslims' would gather in an orchard bordering the Tehran–Chalous road and elect their first leadership, consisting of eight members, namely, Mihdi Âraqi,

Muhammad Sadiq Islami, Âli Dirakhshan, Muhammad Kachou'i, Habibullah Âsgarouladi, Muhsin Labbani Qadirian, Âli Akbar Pourustad and Asadullah Badamchian. Four others were later added, Ayatullah Sayyid Muhammad Husayni Bihishti, Dr Âbbas Shaybani, Javad Maliki and Hasan Ijarehdar. Ayatullah Bihishti took over the political leadership and Âraqi the group's day-to-day operations.

In 1977, the religious opponents of the regime had come out of their torpor and made a comeback within the opposition's folds. Their major achievements were:

– In April, two guerrillas believed to be right-wing Islamists assaulted the Jewish Immigration Agency; both were shot dead, one inside the agency, the other outside. The action was probably carried out by remnants of the Lajivardi group.

– In July, some forty Islamic students made it out of the Tehran University boundaries and went down Takhteh-i Jamshid Avenue chanting "Allah-u Akbar" (God is Great) before being dispersed by the police.

– A new International Islamic University was approved by the Shah for Mashhad in August; investment funds were to be provided by the Office of the Holy Shrine of Imam Riza (A.S.), the Ouqaf and the Pahlavi Foundation.

– On September 17, the Iranian Association of Struggling Clergymen (IASC) issued its first communiqué, asking for the liberation of all political prisoners; a week later the second demanded the return of Ayatullah Khomeini and the freedom of Ayatullahs Taliqani and Muntaziri, Sayyid Mihdi Hashimi and Engineer Lutfullah Maysami.

– Also in September, the nationalist clergyman Sayyid Abu'l Fazl Mousavi Zanjani led the community prayers of the *Âyd-i Fitr* (the holiday marking the end of the fasting month of *Ramadan*) in Tehran's Qaytariyyeh quarter; and Dr Mufatteh inaugurated a series of lectures at Tehran's Quba mosque.

– From October 1-7, Muhammad Muntaziri (the Ayatullah's son), Sayyid Mahmoud Duâ'i (Ayatullah Khomeini's private secretary) and Engineer Muhammad Gharazi (disguised as a *mulla*) led a one week hunger strike in a Paris church.

– On October 7, about one hundred people staged a sit-in at the Shah Âbd ul-Âzim mosque; led by Engineer Bazargan, the movement included members of the LMI and of the religious group of *Bihishti-Âraqi*; it was mentioned by major Tehran newspapers.

But the real strength of the opposition was in its rank and file, first and foremost, the university students. A formidable mass of dedicated and emotional youngsters, always ready to demonstrate or stage sit-ins, the students were an invaluable asset. Next to them came the highly disciplined *Toudeh* party members and the pro-Musaddiq nationalists, both still counting on capable elements. Closing the ranks was a brand-new and highly mobile new urban wave: the *Dihqanzadehs*.

The majority of Iran's 'young wolves' had opted during the seventies for the ranks of opposition, seeing the way into the Iran Inc. pyramid blocked at the top. There was ability without property – therefore they had nothing to lose – a situation, as Burke said: "the conjuncture most redoubtable to society".

17.2. Towards Confrontation

It was against this background of restlessness at home that the Shah arrived in Washington on November 15, 1977 on an official visit. For the Iranian monarch his first meeting with President Carter was crucial. Having got along with seven US presidents, he now had to seduce his eighth. Unfortunately for him, Jimmy Carter, the man who had placed human rights at the top of the American foreign policy agenda, did not subscribe to Dr Kissinger's *realpolitik*. The Shah tried to convince him that the human rights situation in Iran was not as dark as some had painted it: the ICRC was freely visiting Iranian prisons; internal liberalisation was on its way; and, in any case, the Shah would bend over backwards to satisfy new US standards. Hopefully, the Shah said, such concessions on his part would "defuse" friction points between "long-standing allies".

Iranian students did their utmost to mar the Shah's visit. In Iran, they orchestrated large-scale riots at TU and Aryamihr University; at Washington, anti-royalist Iranian students enrolled at American universities clashed daily with the ruthless security forces: over two hundred students were wounded and three hundred arrested.[7] As a protest against excessive police brutality, four thousand Aryamihr University students went on strike; the university chancellor responded by threatening to annul the 1977/78 academic year before things cooled down and the students returned to their classes. In Washington, anti-Shah students easily swept aside the SAVAK phalanxes and the timorous pro-royalist students (some of whom had been brought to Washington at the Iranian Embassy's expense[8]) before clashing with federal policemen, who were forced to use tear gas and baton charges to stop their forceful drive. The tear gas clouds drifted to the White House lawn and both the Shah and Carter had to mop up their tears before the television cameras: a not insignificant victory for the students. Moreover, on December 7, some seventy students booed American athletes taking part in a sporting event at a Tehran stadium (yet another negative signal to the Americans); and on December 9, Iranian students at Rome occupied the Iranian Embassy and, a week later, their colleagues in Denmark took the Copenhagen Embassy.[9]

Less than six weeks after these traumatic events, the Shah might have thought that miracles do happen after all: President Carter and First Lady Rosalyn (accompanied by Secretary of State Cyrus Vance and National Security Adviser Zbigniew Brzezinski) were his guests in his Niavaran Palace. All of the Iran Inc. directors and officers thought that the Shah had achieved yet another feat of *legerdemain* by seducing his eighth American president when the latter toasted him with the following words: "Iran under the great leadership of the Shah is an island of stability in one of the more troubled areas of the world. This is a great tribute to you, Your Majesty, and to your leadership, and the respect, admiration and love which your people give you". On the morrow, it was the petrodollar elite which was celebrating the event. Maybe the Shah would have to keep SAVAK on a shorter leash and give the world further tokens of freedom, but with sustained American backing nothing could go wrong, the regime believed. Even the bomb detonated on December 29 by a SCFKI squad before the Iran-America Society was dismissed as an insignificant event.

Was it the state of overconfidence instilled in royal quarters by the Carter visit or simply carelessness – bred by complacency – that led to the publication on January 7, 1978, of an article entitled 'Iran va Istîmar-i Surkh va Siah' (Iran and the Red and the Black Reactions) in the newspaper *Ittilaât*? It was signed by Ahmad Rashidi Muttlaq, an evident pseudonym.[10]

The article expanded on ideas dear to the Shah (the "Red and Black Reactions" being one of the favourite royal leitmotivs), attacking the 'Red' communists and the 'Black' religious activists, hurling unveiled insults at Ayatullah Khomeini and his family. Even if the piece was a banana skin slipped in by outsiders under the Shah's nose, the court's brains and minds should have known better and stopped the article before it was published.[11]

On January 8, the Qum *Bazaar* and the religious schools closed down as signs of protest; clergyman Nasir Makarim Shirazi, a former student of Ayatullah Khomeini, sent a strong note of protest to the prime minister, and was exiled on the spot. On the morrow, Shaykh Husayn Nouri, another of Khomeini's students, had the courage to harangue a crowd of young religious students with an inflammatory speech. Coming back from the Nouri sermon, religious elements excited armed forces at a Qum police station. Clashes ensued, tear gas filled the air, shooting began and the first blood was drawn when a thirteen year old youth was shot dead. For three hours hit-and-run clashes continued, leading to more casualties, among others three young *tullabs*: Âli Asghar Nasiri (twenty), Murtaza Sharifi (twenty-one) and Muhammad Riza Ansari (nineteen). The 'Black Reaction' had reacted to the insulting article, unleashing forces dormant for fifteen years.

The Qum clashes were a minor incident, but the opposition readily capitalised on the young blood spilled by issuing a flurry of incensed communiqués. Most virulent were those of the IASC and of the Tehran *Bazaar*, the latter calling for a *Bazaar* closedown and a general strike on the Qum martyrs' *chihileh* (February 18). The intelligentsia's mouthpieces all played their part in the mass protests and even Dr Muzaffar Baqa'i (sensing the wind turning) made a comeback on this occasion, issuing a note "vehemently protesting [against] the Qum killings". The regime was not unduly impressed by the opposition's clamours. It had received in great pomp UN Secretary-General Kurt Waldheim on January 9, and Empress Farah departed as scheduled on the 10th for her third US trip in as little as six months.[12] Between February 2 and 5, the Shah duly made his official visit to India. The regime's only crackdown occurred on January 24, when fifteen targeted Tehran *Bazaar* shops (probably owned by anti-royalist traders[13]) were closed *sine die*. The first consequences of the Carter visit also came to light when an important ICRC delegation debarked in Tehran on February 12, with the objective of touring all major Iranian prisons. Everything seemed to have returned to normal.

On February 18, Qum's Ayatullahs, the IASC and the *Bazaar* called for a national day of mourning to commemorate the *chihileh* of the Qum martyrs. Signed appeals were posted at the entrance of every mosque. At the entrance to the Tabriz Mosque of Hajj Mirza Yusuf Aqa Mujtahid, a police officer, Major Majidi, lost patience and tore them down; a young man, outraged by this act, attacked him, but the major shot down his assailant. This incident was all that was required to set Tabriz alight.

For the next thirty-six hours, the fourth largest city in Iran (with around 600,000 inhabitants) erupted like a volcano. The people overwhelmed the security forces. The army had to be called in. It took the tanks until the afternoon of February 19 to restore law and order. By then Tabriz was a devastated city of gutted buildings (e.g. the *Rastakhiz* party offices, the Justice Ministry, the Youth Palace and the Institute of Technology), burnt-out vehicles, littered streets, broken windows: a total of four hotels, nine cinemas, twenty-two supermarkets, twenty-eight cars and seventy-three bank branches (mostly those of the Bank-i Sadirat) and dozens of liquor shops were destroyed in the process. On the human side the official tally was six deaths with one hundred and twenty-five injured and two hundred and fifty arrests,[14] but, according to some Western diplomats, the toll was much higher and the number of "one hundred dead"[15] was put forward.

Everyone was surprised, or rather amazed, by the magnitude of the Tabriz riots. They had a significance unprecedented in modern Iranian history: for the better part of two days the city was virtually in the hands of uncontrolled elements. The regime was left wondering how its security apparatus could have been so easily outflanked by rioters. Even more dumbfounded than the regime was the opposition. In their wildest dreams the counter-elitists couldn't have envisioned such a momentous disruption. None of them thought it possible at such an early stage in the process[16] as neither of the opposition's two battering rams (i.e. the students and the religious-led mobs) were ready then – the students were still afraid to venture off their campuses and the latter had not lasted three hours in their Qum stronghold a month earlier. Even though some Iranian guerrillas might have been on the streets, only the presence of foreign-inspired elements in the Tabriz cauldron can explain the riots' wide successes. It should be borne in mind that a small group of thirty to forty professionally trained men can wreak havoc if assisted by masses of excited followers. A report on the riots by *Le Monde* seems to confirm this hypothesis, as it mentions "les manifestations violentes ont donné l'impression d'être organisées et disciplinées... L'organisation a été assez remarquable des manifestations (les manifestants étant répartis en plusieurs groupes pour échapper à la police)..."[17] Iranian people can do many things, but are poor organisers at best.

The Tabriz events had altered the whole Iranian game. If forces of opposition (foreign-inspired or not) could hold a major city to ransom and turn it into a wreck, it was because the regime – notwithstanding its police, its SAVAK and its armed forces – had lost its iron grip. Failing to see the writing on the wall, the regime reacted routinely, instead of reacting exceptionally to an extraordinary event. It was not the standard dispatch of the Shah's adjudant-general, General Jâfar Shafaqat, at the head of a special inquiry commission to Tabriz, or the dismissal of the governor-general, General Iskkandar Azmoudeh (in place since 1974), and of local SAVAK and police chiefs, which would change anything. If the regime was at a loss confronting these events, so was the liberal opposition: the nationalists and the intellectuals with their human rights grievances had now been outpaced by the Tabriz events. As for the active (and radical) opposition, it had found its footing and the right rhythm: a forty day break between two onslaughts. Moreover, a new wind of hope blew in its sails now it had found out that the Iran Inc. fortress was vulnerable.

As the opposition was recoiling after Tabriz for its next onslaught on the Iran Inc. fortress, the court found no better pastime than to award, on March 12, at the Niavaran Palace, the Order of the Smile to – Empress Farah.[18]

17.3. The Quadruple Vectors

Tabriz was a watershed. Before, confrontation still had a minimal chance of being turned into a compromise and conciliation (although the regime could not envision any reason for compromising): after

Tabriz, it was to be an all-out war between the (now) beleaguered Iran Inc. pyramid and the vast yet uncoordinated opposition. Tabriz had been the first act of 'Sacred Time'. And now was the time for the four main vectors of the Iranian stage to become focused simultaneously, leading to a highly complex four-dimensional nexus of (A) the People, (B) the Powers, (C) the Elites, and (D) Oil, leading to a unique outcome.

(A) The People
Since 1953, people had not been asked their opinion. They had backed the honest Dr Musaddiq *en masse*; when he was removed by force they had lost. Since then they had watched from the sidelines the American-backed Shah give them material welfare, accepting it without any sense of gratitude (taking it as a Danegeld for their silence). Furthermore, the ferocious repression of the 1950s had instilled fear in the majority: fear of intervention, fear of SAVAK, of prison, of torture, of death. And the Shah and his elite had always played on these fears: "Don't get involved and just do as we tell you, or else we'll address SAVAK to you and your family". The hint was enough to make anyone think twice about any further action.

Iranians are loath to risk themselves uselessly, but, after all, they are a 'historical people', a people supposed to pull itself together when ominous danger signs are visible. In the Tabriz aftermath, people had began thinking 'What if?': for the first time in decades change could be envisioned. The smell of 'Sacred Time' was in the air. The first whiffs of rebellion and civil disobedience had been in the air since 1977; in early 1978 they had turned to a breeze and then, at Tabriz, into high winds sweeping all before its path, revealing the strength of opposition of the Iranian people and the world at large. The regime freely publicised the magnitude of the Tabriz disorders, to the point of giving a free hand to local journalists (who took full advantage of it), hoping to scandalise its 'silent majority' – thinking that Iran was either Sweden or Switzerland.

The people of Iran, embarked as they were on the Pahlavi train taking them towards a Great Civilisation, were not sure where exactly the train was taking them. The material benefits of the past decade had been gratifying, pulling them out of the struggle for daily survival. The problem was that there was nothing to replace it with: no ideals, no common endeavours, no dreams (and God knows that

Iranians need to dream). So the common people turned to laziness and dangerous pastimes: alcohol (provided cheap), opium (ditto), pornographic films and cabarets. Encouraged by the regime (for obvious reasons), a general lassitude and apathy was spreading throughout Iranian youth (though fortunately not the elite core of the university students).

The students, being the people's vanguard, were a special breed. In the front line of confrontation since 1953, they had witnessed their heroes die rather than surrender to the enemy. A quarter of century of cumulative struggle and experience against the Pahlavis had made of them irreconcilable foes of the dynasty. Having lost their best and brightest in the battles against SAVAK, they were uncompromising. With their high ideals and youthful incorruptibility, they were the at exact opposite end of the spectrum of the Elite's cynicism and misplaced Machiavellianism. Conscious of their historical responsibilities towards their own people, they were always ready to fight against this Pahlavi regime which they abhorred and which was impeding their natural rise to the top of Iranian society.

The Iranian urban middle classes, although materially better off than ever before, shared the general sentiment of dissatisfaction. They were tired of carrying the weight of the useless Elite, which took all the privileges and shouldered fewer and fewer of its responsibilities (thinking thereby they were smart).

Now that the middle classes had their comfortable lives (a home, an income, vacations, ample savings), they wanted something else.

But in the Iran Inc. protected stadium there was no track provided for middle-class participation. Thus it had no hand on the levers of power, no say in the decision-making process, no position available in the polity: all the seats were reserved for a selected minority.

In this Iranian society, torn apart by too abrupt changes, there were other noteworthy new groups. As for example the *Diqanzadehs*, the urban sons of the *Dihqans* (peasants). They too were a vanguard – for the immense peasant masses.

They too were generally amongst the best and brightest of their class. They had the courage to make the rural-urban leap, to sweat it out and to make it in the city (mostly in the construction business). They had kept their roots back in their villages. They still knew only two masters: a temporal one (the landlord) and a spiritual one (the *mulla*). The first one had been irremediably mauled by the 1963 land reform, and only the latter remained (immovable) to refer to.

As for the millions of peasants scattered among Iran's 60,000 villages, they were still in their state of political torpor, fighting it out with Mother Nature, year in and year out, to make ends meet, without running water, electricity and the other amenities of modern life. The land reform scheme had given them tenure over their land and full ownership of their crops – although they still had to pay the landlord the final instalments of the sale or rent of land – but low produce prices had kept them in economic limbo, with the fittest opting for urban migration. No peasant leader emerged and no political association saw the light. Only Arsanjani could have formed a Peasants' Party, but he was dead and could not be replaced. Rural Iran was light years behind urban Iran; the peasants' chances on the national stage stood not on the basis of their rural millions but rather on their urban thousands – the *Dihqanzadehs*.

Some *Dihqanzadehs* were to be found in the lowest social stratum of the shanty town dwellers. There they joined the other *laissez-pour-comptes*, the destitutes, the retarded, the incapable. Together these formed a whole social sub-group attracted by the lights of the city, but incapable of becoming integrated in the city's social fabric. It was a highly unstable stratum, rootless, propertyless and with very little to lose. Numbering hundreds of thousands, these masses were the price Iran Inc. and its landowning elite were ready to pay to keep the price of real estate buoyant in and around Tehran.

(B) The Powers

Since 1954, the US had single-handedly dominated Iranian political life. It had supported Muhammad Reza Shah against all (even friendly) advice. Its only time of doubt seems to have come in 1958, with the General Qaranay incident. Maybe President Kennedy had a plan for changes in Iran (the Shah not being the Kennedys' type of leader), but, even so, it must have been shifted to the President's second term. In Tehran, the American Embassy took all the crucial decisions. American multinationals had first choice of business ventures in Iran; American banks (especially Chase) received the lion's share of Iranian petrodollar deposits. The Americans failed to see the ever-widening difference between Iran and the Pahlavis; furthermore they thought (erroneously) that controlling the top man meant controlling the whole. With time, the US had become one of the tripods on which the Iran Inc. pyramid rested.

After Tabriz, the American diplomats and agents in Iran should have realised that something had given way, that drastic change in Tehran was needed. But even after a quarter of a century running their 'Iranian Clinic' they were still too inexperienced, and proved it now by failing to realise the magnitude of the events at Tabriz. They thought that they knew everything because they had the money, the agents (CIA and SAVAK, at least) and the power. They couldn't ever imagine that the 'sheepish' Iranians would ever dream of trying to overthrow the awe-inspiring Iran Inc. pyramid. With their arrogance and displaced sense of superiority, they had made no friends in Iran, or very few; and this latter handful had taken advantage of their gullibility to get their dollars. The Americans never seem to understand the East – it doesn't seem to fit into their 'bottom line' theories. Over twenty-five years they had failed to learn what makes the Iranians tick. They were not interested: they had the Shah, the SAVAK and the military machine. That was enough. What did they need the Iranians for?

And they had failed to learn the multiple lessons of Vietnam and to apply them in Iran. Fortunately for the Iranians, in 1978 the Americans were still reeling from the emotional and spiritual shock of the Vietnam War; if not, they could have used their 50,000 nationals stationed in Iran to intervene directly after Tabriz "to protect US military advisers and civilians in danger". The Vietnam Syndrome, however, and the slogan 'No More Vietnams' was perhaps the prime determining motive in American foreign policy. Naturally, had American Marines and GIs intervened in Iran the outcome would have been the same as in Vietnam, for the Iranians would have won eventually anyway, as they always have in the past – but with their brains not with weapons, like the Vietnamese.

The other superpower, the USSR, had never been happy with the Americans ruling the soft Iranian underbelly.

Given economic incentives (i.e. the steel mill, the natural gas) of IGAT I and soon IGAT II), the Soviets kept from interfering too much. They would have relished, however, seeing the Americans somehow ousted from Iran (if only to redress the superpower imbalance there). The Soviet Union didn't have the capability to do it itself, having long since lost its pawns in Iran; furthermore it had backed the wrong strategy in the Third World since it still lived in the "âge archéo-impérial des systèmes d'alliances coûteux et formels", while the West "explore l'âge impérial des réseaux, invisibles et omniprésents".[19] But it could still assist in the expulsion process, engaging its few remaining agents and its disciplined troops, the *Toudeh* rank and file, on the side of opposition.

The third Power in Iran was Great Britain. The British still had a great deal of power in Iran. Three hundred years of continuous intercourse could not be erased in twenty-five years – especially for people as long-term minded as the British. They had endured seeing a fresh, inexperienced superpower unwilling to heed their advice come in and usurp their place, not even allowing them to play second fiddle. After all, the British knew Iran and Iranians as did no one else. Statesmen and scholars such as Lord Curzon, Professor Browne, Sir Reader Bullard, Professor Gibb and Professor Lambton, to name but a few, had spent the better part of their lives studying the land and its inhabitants. In Iran, Great Britain had roots – friends, allies and servants – and more so than any other Power. British hands had always been present in times of danger to straighten out what needed straightening. Now, at a time when the American monopoly over Iran was on the verge of being threatened, it was clear that Great Britain was in the wings waiting to grasp the occasion for a comeback, to regain the position of prominence on the Iranian stage which was her natural role.

In its bid for a place in the Persian sun, the British had a unique weapon: the BBC. 'Radio London', as it was known throughout Iran, was an unique institution whose wavelengths had caught the nimble minds of Iranians with its anti-Reza Shah broadcasts of 1941. Since then, the large majority of Iranians not only listened to its Farsi programmes, but believed whatever it said and believed its word to be official British policy. As Ambassador Anthony Parsons put it in his memoirs:

> ...Even the Shah himself argued that 'the people' were convinced that the views of Radio London were the views of HMG... the Shah [further] argued that the Persian [BBC] broadcasts were helping to convince the people that the British were playing around the opposition ('the people' obviously included himself). I

lost my temper. ...The mullahs themselves believed that they had British support which we were expressing through Radio London...[20]

The BBC, however, was not the only British iron in the fire. Britain could still rely on scores of capable and dedicated Iranian agents such as the *Rashidians*[21] (of *Murdad 28* and Shahinshahr fame); could still rely on first-class Iranologists who had graduated under Professor Lambton; could still rely on widespread support in the population at large, whether urban, rural or tribal; could still rely on the good relations it had kept up with the religious and the *Bazaar* since the early twentieth century (i.e. the Constitutional Movement). But all these joined together did not add up to the power wielded by the BBC, which entered Iranian homes daily and informed all family members about the day's events, analysing the facts, interviewing specialists and telling them about the next day's programmes.

In the wake of Great Britain came the other European powers of West Germany and France. The Germans had the most difficult hand to play as they were *de facto* American allies. Since Von Lilienfeld's departure from Tehran, however, a marked revision in the German approach had come about and the Ten Nights of Poetry at the Goethe Institut were a sign of the new German line. And the Germans had important economic interests to defend, ranking second only to the USA among exporters to Iran (see Table 17.1). The French had also been involved in Iran since the eighteenth century, peaking in the early nineteenth century under Napoleon (with the General Gardane mission). Since then, they had always operated in the shadow of British power. They too had long-standing interests in Iran, especially in archæology, at Shoush (Susa) initiated by Dieulafoy; and in architecture, with André Godard (Reza Shah's chief museum builder, from 1928 until 1939). Politically, the French didn't weigh heavily in Iran, but, nevertheless, their networks (especially hinging on Franco-Iranian matrimonial links) could render valuable services when needed. Finally, they had their unique newspaper institution of *Le Monde* for exceptional occasions.

The last (but not least) foreign player in Iran was Israel. The Israelis had made great strides in just three decades, buying anyone they thought useful, from the old Qajar Elitists needing cash to the minor journalist able to gather relevant information. Money used

Table 17.1. The Western Powers and Japan in Iran (in 1978): Level of Exports, Oil Imports and Number of Nationals in Iran.[22]

Country	Exports ($ millions)	Oil Imports mb/d	Iran's Share	Nationals in Iran
USA	3,684	554	9%	50,000
Gt Britain	1,440	184	12%	10,000
W. Germany	3,381	346	12%	9,000
France	881	209	8%	6,000
Japan	2,719	805	16%	3,500
Total	12,105	2,098		78,500

* Total Western expatriate population in Iran was estimated at around 90,000 individuals in 1978.

came essentially from rich Jewish families and from Mossad.

As in the Powers' cases, Israel had sent its best and brightest to Tehran in the mid-fifties, with Uriel (Uri) Lubrani to head its covert mission. The wily Lubrani was among the first to realise that the Iran Inc. party was over, and to say so, announcing in 1974, "that the Shah's regime might be entering its final days".[23] Under Lubrani, the Israeli policy of total support for the Shah had progressively been reversed, because (1) the Shah had failed to attack Iraq and destroy its military preparations, making it lose a decade or two in its arming process and (2) Lubrani saw no future in the Pahlavi rule.[24]

Many believe that the Israelis had a free ride in Iran on American coat-tails. That was not so. Time and again the Israelis had proposed to the Americans that they let them take the lead in Iran because it was in their sphere of influence and they knew the region better. But the Americans who had failed to listen to their British allies would not pay heed to the Israelis' alarming messages.

With its infiltration of SAVAK, its own large Jewish network in Iran and its separate network of paid Iranians, the Israelis were well-placed to play a major role in Iran. They would bring all their weight into play during the events of 1978/79. And the royalists who were absolutely sure that the Israelis would never support Islamic mobs were in for a surprise.

(C) Elites and Counter-Elites

At Tabriz, ready or not, the opposition had crossed its Rubicon: from then on there was no shying away from total confrontation with Iran Inc., especially because, for the first time since 1963, the regime's vulnerability had been exposed. For many members of the counter-elites it was clearly a note of hope after many years of doubt passed watching Iranian society drowning in the pool of petrodollars. Many counter-elitists saw the first ray of hope and, sensing the wind in its sails, the ship of opposition gained speed and self-confidence.

Having barely mounted the saddle, the petrodollar elite had already lost its mental resources. The fresh elite of the 1970s had joined and then been assimilated into the Pahlavi Elite at the worst time possible. The latter was washed-out, being at the same time too rich and too corrupt, whereas the former thought and dreamt only of petrodollars which it transferred to its Swiss bank accounts. The elite dominating Iran was a cesspool of greed, unscrupulousness and misplaced Machiavellianism, with no inclination to working for a common goal or the common good, only 'me'. In 1978, it was clear that something was wrong within Iran's first class: an aroma of staleness was starting to emanate from its whole structure.[25]

Facing this amorphous and corroding structure, the forces of opposition were full of vitality and hope. The intelligentsia was already left behind by the Tabriz events, but it would still operate as the opposition's mouthpiece. The students and the religious mobs were getting ready to enter the arena, spearheading the opposition's actions in the streets because, in the aftermath of Tabriz, it was clear that henceforward the main battlefield would be Iran's urban streets.

In a contrary position to the regime, the opposition had troops but as yet no leader. Hajj Sayyid Javadi, the journalist critic, had managed to lead the movement during its war of words against the regime, but, with Tabriz, a new chapter had been opened in the struggle and now foot soldiers would be required, and a leader to lead them in battle. The leader would have to be either a guerrilla warrior or a clergyman (from either of the opposition's two main wings); as the majority of the guerrillas had been exterminated by SAVAK, the opportunity lay at the door of the clergy, but here too none of the Grand Ayatullahs seemed to be able wear the shoes.

(4) The Oil Factor

In October 1979, the Consortium Agreement of 1954 came to an end. Consequently, after a quarter of century of calm on the oil front, this crucial national vector made a comeback into the limelight. A complete reappraisal of the Iran-Consortium relationship had become unavoidable before that time, especially because the 1973 Twenty Years Sales Agreement had proven a poor working tool. An attempted revision in August 1976 had ended in stalemate, and by 1977 it was "already 80% outdated and inoperative".[26] The Consortium had perforce to fall back on the 1954 Agreement, which provided for three five-year extensions. A way had to be found out of the quagmire.

The man to find it on the Iranian side was the new NIOC tsar, Dr Iqbal's successor: Houshang Ansari. On the sidelines since August 1977, Ansari was offered the post after Iqbal passed away on November 25. It was under his direction that the first round of preliminary talks began in Tehran on January 30, 1978 between NIOC and the consortium. Led by the BP managing director John Sutcliffe, the Consortiumteam managed to compile an agenda for the second round of talks, envisaged for early March. However, before this second round, Ansari staged a small internal revolution in NIOC by appointing, on February 15, two of his former aides, namely Engineer Farrukh Najmabadi and Dr Hasan Âli Mihran, as his top deputies for technical and administrative affairs respectively.

This abrupt decision incensed the whole NIOC family, from the directors down to the junior managers: it was a political stab in the back for the professional oilmen. Discontented grumblings could heard throughout the industry. Dr Muhammad Âli Nabigh, the highly capable NIOC director for Exploration and Production (and NIOC's natural leader) resigned on the spot; Dr Parviz Mina, NIOC's director for International Affairs (and a company pillar), was eased into early retirement after airing his displeasure in public. Thus, due to the Ansari coup, NIOC was losing two of its ablest professionals in one go (neither Najmabadi nor Mihran were of their calibre). It almost lost its director for Refining, Majid Tabataba'i Diba (the 1972-74 Abadan Refinery general manager), but the latter was put under intense political pressure by the court (as he was related to the Empress) and eventually accepted working under the Najmabadi-Mihran duo. In the process Ansari had lost all of the goodwill he might have had in the company: no one had bothered to tell him that there was slight friction between NIOC and the Ministry of Economy. He had always had a free hand and he was free to do as he pleased.

As scheduled, the NIOC team, led by Dr Mihran, met the Consortiumrepresentative at Tehran from March 4 until 14. This second round of talks failed to yield any palpable result. The third round, held in April, did not improve the situation. A tour of Iran by BP chairman David Steel (accompanied by John Sutcliffe) in June, which included meetings with the Shah and NIOC officials, failed to settle the issue. A fourth round (June 28-July 10) and a fifth one (July 29-August 2) confirmed the deadlock. With the change of government in August 1978, Ansari decided to reshuffle NIOC's top echelon: he discarded his two deputies and replaced them with Tabataba'i Diba as sole deputy; he also named a fresh eleven-man NIOC board of directors, calling to the fore in-house managers,[27] trying to counter the harm he had done in February - but without success.

The sixth round of NIOC-Consortium talks began on September 9 in Tehran. The NIOC team was led by Tabataba'i Diba. For a whole week the two sides reviewed critical issues, and only agreement on minor points were achieved, the six major bones of contention[28] remaining unsettled:

(1) Discounts given to the Consortium

NIOC discounts amounted to 22 US cents per barrel (c/B). From this amount some 8 c/B had to be deducted for the consortium's prepayment of its share (40%) of Khuzistan's oil fields' development costs (in short-term interest-free loans to NIOC) - left unpaid since 1975. In comparison, ARAMCO's discounts were 18-19 c/B: the 4-5 c/B gap proved unbridgeable.

(2) The Most Favoured Nation Clause

NIOC was adamant on this point: it deemed fundamental that any terms given to other exporters should apply to Iran too. The company failed to convince the Consortium on this point.

(3) Consortium liftings

The minimum was set at a level of 3.3m b/d. NIOC proposed a +/- 10% divergence for every quarter; the Consortium offered a 12-13 c/B penalty for underliftings, which proved unsatisfactory to NIOC.

(4) Agreement Life

The Consortium went for the full fifteen years' extension, but settled for the first five years. One of the rare settlements.

(5) NGL Pricing

NIOC was incensed by the gross underpricing of NGL products from Bandar-i Mahshahr, based on the finished cost. NIOC insisted on Gulf posted prices for NGL, with no success.

(6) Abadan Refinery Fuel Oil

This was a headache for NIOC which proposed that the Consortium lift all of it off, but the latter refused. Another unsettled issue.

The sixth round of NIOC-Consortium negotiations ended without a settlement on September 15. At that stage, the Consortium members were not going to bend overbackwards to please NIOC because its Khuzistan oil province was not what it had been. If it had been another Saudi Arabia, the Consortium would have settled for sure, but it was not. It was likely that hints during the negotiations should have awakened the NIOC team to the realities of the moment, but without Dr Nabigh and Dr Mina the Iranians were almost helpless.

If he was meeting little success in the Consortium negotiations, Ansari was indulging in his favourite pastime: wheeling and dealing. He entered into talks with the Bechtel Company of San Francisco (a company which had tried all the tricks to get a foothold in Iran like its Fluor and Parsons sisters, but without any luck so far) and the Munich high-tech outfit of Messerschmitt-Boelkow-Blohm (MBB). Within a four-month span, Ansari engineered three major joint venture agreements involving these two companies:

(1) In June 1978, he formed the Iranian Advanced Technology Company (IATEC), with Iranian institutions (namely NIOC, IDRO, Bank-i Ûmran and the Science and Industry University[29]) holding 65% and MBB 35%.

(2) In July 1978, the Iran Engineering and Construction Company (IECC) was formed, with NIOC (29%), IDRO (22%) and Bechtel (49%).

(3) In September 1978, the Iran Oil Investments Company (IOIC) with an initial capital of $55m, was set up for joint investments in non-oil affairs, with NIOC (50%), Bechtel (30%) and MBB (20%).

The establishment of these joint ventures based on Bechtel and MBB could not hide the fact that Iran's oil question was left unanswered. Ansari could still have attempted to save the Iran Inc. pyramid from the opposition tidal wave, but the chief questions were whether he wanted to, and whether he had the vision to take the drastic steps necessary. His initial NIOC management gambit with Najmabadi and Mihran had shown that even he was more interested in personal affairs then in playing the saviour to a beleaguered Iran Inc.

17.4. Early Skirmishes

On March 21, 1978, the Fifth National Development Plan came to a close amidst a cacophony of contradictory statements.

Instead of the usual triumph, repeating *ad nauseam* the Plan's brilliant achievements in mass media, the regime had taken precautions to hush up the transition to the Sixth Plan.

The Plan and Budget Organisation (PBO) was at a loss over tracking down the myriad uncompleted Fifth Plan projects. The best it could produce was a rough summary of its revenues and expenditures (see Table 17.2).

Table 17.2. Summary of the Fifth Plan's Revenues and Expenditure.[30]
(Figures in $ billions)

Revenues		Expenditures	
Oil & Gas	98.1	Development Projects	49.8
Taxes	17.9	Current Credits	42.5
Loans & Bonds	2.2	Investments Abroad	11.0
Miscellaneous	4.5	Miscellaneous	19.4
Total	122.7	Total	122.7

As for the Sixth Plan, kicked off in August 1976 by the Shah himself with strict orders to the PBO to be "concentrating on basic objectives" and "avoiding temporary showcase projects", it proved yet another planning fiasco. Some 2,500 PBO experts, subdivided into sixty-one sub-committees, had toiled for eighteen months to produce its guidelines. During 1977 the spotlight had been on the Macro-Economic Sub-Committee, headed by macro-economics tsar Firouz Vakil. The PBO's economists, working on a rudimentary model – based on a minimum level of foreign exchange reserves and a double-check of available private and public resources to influence set sectoral growth values and oil production levels – simulated a myriad scenarios: the final choice fell on a $210.7bn envelope (and a preliminary $341bn for the Seventh Plan[30] – optimists never die!) with an average GNP growth rate of 8.6% per annum (see Table 17.3 for preliminary Sixth Plan figures). But the Shah knew that after the Fifth Plan quagmire these figures impressed no one any longer; he ordered all these estimates to be shelved and had the PBO declare that it would henceforward focus on completing the half-finished projects of the Fifth Plan. The proverb 'better late than never' did not apply to this rational decision, which came much too late.

Table 17.3. Summary of the Projected Sixth Plan Revenues and Expenditures.[30]
(Figures in $ billions)

Revenues		Expenditures	
Oil & Gas	128.6	Development Projects	79.6
Taxes	58.8	Current Credits	108.0
Loans & Bonds	10.6	Investments Abroad	3.5
Miscellaneous	12.7	Miscellaneous	19.6
Total	210.7	Total	210.7

By March 1978, development plans were totally eclipsed by social disturbances on Iran's streets. As the regime failed to find an original solution to its planning woes, the imaginative opposition had struck on the *chihileh* idea for disturbances, thus giving its troops the time to breathe before major riots.

The opposition decided to strike at Yazd on the fortieth day after the Tabriz martyrs fell on March 30,. There the religious mobs, mobilised by Ayatullah Saduqi and *Hujjat ul-Islam* Ganjeh'i, spilled into the streets. Violent clashes, centring on Yazd's Pahlavi Square, took place between the people and the armed forces. Many civilian casualties resulted. On the same day riots hit the southern town of Jahrum. Not only had the cycle of *chihilehs* been kept cooking but the religious mobs, not the guerilla groups or the intelligensia, had led the rioting. In the wake of Yazd, some seven other Iranian centres saw popular action on April 2 and 3, with Kermanshah, where the Youth Palace was set ablaze and at least eight bank branches were wrecked, standing out.[31] The official number of killed rioters stood at five, while the opposition claimed seventy martyrs – the truth being, as usual, somewhere in between.

On April 5, as the universities reopened after the *Nourouz* recess, ebullience immediately set in. The students were in no mood for studying. They had smelled blood and found the regime highly vulnerable. Even if other opposition groups suddenly deserted the struggle, they would fight on: never before had they been given such a favourable opportunity. Tehran University (TU) students refused to attend classes, staging daily sit-ins and mini-riots on campus. Other centres, such as Aryamihr and the Polytechnic in Tehran, as well as Tabriz, Isfahan and Mashhad universities, followed suit. The students new *cri de guerre* was "Free our political prisoners!" On May 9, when the *chihileh* of the Yazd martyrs fell, the religious wing was not ready so the task of carrying the anti-regime standard fell on the TU students. And carry it they did. For the whole day the TU campus was the scene of running battles between students and paratroopers; students even dared to go out of the campus boundaries to break cinema windows and wreck bank branches in the neighbourhood, and many casualties resulted when the troops had to open fire. On the Tabriz and Isfahan campuses similar incidents occurred. A total of thirteen martyred students were reported, two of them at Tabriz; as Governor General Shafaqat told the press:

> ...the police having dealt with a maximum of moderation ...was forced to shoot salvos in the air to intimidate the trouble-makers, unfortunately [sic] killing two of them in the process...[32]

It was at this juncture that the long-forgotten Ayatullah Khomeini made a forceful comeback. During his fourteen years at Najaf, the patient clergyman had remained silent; now the time was deemed ripe to speak out, for the opposition's snowball in Iran had developed into a size which now made it unstoppable. Khomeini accorded an historic interview to Lucien Georges of *Le Monde* (the paper always in the right place at the right time!) which was published on April 6 under the title 'Les dernièrs émeuts sont les premices d'une gigantesque explosion'.[33] Khomeini's declarations were those of a leader: no compromise with the Pahlavis or with the Communists, the ultimate goal being the creation of an Islamic state. The seventy-six year old Ayatullah was the first opposition leader to have clearly spelt out his programme. A translation of the *Le Monde* article was widely circulated in Tehran. Not only had he solidly erected his tent amidst the opposition ranks, but he had also stolen a march on all of the other senior clergymen who might have competed with him for the leadership of the religious crowds – the Grand Ayatullahs of Qum, Shariâtmadari, Gulpaygani and Marâshi Najafi; the Ayatullahs Khwu'i at Najaf and Qumi[34] at Mashhad; and the Imam Musa Sadr, the charismatic leader of Lebanon's *Shiîtes*.

So far the regime had made little attempt to counter the opposition's punches. In early spring, however, it decided to take the offensive by forming the *Kumiteh Iqdam-i Milli* (the National Action Committee – NAC) and placing the revenant Âbd ul-Majid Majidi at its head. Public opinion soon recognised the NAC for what it really was: a covert paramilitary organisation for harassing opposition leaders.[35] Soon the bombs placed outside the homes of Engineers Mihdi Bazargan, Dariush Furouhar, Dr Karim Sanjabi and Engineer Rahmatullah Muqaddam Maragheh'i, as well as the beatings of Dr Lahiji (the lawyer) and Dr Payman (the dentist) were linked to NAC. In parallel with the formation of the NAC, the Shah, probably advised by Ardashir Zahidi,[36] ordered the creation of two other five-member committees: the first to whip up royalist demonstrations (headed by General Husayn Fardoust, with General Ghulam Riza Uvaysi, courtier

Amir Aslan Afshar, Grand Master of Ceremonies, businessman Ahanchian and General Parviz Khusrouvani); the second to deal with propaganda (headed by former editor Amin Ashrafi, with the influence-peddler Byuk Sabir, the courtier Amir Muttaqi, deputy Court Minister, and two former *Majlis* deputies, Shams Qanatabadi, Ayatullah Kashani's lieutenant, and Dr Hasan Matin[37]). Neither of the committees would succeed: the first had no troops to lead and the second was far too mediocre to perform any useful propaganda.

Two incidents might have been approved by the above committees. The first occurred at Qum on May 10, when paratroopers of the *Nouhid* division, on a punitive mission, shot dead two young *tullabs* in the house of Ayatullah Shariâtmadari (an inviolable sanctuary according to tradition); one of them, twenty-two year old Sattar Kashan had a long career of anti-royalist activities.[38] The second incident happened on May 18, when special police forces surrounded some two hundred hikers on the slopes above Tehran, attacked them with ropes and gave them a sound thrashing.

While using the stick of his newly formed action groups, the Shah decided in mid-May to open a liberalisation campaign to please what he called "his silent majority": he launched the *Faza-yi Baz-i Syasi* (the Open Political Horizon). Imagining that he had nothing to lose and everything to win at this stage by letting the people vent their frustrations, the Shah bestowed a liberty which was a *de facto* reality since Tabriz. The act's only tangible benefit for the people was the flow of books flooding Tehran's streets.[39] At Najaf, Ayatullah Khomeini was quick to pounce on the opening offered by the royal declaration with a message rapidly copied and distributed through Tehran: "Who is he [the Shah] to afford freedom? Freedom is the people's: it was bestowed by God, and thus allowed by Islam".[40] In the same message, he asked the people to commemorate the 1963 martyrs on June 5 (a date the religious leader carried in his heart). The Tehran Association of Struggling Clergymen (TASC) and the Tehran *Bazaar* issued a communiqué calling for business closures on June 5. From Mashhad, Ayatullah Qumi called for a general strike, and the LMI published a leaflet entitled *Civil Servants: Now it is up to You!*, exhorting bureaucrats to strike *en masse*. The whole *Bazaar* was closed down, but the number of strikers on June 5 remained low and the regime failed to take the threat seriously. It should have done, however, because it was clear that the LMI dons were trying to destabilise the weakest leg of the Iran Inc. tripod: its bureaucracy. The Shah should have foreseen that he could live without the *Bazaar* and the mosques, but it was vital for him to keep his Iran Inc. tripod intact. On US support he would wager anything, on his armed forces as well, but the bureaucracy needed special attention, especially when the opposition was trying to lure away his civil servants.

Then, on June 6, Muhammad Reza Shah made an important blunder: he sacked SAVAK's top two men. SAVAK's chief, General Nîmatullah Nasiri, was appointed Ambassador to Pakistan and left on June 17; his number two, General Âli Mûtazid, was made Ambassador to Syria, leaving on August 5. Nasiri was replaced at SAVAK by his number three, General Nasir Muqaddam. The sacking of Nasiri was catastrophic: on the one hand it sent shockwaves through the Iran Inc. pyramid as every officer ran for cover, for, if the trusted Nasiri could be dismissed, no one was safe; and on the other, it sent waves of jubilation through the ranks of the opposition, who had always considered Nasiri the hated symbol of the regime. The Shah should have known better than to dismiss his trusted lieutenants, for, if he thought thereby to place the blame on them, he was in for a surprise, and if he thought that he was thus gaining time he was in for yet another surprise, since, as Sir Winston Churchill said: "You cannot feed all around to the crocodiles in the hopes that they'll eat you last".

A few weeks later, it was the turn of the *Baha'i* businessman Huzhabrullah Yazdani to be arrested. The fifty-three year old Simnani had benefited during his meteoric business career from the backing of General Ayadi at court.[41] The former shepherd had diversified into industry (purchasing the Isfahan Sugar Factory and placing Jahangir Kia at its head) and finance (his purchase of his Bank-i Sadirat shares had created a furore, forcing him to resell them). In May 1978, Yazdani was back for an encore with his acquisition of 54% of Iranians' Bank shares, paying Citibank $12.85million for 25% of them (the US bank only retaining a 5% token). In August he was indicted for "land-grabbing" and released on a Rls1600m ($23m) bail. But the Shah had thus upset his strong *Baha'i* wing and all the other (Armenian, Jewish and Zoroastrian) minorities without pleasing anyone, least of all his opposition. As Bismark put it: "Never try to please the opposition, the opposition is never pleased".

While trying to please the opposition, the Shah was also looking around for fresh alternatives. One candidate was the former prime minister Dr Âli Amini. Although aged seventy-three, Amini still had to be reckoned with, especially as he was at the head of the old Qajar Elite (which, since Âlam's death, seemed united again). During the summer, he was back in the headlines, giving interviews to all and sundry; in a July 27 outburst he had even proposed "a Government of national unity to safeguard freedom", with himself (of course) at its head. Another candidate was the highly ambitious Dr Houshang Nahavandi. Only forty-eight years old, Nahavandi had formed his own group in early spring with the Shah's tacit assent, dubbed Study Group for Investigating Iranian Problems stemming from the 'Shah-People' Revolution. Thus Nahavandi hoped to duplicate Mansur's feat of the 1960s, but, unfortunately for him (incidentally he had been the youngest minister in Mansur's ill-fated cabinet at the age of thirty-four), the 1970s were not propitious for such transparent endeavours. When Nahavandi proposed to the fossilised *Rastakhiz* party that his study group should form its third wing, he was politely but firmly rebuffed. Having an official monopoly, the unique party would not act as a ladder to outsiders' ambitions, especially now that it had ambitions of its own, aiming to recruit 'young, intellectual civil servants' as its new blood. The only problem was that the party apparatchiks would neither split party funds (generously provided by the government at the rate of Rls2000m per annum) nor share effective power with the newcomers. In any case the massive state subsidy was theirs to munch at, whether the youngsters joined or not.

Fortunately for the regime, the months of June and July were rather calm, as though the opposition were tiring of not gaining a palpable result for its sacrifices. Even the successful cycle of *chihilehs* lapsed without anyone paying notice, as on June 18 the fortieth day after the death of the May 9 martyrs was not commemorated. The only events worth mentioning were more troubles in the illegal house-building movement outside city limits (encouraged by leftist guerrillas), an open letter to the Prime Minister signed by one hundred and eighty-four journalists protesting against censorship (a sure sign that the Misbahzadeh-Masûdi duo was losing its grip on the press), and, finally, the news that the Shah had secretly ordered that "all business dealings by members of the royal family should be stopped"[42]. This was yet another move that came much too late to do any good, especially as the family had still had the time to transfer their assets abroad, and did so in the breathing space.[43]

Meanwhile the universities were buoyant with students continuously pouring fuel on the fire. On June 1, widespread disorders in the TU dormitory at Amirabad resulted in clashes with security forces: one student was killed and six arrested and held incommunicado.[44] At Tabriz University clashes between police and students were frequent; a young female student who took refuge in the rector's room was bayoneted in front of the Rector himself. The latter, Dr Murtazavi, took the first plane to Tehran to hand over his resignation to the Minister of Education:[45] there were still rectors with backbone in Iran.

The last minor event of June was the dissenting voices of two deputies in the *Majlis*: those of Ahmad Bani Ahmad (a centrist deputy from Tabriz) and Muhsin Pizishkpour, the extreme-rightist leader of the former Pan-Iranist party (a deputy from Khurramshahr). The regime was first taken aback by this mini-revolt in its *Rastakhiz* assembly, its two hundred and sixty-eight members having been thoroughly filtered. On June 29, Minister of Information Dariush Humayoun gave in to the pressure by officially announcing that "political parties other than Rastakhiz would be tolerated".

Four former Pan-Iranists – Dr Muhammad Riza Âmili Tihrani, Dr Husayn Tabib, Parviz Zafari and Manouchihr Yazdi – rallied behind their leader Pizishkpour to reform the Pan-Iranist Party and jump into the political fray. Maybe the regime had calculated that setting the extreme right free (the five and Bani Ahmad being a minority of six against a majority of two hundred and sixty-two) might help it at this juncture; if so, it should have appreciated that a first crack (however minor) in the Iran Inc. monolith at that time was extremely detrimental to its external image and its morale.

In July, with the universities closed down, things were calm, with the only noises coming from the *Majlis*. During the last week of July, however, the Navvab Religious School at Mashhad staged violent riots which compelled the security forces to intervene and resulted in some forty casualties.[46] During the month secret comings and goings between Tehran and Qum had been going on, for the regime was trying for a *modus vivendi* with the conservative troika at Qum (led by Ayatullah Shariâtmadari). The conservative clergymen wanted free elections or at least the Shah's official assurance that they would be totally free. On Constitution Day, August 5, the Shah obliged, declaring that the 1979 *Majlis* elections "would be 100% free". Muhammad Reza Shah had lost a golden opportunity to cast the whole opposition into disarray by proposing free elections for the autumn of 1978. One after the other, chances to grab the offensive from the opposition passed away, and, if the Shah didn't seem realise that, neither did any of his top advisers.

17.5. Tilting Scales

Among the larger Iranian cities, Isfahan had been amongst the most buoyant since early spring. Being a traditionally religious city with a large university and a unique cultural heritage, Isfahan was a special case. In April and May, university students had repeatedly clashed on campus with special security commandos. On June 15 a revolt by political prisoners in an Isfahani jail had resulted in the death of one of them, Murtaza Baba'i.[47] Then on August 5, on Constitution Day, people had spilled into the streets creating havoc although police were able to re-establish order in a few hours. Isfahan though, was still ebullient and on August 11 the city erupted in a way similar to Tabriz on February 19: bank branches were destroyed, liquor shops ravaged and cinema windows shattered. People even assaulted the Shah Abbas Hotel and damaged parts of it. Large trees in the main avenues were felled to hamper the circulation of army vehicles. Officially the day's toll was four dead (unofficially four times that) and sixty-six injured. The whole city was running out of control as dusk fell. There was no alternative left but to impose martial law: curfew was declared at 20:00 (until 06:00), with General Riza Naji appointed as martial law commander. On the morrow martial law was extended to Najafabad, Shahriza and Humayounshahr, three towns in the vicinity of Isfahan (and always in harmony with it). Shiraz almost made the list, but last minute machine-gunning of rioters at the New mosque brought calm to the southern city. For the religious branch of the opposition the happenings at Isfahan were a real victory: it had forced the regime to declare martial law and station the army on the streets – a measure the regime was always been reluctant to take, with the last time this had occurred being in June 1963.

By forcing the establishment of martial law the Isfahani religious activists, prominent among whom were the Ayatullahs Tahiri and Khadimi (both with secret links to Khomeini), had with one shot achieved two major triumphs for their colours: a decisive victory against the regime and a first place for the religious sector among the opposition's ranks. The idiosyncracies of Isfahan and its people had helped in creating disorder on a large scale. Again, the armed forces had been totally unable to quell the riots; in the five and a half months since Tabriz they had failed utterly to adapt themselves to the new environment. Isfahan was thus the first time that the opposition forces had scored against the regime during the summer, forcing the latter on to the defensive.

On the evening of August 19, the Rex Cinema at Abadan was set ablaze. With all the exit doors locked and no key available to open them, the movie-house turned into an inferno within minutes. Firefighters were slow to arrive and, once on the spot, they failed to find a functioning water hydrant. When a door was finally broken down it was far too late: some three hundred and seventy-seven people inside had been burnt to death. Only half a dozen spectators had been able to flee via the roof.

A catastrophe of unprecedented proportions had hit Abadan: the town was horrified, a whole nation was shocked. People across Iran were emotionally overwhelmed by the Abadan tragedy. It could have been their town, their cinema, their family! The question on all lips was 'Who could have done it?'

Well, either the opposition or the regime. The opposition's minds and pens were the first to shoot: they dubbed the Rex tragedy "the Shah's private barbecue". Muhammad Reza Shah had the misfortune (or imprudence) to use the expression "*Vahshat-i Buzurg*" (the Great Terror) at a press conference in Saâdabad Palace on August 17, accusing "the Communists of offering the Great Terror".[48] Journalist Hajj Sayyid Javadi, always ready, exploited the royal blunder in a scorching editorial ending with this scathing attack:

> ...The perpetrator of the Great Terror, Great Frauds, Great Prisons and Great Tortures should be brought to trial and sentenced for his abominable crimes...[49]

This conclusion should be compared to the mild (and polite) criticism of Sayyid Javadi's initial letters (of 1976) in order to measure the formidable ground covered in the people's minds during the past months. Naturally, the majority of the people came to believe the opposition, distrustful as they were of any declaration emanating from official mouthpieces.

After the Abadan fiasco, Premier Amuzigar had to go. His exit was long overdue, for he should have resigned after Tabriz. Amuzigar had totally failed in his post-Huvayda mission, and the short year in which he had held power had not been propitious for the regime he was supposed to shore up; neither a very able technocrat nor a born politician, Amuzigar had not even been able to retain the *status quo*. On August 22 he was told that his time was up and two days later he tendered his resignation, being replaced by Engineer Jâfar Sharif Imami.

In 1978, the Muslim fasting month of *Ramadan* happened to begin on August 6. Tehran's leading religious leaders had prepared themselves to deliver suitable nightly sermons in their respective mosques. For example, at the Quba mosque, Dr Mufattih had invited prominent speakers such as Bazargan, Dr Mumkin, and his younger colleagues Khamneh'i and Bahunar. Night after night in the mosques, attendance grew noisier. From August 15, scuffles occurred between religious crowds coming out of the mosques (e.g. the Lurzadeh, the Imam Husayn and the Azarbayjani mosques). The religious sector was flexing its muscles.

It was during this *Ramadan* upswing that the religious faction lost their main underground leader, Sayyid Âli Andarzgou,* on August 24. On his way to visit Hajj Akbar Salihi, a Tehran *Bazaar* merchant, Andarzgou was intercepted by SAVAK agents on Iran Street and shot dead. On August 26, for the commemoration of Imam Âli's (A.S.) martyrdom, religious crowds took to the streets in Tehran, Qum (where at least ten people were injured) and Mashhad.

* SAYYID ÂLI ANDARZGOU (1939–1978), son of preacher Sayyid Asadullah; attended religious schools; joined Sadiq Amani's group in the Tehran *Bazaar* (1962); took part in Premier Mansur's assassination (1965); only group member able to escape; sentenced to death *in absentia*; formed major religious guerrilla group, became expert in disguises (1965–1978); travelled widely to Afghanistan and

Lebanon; married (1970) and had four sons; barely escaped when betrayed by traitor Majid Fayyaz; received anti-tank weapons from Palestinian *Al Fath* (early 1978); fell to SAVAK bullets on August 24, 1978.

Encouraged by the *Ramadan* developments, the Tehran religious leaders decided to count their troops on the last day of the month, the holiday of *Âyd-i Fitr*. All Muslims were invited to attend mass prayers led by Dr Mufattih on the hills of Qaytariyyeh. Thousands showed up. After the prayers, the flock began its slow descent towards the city centre, chanting religious slogans, amassing further thousands along its way, while police forces looked on without intervening. A crowd estimated at around 150-200,000 people made it to Tehran University to listen to the sermon of *hujjat ul-Islam* Hadi Ghaffari, the son of the martyred Ayatullah Ghaffari. The day ended without a single shot being fired and no windows being broken. With this unprecedented peaceful march through Tehran, the religious party had scored on all sides by proving to the world that the masses followed them and that they, in turn, could manage them. By their remarkable feat of September 4, the religious had propelled their leaders to the front line of opposition.

Carried away by their unexpected success, the religious sector decided to follow through with an encore on September 7, for they were used to pushing their luck to the hilt. Invited by the Tehran Association of Struggling Clergymen (TASC), some 300,000 to 400,000 people spread across Shah Reza Avenue on that Thursday. Police and army trucks were parked along the avenue, standing idly by while people pushed roses into their gun barrels. Although the slogans were already more radical than on the *Âyd* march, the major refrain concerned Khomeini's leadership, for example: "Iran is our country, Khomeini our leader". Again the whole march was a peaceful success. The religious leaders decided to hold the next one on the following day and passed word at the end of the day that on Friday September 8 the mass march would begin at Zhaleh Square. During the night of September 7, Tehran was ebullient: groups of youngsters dressed in loose shirts, blue jeans and tennis shoes criss-crossed the streets, preceded by the usual swarm of motorcycles. They carried banners and chanted slogans. Tehran was celebrating Sacred Time;

its streets belonged to Iran's youth (mainly students), and everything was possible.

While Iran's youth was celebrating on the streets, the Iran Inc. top echelon, having woken up to the ominous threat of the marches' cycle, was gathered around the Shah in Niavaran Palace in an *ad hoc* security council. The hawks, led by Ardashir Zahidi (who had arrived from Washington on September 5, with the latest American directives), General Uvaysi and Dr Nahavandi, argued that only an iron fist could now stop the snowballing marches; on the other hand, Premier Sharif Imami pleaded for restraint and a gradual reply. The hawks won the decision: martial law would be imposed in Tehran at 06:00 on the morrow, with General Uvaysi in charge of enforcing it. Sharif Imami tendered his resignation, which was flatly refused by the Shah.[50] Uvaysi and Nahavandi drafted the martial law communiqué: a real declaration of war.

At 06:00 the martial law communiqué was read on Tehran Radio and was reread on the 07:00 and 08:00 news: all demonstrations were forbidden. People nevertheless continued to assemble around Zhaleh Square. Armed troops also converged on the square, taking up position; they were units of the First and Second Imperial Guards Regiments. At 08:00 Shaykh Yahya Nouri (known as Âllameh Nouri, a former pupil of Khomeini) delivered his sermon. Right after the harangue, through a loudspeaker a senior officer asked the thousands strong crowd to disperse peacefully according to the martial law regulations. No one moved. A first salvo was fired in the air. The crowd retreated, then re-formed. The second salvo was fired directly into the crowd: "Un véritable peloton d'exécution" wrote Yvon Berges, the special *Le Figaro* reporter, who was present.[51]

The war had erupted between the people and the army. This was a rude awakening for the people after the two previous peaceful marches. For the whole day running battles would be fought in the east of Tehran: army bullets against the people's Molotov cocktails. A group of youngsters tried to subdue a Chieftain tank, but were mown down to the last man. Machine-gun fire could be heard from the city centre; ambulance sirens wailed continuously; helicopters criss-crossed the skies shuttling officials between centres of decision-making. An air of oppression hung over the whole capital. On the evening of September 8, Tehran was in a dark mood. After all the bloodshed during the day – a record in Iranian history, with an official figure of fifty-eight deaths and two hundred and six wounded[52] and a figure of a hundred and sixty-nine deaths mentioned at the Council of Ministers[53] – the war was on. Iran's 'Black Friday' was a new quantum leap in the escalation of violence.

"Carter has double-crossed us," said the youth leaders, who had believed that the US President would never allow the Shah to order his troops to shoot them down. Iranian public opinion was shocked too; the silent majority, filled as it was with bourgeois inhibitions, tended to sympathise with the victims. Opposition leaders plunged underground, fearing a wave of repression which never came, with only Dr Mufattih and Bazargan being briefly detained. On the evening of Black Friday martial law was declared in eleven major Iranian cities: Ahvaz, Abadan, Tabriz, Mashhad, Shiraz, Qum, Kermanshah, Karaj, Qazvin, Kazirun and Jahrum. Practically all of Iran was under martial law, the army controlling its streets.

On September 9, the Shah cancelled his scheduled visit to Eastern European countries and his Court Minister Huvayda resigned, finally mustering the courage to leave (he was replaced a fortnight later by eighty-six year old Âli Quli Ardalan[54]). The next day President Carter talked for half an hour on the telephone with the Shah, reassuring the latter of "continuous American support". At that critical stage, clear directives from Washington were more necessary than any verbal support, especially now that the Shah had begun to doubt the wisdom of his 'iron fist' policy. He should have borne in mind that in general (and particularly in Iran) mildness after a harsh action leads to the worst of both extremes. The hawks, led by General Uvaysi, aware of the royal doubts, pressed him to let them ride the tiger – to exhaustion if necessary.

To the series of dramatic events befalling Iran from early August, an act of God was to be added on September 16. On that Saturday, at 19:45, an earthquake (7.7 Richter) destroyed the historic town of Tabas, located on the southern fringes of the Dasht-i Kavir desert. The Nayband fault had slipped along 75 of its 225 kilometres fracture, occasioning shocks lasting a full four minutes. Very few people in Tabas survived the jolts and the toll in human lives was reported at between 18,000 and 26,000. Generally acts of God do not impinge on domestic policies, but Tabas did, for three main reasons:

(1) The blame was shifted to Empress Farah's door, people arguing that had she not ordered the town to be classified as an

'historic site', Tabas inhabitants could have built themselves stronger houses instead of having to obtain special permits to do so.

(2) The national struggle between the regime and the opposition was transferred to Tabas as official services (the Red Lion and Sun, the army, the Imperial Social Services and the Empress Farah Charity Foundation) competed with the voluntary elements (mostly students and religious groups). The motivated popular groups did a better job than the apathetic official services.

(3) Psychologically, Iranians were inclined to believe that the Tabas catastrophe fell in line with the regime's ill-starred streak. "People might even believe", Premier Sharif Imami said ironically, "that we were responsible for the quake".[55] The remark was not as funny as he had intended it to sound.

Within forty days, the four major events at Isfahan, Abadan, Black Friday and Tabas, had decisively tilted the scales in favour of the opposition. Public opinion tended to be more favourable to the latter, because it played its trumps much better than the regime, having brains on its side. More important even was that the people, having shed their reserve, were squarely behind them. The students, the lower *Bazaar* hands, the unemployed, the *Dihqanzadehs*, leftist elements – all were in the streets, having made the transition to Sacred Time. The "peuple" were as Robespierre had pictured it: "Le peuple irrite qui sort de son repos majestueux quand les oppresseurs ont comble la mesure de leurs crimes".[56] This was an Iranian people ready to stand up to a petrodollar elite it execrated, ready to fight against a regime that was foreign to it, ready to shed its blood for change (in any direction). A dazed Michel Foucault was wondering about the circumstances which had brought it about: "Quel arrachement pour qu'un homme puise réelement préférer le risque de la mort à la certitude d'avoir à obéir".

Facing these people who were ready to die was a naked elite, too long hidden in SAVAK's robes, devoid of self-confidence (but still arrogant), totally corrupt and disorganised. "There is no policy, no control centre", Huvayda confided to his friend Raji on August 5.[57] A few months earlier Raji had noted: "We are all Chiefs; there are no Indians".[58] These remarks were substantiated by US Ambassador Sullivan's shrewd observation:

> ...In his home [Ardashir Zahidi's] I found a rather tatterdemalion remnant of the figures who had participated in that 1953 [coup] action. But in assaying them, I found them would-be leaders without troops. Those they had led in 1953 were, in 1978, on the other side of the barricades...[59]

They had sufficient troops, however, as the 500,000-strong armed forces were more than enough. And they had done their job on Black Friday (with only three deserters[60]). For the sinking regime, the problem was not so much at the bottom as it was at the very top.

17.6. Poor Alternatives

On August 24, when Sharif Imami became prime minister, he shed all his former responsibilities at the Senate and the Pahlavi Foundation. Three days later he presented the *Majlis* with his so-called Cabinet of National Reconciliation. The new cabinet did not deserve such an appellation, for it consisted of six former Amuzigar ministers, five former civil servants, and only two newcomers who piqued public attention: General Âbbas Qarabaghi (at Interior) and the Pan-Iranist Muhammad Riza Âmili Tihrani (at Information). But his cabinet was secondary, for all the spotlights were on Sharif Imami himself.

With his religious origins, his technocratic background, his aristocratic wife, his strong masonic links and his long career in Iranian politics, the sixty-eight year old Sharif Imami was the elite's best trump card. His peers hoped that he would be their *deus ex machina*, stopping the opposition's successes and leading the counterattack. Morale amongst the petrodollar elite soared: Sharif Imami was the man to engineer a U-turn. From the outset, the Premier had one master strategy: make concessions to satisfy as many constituencies as possible in order to cut the grass from under the opposition's feet. At the close of August, he had to supervise the three-day visit (August 29-31) of Chinese Chairman Hua Ko Feng, trying to capitalise on this in the domestic sphere.

At the beginning of September, Sharif Imami launched his train of concessions. He ordered that:

(1) the Imperial calendar be shelved and the *Hejira*-based one be reinstated as Iran's official calendar;

(2) a programme for releasing political prisoners be set up, with the first batch of three hundred freed on September 11. Religious personalities such as the Ayatullahs Qumi and Pasandideh (Khomeini's elder brother) and Nasir Makarim Shirazi were recalled from internal exile;

(3) all political parties be free to enter the fray. The Pan-Iranist party was the first out, followed by Dr Baqai's Toilers party. Javad Âlamir Davallou, Iran's king of porno magazines (and exclusive *Le Monde* correspondent in Iran), created his *Dimukrat* (Democrat) Party. The most serious new entry was the Party for the New Society, formed on September 5 by Nahavandi and six of his fellow ministers: Ganji, Mûtamidi, Furoughi, Bahiri, Vadiî and Azmoun. The last party of importance to be formed was Beh Azin's Democratic Association of the Iranian People (October 19);

(4) the *Rastakhiz* Party's Rls2,000m allocation be suspended. Fundless, the party folded on October 3, after its secretary Javad Sâid resigned on October 1;

(5) Iran's six casinos be closed down. The Pahlavi Foundation (whose chief custodian had been Sharif Imami) owned three of them and held a minority interest in the fourth.

(6) costly showcase projects (e.g. the Rls5,000m Cultural Centre at Tabriz) and programmes (e.g. the controversial Shiraz Art Festival) be scrapped;

(7) a tax reduction be given to all civil servants and a health insurance scheme covering all of them be formulated (it was ready a month later);

(8) prices of major public services such as electricity, water, telephone and gas be slashed;

(9) *Majlis* debates, starring Bani Ahmad and Pizishkpour, be televised live to Iranian audiences;

(10) some 300,000 youngsters be exempted from compulsory military service;

(11) the Anti-Profiteering Court be disbanded and its head Rasul Rahimi arrested;

(12) a ban be implemented on all pornographic publications (on September 3).

Never before had a Pahlavi cabinet given so many concessions simultaneously: Iran Inc. had, through Sharif Imami, thrown out as much ballast as it could in order to regain some altitude. But Sharif Imami's train of concessions was too little too late. It might have gained sympathy if it had been proposed in early spring but not in late summer; as usual, Iran Inc. was a step behind, reacting to events instead of acting of its own volition. Black Friday on September 8 would come to totally spoil any initial goodwill Sharif Imami might have gained from his opening gambit. Moreover, it might well have been his initial attempt at conciliation that had led to the religious sector taking risks on September 4 and setting in motion the snowball of protest which had to be destroyed on September 8.

Undeterred by Black Friday, Sharif Imami pressed ahead. On September 10, he presented his programme to the *Majlis*, with three priorities: (1) the agricultural sector; (2) fight against inflation; and (3) anti-corruption measures. Both the *Majlis* and the Senate gave him their votes of confidence on September 17 and 19 respectively. Interestingly enough, in his confirmation as premier on August 27 there had been sixteen votes against him and on September 17, for his programme, twenty-two votes against: thus Black Friday had only turned around six deputies. Notwithstanding Black Friday, Tehran's International Fair was held, as every previous year, in September, and the Bank-i Milli Iran commemorated its fiftieth birthday.

On September 12, Sharif Imami launched his anti-corruption campaign by having former health minister Dr Shujâ ul-Din Shaykhulislamizadeh (a Farah protégé) and two of his former deputies – Dr Asadullah Aram Nili (a Jam Hospital shareholder) and Riza Niqabat – arrested. The health department trio was accused of having offered the Texas software firm of Electronic Data Services (EDS) a multi-million dollar (open-ended) contract for computerising Iran's social services without engaging in competitive bidding.[61] Also under arrest were Rasul Rahimi (see above), Âli Asghar Qazazzian (a major fruit importer) and Muhammad Âli Naqibzadeh (a major truck company owner). Two days later, two other former ministers, Mansur Rouhani and Firaydoun Mahdavi, were jailed. Towards the end of September, a renowned member of Tehran's underworld, Rahim Âli Khurram was also arrested. It was not with this half-dozen arrests that Sharif Imami could hope to quench the people's thirst for justice. But that was as far as Sharif Imami dared to go: he was barred from inculpating his peers, let alone his superiors (namely the Pahlavi family). In this respect, the furthest he dared go was to have *Rules of Conduct for the Royal Family* published on September 26. This was a useless move and a detrimental one, because it officially implied that members of the royal family had not had irreproachable conduct in the past (a fact known by everyone, but never publicised). So, all in all, Sharif Imami's anti-corruption drive ended up a total failure, having done more harm than good.

That even Iran Inc. officers had lost hope after Black Friday was underlined by the fact that capital transfers abroad were sky-rocketing. Exchange controls being non-existent in Iran since 1974, one of the Shah's pet policies, banks were stampeded by millionaires wanting to send their funds to either Switzerland or America. A local newspaper reported $1,600m sent abroad in the three weeks following Black Friday;[62] *Le Monde* mentioned an average of $50m daily such funds for the months of September and October.[63] 'Better sooner than never' seemed to be the new dictum of panic-stricken elite members wanting to save their cash; if they thought already of their golden exile, it was because in their minds they had already lost the game. For Sharif Imami, their champion, that was not a good sign.

While Sharif Imami was launching his first offensive, at Tripoli in Libya, the charismatic Iranian religious leader Imam Musa Sadr was vanishing into thin air on August 31. He was supposed to go abroad with a Lebanese cleric, Shaykh Muhammad Yâqub, and a journalist, Âbbas Badr ul-Din, for a one week visit, but Imam Sadr never boarded the Alitalia flight 881 to Rome on August 31, and on September 3 his luggage was still at Tripoli's Hotel Rivage.[64] The Imam Sadr mystery was born (and has so far there has been no satisfactory solution). His interesting speeches, which had trickled through to Iran on magnetic cassettes, had been well-received by the younger intelligentsia. His extraordinary appearance at this crucial time, when his popularity in Iran was on the rise, was most disturbing: Iran had lost a young, dynamic and intelligent religious leader.

Iran's other religious leader in exile, Ayatullah Khomeini, fared much better than Sadr. His messages reached Iran, where they were photocopied and widely distributed. The only problem was that analphabetes could not read them, so that his movement fell back on cassettes, which were intelligible to everyone; also the message came to them directly from Khomeini's lips (no question on authenticity). On September 27 the Iraqi security forces surrounded his Najaf house (possibly in accord with Tehran), placing him under virtual house arrest, and tensions ran high in Iran, with dozens of protest telegrams piled up on Iraqi President Al Bakr's desk. The bar to his free movement was lifted on October 1, but Khomeini had decided to leave Iraq. Four days later he first went to nearby Kuwait, only to be refused entry, then boarded an aeroplane to Paris. In the French capital, the religious leader passed the first nights in a Cachan flat before transferring to the small pavilion at Neauphle-le-Château. For Khomeini the move from Najaf to Neauphle was a blessing in disguise because the international mass media were at arm's length; during his first month at Neauphle he gave no fewer than sixteen major interviews, and the French media reported daily on his activities. Moreover his troika of advisers cum translators – Abu'l Hasan Bani Sadr, Dr Ibrahim Yazdi and Sadiq Qutbzadeh – were with him to tackle the press. The paraphernalia of modern communications were soon available at Neauphle and links to and from Tehran were easily established. Soon the flow of information arriving from Iran was monitored and directives were sent to troops in the field: the Neauphle headquarters were soon humming twenty-four hours a day.

A three-point message was sent by Sharif Imami to Khomeini, the gist of which was: (i) hundreds of Muslim lives had already been lost during the troubles; (ii) Khomeini would not bring the Shah down; (iii) if he returned to Iran, he would be arrested.[65] It totally failed to impress the Ayatullah.

After a calm September (people were recovering from the shock of Black Friday), Iran's provinces erupted once again during October. It first began in the western parts, at Kermanshah and Riza'iyyeh (October 1) and on the same day Colonel Zamanipour, head of Mashhad's police station no. 6, was shot dead by a SCFKI squad. On October 11, a Bell Helicopters bus was fire-bombed at Isfahan, causing three Americans to be injured (the act being avenged by the religious *Guruh-i Touhdi-i Saff*[66]). On October 16, Kerman's Jamî mosque was set on fire by a group of gypsies (disguised SAVAK elements). On October 22 at Qum, "demonstrators shot back for the first time".[67] Then, during the last week of October, three towns exploded: Zanjan, where 15,000 youths created havoc for two days; Amul, leading to the creation of the 'Amul commune'; and Paveh, which was besieged by some 2,000 Jaf tribesmen under Salar Jaf (for six days) after disorders had occurred in the town.

The BBC's daily Persian broadcasts kept the nation informed of the developments in each provincial sector. Here again, as in the case of cassettes, the spoken word had a much wider impact than the printed. And the BBC's coverage of the Iranian events was a marvel of reporting: everything was there, nicely packed, ready for consumption – the day's events, riots and casualties followed by the reactions, the comments and the analyses, and then came the interviews with both government personalities and the opposition's leaders; even future demonstrations were reported. To know what was going on in Iran, Iranians (whether royalists or anti-) had no choice but to tune to the BBC. No news item was classified unless confirmed by the BBC. It was the BBC reports which let the Iranians know that their government had lost control over the provinces.

Besides the loss of provincial control, Sharif Imami's flanks were being endangered by a far more ominous threat: industrial and bureaucratic strikes. When 1,700 workers of the Chitsazi Bihshahr, a Bihshar group subsidiary, walked out, no one saw the writing on the wall. Sensing the loss of authority, the workers, supported and encouraged by opposition forces (mainly leftists), became bolder by the day. In early September, the Tabriz machine tools plant led a fresh wave of strikes even though a similar action in April had failed to trigger the wave. The Iran-Transfo of Ray, the Arak machine tools factory and the NISIC steel direct reduction unit at Ahvaz followed suit. Then, on September 10, the bug got into NIOC when worker at the Tehran Refinery went on strike. In its wake, other NIOC divisions in the south and Tehran went on strike asking for better pay, with top management agreeing that their demands were reasonable.[68] Here again Sharif Imami saw the solution in concessions: he opened the national purse and distributed hefty increases (around 40% on average) to NIOC personnel, and was later forced to give between 25-40% to other civil servants as well. Thus Sharif Imami was only buying time, not the bureaucrats.

And these bureaucrats were crucial to the regime because they collectively formed the third leg of the Iran Inc. tripod.

The bureaucrats had mustered the courage to demand higher pay, and they had won the first round (not seeing the top management giving in without satisfaction). Sharif Imami's strategy was wrong;

the only correct strategy would have been to try to show the bureaucracy's middle management that outside the protective envelope of the Iran Inc. pyramid they were lost. But even if he had tried this latter ploy, he would have also failed, because it was Sacred Time, and middle management had forgotten its undeniable material advantages and dared join the strike. Middle managers saw only the corrupt top management and remembered the alienation and the humiliation it had suffered (especially during the four last years, the petrodollars having exacerbated top bureaucrats' arrogance, leading them to ride rough-shod over their subordinates' self-esteem). One of the managers who joined the strikers said: "There is nothing I can say in their defence";[69] he and the likes of him were not casting their votes in favour of the opposition but rather against the regime. Among the junior ranks opting for the strike were many former students (who had not forgotten their university years) and also former nationalists and *Toudeh* members (who had not forgotten their years of purgatory). Every bureaucrat took this unique occasion to settle his own account with the Pahlavi system by going on strike. After all, a bureaucratic sinecure was not a reason for eternal allegiance to the Pahlavis.

The national press too was busy creating mischief. On October 11, the *Tehran Journal* (*Ittilaât*'s English language daily with a circulation of 10,000 copies) printed a picture of Khomeini on its first page. All copies had been snatched before the military got wind of the incident. General Uvaysi was furious: he dispatched two colonels to *Ittilaât* and *Kayhan* respectively to act as official censors. Outraged journalists, finding the intrusion inexcusable, walked out of work. Sharif Imami was compelled to step in and act as arbiter between the military and the journalists. Three days of negotiations led to the signing of the October 15 four point accord assuring the freedom of the press: a victory for the journalists over the military (the Prime Minister did not relish the idea of a total press walk-out at that stage). The victorious journalists returned to their desks to write articles never seen before in Iran: sales of the two Tehran evening papers doubled and trebled. The press had finally entered the fray, and it was not on the side of the regime. Like the bureaucrats who had accounts to settle with their top management, the journalists had old accounts to settle after twenty-five years of censorship.

At NIOC, Sharif Imami's pay rises had bought calm for only a few weeks. On October 11 (simultaneous with the press problems), the oil industry staged a widely followed one day strike. In Abadan, the military reacted angrily by detaining seven of the refinery's strike leaders. Tensions ran high throughout the industry. On October 21, NIOC chairman Hushang Ansari travelled south to try and defuse the tense situation. In Abadan, he was met with a long list of political demands, headed by the release of all political prisoners.

Taken aback, Ansari argued that he was not empowered to deal with political matters; he returned hurriedly to Tehran for alleged consultations and duly took the first plane out of Iran on his way to a golden exile.[70] OSCO's managing director George Link also left Iran for the US in the last days of October (his Chevrolet Impala had been fire-bombed a few weeks earlier). The departure of the oil industry's two top-ranking managers unleashed a new wave of strikes, with oil production in the Khuzistan oil fields nose-diving from its 5.5m b/d level on October 30 to under 1.5m b/d in a matter of days. In Tehran, Sharif Imami correctly prophesied that: "The oil workers' strike will have dire consequences".

By then, it was clear that Sharif Imami had failed in his mission. His strategy of concessions had not even brought about a breathing space. It was during his tenure that the provinces and the bureaucracy had been lost – with the latest casualties being Bank-I Milli on October 28, the southern oil industry on October 30, and Iran Air on November 1. During the last week of October he had made his last concessions by ordering: (1) the release of some 1,126 political prisoners (October 23) and that of Ayatullah Taliqani, Ayatullah Lahouti and Engineer Maysami (October 30); and (2) the dismissal of thirty-four senior SAVAK officers, among them Parviz Sabiti, who escaped with his family to Geneva on one of Iran Air's last flights out of Tehran on November 1.[71] Even though Sharif Imami received yet another vote of confidence in the *Majlis* (with 35 votes against and 7 abstentions), his cabinet's days were numbered. On November 1, Dr Âli Amini was invited to court by the Shah for consultations. On November 3, Amini met Ayatullah Shariâtmadari at Qum. The elder Qajar Elitist advanced his own candidacy on the BBC and told *Le Monde*: "The Shah cannot be saved, but his regime still can". Another possibility envisaged by the Shah and his advisers was a coalition government under veteran Âbdullah Intizam. While Sharif

Imami was waiting for his order to resign and Amini for his premiership, the explosion of two political bombshells on November 4 – the first at Paris and the second at Tehran – derailed all plans.

During October, as the situation degenerated in Iran, Paris had turned into Iran's capital in exile because of Khomeini's magnetism. On October 22, Engineer Bazargan and Dr Minachi had made the pilgrimage to Neauphle to lay the LMI's allegiance at Khomeini's feet. A week later it was Dr Karim Sanjabi, the *Iran* Party leader, and his *Bazaari* right-hand man, Hajj Mahmoud Manian, who met Khomeini; for a whole week negotiations took place and on November 4, the results of the three-point agreement signed by the parties made headlines:

(1) "The present Iranian monarchy ...has lost all its legal and legitimate bases";

(2) "The nationalistic-religious movement will not agree, under any circumstances, to any kind of political combination with the illegal monarchical regime";

(3) "The future nationalistic regime of Iran based on Islamic precepts ...shall be decided by a national referendum".

For Khomeini the compromise was a triumph. By agreeing to a couple of "nationalistic" and "Iran" terms in the text, he had induced Sanjabi to sign a paper trumpeting the Pahlavis' illegitimacy and their replacement by referendum (the two major points to which Khomeini had always stuck). But Khomeini's masterstroke lay in clause two: the ban on any nationalist compromising with the Shah. Khomeini knew the weak link of the opposition to be the nationalists; he was worried in case of an eleventh-hour sell-out to the Shah (when the stakes would be high) and he had grabbed the opportunity to make such a last-minute deal legally costly. On the other hand, Sanjabi, in his haste to link his nationalist wagon to the religious train, had not gained a single iota; on the contrary, he had narrowly restricted his party's future alternatives. His only gain was personal: the religious sector recognised him as the leader of the *Iran* Party and its National Front (with Sanjabi as leader, they had little to fear from the Nationalists).

The second bombshell of November 4 exploded at the doors of Tehran University. Its fuse had been lit some three weeks earlier, when Sharif Imami had decided to simply leave the TU campus off-limits: students were free within the walls, security forces intervening only if they ventured on the streets.

This strange strategy (never recommended in Iran) soon backfired, when the students (legally free on campus) staged a Week of Solidarity with Political Prisoners, beginning on October 28. The Week turned into a political happening: it was Sacred Time; people from all walks of life came to TU to discuss, buy books and pamphlets, and listen to the speeches of freed political prisoners on the (packed) football field. Safar Qahrimani, a man with a record thirty-two years in jail, delivered a highly emotional address before breaking down in tears when he was given a standing ovation; veteran Azadbad Jina'is also moved the TU audience, as did freed SCFKI and SMKI guerrillas. On the Week's third day, the release of Ayatullah Taliqani further exacerbated passions; on the morrow, the students organised a march from TU to his house (some four kilometres east of TU); the peaceful (even silent) crowd on Reza Shah Avenue snowballed to 100-150,000; the military looked the other way, shy of breaking the labile *modus vivendi* on such an exceptional occasion.

It was the students who broke the *status quo* on the morning of Saturday November 4. Emotionally strung up by a week of happenings on the campus, they had to unwind. They did so by taking to Reza Shah Avenue. There they clashed with soldiers, and had to retreat to the safety of the campus. A TV crew recorded the whole scene of kneeling soldiers shooting into the mass of students: the scene was shown on national television the same evening, on the 20:30 news. Iranians had never before seen such images on their TV screens and the outrage was national.

NIRT chief Nasir ul-Din Shah Husayni resigned on the spot, as did the Ministers of Education (Dr Ganji), and of Science and Higher Education (Dr Qazi). The sands of time were running out for Sharif Imami.

On November 5, after the army soldiers had been pulled off the streets in the aftermath of the TU events, Tehran ran out of control. It seems that on that day both the pro- and anti-royalist factions came to the same conclusion – that a chaotic Tehran was beneficial to their cause. SAVAK members hoped, through their brutal actions, to stir up a law and order backlash from the elusive 'silent majority', while some opposition circles let their troops loose, arguing that "the more disorder, the better".

Tehran was soon devastated, with bonfires burning on every corner and square. It was Sacred Time. Bank branches were ruined, although little cash was stolen, and whole buildings were set on fire, such as the Bank-i Milli on the Sharivar 25 Square and the BMW high-rise half a kilometre away;[72] even a wing of the British Embassy was set on fire and partially destroyed. At TU, the students, although still mourning their fallen comrades, celebrated their victory by pulling down the Shah's bronze statue and parading it on Shah Reza Avenue.

At the end of day, the generals ordered their troops to occupy the streets of the battered capital, having been given proof that they were the last rampart before chaos. Now it was time for them to come to the fore to re-establish law and order. The politicians' days were over: even the most seasoned among them – Sharif Imami – had been unable to stem the crisis.

On the evening of November 5, the Prime Minister tendered his resignation. His tenure had lasted seventy-one days and he had failed in every area; only the military remained trustworthy till the end. In his defence, it should be pointed out that Black Friday, which came about not because of a decision made by him, had come at the worst possible time for his strategy. Being left as the last active leg of the Iran Inc. tripod, the military wanted full powers. They were tired of playing second fiddle to incapable civilians. On the telephone the USA's NSC adviser Brzezinski had told the Shah that they would support him "whether he chose a coalition government or a military government".[73]

On the morning of November 6, the generals held all the levers of power. Holding the levers was one thing, exercising power another, and the generals were to experience the gap separating the latter from the former.

17.7. The Shah's Generals

On the morning of November 6 everyone expected General Uvaysi, Tehran's military commander and the 'Butcher of Black Friday', to take full command as prime minister, as he was the army's natural leader and Iran Inc.'s last (and best) chance for survival. Everyone was wrong, for the new prime minister was the unknown, sixty-one year old General Ghulam Riza Azhari. In the Iran Inc. ranks morale sank to a new low. Azhari was an uncharismatic career officer, a lacklustre four-star general with no following. How could the Iran Inc. board have chosen him over Uvaysi? The days of compromise were long over. It was war for power, the popular opposition pitted against the unpopular (but powerful) military. At that stage, the military should have turned to its best and brightest; even Azhari was pleading for Uvaysi. Instead, Uvaysi was given the Labour and Social Affairs portfolio, remaining military commander of Tehran. The harm, however, was done, as at that stage only the figurehead mattered and it was not Uvaysi.

In the Azhari cabinet, besides the Premier and Uvaysi, were five generals, an admiral and three civilians. General Qarabaghi was at Interior, General Âzimi at War, General Rabiî (air force commander-in-chief) at Housing and Urban Development, General Muqaddam (SAVAK chief) at Energy, General Saâdatmand at Information and Admiral Habibullahi (navy commander-in-chief) in charge of Science and Higher Education. As for the three civilians, they were leftovers from the previous cabinet: A.K. Afshar (Foreign Affairs), M.R. Amin (Industry) and K. Mûtamidi (PTT). During November, Azhari added ten civilians (none of them prominent) to his initial cabinet without altering its military nature, although the civilians acquired a numerical majority.

But the generals had lost even before beginning their uphill struggle. Their early loss came about because the Shah decided to address the nation on November 6. In his last speech, a pale and drawn Shah appeared a loser. Gone was the arrogance of yesteryear, gone the veneer, gone the rodomontades, the guile and the condescension, gone the thumb nonchalantly tucked in his gilet. It was a pitiful king, shaken by his people's will, who said:

> ...I have heard your revolutionary message ...I pledge to grant everything for which you have fought hard and for which some of you died ...I commit myself to make up for past mistakes, to fight corruption and oppression ...to grant the people their fundamental rights and liberties...

It was finished. Muhammad Reza Pahlavi would never recover from such a pitiful performance: Iranians detest losers and are pitiless towards supplicating monarchs. The Shah's belated *mea culpa*, his empty promises and even his eleventh-hour gift of all his assets in Iran[74] to the Iranian people had a decidedly negative impact (who advised him to go on TV?). "Nature would be merciful", wrote T.E. Lawrence to Lady Astor, "if she would end us at a climax and not in the decline". To Muhammad Reza Shah nature would indeed be merciless: on November 6 she took the first step of a decline that could not have been worse.

By throwing in the sponge simultaneously with the generals' entry into the ring, the Shah had dealt them an injurious blow. Their supreme and uncontested leader had given up the fight, so how could they carry on? Even the Americans had seen the writing on the wall, proven by Ambassador Sullivan's decision, on November 9, to cable his historic report 'Thinking the Unthinkable' (a typical case of better late than never). The generals nevertheless tried their best, having nothing better to do, and wanting to show the Iranians what their pampered military was capable of. The generals' first action was to close down all centres of unrest: the universities, the high schools and the *Bazaar*. As for the press, they appointed their own censors; but editors rebelled against the colonels sent to rein them in, and some of them, such as Bastani of *Kayhan* and Bullouri at *Ittilaât*, had to be whisked away. The journalists went on strike in protest. On November 6, only *Rastakhiz* published, but by the morrow its journalists had joined the strikers: Iran was without newspapers. The generals had wreaked their revenge for months of gratuitous vilification by the free press; on the other hand, a large majority of the national TV and radio employees had accepted co-operating with them (from the outset in 1967, NIRT cadres had been extra carefully screened and vetted), so that the broadcast media were operating. The generals knew that they could live without the written press and that radio and TV coverage was all they really needed: on this point they were correct.

The generals' second move was to pursue the anti-corruption drive from where Sharif Imami had left off. On November 7, it was the ex-SAVAK chief, General Nasiri, who was arrested and jailed in Jamshidiyyeh prison, to be joined by ex-premier Huvayda two days later.[75] Even for the hardened Iranians these arrests came as a surprise: how could a regime imprison its former key personalities without discrediting itself? There was something rotten in the Iran Inc. structure.

A string of former ministers soon joined the illustrious pair in Jamshidiyyeh such as Azmoun, Humayoun, Vahidi, Valian, Sadaqiani and Taslimi; other detainees were the ex-Tehran police chief General Jâfar Quli Sadri, ex-Tehran mayor Ghulam Riza Nikpay, ex-Imperial Club chief Jamshid Buzurgmihr, ex-Seventh Asian Games tsar Hasan Rasouli, industrialist Husayn Fouladi, ex-deputy Riza Shaykh Baha'i, Sarbanaha, Naqibzadeh and, closing the list, the former Fars province governor (and Princess Ashraf protégé) Manouchihr Pirouz. Arrests, however, did not impress Iranians any longer, for only if the arrestees were brought to trial and sentenced would that indicate a sea change, but even the generals did not dare do that.

Having re-established law and order in the capital (with intermittent flare-ups in the provinces), the generals' next (and crucial) task was to get the bureaucracy operating. Thus the stronger Iran Inc. pillar was trying to get the weaker one back in the fold. Now the basic compartmentalisation of Iran Inc., which had for years protected the top echelon from lower down cross-linking was working against it, because the generals had no links with the bureaucracy's director-generals (the middle managers on whom the whole system hinged). The Gendarmerie had sent questionnaires to be filled in to managers of key industrial facilities in the summer of 1978[76], but such information was useless in times of crisis when (in Iran) only personal connections allow for favours and reciprocal confidence. Even force is of little use as bayonets cannot force people to work for long, especially not technocrats. For example, the generals were powerless to stop electricity technicians cutting Tehran's power whenever they wanted, and they were equally powerless before the thousands of Telephone Company of Iran employees' decision to expel some two hundred expatriates (of Bell Telephone Company experts) from their offices. Where Sharif Imami had failed, it was clear that the generals wouldn't have even half a chance of success. They naturally failed in their awkward efforts to get the bureaucrats back to work. Iran's generals had lost their opportunities in the 1970s, when, flushed with money and power, they should have paid its masterminds to study such eventualities as crowd control, psychological warfare, propaganda and co-operation with other national institutions. But that would have been asking too much from a military elite which relied too heavily on the Americans for its own good.

In the oil industry, however, first they struck gold when the southern oil fields' output rose back to its pre-crisis level of 5.8m b/d within a three week span (see Table 17.4). Another success (this one foreseeable) was wrung from the *Majlis* when Azhari received the deputies' vote of confidence on November 25 (191 for, 27 against and 11 abstentions). But the *Majlis* was not as tame as it had been, for it lifted the parliamentary immunity of Iran's glass tsar Mansur Yasini (who immediately fled to Kuwait with his millions) and ordered Salar Jaf to remain under *Majlis* arrest for his attack at Paveh. Furthermore, the deputies harassed the government with a total of one hundred and forty questions, some eighty protests and even three censure motions. But this *Majlis* razzmatazz was coming much too late to impress anyone: the national assembly was by then totally irrelevant.

Table 17.4. Levels of Oil Production in the Southern Oil Fields for Selected Days of November 1978.

November 6	1,200,000 b/d
November 11	2,000,000
November 14	3,000,000
November 17	3,200,000
November 21	4,000,000
November 24	5,000,000
November 30	5,800,000

Meanwhile the religious opposition, first taken aback by the military takeover, was gearing up once again, prodded from Paris by Khomeini's appeals. Provincial centres were tested anew, with Sari being the first on November 19, followed by Yazd and Shiraz. On November 23, riots near the Imam Riza (A.S.) Shrine at Mashhad turned bloody when troops intervened. Khomeini pounced on the occasion and called for a day of mourning and strikes on November 26. His invitation was widely taken up throughout the country. Riots shook dozens of provincial centres, and completely eclipsed the pilgrimage to Najaf undertaken by Empress Farah (like all other royal initiatives, it came a year or two too late).

These were but rehearsals for the month of Muharram, whose first day coincided with December 1. On the first night of Muharram the religious activists launched a two-pronged offensive. The first was the chanting of "God is Great" from Tehran's rooftops (a fabulous idea, allowing for a riskfree unnerving of patrolling troops). The second was an attempt at breaking the martial law's curfew by sending out thousands of people dressed in white burial sheets. The troops shot into the large crowd assembled around Navvab Street and Shahpour Square, officially causing seven deaths and twenty-five injured (the opposition claimed forty-five martyrs and three hundred and ninety-five wounded[77]). On the morning of December 2, other clashes resulted around Sarchismeh, near the *Bazaar*: the *Kayhan* newspaper was to later report a total of one hundred and ten martyrs on that day alone[78]. This escalation of bloodshed on the streets of Tehran was dangerous for the military, because there was a limit to the blood its soldiers could shed: they were human and Iranian too. As Carlyle put in a nutshell:

> ...Good is grapeshot on one condition: that the shooter also were made of metal!...[79]

From Paris, Khomeini declared war on the military by issuing a national order to soldiers "to desert their garrisons ...their desertion being an act in line with the *Shariâ* (religious code)". The army soldiers (mainly from peasant stock) were strongly influenced by such a religious order, which gave them an iron-clad alibi not to shoot at their fellow citizens: the stream of army deserters began. The guerrilla groups also became bolder for, on December 4, a SCFKI squad attacked a Tehran police station in broad daylight (killing a policeman, wounding an officer) and another group fire-bombed two military trucks in the Nizamabad district. In another incident, an onslaught by armed individuals was repulsed at the War Ministry. These were signs that Tehran was slipping slowly towards a civil war, pitting all the forces of opposition against the military. Rumours of martial training camps being set up in Karaj farms abounded in the capital.

Then came the mourning days of *Tasouâ* and *Âshoura* on December 10 and 11. On December 10, around one million demonstrators (the bulk of whom belonged to the religious-*Bazaar* association) came to march behind Taliqani and Bazargan in Shah Reza Avenue, from the Pich-i Shimiran all the way to Shahyad Square. The masses, chanting religious slogans and "Khomeini is our leader", stretched for kilometres. The whole march, very well-organised, was peaceful.

No soldier was in sight, as the armed troops had formed a Maginot line on Mirdamad Avenue, blocking all roads to the north of the city, where the Shah resided. The demonstrators, however, having no inclination to storm northwards, went all the way to Shahyad, counted themselves, listened to a fifteen point declaration condemning the regime and quietly returned to their homes. The peaceful march of roughly one million Iranians was a formidable feat all by itself: it was unique in Iranian history and ranked among records in world history. The Iranians had thus voted with their feet for the opposition and also proven to the world that they could discipline themselves, given the opportunity.

The massive march on December 11 was almost a repetition of the *Tasouâ* one, with two differences: firstly, the number of marchers increased by around 50% on the previous day (resulting in a crowd estimated at around 1.5m individuals on Shah Reza Avenue) as the leftists and guerrilla group sympathisers joined the religio-nationalist sectors; secondly, slogans took a political, anti-Shah turn as tens of thousands chanted:

> "The Rex at Abadan, the mosque in Kerman, the Holy Quran, the University of Tehran. Who set them all on fire? The Shah did, it was the Shah! Shah, we shall kill you!"[80]

The *Âshoura* demonstration was another peaceful triumph, with helicopters passing overhead to make sure that the marchers didn't change course. The soldiers still waited on Mirdamad, just in case. For the opposition it was a formidable vote of confidence: the people were solidly behind them. The royalists could not have fielded fifty thousand supporters. The Shah's 'silent majority' was in the enemy camp.

To add insult to injury, on the day of *Âshoura*, a number of regime supporters were shot dead. In a first incident at Hamadan, a private, Muhsin Mubashshir Kashani, shot dead the Governor-General Dr Qudratullah Khudayari and was gunned down by the latter's bodyguards. The second incident occurred at the Imperial Guards' barracks at Lavizan (north-east of Tehran). At 13:20, a seven-man team led by a captain and a first lieutenant (with two NCOs and three privates[80A]) stormed the officers' and NCOs' mess. Firing with their six G-3 guns and a single MGA-3 machine-gun, the assailants totally surprised the officers, who returned fire with their handguns after a couple of seconds. When the smoke cleared six of the seven assailants lay dead, only the captain having survived. The incident's tally was fifteen deaths and thirty-nine injured; among the prominent victims were General Husayn Sadri, Colonels Âskari, Najmabadi, Birjandi, Sanaîfar, and Majors Mirhadi and Marjani. Dozens of officers such as Colonel Muhammad Âli Shahsavand fell seriously wounded. The Imperial Guardsmen had paid with their blood for their lack of extra precautions on such a sensitive day in these exceptional times.

The last three weeks of December would be a long agony for the beleaguered generals. It had become clear to them and their masters that their bayonets were incapable of swinging the odds in their favour. Their only success in the oil industry had turned sour in early December when the oil production dwindled once again from its peak of 5.8m b/d on December 1 to a low of 1.2m b/d a fortnight later (see Table 17.5). On December 14, General Azhari went on television to warn the oil workers against further disorders and strikes. The warning had an effect, as oil production inched back up to reach 3.2m b/d on December 23 (see Table 17.5). In the meantime, the veteran seventy-one year old Âbdullah Intizam was placed at the head of NIOC (December 20)[82] and General Azhari suffered a heart attack (December 21), but had remained at his post.[83] Then, on December 23, in Ahvaz, a three man squad ambushed and shot dead OSCO's production manager, the fifty-six year old Texaco executive Paul Grimm. After Link's departure in October, Grimm had been OSCO's top manager in south Iran. His abrupt death had an electric effect on the whole oil industry and the subsequent threat "to kill twenty key OSCO executives if the export of crude wasn't halted" sealed the question of oil production and exports once and for all: within four days output was under 500,000 b/d and exports dropped to nil (see Table 17.5). The generals' sweet oil success had turned sour.

Table 17.5. The Three Phases of Iranian Oil Production (and Exports) During December 1978.[81]

Phase One

December	1	5,800,000 b/d
December	4	4,400,000
December	6	2,700,000
December	14	1,200,000

Phase Two

December	16	1,300,000
December	23	3,183,000

Phase Three

December	24	2,667,000 b/d	Exports:	1,975,000 b/d
December	25	1,703,000		325,000 "
December	26	946,000		500,000 "
December	27	487,000		nil

The Shah had two prominent visitors in December. The first was the American ambassador-at-large George Ball, who resided in Tehran for the first two weeks of December. Within a few days, he realised that "the Shah's decline was irreversible and that the American Government had to arrange for a transfer of power post haste".[84] Ball also advised the transfer of US nationals from Iran, a measure the National Security Council enacted from December 6: five special C-

130 transport aeroplanes were allocated to a shuttle service between Tehran and European airports; logistics being the domain in which the Americans excel, the transfers were very swift and by January 10 State Department spokesman Hodding Carter said that "30,000 Americans had left Iran and that 12,000 were still there".[85] Ball's own recommendation was for the institution of a 'Council of Notables' made up of elder statesmen. Finally, he passed the following judgement on Muhammad Reza Pahlavi:

> ...He had an honourable ambition for his country and worked tirelessly to fulfil it. But that ambition – stimulated by America's short-sighted encouragement – grew more and more excessive and unrealistic...[86]

So, upon Ball's recommendation but mainly due to the Vietnam Syndrome, the Americans had chosen flight over fight: a wise decision. Especially because, since November, the demonstrators had dared take on American targets,[87] and in Tehran it was clear that, if the revolutionaries' prime target was the Shah, the Americans were a not too distant second (having openly supported the Shah's regime for far too long). Another proof of the revolutionaries' animosity against the USA was given on December 24 when the American Embassy was attacked by a large group of youthful demonstrators.[88] After the assailants were repelled by tear gas fired by marine guardsmen, they stormed the unguarded embassy annexe instead and set a couple of cars in its parking area ablaze.

Since the beginning of the disorders in Iran, the Americans and particularly the CIA had had difficulty understanding the whole process. In an August 1978 paper, the CIA had concluded that Iran "is not in a revolutionary or even a pre-revolutionary situation".[89] An anecdote relating to American Air Force Lieutenant-General Eugene Tighe's visit to Tehran in December 1978 was symptomatic of the reasons behind American vicissitudes in Iran:

> ...To get a first-hand view, Tighe dodged his security protection by changing into civilian clothes and climbing out an Embassy window. He had walked around for three hours ...[seeing] one million demonstrators ...whipped into an anti-American frenzy. It was a

> stunning display, showing true emotion or precision organisation, or both...[90]

The Americans simply couldn't understand (even after three full decades in Iran) what was going on. The CIA later looked for excuses, but they were pretty lame:

> Iran was a hard case to get right ...[the] CIA was not set up to jump ahead on a fast-moving situation ...[there was] no intellectual badminton [at the CIA] ...[the] Tehran CIA [unit was] split over [the] Iran situation ...[the CIA] failed to understand how little strength the moderates had...[91]

And Woodward concludes that:

> ...[The CIA thought] that the Shah would take decisive action ...Brzezinski wanted the Shah to use force. Vance opposed force. The President couldn't decide. And the crux was that the Shah would not act unless he was told by the President of the United States what to do...[92]

As author Robinson put it: "The Shah not only believed the Americans would always take care of him, he bet the Peacock Throne on it".[93] The Shah's second visitor was the French President's special envoy Michel Poniatowski. Arriving on December 21, the French envoy was to remain four days at Tehran: "I found a country already in a revolutionary state". He further reminisced about his *tête-à-tête* with the Shah:[94]

> ...he looked sick, exhausted; he only thought about leaving. I proposed [to] him to take care of Khomeini's destiny, [who was] then residing in France. In other words, he [the Shah] was free to act as he liked ...To which he replied: "No, under no circumstances, do protect him at any cost! If anything happened to him there, it would trigger a formidable explosion here, which I would be unable to control.

> My departure from Iran would then be irremediably jeopardised." I then suggested that he still had a modern army, well-equipped to maintain law and order. He said: "I shall never give the order to shoot. If I did, there would be 25,000 dead people tomorrow." I replied: "But, Majesty, if you don't do that today there will be hundreds of thousands killed later on." The Shah remained adamant: "I shall never order to shoot. Given this final decision, my friends and allies should decide upon the course they will follow." On the way back to the Embassy, I concluded: It's the end...

On December 23, sixty-nine academics belonging to the National Organisation of Iranian Academicians (created on October 4, 1978) began a protest sit-in on the sixth floor of the Ministry of Sciences and Higher Education. Nothing would have differentiated this sit-in from dozens of other sit-ins staged in Iran if, from a building across the street, a member of the security forces had not fired a single shot at 14:30 on December 26, which hit Kamran Nijatullahi, a twenty-seven year old assistant professor at Tehran Polytechnic, in the chest. The young man was taken to hospital where he died in the evening. Tehran was shocked by the fact that inoffensive academics staging a sit-in could be shot dead: a whole class of non-*engagé* intellectuals, not especially hostile to the regime, were thus alienated. For Iran's academics Nijatullahi became a hero: he was their revolutionary martyr, their sign of participation. In the early hours of December 27, paratroopers stormed the remaining academics, ending their sit-in (a strategy they should have adopted on the very first night).

On December 30 and 31, Mashhad was shaken by popular riots threatening to overpower the security forces. These were far worse than the former troubles at Mashhad on December 5 and 23. Tanks had to be brought in to subdue the demonstrators; it was even reported that some people were crushed under the tanks' caterpillar tracks. Over three hundred casualties resulted from the two days of violent riots, and some twenty injured demonstrators were said to have died of their wounds later in hospital.[95] When the Mashhad riots ended, General Azhari finally resigned. The tired and sick general departed on January 7 for a well-deserved rest to the US: his agony had lasted fifty-six days (a fortnight less than that of Sharif Imami). Azhari had never been the man for the Herculean task with which he had been confronted; the man who would have relished the challenge (provided that he was given *carte blanche*) was General Uvaysi, who had also decided to leave for the US on January 4 (along with General Muhammad Javad Moulavi, the former Tehran police chief).

17.8. One Last Trump

With the collapse of oil production during the second week of December, the military solution had lived. Now the only thought in the Shah's mind was to secure a safe exit for himself while he still could. The two historical marches of *Tasouâ* and *Âshoura* had destroyed his last illusions about the people over whom he had been allowed to rule for thirty-seven years. He now needed an honest nationalistic statesman to control the situation until his exit. At first Dr Âli Amini and Âbdullah Intizam (the new duo of the old Qajar elite) selected the seventy-three year old Dr Sadiqi, a retired TU professor and former minister under Dr Musaddiq, to play this lame duck role. On December 19, the three men went to meet the Shah. After the meeting, Sadiqi asked for a few days of reflection; on December 25, he asked for another six months to make up his mind[96] (a polite, Iranian way to say no). Sadiqi wisely refused the premiership because he had nothing to gain and everything to lose in this venture. The old professor was not made for revolutionary times: he would have been crushed by the events.

After the collapse of the Sadiqi option, the next available candidate was Dr Shahpour Bakhtiar.* In this case, the go-between was the multi-millionaire royalist politician and contractor Kazim Jaffroudi, whose daughter was married to Bakhtiar's younger son. After meetings with a Shah on the defensive (if not Bakhtiar, then whom?), Bakhtiar undertook to form a government on December 29, as the Shah had agreed to his two main *sine qua non* requests: (1) the Shah's respect for the 1906 Constitution; (2) the Shah's departure from Iran for extended vacations. In a reverse situation to Sadiqi, Bakhtiar had everything to win and little to lose. Witnessing the formidable religious tidal wave on the horizon, he knew (unlike Sanjabi *et alia*) that he stood no chance if it submerged the country. His only chance was to grasp the moment before the regime collapsed and was replaced by a new one. Even though he was sixty-five, he was still fit and in full possession of his faculties. And he was ambitious, for he had always wanted to be prime minister (like his grandfather on his mother's side, Samsam ul-Saltaneh) and had waited so long and made so many political and familial sacrifices for it. Here was his last chance and he was going to take it come what may. From the outset he knew his chances to be slim: "I am here for either five days or five years", he quipped.[97]

* DR SHAHPOUR BAKHTIAR (1913-1991), son of Muhammad Riza Khan Sardar Fatih (executed in 1932); secondary studies in France; served France during the Second World War; took a French wife (four children); doctorate in law (1946); returned to Iran, joined Ministry of Labour, member of *Iran* Party; failed in bid to enter *Majlis*; deputy minister of labour under Dr Musaddiq (July 1952); sidelined after 1953 coup; active in Second National Front, chairman of University Committee, imprisoned several times during the 1960s; managing director of Vatan factory at Isfahan (1971), then of Ductiran (a venture of French interests with the Pahlavi Foundation), and also of Abgineh glass under Mansur Yasini; back to politics, NF speaker (1977-78); Muhammad Reza Shah's last prime minister (January-February 1979); fled to Paris, oversaw ill-fated *Nouzheh* coup (1980), escaped attempted assassination, killed at Paris home, under suspicious conditions on August 6, 1991.

On January 1, Bakhtiar made his first speech on the radio, calling for a government of national unity (of course) and outlining his programme: democracy, justice and socialism.[98] But his secret trump card was the Shah's pledge to leave Iran soon – for he hoped that he would get all the credit for the latter's departure. On January 3, he staged his first press conference at his home at Rustamabad. He spoke before an oversized portrait of Dr Musaddiq, hoping thereby to rally the former leader's clientele. He also attempted to put some distance between himself and the Shah by proclaiming that: (1) oil exports to Israel and South Africa would be ended; and (2) Iran would stop being the Gulf's gendarme (adding that he had told the Americans about these policies three months earlier). On the morrow, he received his premier's decree from the Shah.

As soon as he got wind of Bakhtiar's deal with the Shah, an incensed Dr Sanjabi, furious that his former spokesman had bypassed him and broken the sacrosanct Paris Accord (reached with Khomeini), had him expelled from both the *Iran* Party and the National Front organisations – on December 30 and 31 respectively. Sanjabi then reshuffled the NF executive[99] and called for a general strike on January 7, which was widely followed. All opposition groups were infuriated by Bakhtiar's eleventh-hour betrayal, especially Khomeini who had always feared such a nationalistic compromise with the enemy. From Neauple, the patriarch launched appeals to isolate Bakhtiar and boycott his ministers: he ordered people to stop paying their water, electricity and telephone bills (January 2) and their general taxes (January 6); he also called for a general strike on January 8 (in reply to the NF's strike on the 7th). The LMI also took part in the anti-Bakhtiar campaign, and Taliqani told the *Le Monde* reporter on January 5: "Bakhtiar doesn't stand the slightest chance of success". But the most damaging attack came from a little-known opposition stalwart, the retired Colonel Âzizullah Amir Rahimi, who wrote an open letter to *Kayhan*, of which his main arguments were summarised in a single sentence: "Mr Bakhtiar, people didn't get killed for you to become Prime Minister!"[100]

There was no doubt that the retired colonel had hit the nail on the head and his final argument was difficult to refute.

But Bakhtiar was not a man to be stopped by words. He had jumped off his fence and had had the courage to take on a heavy responsibility with all the odds stacked against him; he would use his undeniable intelligence and capacities to bolster his razor-thin chances. On January 6, he duly presented his cabinet to the Shah: it was a first setback for his supporters as, besides the highly articulate, sixty-one year old Ahmad Mirfindirisky at Foreign Affairs, the ministers were either former technocrats (Manouchihr Kazimi, Dr Muhammad Amin Riahi, Engineer Luft Âli Samimi and Dr Âbbas Quli Bakhtiar, Shahpour's cousin) or unknown quantities (Rustam Pirasteh, Javad Khadim Asadabadi). General Firaydoun Jam, tipped for the War Ministry, declined and left the post to the highly controversial royalist General Jâfar Shafaqat. As for his Minister of Justice, Yahya Sadiq Vaziri, he resigned on January 15. Bakhtiar could count only on his low-profile *chef de cabinet*, his former Labour Ministry colleague, fifty-eight year old Muhammad Mushiri Yazdi. As for Sharif Imami and Azhari, all spotlights were now on Bakhtiar, not on his ministers and the premier, finally cast in his dream role, showed the nation the gamut of his talents.

Bakhtiar's Achilles' heel, however, was his lack of experience in administrative and political affairs (he had passed his professional life in opposition). His main error was paying too much attention to legality, believing his lawfulness to underpin his legitimacy: he was too old to realise that in a revolutionary situation short cuts are precious for time rapidly runs out. His lifting of press censorship on January 6 was in direct line with his promise of freedom. The wave of arrests he launched simultaneously against corrupt individuals failed to impress, as the people were long past this stage. The main personalities detained were: Huzhabrullah Yazdani, the *Baha'i* millionaire; Amir Nasir Diba Tabataba'i, a director-general at the court (for a couple of days); Husayn Bastani Bushiri, a major merchant; Dr Iraj Syasi and Asadullah Mahmoudzadeh, the managers of the Anjuman-i Tavanbakhshi for embezzlement; and Hajj Shaykh Muhammad Riza Mahdavi Kani, the preacher at Tehran's Jalili mosque, on political grounds (detained on January 7 for two days). On the other hand, Bakhtiar expedited the freeing of political prisoners: sixty-five were released on January 10 and one hundred and sixty-two on January 20 (including the whole SMKI leadership: Masûd Rajavi, Musa Khyabani, Mihdi Bukhara'i, Âli Khavari and Bihrouz Haqqi).

On the streets though, disturbances remained a daily fixture, both in Tehran and in the provinces. Yazdis had laid waste the Yazd SAVAK headquarters on January 9, and Bakhtiar took the unexpected decision to lift martial law in Shiraz; he had already delayed the onset of the curfew by two hours (11p.m. instead of 9p.m.), and intended to use Shiraz as a further step to the abolition of martial law nationwide. Forty-eight hours after his Shiraz order, tens of thousands of Shirazis ransacked the Shiraz SAVAK headquarters and lynched its deputy head, an army colonel.[101] Martial law was immediately reinstated in Shiraz, but the harm had been done and the military had been given their first hint that Bakhtiar was far from being infallible.

On January 11, Bakhtiar presented his cabinet to the *Majlis*. He presented his programme in two parts: domestic and foreign, a programme typical of a moderate, right-of-centre government, with, on the domestic side:

– the official disbanding of SAVAK, and indictment of personnel guilty of unlawful acts;

– all political prisoners to be freed, and compensation to be paid to those jailed after *Murdad 28*, plus compensation of the families of those who died in prison, with people killed during the Revolution to be proclaimed martyrs and their families to be compensated;

– a special court to be set up to judge corrupt individuals and profiteers;

– the expulsion of illegal and redundant expatriates;

– the relaxation of martial law, normalisation, the end of the strikes, national reconstruction, co-operation between civil government and religious authorities, free elections, social security, individual liberties and justice;

– decentralisation, commerce and industry to be a private affair (except for oil, gas, petrochemicals and atomic energy), the Ministry of Sciences and Higher Education to be dissolved (with the universities becoming independent) and the PBO assigned a watchdog role.

The idea of paying compensation to the families of dead political prisoners and martyrs was an incredible blunder (showing how little Bakhtiar understood and cared for the people), which was to attract dozens of protests from the parties concerned.

On the foreign side, the programme foresaw:

– the expansion of relations with Islamic countries and a mutual respect policy with neighbours, with special attention to Third World countries;

– co-operation with UN, the defence of human rights and the practice of non-aggression;

– the halting of crude oil exports to Israel and South Africa, the support of the Palestinian cause, and the championing of anti-apartheid.

On January 15, the Senate gave Bakhtiar its vote of confidence with 38 votes for, 1 against and 2 abstentions. On the morrow, the *Majlis* naturally followed suit, with 149 in favour, 43 against and 13 abstentions. These formal procedures were now rather useless for revolutionary winds were blowing throughout the nation.

While Bakhtiar was getting his first taste of power, at Guadeloupe the four Western leaders – Jimmy Carter, James Callaghan, Valéry Giscard d'Estaing and Helmut Schmidt – were staging their summit.

On January 13, the court ministry had announced the formation of a nine member Regency Council (in accordance with Article 42 of the Constitution's Supplemental Laws), set up to take decisions during the Shah's absence. The members were:

– Sayyid Jalal ul-Din Tihrani (eighty-one, doyen and council chairman);
– Dr Shapour Bakhtiar (sixty-six, prime minister);
– Dr Âli Quli Ardalan (seventy-eight, court minister);
– Muhammad Sajjadi (seventy-nine, Senate president);
– Dr Javad Sâid (fifty-seven, *Majlis* president);
– Âbdullah Intizam (seventy-two, NIOC chairman);
– Dr Âbd ul-Husayn Âliabadi (sixty-five, ex-public prosecutor);
– Muhammad Âli Varasteh (sixty-eight, former minister);
– General Âbbas Qarabaghi (sixty-one, chief of General Staff).

The Shah had even attended the council's first meeting, on January 14, and fixed his departure for January 16, after the Bakhtiar cabinet's confirmation by the *Majlis*.

On January 16, at noon, everything was ready for the departure of Muhammad Reza Pahlavi and Farah Diba. The second Pahlavi was leaving his country with, in attendance, 'his' Prime Minister, who had received the investiture of 'his' Senate and 'his' *Majlis*; 'his' Regency Council was in place; 'his' courtiers and generals were present on the tarmac; 'his' NIRT was filming the event from 'his' Mihrabad Airport as he boarded 'his' private jet, Shahbaz. Appearances did not deceive anyone, least of all the Shah himself: he was fleeing for his life (as he had told Poniatowski a month earlier), flushed out of Iran by the very people over whom he had ruled for thirty-seven years and four months. For the sixty year old monarch, 'his' neck was the last thing he could save, not his face. He was leaving behind 'his' crown and 'his' throne, 'his' courtiers, 'his' officers, 'his' trusted servants and 'his' responsibilities. How could he leave? After all that he had been given? He had lost everything, except for 'his' "umpteen billion dollars"[102] which he had amassed in foreign banks since *Murdad 28*. On the Mihrabad tarmac, his eyes filled with tears, he spoke more than thousands of words. At 13:15, 'his' Shahbaz took off, destination: Egypt. "A childish mystic", Oriana Fallaci had written of him, "...a rather sinister megalomaniac in whom the worst of the old and the worst of the new are combined".[103]

The Shah's departure triggered an explosion of joy throughout Iran. In Tehran, people were dancing in the streets.

It was Sacred Time with smiles. The Pahlavi statues still standing were pulled down in Tehran and the major provincial towns.[104] A milestone in the struggle had been reached; all the sacrifices had not been in vain after all. Now leaderless, the battered Iran Inc. monolith might well crumble faster. But Prime Minister Bakhtiar wouldn't receive any credit for sending the Shah "on vacation"; the people believed that they had forced the Shah out; all the opposition forces – whether nationalist, religious or leftist – were incensed by the game Bakhtiar was playing.

The rallying slogan of demonstrations changed from "Death to the Shah" to "Death to Bakhtiar". The revolutionaries were determined not to let Bakhtiar steal away the prize for which they had fought so long, especially after they had ousted the Shah and all was within their grasp.

As the people celebrated, Bakhtiar got down to work. He first ordered the recall of nine ambassadors he held to be either too corrupt or too royalist: among others Parviz Raji (London), Firaydoun Huvayda (UN), Bahram Bahrami (Paris) and Parviz Âdl (Brasília); Ardashir Zahidi had previously tendered his resignation. Simultaneously he got entangled in the NIRT controversy, having estimated "ninety per cent of its employees to be SAVAK agents"; a correct estimate, but a poor political move when the Premier needed all the support he could get. There were top SAVAK managers in key positions in the Prime Minister's Office itself. Bakhtiar finally apologised, but the harm had been done.

These hiccups were minor compared to the departure of Regency Council chairman Sayyid Jalal Tihrani for Paris on January 18. Tihrani was probably on a goodwill mission to meet Khomeini and try to mediate between him and Bakhtiar.

But at Neauphle, Khomeini refused to receive him until he had resigned from the Council and publicly declared it to be illegal.

Tihrani duly complied and met Khomeini on January 21 and 22. Apparently nothing came out of these talks, as Khomeini had no interest in any compromise with Bakhtiar and was, on principle, opposed to compromises. The only result was that the Regency Council was discredited once and for all.

Another institution since long dead but still afloat was the *Majlis*. With the Shah gone, the deputies lost their last inhibitions and, prodded by the threats hurled by Khomeini, began resigning *en masse*. Twenty of them resigned on January 18 and thereafter every day or so another few were added to the list. The *Majlis*, long since irrelevant, was slowly melting away.

In his bid to retain power against all odds, Bakhtiar needed political support. One side to which he turned was the moderate religious hierocracy, especially Ayatullah Shariâtmadari, with whom he was in contact through Ayatullah Muhammad Taqi Qumi.[105] Bakhtiar even had the impudence to declare that "nine out of ten clergymen are on my side". When interviewed, Sayyid Jâfar Bihbahani declared: "Bakhtiar is taking the Revolution on the wrong tracks", and Ayatullah Shariâtmadari had told the BBC that he "refused any allegation of collusion with Bakhtiar". The Prime Minister's game of seducing moderate clergymen, thereby driving a wedge between them and the radicals, never got off the ground, since the moderates were unwilling to commit themselves in these uncertain times.

Bakhtiar then turned to the Americans, who seemed willing to support his bid, for he had no better option. In Washington, the NSC's Brzezinski clearly favoured the Bakhtiar army alternative. In Tehran Ambassador Sullivan was in charge of the political side, and from January 4 the deputy commander of US armed forces in Europe, General Robert Huyser, was in charge of the military side. Selected at the highest level (by the Joint Chiefs of Staff committee), Huyser was sent on a three day mission, which, in the end, took a full month. His direct superior, General Alexander Haig, had tried to block Huyser's selection and, having been overruled, resigned on January 3 (effective date: June 30). Huyser must have followed a number of objectives in Tehran; his first goal was probably to bring to conclusion Erich von Marbod's protracted efforts to settle legally the backlog of major Iranian arms purchases from the US (see Table 17.6); his second goal was likely to have been to gain "control [over] the [Iranian] Generals" and "ask them to transfer their loyalty to Bakhtiar";[107] other final directives for Americans forces still in Iran (e.g. the IBEX project) and the task of finding a strong general (on whom to bank for the future) might well have been part of Huyser's package. As for Sullivan, he had proposed such a solution weeks earlier:

> ...[We] have to attempt to build a secure barricade against the ayatollah ...it might be possible to rally the military behind a National Front government headed by Bakhtiar, Bazargan and others, and thus limit the influence of Khomeini...[108]

The Ambassador was correct, for the Americans had no other solution to stop the tidal wave of religious feeling engulfing Iran. Brzezinski made sure that Sullivan and Huyser had it right by sending them a joint cable on January 19 along the following lines:[109]
(1) US position unchanged, still support Bakhtiar and return to legality;
(2) military support for Bakhtiar is crucial;
(3) unity of [Iranian] armed forces critical for task ahead;
(4) Bakhtiar to widen his spectrum by opening up to opposition;
(5) enlarged coalition would reinforce both government and army.
Bakhtiar, definitely not an Americanophile by nature, could rely on unwavering American support.

Bakhtiar, however, was far less secure with the generals, of whom he was suspicious. His relationship was General Âbbas Qarabaghi, the man appointed by the Shah as the head of the Joint Chiefs of General Staff on January 10, was far from good: between the French-educated *grand bourgeois* and the Iran-educated military commander, there was little in common. There were no *atomes crochus* between Bakhtiar and most of the top generals. The new commander-in-chief of the army, General Âbd ul-Âli Badreh'i, (a trusted royal servant) who had replaced General Âbd ul-Âli Najimi Nai'ni on January 10, was a case in point; as for the displaced Najimi Nai'ni, the only intellectual among the top generals, he kept repeating: "We have to act. If we fail to do so, we shall melt like snow in the sun".[110] Among the twenty or so top generals forming the Army Commanders' Council, prominent (along with the three mentioned above) were: General Husayn Toufanian, General Amir Husayn Rabiî (commander-in-chief of the air force), Admiral Kamal ul-Din Habibullahi (commander-in-chief of the navy), General Nasir Muqaddam (head of SAVAK) and General Mihdi

Table 17.6. Major US Arms Deals with Iran, Settled by Erich von Marbod in Tehran.[106]

Armaments	Supplier	Estimated Value of Contract ($m)
160 F-16	General Dynamics	3,500
16 F-4E	McDonnell Douglas	500
7 AWACS	Boeing International	1,300
4 Spruance destroyers	Litton	1,400
400 AIM-54 (Phoenix) missiles	Hughes	600
Chah Bahar Base (reduced)	Brown & Root	1,000
Total		8,300

Rahimi, the military commander of Tehran and, since January 22, also the head of the Tehran police. On the National Security Council set up on January 15 there were two civilians (Bakhtiar and Mirfindiriski) and eleven generals (Qarabaghi, Badreh'i, Rabii, Habibullahi, Muqaddam, Rahimi, Shafaqat, Muhaqqiqi, Jâfari, Khajeh Nouri and Amini Afshar); but Bakhtiar clearly dominated all the generals intellectually.

The generals failed to heed Najimi Nai'ini's advice: they languished like sitting ducks, incapable of taking the initiative.

They seemed capable only of complaining daily to General Huyser, believing the American general to have full powers and still believing that the Americans were able to stop the rot. They had three basic requests which they wanted Huyser to relay to the White House for them: (i) "the guarantee that the Ayatollah [Khomeini] would not be permitted back in Iran"; (ii) that "the BBC Broadcasts in Iran [should be] stopped"; and, (iii) "an end to the distribution of inflammatory statements from Khomeini".[111] These requests show the collective IQ of Iran's top generals: only regarding the first point could the

Americans try to exert some pressure (with only a remote chance of success), concerning the two others they were powerless. Huyser "never gave [them] a reply" – he probably never relayed the requests to Washington – for "despite repeated statements to the Iranian Generals that he was speaking every day with the President he does not seem to have done so".[112] When Huyser demanded the dispatch of ten thousand US Marines to Tehran, he was rebuked (remember Vietnam). Having departed Tehran on February 3, Huyser reported to President Carter on the morrow that:

> ...everything was going well, that Bakhtiar had every chance of prevailing, that the military was holding together, and that there was no reason for any drastic action to be taken...[113]

With hindsight, it can be concluded that General Haig's judgement of Huyser had been vindicated and that he had resigned justifiably.

The generals' military machine was more or less "holding together", although "signs of lassitude and a lower morale"[114] were beginning to show after five months of martial law. The only problem was created by the unruly *Humafars*, the air force and heliforces' (*Havanirouz*) technicians. The most discontented group among the Iranian armed forces, the *Humafars* (General Khatami's legacy) let their frustrations burst out in early January. On January 11, a *Humafar* tried to shoot the Kermanshah *Havanirouz* Commander; on January 20, the *Humafars* at Hamadan Shahrukhi air base went on a hunger strike; four days later, in their support, four hundred *Humafars* rioted at the Isfahan air base for helicopters (the former Bell Helicopters' site); other *Humafar*-led disorders were reported at Shiraz and Bushire; on January 29, *Humafars* of the Qasr-i Firouzeh air base (east of Tehran) met Ayatullah Taliqani (thus entering the opposition); on January 31, fifty *Humafars* arrested at the Shahrukhi and Vahdati (Dizful) air bases were transferred to the Tabriz air base, the last secure base! The *Humafars* were the first group in the armed forces to rebel: they had the least to lose and had chosen the right time for their move.[115]

While Bakhtiar and Qarabaghi were busy ironing out their differences, Khomeini was steadily forging ahead. On January 12 he had announced the creation of a Revolutionary Council as a counterweight to the Regency Council, but had had the cunning not to disclose its composition (thereby letting all groups believe that its leaders were sitting on it, and he was also able to reshuffle it at will). Tehran University had been reopened in January on Bakhtiar's orders, amidst a whiff of agitation. The leftist guerrillas kept up their hit-and-run attacks; for instance, on January 15, one of their squads executed Major Majid Majidi, the officer who had fired the first deadly shot at Tabriz on February 19, 1978. Religious-led riots continued unabated in the provinces.

However, all the spotlights were once again on Tehran on January 19, when the fortieth day (*Arbâin*) of the martyrdom of Imam Husayn (A.S.) was being commemorated. A crowd estimated at between 500-600,000 marched along Shah Reza Avenue all the way to Shahyad Square. Troops were nowhere to be seen; the march was peaceful and disciplined; tensions were low and main slogans were "Khomeini - leader" and "Death to Bakhtiar". The people had again voted with their feet against the Prime Minister.

The opposition to Bakhtiar were scoring points on all sides. Internationally, the Soviet Press had entered the arena "fulminating [against] the Western media (especially the American and Israeli ones) for their unjustified attacks on the Ayatullah".[116] After Brezhnev's November 19 warning to Carter "against all interference in the internal affairs of Iran", it was the first time that the Soviets were seen to be taking sides; it must have been because their top Iranian analysts (e.g. Vladimir Poliakov and Youri Alexeyev) had concluded that the wind was blowing in favour of Iran's religious leader. Domestically too the opposition was scoring points, for its leaders were profiting from Bakhtiar's laxity about coming forward and delivering public speeches: Ayatullah Bihihshti, in *Kayhan* for a press conference, the SMKI supremo Masûd Rajavi, who addressed a TU mass rally, author Tunikabuni and the SCFKI's Âli Kishtkar, who spoke at various gatherings.

At Neauphle, the lawyer Hasan Nazih (the LMI's special envoy) had been busy, since January 10, preparing for the return of Khomeini to Iran. Through his services, a special Iran Air flight to take Khomeini and his retinue to Tehran had been arranged for January 25. Nazih must have somehow cleared the Ayatullah's return beforehand with Bakhtiar, an old friend of his since the 1950s; and Khomeini's return might well have been part of a wider deal struck between Nazih and Bakhtiar, the latter believing that he could certainly control and possibly compromise with Khomeini. The politicians had failed to clear the project with the military and when the generals got wind of the project their reaction was electric: they sent their tanks to occupy Mihrabad Airport in the early hours of January 24. When Ayatullah Taliqani came the next day to see the special Iran Air jumbo off to Paris he was told that "all flights were postponed because of a strike of air control operators (!)". Outplayed by the generals, Bakhtiar could only call Nazih in Paris and ask him "to have Khomeini's return delayed by a week or two".[117] Khomeini was incensed – he thought that he had been double-crossed, calling Bakhtiar "a traitor". Whatever minor chance of compromise that had been left had now vanished, leaving only one outcome: total confrontation.

On January 25, instead of Khomeini's supporters it was Bakhtiar's who counted themselves on the Tehran streets: his Supporters of the Constitution and of Social Democracy were happily surprised to found out that they numbered between 150,000 and 200,000 on their march to Baharistan Square and the *Majlis* – an unexpected success. The numbers seemed promising, Bakhtiar's only problem stemming from the fact that his mixed bag of a clientele was too well off to fight and endure: nationalist bourgeois, younger army officers, wealthy royalists, second-rank industrialists, middle-aged technocrats and a handful of *Bazaaris*.[118] There were no Indians among them, and Bakhtiar couldn't count on a single massive constituency to use as a solid base (as the religious leaders had with the *Dihqanzadehs*).

The religious activists were taken aback by the success chalked up by Bakhtiar. They responded by creating disorders and clashes around the TU campus on Friday January 26 and launching a march on Shahyad the following day. On January 28, groups of rioters engaged Gendarmerie personnel in 24 Isfand Square in front of the Gendarmerie headquarters, as they were boarding their service buses. From the building's rooftop, guards fired shots to protect their beleaguered colleagues below. Soon pandemonium reigned in the square: the shoot-out lasted for over five hours before order was restored. Result: the worst bloodshed since Bakhtiar had assumed power, with thirty-two martyrs and over two hundred injured.

By this action against the Gendarmes, the religious-led groups had regained their mastery of the Tehran streets[119] and had torpedoed any chance of a compromise.

Simultaneously with the 24 Isfand Square massacre, Tehrani religious leaders, led by Taliqani, began their sit-in at TU's mosque. Their main demand, the re-opening of Mihrabad Airport (thereby clearing the way for Khomeini's return), was the main subject of their first communiqué. During the next day, politicians and generals reviewed the religious opponents' demand and, after being given reassurances, the generals eventually ordered their tanks to evacuate the airport on January 30. At Neauphle, Khomeini had issued another strong message ordering the continuation of "civil disobedience"; in Tehran, Bakhtiar responded by remarking that "the Ayatullah's return will lead to civil war"; in Paris, French President Giscard d'Estaing had arrived at a diametrically opposed conclusion, telling his ministers that:

> ...Khomeini is the only person capable of instituting a stable government, thus forestalling an Iranian civil war...[120]

The French President seemed to know better than the Iranian Premier.

17.9 Endgame

On Thursday February 1, Ayatullah Khomeini debarked at Mihrabad Airport in an Air France jumbo jet (financed by his *Bazaar* supporters). For the patriarch, after some fourteen years in exile, it was a triumph: millions of people lined the Tehran streets to welcome him back. It was an unprecedented event. It was Sacred Time with flowers. At his first public address, at Tehran's Bihisht-i Zahra cemetery, he showed the qualities that had propelled him to the undisputed leadership of the Revolution, for in a very political speech he reminded his supporters that "the basic recipe for our successes was 'unity' (*vahdat-i kalimeh*)" and showed his animosity towards Bakhtiar with his declaration: "I punch his government in the mouth". When Bakhtiar failed to react to such an insult, it was already clear to Iranians that he had lost.

From the cemetery, Khomeini went to his headquarters at the town centre Âlavi primary school and the adjacent Rifah secondary school (both financed by sources within the LMI in the 1960s, to dispense Islamic education). Friday February 2 was a long day of public relations, as thousands upon thousands streamed through the schools to pay their respects to Khomeini.

On February 3, at a press conference, Khomeini outlined his programme of government, which could be summarised in six points:
(1) the organisation of a Revolutionary Council (functional since January 12);
(2) the institution of a provisional government, to be appointed by himself;
(3) a referendum to be held on the issue of the establishment of an Islamic republic to replace the monarchy;
(4) the election of an assembly of experts (*khubrigan*) to draw up a constitution;
(5) the election of a president of the Islamic republic (if so provided for by the new constitution);
(6) the elections of a *Majlis* (ditto), but no Senate.

It was clear, rational and easy to understand. Besides publicising his programme, Khomeini took another jibe at Bakhtiar, finishing with yet another threat: "Don't push us to declare a *jihad* (holy war)".

The initiative and momentum were indubitably with the Khomeini camp; Bakhtiar could only wait to see from which angle the next blow to his weak position would come. Meanwhile, time was not on his side. The first major official to switch to the Ayatullah's side was Tehran mayor Javad Shahristani: he resigned his office, met Khomeini and was reinstated in his post by the latter. Then, on February 4, Khomeini announced the formation of his provisional government (see Point 2 above), with Engineer Mihdi Bazargan* at its head. With this masterly appointment Khomeini had rallied to his colours (1) the technocrats (thus, the bureaucracy); (2) some undecided nationalist elements; (3) the *Bazaar*'s moderate wing; and (4) Iran's academics and non-communist student body. At the same time the Ayatullah had not given anything away, knowing that Bazargan was inoffensive and malleable.

* ENGINEER MIHDI BAZARGAN (1905-1995), born into a Tehran *Bazaari* family; studied at Paris's École Centrale, specialising in thermodynamics; upon return to Iran became lecturer at Tehran University Technical Faculty (1936); got a share of the lucrative construction business (an Elite preserve) for his fellow technocrats (end 1940s); appointed by Dr Musaddiq as first managing director of NIOC (1951-53); joined National Resistance Movement (1954-59); founding member of LMI (May 1961); arrested (1963), court-martialled, sentenced to ten years, spent four in jail (1963-67); managed his profitable consulting businesses, including his Yad company (1968-78); appointed prime minister by Khomeini (February-November 1979); thereafter went into semi-retirement, writing books and pamphlets.

Faced with a *fait accompli*, Bakhtiar could only be cynical: "As long as the Provisional Government is a farce, we shall accept it". Far from being a joke, it was both a deadly rival – as employees' organisations in eleven ministries soon voted to recognise Bazargan's legitimacy over Bakhtiar's legality – and a ready replacement should Bakhtiar take the plunge.

Behind the scenes, though, Bakhtiar and his old friend Bazargan (twenty-five years in the opposition ranks together) were keeping in touch, and the former could truthfully declare that: "Bazargan and I agree on ninety per cent of the issues".[121] The Premier also hinted that, given time, he would stage a referendum to decide upon the country's future regime (a sign that he had accepted some of Khomeini's ideas, see Point 3 above). But the Premier sometimes forgot his political ABC, as when he publicly stated that: "I fought against Hitler and the Pahlavis, I shall stand before Khomeini and Bazargan".[122] Moreover, when asked by a French journalist (in a private interview on February 8) what he would reply if Khomeini asked him once again to resign, he shot back: "Je lui dirais merde".[123] Not a politic answer to an hypothetical question.

After his expression of amity with Bazargan, Bakhtiar had ordered his last round of arrests and fired his last legal shots. On February 3 and 4, the former PBO tsar Âbdul-Majid Majidi and ex-ministers Houshang Nahavandi and Ghulam Riza Kianpour were arrested. Then Bakhtiar forced his last two bills through a decimated (and heavily guarded) *Majlis* on February 6: these bills were for the official disbanding of SAVAK (to be replaced by a newly-created National Intelligence Centre, with no policing role, under the supervision of the Prime Minister's Office) and for the creation of a special court for the trial of former ministers.

Finally, his Foreign Minister, Mirfindiriski, had officially taken Iran out of CENTO.

On the morning of February 8, dozens of air force officers in full dress uniform lined up at Rifah school to present their respects to Khomeini, a momentous event – scooped by *Kayhan* with a front page photograph showing the officers from the back as they saluted Khomeini – and a politically significant one, as, for the first time, a group of officers was switching its allegiance from the Pahlavis (to whom they had sworn an oath) to Khomeini as leader. The air force had proven to be the chink in the armed forces' façade of unity: first the *Humafars*, now the officers. Due to its more technocratic and technical nature, the air force had from the outset been the more liberal of the three arms, nurtured in a nationalist tradition.[124]

The officers' switch could not be unnoticed by the opposition, which had so far taken advantage of the smallest sign of weakness on the other side. But Thursday 8 ended peacefully and on Friday the 9, rival rallies organised by supporters of Bazargan and Bakhtiar – the first at Tehran University and the second at Amjadiyyeh Stadium – showed once again the popular bias favouring the former, as the crowd of 100,000 at TU clearly outnumbered the 40,000 at the sports arena (nevertheless a commendable effort for Bakhtiar's supporters, who had only achieved a meagre 2-3,000 two days earlier). But even these generally peaceful demonstrations could not cover the fact that Tehran was pregnant with the seeds of violence.

The last bastion of the Pahlavi regime still standing in the way of the revolutionary tidal wave was the army, not Bakhtiar. And with a gap having been found in the armed forces' monolith, any incident now could light the popular fuse, which was fully primed to burn out.

The incident that lit the fuse occurred on the evening of February 9 at Tehran's eastern air base of Doushan Tappeh. The cadets and *Humafars* of the base's training centre were tongue-lashed by their commanding officer for having watched on TV a re-run of Khomeini's arrival at Mihrabad Airport.

It was this untimely reprimand that led to the climax of the Revolution. The *Humafars* dug in their heels, confronting the officer. Confrontation led to armed rebellion. Pandemonium set in at Doushan Tappeh when officers and NCOs tried to control the mutinous ranks. Outnumbered by the latter, the former called for reinforcements from the Imperial Guards. By the time the Guardsmen arrived, the

Humafars were well-entrenched. They were also backed by thousands of Tehrani neighbours who, awakened by the fusillade, had come out to see and then side with the mutiny against the abhorred Guardsmen. Some guerrilla leaders, sensing the beginning of a civil war, had come out of their hide-outs to lead the people to battle. In the early hours, the Guardsmen called for more reinforcements to force a decisive encounter. The number of civilians taking to arms was growing by the hour. Even General Qarabaghi himself was looking for fresh troops for Doushan Tappeh; he called on General Âli Nishat, the commander of the crack *Javidan* (Immortals) Guards, asking for three hundred men, only to be told: "General, as you know better than I, the Immortals have a special mission to fulfil!".[125] At 10:00 on February 10, the Guardsmen were forced to retreat from Doushan Tappeh, leaving the whole eastern part of Tehran to the revolutionaries. A combination of *Humafars*, guerrillas and civilians had won the first round, losing only some fifty men during the skirmish.[126]

In east Tehran, the guerrillas decided to storm the barely protected Farahabad machine-gun factory. They easily captured MC-3s and other weapons which they distributed among those who had thrown petrol bombs for them the night before. The armed movement spread all the way to the centre of town by noon and the first police stations were besieged (in order to acquire much needed arms and ammunitions). The generals tried to nip the popular movement in the bud by issuing an ultimatum for a strict 16:30 curfew, with orders to shoot to kill thereafter. Alerted by the news, Khomeini and Taliqani quickly issued messages "not to obey the curfew". Moreover Khomeini "expressed hopes that the army would end its aggression[127] ...[for he] still favoured a peaceful solution ...and had not declared jihad yet".[128]

Khomeini did not know where a civil war would lead, but he knew that a curfew would give the military a chance of redressing a compromised situation; thus keeping the people on the streets was the best alternative available.

The generals, though, had not played their last trump card: the sturdy 16th Armoured Division stationed at Qazvin. Under the command of Generals Nîmatullah Mûtamidi and Manouchihr Malik, the 16th was on its way to Tehran and due to arrive in the early evening to take the capital city in hand. The division's vanguard had just passed Qazvin when an ominous message came from the Chief of Supreme Staff's office: "Mission aborted. Return immediately to Qazvin. We have been betrayed." An order is an order: the 16th returned to its starting point.

Who had betrayed the ultra-secret mission to the opposition, who had found time to take safety measures that brought about the mission's annulment? In his memoirs, General Qarabaghi fingered the Generals Hushang Hatam, Âbd ul-Âli Najimi Na'ini and... Bakhshi Azar as possible traitors;[129] the fact that all three were eased into early retirement on February 19 by General Qaranay without being further punished leaves some doubt concerning all three – with little chance of the real traitor being uncovered some day. The threat used by the opposition must have been deadly serious for the Chief of Staff to have ordered back its last trump card.

Meanwhile, in Tehran, the people had defied the 16:30 curfew and remained on the streets. The soldiers had safely retired to their barracks, where they barricaded themselves in. The most vulnerable bastions of the establishment were the capital's police stations. These were the first target of the guerrillas, who needed victories and arms. The stations were difficult to defend. Besieged by multitudes and firebombed, the stations readily fell one after another during the afternoon and the evening, beginning with number 10 at 17:00. Dozens of guns and some machine-guns were taken and distributed among the people; some were conveyed to mosques to arm the religious militants. Barricades were set up throughout the capital to defend against a last military attempt, which never came; only a few isolated tanks and armoured vehicles circulated in the streets and they were, for the most part, fire-bombed or damaged.

The partial mutiny of February 19 at Doushan Tappeh had degenerated into an armed confrontation pitting the people (led by a handful of guerrillas) against the Pahlavi armed forces. It was the climax of Sacred Time.

During the evening, Tehran Radio issued statements from leading military commanders declaring the army's neutrality: its forces had retired to their barracks and would not take sides in the present political dispute – the generals would sign (twenty-seven signatures) and issue an official declaration of neutrality at 10:30 in the morning of February 11. How could the generals have believed that they could simply just walk away from it all? Just lock their barracks' doors, pretending not to be a party to the ongoing dispute? This was an extraordinary move which could only encourage the guerrillas and their popular troops to carry on their successful drive of conquests, secure in the certainty that the soldiers would not venture on to the streets.

On the morning of February 11, as the guerrillas delivered the last blow to the Gendarmerie headquarters in 24 Isfand Square, two senior royalist officers were shot dead in separate incidents: the commander-in-chief of the army, General Âbd ul Âli Badreh'i, was machine-gunned by a special execution squad, and the deputy commander of the Imperial Guards, General Muhammad Amin Biglari, was shot down by a lone assailant.[130] Throughout the whole day Tehran was the scene of sieges followed by victories for the guerrilla-led masses; one after the other the regime's bastions fell:
– at 12:00, the Âbbasabad garrison;
– at 13:30, the Îshatabad army base;
– at 14:30, the Tehran Radio station, and the SAVAK headquarters at Sultanatabad;
– at 15:00, the round building of *Kumiteh* headquarters;
– at 15:30, the Prime Minister's Office, and the NIRT facilities at Jam-i Jam;
– at 16:00, the Military Academy (where some cadets resisted till their last cartridge);
– at 16:30, the Military School;
– at 17:00, the palaces of Niavaran and Saâdabad;
– at 18:30, the Bagh-i Shah complex (including the barracks of the dreaded *Nouhid* paratroopers[131]);
– at 19:00, Evin prison.

By the early evening of February 11, Tehran was in the hands of its people. They were dazzled, dumbfounded, incredulous, but victorious. They had won: in less than forty-eight hours an army reputed "to be invincible" was smashed. The two glorious days of fighting had ended with fewer than 5,000 casualties: some 654 dead and 2,703 wounded were reported by *Kayhan*.[132] General Taymour Bakhtiar's prophecy that the Imperial Army was a 'paper tiger' without any stomach for a fight had been proven correct. For the second time in their fifty year history the Pahlavi armed forces had crumbled within hours: there was something basically flawed in Reza Shah's institutional legacy.

The real victors of February were the people of Iran.

As Saint-Just, the French revolutionary hero, said: "I hear many individuals now claim that they made the Revolution, they are all wrong; the Revolution was made by the people".[134] So it was in Iran too, it was the people who had made the Revolution. In the people's vanguard were the guerrillas who had led the people to victory against the troops of the abhorred Pahlavi regime (their lifelong dream) and amassed a considerable arsenal in the process.[133] The religious masses had also played their part as shock troops, but, as few of them had experience or military training, they had remained in the guerrillas' shadows. Furthermore, thousands of ordinary citizens had taken up arms and battled against the armed forces.

Finally the duo of Bakhtiar and Qarabaghi had failed to stop the tidal wave of revolutionary fervour: it had smashed their weak dam, as it had wiped out all other obstacles along its path. Notwithstanding his personal talents, the Prime Minister had never got his equations right. Between the military anvil and the people's hammer he had been lucky not to be crushed to death. At the Council of Ministers on January 23, he had sworn with all his ministers "to either face death or defend the Nation's Constitutional Rights"[134] (eventually doing neither). On February 11, he was fortunate to have some of his family literally grab him from the Prime Minister's Office as he was preparing to have lunch. He made it just in time to the Military Academy where a helicopter took him to the north of the city and there he covered his face with oversized sunglasses, so as not to be recognised by the people on his way to a hideout, and later exile to Paris. He had lasted only thirty-eight days as Muhammad Reza Shah's last prime minister. That would be the title he would carry for posterity, certainly not an epithet he would have relished, but Dr Shahpour Bakhtiar wanted so much to be prime minister that such details were irrelevant.

If Bakhtiar had had the time to show his undeniable abilities, Qarabaghi could not show anything. The General eventually made it into exile too. He had been indecisive and lacking energy as the chief of the General Staff. He was a chief in the image of the Iranian Army: found lacking in almost every department.

As the last dam broke and the people of Tehran became the new masters of the capital, the whole edifice of Iran Inc. came crashing to the ground. Now everything was possible. A new order would have to be built from the ground up. A new elite from among the counter-elites would take up the reins of power and, as they would prove incapable of running the country, they would soon be recalled from the levers of power. As for the counter-elites, they all dreamt of finally coming to power after decades of sacrifice, torture and imprisonment.

The old elite dreamt too of eventually making a comeback, when the powers-that-be had realised that they could not govern without their century-old experience. The old elite had carefully let the Shah "get all the credit", hoping that "he would get all the blame"[135] and that its (crucial) role in the Iran Inc. affairs would be readily forgotten.

In any event a new Iran was to be born, an Iran certainly more Iranian than that of the Pahlavis, an Iran born with the people themselves as midwives. Maybe it was the beginning of yet another decline, but thus far it was certainly for the better. The birth and life of this new Iran is another story altogether.

NOTES

1. An anecdote might best illustrate the straws of discontent blowing in the 1977 national winds: 'Asked over the telephone by his pipeline supervisor (in Tehran) to get ready to start one of his compressors at the Fal-i Baba station (in the middle of nowhere, between Ahvaz and Tehran), the young engineer in charge calmly said, "I won't." To which the startled supervisor replied, "You must be joking!" "Not at all. I am dead serious." "Come on. You can't be. Is there anything wrong with you?" "No. Not at all." "So why won't you start the compressor?" "Because I simply don't feel like it." A voice, lost in Iran's wilderness, had just said that he could also take decisions.' Private communication by an NIOC microwave transmission supervisor, who overheard the conversation.
2. *Iran Almanac 1977* (Tehran: Echo of Iran, 1977) p.123. The headlines in the Tehran newspapers were more free publicity for AI.
3. *L'Humanité* newspaper, May 10, 1977. In an article entitled 'Des tapis dans les prisons pour étouffer les cris des détenus politiques', the French newspaper reported that, although the detainees were told by SAVAK not to tell the commission about their tortures and beatings (under threat of reprisals), the prisoners grabbed this unique occasion and spilled the beans to the ICRC delegates, accepting subsequent reprisals for having talked to the "foreigners".
4. A. Parsons, *The Pride and the Fall* (London: Jonathan Cape, 1984) p.56.
5. The young Sultanpour, a radical leftist with links to the SCFKI guerrillas, showed his deep humanitarianism on the Sixth Night, when Firaydoun Mushiri, a poet co-opted by the regime and given a high position in the PTT, took to the pulpit and the attendants turned their backs to him in a deadly silence. Sultanpour stepped

forward, took the microphone and simply said, "My friends, please." They listened to Mushiri. If it had not been for Sultanpour, Mushiri might have suffered injury after this insult.

6. In the Iranian *Shiî* tradition, a death is usually followed by five rituals after the burial:
   (1) the *Khatm* (the End), a public ceremony of mourning;
   (2) the *Sivvum* (the Third), the third day after death;
   (3) the *Haft* (the Week), the seventh day after;
   (4) the *Chihileh* (the Fortieth), forty days after;
   (5) the *Sal* (the Year), a whole year after the death.

7. *Middle East Economic Digest*, December 2, 1977, p.30.

8. Private communication from a couple of Iranian students who had their plane tickets to Washington reimbursed by the embassy.

9. During 1978, three more Iranian Embassies would be occupied by students: (1) at East Berlin (in March); (2) at Brussels (August) and (3) The Hague (August).

10. See *Keyhan International*, March 12, 1979, p.4. After his arrest in March 1979, Mahmud Jâfarian disclosed that the article had been written by Parviz Nikkhwah and sent to the Minister for Information and Dariush Humayoun, after due approval by both the Shah and Court Minister Huvayda.

11. See A. Parsons, op. cit. (note 4), p.61: "...a piece of great foolishness which, even at the time, I believed would not have happened if Alam had still been at the court..."

12. Again the Empress travelled widely through the US, meeting a number of personalities, including former Vice-President Nelson Rockefeller. The fact that author Lesley Blanch had been advanced $50,000 fuelled the rumours in Tehran that some American lobbies were considering an Empress regency in place of the Shah. On the Lesley Blanch book, see P.C. Radji, op. cit., p.92.

13. The fifteen punished shopowners had sent telegrams of condolences to Ayatullah Khomeini upon his son Mustafa's demise. Among the fifteen was a *Bazaar* trader, Hajji Rukhsifat, whose shop would remain closed until February 1979, in itself a twelve-month record.

14. See *Ittilaât*, Bahman 30, 1356, (February 19, 1978). And also, J.-C. Guillebaud, 'Une seule cible...' in *Le Monde*, April 6, 1978, who mentions "officially twelve dead and around two hundred wounded" and quotes an opposition estimate of "approximately seventy dead".

15. *The Economist*, March 4, 1978, p.59.

16. In his memoirs, an Islamist opponent and former political prisoner, Asadullah Badamchian, wrote that: "Most opponents did not believe that an upheaval with such dimensions and such courage could be achieved so soon in the process". Quoted from Badamchian's memoirs, entitled *Asrar-i Pusht-i Pardeh* (Secrets Behind the Curtains) published in *Risalat* newspaper, Isfand 24, 1365, (March 15, 1987), p.3.

17. See *Le Monde*, op. cit. (note 14).

18. *Iran Almanac 1978* (Tehran: Echo of Iran, 1978) p.48.

19. See *Le Monde*, June 25, 1985. where, in a critique of Regis Debray's book *Les Empires contre l'Europe*, A. Fontaine quotes Debray's concise picture of global Western and Eastern (i.e. the Soviet Union) strategies in the world.

20. A. Parsons, op. cit. (note 4), pp.72-3 and 102-3. The Ambassador's precise reports clearly show the regime's paranoia *vis-à-vis* the BBC.

21 By 1978, of the three Rashidian sons, only Asadullah was still alive.

22 For statistics on exports and oil imports from Iran, see F. Fesharaki, 'Revolution and Energy Policy in Iran', *Economist Intelligence Unit*, no. 82, July 1980, pp.6-7,12. And for expatriates in Iran see *Le Nouvel Observateur* magazine, July 9-15, 1978, p.30.

23 See B. Rubin, *Paved With Good Intentions* (Penguin Books, 1984) p.169. The US Embassy in Tehran had ridiculed Lubrani's suggestions.

24 On the deteriorating state of affairs between the Israelis and the Shah see R.K. Ramazani, 'Iran and the Arab–Israeli Conflict' in The Middle East Journal, vol.32, no. 4, autumn 1978, pp.421-8.

25 Film director Muhsin Makhmalbaf would have one of his heroes tell his former associate when leaving him, in the 1983 film *Ârousi-i Khouban*: "And you, you smell bad too, as the former regime used to".

26 *Middle East Economic Survey*, February 13, 1978, p.1. Interview with NIOC's director for International Affairs, Dr Parviz Mina.

27 The new board consisted of Karim Nazhand (Administration), Âbbas Fallah (Corporate Planning), Jahangir Râufi (Exploration and Production), Fakhr Nouri (Finance), Muhammad Âli Muvahid (Legal), Masûd Mudir (International) Âbbas Quli Bakhtiar (Engineering), Hasan Mustafavi Kashani (Commercial), Âli Asghar Irani (Refining), Kayvan Naraqi (Distribution) and Amir Badakhshan (Research).

28 B. Mossavar Rahmani, 'Time to Stand Firm', in *Keyhan International*, September 20, 1978, p.4. In a strongly worded article, Musavvar Rahmani defended NIOC's position. In 1978 Bizhan Musavvar Rahmani was a journalist and sometime assistant to Dr Firaydun Fisharaki, the then top adviser on energy affairs to Prime Minister Amuzigar. In the autumn of 1978 Musavvar Rahmani somehow received a timely Rockefeller Foundation scholarship before going on to Harvard and to the independent US oil company Apache International. His subsequent American career leaves a serious doubt about his exact role during the 1978 NIOC-Consortium crisis.

29 The Science and Industry University new rector was none other than Dr Ahmad Sikhavat, the former head of the Atomic Energy Organisation's research centre.

30 *Iran Almanac 1978* (Tehran: Echo of Iran, 1978) pp.398-404.

31 J.-C. Guillebaud, 'Les Troubles en Iran' in *Le Monde*, April 6, 1978.

32 *Kayhan* newspaper, Urdibihisht 21, 1357 (May 11, 1978); and also *Rastakhiz*, same date.

33 L. George, *Le Monde*, May 6, 1978, p.4.

34 No relation to Ayatullah Muhammad Taqi Qumi of Tehran.

35 H. Muvahhid, *Dou Sal-i Akhar – Rifurm ta Inqilab* (The Last Two Years – From Reform to Revolution), (Tehran: Amir Kabir, 1363 (1984)) p.126.

36 *Asnad-i Laneh Jasousi*, no. 63, p.12.

37 Ibid., p.13.

38 Public opinion attributed the Qum shootings to General Khusroudad, while informed sources mentioned General Shafaât. In March 1979, after his capture, General Âbbas Shafaât confessed that: "General Uvaysi, the then army commander-in-chief, gave me orders to march on Qum to re-establish law and order there". He added that when he arrived at Qum, the killings had already taken place, hinting at a Captain Tukhmihchi as the perpetrator. See *Keyhan International*, March 19, 1979, p.4.

39 Among these books were the complete works of Dr Âli Shariâti, hitherto banned from publication, and a great success amongst the younger generation.
40 R. Khomeini, *Sahifeh-yi Nour* (Tehran: Ministry of Islamic Guidance, 1361 (1982)) Vol. 2, p.67.
41 It must have been on Dr Ayadi's orders that the Shah's secretary Mûinian had written a letter to Bank-i Markazi governor, Hasan Âli Mihran, recommending Yazdani and his ventures. In his reply, dated May 19, 1977, Mihran assured Mûinian that: "(i) Bank-i Markazi would provide Yazdani with a Rls500m ($22m) working capital; (ii) the IMDBI would take part in four joint ventures with a total capital Rls4100m ($58m); (iii) the ADBI (Agricultural Bank) would disburse the needed funds for Yazdani's agricultural projects". A photocopy of these and other letters are reproduced in: H. Arzhangi, *Gharatgari dar Iran* (Tehran: printed by author, 1358 (1979)) pp.75-6.
42 First disclosed by *The New York Times*, July 4, 1978.
43 One of Empress Farah's aunts and her lady-in-waiting is said to have boasted from her exile: "I had plenty of time to transfer all my cash abroad. Only a $10m chunk somehow got lost along the way." Breadcrumbs... It later came to light that the $10m had been shifted by the Bank-i Ûmran money-changer (a relative of the lady in question) to his own Swiss bank account! From a private communication by a close relative of both the lady and the happy money-changer.
44 *Jumbish* weekly, no. 4, Khurdad 20, 1357 (June 10, 1978) p.6.
45 Ibid., p.2.
46 *The Economist*, July 29, 1978, p.57.
47 *Jumbish* weekly, no. 5, Tir 5, 1357 (June 26, 1978), p.4.
48 *Keyhan International*, August 19, 1978, p.1.
49 *Jumbish* weekly, no. 8 (special issue on Abadan's Rex Cinema), Murdad 31, 1357 (August 22, 1978), p.1.
50 *Le Monde*, October 3, 1978.
51 *Le Figaro*, September 11, 1978.
52 *Kayhan*, Sharivar 18, 1357 (September 9, 1978), p.1. These official numbers seem doubtful as the ratio of injured to killed is less than 4 to 1.
53 Private communication from the eldest son of a minister, who had it from his father on September 9.
54 The Ardalan family, dominated by patriarch Hajj Îzz ul-Mamalik Ardalan, was among the lesser families of the old Qajar Elite which had found favour under the Pahlavi dynasty, placing many of its members in the military and bureaucracy. For example, Âli Quli Ardalan had once been Minister for Foreign Affairs (1955–58) and the patriarch's son Abu'l Fath Ardalan was an admiral with full powers over the Iran Electronic Industries and Isiran (the computer joint venture with the American firm of Honeywell).
55 *The Economist*, September 23, 1978, p.84.
56 M. Gallo, *L'Homme Robespierre* (Paris: Librairie Academique Perrin, Presses Pocket, 1968) p.202.
57 P. Radji, *In the Service of the Peacock Throne* (London: Hamish Hamilton, 1983) p.210.
58 Ibid., p.125.
59 W.H. Sullivan, 'Dateline Iran: The Road Not Taken', *Foreign Policy*, no. 40, autumn 1980, p.179.

60 Three guardsmen, including the Cento sharpshooting champion, ran away from Zhaleh Square. They hid in the champion's house. In the evening SAVAK officers encircled it and after a shoot-out captured the three deserters. One of them died of his wounds; the champion survived.
61 See *Newsweek*, March 5, 1979, p.37. The whole EDS affair smelled of heavy corruption. It was rumoured in Tehran that the company's entry into Iran and in the Health Ministry had been lubricated by top influence-peddler Abu'l Fath Mahvi. The EDS affair would make more waves as the Justice Ministry ordered the arrest of two top EDS-Iran managers, P. Schiapparone and W. Gayford.
62 *Iran Post*, October 2, 1978.
63 *Le Monde*, October 31, 1978, p.1.
64 Ibid., September 30, 1978.
65 A. Parsons, op. cit. (note 3), p.87.
66 The Saff group had probably been behind the August 5 blaze which had destroyed the Bakara nightclub in Tehran; it had avenged the August 13 bomb at the Khansalar restaurant which had caused some forty casualties.
67 *The Economist*, October 28, 1978, p.66.
68 Ibid., September 30, 1978, p.73.
69 Private communication from an oil company department head with twenty-four years of service, who threw in his lot with the strike and pulled along at least a dozen of his subordinates.
70 During the summer of 1978, the prudent Ansari had held private dinners (financed out of his own pocket) for local personalities in both Isfahan and Shiraz. He had heard their grievances and realised the depth of the crisis. He had then sold his house and other assets in Iran, and transferred the proceeds abroad. During the trip to Abadan he had realised the game was up.
71 *Kayhan*, Aban 14, 1357 (November 5, 1978), p.1.
72 The setting on fire of the BMW building might have been the work of anti-Zionist elements wanting to thus settle some very old accounts with the Vahabzadeh family. The blaze was so intense that not only was the high-rise burnt to the ground but it also pulled in its fall the adjacent ten-storey high National Iranian Gas Company headquarters.
73 A. Parsons, op. cit. (note 3), p.90.
74 Senior judge, Jamal ul-Din Akhavi, at eighty-five the dean of the Justice Ministry, turned down the job of auditing the royal finances.
75 Recalled from Pakistan on October 7, Nasiri was officially indicted on October 17 and arrested on November 7, whereas Huvayda was taken prisoner in his Vanak high-rise flat on November 9.
76 One of these questionnaires sent in the Qazvin area (no. 201-4-6, dated July 30, 1978) was reproduced by the Iranian Lawyers' Association.
77 *Le Monde*, December 3/4, 1978, p.1.
78 *Kayhan* newspaper was only published a month later, but in its first issue of Day 16, 1357 (January 6, 1979), p.5, it summarised the events of early December and reported some thirty people requiring surgical treatment in the hospitals adjacent to the rioting area on December 2.
79 T. Carlyle, *The French Revolution*, (London: Macmillan, 1921) Vol. II, p.169.
80 Noted by the author on December 11, 1978. In the original all of the slogan's sections were repeated twice.

80A See *Kayhan*, Azar 22, 1359 (December 13, 1980), p.5. One of the NCOs is reported as being second sergeant Ismâil Salamatbakhsh and a private as Nasir ul-Din Umidi Âbid Baba Nazari.
81 The sources for these statistics are NIOC (private communications) and specialised petroleum journals.
82 The reappointment of Intizam, a popular (and honest) politician of the old Qajar Elite mould, to the head of NIOC after an eclipse of fourteen years was in line with the Shah's new policy of appointing old Elite members. But these appointments came much too late to change anything. The Intizam appointment could have changed things at NIOC if it had been made at least eight months earlier. In this case, as in so many others, the regime's gambits were made at a time when it had become too late to have any positive impact.
83 A. Parsons, op. cit. (note 3), p.116.
84 *The International Herald Tribune*, April 21, 1980, p.4. See article 'Carter and the Fall of the Shah', by M. Ledeen and W. Lewis.
85 *Keyhan International*, January 11, 1979, p.3.
86 G. Ball, op. cit. , p.455.
87 *Le Monde*, J. Gueyras: 'Les manifestations prennent un tour anti-Americain'.
88 The next target after the Americans were the Israelis, and on the same day of December 24 the Tehran offices of air carrier El Al were totally destroyed, with the assailants leaving behind pro-Palestinian slogans on the walls.
89 B. Woodward, *Veil: The Secret Wars of the CIA, 1981–1987* (Simon and Schuster, 1987) p.110. The secret service of the number one superpower should be ashamed of such erroneous judgements. Being aware of these, the layman can began to understand the reasons behind the US's global failure. Moreover, on the same page, Woodward quotes another CIA paper dated November 22, 1978: "[The Shah] is not paralysed by indecision ...[and is generally] in accurate touch with reality [*sic*]".
90 Ibid., p.101.
91 Ibid., p.110.
92 Ibid., p.111.
93 J. Robinson, *Yamani – The Inside Story* (Simon and Schuster, 1988) p.210. Quoting: "The Shah not only believed the Americans would always take care of him, he bet the Peacock Throne on it".
94 *Le Nouvel Observateur*, 5 to 11 September 1986, p.30. See article 'Marenches n'a pas tout dit... Entretien avec Michel Poniatowski'.
95 *Keyhan International*, January 17, 1979, p.4.
96 A. Parsons, op. cit. (note 3), p.119.
97 Â. Qarabaghi, *Îtirafat-i Zhiniral* (The General's Confessions), (Tehran: Nashr-i Nay, 1364 (1985)) p.208.
98 Bakhtiar had concluded his first speech with two verses from a poem of Râdi Azarkhashi: "I am the Firebird, unwary of the Fire,
        I am the Wave, not fearful of the Sea"
Public opinion would know him as 'The Firebird' or *Farsi Murgh-i Toufan*.
99 A few days later, the NF executive was reshuffled to yield the following board: Dr Sanjabi (chairman); Dariush Furouhar (spokesman); Abu'l Fazl Qasimi (secretary-general), Dr Mihdi Azar, Dr Asadullah Mubashshir, Dr Shams ul-Din Amir Âla'i and Riza Shayan.
100 *Kayhan*, Day 19, 1357 (January 9, 1978), p.8.

101 Ibid., Day 23, 1357 (January 13, 1978), p.6.
102 The expression is from Senator Edward Kennedy. *The Washington Post* (of January 17, 1979) estimated the Shah's fortune "at $20 billion".
103 Quoted in *L'express*, 18-24 September, 1978, p.54.
104 Two noteworthy incidents occurred in the provinces. The first, a rather comic one, took place in Rasht where troops unbolted three Pahlavi statues to transfer them to the safety of their garrison. The second, a tragic one, unfolded at Ahvaz where commanders of the armoured division let their tanks run wild in the town's streets to soothe their nerves (bashing some two hundred parked cars), and assaulted the Jundishahpour University campus causing some two hundred casualties.
105 Ayatullah Qumi's eldest son, Ahmad, was among the fifty-seven founding members of the *Hizzb-i Susyal Dimukrat* (the Social Democrat party) formed but never launched, by maverick Ministers Dr Razmara and Engineer Javad Khadim Asadabadi.
106 *Keyhan International*, February 5, 1979, quoting a February 4 AP dispatch from Washington D.C.
107 M. Leeden and W. Lewis, op. cit. (note 84).
108 Ibid.
109 Z. Brzezinski, *Power and Principle* (London: Weidenfeld and Nicholson, 1983) p.111
110 See the book: *...Misl-i Barf Ab khwahim shud* (...We Shall Melt Like Snow), (Tehran: Nashr-i Nay, 1365 (1986)) in which the taped proceedings of the Army Commanders' Council meetings held on January 15, 23 and 29, were allegedly reprinted. General Najimi Nai'ni had replaced the departing General Uvaysi on January 3; he thereafter remained on the Council.
111 M. Leeden and W. Lewis, op. cit. (note 84).
112 Ibid.
113 Ibid.
114 Â. Qarabaghi, op. cit. (note 97), pp.205-6.
115 The wily *Humafars* claimed their due after the Revolution and were rewarded for their timely switch to the opposition by being made officers *en masse*, the only thing they had wanted all along and something Khatami should have given them (after some kind of transition period).
116 *Le Monde*, January 24, 1979.
117 *Keyhan International*, January 28, 1979, quoting a January 27 AP dispatch from Paris.
118 Interestingly it was roughly the same clientele that was taking full advantage of the Bakhtiar era to transfer its assets and cash abroad as fast as it could. Many would have the Premier to thank for a sweeter and richer exile.
119 The streets of Tehran had become dangerous for former regime supporters. On January 28, a clergyman turned deputy, Ghulam Husayn Danishi, was shot at but survived (he was executed in March 1979). On January 29, the Gendarmerie General Taqi Latifi was recognised and manhandled by a revenge-thirsty crowd, being fortunate to get off merely wounded (knife wounds) but alive.
120 *Paris-Match*, no. 1549, February 2, 1979, p.61.
121 *Keyhan International*, February 10, 1979, p.2.
122 Ibid.
123 Private communication to the author by the French journalist on the morning of February 10.

124 The subject of the air force's nationalistic tradition is exposed in the memoirs of Gh.R. Musavvar Rahmani, *Khatirat-i Syasi* (Tehran: Ravvaq, 1363 (1984)).
125 Â. Qarabaghi, op. cit. (note 97), pp.338-9.
126 *Keyhan International*, February 12, 1979, p.7.
127 Ibid.
128 See article by P. Balta and D. Pouchin, 'Les religieux ont paru debordés par des groupes de guérila', in *Le Monde*, February 13, 1979.
129 Â. Qarabaghi, op. cit. (note 97), p.111.
130 The General's private chauffeur was the presumed murderer, but the latter swore to the General's family that he could never commit such a crime and that an unknown assailant had put an end to his master's life. The family believed him. (Private communication to the author)
131 The fighting at Bagh-i Shah had been fierce, with the paratroopers putting up a desperate last-ditch defence. One of the paratroopers decided that it was useless when a bullet hit the butt of his G-3 gun. Throwing the gun away, he made straight for home; arriving in his neighbourhood he was carried in triumph by young revolutionaries who thought that he had fought on their side. They asked him to become their military trainer and he readily accepted: the instantaneous switch to popular leader was not that unnatural for an Iranian paratrooper.
132 See *Kayhan*, Bahman 23, 1357 (February 12, 1979), p.2. The tally was drawn from statistics gathered by its reporters in thirty-eight major Tehran hospitals on February 11/12.
133 *Le Monde*, February 13, 1979. See the excellent article by P. Balta and D. Pouchin, 'Les religieux ont paru debordés par des groupes de guérila'. At the Îshratabad camp the ransacking process lasted an hour, with the guerrillas making off with seven truckloads. The breadcrumbs went to their first-line supporters. By the early afternoon the camp had been stripped clean, down to its last air fan.
134 *Kayhan*, Bahman 4, 1357 (January 23, 1979), p.1.
135 See H. Zonis, 'He Got All the Credit, Now He Gets All the Blame' in *The New York Times*, January 14, 1979.

CONCLUSION

On April 1, 1979, the vast majority of the Iranian people, by their historic vote (98.2% of them voted yes), replaced their centuries-old monarchical system with an Islamic republic. Not only had Muhammad Reza Shah been ousted but the Pahlavi dynasty and the whole monarchical past went down the drain with him too. This was an insult which even Shah Sultan Husayn, the last Safavi king, had avoided. From the fall of the latter to that of the last Pahlavi, two and a half centuries later, Iran had come a long way.

At first, the country of the Lion and Sun had gone from the deepest abyss of Afghan dominion to the pinnacle of Nadir Shah's glorious Indian expedition. During the wise rule of Karim Khan Zand, the nation had found time to lick her wounds, only to fall into the lap of the atrocious but indefatigable eunuch Aqa Muhammad Khan Qajar. So, after two exceptional individual leaders, Persia was back under the spell of a family elite: the Qajars. With the rule of these northern tribesmen, Persia entered "the most unromantic and unproductive period of her history".[1] For Persia, the Qajars couldn't have come at a worse time, because the world was in the throes of the Industrial Revolution and Persia had to withstand the aggression of two European superpowers: Great Britain and Russia. The overlong reign of Nasir ul-Din Shah left the country in the ditch, at the mercy of a corrupt Qajar elite and of unscrupulous foreign speculators. The ill-fated Tobacco Concession and the ideas of Sayyid Jamal ul-Din Asadabadi would help trigger the awakening of the Iranian people.

The twentieth century was a long series of popular revolts and sacrifices aiming to bring about reforms and social justice. It began with the shattering Constitutional Movement, which was succeeded by the *Jangali* uprising of Mirza Kuchik Khan; the opponents of the 1919 Agreement, led by Sayyid Hasan Mudarris, came next; the *coup d'état* of February 1921 brought to power leaders who had risen from among the people – Sayyid Zia' ul-Din Tabataba'i and Reza Khan Mir Panj; the revolt of the people of Mashhad in 1935, quelled with bloodshed, was a sign that Reza Shah's reforms were not acceptable to all; during the 1940s, the formidable expansion of the *Toudeh* Party showed the people's strength; the oil nationalisation drive under Dr Muhammad Musaddiq was a clear expression of popular will; the southern tribes' rebellion and the Tehran riots of 1963 were two different expressions of the same popular discontent with Muhammad Reza Shah's rule; the daring acts of Iran's young guerrillas, which began with the historic attack at Syahkal in 1971, opened up yet another popular chapter; finally, the massive explosion of 1978/79 secured the ultimate victory for the people of Iran.

This long chain of revolts and sacrifices was paid for in blood: the long trail of blood left by all these martyrs is the ultimate guarantor of modern Iran. The people of Iran, from their most illustrious members to the forgotten guerrilla fighters, paid willingly to keep this proud nation on her feet: their names and deeds are etched in the common memory of 'Eternal Iran'. The most noteworthy personalities of Iran over the past three centuries have been Nadir Shah Afshar, Karim Khan Zand, Hajj Ibrahim Kalantar, Mirza Taqi Khan Amir Kabir, Âli Asghar Khan Amin ul-Sultan, Sayyid Jamal ul-Din Asadabadi, Hajj Âli Quli Khan Sardar Asad, Mirza Kuchik Khan, Reza Shah Pahlavi, Âbd ul-Husayn Taymourtash, Âli Akbar Davar, Ahmad Qavam, Prince Muzaffar Firouz, Dr Muhammad Musaddiq, Âli Akbar Dihkhuda, Hajj Âli Muhammad, Mutahhar Âli Shah, Fathullah Khan Hayat Davoudi, Ayatullah Taliqani, Ghulam Riza Takhti, Bizhan Jazani, Hamid Ashraf, Samad Bihrangi and, naturally, the Ayatullah Khomeini.

Iran's new leader, Ayatullah Rouhullah ul-Mousavi ul-Khomeini, was born in 1902 in the (then) small hamlet of Khumayn, the youngest of clergyman Aqa Mustafa's three sons – his elder brother Murtaza (nicknamed Pasandideh) was born in 1896, and Nour ul-Din (nicknamed Hindizadeh[2]) in 1898 (he died in 1976) – and three daughters. Khomeini became an orphan in March 1903 when his father was shot dead by the son of a local chieftain named Jâfar Quli Khan (of the Bahrami family) while on his way to Sultanabad (later Arak) to protest against the chieftain's gross exactions.

Aqa Mustafa's widow, Banou Hajar, set out for Tehran to plead her murdered husband's case with Sayyid Muhammad Kamareh'i, a leading Mujtahid with solid court connections.

After much toing and froing, Jâfar Quli proposed 1,000 krans (a fortune in those days) as the blood money, but the bereaved Banou turned it down, asking for *Qisas*, the Islamic law of reciprocity, i.e. Jâfar Quli's death. Eventually she won her case and in 1908 Jâfar Quli had his throat cut at Muhammad Âli Shah's court before Banou

Hajar and her two eldest sons. Rouhullah was not present, but the lesson that perseverance eventually pays off was certainly not lost on him.

The small Rouhullah grew up in the care of his mother and his paternal aunt, Banou Sahibeh. Both Banous passed away in 1918, and the sixteen year old Rouhullah went to Sultanabad to become a religious student under Ayatullah Hai'ri Yazdi, later following the latter to Qum, where he revived the town's *Houzeh Îlmiyyeh*. For the next four decades Khomeini lived the life of a *Houzeh* teacher, marrying Banou Batoul Saqafi in 1929. His whole life could be summarised in one word: Islam. He taught and breathed it.

The unknown Qum *Houzeh* teacher would abruptly become a national leader on June 5, 1962, when he was arrested and massive riots ensued, during which the name of Khomeini became the rallying cry of the demonstrators. Khomeini would never forget this turning point and the dozens of June 5 martyrs. Now, some fifteen years after the tragic June 5 events, he was the uncontested leader of a victorious Revolution. This was a role he amply deserved – for his patience, his single-mindedness, his courage and his political acumen. In 1979, no other Iranian political leader could compare with him.

The people of Iran are indeed 'historic'. Hegel's remark was proven correct time and again during the twentieth century as Iranians came kicking out of their unusual nineteenth-century torpor. Their only low watermark came during the First World War, but the rest of the century was all buoyancy as they got back their province of Azarbayjan in 1946 from the Soviets, nationalised their oil industry in 1951, and finally terminated twenty-five years of American domination with the 1978/79 Revolution.

The people of Iran are unique. They are as capable of the best as of the worst. Patient, enduring and tenacious, they have their limits: woe to the foreigner who came to think of him as always hospitable or docile. With their extra-long memories, Iranians never forget any act of goodwill or any insult. They always get even with their friends and with their enemies, whatever the cost. They are gifted individuals and know it. They are also proud – proud of their long history, their historical legacy, their culture, their beautiful language and their world-renowned poets.

With the Revolution, a new crop of Iranians was rising to the top: the *Dihqanzadehs*, or rather the natural leaders of Iran's massive peasantry. The rule of the majority was about to dawn. The following picture of the *Dihqanzadehs* was drawn in 1949 in one of the concluding dialogues of an extraordinary book entitled *The Diplomat*:[3]

> ...All your decisions [about Iran] discount the Persians themselves... To you the Persian is a stupid peasant who can't decide his own affairs; an uncultured wretch who will take all manner of deceit and oppression and diplomatic twisting. If you do see any signs, any glimmer of revolt, you blame the Russians and take it to the Security Council. But it isn't the Russians. It's the peasant himself who is revolting. Dirty and wretched they may be, opium-ridden and backward and dull, but they are really the people you should fear not the Russians. It may take time and there may be set-backs, but... you cannot stop the Persian from deciding his own affairs. He is not ignorant and stupid to [the fact of] his political situation. He is not so wretched and afraid of revolt. He is not even uncultured: in the language he speaks and the use he makes of it there is more natural culture among the peasants of Iran than you can find among the world's diplomats at the Savoy Hotel. These people have reached the breaking point... These people are desperate...

Three decades after it was made, this prophecy by author James Aldridge became reality: the Iranian peasants, the *Dihqanzadehs*, were unstoppable during the Islamic Revolution of 1978/79 which eventually brought them to power.

The main question then was: can quantity be a substitute for quality? Upon its answer would depend the length of the *Dihqanzadehs'* time in power. Iran's *sans-culottes* will inevitably give way to a new system some day. Possibly, as Carlyle concluded about the French Revolution: "Sansculottism ...is to perish in a new singular system of Culottism and Arrangement"[4]. Or possibly in a deal brokered by a local Napoleon, most probably a *Dihqanzadeh*.

The amalgam of the old Qajar Elite and the new Pahlavi elite (with the Farmanfarmayans at the junction) had finally succumbed to the counter-elites. The elites had thought that they could saddle Muhammad Reza Pahlavi with all the blame and escape unscathed. But even Machiavellianism has its limits. This time around it didn't work out as planned: the revolutionaries failed to play the game and penalised the fallen elites as well. The elitists would be fortunate to keep their lives and their foreign assets untouched. In the era of 'throwaways', Iran was experimenting with a brand new idea: the throwaway elite. The Shah's elite had not lasted two decades before being uprooted and sent scrambling to their golden exile.

The counter-elites clearly deserved to win. They had made the necessary sacrifices, and the best and the brightest minds were clearly on their side (in 1978). They also had the best leader of all across the Iranian political spectrum to lead them against the Shah: Ayatullah Rouhullah Khomeini. With such a leader, there was little doubt that the religious hierocracy would carve out the lion's share of power for itself, leaving the breadcrumbs to the other counter-elites.

With a new elite in the making, it remained to be seen which constituency would form the new counter-elites. From the fallen debris of Iran Inc. three entities – the old Elite, the army and the bureaucracy – were potential candidates. The old Elite was at the end of its tether and yet had no intention of promoting its handful of best and brightest so its chances of success amounted to almost nil; it still had to learn that when you lose the least you can do is to change your first team. The army, after its disastrous rout on February 10 and 11, 1979, would need some purifying fire to cleanse itself in the popular minds; but it was still a constituency to be reckoned with, for it was there to stay and still was the most powerful domestic player. Unlike the old elite, the armed forces would inevitably promote the best and the brightest from within its ranks. As for the bureaucracy, it had little chance of finding a common denominator to form a technocratic elite capable of pulling its weight on the political stage; the bureaucrats' best alternative was a link-up with army elements to foster a meritocratic politico-military platform capable of managing the country – but the creation of such a coalition required vision on both sides.

Any anti-Pahlavi counter-elite not given its share of power by the religious would stick to its counter-elite status, challenging the new elite in place. The nationalists, the communists and the guerrilla groups were prime candidates for such a return to counter-elite status. However, they would all have difficulties explaining to their respective supporters how they had become deadly enemies with their former allies of the anti-Pahlavi coalition. Furthermore they would need an ideology and a capable leadership (both *sine qua non* on their way to future power). The fact that fresh counter-elites could emerge, either arising from political change or renewal among latent forces, should not be discarded.

In any event, family elites were on their way out. In twenty-first century Iran, pedigrees would count for much less than they had during the twentieth. The era of one-man elites (such as Reza Shah and Khomeini) would be the new standard.

The historical role played by the Great Powers in Iran had always been of utmost importance. During the Great Game played by Great Britain and Russia throughout the nineteenth century, Persia and Central Asia were at the centre of their gigantic chessboard. At the outset of the twentieth century, Germany tried to join in but did not last long, although individuals like Wassmuss found the time to make a name for themselves. The Second World War witnessed the entry of the American superpower to the Iranian fray. With their leadership of the 1953 coup against Dr Musaddiq, the US turned Iran into a client state and developed their own 'clinic'. The American adventure in Iran lasted for only a quarter of a century before crumbling down in a bloodless Vietnam. In the meantime, the US had made few long-lasting friendships and had seriously antagonised the leaders of almost every Iranian constituency; when they left in 1979, there was little sorrow and much rejoicing.

As for the Israelis, they were allowed by the Americans to build their own niche in the American 'clinic'. They found time to noiselessly strike alliances among all walks of life in Iranian society – from the highest spheres of the Qajar Elite to the dregs of the Tehran underworld – mostly through Mossad agents. The general problem of Iranian ambivalence towards Israel was, however, never resolved. The ordinary Iranian saw Israel as a welcome ally against the common Arab enemies, but an ally it would like to keep at arm's length.

The Soviets were most powerful in Iran during the turbulent 1940s. Having lost their chance then to capitalise on the *Toudeh* Party's existence and the trade unions (which they controlled), they became powerless in Iran, and thus impotent to oppose America's bid for hegemony in 1953. During the 1960s and 1970s, the Soviet Union satisfied itself with economic deals, hoping for an end to the US hegemony, always willing to join any anti-American coalition.

Always present in Iran were the British. They had many Persian assets. Their most precious one was the long string of outstanding Persian scholars stretching over two centuries with, among many others: Sir Austen Henry Layard, Sir William K. Loftus, Sir Henry Rawlinson, Professor E.G. Browne, Lord Curzon of Kedleston, Godfrey Havard, Sir Reader Bullard, Professor H.A.R. Gibb, Professor A.K.S. Lambton, Sir Laurence Lockhart, Professor Bernard Lewis, Sir Denis Wright and Sir Anthony Parsons. The diplomats and official analysts certainly played an important role too, but the impact of prominent scholars is without doubt of crucial importance; the failure of other Powers to nurture such towering scholars always left them somehow handicapped. Furthermore, in Iran, as elsewhere, the British had time on their side; as the US *chargé d'affaires* in Tehran W. Smith Murray underlined back in 1924: "Great Britain's policy may be said to be geared to centuries, whereas ours is scarcely geared to years. She can wait".[5] Indeed.

The French always tried their very best, but usually performed below their own expectations, basically being incapable of striking deep roots in Iran. They were still more successful than the Germans, though, who were business giants in Iran (heading the list of exporters to Iran during the 1970s) but always political dwarfs. Neutral European countries such as Holland, Switzerland and Sweden (remember the Gendarmerie) always fared well in Iran, as Iranians were reassured that they would not interfere in their domestic affairs.

The dominance of Western Powers over the land of Hazrat Imam Âli (A.S.) inevitably confronted its inhabitants with the phenomenon of Westernisation. A traditional Muslim society, with its millennia-old customs and creeds, was submitted to the charms of Western products: military skills and armaments, democracy and parliamentarianism, all kinds of technology, progress and development. For Persians, the dilemma was that they couldn't do without and they couldn't do with; they had succumbed to the charms, but were wary of its consequences. They wanted to use Westernism without changing their basic spots, and that was not possible. Every new encroachment by Western habits brought about a subtle change in its users. The problem was that the whole of Persian society was not exposed uniformly to the effects of Westernisation: exposure was directly proportional to wealth and degree of urbanisation, so that rich Tehranis were at the one end of the scale and poor peasants at the other. Travels to Europe and America further exacerbated differences, and the Western-educated minority came to form the visible tip of the Iranian iceberg. Here again, there would have been little problem if this minority had been capable of leading the country (preferably on the right tracks) – but it was not.

As a reaction to Westernisation, the *Dihqanzadehs* had chosen a new weapon to fight it: *Shiîte* Islam. The watered-down nationalism used a generation earlier under Dr Musaddiq had not proven solid enough in the anti-Western struggle. The solid Islamic *shariâ* looked much more promising.[6]

George Bernard Reynolds's historic strike at Masjid-i Sulayman in 1908 opened a whole new chapter in Iranian history: that of crude oil and its industry. For its first three decades, the oil question was, seen from the Iranian angle, purely an elitist matter; only the likes of Nusrat ul-Douleh Firouz or Taymourtash mulled over such issues of national importance. In 1933, Reza Shah could order Hasan Taqizadeh to sign the fresh oil agreement with APOC without having to worry about hostile public opinion. It was the turbulent 1940s and the quest for new concessions that pushed an uncensored press to bring the subject of oil to the public's attention. Oil was even linked to the crucial Azarbayjani conundrum. It was during these post-war years that oil entered the national agenda, rising to the top slot with the oil nationalisation of 1951. Within half a century, crude oil had come all the way from an underground mineral resource to become the 'Fourth Vector' on the Iranian socio-political stage.

After *Murdad 28*, oil's impact was not only political but economic. Oil revenues went on increasing at a rapid pace (as output soared), becoming the major item in the national budget. With the price shock of 1973/74, the Shah was given enough petrodollars to drown in: he duly linked the whole Iranian economy to oil revenues. The oil bonanza ushered in the age of consumption in Iran, with the consumer-happy higher and middle classes taking full advantage of goods and services offered. The windfall petrodollars were soon providing over 90% of Iran's hard currencies. Oil income was the new locomotive pulling the whole Iranian economy: Iran had become addicted to its oil exports. When the oil industry sneezed, Iran caught a cold.

The mammoth oil revenues had also altered some basic Iranian balances:

(1) First and foremost, with such massive doses of – more or less assured – petrodollars, anyone could rule over Iran without any risk, for the billions of dollars could lubricate any wheel and cover any mishap;

(2) It created an 'oil export/goods import' cycle of its own of such magnitude that it overshadowed the local economy, and further crushed any attempt at domestic self-sufficiency made at traditional grass roots level. The Tehran *Bazaar* was the indispensable heart of both cycles, thus placed at the crucial crossroads and thus ideally placed to take economic power (leaving political power to the religious hierocracy);

(3) The day-to-day operation of the Iranian oil industry, the goose laying the golden eggs, would pass to Iranian technocrats and managers. Over the past two decades they had been readied to properly manage their own industry without direct foreign presence;

(4) The oil industry's success brought about the steep decline of Iranian agriculture. When any produce of the land could easily and cheaply be imported, then Iran became 'The Neglected Garden'.[7]

The Iranians would be well-advised to ponder one of their own dicta: 'What the Wind Brings, It Also Taketh Away'.

Its natural resources are, however, but one vector of Iran's importance. The real importance of Iran lies in the crucial fact that a major prerequisite of world domination is hegemony over the Persian high plateau. Both Russian Tsar Peter the Great and leading British statesmen had long understood this inescapable fact of global *realpolitik*.

During the nineteenth century, Persia was the key to domination of the Persian Gulf and the gateway to India. During the twentieth, it became one of the two keys over control of the Gulf (Oman was the second) and the ultimate guardian over its mineral riches.

Saudi Arabia and Iraq later became Gulf powers due to their oil riches but they have neither Iran's past nor people; against the right mix of Iranian ingredients, neither stands the shade of a chance of disputing Iran's role of being the balancing power in the region.

The American continent (north, central and south) is the US's area of total domination. A Europe from "the Atlantic Ocean to the Urals" is in the making. Africa is still insignificant in world power terms (except for the mineral riches of South Africa). In East Asia, Japan, China and India are flexing their muscles – the first qualitatively and the other two quantitatively. In this world only one region stands out without any designated owner: the Middle East area, at the junction of the three largest land masses of Europe, Africa and Asia, the area on which the powers-to-be will focus in the twenty-first century, both for its precious underground resources and its unique location. The region's linchpin is Iran: she is (i) the link between Turkey (in Europe) and Pakistan (in Asia); (ii) the southern flank to the new Caucasus and Central Asian republics; (iii) on Russia's path to warm waters; (iv) towering over the north littoral of the Persian Gulf; and (v) potentially a regional power of the first order; and (vi) possibly at the front line of the Third World War.

Immortal because of her universally admired poets and her rich culture, because of her unique people and her special location at the planet's centre of gravity, Iran is assured of living. Her very survival as a single entity is important for humanity. Some of the Powers (especially among the Europeans) have clearly understood their responsibility. Others have not. It is to be hoped that the former will be able to convince the latter. In times of grave danger, the Iranian people will always turn towards their true defenders, as the sunflower naturally turns towards the sun.

In any event, Iran and Iranians deserve better than their present status. For their modern setbacks they only have themselves to blame (not the Powers). Their main fault was not making proper use of their best and brightest talents. In the past two centuries, some of their natural leaders made it to the top, but these represented only a tiny minority of the immense talent at hand. Failing to promote her most promising sons, Iran might well go on declining. Hopefully these future declines will, as in the past, turn out to be declines ...which are, eventually, for the better.

NOTES

[1] G.B. Walker, *Persian Pageant* (Calcutta, 1950) p.71.

[2] Nour ul-Din's nickname of Hindizadeh was due to the fact that the family was originally of Indian origin. In the middle of the nineteenth century (no exact date is available), an Indian Sayyid named Ahmad came from India to settle in the small hamlet of Khumayn. Ahmad's sons Mustafa and Muhammad remained at Khumayn and entered the religious orders like their father. Hindizadeh and his brothers were Sayyid Ahmad's grandsons.

[3] J. Aldridge, *The Diplomat* (London: The Bodley Head, 1949) pp.721-22. Assuredly one of the most profound pieces written on Iran.

[4] T. Carlyle, *The French Revolution* (London: Macmillan, 1925) Vol. 2, p.400.

[5] *The US and Iran – A Documentary History*, ed. by Y. Alexander and A. Nanes, (Aletheia Books, University Publications of America, 1980) p.416.

[6] J. Daniel, 'La Grande Dérive des Croisés', in *Le Nouvel Observateur*, November 9, 1979, pp.46-7.

[7] See the outstanding compendium: Professor K. McLachlan, *The Neglected Garden: the Politics and Ecology of Agriculture in Iran* (London: I.B. Tauris, 1988), in which it is suggested that, in the long run, water (and the produce of the land) might prove more important than crude oil: an unattackable thesis.